# The SAGE Handbook of
# Cultural Sociology

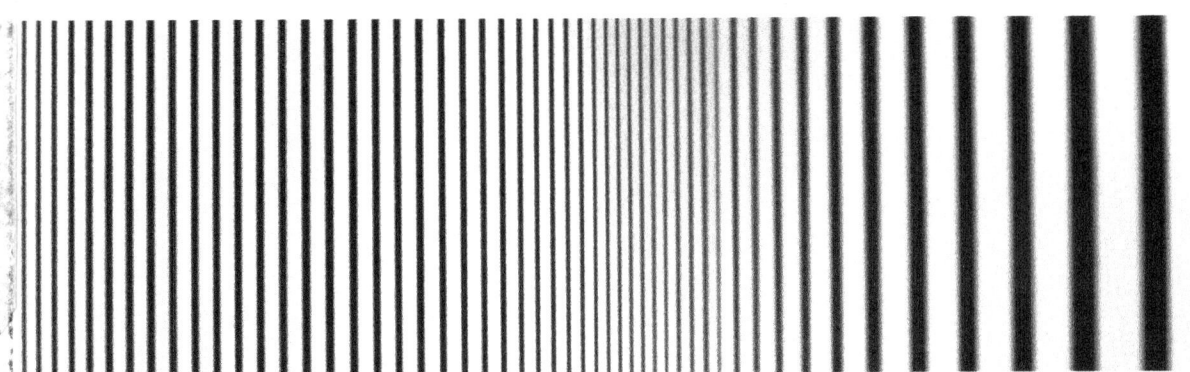

**SAGE** was founded in 1965 by Sara Miller McCune to support the dissemination of usable knowledge by publishing innovative and high-quality research and teaching content. Today, we publish over 900 journals, including those of more than 400 learned societies, more than 800 new books per year, and a growing range of library products including archives, data, case studies, reports, and video. SAGE remains majority-owned by our founder, and after Sara's lifetime will become owned by a charitable trust that secures our continued independence.

Los Angeles | London | New Delhi | Singapore | Washington DC | Melbourne

# The SAGE Handbook of
# Cultural Sociology

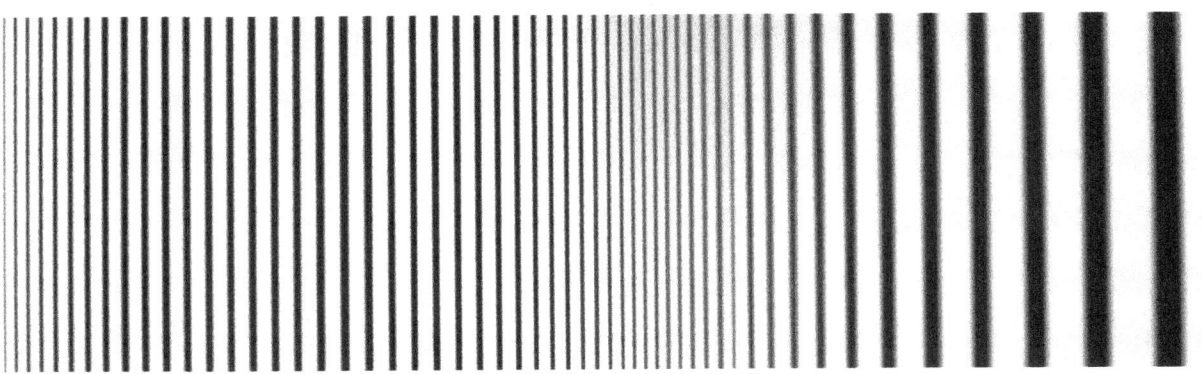

Edited by

David Inglis and
Anna-Mari Almila

Los Angeles | London | New Delhi | Singapore | Washington DC | Melbourne

Los Angeles | London | New Delhi
Singapore | Washington DC | Melbourne

SAGE Publications Ltd
1 Oliver's Yard
55 City Road
London EC1Y 1SP

SAGE Publications Inc.
2455 Teller Road
Thousand Oaks, California 91320

SAGE Publications India Pvt Ltd
B 1/I 1 Mohan Cooperative Industrial Area
Mathura Road
New Delhi 110 044

SAGE Publications Asia-Pacific Pte Ltd
3 Church Street
#10-04 Samsung Hub
Singapore 049483

Editor: Chris Rojek
Editorial Assistant: Matthew Oldfield
Production editor: Sushant Nailwal
Copyeditor: Rosemary Campbell
Proofreader: Sharon Cawood
Indexer: Caroline Eley
Marketing manager: Michael Ainsley
Cover design: Wendy Scott
Typeset by: Cenveo Publisher Services
Printed and bound by CPI Group (UK) Ltd,
Croydon, CR0 4YY

At SAGE we take sustainability seriously. Most of our products are printed in the UK using FSC papers and boards. When we print overseas we ensure sustainable papers are used as measured by the PREPS grading system. We undertake an annual audit to monitor our sustainability.

Editorial arrangement © David Inglis and Anna-Mari Almila 2016

Chapter 1 © David Inglis 2016
Chapter 2 © Paul K. Jones 2016
Chapter 3 © David Inglis 2016
Chapter 4 © Colin Loader 2016
Chapter 5 © David Inglis 2016
Chapter 6 © Eduardo de la Fuente 2016
Chapter 7 © Gisèle Sapiro 2016
Chapter 8 © Norman K. Denzin 2016
Chapter 9 © Karen A. Cerulo 2016
Chapter 10 © Anna-Mari Almila 2016
Chapter 11 © Pertti Alasuutari 2016
Chapter 12 © Ilana F. Silber 2016
Chapter 13 © Rudi Laermans 2016
Chapter 14 © Marco Santoro 2016
Chapter 15 © Chandra Mukerji 2016
Chapter 16 © Dick Houtman and Peter Achterberg 2016
Chapter 17 © Thomas S. Eberle 2016
Chapter 18 © Julien Duval 2016
Chapter 19 © Jonathan Roberge 2016
Chapter 20 © Nick Crossley 2016
Chapter 21 © John Hughson 2016
Chapter 22 © David Inglis 2016
Chapter 23 © Janet Stewart 2016
Chapter 24 © Mary Kosut 2016
Chapter 25 © Bethany Bryson 2016
Chapter 26 © Laura D. Edles 2016
Chapter 27 © Rachel Hurdley 2016
Chapter 28 © Tia DeNora 2016
Chapter 29 © Nick Stevenson 2016
Chapter 30 © Hank Johnston 2016
Chapter 31 © Eric Taylor Woods 2016
Chapter 32 © Ronald N. Jacobs 2016
Chapter 33 © Brad West 2016
Chapter 34 © Paul Jones 2016
Chapter 35 © Tatiana Signorelli Heise and Andrew Tudor 2016
Chapter 36 © Nail Farkhatdinov and Sophia Krzys Acord 2016
Chapter 37 © Anna-Mari Almila 2016
Chapter 38 © Andy Bennett 2016
Chapter 39 © Dominik Bartmanski 2016
Chapter 40 © Frederick F. Wherry 2016
Chapter 41 © David Wright 2016
Chapter 42 © Sonia Bookman 2016
Chapter 43 © Matthias Varul 2016

Apart from any fair dealing for the purposes of research or private study, or criticism or review, as permitted under the Copyright, Designs and Patents Act, 1988, this publication may be reproduced, stored or transmitted in any form, or by any means, only with the prior permission in writing of the publishers, or in the case of reprographic reproduction, in accordance with the terms of licences issued by the Copyright Licensing Agency. Enquiries concerning reproduction outside those terms should be sent to the publishers.

**Library of Congress Control Number: 2015952092**

**British Library Cataloguing in Publication data**

A catalogue record for this book is available from the British Library

ISBN 978-1-4462-7197-1

# Contents

| | | |
|---|---|---|
| *List of Figures* | | ix |
| *List of Tables* | | x |
| *Notes on the Editors and Contributors* | | xi |
| *Acknowledgements* | | xix |
| 1. | Introduction: Culture/Sociology/Sociology of Culture/Cultural Sociology<br>*David Inglis* | 1 |
| **PART I** | **SCHOOLS OF THOUGHT** | 9 |
| 2. | Marxist Cultural Sociology<br>*Paul K. Jones* | 11 |
| 3. | Max Weber's Presences: On the Cultural Sociology of the Long-Term<br>*David Inglis* | 26 |
| 4. | The Cultural Sociology of Alfred Weber and Karl Mannheim<br>*Colin Loader* | 48 |
| 5. | Durkheimian and Neo-Durkheimian Cultural Sociologies<br>*David Inglis* | 60 |
| 6. | A Qualitative Theory of Culture: Georg Simmel and Cultural Sociology<br>*Eduardo de la Fuente* | 78 |
| 7. | Bourdieu's Sociology of Culture: On the Economy of Symbolic Goods<br>*Gisèle Sapiro* | 91 |
| 8. | Symbolic Interactionism's Contribution to the Study of Culture<br>*Norman K. Denzin* | 105 |
| 9. | Cognition and Cultural Sociology: The Inside and Outside of Thought<br>*Karen A. Cerulo* | 116 |
| 10. | Actor Network Theory and Its Cultural Uses<br>*Anna-Mari Almila* | 131 |
| 11. | Neoinstitutionalist Sociology<br>*Pertti Alasuutari* | 144 |

12. The Cultural Worth of 'Economies of Worth': French Pragmatic Sociology from a Cultural Sociological Perspective 159
*Ilana F. Silber*

13. Systems Theory and Culture: Drawing Lessons from Parsons and Luhmann 178
*Rudi Laermans*

14. The 'Production of Culture Perspective' in Perspective 193
*Marco Santoro*

15. Cultural Historical Sociology 214
*Chandra Mukerji*

## PART II   METHODOLOGICAL APPROACHES 223

16. Quantitative Analysis in Cultural Sociology: Why It Should Be Done, How It Can Be Done 225
*Dick Houtman and Peter Achterberg*

17. Qualitative Cultural Sociology 237
*Thomas S. Eberle*

18. Multiple Correspondence Analysis 255
*Julien Duval*

19. Hermeneutics and Cultural Sociology 272
*Jonathan Roberge*

20. Social Network Analysis 282
*Nick Crossley*

21. Ethnography and the Sociology of Culture 294
*John Hughson*

## PART III   DISCIPLINARITY AND INTERDISCIPLINARITY 305

22. Sociology and Cultural Studies: A Close and Fraught Relationship 307
*David Inglis*

23. Visual Culture Studies and Cultural Sociology: Extractive Seeing 322
*Janet Stewart*

24. Queering Gender, Art and Culture in the Age of Media Convergence 335
*Mary Kosut*

## PART IV  CULTURE AND SOCIETY 347

25. Symbolic Boundaries 349
    *Bethany Bryson*

26. Cultural Sociology of Religion and Beliefs 363
    *Laura D. Edles*

27. Everyday Life: The Making of a Sociological Topic, Then Making it
    'Cultural Sociology' 372
    *Rachel Hurdley*

28. 'Turn, Turn, Turn!' Musicalizing Cultural Sociology with the 'in Action'
    Perspective 390
    *Tia DeNora*

## PART V  CULTURE AND POLITICS 401

29. Cultural Citizenship 403
    *Nick Stevenson*

30. Dimensions of Culture in Social Movement Research 414
    *Hank Johnston*

31. Cultural Nationalism 429
    *Eric Taylor Woods*

32. Cultural Sociology of News Media 442
    *Ronald N. Jacobs*

33. Cultural Memory 455
    *Brad West*

## PART VI  ARTS AND AESTHETICS 463

34. (Cultural) Sociologies of Architecture? 465
    *Paul Jones*

35. For a Sociology of the Cinema 481
    *Tatiana Signorelli Heise and Andrew Tudor*

36. Witnessing Culture: Museums, Exhibitions and the Artistic Encounter 496
    *Nail Farkhatdinov and Sophia Krzys Acord*

37. Cultural Sociology of Fashion: On the Sartorial, Symbolic and Social 510
    *Anna-Mari Almila*

| 38. | Popular Music and Cultural Sociology<br>*Andy Bennett* | 527 |
| | | |
| 39. | Iconicity<br>*Dominik Bartmanski* | 538 |
| | | |
| 40. | The Cultural Sociology of Markets<br>*Frederick F. Wherry* | 553 |

**PART VII   CULTURE AND CONSUMPTION** 565

| 41. | Cultural Consumption and Cultural Omnivorousness<br>*David Wright* | 567 |
| | | |
| 42. | Cultural Sociology: Brands<br>*Sonia Bookman* | 578 |
| | | |
| 43. | Cultural Sociology of Ethical Consumption<br>*Matthias Varul* | 590 |

*Index* 599

# List of Figures

| | | |
|---|---|---|
| 9.1 | 'Cute' marketing mascots | 123 |
| 14.1 | Citations per year of four key works on the production of culture and three key works on omnivorousness, 1976–2014 | 194 |
| 14.2 | The six-facets model: a graphic representation | 200 |
| 16.1 | Distinguishing class voting (path 2 × path 3) from cultural voting (path 4 × path 5) | 230 |
| 16.2 | Type of informational provision (x-axis) and predicted support for hydrogen technology (y-axis) for respondents with minimum and maximum levels of stewardship | 233 |
| 18.1 | Variants of the dominant taste (a simplified version of Bourdieu (2010 [1979]: 259): only the modalities which most contribute to axes are represented) | 257 |
| 18.2 | The fractions of the dominant class in the space of lifestyles | 258 |
| 18.3 | The choice of scale | 260 |
| 18.4 | The ten occupational groups (representation after standardization) | 261 |
| 18.5 | The determination of axis 1 | 262 |
| 18.6 | The ten occupational groups in the plane of axes 1–2 | 263 |
| 18.7 | The variables in the plane of axes 1–2 | 264 |
| 20.1 | The network structure of Sheffield's post-punk music world, 1976–1980 | 286 |
| 20.2 | Paul Shaft's ego-net | 289 |
| 20.3 | Paul Shaft's ego-net merged with Paul Bower's | 291 |
| 20.4 | Visualising a two-mode network | 292 |
| 30.1 | Analytical dimensions of social movement research | 415 |

# List of Tables

| | | |
|---|---|---|
| 18.1 | School leaving age and monthly salary for ten occupational groups | 259 |
| 20.1 | An adjacency matrix | 285 |
| 20.2 | Core–periphery density matrix | 287 |
| 20.3 | A hypothetical incidence matrix: dancers and studios | 291 |

# Notes on the Editors and Contributors

## THE EDITORS

**Almila, Anna-Mari** is Post-Doctoral Research Fellow in Sociology of Fashion at London College of Fashion, University of the Arts London. She holds degrees in Art and Design (Clothing) and Sociology. She is the editor of *The Ashgate Research Companion to Veils and Veiling Practices* (forthcoming), and the author of *Veiling in Fashion: Space and the Hijab in Minority Communities* (forthcoming with I.B. Tauris). She writes in the fields of sociology of fashion, fashion and materiality, pre-modern fashion, cultural sociology, historical sociology, fashion and globalization, fashion and space, and fashion and equality. Her current research includes investigation of the cultural worlds of women in the global wine industry, and this work will be published in a book she is co-editing, *The Globalization of Wine* (forthcoming with Bloomsbury).

**Inglis, David** is Professor of Sociology at the University of Exeter, UK. He holds degrees in sociology from the universities of Cambridge and York. He writes in the areas of cultural sociology, the sociology of globalization, historical sociology, the sociology of food and drink, and social theory, both modern and classical. He has written and edited various books in these areas, most recently *An Invitation to Social Theory*, published by Polity (second edition, 2016). He is founding editor of the Sage/BSA journal *Cultural Sociology*. His current research concerns the sociological analysis of the global wine industry.

## THE CONTRIBUTORS

**Achterberg, Peter** is Professor of Sociology at the Department of Sociology, Tilburg School of Social and Behavioral Sciences, Tilburg University, The Netherlands. Peter is a cultural sociologist with a general interest in studying cultural, political, and religious change in the West. Much of his work deals with the question of how people attribute meaning to the changing world surrounding them, whether these meanings have consequences for their behaviour, and, of course, how these (changing and differing) meanings can be explained. He has published in a wide range of journals, from *Public Opinion Quarterly* to *Public Understanding of Science*, from *Crime and Delinquency* to *Social Forces*, and from *Journal for the Scientific Study of Religion* to *International Journal of Hydrogen Technology*.

**Acord, Sophia Krzys** is Acting Director of the Center for the Humanities and the Public Sphere, and Lecturer in Sociology, Criminology & Law, at the University of Florida. She holds a PhD from the Sociology of the Arts (SocArts) research group at the University of Exeter, UK, and managed the Andrew W. Mellon Foundation-funded Future of Scholarly Communication Project at the Center for Studies in Higher Education, University of California, Berkeley. Her research examines the production of knowledge in the arts and humanities, and she has published work in cultural sociology, the sociology of the arts, museum studies, qualitative research methods, and mobile technologies. She was founding editor of the journal Music and Arts in Action and works actively to apply the cultural sociological study of the arts to public program building in the arts and humanities disciplines.

**Alasuutari, Pertti, PhD,** is Academy Professor at the University of Tampere, School of Social Sciences and Humanities. He is editor of the *European Journal of Cultural Studies*, and his research interests include global and transnational phenomena, media, social theory, and social research methodology. He has published widely in international journals, and his books include *The Synchronization of National Policies* (Routledge 2016), *Social Theory and Human Reality* (Sage 2004), *Rethinking the Media Audience* (Sage 1999), *An Invitation to Social Research* (Sage 1998), and *Researching Culture: Qualitative Method and Cultural Studies* (Sage 1995).

**Bartmanski, Dominik** earned his Ph.D. at Yale University and currently works at sociology department at Technical University of Berlin, Germany. He writes in the fields of material culture, music sociology, urban sociology and social theory. In his dissertation and current work he develops a theory of iconicity as a key form of cultural signification. His recent publications include the book "Vinyl: The Analog Record in the Digital Age" (Bloomsbury, 2015, co-authored with Ian Woodward) and articles in *Journal of Consumer Culture, Journal of Sociology, European Journal of Social Theory, Sociologica, Czech Sociological Review* and *Acta Sociologica*. He is currently working on another book project "Labels: Making Independent Music" (to be published by Bloomsbury in 2017).

**Bennett, Andy** is Professor of Cultural Sociology at Griffith University in Queensland, Australia. He has authored and edited numerous books including *Music, Style and Aging, Popular Music and Youth Culture, Cultures of Popular Music, Remembering Woodstock*, and *Music Scenes* (with Richard A. Peterson). He is also a Faculty Fellow of the Center for Cultural Sociology at Yale University.

**Bookman, Sonia** is assistant professor of Sociology at the University of Manitoba. She completed her PhD at the University of Manchester. Her most recent research on the social and cultural implications of brands and branding appears in *Cultural Sociology, European Journal of Cultural Studies, Social & Cultural Geography* and *Space and Culture*. She is currently working on a project that examines the connections between film and urban re-imaging, and regularly teaches a graduate course on Consumer Culture.

**Bryson, Bethany** focuses on the intersection of culture and inequality, especially where culture mediates economic disparities in gender and race. For example, "Own It!" (with Alexander Davis and Laura Rogers, *Cultural Sociology*, 2014) is a study of masculinity and heteronormativity in television fashion makeover shows. Bryson is also the author of *Making Multiculturalism* (Stanford University Press, 2005) and "Anything but Heavy Metal" (*American Sociological Review*, 1993). She teaches at James Madison University, where current research includes (1) quantitative research using sex and gender as a dependent variable and (2) articulating the (less-polarized and increasingly powerful) political affiliations of African-American, Latinx, and female voters in the United States.

**Cerulo, Karen A.** is Professor and former Chair of the Sociology Department at Rutgers University. Her research interests include culture, cognition, symbolic communication, media, technology, and social change. Professor Cerulo's articles appear in a wide variety of journals. She is the author of three books: *Identity Designs: The Sights and Sounds of a Nation,* winner of the ASA Culture Section's award for the Best Book of 1996 (Rose Book Series of the ASA, Rutgers University Press); *Deciphering Violence: The Cognitive Structure of Right and Wrong* (Routledge); and *Never Saw It Coming: Cultural Challenges to Envisioning the Worst* (University of Chicago Press). She has edited a collection entitled *Culture in Mind: Toward a Sociology of Culture and Cognition* (Routledge) and co-authored a book entitled *Second Thoughts: Sociology Challenges Conventional Wisdom* (Sage), now in its sixth edition. Currently, Professor Cerulo is at work on a book entitled *Dreams of a Lifetime: The Sociocultural Dimensions of Our Imaginings.*

**Crossley, Nick** is a Professor of Sociology at the University of Manchester and co-founder/co-director of the Mitchell Centre for Social Network Analysis. His current work is focused upon 'music worlds', and in particular their network structures. His most recent book is Networks of Sound, Style and Subversion: the Punk and Post-Punk Worlds of Manchester, London, Liverpool and Sheffield (Manchester University Press 2015).

**de la Fuente, Eduardo** is Senior Lecturer in Creativity and Innovation at James Cook University, Australia. He has published a monograph entitled *Twentieth Century Music and the Question of Modernity* (Routledge, 2011) and co-edited two collections: *Philosophical and Cultural Theories of Music* (Brill, 2010) and *Aesthetic Capitalism* (Brill, 2014). He has published articles and essays on everyday aesthetics, music and art, urban life, landscape and the writings of social theorist Georg Simmel. He is Treasurer and immediate Past-President of the International Sociological Association's Research Committee for the Sociology of the Arts, is a Faculty Fellow at the Yale Centre for Cultural Sociology and sits on the Editorial Board of *Thesis Eleven.*

**DeNora, Tia** is Professor of Sociology in SPA (Sociology, Philosophy and Anthropology) at Exeter University where she directs the SocArts Research Group. Her main area of research is music sociology where, most recently, she has completed a longitudinal study of music and wellbeing in collaboration with Gary Ansdell, a music therapist. She is the author of *Beethoven and the Construction of Genius, Music in Everyday Life, After Adorno: Rethinking Music Sociology, Music Asylums, Making Sense of Reality: Culture and Perception in Everyday Life,* and - forthcoming in 2016 - *Musical Pathways for Recovery* (with Gary Ansdell). With Gary Ansdell, she co-edits the Ashgate Series in Music & Change.

**Denzin, Norman K.** is Distinguished Professor of Communications, College of Communications Scholar, and Research Professor of Communications, Sociology, and Humanities at the University of Illinois, Urbana-Champaign. Denzin is the author or editor of more than two dozen books, including *Indians on Display; Custer on Canvas; The Qualitative Manifesto; Qualitative Inquiry Under Fire; Searching for Yellowstone; Reading Race; Interpretive Ethnography; The Cinematic Society; The Voyeur's Gaze;* and *The Alcoholic Self.* He is past editor of *The Sociological Quarterly,* co-editor (with Yvonna S. Lincoln) of four editions of the *Handbook of Qualitative Research,* co-editor (with Michael D. Giardina) of eight plenary volumes from the annual Congress of Qualitative Inquiry, co-editor (with Lincoln) of the methods journal *Qualitative Inquiry,* founding editor of *Cultural Studies/Critical Methodologies* and *International Review of Qualitative Research,* and editor of three book series.

**Duval, Julien** is researcher at the French National Center for Scientific Research (CNRS), where he is a member of the European Center for Sociology and Political Science (CESSP), Paris. His publications deal with journalism, cinema, the welfare state and correspondence analysis. He has coedited *The Rouledge Companion to Bourdieu's* Distinction (with Philippe Coulangeon, Routledge, 2014) and, among other books and papers, he has published "Economic Journalism in France" (in Rodney Benson and Erick Neveu (eds), *Bourdieu and the Journalistic Field,* Polity, 2005), "A heuristic tool (in Mathieu Hilgers and Eric Mangez (eds), *Bourdieu's Theory of Social Field*, Routledge, 2014), *Critique de la raison journalistique* (Le Seuil, 2004), "L'art du réalisme. Le champ du cinéma en France au début des années 2000" (*Actes de la recherché en sciences sociales*, n°161-162, 2006).

**Eberle, Thomas S.** is Professor Emeritus of Sociology and former Co-director of the Research Institute of Sociology at the University of St. Gallen, Switzerland. He also taught at several other universities. He served as president of the Swiss Sociological Association from 1998 to 2005 and as Vice-president of the European Sociological Association (ESA) from 2007 to 2011 and was a member of many national and international committees. He was a founding member as well as chair of the ESA-research networks 'Qualitative methods' and 'Sociology of Culture'. His major research areas are the sociology of culture and of communication, of knowledge and of organization, as well as interpretive sociology, phenomenological sociology, methodology, and qualitative methods.

**Edles, Laura D.**, Ph.D., is Professor of Sociology at California State University, Northridge. Her interests include culture, theory, religion, and race/ethnicity. She is the author of *Symbol and Ritual in the New Spain: The Transition to Democracy after Franco* (Cambridge University Press, 1998); *Cultural Sociology in Practice* (Blackwell Publishers, 2002); and co-author of *Sociological Theory in the Classical Era* (Sage, 2004/2009/2015), *Sociological Theory in the Contemporary Era* (Sage, 2006/2010/2015), and *Classical and Contemporary Sociological Theory* (Sage, 2007/2011/2016).

**Farkhatdinov, Nail** is Senior Research Fellow of the Center for Fundamental Sociology at the National Research University Higher School of Economics, Russia. He was awarded PhD from the University of Aberdeen, UK. His doctoral thesis was focused on the analysis of contemporary art experience from cultural sociological perspective driven by video-based ethnographic methodology. His main research interests include social aspects of aesthetic experience, the impact of digital technologies upon art worlds, application of qualitative methodologies to the study of arts and culture. He is an author of publications in sociology of the arts and cultural sociology in Russian and English. He is also a visiting lecturer in Sociology of Arts at the Moscow School of Social and Economic Sciences (Manchester University). From 2015 he is a member of editorial board of an international academic journal Russian Sociological Review.

**Heise, Tatiana Signorelli** is Lecturer in the University of Glasgow's School of Modern Languages and Cultures, where she teaches on Latin American Cinema and Film and Television courses. She is the author of *Remaking Brazil: Contested National Identities in Contemporary Brazilian Cinema* and she has published on various aspects of Latin American cinema and documentary activism. Her current research focuses on post-dictatorship cinemas.

**Houtman, Dick** is Professor of Sociology of Culture and Religion at the Centre for Sociological Research (CeSO), University of Leuven, Belgium. His principal research interest is cultural change in the West since the 1960s. Most of his publications address the spiritual turn in the religious realm and the emergence and maturation of a new political culture and its profound electoral consequences. His most recent books are *Things: Religion and the Question of Materiality* (edited with Birgit Meyer, 2012), *Farewell to the Leftist Working Class* (with Peter Achterberg & Anton Derks, second edition 2012), *Paradoxes of Individualization: Social Control and Social Conflict in Contemporary Modernity* (with Stef Aupers & Willem de Koster, 2011), *Religions of Modernity: Relocating the Sacred to the Self and the Digital* (edited with Stef Aupers, 2010), and *Class and Politics in Contemporary Social Science: 'Marxism Lite' and Its Blind Spot for Culture* (second edition 2009).

**Hughson, John** is Professor of Sport and Cultural Studies at the University of Central Lancashire. He is the author of *England and the 1966 World Cup: A Cultural History* (Manchester University Press, 2016) and *The Making of Sporting Cultures* (Routledge, 2009). He is the principal author of *The Uses of Sport: A Critical Study* (Routledge 2005) and co-author of *Confronting Culture: Sociological Vistas* (Polity 2003). Hughson is the co-editor of *The Sociology of Art: Ways of Seeing* (Palgrave 2005) and *Sport in the City: Cultural Connections* (Routledge, 2011). He is a member of the editorial boards for the academic journals *Cultural Sociology* (Sage) and *Ethnography* (Sage).

**Hurdley, Rachel** is Senior Research Fellow in the College of Arts, Humanities and Social Sciences. Her research explores how everyday interactions, small things and ephemeral practices organize meaning. She has examined how workplaces and homes organize and are organized to produce cultures of belonging and identity. In parallel social worlds, people without those resources practise ephemeral homes and intimacies, calling into question dominant theories of culture and personhood. Research sites include mantelpieces, corridors, sofas, office desks, pin boards, drawings and the few remaining smokers' corners. She is currently making a Cabinet of Curiosity, to collect those inside and outside academia with an interest in materiality, from dust, lists and pencils to screens, stories and rust. In her real life, she keeps hens and plays mind games with three collie dogs.

**Jacobs, Ronald N.** is Professor of Sociology at the University at Albany, State University of New York. He is a cultural sociologist who studies media, politics, and civil society. His most recent books include *The Space of Opinion* and *The Oxford Handbook of Cultural Sociology*. He is co-editor of the *American Journal of Cultural Sociology*.

**Johnston, Hank** is Professor of Sociology at San Diego State University. His research focuses on protest performance in different state systems, cognitive/interpretative dimensions of collective action, and the cultural analysis of mobilization processes. He is founding editor and publisher of *Mobilization: An International Quarterly,* the leading journal of research on protest and social movements. He edits the *Mobilization* Series on Protest, Social Movements, and Culture with Ashgate Publishers. Recently he has published *What is a Social Movement* (Polity 2014), *States and Social Movements* (Polity 2012), *Violent Protest in the Neoliberal State,* (with Seraphim Sepheriades, Ashgate 2011), and *Culture, Social Movements, and Protest* (Ashgate, 2009).

**Jones, Paul K.** is Associate Professor of Sociology at the Australian National University. He is the author of *Raymond Williams's Sociology of Culture: a critical reconstruction* (Palgrave, 2004), lead author of *Key Concepts in Media and Communications* (Sage, 2011) and author of numerous articles in cultural sociology and related fields. He is a member of the editorial board of *Cultural Sociology*. He is currently working on a sociological reframing of approaches to populism, demagogy and cultural populism.

**Jones, Paul** is a Senior Lecturer in Sociology at the University of Liverpool. His research centres on the political economy of the urban; recently this has included studies of architecture and the built environment, digital models, regeneration photography, and – with Michael Mair – the Private Finance Initiative, supermarkets, and state reform.

**Kosut, Mary** is an Associate Professor of Sociology, Media Society & the Arts, and Gender Studies at Purchase College, State University of New York. She is co-author of *Buzz: Urban Beekeeping and the Power of the Bee* (New York University Press, 2013), editor of *The Encyclopedia of Gender in Media* (Sage, 2012) and co-author of *The Body Reader: Essential Social and Cultural Readings* (New York University Press, 2010). Her work has recently appeared in *Ethnography, Cultural Sociology, Humanimalia, Visual Studies,* and *Cabinet Magazine*. She lives in New York City and is co-founder of GCA, an art exhibition space in Bushwick, Brooklyn.

**Laermans, Rudi** is Professor of Sociological Theory at the Faculty of Social Sciences of KU Leuven/University of Leuven, Belgium. His research and publications are situated within the domains of social theory, cultural policy and the sociology of arts. In 1999, he published in Dutch an introduction to sociology from a Luhmannian point of view (*Communicatie zonder mensen* ('Communication without people') Amsterdam: Boom), which was followed in 2012 by a more general introduction (*De maatschappij van de sociologie* ('The society of sociology'). Amsterdam: Boom). In 2015 appeared his study of contemporary dance, *Moving Together: Theorizing and Making Contemporary Dance* (Amsterdam: Valiz).

**Loader, Colin** is professor emeritus of history at the University of Nevada, Las Vegas. Among his books and articles on the history of German sociology are *The Intellectual Development of Karl Mannheim, Karl Mannheim's Sociology as Political Education* (with David Kettler), and *Alfred Weber and the Crisis of Culture, 1890-1933*.

**Mukerji, Chandra** is Distinguished Professor Emeritus of Communication and Science Studies at the University of California, San Diego. Her publications include From Graven Images, Rethinking Popular Culture (with Michael Schudson). Territorial Ambitions and the Gardens of Versailles, and Impossible Engineering.

**Roberge, Jonathan** is an Assistant Professor at the Centre Urbanisation Culture Société of the Institut National de la Recherche Scientifique in Quebec City, Canada. The director of the Canadian Research Chair on New Digital Environments (NENIC lab), he is also a Faculty Fellow at the Center for Cultural Sociology (Yale University). He has written extensively on hermeneutics in established periodicals, among which are Thesis Eleven and Social Semiotics. Recently, he gave interviews for major media outlets on topics related to culture and technology such as the increasing presence of algorithms, bits and codes in the circulation of meaningful artifacts.

**Santoro, Marco** is associate professor of Sociology at the Department of Philosophy and Communication of the University of Bologna. He works on the sociology and history of intellectuals, on cultural production and consumption, and on the political dimensions of mafias.

**Sapiro, Gisèle** is Professor of sociology at the Ecole des Hautes Etudes en Sciences Sociales and Research director at the CNRS (Centre européen de sociologie et de science politique, Labex Tepsis). She is a member of Academia Europaea. Her interests include the sociology of intellectuals, of literature, of translation and of world literature, as well as the history and the epistemology of the Social Sciences and the Humanities. The author of *La Guerre des écrivains, 1940–1953* (1999; English: *French Writers' War*, 2014), *La Responsabilité de l'écrivain* (2011) and *La Sociologie de la littérature* (2014), She has also (co)edited *Pour une histoire des sciences sociales* (2004), *Pierre Bourdieu, sociologue* (2004), *Translatio* (2008), *Les Contradictions de la globalisation éditoriale* (2009), *L'Espace intellectuel en Europe* (2009), *Traduire la littérature et les sciences humaines* (2012), *Sciences humaines en traduction* (2014, online). She is editing the *Dictionnaire international Pierre Bourdieu* (forthcoming).

**Silber, Ilana F.** is Associate Professor in the Department of Sociology and Anthropology at Bar-Ilan University, Israel. Her major fields of interest are sociological theory, the sociology of culture, religion, gift-giving and philanthropy, to which she also brings a cross cutting engagement with comparative historical and interpretative cultural analysis. Related publications include: (2014) 'Boltanski and the Gift: Beyond Love, Beyond Suspicion…?' in S. Susen and B. Turner ed. *Boltanski*. London, New York: Anthem, 2014; 'Emotions as Regime of Justification? The Case of Philanthropic Civic Anger', *European Journal of Social Theory* 14, 2 (2011): 301-320; 'Towards a Non-Unitary Approach to Sociological Theory', *European Journal of Social Theory* 10, 2 (2007): 220-232; 'Bourdieu's Gift to Gift Theory: An Unacknowledged Trajectory,' *Sociological Theory* 27, 2 (2009): 173-190; 'Pragmatic Sociology as Cultural Sociology: Beyond Repertoire Theory?' *European Journal of Social Theory* 6, 4 (2003) : 425-447.

**Stevenson, Nick** is a Reader in Cultural Sociology at the University of Nottingham. He is the author of *Culture, Ideology and Socialism* (Avebury, 1995), *Understanding Media Cultures* (Sage, 1995), *The Transformation of the Media* (Longman, 1999), *Making Sense of Men's Lifestyle Magazines* (along with Kate Brooks and Peter Jackson (Polity, 2001), *Culture and Citizenship* (Sage, 2001), *Cultural Citizenship* (Sage, 2003), *David Bowie* (Polity, 2006), *Education and Cultural Citizenship* (Sage, 2009), *Freedom* (Routledge, 2011). He is currently working on a book on human rights and culture.

**Stewart, Janet** is Professor in Visual Culture and German at Durham University, where she was founding Director of the Centre for Visual Arts and Culture. She is the author of two monographs, *Fashioning Vienna: Adolf Loos's Cultural Criticism* (2000) and *Public Speaking in the City* (2009) and has published widely on Austrian and German literature and visual culture, cultural sociology and urban history. Her current research project, Curating Europe's Oil, develops her interests in modernity and visual culture in a new context, connecting them to the study of energy.

**Tudor, Andrew** is Professor Emeritus in the Department of Theatre, Film & Television of the University of York, where he was formerly Professor of Sociology. He has published widely on the sociology of film and in cultural studies, including *Theories of Film, Image and Influence: Studies in the Sociology of Film, Monsters and Mad Scientists: a Cultural History of the Horror Movie* and *Decoding Culture: Theory and Method in Cultural Studies*. His current interests are in the application of Bourdieu's field theory to the cinema.

**Varul, Matthias** is an independent Cultural Sociologist and Social Theorist who focuses on the moral and religious implications and dimensions of capitalist practices of production, exchange and consumption. He is particularly interested in gauging the potential of consumer cultures for dialectical transcendences of capitalism, both utopian and dystopian.

**West, Brad** is an Associate Professor in the School of Communication, International Studies and Languages at the University of South Australia. Working mainly from a cultural sociological perspective his research focuses on the interrelationship between ritual and collective memory. He is the author of *Re-enchanting Nationalisms* (2015, Springer) which outlines the power of new commemorative forms to reimagine national identity in culturally relevant ways and foster political and institutional change.

**Wherry, Frederick F.** is Professor of Sociology and Co-Director of the Center for Cultural Sociology, Yale University.

**Woods, Eric Taylor** is Senior Lecturer (Associate Professor) in Sociology at the University of East London. His research encompasses cultural, historical and political sociology, with particular interest in nationalism, colonialism, reconciliation and religion. His recent books include: A Cultural Sociology of Anglican Mission and the Indian Residential Schools in Canada: The Long Road to Apology (Palgrave, 2016); The Cultural Politics of Nationalism and Nation-building: Ritual and Performance in the Forging of Nations (Routledge, 2014); and Nationalism and Conflict Management (Routledge, 2012).

**Wright, David** teaches in the Centre for Cultural Policy Studies at the University of Warwick. His research interests are in popular culture, cultural policy, cultural work and the politics of cultural participation. His most recent book is *Understanding Cultural Taste* (Palgrave, 2015).

# Acknowledgements

We wish to thank all the contributors to this volume for producing what we feel are consistently excellent summaries and analyses of the major domains of sociology's confrontation with cultural matters. We also extend our deep appreciation to various colleagues at SAGE who have made the production process such a smooth one – these include Judi Burger and Matthew Oldfield and various others. Each of the editors would also like to thank the other in a manner that avoids mutual self-congratulation. Finally, sincere gratitude is owed to the Ts and Bs for their never-ending support.

# Introduction: Culture/Sociology/ Sociology of Culture/ Cultural Sociology

David Inglis

The field of cultural sociology has blossomed remarkably over the last several decades. Concerns with 'culture', and analytical orientations which foreground cultural matters in their analysis of human social life, have gone from being relatively marginalised in the discipline of sociology, to enjoying in recent years an importance and centrality that would probably have been unthinkable a few decades previously. If at certain times and places in the past sociology was thought to be primarily the study of 'society', or the 'social' dimensions of human life, while it was anthropology that took 'culture' as its central focus, today no one could plausibly claim that sociology was not profoundly oriented towards both the social and cultural elements of human existence. Nor could they convincingly say that specifically 'cultural' approaches to such matters, which seek to complement or go beyond older analytic traditions in sociology, are any longer peripheral within the discipline. Cultural sociology is now a field of sociology that exhibits the vibrancy, multiplicity and lively fractiousness that characterise an intellectual domain constantly growing and mostly in good health.

Within the intellectual terrain this Handbook covers, there are disputes as to whether we are dealing more with 'cultural sociology' or 'sociology of culture', a terminological division explained in more detail below. For the purposes of non-sectarian balance and comprehensiveness, we have included here chapters on material that falls more obviously under one heading or the other. Nonetheless, if we use the phrase 'cultural sociology' in a broad way, to encompass all types of sociological engagements with culture, the field can be characterised in various different ways as follows.

One can depict it simply as a sub-field within sociology. One can understand it as a challenge to what are conceived by its proponents as older, more staid and conventional forms of sociology, and thus as a set of mechanisms for rejuvenating existing fields of study, creating new problems, research questions and methods of analysis (for example, in the sociology of religion – see Chapter 26; also in general, Back et al., 2012). One can view it as a privileged meeting-point between different sociological sub-fields, where, for example, political sociology and historical sociology meet in novel and productive ways (Chapters 15, 30, 31; Friedland and Mohr, 2004). One can think about it as a location where social scientific foci and methods particularly meet and meld with ideas from the humanities. One can praise its success in learning from, or lament its failure to engage fully with, neighbouring intellectual fields like cultural studies (Chapter 22), visual studies (Chapter 23) and gender studies (Chapter 24) (Wolff, 1999).

One can view its undoubtedly multiplicitous and diverse nature as a great strength, and as testament to a vital proliferation of intellectual energies, or conversely as a notable weakness, where different sorts of people, all apparently talking about 'culture', in fact lack a common language and thus talk past each other. One can criticise it as particularly prey to passing intellectual fashions and fads (Patterson, 2014). One can accuse it of relative superficiality vis-à-vis other types and domains of sociology and of being sometimes methodologically suspect (Rojek and Turner, 2000).

One can regard it not as a coherent intellectual field at all, but rather as a loosely bounded site of messy combat between rival sociological paradigms and orientations. One can praise it as a cosmopolitan space of transnational discursive interchange, or as sadly bound by the parochial concerns of each of the national sociological spaces within which cultural sociology is practised. One can regard it as too closely reflecting the typical concerns and institutional structures of each national sociological field. One can write it off as a primarily American and British set of concerns and orientations (each of these national fields being quite different from the other), which have problematic relationships with other sites of sociological and extra-sociological knowledge production around the world.

In sum, there is absolutely no uncontroversial consensus view as to what cultural sociology is, what it does or what its benefits and disadvantages may be, either to wider sociology or to the sum of human (self-)understanding.

Nonetheless, sociology tells us that usually in the midst of apparent chaos there are in fact certain discernible patterns and recurring motifs. So although cultural sociology can be construed as 'a field that embraces everything from the application of theories of narrative to the study of social movements through to ethnographic studies of youth subcultures' (de la Fuente, 2007: 123), and may seem to involve anything and everything, there are still clear patterns to be identified. This applies both at the level of the epistemological foundations of the field, and of the various institutional bases within which it operates (and sometimes helps transform). This book is both a depiction of those patterns, epistemological and institutional, and also an attempt to map many of the most important, productive and telling contributions to the field.

It is testament to the burgeoning popularity since the 1970s of studying 'culture' in some social scientific manner or another, that it has become an apparently endlessly repeated cliché both to note that 'culture' is an exceptionally polysemic and complex word, which appears in 19th-century Europe for specific socio-historical reasons, and also to invoke Raymond Williams' (1976) classic statement on such matters. As what 'culture' means varies – either modestly or hugely – from one linguistic or organisational context to another, then obviously what counts as 'cultural sociology' will also vary across settings.

This is certainly the case in terms of variance between different national contexts of sociological production. Obviously whether something called 'cultural sociology' exists in a particular national setting or not, and the degree to which it thrives or struggles, depends on both the long-term intellectual history of that environment, and past and current institutional arrangements (e.g. see for Japan, Satō (2013); for Germany, Göttlich (2013)).

'Cultural sociology' in the UK is in many ways very different from that in the US. Much of sociology as a whole in the UK today is concerned with discernibly cultural matters, even if many practitioners would not describe themselves as cultural sociologists or sociologists of culture. This is in part due to the strong, if uneven and contested, influence in certain sectors of the sociology of European Marxist theory and its inflection by the Birmingham School of cultural studies (Chapter 22). The 'cultural turn' of the 1980s – involving increasing scholarly interest in both the symbolic and affective aspects of human agency and identities, and post-structuralist and post-modernist philosophical and literary theorisations of these – was particularly strong in UK sociology (Chaney, 2002). This led both to a widespread 'culturalisation' of sociological thinking and practice in the 1990s, to the extent that in Britain one could argue that 'cultural sociology' refers to major swathes of sociology per se, rather than to a defined sub-field as such. It also involves the reworking in more explicitly 'cultural' directions of existing areas of study, notably social class analysis, which took on a strongly Bourdieu-inspired hue in the 1990s (for Bourdieu, see Chapters 7, 18, 41).

By contrast, in the US both 'cultural sociology' and the 'sociology of culture' exist more as defined sub-fields, which exist in complex relationships with other sociological sub-fields and the discipline more broadly. The story of these sub-fields is usually narrated by participants in one of two ways, and that is to a significant extent dependent on whether a particular author self-identifies as a 'cultural sociologist' or 'sociologist of culture'. A thumbnail sketch would depict 'sociology of culture' as encompassing epistemological and methodological orientations for the most part drawing from, and comfortable with, the customary ways of thinking and doing in 'mainstream' sociology, applying these to what seem like explicitly 'cultural' subjects and domains. The epitome of US 'sociology of culture' is the 'production of culture' school, which since the 1970s has applied ideas drawn from the sociologies of work and organisations to cultural industries, often using the quantitative methods favoured in recent American sociology (Chapter 14).

From the point of view of sociologists of culture, their sub-field has gone from a situation of marginalisation to prominence in US sociology over the last four decades (Crane, 1994). Conversely, 'cultural sociologists' are more likely to regard their brand of cultural sociology as a movement different from, and often formulated in critique of, and in resistance against, both 'sociology of culture' and the mainstream American sociology that lies beyond it. Self-identifying 'cultural sociologists' tend to regard the specifically American version of the 'cultural turn' in the social sciences as having both created a set of new methodological possibilities (Bonnell and Hunt, 1999), and made cultural sociology possible as 'an important and intellectually rich subfield in a discipline in which "culture" had not been a founding concept and had relatively little history of explicit theoretical and empirical development' (Jacobs and Spillman, 2005: 2).

The most forceful expression of 'cultural sociology' as critique of both 'sociology of culture' and mainstream sociology is the Yale School, involving Jeffrey C. Alexander and his associates, and their 'strong program' of neo-Durkheimian sociology. This strongly rejects what it sees as the unacceptable reduction of culture to social structural and organisational factors in 'sociology of culture' paradigms and mainstream American sociology, and instead insists on the relatively autonomous power of cultural forms to shape social life (see Chapter 5).

To the uninitiated, the terms 'cultural sociology', 'sociology of culture' and 'cultural studies' may seem like innocuous labels describing much the same things, but they are in fact terms used for often highly polemical processes of academic differentiation and labelling, of self and of others. Such disputes help to constitute and reproduce the entire set of relations involving all of those who believe themselves to be involved in one sort of sociological analysis of culture or another. But the labels mean different things in different places or may even be meaningless, as Heinich (2010) implies for the French situation, where the term 'sociology of art' seems far more pertinent in describing what scholars actually do, and think of themselves as doing, than allegedly ethnocentric Anglo-American terms like 'cultural sociology'.

Conversely, it would be wrong to assert that such processes are organised only or mostly on national bases. The circulation of the themes and procedures pioneered by Bourdieu in the French context across many different national sociologies shows the capacity of ideas to travel across borders, even if they are then indigenised and reworked in light of more local needs (Robbins, 2008). In a certain sense, there is a 'British Bourdieu', an 'American Bourdieu, a 'German Bourdieu', and so on, and often more than one appropriation of his work within particular national sociologies, as well as subsequent appropriations of each of these in other contexts – the taking-up of British understandings of Bourdieu in Australia being a good case in point.

The works of other key thinkers, which have become what Crane (2010) calls 'free-floating paradigms' that act as central intellectual reference points for scholars in many different geographical and institutional locations, include the writings of structuralists and post-structuralists like Lévi-Strauss, Barthes, Foucault, Lyotard, Butler and Baudrillard; critical theorists like Adorno, Gramsci and Habermas; hermeneuticians like Geertz; Science and Technology Studies figures like Latour and Haraway; and cultural studies figures like Raymond Williams. All of these figures are now canonised in an international intellectual terrain also drawn upon by humanities scholars, albeit in somewhat different ways from sociologists. More generally, one might add that the planetary diffusion, and concomitant reformulation, of cultural sociology is itself a cultural process worthy of reflexive self-analysis (Jacobs and Spillman, 2005).

The remarks above show that one important feature of 'cultural sociology' is that those who think that they are involved in the doing of it, are engaged in ongoing debates about what the term refers to, what 'culture' should be understood to mean, and what this means for developing and using appropriate modes of sociological investigation. 'Cultural sociology' is therefore a field both characterised by, and to a large extent generated and reproduced by, disputes between different schools of thought, and associated methodological orientations, as to what culture 'is' and how to study it, ranging from positivist approaches using large-scale quantitative methods, to interpretive readings of texts and ethnographic studies of small-scale groups (Goldfarb, 2005; de la Fuente, 2007). Disputes over the meaning of 'culture', and the ramifications of such definitions for sociological practice, are the life blood of the field, producing 'productive ambiguities' which generate further debate, controversy and (hopefully) intellectual innovation (Jacobs and Spillman, 2005).

Definitions of, and orientations towards studying culture are many and manifold in the field, but beneath the apparent chaos, certain broad patterns emerge when we consider the key fracture lines between different positions and schools of thought. These lines of fracture can be captured in seven sets of central questions, which animate both the field itself and this Handbook's representation of it:

1  *Questions concerning the term 'cultural sociology' (and 'sociology of culture'), and how people in the field understand it and themselves*

Is 'cultural sociology' the best term to describe the intellectual constellation we are dealing with? Is 'sociology of culture' a more accurate term, or one so negatively defined by self-identifying 'cultural sociologists' that it is now highly problematic? Are there more appropriate terms to use? (Certainly this is a field that above all involves disputes about how to name and describe itself.)

Should 'cultural sociology' be construed primarily as the study of what seem obviously 'cultural' domains of human activity, such as music (Chapters 28, 38), news media (Chapter 32), architecture (Chapter 34), cinema (Chapter 35), museums and art galleries (Chapter 36), fashion (Chapter 37)?

Should cultural sociology be regarded as a *special kind* of sociological perspective, foregrounding matters of discourse, symbolism, affect and so on, in analysing potentially *any* aspect of human existence? Is cultural sociology essentially an analytic perspective (or set of perspectives), rather than something defined by its 'cultural' subject matter and the substantive topics it studies?

2  *Questions about what 'culture' is*

What are we talking about when we speak of 'culture' – language, symbols, artefacts, values, beliefs, norms, practices, cognitive maps (Chapter 9), representations, symbolic boundaries (Chapter 25), discourses, repertoires…? All of these, or just some? How do we fit them together?

What should get counted as 'culture' and 'cultural', and what should not? Does it make sense to say that some things are 'less cultural' or 'more cultural' than others?

Is cultural sociology essentially centred on the analysis of human *meaning-making*, or something else (Spillman, 2002)?

Is 'culture' different from 'society' or the 'social'? If so, how and why? Or are they the same thing, and are they mutually embedded? Should we meld them together or separate them out?

Should 'culture' be seen as shaped by 'society' (e.g. social structures, institutional contexts, social networks, forms of power, etc.), or should causality be understood as running the other way, from 'culture' to 'society'?

Is culture a 'thing' in itself (a neo-Durkheimian position – see Chapter 5), or merely a word certain interested parties – including sociologists – impose onto a more complex reality (a position associated sometimes with Actor Network Theory – see Chapter 10)?

Is 'culture' one variable amongst others (e.g. the political, the economic), or is culture a constitutive element of *all* aspects and domains of human life?

Can we still speak of unitary 'cultures', within which all group members think and act in generally the same ways, or should we see culture rather as bundles of practices and cognitions (Chapter 9) enacted by individuals in everyday settings (Lizardo, 2011)?

Which metaphors should we use to describe what culture 'is' and does? Is culture best construed as a 'toolkit' upon which individuals selectively draw (Swidler, 2001)? Is it a series of 'culture structures' which exist beyond the consciousness of individuals and which profoundly underpin their actions (Chapter 5)? Is it something else again?

3  *Which intellectual sources and resources should scholars in the field draw upon?*

Which classical sociological authors and paradigms are still worth drawing upon today? Which classical analytical orientations – including Marxist (Chapter 2), Weberian (Chapter 3), Durkheimian (Chapter 5), Simmelian (Chapter 6) and Symbolic Interactionist (Chapter 8) streams, as well as the sociologies of culture proposed by Alfred Weber and Karl Mannheim (Chapter 4) – constitute living traditions today? And which of the classics are construable as analytic dead-ends, as some contemporary positions, like Actor Network Theory, like to allege (Chapter 10)?

Which streams in more recent sociological thinking and research – such as cognitive sociology (Chapter 9), neo-institutionalism (Chapter 11), the new French pragmatic school (Chapter 12), systems theory (Chapter 13), and theories of agency and practice (Chapter 28) – should cultural sociology draw upon and contribute to?

4  *Questions of disciplinarity*

How does culture relate to core sociological issues of individual and collective action and agency?

Can a focus on cultural matters help to overcome key problems of sociological thought, such as the structure/agency relationship?

How should one understand the relationships between culture and social power?

### 5  Questions of interdisciplinarity

What new things does cultural sociology tell us about, for example, economic phenomena and markets (Chapter 40), that other sorts of sociology and social science do not or cannot see?

Given that cultural sociology studies domains that other disciplines also examine – e.g. media (Chapter 32 – an area also investigated by communications and media studies) – how does cultural sociology relate to those disciplines, and what can it say that differs from their insights?

Given that there exists today a series of inter- and trans-disciplinary intellectual fields – such as Memory Studies (Chapter 33), Material Culture Studies (Chapter 39) and Science and Technology Studies (Chapter 10), what does cultural sociology contribute to them, and what does it productively take from them?

### 6  Questions of method and methodology

How can cultural sociology engage with macro-level (Chapter 11), meso-level and micro-levels (Chapter 8) of analysis?

Should one regard the most important analytic foci for cultural sociology as the *production*, *distribution* and *consumption* of culture, or are there better terms we can use to focus our attention (see Chapters 41, 42, 43; Griswold, 1987)?

Should cultural sociology be especially attuned to the analysis of the dynamics of everyday life, what would that involve both epistemologically and methodologically, and what insights has it or could it yield? (Chapter 27)

What are the most appropriate methodological strategies for cultural sociology in general, and for dealing with particular phenomena and research problems? Does cultural sociology need special methodologies and methods, given the allegedly special nature of its 'cultural' subject matter, or can it draw directly on existing techniques used in other areas of sociology? (See all the Chapters in Part II of the Handbook, covering both quantitative and qualitative possibilities.)

### 7  The extra-academic purposes of cultural sociology

Beyond its scholarly contributions, what does cultural sociology contribute to 'real-world' matters of politics and citizenship (Chapter 29), and how can it effectively intervene in particular socio-political domains and discourses?

As with any intellectual constellation, cultural sociology constantly demands, generates and faces the question *what comes next*? And the answer is provided by differing manifestoes and diagnoses which pinpoint what they define as the current pathologies of the field and the way to solve them. In a recent diagnosis of cultural sociology in the US, Patterson (2014) notes some problems that arguably apply to all national versions of cultural sociology at the present time: a tendency towards the production of agenda-setting proclamations which are overly dismissive of other positions and of earlier forms of analysis, and which unwisely seek to throw out perfectly serviceable concepts for the sake of fashion, and an over-emphasis on some issues and the partial or complete omission of others. One could add to this list of woes the quite noticeable parochialism of nationally-based cultural sociologies, where scholars often fail to engage with relevant work produced in other countries (US sociology arguably being a particularly striking culprit in this regard). One can also note here the industrial (over-)production of orthodox types of analysis, which keep reproducing standard ways of thinking without any clear indication of conceptual innovation. The 'Bourdieu industry' which has sprung up in UK, US, Canadian, Australian, Nordic and Netherlands sociologies over the last few decades is now at a point where there may seem little more to be usefully added about class, consumption and alleged omnivorousness in tastes (Chapter 41), because such matters have been so exhaustively documented and debated already in a wide and apparently ever expanding range of national contexts. But the industry will trundle on for a good while yet, in part because it is so important in generating sociological careers.

It is natural enough that in a period where Bourdieu-inspired sociology is so dominant in many national cultural sociological (or perhaps more accurately, sociology of culture) fields, that some scholars should seek to overthrow that hegemony. If the field is to continue, these are necessary rebellions and attempted revolutions, of the kind Bourdieu himself analysed so acutely in particular cultural fields. But current attempts posthumously to dethrone Bourdieu – which are particularly to be found in British cultural sociology today – also bring the risk of throwing out various babies with the bathwater.

Perhaps the most-cited figures in cultural sociological circles across the world are Bourdieu and Howard S. Becker, the former known for his work on fields of cultural production and means of cultural consumption, and the latter famous for analyses of the 'art world'. Although strongly critical of each other, they are now put together by some critics as exemplifying all that is wrong about a sociological understanding of culture which fails to grasp the latter's distinctive aesthetic properties and the 'affordances' by which cultural objects can 'make a difference' in social life, either by assisting human agency or through their own capacities to act. Such themes can be found in the contemporary works of action theorists like DeNora (Chapter 28) and Actor-Network Theorists such as Hennion (Chapter 10). For DeNora, what needs to happen now is a move away from a conventional sociology *of* music towards a sociology *with* music which does not ignore music's 'discursive and material powers'. A 'new sociology of art' (and by implication, 'culture' more broadly – de la Fuente, 2007) has appeared over the last decade or so, and aims to show how people use cultural objects, and how these in turn affect people and make possible particular forms of practice. This resonates with claims that it is no longer good enough to try to connect the 'social' and 'aesthetic' domains of human activity, because to use such terms already implies the primacy of a possibly mythical realm of 'the social' over aesthetics and meaning. Cultural forms must now be seen as much more than just a proxy of the supposedly determining 'social' realm.

While in their own ways in the 1960s and 1970s Bourdieu and Becker aimed to 'demystify' the role of art and culture in social life, today's critics argue that their analytic orientations destroy what is actually specifically 'cultural' about culture, namely the aesthetic and agential specificities of cultural objects, and the possibility that aesthetic value is more than a hidden expression of social power relations (Born, 2010). Many contemporary critics draw upon the work of a newly-consecrated intellectual authority figure, namely the Actor-Network theorist Bruno Latour (see Chapter 10), who dismisses the previous generation of critical sociologies of culture:

> Apart from religion, no other domain has been more bulldozed to death by critical sociology than the sociology of art. Every sculpture, painting, *haute cuisine* dish, techno rave, and novel has been explained to nothingness by the social factors 'hidden behind' them. (2005: 236)

But there are several problems associated with these contemporary turns towards 'aesthetics' and 'objects'. In the first place, as the sociologist of art Janet Wolff (2008) notes, while it may well be a laudable enterprise to seek to construct a new kind of 'sociological aesthetics' which does not reduce – as Bourdieu, Becker and the 'production of culture school' allegedly do – the aesthetic elements of objects simply to considerations of power and social structure, it is very easy for this project inadvertently to revert back to false aesthetic universalisms that sociologists very effectively pulled apart a generation ago. The challenge is to build upon the achievements of one's predecessors, while acknowledging the inevitable flaws in their thinking, while also not relinquishing in fits of over-enthusiasm the better, and most likely invaluable, elements of their analytic procedures. Likewise, a focus on the powers of cultural objects and on the alleged efficaciousness of human agency beyond social-structural constraints, not only runs the risk of in the near future looking rather faddish, being beholden to the current fashion for Actor-Network Theory in certain circles, but it also potentially means obscuring or ignoring altogether understanding of the sorts of power relations which in their own different ways Bourdieu and Becker were so effective at discerning.

Current attempts to find some sort of middle path between the older approaches and the newer, and between considerations of power and social structure on the one side, and forms of agency on the other, seem sensible but as yet inchoate and conceptually under-developed (Prior 2011; Schwarz, 2013). This question then should be posed: what will a post-Bourdieu terrain of cultural sociology look like, when it seems that wholly to ditch Bourdieusian concerns would be unwise? After all, Bourdieu did not have an exclusive patent on central sociological issues of class, power and inequality, as some of his critics rather perversely seem to imply. Can there in fact be a truly *post-Bourdieu* cultural sociology at the present time and in the near future? Of all the major thinkers of the (recent) past, Bourdieu's influence will remain most unavoidable for many years to come. What the future of cultural sociology might look like after Bourdieu's influence has definitively waned might possibly be more effectively guessed at after one has read all of the richly diverse materials that we have sought to present together in this book.

## REFERENCES

Back, L. et al. (2012) *Cultural Sociology: An Introduction*. Oxford: Wiley-Blackwell.

Bonnell, V.E. and Hunt, L. (1999) *Beyond the Cultural Turn*. Los Angeles: University of California Press.

Born, G. (2010) 'The Social and the Aesthetic: For a Post-Bourdieuian Theory of Cultural Production', *Cultural Sociology*, 4(2): 171–208.

Chaney, D. (2002) *The Cultural Turn*. London: Routledge.

Crane, D. (1994) 'Introduction: The Challenge of the Sociology of Culture to Sociology as a Discipline', in D. Crane (ed.), *The Sociology of Culture: Emerging Theoretical Perspectives*. Oxford: Blackwell. pp. 1–20.

Crane, D. (2010) 'Cultural Sociology and Other Disciplines: Interdisciplinarity in the Cultural Sciences', *Sociology Compass*, 4(3): 169–79.

de la Fuente, E. (2007) 'The Place of Culture in Sociology: Romanticism and Debates about the "Cultural Turn"', *Journal of Sociology*, 43(2): 115–30.

Friedland, R. and Mohr, J. (eds) (2004) *Matters of Culture: Cultural Sociology in Practice*. Cambridge: Cambridge University Press.

Goldfarb, J.C. (2005) 'Dialogues, Culture, Critique: The Sociology of Culture and the New Sociological Imagination', *International Journal of Politics, Culture and Society*, 18: 281–92.

Göttlich, U. (2013) 'Cultural Studies and Sociology of Culture in Germany: Relations and Interrelations', *Culture Unbound*, 5: 33–41.

Griswold, W. (1987) 'A Methodological Framework for the Sociology of Culture', *Sociological Methodology*, 17: 1–35.

Heinich, N. (2010) 'What Does "Sociology of Culture" Mean? Notes on a Few Trans-Cultural Misunderstandings', *Cultural Sociology*, 4(2): 257–65.

Jacobs, M.D. and Spillman, L. (2005) 'Cultural Sociology at the Crossroads of the Discipline', *Poetics*, 33(1): 1–14.

Latour, B. (2005) *Reassembling the Social: An Introduction to Actor-Network Theory*. Oxford: Oxford University Press.

Lizardo, O. (2011) 'Pierre Bourdieu as a Post-Cultural Theorist', *Cultural Sociology*, 5(1): 1–22.

Patterson, O. (2014) 'Making Sense of Culture', *Annual Review of Sociology*, 40(1): 1–30.

Prior, N. (2011) 'Critique and Renewal in the Sociology of Music: Bourdieu and Beyond', *Cultural Sociology*, 5(1): 121–38.

Robbins, D. (2008) 'French Production and English Reception: The International Transfer of the Work of Pierre Bourdieu', *Sociologica*, 2: doi: 10.2383/27720.

Rojek, C. and Turner, B.S. (2000) '*Decorative Sociology*: Towards a Critique of the Cultural Turn', *The Sociological Review*, 48(4): 629–48.

Satō, K. (2013) 'Sociology of Culture in Transition', *International Journal of Japanese Sociology*, 22: 32–40.

Schwarz, O. (2013) 'Bending Forward, One Step Backward: On the Sociology of Tasting Techniques', *Cultural Sociology*, 7(4) 415–30.

Spillman, L. (2002) 'Introduction: Culture and Cultural Sociology', in L. Spillman (ed.), *Cultural Sociology*. Oxford: Blackwell. pp. 1–15.

Swidler, A. (2001) *Talk of Love: How Culture Matters*. Chicago: University of Chicago Press.

Williams, R. (1976) *Keywords*. London: Croom Helm.

Wolff, J. (1999) 'Cultural Studies and the Sociology of Culture', *Contemporary Sociology*, 28(5): 499–507.

Wolff, J. (2008) *The Aesthetics of Uncertainty*. New York: Columbia University Press.

PART I
# Schools of Thought

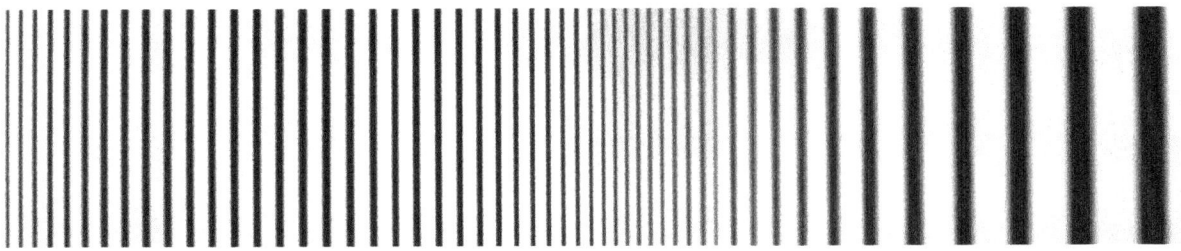

# Marxist Cultural Sociology

Paul K. Jones

## INTRODUCTION: MAPPING MARXISMS

How one maps the legacies of Marxian thought has been a core issue in the very formation of some, if not all, versions of cultural sociology. The act of mapping/defining usually plays a significant role in the approach being advocated.

Perhaps the readiest negative stereotypypical mapping would center on a Marxism understood as a preoccupation with economistic or interest-driven concerns at the expense of a separate and distinct 'culture'. From this point of view, Marxist cultural sociology amounts to little more than a simplistic reading of Marx's famous base and superstructure metaphor whereby all matters cultural (and 'ideological') are functionally dependent on an 'economic' determinant in the same way that a building's superstructure is dependent on its foundational infrastructure, its base (Marx, 1950). The shorthand for this failing varies: economism, reductivism, reflectionism, 'vulgar Marxism', but, following Márkus (1995), I will use 'functional causality' to characterize this real, but not at all universal, Marxian tendency.

A more prominent critique moves from the assumption that any Marxian sociological position is necessarily also a Leninist or even Stalinist political one. Unusually amongst the theoretical traditions under examination in this volume, 'Marxism' (usually Marxism-Leninism) assumed the status of state orthodoxy in multiple nation-states. These states were almost always authoritarian and prevailed for more than half the 20th century, most notably during the Cold War (c.1947–1991), but also, depending on one's definition, from the 1920s to the present. The subordination of aesthetico-cultural innovation in the name of 'the party' has thus become a paradigmatic case of the subordination of intellectual autonomy to instrumental political purposes – its best known shorthand expletive is 'Stalinist!'. Indeed without this heavy burden of 'orthodox Marxism', the negative stereotype of 'base and superstructure' would likely be less prominent.[1]

Thus the past and present role of 'Marxism' in cultural sociology depends very much on how generations of intellectuals dealt with the model of 'the vanguard party' and alternatives to it.

*Inside* societies where the party had attained state power, there was plainly the dilemma of whether to aid the party-state or not. Either course, it eventuated, risked becoming disaffected by the loss of intellectual freedom.

*Outside* those societies the initial problem for many Marxian intellectuals arose as one of explaining revolutionary failure in the West. The proletariat had neither risen up as expected nor succeeded in the uprisings that had occurred, most notably in Germany. This was perceived as a problem of (class) 'consciousness' and thus questions of culture rose to the fore as an explanatory analogue in understanding such processes of consciousness (Anderson 1976). As the failure and horrific severity of state-party authoritarianism became widely understood (and accepted as such), alternatives to the vanguard party were sought by Marxist intellectuals, especially in the West. Many attempted 'de-Stalinization' in countries like France and Italy, which had large and electorally significant communist parties, but many too abandoned the vanguard party model completely and embraced other critical intellectual roles. The modernist aesthetic avant-gardes' practice of leading by example rather than fiat, explicitly entertained by Adorno as early as 1936, was frequently an inspiration (Buck-Morss, 1977, 41).

Each of these options was entwined with intellectual reassessments of the 'revolutionary class character' of the proletariat and, for many in later years, the increasing attractions of 'new social movements' from the 1960s as preferred or additional agents of progressive transformation.

Again the question of culture came to the fore in the context of such rising rights and identity-based social movements. Amidst all this, Marxist intellectuals in East and West who had expertise in aesthetic matters, which often took the form of a sociology of art/culture, found their work valued for more than its immediate aesthetic specificity.

The Frankfurt School, initially conceived as an intellectual project working in liaison to some degree with the German labor movement, came to play a pioneering role on many of these fronts (Jay, 1996; Wiggershaus, 1995). Its best known 'first generation' included Theodor Adorno, Max Horkheimer, Herbert Marcuse, Leo Lowenthal and, by association, Walter Benjamin. Their expertise in sociology, aesthetics and philosophy, and their situation during the Nazi period as US-based intellectual refugees from fascism, placed them in an unusually strong position to articulate 'a Marx minus the proletariat' (Buck-Morss, 1977) or indeed minus the vanguard party. For complex reasons, including their reluctance at times to publish in languages other than German, the school's influence was not as widespread as its pioneering developments might at first suggest. Only with leading 'second generation' critical theorist, Jürgen Habermas, did rapid translation of their work from German become routine.

This chapter will track these normative tensions and their legacies for cultural sociology. It is also partly framed as a gentle corrective to the polemical characterizations of 'cultural Marxism' in the manifestos of the Strong Program (SP) in US cultural sociology. Thus the chapter surveys: debates about Marx's own work, key features of 'Western Marxism' including the Russian debates over formalist poetics and their legacy, the tensions between Stuart Hall and Raymond Williams during the heyday of Birmingham cultural studies, the SP itself and a final sketch of indicative common ground between cultural sociology and 'cultural Marxism'.

## A CULTURALIST MARX AND THE RISE OF A WESTERN MARXIST SOCIOLOGY OF CULTURE

Beyond his own lifetime (1818–1883), Marx's writings were published episodically, initially under the direction of Engels (his frequent co-author) and the German Social Democratic Party, until the archive was sold to institutes in Moscow and London in 1938. The overall reception pattern, accentuated in non-German languages, was that Marx's political journalism and writings on political economy became known first and established his reputation. The role of communist parties was crucial in acting as another layer of editorial gatekeeping and distribution of Marx's work, often in the form of primers. For example, Raymond Williams' 'Marxism and Culture' chapter in his best known work, the 1958 *Culture and Society* (1990), relies almost entirely on texts by Marx he knew from his (former) communist party membership.[2]

Certainly in English translation, only in the late 1950s and 1960s did another, 'more cultural', Marx fully emerge: that associated with his earlier philosophical writings organized around the concept of alienation and his related reflections on the 'Young Hegelian' philosophers from whom he and Engels broke ranks in 1844–45 in order to declare their historical materialism (Marx, 1975; Marx and Engels, 1976). Despite the association of Marx with aesthetic modernism since the postmodernist surge of the 1980s (e.g. Berman, 1988), a powerful Romantic aesthetic, most likely the influence of Schiller, infused the early writings on alienation (Prawer, 1975). Philosophically, this Romantic norm turned on a model of labor in which subject and object – e.g. worker and product of worker's labor in a craft-like practice – formed a unity. Alienation was primarily defined as the opposite of this unity. In contrast to the dominant understanding of capitalism within the economic writings as 'objectively' exploitative, in this earlier work its subjectively alienating features are more evident.[3]

The arrival of these texts generated enormous scholarly debate which co-existed with the more political debates around party/movement described in the previous section. Much of course turned on the capacity to invoke the textual authority of Marx himself in advocating differing political positions. Leninist vanguardism was legitimated by a number of textual warrants but perhaps the most crucial was the use of Engels' invocation of Marxism as a 'science', understood as a positivist emulation of the natural sciences which so secured a related understanding of predictive certainty (Schwartz, 1995, 171). The party leadership could thus claim, in effect, to know the future and require obeisance accordingly.

While there are some such uses of 'science' in Marx's writings, most famously in the base and superstructure passage of 'The 1859 Preface' (Marx, 1950), the weight of the early work suggested a more nuanced role for Marx's practice of critique. Rather than being the founder of a 'new science', Marx emerged as an author whose critiques, while at times devastating 'unmaskings' of the interests he regarded as operative within the writings of those whom he opposed, nonetheless often demonstrated careful exegetical respect for those same positions. Marx's 'method' of critique began to resemble an emancipatory hermeneutics rather than a rigidly polemical predictive science (Benhabib, 1986); in German terms, it seemed more a cultural science (*kulturwissenschaften*) rather than a natural one (*naturwissenschaften*).

The Hungarian philosopher and cultural critic György Lukács is the foundational figure in most accounts of 'Western Marxism' and, during his lifetime, was one of the most respected Marxian writers on aesthetic matters in the world amongst both Marxian and non-Marxian scholars. He is also the key figure in fostering a 'culturalist' view of Marx.[4] Yet for most of his life Lukács was working in the East, in a Hungary ruled by the communist party where he intermittently played a significant, and much debated, role within that party, including its attempted transformation during the 1956 Hungarian revolution. In his development of the concept of reification in his major 1923 work, *History and Class Consciousness: Studies in Dialectics*, Lukács (1968) had to some degree 'anticipated' the early Marx's position on alienation. It is this work more than any other that established the parallelism between aesthetic matters and class consciousness in the Western Marxist tradition via the alienation problematic. It was a powerful influence on the early Frankfurt School.

Lukács's work is also associated with what became a key non-reductivist approach in Western Marxist sociologies of art: an historical sociology of aesthetic cultural forms, especially those of the novel (Lukács and Williams), drama (Goldmann and Williams) but also music (Adorno).[5] In effect, this approach equated 'genre' and 'form' but struggled to account for what Marx (1973b) had called, quite ahistorically, the 'eternal charms' of the 'classical forms' of Ancient Greece (e.g. the epic). Even when historicized as 'traditions', the temptation was to treat such cultural forms nonsociologically i.e. as having 'transcended' historical epochs (Márkus, 1995).

Lukács was committed to a realist aesthetic (as was the best known British Marxist sociologist of art, Raymond Williams).[6] The most influential aesthetic writings of the Frankfurt School, in contrast, were engaged with the implications of aesthetic modernist avant-gardes such as the Expressionists and Surrealists (Lunn, 1985). Yet it was from another avant-garde, the Futurists, that the most influential of 'formalisms' developed.

## FORMALISM, STRUCTURALISM AND ALTHUSSERIAN SCIENTISM

For a brief 'heroic' period after the 1917 Russian Revolution, an artistic renaissance of a kind flourished in which what is now known as the Russian Futurist aesthetic avant-garde entered an effective allegiance, along with constructivists and suprematists, with the Leninist vanguard. Rejecting neoclassicism and orthodox realism, its members achieved a modest but genuine realization of the avant-gardes' dream of the unification of art and life in which everyday life was transformed (Bronner, 2012: 107–118). Poster art for factories and other forms of public art, including early experimental uses of film, proliferated outside the galleries and museums. In a sense a new division of creative labor was attempted in which art as craft frequently rose to prominence in conjunction with post-representational (frequently Cubist) stylistic experimentation.

Although Russian Futurism had a strongly visual focus, the role of literature was also reworked with its sonic qualities given greater prominence (Pike, 1979). In keeping with the broader craft motif, the specifically literary use of language was increasingly considered a product of the deployment of specific linguistic *devices*. The Romantic normative ideal of craft-like practice was effectively rethought as a matter of achievable technique

(Jakobson, 1997). In literary criticism, or poetics, this emphasis on the determining role of formal linguistic properties, including sound, became fully theorized, drawing on the recent Saussurean revolution in linguistics, including its conception of a self-reproducing linguistic system.

Russian Formalism was thus born. Its leading theoretician was Roman Jakobson who left Moscow in 1920 for Prague and whose work became better known as part of the 'Prague Circle' from 1926. Perhaps the most elaborated application of Russian Formalism was found in Vladmir Propp's 1927 *Morphology of the Folktale* (Propp, 1968). Propp subjected his ethnographic records to a systemic model of functional action in which an orthodox notion of 'character' played no part but, instead, the constancy of folkloric narrative action predominated. Its narrative formula, based on the model of the sentence, became the basis of much subsequent formalist and structuralist 'narrative theory'.

The Formalists, and all the cultural innovators from that brief 'heroic' phase, came under increasing, and for many deadly, political pressure – especially following the rise of Stalin from the mid-1920s. The primary expectation was subordination of creative production to a party orthodoxy which required variants of 'proletarian culture' and 'socialist realism' in a dogmatic and propagandistic manner. Significantly, 'formalism' eventually became a key charge of counter-revolutionary activity used against artists, most infamously towards the composer Dmitri Shostakovitch (Mulcahy, 1984).

The Formalists were also challenged more sympathetically by a Marxian critique from 'the Bakhtin circle' (which included Medvedev and Vološinov). It called for an alternative: a *sociological poetics*. This critique recognized the Formalists' gains, which were explicitly regarded by Bakhtin and Medvedev (1985) as 'the theorization of Futurism'. However, the price of the Formalists' very precise delineatiion of 'specifity' had been a narrow technicism. Rather, the Bakhtin group argued, literature should be seen as one sign system within a Marxian semiology which recognized a socio-historical conception of signification. The Bakhtin Circle's path-breaking work, however, was to remain almost completely unknown for decades.

In 1960s France, one of the most powerful communist parties in Western Europe (until the 1990s), held considerable sway over intellectual life. The debates about Marx's early work coincided with the reception of Claude Lévi-Strauss's introduction of the methodological principles of Prague Circle Formalism into anthropology under the name 'structuralism'. Lévi-Strauss declared this a contribution to the '…theory of superstructures, scarcely touched on by Marx,…' (Lévi-Strauss, 1966, 130).

A key tenet of this approach, popularized later by Roland Barthes but plainly in debt to Propp and other Russian and Prague Formalists, was the methodological 'death of the author'. Although rejecting the label 'structuralist Marxism', party member Louis Althusser and his colleagues practiced just that while insisting on the continuing philosophical relevance of Lenin's writings. Marx's historical materialism was declared a science understood as 'a process without a subject'. The effect of this maneuver was to remove both the significance of 'Marx the author' and especially any 'prescientific' Romantic foibles about alienation and subject/object Marx may have practiced prior to the declaration of the historical materialist position in the unpublished 1845 manuscript of *The German Ideology* (Marx and Engels, 1976; Althusser, 1982).

In effect, this Althusserian movement amongst critical intellectuals, which soon gained considerable followings in the UK and English-speaking world, sought to return Marxian scholarship to the kinds of claims to scientificity practiced by Engels in the wake of Marx's death (Colletti, 1974). Moreover, a practice of 'symptomatic reading' was advocated by Althusserians which claimed to establish evidence in suspect writers of the key failing of the young Marx: 'humanist essentialism', i.e. the problematic of alienation. The 'symptomatic' recognition of this failing, often in the name of intellectual 'rigor', added another layer of gatekeeping to the reception practices of Marxian intellectuals, not only in the case of Marx's work but also of that of their own contemporaries. All work that failed this test of scientific rigor was deemed 'ideological' where 'ideology' was understood as the opposite of 'science'.

While the waning of Althusserianism in France might be dated from the May events in Paris of 1968 (Stedman-Jones, 1989), the contradictions and intellectual authoritarianism of Althusserianism became increasingly evident in English-speaking circles from the mid-1970s. Although Althusser had reserved an autonomous place for some art within his blanket conception of ideology (Althusser, 1971), neither it nor a broader sense of culture played any systematic role in his project. Perhaps unsurprisingly, the subsequent rise of postmodernism and poststructuralism, especially in the USA, prioritized the aesthetic and, to varying degrees, adopted an intellectual stance which owed much to the modernist avant-gardes (Huyssen, 1986). The resultant 'post-Marxist' currents were as much a break with the model of the vanguard party as with the shallow understanding of all Marxian thought as economistic.

## CONCEPTUAL ENTANGLEMENTS: CRITIQUE, IDEOLOGY, HEGEMONY, PRODUCTIVE FORCE

The conceptual legacy of these Marxian developments for cultural sociology is of course immensely complex. Take, for instance, the category of *critique* alluded to above. In the wake of the debates about the young Marx, Marxian critique could no longer be confined so readily to an *unmasking* of social interests 'behind' a work of art, body of ideas or political practice, as some versions of base and superstructure might require. Plainly more than direct functional causality was involved. The practice of critique is also *immanent*, a term that refers to the methodical examination of the phenomenon in question 'from within' in order to reveal possible internal contradictions. Cultural criticism could no longer mean merely to be 'negatively' oppositional but, as Adorno (1984) argued most eloquently, it must maintain sufficient autonomy to practice an immanent analysis. Yet that analysis might necessarily invoke the possibility of social critique as well. The critique of the meaningful 'content' of an artwork, as well as its location within a sociology of forms, reveals a 'truth content' that may well provoke a critical social challenge beyond itself.

An almost identical case can be made for the concept of ideology. Indeed, ideology critique too can be regarded as having an emancipatory immanent as well as 'unmasking' function even when the object of that critique is 'bourgeois ideology' or 'bourgeois culture' (Frankfurt Institute for Social Research, 1973: 182–205). Such Marxian ideology critique can redeem normative content or principles of an emancipatory kind within art and ideologies as well as expose their social limitations and potentially legitimative roles. While art can be made to serve, say, the legitimation of nationalist interests – as the history of Romanticism tells us – that same art can be a source of social critique due to its redemptive potential (Löwy and Sayre, 2001).

This was the strategy of Williams' *Culture and Society* (1990) (Jones, 2004). It also became the centerpiece of the public sphere thesis advanced by key second-generation Frankfurt School figure, Jürgen Habermas. He later described its first major formulation as 'moving within the circle of a classical Marxian critique of ideology' (Habermas, 1993, 463). Habermas (1989) subjects to an emancipatory ideology critique a core 'category of bourgeois society', a public sphere where public opinion should form, as a means of highlighting the shortfall between promise ('truth content') and actuality. 'The public sphere' was exhaustively reconstructed, criticized and redeemed – too readily redeemed, according to some leftist and feminist critics – and so re-established as a normative benchmark.

Thus emancipatory immanent critique has major consequences for 'base and superstructure'. While an unmasking critique may expose vested interests 'pulling strings' in a very direct functional causality, from the base as it were, an emancipatory critique examines a quite different, less obvious, scenario. As Márkus has put it, in one of the most useful exegetical accounts to date, emancipatory ideologies produce a 'universalizing, totalizing, rationalizing transformation of the constraints of circumstances and material practices into constraints of discourse and representation, a transposition which always depends on the characteristics and requirements of the cultural genre in question, on the mobilizable cultural traditions, and on the concrete use made of them' (1995: 73).

This transposition schema, unlike a functional causality, so recognizes a role for both intellectual/artistic agency and the formal properties of the aesthetico-ideological form, crucially moving towards a more explicitly sociological, rather than philosophical, Marxism. Such a position was evident in the Marxian sociology of cultural forms within the Germanic tradition from Lukács to the Frankfurt School and in the Marxian semiology advocated by the Bakhtin Circle. It was also advocated by Lukács' Paris-based former student, Lucien Goldmann, who explicitly challenged the growing influence there of Lévi-Strauss' structuralism. In a later comment endorsed by Adorno he charged that 'Structuralism seeks structures without demanding that they have meaning' (Goldmann and Adorno, 1976: 146). For similar reasons, Williams later grouped such Marxian alternatives to technicist formalism (including, in effect, himself) as 'social formalists' (Jones, 2004: 94).

Indeed, for most structuralists, a very reduced understanding of 'transposition' was recognized by the concept of *homology*. This was derived from Lévi-Strauss' interpretation of myth amongst indigenous peoples, which in turn borrowed from the binary oppositional principles of structuralist linguistics. Homological analysis was Lévi-Strauss' 'solution' to 'base and superstructure'. Each myth was reducible to a set of formal binary oppositions that were found to have a homological correspondence with a set of binaries located within local 'material constraints' – such as loss of access to fishing territory. The apparent meaningful 'content' of the myth's narrative played very little role. As Lévi-Strauss famously put it, in a dismissal of the relevance of similarities of 'content' in favor of the differences established by structuralist analysis: 'It is not the resemblances but the differences which resemble each other' (Lévi-Strauss, 1973: 149).[7]

Althusser's structuralist Marxism relied on a myth-like expansive conception of ideology which left no space for a dialectical conception of critique or human agency. In contrast, Marx and most other Marxist theorists never extended the concept of ideology beyond that of the ideational forms that were the product of intellectuals – as opposed to popular belief systems (Márkus, 1983; 1987; 1995). The key Marxist figure who might be thought an exception to this critical Marxian delimitation of the concept of ideology to intellectuals, and on whom Althusser claimed to rely, was Antonio Gramsci. Rather, Gramsci developed a separate concept (reworked from Lenin) to account for the circulation and adoption of legitimative ideologies as popular belief: hegemony.[8] For Gramsci too, ideologies themselves, or certainly their elaboration, were quite explicitly the work of intellectuals. For Gramsci it was the referent of the category of 'intellectual' that should be semiotically expanded – in contrast to Althusser's expansion of 'ideology' – so that it operated in both a narrow and a broad sense. Famously he declares in his prison notebooks that 'all men are intellectuals ... but not all men have in society the function of intellectuals' (1971: 9). Intellectual capacity was thus recognized as a general human faculty as well as a specialized occupation – whose purpose, for 'traditional intellectuals', Gramsci redefined as the organization of consent. Hegemonic power was thus constituted by successful popular consent to a ruling ideology which discursively legitimated the product of a complex compromise between the fractions of a ruling economico-political bloc.

As a communist party leader of the 1920s, Gramsci held the rare distinction of having successfully stood for election to a 'bourgeois' parliament. Thus his Marx was also that known to the party faithful. Gramsci drew on the Marx of the political writings such as, most importantly, *The Eighteenth Brumaire of Louis Bonaparte* of 1852 (Marx 1973a), Marx's remarkable analysis of the rise to power of Louis Napoleon following the 1848 French revolution. It provided Gramsci with many of his core subcategories of politico-cultural analysis such as 'fraction' and 'bloc'.

It was this Marx of applied 'conjunctural analysis' of a key historical moment, as the Althusserians usefully named it, who demonstrated the potential sophistication of even a socio-political analysis reliant on a functional causality traced to the base. *The Brumaire*, written well before the much-cited '1859 Preface' (Marx, 1950), demonstrated more than any other text that, for all its limitations as a metaphor, 'base and superstructure' was not merely a positivist declaration of an economistic scientism, nor a bland ontological claim to a simplistic 'materialism' over a metaphysical 'idealism'.[9] Rather, Marx uses it to refer to the role of institutionalized divisions of labor in intellectual and political practice, their social formation and social consequences. Even here 'transposition' as well as functional causality is strongly implied by Marx's thesis of a 'general relationship' concerning 'political and literary representatives of a class' reliant on the reproduction of 'limits in thought' (1973a: 177).

Moreover, Marx's 'base' had never been merely an 'economy' but rather a mode of production constituted by a dialectical relation between productive forces (instrumental/technical means of production plus labor) and relations of production (the social organization of the productive forces). Both Adorno and Benjamin within the Frankfurt School, in their productive disagreement about the rising 'culture industry', and the later Williams (1973; 1977a; 1983) saw the plausibility in extending this notion of the base directly to the field of aesthetic culture. All three experimented with varying conceptions of forces and relations of *cultural* production. This 'production paradigm', as Márkus (1986) calls it, proved especially useful in accounting for both new means of technical reproduction of aesthetic works and for new technical media, understood initially as new means (media) of 'producing' works of art.[10]

But, of these subtler reworkings of elements of base and superstructure, it was Gramsci's debt to the *Brumaire* version that gained influence in English first.[11] So it was unsurprising that the English translation of major sections of Gramsci's *Prison Notebooks* in 1971 had a catalyzing effect on 'Western Marxism' at least as great as that of the early Marx's work and more so than the still sporadic translations from the German Western Marxian tradition.

In effect this left the 'epochal' meaning of the base as the one source of truly reductionist usage, i.e. where the base refers to the mode of production, especially across an 'epoch' such as the history of capitalism, and is proffered as a functional cause of a quite specific cultural work or form. Williams' favorite example of such *epochal reductivism* was Christopher Caudwell's formulation, 'capitalist poetry'.[12] For subsequent debates about the 'Gramscian' legacy in cultural sociology, however, easily the strongest influence was the mid-period work of Stuart Hall within the Birmingham cultural studies project, which in turn owed much to Raymond Williams.

## BIRMINGHAM CULTURAL STUDIES AND RAYMOND WILLIAMS: HEGEMONY, CULTURE AND TRADITION

The heyday of Birmingham cultural studies, usually associated with Stuart Hall's directorship of the Birmingham Centre for Contemporary Cultural Studies (CCCS) in the 1970s, marks an important confluence of the tendencies discussed above. Perhaps more importantly for this volume, it has become a key negative reference point in the very declaration of a cultural sociological stance within US sociology in the self-styled 'Strong Program' (SP) associated with Alexander and colleagues (discussed in the next section). Hall and his collaborators carved a path between the worst excesses of Althusserian structuralist scientism and the potential analytic gains within the then relatively new (in English) formalist principles of semiotic analysis which included the recent translation of a key text from the Bakhtin Circle, Vološinov's *Marxism and the Philosophy of Language* (1973). They relied more heavily, however, on the 1971 translation of *Selections from the Prison Notebooks* of Gramsci (1971) as a means of delimiting the effects of Althusser's reductivisms.

Hall himself conducted a series of remarkable re-readings of key primary texts of Marx (Hall, 1974; 1977a; 1977b; 1977c) which sought to demonstrate the possibilities of a non-reductivist account of the field of culture with, like Gramsci, a rehabilitated notion of base and superstructure based in *The Eighteenth Brumaire* in play. These re-readings of Marx by Hall were usually tied to an elaboration of Gramsci's conception of hegemony.

The contested dimensions of this field of culture were famously understood at Birmingham to be best demonstrated by the innovative stylistic practices of British youth subcultures and by counter-hegemonic critiques of news media practices within a broader popular culture (e.g. Hall and Jefferson, 1976). To this extent the Birmingham agenda was a Gramscian reworking of the 'radical deviancy' literature within British sociology.[13] But the *tour de force* work, *Policing the Crisis* (Critcher et al., 1978), further located these counter-hegemonic practices, as the Birmingham researchers understood them, as a crisis of hegemony within the British state in which thematics around race were the 'signifiers of the crisis'. Hall's work on 'Thatcherism', most of it published in political journalism deliberately modelled on *The Brumaire*, followed directly from this framework.[14]

In this sense, culture became regarded as 'a field of struggle' where hegemony could be 'won or lost'. However, with the notable exception of the 'Lukácsian' ethnographic work of Paul Willis (1977), this formulation shifted the Birmingham agenda decidedly away from the legacy of a Marxist emancipatory critique towards an instrumentalized conception of culture with little to guide it normatively beyond the 'counter' in 'counter hegemonic' (Hall, 1981). Democracy in particular was increasingly treated as no more than a legitimate masking of class power. The key step here lay in Hall's adherence to a functional dependence understanding, albeit Bourdieuian, of homological correspondence.[15]

Yet prior to Birmingham, Hall had legitimately claimed the warrant of Raymond Williams' work for a sociologically expansive understanding of art and creative capacity within a dialectical practice of 'cultural analysis' indebted too, but distinct from, the literary criticism confined to 'great traditions' in which they had both been trained. Here he and Williams' position considerably resembled emancipatory Marxian cultural critique in its 'transposition' sense. This early commonality and its implications have remained obscured by the widespread acceptance of the reductivist Althusserian readings of Williams by Terry Eagleton (1976) and (the later) Hall himself (1980).

Williams, always the popularizing educator of critical expertise, maintained a role for critical evaluation and recognized that the existence of dominant selective traditions (nowadays more typically called canons) entailed the possibility of their contestation by rival selective traditions. Such counter-traditions, he later argued, held a counter-hegemonic capacity (Williams, 1961: 50–59; 1977a: 115–120). However, unlike Hall, Williams' 'counter' in counter-hegemonic' entailed a role for immanent critique.

In the field of literary studies, Williams' counter-traditions were constructed on the criteria of technical excellence within their art *and* their ability to challenge the dominant order by self-consciously recognizing its contradictions. For the cultural analysis advocated by the early Williams of *The Long Revolution* (1961), only major works were capable of moving beyond the 'recording' of such contradictions, so enabling critical recognition and the potentiality of the need for change (Jones, 2004). This dialectical conception thus practiced a form of immanent critique which was more than merely oppositional.

In 1964 Hall had (with Paddy Whannel) closely followed Williams' mode of cultural analysis but stressed its applicability *within* 'popular arts'. Hall made it explicit that such popular arts had a critical capacity that entirely commodified 'mass art' did not. Hall's own selective tradition thus delineated popular art from mass art but required a conception of tradition which included genre-conventions (Hall and Whannel, 1964: 77). The distinction between popular and mass art rested on the popular artist's capacity and opportunity to move beyond the limits of genre conventions and, in so doing, to address popular taste without exploiting it. Chaplin's films meet these criteria for Hall, for example. Significantly, this early Hall avoided an *en bloc* conception of popular culture by recognizing the specificity of those popular traditions and, in another parallel with Williams, the specificity of 'sufficiently open' institutional facilitation of socially diverse popular audiences such as the music hall and configurations of cinema (Hall and Whannel, 1964: 65). Hall's argument was thus able to construct a tradition of works from diverse popular genres.

However, Williams' own work at this point was constrained by a view that 'authentic' popular culture had been destroyed by industrial capitalism and that any counter-hegemonic cultural traditions 'of the people' were 'residual' at best (Boyes, 1993; Jones, 2004). He later acknowledged this as an epochally reductive conception and included a position like the early Hall's in his later influential typology of dominant, residual and emergent cultural forms (Williams, 1973; 1977a).

Now, as we have seen, aesthetic 'tradition' had proven one of the most difficult challenges for both the Marxian sociology of cultural forms/genres and for the Russian Formalists. The chief problem was the issue of historical survival of works, and especially traditions, from earlier 'epochs', most notably ancient Greece. Williams' innovation was elegantly simple but sociologically precise: traditions were a product of selection and construction, but this was not, as the structuralists would have it, a formalist effect of a meeting between diachronic and synchronic structures. Rather, in a classic 'middle range' sociological formulation, Williams positioned traditions as an agential product of 'institutions and formations' (the latter referring to the informal self-organized 'schools' of intellectuals and artists). This framework directly informed his rejection of 'epochal' uses of base and superstructure (Williams, 1973; 1976; 1977a; 1995).

Had these conceptual subtleties been appropriately recognized at Birmingham, much might have been different. Instead, Hall's adoption of Althusserian 'symptomatic reading' and the extraordinarily hectic pace of Birmingham output prevented such a breakthrough. Considerable violence was done to Williams's early position (and effectively to Hall's too) while most of Williams' later work was ignored completely. In the much cited 'Cultural Studies: Two Paradigms' essay, Hall (1980) attempted to reconcile his structuralist influences with his debts to 'culturalism', as he christened the work of British precursors to Birmingham cultural studies, notably Williams. However, this reconciliation was itself an act of 'symptomatic reading'; so Williams' position was reduced to its near opposite. Hall wrongly attributed to Williams a so-called 'anthropological' conception of culture which Hall developed from Williams' use of the phrase 'whole way of life'. While for Williams the relationship between 'whole way of life' and 'the arts' senses of 'culture' was a dialectical one in which the conjunction of the two meanings was pivotal, as it generated the analytic dialectic described above, Hall attributed to Williams a bland descriptivism that he had never advocated.[16] The normative dimension in Williams' practice of immanent critique was treated as 'a literary moral discourse' from which he had recently 'broken'. This was precisely the prescientific/scientific binary Althusser attempted to impose on Marx's work.[17]

Hall's definitional obsession regarding Williams and 'culture' betrayed an Althusserian expectation that only a rigorously norm- (aka 'moral-')free definition of a core 'theoretical object' could qualify a body of knowledge as 'scientific'. An aesthetic dimension of 'culture' thus could not be afforded. Ironically, within Prague Formalism itself, Mukařovský had employed the formalist principle of 'the dominant function' in any given semiotic situation to elaborate just such a normative model of the aesthetic. Williams incorporated Mukařovský's 'aesthetic function' into his 'mature' sociology of culture (Mukařovský, 1979; Williams, 1977a & 1995). Williams' use of Mukařovský's schema confirmed that his conception of culture was sufficiently open to recognize the immanent analysis of popular arts and traditions such that they might be considered, in his terms, not just residual but emergent. Hall's 'Birmingham' position, in contrast, became completely instrumentalized, albeit within his highly complex model of homological functional dependence.

In a little known and very early critique of the Birmingham project, Williams (1977b) pinpointed this instrumentalizing tendency with remarkable precision and then, over the next decade, proceeded to provide a more elaborate account of the risks he saw in such work. This stance culminated in the essay, 'The Uses of Cultural Theory' (1986). For Williams the Althusserian intolerance of 'unscientific' normative principles was itself symptomatic of the consequences of allowing formalist methods to dominate erstwhile normatively critical research. Formalism risked fetishizing analytic techniques, most notably by deprioritizating immanent analysis of meaning in favor of formal properties. Williams called this 'the formalist trap'. As we shall see, this formalist trap still exists for cultural sociology today.

## THE STRONG PROGRAM IN CULTURAL SOCIOLOGY VERSUS WESTERN AND 'CULTURAL' MARXISM

The development of the Strong Program (SP) approach in US cultural sociology by Alexander and colleagues over the last twenty-five years has been deliberately defined against a set of Marxist failings posited in the work of Western Marxism and other 'cultural Marxists', most notably the Birmingham cultural studies project (Alexander and Smith, 2002; Sherwood et al., 1993).[18]

For SP advocates, adequate recognition of cultural autonomy requires 'a sharp analytical uncoupling of culture from social structure' (Alexander and Smith, 2002: 137). It is this which defines a cultural sociology in opposition to a sociology of culture, for without the required uncoupling, culture is necessarily deemed weak in relation to social structure. From this perspective orthodox (party) Marxism is 'the great theoretical animus' but Western Marxism as a whole is also targeted (Alexander and Smith, 2002: 140). Gramsci's project is positioned as the most significant attempt to revise orthodox Marxism's hostility to cultural autonomy (Alexander, 1990: 21).

What is perhaps most notable in this view of the Marxian tradition is the relative inattention to the long engagement between Western Marxism and the sociology of art.[19] Indeed 'the aesthetic', frequently the ostensible concern of a sociology of culture, plays a marginal role at best in the SP manifestos. The culture so dramatically rendered autonomous is understood almost exclusively in an 'anthropologicial' sense. Indeed it is Geertz's advocacy of 'thick description' within anthropology (itself inspired by literary theory) that often forms the turning point in the SP manifestos. While the important, initially Goffmanesque, performative-aesthetic dimension of all practices is a major feature of SP, the aesthetic 'in dominance' as art, and its normative claims, has only very recently become a SP focus (Alexander and Smith, 2010).

Nonetheless, shorn of their 'openly polemical' performances of differentiation (Alexander and Smith, 2002: 136) which lead to too easy dismissals of Hall's most sophisticated work, the SP manifestos do provide powerful correctives to the Gramscian 'cultural Marxism' of Birmingham cultural studies. They rightly point to its eventual subordination, even in *Policing the Crisis*, to the instrumental logic recounted in the previous section (Alexander and Smith, 2002: 140). The SP critiques are indebted here not to Williams but to the powerful critique of Gramsci by Cohen and Arato (1992). The latter's magnum opus provided a compelling case that, for all its revisionist complexity, Gramsci's own project had no alternative goal to bourgeois hegemony but a proletarian hegemony led by the ultimate organic intellectual, the vanguard party.[20] Civil society – the arena of cultural and political autonomy from the state and, on some accounts, the market – was unlikely to have survived as even a 'relatively autonomous' realm should a counter-hegemonic bloc have prevailed. Indeed, as SP consolidated as an empirical project, it was civil society, refigured as a civil sphere, that provided the key conceptual scaffolding for its more discrete analyses and Alexander's own (2006) magnum opus, *The Civil Sphere*.

At least initially, the SP's methodological alternative was characterized as a 'structuralist hermeneutics'. The core point of its methodological differentiation is the characterization of its opposite, a sociology of culture, as entirely context-driven with no capacity for immanent analysis of culture as such:

> Sociology cannot be the study merely of contexts. ... it must also be the study of *texts*. I do not mean, as the ethnomethodological critique of "normative sociology" would have it, simply formal or written texts. I mean, much more, unwritten scripts, the codes and narratives whose hidden but omnipresent power Paul Ricoeur suggested in his influential argument that 'meaningful actions must be *considered* as texts'; if they are not, the meaning-*full* dimension of action cannot be objectified in a manner that allows it to be submitted to sociological study. (Alexander, 1996: 3)[21]

Everything turns, of course, on how these unwritten scripts are understood and analyzed. Despite the invocations of Ricoeur's hermeneutics, the core step here is 'the felicitous but not altogether accidental congruence between Durkheim's opposition of the sacred and the profane and structuralist theories of sign-systems' which enables 'insights from French theory to be translated into a distinctively sociological discourse and tradition, much of it concerned with the impact of cultural codes and codings' (Alexander and Smith, 2002: 146).

It is ironic then that Hall (1978) claimed almost exactly the same genealogy in the lead essay for the CCCS's highly influential *On Ideology* collection, the very volume Williams (1977b) had openly challenged. The methodological result for both projects is also similar – the establishment of systems of binary oppositional codings as a major analytic moment. The SP practice certainly locates these at a more fundamental level, as necessary components of the discourses of the civil sphere, while Hall follows Bourdieu (in the case of post-traditional societies) by working from binary oppositions that are institutionally given – such as those in parliamentary politics (Bourdieu, 1991). It is from this framework that Hall builds his own model of functionally dependent homological correspondence.

Thus while a typical SP analysis would reveal a binary opposition between the codings of sacred and profane in contemporary public discourse, especially those involving the 'moral pollution' of a rival Other, Hall more typically addressed the binarizing ethical norm that requires 'balance' of viewpoints and sources in journalistic reportage of political debate. In this Bourdieuian structuralist homology, the nearest Hall came to the critical Marxian model of transposition, he argued that the normative logic of the journalistic field 're-presented' a second set of binary oppositions from another field, here parliamentary politics (Hall et al., 1976) and thus its autonomy was at best 'relative'. This position, as we have seen, is quite vulnerable to the SP charge of instrumentalism - which in turn echoes Williams's 'formalist trap'. The SP's own 'uncoupling' imperative of course prevents such a homological correspondence.

Still, as we have seen, the SP also draws on a binary coding analysis. Its 'structuralist hermeneutic' is underwritten by Ricouer's (1971) 'model of the text'. However, the same Ricoeur had in 1963 recommended limits be placed on any extension of the Lévi-Straussian binary oppositional codings, beyond Lévi-Strauss' anthropological usage, to cultural locales where 'myth' was subject to reflective practice. By this Ricoeur meant cultures where 'myth' was not totally ritualized but marked by disembedded practices of tradition and interpretation, as in the academy. In such situations there was a surplus of meaning that such binarizing analysis could not capture (Ricoeur, 1974). Once again, 'tradition' emerges as a conceptual and methodological challenge for cultural sociology. The more immediate problem for the SP is its violation of this Ricoeurian warning.

Similarly vulnerable to social formalist critique is the remarkably open-ended SP commitment to the structuralist analysis of narrative, and the generation of 'formal models' from such a practice. With such an approach, it is declared, 'cultural autonomy is assured' (Alexander and Smith, 2002: 147). The narrative analysis SP appropriates is heavily indebted to the technicism of Russian Formalism, as is the work of the favored SP narrative theorist, Northrop Frye. Frye's work has been much criticized for its ahistorical features.[22] Now, the SP's conception of narrative is offered as an alternative to the inadequate notion of 'context' that is said to inform the sociology of culture. However, as we saw, the concepts of genre/form and the related, if problematical, conception of tradition- not mere 'context' - are the key Western Marxian categories in which the socio-historical meets the aesthetic in a decidedly non-reductive way.

There is then a general problem with the claimed gains over the Marxian tradition in the SP. Its characterization of that body of work is far too reductive, effectively overlooking the most relevant Marxian work entirely.[23] Like Hall's treatment of Williams, its manifestos lack an explicit means of recognizing aesthetic culture's emancipatory potential. Undoubtedly, the SP would be very prone to Williams' charge of a 'formalist trap' – where normativity is effaced by technicism - were the SP manifestos not also very normatively driven. Moreover, they announce an empirical research program rather than a perfectly self-contained theoretical edifice – and thus justly point to their empirical studies already undertaken.

## CONCLUSION: AESTHETIC TRADITION REDUX

The question propelling contemporary cultural studies should not be how to demystify culture by showing that it 'really' represents something else, but rather how culture allows contemporary actors continually to remystify their social worlds. We must study how, despite the continuing disappointments and degradations of the modem world, persons manage to maintain their beliefs in transcendent values and 'true' solidarity, how they still fear evil and persevere in their pursuit of the good, and how they engage in ritual renewal rather than merely strategic behavior. Only if these processes are fully faced can they be fully understood. (Sherwood et al., 1993: 375)

We saw earlier that culture came to play an increasing role in Western Marxism during the deepening crisis of Marxism's political legacy and/or misappropriation by Leninism and Stalinism. A Marxism 'without the proletariat' and vanguard party emerged as early as the 1930s but from the 1960s other forms of collective agency and action, (new) social movements focused initially on race, civil rights and gender, were increasingly recognized. In the Birmingham cultural studies project, youth subcultures that broke with orthodox working-class 'style', always male-dominated albeit often with reinvented masculinities, drew comparable intellectual attention.

The usual SP hyperbole about cultural Marxism aside, the appeal to solidarity in the manifesto extract above is remarkably consistent with this shift in Marxian and comparable sociological thinking.[24] A significant stream of SP work has also been directed towards such social movements, with Alexander's *The Civil Sphere* (2006) providing a highly detailed account of the US civil rights movement as a demonstration of the SP's superiority over existing approaches in social movement studies. In a landmark and now much emulated text, Eyerman and Jamison (1998) commenced a major rethinking of the relation between aesthetic 'tradition' and social movements by focusing on the mobilizing role of musical traditions in the US civil rights movement.[25]

Eyerman and Jamison's central concept of 'tradition' was directly indebted to Raymond Williams' conceptualization. Traditions become mobilizable resources whose activation by social agents realizes the immanent potential that the critical Marxian sociology of genres sought to recognize and which Williams saw as 'emergent'. Yet such an application to popular traditions was anticipated, as we saw, by the early Stuart Hall. In so highlighting the utility of this core Marxian 'sociology of art and culture' concept, Eyerman and Jamison demonstrated the limitations of the exclusion of such a dimension from the SP manifestos.

This foregrounding of the emergent role of aesthetic tradition in social movements is also highly consistent with a lesser known aspect of Habermas' public sphere thesis although, as Eyerman and Jamison note (1998: 35), tradition's critical potential is underestimated by him. A major strain of contemporary cultural sociology now works with the concept of a proto-political aesthetic public sphere, a concept Habermas (1989) developed but largely abandoned in his later work (McGuigan, 2005; Jacobs, 2006; 2010; Jones, 2007).[26] This arena, where aesthetic cultural criticism and debate are in dominance, marks out the social domain where immanent cultural criticism practices the critique and interpretation of traditions, forms and works and thus often invokes social critique. It also sociologically locates the Ricoeurian differentiation of such interpretation and tradition from 'myth'. Such work on aesthetic traditions and public spheres recognizes the critical and at times solidarizing power of the aesthetic in dominance as well as its performative, but less often dominant, role in all 'culture'. The growing cultural sociology of aesthetic public spheres and traditions thus provides an immanent corrective to the SP's hyperbolic manifestos. The latter had placed the SP on the precipice of 'the formalist trap'.

So, must cultural sociology be defined against all 'cultural Marxism'? Is it really the case that in order to 'grasp the nettle of cultural autonomy' it must 'quit the "sociology of culture"-driven project of "Western Marxism"' (Alexander and Smith, 2002: 140)? Plainly not. The hyperbolic requirements of manifestos meant that SP advocates overlooked or understated their commonalities with not only the Birmingham project but also, and perhaps more significantly, with the non-Leninist elements of the Western Marxist tradition. Indeed one of the places where the legacy of Marxian cultural sociology thrives today is within the Strong Program.

## NOTES

1. For examples of both 'orthodox' tendencies see the opening chapters in the still excellent overview by Laing (1978).
2. Williams (1990) cf Williams (1979). The fact that from such thin resources Williams was able to mount a devastating critique of Leninism seems to have gone unnoticed by many commentators.
3. This norm manifests strongly within the Marxian sociology of culture of the later work of Raymond Williams. There he highlights the significance of craft-like artisanal *relations of cultural production* in his cultural production typologies. Williams (1995) cf Jones (2004) and Hesmondhalgh (2007).
4. E.g. Anderson (1976) and Merquior (1986). During his student years in Berlin Lukács was well known to key German sociological figures such as Simmel and (Max) Weber.
5. See Wolff (1993) for comparable attention to the visual arts.
6. On the controversy over Lukács' shifting between critical and orthodox views on this question see Johnson (1984).
7. Confusingly, Goldmann employed the term homology for his own version of sociological transposition in his sociology of literature.

8   Althusser claimed the warrant of Gramsci's hegemony in formulating his notorious notion of ideological state apparatuses (1971: 137). For Gramsci the category of 'state' could also be understood in narrow (governmental) and expansive (state + civil society) senses, like that of intellectual. The latter sense was the chief terrain of his innovative conception of hegemony, the arena of consent, while the former was coercive. Althusser steamrollered this distinction with his mechanistic apparatus formulation.
9   It is difficult to overestimate the confusions created by the latter, especially in subsequent discussions of 'materialism', perhaps the most relevant example being in the work of Terry Eagleton (1989).
10  E.g. Adorno (1978; 1999) cf Buck-Morss (1977: 33), Benjamin (2008) and Williams (1989).
11  Although the clear rival in influence would be the 1970 English translation of the Benjamin 'Work of Art' essay.
12  Jean Cohen (1982) has justly pointed to the problematic role of such an epochal usage in *The Eighteenth Brumaire* too. For all the sophistication of his detailed class analyses of France 1848–1951, Marx wished to further argue that the state of development of France's mode of production determined the final outcome. The Althusserians referred to this as over-determination or economic determination 'in the last instance'. So, national as well as epochal modes of production may generate dubious uses of 'the base'.
13  E.g. Taylor and Taylor (1972). The key link here was Stan Cohen's (2002) concept of moral panic which Hall reworked into a Gramscian/Vološinovian form (cf Jones & Holmes, 2011; Rojek, 2003: 116-119).
14  Many of these are collected in Hall and Jacques (1983).
15  See next section for more detail.
16  As Williams (1979) made plain, the phrase was a contestative immanent appropriation from T.S. Eliot's *Notes Towards the Definition of Culture* (1948). Hall instead followed the precedent of Terry Eagleton's polemical Althusserian critique of Williams (Eagleton, 1976) which had in turn followed the Althusserians' treatment of Marx and Lukács' lockstep. Hall's (1980) tendentious reading of 'The Analysis of Culture' chapter of *The Long Revolution* (Williams, 1961) is quite remarkable for its ellipses and conflations. For a detailed critique see Jones (2004). In a sad further irony, both Paul Gilroy (1987) and Hall (1993) later claimed that this 'definition of culture' as 'whole way of life', to which Hall had reduced Williams' position, was latently racist.
17  However, at least Althusser was prepared to declare the later Marx 'scientific'. Eagleton (1976) and Hall (1980) were not so generous to the later Williams, though Hall continued to claim him as a major influence and Eagleton later partly recanted.
18  It has also been defined against elements of the US functionalist tradition in sociology.
19  A significant exception is Smith (2001), a text which sits largely separate from the SP manifestos.
20  The model of the organic intellectual was much discussed at Birmingham and features prominently in Hall's later reflections on the Birmingham project (e.g. Hall, 1996). Yet Williams, whose early biographical trajectory was the very model of a Gramscian organic intellectual 'rising' from the subaltern, never embraced the term, even in his explicit reflections on the sociology of intellectuals (1995). It would seem Williams' early recognition of the failings of Leninism tempered his adoption of the Gramscian concept of hegemony.
21  This is one of many points where the intellectual crimes with which the SP manifestos charge cultural Marxism seem to be more suited to a characterization of elements of US functionalist sociology.
22  See for example the critiques in Swingewood (1987) and Williams (1977a).
23  For a similar assessment on this point see Amsler and Hanrahan (2010)
24  While Williams abandoned the vanguard party model quite early, he never shifted in his commitment to a central agential role for working-class solidarity.
25  Cf. Roy, 2010; Rosenthal and Flacks, 2012.
26  See also the extended footnoted discussion of this concept and indeed Williams in Alexander, 2006: 581–582

# REFERENCES

Adorno, T. (1978) 'On the Social Situation of Music', *Telos* 35(Spring): 128–164. First published 1932.

Adorno, T. (1984) 'Cultural Criticism and Society', in *Prisms*. Cambridge, MA: MIT Press. First published 1955.

Adorno, T. (1999) 'Adorno to Benjamin 18 March 1936', in H. Lonitz and N. Walker (eds), *T.W. Adorno and W. Benjamin: The Complete Correspondence*. Cambridge: Polity. pp. 127–134.

Alexander, J. (1982) *Theoretical Logic in Sociology, Volume Two. The Antinomies of Classical Thought: Marx and Durkheim*. London: RKP.

Alexander, J. (1990) 'Analytic Debates: Understanding the Relative Autonomy of Culture', in J. Alexander and S. Seidman (eds), *Culture and Society: Contemporary Debates*. Cambridge: Cambridge University Press.

Alexander, J. (1996) 'Cultural Sociology or Sociology of Culture?', *Culture: Newsletter of the Sociology of Culture Section of the American Sociological Assn*, 10(3–4): 1–5.

Alexander, J. (2006) *The Civil Sphere*. New York: Oxford University Press.

Alexander, J. and Smith, P. (1993) 'The Discourse of American Civil Society: A New Proposal for Cultural Studies', *Theory and Society*, 22(2): 151–207.

Alexander, J. and Smith, P. (2002) 'The Strong Program in Cultural Theory: Elements of a Structural Hermeneutics', in J. Turner (ed.), *Handbook of Sociological Theory*. New York: Kluwer Academic. pp. 135–150.

Alexander, J. and Smith, P. (2010) 'The Strong Program: Origins, Achievements and Prospects', in J.R. Hall, L. Grindstaff and M. Lo (eds), *Handbook of Cultural Sociology*. New York: Routledge. pp. 13–24.

Althusser, L. (1971) *Lenin and Philosophy and other Essays*. Trans. B. Brewster. New York: Monthly Review Press.

Althusser, L. (1982) *For Marx*. Trans. B. Brewster. London: Verso.

Amsler, S. and Hanrahan, N. (2010) 'Re-imagining Critique in Cultural Sociology'. in J.R. Hall, L. Grindstaff and M. Lo (eds), *Handbook of Cultural Sociology*. New York: Routledge: 64-73.

Anderson, P. (1976) *Considerations on Western Marxism*. London: NLB.

Bakhtin, M. and Medvedev, P. (1985) *The Formal Method in Literary Scholarship: A Critical Introduction to Sociological Poetics*. Trans. A. Wehrle. Cambridge, MA: Harvard University Press. First published 1928.

Benhabib, S. (1986) *Critique, Norm and Utopia: A Study of the Foundations of Critical Theory*. New York: Columbia University Press.

Benjamin, W. (2008) 'The Work of Art in the Age of its Technological Reproducibility', in *The Work of Art in the Age of its Technological Reproducibility and Other Writings on Media*. Cambridge, MA: Belknap Press. pp. 19–55.

Berman, M. (1988) *All that is Solid Melts into Air: The Experience of Modernity*. New York: Penguin.

Bourdieu, P. (1991) 'Delegation and Political Fetishism', in J. Thompson (ed.), *Pierre Bourdieu, Language and Symbolic Power*. Cambridge, MA: Harvard University Press.

Boyes, G. (1993) *The Imagined Village: Culture, Ideology and the English Folk Revival*. Manchester: Manchester University Press.

Bronner, S. (2012) *Modernism at the Barricades: Aesthetic, Politics, Utopia*. New York: Columbia University Press.

Buck-Morss, S. (1977) *The Origin of Negative Dialectics: Theodor Adorno, Walter Benjamin and the Frankfurt Institute*. New York: Free Press.

Claudin, F. (1975) *The Communist Movement: From Comintern to Cominform*. London: Penguin.

Claudin, F. (1978) *Eurocommunism and Socialism*. London: NLB.

Cohen, J. (1982) *Class and Civil Society: The Limits of Marxian Critical Theory*. Oxford: Martin Robertson.

Cohen, J. and Arato, A. (1992) *Civil Society and Political Theory*. Cambridge, MA: MIT Press.

Cohen, S. (2002) *Folk Devils and Moral Panics*. London: Routledge. (1st edn, 1972.)

Colletti, L. (1974) 'Lucio Colletti: A Political and Philosophical Interview', *New Left Review*, 1(86): 3–28.

Critcher, C., Hall, S., Jefferson, T., Clarke, J. and Roberts, B. (1978) *Policing the Crisis: Mugging, the State and Law & Order*. London: Macmillan.

Eagleton, T. (1976) 'Criticism and Politics: The Work of Raymond Williams', *New Left Review*, 1(95): 3–23.

Eagleton, T. (1989) 'Base and Superstructure in Raymond Williams', in T. Eagleton (ed.), *Raymond Williams: Critical Perspectives*. Cambridge: Polity.

Eliot, T.S. (1948) *Notes Towards the Definition of Culture*. London: Faber.

Eyerman, R. and Jamison, A. (1998) *Music and Social Movements: Mobilizing Traditions in the Twentieth Century*. New York: Cambridge University Press.

Frankfurt Institute for Social Research (1973) *Aspects of Sociology*. London: Heinemann. First published 1956.

Gilroy, P. (1987) *There Ain't No Black in the Union Jack*. London: Hutchinson.

Goldmann, L. and Adorno, T. (1976) 'Goldmann and Adorno: To Describe, Understand and Explain', in L. Goldmann (ed.), *Cultural Creation in Modern Society*. St Louis: Telos Press. First published 1971.

Gramsci, A. (1971) *Selections from the Prison Notebooks*. Ed. Q. Hoare and G. Smith. London: Lawrence and Wishart.

Habermas, J. (1989) *The Structural Transformation of the Public Sphere*. Cambridge, MA: MIT Press. First published 1962.

Habermas, J. (1993) 'Further Reflections on the Public Sphere', tr. T. Burger, in C. Calhoun (ed), *Habermas and the Public Sphere*. Cambridge, MA: MIT Press. pp. 421–63.

Hall, S. (1974) 'Marx's Notes on Method: A "Reading" of the "1857 Introduction"', *Working Papers in Cultural Studies*, 6: 132–171.

Hall, S. (1977a) 'Culture, the Media and the "Ideological Effect"', in J. Curran, M. Gurevitch and J. Woollacott (eds), *Mass Communication and Society*. London: Edward Arnold/Open University Press. pp. 315–418.

Hall, S. (1977b) 'The "Political" and "Economic" in Marx's Theory of Classes', in A. Hunt (ed.), *Class and Class Structure*. London: Lawrence and Wishart, pp. 15–60.

Hall, S. (1977c) 'Rethinking the "Base-and-Superstructure" Metaphor', in J. Bloomfeld (ed.), *Class, Hegemony and Party*. London: Lawrence and Wishart. pp. 43–72.

Hall, S. (1978) 'The Hinterland of Science: Ideology and the "Sociology of Knowledge"', in Centre for Contemporary Social Studies (CCCS), *On Ideology*. London: Hutchinson.

Hall, S. (1980) 'Cultural Studies: Two Paradigms', *Media, Culture and Society*, 2: 57–72.

Hall, S. (1981) 'Notes on Deconstructing "the Popular"', in R. Samuel (ed.), *People's History and Socialist Theory*. London: Routledge. pp. 227–240.

Hall, S. (1993) 'Culture, Community, Nation', *Cultural Studies*, 7(3): 349–363.

Hall, S. (1996) 'Cultural Studies and Its Theoretical Legacies', in D. Morley and K. Chen (eds), *Stuart Hall: Critical Dialogues in Cultural Studies*. London: Routledge. pp. 262–275.

Hall, S., Connell, I. and Curti, L. (1976) 'The "Unity" of Current Affairs Television', *Working Papers in Cultural Studies*, 9: 51–94.

Hall, S. and Jacques, M. (eds) (1983) *The Politics of Thatcherism*. London: Lawrence and Wishart.

Hall, S. and Jefferson, T. (eds) (1976) *Resistance Through Rituals: Youth Subcultures in Post-war Britain*. London: Hutchinson.

Hall, S. and Whannel, P. (1964) *The Popular Arts*. London: Hutchinson.

Hesmondhalgh, D. (2007) *The Cultural Industries*. London: Sage. (1st edn, 2002.)

Huyssen, A. (1986) 'Mapping the Postmodern', in *After the Great Divide: Modernism, Mass Culture, Postmodernism*. Bloomington: Indiana University Press. pp. 179–221.

Jacobs, R. (2006) 'American Television as a Global Public Sphere', Paper presented to the Congress of the International Sociological Association, July.

Jacobs, R.N. (2010) 'Entertainment Media and the Aesthetic Public Sphere', in J. Alexander, R. Jacobs and P. Smith (eds), *The Oxford Handbook of Cultural Sociology*. New York: Oxford University Press. pp. 318–340.

Jakobson, R. (1997) *My Futurist Years*. Ed. B. Jangfeldt. Trans. S. Rudy. New York: Marsilio.

Jameson, F. (1974) *The Prison-House of Language: A Critical Account of Structuralism and Russian Formalism*. Princeton: Princeton University Press. First published 1972.

Jay, M. (1996) *The Dialectical Imagination: A History of the Frankfurt School and the Institute of Social Research, 1923–1950*. Berkeley: University of California Press. First published 1973.

Johnson, P. (1984) *Marxist Aesthetics*. London: Routledge and Kegan Paul.

Jones, P.K. (2004) *Raymond Williams's Sociology of Culture*. Houndmills: Palgrave Macmillan.

Jones, P.K. (2007) 'Beyond the Semantic "Big Bang": Cultural Sociology and an Aesthetic Public Sphere', *Cultural Sociology*, 1(1): 73–95.

Jones, P.K. and Holmes, D.C. (2011) 'Moral Panic' in *Key Concepts in Media and Communications*. London: Sage. Pp. 154-159.

Laing, D. (1978) *The Marxist Theory of Art: An Introduction*. Hassocks England: Harvester.

Lévi-Strauss, C. (1966) *The Savage Mind*. London: Weidenfeld & Nicholson.

Lévi-Strauss, C. (1973) *Totemism*. Harmondsworth: Penguin. (1st edn, 1962.)

Löwy, M. and Sayre, R. (2001) *Romanticism Against the Tide of Modernity*. Trans. C. Porter. Durham: Duke University Press.

Lukács, G. (1968) *History and Class Consciousness: Studies in Dialectics*. London: Merlin.

Lunn, E. (1985) *Marxism and Modernism: Lukács, Brecht, Benjamin, Adorno*. London: Verso.

McGuigan, J. (2005) 'The Cultural Public Sphere', *European Journal of Cultural Studies*, 8(4): 427–443.

Márkus, G. (1983) 'Concepts of Ideology in Marx', *Canadian Journal of Political and Social Theory*, 7(1–2): 84–103.

Márkus, G. (1986) *Language and Production: a critique of the paradigms*. Dordrecht, Holland: D.Reidel.

Márkus, G. (1987) 'Ideology, Critique and Contradiction in Marx: An Answer to J. Larrain', *Canadian Journal of Political and Social Theory*, 11(3): 74–88.

Márkus, G. (1995) 'On Ideology-Critique, Critically', *Thesis Eleven*, 43: 66–99.

Marx, K. (1950) 'Preface to a Contribution to the Critique of Political Economy (aka 'The 1859 Preface'), in K. Marx and F. Engels, *Selected Works. Vol. 1*. London: Lawrence and Wishart.

Marx, K. (1973a) 'The Eighteenth Brumaire of Louis Bonaparte', D. Fernbach (ed.), *K. Marx, Surveys from Exile: Political Writings, Vol. 2*. London: Penguin.

Marx, K. (1973b) 'Introduction' (aka 'The 1857 Introduction'), in *Grundrisse*. London: Penguin.

Marx, K. (1975) 'Economic and Philosophical Manuscripts of 1844', in K. Marx and F. Engels, *Collected Works. Vol. 3, 1843–1844*. London: Lawrence and Wishart.

Marx, K. and Engels, F. (1976) 'The German Ideology', in K. Marx and F. Engels, *Collected Works. Vol. 5, 1845–1847*. London: Lawrence and Wishart.

Merquior, J. (1986) *Western Marxism*. London: Paladin.

Mukařovský, J. (1979) *Aesthetic Function, Norm and Value as Social Facts*. Ann Arbor: University of Michigan. First published 1936.

Mulcahy, K. (1984) 'Official Culture and Cultural Repression: The Case of Dmitri Shostakovich', *Journal of Aesthetic Education*, 18 (3): 69–83.

Pike, C. (1979) 'Introduction', in C. Pike (ed.) *The Futurists, the Formalists and the Marxist Critique*. London: Ink Links.

Prawer, S. (1975) 'What Did Karl Marx Think of Schiller?' *German Life and Letters*, 29 (1): 122-137.

Propp, V. (1968) *Morphology of the Folktale*. Trans. L. Scott. Austin: University of Texas Press.

Ricoeur, P. (1971) 'The Model of the Text: Meaningful Action Considered as a Text', *Social Research*, 38: 529–562.

Ricoeur, P. (1974) 'Structure and Hermeneutics', in *The Conflict of Interpretations*. Evanston: Northwestern University Press. First published in 1963.

Rojek, C. (2003) *Stuart Hall*. London: Routledge.

Rosenthal, R. and Flacks, R. (2012) *Playing for Change: Music and Social Movements*. Boulder, CO: Paradigm.

Roy, W.G. (2010) *Reds, Whites, and Blues: Social Movements, Folk Music and Race in the United States*. Princeton N.J.: Princeton University Press.

Schwartz, J. (1995) *The Permanence of the Political: A Democratic Critique of the Radical Impulse to Transcend Politics*. Princeton N.J.: Princeton University Press.

Sherwood, S., Smith, P. and Alexander, J. (1993) 'The British are Coming ... Again! The Hidden Agenda of "Cultural Studies"', *Contemporary Sociology*, 22(3): 370–375.

Smith, P. (1998) 'The New American Cultural Sociology: An Introduction', in P. Smith (ed.), *The New American Cultural Sociology*. Cambridge: Cambridge University Press.

Smith, P. (2001) *Cultural Theory: An Introduction*. London: Blackwell.

Stedman-Jones, G. (1989) 'The Rise and Fall of French Marxism', in L. Appignanesi (ed.) *Ideas from France: The Legacy of French Theory (ICA Documents)*. London: Free Association Books.

Swingewood, A. (1987) *Sociological Poetics and Aesthetic Theory*. New York: St Martins Press.

Taylor, I. and Taylor, L. (eds) (1972) *Politics and Deviance: Papers from the National Deviancy Conference*. Harmondsworth: Penguin.

Vološinov, V. (1973) *Marxism and the Philosophy of Language*. New York: Seminar Press. First published 1930.

Wiggershaus, R. (1995) *The Frankfurt School: its Histories, Theories And Political Significance*. Cambridge, Mass: MIT Press.

Williams, R. (1961) *The Long Revolution*. London: Chatto and Windus.

Williams, R. (1973) 'Base and Superstructure in Marxist Cultural Theory', *New Left Review*, 1(82): 5–16.

Williams, R. (1976) 'Developments in the Sociology of Culture', *Sociology*, 10: 497–506.

Williams, R. (1977a) *Marxism and Literature*. Oxford: Oxford University Press.

Williams, R. (1977b) 'The Paths and Pitfalls of Ideology as an Ideology', *Times Higher Education Supplement*, June 10: 13.

Williams, R. (1979) *Politics and Letters: Interviews with New Left Review*. London: NLB.

Williams, R. (1983) *Keywords: A Vocabulary of Culture and Society*. London: Flamingo.

Williams, R. (1986) 'The Uses of Cultural Theory', *New Left Review*, 1(158): 19–31.

Williams, R. (1989) 'Marx on Culture', in *What I Came To Say*. London: Hutchinson. pp. 195–225.

Williams, R. (1990) *Culture and Society*. London: Hogarth. First published 1958.

Williams, R. (1995) *The Sociology of Culture*. Chicago: University of Chicago Press and Shocken Books.

Willis, P.E. (1977) *Learning to Labour: How Working Class Kids Get Working Class Jobs*. Farnborough, UK: Saxon House.

Wolff, J. (1993) *The Social Production of Art*. (2nd Edn). London: Macmillan.

# Max Weber's Presences: On the Cultural Sociology of the Long-Term

David Inglis

Imagine that hanging from the ceiling of my study there are violins, pipes and drums, clarinets and harps. Now this instrument plays, now that. The violin plays – that is my religious value. Then I hear harps and clarinets and I sense my artistic value. Then it is the turn of the trumpet and that is my value of freedom. With the sound of pipes and drums I feel the values of my fatherland. The trombone stirs the various values of community, solidarity. There are sometimes dissonances. Only inspired men are able to make a melody out of this – prophets, statesmen, artists, those who are more or less charismatic. I am a scholar who arranges knowledge so that it can be used. My instruments are to be found in bookcases, but they make no sound. No living melody can be made out of them. (Max Weber, quoted in Hennis, 1988: 165)

## INTRODUCTION

It is fitting that when Max Weber (1864–1920) was asked by a colleague to describe the nature of his intellectual activities, he should have outlined a metaphor drawn from the world of the arts. Indeed his early death prevented him from realising a project to write a comprehensive study of all the major arts (Turley, 2001: 637). His great interest in the arts was not merely because he was an eminent member of the German *Bildüngsburgertum*, the highly educated bourgeoisie of the later 19th and early 20th centuries (Ringer, 1990). It was also because of the centrality of the arts, and culture more generally, in his scholarly endeavours. Although subsequently represented, especially in Anglophone sociology, as primarily an analyst of bureaucracy and rational forms of organisation more generally, or as a methodologist of the social sciences, it remains the case that he should be acknowledged as a major cultural sociologist or sociologist of culture. This is so in terms both of his methodological considerations, which set out principles and concepts which are still used by and useful for present-day sociological analysts of cultural forces and materials, and also of his substantive contributions to the understanding of long-term cultural developments which were regarded through distinctive sociological lenses.

This chapter cannot possibly capture all of the empirical and conceptual richness of Weber's writings, for they are too diverse, and often exist in fragmentary form, to allow one to form a comprehensive and definitive picture of them, especially in a limited space such as this (for a synoptic overview in English of central themes in Weber's treatment of cultural matters, see Schroeder (1992); for comprehensive contextualisation of Weber's writings in his biographical circumstances, see Radkau (2009)). Nor can this chapter depict all of the vast secondary literature, in German, English and other languages, concerning the multiple dimensions of Weber's writings, and the varying interpretations of, and polemics over, them, that have appeared since the explosion of interest in Weber first occurred in various national contexts in the 1960s (Roth, 1977; Swedberg, 2003).

Nonetheless, this chapter will outline what seem from the point of view of contemporary cultural sociologists to be Weber's most telling and productive analytic procedures and substantive claims, considering how these have already impacted upon, or could in future fruitfully inform, cultural sociological studies. What follows is a selective interpretation of what is still useful and living in Weber's legacy, as defined by the interests and needs of cultural sociologists at the present time. This is quite appropriate in the case of Weber: although the works of all authors retrospectively defined as sociological 'classics' are interpreted, defined and fought over in specific, historically-determined ways by later exegetes, one of Weber's central methodological precepts was that any analysis of the past is thoroughly informed and shaped by the values, ideals and points of view of those in the present. Weber forcefully argued that such a state of affairs is unavoidable: we are condemned to look at the past – including the history of the discipline of sociology – in light of our own particular location in time, but good social science rests upon acknowledgement of that fact, bringing the values we project onto the past into the full light of (self-)scrutiny. Consequently, the narration that unfolds here will move from considering themes and concepts in Weber's writings that previous generations of scholars have found interesting and productive, towards considering what analysts today find compelling and worth rehabilitating in his writings.

As we will see, while earlier generations have found his analyses of rationalisation processes and forms of rational organisation particularly appealing, and while Pierre Bourdieu in the 1970s took inspiration from Weber's writings on religio-cultural orthodoxy and heterodoxy, students writing in the last twenty years have found his points about the interplay of culture and technology, and about the 'inner logic' of cultural forms, to be especially fecund. These latter points now stand in addition to the more standard claims often made for Weber's continuing relevance to sociology in general, and forms of sociology concerned explicitly with cultural matters more particularly. Such points were well summarised by Nick Gane (2000: 811) some time ago, namely that Weber's understanding of modernity 'offers an alternative to that forwarded by Marxist theory', not least because he remains today probably 'the most important theoretical opponent of Marx' (Mommsen, 1977: 374); that his work 'emphasises the importance of ideas, beliefs or "ideal interests" alongside material interests for understanding historical change, and fits neatly within the recent cultural turn in sociological theory'; and finally that his account of the 'progressive rationalisation and disenchantment of the modern world informs some of the main lines of contemporary social and cultural critique, including Frankfurt School critical theory and certain strands of postmodern theory' (see Gane (2002) for resonances between Weber and postmodernism).

Therefore beyond the stereotype often offered of Weber in undergraduate courses, where he seems to be simply a doom-laden prophet of modernity as a 'polar night of icy darkness and hardness' (Weber, 1991c [1946]: 128), we can say that the central appeal of Weber at the present time is that he seems to offer various attractive vistas for future research, all embedded within a sociological framework – or set of frameworks – focused on meaning and the human creation of meaningful cultural forms, the central analytic focus of research that regards 'cultural sociology' – possibly as opposed to the 'sociology of culture' – as essentially an exercise in reconstructing and analysing processes of meaning creation, and how meanings impact upon actions, practices and institutions in myriad different ways. At the same time Weber offers ways of systematically connecting meaning-making processes to phenomena of social power and domination, thus avoiding any tendencies towards an illegitimate idealism in a cultural sociological approach to analysing the dynamics of meaning in social life (Lima Neto, 2014). In that sense, Weber seems to offer much of interest to contemporary scholarship. We now turn to consider more specifically what that promise might entail.

## CONTEXTS AND THEMES

Weber's work, and the key themes which it responded to, were inevitably greatly marked by the context in which it was created, a fact that Weber himself was highly aware of. The social and intellectual conditions of Wilhelmine Germany included the development of large industry and the formation of economic monopolies; the exponential growth of bureaucratic forms of organisation in the public and private sectors; rapid urbanisation and the unsettling of traditional forms of life in the countryside; diverse class struggles and the mediation of these in politics and cultural life; the rise of mass social movements, especially socialist parties and trades unions; the appearance of a rudimentary welfare state intended by the authorities to dampen down class-based social frictions; the beginnings of organised women's demands for formal political equality with men; and international tensions between a newly imperial Germany and its older imperial rivals, Britain and France (Mommsen, 1977). Among the *Bildungsburgertum* in general, and its academic and intellectual professionals more specifically, there was a widespread air of pessimism about contemporary cultural conditions, with standards in cultural life, and therefore in the quality of life per se, felt to be in decline, in large part due to the rise of a mass culture characterised by a lack of subtlety and feeling (Liebersohn, 1988). Weber's writings obviously reflect, thematise and contribute to the intellectual culture of his time in many subtle ways, but we can say in summary fashion that he was dealing with, and in many ways innovatively contributing to, central German intellectual themes of the time, ranging from working out a post-Kantian methodology for the social scientific study of past and present social and cultural conditions, to conceptualising in a post-Romantic manner the apparently highly alienating nature of modern urban existence, themes and concerns also taken up by contemporaries such as Georg Simmel (Hennis, 1988). Raymond Aron (1971: 92) neatly summed up some of the intellectual resources current at the time that Weber was influenced by, drew upon and contributed to the development of. There was in his thinking:

> ... a Darwinian component (the struggle for life), a Nietzschean component (not the happiness of mankind, but the greatness of man), an economic component (the persistent scarcity of wealth – the ineradicable poverty of peoples), a Marxist component (each class has its own interests and the interests of any one class, even the dominant one, do not necessarily coincide with the lasting interests of the national community), and finally a national component, i.e. the interest of the nation as a whole, must outweigh all others ...

Obviously the intellectual materials Weber was working within and with were diverse and related to each other in subtle, perhaps sometimes contradictory ways, eluding attempts definitively to say this or that understanding of his work reflects the 'real' Weber. Moreover, given the fragmentary and often unfinished nature of his *oeuvre*, it has been open to multiple subsequent interpretations by succeeding generations of scholars, with disputes arising within particular generations about what 'really' are Weber's key concerns (Clegg, 2005). One can create a taxonomy of 'phases' of reception of his work, both in Germany and abroad, centred upon key interpretative contributions by influential scholars and the appearance of new translations of hitherto neglected, or allegedly hitherto badly translated, texts. For example, in the late 1970s, Roth (1977) proposed that between the 1930s and the 1950s, Talcott Parsons' presentation of Weber, including through the widely used translation of the *Protestant Ethic* study (Weber, 1930 [1904–5]), dominated American understandings of Weber as an anti-Marxist theorist of social action and modern rationalisation processes (for an alternative, modern translation see Weber (2010 [1904–5])). Nonetheless, Gerth and Mills' selection of Weber's writings, *From Max Weber* (1991b [1946]), also made a notable impact, even until the present day. The dominance of Parsons' presentation was challenged by an important reinterpretation of Weber by Bendix (1960), which emphasised the latter's contributions to comparative historical sociology, and this interpretation was in turn replaced by multiple understandings forwarded by diverse scholars from the mid-1960s onwards, with Weber variously appearing more close to or distant from Marx. More contemporary interpretations often focus on the history of the production and reception of key texts. For example, Whimster (2007) considers the most important and productive phase of Weber's scholarly life to have been from 1910 to 1914, when he was planning and drafting both the massive work that would eventually appear in unfinished form as *Economy and Society* (Weber, 1978) and also the research on the economic ethics of the world religions. *Economy and Society* was edited posthumously by Weber's wife Marianne, obscuring changes over time in the meaning and use of key concepts, and thus involving a 'plastering over of caesuras' in the text, leading to much confusion later on as to the precise evolution of Weber's thinking (Mommsen, 2000: 366).

It is in light of these various complications and ambiguities that we must consider what are taken by different schools of thought to be Weber's central themes and most important concepts. As Kemple (2008: 385) points out

> The grand themes of Max Weber's massive writings have become canonical references, if not ritualistic clichés. Thus we have the rise of industrial capitalism, the bureaucratic legitimation of power, the disenchantment of cultural world-views, the

fragmentation of values, and the spread of an ascetic work ethic and other forms of disciplined conduct.

One could add to the standard litany of key themes and analytic dispositions the following concerns: Weber's methodological injunction to see sociology as 'the interpretive understanding of social action' (Alexander, 1983: 30), involving the famous four types of action: instrumentally-rational, value-rational, affectual and traditional; the analysis of types and forms of domination and legitimation (charismatic, traditional and legal-rational, the latter being most forcefully expressed in forms of bureaucratic control); and the assigning of special importance to the ways that the actor understands her actions, involving the use of *Verstehen* by the analyst (Scaff, 1981)

The standard mid- to late-20th century Anglophone interpretation of Weber's central substantive concerns is crystallised in remarks like those of Ritzer (1975: 628) that 'the bulk of Weber's work examines the development of rationality in the Occident and the barriers to that development in the rest of the world'. A similar perspective was offered by Kolegar (1964: 360), with the claim that:

> ... a leitmotif of all his studies ... [was] the concept of rationalization, the part played by rationality in all areas of social life, especially in the Western societies of modern times. Seen as a historical process, thoroughgoing rationalization of all institutional areas is the inescapable fate of the Western world. Rationality thus becomes the guiding principle around which Weber's sociology is built. And although the dynamic aspect of rationality, its progressive extension into all areas of life and its increasing preponderance as the ethos of modern society, dominate Weber's work, even the conceptual-methodological and taxonomic parts of his work are permeated with this ordering principle.

On this sort of view, the apparent focus of the comparative, historical-sociological studies of the major world religions involves showing how highly methodical, systematic and calculating ways of acting, thinking, relating and organising came to predominate in Western Europe, ultimately furnishing the basis for highly rationalised modern capitalism and industrialism. But such dispositions did not develop so markedly outside of Europe, most notably for Weber in China and India, these being places whose major cultural orientations had a conservative rather than revolutionary set of effects on social institutions.

Yet as Swedberg (2003: 297) notes:

> What fascinated many earlier students of Weber [before the 1970s] ... was not so much capitalism per se as the process of rationalization and the place of capitalism in this. It was well understood that Western society was capitalistic, but capitalism was typically seen as part of a much larger process that not only encompassed the economy but also art, law, science ...

Thus what may be taken as one of Weber's original *problematiques*, namely 'capitalism', a focus obviously produced by his – and the wider German intelligentsia's – often complicated relationships to the work of Marx, was massaged away in favour of a less obviously politically charged focus on 'rationalisation', partly through Parsons inserting a separate text dealing with rationalisation at the front of his translation of the *Protestant Ethic* study, making the latter seem more like a general treatise on Occidental rationality, rather than as a contribution to post-Marx debates on the nature of the development of capitalism per se.

What 'really' are the key concerns of Weber's studies remains disputed and is likely to remain so (Tenbruck, 1980). But even if we accept the claim that the overall guiding theme throughout his *oeuvre* is rationalisation, with the study of modern capitalism nested within it, this still has to be nuanced. Thus Barbalet (2000: 331) argues that we must relinquish the orthodox earlier understanding of Weber's key concerns as revolving around the simple notion of the characteristically modern 'subordination of individual lives to compelling and comprehensible external forces of rationalization', and recognise that instead Weber was actually concerned with analysing the nature, and reasons for the historical appearance, of tensions between these impersonal forces on the one side, and on the other side processes of *Beruf*, the individual person's cultivation of their self-hood and their 'personality', involving the creation and enacting of self-defined purposes and values, and in so doing coming to higher levels of self-consciousness, these being classic themes of German moral and political philosophy since the times of Kant and the Romantics. The challenges of being a fully-formed and self-forming individual in bureaucratic, rationalistic, modern mass society were also of great significance to another pioneer of cultural sociology, Georg Simmel (see Chapter 6). Regardless of whether this contemporary interpretation holds more water than its predecessors, it remains the case that the individual, and their beliefs, values and innermost constitution, lies at the heart of most of Weber's sociology, but at the same time the core 'personality' is understood as existing within, and being made possible by, complex cultural configurations, which historically have been shaped by either magic or systematic religious systems, but which in modernity are thoroughly informed by the rationalistic worldview offered by the natural sciences. The individual and culture seem equally important to Weber, and we might say that the ways in which the two concepts interact with each other in particular empirical contexts is one of the key orientations of his brand of cultural sociology. The focus on the individual actor – albeit always one located within cultural forces – differentiates Weber's approach in notable ways from any Durkheim-inspired conception of culture, which emphasises the extra-personal nature of cultural forms and forces.

## WEBER ON 'CULTURE'

It is sometimes remarked that at least some of the time Weber was practising 'cultural sociology', and such claims can be the basis for saying that he is both a foundational figure for contemporary cultural sociology and a possible future inspiration for it. While true in a very broad sense, such claims are ahistorical if they are not sensitively attuned to the specific configurations of knowledge production within which Weber operated and to which he contributed. What was meant by 'cultural sciences' (*Geisteswissenshaften* or *Kulturwissenschaften*) in Weber's time and place bears some resemblance to what we today might mean by 'cultural sociology' but there are of course important differences too.

Simplifying matters, we can say that in the late-19th-century German academy, much discussion centred upon the assumed division between the 'natural' and 'cultural' sciences. Under the influence of the ideas of philosophers like Dilthey and Rickert, the cultural sciences were felt properly to be centred upon ideographic methods, as opposed to the nomothetic methods of the natural sciences. Therefore the former were engaged in the understanding of 'cultural complexes and subjective motives' which could not be reduced to, or be understood in light of, any putative 'laws' of human social life (Parsons, 1965: 172). Moreover, German intellectual life of the time was very much influenced by post-Romantic philosophy, as well as by its ostensible opponent, Kantian rationalism (Koch, 1993). By the end of the century, Nietzsche's ideas about power, the alleged Death of God and the need for a fundamental re-evaluation of values were also influential (Turner, 2011). Moreover, impressive empirical, social scientific (*Sozialwissenschaften*) bodies of work existed in jurisprudence and economics. It is within this complex constellation of ideas and influences that Weber's methodological essays should be located (Bruun, 1972). One also has to attend to the fact that Weber's views altered over time – for example, after about 1909 the term *Kultur* recedes in his writings as a description of what is being studied, and he begins to use the word *Soziologie* more, and to focus on forms of social action which are oriented to the various legitimate forms of order identified as charismatic, traditional and legal-rational domination (Walker, 2001). However, for our purposes here we can say that an important task for Weber was to develop a form of investigation that was simultaneously *interpretative* (why did people subjectively act as they did?) and *explanatory* (why did certain processes happen in history, and not others?).

Weber worked with a broader understanding of *Kultur* than did his predecessors in the *Geisteswissenshaften*. 'Culture' for Weber includes not just 'high culture' like the legitimate arts, but also the religious and spiritual beliefs of all social strata, and the modern scientific worldview which is taken to be strongly constitutive of modern social life. This is a broad vision of what 'culture' is and does. Weber existed before the sequestration of knowledge into separate domains like the sociology *of* religion, the sociology *of* media, the sociology *of* culture, and so on. Nonetheless, his *Kultursoziologie* is not co-extensive with the human sciences in general; not all investigations are for him 'culture sociology', for various questions and domains lie outside of that approach's purview (Schroeder, 1992: 164). *Kultursoziologie* is a hybrid enterprise in that it understands *Kultur* in two different but related senses: in a humanistic, *Geisteswissenshaftliche* sense, referring to sophisticated products of the human spirit (*Geist*), and a more 'anthropological', *Sozialwissenschaftenliche* sense, referring to ways of thinking and of living. *Kultursoziologie* studies such cultural domains as religion, systems of law, and music. It studies not a putative cultural 'superstructure', in the mode of classical Marxist analysis, but rather cultural 'matrices' or constellations (Walker, 2001). It differs from the practices of the *Geisteswissenshaften* in that it seeks not to determine whether particular cultural artefacts, notably works of art, are 'good' or 'bad'. Instead, analysts do not make such value judgements, but do study social actors' valuations of such products.

Weber's orientation to studying culture is rooted in certain basic ontological and epistemological assumptions. In a typical post-Kantian sense, Weber holds that the world in itself is both infinite and meaningless; humans alone create meaning; and so they project meaning onto the world in order to make it liveable for themselves. '"Culture" is a finite segment of the meaningless infinity of the world process, a segment on which human beings confer meaning' (Weber, 1949: 81).

Therefore the 'transcendental presupposition of every cultural science ... is that we are cultural beings, endowed with the capacity and the will to take a deliberate attitude towards the world and to lend it significance' (Weber, 1949: 81). The elementary material of human existence is

> subjective activity creating meaning ... [Contrary to Kant's view] the potency creating meaning is not the human mind with its pure intuitions, but divergent values that come into conflict in and through human action ... [T]he way in which [an individual person's] conscience reacts to empirical stimuli is not merely rational, but above all culturally conditioned. (Lima Neto, 2014: 930)

In other words, the human is a culture-creating animal. The empirical world has to be mastered through the development and use of cultural solutions to the problems it throws up for individuals and groups.

Culture is created both by groups and by individuals, and in particular by individuals endowed – or thought to be endowed by peers and followers – with high levels of charisma. This focus on individual culture-creators, especially prophets and preachers, is a distinctive feature of Weber's approach, marking it off from the collectivist orientation of both Marxist and Durkheimian sociologies, which stress that culture is made by groups, these being social classes in the Marxist case. And it is specific *types* of individuals – e.g. followers of a particular religion, especially religious specialists like priests who codify the original teaching of charismatic prophet figures – who are the 'carriers' of particular ideas and values, transporting and (often unintentionally) transforming them over time. In turn, it will be particular types of individuals – living certain kinds of lifestyles – who will be attracted to or repulsed by certain ideas and values. In all such cases, while Weber agrees with Marx that social classes have special relations with particular sets of values and ideas, he rejects a crude Marxist understanding that classes as a whole somehow create those cultural forms and ways of thinking. This is a mystification of what really goes on, namely that particular types of individuals, who may or may not be part of a particular class grouping, create and disseminate ideas that are more or less resonant with the lifestyles of people in a particular class or, in circumstances of some social complexity, of sub-groups (Bourdieu would later call these 'fractions') within that class.

Here we see two important points. First, Weber homes in on what today would be called *cultural producers*, a focus that some regard as having already been implicit in Marx's account of the generation of ideologies (Williams, 1981), but which, more importantly, has become a key concept in various contemporary schools of thought in the sociology of culture, most obviously the 'production of culture' school developed by Richard A. Peterson and others in the US from the 1970s onwards (see Chapter 14), and also in the sociologies of art offered variously by Bourdieu and Howard S. Becker. How and why particular types of workers make particular sorts of cultural products – considered in a way that does not make value judgements about the aesthetic goodness or badness of such work – can be said to have been pioneered by Weber, even if in the cases of the 'production of culture' school and Becker, the more immediate inspirations were American industrial and organisational sociology of the post-World-War-II period, although these latter were in turn partly stimulated by the reception of Weber's writings on the nature of rational organisations. In sum, Weber pioneered a careful typology of different kinds of cultural producers and disseminators (these would be called 'mediators' or 'intermediaries' today), the organisational contexts within which they work, and how such contexts both make possible and might be changed by certain kinds of products and production. It is worth noting that the 'production of culture' school focuses more on how contexts shape production, rather than on how production processes themselves might alter such contexts, a disposition Weber was led to by his emphasis on charismatic and prophetic types of producers, as well as more bureaucratic producers whose productions reinforce rather than alter the organisational status quo.

Another important point here concerns Weber's rejection of any metaphysical conception of 'classes' simply generating worldviews and ideas, without any further specification by the analyst of what specific types of actors are doing the producing, disseminating and receiving of cultural forms. This is part of his broader scepticism towards what he regards as the unacceptably mystified and cumbersome categories of some elements of Marx's theorising. He strongly criticised collective concepts like 'will of the people', 'class interest', 'state' and so on, which he regarded as sloppy, imprecise and metaphysical terms that had infected intellectual life from the time of, and in part due to the influence of, the *Communist Manifesto*. The aim of legitimate social analysis was instead to decompose the sorts of collective terms used in political discourse into 'individual, historical components of action' (Scaff, 1981: 1277).

Relatedly, he famously depicted social stratification as involving not just classes but also status groups and political factions ('parties') too, as well as defining class in terms of an individual's 'life-chances' and market opportunities rather than in terms of a person's relations to property and the current mode of production, as had Marx (Weber, 1991a [1946]). This model produces a more complex understanding of social stratification and power differentials than Marx had, with specifically 'cultural' factors cross-cutting class divisions. Weber denied what he took to be Marx's contention that membership of a class is the primary way an individual in a class-based society will think about themselves. There are many other culturally mediated identities people may have. In relatively complex societies there exist phenomena such as groups being divided up – and set into hierarchies – on status rather than just class lines, symbolic boundaries being drawn between such groups in ways that are irreducible to class-based structures, and symbolic divides operating between sub-groups located *within* particular classes.

All of these themes inform both Bourdieu's (1984) reworking of the conception of social classes, and their cultural orientations, in the landmark study *Distinction* (see Chapter 7), and also post-Bourdieu studies of systems of symbolic classifications and their role in the maintenance of social hierarchies. These studies hybridise Weber's concerns with the complexities of class and status with a Durkheimian focus on symbolic boundaries and group-based classification systems (e.g. Lamont and Fournier, 1993). Nonetheless, Weber's original focus was far from the Durkheimian emphasis on cultural systems and the systematicity of cultural forms (for example, the sacred/profane distinction, allegedly at the root of culture, renders the world into systematic sets of properties, like good/bad, friend/enemy, and so on). For Weber, culture produced and re-produced by individuals and types of individuals, and under certain circumstances (that have to be carefully specified and grounded in empirical evidence), can have profound effects, but the consequences will be unevenly spread through time and social and geographical space. A set of ideas or values only becomes systematised if certain people engage in work to make it so; rival systematisers may be at work at the same point in time, or may later on produce alternative systematisations, and without groups of workers like priests attempting to codify ideas and values, the latter will likely fragment again and dissipate. This historical and empirical approach to culture's systematic properties is very far from Durkheim's notions about all culture being systematically organised, and is probably a reason why Weber is regarded in somewhat negative ways by contemporary neo-Durkheimians like Jeffrey C. Alexander and his associates in the 'Yale School' of cultural sociology (Alexander, 2003).

The issue of the degree of the systematisation or fragmentation of a particular cultural constellation is an empirical, historical issue for Weber and not one that can be decided conceptually. This points to other important features of how Weber conceptualises 'culture'. Some cultural forms – notably the world religions and the modern natural scientific worldview – are traced over the course of several millennia, requiring a mastery of a range of specialist areas of study and of a huge amount of empirical data. Such a long-term approach – the diametric opposite of the primarily synchronic analysis of mainstream Durkheimian approaches – leads to a vision of culture as something more unstable than stable, involving mostly change over time rather than continuity. These, however, are claims based on empirical observations, rather than a priori analytic assumptions. For the agnostic Weber, culture 'can act as a force either for continuity or for change, in either its material or ideal aspects' (Walker, 2001: 46), and is not analytically tied to the maintenance of social order over time, as it often is in Durkheimian and Marxist approaches. But empirically speaking, it is the case that certain cultural forms, certain ways of organising them, and some of their interrelations with social configurations, do indeed promote social stasis rather than movement, as the conservative effects of the ethics and ideals of the Confucian literati on classical Chinese society for many centuries testifies in one of Weber's most absorbing case studies of such matters (Schroeder, 1992).

Weber's long-term historical perspective therefore envisages not reified, unified, singular 'cultures', conceived of in the manner of a simplistic anthropology, but rather diverse and constantly – if often slowly – shifting constellations of human action and attributions of meaning to the world, with changes happening usually not through the deliberate intent of actors but through the unintended consequences of action, the latter being a constant theme in Weber's writings (as it had been, in fact, of Kant's and Marx's before him) (Symonds and Pudsey, 2008). Cultural innovators are succeeded by systematisers, whose efforts may persist for centuries or be usurped quickly by new innovating cultural producers. Given the flexible, mutable and mutating nature of culture, it takes constant work by those who strive to maintain traditional ways of thinking and doing things to keep things as they apparently always have been, even if mostly such work does not appear to them as such, for it would usually only appear so to the analyst living many years after the fact.

Although often presented as a sociology which is centred on individuals' meaningful understandings of the world, Weber's historical approach is not a one-dimensional phenomenology of how things seemed to particular people at particular times. It involves analysis of the deep-rooted cultural underpinnings of individuals' actions, excavating levels of meaning that such individuals could not possibly have been fully aware of (Turley, 2001). This points to a need for us to avoid misconceiving of what the famous *Verstehen* method of studying action involves. It seeks to reconstruct not the empirical motives of particular individuals; it is not an empirical psychology of action – but rather the interpretation of the broader meaning of actions that happened among particular types of people at particular times and places. It concerns less what a particular Puritan thought and did and more the cultural universe within which such a person's thinking and activities took place and made sense. It therefore involves ideal-typical reconstructions of particular worldviews, common to certain types of individuals, including cultural producers (Herva, 1988).

Ideal types may be reconstructions of particular sets of values or worldviews, such as the 'Protestant Ethic' and the 'Spirit of Capitalism', or can be models of particular ways of organising and controlling people, like 'bureaucracy'. Given that social and historical reality is both infinitely complex and in itself in a certain way 'meaningless' (in the sense that there is no one single 'meaning of life' or objective meaning of human historical development), then tools must be fashioned to allow the analyst to make some sense out of the morass of data she has in front of her. Ideal types are theoretical constructs which operate as 'epistemological tool[s] for rationally structuring a great variety of empirical data' (Mommsen, 2000: 371). The ideal types are created, and thus the data selected, organised and interpreted, in light of the particular interests, and the deeper cultural values which underpin them, driving the research questions to be answered. If we accept for the moment that Weber was centrally interested in the history of the rationalisation of culture in the West, then following his logic we would say the following: that he lived in a time and place where the rationalisation of culture and social life seemed to be a pre-eminent fact of life, and a cause for some concern vis-à-vis negative effects on the capacities of individuals to be fully self-forming and autonomous persons. Thus his research questions as to why this has come about are self-consciously to be understood by him as products of that time and place. The questions to be posed compelled him to produce a range of ideal-typical models that allowed him to select and organise empirical, historical data about increasing rationalisation over time. The models allowed him to see how there had been in a wide range of different social spheres an overall movement, albeit at different speeds and unevenly, from less rationalised to more rationalised forms of culture and therefore forms of social interaction and organisation too. Being self-aware about the values one brings to one's studies (here, concerns about the over-rationalisation of modern life) should drive what models and which data are generated and used. A lack of such self-awareness, however, means that the values infiltrate the scientific procedures of investigation, undermining the systematic nature of the analysis, and confusing one's 'political' orientations (i.e. one's particular, personal value positions) with one's scientific, analytic work. In essence, the cultural forces and dispositions of one's own epoch and social group shape what you want to study, and only self-awareness of this can control for this fact and turn it into a virtue rather than a serious problem.

This is the epistemological background to what one may call Weber's nominalist view of culture. He remarks that 'empirical reality becomes "culture" to us because and insofar as we relate it to value ideas. It includes those segments and only those segments of reality which have become significant to us because of this value-relevance' (Weber, 1949: 76). In this sense, it is the analyst's values, underpinning (hopefully in a self-aware manner) her research interests and questions, which shape the selection of phenomena to be examined, and it is this set of selected phenomena – accessed through data – which the analyst then calls 'culture', the object of her cultural sociological investigation. An analyst living in one time and place will have values and interests specific to that context, and their necessarily and unavoidably 'one-sided viewpoint' drives which data 'are selected, analyzed and organized for expository purposes' (Weber, 1949: 72). In that sense, cultural sociology is an approach which analyses 'the phenomena of life in terms of their cultural significance', that significance being wholly relative to that sociologist and their particular social context (Weber, 1949: 76). As values change, so too will cultural sociology's interests and research question, and thus the definition of what counts as the 'culture' to be analysed (Burawoy, 2012). Weber adds that while values underpin and drive what science looks at, there cannot be a science of values in the sense that one could ever finally decide as to which values are superior to others. An ineluctable part of the human condition is that there are different, usually clashing values, especially in a modern and differentiated society, and that one must simply choose which 'god' to believe in, for there is no objective analysis possible of whether one set of ideals is better than another. The most that science can do is to trace out the (usually unintended) consequences of what has happened when particular people have tried to put their particular ideals into practice.

## WEBER'S ANALYTIC TOOLS

In this section we will consider four essential aspects of Weber's analysis of cultural change and how it shapes and is bound up with social change more broadly, the latter understood in terms of changes in forms of social action, of organisation and of domination by some groups over others. The four themes are the relations between 'material' and 'ideal' factors in explaining change; the nature of 'elective affinities'; the interplay of charisma, routinisation and rationalisation; and the relations which historically have pertained between different 'value spheres' (all themes pursued by Schroeder, 1992).

### *'Material' and 'Ideal' Factors*

We have already seen the great analytic divergences between Weber and Marx as to the nature of class and stratification. Weber opposed Marx in various other ways too (Mueller, 1982). One notable aspect here is that Marx's assumption that capitalism is a material system of production which first came into existence in the West alone in the early modern period is strongly criticised by Weber. The latter contended instead that there were various types of capitalism which had existed beyond modern and Western contexts. All of these involve social action oriented towards profit-seeking. While Weber's category of modern, rational capitalism is understood to be 'modern' and Western in essence, his other types of capitalism, namely 'political capitalism' (involving the pursuit of profit through the use of force and naked domination) and 'traditional-commercial capitalism' (involving the sorts of trade and monetary deals that have existed in many parts of the world for millennia), were intended to capture the historical fact, as Weber saw it, that 'capitalism' has had various different forms in different times and places, and that the uniqueness of modern capitalism rests in its highly rationalised nature, being centred around the systematic pursuit of profit, rather than the more haphazard approach to profit maximisation characteristic of earlier versions of capitalistic activity. Moreover, the various types of capitalism were not to be conceived, as Marx did, as socio-economic 'systems', but rather as specific configurations of meaningful social actions.

Capitalism, then, is not just a set of economic 'material' factors of production, but involves an interplay of the material and the ideational, the economic and the cultural. Weber argued that a cultural phenomenon like a religious doctrine could be an important factor in its own right in stimulating economic developments, for the cultural and economic were always bound up with each other in complex ways. Indeed Weber's insistence on combining in a sophisticated way 'economic' and 'cultural' dimensions of human life makes it a predecessor of contemporary understandings of 'cultural economy', which similarly want to tie together rather than separate these two dimensions of human existence (Hinde and Dixon, 2007). More specifically, Weber's (1966) studies of the main world religions attempted to show that economic actions were in fact motivated, at least initially, by religious beliefs. For example, Weber argued that the mind-set associated with Chinese Confucianism encouraged forms of social action oriented towards traditionalism and a desire to preserve the status quo. Christianity, by contrast, has inherently within it a 'world-transformative' capacity, which is – at least in some of its many variations, especially in the case of Protestant Puritanism – oriented towards altering social conditions. Thus one of the reasons why modern capitalism developed in the West and nowhere else was *partly* because of the inherently dynamic nature of the religious-cultural factors associated with Christianity. *The Protestant Ethic* (1930 [1904–5]) study was an attempt to show how Protestantism's religion of self-denial and hard work helped to shape the cultural context of early capitalist entrepreneurs, who in like fashion denied themselves pleasure and reinvested the profits they made in order to make even more profits – the systematic pursuit of profit that Weber defines as the major characteristic of modern, rational capitalism. Protestant thought was thus a very significant – but certainly not the only – feature of the development of capitalism

Weber's orientation to such matters was far too complex to be labelled as simply a form of analytic idealism, where 'ideal' factors (ideas, values, cultural dispositions, etc.) simply drive and shape 'material' and 'social' circumstances. Weber was of the view that ideal factors are indeed highly efficacious, because they do have the (circumscribed and partial) power to change or maintain the patterns of social life. Thus he assumes that a basic element of the human condition involves 'the metaphysical needs of the human mind, as it is driven to reflect on ethical and religious questions, driven not by material need but an inner compulsion to understand the world as a meaningful cosmos and take up a position toward it' (Weber, 1978: 499). In other words, the creation of ideas is not simply driven by basic material needs, but by the human's desire to find meaning in the world, posing answers to great metaphysical questions like 'why does the world exist?', 'what is the purpose of life?', 'how can I be redeemed?', and suchlike. Given this, the ideal realm of values and beliefs is quite as 'real' as the material forms of production that Marx had put forward as the elementary basis of human life (Walker, 2001).

The famous 'switchmen' metaphor which Weber deployed can be read as a straightforward statement of analytical idealism, whereby it is sets of ideas alone which motivate world-changing (or world-conserving) forms of action. But closer consideration of it reveals, as ever, a more complex orientation:

> Not ideas, but material and ideal interests, directly govern men [and women's] conduct. Yet very frequently the 'world images' that have been created by 'ideas' have, like switchmen, determined the tracks along which action has been pushed by the dynamics of interest. 'From what' and 'for what' one wished to be redeemed and ... 'could be' redeemed, depended upon one's image of the world. (Weber, 1991d [1946]: 280)

Thus it is not 'ideas' per se but 'interests', both material (e.g. gaining wealth and power) and ideal (e.g. gaining higher status, achieving religious salvation), which drive people's actions. But when people act upon what they think of as their interests, their actions are themselves guided and channelled by 'ideas', because these create particular images of the world (e.g. telling one what the universe or the gods are like, or how to serve God) that can deeply impact upon how self-interested actions are actually carried out. Working within a strongly Protestant cultural context guides the interested actions of an individual in ways very different from the actions she would have carried out if she lived within a markedly Hindu social world, for example. Thus on Weber's elaborate way of thinking about such matters, there are different types of interest (and certainly not only the wholly calculating type of self-interest imagined by modern economists to be typical of all individuals); diverse interests drive different types of action; and cultural images of the world channel and steer those actions. As Swedberg (2003: 294) summarises the point, 'the orientation of an actor is driven by his or her interests, and the course that the action will take will be shaped by existing world images'.

Obviously a focus on ideas and world images driving actions needs to consider how the former can lead to either transformative or conservative forms of action and social organisation. For Weber, over time originally novel and transformative ideas and world images become crystallised into institutions, such as legal systems or ways of organising family relationships. Institutions become grounded in the interests of the actors operating within them, especially the most powerful and privileged actors, and so become difficult to alter in other than incremental ways – thus one lawyer would find it next to impossible to transform on her own the whole massive legal apparatus she is constrained to operate within. Nonetheless, institutions sometimes can be altered by new ideas which unleash novel, transformative cultural forces, the case of Protestantism's unleashing of new ways of thinking and acting in early modern north-western Europe being a major case in point for Weber (Swedberg, 2003).

It is no surprise that, from a Weberian perspective, ideas and world images are strongly involved in shaping the nature of social groups and associations in a particular society, and that such influences can last for centuries. This is arguably the case in the contemporary US, where the social structure remains deeply influenced by the ideas and practices of the Protestant sects which colonised the country several centuries before (Kalberg, 2009).

This also points to a broader issue: that there is not one singular form of 'modernity' or 'capitalist modernity', as classical Durkheimian and Marxist viewpoints would have it, but instead different, culturally-shaped varieties of rationalised modernity, with 'American' modernity being very different from, for example, 'Turkish' modernity, as each was born out of contrasting religious and cultural complexes. The ongoing debate today about the nature of 'multiple modernities' is in part animated by the Weberian insistence on the importance of specific cultural inheritances in different parts of a modernised world, even if, ironically, Weber's more doom-laden pronouncements concerning the rise to prominence of one single, greyly uniform modern rational culture suggested that this would spread everywhere around the world in an undifferentiated manner (Eisenstadt, 2000).

If Weberian logic – rather than some of his more miserabilist statements about the emerging cultural conditions of his own time – stresses multiplicity rather than uniformity, likewise is it the case that his understanding of how to explain social and cultural change emphasises that there can never be just one explanation of an event, or conclusive proof that just one set of factors was responsible for 'causing' certain things to happen. He firmly stood against the idea, to be found in cruder forms of Marxism, that 'anything, call it technology or the economy, is the "last" or "final" or "actual" cause of anything' (Weber, 2005 [1910]: 31). There were always multiple causes; and since the explanation one could give was always from a one-sided viewpoint which stressed some aspects and omitted others, there were always multiple possible explanations of why certain things happened as they did. It is in this sense that we should understand his famous remark at the end of the Protestant Ethic study, that it was

> ... not my aim to substitute for a one-sided materialistic an equally one-sided spiritualistic causal interpretation of culture and of history. Each is equally possible, but each, if it does not serve as the preparation, but as the conclusion of an investigation, accomplishes equally little in the interest of historical truth. (Weber, 1930 [1904–5]: 183)

Thus he was not interested in *mono-causal* explanations, but *poly-causal* ones, which attempt to model the complexities of the actual situation under study, as far as empirical evidence will allow (Bendix, 1960; Parsons, 1965; Roth and Schluchter, 1979; Collins, 1986). Whether in his conceptual and empirical work he actually achieved such an aim is a matter for dispute. One of the reasons Alexander (1983) rejects Weber as a useful guide for contemporary (cultural) sociology is that he regards Weber's ambition to provide a multi-dimensional approach to sociological explanation as going unrealised, for Weber ends up toppling into a one-dimensional approach that, under the twin influences of Marx's and Nietzsche's accounts of power on the one hand, and on the other hand the pessimistic outlook on life typical of German intellectuals of the time, ends up over-emphasising in its explanations of concrete phenomena both forms of social power and suffocating modern rational culture. In this way, Weber's attempt to give to cultural forms and forces analytic autonomy from material and power factors fails, in a manner that the later Durkheim's work in fact singularly achieves (Alexander, 2003).

## Elective Affinities

The notion of 'elective affinities' (*Wahlverwandtschaften*), was taken by Weber from Goethe's novel of the same name.

It performs various roles in Weber's analysis of culture. In the first place, as we have seen, Weber was of the view that one single, completely exhaustive causal explanation of any event or phenomenon was impossible. History is instead the result of the complex interplay of an infinite number of forces, of various different types. Thus one could never say simply that 'X led to Y' – that, for example, the rise of the bourgeoisie led to the creation of capitalist industry. Such statements greatly oversimplify complex cultural and social constellations, to the point of being useless or even dangerous.

But explanation still has to be attempted, to tell at least one plausible story, out of many possible ones, as to why certain things have happened as they did. 'The investigator can create concepts and typologies that can be shown to exist in complex interrelationships to one another' (Koch, 1993: 132). One can therefore create ideal types, such as 'Protestant Ethic' and 'Spirit of Capitalism', and show not that one 'led' to the other in any simple way, but that two sets of phenomena can have reciprocal influences on each other, and can exist in relations of mutual reinforcement. The notion of 'elective affinities' therefore is used to depict and understand conditions of mutual support between two ideal-typical entities, be these sets of ideas, types of actions and practices, or social institutions.

This allows us to identify, for example, the affinities and mutually reinforcing relations that exist between the lifestyle of a particular social group and a particular cultural form or constellation, such as a particular kind of religious idea or activity, or a specific kind of novel or music. Thus certain religious ethics and dispositions tend to be adopted by particular social groups because they fit comfortably within the overall lifestyle of the group. Aristocratic groups tend to be attracted to and adopt types of religion that are very formal and have highly elaborate rituals, leaving more 'enthusiastic' and emotional forms of worship to groups lower in the social hierarchy. This is because the lifestyle of aristocracies is itself highly formal, being based around elaborate codes of politeness, etiquette and self-control, so naturally enough such groups would tend to favour formalistic types of worship. By contrast, groups of slaves and ex-slaves, whose lifestyle involves no such concerns but is based around taking one's pleasures while they are available, favour more wild, ecstatic and even orgiastic forms of religious practice (Collins, 1986: 136).

The notion of elective affinities also allows one to analyse situations where two sets of phenomena exist in tension with or antipathy to each other. As Weber saw it, as modern rational capitalism became ever more dominant in the modern West, it increasingly marginalised religious and spiritual dispositions which were antithetical to its harder, calculating mind-set, especially the Christian idea of universal brotherhood, which expressly went against the notion of using other people as mere tools for one's own profit-making (Gronow, 1988). Such an analysis allows us to see certain cultural contradictions more clearly (Bell, 1976) – such as the ironic situation of 19th-century American and European capitalists praying in churches and paying apparent homage to Christian notions of universal brotherhood, while ruthlessly exploiting their fellow human beings.

More generally, the notion of elective affinities animates much work in the contemporary sociology of consumption, especially that inspired by Bourdieu (1984), whose account of why the habitus (itself indebted to Weber's notion of group lifestyle and mentality) of particular fractions of classes predisposes them to like certain cultural products and to feel antipathy towards other sorts of products (Bryson, 1996).

## Charisma, Routinisation and Rationalisation

As noted above, it is possible to say that the history of the rationalisation of Western culture was one of Weber's central foci, if not his main one. Making possible such an analysis is a fundamental set of concepts, namely the typology of different types of rational action: traditional action (doing things on the basis of habit and habituation), affectual action (doing things on the basis of emotional responses to circumstances), formal rational action (involving the rational calculation of means to ends, based on universally applied rules, regulations and laws) and substantively rational action (entailing a choice of means to fulfil ends which are guided by a larger system of human values, such as a religious belief system).

For Weber there is a fundamental logical incompatibility between formal and substantive rationality and the actions they entail, because the former is indifferent to substantive values. An 'increase in one type necessarily leads to a decrease in the other type' (Gronow, 1988: 326). The upshot of this is that there could be situations based completely around rational economic action which was wholly irrational in the substantive terms of particular ideals and values – and indeed modern capitalism is precisely such an economic order, because the efficient pursuit of profit is pursued with blind indifference to substantive considerations such as 'brotherly love' or the equitable redistribution of wealth. Unlike the mainstream of 19th-century social thought, which assumed a natural coupling of increasing rationalisation of social life and social and moral 'progress', Weber's understanding of the antinomies of rationality and action suggests that a very formally rationalised social order is not necessarily 'better', substantively speaking, than a less rationalised one, and indeed may in some ways be evaluated as 'worse'. He thus separates out 'material' from 'cultural' progress – the former involves a highly formally rationalised social order centred around systematic profit-seeking on the one side, and increasingly rigid forms of bureaucratic domination and control on the other, while the latter involves the retreat of substantive values from the various spheres of public life into the purely personalised recesses of individual personalities (Kolegar, 1964). In essence, the various types of substantive rationality – both religious beliefs and secular ideals – become a matter of personal conscience without much social efficacy, and are 'individualised' and 'privatised', themes later taken up by certain scholars dealing with the contemporary sociology of religion (Beck, 2010). Weber also noted that it is the task of the social sciences 'to pay particular attention to [formal rationality's and bureaucratic organisation's] progressive expansion into social activities in ... all life spheres alike' (cited at Mommsen, 2000: 374) – thus formal rationality and rational control seep into every aspect of social life, 'colonising' them in ever more systematic fashions (a theme later taken up by Habermas (1984 [1981]; 1987 [1984])).

Such trends are identified by Weber within a two-fold analysis, encompassing both the very long-term history of rationalisation processes in the (so-called) 'West' from the time of the Hebrew prophets and ancient Greek philosophers onwards, and also the comparing of that history to developments that occurred over time in China and India, as well as to some degree in the Islamic world. While in both the West, India and China there were long-term trends towards an increased rationalisation of ideas and belief systems, it was only within the West that there were particularly profound rationalisation processes encompassing both 'ideal' and 'material' aspects of life, leading eventually in Weber's time to the separation of material from ideal phenomena, leaving a highly rationalised scientific, capitalistic and bureaucratic social world set loose from cultural values which had been reduced to purely personalised individual dispositions rather than socially significant and transformative ideals (Walker, 2001). The uniqueness of the West in this regard was due to a very complex array of factors that came together in distinctive ways over several millennia, such as the invention of experimental science in ancient Greece, the development of particular kinds of rational organisation in the Roman Empire, the bureaucratic sophistication of the medieval Catholic Church, and the especially socially transformative characteristics of certain kinds of ancient Judaism and Christianity (Collins, 1986) – in other words, a complicated array of more 'cultural' and more 'social' phenomena, interacting in highly complicated, yet still patterned, ways over long periods of time.

Central concepts which Weber deployed to understand rationalisation processes in both the West and other parts of the globe were 'charisma' and 'routinisation'. A social order centred upon principles of formal rationality is characterised by a legal-rational form of domination, of which bureaucratic control of people and things is the pre-eminent expression. Weber 'contrasts the permanence, rules and impartiality of bureaucratic authority with the changing, arbitrary and personal characteristics of charismatic leadership ... [and] opposes the "everydayness" and economic concerns of the bureaucratic and traditional authorities with the "extraordinary" features and otherworldly indifference of the revolutionary nature of the charismatic leader' (Adair-Toteff, 2005: 189). Thus charisma – involving a particular person's possession of charismatic qualities, as these are perceived by his or her followers – is set up as the antithesis of both bureaucratic and traditional forms of domination and control of persons. The charismatic leader has power over a group of disciples not because s/he holds a particular bureaucratic office, or because there is habitual deference offered by followers to a person or group defined by tradition, custom and habit as a leader, but because s/he seems to have a particular set of unique qualities, especially in terms of being able to provide convincing answers to life's great existential questions and to offer a better life now, or in the future, or in the afterlife. But in line with Weber's account of action being driven by interests, people follow the charismatic leader not just because s/he is somehow extraordinary but also because s/he offers a message or concrete consequences that seem particularly appealing to people living a particular lifestyle (another case of elective affinities at work):

> The charismatic leader gains and maintains authority solely by proving his strength in life. If he [sic] wants to be a prophet, he must perform miracles; if he wants to be a war lord, he must perform heroic deeds. Above all, however, his divine mission must 'prove' itself in that those who faithfully surrender to him must fare well. If they do not fare well, he is obviously not the master sent by the gods. (Weber, 1991e [1946]: 249)

It therefore becomes clear why Weber (clearly echoing Nietzsche) thinks that charismatic individuals and the authority they can apparently create purely from their own inner resources and rhetorical powers, can be sometimes strongly socially transformative: 'charismatic domination means a rejection of all ties to any external order in favour of the exclusive genuine mentality of the prophet and hero. Hence, its attitude is revolutionary and transvalues everything; it makes a sovereign break with all [existing] traditional or rational norms' (Weber, 1991e [1946]: 250).

Such charismatic individuals are clearly culture creators and radical innovators, signifying Weber's interest in the irreducible *individuality* of certain 'great' cultural figures, which can be construed either as a useful antidote to structural accounts of creation which stress that 'creative' individuals are themselves products of particular social-structural conditions, or as an unfortunate feature of post-Romantic thinking which swallows wholesale, and in a markedly un-sociological fashion, the Romantic myth of 'heroes' whose destiny is to 'change the world' – an apparent naivety of Weber's criticised by Bourdieu (Hutt, 2007). But the logic of Weber's argument does not suggest that charismatic figures appear completely out of the blue. The charismatic leader certainly has some purely personal *daemonic* qualities, but s/he often appears in unsettled and chaotic periods when the audience s/he aims at is suffering particularly from anguish and doubt (Adair-Toteff, 2005). Moreover, the religious charismatic can only appear within contexts where earlier religious beliefs and ideals are conducive to and allow the kinds of innovations they offer. Jesus' career as a charismatic leader was made possible by an 'inner logic' intrinsic within Judaism itself, a logic centred around the working out of tension-filled relations between a God removed from the world and the this-worldly needs of believers. In other words, Jesus' career and cultural innovations were made possible by certain cultural logics that pertained within a particular type of religion – that is, within a particular sort of *cultural material* – itself. These furnished him with a capacity to innovate conceptually and thus to revolutionise socially, in ways that would have been impossible for someone operating within a Hindu or Confucian context – the cultural materials available in those contexts were not at all conducive to the type of innovation Jesus was able to create, and indeed would have made such innovation impossible. Here we encounter a key aspect of Weber's claims about the irreducibility of 'culture' to other, material or social, factors: the virtuoso culture creator, be it a prophet or an artist, is both made possible and facilitated, but also powerfully constrained, by the inner logics of cultural materials, which can be played with to create new things, but which nonetheless possess their own special forms of resistance and forbid certain possibilities while allowing others to flourish. This applies as much to religious visionaries as it does to, for example, musicians, as we will see below.

Weber's eye was highly attuned to paradoxes and the unintended consequences of ideas and the social actions they stimulate (Symonds and Pudsey, 2008). One particularly striking paradox he pointed to involves the consequences of charismatic preaching. As Schroeder (1992) points out, although Weber did not spell the point out sufficiently, his empirical analyses show that what was at first charismatic can be either a person or a set of ideas. In both cases, the originally charismatic elements become routinised, becoming part of everyday existence for adherents, and becoming subject to ever more bureaucratic forms of administration. The shift from the charismatic dynamics of the very earliest years of Jesus' ministry to the elaboration of the massive rational organisational structures of the medieval Catholic Church is a paradigmatic case here. Moreover, originally innovative and inspirational ideas are adapted to fit the changing needs of particular sets of adherents and their lifestyles, another case of elective affinities at work.

A further paradoxical outcome of charismatic action is that it unleashes rationalising forces which can eventually contribute to creating a situation where the substantive values embodied in the preaching can be seriously undermined, transformed or destroyed. The famous Weberian phrase 'disenchantment of the world' refers to the increasing elimination of magical ways of thinking from the world in favour of rational systems of thought. The term is often thought to refer to the elimination of magical thought in Western modernity by the twin forces of natural scientific rationality and bureaucratic domination. But for Weber the disenchantment of the world has been going on in the West since the time of the Hebrew prophets, for they engaged in 'rational prophecies' which broke down magical ways of thinking – which are always socially conservative in Weber's view – in favour of promoting more rationally systematic forms of thought and conduct. Thus in the name of substantive religious values Hebrew prophets and then some Christian figures unintentionally promoted forms of theoretical rationality which were socially transformative in the direction of creating an ever more rationalised cultural sphere, which in turn impacted on social relations by 'break[ing] down the traditional sacred rules. Prophecies have released the world from magic and in doing so have created the basis for our modern science and technology, and for capitalism' (Weber, 1927: 265).

Weber juxtaposes the charismatic potentials of prophets with the bureaucratic and rationally systematising activities of priests, who write down the sacred words and turn them into quasi-legal sets of regulations. In so doing, he pointed to two important issues – first, that the tension and rivalry between these two types of religious actor constitutes a *field* characterised by competition over who can legitimately speak for the 'true' religion; and second, that it is above all professional groups, both religious functionaries and secular officials like lawyers and book-keepers, who are the 'carriers' and promoters of rationalisation processes, with programmes of professional training and education particularly fostering the increased rationalisation of particular ideas, practices, and institutions – a feature of social life in general, and Western modernity in particular, that Marx had underplayed (Ritzer, 1975).

One of the greatest ironies in world history was for Weber the fact that it was the rational prophecy embodied in Protestant Puritan ascetic doctrines which had a particularly powerful effect on deepening and speeding up the rationalisation processes that had been going on for many centuries both within Judeo-Christian religion itself and within the institutions of the Western world. Protestant doctrine may have helped to develop the spirit of modern capitalism, but in so doing it also helped to form highly rational forms of conduct, especially to do with the self-controlled and self-denying pursuit of profit-for-profit's sake, and over time these would lose their original religious and charismatic character, and become routinised and secularised. Rational prophecy in its Protestant form helped unleash modes of rationality in thought and action which would lose sight of their initially prophetic provenance. The Protestant ideas of 'duty' and 'calling' to fulfil God's demands lost their charismatic hues and took on the grey qualities of everyday life and fostered compulsions to act without fully knowing why one does so: modern rational capitalism becomes the mechanical expression of 'dead religious beliefs', a system of action in which 'the pursuit of wealth, stripped of its religious and ethical meaning, tends to become associated with purely mundane passions' (Weber, 1930 [1904–5]: 124).

It is in that light that Weber writes of the *stahlhartes Gehäuse* that modern capitalism has created, a concept that Talcott Parsons famously translated as the 'iron cage', but which could be more accurately rendered as 'shell as hard as steel'. As Baehr (2001) notes, unlike the natural element iron, steel is a 'product of human fabrication ... both hard and potentially flexible ... [W]hereas a cage confines human agents, but leaves their powers otherwise intact, a "shell" suggests that modern capitalism has created a new kind of being', a hybrid creature quite different from the sort of humans who lived in pre-modern times, but one ironically created in large part by the rational prophesying work of the Judeo-Christian prophets over the last three millennia. For Weber, modern dilemmas have very ancient roots.

Many scholars have taken up Weber's initial insights to analyse the cultural and social conditions of our own times (Motta, 2011). For example, Ritzer's (2008) diagnosis of late 20th-and early 21st-century rationalisation dynamics describes the latter as 'McDonaldization' processes, involving the four key factors of calculation, predictability, efficiency and control, all elements of thought and practice highlighted by Weber. 'McDonaldization' is seen to involve the rationalisation not just of forms of production and distribution – as in the original case of food created for and prepared in fast food restaurants – but also spaces and objects of all sorts. The spirit of Weber's writings on rationalisation inform Ritzer's (2004) account of globalisation, which is seen to involve 'non-things' – culturally weightless objects recognised everywhere, like the Visa sign and credit cards – being used by people in uniform ways, in homogenised consumer environments that are all the same the world over (Augè, 1995).

However, in the application of the spirit or the letter of Weber's writings, one must be attuned to differences between the form of modernity which he thought was prevalent in his times, and the nature of modernity we may take to be characteristic of our own epoch. For example, in the early 20th century the figure of the bureaucrat was characterised by uniformity and conformity. But under a neo-liberal form of capitalist social order, characterised by the encouragement of self-conscious competition between organisations and between individuals, the white collar worker in service industries like IT is compelled to perform and present supposedly unique forms of individuality and individual creativity (Clegg, 2005). Such dynamics would likely not have surprised Weber greatly, for they are analysable in his terms as hybrids of bureaucratic and charismatic forms of authority and action. In a cultural context where Information Technology is so important, it is not surprising that the type of charismatic figure set up as exemplary figure to be followed should be the likes of Steve Jobs, whose charisma, as perceived by those who set him up as some kind of guru, may be understood as an admixture of capitalist profit-seeking and quasi-messianic 'giftedness'. A Weberian approach is easily able to bring a scalpel-like precision to the analysis of those set up as culture-heroes by particular social groups within specific cultural contexts, laying bare the pretensions of both leaders and followers as a result.

One should also note that Weber's original notion of the routinisation of charisma lends itself to being inverted – as Weber arguably did himself, in terms of analysing the nature of religious revivals like the Reformation – so that another notion is created, namely the *charismaticisation of routine*. Here one would examine how particular individuals, groups or sets of ideas work to reinvigorate, and in so doing perhaps transform, the ideals and aspiration of targeted audience groups (Lee, 2010). For example, the cadres of Green social movements and protest groups have been sometimes very successful in galvanising supporters through effective rhetorical and emotional work which awakens or re-awakens moral conscience and spiritual responses about 'Nature', the environment, non-human animals and so on (Lindholm and Zuquete, 2010). But as Weber was well aware, any successful galvanisation of support is always likely over time to lapse back again into routinisation of thought and practice, as the bureaucratisation of Green political parties and other groups, and concomitant claims by critics that they have become mere rational capitalist businesses or just like any other routine political party, amply attest.

A Weberian focus on the interplay of charisma and routine lays the foundation for a sociology of 'authenticity', an especially valued phenomenon in modern, rational cultural contexts where actors think that everyday reality is centred around either dull bureaucratic compulsion or the fraudulent practices perpetrated by those who have only profit in mind. Performances and presentations of charisma rejuvenate and re-energise life for certain audiences, endowing them with revitalised substantive purposes, but such revitalisation and perception of authenticity is always precarious (Osbaldiston, 2013). Moreover, authenticity itself is manufactured within rationally organised industrial capitalist contexts, cultural producers having to engage in effortful work to prevent the authenticity being damaged by consumers coming to realise this fact – a theme taken up by the 'production of culture' school which itself owes significant debts to Weber (Peterson, 1999).

## *Value Spheres*

The final key concept of Weber's that we will consider here is that concerning 'value spheres'. Weber identifies five central spheres of social existence: the political, economic, aesthetic, erotic and the intellectual, the latter encompassing religion, science and philosophy. These can either overlap with each other in particular ways, thus reinforcing each other in specific manners, or may be differentiated from each other, a situation which is characteristic of modern social formations only. Whether the value spheres overlap or not has great consequences both for what happens inside each of them and for the wider social fabric (Schroeder, 1992).

When particular value spheres overlap, as they do in one way or another in all pre- and non-modern contexts, this tends to produce conservative ideas and forms of action. For example, in classical China, the Confucian literati held power in both the political sphere, operating as State bureaucrats, and the intellectual sphere, operating there as the producers and holders of knowledge about the universe's workings, and consequently the political and intellectual realms reinforced each other, creating no revolutionary ideas or actions and leaving the economic sphere to function through traditional forms of action. On Weber's view, this is the sort of situation that meant that, in the long term, industrialism and modern capitalism could not have appeared in China. By contrast, it was the increasingly marked differentiation of the various value spheres in the West which was both partial cause, and then further consequence, of the rise of rational capitalism. From the 16th century onwards, there was a withdrawal of religion from the other value spheres, and a transformation and then diminishment of its power in the intellectual sphere, and this further fostered rationalised secular cultural dispositions in all the various domains of Western life. This was one of the major foundations for the rapid and strong development of rationalised institutions in all aspects of existence.

The differentiation of the value spheres had various far-reaching consequences. Once each becomes autonomous of the others, it means that it operates according to its own specific logics. Activity within each sphere – especially the aesthetic and intellectual ones – becomes centred upon working with the specific 'cultural materials' associated with that sphere and working out their 'inner logics' in innovative ways, such work now being largely free from interference from priests and State officials, whose sphere of duty is now limited mostly to their own value spheres. What follows from such differentiation is that 'what is rational from one point of view may be irrational from another' (Barbalet, 2000: 331), because each sphere works with a rationality and logic that is very different from those that pertain in the others.

Thus contrary to Weber's bleak pronouncements about the dominance of formal rationality throughout all of modern social life, the analysis of value spheres potentially points in another direction – that of modernity as a constellation of multiple and separate rationalities and domains of action. The difficulties each sphere has in communicating with, and understanding the activities going on in the others, is a theme taken up by Niklas Luhmann (1982).

Weber noted that the world of art and aesthetics was the last of the value spheres to be systematically rationalised (Harrington, 2004). The nature and consequences of the 'relative autonomy' of art from other spheres of life thus becomes a major focus for sociology. Kemple (2005) proposes that in scattered places in his writings where Weber observes the modern aesthetic sphere, he offered what can today be reconstructed as a 'sociological aesthetics'. This is a 'value-free' enterprise in that it does not 'adjudicate matters of taste or temperament, nor can it assess the cultural or ethical value of the subject matter of artworks' (2005: 10). Instead such a project

> observe[s] and analyse[s] the emergence of new cultural media and innovative aesthetic forms in view of the social foundations and economic conditions that make them possible ... [thus] determining what is distinctive about the aesthetic sphere of modernity ... [Weber does] not just explain how class interests or new technologies transform the subject matter of art and thus what may count as art, but ... pose[s] broader questions concerning ... the social conditions within which new aesthetic forms acquire cultural value and significance. (Kemple, 2005: 11–12)

A particularly striking example of Weber's style of analysis in this regard comes from a lecture given in 1910. Weber notes:

> ... if we ask whether what is called modern technology in the ordinary meaning of the word does not stand in some relationship with formal-aesthetic values ... then ... we must undoubtedly answer yes to this question, insofar as very definite formal values in our modern artistic culture could only be born through the existence of the modern metropolis: the modern metropolis with its railways, subways, electric and other lights, shop windows, concert and catering halls, cafés, smokestacks, and piles of stone, the whole wild dance of sound and colour impressions that affect sexual fantasy, and the experiences of variations in the soul's constitution that lead to a hungry brooding over all kinds of seemingly inexhaustible possibilities for the conduct of life and happiness. Partly as a protest, a specific means of

fleeing from this reality: the highest aesthetic abstractions, the deepest forms of dream, or the most intense forms of frenzy; and partly as an adaptation to this reality: apologies for its own fantastic and intoxicating rhythms. (Weber, 2005 [1910]: 29)

With such remarks, argues Kemple (2005: 13), Weber 'appears to perform sociology itself as an art form, that is, to articulate the sociological imagination as both a scientific method and an expressive mode of aesthetic experimentation'. Thus we should place Weber among those sociologists such as Simmel, Howard S. Becker and Robert Nisbet (2005) who have regarded sociology not just as a way of reflecting upon art's nature and roles in modernity, but as itself an aesthetic form which creates verbal pictures of modern social dynamics, including vivid representations of how modern aesthetics is made possible within a sphere that is indirectly affected and made possible by other value-spheres, such as that of science and technology.

## WEBER TODAY

The preceding discussion has illustrated many of the debts contemporary cultural sociology and sociology of culture owe to Weber's pioneering work. In many ways the 'production of culture' school (see Chapter 14) can be regarded as working out, in painstaking empirical ways, some of Weber's observations about the creation of culture on the one side and the nature of modern rational organisations on the other. This is because Weber 'provides the researcher [with] a way to acknowledge the rational, capitalistic ... and structural elements' of modern contexts of cultural production (Turley, 2001: 650). He shows how in such contexts, different sorts of people are at work, such as entrepreneurs, bureaucrats and manual workers, each endowed with specific sorts of predictable relations between them, of both co-operation and value-driven conflict, involving aggressive profit-seeking and bureaucratic conservatism, the latter being driven by pride in possessing certain skills and the need to maintain a certain type and degree of honour and self-worth (Swedberg, 2003). All of these sorts of dynamics have been uncovered in contemporary cultural industries by production of culture scholarship in recent years (Peterson and Anand, 2004).

The major and varied influences of Weber on Bourdieu's accounts of cultural production, mediation and consumption also cannot be underestimated (Hutt, 2007). In Bourdieu's view, 'one may – and should – use Weber against Weber to go beyond Weber' (1988: 780). In his conception of social class, in his understanding of the affinities between certain lifestyles and particular cultural objects, in his conception of the relative autonomy of cultural fields, in his attempt to create a nuanced understanding of the relations between ideal and material interests in social action, and in his stress on the importance of symbolic forms in maintaining and legitimating power relations, the mark of Weber on Bourdieu's writings is clear. Bourdieu (1987 [1971]) was particularly inspired by Weber's sociology of religion. He found within it various themes he found conducive for developing an understanding of the dynamics operative within fields of cultural production and consumption. On Bourdieu's interpretation, religions are fields of struggle, involving more orthodox and heterodox groupings, each trying to win control over the monopoly of the legitimate exercise of power over lay groups. Such fields are populated by different types of specialist religious producer engaged in the production and distribution of religious goods. Elective affinities come into existence between particular sorts of producers and their audiences. Two particularly important types of actor are prophets who must seek authority through charismatic means, and priests who possess legitimacy by virtue of holding an office that is generally respected. All of these themes were transposed by Bourdieu onto the analysis of the emergent autonomous fields of painting and literature in 19th-century France (Bourdieu, 1993, 1996).

An important break which Bourdieu made with Weber concerns the latter's understanding of charisma. For Bourdieu, Weber overemphasises the unprecedented and apparently unique nature of charismatic individuals, and he replaces it with the view that charisma is only ever perceived by audiences, does not somehow rest in the person themselves, and therefore is created and licensed by the particular field and its power dynamics within which such persons act. We must therefore investigate the mechanisms whereby operates the social production of charismatic leaders, culture creators, 'great artists', and suchlike figures. This is in line with Bourdieu's broader social structuralist epistemology, partly inherited from Durkheim, which insists on seeing actors as products of underlying structural forces and as occupying and expressing particular positions in a field according to the type and amount of capital they possess. But it is precisely this move, involving the downgrading of concrete individuals to structural positions, which Bourdieu's critics focus on as one of the least appealing aspects of field theory, with Bourdieu seen to have unwisely ditched the Weberian focus on specific individual actors and their irreducibly unique actions (Becker and Pessin, 2006; Bottero and Crossley, 2011). Bourdieu's appropriation of Weber to Marxian and Durkheimian concerns has thus been viewed by some as highly problematic.

A more recent line of inquiry by other scholars has concerned Weber's treatment of the history of music. This was one part of his broader study of rationalisation in the West, and up until recently was presented as being primarily about the increasingly rational organisation of music and musical practices (Martin, 1995). If considered in that way, then Weber's (1958) major contribution to the sociology of music is to have shown that Western music developed into much more rational forms than the music of other civilisations (a claim disputed by Turley, 2001). The history of music is based upon a fundamental tension between the irrationality of sounds and human attempts to create rational systems out of them – it is this tension that has allowed for and driven musical creativity and innovation over the centuries. From the Middle Ages onwards, Western music involved a 12-tone scale, unlike in places such as India and China which had a different set of scales and chords. Western composers developed their music on the basis of rational experimentation with the permutations possible within the 12-tone scale. As a result, Western music developed in ways that derived logically from the initial scale patterns. In addition, Western music over the last several hundred years has been *polyvocal* in character, whereas the musical culture of other societies has generally been *univocal*. In the former case, different 'voices' (either human or those of instruments) each play simultaneously, each having its own melody. Western musical composition has developed on the basis of finding ways of organising the different voices so that they are related to each other harmoniously. According to the Weberian diagnosis, the orchestra is a cultural phenomenon unique to the modern West. Its characteristics are a 'bureaucratic' rational organisation of the different sections (wind, strings, etc.). The ways of composing for this type of musical organisation are inevitably more about rule-following and procedures for attaining harmony than are other types of music-making. Thus the highly rationalistic character of Western art, at least in its musical forms but also to some extent in its architectural forms too, is expressive of a wider rational culture (Feher, 1987).

While the details of Weber's account can be questioned, his study of music illustrates well the general methodological principles underpinning his studies, namely that one should 'identify a process with many dimensions and try to incorporate [as many of] these dimensions [as possible] into the explanation', thus producing a sophisticated, multi-dimensional, poly-causal understanding of the phenomena in question (Turley, 2001: 639). In his account of the history of Occidental music, Weber connects the 'cultural material' of music and the problems it posed to composers, with a diverse range of social, material and cultural factors, including religious institutions within which musical creators operated, the craft guilds within which instrument makers worked, the instruments they produced for evolving markets of producers and consumers, and the economic relations – such as being hired to play at royal courts – within which instrumentalists functioned. By connecting these disparate factors and phenomena, Weber is able to show how people, objects, cultural materials, and political and economic arrangements all related to each other. Thus whether or not we accept the contention that the interaction of all these things was ultimately responsible for the overall rationalisation of music and music-playing, nonetheless the multi-modal methodology remains appealing. It was taken up in part by Norbert Elias (1978) in his study of the social conditions within which Mozart was constrained to produce his works, and it influenced Adorno (2015 [1976]: 67), who partly in a Weberian spirit claimed that the sociology of music 'should take its bearings from the social structures that leave their imprint on music, and ... musical life'. Nonetheless, much remains in potential to be developed by other scholars in the future.

A particularly promising avenue is opened up when one considers that Weber's willingness to connect cultural forces, cultural materials possessed of certain 'inner logics', and social relations to the creation and use of technologies, resonates at the present time with the newer Science and Technology Studies (STS) and Actor-Network Theory (ANT) orientations in cultural sociology (Maley, 2004; see Chapter 10). Darmon (2015: 21) argues that Weber's overall analytic orientation 'accounts for music as a cultural domain of action, engagement and relations, starting from the matter of music [i.e. the cultural material of music], its sounds, technologies, instruments and logics of organization'. His approach gives us clues as to how to connect the organisation of 'sound material', and the inner dynamics of its development, to many other social and material factors, trying to keep them all in dynamic interplay rather than subordinating them to a mono-causal explanation. Weber thus should figure as an important inspiration for 'new sociologies of art' (de la Fuente, 2007), which attempt to take the realm of aesthetics as a partly autonomous social sphere and not to reduce it, as Bourdieu's critics claim he did, to a more foundational social realm of power and social interests. The 'encounters' between culture makers and the inner logics of cultural materials is a Weberian theme that today is highly productive (Darmon, 2015: 30). This is in part because Weberian ideas can help us to develop more aesthetically sensitive forms of analysis, while still retaining the classically sociological focus on power foregrounded by Bourdieu, which itself stems partially from Weber (Prior, 2011).

Moreover, Weber's accounts of the development of musical technologies remain highly suggestive for a field increasingly oriented towards considering the role of non-human actants in cultural production, distribution and consumption. This is because Weber linked the development of musical technologies to cultural, social, political, economic and even climactic factors, the latter being particularly interesting for cultural sociologists in a time of climate change. For example, the piano developed in the colder climes of Northern Europe, among a largely house-bound bourgeoisie. It was from within that type of lifestyle that there emerged demand for certain kinds of instruments which could play music notated in certain ways. An increasingly rationalised capitalism produced both music and mass-manufactured pianos for such an audience. Technological innovations were stimulated by the demands of that lifestyle and the increasingly varied climactic conditions in which it played out – thus the Steinway company invented iron piano frames to replace the earlier wooden type, to serve European clients in tropical colonial contexts where the wooden frames would be liable to warp (Turley, 2001). Through such considerations we can see how Weber's multi-dimensional mode of analysis seems to be particularly appealing to scholars today who want to try to develop understandings of phenomena which go beyond older disciplinary and sub-disciplinary specialisms and the forms of blindness to multi-causality which they entail.

## CONCLUSION

Max Weber pointed out how the ghosts of belief-systems past continued to stalk the cultural landscapes of the present, albeit in often radically transformed guises from their original incarnations. It is therefore appropriate that the shade of Weber himself prowls the terrain of contemporary sociological investigations of culture. His presences take many forms, which have been presented throughout this chapter. From being primarily considered as a theorist of rationalisation processes and rational forms of organisation, the roles of Weber in sociology in general, and cultural sociology in particular, have multiplied over the years, such that there are now many Webers, all equally plausible. These include the Weber who influenced much of Bourdieu's field theory, the Weber who supplied the analytical tools for the 'production of culture' school, the cultural-historical-sociological Weber (see Chapter 15), Weber the analyst of the relative autonomy of culture, Weber the STS and ANT thinker *avant la lettre*, and so on. The many incarnations exist in a potentially infinite list that stretches out into the future to encompass as yet uninvented Webers who nonetheless exist in potential, waiting to be brought into being by future scholarly generations. Weber's presences continue to multiply, as more is understood of the complexities of his life's work and as new exegetes, equipped with novel orientations and concerns generated by their own time and place, find new forms of significance and potentiality in his writings. It is not too great an exaggeration to say that in sociology's engagements with cultural matters most, if not all, roads ultimately lead to Weber, not just back to him but forward to him as well – hence the sustained attention he has been given in this chapter. He is not just a foundational figure for cultural sociology and the sociology of culture – he is perhaps *the* most important of the classical thinkers for how these fields have developed over the last hundred years.

As we have seen, some scholars today see his ongoing usefulness for these fields as being made possible by decoupling his concerns with cultural materials and their 'inner logics' from the grand account of millennia of rationalisation in the West. That makes sense in one way, but such a move also risks losing one of the greatest benefits of Weber's approach to cultural matters, namely its connecting of contemporary cultural forces and forms of production to hundreds and thousands of years of cultural and social change. This is precisely the kind of broad analytical vision that the social sciences always need to embrace in order to avoid both fetishizing the supposed uniqueness of the present and succumbing to a historical parochialism of a type which is detrimental to the kind of scholarly ambition and global grasp of materials which Weber still today so acutely embodies (Inglis, 2014).

# REFERENCES

Adair-Toteff, C. (2005) 'Max Weber's Charisma', *Journal of Classical Sociology*, 5(2): 189–204.

Adorno, T. (2015 [1976]) 'Sociology of Music', in J. Shepherd and K. Devine (eds), *The Routledge Reader on the Sociology of Music*. London: Routledge. pp. 67–72.

Alexander, J.C. (1983) *Theoretical Logic in Sociology, Volume III: The Classical Attempt at Theoretical Synthesis: Max Weber*. Los Angeles: University of California Press.

Alexander, J.C. (2003) *The Meanings of Social Life: A Cultural Sociology*. New York: Oxford University Press.

Aron, R. (1971) 'Max Weber and Power-politics', in Otto Stammer (ed.), *Max Weber and Sociology Today*. New York: Harper and Row. pp. 85–94

Augè, M. (1995) *Non-Places: Introduction to an Anthropology of Supermodernity*. London: Verso.

Baehr, P. (2001) 'The "Iron Cage" and the "Shell as Hard as Steel": Parsons, Weber, and the *Stahlhartes Gehäuse* Metaphor in the Protestant Ethic and the Spirit of Capitalism', *History and Theory*, 40(2): 153–69.

Barbalet, J.M. (2000) '"Beruf", Rationality and Emotion in Max Weber's Sociology', *European Journal of Sociology*, 41(2): 329–51.

Beck, U. (2010) *A God of One's Own: Religion's Capacity for Peace and Potential for Violence*. Cambridge: Polity.

Becker, H.S. (1984) *Art Worlds*. Los Angeles: University of California Press.

Becker, H.S. and Pessin, A. (2006) 'A Dialogue on the Ideas of "World" and "Field"', *Sociological Forum*, 21(2): 275–86.

Bell, D. (1976) *The Cultural Contradictions of Capitalism*. New York: Basic Books.

Bendix, R. (1960) *Max Weber: An Intellectual Portrait*. New York: Doubleday.

Bottero, W. and Crossley, N. (2011) 'Worlds, Fields and Networks: Becker, Bourdieu and the Structures of Social Relations', *Cultural Sociology*, 5(1): 99–119.

Bourdieu, P. (1984) *Distinction: A Social Critique of the Judgment of Taste*, London: Routledge.

Bourdieu, P. (1987 [1971]) 'Legitimation and Structured Interests in Weber's Sociology of Religion', in S. Lash and S. Whimster (eds), *Max Weber: Rationality and Modernity*. London: Allen and Unwin. pp. 119–36.

Bourdieu, P. (1988) 'Vive la Crise! For Heterodoxy in Social Science', *Theory and Society*, 17(5): 773–87.

Bourdieu, P. (1993) *The Field of Cultural Production*. Cambridge: Polity.

Bourdieu, P. (1996) *The Rules of Art: Genesis and Structure of the Literary Field*. Stanford: Stanford University Press.

Bruun, H.H. (1972) *Science, Values and Politics in Max Weber's Methodology*. Copenhagen: Munksgaard.

Bryson, B. (1996) '"Anything But Heavy Metal": Symbolic Exclusion and Musical Dislikes', *American Sociological Review*, 61(5): 884–99.

Burawoy, M. (2012) 'From Max Weber to Public Sociology', in H.G. Soeffner (ed.), *Transnationale Vergesellschaftungen*. New York: Springer. pp. 741–55.

Clegg, S.R. (2005) 'Puritans, Visionaries and Survivors', *Organization Studies*, 26(4): 527–45.

Collins, R. (1986) *Max Weber: A Skeleton Key*. Newbury Park, CA: Sage.

Darmon, I. (2015) 'Weber on Music: Approaching Music as a Dynamic Domain of Action and Experience', *Cultural Sociology*, 9(1): 20–37.

de la Fuente, E. (2007) 'The "New Sociology of Art": Putting Art Back into Social Science Approaches to the Arts', *Cultural Sociology*, 1(3): 409–25.

Eisenstadt, S.N. (2000) 'Multiple Modernities', *Daedalus*, 129(1): 1–29.

Elias, N. (1978) *The Civilizing Process: The History of Manners*, Vol. 1. Oxford: Blackwell.

Feher, F. (1987) 'Weber and the Rationalization of Music', *The International Journal of Politics, Culture and Society*, 1(2): 147–62.

Gane, N. (2000) 'Max Weber Revisited', *Sociology*, 34(4): 811–16.

Gane, N. (2002) *Max Weber and Postmodern Theory: Rationalization versus Re-enchantment*. London: Palgrave.

Gronow, J. (1988) 'The Element of Irrationality: Max Weber's Diagnosis of Modern Culture', *Acta Sociologica*, 31(4): 319–31.

Habermas, J. (1984 [1981]) *Theory of Communicative Action, Vol. One: Reason and the Rationalization of Society*. Boston: Beacon Press.

Habermas, J. (1987 [1984]) *Theory of Communicative Action, Vol. Two: Liveworld and System: A Critique of Functionalist Reason*. Boston: Beacon Press.

Harrington, A. (2004) *Art and Social Theory*. Cambridge: Polity.

Hennis, W. (1988) *Max Weber: Essays in Reconstruction*. London: Allen & Unwin.

Herva, S. (1988) 'The Genesis of Max Weber's "Verstehende Soziologie"', *Acta Sociologica*, 31(2): 143–56.

Hinde, S. and Dixon, J. (2007) 'Reinstating Pierre Bourdieu's Contribution to Cultural Economy Theorizing', *Journal of Sociology*, 43(4): 401–20.

Hutt, C. (2007) 'Pierre Bourdieu on the "Verstehende Soziologie" of Max Weber', *Method & Theory in the Study of Religion*, 19(3/4): 232–54.

Inglis, D. (2014) 'What is Worth Defending in Sociology Today? Presentism, Historical Vision and the Uses of Sociology', *Cultural Sociology*, 8(1): 99–118.

Kalberg, S. (2009) 'Max Weber's Analysis of the Unique American Civic Sphere: Its Origins, Expansion, and Oscillations', *Journal of Classical Sociology*, 9(1): 117–41.

Kemple, T.M. (2005) 'Instrumentum Vocale: A Note on Max Weber's Value-Free Polemics and Sociological Aesthetics', *Theory, Culture & Society*, 22(4): 1–22.

Kemple, T.M. (2008) 'Review: Re-Reading Max Weber', *Minerva*, 46(3): 385–9.

Koch, A.M. (1993) 'Rationality, Romanticism and the Individual: Max Weber's "Modernism" and the Confrontation with "Modernity"', *Canadian Journal of Political Science*, 26(1): 123–44.

Kolegar, F. (1964) 'The Concept of "Rationalization" and Cultural Pessimism in Max Weber's Sociology', *Sociological Quarterly*, 5(4): 355–73.

Lamont, M. and Fournier, M. (1993) *Cultivating Differences: Symbolic Boundaries and the Making of Inequality*. Chicago: The University of Chicago Press.

Lee, R.L. (2010) 'Weber, Re-Enchantment and Social Futures', *Time and Society*, 19(2): 180–92.

Liebersohn, H. (1988) *Fate and Utopia in German Sociology, 1870–1923*. Cambridge, MA: MIT Press.

Lima Neto, F. (2014) 'Cultural Sociology in Perspective: Linking Culture and Power', *Current Sociology Review*, 62(6): 928–46.

Lindholm, C. and Zuquete, P. (2010) *The Struggle for the World: Liberation Movements for the 21st Century*. Stanford: Stanford University Press.

Luhmann, N. (1982) *The Differentiation of Society*. New York: Columbia University Press.

Maley, T. (2004) 'Max Weber and the Iron Cage of Technology', *Bulletin of Science, Technology & Society*, 24(1): 69–86.

Martin, P. (1995) *Sounds and Society: Themes in the Sociology of Music*. Manchester: Manchester University Press.

Mommsen, W.J. (1977) 'Max Weber as a Critic of Marxism', *Canadian Journal of Sociology*, 2(4): 373–98.

Mommsen, W.J. (2000) 'Max Weber's "Grand Sociology": The Origins and Composition of Wirtschaft und Gesellschaft: Soziologie', *History and Theory*, 39(3): 364–83.

Motta, R. (2011) 'Max Weber's Vocation: Some Remarks Concerning the Disenchantment of the Disenchanter', *Social Compass*, 58(2): 153–61.

Mueller, G.H. (1982) 'Socialism and Capitalism in the Work of Max Weber', *British Journal of Sociology*, 33(2): 151–71.

Nisbet, R.A. (2005) *Sociology as an Art Form*. New York: Transaction.

Osbaldiston, N. (ed.) (2013) *The Culture of the Slow: Social Deceleration in an Accelerating World*. London: Palgrave.

Parsons, T. (1965) 'Max Weber 1864–1964', *American Sociological Review*, 30(2): 171–5.

Peterson, R.A. (1999) *Creating Country Music: Fabricating Authenticity*. Chicago: University of Chicago Press.

Peterson, R. and Anand, N. (2004) 'The Production of Culture Perspective', *Annual Review of Sociology*, 30: 311–34.

Prior, N. (2011) 'Critique and Renewal in the Sociology of Music: Bourdieu and Beyond', *Cultural Sociology*, 5(1): 121–38.

Radkau, J. (2009) *Max Weber: A Biography*. Cambridge: Polity.

Ringer, F.K. (1990) *The Decline of the German Mandarins: The German Academic Community, 1890–1933*. Middletown: Wesleyan University Press.

Ritzer, G. (1975) 'Professionalization, Bureaucratization and Rationalization: The Views of Max Weber', *Social Forces*, 53(4): 627–34.

Ritzer, G. (2004) *The Globalization of Nothing*. Los Angeles: Pine Forge Press.

Ritzer, G. (2008) *The McDonaldization of Society*. Los Angeles: Pine Forge Press.

Roth, G. (1977) 'Max Weber: A Bibliographical Essay', *Zeitschrift fur Soziologie*, 6(1): 91–102.

Roth, G. and Schluchter, W. (1979) *Max Weber's Vision of History: Ethics and Methods*. Berkeley: University of California Press.

Scaff, L.A. (1981) 'Max Weber and Robert Michels', *American Journal of Sociology*, 86(6): 1269–86.

Schroeder, R. (1992) *Max Weber and the Sociology of Culture*. London: Sage.

Swedberg, R. (2003) 'The Changing Picture of Max Weber's Sociology', *Annual Review of Sociology*, 29: 283–306.

Symonds, M. and Pudsey, J. (2008) 'The Concept of "Paradox" in the Work of Max Weber', *Sociology*, 42(2): 223–41.

Tenbruck, F.H. (1980) 'The Problem of Thematic Unity in the Works of Max Weber', *British Journal of Sociology*, 31(3): 316–51.

Turley, A.C. (2001) 'Max Weber and the Sociology of Music', *Sociological Forum*, 16(4): 633–53.

Turner, B.S. (2011) 'Max Weber and the Spirit of Resentment: The Nietzsche Legacy', *Journal of Classical Sociology*, 11(1): 75–92.

Walker, G. (2001) 'Society and Culture in Sociological and Anthropological Tradition', *History of the Human Sciences*, 14(3): 30–55.

Weber, M. (1927) *General Economic History*. Trans F.H. Knight. London: Allen & Unwin.

Weber, M. (1930 [1904–5]) *The Protestant Ethic and the Spirit of Capitalism*. Trans T. Parsons. London, Boston: Unwin Hyman.

Weber, M. (1949) 'Objectivity in Social Science and Social Policy', in E. Shils and H. Finch (eds), *Max Weber on the Methodology of the Social Sciences*. Glencoe: Free Press, pp. 50–112.

Weber, M. (1958) *The Rational and Social Foundations of Music*. Carbondale: Southern Illinois University Press.

Weber, M. (1966) *The Sociology of Religion*. London: Methuen.

Weber, M. (1978) *Economy and Society: An Outline of Interpretive Sociology*. Berkeley: University of California Press.

Weber, M. (1991a [1946]) 'Class, Status, Party', in H.H. Gerth and C.W. Mills (eds), *From Max Weber*. London: Routledge. pp. 180–95.

Weber, M. (1991b [1946]) *From Max Weber*. H.H. Gerth and C.W. Mills (eds). London: Routledge.

Weber, M. (1991c [1946]) 'Politics as a Vocation', in H.H. Gerth and C.W. Mills (eds), *From Max Weber*. London: Routledge. pp. 77–128.

Weber, M. (1991d [1946]) 'The Social Psychology of the World Religions', in H.H. Gerth and C.W. Mills (eds), *From Max Weber*. London: Routledge. pp. 267–301.

Weber, M. (1991e [1946]) 'The Sociology of Charismatic Authority', in H.H. Gerth and C.W. Mills (eds), *From Max Weber*. London: Routledge. pp. 245–52.

Weber, M. (2005 [1910]) 'Remarks on Technology and Culture', *Theory, Culture & Society*, 22(4): 23–38.

Weber, M. (2010 [1904–5]) *The Protestant Ethic and the Spirit of Capitalism*. Trans S. Kalberg. New York: Oxford University Press.

Whimster, S. (2007) *Understanding Weber*. London: Routledge.

Williams, R. (1981) *Culture*. London: Fontana.

# The Cultural Sociology of Alfred Weber and Karl Mannheim

Colin Loader

## INTRODUCTION

In September 1928 Karl Mannheim delivered a paper on 'Competition as a Cultural Phenomenon' at the Sixth Congress of the German Sociologists in Zurich, Switzerland. Mannheim's paper addressed the issue of culture sociologically, anticipating the strategy of his best known work, *Ideology and Utopia*, which, like his Zurich paper, would be published the next year. Among those in his audience was his primary sponsor at the University of Heidelberg, Alfred Weber. Weber understood that Mannheim's paper represented a distancing from his own approach to the sociology of culture, which he had been developing in a series of writings over almost two decades. In the most recent of those works before Zurich, he distinguished his methodological approach from that of his late brother Max. Now it appeared that Mannheim was moving toward Max's formulation. The confrontation between the two continued the next year back in Heidelberg, where they conducted a joint seminar on Georg Lukács's *History and Class Consciousness*. This chapter traces the development of the cultural sociologies of Weber and Mannheim, leading to their clash in the late 1920s.

## ALFRED WEBER'S CULTURAL SOCIOLOGY

Alfred Weber first formulated his cultural sociology in the decade before World War I. Attention to culture as a central sphere of human activity increased dramatically with the rapid industrialization of Germany and the expansion of the bureaucratic imperial state. Those who turned their attention to culture represented a spectrum of world views, from anti-modern traditionalists to liberal academics (Lichtblau, 1996). The latter, which included Weber, his brother Max, Werner Sombart, and others of their generation of political economists, found themselves at odds with the academic establishment's view that the nation formed an organic unity of meaning and values, which were embodied in the imperial state and arbitrated by the academic elites whose identity was tied to the state (Ringer, 1969). The state's organic unity presupposed the subordination of the divisive sphere of civil society, which consisted of conflicting material interests and the political parties that represented them. Many in Weber's generation, following the lead of Ferdinand Tönnies, replaced the hierarchical imperial dualism of state and civil society with a successive one in which an organic traditional community (*Gemeinschaft*) gave way to a rational, atomistic society (*Gesellschaft*). The imperial state was now included with civil society as part of the *Gesellschaft*. In so doing, these thinkers transformed the officialdom, which included themselves, from an educated provider of national values into functionaries of the bureaucratic state (Loader, 2012).

Alfred Weber accepted much of this model but not its successive arrangement. Instead he argued that two processes – an organic cultural one centered on the 'soul' (the inner unity that precedes acts of feeling, thinking, and willing) and a linear civilizational one based on rational intellect, or 'spirit' (*Geist*) – operated side by side influencing one another. Weber assigned the role of the creation of meaning to the cultural sphere. With the decline of religious institutions, which had formed the center of the cultural sphere in the past, the question for him then became: what would replace religion at the center of cultural activities? To answer that question it became necessary to understand the relationship of the cultural and civilizational processes. This was the task of the sociology of culture that he proposed.

In 1912 he gave an address to the Second Congress of German Sociologists on 'The Sociological Concept of Culture', his initial formal presentation of the discipline (A. Weber, 2000 [1913]). World War I diverted his attention to political matters and he did not follow up on this lecture until 1920, when he published his most definitive account, 'Fundamentals of Cultural Sociology: Social Process, Civilizational Process and Cultural Movement' (A. Weber, 2012 [1920]). This article continued the basic format of the earlier address, adding some new components in an attempt to make the discipline more precise. He added a third process, the social, to the original two, and he changed his term 'cultural process' to 'cultural movement'.

Before the war, Weber had been more concerned with describing the relationship of the cultural and civilizational processes in general rather than exploring their interaction in historical units. In the 1920 account he addressed these units, which he labeled 'historical circles' or 'historical bodies'. Although Weber did not consistently maintain the difference between these two terms, 'historical circles' appear to refer to larger units such as the ancient Near East. 'Historical bodies' are subunits of the circles, for example, ancient Egypt and Babylonia. Weber focused on historical bodies as the realm in which the social process, the civilizational process, and cultural movement interact (A. Weber, 2012 [1920]: 166–70).

The social process did not play a major role in Weber's sociology. He described it as the social objectification of unchanging natural forces of drives and will. The form and development these take, which are influenced by natural conditions such as geography and climate, are essentially those of the human body: from youth to 'senile torpor', a cyclical pattern that contradicts his labeling it as a process (A. Weber, 2012 [1920]: 170–74).

Weber defined the civilizational process as the intellectual and technical mastery of the external world. It is utilitarian, instrumental, and analytical as it progressively uncovers mechanistic relationships of objects to one another. It consists of abstract theories of nature, such as Euclidian geometry, as well as technological innovations, such as the steam engine. It operates with the logic of causality, and those who participate in it discover patterns rather than create meaning. Its capacity for objectification allows it to be a communicative medium between historical bodies, all of which to some degree participate in it. Its pattern of development, however, is very different from that of the historical bodies. It is one of universal progress. Although the civilizational process does not move at a uniform speed through history, sometimes stagnating, other times moving methodically, and still other times advancing rapidly, it progresses inexorably toward the objective domination of material existence. The three phenomena that his brother Max identified as the central elements of the Western rationalization process – modern science, the legal-rational bureaucratic state, and modern capitalism – were all assigned by Alfred to the civilizational process (A. Weber, 2012 [1920]: 174–81). Alfred recognized the importance of the civilizational process for the material progress of humanity, but he criticized thinkers such as Hegel, Marx, and Comte, who characterized the entirety of human mental activity in terms of 'intellectualized' analytical concepts (A. Weber, 2012 [1920]: 196–197).

Strongly influenced by vitalism (*Lebensphilosophie*), Weber stressed the importance of the intuitive, creative faculty, which he identified as constituting the cultural movement of a historical body. The latter possesses an inherent destiny expressed through its soul. One may separate parts of it, but that does not destroy its inherent configuration. Weber was especially concerned with the monadically organic relationship between the soul of an individual and the soul of the larger historical body. Individuals, especially creative individuals, are the authors of cultural works and ideas that give expression to the center of the lived experience of the supraindividual unity. The soul aspires to a unity of meaning in face of the realignments brought about by the social and civilizational processes. The individual expresses his/her soul by producing symbols, and the changing configuration of meaning through these symbols organized around a center comprises a culture. Unlike the civilizational process, cultural movement does not extend beyond historical bodies. Whatever unity the historical body possesses is limited to it (A. Weber, 2012 [1920]: 182–6).

Weber believed that a crisis of culture arises when individuals are not able to engage in this creative endeavor. This disruption most likely takes the form of relativism, which he defined as the inability of the larger cultural soul to configure itself. He attributed the crisis of his era to the overvaluation of human faculties connected with the civilizational process, in part due to the significant technical mastery of nature and the spread of rationalism in the 19th century. In seeking knowledge simply in the sphere of intellect, thinkers such as the Marxist Georg Lukács – who was a critic of Weber's cultural sociology (Lukács, 1915) – viewed history as a teleological process that can be rationally analyzed and, in so doing, they largely conflated the intellect (*Geist*) and the soul to the detriment of the latter. As a result, cultural movement and the life forces it configures were largely ignored. Weber labeled such an approach 'intellectualism' (A. Weber, 2000 [1913]: 63–4). He believed that the cultural sociology he advocated would allow one to understand the relationship of the cultural soul to other activities. It would bring the realization that every new interaction of the social and civilizational processes with a historical body would require a new cultural configuration. Given the criticism of impreciseness by reviewers such as Lukács, Weber understood that a more detailed explication of the methodology of his new discipline would be necessary to win adherents.

He attempted that explication in 1927, the year before the Zurich Congress, with a methodological introduction to a collection of his earlier essays (A. Weber, 2000 [1927]). Central to his discussion was the need to distinguish his approach from that of his brother Max, whose posthumous *Economy and Society* had appeared in 1921. He noted that Max, in order to achieve a conceptual exactness, sacrificed any attempt to grasp phenomena as belonging to a totality. He acknowledged the value of Max's ideal-typologies, but added that such an emphasis on pure conceptual formation through exaggeration and isolation is designed to consider social structure, its movement, and all transpersonal forces strictly through 'the social intentions, attitudes and reactions of individuals'. Such an approach divorces the parts (individuals) from the larger organic totality that culture represents and, thus, cannot capture the unity of historical bodies in its concreteness. Alfred claimed that his method can examine totalities in their complexity while consciously preserving them as unities (A. Weber, 2000 [1927]: 52–4).

Max believed that when human beings act, they do so in a world that makes sense to them according to the meaning that they have given it. Because action is ultimately individual, so is the meaning. However, action takes place in a social context. If individuals decide on a certain course, they have to anticipate how others will respond to that course. They try to make sense of others' actions, just as cultural scientists might try to make sense of theirs. This position has an important corollary: it assumes that one can make sense of all social action. All understanding is to some degree rational. A social relationship, then, involves a 'plurality of actors' who take account of the orientations of one another. Thus, all larger structural forms are built out of components consisting of individual action (M. Weber, 1978: 2–27).

While Max started with the individual and worked out, Alfred started with the totality and worked in. The cultural sociologist interprets the interaction of the civilizational and social processes and cultural movement in 'the completely concrete, unique constellation of a historical moment'. His method is akin to phenomenological 'intuition', but differing in that it is not only intuitionistic and synthetic, but also consciously analytic. Analysis of the cultural sphere consists of clarifying how 'the always creative, psychic human power' is located in the 'life substance' in a historical body according to its social, civilizational, and cultural attributes. Sociological analysis investigates the 'sociological constellations and their transformations in the historical process' to clarify their patterns and conditions. It does not attempt to arrive at 'an exhaustive causal explanation' (A. Weber, 2000 [1927]: 44–7).

Weber's discussion of the ancient Egyptian historical body provides an example of his methodology. He wrote that the Egyptian world created a series of innovations, but that these took place within an unchanging structure and did not produce any significant transformation. He asked how this structure arose and why it did not change until the time of Akhenaten. His answers pointed to the interaction of the civilizational and social processes with the cultural aspiration (A. Weber, 2000 [1926]).

Weber argued that when the Old Kingdom was established over the earlier tribal societies, a unique sociological constellation was created by civilizational technology that would last a millennium. The central component of this technology was a canal system constructed by the early pharaohs that exploited the regularities of nature such as the weather and the Nile River flooding to create a stable agricultural economy and a non-nomadic farming people. Other innovations, such as the calendar and writing, were introduced in conjunction with the canals. These developments allowed for a centralization of power and the growth of a rational bureaucracy that, with its 'hierarchy of scribes', became the center of the new system. When new social strata arose, such as an officer corps and priesthood, they were integrated into the bureaucratic system. The religion of the earlier tribal society had been a totemism of nature gods. As centralization took place, the primitive assemblage of local gods was also centralized, with the pharaoh as the central god. The pharaoh was identified with the canal system as the other gods had been identified with aspects of nature. The result was a 'marriage' of civilizational technology, a bureaucratic apparatus, and the old primitive religiosity, resulting in a new cultural expression whose visible form was constancy. The progress usually associated with the process of civilization was arrested and innovations became simply more refined ways of repeating the old form (2000 [1926]: 211–12, 217–19, 227–36).

Systemic change came, Weber wrote, not from a weakening of ties to the primitive religion, but as an innovation of the Pharaoh Akhenaten. Deeming the old religious forms to be inadequate for establishing his domination beyond Egypt proper to the rest of the empire, Akhenaten initiated a monotheistic cult by elevating a minor god to the supreme position and associating himself with the new deity. This act shattered the traditional 'life-aggregation'. For Weber, the cultural creation of Akhenaten demonstrated the importance of elites in shaping the meaning of a historical body (2000 [1926]: 248–51).

Weber believed that the cultural elites of his day faced a different task. Rather than a new configuration of cultural meaning where stasis had prevailed, they had to provide meaning for the rapid changes Germany was undergoing. They were charged with creating an organic cultural unity of values that would not succumb to the pluralism of republican civil society. He believed that those he terms 'spiritual leaders' could aid the political leadership of the republic in giving direction to the institutions of the civilizational sphere. However, these spiritual leaders faced their own crisis arising from the civilizational process – the hyperinflation of the early 1920s. Weber's account of the situation, *The Distress of the Spiritual Workers*, was his most specific application of his cultural sociology to the concrete reality of his time (1999 [1923]).

In his study he described the toll that the inflation took on spiritual workers, whose income had been largely independent of immediate economic circumstances. They came from the upper strata of the bourgeoisie that had amassed significant capital, or they were high state officials or academics with dependable incomes. In addition to security and independence, their position also conferred social and cultural status. Thus, their material support and social status allowed them to be the shapers of meaning for the historical body. This situation changed when the hyperinflation depleted their wealth. Those on salary saw their incomes plummet from seven times that of a manual worker to almost equal their wages. This economic leveling contributed to a leveling of status (1999 [1923]: 607–13).

These intellectuals were part of a larger public, the cultivated elites, which in turn was intertwined with the other strata of the social order. The larger cultivated public also suffered hard times in the inflation, and, as a result, its demand for the cultural products of the spiritual elite was reduced. In addition, the cultural infrastructure upon which spiritual workers depended, such as libraries, institutes, research facilities, and museums, lost a considerable amount of their financial support. The place of this cultivated public was taken by a larger mass audience that was less discerning, and the cultural creations of the spiritual elites had to compete with those aimed at this larger audience. The increased influence of industrial magnates in the cultural sphere accompanied this process. Intellectuals were forced to cater to the wishes of these 'industrial princes', further demeaning their creative abilities and casting doubt on the value of pure intellectual products that had not become commodities. The result was a loss of intellectual freedom, which further deprived intellectuals of their status and influence (1999 [1923]: 603–8, 613–16).

Weber believed that this shift in publics doomed the old type of intellectual. But he held out the hope that an alternative to it, the 'worker intellectual', would appear. This type would ascend from and address itself to the growing stratum of white-collar workers. It would combine a spiritual orientation with a more practical vocation. These individuals would resemble, and include, lawyers, doctors, and engineers in that they were essential to modern society and they also retained a strong spiritual component. He believed that this new type of spiritual worker also would be able to grasp and formulate the 'public spirit', which no longer sat in official chambers but rather in the organs of the democratic state, in the press and the parties (1999 [1923]: 607–8, 621–4, 627).

Weber's model here was an organic one in which conflict was overcome through cultural production. He believed that current intellectual elites, despite the material pressures placed upon them, were capable of producing an organic meaningful unity for their time. He hoped that the new worker intelligentsia would be able to preserve this unity in the future (1999 [1923]: 608, 627). His cultural sociology had an explicitly political agenda – to reconcile an organic unity of meaning with the pluralism of parliamentary democracy. The ability of the cultural elite to transcend the divisions of civil society made his 'spiritual leaders' socially free-floating in the manner often incorrectly attributed to Karl Mannheim's well-known concept of the intelligentsia.

## KARL MANNHEIM'S CULTURAL SOCIOLOGY

When Mannheim left his native Budapest and settled in Heidelberg in the early 1920s, he did so under the sponsorship of Alfred Weber and Emil Lederer. Although he used his earlier association with Georg Lukács as cultural capital in Heidelberg, he never followed Lukács into Marxism. His most significant publication while in Hungary, a lecture titled 'Soul and Culture', used the terminology of Georg Simmel, another thinker deeply influenced by vitalism (2012 [1918]). By the 1920s 'soul' and 'culture' were two of the most central terms of Alfred Weber's cultural sociology and, accordingly, Mannheim became a member of Weber's seminar on that subject. During this period Mannheim composed two book-length manuscripts that addressed his questions concerning this new discipline. He evidently was not satisfied with his answers, because the two were never published during his lifetime.

In the first of these manuscripts, 'The Distinctive Character of Cultural-Sociological Knowledge' (1982 [1922]), Mannheim introduced his version of Alfred Weber's historical body, the collective 'context of lived experience'. As did Weber, he focused on the relationship of the individual experiential subject (the soul) to the larger communal lived experience. The context of lived experience forms an atheoretical, organic totality that can never be conceptually grasped in its entirety. Because this context includes not only the world views of its individual and collective subjects but also the social reality in which these subjects function, cultural products and social relationships are connected to one another in a reciprocal relationship. Mannheim designated the world view, which can be comprehended for a 'variety of spheres of objectification', as the element of the context of lived experience that can be conceptualized. This conceptualization depends on the 'attitude' (*Einstellung*) of the interpreter and on the objectification of the context on which s/he focuses (1982 [1922]: 50, 65, 70–4, 77, 91–2, 97). Mannheim identified 'displacement' (*Verschiebung*), the understanding of one level of conceptualization from the standpoint of another, as a way to examine the 'intermeshing' of these concepts in the context of lived experience. Displacement clarifies these concepts by providing a certain perspective, a degree of 'distance' between them (1982 [1922]: 63–4, 81–4, 88–96).

For Mannheim, cultural sociology must focus on the dynamics of history. It assembles types that are not immanently construed but are imputed from individual cultural products. And it is not teleological. What comes later is not viewed as 'higher'. He envisioned a threefold program for this cultural sociology: arranging cultural products into cultural spheres and tracing the development of these spheres; tying those spheres to a world view, which is imputed to a context of lived experience; and charting the transition from one world view to another. Central to this program is identifying the social groups that are bearers of certain cultural formations. He distinguished these 'cultural bearers' from 'cultural creators' who have a certain degree of autonomy from the groups. Thus he can focus on the social groups that bear culture while allowing for the creativity of certain individuals. He also noted, anticipating his later essay on generations (1952 [1928]), that contemporaneous groups do not all live in the same time. For example, bearers of the world view of the nobility might continue to exist even though the nobility itself had been replaced by the bourgeoisie as the main cultural bearer. Cultural sociology arranges these contexts of lived experience and the social groups that are part of them in a discontinuous and dialectical relationship (1982 [1922]: 113–18, 123–30).

This early version of cultural sociology was compatible with that of Alfred Weber. The discontinuity of the cultural sphere and the organic unity of the context of lived experience were central in Weber's cultural sociology. Mannheim's second long manuscript, 'A Sociological Theory of Culture and Its Knowability (Conjunctive and Communicative Thinking)' (1982 [1924]: 141–288), appears to follow the same pattern, as does a published article the same year on historicism (1952 [1924]). In the former he used Weberian language to draw a distinction between 'communicative' and 'conjunctive' knowledge. Disciplines based on communicative knowledge seek supratemporal, universal systems that progress unilinearly. Objects are divorced from sociohistorical contexts and addressed quantitatively. Conversely, conjunctive knowledge is limited to a given historical context, which it seeks to understand qualitatively.

In this manuscript and in the article on historicism Mannheim used Weber's central terminology – 'civilizational' and 'cultural' – to describe the difference (1982 [1924]: 207, 259).

Mannheim presented two types of conjunctive knowledge – understanding and interpretation. He defined understanding as an essentially pre-theoretical activity that penetrates 'into a communally bound experiential realm, into that realm's meaningful products and their existential bases'(1982 [1924]: 243 translation modified). Interpretation, on the other hand, is a theoretically reflective examination of that which is understood. His primary unit of interpretation is the 'world aspiration' (*Weltwollung*), the collectively conjunctive will of a historical group to realize the goals articulated by its world view.

In his earliest Hungarian work, Mannheim had described the 'work' as the product of an individual that allows him/her to participate in a totality of meaning, a position very much like that of Alfred Weber. Now he added collective works – such as language, institutions, customs, and self-regulating social relations – as objectifications of collective aspirations. Earlier he had focused on the alienation of individuals from one another because of their alienation from the larger totality. Now the definition of the totality itself became problematical and complex. The problem of individual alienation became subordinate to the problem of pluralism. The central task of cultural sociology ceased to be determining the relation of individual subjects to a totality via their works but rather the relationship of collective subjects to one another.

Near the end of this manuscript Mannheim combined both of these relationships in the concept of a 'cultivated culture' (*Bildungskultur*), which he defined as 'a culture that has been rendered relatively independent from the particular, narrowly bounded life community and its existential connectedness' (1982 [1924]: 266). This culture arises from a widening of the community as well as a mixing of social spheres. Here 'group communities' within the same 'framing-society' interact with one another, working out their various tendencies, world aspirations, and germs (*Keime*). These germs, which are restricted in the life-communities due to their strong existential ties, are developed toward their full potential by the participants in the cultivated culture. Mannheim indicated that cultivation means an increased sensibility to other world aspirations that are not present in the context of lived experience from which the individual comes. Cultivated culture is therefore 'polyphonic and dialectical in constitution' (1982 [1924]: 267). Its members continually rework tendencies of their original existential communities, but they cannot generate new germs and tendencies. They are not completely 'free-floating', but only relatively so. To a certain extent cultivated culture resembles communicative thinking in that it is removed from specific communities, achieving a certain distance. But its germs always originate in those specific communities and thus it remains conjunctive. It represents the highest stage of conjunctive thinking, achieving a reflective comprehension that entitles it to be labeled a human science (1982 [1924]: 267–9). This last sentence has echoes of those critics of Alfred Weber who argued that his reliance on intuition to investigate culture prevented his cultural sociology from becoming a social science.

Mannheim's concept of cultivated culture is indicative of the tension that was growing between his view of culture and that of Weber. The language, with its emphasis on organic potentially, its distinction between cultural and civilizational, is Weber's, but the introduction of a dialectical relationship is not. This element of pluralism would be developed and given a political dimension in the following six years, leading to the confrontation between the two men. On seeing Mannheim's habilitation proposal on conservatism, Weber wrote to his partner Else Jaffé that Mannheim was in a different world than he, one under the gravitational pull of Georg Lukács (Demm, 1999: 30).

## MANNHEIM'S TRANSITION TO THE SOCIOLOGY OF KNOWLEDGE

Mannheim's full habilitation thesis only surfaced in the 1980s, but a shortened version of it, titled 'Conservative Thought', appeared in 1927 (1953 [1927]). In addition to a political focus, Mannheim's writings on conservatism offer the best example of the application of his methodology. He now labeled that methodology 'the sociology of knowledge', a term borrowed from Max Scheler, with the indication that it was a more specialized application of cultural sociology. He wrote: 'All of cultural sociology rests upon the problem of imputation. This problem forms its methodological axis'. Because all imputations are essentially constructions, they must be 'grounded in the substance of matter' (1986 [1925]: 40). Imputation must, therefore, work through a series of heuristic levels without attempting to assert a causal priority among them. They are simply connected (*verbunden*). The same methodology will hold true for other world aspirations. At the first level the sociologist identifies a world view by tracing particular cultural formulations. Here conservatism was distinguished from traditionalism, a non-reflective aversion to change. Conservatism is traditionalism that has become historically conscious in response to the liberal world aspiration of the Enlightenment. Traditionalists were forced to become conservatives, to position themselves reflectively in the course of history.

At the second level of imputation the sociologist identifies an intellectual stratum whose commitment to the world view makes it a world aspiration. In other words, the world view is examined through its components that appear in the works of individual thinkers, in the case of conservatism, Justus Möser, Gustav Hugo, Friedrich von Savigny, and Adam Müller. Finally the members of the intellectual stratum are tied to specific social strata: Möser to the provincial nobility, Hugo and Savigny to the bureaucracy, non-noble and noble respectively, and Müller to unattached intellectuals in league with the landed nobility. These social strata were the bearers of the conservative world aspiration. But there is no simple identification of the intellectual strata with the social strata, for there were other possible combinations of both. For example, some bureaucrats, especially non-noble ones, and unattached intellectuals supported a version of liberalism. Finally, the four thinkers are placed not only in relationship to one another and to the various social strata to which they were connected, but also to events and competing world aspirations that forced adjustments in the formulations of the world aspiration. In a static world conservatism is unnecessary; traditionalism suffices. But the historical context had become dynamic as a differentiation of social strata took place, each with their own aspirations. This dynamic element means that the interpretation of world aspirations must avoid remaining static.

Mannheim wrote that social differentiation took on an increasingly political character, forming a constellation of antagonistic world aspirations. Conservatism was traditionalism that was not only becoming historically conscious but also becoming political. Political polarization became the focal point of Mannheim's writings in the mid-1920s, including 'Competition as a Cultural Phenomenon', the paper he delivered in Zurich in 1928. Here he followed Alfred Weber in differentiating a civilizational sphere from a cultural one and assigning meaning and values to the cultural sphere. However, he described this sphere not as an organic unity but as a 'polarized' competition between social groups organized into parties and striving to determine the 'public interpretation of existence'. Conservatism is joined now by liberalism and socialism as parties that are defined by their commitment to 'intellectual currents', in other words their world aspirations (1990 [1929]: 56–8, 67–70).

In the discussion that followed, Weber objected to Mannheim's 'intellectualism', the division of an organic unity into analytical categories. He accused Mannheim of following Marx's example by depicting pluralistic fragmentation and conflict rather than any kind of unity in the cultural sphere. Instead, Weber advocated 'spiritual creativity' – the ability to create a cultural synthesis of meaning. The next year the two men held a joint seminar in Heidelberg on Lukács's *History and Class Consciousness*, although Lukács was secondary to their views of one another's work. Weber repeated his charge of intellectualism, arguing that such analytical categories, whether portrayed as material interests or interpretations of existence, mean the fragmentation of the larger organic sphere of meaning. Acknowledging his vitalist premises, Weber argued that only spiritual creativity can create a unity of meaning between the larger culture and the soul of the individual (Mannheim and Weber, 2001 [1929]: 112–13, 122).

Mannheim responded to Weber by denying that his approach could be accurately labeled as intellectualistic. Rather, he and Weber were presenting different conceptions of rationality. His approach was 'functionalist', and was oriented toward the more modern model of 'achievement' in which 'the rationally achievable and controllable comes ever more to the fore'. Weber, on the other hand, was engaging in a 'morphological' attempt to rescue the irrational, which was oriented to the model of 'growing', and which attempted to leave a 'substantial being' untouched other than nurturing it. Adding a touch of irony, Mannheim declared that the sociological methodology representing his approach was that of Max Weber (2001 [1929]: 113, 117–20).

Mannheim's pitting Alfred Weber against his brother continued in *Ideology and Utopia*, which worked out many of the implications of the structure of the cultural realm, including the role of intellectuals in its polarization. He used the categories of 'ideology' and 'utopia' to impute in ideal typical form the world aspirations competing to determine the public interpretation of reality. To the three introduced in his Zurich paper – liberalism, conservatism, and socialism – he added an additional one, fascism, or chiliasm (Mannheim, 1968 [1929]: 91–114, 190–222).

The difference between ideologies and utopias lies largely in how they are viewed. Ideologies are viewed from the perspective of their opponents, who 'unmask' their claims to universality by declaring that they are limited to the specific social group's perspective. Ideology is not determined by the active subject making a claim to universality, but by opponents who refute that claim (Mannheim, 1968 [1929]: 57–62). Utopias, on the other hand, are viewed from the perspective of active subjects, whose aspiration is to change the world by gaining universality. Utopias do not recognize any claims by opponents that they are socially limited, for if they did they would cease to be utopian. It is this utopian challenge to the status quo in order to establish one's aspiration as universal that propels history forward. Although utopias are able to initiate change, they can never have complete success, for they will in turn be challenged by other utopian aspirations connected to other social positions, giving rise to new historical configurations (Mannheim, 1968 [1929]: 130–31, 176).

Here one can point to Mannheim's distinction between the terms 'existentially connected' (*seinsverbunden*) and 'existentially bound' (*seinsgebunden*) – which is negated in the English translation by the rendering of both terms as either 'existentially conditioned' or 'situationally determined'. He used the term 'existentially connected' to indicate that world aspirations arise from specific social groups. However, this term does not address the relationship of world aspirations to one another or attempt to assign a truth value to them. The latter is the role of the term 'existentially bound', which indicates that a certain perspective cannot claim validity for an entire era but is limited (bound) to the social group to which it is connected. The tactic of ideological unmasking exposes not only the existential connection of opponents' world views, but also their limitation (bondedness).

Mannheim asserted that all world aspirations, including the Marxist claim to the universality of the proletariat, are both existentially connected and existentially bound (66). The task of the sociology of knowledge is to overcome this limitation so that 'the discovery of the existential *connectedness* of the views at hand will be seen as the first step to the solution of existential *bondedness* itself' (1968 [1931]: 271, translation modified). This last quotation is from Mannheim's 1931 summary of the sociology of knowledge, and it was anticipated almost a decade earlier by a similar statement in 'A Sociological Concept of Culture and Its Knowability' in which he described the cultivated culture as 'a culture that has been rendered relatively independent from the particular, narrowly limited life community and its *existential connectedness*. It is just as conjunctively determined as the original culture, although not as strictly *bound to existence*' (1982 [1924]: 266, translation modified and italics added).

In *Ideology and Utopia* Mannheim introduced the concept of relationism, which rejects the possibility of universal truth in favor of a historically changing one and incorporates the interrelationships and competition of world aspirations, providing more orientation by making sense of and even promoting change in the political arena. And because this judgment of success has to be made retroactively (1968 [1929]: 69–72, 85, 94–5, 234), relationism means the postponement of certainty. One struggles for one's convictions, believing that the future will judge them to have provided the best grasp of the pluralistic political spectrum and promotion of constructive change. Relationism allows the 'existential transcendence' of ideologies and utopias to be replaced with an 'existential congruence' informed by a 'sociologically fully clarified consciousness'. Mannheim hoped that relationism would preserve the utopian's commitment to change, not in spite of ideological unmasking but in conjunction with the extension of unmasking in the sociology of knowledge.

Mannheim assigned this task to the 'relatively socially unattached [or free-floating] intelligentsia', a term he attributed to Alfred Weber, although Weber did not use it in his published writings. It was the successor to the above-described concept of cultivated culture. Mannheim's intelligentsia is not free from existential connections, being only '*relatively* classless' (1968 [1929]: 137), and thus is not capable of a universal truth or the establishment of an organic cultural totality. Members of the intelligentsia stem from increasingly diverse social backgrounds and represent many political groups and commitments, but their intellectualism keeps them from being fully integrated into these groups. This degree of 'distance' gives each of them a looser connection to the group and hence a broader perspective. Together they form a microcosm of the larger sociopolitical conflict and not simply one part of it. At the same time, as intellectuals they share a common medium and possess the communicative ability that allows them to exchange perspectives with one another. This combination provides better orientation in the pluralistic world (1968 [1929]: 138–43).

Here it helps to recognize that 'free-floating' is not the antonym of 'existentially connected' but of 'existentially bound'. Although individual members of the intelligentsia might be *individually* existentially connected and thus limited by their social connections, their communicative abilities allow them *as a group* to escape those limitations. Their exchange of perspectives with one another fosters a better understanding of the interrelationships of their different world aspirations. Their social heterogeneity prevents them from becoming existentially bound as a group, even though individually they are somewhat bound. The intelligentsia does not float above social conflict but rather incorporates it.

Mannheim did not believe that the intelligentsia can bring change by themselves, for they are not really political actors. The latter are motivated by the political commitment of a group to change the world according to their world aspiration. Instead, the intelligentsia's task is to help politicians become relational thinkers and understand the ramifications of their decisions, which allows them to develop the means to orient themselves in the changing world (1968 [1929]: 151–5). Thus, the 'synthesis' they achieve is a 'dynamic' one in which conflict among commitments is clarified and to some degree reconciled but never transcended in an organic unity. Unlike Alfred Weber, who, because he believed that the spiritual leadership could rise above pluralistic conflict, blurred the relationship between the elites of culture and political parties, Mannheim, like Max Weber in his vocation essays, sharply delineated the roles of the politician and the scientist, limiting the role of the latter.

Mannheim recognized that the decentered political and economic sphere is accompanied by a decentered cultural sphere. The latter cannot form an organic totality, but rather is characterized by conflict, the struggle for cultural hegemony, in which intellectuals play the more restrained role of advisors rather than the creative role postulated by Alfred Weber. Although his intelligentsia can clarify temporary constellations within the competition and provided a medium for communication between the competing groups, they cannot grant a privileged position to any of those groups. In contrast to Alfred's belief, they cannot become 'spiritual leaders'.

Mannheim and Weber physically parted ways in 1930 when Mannheim left Heidelberg to accept the chair of sociology at the University of Frankfurt. In doing so he changed his overall strategy. The gridlock of the political system convinced him to replace his focus on the relationship of the intelligentsia to party leaders with one of teachers of sociology to their students. In his inaugural lectures at Frankfurt he investigated the role that a new sociological 'attitude' could play in the civic education of those students, and the concept of cultivation, in a revised form, assumed a renewed importance.

In articulating that concept Mannheim writes: 'By cultivational knowledge [*Bildungswissen*] ... we shall understand the tendency towards a coherent life-orientation, with a bearing upon the overall personality as well as the totality of the objective life-situation insofar as it can be surveyed at the time' (2001 [1930]: 154). Individuals' potential to orient themselves in conjunction with others, i.e. the active reflexivity of the subject, takes priority over the passive non-reflexivity of the object.

In formulating the essentials of the sociological attitude, Mannheim depended on two dialectically related concepts, 'enactment' and 'distantiation'. Subjects enact worlds, which change both themselves and these worlds within which they act. At the same time they perceive both themselves and those worlds as objects, thus creating a distance that leads to yet more enactments. The claim that distantiation can be turned into an enactment that leaves the agent capable of further enactments at a higher level of self-control is the central argument of the sociological project. Sociology is practice, not contemplation. To distance is to objectify, but not to the degree that one becomes a neutral observer removed from the situation.

Expansion does not mean abandonment of a specific historical location. In moving beyond the confines of a specific community (group), one does not become the purely communicative subject of positivistic social science. Distantiation means self-reflexivity – that is, making facts out of one's norms, not simply accepting their validity as given – by placing oneself as a subject into a context so that one is object as well as subject (Mannheim, 2001 [1930]: 103). In the language of his earlier sociological theory of culture, neither the purely conjunctive subject in his concrete subjectivity, nor the purely communicative subject in her abstract universality, is self-reflexive. The distinction between being bound and distantiation runs parallel to the earlier one between the communal culture and the cultivated culture. Members of the communal culture are not able to distance themselves because it is not necessary that they do so. Only when one regards oneself ironically as something that could be something else does one become open to the idea of one's own transformation. One can then adopt a sociological attitude.

Mannheim's advocacy of the sociological attitude as the central component of a modern cultivation necessitated a rethinking of the relationship between sociology as an academic discipline and the larger public. This meant a modification of his earlier notion of cultivated culture, which was based on the premise of an organic public. Previously expansion had been the role of the cultural elite; now he proposed that it should be a quality of all citizens. The intellectual now became more important as teacher of the sociological attitude than as the mediator between political parties. He or she had to instill the ethic of responsibility in all citizens.

## MANNHEIM AND WEBER AFTER WEIMAR

In 1935 Alfred Weber and Karl Mannheim came together symbolically when both, having been driven into exile by the National Socialists – Weber into forced retirement in Heidelberg, Mannheim to London – had books published by the firm of A.W. Sijthoff in Leiden, Netherlands. The two books took on similar tasks. In *Cultural History as Cultural Sociology* Weber wrote that the main task of cultural sociology was to answer the question: 'where do we find ourselves in the stream of history?' (1997 [1935]: 61) In *Man and Society in an Age of Reconstruction* Mannheim described his work as 'an attempt at self-enlightenment, made for the benefit of those who have actually lived through these experiences' (1940 [1935]: 3). But despite the similarity of the task, the two books reiterated that the two men were headed in different directions.

Weber urged historians to become cultural sociologists, to focus on the interaction of the social, civilizational, and cultural spheres. But rather than continuing the methodological specificity of his earlier article on Egypt and Babylonia, his book offered a vast sweep of 'cultural physiognomies' that can only be described as a meta-history. The bulk of his book dealt with the appearance of the 'third person', characterized by a greater control over nature, the emergence of world religions, and a truly historical humanity (Weber, 1997 [1935]: 41–4, 84–92). The third person reached its highest form in the late 18th-century West with the monadic relationship between creative individuals such as Goethe and Schiller and the organic historical body of the nation (1997 [1935]: 328–41, 390–404, 422–6). As the 19th century progressed, the civilizational process became dominant and the ties between the individual and the larger unity weakened, resulting in a time of cultural crisis. Weber concluded by wondering if this crisis could be resolved, if a new life-aggregation and culture could break out of the chaos. A 'fourth person', a fragmented being incapable of cultural synthesis and without freedom, would prevail if the third person could not be revitalized (1997 [1935]: 439–450).

Mannheim also saw 'organic publics' giving way to 'disintegrated' ones. The former provide individuals with orientation to some larger totality of meaning and coherence through forms of 'substantial irrationality', such as tradition and religion. Although these orienting elements are not rational, they do not preclude 'functionally rational' actions directed toward specific ends in subordinate forms. The organic public, which very much resembles Alfred Weber's, can also have a certain amount of diversity among the elites, provided that differentiation is informed by an organic cultural center (Mannheim, 1940 [1935]: 53, 96–7). And, like Weber, Mannheim wrote that the dangers to that public take the form of a technological progress that increasingly divides society along functionally rational lines, weakening the ability of substantially irrational institutions to provide larger meaning. Mannheim terms this lack of normative and moral certainty 'functional irrationality' (1940 [1935]: 53, 67, 97).

Here Mannheim departed from Weber by introducing an alternative to both the organic and disintegrated publics, a public 'organized' by social planners in conjunction with the public that is being planned. Planner and planned share a 'substantial rationality', a self-reflexive cognition, to replace the lost substantial irrationality. Through 'thinking that plans' (*planendes Denken*) individuals in a society gain knowledge not only of themselves but also of the factors that influence their conduct, as well as the ability to shape both those factors and themselves (1940 [1935]: 63, 210–13). The planners are not identical with the cultivated culture, the free-floating intelligentsia, or the sociological educator, but they do represent the continuity of a commitment to a sociological reflexivity that understands and engages a pluralistic society rather than yearning for the preservation of a supposed organic unity, as Alfred Weber did.

Although both men are acknowledged to be pioneers in the field of cultural sociology, their influence on current work does not match that of Max Weber or Georg Simmel. Alfred Weber gained little attention before the 1990s, the most important exception being Eckert (1970). Since then there have been a number of monographs (Demm 1990, 1999; Kruse 1990; Blomert 1999; Widdig 2001: 182–90; Loader 2012), but the emphasis has been biographical and historical rather than methodological. Mannheim has received more attention, the most important book-length monographs being those of Simonds (1978), Loader (1985), Woldring (1986), Ketter and Meja (1995), Loader and Kettler (2002), Laube (2004), and Kettler, Loader, and Meja (2008).

# REFERENCES

Blomert, R. (1999) *Intellektuelle im Aufbruch: Karl Mannheim, Alfred Weber, Norbert Elias und die Heidelberger Sozialwissenschaften der Zwischenkriegszeit*. Munich: Carl Hanser.

Demm, E. (1990) *Ein Liberaler in Kaiserreich und Republik. Der politische Weg Alfred Webers bis 1920*. Boppard: Harald Boldt.

Demm, E. (1999) *Von der Weimarer Republik zur Bundesrepublik. Der politische Weg Alfred Webers 1920–1958*. Düsseldorf: Droste.

Eckert, R. (1970) *Die Geschichtstheorie Alfred Webers*. Tübingen: Kyklos.

Kettler, D. and Meja, V. (1995) *Karl Mannheim and the Crisis of Liberalism: The Crisis of These New Times*. New Brunswick, NJ: Transaction.

Kettler, D., Loader, C. and Meja, V. (2008) *Karl Mannheim and the Legacy of Max Weber*. Aldershot: Ashgate.

Kruse, V. (1990) *Soziologie und 'Gegenwartskrise': Die Zeitdiagnosen Franz Oppenheimers und Alfred Webers*. Wiesbaden: DUV.

Laube, R. (2004) *Karl Mannheim und die Krise des Historismus*. Göttingen: Vandenhoeck and Ruprecht.

Lichtblau, K. (1996) *Kulturkrise und Soziologie um die Jahrhundertwende: Zur Genealogie der Kultursoziologie in Deutschland*. Frankfurt: Main: Suhrkamp.

Loader, C. (1985) *The Intellectual Development of Karl Mannheim: Culture, Politics and Planning*. Cambridge: Cambridge University Press.

Loader, C. (2012) *Alfred Weber and the Crisis of Culture, 1890–1933*. New York: Palgrave Macmillan.

Loader, C. and Kettler, D. (2002) *Karl Mannheim's Sociology as Political Education*. New Brunswick, NJ: Transaction.

Lukács, G. (1915) 'Zum Wesen und zur Methode der Kultursoziologie', *Archiv für Sozialwissenschaft und Sozialpolitik*, 39: 216–22.

Mannheim, K. (1940 [1935] *Man and Society in an Age of Reconstruction*. E. Shils (trans.). New York: Harcourt, Brace.

Mannheim, K. (1952) *Essays in the Sociology of Knowledge*. P. Kecskemeti (ed. and trans.). London: Routledge and Kegan Paul.

Mannheim, K. (1952 [1924]) 'Historicism', in Mannheim, K. (1952) *Essays in the Sociology of Knowledge*. P. Kecskemeti (ed. and trans.). London: Routledge and Kegan Paul, pp. 33–83.

Mannheim, K. (1952 [1928]) 'The Problem of Generations', in Mannheim, K. (1952) *Essays in the Sociology of Knowledge*. P. Kecskemeti (ed. and trans.). London: Routledge and Kegan Paul, pp. 276–322.

Mannheim, K. (1953) *Essays on Sociology and Social Psychology*. P. Kecskemeti (ed. and trans.). London: Routledge and Kegan Paul.

Mannheim, K. (1953 [1927]) 'Conservative Thought', in Mannheim, K. (1953) *Essays on Sociology and Social Psychology*. P. Kecskemeti (ed. and trans.). London: Routledge and Kegan Paul, pp. 74–164.

Mannheim, K. (1965) *Ideologie und Utopie*, 5th edn. Frankfurt/Main: G. Schutle-Bulmke.

Mannheim, K. (1968 [1929]) *Ideology and Utopia: An Introduction to the Sociology of Knowledge*. L. Wirth and E. Shils (trans.). New York: Harcourt, Brace and World.

Mannheim, K. (1968 [1931]) 'The Sociology of Knowledge', in Mannheim, K. (1968 [1929]) *Ideology and Utopia: An Introduction to the Sociology of Knowledge*. L. Wirth and E. Shils (trans.). New York: Harcourt, Brace and World, pp. 237–80.

Mannheim, K. (1970) *Wissensoziologie*. K.H. Wolff (ed.). Neuwied: Luchterhand.

Mannheim, K. (1980) *Strukturen des Denkens*. D. Kettler, V. Meja, and N. Stehr (eds). Frankfurt/Main: Suhrkamp.

Mannheim, K. (1982) *Structures of Thinking*, D. Kettler, V. Meja, Volker and N. Stehr (eds). London: Routledge and Kegan Paul.

Mannheim, K. (1982 [1922]) 'The Distinctive Character of Cultural Knowledge', in Mannheim, K. (1982) *Structures of Thinking*, D. Kettler, V. Meja, Volker and N. Stehr (eds). London: Routledge and Kegan Paul, pp. 31–139.

Mannheim, K. (1982 [1924]) 'A Sociological Theory of Culture and Its Knowability (Conjunctive and Communicative Thinking)', in Mannheim, K. (1982) *Structures of Thinking*, D. Kettler, V. Meja, Volker and N. Stehr (eds). London: Routledge.

Mannheim, K. (1984 [1925]) *Konservatismus. Ein Beitrag zur Soziologie des Wissens*. D. Kettler, V. Meja, and N. Stehr (eds). Frankfurt/Main: Suhrkamp.

Mannheim, K. (1986 [1925]) *Conservatism: A Contribution to the Sociology of Knowledge*. D. Kettler, V. Meja, and N. Stehr (eds). London: Routledge and Kegan Paul.

Mannheim, K. (1990 [1929]) 'Competition as a Cultural Phenomenon', in Meja, V. and Stehr, N. (eds) (1990) *Knowledge and Politics: The Sociology of Knowledge Dispute*. London: Routledge, pp. 53–85.

Mannheim, K. (2001) *Sociology as Political Education*. D. Kettler and C. Loader (eds). New Brunswick, NJ: Transaction.

Mannheim, K. (2001 [1930]) 'An Introduction to Sociology', in Mannheim, K. (2001) *Sociology as Political Education*. D. Kettler and C. Loader (eds). New Brunswick, NJ: Transaction, pp. 1–78. (Also in Endress, M. and Srubar, I. (2000) *Karl Mannheims Analyse der Moderne. Mannheims erste Frankfurter Vorlesung von 1930. Edition und Studien (Jahrbuch für Soziologiegeschichte 1996)*. Opladen: Leske and Budrich.)

Mannheim, K. (2012 [1918]) 'Soul and Culture', A. Wessely (trans.), D. Kettler (introduction), *Theory, Culture and Society*, 29(7–8): 279–301.

Mannheim, K. and Weber, A. (2001 [1929]) 'The Intellectualism Dispute: Protocols of the Joint Meetings of the Seminars of Professor Alfred Weber and Dr. Karl Mannheim. Heidelberg, February 21 and 27, 1929', in Mannheim, K. (2001) *Sociology as Political Education*. D. Kettler and C. Loader (eds). New Brunswick, NJ: Transaction, pp. 109–29.

Meja, V. and Stehr, N. (eds) (1990) *Knowledge and Politics: The Sociology of Knowledge Dispute*. London: Routledge.

Ringer, F.K. (1969) *The Decline of the German Mandarins*. Cambridge, MA: Harvard University Press.

Simonds, A.P. (1978) *Karl Mannheim's Sociology of Knowledge*. Oxford: Oxford University Press.

Weber, A. (1990 [1929]) 'Contribution to 'Discussion of Karl Mannheim's "Competition" paper at the Sixth Congress of German Sociologists (Zurich, 1928)', in Meja, V. and Stehr, N. (eds) (1990) *Knowledge and Politics: The Sociology of Knowledge Dispute*. London: Routledge, pp. 89–90.

Weber, A. (1997 [1935]) *Kulturgeschichte als Kultursoziologie*, E. Demm (ed.). Vol. 1, *Alfred-Weber-Gesamtausgabe*. Marburg: Metropolis Verlag.

Weber, A. (1999 [1923]) *Die Not der Geistigen Arbeiter*, in Alfred Weber (1999), *Politische Theorie und Tagespolitik, 1903–1933*, in E. Demm (ed.). Vol. 7, Alfred-Weber-Gesamtausgabe. Marburg: Metropolis, pp. 601–39.

Weber A. (2000) *Schriften zur Kultur- und Geschichtssoziologie, 1906–1958*, R. Bräu (ed.). Vol. 8, *Alfred-Weber-Gesamtausgabe*. Marburg: Metropolis Verlag.

Weber, A. (2000 [1913]) 'Der Soziologische Kulturbegriff', in Weber, A. (2000) *Schriften zur Kultur- und Geschichtssoziologie, 1906–1958*, R. Bräu (ed.). Vol. 8, *Alfred-Weber-Gesamtausgabe*. Marburg: Metropolis Verlag, pp. 60–82.

Weber, A. (2000 [1926]). 'Kultursoziologische Versuche: Das alte Aegypten und Babylonien', in Weber, A. (2000) *Schriften zur Kultur- und Geschichtssoziologie, 1906–1958*, R. Bräu (ed.). Vol. 8, *Alfred-Weber-Gesamtausgabe*. Marburg: Metropolis Verlag, pp. 203–52.

Weber, A. (2000 [1927]) 'Einleitung: Aufgaben und Methode', in Weber, A. (2000) *Schriften zur Kultur- und Geschichtssoziologie, 1906–1958*, R. Bräu (ed.). Vol. 8, *Alfred-Weber-Gesamtausgabe*. Marburg: Metropolis Verlag, pp. 35–59.

Weber, A. (2012 [1920]) 'Fundamentals of Cultural Sociology: Social Process, Civilizational Process, and Cultural Movement', in Loader, C. (2012) *Alfred Weber and the Crisis of Culture, 1890–1933*. New York: Palgrave Macmillan, pp. 165–204. (Also in Weber A. (2000) *Schriften zur Kultur- und Geschichtssoziologie, 1906–1958*, R. Bräu (ed.). Vol. 8, *Alfred-Weber-Gesamtausgabe*. Marburg: Metropolis Verlag, pp. 147–86.)

Weber, A. (2015) 'The Sociological Concept of Culture', C. Loader (trans.), *Cultural Sociology*, 9(2): 256–70. (Also in Weber A. (2000) *Schriften zur Kultur- und Geschichtssoziologie, 1906–1958*, R. Bräu (ed.). Vol. 8, *Alfred-Weber-Gesamtausgabe*. Marburg: Metropolis Verlag, pp. 60–82.)

Weber, M. (1978) *Economy and Society*. G. Roth and K. Wittich (eds). Berkeley and Los Angeles: University of California Press.

Widdig, B. (2001) *Culture and Inflation in Weimar Germany*. Berkeley and Los Angeles: University of California Press.

Woldring, H (1986) *Karl Mannheim: The Development of His Thought*. New York: St. Martin's.

# Durkheimian and Neo-Durkheimian Cultural Sociologies

David Inglis

## INTRODUCTION

This chapter concerns the work of one of the foundational figures in sociology, Émile Durkheim [1858–1917], and the uses made of some of his ideas by later sociological analysts of culture. Ideas drawn from his later works are arguably more complex, interesting and longer lasting than those from his earlier writings. While controversies still go on today about exactly what Durkheim was trying to achieve in his later works (Rawls, 1996), the most dominant contemporary interpretation holds that the late masterwork, *The Elementary Forms of Religious Life* (Durkheim, 2001 [1912]), is a foundational text for a kind of *cultural sociology* which is distinctive from, and analytically superior to, approaches that could be put under the collective heading *sociology of culture* (Alexander, 2003). As Emirbayer (1996b: 115) puts it, we should attend to 'the truly radical nature of Durkheim's later turn toward cultural analysis', as opposed to the more conventional sociological frameworks of his earlier work. This is because his 'newfound understanding ... of the internal complexity and causal significance of cultural structures' – which are at least partly autonomous of, and have the power profoundly to affect, social structures, patterns and individuals' actions – is a major revolution, not only in his own thought but in the social sciences more generally, an achievement at least on par with Saussure's revolutionary reconstruction of linguistics at around the same time.

This chapter will review the genesis and development of Durkheimian and Durkheim-inspired analysis of culture. It begins with a consideration of a major anticipation of, and influence on, Durkheim's thinking, namely the ideas of Fustel de Coulanges on the constitutive nature of religion in social life. It then turns to depict the central elements of Durkheim's approach to cultural analysis, especially in his later work. It considers the appropriation and uses made of that work throughout the 20th century, especially in France and the US. The chapter ends with consideration of a major school of neo-Durkheimian thought, the version of cultural sociology as a 'strong program' forwarded by Jeffrey C. Alexander and associates, and reflects on what might be the future direction of Durkheimian analysis.

## BEFORE DURKHEIM: FUSTEL DE COULANGES ON CULTURE

Before turning to Durkheim, we must first consider a major anticipation of, and influence upon, his ideas. Numa Denis Fustel de Coulanges (1830–1889), French historian and proto-sociologist, pioneered a structuralist analysis of social institutions which influenced subsequent sociologists, including most notably Durkheim. His major work, *The Ancient City* (2001 [1864]), concerned the social orders of ancient Greece and Rome. The city-states of Greece and early Rome were understood as social systems governed in all respects by religious principles. State, society and religion were synonymous. Religio-political boundaries strongly divided members of a polity from those defined as outsiders. From the study of the earliest phases of these societies, Fustel came to regard religion as the elementary social fact from which all others – family life, sexual and gender mores, economic and political organization – derived, and religious change as the motor of wider societal shifts. As changes occurred at the level of religious beliefs, the wider social structure was profoundly affected. How religion was organized structured how every other facet of life within a particular polity was organized too.

We can see here the beginnings of the notion that 'culture' – understood as sets of values, ideas and ideals beyond more narrowly-conceived 'religious' phenomena – has the power to affect, or even wholly generate, forms of social structure and organization, rather than vice versa, as in orthodox Marxist understandings of how specific sorts of socio-economic structures create particular sorts of cultural forms. Fustel's position is that of cultural determinism, where culture is the factor in human life which creates and regulates everything else. An important problem for later thinking about such matters involves trying to find a way to assert culture's generative powers, including the ability to structure rather than be structured by social structures, without toppling into a simplistic deterministic position whereby culture is asserted simply to be the root of all things.

Fustel was less concerned with the substantive properties of a particular set of religious beliefs and more with the formal properties shared by all ancient Greek and Roman religions. At the heart of all belief systems, and thus the linchpin of all socio-political constellations generated by such religious forms, was the *pyrtaneum*, the sacred hearth and fire which symbolized all the sacred phenomena of a particular community, including the gods, the dead ancestors, and revered heroes of the past. The cult of the *pyrtaneum* involved 'a daily worship and beliefs that had a powerful influence over the [individual's] soul' (2001 [1864]: 166). Moreover, the sacred centre-point of community life was the *pyrtaneum* and the rituals surrounding it.

Fustel's analysis highlights not the specific contents of any particular polity's *pyrtaneum*-centred belief set, but rather the importance of the *pyrtaneum* form per se in the generation and maintenance of community in general. If a socio-political body like a city-state lacks a *pyrtaneum*, it cannot exist as a coherent entity for long, for there will be no shared values among the citizenry. Additionally, when a *pyrtaneum* does exist, it must be tended by ongoing rituals and observances, in order for its revered power over both individual minds and social structures to be regularly revivified and reignited. In times when these rituals have fallen into mere traditional observance and lip-service rather than awe-filled reverence, social relations between individuals in the community tend towards diffuseness and dysfunctionality. Without a constantly ritually invoked sense of sacred purpose, social collapse will follow among people who have come to lack a strong sense of who they are and what their community means to them (2001 [1864]: 304).

In other words, without a constantly revivified sense of the sacred, which must animate both individual lives and ways of thinking, as well as the nature and operation of social organization, anomie will ensue and social relations will degenerate into meaninglessness, hopelessness and barbarity. We can see here the beginnings of the idea that culture works both to set limits to otherwise potentially boundless human aspirations, locating them within social frameworks that allow them to be plausibly realized, and to foster bonds of fellow-feeling among individuals and family groups that otherwise would have no strong sense of commonality among them and would lack the means to cooperate peacefully with each other. All of these themes in Fustel were later taken up and expanded upon by Durkheim, whom Fustel taught in the early phases of the latter's intellectual career (Lukes, 1973).

## THE EARLIER DURKHEIM ON CULTURE

In the early work *De La Division du Travail Sociale* (often translated as *The Division of Labour in Society*) (Durkheim, 1984 [1893]), Durkheim held the view that it is social structural factors which shape the forms cultural phenomena take. More particularly, it is the specific form that the division of labour takes that dictates the nature of a society's corresponding culture. In another earlier work,

*Suicide* (1951 [1897]: 387), Durkheim argued that:

> Given a people, consisting of a certain number of individuals arranged in a certain way, there results a determinate set of collective ideas and practices ... [A]ccording to whether the parts composing it are more or less numerous and structured in this or that way, the nature of collective life necessarily varies and, in consequence, so do its ways of thinking and acting.

Thus the shape of a particular society – its particular form of division of labour – determines the nature of the corresponding culture. Culture in its most basic form is essentially religious in nature (Lukes, 1973: 152). In a very simple society, culture – in the form of the *conscience collective*, the ideas and values held by all members of a social entity – *is* religion and vice versa. Only in a more complex society does culture come to involve anything more than religion. When social structures develop through processes of structural differentiation, becoming increasingly more complex, then 'religion tends to embrace a smaller and smaller sector of social life. Originally, it pervades everything: everything social is religious ... political, economic scientific functions gradually free themselves from religious control, establish themselves separately and take on a more and more openly' secular character (Durkheim, 1972: 245). It is only when a certain level of social structural complexity has been reached that there can exist within culture a separate realm of 'art' and other forms of cultural production not explicitly 'religious' in nature (Inglis and Hughson, 2005).

One problem of modern society's cultural expression was 'anomie' or 'norm-lessness'. Without strongly held shared beliefs, modern individuals feel dislocated from the society of which they were part. Connected with this was the possibility of individuals' desires going unchecked, leaving them wanting things they could never possibly have, and thereby creating serious forms of personal anguish and social strain. The theme of culture's power to constrain otherwise potentially infinitely spiralling desires, and to adjust individuals' life expectations to the social reality they have to operate within, was later taken up by Pierre Bourdieu (1977) in his influential conception of *habitus*. The allegedly unquenchable desires made possible by and expressed within dysfunctional forms of modern individualism were later taken up by conservative sociological and semi-sociological authors, such as Daniel Bell (1976) and Christopher Lasch (1991 [1979]), in their critiques of the apparently socially destructive nature of modern hedonism. Contemporary communitarian social and political philosophers, who advocate a return to more tightly integrated communities governed by authoritative morals and norms, also echo some of these earlier Durkheimian concerns (Hookway, 2015).

The more positive side of modern culture for the early Durkheim is based around a certain sort of *individualism*, with the worth and value of each individual being recognized and celebrated. This individualism, far from promoting antipathy by individuals towards the wider society, promotes new forms of social solidarity. The modern 'cult of the individual', which stresses the value of each individual person as an object of care and veneration, would operate as the cultural means whereby there could be a reduction of friction between the different parts of a complex division of labour. Despite his apparent naivety here, Durkheim was arguably quite prophetic in one sense. Contemporary scholars in the 'world polity' school of thought have shown how the cult of the individual is a useful means to understand the extraordinary proliferation of human rights discourses, laws and institutions – all centred around the sacredness of the individual and her rights – across the world since 1945 (Elliott, 2008; Alasuutari, this volume).

Durkheim and his collaborator Marcel Mauss (1872–1950), in an important essay from 1903, argue that a society's cultural fabric is made up of a set of *collective representations* (Durkheim and Mauss, 1969 [1903]). These are the ways in which reality is made sense of collectively by the members of a society. The sense they have of their world derives from the ways in which their minds have been culturally shaped in the socialization process that begins at birth and which makes each person truly a 'member' of a certain society. Collective 'classifications' are the socially created lenses through which people make sense of reality and the world around them, the frameworks through which they think and the bases on which they act. Systems of collective classifications specify what is perceivable and not perceivable, thinkable and not thinkable, by all members of a particular society or group. Culture, in the form of collective representations, transforms the world as perceived by the human senses into a realm mediated by and centred on symbols (Lukes, 1973: 424). The classification mechanisms in human minds are not inborn in each individual, as Kant had argued. Rather, because minds are at birth inchoate blank slates, classificatory mechanisms are implanted in the mind by social means, and such mechanisms are the cultural forms prevalent in each particular society (for a critique of Durkheim's assumptions here, see Bergesen, 2004).

## FROM RELIGIOUS SOCIOLOGY TO CULTURAL SOCIOLOGY

Contemporary sociologists who champion the utility of Durkheim's later works today argue that there is a fundamental break between his earlier and later works, for in the latter culture ceases to be seen simply as a product of social structures and instead becomes understood – especially in its specific form of religious beliefs and rituals – as a *sui generis* entity with the power to affect social life in general, and forms of social organization, patterning and individuals' actions in particular (Alexander, 2003; Emirbayer, 1996a, 1996b).

Durkheim in the later part of his career turned to so-called 'primitive' societies with a low level of the division of labour to make this argument, in particular focusing on the religious-cultural aspects of Australian aboriginal societies. From analysis of such a 'simple' type of society, he believed that the most general and basic aspects of *all* societies could be deduced – a typical 19th-century social scientific assumption, subsequently often criticized by later thinkers (McKinnon, 2014).

Durkheim's central claim in what is widely understood to be his masterpiece, and the central work of his later period, *The Elementary Forms of Religious Life* (2001 [1912]), is that the main building blocks of all societies are essentially 'religious' ideas, morals, values and forces. It is these that are the crucial elements of any social order. How Durkheim developed a vocabulary to describe such matters is regarded by some interpreters as involving a fundamental break not only with the positivist and materialist tenor of his earlier work, but with 'mainstream' sociology more generally. Durkheim has arguably moved in *The Elementary Forms* from a *sociology of religion*, to a *religious sociology* – the former connoting the use of standard sociological ideas and methods to define and research religion, the latter referring to a new kind of sociology which is profoundly affected in its basic conceptual fabric by the phenomena, here religious, which it takes as its theme (Alexander, 1986). Religion is not just an object of sociological scrutiny, although it continues to be that, but becomes the means through which to create new concepts, themes, orientations and insights into the fundamental nature of human social life. The opposition between sociology *of* religion and *religious* sociology directly maps onto the contemporary distinction between sociology *of culture* and *cultural* sociology. For those who understand the latter to be fundamentally different from the former, the former term refers to the set of approaches which use (what are taken to be) standard sociological ideas and methods to define and research 'culture' – treating it as a dependent variable, subordinate to more primary variables such as social structure and power inequalities, rather than as an autonomous sphere in its own right. The term *cultural sociology*, by contrast, points to a perspective which is fundamentally shaped by the phenomena – here cultural, understood in light of the ideas of the later Durkheim's study of religion – which it takes as its central focus. Therefore one of the key differences between *sociology of culture* and *cultural sociology* is that the latter is founded on the later Durkheim, while the former has strong affinities with the positivism and materialism of Durkheim's earlier work (for extended treatment of these divisions by proponents of this sense of cultural sociology, see Alexander and Smith, 2003).

As Emirbayer (1996b: 115), another advocate of this sort of understanding of Durkheim's religious and cultural sociologies, summarizes it, the significance of the later Durkheim for contemporary cultural sociology is huge, because he provides highly

> ... useful tools for investigating symbolic structures and processes in the modern world. His 'religious' sociology opens up new possibilities for analyzing the cultural environment of action, which he regards as theoretically, if not empirically, independent of other (social structural and social-psychological) environments. [He gives] key insights as to the enduring significance, even in the modern world, of 'sacred' ideals, images, and symbols; the importance in cultural life of the polarity of the 'sacred' and the 'profane'; the recurrence of pivotal moments of 'collective effervescence' – or cultural 'renaissances' as he termed them – in the developmental history of the sacred; the emergence during these renaissances of conflicts over the very meaning and legitimate definition of sacred ideals; and ... the value of examining such conflicts from a multidimensional point of view, with an emphasis not only upon the bearers of symbols and the concrete circumstances of their struggles, but also upon the internal logic and organization of the symbolic forms themselves.

Whatever one's particular take on its subsequent significance, and despite the many flaws in its arguments which critics have pointed to over the years, most scholars would admit that *The Elementary Forms* is an extraordinarily complex and rich work, so much so that it is very difficult to summarize in a small space its multiplicitous arguments, productive ambiguities and manifold implications for a whole series of fields that would later become institutionalized as the sociology of knowledge, the sociology of religion, and the sociology of science, as well as cultural sociology. Nonetheless, a brief summary has to involve at least these points:

1 Religion involves, in an occluded form, the worship of society itself. '[R]eligion is above all a system of notions by which individuals imagine the society to which they belong and their obscure yet intimate relations with that society ... [A]cts of worship ... strengthen the ties that bind the individual to his [sic] society, since god [or the gods] is merely the symbolic expression of society' (Durkheim, 2001 [1912]: 170–1). Durkheim has a complex conception of a two-fold relationship where religion *is* society, and society *is* religion (2001 [1912]: 314; Pecora, 2006). Given that 'religion does not know itself. It knows neither what it is made of nor what needs it satisfies', it follows that it is the job of the analyst to uncover the *deep significance* of cultural forms and practices whose surface-level meanings may well be different from their more essential, subterranean ones (Durkheim, 2001 [1912]: 325).

2 The society/religion complex is a social and cultural universal. 'However complex the external manifestations of religious life, it is essentially unitary and simple. Everywhere it answers to the same need and derives from the same state of mind. In all its forms its purpose is to raise man [sic] above himself and make him live a life superior to the one he would lead if he were only to obey his individual impulses. Beliefs express this life in terms of representations; rites organize it and regulate its functioning' (2001 [1912]: 309).

3 Durkheim emphasizes the centrality of the distinction between the *sacred* and the *profane* in all social life. These are 'two distinct realities, separated by a clearly drawn line of demarcation' (2001 [1912]: 169). 'They repel and contradict each other with such force that the mind refuses to think of them at the same time' (2001 [1912]: 182). The social power of the sacred is such that religion very often 'represents the triumph of good over evil, life over death, the powers of light over the powers of darkness ... [social] reality is no different. If the relation between these opposite forces was reversed, life would be impossible' (2001 [1912]: 316).

4 Religion, and thus society, operate around a series of binary oppositions. 'Religious forces are of two kinds. Some are benevolent, guardians of the physical and moral order ... On the other hand, there are negative and impure powers that produce disorder ... and instigate sacrilege ... Man's [sic] only feeling[s] for them [are] fear [and] horror ... all religious life gravitates around two opposite poles, which share the opposition between pure and impure, holy and sacrilegious, divine and diabolical ... any contact between them is considered the worst of profanations' (2001 [1912]: 304–5).

5 Yet the relationships between the pure and impure are ambiguous, because they are so closely related. Disgust and horror can mingle with respect towards impure things. And pure things can invoke a sense of dread. It can be unclear as to whether something is regarded as special because it is viewed either as impure or as holy. Impure things can become holy things if the circumstances in which they are embedded change – for example, parts of a corpse can, after a long enough time has passed after death, come to be seen as holy relics. Conversely, if handled inappropriately, holy things can be polluting. In general terms, 'the pure and impure are not two separate genera but two varieties of the same genus that includes all sacred things. There are two kinds of sacred, one auspicious, the other inauspicious ... there is no discontinuity between the two forms ... the same object can pass from one to the other without changing its nature. The pure can be made impure, and vice versa' (2001 [1912]: 306) (For a discussion of how Durkheim's consideration of the ambiguity of the sacred has been unwisely ignored by later sociologists, see Kurakin, 2013).

6 Reality is thoroughly created by cultural forms, while social life is made possible by shared symbols. 'The whole social world seems populated by forces that in reality exist only in our mind. We know how the soldier feels about the flag, though it is merely a scrap of cloth ... [O]ur representation of the external world is ... just a tissue of hallucinations: the smells, tastes and colours that we attribute to bodies are not there, or at least not [in] the way we perceive [them to be]' (Durkheim, 2001 [1912]: 172). 'Collective representations of things often attribute to them properties that are not inherent [in them] ... They can turn the most ordinary object into a sacred and very powerful being ... though purely ideal, [collective representations] determine man's [sic] conduct as imperatively as [do] physical forces' (2001 [1912]: 173).

7  Collective classification systems reflect the morphology of a given society and are generated by the latter. '[L]ogical understanding is a function of society, since it adopts the forms and attitudes society imprints on it' (Durkheim, 2001 [1912]: 180). This applies to all social orders. Modern scientific explanations 'are not inherently different from those that satisfy primitive thought … the same method by which the mind places things in relationship [with each other] does not essentially differ' (2001 [1912]: 181–2). Modern society's faith in science 'is not essentially different from religious faith. The value that we ascribe to science depends … on the idea that we, collectively, have of its nature and role in life' (2001 [1912]: 334). (For a famous analysis of the logic and rationality of 'primitive' classification systems, see Lévi-Strauss, 1994.)

8  Once cultural systems have been created, they become semi-autonomous, or sometimes wholly autonomous, of the social realities from which they originally emerged. Culture comprises 'a whole world of feelings, ideas, and images that, once born, obey their own laws. They are mutually attractive and repellent, they fuse, segment and proliferate without being directly ordered and required to do so by the state of underlying reality. The life thus conjured up enjoys such great independence that it sometimes plays out in aimless, useless manifestations for the sole pleasure of affirming itself' (Durkheim, 2001 [1912]: 319). This point about the autonomy of culture from social structure will be crucial in later Durkheim-inspired cultural sociology, as we will see below.

9  Taboos and profanations are as much part of modern cultural life as they were of previous epochs: 'Even today, with all the freedom we grant each other, it would be sacrilege for a man to deny progress and flout the humanistic ideal to which modern societies are attached … [T]here is a principle that even peoples most enamored of free enquiry tend to place above discussion and to regard as untouchable, or sacred: that is the principle of free enquiry' (Durkheim, 2001 [1912]: 161). Thus modern social orders are in principle quite as based around taboos and ritualized structures as are non-modern ones, a key point taken up in later analyses of modern secular civil religions.

10  Social revolutions are always also cultural revolutions, where the old cultural order of sacred/profane is inverted and reinvented. For example, in the French revolution, 'things that were purely secular in nature were transformed … into sacred things: homeland, liberty and reason' (Durkheim, 2001 [1912]: 161), and this was the most important revolutionary transformation begun in 1789. Here we see Durkheim's focus on how the symbols and rites of modern, secular, civil life perform the same roles in social life as symbols and rites in non-modern social contexts, that of binding individuals together and periodically re-energizing the social order by stimulating feelings of shared purpose.

11  Durkheim emphasizes the importance of the totem for group life. A totem is a particular social group's 'flag … the sign by which each clan distinguishes itself from others, the visible mark of its personality, a mark that embodies everything that belongs to the clan in any way' (2001 [1912]: 154). 'A clan is essentially a union of individuals bearing the same name who rally around the same sign. Take away the name and the sign that makes it tangible, and the clan can longer even be imagined' (2001 [1912]: 178). 'Religious force is nothing but the collective and anonymous force of the clan [i.e. social group or 'society'], and because this can be imagined only in the form of the totem, the totemic emblem is like the visible body' of the group itself (2001 [1912]: 166). In Aboriginal Australia, the totem tends to be a simple, natural object, such as a plant or animal. It has to be a concrete object, rather than an abstract one, so that the human mind can easily grasp it. The 'sign takes the place of the object, and the emotions it arouses are attached to that sign. The sign is loved, feared, and respected; the sign is the object of gratitude and sacrifice. The soldier who dies for his flag, dies for his country; but in his mind the flag comes first … We forget that the flag is only a sign, that it has no intrinsic value but serves only to recall the reality it represents; we treat it as if it were that reality' (2001 [1912]: 165). With these remarks, Durkheim comes close to the contemporaneous reflections of Saussure on the arbitrary nature of signs and signification processes. (For a present-day, Durkheim-inspired take on iconic objects, see Chapter 39)

12  Durkheim stresses the crucial importance of group *collective effervescence* in maintaining social life over time. '[E]very festival, even one purely secular in nature, has certain features of the religious ceremony, for it always has

the effect of bringing individuals together, setting the masses in motion' (2001 [1912]: 285). 'To reaffirm feelings that might fade if left to themselves, it is enough to bring those who share them together into a closer and more active relationship' (2001 [1912]: 157). When the group is together in a festival-like situation, 'passionate energies' and an 'unusual surplus of forces' are unleashed, electrifying all present. 'People live differently and more intensely than in normal times' (2001 [1912]: 158). 'Once the individuals are assembled, their proximity generates a kind of electricity that quickly transports them to an extraordinary degree of exaltation' (2001 [1912]: 162). An individual is 'transported into a special world [i.e. of the sacred] entirely different from the ordinary, a setting populated by exceptionally intense forces that invade and transform him' (2001 [1912]: 164). 'Once we are acquitted of our religious duties, we re-enter profane life with more courage and enthusiasm … our forces have been reinvigorated' (2001 [1912]: 284–5). As no society can exist which does not gather individuals together to 'sustain and reaffirm the collective feelings and ideas that constitute its unity', then all social orders must do the same. There is therefore no essential difference between such events in aboriginal Australia, in Christianity or in modern secular societies which must have periodic 'meeting[s] of citizens commemorating the institution of a new moral charter or some great event in national life' (2001 [1912]: 322).

13 Durkheim also makes a distinction between 'joyous festivals … [and] sad festivals, whose purpose is either to cope with a catastrophe or … to recall and deplore it' (2001 [1912]: 289). Mourning at such rites is not so much an effect of individual grief but a social role that people are obliged to perform. Here we see the theme of the construction and ritualized maintenance of social and cultural trauma, which will be taken up by later Durkheim-inspired scholarship (Alexander, 2012).

14 Durkheim also points to the apparently unavoidable nature of scapegoating. During negative rites, the group feels 'a need to find a victim on whom to discharge the collective pain and anger at any price … this victim is sought outside the group' (2001 [1912]: 298). Thus group affirmation is achieved not just through positive celebration of sacred symbols, but also through negative activities such as demonizing others.

## AFTER DURKHEIM

Durkheim died in 1917, never finishing a project to establish a systematic sociology of morals, a project that later interpreters nonetheless have sought to piece together and reconstruct. The so-called 'Durkheim School', made up of close collaborators and those influenced by him, and centred around the journal *L'Annee Sociologique*, produced many interesting studies in the shadow of the master, many of which could now be dubbed as exercises in cultural sociology. These included the analysis of money as a symbolic system and its roots in religious practices (Simiand, 1934), the evolution of religious symbolism (Hubert and Mauss, 1909), and analysis of the cultural dynamics underpinning the Indian caste system (Bouglé, 1971).

Particularly notable in this context are Maurice Halbwachs' (1992) studies of collective memory, which showed how particular groups or whole societies use rituals and forms of memorialization to produce the ongoing remembrance of certain past events, whilst effacing others. Everyday forms of commemoration (e.g. iconic pictures of past Presidents on bank notes) work to produce collective memories of particular events and persons defined to be central to the history of the group, operating in the periods in between the grand, explicitly formalized ceremonies (such as the 4th of July in the US, and the 14th of July in France) of the kind that Durkheim had considered in Aboriginal Australia (Coser, 1992). Such work has inspired the contemporary interdisciplinary field of memory studies, and also is a reference point for analyses of how events that are defined as collective cultural traumas are managed and memorialized by particular social groups (Alexander, 2012).

One can also note the remarkable, if diffuse, influence of Durkheim on the *Annales* school of history and historical sociology developed by Marc Bloch and Lucien Febvre, and on the history of 'mentalities' (a phrase that bears the imprint of Durkheim's original understanding of collective classifications) pioneered by French historians like Emmanuel Le Roy Ladurie and Philippe Ariès (Emirbayer, 1996a). The work of Michel Foucault obviously is part of the intellectual universe of French historiography, being influenced by Durkheiman themes of collective classificatory systems in diffuse ways, but coupling these with Nietzschean concerns about power and the constitution of the self. Foucauldian and neo-Durkheimian themes have come together at the present time in the emergent field of historical cultural sociology, where the genealogical methods of the one exist in conjunction with the focus on collective representations of the latter (Mukerji, 2007, Chapter 15)

Different strands of Durkheim's thought were taken up in multiple ways by later sociologists Karl Mannheim (1887–1947) brought together Durkheimian themes with Marxist and Weberian orientations, in order to produce a sociology of knowledge, defined as 'a theory of the social ... determination of actual thinking' (1985 [1936]: 267). Mannheim sought to relate certain styles of thought to the shape of the social conditions that produced them. Mannheim (1985 [1936]: 4) argues that if a group of people is to realize its aims, it has to struggle with its environment, both the natural environment of physical nature and the social environment comprised of other groups of people. The particular ways in which those struggles occur determines the ways in which the group conceives the world around it, the 'worldview' (*Weltanschauung*) characteristic of that group. It is therefore collective activity, oriented towards the survival of the group, which produces the particular worldview which characterizes the group's culture. The way a group or society *acts* is the basis and generator of how it *thinks*. Mannheim's particular innovation is to apply Durkheim's views on the social generation of culture away from the level of a whole 'society', to the study of particular groups *within* a society. Mannheim generally agrees with Marx that such groups are classes. Thus the social conditions of each class are regarded as producing the particular worldview of that class. Mannheim (1956: 184) argues that in societies where 'the political and social order basically rests upon the distinction between "higher" and "lower" human types, an analogous distinction is also made between "higher" and "lower" objects of knowledge or aesthetic enjoyment'. Where there is a class division between rulers and ruled, culture will be divided along those lines. There will be a culture of the ruling classes that is defined as 'high', and a culture of the lower class(es) that is defined as 'low'. There is in fact nothing intrinsically superior about the products of the 'high' culture. They are only regarded as 'high' because the ruling class has defined them that way. There is also nothing intrinsically inferior about the cultural objects used or enjoyed by the lower classes. Their inferiority results from them being defined as inferior by higher classes.

Such ideas as to the *relativity of cultural value* became central in later sociologies of culture, most notably in the work of Pierre Bourdieu (1992). Mannheim's synthesis of Durkheimian, Marxist and Weberian themes therefore both anticipates Bourdieu, and implicitly informs the latter's highly influential understanding of the relationships between cultural forms and social power (Brubaker, 1985). In Bourdieu's work, collective classifications become rooted in the habitus of particular social classes. A particular class-based group's classifications both classify the world for people within that class, and in turn such classifications are then used by other groups to classify, in cultural hierarchies, that class-based group and the people within it. In Bourdieu's formulation, a person's cultural tastes both classify things and classify the classifier herself in turn.

One of the most influential interpreters of Durkheim in the second half of the 20th century was Talcott Parsons. In the book *The Social System* (1951) and elsewhere, Parsons argues that sociology should focus on the relations between the *social system*, the *cultural system*, and the *personality system*. The sociological study of culture is defined as 'the analysis of the interdependence and interpenetration of social and cultural systems' (Parsons, 1961: 991). Thus sociology looks at the relationships between *culture* and *society*, where the former means *values* (i.e. norms, beliefs and ideas) and the latter means *patterns of social interaction*. The cultural system contains the most general and abstract values of a society (e.g. a belief in God or democracy). From these values are derived more concrete *norms*, that guide interactions in the social system. The relation between cultural and social systems is therefore characterized by the former guiding the latter. The cultural system patterns the *personality system*, the ways people in a particular society, or sub-section thereof, typically think and feel. Parsons argues that it is culture that motivates people to act, by constructing their ideas as to what they want and how to get it. From this viewpoint, it is 'the structure of cultural meanings [that] constitutes the "ground" of any system of action' (Parsons, 1961: 963). It is values that drive action. How any society works is absolutely dependent on a cultural context characterized by *value consensus*: most people in a particular society must share the same values and act in regular ways on the basis of them. Thus social order is maintained over time. One of the usual criticisms of this position, is that it seems to make actors out to be 'cultural dopes', obeying the 'instructions' of culture in automatic ways (Wrong, 1980 [1961]). Critics see Parsons as having set up the polar opposite of Marx's alleged economic determinism, namely a cultural determinism. Parsons' interpretation of Durkheim's original focus on shared values and ideals smothers both individual scope for action and the conflicts which Marxist and Weberian sociologies emphasize as being at the heart of social life. One of the main efforts of neo-Durkheimian cultural sociologists working today, most notably Jeffrey Alexander, has been to reinterpret the significance of Durkheim beyond Parsons' framing of the latter as a theorist of cultural consensus.

## EXTENDING DURKHEIM

One important step in that direction was taken in the 1950s and 1960s by Parsons' sometime collaborator Edward Shils (1975). In *The Elementary Forms*, Durkheim had made some comments about the relevance of his analysis of Aboriginal religion to the operation of modern societies, but these had not been systematically pursued. Shils (1961) developed an account of the role of sacred beliefs in modern societies which added some nuance to the basic Durkheimian framework, which after all had been generated on the basis of Durkheim's engagement with pre-modern religion and thus lacked consideration of the differences between pre-modern and modern forms of the social forms of the sacred. Shils was also concerned to demonstrate the enduring 'religious' foundations of modern life, in opposition to Marxists, Weberians and others who seemed to overestimate the centrality of political ideologies in the constitution of modern cultures. Thus Shils' intervention was two-fold – to show the ongoing relevance of Durkheim's understanding of the sacred for modern societies, but nuancing it so that the framework fitted modern social conditions more carefully than Durkheim himself had been able to work out (for extended discussion, see Lynch, 2012).

Shils analyses the nature of the relationships pertaining between a society's sense of the sacred, the nature of authority in that society, and the various social institutions – such as parliaments and political systems, the economy and the media – all of which are the structural features of that society. Shils asserts that all societies, including modern ones, have a central value system, which he refers to as the 'sacred centre'.

> The centre ... is a phenomenon of the realm of values and beliefs. It is the centre of the order of symbols, of values and beliefs, which govern the society. It is the centre because it is the ultimate and irreducible; and it is felt to be such by many who cannot give explicit articulation to its irreducibility. The central zone partakes of the nature of the sacred. In this sense, every society has an 'official' religion, even when that society or its exponents and interpreters, conceive of it, more or less correctly, as a secular, pluralistic and tolerant society. (1961: 117)

For Shils, the sacred is not purely a set of ideas and symbols, for these are always concretely interwoven into social institutions. Central institutions, such as for example monarchies and state churches, are touched by, and thereby legitimated by, the sacred. Institutions are regarded by citizens as sacred as they embody the sacred values. Moreover, when people regard and engage with the awesome face of institutional power, the concentrated and apparently massive quality of that power gives those institutions a sacred aura. For example, when someone goes to a state's capital and looks upon the huge, imposing buildings of the state – the central law courts, the parliament house, the monarch's or president's palace – the monumental qualities of those edifices conjure up feelings not just about the great power of the state but also of the values it supposedly upholds, such as the freedom of the nation, the rights of the people, the power of the sovereign, and so on. And it is not surprising that it is within these edifices, or in front of them, that the solemn rituals of the state are performed regularly, allowing for the ongoing presentation not just of the might and majesty of the state and the personnel who run it and embody it, but also of the sacred values that are embodied in, and re-energized by, such rituals themselves.

Shils' focus is on social and cultural centres and peripheries, a focus on the latter being mostly absent from Durkheim's earlier considerations, and arguably from Parsons' purview too. If the sacred symbols and ideas of a society are the cultural centre, then the social centre is made up of the institutions touched and legitimated by the sacred, and the elite groups who run and control those institutions. The sacred legitimates those elites either directly or indirectly. This focus on elites and their legitimation by sacred values illustrates Shils' combining of Durkheimian and Weberian themes.

Shils' intention was to provide a more nuanced understanding of the sacred in modernity than Durkheim had been able to offer. One issue, which had also engaged Halbwachs (see above), was how social solidarity was maintained in between the periods of the major social rituals. Shils argued that sacred values are only one basis of social integration, and there were others that were more prosaic, like forms of professional pride and individual ambition. Drawing again on Weber, Shils also noted that the embodying of sacred values into institutions is never complete or perfect. There often occurs a certain routinization of the institutionalization of values, such that institutions do not seem particularly sacred to those within them or affected by them. More importantly, most sacred orders have idealistic aspects – for example, modern democratic societies have aspirations to be truly, rather than just imperfectly, democratic. The idealistic elements can never be fully institutionalized. What that means is there is always the possibility of institutions being seen to be flawed, letting down and corrupting the sacred values rather than embodying and upholding them. These flaws can be exploited by social critics, who can try to persuade 'ordinary people' – i.e., those at the social periphery, occupying non-elite positions – that the elites have let down the nation's most important values. If this persuasion is successful, then crisis, reform and even revolution can come onto the socio-political agenda. Sacred ideals are therefore resources for would-be revolutionaries as well as for the guardians of the status quo.

Moreover, the presence and performance of the sacred in, for example, major state rituals, can provoke resentment as well as devotion from people in peripheral positions. A royal wedding can provoke outbursts of anti-monarchist sentiment as well as reinforcing beliefs among the populace as to the legitimacy and desirability of monarchical rule. What this points to is the uneven nature of assent in modern societies to elites' definitions of what the sacred values of society are. The socially central people may define, control and be legitimated by the sacred centre, but how the socially peripheral people respond to the sacred is an open question, and depends on continuous efforts by elites to adequately embody the sacred in the institutions they run. Here Shils points towards a theme later to be taken up by Jeffrey Alexander and his school – what can elites do to ensure the convincing *performance* of sacredness and thus legitimate power, when in a modern society there are no guarantees that such performances will 'work'?

In one way, it seems obvious that elites will struggle more in modern than in pre-modern societies to elaborate successful performances of power, legitimacy and sacralization. This is because modern societies typically involve more social groups and higher levels of complexity than pre-modern ones, so more can go wrong in the performance and the potential for failed performances is higher. This is a point emphasized by Alexander and his associates (see below). But in an interesting move, Shils argues in somewhat the opposite direction. Pre-modern societies left more people at the social periphery than do modern ones. Think of ancient Egypt, for example, where a tiny priestly and royal elite controlled the sacred centre, leaving the overwhelming majority of the peasant population out of contact with the official religion and political ideology. In such a society, where the sacred barely touches the social periphery, an alternative, unofficial, and potentially oppositional sacred, or multiple sacreds, can appear among the populace. Thus in a highly centralized civilization like ancient Egypt – which notably is a pre-modern society very unlike Durkheim's conception of Aboriginal Australia – the scared centre may hardly count as a centre at all, but rather as the preserve of narrow elites only. By contrast, for Shils modern societies are far more effective at pulling in socially peripheral groups towards the sacred centre controlled by elites.

> [I]n the modern societies of the West, the central value system has gone much more deeply into the heart of their members than it has ever succeeded in doing in any earlier society. The 'masses' have responded to their contact with a striking measure of acceptance. (1961: 125)

For example, in 20th-century Britain, the media performed a very effective job of bringing the working classes into forms of participation in events such as the Coronation of Queen Elizabeth II and the marriage of Prince Charles to Diana Spencer, through massive and sustained coverage of such events. In that way, the socially peripheral people of the 20th century were, paradoxically, brought into more sustained contact with elites' sacred centre – in this case, the values of monarchy and being a subject of the monarch – than were British lower-class people of earlier centuries. Despite more social complexity and more diverse political opinions, including oppositional ones, the 20th-century lower classes were more systematically brought into the sacred system than were their counterparts in earlier phases of modernity, despite there being theoretically more opportunities in the later period for the performance of the sacred to go 'wrong', and to cultivate resistive viewpoints. Shils here seems to be pointing to the remarkable resilience of at least some sacred centres – not only have they adapted, or been actively adapted by elites, to fit the modern media age, they have also been able to absorb effectively the resistive and oppositional viewpoints that the rituals in which they are performed may themselves stimulate. Thus the social sacred seems to have notable capacities to absorb and neutralize the critique it will inevitably provoke, by bringing peripheral groups ever more into its orbit, and thus muffling protests from such groups that would be more efficacious if they existed symbolically and practically completely outside of its influence. The social sacred can be made to work to drown out resistance to it, as the feeble anti-monarchist movements in the UK, Sweden, the Netherlands and other national societies attest. More generally, Shils' contribution remains interesting today as it simultaneously shows that modern societies can have multiple, competing forms of the sacred all existing at one time, as well as how in particular national spaces, a dominant state-sanctioned sacred can continue to marginalize or submerge oppositional voices and practices, in ways that seem as much 'pre-modern' as modern.

While Shils was concerned with modern societies in general, Robert Bellah (1967) was more specifically concerned with the US, and what he termed its 'civil religion'. Lynch (2012: 37) usefully summarizes Bellah's views of American civil religion thus:

> [I]t is constituted around the sacred values of universal human rights and freedom, enshrined in the principles of democratic society, in which freedom is viewed in positive moral terms as the freedom to pursue a just and civically responsible life. This system of sacred values finds expression in particular sacred texts such as the Declaration of Independence, the Constitution, seminal speeches such as the inaugural presidential addresses of George Washington and J.F. Kennedy, and rituals such as the celebration of Thanksgiving and Memorial Day, as well as through material forms such as the American flag and national cemeteries. Through participation in the symbolic and ritual world offered by this civil religion, Americans are able to experience themselves as part of a national collective, oriented towards sacred values of freedom, democracy and justice.

Bellah's characterization of civil religion has been very influential in the analysis of American social and political life. One of the questions it raises is the degree to which this cultural sacred actually informs contemporary American life, and in which ways. In an empirically-based study carried out in the early 1980s, *Habits of the Heart* (1988), Bellah's research group investigated those 'ordinary practices of life' in communities beyond the big cities that Alexis de Tocqueville in the early 19th century had called the 'habits of the heart' of ordinary Americans. Tocqueville's original analysis concluded that American life was torn between too much individualism – a concern also of Durkheim – and a tendency towards the individual being subsumed into a mass of people. Bellah and his colleagues argued that it is the former problem, that of too much individualism and a decline in community participation, that is the main dilemma in contemporary America. As Bellah (1988: 285) phrases it, the 'American dream is often a very private dream of being the star, the uniquely successful and admirable one, the one who stands out from the crowd of ordinary folk who don't know how'. If everyone is dreaming in their own personal way and acting in a self-centred manner, what happens to the bases of community life?

The Bellah team emphasized that the centrifugal forces of individualism are an important feature of American life today, especially among the suburban middle classes. In the suburbs, the main source of information and entertainment is the television, not the community hall. The people interviewed did experience a 'profound yearning for the idealized small town' that is part of American mythology (Bellah et al., 1988: 282). But this recognition of the importance of civic participation often remained at the level of desire rather than of practice. Nonetheless Bellah and the other researchers found that the religious and political traditions of early America had not completely died out. Even in modern America, land of the automobile and 24-hour television, 'somehow families, churches [and] a variety of cultural associations ... do manage to communicate a form of life' that vaguely corresponds to the civic society described more than one hundred and fifty years before by Tocqueville (Bellah et al., 1988: 282). For example, the local church retains its role as a centre of community life in many places. The ceremonies of American civil religion, such as Thanksgiving and the 4th of July, provide a 'shared rhythm' to the lives of otherwise separated family groups. Bellah finds evidence of the continuance of 19th-century America's habits, and the civil religion which animates them and ensures their reproduction, into the 21st century. Even 'the mass media, with their tendency to homogenize feelings and sensations, cannot entirely avoid transmitting' such ideals 'in however muted a form' (Bellah et al., 1988: 282). While some TV programming exhibits the highly materialistic, self-interested vision of the American Dream, there are also many shows which emphasize the importance of community association and civic participation. Deep currents of American civil religion apparently continue to run through what seem like the shallows of American television.

Returning to more analytical concerns, Bellah makes a number of points which are important for the refinement of the original Durkheimian ideas. First, according to Bellah, American civil religion is about republican conceptions of citizenship and civic and political participation. But this vision is theoretically incompatible with, and exists in empirical contexts in some friction with, a liberal political philosophy of maximum freedom for individuals and minimal state interference in their lives, in both political and economic terms.

Thus the US was founded with two competing cultural sacreds, testifying to the multiple nature of the sacred in modern societies, as well as to the possibility – under-emphasized by Shils – that central institutions could embody more than one sacred, with complicated consequences. For example, the US Supreme Court routinely has to make decisions which navigate awkwardly between republicanism and liberalism. Some institutions may embody mostly one form of the sacred, while other institutions embody mostly the other, bringing them into latent or explicit conflict.

Second, Bellah also raises an important point about how the sacred can be put to use by different interested parties, a point also gestured to by Shils. Bellah notes that American civil religion is partly secular, but nonetheless has a directly transcendent and theological element, captured in the phrase 'one nation under God'. An abstract Judeo-Christian God stands in judgement upon the nation. This allows for certain individuals and groups to engage in social critique, criticizing the current institutionalization of the sacred values. They have a powerful rhetorical move at their disposal – the way society and its institutions are currently organized falls short of the sacred values, such that there is only imperfect democracy, imperfect citizenship for people of all ethnicities, and so on. This shortfall is shameful in the eyes of God. Therefore reform will have to take place to make social reality once again live up to the ideals. This is the essential strategy afforded to and used by reformers like Martin Luther King and the civil rights movement: a revivification of reality in the direction of the sacred, so that human reality may once again approach Godlike perfection. This explains the tenor of much American political rhetoric, – one makes appeal to values perceived to be higher than their current institutionalization, so that current institutions can be thoroughly modified in a movement that preserves their essentially good core but purges them of the pollution of their current imperfections, stains put there by corrupt personnel who must be swept from office. Because of the transcendent theological nature of the American sacred, a particular institutionalization of it can always be challenged and potentially overthrown. The volatile energies of the sacred can be tapped into by reformers who know how to deploy such energies. It is that sense of the idealistic and open-ended nature of the sacred in American society – and perhaps by extension in other modern national societies – that has in large part animated the neo-Durkheimian cultural sociology to which we turn our attention in the final section of this chapter.

# NEO-DURKHEIMIAN CULTURAL SOCIOLOGY

Since the mid-1980s, a form of neo-Durkheimian cultural sociology has been developed by the American sociologist Jeffrey C. Alexander and his associates, such as Ron Eyerman and Philip Smith. Based at the Yale Center for Cultural Sociology which was founded in the early 2000s, Alexander, his colleagues at Yale and other locations, and their PhD students, have promoted what they call the 'strong program' in cultural sociology, which draws on diverse sources from the social sciences and humanities, but the foundation stone of which is an account of autonomy of culture from social structure which is inspired by Durkheim's statements in *The Elementary Forms*. The 'strong program' challenges what it regards as overly reductionist forms of analysis, especially the 'production of culture' school (see Chapter 14) and Bourdieusian sociology of culture (see Chapter 7), for both are taken to sacrifice culture's capacities to shape social life on the altar of structuralist considerations of social institutions and forms of power. The 'strong program' argues that such positions also radically underplay the *meaningful* nature of social life, and how cultural forms are themselves strongly patterned and structured in the sorts of ways pointed at by the later Durkheim.

In early statements of his position, Alexander (1986) argued that the later Durkheim had established not a sociology *of* religion but rather a 'religious sociology', one which took the partly autonomous and meaning-making capacities of 'religious' cultural forms seriously. On this reading, 'Durkheim's challenge is to develop a cultural logic for society: to make the symbolic dimension of every social sphere a relatively autonomous domain of cultural discourse interpenetrated with the other dimensions of society' (Alexander, 1988a: 188). What this in turn means is a positing of the centrality of meaning in all types of society, including modern, apparently wholly 'secular' ones. Alexander takes thinkers like Max Weber to task for apparently believing that modern, industrial capitalist social orders were ever more devoid of meaning. Durkheim, by contrast, is taken to show that meaningful cultural patterns are as central to such societies as they are in pre- and non-modern social orders. While criticizing Talcott Parsons' interpretation of Durkheim for oversimplifying Durkheim's real conceptual achievements, nonetheless Alexander's positing of culture's centrality to modern social orders owes something to Parsons, as well as to Shils and Bellah, whom Alexander presents as important pioneers in the struggle to create, out of Durkheim's religious sociology, a genuinely *cultural* sociology.

In a now well-known statement of his more mature position on what cultural sociology is and does, Alexander (2003: 3–4) noted that:

> ... the task of a cultural sociology ... is to bring the unconscious cultural structures that regulate society into the light of the mind. Understanding may change but not dissipate them, for without such structures society cannot survive. We need myths if we are to transcend the banality of material life. We need narratives if we are to make progress and experience tragedy. We need to divide the sacred from profane if we are to pursue the good and protect ourselves from evil.

Cultural sociology, then, aims to reveal the sorts of cultural structures that underpin social existence and animate it. Alexander strongly rejects understandings of culture that have been dominant, in American sociology in particular, over the last several decades. Among US sociologists

> ... there is decided reluctance to allow culture to itself be seen in a structural way. It must be something constantly in flux, reflecting the freedom and subjectivity that mark the distinctiveness of humankind. It must be rooted in an ever evolving existential search for meaning. It must grow out of the pragmatics of problem solving and boundary making, the situated exigencies of speech, the need for reciprocity, for taking the role of the other. (Alexander, 2007: 644)

All of these sorts of views, which Alexander labels as variants of the over-arching category of 'sociology *of* culture', can discern 'the significant *effects* of collective meanings'. But what they cannot do, which is precisely what a genuinely cultural sociology seeks to do, is to 'interpret ... collective meanings [and] trac[e] the moral textures and delicate emotional pathways by which individuals and groups come to be influenced by them'. 'Sociology of culture' approaches merely seek to 'explain what *created* meanings ... [and] to expose how the ideal structures of culture are formed by *other structures* – of a[n allegedly] more material, less ephemeral kind' (Alexander, 2003: 5). In other words, 'culture' is explained – or rather, explained away – by other, supposedly 'harder' variables. But for Alexander 'culture is not a thing but a dimension, not an object to be studied as a dependent variable but a thread that runs through, one that can be teased out of, every conceivable social form' (2003: 5). How the human world actually works involves an opposite causal trajectory, not from 'society' to 'culture', but vice versa, from meaningful cultural structures to social institutions and practices. Every action is seen to be embedded in a horizon of affect and meaning, while institutions always have a powerful and efficacious cultural foundation.

Alexander takes Bourdieu's work to be the epitome *par excellence* of a 'sociology of culture' approach.

> Bourdieu's sociology is irredeemably flawed, in theoretical as well as in empirical terms ... It distorts the nature of action and order and misunderstands the basic institutional and cultural structures ... [and] the moral and human possibilities, of contemporary life ... The result is that Bourdieu strategizes action (reincorporating behaviorism), subjects it to overarching symbolic codes (reincorporating structuralism), and subjugates both code and action to an underlying material base (reincorporating orthodox Marxism). (Alexander, 1995: 130–1)

This now-famous attack on Bourdieu is either a devastating critique of the shortcomings of the latter's sociology, or an unfair and greatly over-stated polemic which, deliberately or not, omits consideration of the subtleties of Bourdieu's overall theory of practice and its application to explicitly 'cultural' matters such as the operation of fields of cultural production.

Regardless of how compelling Alexander's criticisms of Bourdieu may be, the former's point may well still hold, namely that social contexts do not simply determine the content and significance of cultural forms, but rather refract these in meaningful ways (Alexander and Smith, 2003). Likewise, Alexander's point about how 'sociology of culture' approaches in general tend to downplay or ignore the meaningful, and therefore emotional dimensions of culture and social life, is an important one.

> Cultural sociology makes collective emotions and ideas central to its methods and theories precisely because it is such subjective and internal feelings that so often seem to rule the world. Socially constructed subjectivity forms the will of collectivities; shapes the rules of organizations; defines the moral substance of law; and provides the meaning and motivation for technologies, economies, and military machines. (Alexander, 2003: 5)

One of the central planks of the 'strong program' is its assertion of the autonomous nature of culture vis-à-vis social structures and social power. Cultural sociology involves the analytical move of decoupling culture from social structure, so that the cultural forms and patterns involved in the particular subject matter being studied may be seen clearly (Kane, 1991). Alexander is able to justify theoretically the autonomy of culture with reference to arguments taken from Durkheim and Saussure. In the case of the latter, if meanings are arbitrary, so they must perforce have a certain autonomy from forms of social determination. In the case of the former, the fact that culture is centred around binary structures like good/evil and pure/impure, also means that it is relatively autonomous of 'social' factors. The central binary animating all social life is the opposition between the sacred and the profane, which

> not only defines what people care about but establishes vital safeguards around the shared normative 'good' ... [and] places powerful, often aggressive barriers against anything that is construed as threatening the good, forces defined not merely as things to be avoided but as sources of horror and pollution that must be contained at all costs. (Alexander, 2003: 32)

Once the analyst has made the move of isolating the cultural patterns and structures that s/he discerns to be at work in the area she is investigating, then she can move to examine how those particular cultural phenomena have, in the specific empirical contexts within which they are located, 'concrete autonomy'. Thus one looks to see how the cultural phenomena concretely interact with other phenomena, including institutions and actions. Cultural sociology seeks to go beyond purely abstract claims about culture's capacities to shape and motivate other phenomena, by anchoring accounts of causality in specific actors and forms of agency. The degree to which cultural sociology has been able to do this convincingly remains an open question (McLennan, 2004).

As Alexander and his associates developed their version of cultural sociology, they added to the Durkheimian foundations other analytical and methodological elements which they felt compensated for gaps and absences in Durkheim's original views. By adding in themes pursued by later Durkheim-inspired scholars such as Lévi-Strauss (1994) and Mary Douglas (1966) on the structural dimensions of cultural forms, by analysts of social liminality and ritual like Victor Turner (1969), and by hermeneuticians such as Dilthey (1991 [1883]), they assembled a form of analysis which took in many themes and concepts from across the range of non-positivist social science. One particularly important resource was the interpretative anthropology of Clifford Geertz, which is predicated on the view that culture is a rich and complex text, with subtle patterning influences on social life. The combination of Durkheim and Geertz leads to the claim that cultural sociology is a kind of 'structural hermeneutics', which examines the structured nature of cultural forms, understanding these as texts to be deciphered and their structural properties revealed. But Geertz's (1973) bravura readings of particular cultural/social texts, most famously the Balinese cockfight, are themselves criticized for lacking specification of how precisely culture influences the concrete actions of individuals, something that cultural sociology is intended to be able to provide.

Added to these social scientific resources are ideas taken from the literary humanities, this addition being a particularly striking example of analytical, cross-disciplinary bricolage. Combined with the Durkheimian focus on cultural structures are literary studies of narrative and narrative form, such as those offered by Northrop Frye (1957). Culture is seen to involve archetypal narrative forms like the morality play and the tragedy, which dramatize the key binaries like good and evil for particular social groups. Literary tropes like irony are focused on by cultural sociologists, examining how such devices are used by particular actors for the purposes of social critique (Guhin, 2013).

By the late 1980s, much of the analytical apparatus of cultural sociology was already fairly well formed, and one of the most enduring and well-cited studies created within that framework dates from that time. Alexander's (1988a) analysis of the Watergate scandal and the subsequent American governmental hearings provoked by it, is a modern classic of cultural sociology. The structural hermeneutic approach is deployed to show how and why Watergate became a symbol of such profound impurity and evil in and for the American body politic. On this analysis, the hearings were a sort of sacred process within secular political life, involving the invoking by the prosecutors of the Watergate conspirators of a set of mythical ideals such as 'Democracy' and 'Liberty'. The Republican Party, which in effect was on trial for the misdemeanours of its President in office, desperately tried to prevent a symbolic move in the hearings from the level of the politically profane to the sacred level of core American values. But once these were successfully brought into play by the prosecutors, the hearings became a sacred drama in which the future of 'America' itself lay in the balance. Clearly echoing earlier Durkheimian analyses like that of Shils, Alexander argues that the hearings strengthened rather than weakened the key cultural structures of the American polity. This is because at work were purification processes which enforced 'the strength of the symbolic, sacred center of society at the expense of ... [an empirically-existing political] center which is increasingly seen as ... profane and impure'

(1988a: 195). While the perpetrators were polluted and expelled from the body politic, the sacred drama's heroes – such as the prosecutors and the journalists who exposed the scandal – were 'purified in the resacralization process through their identification with the Constitution, norms of fairness and citizen solidarity' (1988a: 205). According to Alexander's examination of events, the eventual outcome of the drama was 'increased faith in the political "system" even while the distrust it produced continued to undermine public confidence in particular institutional actors and authorities' (1988a: 213). Empirical politics was profaned while the underlying, deep cultural sources of politics were rejuvenated.

While Alexander has strenuously defended such a cultural sociological approach as being thoroughly grounded both in empirical data – such as court transcripts, official documents, and so on – and in a rigorous set of methodological procedures to deal with them, one might still object that, *à la* Geertz, such readings are still ultimately bravura exercises in interpretation which other analysts might struggle to carry out themselves or indeed to replicate, and that the analysis is based on the strong assumption that there *are* and *must be* cultural structures underpinning the observable empirical phenomena. Alexander (2007) has countered such accusations by making recourse to a classic Durkheimian position – that cultural structures are 'social facts', existing 'out there' in the world, can be demonstrated to exist, and are not merely the projections of the cultural sociologist onto the phenomena she is investigating. But it is precisely the alleged 'thingness' of culture that has been criticized by some (notably McLennan, 2004) as a kind of fetish, which comes to contradict Alexander's broader social-theoretical project, namely to create a truly multi-dimensional social science which refuses to reduce any set of factors to any other. For some critics, Alexander unintentionally ends up with a highly problematic cultural idealist position, involving 'the exaggerated elevation of something called Culture to a near-sacred interpretative status' (McLennan, 2004: 80).

That criticism may have been dealt with in part by more recent work on what Alexander has called 'cultural pragmatics'. This moves from the level of cultural structures to the analysis of concrete forms of action. Cultural pragmatics understands social interactions as involving performances which are aimed at generating forms of solidarity between actors and audiences. An actor's performance is 'successful' when people in a given audience view it as somehow 'authentic', with the result that there is an affective 'fusing' of performers and those on the receiving end of their messages (Alexander et al., 2006).

There are six central properties of social performances (Alexander, 2004a). These are: (1) a system of collective representations, i.e., the broad cultural background against which performances occur and upon which they draw; (2) an actor or group of actors who enact certain culturally-defined scripts and endeavour to make their performances convince their intended audiences; (3) audiences, who may view actors' performance as authentic, but only if these make sense vis-à-vis the background collective representations and are emotionally and cognitively satisfying; (4) means of symbolic production, such as public arenas for performances and resources for enacting of scripts; (5) *mise-en-scène*, the process by which the previous dimensions are orchestrated, hopefully to produce effects which work well for the chosen audience; and (6) power relations, which thoroughly penetrate all aspects of performances, such as which collective representations are particularly salient and which are subordinated, which actors are socially sanctioned to perform and which not, the degree to which audience members are able to dispute or undermine performances, and so on. This latter factor is included to pre-empt criticisms that this version of cultural sociology lacks an adequate understanding of power dynamics.

As Alexander (1988b: 14) already noted in an earlier work, in complex modern societies in particular, 'the fact of ritual process is separated from any expectations about consensual outcome'. Performances are more likely to fail than succeed in societies where collective representations are multiple, overlapping, complex and potentially contradictory, and where audiences themselves are multiple and heterogeneous. Performances probably fail if 'any of the elements that compose them are insufficiently realized, or if the relation among these elements is not articulated in a coherent or forceful way' (Alexander, 2004b: 92). Nonetheless, some performances do succeed, and have profound consequences for social order – the oratory of Martin Luther King is an obvious example of how an actor succeeded in mobilizing collective representations (involving the sacred terms of 'American democracy') to win over new audiences (here, Northern white voters who were won over to the Civil Rights movement's cause) (Alexander, 2006).

The performance perspective has also been applied to less overtly political, and more apparently straightforwardly 'artistic' domains, such as music. For McCormick (2009: 7), music is a form of social performance in which 'actors, individually or in concert, display for others the meaning of their social situation'. Music is therefore a cultural communication process, played out against the backdrop of, and drawing upon, systems of collective representations. These are 'conjured [by musical actors] to construct the context of performance and ... in turn guide the interpretation of performances enacted within' that context (McCormick, 2009: 7). Far from musical contexts being inert structural conditions within which particular styles of performance are demanded and generated – the charge McCormick's cultural sociology of music makes against both 'production of culture' and Bourdieusian approaches – they are in fact 'the result of an ongoing process of cultural construction', which is re-created by musical actors as they perform music (McCormick, 2009: 7).

Alexander's *magnum opus* of cultural sociology is *The Civil Sphere* (2006), which constitutes a major contribution not just to cultural sociology but to political sociology and socio-political theory too. In that work, Alexander argues that civil society should be conceived in cultural sociological terms, as a sphere that is 'analytically independent, empirically differentiated, and morally more universalistic vis-à-vis the state, and the market and from other social spheres as well' (2006: 31). It is a sphere of social solidarity – a central Durkheimian theme – that is centred not on self-interest or power relations but universalistic moral feelings and sympathies for others. Such feelings are not the simple products of the 'uncivil spheres' of the market and state, but rather should be understood as having an autonomous cultural existence of their own. In particular empirical contexts, the civil sphere is 'always limited by, and interpenetrated with, the boundary relations of other, non-civil spheres' (Alexander, 2006: 31). The latter's power, and the forms of discrimination and prejudice that they can involve against particular disadvantaged groups, is pushed back when the civil sphere effectively 'invade[s] uncivil spheres, to demand certain reforms', the latter involving 'repairs that aim to mend the social fabric' (2006: 33).

The civil sphere is made of profound cultural structures. As Alexander (2006: 644) puts it:

> ... while deeply rooted in institutional exigencies, and directed toward real pragmatic problems of the most grave and also the most banal kind, a binary discourse ... inform[s] and organize[s] the patterned conflicts and understandings of civil spheres. The content of this symbolic language is rich and complex but at bottom rather simple, its binaries repeated endlessly wherever the aspirations and realities of civil society come into play ... [The civil sphere involves a central] code, detailed yet at the same time generic, composed of layered sets of symmetrically equivalent binaries such as truth/lies, rational/irrational, open/secretive. In both its positive and negative references, these binaries seem ... to be accepted by both sides in ... polarized political conflict[s], as well as by the representatives of institutional elites, whether religious, economic, or journalistic. The code [is usually] never thematized as such [but rather] presented as descriptive, not proscriptive; as denotive, not connotative; as natural, not performative. (2006: 644–5)

On this reading of the civil sphere as a deep cultural resource, subordinated groups can effect social change by creating social movements which engage in symbolically-charged performances. These are projected to various audiences outside the movement, encompassing both more subordinated and more powerful groups. Successful performances are those which notably expand for such audiences who counts as 'we' and 'us'. If other groups come to regard the suffering of those whom the social movement claims to speak for as 'our own' suffering, then the moral horizons of those groups expand and solidarity between groups increases. One of the most striking examples Alexander offers in this regard is how over time, through complex processes within the civil sphere, the Holocaust became redefined not as a specifically 'Jewish' matter but as an emblem of suffering 'humanity' as a whole. The parameters of the binary us/them were altered over time, in favour of more universalistic understandings of who, for broader American and European societies, counts as 'us'. Such an analysis indicates the broadly positive tone of Alexander's political diagnoses that draw upon and animate his cultural sociology, with the autonomous cultural structures of the civil sphere being understood to contain powerful resources for under-dog groups to gain respect and recognition from those who formerly oppressed them. This resonates with the generally optimistic tenor of Durkheim's own political outlook, as it was reflected in his sociological analysis of modern social conditions.

## CONCLUSION

The Durkheimian stream within the sociological analysis of culture is a major analytic tradition. From the original writings of Durkheim, and indeed of Fustel de Coulanges before him, it has mutated over time in diverse ways, being appropriated by sociological thinkers as diverse as Parsons and Bourdieu. It has proven to be particularly appealing to certain sociologists working in the US context and analysing that country's civil religion, such as Shils, Bellah and more recently Alexander. This is not surprising, in that Durkheim's original reflections were very much centred on and influenced by the version of secular civil religion instigated by the French Revolution, a civil religion that bears many strong resemblances to its American counterpart. Given the strong affinity between these two national socio-political contexts, it is understandable that American sociologists would find in Durkheim a very useful resource for understanding the operations of the national scene they are part of and are oriented to in their studies. But just as Durkheim's work can be regarded as a series of reflections on the particularity of the French national context, which are then problematically elevated to the status of universal principles alleged to apply to all forms of culture and social order everywhere, so too does American 'cultural sociology', stretching from Shils to Alexander, run the risk of creating a general model of cultural dynamics which is based on the particularities of the American situation in a more subterranean and unacknowledged manner than one might wish (Roudometof, 2007). Not only does this raise problems of the universalization of socio-cultural specificities, it also perhaps reproduces national frames of reference in a period when sociologists are encouraged to relinquish forms of methodological nationalism and to turn their gaze to trans-national processes that move across and transform national borders, cultural and otherwise (Beck, 2000). While Durkheimian sociology has historically been primarily methodologically nationalist in orientation, that is a historical accident and it need not be so. Indeed, towards the end of *The Elementary Forms*, Durkheim outlines an account of what today could be called 'cultural globalization', noting how over time the religious-cultural traditions of different groups fuse and create new cosmopolitan cultural forms (Inglis and Robertson, 2008). This suggests that the next phase of analytic innovation should involve the adumbration of a Durkheimian *global cultural sociology*, which builds on previous developments in Durkheimian thought but takes them in the direction of a more global, planet-spanning vision – one which Durkheim himself in fact possessed.

## REFERENCES

Alexander, J.C. (1986) 'Rethinking Durkheim's Intellectual Development II: Working Out a Religious Sociology', *International Sociology*, 1(2): 189–201.

Alexander, J.C. (1988a) 'Culture and Political Crisis: "Watergate" and Durkheimian Sociology', in J.C. Alexander (ed.), *Durkheimian Sociology: Cultural Studies*. Cambridge: Cambridge University Press. pp. 187–224.

Alexander, J.C. (1988b) 'Introduction: Durkhemian Sociology and Cultural Studies Today', in J.C. Alexander (ed.), *Durkheimian Sociology: Cultural Studies*. Cambridge: Cambridge University Press. pp. 1–22.

Alexander, J.C. (1995) *Fin de Siècle Social Theory*. London: Verso.

Alexander, J.C. (2003) *The Meanings of Social Life*. Oxford: Oxford University Press.

Alexander, J.C. (2004a) 'Cultural Pragmatics: Social Performance between Ritual and Strategy', *Sociological Theory*, 22(4): 528–73.

Alexander, J.C. (2004b) 'From the Depths of Despair: Performance, Counterperformance, and "September 11"', *Sociological Theory*, 22(1): 88–105.

Alexander, J.C. (2006) *The Civil Sphere*. Oxford: Oxford University Press.

Alexander, J.C. (2007) 'On the Interpretation of The Civil Sphere: Understanding and Contention in Contemporary Social Science', *Sociological Quarterly*, 48: 641–59.

Alexander, J.C. (2012) *Trauma: A Social Theory*. Cambridge: Polity.

Alexander, J.C. and Smith, P. (2003) 'The Strong Program in Cultural Sociology: Elements of a Structural Hermeneutics', in J.C. Alexander, *The Meanings of Social Life*. Oxford: Oxford University Press.

Alexander, J.C., Giesen, B. and Mast, J. (2006) *Social Performance: Symbolic Action, Cultural Pragmatics, and Ritual*. Cambridge: Cambridge University Press.

Beck, U. (2000) 'The Cosmopolitan Perspective: Sociology of the Second Age of Modernity', *British Journal of Sociology*, 51(1): 79–105.

Bell, D. (1976) *The Cultural Contradictions of Capitalism*. New York: Basic Books.

Bellah, R. (1967) 'Civil Religion in America', *Daedalus*, 96(1): 1–21.

Bellah, R. et al. (1988) *Habits of the Heart*. London: Hutchinson.

Bergesen, A.J. (2004) 'Durkheim's Theory of Mental Categories: A Review of the Evidence', *Annual Review of Sociology*, 30: 395–408.

Bouglé, C. (1971) *Essays on the Caste System*. Cambridge: Cambridge University Press.

Bourdieu, P. (1977) *Outline of a Theory of Practice*. Cambridge: Cambridge University Press.

Bourdieu, P. (1992) *Distinction: A Social Critique of the Judgement of Taste*. London: Routledge.

Brubaker, R. (1985) 'Rethinking Classical Theory: The Sociological Vision of Pierre Bourdieu', *Theory and Society*, 14: 745–75.

Coser, L.A. (1992) 'The Revival of the Sociology of Culture: The Case of Collective Memory', *Sociological Forum*, 7(2): 365–73.

Dilthey, W. (1991 [1883]) *Wilhelm Dilthey, Selected Works. Vol. I: Introduction to the Human Sciences*. Princeton: Princeton University Press.

Douglas, M. (1966) *Purity and Danger*. London: Routledge and Kegan Paul.

Durkheim, E. (1951 [1897]) *Suicide*. New York: The Free Press.

Durkheim, E. (1972) *Emile Durkheim: Selected Writings*. A. Giddens (ed. and trans). Cambridge: Cambridge University Press.

Durkheim, E. (1984 [1893]) *The Division of Labour in Society*. Basingstoke: Macmillan.

Durkheim, E. (2001 [1912]) *The Elementary Forms of Religious Life*. M.S. Cladis (trans). Oxford: Oxford University Press.

Durkheim, E. and Mauss, M. (1969 [1903]) *Primitive Classification*. London: Cohen and West.

Elliott, M. (2008) 'Human Rights and the Triumph of the Individual in World Culture', *Cultural Sociology*, 1(3): 343–63.

Emirbayer, M. (1996a) 'Durkheim's Contribution to the Sociological Analysis of History', *Sociological Forum*, 11(2): 263–84.

Emirbayer, M. (1996b) 'Useful Durkheim', *Sociological Theory*, 14(2): 109–30.

Frye, H.N. (1957) *Anatomy of Criticism*. Princeton: Princeton University Press.

Fustel de Coulanges, N.S.D. (2001 [1864]) *The Ancient City*. Kitchener: Batoche Books.

Geertz, C. (1973) *The Interpretation of Cultures*. New York: Basic Books.

Guhin, J. (2013) 'Is Irony Good for America? The Threat of Nihilism, the Need for Romance, and the Power of Cultural Forms', *Cultural Sociology*, 7(1): 23–38.

Halbwachs, M. (1992) *On Collective Memory*. Chicago: University of Chicago Press.

Hookway, N. (2015) 'Moral Decline Sociology: Critiquing the Legacy of Durkheim', *Journal of Sociology*, 51(2): 271–84.

Hubert, H. and Mauss, M. (1909) *Melanges d'Histoire des Religions*. Paris: Alcan.

Inglis, D. and Hughson, J. (2003) *Confronting Culture: Sociological Vistas*. Cambridge: Polity.

Inglis, D. and Hughson, J. (2005) *The Sociology of Art: Ways of Seeing*. Basingstoke: Palgrave.

Inglis, D. and Robertson, R. (2008) 'The Elementary Forms of Globality: Durkheim and the Emergence and Nature of Global Life', *Journal of Classical Sociology*, 8(1): 5–25.

Kane, A. (1991) 'Cultural Analysis in Historical Sociology: The Analytic and Concrete Forms of the Autonomy of Culture', *Sociological Theory*, 9(1): 53–69.

Kurakin, D. (2013) 'Reassembling the Ambiguity of the Sacred: A Neglected Inconsistency in Readings of Durkheim', *Journal of Classical Sociology*, published online 18 November.

Lasch, C. (1991 [1979]) *The Culture of Narcissism: American Life in an Age of Diminishing Expectations*. New York: W.W. Norton.

Lévi-Strauss, C. (1994) *The Savage Mind*. Oxford: Oxford University Press.

Lukes, S. (1973) *Emile Durkheim, His Life and Work: A Historical and Critical Study*. Harmondsworth: Penguin.

Lynch, G. (2012) *The Sacred in the Modern World: A Cultural Sociological Approach*. Oxford: Oxford University Press.

Mannheim, K. (1956) *Essays on the Sociology of Culture*. London: Routledge.

Mannheim, K. (1985 [1936]) *Ideology and Utopia*. Orlando: Harcourt, Brace, Jovanovich.

McCormick, L. (2009) 'Higher, Faster, Louder: Representations of the International Music Competition', *Cultural Sociology*, 5(1): 3–30.

McKinnon, A. (2014) 'Elementary Forms of the Metaphorical Life: Tropes at Work in Durkheim's Theory of the Religious', *Journal of Classical Sociology*, 14(2): 203–21.

McLennan, G. (2004) 'Rationalizing Musicality: A Critique of Alexander's "Strong Program" in Cultural Sociology', *Thesis 11*, 79: 75–86.

Mukerji, C. (2007) 'Cultural Genealogy: Method for a Cultural Sociology of History or Historical Sociology of Culture', *Cultural Sociology*, 1(1): 49–71.

Parsons, T. (1951) *The Social System*. New York: The Free Press.

Parsons, T. (1961) 'Introduction – Part Four – Culture and the Social System', in T. Parsons et al. (eds), *Theories of Society*, Vol. II. Glencoe: Free Press.

Pecora, V.J. (2006) *Secularization and Cultural Criticism*. Chicago: University of Chicago Press.

Rawls, A. (1996) 'Durkheim's Epistemology: The Neglected Argument', *American Journal of Sociology*, 102(2): 430–82.

Roudometoff, V. (2007) 'The Civil Sphere (Review)', *Mediterranean Quarterly*, 18(2): 145–8.

Shils, E. (1961) 'Centre and Periphery', in Polanyi Festschrift Committee (eds), *The Logic of Personal Knowledge: Essays Presented to Michael Polanyi*. London: Routledge and Kegan Paul. pp. 117–30.

Shils, E. (1975) *Center and Periphery: Essays in Macro-Sociology*. Chicago: University of Chicago Press.

Simiand, F. (1934) 'La Monnaie, Réalité Sociale', *Annales Sociologiques*, Series D, *Sociologie économique*: 1–58.

Turner, V. (1969) *The Ritual Process: Structure and Anti-Structure*. Chicago: Aldine.

Wrong, D. (1980 [1961]) 'The Oversocialized Conception of Man in Modern Sociology', in R. Bocock et al. (eds), *An Introduction to Sociology: A Reader*. Glasgow: Fontana.

# A Qualitative Theory of Culture: Georg Simmel and Cultural Sociology

Eduardo de la Fuente

## INTRODUCTION: SIMMEL AS QUALITATIVE SOCIAL AND CULTURAL THEORIST

Georg Simmel (2010: 160) famously predicted: 'I know that I will die without spiritual heirs (and that is at it should be)'. The prediction has proven correct. Part of the explanation lies in the difficulties associated with absorbing Simmel's thought into mainstream social science. His style can be oblique; and his mode of analysis sometimes jumps from discipline to discipline, which can range from sociology to aesthetics and economics, from philosophy to group psychology and the study of material forms. As Weber (1972: 161) famously said of the method employed in *The Philosophy of Money* (Simmel, 1978) – and he wasn't alone in forming such judgements of Simmel's style of analysis (see Durkheim, 1965) – it explored the topic through 'totally heterogeneous subject matters' (for example, money from the perspective of history, aesthetics, psychology, epistemology and material culture), and the 'specialist' interested in 'questions of facticity' might be led to throw the book 'in the corner and [be] finished with it'. Wolff (1965: viii) was more positive and suggested that what Simmel's mode of analysis betrays is a desire to think 'our sense of life as we catch ourselves in the act of sensing it'.

Wolff's reference to thinking life as we catch ourselves in the act of sensing it is a quintessential feature of what I am here calling a *qualitative theory of culture*. The understanding of the qualitative that I am employing is different to the common-sense understanding in the social sciences. I take the qualitative to connote much more than approaches such as interviews or narrative and textual analysis. From a conceptual perspective, the qualitative is about categories such as the 'interesting' and the 'boring' (Davis, 1971; Conrad, 1999), the dividing line between 'new' things and things that are 'crumbling' (Riegl, 1982; Dekkers, 1997), and many other situations where things and events depend for their character on relational and dynamic properties. Qualities often involve the play of contrast, rely on the ability to sense significant differences and are often linked to transformational experiences (i.e., changes in moods or the alteration of energy levels). In other words, when qualities change we change with them.

In this respect, something like colour is a quintessentially qualitative phenomenon. Colour involves a spectrum of sensory possibilities and these, in turn, depend on lighting and background for their sharpness and potency. As a recent popular book on the subject proposes: 'colours ... don't really exist ... our minds create them as an interpretation of vibrations that are happening around us' (Finlay, 2004: 4). Yet the same author writes that, even if it is our 'brains' and our 'languages' that help us to identify a colour called 'red', there is a materiality attached to red as what we are seeing is a 'portion of the electromagnetic spectrum' and the absence of 'wavelengths' that would dampen the redness of what we are seeing (Finlay, 2004: 4). But, as is often the case with qualitative conditions, the material dimension is closely linked to the cultural and the psychological-cum-perceptual one. Red is the 'colour of love', as well as a 'traffic sign which means we have to stop' (Finlay, 2004: 4–5).

The parallels between something like colour and social life are not entirely irrelevant to a discussion of Simmel's work. As one commentator puts it, the 'figure-ground' idea is an important conceptual instrument by which Simmel conceives of 'individuality as a pattern whose pronouncedness must be seen against the background of what it is not'; adding this is why Simmel was interested in *chiaroscuro* 'since Rembrandt used that technique for the purpose of intense individualization' (Lipman, 1965: 124). Indeed, one of the central arguments of *Rembrandt: An Essay in the Philosophy of Art* is that Rembrandt's portraits succeed precisely because their 'generality' emerges out of the 'unity of inner life' (Simmel, 2005: 94). The point of contrast is Renaissance portraiture, which Simmel (2005: 87, 95) characterizes as rendering the individual in terms of '*typical*' and '*sociological*' properties, a form of abstraction that fails to capture the individual as '*immanent* generalization'. Again, the contrast could be said to be between a quantitative logic that abstracts and one that is sensitive to the qualities of specific things.

Does the hypothesis that Simmel is fundamentally a theorist of the qualitative alter our image of him? If nothing else it may lead to a new appreciation of his status as theorist of culture. As Weingartner (1965: 33) wrote some decades ago, underpinning this 'energetic, many-sided thinker who turned from one field to another as his interests led him' was the fact that 'Simmel's world was the world of culture'. The same author claims that the concern with the products of culture, and how to make them intelligible, is, as is often the case with Simmel's thought, a double-sided affair. On the one hand, it led to a study of the 'similarities' and 'differences' present in the 'network of relations holding among the elements of culture'; on the other, there was a desire to render the world of culture and its manifold products significant and meaningful through a linking of cultural forms to a 'philosophy of life and a philosophy of experience' (Weingartner, 1965: 34). This image of Simmel's forays into cultural analysis accords with Pyyhtinen's (2010: 38–39) depiction of his style of analysis as both relational and designed to 'enliven' the social: 'For Simmel, the totality of the world does not mean absolute, substantial unity, but endless entities connected to one another by reciprocal relations ... In the last instance, the social too appears for him under the sign of life'.

Arguably, a greater focus on Simmel as qualitative theorist may also make partial readings of his writings on culture less likely. As we will see in the next section, Simmel-reception has been far too prone to one-sided interpretations of his sociology, philosophy, aesthetics and cultural analyses. There have also been attempts to understand his work by locating their source in other authors and extrinsic problematics. There is no denying that Simmel was heavily influenced by currents as diverse as Darwinism, Neo-Kantianism, Nietzsche and Schopenhauer, and Vitalism. But, his style of analysis is not reducible to so-called influences. As the perceptive Simmel-interpreter, Davis (1973: 325) notes Simmel does, for example, have a Kantian core that is evident in the notion that the mind organizes the variety of sense-data into 'unities'; but, to the extent that 'Simmel's world possesses many such centres of organization ... [it] looks more like Leibniz's *Weltanschauung* of self-actualizing monads or, even, the primitives' animistic worldview'.

Such multi-dimensionality is a desirable quality amongst theories and methods aspiring to the status of a cultural sociology. One of the first books to champion a return to Simmel in the last few decades, Robertson's (1978: 7) *Meaning and Change*, defines cultural sociology thus:

> Cultural sociology is certainly not a school or a particular theoretic tendency. Rather it is a style of analysis – a standpoint that insists on the salience of concern with life as well as with society, concern with the role of ideas and symbols ... and a number of other matters which are best exposed by way of detailed case-studies.

Simmel fits this vision of a cultural sociology extremely well. Simmel also often seems to be the target of the type of criticisms that Robertson claimed frequently accompanied cultural sociological forms of analysis. The latter notes that even in an era where there is routine recognition that the 'soft variables' are not be separable from the 'hard variables' of society and economy, 'Cultural sociologists are still charged with being too "humanistic", too "philosophical" or whatever' (Robertson, 1978: 6). As we shall see, sometimes Simmel-supporters have also been prone to emphasizing his fragmentary or non-causal mode of exposition and thereby have tended to reinforce the image of theorists of culture as unduly 'humanistic' and 'philosophical'.

If I had to give the type of qualitative cultural analysis Simmel practices a characterization I would suggest that his account of culture is fundamentally *textural*. Textural analysis is necessarily fine-grained and attentive to the surfaces, materialities and substances of the world. The kinds of textures I have in mind are discussed in the essay on 'The Ruin' (Simmel, 1965a). There Simmel (1965a: 261) suggests 'so long as we can speak of a ruin at all and not a mere heap of stones' it is because the 'crumbling power of nature' has not sunk the products of human culture 'into the formlessness of mere matter'. Textures matter because they manifest the interplay of constancy and dynamism, materiality and spirit, substance and style. I will not be arguing that Simmel's cultural sociology resolves all the *aporias* present within the field. But I do think such an approach deepens our sense of what we mean by such basic concepts as culture, meaning and connectedness.

## NEITHER MONET NOR CEZANNE: A SHORT HISTORY OF SIMMEL-RECEPTION

As intimated above, Simmel scholarship has often been mired in one-sided interpretations of his intentions and achievements. It has also been prone to the cycles of fashion – something not altogether unusual in fields such as social and cultural theory, cultural studies and cultural sociology. But, in Simmel's case, the interpretations also seem to be coloured by reactions – past and present – to 'the powerful impression of this spiritual personality' (Worringer, 1997: xvii). The latter formulation was used to describe Simmel by Worringer (1997), the author of one of the most important books in 20th-century art history: *Abstraction and Empathy*. Wanting to discount the notion that *Abstraction and Empathy* was a kind of manifesto for abstract artistic tendencies (it was first published in 1908, i.e. a year after Picasso's *Les Demoiselles d'Avignon*), Worringer traces the birth of his book to a fortuitous encounter with 'the Berlin philosopher, Georg Simmel' in the Trocadéro Museum while he was still a graduate student. The two never actually speak but

> it was the ensuing hours spent in the halls of the Trocadéro with Simmel, in a contact consisting solely in the atmosphere created by his presence, that produced in a sudden, explosive act of birth the world of ideas which then found its way into my thesis and first brought my name to the public. (Worringer, 1997: xvii)

Worringer (1997: xx) tells us that serendipity continued to play a role as, years later, it was Simmel who 'after reading the book, wrote the exciting letter' that made him feel as if his thesis had been validated. As Mary Shields (1999: 218) notes, the common post-Nietzschean intellectual paradigm that both Worringer and Simmel shared was concerned with the tension between the 'stream of life' and the cultural forms which 'harden', thereby losing 'their inner vitality and reason for existence'. In *Abstraction and Empathy* this manifests itself in the dialectic between a geometric art that 'tears' or *abstracts* an object 'out of the flux of happening' and figural representations which – in terms of their psychological disposition – could be said to *empathize* with the 'phenomena of the external world' (Shields, 1999: 218). In his 'The Conflict in Modern Culture', originally published in 1918, Simmel (1971: 375) suggests: 'We speak of culture whenever life produces certain forms in which it expresses and realizes itself'. But, even if they emerge from life processes, these forms are self-enclosed – abstractions, if you like – that 'do not share the restless rhythm of life, its ascent and descent, its constant renewal, its incessant divisions and reunifications' (Simmel, 1971: 375).

Simmel's dialectic of 'life' and 'form' has given rise to all sorts of misunderstandings and one-sided readings of his work. Again, the tone was set early on and by those who knew him personally. In a famous obituary, Lukacs (1991: 147) – who, like Worringer, had attended Simmel's lectures – dubbed Simmel the 'Monet of philosophy who has not yet been followed by a Cezanne'. The author continues by suggesting that, like the Impressionists, Simmel possessed a 'brilliance' and 'lightening grasp'; an 'ability to see the smallest and most inessential phenomenon of daily life so sharply' (Lukacs, 1991: 145, 146). But the weakness present in any philosophical or sociological 'intensified apperception of life', according to Lukacs (1991: 146), is that it has a 'missing centre' and suffers from an 'inability to make ultimate, absolute decisions'. Impressionisms are always a 'transitory form' and Lukacs (1991: 146–147) implies that Simmel's writings could only but prepare the way for 'a new classicism which renders eternal the fullness of life'.

Needless to say, what some social and cultural theorists regard as a deficiency others will consider an asset, if not a source of intellectual redemptiveness. Thus, in the 1980s,

Simmel-as-Impressionist made a comeback. In two elegant and rhetorically persuasive books, *Sociological Impressionism* and *Fragments of Modernity*, Frisby (1981; 1985) did much to resurrect this image of Simmel. In *Sociological Impressionism*, the author writes: 'If my interpretation of Simmel is somewhat different from that which is usually offered to us, namely as a 'formal', 'systematic' sociologist, then this is, in part, due to the reconstruction of the central motifs in Simmel's work' (Frisby, 1981: viii). By 'formal' and 'systematic', Frisby means something remarkably like the Classicism that Lukacs opined Simmel had never attained.

A central motif in this wave of Simmel-reception was the notion, outlined in Chapter 3 of Frisby's (1981) *Sociological Impressionism*, that Simmel resembled the figure of the *flaneur* discussed by Charles Baudelaire and, after him, by Walter Benjamin. The argument that Simmel constituted a type of sociological *flaneur* rested on highlighting the following features of his thought: 'his conscious essayism, his preoccupation with the fragmentary, his tendency not to reveal himself in his writings, his aestheticization of reality and distance from it and the centrality of the work of art as a model for his own essays' (Frisby, 1981: 78). At last, sociology had found a classical figure who pre-empted the 'cultural turn'. The governing assumption within this strand of Simmel-reception-cum-appreciation was that Simmel was more *modernist theorist* than *theorist of modernity*. Frisby's (1985: 4) thesis was stated as such: 'Simmel wrote frequently upon the literary and artistic movements of his time ['naturalism', 'art nouveau', Böcklin, Rodin, Hauptmann, George, Ernst and Rilke] ... More importantly, it is not difficult to see aesthetic movements such as impressionism manifesting themselves in Simmel's own style and mode of presentation'.

What was interesting about the Simmel-reception of the 1980s was that it was so heavily and self-consciously driven by the concerns of the day. The debate Habermas (1981) launched regarding 'Modernity versus Postmodernity' had led to a re-evaluation of terms such as modern, modernity and modernism. In this respect, Frisby's *Sociological Impressionism* and *Fragments of Modernity* should be read together with Berman's (1983) *All that is Solid Melts into Air* and Scaff's (1989) *Fleeing the Iron Cage*. While the latter were about Marx and Weber respectively, the narrative was similar to the Simmel-revival one: the argument was that classical sociologists were much more complex and more attuned to aesthetic modernism than previously realized.[1]

An undoubted benefit of the explosion of interest in Simmel in the 1980s and 1990s was also the sheer volume of his writings that became available to Anglophone sociology scholars and students of culture. Good examples are provided by the 1991 special volume of *Theory, Culture & Society* on Simmel (Volume 8, number 3); and by Frisby and Featherstone's (1997) collection, *Simmel on Culture*, which formed part of the *TCS* book series. These enlarged the capacity of English-language scholars to engage with Simmel's thought substantially. They also served to fuel the Simmel as Impressionist-cum-Aesthete image. Thus, in his influential essay 'The Aestheticization of Everyday Life', Featherstone (1991: 76) lists Simmel amongst those theorists whom we might use to understand 'how the urban landscape has become aestheticized and enchanted' and why, in varying degrees, urban dwellers turn to 'fashionable clothing, hairstyles, make-up ... or hold their bodies in particular stylized ways'. Highmore's (2002: 38–9) *Everyday Life and Cultural Theory* devotes a chapter to Simmel, alongside chapters on Surrealism, Mass-Observation, Benjamin and Lefebvre, and follows the Frisby narrative closely when it observes: 'Simmel's diagnosis of modernity is one in which the everyday registers diverse and contradictory experiences ... I would suggest that such an aesthetics should be seen as part of an aesthetic avant-gardism in which the everyday is rendered as vivid'. But even more inventive readings were to come. In *Postmodern(ized) Simmel*, Deena and Michael Weinstein (1993: 17, 167) refer to aesthetics 'as an unfortunate choice of words' and link Simmel with the prosaic events and spaces of postmodern culture: 'Going shopping, going to the mall, is like watching television – a form of play within a field of signifiers ... One can drift from shop to shop, examining products, imagining what one might do with them ... Life becomes immanent to the sensuous forms in which it participates'. In short, Simmel was a kind of precursor to the postmodern notion that image and reality, desire and commodity, are one and the same.

Predictably, there was a reaction by those who wanted to hold on to Simmel-as-formal-sociologist. Zerubavel (1999), who has been at the forefront of a mode of cultural sociology labelled 'cognitive sociology' has argued that Simmel was at the head of a tradition of 'social pattern analysis' and cites approvingly Coser's formulation that Simmel's programmatic sociology suggests the following: 'The sociologist is concerned with *King* John, not with King *John*' (Zerubavel, 2007: 133). Zerubavel's comments on the significance of form to Simmel's sociology were not merely casual observation. He had used essays such as 'The Picture Frame' (Simmel, 1994) to great effect in his account of how we make distinctions in everyday life and Simmel plays an important role in his analysis of the 'rigid', 'fuzzy' and 'flexible' mind-sets (Zerubavel, 1991). The turn against Impressionistic/cultural-studies-Simmel also came from the translators of one of his important texts on an art historical topic: *Rembrandt: An Essay in the Philosophy of Art* (Simmel, 2005). Scott and Staubmann, (2005: xviii) make the point that, in many respects, Simmel is the 'antithesis of modern sociocultural analysis' and that his 'insistence on the autonomy of the aesthetic sphere and his meticulous avoidance of reference to social, cultural, or autobiographical context seem hopelessly retrograde'. Another interesting piece of commentary on Simmel-reception came from Green (1988), in a book, paradoxically, arguing for a rapprochement of literary methods and sociological theory. The author argues that an interest in art, styling and everyday artefacts is not in and of itself 'sufficient basis' for describing a mode of analysis as a species of *aesthetic sociology*:

> There is no doubt of Simmel's involvement with aesthetics. He wrote extensively on art and the aesthetic attitude to life. Also, his style of life was marked by aestheticism: exquisite domestic décor, weekly gatherings of gifted and beautiful people, a passion for collecting objects d'art, especially from Japan, and acute sensory sensitivity ... [But] [a]esthetics can be written about in nonaesthetic modes, and the analogical extension of art collecting to Simmel's collection of examples is only metaphorically persuasive. (Green, 1988: 96–97)

The answer of course lies somewhere in the middle. Simmel's attention to aesthetic topics impacts the way he sees society (for example, it presents us with a sociology of things that otherwise go unnoticed); and his interest in social form produces an aesthetic theory of patterns (for example, his discussion of symmetries or on the model of individuation present in Rembrandt's paintings). The correction to relativistic and fragmentary Simmel was therefore necessary, including amongst aesthetically-minded sociologists. As the sociologist of the arts and scholar of classical civilizations, Tanner (2003: 32) noted, the tendency to emphasize Simmel's 'anticipating of important themes in postmodern theory' is as incorrect as the tendency to emphasize the more 'specifically sociological aspects of his thought'. He adds that what is perhaps most 'interesting about Simmel is that he treats aesthetic form as a deep generative phenomenon within the social order and conversely sociological principles of ordering as aesthetically generative from within art rather than external determinants' (Tanner, 2003: 32).

A field where Simmel has arguably started to play a different kind of role to the one implied by the Monet/Cezanne dichotomy is in management and organization studies. Pierre Guillet de Monthoux (2000: 51), a doyen of the new type of management theory, has suggested: 'I think Georg Simmel, who started by writing on Raphael and ended with Rembrandt, could inspire further investigation into ways to manage ... organizations than Max Weber'. One of the main advocates for research into 'organizational aesthetics', the Italian scholar Antonio Strati (1999; 2014: 115), has written of Simmel's (1997a) 'Sociology of the Senses' that it 'beautifully' evokes the role played by the senses, such as sight, in organizational life: 'Looking at each other ... involves a social relation of specific intensity and proximity ... These interactions ... have the capacity to coalesce individuals into some sort of association within the organization ... they are embedded in the routine of workplace social relations'. There are countless other examples. In 2009, the Standing Conference on Organizational Symbolism (SCOS), an academic group at the forefront of reflecting upon the importance of artefacts and symbols to organizational practices, focused its conference theme on Simmel's (1997b) essay 'Bridge and Door', liberally quoting from the author in its Call for Papers (http://www.scos.org/2009/). The Simmel to be found in contemporary organization studies is often a formalist-aestheticist hybrid.

We might suggest that Simmel is – contra Lukacs' famous duality – neither the Monet nor Cezanne of a philosophy and sociology of culture. If one wanted to connect him to his painterly contemporaries, one might say that Simmel sought to juggle the feeling for colour, the interest in everyday scenes and the expressive style of a Van Gogh, with the more formalistic and metaphysical motifs of a Gaugin. In any case, what seems clear is that Simmel's legacy got entangled in an unhelpful binary between an aesthetic and formal approach, which perhaps says more about the social sciences and cultural analysis during the last few decades than it does about his own thought. As a former student of Simmel suggested: 'whoever speaks of forms moves in the fields of aesthetics. Society, in the last analysis, is a work of art' (Salz, 1965: 236). We might suggest that Simmel is both a microsociologist of everyday life and a metaphysician of the patterns and rhythms that recur in life more generally. Simmel's ideas demand such a double-sided interpretation of his work.

## CULTURE AS CRYSTALLIZATION, CULTIVATION AND CRISIS

Part of the difficulty in pinning down Simmel's theory and method for studying culture is that his writing career took place during a period when disciplinary and other intellectual grids were not yet set in stone. As Frisby (1997: 1–2) points out, Simmel's writings on cultural themes span 'more than two decades' and were written against a background of the concept being linked to a range of knowledge bases:

> [I]n the sphere of theorizing about culture, it should not be forgotten that the epithet 'culture' ... was applied in Simmel's lifetime to a whole range of disciplines and theoretical practices: to the philosophy of culture ... to the historic study of culture ... to the development of a sociology of culture ... to the development of a psychology of culture ... to a critique of contemporary culture ... as well as the more general references to the cultures of peoples ... social classes ... and so on. (Frisby, 1997: 2)

In his precautionary note about the multiple connections of the term culture, Frisby (1997: 2–3) adds that the academic setting that Simmel's writings would have been received in (which is not to say that Simmel wrote primarily for academic readers) included 'contested attempts to establish academic disciplines around the sciences of culture, be they historical, philosophical, sociological, anthropological, psychological and so on'; as well as the 'all-encompassing foundations for [the] human sciences' denoted by Dilthey's term *Geisteswissenschaften* and Rickert and Windelband's espousal of a *Kulturwissenschaften*. As is often the case with Simmel's writings about specific concepts, locating singular definitions is largely out of the question. Frisby points to three major conceptualizations of culture and connects them with different periods in Simmel's work. The three understandings of culture are: (1) culture as 'condensation, coalescence and crystallization'; (2) 'cultivation' or culture as 'purposeful' creation; and (3) culture as 'disharmony' or imperfect fit 'between life and form and between subjective and objective culture' (Frisby, 1997: 4–5).

The first of these is found in those writings where Simmel distinguishes between form and its contents, and the underlying assumption is that as the 'contents of experience take on a structure' they assume an independent form that 'condenses or coalesces into something other than mere content' (Frisby, 1997: 4). A good example is contained in Simmel's (1950) discussion of sociability. The author suggests that for sociable interaction to become 'society without qualifying adjectives' (i.e., more than the type of historical examples provided by the brotherhood of knights, medieval guilds, bourgeois associations and other collectives that evolved into something other than their original purpose), what was needed was for the 'content' of interaction to be transformed into 'pure sociability' or the 'feeling of being sociated' for its own sake (Simmel, 1950: 43–44). Simmel speaks of 'thresholds' needing to be crossed; of a dynamic process he labels the 'autonomization of contents'; and of the final result being the 'play-form' of sociability. The analogy here is with art, although similar processes could be said to exist in the fields of science, religion, economics, and so on. In the case of art, the original wresting of contents from life takes the shape of drawing, symbolization and acoustic manipulation designed to serve practical purposes. These original contents become purely aesthetic once they re-enter art as the media and materials for activities detached from their original purposes (for example, musical sounds that no longer directly serve ritual or ceremonial needs). It should be said that for Simmel the parallels between art and sociability are not entirely analogical (see de la Fuente, 2008). He refers to sociability's 'artful' qualities including performing one's social duties 'ironically', 'playfully', 'charmingly' and in an 'attractive manner' (Simmel, 1950: 51). But, in the end, for social interaction to crystallize into its pure form of sociable gatherings, coquetry and conversation, dining and the pleasure of attending salons, it has to be more than mere etiquette and it can't seem unduly 'artificial' (Simmel's example is the type of sociabilities engendered during the *Ancien Régime*). As Simmel (1997c: 131) says in 'Sociology of the Meal': 'in so far as the meal becomes sociological matter, it arranges itself in a more aesthetic, stylized and supra-individually regulated form'. The meal only becomes sociable dining when 'both the physical act of eating disappears' and 'external prescribed *good form*' are rendered less important (Simmel, 1997c: 132).

Culture as 'cultivation' is directly addressed by Simmel in several of his writings. The fragment, 'Meaning of Culture', which appears in Lawrence's (1976) collection, *Georg Simmel: Sociologist and European*, starts from the premise that in many respects human activity and nature are not fundamentally different. Both human activity and natural phenomena involve 'causally determined development in which each stage ... [is] explicable in terms of the configuration and dynamic forces of the preceding situation' (Simmel, 1976: 243). 'Natural development' only becomes 'cultural development' when it acquires a 'new evolutionary energy' which is more than 'psycho-physical constitution, heredity and adaptation' to given forms of 'existence' (Simmel, 1976: 243). Simmel gives the example of a wild pear tree as compared to those that are grown for edible, ornamental and aesthetic purposes. He suggests that the distinguishing characteristic of the latter – that is, of a pear tree that is no longer simply bound by causal development – is that it is 'cultivated'. Cultivation implies, for him, unleashing 'latent' forms and 'energies'. The cultivated form is culture and no longer nature as 'cultivation develops its object to that perfection which is predetermined as a potential of its essential underlying tendency' (Simmel, 1976: 245). The cultured version of an entity is therefore one that emanates from a 'teleological intervention', one which 'requires a technique' and some type of 'procedure directed by the will' – all of which Simmel (1976: 244–245) claims can only be pursued by a being or agent which bears the traits of the 'human soul'.

Culture as cultivation points to an understanding of culture that we have to some extent lost. Raymond Williams (1976: 77) claims in *Keywords*: '*Culture* in all its early uses was a noun of process: the tending *of* something, basically crops or animals'. He adds that by the time the word had become common usage – which was not until the 19th century – there was a degree of 'habituation to the metaphor ... of human tending' and also an 'extension of particular processes to a general process' (Williams, 1976: 77). Thus, by the time commentators were speaking of the culture of a people, they actually meant cultivation writ large. The cultivation theory of culture was arguably left behind as social theory, along with modern intellectual culture more generally, became interested in, and defined by, the rationalization and disenchantment of the world. An author who has championed a return to a cultivation view of culture is Eugene Halton (1995). He argues that recent cultural theory has tended towards what he terms the *doughnut theory of culture*, a conception of culture as convention, code or context, one that tends to see 'culture as abstract, depersonalized system', a mode of thinking that 'denies the living source of culture as *cultus*' (Halton, 1995: 104). Halton not only argues for a more embodied and *earthy* theory of culture but also one that reconnects culture and biology, meaning and process. Emphasizing the sense in which culture meant to 'till, cultivate, dwell or inhabit', Halton (1995: 104–105) argues that culture has to regain the 'fertile, seminal, and gestational meanings it once carried'.

The preceding discussion of what has gone wrong with cultural theory alerts us also to what Frisby identifies as the third conception of culture in Simmel's work: namely, the crisis or disharmony of modern or overly intellectualized-cum-objective life. In his discussion of culture as cultivation, Simmel (1976: 245) identifies *technique* as one of the primary ways in which the human will directs the cultivation process. But, already in the 'Meaning of Culture', there is discussion of how the spiritual and subjective guiding of energies results in something external to humans. The fundamental contradiction of culture is therefore that while 'cultivatedness is a spiritual state', cultivation is only 'attained by the use of purposively formed *objects*' (Simmel, 1976: 246). The latter gives rise to what Simmel (1976: 249) terms an 'objective culture', a type of culture he fears eventuates in 'any highly developed epoch based on [a] division of labour'. The independent development of objective culture results in an imbalance that troubled many philosophers and social theorists of the latter part of the 19th and early part of the 20th century:

> [As] [o]bjects become more perfect, more intellectual, they follow more and more obediently their own inner logic of material expediency. But real culture, that is, subjective culture, does not progress equally ... historical development tends increasingly to widen the gap between concrete creative cultural achievements and the level of individual culture. The disharmony of modern life, in particular the intensification of technology in every sphere combined with deep dissatisfaction with it, arises largely from the fact that things become more and more cultivated but people are capable only to a lesser degree of deriving from the improvement of objects an improvement of their subjective lives. (Simmel, 1976: 249)

Culture can therefore become cultivation gone awry. The ideal situation is one where 'By cultivating objects, that is by increasing their value beyond the performance of their natural constitution, we cultivate ourselves' (Simmel, 1997d: 37). For Simmel, an imbalance arises between subjective and objective culture when the former fails to keep pace with the cultivation and independent development of things. He suggests:

> If one compares our culture with that of a hundred years ago, then one must surely say ... that the things that determine and surround our lives, such as tools, means of transport, the products of science, technology and art, are extremely refined. Yet individual culture ... has not progressed at all to the same extent; indeed, it has frequently declined ... Just as our everyday life is surrounded more and more by objects of which we cannot conceive how much intellectual effort is expended

in their production, so our mental and social communication is filled with symbolic terms, in which comprehensive intellectuality is accumulated, but of which the individual mind need make only minimal use. (Simmel, 1997d: 38–39)

These themes are more fully fleshed out in Simmel's (1971) 'The Conflict in Modern Culture'. They certainly bring his discussion of modern culture close to the kinds of critique of capitalism and mass culture that were prevalent at the end of the 19th and well into the 20th century. Frisby (1997: 24) suggests that, in this respect, Simmel laid the foundation for a critique of modern tendencies that was to be developed 'by his students such as Georg Lukacs, Ernest Bloch and Siegfried Kracauer, as well as those in the Critical Theory tradition'.

Without doubt there is a pessimistic streak in Simmel's critique of modern culture and the picture of alienated individual subjectivity it paints in the face of an ever-expanding objective culture. All the individual can fall back on in areas as diverse as economic, technological or artistic life, is for the 'individual mind … [to] enrich the forms and contents of its own development … by distancing itself still further from that culture and developing its own at a much slower space' (Simmel, 1997d: 39). This seems to pre-empt what we now call 'slow culture' (Osbaldiston, 2013). It also offers a possible critique of things like branding and the general tendency to desire commodities for their aesthetic or stylistic appeal. In an essay entitled 'Style and the Perfection of Things', Celia Lury (2002: 202, 205) argues that Simmel's critique of objective culture swamping subjective culture can be both used to explain both the 'stylistic autonomy' now associated with 'companies such as Nike, Philips, Ford, Sony, and Apple' and to sharpen our focus 'on the paradox that while objects may be said to be more and more design intensive, they are less and less a matter of taste'.

## SIMMEL AS AESTHETIC ECOLOGIST

However, Simmel is no Plato-like critic of either aesthetic forms or their debasement under modern conditions. As I have argued elsewhere, his version of sociological aesthetics is not tied to the epochal argument that aestheticization is tied to changes in economy, technology, the 'end of politics' or any other of the usual tropes associated with post-modernity (de la Fuente, 2007). In his account of how social and aesthetic forms become entangled, the relationship between 'micro' and 'macro' is often left deliberately open, if not unresolved; and given the prevalence of non-commodified social forms that are presented as examples of social aesthetic organization – for example, sociability and the meal – it is fair to say that, in Simmel's thought, aestheticization seems to be a potential development within all forms of human organization. As his 1896 essay, entitled 'Sociological Aesthetics' argues, 'Even the lowest, intrinsically ugly phenomenon can be dissolved into contexts of colour and form, of feeling and experience, which provides significance' (Simmel, 1968: 69). Simmel (1968: 70) adds that any phenomenon that involves contrast, comparability and the generation of value, which he here describes as 'the moulding of the inspired out of the dull and the refined out of the raw', involves the aesthetic apprehension and ordering of reality. Needless to say the aesthetic apprehension of social reality is not an inherently positive or ethical development. In his discussion of why symmetry plays such an important role in human affairs, and why in some respects it is the initial or primal step in ordering the world aesthetically, Simmel (1968: 72) suggests that 'the tendency to organize all of society symmetrically … is shared by all despotic regimes', as well as in the world-view of rationalism, machines that function effectively, factory manufacturing systems and socialistic planning. Symmetrical patterns appear in a somewhat positive light in 'The Aesthetic Significance of the Face' (Simmel, 1965b). Simmel (1965b: 279–281) suggests that the reason why the face is able to generate a sense of aesthetic unity, and in turn function as a mechanism for the 'veiling and unveiling of soul', is because the 'face consists of two halves which are similar to one another'. Aesthetic patterning is therefore central to processes of socio-political and individual-psychic ordering but not reducible to either one.

Such an expansive conception of the role of aesthetic patterns and experience in human life is not reducible to either the 'micro' instances that Simmel is justifiably famous for analysing nor to the kind of 'macro' entities that social scientists often cling to (for example, capitalism, metropolitan life or the division of labour). The latter can certainly increase the tendency for phenomena to be aestheticized but Simmel seems to share the view of someone like psychologist Jan Valsiner (2008: 67) that 'our everyday life contexts … are saturated with highly repetitive patterns of visual and auditory kinds' (see also de la Fuente, 2014). In this respect, it is interesting that Simmel (1997a) offered the first foray into the 'Sociology of the Senses' within the social sciences and that he saw vision and hearing as playing contrasting, if somewhat complementary, functions in social interaction. The senses shape the degree of openness or capacity for exchange that individuals or groups attain with respect to the world at large (de la Fuente and Walsh, 2013). Everything is interconnected for Simmel (1994: 11) and sense-perception, as well as the endless pulsations of life-energies, mediate how interconnections do their work: 'each thing is a transitional point for continuously flowing energies and materials, comprehensible only as an element of the entire natural process'. Elsewhere, Simmel (1997b: 174) offers the maxim that the human is the 'connecting creature'.

How then to make sense of this world in which culture is relation, patterning, connection, the ordering of perception and the ceaseless flow of life-energies? In a forthcoming publication, I argue that Simmel's cultural sociology bears a certain resemblance to the tradition of ecological thought in the social sciences that stretches from Bateson (1973) to Gibson (1966; 1979) and Ingold (1993; 2000), and which sees aesthetic perception as 'not reducible to either the internal mechanisms of the perceiving subject nor to properties of the external environment but rather to the complex interplay of both' (de la Fuente, forthcoming: 3). What Simmel shares with such authors is the sense that aesthetic qualities are not reducible to either internal-subjective or external-objective processes. As Gibson (1979: 139) puts it, in *The Ecological Approach to Visual Perception*, 'awareness of the world and of one's complementary relations to the world are not separate'. The type of unity represented by aesthetic environments, and the dynamic organization of perception such environments embody, is a theme present in Simmel's thought. I discuss some of these writings and their parallels with ecological socio-aesthetic thinking below.

Simmel shares the view of writers such as Bateson and, after him, Goffman (1974) and Zerubavel (1991) that what separates playful gestures from actual combat, metaphors from literal expressions, jokes from actual statements, is the framing of experience. As Simmel (1994: 12) suggests in 'The Picture Frame', the 'qualities of the picture frame reveal themselves to be those of assisting and giving meaning to [the] inner unity of the picture'. But, while the primary function of the frame is to separate the artwork from the world and to direct the eye (and therefore exclude all other senses), framing is not simply a cognitive or ideational activity. Simmel (1994: 12) claims that the frame helps to direct 'the gaze, [which] like bodily movement, moves more easily from higher to lower'; and that it is because the picture plane replicates aspects of embodiment that the 'coherence of the picture is subjected to centrifugal dispersal'. The picture frame could be said to constitute a type of mini-aesthetic ecology where viewer and picture, picture and the rest of the space surrounding it are bounded in very specific ways. And, the qualities of this framing differs from those of furniture or utensils because – as Gibson (1966: 224) puts it – despite involving 'modifications of pre-existing surfaces' only a painting is 'made for the explicit purpose of being looked at'.

Simmel's interest in the aesthetic ecology of things, and how this structures agential experience, is also very evident in the essay 'The Handle' (1965c). There he writes that what makes a 'utensil', a 'vessel' or a 'vase' theoretically interesting is that it 'stands in two worlds at once' and, unlike paintings and other images, such objects are meant to be 'handled, filled and emptied, proffered, and set down here and there' (Simmel, 1965c: 267). It is by virtue of being 'held in the hand' that these objects are 'drawn into the movement of practical life'; and the relationship between 'handle' and 'vessel' is compared to a 'man's arms which, having grown as part of the same organizational process as his torso, also mediate the relationship of the whole being to the world outside it' (Simmel, 1965c: 267, 269). Simmel's (1997e: 214) formulation that a 'chair exists so that one can sit on it, a glass in order that one can fill it with wine and take it in one's hand' echoes what theorists such as Gibson and Norman have termed *affordances*. Gibson (1979: 127) coined the term to capture what the environment 'offers the animal, what it *provides* or *furnishes*'; whereas a design theorist, Norman (2002: 9) suggests affordances 'provide strong clues to the operations of things', adding that a 'psychology of causality is ... at work as we use everyday things'. A negative exemplar for the latter is French artist Jacques Carelman's *Coffeepot for Masochists*, which because it has the handle and spout in close proximity is basically impossible to use (Norman, 2002; 2005). *Coffeepot for Masochists* exemplifies Simmel's (1965c: 272) claim that the 'handle and spout correspond to each other visually as the extreme points of a vessel's diameter and ... must maintain a certain balance' so that they can play their respective *teleological* roles. This is because the handle and spout have contrasting 'centripetal' and 'centrifugal' affordances. The handle and spout exemplify how the shape, design and ornamentation of objects 'seize the totality of our energy by means of such particular faculties and enlist into their service' (Simmel, 1965c: 274).

Such depth of insight notwithstanding, it is possible to see Simmel's account of objects – from the vantage point of contemporary material culture studies – as treating material forms 'as far too self-evident' and as possessing an '*a priori* asymmetry between the capabilities of humans and nonhumans' (Pyyhtinen, 2010: 129–130). The same (overwhelmingly sympathetic) critic admits that Simmel's analysis of objects often treats them as 'essentialized, external, and simply imposing their causal laws upon us' (Pyyhtinen, 2010: 112) However, it is arguably less possible to accuse Simmel of such asymmetries or of perpetuating subject-object dualisms in the case of his analysis of landscape. As the translator of Simmel's (2007) 'Philosophy of Landscape' notes, this essay allowed 'Simmel to bring hitherto underexposed strands in his work concerning the oneness of humanity and nature within the all-pervading Life that continuously creates, sustains and reforms them' (Bleicher, 2007: 20). This is not surprising. Landscape is something that forces us to negotiate socially mediated dualisms such as between proximity and distance, observation and inhabitation, eye and land, culture and nature (Wylie, 2007: 2–11).

Ecological authors, like Gibson (1979: 127–128), have argued that landscape provides 'surfaces of support' for activities such as climbing, falling, hiding, walking, running, swimming and colliding with; and Ingold (2000: 207) has emphasized that landscape is not a 'totality that you or anyone else can look at, it is rather the world in which we stand'. The central idea here is that landscape is an environment that produces a sense of immersion, a perspective that Simmel himself advocates in 'The Philosophy of Landscape'. For the latter, the uniqueness of landscape is not what it affords to the eye through vision but rather something emotional and psychic that is neither 'inside' nor 'outside' the perceiving subject: namely, mood as the primary 'quality inherent in landscape' (Simmel, 2007: 27). Simmel (2007: 28) contends that mood is much more than whether a landscape is 'cheerful or serious, heroic or monotone, exciting or melancholic' as these are all emotional abstractions; rather mood is the 'fusion' that the 'unifying powers of Soul' are able to form 'in and through landscape'. Landscapes also have a temporal or dynamic element to them and these temporalities and processes are distinct from human-centred ones (Ingold, 1993). As Simmel (1965a: 260) suggests with respect to the ruin: 'the same forces which give a mountain its shape through weathering, erosion, faulting, and the growth of vegetation, here do their work on old walls'. In other words, aesthetic ecologies are being fashioned all the time even if the time it takes is slow and to some extent imperceptible. Simmel (1965a: 263) suggests that even a house that is designed to fit in, or built from local materials, still 'stems from another order of things'. By comparison, the 'ruin orders itself into the surrounding landscape without a break, growing together with it like tree and stone' (Simmel, 1965a: 263).

## CONCLUSION: SIMMEL'S LEGACY AS THE STUDY OF EVERYDAY TEXTURES

In this chapter, I have reviewed past and existing interpretations of Simmel's thought, as well as his puzzling absence from mainstream cultural sociological debates. One would think that a philosopher and sociologist of culture who was amongst the first to pen analyses of fashion, adornment, ruins, adventures, the Alps and coquetry, would command a central place in the cultural sociology pantheon. Yet a recent Reader in the field contains only one selection of his work: 'The Metropolis and Mental life' (Spillman, 2002), a piece that is hardly representative of his philosophy of culture or his interest in everyday aesthetics. Part of the problem still lies with definitions of culture that seem to preclude Simmel's involvement in the discipline. If the task of the sociologist is to study culture as power or as identity-shaper then Simmel will not be your natural starting point. Simmel has so far not fared well even amongst those who might see an echo of his theoretical universe in their own projects. Thus, for example, the Yale Strong Program has argued that a form of knowledge worthy of the name cultural sociology needs to recognize that culture 'possesses a relative autonomy in shaping actions and institutions, providing inputs every bit as vital as more material and instrumental forces' (Alexander and Smith, 2003: 12). But, its dominant tropes have so far been code, myth and narrative, ritual, performance, and most recently 'iconicity' – see Alexander and Bartmanski (2011)). No doubt there is room for synergies to be generated with a Simmelesque framework amongst those championing the autonomy of culture; although, so far, Simmel seems to have provided more inspiration for the Goffmanesque, Latourean and material culture end of culture studies (Zerubavel, 1991; Miller, 2005; Pyyhtinen, 2010), as well as amongst those interested in the sociology and anthropology of the senses (Vannini et al., 2011). As mentioned earlier, the centrality of Simmel to organizational studies after that discipline's 'cultural turn' is also encouraging.

However, to return to the central theme of this chapter: what if Simmel's greatest contribution to a theory of culture is to emphasize the qualities of things and experiences? By focusing on symmetry, play and artifice, immersion, separating and connecting, and the spatio-temporal patterns of everyday life, Simmel's account of culture and cultural forms could be said to enlarge and deepen what we understand by meaning. His writings do so in two significant respects: firstly, they suggest that meaning is as much about sensory and psychic connection as it is about the power of things like myth or story-telling; and, secondly, the analyses point to how the metaphysical is always already present within the micro-logical. As Simmel (1997c: 135) concluded one of his essays: 'The indifference and banality of the field with which these remarks are concerned should not deceive us into believing the paradoxical depth' of life and culture 'is not equally alive within it'. The textures of everyday life are inseparable from the deeper meanings lurking in the interplay of 'life' and 'form'.

What Simmel's interest in the aesthetic textures of everyday life promises to achieve is to facilitate a move beyond seeing art and society, aesthetics and social life as separate entities (Davis, 1973; de la Fuente, 2008). Despite all the talk of forms operating as autonomous or self-organizing monads, Simmel's philosophy of culture is one in which form detaches itself from life but, in the end, needs to share some of its substance and energies if it is to allow us to achieve a sense of balance through culture. Is it too much of a stretch: Simmel as a metaphysician of balance, if not 'grace' (on such a possibility see Podoksik (2007))? I think that one of the heirs to Simmel's thought is, as suggested earlier, Bateson (1973: 101), who sees art as 'part of man's quest for grace; sometimes his ecstasy in partial success, sometimes his rage and agony at failure'. Bateson suggests in *Steps to an Ecology of Mind* that the most important 'psychic information' that we can divine from art is not what it 'represents' but rather the 'very rules of transformation' that govern whether something is made of wood or stone, symmetrically organized or understylized (Bateson, 1973: 103).

In the end, what also interested Simmel about symmetry and asymmetry, frames and handles, landscapes and ruins, was that they represented different types of unity and different ways of channelling consciousness and life-energies for higher purposes. Frames keep extraneous things at bay; handles ask us to grasp things and suggest specific practical activities; and landscapes invite immersion and movement or dwelling. Ruins remind us of the inevitability, and beauty, of processes of decay. Whether we call the experience afforded by such things 'grace', 'fusion', 'flow' or 'transcendence' matters very little. What matters is that culture possesses the ability to re-awaken the animating spirit that gave rise to cultural forms in the first place. Through his philosophy of culture and analyses of specific cultural forms, Simmel reminds us of what needs reminding.

## REFERENCES

Alexander, J. C. and Bartmanski, D. (eds) (2011) *Iconic Power: Materiality and Meaning in Social Life*. London: Palgrave Macmillan.

Alexander, J. C. and Smith, P. (2003) 'The Strong Program in Cultural Sociology: Elements of a Structural Hermeneutics', in J. C. Alexander (ed.), *The Meanings of Social Life: A Cultural Sociology*. Oxford: Oxford University Press.

Bateson, G. (1973) *Steps to an Ecology of Mind: Collected Essays in Anthropology, Psychiatry, Evolution, and Epistemology*. London: Paladin.

Berman, M. (1983) *All that is Solid Melts into Air: The Experience of Modernity*. London: Verso.

Bleciher, J. (2007) 'Introduction to Georg Simmel "The Philosophy of Landscape"', *Theory, Culture & Society*, 24(7–8): 20–21.

Conrad, P. (1999) 'It's Boring: Notes on the Meanings of Boredom in Everyday Life', in B. Glassner and R. Hertz (eds), *Qualitative Sociology as Everyday Life*. Thousand Oaks, CA: Sage. pp. 123–135.

Davis, M. S. (1971) '"That's Interesting!" Towards a Phenomenology of Sociology and a Sociology of Phenomenology', *Philosophy of the Social Sciences*, 1(4): 309–344.

Davis, M. S. (1973) 'Georg Simmel and the Aesthetics of Social Reality', *Social Forces*, 51(1): 320–329.

Dekkers, M. (1997) *The Way of all Flesh: A Celebration of Decay*. London: Harvill Press.

de la Fuente, E. (2007) 'On the Promise of a Sociological Aesthetics: From Georg Simmel to Michel Maffesoli', *Distinktion: The Sandinavian Journal of Social Theory*, 15: 93–112.

de la Fuente, E. (2008) 'The Art of Social Forms and the Social Forms of Art: The Sociology-Aesthetics Nexus in Georg Simmel's Thought', *Sociological Theory*, 26(4): 344–362.

de la Fuente, E. (2014) 'Why Aesthetic Patterns Matter: On Art and a Qualitative Social Theory', *Journal for Theory of Social Behaviour*, 44(2): 168–185.

de la Fuente, E. (Forthcoming) 'Frames, Handles and Landscapes: Georg Simmel and the Aesthetic Ecology of Things', in T. Kemple and O. Pyyhtinen (eds.), *The Anthem Companion to Georg Simmel*. New York: Anthem Press.

de la Fuente, E. and Walsh, M. J. (2013) 'Framing through the Senses: Sight and Sound in Everyday Life', in M. Andersen et al. (eds), *Transvisuality: The Cultural Dimension of Visuality*. Liverpool: University of Liverpool Press. pp. 207–222.

de Monthoux, P. G. (2000) 'The Art Management of Aesthetic Organizing', in S. Linstead and H. Höpfl (eds), *The Aesthetics of Organization*. London: Sage. pp. 35–58.

Durkheim, E. (1965) 'Sociology and its Scientific Field', in L. Coser (ed.), *Georg Simmel*. Englewood Cliffs, NJ: Prentice Hall. pp. 43–49.

Featherstone, M. (1991) 'The Aestheticization of Everyday Life', *Consumer Culture and Postmodernism*. London: Sage. pp. 65–82.

Finlay, V. (2004) *Colour: A Natural History of the Pallette*. New York: Random House.

Frisby, D. (1981) *Sociological Impressionism: A Reassessment of Georg Simmel's Social Theory*. London: Heinemann.

Frisby, D. (1985) *Fragments of Modernity: Theories of Modernity in the Work of Simmel, Kracauer and Benjamin*. Cambridge: Polity.

Frisby, D. (1997) 'Introduction to the Texts', in D. Frisby and M. Featherstone (eds), *Simmel on Culture: Selected Writings*. London: Sage. pp. 1–28.

Frisby, D. and Featherstone, M. (eds) (1997) *Simmel on Culture: Selected Writings*. London: Sage.

Gibson, J. J. (1966) *The Senses Considered as Perceptual Systems*. Boston: Houghton Mifflin.

Gibson, J. J. (1979) *The Ecological Approach to Visual Perception*. Boston: Houghton Mifflin.

Goffman, E. (1974) *Frame Analysis: An Essay on the Organization of Experience*. London: Harper and Row.

Green, B. (1988) *Literary Methods and Sociological Theory*. Chicago: University of Chicago Press.

Habermas, J. (1981) 'Modernity versus Postmodernity', *New German Critique*, 22(1): 3–14.

Halton, E. (1995) *Bereft of Reason: On the Decline of Social Thought and Prospects for its Renewal*. Chicago: University of Chicago Press.

Highmore, B. (2002) *Everyday Life and Cultural Theory: An Introduction*. London and New York: Routledge.

Ingold, T. (1993) 'Temporality of the Landscape', *World Archaeology*, 25(2): 152–174.

Ingold, T. (2000) *Perception of the Environment: Essays on Livelihood, Dwelling and Skill*. London: Routledge.

Lawrence, P. A. (ed.) (1976) *Georg Simmel: Sociologist and European*. New York: Barnes and Noble Books

Lipman, W. (1965) 'Some Aspects of Simmel's Conception of the Individual', in K. H. Wolff (ed.), *Essays on Sociology, Philosophy and Aesthetics*. New York: Harper Torchbooks. pp. 119–138.

Lukacs, G. (1991) 'Georg Simmel', *Theory, Culture and Society*, 8(3): 145–150.

Lury, C. (2002) 'Style and the Perfection of Things', in Jim Collins (ed.), *High-Pop: Making Culture into Popular Entertainment*. Oxford: Wiley-Blackwell. pp. 201–224.

Miller, D. (2005) 'Materiality: An Introduction' in D. Miller (ed.) *Materiality*, Durham, NC: Duke University Press: 1–50.

Norman, D. (2002) *The Design of Everyday Things*. New York: Basic Books.

Norman, D. (2005) *Emotional Design: Why We Love (or Hate) Everyday Things*. New York: Basic Books.

Osbaldiston, N. (ed.) (2013) *Culture of the Slow: Social Deceleration in an Accelerated World*. London: Palgrave Macmillan.

Podoksik, E. (2007) 'In Search of Unity: Georg Simmel on Italian Cities as Works of Art', *Theory, Culture & Society*, 29(7–8): 101–123.

Pyyhtinen, O. (2010) *Simmel and 'The Social'*. Basingstoke: Palgrave Macmillan.

Riegl, A. (1982) 'The Modern Cult of Monuments: Its Character and its Origins', *Oppositions*, 25(Fall): 20–51.

Robertson, R. (1978) *Meaning and Change: Explorations in the Cultural Sociology of Modern Societies*. Oxford: Basil Blackwell.

Salz, A. (1965) 'A Note from a Student of Simmel's', in K. H. Wolff (ed.), *Georg Simmel: Essays on Sociology, Philosophy and Aesthetics*. New York: Harper Torchbooks. pp. 233–236.

Scaff, L. (1989) *Fleeing the Iron Cage: Culture, Politics, and Modernity in the Thought of Max Weber*. Berkeley and Los Angeles: University of California Press.

Scott, A. and Staubmann, H. (2005) 'Editors' Introduction', in G. Simmel, *Rembrandt: An Essay in the Philosophy of Art*. New York: Routledge. pp. xi–xix.

Shields, M. (1999) 'Max Weber and German Expressionism', in S. Whimster (ed.) *Max Weber and the Culture of Anarchy*. London: Palgrave. pp. 214–231.

Simmel, G. (1950) 'Sociability: An Example of Pure or Formal Sociology', in K. H. Wolff (ed.), *The Sociology of Georg Simmel*. New York: Free Press. pp. 40–57.

Simmel, G. (1965a) 'The Ruin', in K. H. Wolff (ed.), *Georg Simmel: Essays on Sociology, Philosophy and Aesthetics*. New York: Harper Torchbooks. pp. 259–266.

Simmel, G. (1965b) 'The Aesthetic Significance of the Face', in K. H. Wolff (ed.), *Georg Simmel: Essays on Sociology, Philosophy and Aesthetics*. New York: Harper Torchbooks. pp. 276–281.

Simmel, G. (1965c) 'The Handle', in K. H. Wolff (ed.), *Georg Simmel: Essays on Sociology, Philosophy and Aesthetics*. New York: Harper Torchbooks. pp. 267–275.

Simmel, G. (1968) 'Sociological Aesthetics', in P. E. Etzkorn (ed.), *Georg Simmel: The Conflict in Modern Culture and other Essays*. New York: Teachers College Press. pp. 68–80.

Simmel, G. (1971) 'The Conflict in Modern Culture', in D. Levine (ed.), *Georg Simmel on Individuality and Social Forms*. Chicago: University of Chicago Press. pp. 375–393.

Simmel, G. (1976) 'Meaning of Culture', in P. A. Lawrence (ed.), *Georg Simmel: Sociologist and European*. New York: Barnes and Noble Books. pp. 243–249.

Simmel, G. (1978) *The Philosophy of Money*. London: Routledge.

Simmel, G. (1994) 'The Picture Frame: An Aesthetic Study', *Theory, Culture & Society*, 11: 11–7.

Simmel, G. (1997a) 'Sociology of the Senses', in D. Frisby and M. Featherstone (eds), *Simmel on Culture*. London: Sage. pp. 137–169.

Simmel, G. (1997b) 'Bridge and Door', in D. Frisby and M. Featherstone (eds), *Simmel on Culture*. London: Sage. pp. 170–174.

Simmel, G. (1997c) 'Sociology of the Meal', in D. Frisby and M. Featherstone (eds), *Simmel on Culture*. London: Sage. pp. 130–136.

Simmel, G. (1997d) 'The Concept of Culture', in D. Frisby and M. Featherstone (eds), *Simmel on Culture*. London: Sage. pp. 36–39.

Simmel, G (1997e) 'The Problem of Style' in D. Frisby and M. Featherstone (eds), *Simmel on Culture*. London, Thousand Oaks and New Delhi: Sage. pp. 211–217.

Simmel, G. (2005) *Rembrandt: An Essay in the Philosophy of Art*. New York: Routledge.

Simmel, G. (2007) 'The Philosophy of Landscape', *Theory, Culture & Society*, 24(7–8): 20–29.

Simmel, G. (2010) *The View of Life: Four Metaphysical Essays with Journal Aphorisms*. Chicago: University of Chicago Press.

Spillman, L. (ed.) (2002) *Cultural Sociology*. Oxford: Blackwell.

Strati, A. (1999) *Organization and Aesthetics*. London: Sage.

Strati, A. (2014) 'The Social Negotiation of Aesthetics and Organizational Democracy', in P. Murphy and E. de la Fuente (eds), *Aesthetic Capitalism*. Leiden: Brill. pp. 105–127.

Tanner, J. (2003) 'Introduction: Sociology and Art History', *The Sociology of Art: A Reader*. London and New York: Routledge. pp. 1–26.

Valsiner, J. (2008) 'Ornamented Worlds and Textures of Feeling: The Power of Abundance', *Critical Social Studies*, 1: 67–78.

Vannini, P., Waskul, D. and Gottschalk, S. (2011) *The Senses in Self, Society and Culture: A Sociology of the Senses*. London and New York: Routledge.

Weber, M. (1972) 'Georg Simmel as Sociologist', *Social Research*, 39: 155–163.

Weingartner, R. H. (1965) 'Form and Content in Simmel's Philosophy of Life', in K. H. Wolff (ed.), *Essays on Sociology, Philosophy and Aesthetics*. New York: Harper Torchbooks. pp. 33–60.

Weinstein, D. and Weinstein, M. (1993) *Postmodern(ized) Simmel*. London and New York: Routledge.

Williams, R. (1976) *Keywords: A Vocabulary of Culture and Society*. London: Croom Helm.

Wolff, K. H. (1965) 'Preface', in K. H. Wolff (ed.), *Essays on Sociology, Philosophy and Aesthetics*. New York: Harper Torchbooks. pp. vii–xiii.

Worringer, W. (1997) *Abstraction and Empathy: A Contribution to the Psychology of Style*. Chicago: Elephant.

Wylie, J. (2007) *Landscape*. London and New York: Routledge.

Zerubavel, E. (1991) *The Fine Line: Making Distinctions in Everyday Life*. New York: The Free Press.

Zerubavel, E. (1999) *Social Mindscapes: An Invitation to Cognitive Sociology*. Cambridge, MA: Harvard University Press.

Zerubavel, E. (2007) 'Generally Speaking: The Logic and Mechanics of Social Pattern Analysis', *Sociological Forum*, 22(2): 131–145.

# Bourdieu's Sociology of Culture: On the Economy of Symbolic Goods

Gisèle Sapiro

## INTRODUCTION

Pierre Bourdieu constituted the sociology of culture as a specialty of the sociological discipline at a time when culture was becoming a site of public intervention in France and elsewhere, with the development of cultural politics (Dubois, 1999; Bustamante, 2015), and when 'Cultural Studies' was just emerging in the UK. As a specific research domain, the sociology of culture encompasses the sociology of art, that is to say, the conditions of production and circulation of cultural works, and the sociology of cultural practices. While the concept of 'field' implies the relative autonomy of cultural universes, endowed with their particular rules and specific stakes, the concept of 'habitus' aims to account for differences that one may observe between the cultural practices of different social groups and their (relative) harmony within each one of these groups. However, far from being confined to this domain, culture occupies a central place in Bourdieu's reflections upon both the economy of symbolic exchanges and social structure, which he rethinks and reconfigures in introducing the concept of 'cultural capital'. If his theory thus belongs to 'Cultural Sociology' in a global sense, Bourdieu never subscribed to culturalist theses that tend to essentialize culture. His approach is relational and dynamic, and aims, following Durkheim, to explain 'the social by the social'. His reflection on the symbolic dimension of exchanges drove him to rethink the theory of domination.

## THE ECONOMY OF SYMBOLIC GOODS

The analysis of the economy of symbolic goods developed by Bourdieu is anchored in a criticism of an economism that reduces exchanges to agents pursuing their maximum interest. His first studies on pre-capitalist societies, Kabylia and Béarn, and then his research on the literary, artistic, religious and scientific fields, highlighted the symbolic dimension of exchanges, which functions to render them unrecognizable as such. The 'economism' that came to prevail from the 18th century onwards is nothing more than a particular form of the economy of practices and exchanges and, if it has imposed itself as a dominant paradigm with a triumphant capitalism, certain universes, such as the fields of cultural and scientific production, continue to function in large part according to the principles governing pre-capitalist economies, while the case of paternalism demonstrates that such disavowed forms of domination still subsist at the very heart of the economic field. This theory was successively reformulated throughout all of his work, from *Outline of a Theory of Practice* (1977 [1972]), through *The Logic of Practice* (1990 [1980]), to *Practical Reason* (1998), where we find it in its most developed and synthetic version. His works on literature, art, religion and science, fields wherein prevails 'the interest in disinterestedness' provide paradigmatic illustrations of the theory.

Bourdieu's reflection on the symbolic dimension of exchanges and of power relations in society is born of his observation of pre-capitalist societies. In the pre-capitalist economy, where the reproduction of modes of domination is uncertain, political authority stems from the lack of symmetry of exchanges, that is to say, from practices of ostentatious redistribution, but also from a set of strategies oriented towards the domination of persons, via mechanisms specific to symbolic violence (Bourdieu, 1977 [1972]; 1990 [1980]). This observation drove Bourdieu to refute an 'economistic' approach that reduces exchanges to material interests. Symbolic capital is a kind of credit in the broad sense, based on the belief of the group. The sense of honour and gift practice are two paradigmatic examples of the mode of functioning of the economy of symbolic goods: they are founded on the refusal of calculation, of the logic of price, which are at the core of economism. It does not suffice to objectivize the reality of exchange as does Lévi-Strauss (1969) with the 'gift and counter-gift' pattern, for instance, as this pattern is masked by the temporal interval that also introduces uncertainty with respect to reciprocity.

Thus the foremost property of the economy of symbolic goods consists in the denial of the economic economy, that is to say, of calculation in terms of self-interest: economic interest is 'repressed', 'censured'. The second property, correlated with the first, is the transformation of economic acts into symbolic acts: this alchemy requires a constant investment on the part of agents in order to euphemize the 'interested' nature of the exchange, an investment not attributable to cynical strategy, but rather one that proceeds from a set of dispositions to adopt formal conventions, to dissimulate expectations of reciprocity when giving a gift, for example, or to mask prices (like when one removes the price label from an object that one intends to offer someone). By displacing the explanation of the act from intention to the dispositions of agents, Bourdieu means to recall the role of the socialization process in transmitting these instituted practices, the transgression of which exposes the agent to sanction or blame.

The 'collective work of repression' (Bourdieu, 1998: 121) is not possible unless agents share the same schemes of perception and appreciation. As a result of this constant work of transfiguration, the economy of symbolic goods is an 'economy of imprecision and indeterminacy', which rests upon the 'taboo of making things explicit'. The practices that partake in this economy are, by consequence, 'always ambiguous, two-sided, and even apparently contradictory (for example, goods have a price and are "priceless")' (Bourdieu, 1998: 121). The third property of the economy of symbolic goods is that it is in the very course of their circulation that they accumulate symbolic capital, a type of capital whose efficacy stems from the entourage's perception (that of the clan, the tribe, or the field) of a particular characteristic such as wealth, the value of being warlike, or cultural value. Again in this case, symbolic value is recognized on the basis of shared categories of perception and judgement. Whereas in Kabylia, symbolic capital took the form of honour, it is cultural capital that paradigmatically embodies this value in modern, capitalist societies.

## THE SYMBOLIC VALUE OF CULTURAL CAPITAL

During the 1960s, a period of rapid growth in the number of students attending university in France, Bourdieu undertook a study of 'students and culture' that eventually became *Les Héritiers (The Inheritors)*, co-authored with Jean-Claude Passeron and published in 1964. Analysing the causes of inequalities with respect to education, this work revealed the impact of inherited cultural capital on academic success. The calculation chances was done by relating the proportion of students from different social categories to the share of these categories within the entirety of the French population: thus the chance of obtaining access to higher education ranges from 1% for the children of agricultural workers, or 1.4% for the children of labourers, to 60% for the children of liberal professionals and senior managers. Why does inherited cultural capital have such an impact? It is, as the authors explain, because the culture taught at school resembles most the culture of the dominant classes. But it is also because teachers tend to praise general knowledge that is not transmitted through the educational system, celebrating it as a culture that seems to be 'free', but which in fact is the fruit of a long process of inculcation undertaken within the family. Indeed, cultural education is inscribed in time and in bodies, for it is 'incorporated' by children that were exposed to it from a very young age. Instead of 'correcting' these initial inequalities, teachers unwittingly reinforce them. This unequal social power dynamic finds itself legitimated by the ideology of 'giftedness', which explains scholarly success by innate abilities and by personal merit. This pedagogical arbitrariness is at the origin of 'social reproduction, given the role that the school henceforth plays in this process' (Bourdieu and Passeron, 1990 [1970]). The universalization of education and of the meritocratic ideal have indeed modified the mode of reproduction, which transformed from an unmediated form – families designate their heirs – into what Bourdieu would call in *The State Nobility*, 'the mode of reproduction with an educational component' (Bourdieu, 1996a).

Distinguishing his approach from the Marxist conception that bases class differences solely upon the possession of material means of production, Bourdieu thus developed a theory of symbolic violence, exerted through the possession and imposition of 'cultural capital'. This approach is informed by Weber's theory of legitimacy, which Bourdieu redefines with a more critical tone, in the framework of a theory of symbolic domination. His conception of 'symbolic power' partakes in the rationalist neo-Kantien tradition, which considers, contrary to the empiricist tradition, that our worldview is structured by categories of perception. This is a tradition which was developed in the 20th century in its sociological version in the works of Durkheim and Mauss, and in its philosophical version in the works of Cassirer. Following Marx and Weber, Bourdieu recalls, however, that these categories are not neutral but fulfil ideological functions, and underlie the mechanisms of social domination (Bourdieu, 1977). For Bourdieu, the potency of symbolic power resides in its internalization within the body, in the form of dispositions that come to constitute the 'habitus'. It reveals itself, for instance, in linguistic exchanges, which are the fruit of an encounter between various linguistic habitus and markets that confer meaning upon them (Bourdieu, 1993a). Language is indeed the site of the expression of 'common sense' or 'shared meanings', that is to say, of those schemes of perception and of classification inculcated through education. These schemes underlie logical conformism, and separate between social groups, between sacred and profane forms of knowledge. The site of interaction between thought and body, language is the principal medium of both communication and of everyday domination through 'symbolic violence'. This 'soft' violence relies upon the complicity of the 'dominated' as they share the schemes of perception and evaluation of the dominant, and they have thereby interiorized their 'inferiority' as 'natural' in the face of the legitimacy that they grant the dominant. The efficacy of that violence is bound up in the fact that it is unrecognized - or "misrecognized" - as such.

In the 1960s, Bourdieu also carried out a number of studies on new cultural practices, such as photography (Bourdieu, Boltanski, Castel, Chamboredon, 1990 [1965]), and on museum visiting (Bourdieu, Darbel, Schnapper, 1990 [1966]), which appears to be strongly determined by cultural capital, in a period during which the policy implemented by the minister of Cultural Affairs, André Malraux, aimed to foster universal access to culture. These surveys gave rise to reflections upon the principles of hierarchization of cultural practices, according to a relational and non-essentialist approach: the same practice can become banal and lose its distinctive character when it is adopted by a large number of people, whereas cultural products typically considered as 'popular', such as jazz and the crime novel, can undergo a process of valorization and legitimation due to their appropriation by fractions endowed with cultural capital.

The results of these studies of the modes of legitimation of class domination were extended and generalized in the inquiry on taste and lifestyles which is at the core of Bourdieu's major work, *Distinction* (1984 [1979]). In the midst of an intellectual conjuncture within which two dominant paradigms – Structuralism and Marxism – came up against one another, Bourdieu adopted their common relational approach, which he combined with a topological one – based upon the notion of positions that agents occupy within a hierarchized social space – thereby entirely renewing the analysis of social classes. Against the Marxist theory of reflection that posits culture as a mere superstructure of economically determined power relations, he demonstrates the relative autonomy of fields of cultural production, a factor that engendered, alongside the ideal of educational meritocracy, a distinct species of capital, 'cultural capital'. The social structure appears thus as a chiastic pattern, according to the overall amount and composition of capital: the vertical hierarchy resulting from the overall amount of capital crosses a horizontal distribution of agents according to the amount of cultural capital as opposed to economic capital which they possess. Unlike studies of social stratification that adopt fixed criteria of hierarchization according to income, in this view, the social structure emerges as a dynamic space, a space of symbolic struggles over the definition of cultural legitimacy.

To apprehend the relations between classes and fractions of classes, Bourdieu introduces the method of structural analysis that consists in identifying the systems of differential gaps endowed with cultural significance. Thus the dominant classes, which differ from the dominated classes by the overall amount of capital of all types in their possession, distinguish themselves from these lower classes by expressing, in their tastes, as in their lifestyles, their distance from necessity. However, the different dominant fractions also differentiate themselves from one another through their cultural practices and preferences according to the composition of their capital. Those most endowed with cultural capital (professional and artistic intellectuals) occupy a dominated position in the field of power, with respect to the holders of economic and political power, while those who practice liberal professions situate themselves in an intermediary position between those two poles. For example, mountain climbing, the frequenting of museums, the preference for Goya or Kandinsky, listening to the *Art of the Fugue* and a taste for exotic cuisines, characterize the lifestyle of professors of higher education, which stands out from other fractions of the dominant classes, such as industrial bosses, who are better endowed with economic capital, but less so with cultural capital. The different fractions of the dominant class differentiate themselves not only by their lifestyles and their preferred objects of consumption (Goya versus Renoir), but also through their categories of judgement and their modes of artistic appropriation: those most endowed with cultural capital but least possessed of economic capital opposie material appropriation with symbolic appropriation through a pure and 'disinterested' mode of contemplation in museums, which corresponds to their broader ascetic dispositions. The Kantian theory of disinterested aesthetic pleasure therefore concerns solely one mode of appropriation of artworks among others, the most distinguished and most distinctive in fact, which is the product of the field of cultural production's claims for autonomy (see below). We find similar principles of differentiation within the dominated classes, between, for example, the small intellectual bourgeoisie (primary school teachers, librarians, etc.), which display their 'cultural good will' in their cultural practices, and the small business bourgeoisie, who are more interested in material goods like cars. The concept of 'habitus' designates this system of ethical and aesthetic dispositions acquired over the course of education by the internalization of social structures, which, in turn, structure the perceptions, judgements and practices of social groups.

According to Bourdieu, cultural capital exists in three forms: incorporated in the form of dispositions (habitus) as a result of the processes of familial and educational transmission; objectified in artworks, literary works, monuments, etc.; and institutionalized through scholarly titles, which confer symbolic power upon it in the matrimonial marketplace, the labour market, and so on. Cultural capital is all the more effective given that, unlike economic wealth, it is misrecognized as such and thus recognized as legitimate, which generates its symbolic value. This notion of cultural capital is different from the idea of human capital developed in the 60s by Gary Becker (1993), which only measures the returns made on educational investments as manifested in monetary profits or in benefits that can be directly converted into money, without assessing 'the differential chances of profit which the various markets offer these agents or classes as a function of the volume and the composition of their assets' and without contextualizing these investments within 'the system of strategies of reproduction' (Bourdieu, 1984 [1979]: 3). Cultural capital and, more generally, symbolic capital, appear as a mode of legitimation of social domination in capitalist societies.

## THE FIELDS OF CULTURAL PRODUCTION: FOR A SCIENCE OF ARTWORKS

The concept of field apprehends art worlds or fields of cultural production as social universes endowed with relative autonomy, in that they are regulated by their own rules, which reflect their history and determine the conditions of accumulation of the field's specific type of capital. This concept works to avoid a double obstacle. Against the romantic ideology of the 'uncreated creator', which finds its most accomplished expression in Sartre's notion of 'creative project', and which underlies the purely hermeneutic approach to artworks, it recalls the fact that cultural producers do not escape the constraints that regulate the social world. A sociology of artworks is justified in asking: 'But who created the creators?' (Bourdieu, 1990 [1980]), that is to say, through which processes is the symbolic value of artworks created? However, against Marxist sociology, which reduces the artwork to the social characteristics of its public or its author, and against the economistic approach which is interested solely in the material conditions of the production and consumption of cultural industries, Pierre Bourdieu affirms that we cannot account for cultural fields without taking into consideration their relative autonomy and their principal property, which is belief.

From a methodological point of view, such an approach aims to transcend the traditional opposition between internal and external analyses. The internal analysis focuses on deciphering the meaning of artworks, rather than on the creative acts which produced them. Inversely, the external analysis tends to reduce artworks to their conditions of production and reception. While the internal analysis is interested in the structure of artworks, the external analysis focuses rather on their social function. The concept of field works to connect these two dimensions, taking into account the mediations that occur between these two orders of phenomena.

The concept of field was first coined by Bourdieu in an article entitled, 'The Intellectual Field and the Creative Project', published in 1966 in Sartre's journal, *Les Temps Modernes*. However, Bourdieu eventually renounced that initial theorization, which he came to consider as too interactionist, in favour of a more objectivist and topological conception of the field, developed in a number of articles that appeared between 1971 and 1991: 'The Market of Symbolic Goods' in 1971 (a shortened English version appeared in the journal *Poetics* in 1985), 'Some Properties of Fields' and 'But Who Created the Creators?' in *Sociology in question*, published in 1984 (1993c), 'The Field of Cultural Production' (1993b), 'Le champ littéraire' (1991). Most of these studies were assembled and reworked in his major book *The Rules of Art* (1996b [1992]) (see also the collection which appeared in English under the title *The Field of Cultural Production* (Bourdieu, 1993b)). If his initial works dealt mainly with the French literary field in the 19th century, in the 1980s Bourdieu began a research project on Manet and on the notion of 'symbolic revolution', which he developed in a course at the College de France and in a book co-authored with Marie-Claire Bourdieu, his wife, a work whose unfinished manuscript was published after his death in the same volume as these lectures (Bourdieu, 2013b). Bourdieu also took an interest in music, albeit in a more sporadic fashion (see notably Bourdieu, 2001). One should include among his works on culture, his articles on religion, *haute couture*, and sports, which played a non-negligible role in the construction of his field theory. The case of the religious field was instrumental in his reflections, inspired by Weber, upon the processes of formation of a body of specialists that characterizes the emergence of fields, and upon the ideal typical opposition between priests and prophets, which underscores an opposition between orthodoxy and heresy that he later transposed to fields of cultural production (Bourdieu, 1991 [1971]; 1987 [1971]). The sports field also illustrates the cleavage between professionals and amateurs and raises, like cultural products, the question of the production of a diversified and socially hierarchized cultural supply (Bourdieu, 1990 [1980]: 173–95). Throughout his reflections upon the field of *haute couture*, Bourdieu analyses the process of production of the belief in the fetish of the brand name, comparing it to the functioning of magic according to Mauss, as well as the opposition between 'Right Bank' (Balmain) and 'Left Bank' (Scherrer), which is ideal typical of the structural opposition between the dominant and the dominated poles of the field (Bourdieu, 1990 [1980]: 196–206).

According to its objectivist and relational definition, which is inspired by the concept of magnetic field in physics (including the principles of attraction and repulsion), the notion of field simultaneously designates the field of positions which define themselves with respect to one another according to the unequal distribution of a specific form of capital, and a space of position-takings inscribed in a particular history, which also assume meaning with respect to one another. These two spaces are in a homologous relationship. Indeed, if the space of possibilities presents itself to the creators in the form of a choice to make between options constituted more or less as such over the course of its history (rhymes or free verse, for example), these aesthetic choices are correlated with the positions that their authors occupy in the field, according to the overall amount and composition of the specific symbolic capital they hold, that is to say, to the degree and the type of recognition that they have acquired as well as to their ethical-aesthetic dispositions. In order to understand this distribution of specific capital, one has to relate it to the principal oppositions that structure the literary field.

The first opposition is no more than the specification in the field of a cleavage that structures the social space and that is also observable in all social fields: it opposes the 'dominants' to the 'dominated,' according to the overall amount of specific capital they hold in that field, which is, in this case, the capital of recognition. This cleavage overlaps in general the opposition between 'old' and 'young', between established writers or artists and newcomers. It may be illustrated on the one side by the members of the Académie Française, a selective Old Regime literary institution which co-opts only a few older writers, and the avant-garde, on the other (the Surrealists, for example). While the dominant have an interest in the conservation of the state of power relations as they are, the dominated, who work to subvert them, break with established codes and conventions. Drawing elements from Weber's theory of religion, to reflect upon these confrontations in a field regulated by an *illusio* – i.e. the belief in the game – Bourdieu uses the notions of orthodoxy and heterodoxy. Like sects assembled around a prophetic figure, the avant-garde movements appear as heterodox in their attempts to subvert the writing conventions of their epoch, provoking more or less intense reactions on the part of the defenders of orthodoxy, which are comparable to those of priests, representatives of the established Church. The struggles between the defenders of orthodoxy and the heretics are recurrent and largely constitutive of the history of the field. The principle of 'originality' that has regulated the world of letters since the Romantic period means that the competing struggles for the imposition of the legitimate definition of literature assume an open and sometimes violent form, as reflected in the genre of 'manifestoes'.

The second opposition is more specific to fields of cultural production, and defines their relationships with external constraints. It distinguishes different types of recognition, symbolic or temporal, according to the degree of autonomy with respect to demand, whether it is a question of audience expectations or of ideological demands. According to the heteronomous logic, the value of a work comes down to either its commercial value, indicated by sales figures (best sellers, for example), or to its pedagogical value, according to moral or ideological criteria (including of course religious ones). On the other side, the autonomous logic prizes the purely aesthetic value of the work, a value that only specialists, such as artists' peers and critics, are able to appreciate. The recognition by peers thus becomes the criteria of accumulation of the specific symbolic capital within a field.

According to Bourdieu, the science of art works requires three operations: (1) the analysis of the position of the literary field within the field of power (its relative degree of autonomy) and its evolution through different socio-historical conjunctures; (2) the analysis of the structure of the literary field according to objective relations between individuals and groups vying for the acquisition of specific capital; and (3) the analysis of the habitus of these individuals and of their social trajectories, as the effect of the field does not exert itself mechanically but is mediated by the space of possibilities as they present themselves to agents according to their dispositions.

## THE MARKET OF SYMBOLIC GOODS: A REVERSED ECONOMY

Literary production achieved autonomy from the demands of the dominant classes and from the wider audience by asserting the supreme importance of the judgement of specialists. In an article published in 1971, Bourdieu (1985) set out to study the conditions of emergence of a 'market of symbolic goods', a process correlated to that of the autonomization of the literary and artistic fields with respect to patronage and sponsorship. The appearance of specific bodies in charge of the diffusion of artworks (publishers gallery owners) and of specific authorities endowed with the power of consecration (academies, painting salons, prizes), which produce value in this market, rendered it impossible to assess cultural goods according to purely economic criteria (sales figures, painting prices) and ensured that their economic value would be 'mediated' by their symbolic value. Aesthetic judgement concomitantly became a specific form of specialization: literary critics, art critics and music critics participate in the valorization process enacted upon artworks, asserting, in the face of laypersons, their monopoly as competent authorities concerning their particular domain of creation. As Bourdieu reveals in *The Rules of Art* (Bourdieu, 1996 [1992]), these different authorities contributed to the formation, from the middle of the 19th century onwards, of a small-scale pole of production of cultural goods, which proclaimed the supremacy of aesthetic value over the criteria of economic success prevailing at the pole of large-scale production (indicated by short-term sales figures). It can thus be described as a 'reversed economy', based upon the denial of the economic dimension of the activity of creation (Bourdieu, 1993b).

The dissociation between aesthetic value and economic value, which characterizes the pole of small-scale production within this market of symbolic goods, and which underlies the process by which the fields of cultural production achieved relative autonomy, takes on various forms according to the specific medium and in differing configurations, from the Romantic figure of the dandy to the sacralization of the 'cursed artist', but they are all the expression of the artist's ethic of disinterestedness, or at least, of his refusal to submit to the external constraints (economic, political, moral) that society attempts to impose upon him. If the entrepreneurial models of Balzac and Beethoven remins us that artistic careers do not escape such constraints, they also display the work of negotiation that is required in order to impose oneself without making concessions to social expectations (Bourdieu, 2001). However, these negotiations are most often taken up by an intermediary, a publisher, an art dealer, a literary agent, who, while working to extricate the artist from any suspicion of self-interest that acts of self-promotion inevitably imply, participates in the chain of "production of the belief" in the artwork, a point expressed in the title of the 1977 article that Bourdieu dedicated to the relationship between the writer and the publisher (Bourdieu, 1977). Like the fashion designer's signature, the publisher affixes their brand-name to the artwork, helping to confer value upon it through a 'magical' operation consisting in the transference of symbolic capital. This symbolic exchange ensures that the relationship between the author and the publisher cannot be reduced to a simple contract: strongly personalized, it oscillates between the enchantment of relationships founded upon elective affinities, and the resentment that the resulting dependency and forms of exploitation generate.

This complex relationship between the author and her publisher, and between the artist and the art dealer, is tribute to the fact that the economy of symbolic goods hinges often upon the disinterested investment not only of the creator but also of the intermediary who bets upon his artworks. Indeed, this investment, founded upon the belief in the artwork itself, is marked by uncertainty and risk, especially for innovative works that have difficulty establishing themselves on the market. In economic terms, there are often deficit-producing investments, which bet upon long-term gains. Indeed, one of the characteristics of the economy of symbolic goods is temporality: gaining recognition for an artwork requires time and constitutes a long-term process. During the term of the consecration process – if it occurs – symbolic value may be converted into commercial value. Sometimes punctuated by prizes, this process can continue until the work enters into the academic pantheon, whereupon it becomes consecrated as a classic (often well after the death of the author), but there is nothing linear or guaranteed about this. Despite the risk and possible loss, this long-term investment on the part of the intermediary is not totally disinterested: it brings them symbolic gratifications such as the esteem and recognition of the literary and artistic milieu for their capacity for discernment and courage, therefore helping to maintain and reinforce their 'credit', that is, their symbolic capital. However, these risky bets require a complex economy of equalization which consists in compensating the losses linked to one artwork via gains obtained upon other artworks, either those which are already consecrated, or those which partake in the large-scale production network, according to a formula that large publishers often practice. This economy also often relies upon public or private support (philanthropic foundations, sponsorship, etc.), which are a number of modern forms of patronage testifying to the social recognition artistic creation has acquired. The smallest publishers also rely on volunteering, which is the most extreme form of disinterested investment on the part of intermediaries and the purest expression of their belief in this investment.

## THE 'SYMBOLIC REVOLUTIONS'

Bourdieu's concept of 'symbolic revolution' designates the redefinition of a space of possibilities which innovative works accomplish. It was in his lectures on Manet that Bourdieu most extensively reflected upon the conditions of symbolic revolutions (Bourdieu, 2013b). In this research he reconstructs the academic system which had a monopoly upon artistic training and on the art market in Manet's time. This academic system functioned like an organized body ('corps') bent upon its own reproduction. Careers were delineated by the entrance examination at the École des Beaux Arts, apprenticeship learning in the ateliers, prizes, exhibitions at the Salon, which gave access to the market, and commissions by the State for the best artists involved. The academic aesthetic derived from this system: it praised technical mastery (perspective, relief, chiaroscuro, etc.), legibility (the message), reference to history (which in turn founded a hierarchy of genres, with historical subjects at the top of the hierarchy) and a certain kind of visual 'finish' in the paintwork. Manet destroyed this aesthetic code, which was sustained by a State monopoly. However, against a heroic and idealistic vision, Bourdieu seeks to reinsert this symbolic revolution in the social history that produced it, without reducing aesthetic stakes to socio-economic and political stakes. Such a history combines technical evolutions (such as the invention of the colour tube that allows for outdoor painting) and morphological factors, in particular the growth of the population of artists excluded from the system and bearing an anti-academic attitude, who would go on to invent the bohemian lifestyle and create a parallel system: that of the society of artists. Another consequence of this symbolic revolution is the emergence of a field of critics, at the intersection of the literary and artistic fields, which fostered the rise of a counter-legitimacy that challenged the monopoly of the academy. All of these factors rendered possible, without necessitating it, the revolution accomplished by Manet. He was not the first to call into question the academic aesthetic: the Romantics (e.g. Delacroix), the Realists (e.g. Courbet) and the Impressionists (notably Monet with whom he was close), all contributed to that revolution. What can explain the fact that it was Manet who contributed to such an extent to its fully fledged accomplishment?

Bourdieu replaces the traditional hermeneutic approach with a 'dispositionalist theory of action'. Art history (or the history of literature) is the fruit of an encounter between a space of possibilities – a field – and the singular trajectory of a particular agent. Sociological analysis must take into account Manet's dispositions, which expressed themselves in his elegant corporeal hexis, among other things; the important economic, social and cultural resources that this son of a first-instance court judge possessed, as an inheritor of a long line of legal professionals, who deviated from the career that his family had intended for him in order to become a painter; his training within the academic system; his deep knowledge of the history of art; the liberty that his private income and his dense social network conferred upon him. These networks included the high society salons, on the one hand (amongst which there was that of his wife), and cafés and bohemian milieux on the other, wherein his first circle of admirers was recruited. That extraordinary concentration of assets, combined with what Bourdieu called a 'cleft habitus', torn between the two poles of the 'field of power' (economic and cultural), and underlying his double rejection of the academic system and of the bohemian way of life, predisposed Manet to accomplish the revolution that ultimately gave birth to the autonomous artistic field. This was a revolution that, like all 'symbolic revolutions', was defined less by the destruction it accomplished, than by the integration of that which preceded it. The rupture was carried out within a form of continuity, as illustrated by the practice of 'pastiche' to which Bourdieu devoted a great deal of attention.

As Bourdieu emphasizes, in order to understand the symbolic revolution accomplished by Manet, we first have to abandon our categories of aesthetic perception, which are the fruit of this very revolution, and to reconstitute the mental world of 'academicism', which was codified into a system. We have to 'de-normalize' the effects produced by this revolution, to become 'unfamiliar' with the presuppositions of modern art, which today are so taken for granted that one cannot conceive of things being otherwise. This injunction is more than a methodological proposition, for it opens the way for a historical sociology of the perception and reception of artworks.

In the third part of *The Rules of Art*, Bourdieu (1996 [1992]) investigates the historical genesis of pure aesthetics since Kant and his theory of disinterested aesthetics pleasure. This aesthetic attitude was embodied in institutions such as museums where artworks are isolated, sanctified and fetishized. Bourdieu denounces the anachronism that consists in acting as if this mode of reception had always existed and as if it was universal. Unlike most works in art history that commit this error, the book by Michael Baxandall (1988) on 'the Period Eye' offers, according to Bourdieu, an alternative model, by showing how the eye is fashioned by religion, education and business, that is to say, by the dispositions and schemes of perception proper to the merchant habitus of the Quattrocento period. The work of reconstructing the code that allows for the researcher's act of deciphering must not lead him or her to project that operation upon the emic perception of agents, which do not need such a method to apprehend artworks. The theory of perception in favour of which Bourdieu argues, relies upon the idea that the 'first perception is practical, with neither theory nor concept' (Bourdieu, 1996 [1992]: 433).

## A RESEARCH PROGRAMME

Bourdieu's theory, as well as his empirical works, which were often conducted in research teams, have functioned as a research programme – in the sense of Imre Lakatos – for his students, within his research centre[1] and beyond this circle, in France and abroad, in sociology, in literary studies and in political science in particular, but less so in art history. It is impossible in the framework of this chapter to give a complete inventory of all these works. We shall here just trace Bourdieu's impact on the sociology of culture, the types of appropriation to which his theory was subjected, and the questions it has raised. It is certainly in the sociology of education that Bourdieu's earlier works had the greatest impact, at least in the beginning. In sociology, the notion of 'cultural capital' is the one which has had the greatest success, especially in the United States (Sallaz and Zavisca, 2007), while the concept of field was appropriated more in literary studies and political science. In 1983 the Dutch journal *Poetics* published an article by Bourdieu entitled 'The Field of Cultural Production or: The Economic World Reversed'. From 1990 onwards, published under the guidance of Paul DiMaggio and Kees Van Rees, the journal had shifted away from its previous more narrow focus on literary culture and broadened its remit by printing a number of works in the sociology of culture that referred to Bourdieu, and by bringing into one location research on both cultural practices and fields of cultural production – domains of inquiry that are even today still too often separated.

The success of the concept of 'cultural capital' is above all attributable to the vast impact of

*La Distinction* in France, and then internationally, after the first translations into German, Italian and English (Sapiro, 2014). Paul DiMaggio's study of the dominant classes in Boston and the uses they made of high culture in order to establish the boundaries of their group, was one of the first attempts to test Bourdieu's analytical model as regards American society (DiMaggio, 1982). The English translation of *La Distinction*, published by Harvard University Press in 1984, strongly contributed to the development of the sociology of culture in the United States. In 1986, a research network was created within the American Sociological Association (ASA), at the instigation of Vera Zolberg, one of the first importers of Bourdieu's sociology of art in the United States, Gary Alan Fine, Richard Peterson, and some others (Santoro, 2008). An extensive debate took place as to the indicators of cultural capital, and their relevance for analysing American society (Lamont and Lareau, 1988; Holt, 1997). Responding to a number of reservations articulated by American researchers with respect to the 'transposability' of this model to the United States, Holt (1997) showed that most of them used as indicators of the 'objectivized' forms of cultural capital, which are less distinctive in contemporary American society than are their incorporated forms (attitude towards culture, modes of consumption). In her book entitled *Money, Morals, and Manners: the Culture of the French and American Upper-Middle Class*, Michèle Lamont (1992) compared the formation of borders between social groups in France and the United States through qualitative methods – in-depth interviews during which she asks her respondents to position themselves with respect to the cultural practices of other social groups – and concludes that there are differences between the two countries with respect to the role of legitimate culture, less generative of disdain towards lower classes and their tastes in the United States, as well as in terms of the porousness of social boundaries, which is greater in the United States. According to Holt (1997), however, this study is based upon the explicit judgements gathered amongst research subjects, and as a result underestimates the gap between discourses – which are strongly redolent of the cultural relativism and egalitarian values that prevail in American society – and practices, obfuscating the implicit character of the ways of distinguishing things described by Bourdieu. A number of research projects undertaken in the United States have tested cultural capital as an indicator of an elevated social position, without calling into question the differentiation between cultural capital and economic capital which is at the heart of the analysis of the social space in *La Distinction*. Yet the question is whether or not this differentiation, which results in France from the Republican meritocratic educational system, can be observed in other societies.

Beyond the question of international comparisons, there is the issue of changes over the course of time. Richard Peterson (Peterson & Kern, 1996) developed the notion of 'omnivorism' to account for the eclecticism of the practices of the dominant classes in the US, in opposition to the 'univorism' of the dominated classes, whereas for Bernard Lahire (2004), the eclecticism of practices seriously problematizes the notion of 'habitus' at a group or social-class level. However, large quantitative studies on cultural practices show, with the help of Multiple Correspondence Analysis (see Duval, Chapter 18 in this volume), the persistence of social differences with respect to cultural practices in the UK (Bennett et al., 2009), Denmark (Prieur and Savage, 2013), Norway (Rosenlund, 1996; 2009), Portugal (Pereira, 2011), and France (Coulangeon, 2011). Furthermore, one can ask whether the opposition omnivore/univore does not rest above all upon a tendency to fix categorizations in place: for example, classifying jazz and the crime novel in lowbrow or middlebrow culture, without examining the processes of legitimation of these genres and their subdivision into an experimental or intellectual segment, a traditional one and a popular one. Moreover, it can be observed that readers of crime novels do not read romantic novels, and this division cannot be explained solely by gender because it applies just as much to female readers of crime novels belonging to the educated middle or upper classes as it does to male readers. One also has to question these classifications themselves: the univorism imputed to the unprivileged classes is partly due to the fact that popular music genres are regrouped into a large and catch-all type of category, the 'pop rock' category, blending rock, punk, rap and pop music, while these practices are in fact quite socially differentiated (Prieur and Savage, 2013). It has also been frequently noted that dominant classes appropriate popular products in a distanced or ironical fashion, which marks their difference from the unprivileged classes. One might also hypothesize that univorism characterizes the strongest and most exclusive investments (contemporary music, punk, hard rock), which constitute a form of distinction in certain milieux, dominant as well as dominated. They lead to a form of specialization (knowledge of music groups, of their history, of types of recording, of writings by critics, etc.), which cannot be assimilated with straightforward fan practices and which constitute veritable forms of cultural capital in their own right.

Comparisons between countries and over time have raised a number of heuristic questions, calling for the extension of the original research programme (Coulangeon and Duval, 2014). What are the comparative indicators of cultural capital in different societies? Has the differentiation of economic and cultural capital occurred everywhere? Do age, sex and 'race' directly impact upon cultural practices? A team of researchers which conducted a large survey in the UK showed that, without calling into question the relevance of the notion of class to account for discrepancies in this domain, as members of the working class engage minimally in activities traditionally defined as 'cultural' (besides watching television), one observes correlations between musical tastes and age, as well as between reading practices and sex (Bennett et al., 2009). Moreover, the relative decline of traditional literate culture in the face of the rise of scientific and technological capital, calls for an examination of new forms of cultural capital, and even of what some scholars call 'informational capital' (Prieur and Savage, 2013). One observes in particular the emergence of what can be called 'cosmopolitan' cultural capital, which involves a growing attention to issues of social and cultural diversity (Prieur and Savage, 2013). This raises the issue of the conditions of transmission and reproduction of cultural capital in the era of globalization.

Concerning the sociology of artworks, the programme was developed in France and abroad by both Bourdieu's students (Remy Ponton, Christophe Charle, Gisèle Sapiro in France, Sergio Miceli in Brazil, Anna Boschetti in Italy) and also by some of his colleagues, such as Vera Zolberg in the United States (1990), Joseph Jurt (1995) in Germany, and Itamar Even-Zohar (1990) in Israel. Most of these works deal with literature, but new research is now emerging in the fields of cinema, art, music and dance (Duval and Mary, 2006; Lizé and Roueff eds., 2010; Sapiro, Pacouret and Picaud eds., 2015). Prosopographic surveys were conducted on French writers in the second half of the 19th century and the first half of the 20th century, combined with studies of authorities and/or schools and literary movements (Ponton, 1977; Sapiro, 2014). Following Bourdieu's analyses of Flaubert and Baudelaire, other studies have focused on a central figure credited with having brought about a symbolic revolution that transformed a particular field: Sartre (Boschetti, 1988 [1985]), Beckett (Casanova, 2006 [1997]), Apollinaire (Boschetti, 2001), Mallarmé (Durand, 2008). Research projects were also undertaken on the German literary field at different periods (Joch and Wolf, 2005; Tommek and Bogdal, 2012), as well as on the Egyptian literary field (Jacquemond, 2008 [2003]).

The fields of cultural production are situated between the State and the market, which respectively exert more or less constraint upon them according to the type of government and economic conditions. While the market can help these fields to acquire autonomy from the State, the State can, in turn, protect them from economic constraints through financial support (Sapiro, 2003b). Research on Communist regimes, where the power of consecration was monopolized by a body controlled by the Communist party, the Writers' Union, has shown, however, that forms of relative autonomy exist even in contexts of great heteronomy and dependence upon the State (Dragomir, 2007). By the same token, autonomous logics can be found even in the fields of cultural production that depend most upon the market, such as cinema, which is also structured according to the opposition between the pole of large-scale production and the pole of small-scale production (Duval, 2006). This latter segment is strongly supported in France by the State, like the pole of small-scale production in the publishing field. While Bourdieu (1996 [1992]) analysed the process whereby the pole of small-scale production in the literary field achieved autonomy from the rule of the market, the study of literary trials offers a fertile ground for understanding the heteronomous logics that continue to weigh upon literature and the social expectations to which it is subjected, as well as the process through which, starting in the 20th century, its autonomy from the State was progressively recognized (Sapiro, 2011). The process of autonomization that the literary field underwent must furthermore be understood with respect to the division of intellectual labour that intensified in the 20th century (Sapiro, 2003a).

Studies of the politicization of the intellectual field in times of crisis, which entail a loss of autonomy – as in the case of the Dreyfus Affair (Charle, 1990), and to an even greater extent in the case of the French literary field under the German Occupation (Sapiro, 2012b; 2014) – reveal that political position-taking is significantly related to the positions agents occupy in their particular fields of reference. These results confirm the effect of refraction exerted by the field upon external constraints. This structural homology between positions in the literary or intellectual field, and position-taking in the political field, also manifests itself in the forms of politicization at the different poles of the literary or intellectual field, according to the overall amount of specific capital (opposing dominant or established writers to dominated ones), the degree of autonomy, and, in the case of the broader intellectual field, the degree of specialization (Sapiro, 2003b, 2009a).

The question of the geographical limits of fields, in particular in a post-colonial context, was raised by transnational analytical approaches (Ducournau, 2011). While many studies on fields limit themselves to the national context, fields are not necessarily circumscribed within the boundaries of the nation-state (Bourdieu, 1985b). Their contours are not given, but are a matter of struggles, and it is precisely the researcher's job to trace them. The nationalization of the fields of cultural production is a historical fact linked to the construction of national identities (Sapiro, forthcoming). However, these national cultures were formed in relation to one another (Thiesse, 1998), and rapidly came to constitute an international space regulated by authoritative bodies such as the League of Nations, which was later transformed into the United Nations, and, for the domains of science and culture, the International Institute of Intellectual Cooperation, taken over after the war by UNESCO, these bodies fostering the circulation of organizational models and persons between countries (Sapiro, 2009b). In parallel, markets were formed, with borders largely transcending those of the nation-state, thanks to processes of colonialism and the hegemonic ambitions of nation-states (for example, linguistic areas constituted spaces of circulation of the printed word in vehicular languages such as English, French, Spanish, Portuguese and Arabic). The emergence of more or less autonomous transnational spaces depends, however, upon the existence of sites of exchange and of specific consecrating authorities – which differentiates them from a market – such as the Nobel Prize for Literature (Casanova, 2004 [1999]). Relatedly, the relative autonomy of national literary fields is demonstrated by the fact that works which have already been consecrated in transnational spaces or in other national fields often take a long time to be received and legitimated in particular national contexts (Casanova, 2004 [1999]).

In this regard, translations offer a privileged site of observation of the political, economic and cultural logics that bear upon the global publishing market. While analysing the flows of translations reveals the asymmetry of exchanges between languages (Heilbron, 1999), taking into account the structure of the publishing field (Bourdieu, 2008 [1999]) allows one to distinguish a pole of large-scale circulation, largely dominated by the English language, from a pole of small-scale circulation, wherein a real cultural diversity exists, as measured through the number of original languages of translated texts (Sapiro, 2008; 2010; 2015a). At this pole of small-scale circulation, while translations can be a mode of accumulation of symbolic capital for a publishing house at its inception, a prestigious publisher such as Gallimard can greatly increase the symbolic capital of the authors it translates in the transnational literary field (Sapiro, 2015b). The transfer of symbolic capital can also be observed between authors and translators: while translating a writer who is already internationally consecrated enlarges the symbolic capital of a translator, a renowned translator can help attract attention to an unknown author (Casanova, 2010). And if one observes a tendency towards mimetic isomorphism in the choice of translations (Franssen and Kuipers, 2013), this imitation is neither automatic nor random, for it depends upon publication strategies and the symbolic capital of agents invested in the transference, such as publishers, translators, literary agents (Sapiro, 2015c). The concepts of field, habitus and strategy are also heuristic tools for understanding the logics at work in importation and reception processes (Bourdieu, 2002). The study of the social conditions of the circulation of cultural products requires that we link three levels of observation: on the macro level, the flow of symbolic goods and the roles of international bodies; on the meso level, the structure of national fields, and political and economic constraints; on the micro level, the strategies of agents like publishers, translators and literary agents (Sapiro, 2012c). (For an example of the importation of literary works from Eastern Europe to France during the Communist period, see Popa (2010).)

The theory of fields therefore allows us to connect a comparative approach between national fields to the study of the international circulation of models (publishing models, publishers' lists, editing practices) and of individuals (migrants, exiles, visitors), which bring about similarities between them. But it also requires us to take into account the unequal power relations between national fields (Casanova, 2004 [1999]) and the phenomenon of cultural hegemony that help us to explain the generation of mimetic strategies.

## CONCLUSION

Bourdieu's sociology of culture, founded upon a theory of the economy of symbolic exchanges, the habitus and the autonomization of fields, has led to a vast research programme concerned with cultural practices and fields of cultural production. It is a comparative approach that prevails in the study of cultural practices, involving comparison of the distribution of cultural practices between social groups, and international comparisons of factors of differentiation in the social space. Research on the fields of cultural production has evolved from the study of their specific mode of functioning and their relations with the political, economic and religious fields, on a national level (involving relations of dependence, constraint or autonomy), to the study of transnational fields and of the inter-cultural circulation of artworks, as well as analysis of their reception in specific contexts. However, comparative research on fields of cultural production has concentrated on 19th-century Europe (Charle, 2015 [1996]; Thiesse, 1998), while surveys about cultural practices have taken little interest in their international circulation. These gaps constitute paths for future research projects. Additionally, new research objects such as cultural festivals offer the opportunity to decompartmentalize studies of fields and studies of cultural practices, on the condition that we investigate these new forms of cultural mediation not only through the prism of the profile and modes of cultural consumption of the publics who attend such events, but also through that of the production of value and the role that these forms of mediation play in mechanisms of consecration (Sapiro, Picaud, Pacouret, Seiler, 2015). In this way, the original Bourdieusian programme can be at once renewed, extended and replenished.

Translated by Jasmine Van Deventer and Gisèle Sapiro. The translation was funded by Labex TEPSIS.

## NOTE

1   The Centre de Sociologie Européenne, directed by Raymond Aron, and of which Bourdieu was the co-director, and, after the break with Aron, the Centre de Sociologie de l'Éducation et de la Culture, renamed in 1997 as the Centre de Sociologie Européenne, became in 2010 the Centre Européen de Sociologie et de Science Politique (http://www.cessp.cnrs.fr/)

## REFERENCES

Baxandall, M. (1988 [1972]) *Painting and Experience in Fifteenth-Century Italy*. 2nd edn. Oxford: Oxford University Press.
Becker, G. (1993 [1964]). *Human Capital. A Theoretical and Empirical Analysis, with Special Reference to Education*. Chicago: The University of Chicago Press.
Bennett, T., Savage, M., Silva, E., Warde, A., Gayo-Cal, M. and Wright, D. (2009) *Culture, Class, Distinction*. New York: Routledge.
Boschetti, A. (1988 [1985]) *The Intellectual Enterprise: Sartre and 'Les Temps modernes'*. Trans. R. McCleary. Evanston: Northwestern University Press.
Boschetti, A. (2001) *La Poésie partout. Apollinaire, homme-époque (1898–1918)*. Paris: Seuil.
Bourdieu, P. (1966) 'Champ intellectuel et projet créateur', *Les Temps modernes*, 246: 865–906.
Bourdieu, P. (1977) 'Sur le pouvoir symbolique', *Annales. Économies, Sociétés, Civilisations*, 3: 405–41.
Bourdieu, P. (1977 [1972]) *Outline of a Theory of a Practice*. Trans. R. Nice. Cambridge, MA: Polity.
Bourdieu, P. (1984 [1979]) *Distinction: A Social Critique of the Judgement of Taste*. Trans R. Nice. Cambridge, MA: Harvard University Press.
Bourdieu, P. (1985a) 'Effet de champ et effet de corps', *Actes de la recherche en sciences sociales*, 59: 73.
Bourdieu, P. (1985b) 'Existe-t-il une littérature belge? Limites d'un champ et frontières politiques', *Études de lettres*, III: 3–6.
Bourdieu, P. (1985 [1971]) 'The Market of Symbolic Goods', *Poetics*, 14(1–2): 13–44.
Bourdieu, P. (1987 [1971]) 'Legitimation and Structure Interests in Weber's Sociology or Religion', in S. Whimster and S. Lash (eds), *Max Weber, Rationality and Modernity*. London: Allen and Unwin. pp. 119–36.
Bourdieu, P. (1990 [1980]) *The Logic of Practice*. Trans. R. Nice. Cambridge, MA: Polity.
Bourdieu, P. (1991a), 'Le champ littéraire', *Actes de la recherche en sciences sociales*, 89: 3–46.
Bourdieu, P. (1991b [1971]) 'Genesis and Structure of the Religious Field', *Comparative Social Research*, 13: 1–44.
Bourdieu, P. (1993a [1982]) *Language and Symbolic Power*. Ed. J. Thompson, Trans. G. Raymond. Cambridge, MA: Harvard University Press.
Bourdieu, P. (1993b) *The Field of Cultural Production*. Ed. R. Johnson. Cambridge: Polity.
Bourdieu, P. (1993c [1984]) *Sociology in Question*. Trans. R. Nice. London: Sage.
Bourdieu, P. (1996 [1992]) *The Rules of Art*. Trans. S. Emmanuel. Cambridge: Polity Press.
Bourdieu, P. (1998 [1994]), *Practical Reason. On the Theory of Action*. Trans. R. Johnson. Stanford: Stanford University Press.
Bourdieu, P. (2001) 'Bref impromptu sur Beethoven, artiste entrepreneur', *Sociétés and Représentations*, 11: 13–8.
Bourdieu, P. (2002 [1989]) 'The Social Conditions of the International Circulation of Ideas', in R. Shusterman (ed.), *Bourdieu: A Critical Reader*. Oxford and Malden, MA: Blackwell.
Bourdieu, P. (2008 [1999]) 'A Conservative Revolution in Publishing', *Translation Studies* 1(2): 123–53.

Bourdieu, P. (2013a) 'Séminaires sur le concept de champ, 1972–1975', *Actes de la recherche en sciences sociales*, 200: 4–37.

Bourdieu, P. (2013b) *Manet. Une révolution symbolique*. Paris: Seuil-Raisons d'agir.

Bourdieu, P. and Passeron, J. (1979 [1964]) *The Inheritors, French Students and their Relation to Culture*. Trans. R. Nice. Chicago and London: The University of Chicago Press.

Bourdieu, P. and Passeron, J.C. (1990 [1970]) *Reproduction in Education, Society and Culture*. Trans R. Nice. London: Sage.

Bourdieu, P., Boltanski, L., Castel R. and Chamboredon, J. (1990 [1965]) *Photography: A Middle-brow Art*. Trans. S. Whiteside. Cambridge: Polity.

Bourdieu, P., Chamboredon, J.C. and Passeron J.C. (2005 [1968]) *The Craft of Sociology*. Ed. B. Krais, Trans. R. Nice. New York: de Gruyter.

Bourdieu, P., Darbel, A. and Schnapper, D. (1990 [1966]) *The Love of Art: European Art Museums and their Public*. Trans. C. Beattie and N. Nerriman. Cambridge: Polity Press.

Casanova, P. (2004 [1999]) *The World Republic of Letters*. Trans. M.B. DeBevoise. Cambridge, MA: Harvard University Press.

Casanova, P. (2006 [1997]) *Samuel Beckett: Anatomy of a Literary Revolution*. Trans. G. Elliott. London: Verso.

Casanova, P. (2010) 'Consecration and Accumulation of Literary Capital: Translation as Unequal Exchange', in *Critical Readings in Translation Studies*. Trans. Siobhan and M. Baker. London and New York: Routledge. pp. 286–303.

Casanova, P. (2015 [2011]) *Kafka, Angry Poet*. Trans. C. Turner. Seagull Books.

Charle, C. (1990) *Naissance des 'intellectuels'*. Paris: Minuit.

Charle, C. (2015) *La Dérégulation culturelle. Essai d'histoire des cultures en Europe au XIXe siècle*. Paris: PUF.

Coulangeon, P. (2011) *Les Métamorphoses de la distinction. Inégalités culturelles dans la France d'aujourd'hui*. Paris: Grasset.

Coulangeon P. and Duval J. eds (2014), *The Routledge Companion to Bourdieu's Distinction*. London: Routledge.

DiMaggio, P. (1982) 'Cultural Capital and School Success: The Impact of Status Culture Participation on the Grades of U.S. High School Students', *American Sociological Review*, 47: 189–201.

Dragomir, L. (2007) *Une institution littéraire transnationale à l'Est: l'exemple roumain*. Paris: Belin.

Ducournau, C. (2011), 'From One Place to Another: The Transnational Mobility of Contemporary Francophone Sub-Saharan African Writers', *Yale French Studies*, 120: 49–61.

Dubois, V. (1999) *La Politique culturelle. Genèse d'une catégorie d'intervention publique*. Paris: Belin.

Durand, P. (2008) *Mallarmé*. Paris: Seuil.

Duval, J. (2006) 'L'art du réalisme. Le champ du cinéma français au début des années 2000', *Actes de la recherche en sciences sociales*, 161–2: 96–115.

Duval, J. and Mary, P. (eds) (2006) 'Cinéma et intellectuels. La production de la légitimité artistique', *Actes de la recherche en sciences sociales*, 161–2.

Even-Zohar, I. (1990) 'Polysystem Studies', *Poetics Today*, 11(1).

Franssen, T.P. and Kuipers, G. (2013) 'Coping with Uncertainty, Abundance and Strife: Decision-Making Processes of Dutch Acquisition Editors in the Global Market for Translations', *Poetics*, 41(1): 48–74.

Heilbron, J. (1999) 'Towards a Sociology of Translation Book Translations as a Cultural World-System', *European Journal of Social Theory*, 2(4): 429–44.

Holt, D.B. (1997) 'Distinction in America? Recovering Bourdieu's Theory of Tastes from his Critics', *Poetics*, 25: 93–120.

Jacquemond, R. (2008 [2003]) *Conscience of the Nation: Writers, State, and Society in Modern Egypt*. Trans. D. Tresilian. New York and Cairo: American University in Cairo.

Joch, M. and Wolf, N. (eds) (2005) *Text und Feld. Bourdieu in der literaturwissenchaftlichen Praxis*. Tubingen: Max Niemeyer Verlag.

Jurt, J. (1995) *Das literarische Feld. Das Konzept Pierre Bourdieus in Theorie und Praxis*. Darmstadt: Wissenschaftliche Buchgesellschaft.

Lahire, B. (2004) *La Culture des individus. Dissonances culturelles et distinction de soi*. Paris: La Découverte.

Lamont, M. (1992) *Money, Morals, and Manners: The Culture of the French and the American Upper-Middle Class*. Chicago: The University of Chicago Press.

Lamont, M. and Lareau, A. (1988) 'Cultural Capital: Allusions, Gaps and Glissandos in Recent Theoretical Developments', *Sociological Theory*, 6(2): 153–68.

Lévi-Strauss, C. (1969 [1949]). *The Elementary Structures of Kinship*. Boston: Beacon Press.

Lizé, W. and Roueff, O. (eds) (2010) 'Les partitions du goût musical', *Actes de la recherche en sciences sociales*, 181–182 (special issue).

Pereira, V.B. (2011) 'Experiencing Unemployment: The Role of Social and Cultural Capital in Mediating Economic Crisis', *Poetics*, 39(6): 469–90.

Peterson, R. A. and Kern, R. M. (1996) 'Changing Highbrow Taste: From Snob to Omnivore.' *American Sociological Review*, 61(5): 900-907.

Ponton, R. (1977) *Le Champ littéraire de 1865 à 1906 (recrutement des écrivains, structures des carrières et production des œuvres)*, Doctoral thesis. Paris: Université Paris V.

Popa, I. (2010) *Traduire sous contraintes. Littérature et communisme (1947–1989)*. Paris: CNRS Éditions.

Prieur, A. and Savage, M. (2013) 'Emerging Forms Of Cultural Capital', *European Societies*, 15(2): 246–67.

Rosenlund, L. (1996) 'Cultural Changes in a Norwegian Urban Community: Applying Pierre Bourdieu's Approach and Analytical Framework', *International Journal of Contemporary Sociology*, 33(2): 211–236.

Rosenlund, L. (2009) *Exploring the City with Bourdieu: Applying Pierre Bourdieu's Theories and Methods to Study the Community.* Verlag: VDM.

Sallaz, J. and Zavisca, J. (2007) 'Bourdieu in American Sociology, 1980–2004', *Annual Review of Sociology*, 33: 21–41.

Santoro, M. (2008) 'Culture As (and After) Production', *Cultural Sociology*, 2(1): 7–31.

Sapiro, G. (2003a) 'Forms of Politicization in the French Literary Field', *Theory and Society*, 32: 633–52.

Sapiro, G. (2003b) 'The Literary Field between the State and the Market', *Poetics*, 31(5–6): 441–61.

Sapiro, G. (2008) 'Translation and the Field of Publishing: A Commentary on Pierre Bourdieu's "A Conservative Revolution in Publishing" from a Translation Perspective', *Translation Studies*, 1(2): 154–67.

Sapiro, G. (2009a) « Modèles d'intervention politique des intellectuels : le cas français. » *Actes de la recherche en sciences sociales*, 176-177: 8–31.

Sapiro, G. (2009b) « L'internationalisation des champs intellectuels dans l'entre-deux-guerres : facteurs professionnels et politiques. » In: G. Sapiro (ed.) *L'Espace intellectuel en Europe, XIXe–XXIe siècles: de la formation des Etats-nations à la mondialisation*. Paris: La Découverte, 111–146.

Sapiro, G. (2010) 'Globalization and Cultural Diversity in the Book Market: The Case of Translations in the US and in France', *Poetics*, 38(4): 419–39.

Sapiro, G. (2011) *La Responsabilité de l'écrivain. Littérature, droit et morale en France (XIX<sup>e</sup>–XXI<sup>e</sup> siècle)*. Paris: Seuil.

Sapiro, G. (2012a) 'Autonomy Revisited: The Question of Mediations and its Methodological Implications', *Paragraph*, 35, http://www.euppublishing.com/doi/abs/10.3366/para.2012.0040

Sapiro, G. (2012b) 'Structural History and Crisis Analysis: The Literary Field during WWII', in P.S. Gorski (ed.), *Bourdieu and Historical Analysis*. Durham: Duke University Press.

Sapiro, G. (2012c) 'Comparaison et échanges culturels: le cas des traductions', in *Faire des sciences sociales*, vol. 2, *Comparer*. Paris: Editions de l'EHESS. pp. 193–221.

Sapiro, G. (Forthcoming [2013]) 'Field Theory from a Transnational Perspective', in T. Medvetz and J. Sallaz (eds), *Oxford Handbook of Pierre Bourdieu*. Oxford: Oxford University Press.

Sapiro, G. (2014) 'The International Career of *Distinction*', in P. Coulangeon and J. Duval (eds), *The Routledge Companion to Bourdieu's Distinction*. London: Routledge.

Sapiro, G. (2014 [1999]) *The French Writers' War, 1940–1954*. Trans. V.D. Anderson and D. Cohn. Durham: Duke University Press.

Sapiro, G. (2015a) 'The World Market of Translation in the Globalization Era: Symbolic Capital and Cultural Diversity in the Publishing Field', in L. Hanquinet and M. Savage (eds), *Routledge International Handbook of the Sociology of Art and Culture*. London: Routledge.

Sapiro, G. (2015b) 'Strategies of importation of foreign literature in France in the 20th Century: the case of Gallimard, or the making of an international publisher.' In: S. Helgesson, P. Vermeulen, *Institutions of World Literature: Writing, Translation, Markets*. London: Routledge: 143–159.

Sapiro, G. (2015c) 'Translation and Symbolic Capital in the Era of Globalization: French Literature in the United States', *Cultural Sociology*, 9(3): 320-346.

Sapiro, G., Pacouret, J. and Picaud, M. (eds) (2015) 'La culture entre rationalisation et mondialisation', *Actes de la recherche en sciences sociales*, 206–7 (special issue).

Sapiro, G., Picaud, M., Pacouret, J. and Seiler, H. (2015) 'L'amour de la littérature: le festival, nouvelle instance de production de la croyance. Le cas des Correspondances de Manosque', *Actes de la recherche en sciences sociales*, 206–7: 108–37.

Thiesse, A. (1998) *La Création des identités nationales. Europe (XVIIIe–XXe siècles)*. Paris: Seuil.

Tommek, H. and Bodgal, K. (2012) *Transformationen des literarischen Feldes in der Gegenwart. Sozialstruktur, Medien-Okonomien, Autorpositionen*. Heidelberg: Synchron.

Zolberg, V. (1990) *Constructing a Sociology of the Arts*. New York: Cambridge University Press.

# Symbolic Interactionism's Contribution to the Study of Culture

Norman K. Denzin

The study of culture has been given its most powerful expression ... in the tradition of symbolic interactionism. (Carey, 1989: 96, paraphrased)

## INTRODUCTION

In this chapter I attempt a reading of that complex contemporary theoretical formation, symbolic interactionism, and its contributions to the study of culture. Symbolic interactionism, the study of culture and American cultural studies exist within competing fields of discourse (see Reynolds and Herman-Kenney, 2003). These discourses are moving in several directions at the same time.[1] This has the effect of simultaneously creating new spaces, new possibilities and new formations for these perspectives, while closing down others. Anticipating my conclusions, I will call for a critical, interpretive, interactionist approach to the study of culture. This approach sees culture as a process, as a performance (Conquergood, 2013).

My discussion unfolds in four parts. I first make explicit the critical assumptions that define the symbolic interactionist framework. Then I turn to the media and the processes that structure the representation, production, distribution and consumption of cultural objects. I then outline a set of interpretive criteria that can be used in the study of culture. I conclude with an extended treatment of performance and the interpretation of culture within the symbolic interactionist tradition.

There is considerable appeal for a critical interactionist approach to the study of culture. This is a period of ferment and explosion. It is defined by breaks from the past, a focus on previously silenced voices, a turn to performance texts and a concern with moral discourse, with critical conversations about democracy, race, gender, class, nation, freedom and democracy. These are traditional foundational concerns within the interactionist community.

Indeed, at this time, there is a pressing demand to show how the practices of a critical, interactionist approach to cultural studies can help change the world in positive ways. It is necessary to examine new ways of making the practices of critical cultural inquiry central to the workings of a free democratic society. Further, there is a need to bring these practices more centrally into the field of interactionist inquiry. This is my agenda, to show how the discourses of cultural studies can be put to critical advantage by interactionist researchers. Some term this the eighth moment of inquiry (Denzin and Lincoln, 2000: 2, 12).[2]

## SYMBOLIC INTERACTIONISM

Symbolic interactionism is that unique American sociological and social psychological perspective that traces its roots to the early American pragmatists, James, Dewey, Peirce and Mead. It has been called the loyal opposition in American sociology, the most sociological of social psychologies. In its canonical form (Blumer, 1969), symbolic interactionism rests on the following root assumptions. First, 'human beings act toward things on the basis of the meanings that the things have for them' (Blumer, 1969: 2). Second, the meanings of things arise out of the process of social interaction. Third, meanings are modified through an interpretive process which involves self-reflective individuals symbolically interacting with one another (Blumer, 1969: 2). Fourth, human beings create the worlds of experience in which they live. Fifth, the meanings of these worlds come from interaction, and they are shaped by the self-reflections persons bring to their situations. Sixth, such self-interactions are interwoven with the social. Seventh, joint acts, their formation, dissolution, conflict and merger, constitute the fabric of everyday social life. A society consists of the joint or social acts produced by interacting individuals. Eighth, a complex interpretive process shapes the meanings things have for human beings. This process is anchored in the cultural world, in the 'circuit of culture' where meanings are defined by the mass media, including advertising, cinema and television. This process is based on the *articulation* or interconnection of several distinct and contingent processes (du Gay et al., 1997: 3).

## CIRCUITS OF CULTURE AND POLITICAL ECONOMY

In the circuits of cultural meaning, five interconnected processes – representation, identification, production, consumption and regulation – mutually influence one another (du Gay et al, 1997: 3). Cultural objects and experiences are *represented* in terms of salient cultural categories. These categories are directly connected to social and personal *identities*. These identities are attached to representations of family, race, age, gender, nationality and social class. These objects and identities are in turn located in an on-going political economy.

A political economy is a complex, interconnected system. It structures the *production*, *distribution* and *consumption* of wealth in a society. It determines the Who, What, When, Where, Why and How of wealth and power in everyday life; that is, who gets what income, at what time, in what places, for what labour, and why? This economy regulates the production, distribution and consumption of cultural objects. It does so by repeatedly forging links between cultural objects (cars, clothing, food, houses), their material representations, and the personal identities of consumers as gendered human beings (see discussion below).

## THE RESEARCHER AND THE CIRCUITS OF CULTURE

The symbolic interactionist researcher is not an objective, politically neutral observer who stands outside and above the study of these media processes and the circuits of culture. Rather, the researcher is historically and locally situated within the very processes being studied. A gendered, historical self is brought to this process. This self, as a set of shifting identities, has its own history with the situated practices that define and shape the consumption of cultural goods and commodities.

In the social sciences today there is no longer a God's eye view which guarantees absolute methodological certainty. All inquiry reflects the standpoint of the inquirer. All observation is theory-laden. There is no possibility of theory- or value-free knowledge. The days of naive realism and naive positivism are over. In their place stand critical and historical realism, and various versions of relativism. The criteria for evaluating research are now relative. This is the non-foundational position.[3] Each process within the circuit of culture becomes a nodal point for critical, interpretive consumer research. Critical researchers seek to untangle and disrupt the apparently unbreakable economic and ritual links between the production, distribution and consumption of commodities. Critical researchers are constantly intervening in the circuits of culture, exposing the ways in which these processes over-determine the meanings cultural commodities have for human beings. The moral ethnographer becomes visible in the text, disclosing, illuminating and criticizing the conditions of constraint and commodification that operate at specific points in these circuits.

Complex discursive and ideological processes shape the rituals of cultural production and consumption. Each historical period has its racially preferred gendered self. These selves are announced and validated through these circuits of representation, identification and consumption. The cultural studies scholar interrogates these formations and the circuits they forge. A single question is always asked, namely 'How do these structures undermine and distort the promises of a radically free democratic society?' Phrased differently, 'How do these processes contribute to the reproduction of systems of racial and gender domination and repression in the culture?'

## EXPERIENCE AND ITS REPRESENTATIONS

Of course it is not possible to study experience directly, so symbolic interactionists study representations of experience, interviews, stories, performances, myth, ritual and drama. These representations, as systems of discourse, are social texts, narrative, discursive constructions. Bruner (1984) clarifies this situation, making needed distinctions between three terms: reality, experience and expressions of experience. *Reality* refers to 'what is really out there' (1984: 7). *Experience* refers to 'how that reality presents itself to consciousness' (1984: 7). *Expressions* describe 'how individual experience is framed' (1984: 7). A 'life experience consists of the images, feelings, sentiments ... and meanings known to the person whose life it is ... A life as told ... is a narrative' (Bruner, 1984, 7). The meanings and forms of experience are always given in narrative representations. These representations are texts that are performed, stories told to others. Bruner is explicit on this point, representations must 'be performed to be experienced' (1984: 7).

In these ways symbolic interactionists deal with performed texts, rituals, stories told, songs sung, novels read, dramas performed. Paraphrasing Bruner (1984: 7), experience is a performance. Interactionists study how people perform meaningful experience. The politics of representation is basic to the study of experience. How a thing is represented often involves a struggle over power and meaning. While interactionists have traditionally privileged experience itself, it is now understood that no life, no experience can be lived outside of some system of representation. Indeed, there is no escaping the politics of representation (Hall, 1997).

This narrative turn suggests that symbolic interactionists are constantly constructing interpretations about the world, giving shape and meaning to what they describe. Still, all accounts, all interpretations reflect the point of view of the author. They do not carry the guarantee of truth and objectivity. For example, feminist scholars have repeatedly argued (rightly we believe) that the methods and aims of positivistic social psychology are gender-biased, that they reflect patriarchal beliefs and practices.

## THE STUDY OF CULTURE AND THE ORIGINS OF CULTURAL STUDIES

At one level, cultural studies is a name for a movement that began in the early 1970s in the academy. Cultural studies' 'myths of origin' were made in Britain, and their founding fathers were Raymond Williams, Richard Hoggart, E. P. Thompson and, subsequently, Stuart Hall (Hay, 2013). The legacies of these figures is enduring, and includes a commitment to a Marxism without guarantees, a rejection of positivism and functional social theory, and a conception of culture that is political.

The culture in cultural studies is not aesthetic, or literary, it is political, and located in the domain of the popular, or the everyday. The object of study is how culture, as a set of contested interpretive, representational practices, embraces and represents 'a particular way of life, whether of a people, period or a group' (Williams, 1976: 90). Popular, everyday cultural practices are treated as social texts. It is understood that nothing stands outside textual representation. Texts, however, involve material practices, structures, flows of power, money and knowledge.

The interpretive and critical paradigms, in their several forms, are central to this project. The field of cultural studies now has its own journals, scientific associations, conferences and faculty positions (see Hay, 2013).[4] The movement has made significant in-roads into virtually every social science and humanities discipline. The transformations in cultural studies that gained momentum in the 1990s continue into the new century. Today few look back with skepticism on the narrative cultural turn. It is now understood that writing is not an innocent practice. Men and women write culture differently. Sociologists and anthropologists continue to explore new ways of composing ethnography, and more than a few are writing fiction, drama, performance texts and ethnographic poetry.

There are those who would marginalize cultural studies, equating it with Marxist thought and chastising it for not paying adequate homage to sociology's founding fathers, including Weber and Durkheim. Others would seek a preferred, canonical, but flexible version of the project. Within this framework there are attempts to establish a set of interpretive practices fitted to specific projects.[5] Still others would ironically equate cultural studies with identity politics and critical readings of popular culture. Some would critique the formation from within, distinguishing semiotic, political economy, empiricist and material approaches to the field's subject matter. Still others challenge cultural studies to take up the problems of feminism, gender, racism, colonialism and nationality.

Popular culture is conceptualized as a site of constant negotiation, consent and resistance, as a site where identity and meaning collide. Culture is the place where persons struggle over the control, regulation and distribution of the resources that mediate identity, agency and desire (Giroux, 2000: 25). Meaning is always contextual, structural and anchored in historical processes (Hall, 1996b). Culture cannot be separated from politics, or political economy (see below), nor can cultural studies be reduced to the study of the popular. The performative practices of culture are pedagogical and ethical, they are central to the practices of cultural politics (Giroux, 2000: 158).

A performance-based cultural studies examines how people create and recreate themselves through their performative acts, through social acts that put the self in play in concrete situations (Diawara, 1996: 304). These interactional, cultural processes, in turn, embody class, gender and racial divisions and relationships. These relationships involve the exercise of power. This performance approach critiques racism, sexism and homophobia (Diawara, 1996: 305). It seeks new versions of the public sphere, black, feminist, transnational, queer hybridities, new spaces of consumption, performance and desires.

## CULTURAL CONSUMPTION

The consumption of cultural objects refers to more than the acquisition, use and disvestment of goods and services. Cultural consumption represents a site where power, ideology, gender and social class circulate and shape one another. Consumption involves the study of particular moments, negotiations, representational formats and rituals in the social life of a commodity. The consumption of cultural objects by consumers can empower, demean, disenfranchise, liberate, essentialize and stereotype. Consumers are trapped within a hegemonic marketplace. Consumers who challenge or resist these hegemonic marketing and consumption practices find themselves located in an ever-expanding postmodern market tailored to fit their individual needs. After Smythe (1994: 285), I understand that the basic task of the mass media is to 'operate itself so profitably as to ensure unrivalled respect for its economic importance in the [larger cultural and social] system' (Smythe, 1994: 285).

The prime goals of the mass media complex are four-fold, to create audiences who: (1) become consumers of the products advertised in the media; while (2) engaging in consumption practices that conform to the norms of possessive individualism endorsed by the capitalist political system; and (3) adhering to a public opinion that is supportive of the strategic polices of the state (Smythe, 1994: 285). At this level the information technologies of late capitalism function to create audiences who use the income from their own labour to buy the products that their labour produces (Smythe, 1994: 285). The primary commodity that the media produce 'is audiences' (Smythe, 1994: 268). The fourth goal of the media is clear, to do everything it can to make consumers as audience members think they are not commodities.

## INTERPRETIVE CRITERIA IN THE EIGHTH MOMENT

In what I call the eighth moment of inquiry, the criteria for evaluating critical qualitative cultural studies work are moral and ethical. The following understandings structure this process. First, this is a political, ethical and aesthetic position. It blends aesthetics, ethics and epistemologies.[6] It understands that nothing is value-free, that knowledge is power. Further, those who have power determine what is aesthetically pleasing and ethically acceptable. Thus this position erases any distinction between epistemology, aesthetics and ethics.

Second, in a feminist, communitarian sense, this aesthetic contends that ways of knowing (epistemology), are moral and ethical (Christians, 2000). These ways of knowing involve conceptions of who the human being is (ontology), including how matters of difference are socially organized. The ways in which these relationships of difference are textually represented answer to a political and epistemological aesthetic which defines what is good, true and beautiful.

All aesthetics and standards of judgment are based on particular moral standpoints. There is no objective, morally neutral standpoint. Hence, for example, an Afrocentric feminist aesthetic (and epistemology), stresses the importance of truth, knowledge and beauty. Such claims are based on a concept of storytelling, and a notion of wisdom that is experiential and shared. Wisdom so conceived, is derived from local, lived experience, and expresses lore, folktale and myth (Collins, 1991).

Third, this is a dialogical epistemology and aesthetic. It involves a give and take and on-going moral dialogue between persons. It enacts an ethic of care, and an ethic of personal and communal responsibility (Collins, 1991: 214). Politically, this aesthetic imagines how a truly democratic society might look, including one free of race prejudice and oppression. This aesthetic values beauty and artistry, movement, rhythm, colour and texture in everyday life. It celebrates difference and the sounds of many different voices. It expresses an ethic of empowerment.

Fourth, this ethic presumes a moral community that is ontologically prior to the person. This community has shared moral values, including the concepts of shared governance, neighbourliness, love, kindness and the moral good (Christians, 2000: 144–9). This ethic embodies a sacred, existential epistemology that locates persons in a noncompetitive, nonhierarchical relationship to the larger moral universe. This ethic declares that all persons deserve dignity and a sacred status in the world. It stresses the value of human life, truth-telling and nonviolence (Christians, 2000: 147).

Fifth, this aesthetic enables social criticism and engenders resistance (see below). It helps persons imagine how things could be different. It imagines new forms of human transformation and emancipation. It enacts these transformations through dialogue. If necessary, it sanctions nonviolent forms of civil disobedience (Christians, 2000: 148).

Sixth, this aesthetic understands that moral criteria are always fitted to the contingencies of concrete circumstances, assessed in terms of those local understandings that flow from a feminist, communitarian morality (Christians, 2000). This ethic calls for dialogical research rooted in the concepts of care and shared governance. How this ethic works in any specific situation cannot be given in advance.

Seventh, properly conceptualized, consumer research becomes a civic, participatory, collaborative project, a project that joins the researcher with the researched in an on-going moral dialogue. This is a form of participatory action research. It has roots in liberation theology, neo-Marxist approaches to community development, and human rights activism in Asia and elsewhere (Kemmis and McTaggart, 2000: 568). Such work is characterized by shared ownership of the research project, community-based analyzes, and an emancipatory, dialectical and transformative commitment to community action (Kemmis and McTaggart, 2000: 568, 598). This form of consumer research 'aims to help people recover, and release themselves, from the constraints embedded in the social media' (Kemmis and McTaggart, 2000: 598). This means that the researcher learns to take on the identities of consumer advocate and cultural critic. Accordingly, eighth, this ethic asks that interpretive work provide the foundations for social criticism and social action. These texts represent calls to action. As a cultural critic, the researcher speaks from an informed moral and ethical position. He or she is anchored in a specific community of moral discourse. The moral ethnographer takes sides.

## MORAL CRITICISM AND TAKING SIDES

Taking sides is a complex process (Hammersley: 2001), involving several steps. First, researchers must make their own value positions clear, including the so-called objective facts and ideological assumptions that they attach to these positions. Second, they identify and analyze the values and claims to objective knowledge which organize positions that are contrary to their own. Third, they show how these appeals to ideology and objective knowledge reflect a particular moral and historical standpoint. Fourth, they show how this standpoint disadvantages and disempowers members of a specific group.

Fifth, they next make an appeal to a participatory, feminist, communitarian ethic. This ethic may represent new conceptions of care, love, beauty and empowerment. Sixth, they then apply this ethic to the specifics of a concrete case, showing how it would and could produce social betterment. Seventh, in a call to action, researchers engage in concrete steps which will change situations in the future. They may teach consumers how to bring new value to commodities and texts that are marginalized and stigmatized by the larger culture. They will demonstrate how particular commodities or cultural objects negatively affect the lives of specific people. They indicate how particular texts directly and indirectly misrepresent persons and reproduce prejudice and stereotypes.

Eighth, in advancing this utopian project, the critical researcher seeks new standards and new tools of evaluation. For example, Karenga (1997), a theorist of the Black Arts Movement in the 1970s, argued that there were three criteria for black art. Such art, he said, must be functional, collective and committed. Functionally, this art would support and 'respond positively to the reality of a revolution' (1997: 1973). It would not be art for art's sake, rather it would be art for our sake, art for 'Sammy the shoeshine boy, T. C. the truck driver and K. P. the unwilling soldier' (Karenga 1997: 1974). Karenga told blacks that

> [W]e do not need pictures of oranges in a bowl, or trees standing innocently in the midst of a wasteland ... or fat white women smiling lewdly ... If we must paint oranges or trees, let our guerrillas be eating those oranges for strength and using those trees for cover. (1997: 1974)

According to Karenga, taken collectively, black art comes from the people, and must be returned to the people, 'in a form more beautiful and colorful than it was in real life ... art is everyday life given more form and color' (1997: 1974). Such art is committed, it is democratic, it celebrates diversity, and personal and collective freedom. It is not elitist.

## THE NARRATIVE PERFORMANCE TURN

The narrative performance turn moves in three directions at the same time. First, interactionist scholars formulate and offer various narrative versions, or stories, about how the social world operates. Second, scholars study narratives and systems of discourse, arguing that these structures give coherence and meaning to the world. A system of *discourse* is a way of representing the world. A complex set of discourses is called a *discursive formation*. The traditional gender belief system in American culture, with its focus on patriarchy and a woman's place in the home, is an instance of a discursive formation. Discursive formations are implemented through discursive practices, for example patriarchy and the traditional etiquette system. They are embedded in competing discourses. As such they are connected to struggles over power, that is, who has the power to determine which term will be used? Power produces knowledge. Regimes of truth can be said to operate when discursive systems regulate relations of power and knowledge. This leads to the performance turn.

A radical performative discourse revolves around specific acts of resistance and activism. These acts are public interventions. That is, performance is used subversively, as a strategy for awakening critical consciousness and moving persons to take human, democratic actions in the face of injustice (Madison, 2010: 1). These explicit acts of activism imply an embodied epistemology, a poetic reflexive performing body moving through space, an ethical body taking responsibility for its action.

In moving from fieldwork and inquiry to page and then to stage and performance, researchers as advocates resist speaking for the other (Spry, 2011). Rather they assist in the struggles of others, staging performance events, screening and re-presenting history, offering new versions of official history, performing counter-memories, exposing contradictions in official ideology, reflexively interrogating their own place in the performance, thereby taking ethical responsibility for the consequences of their own acts and performances (Madison, 2010: 11).

In these ways, staged ethnography, ethnodramas and performance autoethnogaphies do the work of advocacy (see Saldana, 2011). The performance is not a mirror; it is, as Madison argues, after Bertolt Brecht, the hammer that breaks the mirror, shatters the glass and builds a new reality (Madison, 2010: 12). In their performances autoethnographers incite transformations, cause trouble, act in unruly ways. They self-consciously become part of the performance itself, the instrument of change. Performance now becomes a moral, reflexive act – more than a method, an ethical act of advocacy.

Radical performances are acts of activism; that is, they are radical acts that confront root problems, not just surface manifestations of social injustice. Beneath the sources of daily injustices lies a deeper level of overriding root causes. Madison is explicit concerning these underlying causes or sources: 'troubling local human rights and social justice activism are *the machinations of neoconservatism [and neoliberalism] and a corporate global political economy that affects small stories everywhere*' (Madison, 2010: 19, emphasis in original). Radical performances are located in these small stories. Trapped in the same small and large spaces, we struggle to get free.

Acts of activism use performance as the vehicle for getting free, as the way of contesting official history and the status quo. A double reflexivity is at work. The performance text uses performativity as a method for making a slice of contested reality visible. The performance is intended to bring the audience and/or Spec-Actors into a state of critical reflexivity concerning the events under discussion. The act of witnessing (and performing) utopian performatives is itself a performative, interpretive act, somehow the world *can* be a better place. The coyote trickster leads us into this new space (Conquergood, 2013: 27). The intent is to create a counter-memory, an alternative history of the present.

Conquergood (1998: 26) and Diawara (1996) are correct. We must find a space for the study of culture that moves from textual ethnography to performative (auto) ethnography.[7] 'Performance-sensitive ways of knowing' (Conquergood, 1998, 26) contribute to an epistemological and political pluralism that challenges existing ways of knowing and representing the world. Such formations are more inclusionary and better suited for thinking about postcolonial or 'subaltern cultural practices' (Conquergood, 1998: 26). Performance approaches to knowing insist on immediacy and involvement. They consist of partial, plural, incomplete and contingent understandings, not analytic distance or detachment, the hallmarks of the textual and positivistic paradigms (Conquergood, 1998: 26).

Building on Diawara (1996: 304), this performative approach will create a multi-racial approach to the study of culture Consistent with the pragmatic, interactionist tradition, performance ethnography studies the ways in which people, 'through communicative action, create and continue to create themselves' (Diawara, 1996: 304). This performative approach puts culture into motion. It examines, narrates and performs the complex ways in which persons experience themselves within the shifting ethnoscapes of today's global world economy.

The multiple ways in which we can understand performance, include: as imitation or *mimesis*; as *poiesis* or construction; as *kinesis*, or motion, interruption, transgression (Conquergood, 1998: 31). Each performance has elements of mimesis and imitation, or dramaturgical staging. Quickly, a performer and a performance moves into a liminal space of construction, emergence, the unpredictable. Viewed as imitative, emergent, liminal struggles, and interventions, performances always have the potential of transformation. A performance is always everything at once.

A performance is an interpretive event involving actors, purposes, scripts, stories, stages and interactions (Goffman, 1959). Cultural performances are encapsulated contingent events, embedded in the flow of everyday life. I wish performance in the singular, following Kirshenblatt-Gimblett (2001), to be used 'as an organizing concept for examining phenomena that may or may not be a performance in the conventional sense of the word ... [including] museum exhibitions, tourist environments and the aesthetics of everyday life' (2001: 218). A performance text can take several forms: dramatic texts, such as a poem, or play; natural texts – transcriptions of everyday conversations; or ethnodramas – dramatic, staged and improvised readings.

Performance is an act of intervention, a method of resistance, a form of criticism, a way of revealing agency (Alexander, 2003). Performance becomes public pedagogy when it uses the aesthetic, the performative, to foreground the intersection of politics, institutional sites and embodied experience. In this way, performance is a form of agency, a way of bringing culture and the person into play.

Performances are embedded in language. That is, certain words do or accomplish things, and what they do, performatively, refers back to meanings embedded in language and culture. Schechner contends that we inhabit a world where cultures, texts and performances collide. Such collisions require a distinction between '"as" and "is"' (Schechner, 1998: 361). As fluid on-going events, performances 'mark and bend identities, remake time and adorn and reshape the body, tell stories and allow people to play with behavior that is restored, or "twice-behaved"' (Schechner, 1998: 361). The way a performance is enacted describes performative behaviour, 'how people play gender, heightening their constructed identity, performing slightly or radically different selves in different situations' (Schechner, 1998: 361).[8] This view of the performative makes it 'increasingly difficult to sustain any distinction between appearances and facts, surfaces and depths, illusions and substances. Appearances are actualities' (Schechner, 1998: 362). Performance and performativity intersect in a speaking subject, a subject with a gendered and racialized body.

Clearly performativity and performance exist in a tension with one another, in a tension between *doing*, or performing, and the *done*, the text, the performance. Performance is sensuous and contingent. Performativity 'becomes the everyday practice of *doing* what's *done*' (Pollock, 1998b: 43, emphasis in original). Performativity is '*what happens* when history/textuality sees itself in the mirror – and suddenly sees double; it is the disorienting, [the] disruptive' (Pollock, 1998b: 43). Performativity derives its power and prerogative in the breaking and remaking of the very textual frameworks that gave it meaning in the first place (Pollock, 1998b: 44). An improvisatory politics of resistance is anchored in the spaces where the doing and the done collide.

## THE CALL TO PERFORMANCE IN THE STUDY OF CULTURE

The call to performance in the study of culture concerns five questions, and each question pairs performance with another term (Conquergood, 1991: 190; 1998; Schechner, 1998: 360). Each pair is predicated on the proposition that if the world is a performance, not a text, then today we need a model of social science which is performative. This means it is necessary to rethink the relationship between: performance and cultural process; performance and ethnographic praxis; performance and hermeneutics; performance and the act of scholarly representation; performance and the politics of culture (Conquergood, 1991: 190).

All pragmatists and ethnographers who have studied Dewey would agree with the first pair, culture is a verb, a process, an on-going performance, not a noun, or a product or a static thing. Performances and their representations reside in the centre of lived experience. We cannot study experience directly. We study it through and in its performative representations. Culture, so conceived, turns performance into a site where memory, emotion, fantasy and desire interact with one another (Madison, 1998: 277). Every performance is political, a site where the performance of possibilities occurs (Madison, 1998: 277).

The second cluster brings performance and ethnographic praxis into play, highlighting the methodological implications of thinking about fieldwork as a collaborative process, or a co-performance (Conquergood, 1991: 190). The observer and the observed are co-performers in a performance event. The third pair connects performances to hermeneutics, and privileges performed experience as a way of knowing, as a method of critical inquiry, and as a mode of understanding. Hermeneutics is the work of interpretation and understanding. Knowing refers to those embodied, sensuous experiences which create the conditions for understanding. The fourth and fifth pair question the unbreakable link between hermeneutics, politics, pedagogy, ethics and scholarly representation. Conquergood (1991: 190) remains firm on this point. We should treat performances as a complementary form of research publication, an alternative method or way of interpreting and presenting the results of one's ethnographic work.

Performances deconstruct, or at least challenge, the scholarly article as the preferred form of presentation (and representation). A performance authorizes itself, not through the citation of scholarly texts, but through its ability to evoke and invoke shared emotional experience and understanding between performer and audience.

Performances become a critical site of power and politics in the fifth pair. A radical pedagogy underlies this notion of performative cultural politics. Foucault reminds us that power always elicits resistance. The performative becomes an act of doing, an act of resistance, a way of connecting the biographical, the pedagogical and the political.

The concepts of militant utopianism and educated hope are realized in the moment of resistance. This utopianism and vision of hope moves from private to public, from biographical to institutional, linking personal troubles with public issues. This utopianism tells and performs stories of resistance, compassion, justice, joy, community and love.

As pedagogical practices, performances make sites of oppression visible. In the process, they affirm an oppositional politics that reasserts the value of self-determination and mutual solidarity. This pedagogy of hope rescues radical democracy from the conservative politics of neo-liberalism. A militant utopianism offers a new language of resistance in the public and private spheres. Thus performance pedagogy energizes a radical participatory democratic vision for this century.

## BRINGING THE CULTURAL CONSUMER BACK IN

Critical consumer research in the eighth moment of inquiry will use the interpretive criteria outlined above. It will take sides. It will bring the cultural consumer back in, guiding consumers in the development of collective and individual forms of resistance to the consumption cultures of postmodernism. Through storytelling, performance texts, rich local ethnographies and ethnoscapes, researchers show consumers how to find their own cultural homes within the shifting hegemonic structures of global and local capitalism.

Scholars show persons how to fashion their own *grounded aesthetics* within the spaces of the everyday world. This grounded aesthetic is at once political and personal. It deconstructs the images, appearances and promises of happiness, the commodity aesthetics that are used to make objects attractive to the consumer. Like bricoleurs, persons use cultural commodities as symbolic resources for the sensuous, embodied construction of social and personal identity. These images, commodities and sounds are fashioned into interpretive bricolages. They are invested with particular aesthetic meanings which are 'grounded' within the everyday lives of individuals. These meanings are experienced in the arenas of home and work, and leisure.

These aesthetic practices speak to the complex interplay between resistance and consumption, between desire and pleasure. They articulate the many different ways in which consumers creatively use the resources of popular culture for personal and group empowerment. This grounded aesthetic functions both as a vehicle and as a site of resistance.

In the arena of consumption and race, for example, race scholars deconstruct negative racial images. They turn these negative images into positive representations. They invent new cultural images and slogans. In these moves a racially grounded practical aesthetic is formulated. In the sensuous enactment of this aesthetic, the consumer becomes an active player in the construction of new racial identities. This aesthetic helps persons, as active consumers, give new meanings to the structural and cultural formations that circulate through their daily lives. This aesthetic applies to each nodal point within the circuit of culture. It shows active consumers how critically and creatively to evaluate the processes which structure representation, commodification, identification, production and consumption.

## IN CONCLUSION: THE CALLING OF SYMBOLIC INTERACTIONISM

There is a pressing need for a critical theory of society and consumer behaviour which combines historical, sociological, cultural and political analysis. Symbolic interactionism provides this theory. I believe that a more radical consumer research agenda can advance this project. This theory and this project dreams of a radically democratic society where individuals 'freely determine their needs and desires' (Harms and Kellner, 1991: 65). In the eighth moment of inquiry this society comes into focus through the use of the kinds of interpretive practices outlined above.

I am convinced that critical interpretive interactional studies have a moral and political role to play today. I too am concerned with how our patterns, practices and philosophies of cultural consumption estrange us from and threaten our place in the 'natural' world. I believe we need to craft new interpretive methods of inquiry. We need to develop new ways of evaluating critical qualitative work. The problem is clear: critical inquiry work must be focused around a distinct set of moral and political goals which are connected to a clearly defined set of interpretive practices. This is the calling of symbolic interactionism.

## NOTES

1. Within interactionism, there are competing and overlapping perspectives, or idioms, ranging from theoretical traditionalists to empiricists, constructivists, humanists, neo-pragmatists, dramaturgical and grounded theorists, feminists, ethnomethodologists, existential interactionists, poststructuralists, postmodernists, and even a psychoanalytic wing.
2. Denzin and Lincoln (2011: 3) define the eight moments of qualitative inquiry, all of which operate in the present, as: the traditional (1900–1950); the modernist (1950–1970); blurred genres (1970–1986); the crisis of representation (1986–1990); postmodern or experimental (1990 to 1995); post-experimental (1995–2000); the methodologically contested present (2000–2010); and the future (2010–).
3. There are three basic positions on the issue of evaluative criteria: foundational, quasi-foundational and non-foundational. Foundationalists apply the same positivistic criteria to qualitative research as are employed in quantitative inquiry, contending that is there is nothing special about qualitative research that demands a particular set of evaluative criteria. Quasi-foundationalists contend that a set of criteria unique to qualitative research must to be developed (see Smith and Deemer, 2000). Non-foundationalists reject in advance all epistemological criteria.
4. Journals include *Cultural Studies*, *European Journal of Cultural Studies*, *International Journal of Cultural Studies*, *Cultural Studies – Critical Methodologies*, *Representations*.
5. For Grossberg (2010), these practices, or interpretive principles, involve a self-reflexive, interdisciplinary project which always detours through theory. This version of cultural studies maintains a commitment to political praxis and radical contextualization, including anti-reductionist, anti-essentialist ontologies.
6. Definitions – Aesthetics: Theories of beauty; Ethics: Theories of ought, of right; Epistemology: Theories of knowing.
7. Cultural studies, in a generic sense, represents a body of work concerned with culture and power, with politicizing theory, theorizing politics, with the political nature of knowledge production, an orientation to the texts and contexts of the object of cultural analysis, a commitment to a theory of articulation, and to the belief that theory offers a necessary explanatory framework for the object of inquiry

    In turn, the present performative, interpretive interactionist version of cultural studies focuses on four interrelated issues: the study of personal troubles, epiphanies and turning point moments in the lives of interacting individuals; the connection of these moments to the liminal, ritual structures of daily life; the intersection and articulation of racial, class and sexual oppressions with turning point experiences; and the production of critical pedagogical performance texts which critique these structures of oppression while presenting a politics of possibility that imagines how things could be different (see also Denzin, 1992: 80–1).

8  Schechner (1998: 362) observes that this is the 'performative Austin introduced and Butler and queer theorists discuss'.

## REFERENCES

Alexander, J.C. (2003) The Meanings of Social Life: A Cultural Sociology. Oxford: Oxford University Press.

Blumer, H. (1969) Symbolic Interactionism: Perspective and Method. Englewood Cliffs, NJ: Prentice-Hall.

Bruner, E.M. (1984) 'The Opening Up of Anthropology', in Edward M. Bruner (ed.), Text, Play, and Story: The Construction and Reconstruction of Self and Society. Proceedings of the 1983 annual meeting. Washington, D.C.: American Ethnological Society. pp. 1–16.

Bruner, E. M. (1986) 'Experience and Its Expressions', in V. M. Turner and E. M. Bruner (eds), The Anthropology of Experience. Urbana: University of Illinois Press. pp. 3–30.

Blumer, H. (1969) Symbolic Interactionism: Perspective and Method. Englewood Cliffs, NJ: Prentice-Hall.

Carey, J. (1989) Communication as Culture. New York: Routledge.

Christians, C. (2000) 'Ethics and Politics in Qualitative Research', in N. K. Denzin and Y. S. Lincoln (eds), Handbook of Qualitative Research, 2nd edn. Thousand Oaks, CA: Sage. pp. 133–55.

Collins, P. H. (1991) Black Feminist Thought. New York: Routledge.

Conquergood, D. (1985) 'Performing as a Moral Act: Ethical Dimensions of the Ethnography of Performance', Literature in Performance, 5(1): 1–13.

Conquergood, D. (1991) Rethinking Ethnography: Towards a Critical Cultural Politics. Communication Monographs, 58(2): 179–94.

Conquergood, D. (1992) 'Ethnography, Rhetoric and Performance', Quarterly Journal of Speech, 78: 80–97.

Conquergood, D. (1998) 'Beyond the Text: Toward a Performative Cultural Politics', in S. J. Dailey (ed.), The Future of Performance Studies: Visions and Revisions. Annandale, VA: National Communication Association. pp. 25–36.

Conquergood, D. (2002) 'Performance Studies: Interventions and Radical Research', The Drama Review, 45: 145–56.

Conquergood, D. (2005) 'Rethinking Ethnography: Towards a Critical Cultural Politics', in D. S. Madison and J. Hamera (eds), The Sage Handbook of Performance Studies. Thousand Oaks: Sage. pp. 351–65.

Conquergood, D. (2013) Dwight Conquergood: Cultural Struggles, Performance, Ethnography, Praxis, ed and with an Introduction by E. P. Johnson. Ann Arbor. University of Michigan Press.

Denzin, N.K. (1992) Symbolic Interactionism and Cultural Studies: The Politics of Interpretation. Oxford: Blackwell.

Denzin, N. K. (2003) Performance Ethnography: Critical Pedagogy and the Politics of Culture. Thousand Oaks, CA: Sage.

Denzin, N.K. and Lincoln, Y.S. (2000) 'Introduction: The Discipline and Practice of Qualitative Research', in N.K Denzin and Y.S. Lincoln (eds) Handbook of Qualitative Research, 2nd edition. Thousand Oaks: Sage. pp. 1–29.

Denzin, N. K. and Lincoln, Y. S. (eds) (2011) Handbook of Qualitative Research, 4th edn. Thousand Oaks, CA: Sage.

Diawara, M. (1996) 'Black Studies, Cultural Studies: Performative Acts', in J. Storey (ed.), What Is Cultural Studies. London: Arnold. pp. 300–6.

du Gay, P., Hall, S., James, L., Mackay, H. and Negus, K. (1997) Doing Cultural Studies: The Story of the Sony Walkman. London: Sage.

Giroux, H. (2000) Impure Acts: The Practical Politics of Cultural Studies. New York: Routledge.

Goffman, E. (1959) The Presentation of Self in Everyday Life. New York: Doubleday.

Grossberg, L. (1997a) Bringing It All back Home: Essays in Cultural Studies. Durham, NC: Duke University Press.

Grossberg, L. (1997b) Dancing In Spite of Myself: Essays on Popular Culture. Durham, NC: Duke University Press.

Grossberg, L. (2010) Cultural Studies in the Future Tense. Durham: Duke University Press.

Hall, S. (1980) 'Cultural Studies: Two Paradigms', Media, Culture & Society, 2: 57–72.

Hall, S. (1992) 'Cultural Studies and its Theoretical Legacies', in L. Grossberg, C. Nelson and P. Treichler (eds), Cultural Studies. New York: Routledge. pp. 277–94.

Hall, S. (1996a) 'Introduction', in S. Hall, D. Held, D. Hubert and K. Thompson (eds), Modernity: An Introduction to Modern Societies. Cambridge, MA: Blackwell. pp. 3–18.

Hall, S. (1996b) 'Gramsci's Relevance for the Study of Race and Ethnicity', in S. Hall, Critical Dialogues in Cultural Studies, ed by D. Morley and K-H. Chen. London: Routledge. pp. 411–40.

Hall, S. (1996c) 'What Is This "Black" in Black Popular Culture?', in S Hall, Critical Dialogues in Cultural

*Studies*, ed by D. Morley and K-H. Chen. London: Routledge. pp. 465–75.

Hall, S. (1997) Representation: cultural representations and signifying practices. London and Thousand Oaks, California: Sage.

Hammersley, M. (2001) 'On "Systematic" Reviews of Research Literatures: A 'narrative' response to Evans & Benefield', *British Educational Research Journal*, 27(5): 543–54.

Harms, J. and Kellner, D. (1991) 'Critical Theory and Advertising', *Current Perspectives in Social Theory*, 11: 41–67.

Hay, J. (2013) 'Editorial Introduction', *Communication and Critical/Cultural Studies*, 10(1): 1–9.

Karenga, M. (1997) 'Black Art: Mute Matter Given Force and Function', in H. L. Gates and N. Y. McKay (eds), *The Norton Anthology of African American Literature*. New York: W. W. Norton and Company. pp. 1973–77.

Kemmis, S. and McTaggart, R. (2000) 'Participatory Action Research', in N. K. Denzin and Y. S. Lincoln (eds) *Handbook of Qualitative Research*, 2nd edn. Thousand Oaks, CA: Sage. pp. 567–606.

Kirshenblatt-Gimblett, B. (1998) *Destination Culture: Tourism, Museums, and Heritage*. Berkeley: University of California Press.

Kirshenblatt-Gimblett, B. (2001) 'Performing Live: An Interview with Barbara Kirshenblatt-Gimblett', *Tourist Studies*, 1(1): 211–32.

Madison, D. S. (1998) 'Performances, Personal Narratives, and the Politics of Possibility', in S. J. Dailey (ed.), *The Future of Performance Studies: Visions and Revisions*. Annandale, VA: National Communication Association. pp. 276–86.

Madison, D. S. (2005) *Critical Ethnography*. Thousand Oaks, CA: Sage.

Madison, D. S. (2010) *Acts of Activism: Human Rights as Radical Performance*. Cambridge: Cambridge University Press.

Madison, D. S. (2012) *Critical Ethnography*, 2nd edn. Thousand Oaks, CA: Sage.

Madison, D. S. and Hamera, J. (2006) 'Introduction: Performance Studies at the Intersections', in D. S. Madison and J. Hamera (eds), *The Sage Handbook of Performance Studies*. Thousand Oaks, CA: Sage. pp. xi–xxv.

Pollock, D. (1998a) 'Performing Writing', in P. Phelan and J. Lane (eds), *The Ends of Performance*. New York: New York University Press. pp. 73–103.

Pollock, D. (1998b) 'A Response to Dwight Conquergood's Essay: "Beyond the Text: Towards a Performative Cultural Politics"', in S. J. Dailey (ed.), *The Future of Performance Studies: Visions and Revisions*. Annandale, VA: National Communication Association. pp. 37–46.

Reynolds, L. T. and Herman-Kenney N. J. (eds) (2003) *Handbook of Symbolic Interactionism*. Lanham, MD: Rowman Littlefield.

Saldana, J. (2011) *Ethnotheatre: Research from Page to Stage*. Walnut Creek: Left Coast Press.

Schechner, R. (1998) 'What Is Performance Studies Anyway?', in P. Phelan and J. Lane (eds), *The Ends of Performance*. New York: New York University Press. pp. 357–62.

Schechner, R. (2013) *Performance Studies: An Introduction*, 3rd edn. New York: Routledge.

Smith, J.K. and Deemer, D.K. (2000) 'The problem of criteria in the age of relativism', in N.K. Denzin and Y.S. Lincoln (eds.), Handbook of Qualitative Research, 2nd ed. Sage: Thousand Oaks, California. pp. 877–96.

Smythe, D. (1994) *Counterclockwise: Perspectives on Communication: Essays Honoring Dallas W. Smythe*, ed T. Guback. Boulder, CO: Westview Press.

Spry, T. (2011) *Body, Paper, Stage: Writing and Performing Autoethnography*. Walnut Creek, CA: Left Coast Press.

Williams, R. (1976) *Keywords*. London: Fontana.

# Cognition and Cultural Sociology: The Inside and Outside of Thought

Karen A. Cerulo

## INTRODUCTION

Cognition has long been part of the sociological conversation. But over the past 25 years, interest in the topic has intensified, with cultural sociology, in particular, taking a cognitive turn (see e.g. Cerulo 2010; DiMaggio 1997). The current approach to cognition is notable because, for the first time, sociologists are reaching across disciplinary lines and joining in dialog with cognitive anthropologists, cognitive psychologists, neuroscientists, and philosophers. As such, the contemporary sociological literature on culture and cognition resides at a dynamic intersection of several academic fields.

In this chapter, I briefly highlight the intellectual roots of culture and cognition as a field. (For more detailed accounts, see e.g. Cerulo 2002; 2006; 2010; DiMaggio 1997; Zerubavel 1997). I then describe recent changes in sociologists' approach to cognition, highlighting a turn toward embodied cognition and proposing several areas ripe for productive interdisciplinary dialog.

## THE ROOTS OF CULTURE AND COGNITION RESEARCH

Culture and cognition, as a field, can be traced to various literatures, including symbolic interactionism, social constructionism, the sociology of knowledge, sociolinguistics, and ethnomethodology. George Herbert Mead was a primary contributor here, writing of mind, its formation, and its role in the development of self. In a challenge to 'Dualism', which conceived of mind and body as separate entities, and 'Materialism', which equated the mind with the physiological properties of the brain, Mead argued for a synthesis of ideas. He was, in many ways, the first modern theorist to centralize issues of embodied cognition. Mead argued: 'objectively observable behavior finds expression within the individual, not in the sense of being in another world, a subjective world, but in the sense of being within his organism', (1962[1934]: 5). He speaks of the central nervous system, neurons and traces as integral to understanding thought. He speaks also of the senses as important to information apprehension.

At the same time, he notes that such physiological components are necessary but insufficient to a full understanding of cognition. For Mead, the brain enables thinking, but the substance of thought emerges from dynamic social interaction. Thus thought must be considered *in situ*. Cognition can only be fully understood by connecting physiological capacities to the behaviors and exchanges of those in the social groups or communities in which thinking occurs.

From our current vantage point, Mead's attention to the 'inside' and 'outside' of thought (1962[1934]: 7) may well have been his most key insight. To be sure, other important social thinkers discuss cognition. But the mind–body link initiated by Mead lost centrality in these works. Karl Mannheim (1936), for example, preferred to focus on the important link between social interaction and cognition. Manheim was especially interested in the collective mind and the building of shared knowledge. He argued that a group or community's thoughts and understandings were formed by group members' social locations, generation, and the context or situation of action. Thus for him thinking is a relational phenomenon – a product of multiple perspectives that traverse space and time. Decades later, Peter Berger and Thomas Luckmann probed the culturally constructed elements of thought. Leaning heavily on philosopher Alfred Schutz, Berger and Luckmann argued that a collective mind emerges from a group or society's 'stock of knowledge…the facts a group recognizes, the beliefs it espouses, and the routine performances, logics, and symbols by which these facts and beliefs are created and sustained' (1967: 41–46). For Berger and Luckmann, the stock of knowledge functions as a pocket dictionary of culture – one used to negotiate our mental images of the everyday world. Still other scholars began exploring the ways in which social and cultural elements organize cognition. Erving Goffman's classic *Frame Analysis* (1974) approached frames as conceptual tools derived from one's local cultural context. These frames become mechanisms that define and arrange individuals' awareness and understanding of social experience. Similarly, Eviatar Zerubavel's *Social Mindscapes* (1997) identifies and maps the interpretative procedures (e.g. lumping, splitting) and cultural tools (e.g. cognitive lenses) by which members of cultural communities organize thought and give meaning to situations.

In contrast to symbolic interactionists and social constuctionists, sociolinguists were unwilling to background the mind–body connection. Indeed, they embraced the connection explicitly, fully engaging the physicality of thought. For example, Noam Chomsky's work (1968; 1978) on transformational and generative grammar centralized the brain. Chomsky argued that brains hold a set of innate linguistic competences that channel cognition, communication, and comprehension. These competences, called 'deep structures', emerge from a universal grammar that is common to all spoken and written language forms; they constitute rules that guide how words can be combined to create grammatically correct and sensible ideas. As such, deep structures, the physiological components that build mind, are critical to human cognition. In tandem with deep structures, Chomsky considered the role of culture and environment in language and thought. These factors prove relevant in the 'performance' of language. In performance, individuals transform deep structures by re-arranging a sentence's outward form, creating more variable surface structures that coincide with cultural contexts of action and community traditions.

Aaron Cicourel's (1974) work on cognition also foregrounded the mind–body link. Language forms the cornerstone of his theory, but Cicourel also considered the role of human senses in cognition. He argued that sight, touch, gestures, and body movements often take control of the communication experience – particularly when language is unavailable; he contended that people use these interpretive avenues to develop a 'sense' of social structure – one that organizes their perceptions of social structure and guides their actions within it. For Cicourel, the mind is a product of the senses, and the senses are contingent on the body's situation.

The mind–body connection was solidified in Pierre Bourdieu's writings on 'habitus'. Bourdieu defines the habitus as a system of 'durable, transposable dispositions' that are products of a culturally situated mind–body. The habitus organizes social fields of action, and enables individuals, groups, or communities to perceive and understand their environment, and to negotiate and recreate action. In essence, the habitus allows individuals to practice culture without 'in any way being the product of obedience to rules', to be 'collectively orchestrated without being the product of the orchestrating action of a conductor' (1977: 72; see also 2000). Bourdieu's theory draws an important connection between mind and body. Bourdieu's body is not simply a vehicle of action. Rather, he views thought and action as embodied – internalized through our material physical being. In this way, the structures of the habitus are physically grounded and pre-reflexive.

## *Meanwhile … in Cognitive Science*

The 1950s saw the formal establishment of cognitive science as a discipline. Linguists, mathematicians, neurologists, philosophers, psychologists and others joined in developing theories of mind built upon complex representations and computational procedures. Noam Chomsky, George Miller, John McCarthy, Marvin Minsky, Allen Newell, and Herbert Simon are often identified as the 'fathers' of the movement. (Gardner (1985) offers a good history of the field.)

While sociologists such as Cicourel and Bourdieu were theorizing the physicality of thought, cognitive scientists argued that they were watching thought. By the 1990s, Pet-Scans, CT-Scans, fMRIs and related technologies made brain activity visible, allowing cognitive scientists to observe and track neural operations. These pictures, many argued, meant that cognitive scientists were witnessing thinking (and feeling) in action. The power of pictures made the brain and all its processes seem directly accessible. This gave cognitive scientists enormous authority in the public discourse on cognition – so much so that anthropologists, political scientists, and economists began to engage with the new science of the mind. Together, these disciplines helped solidify an intellectual turn toward cognition. Among social scientists, only sociologists clung to the sidelines of the discussion.

Then came a turning point. In his classic essay 'Culture and cognition', Paul DiMaggio urged sociologists to take a fresh look at cognitive science: 'Cognitivists have developed ingenious empirical techniques that permit strong inferences about mental structures, going far toward closing the observability gap between external and subjective aspects of culture' (1997: 266). Others joined DiMaggio in passionately pleading for interdisciplinary dialogue, with some suggesting that the sociology of cognition be aggressively re-theorized (see e.g. Bergesen 2004a; 2004b; Brubaker et al. 2004; Cerulo 1995a; 1995b; 1998; 2002; 2006; 2010; Howard and Renfrow 2003; Ignatow 2007; Massey 2002; Shepherd 2011; Wuthnow 2007). The result is an exciting line of new research that brings sociology toe-to-toe with both cognitive science and other social sciences. Sociologists are 'continuing' stories that focus solely on the brain operations; they are elaborating these processes by linking brain, body, and mind – considering thought, feeling, and action in varying cultural contexts. In this way, such works begin to explore the socioculturally embodied nature of thought.

Elsewhere, I have reviewed works that attempt to merge sociology and cognitive science with reference to processes such as framing, schematization, and cognitive styles (e.g. automatic vs. deliberate and hot vs. cold cognition (see Cerulo 2002; 2010; 2015)). Here, I entertain some new points of intellectual intersection, focusing on three specific themes: (1) habituation and attention; (2) attachment and nurturing; (3) serialization and sequencing. I choose these themes because they provide clear mind–brain–body links, allowing us to better outline an agenda for the study of embodied thought.

## CONTINUING THE STORY: HABITUATION, ATTENTION, AND DISTORTION

Cognitive scientists define habituation as a decrease in synaptic transmission; it is the likely result of repeated exposure to the same thing. When habituation occurs, neurons in the brain send out less information – i.e. fewer signals to brain synapses. As a result, chemical activity in the brain decreases and attention to stimuli wanes. In essence, we begin to 'tune out' of the external world, putting the familiar on the neural 'back burner'. (See Thompson (2009) for a useful review of neurological and psychological understandings of habituation.) In contrast, attention involves directed concentration on some particular aspect of one's environment. Our brains can be drawn to attention by novel stimuli – i.e. sudden movements or unexpected noises. These stimuli activate the brain's stem, parietal and temporal cortices. Attention can also be initiated from within – by a memory or a goal orientation. Here, the brain's frontal cortex and basal ganglia prove most active, focusing our thoughts on specific issues or elements.

These processes – habituating to the familiar and attending to the novel – are characteristics of normally functioning brains. Indeed, they can be witnessed among babies as young as six months old. For example, Hamlin, Wynn, and Bloom (2007) found that infant brains innately understand the 'physics' of their environment – i.e. what is or is not materially possible regarding the movement of people and objects. Moreover, they appear to have distinct expectations regarding such movement. Thus when infants are shown actions that contradict those expectations – for example, a toy car or airplane that appears to move *through* a solid object – they are far more attentive and less likely to habituate than they are when shown actions that meet expectations – i.e. a toy moving *around or behind* a solid object. Interestingly, a similar pattern emerged when Hamlin and colleagues examined infants' understanding of the socialness of their environment, something we typically view as culturally variable rather than innate. Morality provides a case in point. Hamlin and colleagues note that babies, again even those as young as six months old, are more attentive to people and objects that appear to violate morality norms. Thus infants exposed to puppets engaging in anti-social versus pro-social behaviors, paid more active attention to the former while habituating to the latter. This work exemplifies a line of inquiry that links attention and habituation to innate knowledge structures. (Many argue that these knowledge structures are a product of evolution and the need for species survival.) Cognitive scientists believe that human brains are wired to recognize certain patterns of action. When behaviors and images conform to these knowledge structures, our neurons are less likely to fire than in instances where such structures are challenged.

The physiology or inside elements of attention and habituation are important to understand, but physiology is only part of the story. Several sociologists are continuing this story – identifying the sociocultural aspects of these processes. The innateness or source of certain knowledge structures and neural processes is not the central focus of such works nor is it necessarily in contention. More important to sociologists are (a) the contextually based factors most likely to trigger, facilitate or constrain such neural responses, and (b) the mechanisms by which these effects, once triggered, are enacted and experienced. For example, Cerulo (1988; 1995a) uses persuasive communications to explore the connections between message design, attention and habituation. Her work identifies culturally established design formats that reside in creative spaces – what she calls 'normal designs'. She also identifies techniques of distorting the visual and auditory aspects of these typologies in ways that either heighten attention to a message or trigger habituation to it. Cerulo identifies four specific types of distortion. 'Semantic distortion' disrupts the normative meaning carried by message elements. 'Syntactic distortion' disrupts normative combinations of message elements. 'Sequential distortion' disrupts normative temporal orderings of message elements. 'Noise' involves the simultaneous distortion of semantic, syntactic or sequential message elements. Cerulo shows that semantic, syntactic and sequential distortion represent moderate disruptions; messages constructed in this way become 'eye or ear catching' and hold great potential to activate one's senses, thus heightening receivers' attention to and comprehension of a message. In contrast, normal designs represent high familiarity and predictability; such messages are likely to trigger habituation in receivers. Noise represents extreme disruption, a barrage of conflicting signals that create confusion and discomfort; when confronted with noise, receivers are likely to withdraw from the message.

Similar findings are suggested by other media scholars. Whittock (1990), for example, contends that syntactic distortion helps filmmakers create attention-getting metaphors that maximize viewers' attention to certain film scenes. Those studying television ads find that receivers' attention to and recall of such ads is heightened via the juxtapositoning of unexpected images (see e.g. Arias-Bolzmann, Chakraborty, and Mowen 2000; Leiss, Kline, and Jhally 1990). Metallinos (1988) studied viewer attention to still advertising images. He found that extreme distortion or noise (exemplified by blurred images) was associated with decreased viewer attention, comprehension and retention of material. In sum, this literature shows that responses to distortion, while neural and sensual in nature, are also culturally and contextually situated. To effectively facilitate attention or constrain habituation, communicators must be familiar not only with neural operations, but with the existing design norms that readers/viewers inhabit, the ways in which readers/viewers apprehend and experience messages, and the acceptable boundaries of design distortion. Moreover, since moderate distortion diminishes habituation and heightens attention, one must become familiar with the values at work in any message's target audience. Heightening attention to negative or offensive messages can result in receivers' rejection of a message, thus defeating communicators' goals. Knowing this, using distortion to alter neural responses must be viewed as more than a simple stimulus-response effect. Rather, habituation and attention must be explored as part of a complex puzzle – one involving what is said, how it is organized, the context in which a message is delivered, and the embodied emotions elicited by information content and structure.

Like media scholars, students of religion have also explored expectations and distortion, and their links to attention and habituation. In this regard, sociologists and cultural anthropologists examine the factors that enhance the recall and memory of religious stories and myths. Here, distortions in the form of 'domain violations' prove important. Domain violations are ideas and narratives that contradict the expectations operating in certain cultural and cognitive domains. Wuthnow (2007) observes that these violations are a typical feature of religious doctrine. Consider that most people worship a deity that greatly resembles a human being; at the same time, such gods are also assumed to be eternal and omnipresent. Similarly, many of religions' most central human figures possess supernatural abilities. These contradictory characteristics present a clear domain violation. When we reflect on Moses' power to part the ocean, the resurrection of Jesus, the Virgin Birth, Mohammed's ability to decipher the speech of a wolf, God's omnipresence, etc., all violate our expectations of bodily capacities and our understanding of how the material world works.

According to some, domain violations are what make religion so powerful. Laboratory studies suggest that domain violating stories persist because their characteristics are more memorable than concepts and images that conform to cultural expectation. Subjects habituate to the expected and familiar when presented with religious stories; in contrast, they sense and attend to elements of stories that break with expectation (see e.g. Boyer 2001; Boyer and Ramble 2001; McCabe and Peterson 1990). Wuthnow (2008) adds a different type of empirical support on this topic. During in-depth interviews, Wuthnow asked 77 respondents to report any recollections they had from prayers offered during recently attended worship services. The prayers that proved most memorable to respondents were those containing language that referenced a domain violation. But Wuthnow notes that the form of these violations was quite different from the ones established in more historic religious images. In these contemporary prayers:

> the domain violation was not a literal transgression of the known, natural world by a supernatural being who enters in tangible form to divert hurricanes, regenerate amputated limbs, or perform other magical feats. Instead, the language juxtaposed two domains – the human and the non-human – in a rather particular way. The human side in this pairing was described as a concrete person, rather than as an abstract concept or category of people, thus implying (but usually not stating) that the interviewee could identify with the person for whom prayer was offered. But, more importantly, the human side was described as fragile, weak, small, childish, vulnerable, or lacking in understanding. In contrast, the non-human or divine side was often described as strong, big, or powerful, but otherwise left rather vague. (2008: 504)

These data suggest that domain violations may be tempered by the sociocultural context in which the prayer is offered. But like the distortions found in persuasive communications, domain violations cannot be extreme; they must be tempered – unexpected yet believable with reference to the cultural norms embodied in contemporary action.

Comedy provides another venue for studying expectations and distortions, and their links to attention and habituation. Here, scholars explore how comedic 'incongruities' can avoid habituation and elevate attention. Incongruities refer to elements of a comedic message that seem out of place in relation to other message components. Incongruities are funny because they change the relationship between a culturally established sign and its referent. As Simon Weaver (2011: 265) explains (and here, note the language of embodiment): 'in the case of humour that impacts on identity in the habitus [for example], concepts of self and identity can be *pulled* from each other through the incongruity of the joke and realigned'. In this way, the joke *snaps* one to attention, forcing receivers to rethink and deliberate over the material just heard. Like distortions and domain violations, incongruities '"*stretch*" but do not "break" habitus boundaries, beliefs, and constitutive discourse' (2011: 257, my emphasis). Incongruities 'play' with normal cultural meanings and force an embodied reaction – active attention in the body and brain. The power of humor in this regard underpins Cate Watson's (2014) suggestion that humor enters the scholarly research endeavor. Watson contends that laughter and humor can provide researchers with the sort of mental jolt that could trigger innovative paradigm shifts.

In one final arena – organizational communication strategies – sociologists are teaching us much about the relationship between cultural expectations, their distortions, and attention and habituation. These scholars believe that heightened attention, as well as recall and creativity, emerge from a 'shaking-up' of communication and interaction routines. Routines can be shaken up by distorting the expectations of discourse. For example, in examining the discourse emerging from a shipyard union dispute, Ignatow (2004) studied the strategies by which movement leaders tried to influence constituents' actions. Some used metaphors that cast familiar images in incongruous ways – i.e. equating the government with murderers and butchers, etc. Ignatow argues that the use of disruptive metaphors represents purposive communication designed to capture attention, activate emotions, and sway constituents toward leaders' desired actions.

One can also shake up routines by distorting interaction rituals. In this regard, Eisenberg (1990: 139) theorizes an interactive style called 'jamming'. In the workplace, argues Eisenberg, two forms of interaction are typically studied: intimate, highly disclosive relationships and cold non-disclosive relationships. Jamming represents a third form of interaction. Jamming heightens attention among interactants by distorting or 'dramatically altering the figure-ground relationship in which personality, social role and life history provide the context for understanding a person's actions'. The process allows us to 'set aside what we know about the details of another person's personality in order to create the possibility for seemless coordination'. We attend to one another in a less historical way, much as musicians do when engaged in a spontaneous jam session. As a result, jamming represents an unconventional way to elicit mutual attention and coordinate behaviors among members of a group or organization – even when those individuals share limited consensus. The practice encourages new modes of performance and reconfigures patterns of action – something that may be more and more critical as contemporary actors move through increasingly diverse social settings. (Also see Lee (1998) and Ocasio (2012) for related work in this area.)

One final means of shaking up communication and interaction routines involves the distortion of mind–body operations. In laboratory studies, Huang and Galinsky (2011) asked individuals to produce stories that described happy memories. Some individuals were asked to do so in a state of 'mind–body dissonance' – i.e. recounting happy moments while either frowning or listening to sad music. Others were asked to create such stories in a state of 'mind–body consonance' – i.e. recounting happy moments while smiling or hearing happy music. People were more likely to attend to, engage with and remember information created in the mind–body dissonance condition. Huang and Galinsky note the importance of these findings for issues such as innovation and group performance. They argue that the 'ability to display bodily expressions that contradict mental states may be an important foundation for the capacity of humans to embrace atypical ideas' (2011: 351). Forcing ourselves to remember one emotion while being prompted to feel another creates a level of discomfort that snaps us to attention.

Distortion, domain violation, incongruency, jamming, mind–body dissonance: all are similar ideas. While the terminology differs, each approach makes the case that brain-based experiences of habituation and attention can only be fully understood by considering brain, body and mind *in situ*, attending to the structures and norms at work in the sociocultural contexts by which thought is stimulated. This line of research is fruitful, and the coordination of ideas could yield important contributions.

## CONTINUING THE STORY: NURTURANCE, ATTACHMENT AND CULTURAL TRIGGERS

Within cognitive science, there is a large and well-established literature addressing the nurturing response in humans. The need to nurture is believed to be hardwired in human brains, with normally functioning brains displaying innate sensitivity to signs of suffering and need – especially those displayed by children, and in some cases, small animals. Here too, most cognitive scientists argue for an evolutionary basis to humans' propensity to protect and nurture, viewing the response as a facilitator of species survival.

Cognitive scientists also suggest certain qualifications to the nurturing response. Some external stimuli are more successful than others at triggering the reaction. Among these triggers, 'cuteness' is primary. Indeed, the nurturing response is overwhelmingly reserved for 'cute' children and animals. Cuteness is typically defined on the basis of infant-like traits, features ethologist Konrad Lorenz (1971) referred to as a 'baby schema'. Characteristics of cuteness include large eyes, round faces, small body size (particularly proportional to head size), small hands and feet, etc. Cuteness may also include playful actions – giggling, skipping, etc. In recent years, fMRI analysis allows us to see the brain activity elicited when normally functioning brains encounter cuteness. Cuteness activates the nucleus accumbens, a brain region associated with emotional responses and especially important with regard to motivation, pleasure, and addiction (Glocker et al. 2009: 9115; also see Decety 2011 and Sherman and Haidt 2011 for good reviews of this literature).

Evolution and the need for survival may indeed play a role in our propensity to nurture cute entities. But a full understanding of this phenomenon must include detailed sociocultural analysis as well. Nurturing, as a response to cuteness, is not automatic. Rather, our attention to and emphasis of cuteness exhibits cultural variability, making it a story of both inside and outside effects. Some Asian cultures, for example, seem to centralize cuteness more than other cultures (see e.g. Cho 2012; Kinsella 1995; 1997; Locher 2007; McVeigh 2000; Yano 2009). Existing studies also show that cuteness is more likely to elicit the nurturing response in females and Asians than it is in males and Caucasians (see e.g. Proverbio et al. 2011; Volk 2009; Yano 2009). And like attention and habituation, feelings of nurturance and attachment can be constrained or enhanced by varying symbolic representations of cuteness. Indeed, this evolutionary-based response can be culturally manipulated such that representations of inanimate objects or fictional entities can trigger the same feelings of nurturance and attachment as do real infants and small animals. Sociologists are critical to identifying the strategies involved in this process as well as exploring the culturally variable ways in which cuteness and nurturing are experienced.

Cartoon animators have long been sensitive to the triggering power of cute representations. Indeed Stephen J. Gould (1980) discusses historical changes in the development of 'Mickey Mouse', arguing that Disney attempted to increase the character's popularity by making the images of Mickey Mouse look more and more infant-like over time. Advertisers have applied the power of cute even more aggressively, using cute representations to link the nurturing response to active consumerism. Many companies consciously work to produce 'mascots' that mimic – indeed exaggerate – the characteristics of cuteness. These tactics help us experience the product in a very positive way. 'Cute gives consumer goods warm and cheerful personalities', argue Granot, Alejandro, and La Toya, 'After the production process has depersonalized goods, cute designs attempts to re-personalize them' (2014: 82). In executing this process, marketers do note simply rely on realistic images of babies and small animals. Rather, they transform babies, small animals – even creatures and objects that typically elicit fear or disgust – to lovable, vulnerable, cute entities in need of our protection. We attach to the objects, we embrace, even experience their vulnerability, and we welcome them into our sphere of action. In this way, companies create strong brand loyalty (Bellfield et al. 2011; Cayla 2013; Connell 2013).

Those studying the creation of commercial mascots have identified specific strategies that crystalize representations of cuteness and thus maximize the nurturing response. These strategies involve (a) suppressing realistic detail, (b) exaggerating the cues of cuteness, and often (c) juxtaposing cuteness cues with images previously defined as ugly and dangerous (one might think of this latter strategy as a form of syntactic distortion.) The history of some well-known mascots helps to illustrate these strategies. The *Gerber* baby, for example, was the product of a national contest held in 1928. Dorothy Hope Smith, the winning artist, submitted a charcoal sketch of the baby, promising a more detailed oil painting should the entry be selected. Smith's drawing won the contest, but *Gerber* declined the detailed oil painting. Instead, they retained the original sketch, making only minimal adjustments. (The image can be found at: https://www.gerber.com/why-gerber/meet-the-gerber-baby) The sketch accentuates the elements of cuteness – large eyes, rounded face, petit nose and mouth. Details that might be part of a 'real' baby face are masked by the drawing's low definition. The *Gerber* baby was introduced to the public in 1928 and the mascot was immediately embraced. Buyers responded to the baby's cuteness and, via the mascot, attached to the manufacturer. The *Gerber* baby, along with other masterful marketing techniques, kept *Gerber* well ahead of other baby food companies, and the mascot served as the official company trademark from 1931 through 2012 (Bentley 2005; Gerber.com 2014). The representational strategies itemized here mark the development of other popular mascots as well. For example, in 1965 Pillsbury introduced 'Poppin' Fresh' a boy made out of dough. Martin Nodell of Chicago's Leo Burnett advertising agency designed the original image. The medium of dough made it possible for Nodell to feature nothing but the marks of cuteness – large eyes, round body and face, and a disproportionate small body (see Figure 9.1A). The doughboy is also placed in social situations that allow his playful characteristics to shine. The cuteness profile created immediate attachments with the buying public. As a result, Poppin' Fresh has starred in over 600 commercials featuring over 50 different Pillsbury products. A Poppin' Fresh toy, created in 1972 was named 'toy of the year' and Pillsbury reports that consumers react to Poppin' Fresh in ways usually reserved for other humans; the mascot receives about 200 fan letters per week and 1500 weekly requests for signed photos (Goodsell 2011).

Other advertising campaigns have put the power of cuteness to its most demanding tests. Some marketers transform entities that typically generate fear or disgust – lizards, meerkats, human organs, etc. – into lovable images that beckon nurturing. This transformation typically entails much fine-tuning, involving a series of creative iterations. For example, *Geico* Insurance catapulted its brand to visibility and popularity by introducing the *Geico* gecko. (The image can be found at https://www.geico.com/about/commercials/#.VhKtaysT26h) The marketers began with a lizard, an animal many cognitive scientists argue elicits an evolutionary-based fear in humans (see e.g. Ohman and Mineka 2001), and transformed it into a precious company spokesperson. The transformation occurred when the designers introduced elements of cuteness (i.e. big eyes, small hands, etc.) to the animated representation of the gecko. The design process involved much trial and error. In a press interview, the creators of the gecko reported that they worked and reworked the gecko image, giving it 'bigger, more-expressive eyes, more humanlike movements, a shorter body'. When finally perfected and presented to the public, the mascot garnered both public popularity and high effectiveness ratings (Howard 2006). In the United Kingdom, *ComparetheMarket.com* followed a similar strategy. The company adopted a meercat, a typically unattractive, weasel-like predator and, by transforming its features, created the cute and

A: Poppin' Fresh Pillsbury Doughboy

B: The Myrbetriq Bladder

**Figure 9.1 'Cute' marketing mascots**

markings of cuteness (see them at http://www.sato-pharmaceutical.com/us/usa/satochan/index.html). In 2014 *Astellas* created an animated bladder to help sell its new bladder control drug Myrbetriq. In commercials, the mascot, boasting all the elements of cuteness, successfully garners the nurturing response of its female owner. *Astellas* hopes the same is true of the women in the viewing audience (see Figure 9.1B)

The manipulation of cuteness has implications that reach beyond marketing and consumption. Early research shows that perceptions of cuteness can influence certain performance levels as well. Bellfield et al. (2011) found that including cute stimuli on survey instruments significantly increases the response rates of survey subjects. Similarly, exposure to cute stimuli before the performance of certain tasks results in increased care and dexterity while performing the task (Nittono et al. 2012; Sherman, Haidt, and Coan 2009). Cuteness also plays a role in the economics of giving. When endangered species conform to the elements of cuteness, people are more likely to contribute to the species' survival (Estren 2012). In all these studies, cute representations call forth a nurturing response associated with greater care and attention to decision making and task completion.

Additional work is required before we fully understand the impact of cuteness on the propensity to nuture. While the response may be hard-wired, such reactions, and the ways in which they are experienced must be considered in their cultural context. Gender, racial and ethnic variations must be thoroughly examined, as well as the varying ways in which cuteness is visualized cross-culturally. While the basic elements of the cuteness typology appear in most cute images, some characteristics seem more important in some cultures than in others. The work in this area is sparse, but current findings beckon additional research.

lovable 'Aleksandr Orlov' as its company mascot. (See the image at http://www.comparethemarket.com/meerkat/movies/meerkats-in-hollywood/) The introduction of the mascot dramatically increased public attachment to the company as well as the company's presence in the marketplace (Patterson, Khogeer and Hodgson 2013). Indeed, Aleksandr Orlov became so popular that *ComparetheMarket.com* introduced 'Oleg', a baby meercat – with a stuffed version available for 'adoption' on the company's website. Drug companies have embraced this approach as well. In 1959, Sato Pharmaceutical created Sato-chan and Satoko-chan, sibling elephants with all the

## CONTINUING THE STORY: SERIAL POSITION EFFECTS, SEQUENCING, PERSPECTIVE, AND DECISION-MAKING

Cognitive scientists have studied extensively a phenomenon known as 'serial position effects'. Serial position effects address the links between the order of information in an input string and the tendency of normal brains to either recall or release the information. Research reveals both a 'primacy effect' – the inclination to remember the earliest information one receives – and a 'recency effect' – a tendency to remember the most recent information one receives.

In normally functioning brains, the primacy effect seems most powerful, with people recalling 70% of the stimuli to which they are exposed. Some speculate that the brain has time to 'rehearse' early information, giving such material the best chance of being stored in one's long-term memory. When exposed to information, subjects also recall about 60% of the exit material. Many argue that these items are still in the working or short-term memory, making them easier to recall. Despite the fact that more brain areas are activated in processing information in the middle of an input string (as revealed by fMRI), people are less likely to recall middle data than they are data at the beginning or end of informational strings (see e.g. Baddeley and Warrington 1970; Fischler, Rundus, and Atkinson 1970; Howard and Kahana 2001; Murdock 1962; Troyer 2011; Zhang et al. 2003).

The neural operations involved in processing serialized information are important and well documented – but there is more to this story. Cognitive science has outlined the 'inside' dimensions of primacy and recency effects – but what are the 'outside' dimensions? Here several sociologists have been working to identify the sociocultural aspects that enable or constrain primacy and recency effects. By focusing on conventions surrounding the sequencing of information, as well as informational contexts and themes, cultural sociologists have been able to isolate elements that can both influence sequence selection and maximize or minimize primacy and recency effects. Others in the field are also bringing the body into this discussion, theorizing the physicality of informational sequence processing (Ignatow 2007). If we attend to the various pieces of this dialogue – brain, body and mind – we emerge with a more inclusive picture of information processing.

Cerulo has explored this issue with regard to media messages – particularly those designed to elicit moral judgments. Her work on media coverage of violence initiated this line of study. Cerulo (1998; 2000) identified four informational sequences by which storytellers routinely present accounts of violence: victim sequences, performer sequences, contextual sequences, and doublecasting sequences. She found that these message sequences were systematically chosen by those crafting accounts of violence, with their choices linked to storytellers' perceptions of audience morality. Storytellers favored victim sequences for accounts of heinous violence, performer sequences for accounts of justifiable violence, and contextual or doublecasting formats for accounts of ambiguous violence. Entry points were especially important in defining the senders' intended meaning. But did storytellers' sequence choices resonate with audience assessments of violence? Not always. Cerulo's research showed that sequencing's effect on audience reception varied according to the degree of consensus surrounding the 'rightness' or 'wrongness' of acts. While sequencing greatly influenced evaluations of acts about which there was low moral consensus (especially the informational entry point to the sequence), it had little impact on the evaluation of acts about which there was high moral consensus. King (2014) found a similar pattern in analyzing sympathy toward variably raced protagonists in film, and Prince (2006) noted the pattern in people's evaluations of violence in religious films. In their analysis of media accounts of school shootings, Muschert and Janssen (2012) show something more. Their work indicates that the sequencing of violent accounts systematically varies over the 'life' of a story. When reporting school shootings, storytellers initially choose sequences that attribute clear blame to the shooters. But over time journalists tend to highlight contextual elements of the shooting, thereby humanizing the shooter and taking the spotlight off the shooter's criminal actions. Muschert and Janssen conclude that 'school shootings may ultimately be remembered as horrible events, but the youthful nature of the offenders and other contexts of the events will tend to mitigate the shooters' moral culpability' (2012: 181; see also Schildkraut 2012).

The effects of informational sequencing are not confined to issues of violence. Sequences appear important to other moral judgments as well. Cerulo and Ruane (2014) analyzed 183 celebrity apologies offered between October 2000 and October 2012. They studied elements of the apology itself as well as public reaction to the apology. The researchers found that *how* one organizes a plea for pardon – e.g. the sequencing of apology elements – is as important to forgiveness as *what* one says. The most successful apologies were those that began with a focus on the victim or wounded party and ended with either an additional focus on the victim, an expression of sorrow, or a promise of corrective action. This finding held true even when the researchers controlled for the socio-demographics of the offender, the victim, and the characteristics of the offense. In analyzing the findings, Cerulo and Ruane argue that what one says first in a public plea for forgiveness 'primes' those hearing or seeing the apology; first words trigger different associative pathways in the brain and activate different cultural scripts of atonement. (Priming is a process by which a word, image or action triggers a certain line of thinking or activates a memory (see e.g. Abelson

1976)). Apology exit points must 'fulfill' audience expectations; they must deliver the correct conclusions to the atonement scripts invoked by one's first words. Failing to do so appears to damage one's effectiveness. For example, apologies initiated with reference to victims prioritize the 'object' of the offense and the negative impact of the offender's sin. That focus triggers central cultural scripts of compassion and sympathy. When someone has been wronged – perhaps someone similar to those reading, hearing, or viewing the statement – the audience will care little about the elements surrounding the offense, its context, or the characteristics of the offender. Sympathy desires commensuration not explanation. Thus those who enter an apology via the victim will be primed for clear statements of restitution or atonement; they will expect this as the apology's logical conclusion. If one's plea ends with a different reference point, one's message will not resonate with audiences and forgiveness may be difficult to achieve. In such situations, the mind was primed for a script of atonement – but that script was never completed.

The study of sequencing allows us to consider not only neural activity and cultural convention, but the role of the body in grounding interpretation. This is because one's point of entry into a discourse or narrative establishes perspective. Entry points place us in the action. Maurice Merleau-Ponty (1962: 68) referred to this as the 'point-horizon structure'. Readers and viewers come to inhabit the entry point, grasping all other elements of a story from that position. Whether one is processing verbal, visual or aural material, informational entry points establish an embodied point of view. A number of studies illustrate the links between entry points, perspective, and assessment. In researching crime narratives, researchers show that narrative entry points provide a perspective on offenders' guilt or innocence (Hirschfield and Simon 2010), and entry points influence audience assessments of crime spaces and the likelihood that their neighborhood might be an active site of crime (Wallace 2008). In related work, research shows that narrative entry points can trigger either legitimation or delegitimation schemas in response to acts of terrorism (Robinson 2008); entry points can trigger emotional codes that encourage audience members to feel in certain ways as they reflect on acts of terrorism (Loseke 2009). Narrative entry points can mediate children's moral reasoning about the rightness or wrongness of certain acts (Jones 2008; 2012; Krcmar and Vieira 2005; Vieira and Krcmar 2011). Entry points prove influential in the socioeconomic realm as well. Richardson (2009) shows that variable entry points can make the difference in pro-labor versus pro-management evaluations of labor strikes.

Ignatow (2007) underscores the physicality surrounding narrative entry points and their impact on both cognitive assessments and emotional responses. He contends that processing informational sequences exemplifies 'embodied cognition' – thought that is guided by aspects of the body. For example, in reflecting on the impact of victim entry sequences in stories of violence, Ignatow argues that these mental representations gain their impact because they are stored in the long-term memory, not simply as an 'amodal schema or feature list' but as simplified patterns of 'neural associations gleaned from firsthand or vicarious perceptual and sensory experiences'. We sympathize with the victim because the sequential structure involved in the storytelling 'stimulates a subset of emotional, bodily and cognitive states, and perhaps even cognitive memories, of personal or vicarious experiences of victimhood' (2007: 126; see also Ignatow 2009; 2014).

The embodied nature of thought can be clearly witnessed in research on video game experiences. As technology advances, video game designers are able to make game experiences seem more and more realistic. Such realism creates physical perspective and increases players' sense of 'presence' – i.e. their sense of involvement and immersion in the game environment. When present in a video game, players are not simply imagining situations or reacting to descriptions of places and actions. Rather, players feel they are physically inside the game world, co-present with the world's objects and actors, and sensorily aware of embodied others (Tamborini and Bowman 2009). (This idea, of thought emerging from bodies situated in interactive settings, fits well with Shepherd's (2014) idea of a process model of thought.) Realism and presence give gamers a point-horizon on game behaviors and that perspective both facilitates embodied cognition and influences performance and emotional responses. Knowing this, it is not surprising to learn that feelings of increased presence among violent video game players are associated with greater feelings of aggression and increases in aggressive responses (see e.g. Ivory and Kalyanaraman 2007; Krcmar, Farrar, and McGloin 2011; Nowak, Krcmar, and Farrar 2008; Persky and Blascovich 2008).

Sequencing and the creation of perspective – these strategies situate thought in space and move us through unfolding events. As such, these strategies necessarily acknowledge the physicality of thought. Work in this area offers an exciting site for future research on the sociocultural side of embodied cognition.

## EMBODIMENT IS THE WORD

In this chapter, I have focused on three sets of cognitive processes: habituation and attention, the nurturing response, and serial position effects. I have summarized cognitive scientists' descriptions of the 'inside' of these processes – the neural activity at work when these processes ensue. I have also described sociological research on the 'outside' of these processes – the strategies (i.e. distortion, domain violation, incongruence, cuteness representation, sequencing, perspective, presence, etc.) by which neural activity can be triggered, facilitated, or constrained. The processes discussed in this chapter enhance the opportunity for interdisciplinary dialog; they present exciting empirical opportunities to further explore the ways in which brains, bodies, representations, and social contexts simultaneously contribute to thought and the behaviors that may flow from it. The areas I explore here are not unique in this sense. Similar opportunities exist in the study of dual process models of thought, priming, memory, and recall, etc. What should be clear from my review of the literature is the fact that scholars across a wide variety of disciplines are focusing on similar problems and puzzles. The terminology may differ, as does the attention ratio to the inside and outside facets of thought. Yet, the similarities of these inquiries beckon a more effervescent dialog.

How can we facilitate better interdisciplinary discussion? One possibility rests in our point of departure. There is much to suggest that embodiment represents a fruitful starting point. At present, there appears to be enormous interdisciplinary convergence on the embodiment of thought. Linguists such as Lakoff, Johnson, or Núñez argue that the body's experience feeds the brain, and thus, the cognitive structures we use to think – metaphor being a case in point (see e.g. Lakoff and Johnson 1999). The philosopher Andy Clark (1997; 2008) explores the 'doing' of thought and the key role of the body therein. Biologist Francisco Varela along with philosopher Evan Thompson and psychologist Eleanor Rosch (1991) apply a phenomenological perspective to thought, considering cognition as a product of the body's engagement with the environment. Anthropologist Maurice Bloch (2012) follows a similar path, emphasizing the circularity of inside and outside thought. Physicist David Bohm (1994) proposed an approach to thought involving feelings, sense, body, and sociality. Robotics engineer Rodney Brooks (1990) considers the body's sensory-motor coupling as the basis of thought. Such moments of convergence can be important.

Sociologists are, unfortunately, the last to this particular interdisciplinary party. But, increasingly, sociologists of culture are beginning to theorize the issue. Bergesen (2004a) began this trend, arguing that sociologists should acknowledge a set of pre-existing neural capacities that lead to various thought products once coming into contact with the sociocultural environment. Two years later, Cerulo (2006) explored the ways in which an inside neural process (graded membership) could influence the way we apprehend the world around us, especially as it relates to constructing cultural evaluative mechanisms. In recent years, the theorizing of embodied cognition has become even more aggressive and exciting. Some offer embodied cognition 'readings' of existing works and suggest new ways of incorporating the perspective into empirical inquiry (Ignatow 2007). Others suggest procedural theories of embodied culture and cognition (Lizardo 2012; also see 2007). And still others explore the 'fast and "hot" cognitive-affective complexes that play a key role in everyday decisions' (Vaisey and Lizardo 2010; 1600). Moreover, sociologists are now actively dialoging about a new sociology of culture and cognition – one that considers different ways to study brain, body, and mind in tandem (Cerulo 2014; Danna 2014; Ignatow 2014; Lizardo 2014; Pitts-Taylor 2014; Shepherd 2014).

As we start down this path, I offer some seemingly odd advice: think small. This is because each discipline has elements with which it cannot part – even if those elements are abhorrent to those working in other fields. Sociologists, for example, will always maintain some elements of constructionism in their cannon and will likely never embrace cognitive scientists' propensity to reduce all neural reactions to evolution and species survival. Cognitive scientists, in turn, are not likely to stray from their evolutionary stance, nor are they likely to ever take more than a minimal interest in constructionism. Thus if we attempt to link our research by standing on our disciplinary cornerstones, our reach will always be too short. On the other hand, with sufficient effort, we could successfully identify specific issues of interest that transcend disciplinary-linked concerns. In these areas, sociologists and cognitive scientists can share a similar focus and, as Danna (2014) suggests, 'make explicit links to already established knowledge from other fields'. These are the places from which to build cross-disciplinary dialogue.

Theorizing is valuable. But empirical work is also necessary in this project. This chapter offers some areas in which empirical work might ensue. And happily, some recent projects offer other promising ideas for the measurement required for good empirical work in this area (e.g. Bail 2014;

McDonnell 2014; Mische 2014; Vaisey 2008; 2009). The pieces are in place for a new turn in the sociology of culture and cognition, and the field is ripe for growth. Flexible thinking and systematic empirical inquiry will build a comprehensive picture of the complex interaction between brain, mind, and body.

# REFERENCES

Abelson, Robert P. 1976. 'Script processing in attitude formation and decision making'. In J.S. Carroll and J.W. Payne (eds) *Cognition and Social Behavior* (pp. 33–35). Hillsdale, NJ: Erlbaum.

Arias-Bolzmann, Leopoldo, Goutam Chakraborty, and John C. Mowen. 2000. 'Effects of absurdity in advertising: The moderating role of product category attitude and the mediating role of cognitive responses'. *Journal of Advertising* 29(1): 35–49.

Baddeley, A. D. and Elizabeth K. Warrington. 1970. 'Amnesia and the distinction between long- and short-term memory'. *Journal of Verbal Learning and Verbal Behavior* 9(2): 176–189.

Bail, Christopher A. 2014. 'The cultural environment: Measuring culture with big data'. *Theory and Society* 43(3–4): 465–484.

Bellfield, John, Chloe Bimont, Jeanette Blom, Curt J. Dommeyer, Kaitlin Gardiner, Erin Mathenia, and Jenny Soto. 2011. 'The effect of a cute stimulus on personally-initiated, self-administered surveys'. *Marketing Bulletin* 22(1): 1–9.

Bentley, Amy. 2005. 'Feeding baby, teaching mother: Gerber and the evolution of infant food and feeding practices in the United States'. In A. V. Avakian and B. Haber (eds) *From Betty Crocker to Feminist Food Studies* (pp. 62–88). Amherst: University of Massachusetts Press.

Berger, Peter L. and Thomas Luckmann. 1967. *The Social Construction of Reality: A Treatise in the Sociology of Knowledge*. Garden City, NY: Anchor Books.

Bergesen, Albert, 2004a. 'Durkheim's theory of mental categories: A review of the evidence'. *Annual Review of Sociology* 30: 395–408.

Bergesen, Albert, 2004b. 'Chomsky vs. Mead'. *Sociological Theory* 22: 257–370.

Bloch, Maurice. 2012. *Anthropology and the Cognitive Challenge*. Cambridge: Cambridge University Press.

Bohm, David. 1994. *Thought as a System*. New York: Routledge.

Bourdieu, Pierre. 1977. *Outline of a Theory of Practice*. Cambridge: Cambridge University Press.

Bourdieu, Pierre. 2000. *Pascalian Meditations*. Stanford: Stanford University Press.

Boyer, Pascal. 2001. *Religion Explained: The Human Instincts that Fashion Gods, Spirits and Ancestors*. London: Vintage.

Boyer, Pascal and Charles Ramble. 2001. 'Cognitive templates for religious concepts: Cross-cultural evidence for recall of counter-intuitive representations'. *Cognitive Science* 25: 535–564.

Brooks, Rodney A. 1990. 'Elephants don't play chess'. *Robotics and Autonomous Systems* 6(1): 3–15.

Brubaker, Rogers, Mara Loveman, and Peter Stamanov. 2004. 'Ethnicity as cognition'. *Theory and Society* 33: 31–64.

Cayla, Julien. 2013. 'Brand mascots as organizational totems'. *Journal of Marketing Management* 29(1–2): 86–104.

Cerulo, Karen A. 1988. 'What's wrong with this picture?' *Communication Research* 15: 93–101.

Cerulo, Karen A. 1995a. 'Designs on the White House: TV ads, message structure, and election outcome'. *Research in Political Sociology* 7: 63–88.

Cerulo, Karen A. 1995b. *Identity Designs: The Sights and Sounds of a Nation*. The Arnold and Caroline Rose Book Series. New Brunswick, NJ: Rutgers University Press.

Cerulo, Karen A. 1998. *Deciphering Violence: The Cognitive Structure of Right and Wrong*. New York/London: Routledge

Cerulo, Karen A. 2000. 'The rest of the story: Sociocultural patterns of story elaboration'. *Poetics* 28(1): 21–45.

Cerulo, Karen A. 2002. *Culture in Mind: Toward a Sociology of Culture and Cognition*. New York: Routledge.

Cerulo, Karen A. 2006. *Never Saw It Coming*. Chicago: University of Chicago Press.

Cerulo, Karen A. 2010. 'Mining the intersections of cognitive sociology and neuroscience'. *Poetics* 38(2): 115–132.

Cerulo, Karen A. 2014. 'Continuing the story: Maximizing the intersections of cognitive science and sociology'. *Sociological Forum* 29(4): 1012–1019.

Cerulo, Karen A. 2015. 'Culture and cognition'. *Emerging Trends in Sociology*, R. Scott and S. Kosslyn (eds). Hoboken, NJ: John Wiley and Sons. http://onlinelibrary.wiley.com/doi/10.1002/9781118900772.etrds0063/abstract

Cerulo, Karen A. and Janet M. Ruane. 2014. 'Apologies of the rich and famous: Why we care and why we forgive'. *Social Psychology Quarterly* 77(2): 123–149.

Cho, Sookyung. 2012. 'Aesthetic and value judgment of neotenous objects: Cuteness as a design factor and its effects on product evaluation'. Dissertation: The University of Michigan.

Chomsky, Noam. 1968. *Language and Mind*. Boston: M.I.T./Harcourt, Brace & World.

Chomsky, Noam. 1978. *Topics in the Theory of Generative Grammar*. Boston: Mouton De Gruyter.

Cicourel, Aaron. 1974. *Cognitive Sociology: Language and Meaning in Social Interaction*. New York: Free Press.

Clark, Andrew. 1997. *Being There: Putting Mind, Body, and World Together Again*. Cambridge, MA: MIT Press.

Clark, Andrew. 2008. *Supersizing the Mind: Embodiment, Action, and Cognitive Extension*. New York: Oxford University Press.

Connell, Paul M. 2013. 'The role of baseline similarity to humans in consumer responses to anthropomorphic animal images'. *Psychology and Marketing* 30(6): 461–468.

Danna, Karen. 2014. 'The study of culture and cognition'. *Sociological Forum* 29(4).

Davidson, Denise. 2014. 'Recognition and recall of irrelevant and interruptive actions in script-based stories'. *Journal of Memory and Language* 33(6): 757–775.

Decety, Jean 2011. 'The neuroevolution of empathy'. *Annals of the New York Academy of Sciences* 1231: 35–45.

DiMaggio, Paul. 1997. 'Culture and cognition'. *Annual Review of Sociology* 23: 263–287.

Eisenberg, Eric M. 1990. 'Jamming transcendence through organizing'. *Communication Research* 17(2): 139–164.

Estren, Mark J. 2012. 'The neoteny barrier: Seeking respect for the non-cute'. *Journal of Animal Ethics* 2(1): 6–11.

Fischler, Ira, Dewey Rundus, and Richard C. Atkinson. 1970. 'Effects of overt rehearsal procedures on free recall'. *Psychonomic Science* 19(4): 249–250.

Gardner, Howard. 1985. *The Mind's New Science: A History of the Cognitive Revolution*. New York: Basic Books.

Gerber.com. 2014. 'Meet the Gerber baby'. https://www.gerber.com/our-story/meet-the-gerber-baby (accessed on August 11, 2014).

Glocker, Melanie L., Daniel D. Langleben, Kosha Ruparel, James W. Loughead, Jeffrey N. Valdez, Mark D. Griffin, Norbert Sachser, and Ruben C. Gur. 2009. 'Baby schema modulates the brain reward system in nulliparous women'. *Proceedings of the National Academy of Sciences* 106(22): 9115–9119.

Goffman, Erving. 1974. *Frame Analysis: An Essay on the Organization of Experience*. London: Harper and Row.

Goodsell, Suzy. 2011. 'The creation of Poppin' Fresh'. http://blog.generalmills.com/2011/09/the-creation-of-poppin-fresh/ (accessed August 11, 2014).

Gould, Stephen Jay. 1980. 'A biological homage to Mickey Mouse'. In *The Panda's Thumb: More Reflections in Natural History* (pp. 95–107). New York: W.W. Norton and Company.

Granot, Elad, Thomas Brashear Alejandro, and M. Russell La Toya. 2014. 'A socio-marketing analysis of the concept of cute and its consumer culture implications'. *Journal of Consumer Culture* 14(1): 66–87.

Hamlin, J. Kiley, Karen Wynn, and Paul Bloom. 2007. 'Social evaluation by preverbal infants'. *Nature* 450(7169): 557–559.

Hirschfield, Paul J. and Daniella Simon. 2010. 'Legitimating police violence: Newspaper narratives of deadly force'. *Theoretical Criminology* 14(2): 155–182.

Howard, Judith A. and Daniel G. Renfrow. 2003. 'Social cognition'. In J. Delamater (ed.) *Handbook of Social Psychology* (pp. 259–281). New York: Kluwer Academic/Plenum Publishers.

Howard, Marc W. and Michael J. Kahana. 2001. 'A distributed representation of temporal context'. *Journal of Mathematical Psychology* 46(3): 269–299.

Howard, Theresa. 2006. 'Gecko wasn't first choice for Geico'. *USA Today* (July 16). http://usatoday30.usatoday.com/money/advertising/adtrack/2006-07-16-geico_x.htm

Huang, Li and Adam D. Galinsky. 2011. 'Mind–body dissonance conflict between the senses expands the mind's horizons'. *Social Psychological and Personality Science* 2(4): 351–359.

Ignatow, Gabriel. 2004. 'Speaking together, thinking together? Exploring metaphor and cognition in a shipyard union dispute'. *Sociological Forum* 19(3): 405–433.

Ignatow, Gabriel. 2007. 'Theories of embodied knowledge: New directions for cultural and cognitive sociology?' *Journal for the Theory of Social Behaviour* 37(2): 115–135.

Ignatow, Gabriel. 2009. 'Culture and embodied cognition: Moral discourses in Internet support groups for overeaters'. *Social Forces* 88(2): 643–669.

Ignatow, Gabriel. 2014. 'Ontology and method in cognitive sociology'. *Sociological Forum* 29(4).

Ivory, James D. and Sriram Kalyanaraman. 2007. 'The effects of technological advancement and violent content in video games on players' feelings of presence, involvement, physiological arousal, and aggression'. *Journal of Communication* 57(3): 532–555.

Jones, Steve. 2008. 'Against what you did: Interpersonal distances and morality in *Decalogue 5*'. *Cinemascope* 4(11): 1–10.

Jones, Steve. 2012. 'Mindful violence? Responses to the Rambo series shifting aesthetics of aggression'. *New Review of Film and Television Studies* 10(4): 464–479.

King, Neal. 2014. 'Dead-end days: The sacrifice of displaced workers on film'. *Journal of Film and Video* 56(2): 32–44.

Kinsella, Sharon. 1995. 'Cuties in Japan.' In B. Moeran (ed.) *Women, Media and Consumption in Japan* (pp. 220–254). Honolulu: University of Hawaii Press.

Kinsella, Sharon. 1997. 'Comments on McVeigh (1996)'. *Journal of Material Culture* 2(3): 383–385.

Krcmar, Marina and Edward T. Vieira Jr. 2005. 'Imitating life, imitating television: The effects of family and television models on children's moral reasoning'. *Communication Research* 32(3): 267–294.

Krcmar, Marina, Kirstie Farrar, and Rory McGloin. 2011. 'The effects of video game realism on attention, retention and aggressive outcomes'. *Computers in Human Behavior* 27(1): 432–439.

Lakoff, George and Mark Johnson. 1999. *Philosophy in the Flesh: The Embodied Mind and Its Challenge to Western Thought*. New York: Basic Books.

Lee, Jaesub. 1998. 'Effective maintenance communication in superior-subordinate relationships'. *Western Journal of Communication (includes Communication Reports)* 62(2): 181–208.

Leiss, William, Stephen Kline, and Sut Jhally. 1990. 'Two approaches to the study of advertisements'. In W. Leiss, S. Kline, and S Jhally (eds) *Social Communication and Advertising: Person's Products and Images of Well-Being* (pp. 197–224). New York: Routledge.

Lizardo, Omar. 2007. '"Mirror neurons," collective objects and the problem of transmission: Reconsidering Stephen Turner's critique of practice theory'. *Journal for the Theory of Social Behaviour*, 37(2): 319–350.

Lizardo, Omar. 2012. 'Embodied culture as procedure: Cognitive science and the link between subjective and objective culture'. In A. Warde and D. Southerton (eds) *The Habits of Consumption. COLLeGIUM: Studies across Disciplines in the Humanities and Social Sciences*, Volume 12 (pp. 70–86). Helsinki: Helsinki Collegium of Advanced Studies.

Lizardo, Omar. 2014. 'Beyond the Comtean schema: The sociology of culture and cognition versus cognitive social science'. *Sociological Forum* 29(4).

Locher, Christine. 2007. *The Cult of Cuteness in Japanese Youth Culture*. Munich: GRIN-Verlag.

Lorenz, Konrad. 1971. *Studies in Animal and Human Behavior*. Cambridge, MA: Harvard University Press.

Loseke, Donileen R. 2009. 'Examining Emotion as Discourse: Emotion Codes and Presidential Speeches Justifying War'. *The Sociological Quarterly* 50(3): 497–524.

Mannheim, Karl. 1936. *Ideology and Utopia*. London: Routledge.

Massey, Douglas S., 2002. 'A brief history of human society: The origin and role of emotion in social life'. *American Sociological Review* 67(1): 1–29.

McCabe, Allyssa and Carole Peterson. 1990. 'What makes a narrative memorable?' *Applied Psycholinguistics* 11(1): 73–82.

McDonnell, Terence E. 2014. 'Drawing out culture: Productive methods to measure cognition and resonance'. *Theory and Society* 43(3–4): 247–274.

McVeigh, Brian J. 2000. 'How Hello Kitty commodifies the cute, cool and camp: 'Consumutopia' versus 'control' in Japan'. *Journal of Material Culture* 5(2): 225–245.

Mead, George Herbert. (1962[1934]). *Mind, Self and Society: From the Standpoint of a Social Behaviorist*, C. W. Morris (ed.). Chicago: University of Chicago Press.

Merleau-Ponty, Maurice. 1962. *Phenomenology of Perception*. Trans. Colin Smith. London: Routledge and Kegan Paul.

Metallinos, Nikos. 1988. 'Figure/ground anomalies in commercial television: A diagnostic study'. In R. A. Braden, D. G. Beauchamp, L. Miller, and D. M. Moore (eds) *About Visuals: Research, Teaching and Applications* (pp. 291–303). Troy, NY: International Visual Literacy Association.

Mische, Ann. 2014. 'Measuring futures in action: Projective grammars in the Rio+ 20 debates'. *Theory and Society* 43(3–4): 437–464.

Murdock, Bennet. 1962. 'Serial position effect of free recall'. *Journal of Experimental Psychology* 64(2): 482–488.

Muschert, Glenn W. and Leah Janssen. 2012. 'Deciphering rampage: Assigning blame to youth offenders in news coverage of school shootings'. *Studies in Media and Communications* 7(2): 181–200.

Nittono, Hiroshi, Michiko Fukushima, Akihiro Yano and Hiroki Moriya. 2012. 'The power of Kawaii: Viewing cute images promotes a careful behavior and narrows attentional focus'. *PloS one* 7(9): e46362.

Nowak, Kristine L., Marina Krcmar, and Kirstie M. Farrar. 2008. 'The causes and consequences of presence: Considering the influence of violent video games on presence and aggression'. *Presence: Teleoperators and Virtual Environments* 17(3): 256–268.

Ocasio, William. 2012. 'Situated attention, loose and tight coupling, and the garbage can model'. *Research in the Sociology of Organizations* 36: 293–317.

Ohman, Arne and Susan Mineka. 2001. 'Fears, phobias, and preparedness: Toward an evolved module of fear and fear learning'. *Psychological Review* 108(3): 483–522.

Patterson, Anthony, Yusra Khogeer, and Julia Hodgson. 2013. 'How to create an influential anthropomorphic mascot: Literary musings on marketing, make-believe, and meerkats'. *Journal of Marketing Management* 29(1–2): 69–85.

Persky, Susan and Jim Blascovich. 2008. 'Immersive virtual video game play and presence: Influences on aggressive feelings and behavior'. *Presence: Teleoperators and Virtual Environments* 17(1): 57–72.

Pitts-Taylor, Victoria. 2014. 'Cautionary notes on navigating the neurocognitive turn'. *Sociological Forum* 29(4).

Prince, Stephen. 2006. 'Beholding blood sacrifice in *The Passion of Christ*': How real is movie violence'. *Film Quarterly* 59(4): 11–22.

Proverbio, Alice Mado, Valeria De Gabriele, Mirella Manfredi, and Roberta Adorni. 2011. 'No race effect (ORE) in the automatic orienting toward baby faces: When ethnic group does not matter'. *Psychology* 2(9): 931–935.

Richardson, John G. 2009. 'Mill owners and wobblies: The event structure of the Everett Massacre of 1916'. *Social Science History* 33(3): 183–215.

Robinson, Laura. 2008. 'The moral accounting of terrorism: Competing interpretations of September 11, 2001'. *Qualitative Sociology* 31(3): 271–285.

Schildkraut, Jaclyn. 2012. 'Media and massacre: A comparative analysis of the reporting of the 2007 Virginia Tech shootings'. *Fast Capitalism* 9(1): 1–22.

Shepherd, Hana. 2011. 'The cultural context of cognition: What the implicit association test tells us about how culture works'. *Sociological Forum* 26(1): 121–143.

Shepherd, Hana. 2014. 'What a sociology of culture and cognition should look like: A process-based account of culture'. *Sociological Forum* 29(4).

Sherman, Gary D. and Jonathan Haidt. 2011. 'Cuteness and disgust: The humanizing and dehumanizing effects of emotion'. *Emotion Review* 3(3): 245–251.

Sherman, Gary D., Jonathan Haidt, and James A. Coan. 2009. 'Viewing cute images increases behavioral carefulness'. *Emotion* 9(2): 282–286.

Tamborini, Ron and Nicholas D. Bowman. 2009. 'Presence in video games'. In C. C. Bracken and P. Skalski (eds) *Immersed in Media: Telepresence in Everyday Life* (pp. 87–109). New York: Routledge.

Thompson, Richard F. 2009. 'Habituation: A history'. *Neurobiology of Learning and Memory* 92(2): 127–134.

Troyer, Angela K. 2011. 'Serial position effect'. In the *Encyclopedia of Clinical Neuropsychology* (pp. 2263–2264). New York: Springer.

Vaisey, Stephen. 2008. 'Socrates, Skinner, and Aristotle: Three ways of thinking about culture in action'. *Sociological Forum* 23(3): 603–613.

Vaisey, Stephen. 2009. 'Motivation and justification: Toward a dual-process theory of culture in action'. *American Journal of Sociology* 114: 1675–1715.

Vaisey, Stephen and Omar Lizardo. 2010. 'Can cultural worldviews influence network composition?' *Social Forces* 88(4): 1595–1618.

Varela, Francisco, Evan Thompson, and Eleanor Rosch. 1991. *The Embodied Mind: Cognitive Science and Human Experience*. Cambridge, MA: MIT Press.

Vieira, Edward T. Jr and Marina Krcmar. 2011. 'The influence of video gaming on children's moral reasoning about violence'. *Journal of Children and Media* 5(2): 113–131.

Volk, Anthony A. 2009. 'Chinese infant facial cues'. *Journal of Evolutionary Psychology* 7(3): 225–240.

Wallace, Aurora. 2008. 'Things like that don't happen here: Crime, place and real estate in the news'. *Crime, Media, Culture* 4(3): 395–409.

Watson, Cate. 2014. 'A sociologist walks into a bar (and other academic challenges): Towards a methodology of humour'. *Sociology* 48(4): 1–14.

Weaver, Simon. 2011. 'Definitions of the humorous in Chris Rock and Russell Peters fan blogs: A discussion of the problem of incongruity'. *Participations: Journal of Audience and Reception Studies* 8(2): 257–275.

Whittock, Trevor. 1990. *Metaphor and Film*. New York: Cambridge University Press.

Wuthnow, Robert. 2007. 'Cognition and religion'. *Sociology of Religion* 68(3): 341–360.

Wuthnow, Robert. 2008. 'Teach us to pray: The cognitive power of domain violations'. *Poetics* 36(5–6): 493–506.

Yano, Christine R. 2009. 'Wink on pink: Interpreting Japanese cute as it grabs the global headlines'. *The Journal of Asian Studies* 68(03): 681–688.

Zerubavel, Eviatar. 1997. *Social Mindscapes: An Invitation to Cognitive Sociology*. Cambridge, MA: Harvard University Press.

Zhang, Da Ren, Zhi Hao Li, Xiang Chuan Chen, Zhao Xin Wang, Xiao Chu Zhang, Xiao Mei Meng, Sheng He, and Xiao Ping Hu. 2003. 'Functional comparison of primacy, middle and recency retrieval in human auditory short-term memory: An event-related fMRI study'. *Cognitive Brain Research* 16(1): 91–98.

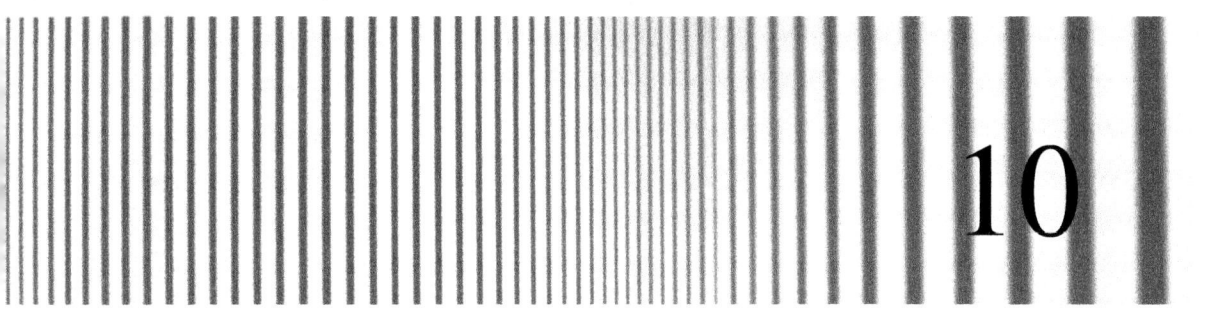

# Actor Network Theory and Its Cultural Uses

Anna-Mari Almila

## INTRODUCTION

This chapter traces the history of what has come to be known as Actor Network Theory (ANT). Beginning in Parisian intellectual circles in the late 1970s and early 1980s, ANT grew quickly in popularity, but also drew fierce criticism, and this resulted in what its creators have called various misunderstandings (see Latour, 1996 [1990]; Law, 1997). Despite their efforts to clarify their concepts and thinking, these early contributors found themselves unable to 'control' ANT when other, newer scholars took it on and developed it in novel ways. Therefore the story of ANT is not one great narrative but several small ones (Law, 2007). In this chapter, I aim to set out an account that starts with the early forms of ANT, considers its ontological and methodological principles and central concepts, and then turns to consider recent developments in terms of ANT's relevance for cultural sociology today. Yet if we are to believe ANT scholars, this task is not in fact possible to accomplish. This is for two reasons: first, ANT is not one, stable thing (which can of course be said of any school of thought), and second, ANT is not an abstract set of principles but instead is a body of empirical knowledge. In other words, ANT should be done, not explained.

## INTELLECTUAL BACKGROUND OF ANT

ANT (also sometimes called Sociology of Translation (Callon, 1980; 1986b), Co-Word Analysis (Callon et al., 1986), Actor-Network Theory (AT) (Latour, 1996 [1990]), Actant-Rhizome Ontology (Latour, 1999) and (a form of) Material Semiotics (Law, 2007)) began as a branch of Science and Technology Studies (STS) at the École Nationale Supérieure des Mines de Paris, where Michel Callon and Bruno Latour, and John Law who was visiting the institution, were the most central scholars contributing to its formulation. Callon's (1980; 1986a; 1986b) work in the 1980s was particularly influential in developing the terminology that became established in ANT, while Latour's (1987; 1993 [1991]; 1996 [1990]; 2000 [1997]) more philosophical writings have come to be associated with the sometimes controversial ontological ideas ANT is based upon. Law has been especially important for the introduction of ANT for English-speaking audiences, particularly in the UK (Munro, 2009).

The term 'actor-network' was coined by Callon (1986a), who used it in the context of a study of 'electric vehicle' (VEL) and all the political, social, economic and technological struggles involved in its design, development and eventual failure in

France in the 1970s. His focus was on the formulation of 'actor-worlds', and on whether such processes of formulation were successful or not. Some fundamental ontological principles – that the relations between actors matter more than the actors themselves, and that actors in networks are heterogeneous in nature instead of being only human – were introduced by Latour (1987; 1988 [1984]) in the context of his study of science and politics in laboratories. His fundamental point was that science is political to its roots, and that an actor who seems 'great' is only actually a spokesperson, a result of a network of actors rather than 'great' in his or her own right. This echoed Callon and Latour's (1981) earlier argument, in which they drew on Hobbes' *The Leviathan* (1978 [1651]), about a social contract upon and through which a spokesperson gains the right to speak for an entity.

Callon and Latour (1981) drew the central ANT concept of 'translation' from the philosopher Michel Serres (1974), who wrote about the borders of order and disorder, where translations happen across borders, linking, changing and betraying things. Callon (1986b) further formulated the methodological principles of agnosticism, general symmetry and free association upon which ANT research came to be established. The point of these principles is that in formulating networks, which might either become durable or not, all sorts of actors – humans, artefacts, natural elements, technology – are necessary. This was vividly demonstrated by Law (1986) in his analysis of the early modern Portuguese maritime empire, the establishment of which was dependent on actors as diverse as navigation techniques and documents, vessels suitable for long-distance sea fare, winds and sea streams, and the recruitment and drilling of humans. I shall explore the central concepts of ANT in detail below, here it is enough to say that the initial formulation of ANT happened in a very concentrated form and in a relatively short time, largely led by Callon and Latour, who have remained the most influential names within this school of thought.

In many ways, ANT follows the general lineaments of post-structuralist thought. Foucault's (1973 [1963]; 1977 [1975]; 2001 [1966]; 2002 [1969]) ideas on the production of knowledge, discourses and the significance of the body, remain influential among ANT scholars (e.g. Dugdale, 1999; Hetherington, 1999; Latour, 2005; Mol and Law, 2004). Particularly for those interested in gender (e.g. Dugdale, 1999; Mol, 1999; 2002), but also for others (e.g. Latour, 1993 [1991]; Law, 1999), Haraway's (1989; 1990; 1991) feminist critique of the creation of scientific knowledge has also been influential. The common element for these approaches is a critical approach to how (scientific) knowledge is constructed, and what its broader consequences are. Furthermore, Deleuze's (2001 [1968]) philosophy has influenced particularly Latour (1988 [1984]; 1993 [1991]; 2005) and Callon (1990; and Latour, 1981), but also later generations of ANT scholars (e.g. Murdoch, 1998; Schillmeier, 2008).

Law (2007) argues that at some point in the late 1980s or early 1990s, ANT had become a recognizable entity in social theory, and thus to a certain extent had become fossilized. This 'text-book version' of ANT is what summary chapters usually recall, and partly this is the case also here. I do not seek to give any decisive summary of ANT, but rather to show how ANT came to be, and which of its principles came to matter most, particularly in terms of cultural topics in sociology. What follows is an attempt to introduce the most frequently occurring concepts and terms, and to describe the ontological and epistemological principles upon which there is most agreement among ANT scholars, despite differences of emphasis that exist between them.

## ONTOLOGICAL FOUNDATIONS

> Actor-network is, has been, a semiotic machine for waging war on essential differences. (Law, 1999: 7)

The first and most important principle of ANT, and one which all ANT scholars seem to agree upon, is the rejection of what they call 'essentialism'. Latour (2005) sees sociology as fundamentally flawed in its study of 'the social'. He makes two main claims in this regard. First, drawing from Gabriel Tarde (2000 [1899]), he argues that 'the social' is a type of connection, instead of, contra the claim of Durkheim, 'a thing'. Second, and following from this, he argues for a *sociology of translation* instead of a sociology of 'the social', for he sees sociology's understanding of 'the social' as essentialist and therefore erroneous. What such a sociology actually means in methodological and conceptual terms, I will discuss later on. Here I will concentrate on the ontological basis of ANT. According to Latour (1996 [1990]: 370), ANT 'aims at accounting for the very essence of societies and nature. It does not wish to add social networks to social theory but to rebuild social theory out of networks. It is as much an ontology or a metaphysics, as a sociology.' In his later work (since the 1990s), Latour's debt to Tarde, who was critical of a structural understanding of 'the social', including Durkheim's, and instead understood society as an effect or evidence of interactions, is clear (Santana-Acuña, 2015). It is equally obvious why Latour is highly critical of Durkheimian sociology, which became established within the discipline instead of the alternative vision offered by Tarde.

A key 'essentialist' way of thinking that ANT scholars reject involves assumptions about the nature of actors. This rejection happens especially in terms of the presumed different kinds of characteristics of actors such as individuals and institutions. Differences between an individual and an institution are not about size, but about power relations: no actor is 'bigger' than another per se (Callon and Latour, 1981; for an extended discussion of the complex understandings of 'power' within ANT see Munro, 2009). Defined only by relations between them, actors must be understood as 'materially heterogeneous', meaning that all types of actors have a similar status in the eyes of an ANT scholar (Law, 1997). Instead of (human) subjects and (material, non-human) objects being considered separate, and the heterogeneity of the world considered as something simply to be controlled and ordered by humans, the division between 'subject' and the 'world' must be broken down, and the whole world understood as heterogeneous (Hetherington, 1999). This means treating all actors symmetrically, with no preference for, or attribution of presumed characteristics to any particular kind of actors (Callon, 1986b).

This leads us to one of the most controversial elements of ANT: the nature of agency. 'Actor' does not refer to what it is most commonly understood to mean in sociology, that is, a person with independent agential capacity in relation to social or linguistic structures or contexts (Passoth et al., 2012). ANT seeks to go beyond divisions between different kinds of actors, with a focus on 'movement' and interactions (Latour, 1999). An actor, in such a view, refers to 'something that acts or to which activity is granted by others' (Latour, 1996 [1990]: 374). Material artefacts, according to Law (1986: 237) 'do not, so to speak, stand apart as means or tools to be directed by social interests. Rather they should be seen as forming an integral part of such systems, interwoven with the social, the economic and the rest'. Therefore, ANT sees no differences between human, non-human and non-individual actors. The *intention* of the actor is far less important for ANT than is the *effect* of relations in a network of actors (Latour, 1999). The word 'actant' is often used instead of 'actor' (see e.g. Latour 1996 [1990]), for it stresses the understanding of agency that ANT subscribes to. Actants, claim Gomart and Hennion (1999: 226), 'do not have to choose between obliging and being obliged, domination and submission, individual action and causation'. All forms of activity are open for an actant. Actor – or actant – is 'created' by and through connections, and the networks of connections must be actively performed. Neither actors nor networks merely 'exist'. Performances in, by and through relations are what make networks durable and fixed (Law, 1999).

If we understand actor-networks as generally symmetrical and materially heterogeneous, we must also question certain elements which are often associated with certain kinds of actors. There are no small or large actors per se, distance between actors matters far less than the strength of their inter-connections, and no pre-existing hierarchy of actors defines actor-networks (Latour, 1996 [1990]). The connections and relations between actors are not pre-defined, but may take multiple forms. Therefore networks are 'discursively heterogeneous', meaning that communications between actors are not only verbal and human-defined. Thus materially heterogeneous actors perform discursively heterogeneous activities in constantly mutating networks, and one – the actor – cannot exist without the other – the network (Law, 1999; 2007). In Callon's (1987: 93) words, '[a]n actor-network is simultaneously an actor whose activity is networking heterogeneous elements and a network that is able to redefine and transform what it is made of'.

One ontological element of ANT particularly stressed by Latour (1987; 1988 [1984]) is that of politics. He sees, for example, the making of science as a constant political battle, a 'war' in the laboratory setting where many different kinds of actors participate in the ongoing warfare. The concept of 'ontological politics' was later taken up by Annemarie Mol (1999), who saw the construction of reality as a political battle. Since reality is not given, but multiple, and as reality is not unchanging, different realities co-exist and are performed simultaneously. These performances and realities are 'political' in the sense that they construct particular kinds of realities. Thus, for example, medical statistics, by differentiating between, say, men, women and pregnant women, *make* these categories rather than just describe pre-existing 'real things', and moreover make these categories *biological*. This in itself is a highly political act of constructing gender. It is an act of ontological politics, of meaning-making that establishes fundamental categories of difference.

## SOME CENTRAL CONCEPTS

While Latour is probably the main philosophical writer concerned with the ontology of ANT, many of the theoretical concepts associated with the group of scholars under the ANT banner come from Callon's work. I do not discuss them all here, as the concepts and their changing names that have appeared within the ANT literature would probably fill a whole chapter in themselves. Instead I concentrate on three central concepts: actor-network, translation and performativity.

Actor-network, or actor-world, was discussed in detail by Callon (1986a) in the context of the already-mentioned VEL (electric vehicle) and its 'failure' in France in the 1970s. His argument about actor-world starts with the basic statement that science and the social world change each other through a variety of actors. The essential point, already discussed, is that non-human actors also are part of actor-worlds, and that these worlds are 'equal' in the sense that all actors, of whatever type, are considered important. Actors range from electrons to societies. So what would usually have been considered as an object – the VEL – is the actor-world according to which all the relevant actors are organized. Actor-network refers to the dynamics and structure of the actor-world. Each entity, or actor, has a network it draws upon. But actors and entities are complex in themselves. Therefore actor-world is 'simplified' through encompassing necessary elements only. For example, one does not need to understand everything about road-building and planning to understand how roads are relevant for a VEL. Here the concept of 'punctualization' is relevant: it refers to a process which 'converts an entire network into a single point or node in another network' (Callon, 1990: 153). Any durable actor-world formed of entities is based on durable and simplified networks: '[a]n actor-world is a network of simplified entities which in turn are other networks' (Callon, 1986a: 32). This is what Latour (1996 [1990]) means when he argues that actants are 'networky' by character. Through punctualization, complex networks are converted into simplified points, that is, into actors/actants in other networks. This is why the actor/actant cannot exist without the network and vice versa. Actor-world and actor-network describe the same phenomenon, but draw attention to its different aspects – self-sufficiency in the case of actor-world, and structure in the case of actor-network (Callon, 1986a).

The actor-world of the VEL in fact failed to become durable, despite the enormous political, economic and technological efforts involved in its development, because the primary political actor involved in its development failed to *translate* the relationships and roles of different actors according to its desires (Callon, 1986a). Translation, argues Law (1997), is about both similarity and difference. This means that when the process of translation happens, some elements change and some do not. 'Translation builds an actor-world from entities. It attaches characteristics to them and establishes more or less stable relationships between them' (Callon, 1986a: 25–6). In order for a translation process to be successful, the actor-world must be capable of defining and enrolling actors and entities. As there is always resistance to translation, a durable actor-world only follows a successful process of isolating or excluding entities that seek to distance actors from the actor-world. To translate is to speak for others, define others, make oneself their spokesman, and thus to control others (Callon, 1986b). But for Law (1999: 8) translation is 'the process ... of making two things that are not the same, equivalent', so that they can communicate and form connections. He sees translation as a concept that does not necessarily tell us about how links between actors are established. Both Callon and Law consider translation important for the formulation of networks, but their interpretation of the concept differs significantly. While Callon's ideas have everything to do with politics within actor-worlds, for Law power relations are far less central, and he doubts the concept's capacity for actually explaining the nature of processes of network-construction. Indeed, Law (1999) suggests that translation is always *performative*, as translation is never faithful but is always also betraying what is being translated. The actor doing the translation is fundamentally involved in the processes of reality-making.

The concept of performativity was later used by Callon (2006) as a solution to what he saw as a 'problem of contradiction'. According to Law and Urry (2004), all sciences enact the world they describe. They never only describe, but are always fundamentally involved in making realities. For Callon (2006), this presents a problem about scientists' tasks and roles. He asks: 'How can a discourse be outside of the reality that it describes and simultaneously participate in the construction of that reality as an object by acting on it?' (Callon, 2006: 7) In this, he draws upon J. L. Austin's (1976 [1962]) work on performative speech acts, and particularly on Austin's consideration of whether all speech acts are performative. Performativity, the basic idea that 'any discourse acts on its object' (Callon, 2006: 8), is taken somewhat further in the ANT take on the concept. Callon (2006: 12) explains:

> When I say: 'this thread breaks', I am referring to all the actions that cause the break in the thread and that cause my statement to be true, to actually happen (or not). It is because the statement describes a singular course of action still to happen – and not a preexisting word out there – that it is performative.

Descriptions are therefore not about pre-existing realities, but about realities in-the-making. Performativity is a necessary concept to explain the tension between describing and making – otherwise the scholar's only role would be to distance and describe something that already existed.

## METHODOLOGICAL IMPLICATIONS

Is ANT a 'theory'? Many ANT scholars say emphatically no. Latour (1999: 20) states that ANT is 'a method and not a theory'. According to Law (2007), ANT is not a theory, but a description of things. Law (1999) is concerned with the loss of potential for 'tension' and 'openness' in the process of turning ANT into an explainable and rigid 'theory'. He argues that adding the affirmative term 'theory' to the inherently tension-filled phrase 'actor-network' serves to create unnecessary consistency, and indicates a loss of tension. But this tension is for him a desirable element of ANT, and therefore he resists what he sees as the fossilization of ANT when it is conceived of as a 'theory'. Callon (1999) argues that the fact that ANT is *not* a theory is precisely its strength. According to him, 'ANT is based on no stable theory of the actor; rather it assumes the *radical indeterminacy* of the actor' (Callon, 1999: 181). For Callon, this is no reason for criticism, but rather a cause for celebration of ANT's flexibility. Due to its undefined character, he argues, ANT is a more useful tool than many other, more rigidly 'theoretical' ways of making sense of the world.

One important characteristic of ANT is that it is grounded in multiple empirical case studies. In many ways, ANT cannot be *explained* but must be *done* (Cressman, 2009; Latour, 2005: 141–56; Law, 2007), and this 'doing' is not guided by clear advice on the research methods to be used. However, while ANT does not specify any particular methods of data collection and analysis, but rather sees its role as tracing connections between, or 'following', heterogeneous actors, there are some fundamental methodological principles that are common to ANT studies. Bearing some similarities to ethnomethodology, ANT places the primary importance on actors and their interpretations of reality, but, as has already been seen, it understands the actor in a manner different from the ethnomethodological viewpoint.

ANT scholars also insist on *description* rather than explanation. In Latour's (2005) view, if an explanation is needed in addition to a description of phenomena, then the description is not good enough. He also argues that if an additional theoretical category or frame is needed to explain research findings, then all actors in the network have not yet been recognized. Therefore he firmly resists such standard activities as theoretical framing of data.

Law (1997; 2007) sees ANT as a set of stories to be told, these stories each in their own way clarifying certain conceptual questions central to ANT. The starting point for an ANT study is therefore the assumption that *anything* can happen, and that there is no distinction between reality and its interpretations (Munro, 2009). Such a standpoint derives from three analytical principles.

The first methodological principle is that of *agnosticism*. This means refusing to privilege any particular point of view, or to judge or censor anything. It also involves the principle that actors both speak about and analyse their own social environments, and all the analyses should be given equal status (Callon, 1986b). In other words, it is not the scholar's job to provide an analysis, but to take seriously what actors say and do. Second, there is the principle of *general symmetry*, an idea borrowed and adopted from the sociology of scientific knowledge (Law, 2007). This principle means that when describing elements of an actor-network, all elements should be described in equal terms. According to this principle, when Callon (1986b) describes the different actors in his famous study of scallops, he uses the same terminology to talk about scientists, scallops and fishermen, all of whom he sees as symmetrical elements of an actor-network. The third principle, that of *free association*, requires that the ANT scholar does not presume boundaries between the social and the natural worlds (or the cultural, technological, semiotic or economic worlds for that matter too). As such distinctions and boundaries are effects, not causes, of networks, they are not capable of offering any analytical aid (Crawford, 2005). If agency, as Latour (1996 [1990]) argues, is simultaneously natural, social and semiotic, the researcher must explore how these come together, rather than distinguish between them.

As ANT is something to be done rather than to be explained or defined, and as ANT also offers no frameworks or firm theoretical assumptions, it also uses no set methods of data collection and analysis. Law (2007: 1) calls ANT 'a disparate family of material-semiotic tools, sensibilities and methods of analysis', but also states that since the actor-network being studied in each individual case is (or can be) different from any other actor-network, giving rigid rules about *how* exactly to follow the heterogeneous actors would make very little sense. What an ANT scholar must do is everything and anything that s/he finds suitable, in order to trace the relevant connections, while staying true to the methodological principles at the core of ANT.

## CRITIQUE

It is probably because Latour has been the one ANT scholar who far more than most of his colleagues has tried to establish ANT as a general theory concerning everything, that his work has faced sometimes rather fierce criticism. According to some critics, he has misrepresented those intellectual positions which he claims to oppose, and has dismissed whole intellectual traditions (such as Durkheimian sociology) in simplistic terms (Bloor, 1999). The scientific world, which ANT scholars studied especially in the early days of ANT, has not remained quiet either. Latour is referred to by some critics as one of the members of the 'postmodernist' French intellectual tradition, taken to task by Sokal and Bricmont (1999) for using scientific terminology for their own purposes with no proper contextualization or explanation of their use of it. Furthermore, these critics point out the incomprehensibility and lack of logic that they see in the writings of these postmodernist philosophers and social scientists, Latour included. They suspect that '[t]he goal is, no doubt, to impress and, above all, to intimidate the non-scientist reader' (Sokal and Bricmont, 1999: 3).

Latour has also been accused of, instead of abandoning or going beyond the nature/society distinction as he claims, not making clear enough or fully understanding the conceptual difference between nature and ideas about nature (Bloor, 1999). While the idea of going beyond such a divide sounds innovative, it is in fact, argues Amsterdamska (1990), a tautological method of argument that Latour applies to a variety of phenomena. Such a rhetorical method creates seemingly contradictory statements, but when the arguments are stripped to their core, they are revealed to be the same statement, just turned over and presented as contradictory. In order for this strategy to succeed, the dismissal of the conceptual difference between nature and ideas about it is absolutely necessary, for 'Latour's mode of argument succeeds *only because* he shifts deftly back and forth from the language of representation to the language of "reality"' (Amsterdamska, 1990: 498, emphasis added). Thus what Latour claims to be a radical new way of understanding science and society, is nothing more than an empty, circular argument relying on a rhetorical method.

Unsurprisingly, ANT's principle of attributing symmetrical agency to all sorts of actors has met with much criticism. For Bloor (1999), attributing symmetrical agency to something that only holds causal agency leads nowhere. The problem is that the object of scientific study, such as an electron, responds always in a similar manner under similar conditions. To attribute agency to it would be to assume that the electron performs one thing to one person and another thing to another, which it cannot do. Bloor's fierce criticism of Latour is hardly surprising, since he is one of the leading practitioners of the Strong Programme for Sociology of Scientific Knowledge (SSK), originated at the University of Edinburgh in the 1970s, whose goal was to offer a definitive historical explanation of the production of scientific knowledge, and this was one of the schools of thought that ANT scholars in late 1970s and early 1980s decidedly opposed (Zammito, 2004).

Concerning the nature of agency, it can also be argued that if actors are presumed to have no intrinsic qualities, and if the character of relationships between actors is not important, ANT offers very little explanatory power of the *types* of actions through which networks are created (Amsterdamska, 1990). As Collins and Yearley (1992) point out, ANT's principle of attributing agency to all kinds of actors depends on an 'innocent' point of view towards science. If an expert viewpoint is applied instead, such agency becomes highly questionable, because an expert knows how to manipulate such 'agency' (although never fully, of course). Therefore it remains questionable whether such agency can or should be attributed to an object, and if it is, what the benefits of such an attribution are.

There is also an epistemological-methodological concern raised by Collins and Yearley (1992). All the 'evidence' of agency of non-human actors is in reality gathered through human actions, which is hardly a symmetrical method of data collection. If we are to do symmetrical research where all actors are equal, we must have tools to study something more than our interpretations or measurements of the non-human actors. The sociological and philosophical tools used by ANT are not suitable for penetrating non-human actors and approaching their 'true' characteristics. The only thing that STS *can* talk about, based on the tools at its disposal, is human action, but ANT scholars are reluctant to discuss only that.

As ANT is ontologically political, there are political implications in its application which cannot be ignored. Amsterdamska (1990) argues that by claiming to forget all 'knowledge about knowledge', Latour makes everything highly political. Yet how authority is in fact created cannot be explained using the symmetrical tools he offers. Latour seems to offer tools that trace only the strength of the connections, instead of their character. This means:

> that it no longer matters whether the scientist's victory is assured by the use of arguments or by success in eliminating opponents physically, whether enrolment takes place by performing experiments that convince others or by fraud, whether allies are convinced that a particular course of action is of benefit or whether they are being intimidated or simply bought. (Amsterdamska, 1990: 502)

If all that matters is the strength and durability of the network, then all the moral questions related to power are removed.

A further political critique, related to the process through which ANT itself creates knowledge, concerns the narrative it offers – at least in its Latourian version – for explaining everything, and considering everything in the world as equal. By not having any 'other', by denying 'otherness' to non-human actants, argue Lee and Brown (1994), ANT in effect tries to offer a universal language, and thus to become the spokesperson for all things. However, this is a risk that at least some authors consciously and explicitly try to avoid. Law (1999; 2007) states that he does not try to argue that ANT is right or that others are wrong, but to offer narratives and descriptions that might clarify what ANT can do.

## ANT FOR CULTURAL SOCIOLOGY

Despite all of these critiques, it is nevertheless the case that ANT has influenced certain elements of social thought more generally, especially when technology's and non-human actors' relevance for social existence is considered. Elements of ANT have been applied in a variety of fields, including medical science (e.g. Mol, 2005), media studies (see Couldry, 2008), human geography (e.g. Murdoch, 1998; see also Jóhannesson and Bærenholdt, 2009), archaeology (e.g. Bjornar, 2010), and urban design (e.g. The, 2014), and on such diverse topics as human–animal relations (e.g. Mangelsdorf, 2012), environmental catastrophes (e.g. Roux, 2012), aesthetic consciousness (e.g. Acord and DeNora, 2008; see also Farkhatdinov and Acord in this volume) and iconicity (see Bartmanski in this volume).

In this section, I consider the elements of ANT that cultural sociologists in particular have adapted and been inspired by. The relevance of ANT for cultural sociology cannot be considered unless the sometimes uneasy relationship between cultural sociology (or cultural studies, for that matter) and STS is at least briefly acknowledged. The most important ontological tool on offer for a cultural sociologist here is that of challenging the distinction between culture and technology, but how far has this tool really been used by either side of the supposed divide?

While STS was already developing in the 1979s a cultural view of the production of science, integration of considerations of technology into studies of cultural phenomena took more time to establish. The two fields where technology's role as mediator has been significantly recognized are media studies and music studies (Magaudda, 2014). Both or these areas are quite obvious domains for this kind of scholarship, as both fields obviously have a lot to do with technology. Musicology was one of the first cultural areas where ANT principles came to be established, particularly through the work of Antoine Hennion (1989; 2001; Gomart and Hennion, 1999; Hennion and Grenier, 2000). Later on, as we will see below, considerations of not only technology but also materiality came to be established within certain fields of cultural sociology.

Brown (2011) has argued that ANT has developed in three waves. The first wave was the early STS work of those who established ANT. The second wave, led by Callon (1998; 1999), focused on marketing and management studies. Third-wave scholars are no longer orthodox in their uses of ANT, but rather take on certain basic elements of it, transforming and translating ANT itself in the process. All these waves have been developed and adopted within particular spheres in cultural sociology.

### On Tasting and Mediation

The first wave of cultural uses of ANT can almost exclusively be attributed to Hennion's studies of music. He started by analysing the role of the music producer as a mediator of production and consumption, and in particular treated the studio as an environment equivalent to a scientific laboratory. He argued that the producer is the point where the technological and the social meet, and therefore the appropriate focus of study. While not claiming to 'do' ANT as such, he acknowledged that he comes from the same intellectual background, and the same institution, as Callon and Latour (Hennion, 1989). In his later work, Hennion (2005; 2007; 2013; Gomart and Hennion, 1999;

Hennion and Grenier, 2000) focused on 'amateurs' of music, and different forms of music mediation. Here the amateur is French *amateur*, a lover, someone passionate about the object of her/his interest. Hennion subscribes to certain ANT-like principles in terms of taking technology seriously, and rejecting oppositions such as active/passive, subject/object, agency/structure or dominant/subjugated. He also argues that subjects cannot exist without networks and vice versa (Gomart and Hennion, 1999). He has argued against Bourdieusian understandings of taste, instead considering taste as collective, reflexive and performative. Taste, according to Hennion, is created and expressed in social and material practices, and it formulates individuals' self-understandings. Activities in relation to taste are embodied through repetition, practice and the perfection of skills (Hennion, 2007). In the formulation of taste, he considers the amateur as someone who really *tastes* things. This means that taste is not a label of distinction or anti-distinction, or involved in the expression and production of social locations, but is instead mediated and performed: it is an *act of tasting*. The mediators involved include the community of amateurs the taster is involved with, the material mediators of tasting (for example, wine glasses and decanters), the tasting body and its cultivated skills, and the tasted object and its 'feedback' – what it does, and what it causes the person who is engaged in tasting to do (Hennion, 2005). So if I wear certain high-heeled shoes in a fashion event, my experience of wearing them is mediated through the surrounding community of fashion amateurs, the floor on which I walk wearing the shoes (the sound of the heels on the surface, whether the floor is slippery or not, or whether it is soft or hard), the surrounding room and its spatio-material conditions, my personal history of wearing shoes (can I walk wearing heels? How do I think the shoes look?), and how the shoes feel on my feet and how they make me walk. As Hennion (2005) points out, other things might influence tasting practices as well. The important point is that none of these elements are pre-determined, and all of them participate in the experience of 'tasting', formulating my taste in shoes.

The concept of mediation, since it is very central to Hennion's thinking, deserves some further consideration. Mediations, he argues 'have to be recognized in their own right' (Hennion and Grenier, 2000: 349). When a person looks at a work of art, s/he necessarily reads it in the light of other works of art she is aware of, the specific environment the object is located in (probably a museum or gallery), and the social meanings associated with art appreciation (Hennion and Grenier, 2000). It has been argued that museums have been central to the formulations of ways of looking, and through that to broader formulations of subjectivity, throughout European history (Hetherington, 1999). Therefore they must be considered as important mediators of the ways of looking at art. The fundamental point here is that no form of art is simply an object to be consumed, but is 'created' through the act of looking and the mediators influencing the act (Hennion, 2001). In like manner to the ways that the work of art in a museum or gallery is created through acts of looking, music is created together with the listener and mediators such as musical instruments, amplifiers, acoustics, record players and so forth (Hennion, 2013). We must explore these *acts* of looking, listening and tasting, in order to understand experiences, emotions and passions involved in the processes in question.

Hennion has been criticized for going too far in his rejection of social structures and forms of (inherited) capital, the foci on which Bourdieu (1993; 2010 [1979]) concentrated. His approach risks romanticizing art worlds and art tasting, and ignoring questions to do with power (Prior, 2011; Schwarz, 2013). For critics, Hennion ignores the fact that tasting is not only about processes and techniques of tasting, but also about '(a) durable tastes which are strong enough to persist across situations, independently of the tasting techniques applied; (b) the class/group characteristics of tasting techniques; and (c) the use of tasting techniques as a basis for discrimination and social closure' (Schwarz, 2013: 421). New approaches to the sociology of art, discussed in the end of this section, have sought to integrate Hennion's insights with those of Bourdieu, and to create new ways of analysing and understanding art worlds and individuals involved in them.

## On Markets and Mediation

As already mentioned, work within and oriented to management studies can be considered as the second wave within ANT. Within this tradition, some works analyse the processes of cultural production. Lury (2004) analyses brands as performative objects that mediate supply and demand. She considers the brand as an economic, affective and cultural mediator that organizes and communicates relations between the producer and consumer. A brand is contradictory in many ways. While it is a form of social currency, it is legally protected as private property; while it is an object, it is no one physical thing. Brand mediates the relations between material and virtual products, making objects that are different in their specific characteristics recognizable as parts of the same brand. Therefore, brand is both an actor and a network, and it mediates the relations between human, non-human and non-individual actors.

Drawing inspiration from Lury's analysis of brands, Entwistle and Slater (2014) have considered fashion models' 'looks' as cultural-economic objects which operate as mediators between fashion houses, products and consumers. It is striking that both these studies ignore the music/art tradition of Hennion and others, and place themselves within the economic tradition of ANT only, despite Hennion's elaborate work on cultural-technological mediation. This is probably due to the fact that these analyses rather underplay the technology side of the phenomena they seek to analyse.

Entwistle and Slater (2014) argue that ANT has not achieved the symmetry it claims to seek, namely that between culture and economy. According to them, 'culture appears in ANT largely as an artefact of modernist thought rather than as an empirical aspect of agents' performances' (Entwistle and Slater, 2014: 161). They consider culture as an empirical fact in the sense that actors in fields of cultural production refer to it constantly when making sense of their particular cultural worlds. Therefore, they argue, it is not for the ANT scholar to claim, as they have according to Entwistle and Slater, that culture must be dismissed as an explanatory category, for, according to ANT principles, researchers of a phenomenon must take its participants' views seriously. In the dismissal of 'culture' as a category, ANT scholars are guilty of dismissing the views of individuals participating in fields of cultural production. However, Entwistle and Slater's critique only targets the management wave of ANT, not the whole ANT school of thought (as they imply). Other ANT-inspired cultural sociologists have developed new approaches to understanding cultural practices that go far beyond such criticism.

On a different vein, Herrero (2010) has analysed art auction catalogues as presenters and creators or art value. Drawing from Callon-inspired ANT and Bourdieusian cultural-economic analyses, she argues that market devices such as catalogues mediate and communicate the value attached to art objects. Through such meanings attached to art objects, catalogues also mediate the struggles between human actors engaged in the field or art-buying. Catalogues construct and represent art objects and direct the actions of buyers, and thereby they also mediate how others in the field perceive each buyer and the capitals s/he holds.

## On Art, Materiality and Mediation

Probably the most developed ANT-influenced approach to culture today can be placed within the third wave of ANT. This approach involves taking particular elements of ANT and making use of them for the sociology of art and cultural sociology, without necessarily taking up all of the various facets of ANT. The scholars involved in such developments are often (but not always) influenced by Hennion's ideas about tasting, mediation and performativity. They sometimes locate themselves as critics of Bourdieusian analysis of culture (e.g. Tanner, 2010; Yaneva, 2003), and sometimes seek to critique and extend Bourdieusian analysis with ANT ideas (e.g. Herrero, 2010; Prior, 2008; 2011). Thus, for example, Bennett (2007), drawing on Bourdieu, Foucault and ANT, argues that in analyses of cultural phenomena, it is necessary to consider how 'culture' and 'the social' are historically created as different through institutions that classify knowledges and practices. Yet the construction of culture is socially meaningful and socially acted, and human and non-human actors participate in different ways in such cultural assemblages. Culture and the social are not ontologically different but rather are made different in the public realm through the organization of elements, and it is these processes that study of culture should have as its focus.

In a more pragmatic vein, Prior (2008) argues that while Bourdieu's field analysis is extremely useful for analysing fields of music production, it is underpowered in its capacity to integrate technological elements into the analysis of the construction of the field. As non-human objects are crucial for fields of music production, tools must be developed which enable such elements to be analysed properly. While Prior rejects the idea that independent agency should be attributed to non-human actors, he argues that the cultural and the technological are actively linked, and that music is mediated and created through and by different non-human devices.

Klett and Gerber (2014) draw upon Hennion in their exploration of performative elements of taste, and consider non-human actors as actants which mediate such performances, in order to make sense of the contradictions and interactions involved in the Noise Music scene. Strandvad (2012) argues that in the process of creating an artwork, the subjects involved in making the product, and the product itself, are co-produced simultaneously, and that the product becomes active through the participation of human and non-human actors and networks evolving around and through the process. She demonstrates through an empirical analysis of a (failed) film-making process how the art product, a film in this case, itself came to mediate such connections.

Rubio (2012) argues that in order to understand the processes of art-making, these must be followed using multiple, flexible methods. Since the artwork comes into being through material practices, it is these practices that must be followed in order to understand the process of art-making. His empirical case study of the making of an earthwork sculpture demonstrates that the material practices involved in the process of art-making are multiple, and often beyond the artist's control. His approach to researching the art-creation process makes use of the ANT-inspired idea of following in a detailed way the agencies of human and non-human actors involved in the process. Yaneva (2003) argues that in analyses of art, what is significant is the process of how art comes to be, involving various human and non-human actors, latter of which would contemporarily be understood as tools only. In her analysis of the creation of a chalk art-work on a museum floor, she strikingly demonstrates how the floor emerges as a crucial mediator between different actors, and how 'chalk' changes its nature throughout the process of art-making and experiencing. Griwold and Mangione (2013) explore the materiality of spaces, art objects and human bodies, and argue that the physical shape and characteristics of bodies, gallery spaces and artworks all interact and shape visitor experiences. They argue for the analysis on how the' interactions among objects, words, and bodies in space impact viewers' physical, emotional, and cognitive responses to art.' (345)

All these authors consider the artwork and the different elements of it as actors and mediators in the process of art-making and experiencing (Rubio and Silva, 2013). This echoes the broader programme of the 'new sociology of art' which considers the artwork as an important element to be included in the analyses of art worlds, compensating for the tendency in earlier sociological studies of art to focus on external social forces at the expense of considering the aesthetic properties of art works themselves (de la Fuente, 2007; 2010). Another important element in the work of these authors is a certain methodological flexibility, which follows from the idea that the processes, actions and performances are what must be studied, instead of inert objects and human subjects. These are very ANT-like principles, even if some authors do not announce direct ANT affiliations. It seems to be the case that many ideas which were earlier forcefully rejected by some STS scholars have found a home in certain branches of cultural sociology today.

## CONCLUSION

In this chapter I have presented a narrative as to how ANT was born, formulated, established and criticized, and how some elements of it have found their way into the sociology of art in particular, but also into (some areas of) cultural sociology more generally. What ANT's future as a school of thought in respect to cultural sociology is, is very difficult to say. Not many cultural sociologists subscribe to all the ANT principles or declare direct ANT affiliation. However, the great significance of some of its ideas is likely to continue and increase, as the fundamental importance of technology and materiality for cultural mediation is increasingly recognized. It is perhaps an obvious thing to state that today that which is cultural or social is almost always also technological, and vice versa. Yet this obvious point still needs to be made. There is no music without sound technology and acoustics, there is no fashion without material technology, there is no wine without sophisticated production and glassware technologies, and so on. It is also the case that none of these cultural worlds can be entered without appropriate bodily techniques and cultural knowledge of tasting the particular cultural objects in question. Yet these matters have often been discussed in cultural sociology and cultural studies as if they existed in and through social and linguistic meanings only. While ANT is not the only approach stressing the significance of technology and materiality for cultural practices today (and vice versa), it is its job to keep reminding us that we often consider technology as being outside of the study of culture, and thereby behave as if the distinctions that ANT has argued against actually existed. And that is, of course, how we make them exist, by assuming uncritically that they do so.

## REFERENCES

Acord, S.K. and DeNora, T. (2008) 'Culture and the Arts: From Art Worlds to Arts-in-Action', *The Annals of the American Academy of Political and Social Science*, 619(1): 223–37.

Amsterdamska, O. (1990) 'Surely You Are Joking, Monsieur Latour!', *Science, Technology, & Human Values*, 15(4): 495–504.

Austin, J.L. (1976 [1962]) *How to Do Things with Words*. Oxford: Oxford University Press.

Bennett, T. (2007) 'The Work of Culture', *Cultural Sociology*, 1(1): 31–47.

Bjornar, O. (2010) *In Defense of Things: Archaeology and the Ontology of Objects*. Lanham: AltaMira.

Bloor, D. (1999) 'Anti-Latour', *Studies in History and Philosophy of Science*, 30(1): 81–112.

Bourdieu, P. (1993) *The Field of Cultural Production: Essays on Art and Literature*. New York: Columbia University Press.

Bourdieu, P. (2010 [1979]) *Distinction: A Social Critique of the Judgement of Taste*. London: Routledge.

Brown, S. (2011) 'Actor-Network Theory (ANT)', in M Tadajewski (ed.), *Key Concepts in Critical Management Studies*. London: Sage.

Callon, M. (1980) 'Struggles and Negotiations to Decide What is Problematic and What is Not: The Sociology of Translation', in K. Knorr, R. Krohn and R. Whitley (eds), *The Social Process of Scientific Investigation*. Dordrecht: Reidel. pp. 197–220.

Callon, M. (1986a) 'The Sociology of an Actor-Network: The Case of the Electric Vehicle', in M. Callon, J. Law and A. Rip (eds), *Mapping the Dynamics of Science and Technology*. London: Macmillan. pp. 19–34.

Callon, M. (1986b) 'Some Elements of a Sociology of Translation: Domestication of the Scallops and the Fishermen of St Brieuc Bay', in J. Law (ed.), *Power, Action and Belief: A New Sociology of Knowledge?* London: Routledge. pp. 196–223.

Callon, M. (1987) 'Society in the Making: The Study of Technology as a Tool for Sociological Analysis', in W. Bijker, T. Hughes and T. Pinch (eds), *The Social Construction of Technological Systems*. Cambridge: MIT Press. pp. 77–97.

Callon, M. (1990) 'Techno-Economic Networks and Irreversibility', *The Sociological Review*, 38(1): 138–61.

Callon, M. (1998) 'The Embeddedness of Economic Markets in Economics', in M. Callon (ed.), *The Laws of the Markets*. Oxford: Blackwell, pp. 1–57.

Callon, M. (1999) 'Actor-Network Theory: The Market Test', in J. Law and J. Hassard (eds) *Actor Network Theory and After*. Oxford: Blackwell. pp. 181–95.

Callon, M. (2006) 'What Does it Mean to Say that Economics is Performative?' *CSI Working Papers Series* 005.

Callon, M. and Latour, B. (1981) 'Unscrewing the Big Leviathan: How Actors Macro-Structure Reality and How Sociologists Help Them Do So', in K. Knorr-Cetina and A.V. Cicourel (eds), *Advances in Social Theory and Methodology: Toward an Integration of Micro- and Macro-Sociologies*. Boston: Routledge & Kegan Paul.

Callon, M., Law, J. and Rip, A. (1986) 'How to Study the Force of Science', in M. Callon, J. Law and A. Rip (eds), *Mapping the Dynamics of Science and Technology*. London: Macmillan. pp. 3–15.

Collins, H.M. and Yearley, S. (1992) 'Epistemological Chicken', in A. Pickering (ed.), *Science as Practice and Culture*. Chicago: University of Chicago Press. pp. 301–26.

Couldry, N. (2008) 'Actor Network Theory and Media: Do They Connect and on What Terms?', in A. Hepp, F. Krotz, S. Moores and C. Winter (eds), *Connectivity, Networks and Flows: Conceptualizing Contemporary Communications*. Cresskill: Hampton. pp. 93–110.

Crawford, C.S. (2005) 'Actor Network Theory', in G. Ritzer (ed.), *Encyclopedia of Social Theory*. Thousand Oaks, CA: Sage. pp. 1–4.

Cressman, D. (2009) *A Brief Overview of Actor-Network Theory: Punctualization, Heterogeneous Engineering & Translation*. ACT Lab/Centre for Policy Research on Science & Technology (CPROST) School of Communication, Simon Fraser University.

de la Fuente, E. (2007) 'The "New Sociology of Art": Putting Art Back into Social Science Approaches to the Arts', *Cultural Sociology*, 1(3): 409–25.

de la Fuente, E. (2010) 'In Defence of Theoretical and Methodological Pluralism in the Sociology of Art: A Critique of Georgina Born's Programmatic Essay', *Cultural Sociology*, 4(2): 217–30.

Deleuze, G. (2001 [1968]) *Difference and Repetition*. Trans. P. Patton. London: Continuum.

Dugdale, A. (1999) 'Materiality: Juggling Sameness and Difference', in J. Law and J. Hassard (eds), *Actor Network Theory and After*. Oxford: Blackwell, pp. 113–35.

Entwistle, J. and Slater, D. (2014) 'Reassembling the Cultural', *Journal of Cultural Economy* 7(2): 161–77.

Foucault, M. (1973 [1963]) *The Birth of Clinic: An Archaeology of Medical Perception*. New York: Pantheon.

Foucault, M. (1977 [1975]) *Discipline and Punish*. Harmondsworth: Penguin.

Foucault, M. (2001 [1966]) *The Order of Things: Archaeology of the Human Sciences*. London: Routledge.

Foucault, M. (2002 [1969]) *Archaeology of Knowledge*. London: Routledge.

Gomart, E. and Hennion, A. (1999) 'A Sociology of Attachment: Music Amateurs, Drug Users', *The Sociological Review*, 47(1): 220–47.

Griswold, W., Mangione, G. and McDonnell, T.E. (2013) 'Objects, Words, and Bodies in Space: Bringing Materiality into Cultural Analysis', *Qualitative Sociology*, 36: 343-64.

Haraway, D. (1989) *Primate Visions: Gender, Race and Nature in the World of Modern Science*. London: Routledge and Chapman Hall.

Haraway, D. (1990) 'A Manifesto for Cyborgs: Science, Technology and Socialist Feminism in the 1980s', in L.J. Nicholson (ed.), *Feminism/*

*Postmodernism*. New York: Routledge. pp. 190–233.
Haraway, D. (1991) 'The Biopolitics of Postmodern Bodies: Constitutions of Self in Immune System Discourse', in D. Haraway (ed.), *Simians, Cyborgs and Women: the Reinvention of Nature*. London: Free Association Books. pp. 203–30.
Hennion, A. (1989) 'An Intermediary between Production and Consumption: The Producer of Popular Music', *Science, Technology & Human Values*, 14(4): 400–24.
Hennion, A. (2001) 'Music Lovers: Taste as Performance', *Theory, Culture & Society*, 18(5): 1–22.
Hennion, A. (2005) 'Pragmatics of Taste', in M. Jacobs and N. Hanrahan (eds), *The Blackwell Companion to the Sociology of Culture*. Oxford: Blackwell. pp. 131–44.
Hennion, A. (2007) 'Those Things That Hold Us Together: Taste and Sociology', *Cultural Sociology*, 1(1): 97–114.
Hennion, A. (2013) 'Talking Music, Making Music: A Comparison between Rap and Techno', in D.B. Scott (ed.), *The Ashgate Research Companion to Popular Musicology*. Farnham: Ashgate. pp. 365–76.
Hennion, A. and Grenier, L. (2000) 'Sociology of Art: New Stakes in a Post-Critical Time', in S.R. Quah and A. Sales (eds), *The International Handbook of Sociology*. New York and London: Sage. pp. 341–55.
Herrero, M. (2010) 'Performing Calculation in the Art Market', *Journal of Cultural Economy*, 3(1): 19-34.
Hetherington, K. (1999) 'From Blindness to Blindness: Museums, Heterogeneity and the Subject', in J. Law and J. Hassard (eds), *Actor Network Theory and After*. Oxford: Blackwell. pp. 51–73.
Hobbes, T. (1978 [1651]) *The Leviathan*. London: Pelican Books.
Jóhannesson, G.T. and Bærenholdt, J.O. (2009) 'Actor-Network Theory/Network Geographies', in R. Kitchin and N. Thrift (eds), *International Encyclopedia of Human Geography*, Vol. 1. Amsterdam: Elsevier. pp. 15–19.
Klett, J. and Gerber, A. (2014) 'The Meaning of Indeterminacy: Noise Music as Performance', *Cultural Sociology*, online first: 1–16.
Latour, B. (1987) *Science in Action: How to Follow Scientists and Engineers through Society*. Cambridge, MA: Harvard University Press.
Latour, B. (1988 [1984]) *The Pasteurization of France*. Cambridge, MA: Harvard University Press.
Latour, B. (1993 [1991]) *We Have Never Been Modern*. Trans. C. Porter. Cambridge, MA: Harvard University Press.
Latour, B. (1996 [1990]) 'On Actor-network Theory: A Few Clarifications Plus More Than a Few Complications', *Soziale Welt*, 47: 369–81.
Latour, B. (1999) 'On Recalling ANT', in J. Law and J. Hassard (eds), *Actor Network Theory and After*. Oxford: Blackwell. pp. 15–25.
Latour, B. (2000 [1997]) 'A Well-articulated Primatology: Reflexions of a Fellow-traveller', in S. Strum and L. Fedigan (eds), *Primate Encounters*. Chicago: University of Chicago Press. pp. 358–81.
Latour, B. (2005) *Reassembling the Social: An Introduction to Actor-Network-Theory*. Oxford: Oxford University Press.
Law, J. (1986) 'On the Methods of Long Distance Control: Vessels, Navigation, and the Portuguese Route to India', in J. Law (ed.), *Power, Action and Belief: A New Sociology of Knowledge?* Routledge: Henley. pp. 234–63.
Law, J. (1997) 'Traduction/Trahison: Notes on ANT', The Centre for Science Studies, Lancaster University, Lancaster LA1 4YN.
Law, J. (1999) 'After ANT: Complexity, Naming and Topology', in J. Law and J. Hassard (eds), *Actor Network Theory and After*. Oxford: Blackwell, pp. 1–14.
Law, J. (2007) 'Actor Network Theory and Material Semiotics', version of 25th April 2007, http://www.heterogeneities.net/publications/Law2007ANTandMaterialSemiotics.pdf
Law, J. and Urry, J. (2004) 'Enacting the Social', *Economy and Society*, 33(3): 390–410.
Lee, N. and Brown, S. (1994) 'Otherness and the Actor Network: The Undiscovered Continent', *American Behavioral Scientist*, 37(6): 772–90.
Lury, C. (2004) *Brands: The Logos of the Global Economy*. London: Routledge.
Magaudda, P. (2014) 'The Broken Boundaries between Science and Technology Studies and Cultural Sociology: Introduction to an Interview with Trevor Pinch', *Cultural Sociology*, 8(1): 63–76.
Mangelsdorf, M. (2012) 'Horses – Significant Others, People's Companions, and Subtle Actors', in J. Passoth, B. Peuker and M. Schillmeier (eds), *Agency Without Actors? New Approaches to Collective Action*. Abingdon: Routledge. pp. 196–211.
Mol, A. (1999) 'Ontological Politics: A Word and Some Questions', in J. Law and J. Hassard (eds), *Actor Network Theory and After*. Oxford: Blackwell. pp. 74–89.
Mol, A. (2002) 'Cutting Surgeons, Walking Patients: Some Complexities Involved in Comparing', in J. Law and A. Mol (eds), *Complexities: Social Studies of Knowledge Practices*. Durham: Duke University Press. pp. 218–57.
Mol, A. (2005) *The Body Multiple: Ontology in Medical Practice*. London: Duke Universtiy Press.
Mol, A. and Law, J. (2004) 'Embodied Action, Enacted Bodies: The Example of Hypoglycaemia', *Body & Society*, 10(2): 43–62.

Munro, R. (2009) 'Actor-Network Theory', in S.R. Clegg and M. Haugaard (eds), *The Sage Handbook of Power*. London: Sage.

Murdoch, J. (1998) 'The Spaces of Actor-Network Theory', *Geoforum*, 29(4): 357–74.

Passoth, J., Peuker, B. and Schillmeier, M. (2012) 'Introduction', in J. Passoth, B. Peuker and M. Schillmeier (eds), *Agency without Actors? New Approaches to Collective Action*. Abingdon: Routledge. pp. 1–11.

Prior, N. (2008) 'Putting a Glitch in the Field: Bourdieu, Actor Network Theory and Contemporary Music', *Cultural Sociology*, 2(3): 301–19.

Prior, N. (2011) 'Critique and Renewal in the Sociology of Music: Bourdieu and Beyond', *Cultural Sociology*, 5(1): 121–38.

Roux, J. (2012) 'Agencies' Democracy: "Contribution" as a Paradigm to (re)Thinking the Common in a World of Conflict', in J. Passoth, B. Peuker and M. Schillmeier (eds), *Agency Without Actors? New Approaches to Collective Action*. Abingdon: Routledge. pp. 130–45.

Rubio, F.D. (2012) 'The Material Production of the Spiral Jetty: A Study of Culture in the Making', *Cultural Sociology*, 6(2): 143–61.

Rubio, F.D. and Silva, E.B. (2013) 'Materials in the Field: Object-trajectories and Object-positions in the Field of Contemporary Art', *Cultural Sociology*, 7(2): 161–78.

Santana-Acuña, Á. (2015) 'Social Monads, Not Social Facts: Gabriel Tarde's Tool for Sociological Analysis', in A. Law and E.R. Lybeck (eds), *Sociological Amnesia: Cross-Currents in Disciplinary History*. Farnham: Ashgate. pp. 141–58.

Schillmeier, M. (2008) 'Actor-Networks of Dementia', *Sociological Review*, 56(s2): 139–58.

Schwarz, O. (2013) 'Bending Forward, One Step Backward: On the Sociology of Tasting Techniques', *Cultural Sociology*, 7(4): 415–30.

Serres, M. (1974) *Hermès III: La Traduction*. Paris: Les Éditions de Minuit.

Sokal, A. and Bricmont, J. (1999) *Fashionable Nonsense: Postmodern Intellectuals' Abuse of Science*. New York: Picador.

Strandvad, S.M. (2012) 'Attached by the Product: A Socio-Material Direction in the Sociology of Art', *Cultural Sociology*, 6(2): 163–76.

Tanner, J. (2010) 'Michael Baxandall and the Sociological Interpretation of Art', *Cultural Sociology*, 4(2): 231–56.

Tarde, G. (2000 [1899]) *Social Laws: An Outline of Sociology*. Trans. H.C. Warren. Kitchener, Ont.: Batoche Books.

The, T. (2014) 'Actor-Network Theory Coevolution Framework for Urban Design', in M. Carmona (ed.), *Explorations in Urban Design: An Urban Design Research Primer*. Farnham: Ashgate. pp. 101–22.

Yaneva, A. (2003) 'Chalk Steps on the Museum Floor: The 'Pulses' of Objects in an Art Installation', *Journal of Material Culture*, 8(2): 169-88.

Zammito, J.H. (2004) *A Nice Derangement of Epistemes: Post-positivism in the Study of Science from Quine to Latour*. Chicago: University of Chicago Press.

# Neoinstitutionalist Sociology[1]

Pertti Alasuutari

## INTRODUCTION

The rise of the new institutionalisms (Hall and Taylor, 1996; Schmidt, 2008) can be seen as part of the same 'linguistic', 'constructionist' or – if you like – 'cultural' turn that also resulted in coining the terms 'cultural studies' and 'cultural sociology'. As Powell and DiMaggio (1991) note, new institutionalism developed from several researchers' observation in the 1970s that the world is inconsistent with the ways in which contemporary theories – rational choice and functionalism – asked them to see it. Empirical observations spoke against the assumptions that individuals and organizations make rational choices and that organizations are built because of their beneficial consequences:

> Administrators and politicians champion programs that are established but not implemented; managers gather information assiduously, but fail to analyze it; experts are hired not for advice but to signal legitimacy. Such pervasive findings of case-based research provoke efforts to replace rational theories of technical contingency or strategic choice with alternative models that are more consistent with the organizational reality that researchers have observed. (1991: 3)

For neoinstitutionalist sociology the answer to these mysteries is culture. As initiators and carriers of culture, institutions are shaped by historical factors that limit the understanding of and actual range of options open to decision-makers. Besides, the institutional setup of society constitutes actors, providing them with the 'frames of meaning' that guide their action.

Because of this emphasis on culture and history, neoinstitutionalists do not conceive of societies as universal, machine-like entities that are governed by universal sociological laws. Rather, neoinstitutionalists' objects of research are considered as contingent historical creations. Thus, they approach contemporary society as a culture of modernity.

Despite these shared starting points, new institutionalisms differ in several ways from the bulk of cultural sociological research. To start with, while cultural sociology often deals with art or popular culture and the media or with the everyday life, most of the neoinstitutionalist research deals with macro sociological questions such as organizational change, political or managerial decision-making, and globalization. Secondly, the starting point of new institutionalist economics – i.e. the revision of an underlying premise of *homo economicus* by acknowledging that transaction costs are not zero (North, 1990; Ostrom,

1990) – sounds like reinventing sociology. After all, sociology was born as an antidote to classical economics, stressing that there is more to the social world than utilitarian individuals. Yet the angle from which rational choice theory and functionalism are challenged, combined with what are in standard cultural sociology unconventional objects of research, make institutionalism a refreshing new opening in cultural sociology.

Since mainstream cultural sociology studies informal communities, often engaged in expressive cultural activities, the role of symbols, myths and intersubjective meanings is not surprisingly the key to understanding the social worlds studied. Essentially, the meta-narrative of these studies is that culture is cultural. In contrast, by focusing on formal organizations and by showing that they are no less shaped by a contingent cultural system, new institutionalism directs a frontal attack on rationalist assumptions according to which 'culture' is only relevant when dealing with 'traditional' societies and informal organizations. In that respect new institutionalism is akin to social studies of science, which also scrutinize the cultural foundations of activities that are generally considered as something universal and a-cultural, determined by pure reason.

The objects of research also make understandable the tone in which neoinstitutionalists' research typically discusses the cultural worlds of decision-making and organizational life. Cultural sociological research dealing with people's everyday life normally positions its objects of research as the underdog, sympathizing with their view of life, admiring their creativity in transforming their imposed-on living conditions into a tolerable or even enjoyable life, perhaps even celebrating their cultural resistance (see e.g. Becker, 1967; Hall and Jefferson, 1976; Willis, 1977; 1978). Neoinstitutionalist sociology, instead, approaches its objects of research often with an ironic attitude, thus highlighting the paradox between high-minded expectations or expressed principles and actual practices. In both cases 'culture' reveals or refers to the human side of how things actually work, but it is viewed from practically opposite perspectives.

As is implied above, there is not just one but several new institutionalisms, and given the thrust of interest in this approach, there will be more and more internal divisions in the coming years. In this chapter, however, I am going to concentrate on discussing only those variants that are of particular interest from the viewpoint of cultural sociology. Hence the focus will be on sociological institutionalism, particularly the 'Stanford school' of sociological institutionalism, and its developments and challenges stemming from what has been labelled as constructivist (Hay, 2006) or discursive (Campbell and Pedersen, 2001; Schmidt, 2008) institutionalism. I will first discuss how sociological institutionalism relates to other institutionalisms and introduce its basic ideas. The subsequent sections will then take up some of its problems and how they have been tackled in discursive institutionalist scholarship.

## NEW INSTITUTIONALISMS AND WORLD SOCIETY

The proliferation of new institutionalist scholarship has multiplied the number of its different branches so that by 2011 Colin Hay (2011) ended up adding constructivist institutionalism onto the list in which B. Guy Peters (1999) had already identified seven variants. Of these institutionalisms at least the first three, identified by Hall and Taylor (1996) – rational choice and historical and sociological institutionalism – developed quite independently, unaware of each other. Later, with the surge of interest in new institutionalisms, coupled with texts that introduce and compare its different strands, they formed a field that functions as an incubator of new variants, stemming from mutual cross-fertilization and influences from other scholars and theoretical traditions.

The new institutionalisms share the conviction that the social world and actors' decision-making cannot be properly explained without taking into account the role of institutions in constituting the conditions under which actors make their moves and how they expect others to behave. Yet there are significant differences between these approaches as to how they define the relationship between institutions and behaviour and how they explain the origins and change of institutions. For instance, historical institutionalism stresses the contingent character of the origins of institutions and their critical turning points, while also underscoring that institutions determine a path-dependent trajectory that polities follow in their policymaking. This means that historical institutionalists consider different societies as idiosyncratic systems in which the same component, say the national railway network, may assume quite different roles and meanings (Hall and Taylor, 1996; Schmidt, 2008). Rational choice institutionalism, on the other hand, contends that actors have a fixed set of preferences, the attainment of which they aim to maximize by behaving instrumentally in environments that are shaped by the institutional arrangements. With several actors pursuing their goals, the final outcome may be unintended and collectively sub-optimal. Rational choice institutionalists also stress that actors' moves are premised on their expectations about how others are likely to behave; a point that leads to game-theoretical research designs (Hall and Taylor, 1996; Ingram and Clay, 2000; Schmidt, 2008).

Sociological institutionalism, the research tradition that is of particular interest here, differs from both of the above-mentioned approaches. While historical institutionalism points out national differences and path-dependent policy choices, sociological institutionalism directs attention to global isomorphism, evident in the spread of worldwide models even to countries for which they are not suitable in their present situation. In contrast with rational choice institutionalism, sociological institutionalism stresses that institutions constitute actors instead of just constraining them, and that interests emerge within particular normative and historical contexts (Powell and DiMaggio, 1991: 7). That is why sociological institutionalists argue that agents fairly unthinkingly enact global scripts rather than behave in a truly rational manner.

Sociological institutionalism also defines institutions in a much broader sense than the other two approaches. For it, institutions do not just depict formal rules, procedures or norms, but also symbols, scripts and moral principles that provide the 'frames of meaning' guiding human action (Hall and Taylor, 1996: 947). In other words institutions – or the institutional infrastructure composed of the institutions – are more or less equated with culture and society. This can be seen most clearly in world polity theory (WPT), particularly associated with John Meyer and his disciples, who talk about the contemporary global institutional setup as *world society* or world polity and the cultural models and scripts that carry it as *world culture* (Boli and Thomas, 1999: Lechner and Boli, 2005; Meyer et al., 2009).

Instead of focusing on the differences between nation-states and their policies, WPT raises the point that the current world is 'organized as nation-states, [which] are structurally similar in many unexpected dimensions and change in unexpectedly similar ways' (Meyer et al., 1997: 145). The answer to this mystery is world culture, the culture of world society. It comprises norms and knowledge shared across state boundaries, which are rooted in 19th-century Western culture, but since globalized and carried by the infrastructure of world society (Lechner and Boli, 2005: 6). As a shared cultural frame much larger than states or nations, world culture constitutes the actors, and makes them respond and behave in the same way. World cultural principles and institutions shape the action of states, firms, individuals and other subunits. Within the world polity organized this way many ideas and principles are shared across state boundaries, and the desires and pressures to keep up with global trends are infiltrated to domestic politics through many routes. Consequently, nation-states are more isomorphic than most theories would predict and change more uniformly than is commonly recognized (Meyer et al., 1997: 173).

The story of the global diffusion of models, including the nation-state as a building block of the international political system, and the ideas about how the government and economy of such a state can be best organized, resembles the functionalist account of social development, according to which societies go through the same stages determined by the functional requirements of each stage (Parsons, 1964; 1966). New institutionalism, however, opposes this view, criticizing the 'optimistic functionalism' that explains institutions by their allegedly beneficial consequences. Instead, new institutionalism stresses that institutions may persist even when they serve no one's interests, and that they are end-products of random variation, selection and retention, rather than individual foresight (Powell and DiMaggio, 1991: 4). Instead of treating the idea of functional requirements as a natural explanation for isomorphism found among nation-states, WPT treats it as a justification that actors use to promote global models to countries that have not yet enacted them. Such a justification appeals to policymakers and the general public because the world culture of modernity is 'rationalistic'. As Meyer and colleagues (1997: 162) point out, in the name of (social) science policymakers are consulted about the functional requirements of the modern society, organization and individual, and the linkages among them, which justifies the assumption that there is basically only one right, or research-based way to organize society and its institutions. Almost every aspect of social life is discussed, rationalized and organized, including rules of economic production and consumption, political structure, education, and people's private and public everyday life. 'In each arena, the range of legitimately defensible forms is fairly narrow. All the sectors are discussed as if they were functionally integrated and interdependent, and they are expected to conform to general principles of progress and justice' (Meyer et al., 1997: 162–3).

Sociological institutionalism stresses that rationalism and conformity are the core underlying reasons for actors' willingness to enact the same worldwide models. Rationalism creates a tendency of many actors to be overtly organized because it gives the outer appearance of being rational and efficient. Due to the great belief in and respect for rational planning, actors develop increasingly detailed plans, which policymakers also in peripheral states adopt though they have no need for or resources to implement them (Boli, 1987; Meyer et al., 1997: 244). Decoupling is an inevitable outcome: actors adopt inconsistent structures from different global sources and symbolic frames without substantive meaning. Hence hypocrisy is prevalent.

Such hypocrisy is often pointed out in an ironic tone. For instance, in one article John Meyer (2004) describes how in a rural school in sub-Saharan Africa, a language teacher was giving a lesson.

> She was the only teacher present. It was Friday, and none of the other teachers had bothered to come. The instructor was only semi-literate, and not a single one of her sixth-graders could read the simplest sentence. The Ministry of Education official accompanying us seemed not to notice. He turned to me and said improved textbooks and instruction in science were really needed: 'After all, our children have to compete in the global economy'. (Meyer, 2004: 42)

According to Meyer this excerpt illustrates how Ministry officials at the national level are thinking in terms of world educational fashions, quite out of touch with local problems and realities. That is because leading nations, global institutions like the World Bank, and social movements like human rights campaigns encourage standardized social arrangements around the world, and national governments turn out to be conformist, although their official conformity is often superficial and hypocritical.

## INSTRUMENTAL AND EXPRESSIVE CULTURE

The idea of national uniqueness is also part of world culture. John Meyer (2000) however suggests that the uniqueness of national cultures is expressed in 'expressive culture'. By this concept he depicts areas that are irrelevant from the viewpoint of 'instrumental culture', i.e. from the perspective of rational action. According to him, nation-states do not want to be too unique in, for instance, their divisions of labour, forms of state structure, or educational or medical systems. Instead:

> Uniqueness and identity are thus most legitimately focused on matters of expressive culture: variations in language, dress, food, traditions, landscapes, familial styles and so on. These are precisely the things that in the modern system do not matter, which is to say they have no direct, rational relation to instrumental actorhood. Nation-states and organized ethnic groups within them do not claim to have their own styles of wife- or child-beating, of economic production and so on. Such claims would violate global principles and pressures, and actual traditions along these lines are suppressed in reconstructions or revitalizations of history and tradition. (Meyer, 2000: 245)

Meyer certainly has a point here: worldwide models that can be justified by science and rationality spread more easily. Yet his argument is questionable. What about the fact that practically all nation-states want to express that they belong to the civilized world by establishing the classical European art institutions of opera, ballet and classical music (Adams, 1999)? Although established art is a distance away from activities that are most essential for people's livelihood, in this area too individual and collective actors such as nation-states do not want to appear too different from each other. It is part of the 'nation branding' of a 'civilized' and 'modern' nation to have cultural heroes in the established fields of art: a national poet, sculptor, composer, etc. Those artists are expected to reflect a distinctive style that somehow also reflects 'national culture', but on the other hand the style cannot be too exotic to be recognized as belonging to an international sub-field of the high arts (Alasuutari, 2001). The same goes for individual artists, for instance film directors: they walk a thin line between an idiosyncratic style and the isomorphic pressures of the field (Alvarez et al., 2005).

By using 'pop-rockization' of popular music as his case example, Motti Regev has elaborated on this phenomenon. He notes that the globally institutionalized fields of art 'dictate to aspiring artists, creative workers, and cultural consumers around the world what are the art forms, the stylistic elements, and the aesthetic idioms that should be adopted in order to count as candidates for recognition, participation, and parity in the innovative frontiers of world culture' (Regev, 2013: 11). Consequently, certain institutionalized art forms such as pop-rock spread throughout the world and merge with national traditions. By extending the work by Meyer and others to the realm of expressive culture, Regev refers to this process as expressive isomorphism, leading to aesthetic cosmopolitanism. In the field of popular music this process has led to pop-rockization, by which Regev means the global spread of pop-rock music throughout the world, creating fusions with, and integrating, folklore and traditional elements.

To illustrate this interlacing of the expression of national cultural uniqueness with world-cultural aesthetic cosmopolitanism, Regev mentions two songs, *La Argentinidad al Palo* performed by Argentinean rock band Bersuit Vergarabat, and *Kama Yossi* by Israeli rock auteur Berry Sakharoff. Sung in national languages, engaging in dialogue with earlier moments in local history, both celebrated hit songs stand as expressions of current ethno-national uniqueness, in these cases Argentineness and Israeliness. Yet the sonic elements are easily identifiable. 'The electric and electronic instrumentation, the sophisticated studio production techniques used for their creation and the presence of the stylistic influence of global pop-rock genres, make each of these songs an art work that shares much aesthetic common ground with many songs produced elsewhere in the world' (Regev, 2007: 318). Thus the model of world culture is not confined to the realm of instrumental rationalized culture. Similar isomorphism takes place in expressive culture, when national artists are self-mobilized to create 'their own' version of a global art form, in this case pop-rock, while simultaneously adapting to globally spread aesthetic idioms.

## FROM DIFFUSION TO TRANSLATION AND DOMESTICATION

By regarding the global system as an institutional order ingrained in world culture, WPT marks a stimulating departure from the conventional macro-realist view, which treats the world system simply as a battleground on which national states, blocs or civilizations fight each other while defending their interests. However, WPT's view of culture as constitutive of the actors, considered as agents mindlessly enacting world cultural scripts (Meyer, 2010), overemphasizes a structuralist view of culture at the expense of acknowledgement of actors' creativity, reflexivity and shrewdness. This emphasis on the constitutive role of culture is understandable since WPT developed as a corrective to, and an antipode of, rational choice theory, which treats actors' interests as a self-evident starting point. Yet the disregard of the role of local actors is an obvious problem, which has been addressed and solved in some other strands of neoinstitutionalism.

From the perspective of cultural sociology or anthropology, it can be said that WPT's conception of culture as a set of models or scripts that produce its agents is wanting. In contrasting its view of actorhood with rational choice theory by stressing that actors' choices cannot be deduced from their 'objective interests', in a peculiar way WPT ends up repeating the old imagery of primitive culture as a belief system and as a social organization that functions as a copying machine, producing its members as duplicates programmed by the scripts, norms and beliefs of the culture (see e.g. Mauss, 1979). Although it is a fair point to say that modern individuals or collective actors are in many ways conformists who follow fashions and do not want to look too different from others in their reference group, it is not convincing to explain global isomorphism only by imitation or by scripts which actors are programmed to enact. This kind of insistence on the power of culture leads into considering individuals as cultural dopes. As an early interpretation of primitive cultures, it is obviously an inverse mirror image of the self-conception of the moderns. Later on, several scholars have pointed out that members of indigenous cultures are perfectly capable of strategic action and that rationality is always culturally conditioned (see e.g. Bourdieu, 1977; Sahlins, 1976). In that sense, insisting that the global order is rooted in world culture does not necessarily lead to the assumption that individuals are incapable of strategic action and instead only imitate others. Instead, it is possible to stress that while actors are culturally constituted, they are also capable of affecting the shared views of the world with their own activity.

Vivien Schmidt (2008) has dubbed this view of the relationship between actors and institutions as discursive institutionalism, although she admits that the scholars she lists as its representatives are a diverse group. Methodological orientation is probably the clearest common denominator. While the standard WPT research design scrutinizes the variables – such as memberships in international governmental and non-governmental organizations – that explain the spread of a particular worldwide model to different nation-states, these scholars represent a qualitative case-study approach. From this viewpoint the image of nations as mindless emulators does not hold. Instead, these scholars emphasize the active role of local actors in promoting exogenous ideas. That is, the adoption of new institutional practices requires domestic 'policy entrepreneurs' with the interests and capacity to promote them in a new context (Appel and Orenstein, 2013; Campbell, 2004).

As Maman and Rosenhek (2007) show in their analysis about the adoption of the policy of central bank independence in Israel, even external pressure from actors such as the IMF, the World Bank and the US government is mediated and processed by local actors. In this case local academic economists, who earlier had a marginal role, became key players with the capacity to promote their agenda of institutional reform.

> Their success resulted both from their ability to formulate concrete and authoritative policy and institutional alternatives based on scientifically-accepted theoretical frames, and from a crucial resource held by them: their close ties with leading American economists. The dense network of cross-national academic economists enabled them to gain access to both the Israeli decision-makers and the American administration, which on the basis of inter-state dominance used its coercive power to put pressure on the Israeli government. (Maman and Rosenhek, 2007: 270)

The active role of local actors in the diffusion of ideas and policy models has been noted in a number of studies and research traditions. They do not just enact a ready-made model but rather adapt it to the local conditions and to their own interests. Local actors contest and socially construct the 'success' of a model policy and the 'appropriateness' of the proposed reform (Acharya, 2004; Callon, 1986; Cook, 2008; Cortell and Davis, 2000; Dolowitz and Marsh, 1996; Evans and Davies, 1999). Consequently, the original model is transformed in several ways.

To take an example from consumer culture, in her analysis about the localization of McDonald's to Russia, Caldwell (2004) argues that the active role of Muscovites in incorporating McDonald's into their daily lives complicates the argument that global movements such as McDonaldization (Ritzer, 1996) elide meaning from daily life.

Muscovites have incorporated McDonald's into the more intimate and sentimental spaces of their personal lives: family celebrations, cuisine and discourses about what it means to be Russian today. In so doing, Muscovites have drawn McDonald's into the very processes by which local cultural forms are generated, authenticated and made meaningful. It is by passing through this process of domestication that McDonald's has become localized (Caldwell, 2004: 6).

These studies on the adoption of global ideas to local contexts have also challenged the accuracy of the image of diffusion in capturing what happens when ideas travel. Instead of talking about diffusion, a group of scholars known as Scandinavian institutionalists have suggested that translation is a more adequate metaphor (Czarniawska and Sevón, 2005; Czarniawska-Joerges and Sevon, 1996). The concept of diffusion conveys the impression of 'packages' of ideas, forms or policies flying around and sticking to organizations. This physicalist term implies that nothing happens to these ideas during the process of diffusion, which is not the case as far as the spreading of ideas or forms is concerned. Following Latour's (1986) suggestion (see also Callon, 1986), Scandinavian institutionalists prefer to talk about a process of translation, in which humans have an active role in circulating and shaping ideas. As Latour puts it, according to the model of translation, the spread in time and space of anything is in the hands of people:

> Each of these people may act in many different ways, letting the token drop, or modifying it, or deflecting it, or betraying it, or adding to it, or appropriating it. The faithful transmission of, for instance, an order by a large number of people is a rarity in such a model and if it occurs it requires explanation. (Latour, 1986: 267)

By utilizing the concept of translation, Sahlin-Andersson (1996) explains the circulation of ideas by approaching it from the perspective of local actors: why for instance organizations seek to imitate others. According to her, actors are motivated to making changes in their organization to solve problems, which are constructed through comparing the local situation with that of other organizations. That is why actors want to imitate success: they adopt ideas and strategies from organizations that are judged successful. Such copying is, however, an editing process:

> Imitated 'successes' are formulated and reformulated as they are circulated. Similarities are emphasized while differences that might lead to a conclusion that the imitated prototype does not fit in the local setting are played down. In order to attract attention, imitated prototypes are reformulated in more dramatic terms. In such processes of translation, new meanings are created and ascribed to activities and experiences. (Sahlin-Andersson, 1996: 70)

Scandinavian institutionalism is particularly interested in public or private organizations, but the same principles – defining problems by comparing to others, and copying ideas to be more successful – apply to political decision-making. Nation-states or other polities do not adopt the same models to look similar but rather in order to do well in international competition. That is why political actors produce and use international league tables and comparisons as a means to justify or criticize political reforms.

When talking about political decision-making it is however important to note that although all actors appeal to the best of the nation or another imagined community, politics consists of several parties and stakeholder groups. They are all engaged in suggesting how the facts of, say, an international comparison must be interpreted and what needs to be done, trying to translate their stakeholder interests into the common interest. The political processes triggered by the OECD's Programme for International Student Assessment (PISA) in several countries are a prime example. The results have created heated debates and reform demands in countries whose performance was judged poor (Ertl, 2006; Ringarp and Rothland, 2010; Takayama, 2008; 2010; Waldow, 2009), but also success has political repercussions. Finland's top ranking was a problem for Finnish teachers' trade union in the sense that since the education system appeared to be excellent in international comparison, it was difficult for the teachers to find arguments by which to require more resources for the schools (Rautalin and Alasuutari, 2007). On the other hand, the domestic public praise of the high international ranking gave peace to the Finnish ministry of education to carry through a curriculum reform that ran contrary to how national educational experts had interpreted the reasons behind the country's resounding PISA success (Rautalin, 2014).

When the local-global interplay related to the global circulation of ideas is perceived from this perspective, the issue at hand is no more whether, or how much, models or formats are transformed when they are instituted to different local contexts. Some 'policy formats', such as the national bioethical committee (Syvätera and Alasuutari, 2014), may be internationally codified, so that national organizations dutifully subscribe to the same practices. In some other cases a local version may be unrecognizable in comparison with its international exemplar. What is at stake is not how much original models are modified to local contexts but rather the point that the local process through which policies or ideas are instituted makes them experientially domestic, and such a process of domestication entwines a cosmopolitan consciousness with banal nationalism (Billig, 1995) or localism.

Consider a study that analysed the effects of an R&D project aimed at developing local government cultural activities in Finnish towns and cities (Alasuutari, 2013). One aim of the project, organized by the Association of Finnish Local and Regional Authorities (AFLRA), was to create a statistical standard about how to calculate the costs and profits of cultural activities, so that cities could learn from each other's experiences of good practices. In that sense the project dealt with local government cultural activities in a national comparative perspective, and the final report ALFRA published also placed cities' cultural policy in international perspective, referring to all the global buzzwords like 'creative cities'. Therefore, one could expect that the project would have advanced a broader national or global perspective, but that was not the case. When the final report was released, the media immediately interpreted the results in terms of the cultural framework of competition. Independently of each other, local newspapers uniformly presented the ranking of their city as the headline news of the report. Thus the media reception of the project drew on and enhanced identification with one's city as an imagined community – invigorating banal localism. The framing of the issue was thus similar to the PISA case discussed above, only this time in a city rather than a national context.

While there is a plethora of concepts[2] that captures the transformation of the original when an idea or policy is introduced to a local context, the concept of domestication pays attention to a local field battle as a condition of its acceptability. When an idea, concept, model or a comparison to other entities, becomes part of local politics, local actors and spectators to the political drama retain their sense of agency, and the eventual policy changes do not seem to be mere imitation of what has been done elsewhere.

This phenomenon was substantiated in a study that compared the press coverage of the 2011 Egyptian uprising in British, Finnish and Pakistani newspapers (Alasuutari et al., 2013). The British and Finnish newspapers used several discursive means to bring the events experientially closer to their readers, and through their selection of interviewees sided with the protesters, making their fight against the regime emotionally understandable and sympathetic. In the Pakistani *Daily Times*, on the other hand, the coverage of the Egyptian events was fairly neutral, and it only covered the events as hard news, using the international news agencies as their sources. Yet the neutrality of the coverage did not prevent the Arab Spring from becoming a reference point in Pakistani politics and also forcing the President to take part in the debate that evolved. That is because Pakistani political actors domesticated the Egyptian uprising to Pakistani politics. They tried their best to capitalize the attention and sentiments that the events aroused in the population, bringing ideas and principles evoked by the events to the domestic agenda. Thus ideas, in this case the exemplar of a popular uprising, seem to travel best across borders when they cease to be viewed as exogenous and foreign.

In that sense the persistent parochialism found in the domestication of foreign ideas is not an antithesis of global isomorphism or a 'countervailing force to the pull of globalization' (Gurevitch et al., 1991: 207). These two phenomena are instead intertwined in the domestication of global trends.

## GLOBALIZATION AND SYNCHRONIZATION

Although sociological institutionalism is critical of, and antithetical to, the functionalist idea of modernization as an evolutionary path, many scholars representing WPT picture past and future social change in terms of a linear development towards increasing isomorphism. For instance, Boli (2005) argues that world culture in the post-war era of rapid globalization is increasingly organized, rationalized and ubiquitous. Hence, he thinks, though some countervailing forces are evident, world culture is likely to continue to become further codified, institutionalized and consequential in coming decades. This description of a past and future linear development towards increasing homogenization is in fact quite close to the functionalist theory of modernization. The main difference is the driver of development. For WPT it is not the evolutionary universals of society (cf. Parsons, 1964; 1966) but rather world culture which, once instigated as a set of scripts that constitutes its agents, functions as the Weberian iron cage that determines the future for the entire world society.

Admittedly, Boli (2005, see also Boli and Thomas, 1999) presents a fascinating and convincing account of the institutional formation of world society from the late 19th century onward, with a rapid proliferation of intergovernmental and international non-governmental organizations in recent decades. From this perspective, global social change may be described as constant expansion and incorporation of global organizational standards to ever more regions of the world and pockets of social life. However, the focus on the global spread of all kinds of world models has made this strand of research largely neglect the question of the dynamics that create new ideas and hence guide political changes on a world scale. After all, global change often entails that new ideas replace existing beliefs about reality and rational ways to govern it. The problem is, how new ideas and models come about, why they spread across borders, and how they affect national policies.

In a seminal article on the institutional conditions of diffusion Strang and Meyer (1993) suggest that the process begins with the invention of a worldwide model through theoretical abstraction or 'theorization' followed by diffusion that accelerates when enacting a model becomes an 'institutional imperative' (1993: 495) among potential recipients. Research that digs into the actual practices through which actors create, 'edit' and promote an idea however show that the invention and spread of a policy format cannot be separated from each other. Rather, models are created and codified as global standards in parallel with the process of diffusion. For instance, in the case of national bioethics committees (NBCs), organizations such as the International Bioethics Committee, established as part of the process, redefined and codified the NBC as an institution simultaneously with its spread to ever more countries (Syvätera, 2013). This also suggests that implementing a policy format in a target country is not the end point of global policy changes; rather, actors running national organizations collaborate with their counterparts in other countries through the international organizations in question, exchanging ideas and publishing recommendations to be used as political capital in steering national practices in the relevant area.

Besides, the main attention paid to globally codified policy formats has created a biased picture of nation-states' interdependent decision-making. When viewed from the perspective of policymaking in a national state, interdependence rarely means promoting a single model implemented by other countries. Rather, political actors typically start with an argument about a problem – for instance a deficiency in services or inefficient functioning of a sector – often defined in international comparison. Several solutions, justified by alluding to models adopted elsewhere, are typically proposed, and the eventual policy is adapted to the local conditions, bearing resemblance to several ideas and policies (see e.g. Greener, 2002).

Looking at national policymaking in a cross-national perspective also challenges the impression created by policy diffusion research, according to which new policy models are created in developed economies to solve emergent problems, whereas developing countries follow them. The opposite seems to be true. From an analysis of law-making in six countries, it appears that the more a country is integrated with the global system, the more its parliamentary debates feature references to international comparisons or policies adopted elsewhere (Alasuutari, 2014).

Therefore, instead of thinking about world society as a global system in which the diffusion of world cultural models from the leaders to the laggards drive the development to ever-increasing homogenization, it is better to think of it as an institutional infrastructure within which nation-states keep an eye on what others are doing and synchronize their policies with their neighbours, competitors and others in their reference group. The same goes for regional polities, as well as public and business organizations. In that sense, members of world society behave like a school of fish, which make the same turns and adjust their movements to each other.

This focus on synchronization does not mean that one does not acknowledge or study the travel of ideas, values or catchwords and the codification of models as global standards. In fact, travelling ideas are often the reason that makes nation-states change their policies, but the ways in which states react to new ideas vary so that they hold onto their trajectories. In that sense trendy ideas are like shock waves that make national states make a new turn, not as proof of increasing isomorphism or of a trickle down of models from the centre to the peripheries. Rather, the differences between the ways different states respond to new ideas and buzzwords also serve as a dynamo of constant change, because a local adaptation of a circulating idea can always be marketed as a new solution for others to learn from (Alasuutari and Qadir, 2014a: 9).

The image of synchronization is better than that of diffusion in that it does not imply an assumption of endlessly increasing uniformity. Though fish align their moves with those of others, they retain their distance to each other and yet never become a single fish. Such synchronization of behaviour is based on information received from or about other members of the group, but it is two-way rather than one-way communication: a dialogue through which members update a shared understanding of the world and their position in it. Thus global models are not the starting point but rather an effect and a political tool of synchronization based on international comparison: a high ranking of some countries is represented as a result of particular 'best practices', which are then promoted globally.

The global travel of ideas as an essential element in the synchronization of actions in the global system has also been addressed in a recent discussion on circulation (Appadurai, 2000; Aronczyk and Craig, 2012; Lee, 2002) – a concept that also captures the idea that the flow of ideas is not unidirectional. In a similar vein, Karin Knorr-Cetina (2006; 2007; Knorr-Cetina and Bruegger, 2002) points out that the constant real-time connection between the traders constructs financial markets into a massive global conversation, synchronizing the moves of individual actors.

## POWER AND GOVERNANCE IN THE WORLD POLITY

Although all forms of neoinstitutionalism have a direct bearing on power relations, several authors have argued that WPT elides the question of power and dominance in the global system. Beckfield (2003; 2008) says that WPT views the structure of the world polity as relatively flat, whereas Hall and Taylor (1996: 954) remark that the focus on macro-level processes of diffusion guided by world culture drops the actors involved from sight so that the result begins to look like 'action without agents'. On the other hand, Koenig and Dierkes (2011) argue that while WPT challenges fundamental assumptions of actor-oriented conflict-theoretical approaches by conceptualizing action as highly scripted and actors as culturally constituted, as a theory it can also shed light on the nature of conflicts in the contemporary world. It may explain latent motives for conflict as illustrated by the conflict-generative potential of globally institutionalized principles of state sovereignty and human rights. Furthermore, they maintain:

> the world polity's associational structure and cultural content also account for the emergence of new methods of conflict resolution, as exemplified not only by the role of IGOs in reducing states' propensity to use force in dyadic conflict resolution but also by the global spread of triadic forms of conflict resolution such as reconciliation policies, alternative dispute resolution and the like. (Koenig and Dierkes, 2011: 18)

It is true that WPT scholarship has paid little attention to the question of power and the way in which frames of meaning, scripts and symbols emerge not only from processes of interpretation but also from processes of contention (Hall and Taylor, 1996: 954). Yet, at times the critics miss the point that WPT has particular relevance in elucidating 'community power' discussed by Steven Lukes (2004 [1974]). While the actor-centric approaches to power typically conceive of it as a hierarchical zero-sum game based on different forms of coercion, neoinstitutionalism directs attention to world-cultural values and scripts that make actors voluntarily act in a uniform manner. In WPT the focus is on the models that spread as a consequence of such shared views or standards, but if we ask about the nature of the struggle through which a unanimity or compromise is reached, ideas and beliefs are the primary battleground. This is how Schmidt (2008: 305) characterizes the contribution of discursive institutionalism: it provides insight into

> the questions that political philosophers through the ages have puzzled over, such as the role of ideas in constituting political action, the power of persuasion in political debate, the centrality of deliberation for democratic legitimacy, the construction and reconstruction of political interests and values, and the dynamics of change in history and culture.

This is also what Michel Foucault had in mind when he introduced the neologism of governmentality, which depicts government that guides the comportment of others by acting upon their hopes, desires, or milieux (Foucault, 1991; Inda, 2005). According to Foucault this kind of governance became increasingly crucial for the political elite when the sovereign power of monarchy was gradually replaced by a constellation in which the art of government consists in managing public opinion and the support of several factions of society (Foucault, 2007; 2008). The same has been said about governance at a global scale: national states adopt global standards and policy models not because they are forced to do so but primarily because governments are convinced that it is good for them, and hence global governance works particularly through knowledge production and consultancy (Alasuutari, 2011; Buduru and Pal, 2010; Radcliffe, 2010).

This kind of epistemic governance (Alasuutari and Qadir, 2014) is based on struggles over meaning and over a hegemonic definition of the situation at hand. Or let us say that policy decisions are reached through such struggles. They are not just struggles that consist in facts and ontological claims because actors also appeal to values and principles; they justify policies by bolstering shared values and by suggesting what they oblige us to do. Epistemic governance thus works by acting upon other people's view of reality and their conceptions of what is feasible, acceptable or desirable, but it does not mean that this analytic of governance only applies to subtle influence or 'soft power' (Nye, 2004). Rather, the epistemic governance analytic depicts an approach to studying governance, however rough, violent and easily discernible or 'dislocational' (Foucault, 1977) and subtle it is. Hence governance can be approached as more or less unself-conscious ways by which actors work on people's conceptions of reality. This entails strategies that affect people's wishes and aspirations, but a threat or use of military force and economic constraints are also means to affect people's conceptions of the situation and hence make them adopt a particular line of action. Whether actors use, say, science, money or tanks as their consultants, the objective in utilizing those resources is to convince others of what they want, or should or must do in a given situation.

The so-called governmentality studies have come close to these questions by investigating the rationales and effects of public policies on individuals' mentalities (see e.g. Dean, 1998; Rose, 2000). The analyses show that the self-regulating capacities of subjects, created by different indirect 'technologies of government', are important for governing in liberal democratic societies, even extending to controlling populations beyond the state's purview (Rose and Miller, 1992). But rather than rushing into the effects of a policy, similar questions can be asked about political decision-making: How are decision-makers and the general public led to think that a particular policy must be adopted? What are the means by which political actors try to convince others of the adequate solutions to the problems on the agenda? And how are issues constructed as problems in need of a policy reform?

Scrutiny of the debates and discussion on political issues shows that actors are engaged in what can be called epistemic work, in which they not only appeal to facts but also to commonly shared values. Furthermore, they address their audience as a community with shared interests, such as the nation. Indeed, there seems to be an analytical unity in the techniques by which policymakers generally get convinced of, and in turn try to convince others of, policy solutions. Epistemic work can be targeted on three different aspects of the social world: what is the environment, who are the actors, and what is virtuous or acceptable. In actual practice these three objects of epistemic work appear in combination so that there is no epistemic work that does not entail all three objects. When, for instance, a politician in national politics promotes a reform, she or he would provide sources of authority aimed at convincing the citizens that the current state of affairs is unsatisfactory and that the proposed measures will be effective and in the best interests of the nation. Such an argument obviously appeals to claims about reality, but arguing for a reform on that basis also includes a normative element. And to say anything about what must be done implies actors and what they identify with (Alasuutari and Qadir forthcoming).

Such a discursive institutionalist perspective on politics and power relations enables us to better understand why nation-states in their policies end up reacting to the same global ideas and buzzwords. It is because actors throughout the world share the same world-cultural values and premises, which means that the same arguments and discourses appeal to them. One of these globally shared premises is a strong belief in science and rationality, which is why actors justify their claims by referring to empirical evidence and to the authority of science. It may result at times in scientists as an epistemic community playing a decisive role in decision-making (Carayannis et al, 2011; Haas, 1992; Miller and Fox, 2001), but more generally it means that scientific evidence and authority are key weapons in the political battlefield. Consequently, national states and stakeholder groups all alike resort to knowledge production organizations such as the OECD and the World Bank or various privately funded think tanks.

One would think that increased use of research and evidence leads the way to increasingly scientific planning and organization of society, but in fact it drives the creation of policy fashions. For instance in recent decades there has been a global trend to transform older social forms – traditional bureaucracies, family firms, professional and associations – into the same standard format of a formal organization. For instance traditional charities are now 'nonprofit organizations' (Meyer and Bromley, 2013). From the perspective of political actors, what counts is not whether they believe in a new policy, concept or principle, but whether they think that other actors and so-called 'public opinion' consider it important. Hence individuals who want to influence decision-making need to align with the other actors' views and sentiments, influence others with their own moves, or affect the beliefs about what the 'general public' thinks. In other words, politics is increasingly dependent on impressions and impression management, which leads to 'signalling games' discussed in rational choice institutionalism (Hall and Taylor, 1996: 956).

## DISCUSSION AND CONCLUSION

In this chapter I have introduced new institutionalisms and particularly sociological and discursive institutionalism as approaches to cultural sociology. To reiterate what has been discussed above, there is a tension between different strands of neoinstitutionalism regarding actorhood. The Stanford School scholars have thus far concentrated on studying the diffusion of world culture as scripts that constitute actors as agents. In contrast, discursive institutionalist scholars have conducted case studies about the actual practices through which global ideas are incorporated in local contexts, and these studies have highlighted the key role of local actors and their objectives and skirmishes in the local–global interaction.

Yet these orientations must not be seen as separate schools of thought but rather as developments within neoinstitutionalist sociology. In other words, recent years have witnessed an increased interest in the forms of local–global interaction (Alasuutari and Qadir, 2014b; Drori et al., 2013) and in the 'receptor sites' (Frank et al., 2000; 2007; Larson et al., 2008) of global ideas. Case analyses about the enactment and domestication of global ideas have, in turn, shown that conformity is not the only or primary reason for the fact that nation-states and all kinds of organizations synchronize their moves with their reference groups. Rather, synchronization of national policies seems to be a side effect of local actors utilizing broadly shared ideas and values in justifying their political objectives. In this way the key principle of neoinstitutionalism to not rely on any given assumptions but to study actors' actual conduct in their institutional contexts has led neoinstitutionalist sociology to new observations and questions.

As has been implied in the discussion above, neoinstitutionalist sociology is also akin to the sociology of knowledge and to social studies of science. That is, in neoinstitutionalism existing theories of the social world are not considered simply as contestants of the neoinstitutionalist account but rather as frameworks that people apply in making sense of their environment, which guide their conduct and become real when institutionalized into organizational forms. This is captured well by Meyer and Bromley (2013), who stress the role of science in providing a universalistic basis for rules applicable to the domains of natural and social life alike:

> Scientization rapidly turns the chaos surrounding human life into articulated uncertainties and structures the proper management of the risks involved. As an instance, scientific analyses of childhood and its problems blossom and provide bases for social organization extending to the global level. New organizations arise, and older ones take on responsibilities for dealing with various dimensions of childhood – health, education, consumption behavior, protection from abuse by families and firms, and so on. (Meyer and Bromley, 2013: 370)

As elsewhere, in this instance sociological neoinstitutionalism is also indebted to Michel Foucault's discussion about the power/knowledge couplet. Foucault talks about the way in which the formation of knowledge and the increase of disciplinary power working through surveillance and standardization regularly reinforce one another in a circular process, making possible 'the formation of clinical medicine, psychiatry, child psychology, educational psychology, the rationalization of labour' (Foucault, 1977: 224). The difference is that neoinstitutionalists talk about this phenomenon in a global context, as part of the formation of the worldwide culture of modernity.

As a strand of cultural sociology, the strength of neoinstitutionalism is that instead of focusing on everyday life, art and entertainment, it treats the core areas of modern society such as science, politics and organizational life as cultural phenomena. That does not mean, however, that it is only relevant to those interested in macro-sociological phenomena. Neoinstitutionalist sociology also makes understandable action in local contexts and in the way they are intertwined with global ideas and considerations. Furthermore, as Motti Regev (2013) has shown in the case of popular music, the dynamics of global isomorphism at play in the domain of instrumental culture also apply to expressive culture. In the future, more research needs to and most likely will be done on how fads spreading in different walks of life synchronize social change on a global scale.

## NOTES

1 Some elements of this chapter first appeared in Alasuutari, P. (2015) 'The Discursive Side of New Institutionalism', *Cultural Sociology*, 9(2): 162–84.
2 At least creolization (Hannerz, 1987), glocalization (Robertson, 1992; 2013), hybridization (Pieterse, 1995), indigenization (Friedman, 2004), localization (Acharya, 2004; Bennett, 1999) and translation (Callon, 1986; Kjær and Pedersen, 2001) have been used in this context.

## REFERENCES

Acharya, A. (2004) 'How Ideas Spread: Whose Norms Matter? Norm Localization and Institutional Change in Asian Regionalism', *International Organization*, 58(2): 239–75.
Adams, L. L. (1999) 'Invention, Institutionalization and Renewal in Uzbekistan's National Culture', *European Journal of Cultural Studies*, 2(3): 355–73.
Alasuutari, P. (2001) 'Art, Entertainment, Culture, and Nation', *Cultural Studies/Critical Methodologies*, 1(2): 157–84.
Alasuutari, P. (2011) 'The Governmentality of Consultancy and Competition: The Influence of the OECD', in G. Solinís and N. Baya-Laffite (eds), *Mapping out the Research-Policy Matrix: Highlights from the First International Forum on the Social Science-policy Nexus*. Paris: Unesco Publishing. pp. 147–65.
Alasuutari, P. (2013) 'Spreading Global Models and Enhancing Banal Localism: The Case of Local Government Cultural Policy Development', *International Journal of Cultural Policy*, 19(1): 103–19.
Alasuutari, P. (2014) 'Interdependent Decision-making in Practice: Justification of New Legislation in Six Nation-states', in P. Alasuutari and A. Qadir (eds), *National Policy-Making: Domestication of Global Trends*. London: Routledge. pp. 25–43.
Alasuutari, P. and Qadir, A. (2014a) 'Introduction', in P. Alasuutari and A. Qadir (eds), *National Policymaking: Domestication of Global Trends*. London: Routledge. pp. 1–22.
Alasuutari, P. and Qadir, A. (eds) (2014b) *National Policy-Making: Domestication of Global Trends*. London: Routledge.
Alasuutari, P. and Qadir, A. (2014) 'Epistemic Governance: An Approach to the Politics of Policy-Making', *European Journal of Cultural and Political Sociology* 1(1): 67–84.
Alasuutari, P., Qadir, A. and Creutz, K. (2013) 'The Domestication of Foreign News: News Stories Related to the 2011 Egyptian Revolution in British, Finnish and Pakistani Newspapers', *Media Culture and Society*, 35(6): 692–712.
Alvarez, J. L., Mazza, C., Pedersen, J. S. and Svejenova, S. (2005) 'Shielding Idiosyncrasy from Isomorphic Pressures: Towards Optimal Distinctiveness in European Filmmaking', *Organization*, 12(6): 863–88.
Appadurai, A. (2000) 'Knowledge, Circulation and Collective Biography', *L'Homme*, 156: 29–38.
Appel, H. and Orenstein, M. A. (2013) 'Ideas Versus Resources: Explaining the Flat Tax and Pension Privatization Revolutions in Eastern Europe and the Former Soviet Union', *Comparative Political Studies*, 46(2): 123–52.
Aronczyk, M. and Craig, A. (2012) 'Introduction: Cultures of Circulation', *Poetics*, 40(2): 93–100.
Becker, H. S. (1967) 'Whose Side Are We On', *Social Problems*, 14(3): 239–47.
Beckfield, J. (2003) 'Inequality in the World Polity: The Structure of International Organization', *American Sociological Review*, 68(3): 401–24.
Beckfield, J. (2008) 'The Dual World Polity: Fragmentation and Integration in the Network of Intergovernmental Organizations', *Social Problems*, 55(3): 419–42.
Bennett, A. (1999) 'Hip Hop Am Main: The Localization of Rap Music and Hip Hop Culture', *Media, Culture and Society*, 21(1): 77–91.
Billig, M. (1995) *Banal Nationalism*. London: Sage.
Boli, J. (1987) 'World Polity Sources of Expanding State Authority and Organization, 1870–1970', in G. M. Thomas (ed.), *Institutional Structure: Constituting State, Society, and the Individual*. Newbury Park: Sage Publications. pp. 71–91.
Boli, J. (2005) 'Contemporary Developments in World Culture', *International Journal of Comparative Sociology*, 46(5/6): 383–404.
Boli, J. and Thomas, G. M. (eds) (1999) *Constructing World Culture: International Nongovernmental Organizations Since 1875*. Stanford: Stanford University Press.
Bourdieu, P. (1977) *Outline of a Theory of Practice*. Cambridge studies in social anthropology; 16. Cambridge: Cambridge University Press.

Buduru, B. and Pal, L. A. (2010) 'The Globalized State: Measuring and Monitoring Governance', *European Journal of Cultural Studies*, 13(4): 511–30.

Caldwell, M. L. (2004) 'Domesticating the French Fry: McDonald's and Consumerism in Moscow', *Journal of Consumer Culture*, 4(1): 5–26.

Callon, M. (1986) 'Some Elements of a Sociology of Translation: Domestication of the Scallops and the Fishermen of St Brieuc Bay', in J. Law (ed.), *Power, Action, and Belief: A New Sciology of Knowledge?* London: Routledge and Kegan Paul. pp. 196–223.

Campbell, J. L. (2004) *Institutional Change and Globalization*. Princeton, NJ: Princeton University Press.

Campbell, J. L. and Pedersen, O. K. (2001) 'Introduction', in J. L. Campbell and O. K. Pedersen (eds), *The Rise of Neoliberalism and Institutional Analysis*. Princeton: Princeton University Press. pp. 1–23.

Carayannis, E. G., Pirzadeh, A. and Popescu, D. (2011) *Institutional Learning and Knowledge Transfer across Epistemic Communities: New Tools of Global Governance*. New York: Springer.

Cook, I. R. (2008) 'Mobilising Urban Policies: The Policy Transfer of US Business Improvement Districts to England and Wales', *Urban Studies*, 45(4): 773–95.

Cortell, A. P. and Davis, A. W. (2000) 'Understanding the Domestic Impact of International Norms: A Research Agenda', *International Studies Review*, 2(1): 65–87.

Czarniawska, B. and Sevón, G. (2005) *Global Ideas: How Ideas, Objects and Practices Travel in the Global Economy*. Advances in organization studies, 13. Malmö: Liber and Copenhagen Business School Press.

Czarniawska-Joerges, B. and Sevón, G. (1996) *Translating Organizational Change*. Berlin: Walter de Gruyter.

Dean, M. (1998) 'Administering Asceticism: Reworking the Ethical Life of the Unemployed Citizen', in M. Dean and B. Hindess (eds), *Governing Australia: Studies in Contemporary Rationalities of Government*. Cambridge: Cambridge University Press. pp. 87–107.

Dolowitz, D. and Marsh, D. (1996) 'Who Learns What From Whom: A Review of the Policy Transfer Literature', *Political Studies*, 44(2): 343–57.

Drori, G. S., Höllerer, M. A. and Walgenbach, P. (eds) (2013) *Global Themes and Local Variations in Organization and Management: Perspectives on Glocalization*. New York: Routledge.

Ertl, H. (2006) 'Educational Standards and the Changing Discourse on Education: The Reception and Consequences of the PISA Study in Germany', *Oxford Review of Education*, 32(5): 619–34.

Evans, M. and Davies, J. (1999) 'Understanding Policy Transfer: A Multi-Level, Multi-Disciplinary Perspective', *Public Administration*, 77(2): 361–85.

Foucault, M. (1977) *Discipline and Punish: The Birth of the Prison*. London: Penguin Books.

Foucault, M. (1991) 'Governmentality', in G. Burchell, C. Gordon and P. Miller (eds), *The Foucault Effect: Studies in Governmentality*. Chicago: University of Chicago Press. pp. 87–104.

Foucault, M. (2007) *Security, Territory, Population: Lectures at the Collège de France, 1977–78*. Basingstoke: Palgrave Macmillan.

Foucault, M. (2008) *The Birth of Biopolitics: Lectures at the Collège de France, 1978–79*. New York: Palgrave Macmillan.

Frank, D. J., Hironaka, A. and Schofer, E. (2000) 'The Nation-State and the Natural Environment over the Twentieth Century', *American Sociological Review*, 65(1): 96–116.

Frank, D. J., Longhofer, W. and Schofer, E. (2007) 'World Society, NGOs and Environmental Policy Reform in Asia', *International Journal of Comparative Sociology*, 48(4): 275–95.

Friedman, J. (2004) 'The Dialectic of Cosmopolitanization and Indigenization in the Contemporary World System: Contradictory Configurations of Class and Culture', in D. Nugent and J. Vincent (eds), *A Companion to the Anthropology of Politics*. Malden: Blackwell. pp. 179–197.

Greener, I. (2002) 'Understanding NHS Reform: The Policy-Transfer, Social Learning, and Path-Dependency Perspectives', *Governance*, 15(2): 161.

Gurevitch, M., Levy, M. R. and Roeh, I. (1991) 'The Global Newsroom: Convergences and Diversities in the Globalisation of Television News', in P. Dahlgren and C. Sparks (eds), *Communications and Citizenship: Journalism and the Public Sphere in the New Media Age*. London: Routledge. pp. 195–216.

Haas, P. M. (1992) Introduction: Epistemic Communities and International Policy Coordination', *International Organization*, 46(1): 1–35.

Hall, P. A. and Taylor, R. C. R. (1996) 'Political Science and the Three New Institutionalisms', *Political Studies*, 44(5): 936–57.

Hall, S. and Jefferson, T. (1976) *Resistance Through Rituals: Youth Subcultures in Post-war Britain*. London: Hutchinson.

Hannerz, U. (1987) 'The World in Creolization', *Africa*, 57(4): 546–59.

Hay, C. (2006) 'Constructivist Institutionalism', in S. A. Binder, R. A. W. Rhodes and B. A. Rockman (eds), *The Oxford Handbook of Political Institutions*. Oxford: Oxford University Press. pp. 56–74.

Hay, C. (2011) 'Ideas and the Construction of Interests', in D. Béland and R. H. Cox (eds), *Ideas and Politics in Social Science Research*. Oxford: Oxford University Press. pp. 65–82.

Inda, J. X. (2005) 'Analytics of the Modern: An Introduction', in J. X. Inda (ed.), *Anthropologies of Modernity: Foucault, Governmentality, and Life Politics*. Oxford: Blackwell. pp. 1–20.

Ingram, P. and Clay, K. (2000) 'The Choice-Within-Constraints New Institutionalism and Implications for Sociology', *Annual Review of Sociology*, 26(1): 525–46.

Kjær, P. and Pedersen, O. K. (2001) 'Translating Liberalization: Neoliberalism in the Danish Negotiated Economy', in J. L. Campbell and O. K. Pedersen (eds), *The Rise of Neoliberalism and Institutional Analysis*. Princeton: Princeton University Press. pp. 219–48.

Knorr-Cetina, K. (2006) 'The Market', *Theory, Culture & Society*, 23(2/3): 551–6.

Knorr-Cetina, K. (2007) 'Global Markets as Global Conversations', *Text and Talk*, 27(5/6): 705–34.

Knorr-Cetina, K. and Bruegger, U. (2002) 'Global Microstructures: The Virtual Societies of Financial Markets', *American Journal of Sociology*, 107(4): 905–50.

Koenig, M. and Dierkes, J. (2011) 'Conflict in the World Polity – Neo-institutional Perspectives', *Acta Sociologica*, 54(1): 5–25.

Larson, E., Johnson, Z. and Murphy, M. (2008) 'Emerging Indigenous Governance: Ainu Rights at the Intersection of Global Norms and Domestic Institutions', *Alternatives: Global, Local, Political*, 33(1): 53–82.

Latour, B. (1986) 'The Powers of Association', in J. Law (ed.), *Power, Action and Belief: A New Sociology of Knowledge?* London: Routledge. pp. 261–77.

Lechner, F. J. and Boli, J. (2005) *World Culture: Origins and Consequences*. Malden: Blackwell.

Lee, B. (2002) 'Cultures of Circulation: The Imaginations of Modernity', *Public Culture*, 14(1): 191–213.

Lukes, S. (2004 [1974]) *Power: A Radical View*, 2nd edn. Houndmills: Palgrave Macmillan.

Maman, D. and Rosenhek, Z. (2007) 'The Politics of Institutional Reform: The "Declaration of Independence" of the Israeli Central Bank', *Review of International Political Economy*, 14(2): 251–75.

Mauss, M. (1979) *Sociology and Psychology: Essays*. London: Routledge and Kegan Paul.

Meyer, J. W. (2000) 'Globalization: Sources and Effects on National States and Societies', *International Sociology*, 15(2): 233–48.

Meyer, J. W. (2004) 'The Nation as Babbitt: How Countries Conform', *Contexts*, 3(3): 42–7.

Meyer, J. W. (2010) 'World Society, Institutional Theories, and the Actor', *Annual Review of Sociology*, 36: 1–20.

Meyer, J. W. and Bromley, P. (2013) 'The Worldwide Expansion of "Organization"', *Sociological Theory*, 31(4): 366–89.

Meyer, J. W., Boli, J., Thomas, G. M. and Ramirez, F. O. (1997) 'World Society and the Nation-State', *American Journal of Sociology*, 103(1): 144–81.

Meyer, J. W., Krücken, G. and Drori, G. S. (eds) (2009) *World Society: The Writings of John W. Meyer*. Oxford: Oxford University Press.

Miller, H. T. and Fox, C. J. (2001) 'The Epistemic Community', *Administration and Society*, 32(6): 668–85.

North, D. C. (1990) *Institutions, Institutional Change, and Economic Performance: The Political Economy of Institutions and Decisions*. Cambridge: Cambridge University Press.

Nye, J. S. (2004) *Soft Power: The Means to Success in World Politics*, 1st edn. New York: Public Affairs.

Ostrom, E. (1990) *Governing the Commons: The Evolution of Institutions for Collective Action*. Cambridge: Cambridge University Press.

Parsons, T. (1964) 'Evolutionary Universals in Society', *American Sociological Review*, 29(3): 339–57.

Parsons, T. (1966) *Societies: Evolutionary and Comparative Perspectives*. Foundations of Modern Sociology Series. Englewood Cliffs: Prentice Hall.

Peters, B. G. (1999) *Institutional Theory in Political Science : The 'New Institutionalism'*. London: Pinter.

Pieterse, J. N. (1995) 'Globalization as Hybridization', in M. Featherstone, S. Lash and R. Robertson (eds), *Global Modernities*. London: Sage. pp. 45–68.

Powell, W. W. and DiMaggio, P. J. (1991) 'Introduction', in W. W. Powell and P. J. DiMaggio (eds), *The New Institutionalism in Organizational Analysis*. Chicago: The University of Chicago Press. pp. 1–38.

Radcliffe, S. (2010) 'Non-rational Aspects of the Competition State – the Case of Policy Consultancy in Australia', *Policy Studies*, 31(1): 117–28.

Rautalin, M. (2014) 'The Role of PISA Publicity in Forming National Education Policy: The Case of the Finnish Curriculum Reform', in P. Alasuutari and A. Qadir (eds), *National Policymaking: Domestication of Global Trends*. London: Routledge. pp. 95–110.

Rautalin, M. and Alasuutari, P. (2007) 'The Curse of Success: The Impact of the OECD PISA Study on the Discourses of the Teaching Profession in Finland', *European Educational Research Journal*, 7(4): 349–64.

Regev, M. (2007) 'Ethno-National Pop-Rock Music: Aesthetic Cosmopolitanism Made from Within', *Cultural Sociology*, 1(3): 317–41.

Regev, M. (2013) *Pop-rock Music: Aesthetic Cosmopolitanism in Late Modernity*. Cambridge: Polity Press

Ringarp, J. and Rothland, M. (2010) 'Is the Grass Always Greener? The Effect of the PISA Results on Education Debates in Sweden and Germany', *European Educational Research Journal*, 9(3): 422–30.

Ritzer, G. (1996) *The McDonaldization of Society: An Investigation into the Changing Character of Contemporary Social Life*, Rev. edn. Sociology for a new century. Thousand Oaks: Pine Forge Press.

Robertson, R. (1992) *Globalization: Social Theory and Global Culture*. London: Sage.

Robertson, R. (2013) 'Situating Glocalization: A Relatively Autobiographical Intervention', in S. Drori, M. A. Höllerer and P. Walgenbach (eds), *Global Themes and Local Variations in Organizational Management*. London: Routledge. pp. 25–36.

Rose, N. (2000) 'Community, Citizenship, and the Third Way', *American Behavioral Scientist*, 43(9): 1395–411.

Rose, N. and Miller, P. (1992) 'Political Power Beyond the State: Problematics of Government', *The British Journal of Sociology*, 43(2): 173–205.

Sahlin-Andersson, K. (1996) 'Imitating by Editing Success: The Construction of Organization Fields', in B. Czarniawska and G. Sevón (eds), *Translating Organizational Change*. Berlin: Walter de Gruyter. pp. 69–92.

Sahlins, M. D. (1976) *Culture and Practical Reason*. Chicago: University of Chicago Press.

Schmidt, V. A. (2008) 'Discursive Institutionalism: The Explanatory Power of Ideas and Discourse', *Annual Review of Political Science*, 11(1): 303–26.

Strang, D. and Meyer, J. W. (1993) 'Institutional Conditions for Diffusion', *Theory and Society*, 22(4): 487–511.

Syvätera, J. (2013) 'Making a Global Policy Model: The Case of "National Bioethics Committee"', Unpublished manuscript.

Syvätera, J. and Alasuutari, P. (2014) 'Converging National with Stakeholder Interests: Establishing a National Bioethics Committee in Finland', in P. Alasuutari and A. Qadir (eds), *National Policy-Making: Domestication of Global Trends*. London: Routledge. pp. 164–180.

Takayama, K. (2008) 'The Politics of International League Tables: PISA in Japan's Achievement Crisis Debate', *Comparative Education*, 44(4): 387–407.

Takayama, K. (2010) 'Politics of Externalization in Reflexive Times: Reinventing Japanese Education Reform Discourses through "Finnish PISA Success"', *Comparative Education Review*, 54(1): 51–75.

Waldow, F. (2009) 'What PISA Did and Did Not Do: Germany after the "PISA-shock"', *European Educational Research Journal*, 8(3): 476–83.

Willis, P. E. (1977) *Learning to Labour: How Working Class Kids Get Working Class Jobs*. Farnborough: Saxon House.

Willis, P. E. (1978) *Profane Culture*. London: Routledge and Kegan Paul.

# The Cultural Worth of 'Economies of Worth': French Pragmatic Sociology from a Cultural Sociological Perspective

Ilana F. Silber

## INTRODUCTION

What used to be called 'the new French pragmatic sociology' is not so new anymore. Twenty-four years since Luc Boltanski and Laurent Thévenot published their landmark treatise *De la Justification: Les Économies de la Grandeur* in 1991 (if less than a decade after it appeared in a belated English translation), this chapter will address French pragmatic sociology from the perspective of its ongoing dialogue with and contribution to cultural sociology.

Adding complexity to the matter at hand, neither cultural nor pragmatic sociology can be seen as united or static currents of sociological research and theory. French pragmatic sociology, also going under the name of 'the sociology of critical capacity' or 'pragmatic sociology of critique', has been garnering increasing attention and *De la Justification* in particular is by now a widely cited work across many fields of sociology and beyond.[1] In the process, the pragmatic sociology of critique has also branched out in various directions, reflecting diverse theoretical emphases and empirical foci of interest. As of cultural sociology at large, it has undergone tremendous expansion, leading to a rich, as well as fluid and quite polemical intellectual scene. Moreover, an active concern with culture and meaning-making appears to have seeped into many fields of sociological research not necessarily identified as cultural sociology proper – making the latter's boundaries increasingly fuzzy and controverted (Binder et al., 2008).[2]

Not making things simpler, the very definition of these two currents is strongly inflected by local, even national traditions of research, to the point of challenging the very possibility of exploring their relation as such. Pragmatic sociology has clear French origins[3] and established a distinct institutional anchor in French academia in the mid-1980s: the Groupe de Sociologie Politique et Morale (GSPM) at the EHESS/CNRS.[4] In contrast, what goes under the name of 'cultural sociology' in the North American context appears to have no clear equivalent in France (Cefaï, 2009a).[5] Main authors identifying themselves as cultural sociologists in the United States have yet few if any evident counterparts as such in France.[6] Symptomatically perhaps, *On Justification* itself hardly uses the word 'culture' (three times only), nor does it discuss the notion at any length. On the other hand, many authors identifying themselves to various degrees with the pragmatic sociology of critical capacities are hardly known outside of France.[7]

With such difficulties in mind, I shall not reach here for an exhaustive depiction of the mutual relation between these two influential strands of current sociology. Rather, my aim will be to clarify French pragmatic sociology's contribution to some key issues of cultural sociological analysis. For that purpose, I find it useful to start by tracing its main theoretical arguments and situating these relatively to two major strands of American cultural sociology in particular (themselves not entirely homogeneous and in ongoing development): what may be loosely labeled 'repertoire theory' on the one hand and the 'strong program', or as it is sometimes called, the Alexander or Yale school of cultural sociology on the other. The idea is to identify French pragmatic sociology's distinctive ways of navigating theoretical dilemmas facing current cultural analysis, and to better demarcate the special strengths and (often self-imposed) limitations of a strand of sociological research that has retained a relatively open-ended, modest character and never claimed to provide a full-blown 'grand theory' to begin with. A following section will briefly survey the increasing application of Boltanski and Thévenot's approach to 'economies of worth' and 'regimes of justification' to various areas of empirical and theoretical research, not necessarily identified with cultural sociology specifically.[8] I shall then conclude with some implications for further intensifying the dialogical, theoretical synergy between pragmatic sociology and cultural sociology, thereby also contributing to a growing, multilayered *cultural* sociology of morality.

## A DISTINCTIVE APPROACH TO CULTURAL ANALYSIS

Three interrelated features of French pragmatic sociology are especially significant for present purposes: a sustained effort to link micro- to macro-sociological, and even more significantly here, macro-cultural analysis; a structured form of 'cultural repertoire' theory; a plural and multilevel, or as I shall term it here 'modular', approach to cultural analysis.

### *A Micro-sociology with a Macro-cultural Thrust*

French pragmatic sociology as it emerged in the mid-1980s was often read as mainly a reaction, and an alternative, to Bourdieu's 'critical sociology'. In the meanwhile, Boltanski as well as Thévenot have insisted on countering any unduly anti-critical interpretation of their approach and elaborated upon their own contribution to critical analysis (Boltanski, 2011 [2009]; Thévenot, 2011a, 2011b). But they also steadily maintained their principled opposition to the more reductionistic aspects of Bourdieu's work, its implied 'hermeneutics of suspicion', and in particular its neglect of actors' own critical and evaluative capacities. In contrast, these very same capacities were made central to their own approach, where systematic attention is drawn to the ways in which actors justify themselves and criticize others – be it while engaged in the ordinary stream of shifting sequences of action, or in intensified situations of dispute and conflict.

Given the importance granted to actors' perceptions, actions and interactions in such a framework, the new French current might seem to favor a micro-sociological perspective. Affinities with Garfinkel's ethnomethodology specifically have often been emphasized,[9] revolving around a similar concern with investigating the practical reasoning, procedures and reflexive 'accounts' which make social life an ongoing, practical accomplishment (Heritage, 1984: 4). But pragmatic sociology also came to focus upon one distinct category of 'practical reasoning', namely the range of arguments and principles of evaluation which individuals deploy in the process of trying to define what may be the most proper or legitimate action or standard of action, and groping for or re-establishing social agreement. Intrinsic to such 'regimes of justification' is the tendency to articulate principles of a broad, generalizing nature, of the kind apt to carry across and beyond shifting concrete situations and contexts. As well known by now, six such main regimes of justification (or 'orders of worth' as they are now often called in English) were thus mapped out by Boltanski and Thévenot in *On Justification*.[10] The point is, for now, that pragmatic sociology sharply departs from any treatment of the 'objective reality of social facts' as an essentially local, detailed, contingent and situation-specific achievement (Garfinkel, 1991: 11) and insists, by contrast, on the systematic exploration of principles of evaluation or 'regimes of justification' that are indeed mobilized within, but also transcend specific, situational contexts.

Pragmatic sociology thus displayed from the very start a principled openness to macro-sociological, and even more precisely, macro-cultural analysis, deeply enmeshed in the exploration of what are commonly seen as micro-sociological aspects of everyday action and interaction.[11] Rephrasing this in cultural sociological terms, it combines sustained sensitivity to ongoing processes of meaning-making and to supra-individual and supra-situational cultural frameworks that structure – in the sense of both enabling and constraining – such processes.

As critics were quick to point out, many questions of importance to sociological theory in general, as well as cultural sociology, were left unanswered. Do regimes of justification (in either their more philosophical or commonsensical discursive expression) operate, to use Clifford Geertz's famous formulation, as 'models for' or 'models of' reality? Or even more basically, how precisely does pragmatic sociology conceive the relation between discourse and practice, or as often phrased in other corners of contemporary sociology, culture and agency? And how does it theorize, if at all, the relation of regimes of action and justification to any social or societal structures, and to organizational and institutional frameworks within and across social spheres, be it at a meso- or macro-sociological level of analysis? On all such scores it must be admitted, French pragmatic sociology remained somewhat enigmatic.

Yet we need to emphasize that the very same macro-cultural thrust just described above comes to the fore again, if now deployed in a diachronic historical perspective and combined with enhanced attention to economic structures and institutions, in Boltanski and Chiapello's study of the *New Spirit of Capitalism* (2005 [1999]). Very briefly, this influential work traces the sequential development of at least three different 'spirits', or modes of justification, in the history of modern capitalism, a history it depicts as propelled, at least in part, precisely by the dynamics of criticism and its dialectical relation to dominant modes of justification. Not only did different phases of capitalism, each with its own defining 'spirit' and system of justification, engender different types of critiques, but critique itself played a role in inducing transformations within capitalism. The critical faculties of human beings and their moral need for justification (of themselves and others) are here again at the very heart of the matter; but now they are perceived as interacting in a complex and largely unintended fashion with extant economic, social and ideological structures, which they both shape and are shaped by.[12]

A similar combination of interest in meaning-making and macro-cultural analysis, with the added ingredient of a more sustained analytical focus on institutions as such, is expressed once again in Boltanski's recent collection of lectures *On Critique*, in which he underscores the 'semantic role of institutions', and 'hermeneutic contradictions' in processes of constitution and critique of an ever-fragile 'reality' (Boltanski, 2011 [2009]). And the same combination is further put to work in his analysis of the rise of the spy novel and detective story in *Enigmes et Complots* (Boltanski, 2012), a study I shall return to later in some more detail.

On a very different front, this sustained macro-cultural thrust also helps distinguish regimes of justification – as relatively independent cultural, conceptual formations cutting across and transcending specific situations and contexts – from the neo-institutionalist idea of 'institutional logics', which are anchored on the contrary (at least in its early versions) in specific organizational and institutional settings, fields or spheres, of which they become a dominant feature (Powell and DiMaggio, 1991; Friedland and Alford, 1991).[13] To that extent, we also need to resist interpretations of French pragmatic sociology that have tended to reduce it to one more form of institutional differentiation theory, be it classically Weberian, neo-institutionalist or otherwise.

Significantly for present purposes, it is this sustained macro-cultural thrust, and related concern with cultural structures and their internal parameters and logics of meaning as such, which help us conceive of French pragmatic sociology as a specific brand of cultural repertoire theory, and which in turn call for a comparison with the 'strong program' of cultural sociology pioneered by Alexander and his colleagues.

## *A Form of Repertoire Theory?*

Shifting now to consider pragmatic sociology's precise understanding of the relation between actors and macro-cultural frameworks makes it easier to highlight significant points of convergence with the rich vein of research on cultural repertoires. Individual actors, in the pragmatic perspective, are not only endowed with an essential competence for evaluation and criticism, but also a flexible capacity to switch codes from one situation to another.[14] Switching codes, however, is not an easy, but rather a delicate and costly task that requires, precisely, such flexible and competent forms of agency. Justification itself, in fact, is never to be taken-for-granted, nor achieved once and for all. On the contrary, it is repeatedly reconfirmed or alternately weakened by confrontation with 'tests' deemed adequate to each respective regime of justification, and with other regimes of justification, this also engineering at times a distinctive set of possible 'compromises'. Not all situations, moreover, answer to regimes of justification (or more broadly put, to the mode of '*justice*'), and some may well tip over into any of the main alternative modes or 'regimes of action' that have been hitherto identified from this theoretical perspective, such as 'violence', '*agapè*' (all-out love and solidarity), 'justesse' or 'familiarity'.

For present purposes, the more important feature of the pragmatic approach is that conflictual situations and efforts at agreement tend to be channeled into and shaped by the agents' access to only a small, limited number of alternative regimes of action and justification coexisting in a state of instability. In other words, far from being completely free and flexible, individuals can only choose from an ultimately limited pool of regimes of criticism and justification that happen to have been made available to them historically, as part of what may best be called – even if the term never appears in *On Justification* or any other pragmatic writings – their 'cultural repertoire'.

In several respects, French pragmatic sociology converges with an expanding body of research, mainly in the context of American cultural sociology, giving weight to the wider 'cultural repertoire' which social actors draw upon while engaged in meaning-making 'on the ground', i.e. in the context of interactive processes (Spillman, 2002: 7). Strong affinities with repertoire theory could already be easily discerned by the early 2000s (Silber, 2003). At that point, not only had the idea of repertoire gained much traction as a key theoretical metaphor in various corners of (mainly American) sociology (see among others, Lamont, 1992; 1999; 2000; Silber, 2001; Steinberg, 1995; 1998; 1999; Swidler, 1986; 2001a; 2002; Tilly, 1979; Traugott, 1995), but the affinities between the two currents had already been made fully explicit in the collaborative collection published by Michèle Lamont and Laurent Thévenot in 2000, *Rethinking Comparative Cultural Sociology: Repertoires of Evaluation in France and the United States* (Lamont and Thévenot, 2000), as evident from the title of that collection itself.

Underpinning the increasing appeal of the idea of repertoires as a key theoretical metaphor, it would seem, is its usefulness in conveying the image of a structure that is both enabling and constraining, limiting but also flexible, and relatively stable yet never utterly static or closed. In addition, it has the advantage of connoting the ready enactment and concrete performance of practical or practicable options, and of allowing for a measure of individual meaning and agency in mobilizing and choosing a specific configuration of cultural resources, while also stressing the public and publically available nature of those resources.

Extant variants of repertoire theory, however, do not form a fully unified front. To begin with, they do not all present the same combination of the central tenets outlined above. In fact, they even differ in the extent to which they take a fully explicit stance in all these matters. Substantial differences may also be noted with regard to other important theoretical issues, such as the relation between cultural repertoires and other social structures, the incorporation of economist or instrumental notions and metaphors (such as cultural 'resources', 'tools' and 'tool-kit', 'supply side'), or the exclusive focus on discourse versus inclusion of non-discursive practices.

Most importantly here, diverse studies of cultural repertoires also differ in their approach to the internal structure of cultural repertoires, i.e. the extent to which they promote a leveling, undifferentiating approach to repertoires' ideational or symbolic contents, or try to establish, on the contrary, some basic principles of internal organization (e.g. a form of hierarchy, an internal 'logic', and/or internal contradictions). Briefly put, one of the earliest and most explicit formulations of repertoire theory, Ann Swidler's seminal argument about culture as 'tool-kit', (Swidler, 1986),[15] also entailed a largely unstructured approach, suggesting no distinctions or principle of internal organization in actors' respective 'cultural tool-kits'. Significantly, if still rarely noticed in current cultural sociology, Swidler herself has since explicitly made effort to correct for this lack of structure in her initial conception, and underscored the need to investigate how culture is organized at various levels (and in particular 'codes', 'contexts' and 'institutions') as both a theoretical issue and an empirical variable (Swidler, 2001; 2002; 2008; 2012; Tavory and Swidler, 2009).[16]

By and large, however, research on cultural repertoires has given little attention, empirically and theoretically, to the issue of their internal structure. One reason for that is probably the obvious theoretical tension between emphasizing plurality and flexibility in the conceptualization of cultural repertoires on the one hand, and trying to endow these very same loose, flexible entities with some form or principle of internal structure on the other; or opting to theorize structuring constraints as external to cultural repertoires themselves. It is thus very significant that French pragmatic sociology, otherwise attuned to repertoire theory in so many ways, happens to display a distinctive and systematic concern not only with the internal ideational contents but also the internal structures of cultural repertoires.

The systematic attention to cultural contents, to the actual pool of specific ideas and ideals extant in cultural repertoires, and to the ways in which they interrelate and partake of identifiable structured formations, is most evident in Boltanski and Thévenot's detailed analysis and comparison of the criteria of equivalence, definitions of the public good, and internal 'logic' of distinct regimes of justification, a project that entails outlining methodically some thirteen parameters of analysis for each regime.[17] But no less noteworthy, as we shall see now, it comes together with an equal attention to the structure of relations not only within but also between regimes of justification themselves, and with a modular approach to distinct domains or levels of cultural analysis.

## A Plural and 'Modular' Cultural Theory

Given the special place the pragmatic sociology of critique assigns to justification by reference to values and conceptions of the common good ('principes supérieurs communs'), it may be said to grant privileged attention to *moral* contents, and as such perhaps even harks back to Durkheim's conception of sociology as the study of 'systems of morality'. But it also allows for a cultural-ideological plurality and flexibility that is rather uncongenial to any classically Durkheimian treatment of morality (see however Rawls, 2012). Not only does this pluralist temper prevent any undue return to overly consensual, functionalist or holistic conceptions, it even leads pragmatic sociology to adopt what it called a 'symmetrical', leveling and detached descriptive approach to all competing regimes of evaluation.[18]

Yet counteracting this pluralizing and leveling thrust, pragmatic sociology's methodical exploration of regimes of justification does posit some very basic structural features. To begin with, as already noted above, tools of justification are not treated in isolation, but as part of broader clusters, regimes of justification, each with its own distinctive and detailed internal 'logic'. Moreover, the relation between the alternative regimes of justification is itself seen as one of tense coexistence in a state of constant, principled tension and contradiction within one and the same repertoire, rather than a chaotic or random absence of structure. It is also precisely this structured pattern of tensions and contradictions that makes it possible for Boltanski and Thévenot to map a limited number of possible, distinct forms of compromises between regimes of justification.

In addition, a most original (if also controversial) feature of this sustained scrutiny of cultural structures is its attempt to distinguish, as well as connect, two very different cultural layers or levels of analysis in the operation of regimes of justification: textual philosophical traditions belonging to what is classically understood as intellectual 'high' culture on the one hand, and regimes of justification, i.e. principles of evaluation as used in everyday life on the other. Each of the six main regimes of justification, or 'cités' (inspirational, domestic, civic, recognitional, industrial, commercial) originally identified by Boltanski and Thévenot, was also said to correspond to a distinct, key text of philosophy or political thought (respectively, Augustine, Bossuet, Rousseau, Hobbes, Saint-Simon, Adam Smith), conceived not only as providing a fuller and more systematic articulation of the very same principles, but also as somehow nurturing and shaping their inchoate awareness and commonsensical application in 'ordinary' life. Moreover, in their analysis of managerial practical guides, Boltanski and Thévenot may even be said to scrutinize regimes of justification at what is in fact a third level of cultural articulation, that of a specific professional elite, lying somewhere in between more inchoate, 'ordinary' commonsense and more rigorous high-brow philosophies.

The weaknesses and dilemmas of such an approach, for those in search of a more rigorous theory of culture, were immediately and still are quite blatant. In particular, it remained unclear what exactly could be the basis for such a linkage between 'high' and 'popular' tools of evaluation, when Boltanski and Thévenot themselves make it clear that most 'ordinary' actors never even read the texts in question. To many, it all seemed one more expression of French 'Cartesian' intellectualism, with no small dose of intellectual provincialism to boot.

Be this as it may, this sensitivity to diverse layers of culture and levels of cultural analysis also partakes of what might best be understood as a phenomenological perspective, quite distinctive in a field now rather pervaded by structuralist, linguistic and discursive or textual models of cultural analysis. True enough, Boltanski and Thévenot's writings clearly reckon with the influence of the turn to linguistics and semiotics, evident in their focus on the study of discursive paradigms and their underlying 'grammars' in particular. Yet all throughout its demarcation of regimes of justification and its analysis of the specific ways in which such regimes proceed, pragmatic sociology also displays important affinities to Peter Berger and Thomas Luckmann's famed *The Social Construction of Reality* (1967) – a work explicitly impregnated with the deep influence of Schütz's phenomenological sociology – a frame of reference much less noticed but perhaps no less important than the oft-mentioned kinship with ethnomethodology.[19] And in such a perspective, regimes of justification may thus be seen, analytically, as operative in, and thereby constituting, a specific level, layer or domain of meaning. In that sense, they are coextant with other domains and parameters of meaning already explored and identified by sociologists, and with which they may interact or overlap, be it Weber's diverse theodicies and bases of legitimacy, Geertz's range of 'cultural systems' (e.g. religion, ideology, commonsense, etc.), or even Goffman's 'interaction order'.

The more general issue at stake here is the need to theorize various modes and levels of meaning-making, and how to do so. This is richly confirmed by Thévenot's own intellectual trajectory, which led him to explore a plurality of regimes of 'engagement', in what he calls a 'below-the-public' level of analysis. Shirking away from the more public and generalizing aspects of dynamics of justification – even as he means to challenge classical micro–macro and relatedly, private–public, dichotomies – the analysis now aims to tackle the plurality of cognitive formats and engagements from the very familiar to the most public, 'unequally ready to be commonized' (Thévenot, 2006; 2007). Moreover, Thévenot in particular also developed an interest in comparative work addressing yet another level of cultural analysis, that of distinctive national patterns and cultural traditions, the importance of which was never denied in previous work with Boltanski, and even at times explicitly acknowledged in other pragmatic writings (e.g. by Boltanski and Chiapello in *The New Spirit of Capitalism* (2005 [1999])), but never much elaborated upon either.[20]

In this respect, there are significant affinities with one major strand of research on cultural repertoires already alluded to above, namely Lamont's series of studies on symbolic boundaries and national cultural repertoires, often oriented to trans-Atlantic comparisons between France and the United States (Lamont, 1992; 2000) if also extending of late to other regions of the world. Indeed, attention to both the internal contents and structures of cultural repertoires similarly arises from Lamont's explorations of the varying importance, precise meaning and interrelation between a specific range of symbolic boundaries, varying within limited bounds across groups and countries. In addition, Boltanski and Thévenot's idea of a plurality of 'orders of worth',[21] each centering on justification by reference to superior values and conceptions of the common good ('*principes supérieurs communs*'), dovetails with Lamont's reassertion, against Bourdieu, of the part played by morality and moral criteria of evaluation. Relatedly, both strands of research opt to take actors' subjective perceptions seriously, and share a similar resistance to any sweeping 'hermeneutic of suspicion', such as tends automatically to anchor all cultural statements in underlying power differentials and individual or group interests.

Last but not least, both approaches share a principled openness to macro-cultural analysis, intervening in the exploration of what otherwise are more commonly seen as micro-sociological aspects of everyday action and interaction. This is precisely what enabled them both to identify influential frames of evaluation and/or justification, not only expressed within, but also reaching beyond discrete situations, institutional spheres or domains of action, and ultimately anchored in higher-order cultural traditions and ideational matrices (be they intellectual, philosophical, religious or political-ideological). From the very start in fact, Lamont diverged from Swidler's originally unstructured approach underscored above, in that it allowed for at least two if not more distinct levels of analysis in cultural repertoires: that of criteria for symbolic boundary work, and that of national cultural traditions (the term employed in her first book at least), with their various co-existing intellectual, religious and other types of cultural and ideological currents. There is even a hierarchy of causality hinted at, with cultural traditions playing a role, if never exclusive,[22] in shaping the tendency to privilege certain types of symbolic criteria of evaluation of others.

These many basic affinities, and shared interests in a macro-cultural, and more specifically national cultural, level of analysis became especially manifest in the early, ambitious collaborative comparative trans-Atlantic project, already mentioned above, *Rethinking Comparative Cultural Sociology: Repertoires of Evaluation in France and the United States* (Lamont and Thévenot, 2000). Gathering detailed case studies dealing with a number of conflictual areas generating intense passion or disagreement in each country – racism, sexual harassment, criteria for proper journalism, publishing policies, environmental issues – the idea was to try to tap the full range of 'cultural tools' (also addressed as 'schemas of evaluation' or 'elementary grammar')[23] deemed to be available across situations, as well as, crucially here, unevenly available across national contexts. Yet far from being just the result of a one-time collaboration, Thévenot's lasting interest in comparative cross-national research comes to the fore again in more recent work comparing the plurality of regimes of engagement coming to expression in France and Russia (Thévenot, 2010; forthcoming).

Significantly, all three facets of pragmatic cultural analysis just noted, including a multi-level, layered approach and attention to national configurations, are deployed again, if in a very different vein, in Boltanski's recent *Enigmes and Complots* (Boltanki, 2012). Describing and trying to explain the rise and enormous expansion of a new form of literary product – detective and spy novels – at a specific point of time in the history of West European polities, France and England in particular, this study could be seen as corresponding to both cultural sociology and a sociology *of* culture (if one accepts for the moment such a problematic distinction), or as I would prefer to state it, a cultural sociology of culture. Significantly here, Boltanski's argument gives pride a place both to macro-institutional transformations (especially evolving forms of the social state), and to concomitant changes in macro-cultural assumptions, having to do with the provision and stabilization of 'reality', and what he sees as the new salience of a distinction between the 'official' and the 'officieux'. We thus see confirmed the phenomenological attention to the social and cultural construction of diverse domains of meaning and layers of experienced reality already alluded to above, now also emerging as macro-cultural conditions shaping, as well as made possible by, actors' capacities of criticism and suspicion.

In more than one way, therefore, French pragmatic sociology appears to have taken to heart the analytical effort to map out the various aspects, levels or spheres constitutive of culture.[24] To that extent, it also appears to converge with otherwise very diverse strands of sociological theory, that increasingly theorize multiple levels of social life as such (if not focusing on 'cultural' structures specifically), each with its own distinctive properties, and variable relations to other identified levels of analysis (e.g. Archer et Maccarini., 2013; DiMaggio, 1997; Gorski, 2013; Jepperson and Meyer, 2011; Silber, 2007; Vandenberghe, 2014), a topic worthy of much more attention.

Yet we now need to highlight a more complex relation to another major current of cultural sociology, the 'strong program' in cultural sociology and Jeffrey Alexander's work in particular, with which French pragmatic sociology displays similar, significant affinities, but also starker divergences (and as I see it therefore, potentially fecund mutual complementarities). In many respects, pragmatic sociology would seem also to be compatible with many, if not all, aspects of the 'strong program' in cultural sociology, and even seems to buttress one of its most central claims in particular, namely, the need to explore 'culture structures' as autonomous, irreducible formations with their own internal contents and principles of organization (Alexander, 1988, 2003; Alexander and Smith, 1993, 1998). In addition, there is a shared empirical interest in situations of intensified dispute, public scandals, major '*affaires*' and crises, and thereby the operation of cultural structures, not only in situations of taken-for-granted agreement and consensus, but also situations of disagreement and conflict (Alexander, 1988; Alexander and Smith, 1993).

However, little dialogue has taken place between pragmatic sociology and the strong program. To proponents of the strong program, pragmatic sociology may seem too logical and argumentative, still smacking ultimately of a problem-solving, situationally instrumental, 'culture-as-tool-kit' approach, and unduly insensitive to the symbolic charge of deeper layers of subjective meanings. Relatedly, its interest in the critical capacity of actors to switch codes and juggle a plurality of logics of critique and justification, conveys a vision of culture too fragmenting and 'flattening', uncongenial to a neo-Durkheimian insistence on a deep, ultimately binary structure of meanings, carrying the spell and pulse of the sacred, and the attendant dynamics of pollution and purification. As such, it fails to appreciate the central, pervasive part played by such binary structures and dynamics of purification in patterns of inclusion and exclusion, as these affect boundaries of collective identity in general and the civil sphere in particular (Alexander, 2006), and even more generally, the unfolding of social performance as shot through with symbolic codes, cultural narratives and dramas (Alexander et al., 2006).[25]

Yet it is not difficult to sense the possibility of a more fruitful encounter between the two approaches. Pragmatic sociology's stress on actors' capacity to valorize, search for agreement, and invoke the common good, is highly relevant to many aspects of Alexander's work in particular, such as his ideas on the civil sphere and civil repair (Alexander, 2006). On the other hand, Alexander's ideas about the public dynamics of felicitous or failed cultural performance (Alexander 2004; Alexander, Giesen and Mast 2006) – what he calls 'cultural pragmatics' – could add an important, fascinating dimension to the study of regimes of critique and justification; it may perhaps even help explain their varying capacity to compete and convince under diverse cultural and structural conditions.

In the same vein, it would be intriguing to explore symbolic processes of pollution and purification, and also symbolic excess, not only with regimes of justification, but also regimes of action, facilitating or hindering their flipping over into any of the other identified regimes of action, or as later added by Thévenot, regimes of engagement. Moreover, binary structures are in fact already implicitly present within each order of worth: if each 'order of worth' as regime of justification entails the possibility for nuanced, graded evaluations and rankings of 'greatness', these also imply the possibility of a binary contrast between the two extremes of the hierarchy of worth, i.e. 'greatness' and its lowly, and therefore potentially 'polluting' opposite, within that specific order of evaluation. Finally, if both strands are bent to lend cultural significance to the world of objects and materiality—be it as tools of proof and testing in the context of French pragmatic sociology, or rather endowed with concentrated cultural power in line with the 'strong program'—we may well agree that a material object's capacity to provide proof may well depend (perhaps in some regimes of justification rather than others), on its symbolic-iconic qualities (Alexander, Bartmanski and Giesen, 2011).

Conversely, importing the idea of regimes of justification and action may contribute to cultural sociology, and the strong program in particular, by enhancing sensitivity to the need for a more plural, multi-level and modular approach to cultural analysis. In sum, not everything culturally significant need be ultimately amenable, or indeed reducible to a binary structure; nor does a relational approach to meaning necessarily imply a binary structure, however especially compelling the latter may be. Moreover, and we may find here the seeds of future research, cultural or iconic power may well itself be connected to the constructive and destructive forces of discursive debates and regimes of justification, or the capacity to override the boundaries between regimes of action, be it by compromise or some other yet unmapped form of cultural process.

Broadening now the argument to all forms of cultural sociology, approaching cultural analysis in a modular fashion also means allowing for the fact that not all situations, nor all aspects and levels of social life, are amenable, or need be subsumed, under one over-riding form of interpretation or logic. In some settings we may well benefit from a more differentiated analysis of a plurality of cultural logics at work, if perhaps not necessarily, or only, in the very ways they were defined and found to work by Boltanski and Thévenot themselves. And if we did hone our tools in some convincing way at one level of analysis, we may well need to slow down and see how it all relates to other levels of cultural analysis, and accept that the relation between various levels themselves may well empirically vary.

## CURRENT APPLICATIONS AND EXTENSIONS

This final section will now briefly survey the growing impact of French pragmatic sociology, and of *On Justification* in particular in various areas of sociological research.

Key ideas of French pragmatic sociology have now become a familiar influence across very diverse fields of sociology worldwide. Modes of reception happen to vary greatly however, and range from merely marginal or 'ceremonial' references to stronger, principled and theoretical applications and extensions, as well as critical discussions (the latter to be taken of course as also a sign of recognition). Most visible perhaps is the reception of *On Justification* in sociologies of the public sphere, i.e. studies touching upon public debate, law, civil society, voluntary organizations and the nonprofit sector (Cefaï, 2009b; Frère, 2006; Eulriet, 2008; 2014; Gladarev and Lonkila, 2013; Lichterman, 2012; Lichterman and Cefaï, 2006; Silber, 2011; Yamagushi and Suda, 2009), urban sociology (Boissonade, 2011; Fuller, 2013), and the environment (Allaire and Blanc, 2003; Blok, 2013; Centemeri, 2014; Chun, 2007; Lafaye et al., 2000; MacNaghten et al., 2015). There is also a significant imprint in sociology of the arts and culture (in the restricted sense of that term) (see especially Heinich, 2002; 2011; 2012); also Dromi and Illouz, 2010; Gielen, 2005; Illouz, 2003; Marontate, 2013; Pardo-Guerra, 2011; Roberts, 2012; Strand, 2014; Ten Eyck and Busch, 2012), as well as more purely theoretical research, social thought and critical theory (see Basaure, 2014; Blokker and Brighenti, 2011b; Boland, 2013; Borghi, 2011; Celikates, 2012; Eagleton-Pierce, 2014; Gonzalez and Kaufman, 2012; Hansen, 2016; Michel, 2014; Roberge, 2011; Wagner, 2001). And no less impressive is the migration of French pragmatic ideas into economic and organizational sociology (broadly understood, including fields of applied research in marketing, consumption, accounting and management) (Annisette and Richardson, 2011; Beckert, 2008 [2004]; Blic, 2000; Bouillé et al., 2014; Fourcade, 2011a, b; Jagd, 2005; 2007; Karpick, 2010; Lane 2014; Latsis, 2006; Lehtonen and Liukko, 2010; Lehoux et al., 2014; Ottosson and Galis, 2011; Patriotta et al., 2011; Pecoraro and Uusitalo, 2014),[26] including sociology of the professions and of the workplace (see Chateauraynaud, 1991; Dodier, 1993; Lemieux, 2000; 2009; Moreira, 2013; Pagnucco, 2012).

By and large, Boltanski and Thévenot's writings appear to be more influential outside than within cultural sociology proper (with all due caveats concerning that label, as already suggested at the beginning of this article). To some extent, this may be a side effect of both currents' own expansion and success, as well as their confluence with the more diffuse 'cultural turn' that made an imprint on so many domains of research. More than once in fact, French pragmatic sociology is simply made use of and referred to as 'cultural sociology'. Moreover, we need take into account complex intersections with a renewed interest in the sociology of morality (see Abend, 2008; 2010; Hitlin and Vaisey, 2010, 2013; Smith, 2003; Tavory, 2011)[27] and the way in which all three trends (in brief, pragmatic, cultural, moral) partly converge and partly compete, while dovetailing with the emerging field of 'valuation studies' (Cefaï et al., 2015; Vatin, 2013).

Here again, we see unfolding continuities and affinities with Lamont's brand of cultural sociology in particular, itself now precisely developing into a broader comparative 'sociology of valuation and evaluation' (SVE) (Lamont, 2012), partaking of the new field of valuation studies in formation. Increasingly concerned with exploring situations of 'heterarchy' or plurarchy, defined as a plurality of criteria/grammars of valuation and evaluation, the SVE project explicitly pursues a theme already central to Boltanski and Thévenot's writings, if one also finding an anchor in American writings such as Michael Walzers' (1983) work on 'spheres of justice' and Friedland and Alford's (1991) influential idea of a plurality of 'institutional logics'.

By and large, it is indeed this idea of a plurality of competing principles of valorization, which seems to find a powerful echo across fields of research and even across disciplines. It appears to coincide with a sweeping interest in the theoretical as well as practical implications associated with multiple orders of worth, and with the dynamic coexistence of a plurality of competing points of view in specific settings. However, it is also an idea that is often put to work independently of other notions of vital importance to French pragmatic sociology, such as critique and justification, or the distinction between regimes of action and justification. And while it is very much in tune with Lamont's interest in states of 'heterarchy' mentioned above, it does not necessarily come with a similar concern with the implications of the analysis for patterns of social inclusion or exclusion.

Numerous works are today exploring the plurality of conflicting principles, competing rationalities and dynamics of debate and compromise in a variety of contexts, too numerous to be surveyed here in any detail, and working with the help of very diverse methodologies, including an increasing use of empirical ethnographic methods.[28] The idea has received a rich echo in research on so-called 'hybrid organizations', such as are increasingly common for example at the interface of non-profit and for-profit universes of action (Mair, 2012; 2015; Rousselière and Vezina, 2009). But ongoing 'justification work', and expressions of dissent and critique, are increasingly identified as endemic (and mainly regarded as creative and constructive) to many types of organizations and institutions (Girard and Stark, 2003; Jagd, 2007; 2011; Messner et al., 2008; Patriotta et al., 2011; Scott and Pasqualoni, 2014; Stark, 2009). In this regard, the influence of French pragmatic sociology is often mediated by Thévenot's special ties to the 'economy of conventions', with an eye to processes of cooperation and coordination, establishment or re-establishment of agreement, or at least reliance on 'common grounds'.[29]

We are therefore witnessing a strong reception of the pragmatic sociology of critique in research targeting a meso-level of analysis, that of organizations and institutions and related field effects reaching beyond discrete organizational units, which was relatively neglected in the early writings of pragmatic sociology. Surveying this rich body of work in-depth is clearly beyond the limits of this chapter, but a recent theoretical contribution worth singling out for attention in that regard is Charlotte Cloutier and Ann Langley's systematic analysis of pragmatic sociology's possible contribution to the study of 'institutional logics' and vice versa (Cloutier and Langley, 2013). Published in a journal of management normally far from the eyes of cultural theorists, their dialogical argument not only maps the complementary strengths and weaknesses of both currents, but also calls for multi-level, multi-tiered explorations of the varying ways in which regimes of justification might interact with institutional frameworks, while also nested within broader, higher-order cultural structures. As such, it alerts us to an important challenge facing the exploration of multiple worths: namely, better theorizing the plurality of conflicting principles or 'cultural logics' not only meeting and competing in, but also cutting across and reaching beyond, specific settings.

Finally, it is crucial to note that multiple orders of worth in this expanding literature are not presented as just a pool of discursive resources put to instrumental or strategic use (the early loose style of repertoire theory with which Boltanski and Thévenot are still often mistakenly associated), but more often, as frames of moral interpretation and evaluation, referring to 'matters that matter', that is, issues and dilemmas that people can deeply care about in either specific contexts or the public sphere at large. In such a perspective, moreover, culture does not necessarily always operate in precisely the same way. Rather than either motivating and/or justifying actors' actions (see e.g. Céfaï, 2009b; Eulriet, 2008; 2014; Frère, 2006; Gladarev and Lonkila, 2013; Lichterman, 2012; Lichterman, 2006; Silber, 2011; Yamagushi and Suda, 2010), or providing a form of scaffolding external to agents' subjectivities, as some have portrayed it, orders of worth may also articulate and even constitute meaning-making in a more basic way, framing or calibrating forms of meaningfulness relevant to a specific setting, or in other words, actually defining for us what is meaningful to begin with.

But there may also be many more ways than hitherto have been mapped in French pragmatic writings and their current applications, as to how individual actors themselves negotiate their relations to worlds of worth and justification – be it in the private or public spheres, in informal situations of interaction with other individuals and objects in their proximate environment, as well as in the context of organizations or more distant macro-political, national or supranational frameworks. In sum, and in more ways than I have been able to fully convey here, the current dissemination of French pragmatic sociological ideas as to the form and contents of orders of worth may be seen as partaking of a *moral cultural turn*, involving a growing interest in a cultural sociology of morality, to which pragmatic sociology and cultural sociology may well bring both converging and complementary insights. Much remains to be explored, as we still need to reach for ways to better combine pragmatic sociology's attention to actors' critical capacities and structured plurality of orders of worth, together with the sensitivity of cultural sociology to the symbolic and moral charge of structured cultural meanings, while also aiming for a multidimensional and layered approach to cultural analysis.

## NOTES

1 A very early version of sections of this article was presented at the 10th Anniversary Conference of the Center for Cultural Sociology on *Advancing Cultural Sociology*, at Yale University, April 25–27, 2014. I also wish to thank David Inglis for a brilliant intellectual initiative and personal encouragement, as well as Jeffrey Alexander, Daniel Cefai, and Ori Schwarz for their comments on the final version. Even if I was only able to react in minimal ways at a late stage of production, they gave me a taste for more.
2 In a recent assessment, *De la Justification* is still 'generally considered to be the single most important sociological treatise of post-Bourdieu French sociology' (Baert and Carreira da Silva, 2010: 43).
3 It is worth noting that none of the articles in this special issue, precisely devoted to underscoring the diversity of forms of cultural sociology, refer to any French pragmatic research.
4 Notwithstanding the somewhat confusing label 'pragmatic', Boltanski and Thévenot state that they were not influenced by American pragmatism in their earlier work (see interview with Boltanski by Juliette Rennes and Simon Susen in Susen and Turner (2014: 591); see also Quéré and Terzi's essay in the same volume). More recently, we witness a more conscious, reflexive effort at an encounter between the two trends, often underpinned by renewed interest in John Dewey's writings and his theory of valuation in particular (see Cefaï et al., 2015; Gonzalez and Kaufmann, 2009; Stavo-Debauge, 2012; Thévenot, 2011a), fermenting other strands of pragmatist sociology in France with a stronger and more explicit anchoring in symbolic interactionism, ethnomethodology and the Chicago School (cf. Isaac Joseph, Louis Quéré, Albert Ogien). For an illuminating discussion of the complex relation between various strands of philosophical pragmatisms and current sociology (in France especially), see Ogien (2014).
5 The GSPM, however, has been recently dispersed, with some of its associated researchers (if not Boltanski and Thévenot themselves) regrouped under the umbrella of the Institut Marcel Mauss at the EHESS. For a recent, updated collective statement of what is also labelled 'sociologie des épreuves', see Barthe et al. (2013). Cultural sociology is not addressed at all in this text, but for referencing Lamont and Thévenot's collaborative volume as an example of pragmatic research with a macro-comparative dimension.
6 See also, addressing misunderstandings around related notions of sociology of culture and cultural studies, with a focus on the arts, Heinich (2010). Symptomatically, if one 'googles' in French 'Boltanski sociologie de la culture', little comes up. 'Sociologie culturelle' is not much used as a term either.
7 This state of affairs appears to apply to all major strands of American cultural sociology, and is all the more paradoxical if one remembers that much of American cultural sociology finds an explicit anchor in a quintessentially French, Durkheimian tradition of sociology. This is especially salient in the case of scholars most closely associated with the 'strong program', but also evident with regard to much research dealing with such Durkheimian themes as symbolic boundaries, civic religion, moral order, collective memory and rituals of solidarity.
8 I cannot but leave aside for now complexities having to do with the differential impact of cultural sociology (and cultural studies, adding another thorny issue) in various European countries, the UK and Germany in particular.

9  This entailed identifying major trends of reception and elaboration of French pragmatic sociology (only in English and French for now, ideally one would need to include other languages), focusing on key ideas developed in *On Justification* in particular. Luckily, we benefit from a special issue of the *European Journal of Social Theory* from 2011 edited by Paul Blokker, devoted to the theoretical developments and empirical applications of French pragmatic sociology. See also the recent, important collection by Simon Susen and Bryan Turner, *The Spirit of Luc Boltanski: Essays on the 'Pragmatic Sociology of Critique'* (2014). However, none of the essays in these two important collections explicitly addresses French pragmatic sociology from the point of view of cultural sociology. Also useful are several recent interviews with Boltanski, Thévenot, Lamont and Alexander, conveying personal accounts of their intellectual trajectories and occasional insights into their mutual perceptions of each other.

10 Garfinkel himself, however, would reject any definition of his approach as 'merely' micro-sociological, and sees himself as ultimately groping for a radically different way of addressing both micro- and macro-structures. His work, in any case, is not referenced in *On Justification*.

11 The list was not presented as exhaustive. Thévenot and collaborators soon demarcated 'ecology' as a possible, additional order of worth (Lafaye and Thévenot, 1993; Thévenot, Moody and Lafaye, 2000), while Boltanski and Chiapello later traced the emergence of a 'project-oriented' cité in *The New Spirit of Capitalism* (2005 [1999])

12 This macro-cultural thrust goes beyond just granting complementary validity to the macro-sociological perspective, as is done by some micro-sociologies or sociologies of action. It is also more principled and systematic than a converging tendency in the sociology of accounts to increasingly acknowledge that accounts need to be contextualized and may reflect culturally embedded normative explanations (Ohrbuch, 1997).

13 Some have sensed an affinity with S.N. Eisenstadt's attention to the part played by latent cultural contradictions, codes and counter-codes in the historical development of civilizations in general and modernity in particular, processes of institutionalization generating alternative counter-cultural codes and orientations leading to their own transformation or demise (Joas and Knoebl, 2009 [2004]: 542)

14 Neo-institutionalist contributions to cultural sociology would deserve separate attention, starting perhaps with John Meyer and associated scholars' studies of variegated cultural changes in relation to world-society and related matters. See for example, dispelling any such institutionally specific conflation (Thornton et al., 2012).

15 Pragmatic sociology, at least in its earlier formulations, does not operate with an altogether classically humanist view of human agency and individual autonomy (Bénatouïl, 1999: 297–301). Early formulations such as the notion of actants, or putting humans and objects on the same level, etc. are not or hardly reiterated with the same weight in later writings.

16 Swidler argues that culture's causal significance lies not in defining the ends of action but rather in providing the components or tools used to construct recurrent strategies of action. This emphasis on practice and action was already apparent in Charles Tilly's influential historical sociological work on repertoires of collective violence, where it had yet no explicit connection to cultural analysis (Tilly, 1979).

17 This was mainly at first by giving weight to the structuring power of institutions and 'anchoring social practices' (Swidler, 2001). More recent writings, however, show a growing interest in contents as well as internal structural aspects of cultural repertoires (rather than only institutional forces or ritualized situations impacting upon them "from the outside," as it were), such as a set of alternative, if also interrelated semiotic codes (Tavory and Swidler, 2009), or even more fundamental 'constitutive rules that define the social location of the sacred power of collective life' (Swidler, 2012). These later developments may be taken to buttress another important facet of her early 1986 statement (if one also relatively underlooked), namely, its convergence (via the distinction between settled and unsettled settings but not only) with a rising tendency to develop a non-unitary approach to "how culture matters," rejecting the idea of one single answer to that vexing question (Silber, 2007: 227).

18 This entails, for example, outlining a regime's conception of the state of being associated with 'greatness'; common human dignity, relevant subjects, objects, apparatus, tests, economy of resources, natural relations between beings, and so on.

19 This has been criticized by Ricoeur, for one, as an overly levelling discussion of the 'political' in particular as belonging to only one (so-called 'civic') among various possible regimes (Ricoeur, 1995).

20 Especially relevant here are Berger and Luckmann's attention to plural modes of legitimization, the coexistence of a plurality of finite provinces of meaning, processes of objectivization, and Berger's related idea of "plausibility structures" (Berger, 1967). The very notion of the social construction of reality is grappled with explicitly by Boltanski in recent writings (Boltanski, 2011

[2009]). See also Thévenot 2001: 59, for a rejection of radical 'constructivism', which should not be mistakenly identified with Berger and Luckmann's approach.

21 Boltanski and Chiapello were ready to acknowledge 'the heavy impact that 'traditions and national political conjunctures' continue to have in 'orienting economic practices and the ideological forms of expression that accompany them', even to the point where the categories they fashioned out of French materials might become perhaps inadequate when brought to other parts of the world (Boltanski and Chiapello, 2005 [1999]. Confirming a cultural interpretative dimension, they connect this national focus to a better chance of successfully taking into account the meaning that people give to their actions: '… les façons dont les personnes s'engagent dans l'action, leurs justifications et le *sens qu'elles donnent à leurs actes*' (Boltanski and Chiapello, 1999: 36, my emphasis).

22 Notions of worlds of worth, orders of worth and regimes of justification are used interchangeably by Boltanski and Thévenot themselves and commentators. Less noticed is that fact that the idea of economies of worth, starring in the title both in French and English, is in fact seldom used thereafter in the text of DJ/OJ itself.

23 Lamont's approach is rather Weberian and multidimensional, identifying a whole configuration of cultural and institutional factors, some more proximate than others, helping to account for the differential prominence of criteria of boundary work in these two national settings.

24 This shifting terminology is perhaps indicative of an indecisive stance towards the instrumentalist connotations of the tool-kit metaphor, mixed as it is here with a vocabulary somewhat rooted in linguistic and literary models of cultural analysis, thus also pointing to unresolved theoretical dilemmas.

25 I diverge here from overly dichotomic arguments contrasting justification and motivation, and positioning French pragmatic sociology as closest to a very loose, unstructured form of repertoire theory that denies cultural structures (such as regimes of justification or other, higher-order levels of macro-cultural analysis) an autonomous causal impact (Beyerlein and Vaisey, 2013; Vaisey, 2009). This approach, moreover, sometimes simplifies the strong program's approach, conflating what Anne Kane would call the analytical as opposed to concrete autonomy of culture structures (Kane, 1991), and overlooking its more nuanced arguments that allow for empirical variability and more situated models of social structure, action and culture (e.g. Alexander and Smith, 1993: 159)

26 Besides such theoretical divergences, Alexander criticizes the orders of worth, and dynamics of compromise between them, for assuming the existence of civil society and political institutions (echoing thus somewhat Ricoeur's critique, see above endnote 18), and failing to account for what Alexander calls the civil sphere, with its inner tension between inclusive and excluding, universalizing and particularizing orientations, over-reaching each and all orders of worth (Alexander, 2000).

27 It would be important further to explore intersections with cultural economic sociology in particular.

28 Most of this new sociology of morality however, hardly relates to French pragmatic sociology, or only critically. See however Dromi, 2012; 2013; Dromi and Illouz, 2010; Majamäki and Pöysti, 2012; Schwarz, 2013.

29 One strand of work which has proved particularly receptive to pragmatic sociology are studies exploring processes of meaning-making 'on the ground', often via ethnographic methods and also written texts, and giving pride of place to actors' subjective perspectives and unfolding encounters with situations and concrete settings. See research by Daniel Cefaï, Paul Lichterman and Nina Eliasoph in particular, all very aware of the relevance of Boltanski and Thévenot's ideas for the exploration of 'civic culture' in particular.

30 Symptomatic perhaps of an often more practical and instrumental orientation, the terminology adopted in English translation differs, and it is the notion of 'economies of worth' which often seeps into this body of research, rather than that of regimes of justification.

## REFERENCES

Abend, G. (2008) 'Two Main Problems in the Sociology of Morality', *Theory and Society* 37: 87–125.

Abend, G. (2010) 'What's New and What's Old about the New Sociology of Morality', in Hitlin S. and Vaisey S. eds. *Handbook of the Sociology of Morality*. New York: Springer, pp. 561–584.

Alexander, J.C. (1988) 'Culture and Political Crisis: Watergate and Durkheimian Sociology', in J. Alexander (ed.), *Durkheimian Sociology: Cultural Studies*. Cambridge: Cambridge University Press. pp. 187–224.

Alexander, J.C. (2000) 'Theorizing the Good Society: Hermeneutic, Normative and Empirical Discourses', *Canadian Journal of Sociology*, 25(3): 271–309.

Alexander, J.C. (2003) *The Meanings of Social Life: A Cultural Sociology*. New York: Oxford University Press.

Alexander, J. C. (2004) 'Cultural Pragmatics: Social Performance Between Ritual and Strategy,' *Sociological Theory*, 22(4): 527–573.

Alexander, J.C. (2006) *The Civil Sphere*. New York: Oxford University Press.

Alexander, J.C. and Smith, P. (1993) 'The Discourse of American Civil Society: A New Proposal for Cultural Studies', *Theory and Society*, 22: 151–207.

Alexander, J.C. and Smith, P. (1998) 'Cultural Sociology or Sociology of Culture? Towards a Strong Program for Sociology's Second Wind', *Sociologie et sociétés*, 30(1): 97–106.

Alexander, J.C., Bartmanski D. and Giesen, B. (2011) *Iconic Power: Materiality and Meaning in Social Life*. New York: Palgrave.

Alexander, J.C., Giesen, B. and Mast, J. (eds) (2006) *Social Performance: Symbolic Action, Cultural Pragmatics and Ritual*. Cambridge: Cambridge University Press.

Allaire G. and Blanc, M. (2003) 'Local/Global Institutional Systems of Environmental Public Action', *Sociologia Ruralis*, 43(1): 17–33.

Annisette, M. and Richardson, A.J. (2011) 'Justification and accounting: Applying sociology of worth to accounting research', *Accounting, Auditing and Accountability Journal*, 24(2): 229–49.

Archer, M. S. (1995) *Realist Social Theory and the Morphogenetic Approach*. Cambridge: Cambridge University Press.

Archer, M.S. and Maccarini, A. M. (eds.), (2013) *Engaging with the World: Agency, institutions, historic formations*. London and New York: Routledge

Baert, P. and Careira de Silva, P. (2010) *Social Theory in the Twentieth Century and Beyond*. Cambridge and Malden, MA: Polity.

Barnett, C. (2014) 'Geography and Ethics III: From Moral Geographies to Geographies of Worth', *Progress in Human Geography*, 38(1): 151–60.

Barthe, Y. et al. (2013) 'Sociologie pragmatique: Mode d'emploi', *Politix*, 103(3): 175–204.

Basaure, M. (2014) 'Axel Honneth and Luc Boltanski at the Epicentre of Politics', in S. Susen and B. Turner (eds), *The Spirit of Luc Boltanski: Essays on the 'Pragmatic Sociology of Critique'*. London: Anthem Press.

Beckert, J. (2008 [2004]) *Inherited Wealth*. Trans. T. Dunlap. Princeton: Princeton University Press.

Beckert, J. and Aspers, P. (eds) (2011) *The Worth of Goods: Valuation and Pricing in the Economy*. New York: Oxford University Press.

Bénatouïl, T. (1999) 'A Tale of Two Sociologies: The Critical and the Pragmatic Stance in French Contemporary Sociology', *European Journal of Social Theory*, 2(3): 379–96.

Berger, P. and Luckmann, T. (1967) *The Social Construction of Reality*. Garden City, N.Y.: Anchor.

Beyerlein, K. and Vaisey, S. (2013) 'Individualism Revisited: Moral Worldviews and Civic Engagement', *Poetics*, 41(4): 384–406.

Biggart, N.W. and Beamish, T.D. (2003) 'The Economic Sociology of Conventions: Habit, Custom, Practice, and Routine in Market Order', *Annual Review of Sociology*, 29: 443–64.

Binder, A., Blair-Loy, M.J.H., Evans, K.N. and Schudson, M. (2008) 'Cultural Sociology and its Diversity', *Annals of the American Academy of Political and Social Science*, 619 (September): Special issue.

Blic de, D. (2000) 'Le scandale financier du siècle, ça ne vous intéresse pas? Difficile mobilization autour du Credit Lyonnais', *Politix*, 52: 157–81.

Blok, A. (2013) 'Pragmatic Sociology as Political Ecology: On the Many Worths of Nature(s)', *European Journal of Social Theory*, 16: 492–510.

Blokker, P. (2009) *Multiple Democracies in Europe: Political Culture in New Member States*. London: Routledge.

Blokker, P. (2011) 'Pragmatic Sociology: Theoretical Evolvement and Empirical Application', *European Journal of Social Theory*, 14: 251–61.

Blokker, P. and Brighenti, A. (2011a) 'An interview with Laurent Thévenot: On Engagement, Critique, Commonality, and Power', *European Journal of Social Theory*, 14: 383–400.

Blokker, P. and Brighenti, A. (eds) (2011b) 'Politics Between Justification and Defiance', *European Journal of Social Theory*, 14: 401–6.

Boisard, P. and Letablier, M.T. (1989) 'Un compromis d'innovation entre tradition et standardization dans l'industrie laitiere', in L. Boltanski and L. Thévenot (eds), *Justesse et justice dans le travail*. Centre d'études de l'emploi. pp. 153.

Boissonade, J. (2009) 'Les apports de la sociologie pragmatique à la transaction sociale', *Pensées plurielles*, 20: 37–50.

Boissonade, J. (2011) 'Le développement durable face à ses épreuves', *Espaces et Sociétés* 147(4): 57–75.

Boland, T. (2013) 'Towards an Anthropology of Critique: The Modern Experience of Liminality and Crisis', *Anthropological Theory*, 13: 222–39.

Boltanski, L. (1999 [1993]) *Distant Suffering: Morality, Media and Politics*. Trans. G.D. Burchell. Cambridge: Cambridge University Press.

Boltanski, L. (2000) 'The Legitimacy of Humanitarian Actions and their Media Representation: The Case of France', *Ethical Perspectives*, 7(1): 3–16.

Boltanski, L. (2007 [1993]) *La souffrance à distance: morale humanitaire, médias et politique*, 2nd edn, with a new chapter and postface. Paris: Gallimard.

Boltanski, L. (2008) 'Autour de *De la justification*. Un parcours dans le domaine de la sociologie morale', in M. Breviglieri, C. Lafaye and D. Trom (eds), *Sens critique, sens de la justice*. Paris: Economica.

Boltanski, L. (2011 [2009]) *On Critique: A Sociology of Emancipation*. Trans. G. Elliott. Cambridge: Polity.

Boltanski, L. (2012) *Enigmes et Complots: Une enquête à propos d'enquêtes*. Paris: Gallimard.

Boltanski, L. (2012 [1990]) *Love and Justice as Competences*. Trans. C. Porter. Cambridge: Polity.

Boltanski, L. and Chiapello, E. (2005 [1999]) *The New Spirit of Capitalism*. Trans. G. Elliott. London: Verso.

Boltanski, L. and Thévenot, L. (eds) (1989) *Justesse et justice dans le travail*. Centre d'études de l'emploi.

Boltanski, L. and Thévenot, L. (1991) *De la justification. Les économies de la grandeur*. Paris: Gallimard.

Boltanski, L. and Thévenot, L. (1999) 'The Sociology of Critical Capacity', *European Journal of Social Theory*, 2(3): 359–77.

Boltanski, L. and Thévenot, L. (2000) 'The Reality of Moral Expectations: A Sociology of Situated Judgment', *Philosophical Explorations*, 3(3): 208–31.

Boltanski, L. and Thévenot, L. (2006 [1991]) *On Justification: Economies of Worth*. Trans. C. Porter. Princeton: Princeton University Press.

Boltanski, L., Claverie, E., Offenstadt, N. and Van Damme, S. (eds) (2007) *Affaires, Scandales et Grandes Causes. De Socrate à Pinochet*. Paris: Stock.

Borghi, V. (2011) 'One-way Europe? Institutional guidelines, emerging regimes of justification, and paradoxical turns in European welfare capitalism', *European Journal of Social Theory*, 14: 321–41.

Bouillé, J., Robert-Demontrond, P. and Basso, F. (2014) 'Mesurer la force persuasive de l'activisme consumériste: une étude expérimentale de la théorie des cités appliquée aux food imitating products', *Recherche et Applications en Marketing*, 29: 79–113.

Breviglieri, M., Lafaye, C. and Trom, D. (eds) (2009) *Sens de la critique, sens de la justice*. Paris: Economica.

Breviglieri, M. and Stavo-Debauge, J. (1999) 'Le geste pragmatique de la sociologie francaise: Autour des travaux de Luc Boltanski et Laurent Thévenot', *Antropolitica*, 7: 7–22.

Breviglieri, M., Lafaye, C. and Trom, D. (eds) (2001) *Sens critique, sens de la justice*. Paris: Economica.

Cefaï, D. (2009a) 'Looking (Desperately?) for Cultural Sociology in France', *Culture*, Newsletter ASA Sociology of Culture.

Cefaï, D. (2009b) 'Comment se mobilise-t-on? L'apport d'une approche pragmatiste à la sociologie de l'action collective', *Sociologie et sociétés*, 41(2): 245–69.

Cefaï, D., Zimmermann, B., Nicolae, S. and Endress, M. (2015) 'Introduction', Special issue on Sociology of Valuation and Evaluation, *Human Studies*, 38(1): 1–12.

Celikates, R. (2012) 'Systematic Recognition and the Practice of Critique: Bourdieu, Boltanski and Critical Theory', in M. Bankowski and A. Le Goff (eds), *Recognition Theory and Contemporary French Moral and Political Philosophy*. Manchester: Manchester University Press. pp. 160–72.

Centemeri, L. (2014) 'Reframing Problems of Incommensurability in Environmental Conflicts through Pragmatic Sociology: From Value Pluralism to the Plurality of Modes of Engagement with the Environment', *Environmental Values*, 24(3): 299–320.

Chateauraynaud, F. (1991) *La faute professionelle. Une sociologie des conflits de responsabilité*. Paris: Métailié.

Chiapello, E. (2013) 'Capitalism and its Criticisms', in P. du Gay and G. Morgan (eds), *New Spirits of Capitalism? Crises, Justifications, and Dynamics*. Oxford: Oxford University Press. pp. 60–81.

Chiapello, E. (2014) 'Financialization and Valuation', *Human Studies*, 38(1): 13–35.

Chun, L. (2007) 'How does Morality Evaluate Public Works? Justifications in a Community-based Environmental Dispute in Shenzhen', *Chinese Sociology and Anthropology*, 40(2): 35–64.

Cloutier, C. and Langley, A. (2013) 'The Logic of Institutional Logics: Insights from French Pragmatist Sociology', *Journal of Management Inquiry*, 22(4): 360–80.

Corcuff, P. (1998) 'Justification, stratégie et compassion: Apports de la sociologie des régimes d'action', *Correspondances*, 51, Bulletin d'information scientifique de l'Institut de Recherche sur le Maghreb Contemporain, Tunis.

Couldry, N. (2010) *Why Voice Matters: Culture and Politics after Neoliberalism*. London: Sage.

Davies, W. (2012) 'Ways of Owning: Towards an Economic Sociology of Privatization', *Poetics*, 40: 167–84.

Delanty, G. (2011) 'Cultural Diversity, Democracy, and the Prospects of Cosmopolitanism: A Theory of Cultural Encounters', *The British Journal of Sociology* 62(4): 633–56.

Dequech, D. (2008) 'Logics of Action, Logics of Justification', *Journal of Economic Issues*, 42(2): 527–35.

Deutschmann, C. (2008) 'Kapitalismus und Geist des Kapitalismus: Ammerkungen zum theoretischen Ansatz Boltanski/Chiapello', in G. Wagner and P. Hessinger (eds), *Ein Neuer Geist des Kapitalismus?* The Netherlands: Springer. pp. 127–44.

DiMaggio P. (1997) 'Culture and Cognition', *Annual Review of Sociology*, 23: 263–87.

Powell W.W. and DiMaggio P. J. (1991) *The New Institutionalism in Organizational Analysis*. Chicago: The University of Chicago Press.

Dodier, N. (1993) *L'expertise médicale*. Paris: Métailié.

Dodier, N. (1993) 'Action as a Combination of "Common Worlds"', *Sociological Review*, 41(3): 556–71.

Dosse, F. (1995) *L'empire du sens: l'humanisation des sciences sociales*. Paris: La découverte.

Dromi, S.M. (2012) 'Penny for Your Thoughts: Beggars and the Exercise of Morality in Daily Life', *Sociological Forum*, 27(4): 847–71.

Dromi, S.M. (2013) 'Uneasy Settlements: Reparation Politics and the Meanings of Money in the Israeli Withdrawal from Gaza', *Sociological Inquiry*, 84: 1–22.

Dromi, S. and Illouz, E. (2010) 'Recovering Morality: Pragmatic Sociology and Literary Studies', *New Literary History*, 41(2): 351–69.

Du Gay, P. and Morgan, G. (eds) (2013) *New Spirits of Capitalism? Crises, Justifications and Dynamics*. Oxford: Oxford University Press.

Eagleton-Pierce, M. (2014) 'The Concept of Governance in the Spirit of Capitalism', *Critical Policy Studies*, 8(1): 5–21.

Edles, L.D. (2002) *Cultural Sociology in Practice*. Oxford and Malden, MA: Blackwell.

Eliasoph, N. and Lo, J. (2012). 'Broadening Cultural Sociology's Scope: Meaning-making in Mundane Organizational Life', in J.C. Alexander, R. Jacobs and P. Smith (eds), *The Oxford Handbook of Cultural Sociology*. New York: Oxford University Press. pp. 763–87.

Eulriet, I. (2008) 'Analysing Political Ideas and Political Action', *Economy and Society*, 37(1): 135–50.

Eulriet, I. (2014) 'The Civil Sphere and De la Justification: Two Models of the Public Sphere', in S. Susen and B. Turner (eds), *The Spirit of Luc Boltanski*. London: Anthem.

Fourcade, M. (2011a) 'Cents and Sensibility: Economic Valuation and the Nature of Nature', *American Journal of Sociology*, 116(6): 1721–77.

Fourcade, M. (2011b) 'Price and Prejudice', in J. Beckert and P. Aspers (eds), *The Worth of Goods: Valuation and Pricing in the Economy*. New York: Oxford University Press.

Fourcade, M and Healy, K. (2007) 'Moral Views of the Market', *Annual Review of Sociology*, 33(1): 285–311.

Frère, B. (2006) 'La sociologie de Max Scheler: Une resource phénoménologique pour un régime d'action philia au coeur de l'économie solidaire', *Social Science Information*, 45: 561–99.

Friedland, R. (2009) 'The Endless Fields of Pierre Bourdieu', *Organization*, 16: 887–917.

Friedland, R. and Alford, R.R. (1991) 'Bring Society Back In: Symbols, Practices and Institutional Contradictions', in W.W. Powell and P.I. DiMaggio (eds), *The New Institutionalism in Organizational Analysis*. Chicago: The University of Chicago Press. pp. 232–62.

Fuller, C. (2013) 'Urban Politics and the Social Practices of Critique and Justification: Conceptual Insights from French Pragmatism', *Progress in Human Geography*, 37: 639–57.

Garfinkel, H. (1991) 'Respecification: Evidence for Locally Produced, Naturally Accountable Phenomena of Order, Logic, Reason, Meaning, Method, etc. in and as of the Essential Haecceity of Immortal Ordinary Society, (I)', in G. Button (ed.) *Ethnomethodology and the Human Sciences*. Cambridge: Cambrige University Press, pp. 10–19.

Gielen, P. (2005) 'Art and Social Value Regimes', *Current Sociology*, 53(5): 789–806.

Girard, M. and Stark, D. (2003) 'Heterarchies of Value in Manhattan-Based New Media Firms', *Theory, Culture & Society*, 20: 77–105.

Gladarev, B. and Lonkila, M. (2013) 'Justifying Civic Activism in Russia and Finland', *Journal of Civil Society*, 9(4): 375–90.

Gonzalez, P. and Kaufmann, L. (2009) 'The Social Scientist, the Public and the Pragmatist Gaze', *European Journal of Pragmatism*, 4(1): 55.

Gorski, P. (2013) 'What is Critical Realism and Why should we Care?' *Contemporary Sociology*, 42(5): 658–670.

Guggenheim, M. and Potthast, J. (2012) 'Symmetrical Twins: On the Relationship between Actor-Network Theory and the Sociology of Critical Capacities', *European Journal of Social Theory*, 15: 157–78.

Hansen, M.P. (2016) 'Non-normative Critique: Foucault and Pragmatic Sociology', *European Journal of Social Theory* 19: 137–145.

Heinich, N. (2002) *L'art en conflit*. Paris: La découverte.

Heinich, N. (2010) 'What does Sociology of Culture Mean? Notes on a Few Transcultural Misunderstandings', *Cultural Sociology*, 4(2): 257–65.

Heinich, N. (2011) 'The Making of Cultural Heritage', *The Nordic Journal of Aesthetics*, 40–1: 119–28.

Heinich, N. (2012) 'Mapping Intermediaries in the World of Art according to Pragmatic Sociology', *European Journal of Cultural Studies*, 15(6): 695–702.

Heinich, N. (2013) 'Avoir un don: Du don en régime de singularité', *Revue du M.A.U.S.S*, 41: 235–40.

Heinich, N. (2014) 'The Art of Inflicting Suffering: Animals and Spectators in the Crucible of Contemporary Art', in R. Hadj-Moussa and M. Nijhawan (eds), *Suffering, Art and Aesthetics*. London: Palgrave Macmillan.

Hennion, A. (2013) 'D'une sociologie de la médiation à une pragmatique des attachements', *SociologieS*, http://sociologies.revues.org/4353

Héritage, J. (1984) *Garfinkel and Ethnomethodology*. Cambridge: Polity Press.

Hitlin, S. and S. Vaisey (2010) *Handbook of the Sociology of Morality*. New York: Springer.

Hitlin, S. and Vaisey S.(2013) 'The New Sociology of Morality', *Annual Review of Sociology*, 39: 51–68.

Huutoniemi, K. (2012) 'Communicating and Compromising on Disciplinary Expertise in the Peer Review of Research Proposals', *Social Studies of Science*, 42: 897–921.

Illouz, E. (2003) *Oprah Winfrey and the Glamour of Misery: An Essay on Popular Culture*. New York: Columbia University Press.

Jagd, S. (2005) 'The "Network Ethic" and the New Spirit of Capitalism in French Sociology of Capitalism', in S. Konordios (ed.), *Networks, Trust and Social Capital: Theoretical and Empirical Investigations from Europe*. Farnham: Ashgate.

Jagd, S. (2007) 'Economics of Convention and New Economic Sociology: Mutual Inspiration and Dialogue', *Current Sociology*, 55: 75–91.

Jagd, S. (2011) 'Pragmatic Sociology and Competing Orders of Worth in Organizations', *European Journal of Social Theory*, 14(3): 343–59.

Jepperson, R. and Meyer, J. (2011) 'Multiple Levels of Analysis and the Limitations of Methodological Individualism', *Sociological Theory*, 29(1): 54–73.

Jetté, C. (2003) *Du don comme principe de justification*. Montréal: Université du Québec.

Joas, H. and W. Knoebl (2009 [2004]) *On Social Theory: Twenty Introductory Lectures*. Trans. from the German by A. Skinner. Cambridge: Cambridge University Press.

Johnson, P. (2011) 'The Embedded Market and Ideology Critique', *Critical Horizons*, 12(3): 302–22.

Kane, A. (1991) 'Cultural Analysis in Historical Sociology', *Sociological Theory*, 9(1): 53–9.

Karpik, L. (2010) *Valuing the Unique: The Economics of Singularities*. Princeton: Princeton University Press.

Kirwan, J. (2005) 'The Interpersonal World of Direct Marketing: Examining Conventions of Quality at UK Farmers' Markets', *Journal of Rural Studies*, 22(3): 310–12.

Kostiner, I. (2003) 'Evaluating Legality: Toward a Cultural Approach to the Study of Law and Change', *Law and Society Review*, 37(2): 323–68.

Krucken, G. and Drori, G.S. (2009) *World Society: The Writings of John W. Meyer*. Oxford: Oxford University Press.

Lafaye C. and Corcuff, P. (1996) 'Légitimité et théorie critique: Un autre usage du modèle de la justification publique', *Mana – Revue de Sociologie et d'Anthropologie*, 2: 217–33.

Lafaye, C. and Thévenot, L (1993) 'Une justification écologique? Conflits dans l'aménagement de la nature', *Revue Française de Sociologie*, 34 (4): 495–524.

Lafaye, C., Moody, M. and Thévenot, L. (1994) 'Aménager un site littoral', *Études rurales*, 133–4: 163–80.

Lafaye, C., Moody, M. and Thévenot, L. (2000) 'Forms of Valuing Nature: Arguments and Mods of *Justification*in French and American Environmental Disputes', in M. Lamont and L. Thévenot (eds), *Rethinking Comparative Cultural Sociology: Repertoires of Evaluation in France and the United States*. Cambridge: Cambridge University Press. pp. 229–72.

Latsis, J. (2006) 'Convention and intersubjectivity: New Developments in French eEconomics', *Journal for the Theory of Social Behavior* 36(3): 255–277.

Lamont, M. (1992) *Money, Morals, Manners: The Culture of the French and American Upper Middle Classes*. Chicago: The University of Chicago Press.

Lamont, M. (1999) *The Cultural Territories of Race: Black and White Boundaries*. Chicago: The University of Chicago Press.

Lamont, M. (2000) *The Dignity of Working Men: Morality and the Boundaries of Class, Race and Immigration*. Cambridge: Harvard University Press.

Lamont, M. (2008) 'Critères d'évaluation et structures culturelles: réflections sur un parcours de recherches', in M. Breviglieri, C. Lafaye, and D.Trom (eds), *Sens de la critique, sens de la justice*. Paris: Economica.

Lamont, M. (2012) 'Toward a Comparative Sociology of Valuation and Evaluation', *Annual Review of Sociology*, 38: 201–21.

Lamont, M. and Thévenot, L. (eds) (2000) *Rethinking Comparative Cultural Sociology: Repertoires of Evaluation in France and the United States*. London: Cambridge University Press.

Lane, C. (2014) *The Cultivation of Taste: Chefs and the Organization of Fine Dining*. Oxford: Oxford University Press.

Lehoux, P. et al. (2014) 'How do Values Shape Technology Design? An Exploration of What Makes the Pursuit of Health and Wealth Legitimate in Academic Spin-offs', *Sociology of Health and Illness*, 36(5): 738–55.

Lehtonen T.-K. and Liukko, J. (2010) 'Justifications for Commodified Security: The Promotion of Private Life Insurance in Finland 1945–90', *Acta Sociologica*, 53: 371–86.

Lemieux, C. (2000) *Mauvaise Presse: Une Sociologie Comprehensive du Travail Journalistique et de ses Critiques*. Paris: Métaillé.

Lemieux, C. (2009) *Le Devoir et la Grâce. Pour une Analyse Grammaticale de l'Action* Paris: Economica.

Lichterman, P. (2012) 'Reinventing the Concept of Civic Culture', in J. Alexander et al. (eds), *Oxford Handbook of Cultural Sociology*. Oxford University Press.

Lichterman, P. and Cefaï, D. (2006) 'The Idea of Political Culture', in R.E. Goodin and C. Tilly (eds), *The Oxford Handbook of Contextual Political Analysis*. Oxford: Oxford University Press.

MacNaghten, P., Davies, S.R. and Kearnes, M. (2015) 'Understanding Public Responses to Emerging Technologies', *Journal of Environmental Policy and Planning* 17(4): 1–19.

Mair, J., Battilana J. and Cardenas, J. (2012) 'Organizing for Society: A Typology of Social Entrepreneuring', *Journal of Business Ethics* 111: 353–373.

Mair, J., Mayer, J. and Lutz, E. (2015) 'Navigating Institutional Plurality: Organizational Governance in Hybrid Organizations', *Organization Studies* 36(6): 713–739.

McLean, A. (2001) 'Cultural Repertoires and the Practices of Collective Identity'. Paper delivered at the Annual Meeting of the American Sociological Association, Anaheim, Ca. August 18–22.

Mailhot, C., Gagnon, S., Langley, A. and Binette, L. (forthc.) 'Distributing Leadership Across People and Objects in a Collaborative Research Project', *Leadership* 10, 3. First published on July 25, 2014. doi:10.1177/1742715014543578

Majamäki, M.H. and Pöysti, V.K. (2012) 'Vocabularies of Gambling Justification Among Finnish and French Players', *European Journal of Cultural Studies*, 15: 496–512.

Marontate, J. (2013) 'Strategies for Studying Multiple Meanings in Conservation Research', *CeROArt* [Online].

Messner, M., Clegg, S. and Kornberger, M. (2008) 'Critical Practices in Organizations', *Journal of Management Inquiry*, 17: 68–82.

Michel, J. (2014) 'Herméneutique, pragmatisme, et critique des institutions', *Social Science Information*, 53(2): 255–73.

Morawaska, E. (2001) 'Cultural Repertoire in a Structuration Process.' Paper delivered at the Annual Meeting of the American Sociological Association, Anaheim, Ca. August 18–22.

Moreira, T. (2013) *The Transformation of Contemporary Health Care: The Market, The Laboratory, the Forum*. London: Routledge.

Nachi, M. (2006) *Introduction à la sociologie pragmatique: Vers un nouveau style sociologique?* Paris: Armand Colin.

Ogien, A. (2014) 'Pragmatisms and Sociologies', *Revue Francaise de Sociologie*, 55(3): 414–28.

Ohrbuch, T. L. (1997) 'Peoples' Accounts Count: The Sociology of Accounts', *Annual Review of Sociology*, 23: 455–478.

O'Mahony, P. (2009) 'Sociological Theory, Discourse and the Cognitive Construction of Participation', *Comparative Sociology*, 8: 490–516.

Ottosson, M. and Galis, V. (2011) 'Multiplicity Justifies Corporate Strategy', *Journal of Cultural Economy*, 4(4): 455–75.

Pagnucco, N.D. (2012) *Qualifying Adjuncts' Academic Worth and the Justification of Adjunct Work*. PhD dissertation, State University of New York at Albany.

Pardo-Guerra, J.P. (2011) 'How Much for the Michelangelo? Valuation, Commoditization and Finitism in the Secondary Art Market', *Cultural Sociology*, 5: 207–23.

Patriotta, G., Gond, J.-P. and Schultz, F. (2011) 'Maintaining Legitimacy: Controversies, Orders of Worth, and Public Justifications', *Journal of Management Studies*, 48(8): 1804–36.

Pecoraro, M.G. and Uusitalo, O. (2014) 'Conflicting Values of Ethical Consumption in Diverse Worlds: A Cultural Approach', *Journal of Consumer Culture*, 14: 45.

Perrin, Andrew J. (2005) 'Political Microcultures: Linking Civic Life and Democratic Discourse', *Social Forces*, 84(2): 1049–82.

Quéré, L. and Terzi, C. (2014) 'Did you say Pragmatic? Luc Boltanski's Sociology from a Pragmatist Perspective', in S. Susen and B. Turner (eds), *The Spirit of L. Boltanski: Essays on the 'Pragmatic Sociology of Critique'*. London: Anthem, pp. 91–128.

Rawls, A. (2012) 'Durkheim's theory of modernity: Self-regulating practices as constitutive orders of social and moral facts', *Journal of Classical Sociology* 12: 479–512,

Ricoeur, P. (1995) 'La place du politique dans une conception pluraliste des principes de justice', in J. Affichard and J-B de Foucauld (eds) *Pluralisme et équité: Penser la justice dans la démocratie*. Paris: Esprit.

Roberge, J. (2011) 'The Aesthetic Public Sphere and the Transformation of Criticism', *Social Semiotics*, 21(3): 435–53.

Roberts, D. (2012) 'From the Cultural Contradictions of Capitalism to the Creative Economy: Reflections on the New Spirit of Art and Capitalism', *Thesis Eleven*, 110: 83–97.

Rousselière, D. and Vezina, M. (2009) 'Constructing the Legitimacy of a Financial Cooperative in the Cultural Sector: A Case Study using Textual Analysis', *International Review of Sociology*, 19(2): 241–61.

Saguy, A.C. and Forrest, S. (2008) 'Culture and Law: Beyond a Paradigm of Cause and Effect', *Annals of the American Academy of Political and Social Science*, 619(1): 149–64.

Sayer, A. (2008) 'Moral Economic Regulation in Organizations: A University Example', *Organization*, 15: 147–64.

Schwarz, O. (2013) 'Dead Honest Judgments: Emotional Expression, Sonic Styles, and Evaluating Sounds of Mourning in Late Modernity', *American Journal of Cultural Sociology*, 1: 153–85.

Scott, A. and Pasqualoni, P.P. (2014) 'The Making of a Paradigm: Exploring the Potential of the

Economy of Conventions and Pragmatic Sociology of Critique', in P.S. Adler, P. du Gay, G. Morgan and M. Reed (eds), *The Oxford Handbook of Sociology, Social Theory and Organization Studies*. Oxford: Oxford University Press. pp. 64–86.

Silber, I.F. (2003) 'Pragmatic Sociology as Cultural Sociology: Beyond Repertoire Theory?', *European Journal of Social Theory*, 6(4): 425–47.

Silber, I.F. (2007) 'Towards a Non-Unitary Approach to Sociological Theory', *European Journal of Social Theory*, 10(2): 220–32.

Silber, I.F. (2011) 'Emotions as Regime of Justification? The Case of Philanthropic Civic Anger', *European Journal of Social Theory*, 14(2): 301–20.

Silber, I.F. (2014) 'Boltanski and the Gift: Beyond Love, Beyond Suspicion…?', in S. Susen and B. Turner (eds), *The Spirit of L. Boltanski: Essays on the 'Pragmatic Sociology of Critique'*. London: Anthem.

Spillman, L. ed (2002) *Cultural Sociology*. Oxford: Blackwell.

Stark, D. (2000) 'For a Sociology of Worth', Working paper, Center on Organizational Innovation, Columbia University.

Stark, D. (2009) *The Sense of Dissonance: Accounts of Worth in Economic Life*. Princeton, NJ: Princeton University Press.

Stavo-Debeauge, J. (2012) 'La sociologie dite "pragmatique" et la philosophie pragmatiste, une rencontre tardive', séminaire *Pourquoi le Pragmatisme?* Villa Vigoni, June 15–18.

Steinberg, M.W. (1998) 'Tilting the Frame: Considerations on Collective action Framing from a Discursive Turn', *Theory and Society* 27: 845–872.

Steinberg, M. W. (1999) 'The Talk and Back Talk of Collective Action: A Dialogic Analysis of Repertoires of Discourse among Nineteenth-Century English Cotton Spinners', *American Journal of Sociology* 105(3): 736–80.

Steensland, B. (2009) 'Restricted and Elaborated Modes in the Cultural Analysis of Politics', *Sociological Forum*, 24(4): 926–34.

Strand, M. (2014) 'Authenticity as a Form of Worth', *Journal for Cultural Research*, 18: 60–77.

Susen, S. (2007) *The Foundations of the Social: Between Critical Theory and Reflexive Sociology*. Oxford: Bardwell Press.

Susen, S, and Turner, B. (eds) (2014) *The Spirit of Luc Boltanski: Essays on the 'Pragmatic Sociology of Critique'*. London: Anthem Press.

Swidler, A. (1986) 'Culture in Action: Symbols and Strategies', *American Sociological Review*, 51: 273–86.

Swidler, A. (2001a) *Talk of Love: How Culture Matters*. Chicago: University of Chicago Press.

Swidler, A. (2001b) 'What Anchors Cultural Practices', in T.R. Schatzki, K. Knorr-Cetina and E. von Savigny (eds), *The Practical Turn*. London: Routledge and Kegan Paul. pp. 74–92.

Swidler, A. (2002) 'Cultural Repertoires and Cultural Logics: Can They Be Reconciled?', *Culture*, Newsletter of the Sociology of Culture Section of the American Sociological Association, Winter: 68.

Swidler, A. (2008) 'Comment on Stephen Vaisey's Socrates, Skinner, and Aristotle: Three Ways of Thinking about Culture in Action', *Sociological Forum* 23(3): 614–618.

Swidler, A. (2012) 'The Axial Age and its Consequences: Problems in Thinking the African Case', in R. Bellah and H. Joas (eds), *The Axial Age and its Consequences*. Cambridge: Harvard University Press.

Symonds, H.W. (ed.) (1990) *The Rhetorical Turn*. Chicago: Chicago University Press.

Taupin, (2015) 'L'apport de la sociologie pragmatique française aux études critiques en mangement', *RAE-Revista de Admnistracao de Empresas*, 55(2): 162–74.

Tavory, I. (2011) 'The Question of Moral Action: A Formalist Position', *Sociological Theory* 29(4): 272–293.

Tavory, I. and Swidler, A. (2009) 'Condom Semiotics: Meaning and Condom Use in Rural Malawi', *American Sociological Review*, 74(2): 171–89.

Ten Eyck, T.A. and Busch, L. (2012) 'Justifying the Art Critique: Clement Greenberg, Michael Kimmelman, and Orders of Worth in Art Criticism', *Cultural Sociology*, 6: 217–31.

Thévenot, L.(2001a) 'Pragmatic Regimes Governing the Engagement with the World', in K. Knorr-Cetina, T. Schatzki and E. von Savigny (eds), *The Practice Turn in Contemporary Theory*. London: Routledge. pp. 56–73.

Thévenot, L.(2001b) 'Organized Complexity: Conventions of Coordination and the Composition of Economic Arrangements', *European Journal of Social Theory*, 4: 405–25.

Thévenot, L.(2002) 'Which Road to Follow? The Moral Complexity of an Equipped Humanity', in J. Law and A. Mol (eds), *Complexities: Social Studies of Knowledge Practices*. Durham and London: Duke University Press. pp. 53–87.

Thévenot, L.(2006) *L'Action au Pluriel. Sociologie des Régimes d'Engagement*. Paris: Editions La Découverte.

Thévenot, L.(2007) 'The Plurality of Cognitive Formats and Engagements: Moving between the Familiar and the Public', *European Journal of Social Theory*, 10(3): 409–23.

Thévenot, L.(2011a) 'Power and Oppression from the Perspective of the Sociology of Engagements: A Comparison with Bourdieu's and Dewey's Approaches to Practical Activities', *Irish Journal of Sociology*, 19 (1): 35–67.

Thévenot, L.(2011b) 'An Interview with Laurent Thévenot: On Engagement, Critique, Commonality and Power',: Interviewed by P. Blokker and

A. Brighenti, *European Journal of Social Theory* 14(3): 383–400.

Thévenot, L. (forthcoming) 'Bounded Justifiability: Three Constructions of Commonality in the Plural', in P. Dumouchel and G. Reiko (eds), *Bounds and Boundaries: New Perspectives on Justice and Culture.* Cambridge: Cambridge University Press.

Thévenot, L., Moody, M. and Lafaye, C. (2000) 'Forms of valuing nature: arguments and modes of justification in French and American environmental disputes', in M. Lamont and L. Thévenot (eds.), *Rethinking Comparative Cultural Sociology, Repertoires of Evaluation in France and the United States.* Cambridge: Cambridge University Press, pp. 229–272.

Thornton , A. et al. (2012) 'Knowledge and Beliefs' about National Development and Developmental Hierarchies: The Viewpoints of Ordinary People in Thirteen Countries, *Social Science Research*, 41: 1053–1068.

Tilly, C. (1979) 'Repertoires of Contention in America and Britain 1750–1830', in John D. McCarthy and M. Zald ed. *The Dynamics of Social Movements.* Cambridge, Mass.: Winthrop Publishers, pp. 126–155.

Traugott, Mark 1995 Repertoires and Cycles of Collective Action, Durham, NC: Duke University Press

Vaisey, S. (2009) 'Motivation and Justification: A Dual-Process Model of Culture in Action', *American Journal of Sociology*, 114(6): 1675–715.

Vandenberghe, F. (2014) *What is Critical about Critical Realism?: Essays in Reconstructive Social Theory.* London and New York: Routledge.

Vatin, F. (2013) 'Valuation as Evaluating and Valorizing', *Valuation Studies*, 1(1): 31–50.

Wagner P. (1999) 'After Justification: Registers of Evaluation and the Sociology of Modernity', *European Journal of Social Theory*, 2(3): 341–57.

Wagner P. (2001) 'Modernity, Capitalism and Critique', *Thesis Eleven*, 66: 1–31.

Walzer, M. (1983) *Spheres of Justice: A Defense of Pluralism and Equality.* New York: Basic Books.

Yamagushi, T. and Suda, F. (2010) 'Changing Social Order and the Quest for Justification: GMO's Controversies in Japan', *Science, Technology and Human Values*, 35: 382–407.

Zug, S. (2014) *The Gift of Water: Bourdieusian Capital Exchange and Moral Entitlements in a Neighborhood of Khartoum.* Berlin: LIT Verlag.

# Systems Theory and Culture: Drawing Lessons from Parsons and Luhmann

Rudi Laermans

## INTRODUCTION: SITUATING PARSONS VERSUS LUHMANN

Within the social sciences, the variety in conceptual frameworks or paradigms inspiring research actually has a Janus-face. Theoretical pluralism can be addressed in a general way by observing differences in epistemological starting-points, social ontologies or definitions of core concepts such as power, organization or indeed culture. However, every crystalized paradigm also involves the names of one or more founders and a handful of adherents who creatively rearticulated the insights of, for instance, Karl Marx, Emile Durkheim or Max Weber. Such an author-centred approach is rather unavoidable when discussing the tradition of systems theory in the social sciences and its eventual relevance for cultural sociology. Although this paradigm can evidently not be reduced to their works, Talcott Parsons (1902–1979) and Niklas Luhmann (1927–1998) effectively stand out as the most innovative and prolific authors. Their mutual relationship is not one of grounder and disciple. Although he was initially influenced by Parsons and adopted some of his master-concepts, Luhmann already in an early stage went his own way. This intellectual independence culminated around the mid-1980s in an autonomous version of systems theory that decisively breaks with the central axioms of Parsonianism. Thus there exist nowadays two main strands of systems theory in the social sciences that are difficult to reconcile, not the least when it comes to the notions of social system and culture. I first briefly introduce the main differences between both approaches and will then present in more detail the views of Parsons and Luhmann respectively.

Parsons and Luhmann concur on the basic definition of a system of whatever sort as consisting of elements that entertain relations with each other and having boundaries differentiating it from an environment. They disagree, however, on the nature of a social system's components. Parsons started as an action theorist who in his first major work *The Structure of Social Action* (1937) tries to synthesize the leading ideas of Durkheim, Weber, Vilfredo Pareto and Alfred Marshall (Parsons, 1967). He subsequently appropriated the concept of system, a theoretical turn codified at length in *The Social System* (1951). Nevertheless, the study tellingly opens with the statement that 'the subject of this volume is the exposition and illustration of a conceptual scheme for the analysis of social systems in terms of the action frame of reference' (Parsons, 1991: 1). That Parsons kept on seeing himself throughout his career as an action theorist may be read off the title of his last book, *Action Theory and the Human Condition* (Parsons, 1978). Luhmann (2013a: 7) therefore once jokingly observed that the complete work of Parsons is a nearly interminable comment to the sentence 'Action is system'. In his early publications Luhmann actually also considers self-referentially networked actions as the proverbial stuff social systems are made off. Yet over the years the notion of communication clearly gains in prominence in his writings. The original German publication in 1982 of Jürgen Habermas' *The Theory of Communicative Action* (Habermas, 1984) partly accelerated this gradual shift, which is sealed in *Social Systems* (1995 [1984]). Relying on the notion of autopoiesis proposed by theoretical biologists Humberto Maturana and Francisco Varela (1980), Luhmann (1995) counter-intuitively conceptualizes social systems as consisting of communications self-producing communications. Communications are commonly interpreted as human actions, but Luhmann indeed regards the basic components of social systems as theoretically non-reducible to the conscious doings of those participating in a communication process. In a word, whereas for Parsons action is the initial given that systems theory may elucidate in a conceptually coherent fashion, Luhmann decidedly frames social systems in his later writings in non-action terms.

Parsons and Luhmann as well markedly differ in their assessment of the theoretical centrality of the problem of social order or systems-equilibrium. Although he repudiates in his later work the expression (Parsons, 1977a: 100–17), the structural-functionalism advocated by Parsons premises the existence of structures or stable patterns, which are deemed necessary for the viability of an action system. In his analysis of social phenomena Parsons therefore concentrates on mechanisms such as social control that have positive consequences or functions for social systems because they further their orderly reproduction. Luhmann dismisses such a Durkheim-inspired approach and finds the one-sided focus on the conditions of systems-equilibrium that Parsons inherited from both Pareto and neo-classical economy theoretically unproductive (see especially Luhmann, 1970: 9–52; 1995: 52–8; 2013: 6–24). Luhmann (1995: 54) argues:

> [The] real theoretical achievement provided by the introduction of functional analysis resides in the construction of problems. This yields the conjunction of functional analysis and systems theory. The classical account of this conjunction interpreted the ultimate problem as that of the system's permanence, or stability. This is not incorrect, but it is inadequate.

Instead of conceptualizing social phenomena primarily from the point of view of their positive contributions to systems-equilibrium, the possible functions of both these phenomena and social structures can be studied in reference to whatever kind of problem is considered theoretically interesting. In other words, functional analysis has to be freed from the traditional focus on social reproduction (which also characterizes the method's adaption in critical sociology).

Something more substantive is involved than the correct methodology of functional analysis. Precisely his interest in the conditions furthering social order incites Parsons to highlight the structuring role of culture or, rather, of shared values and the concrete norms they at once engender and legitimate. Indeed, 'the structure of social systems ... as treated within the frame of reference of action *consists* in institutionalized patterns of normative culture' (Parsons, 1961: 36, emphasis in original). The direct influence of Durkheim is again unmistakable. Parsons' structural-functionalism essentially stands for an overtly culturalist systems approach in which culture also possesses system-properties, including the tendency towards equilibrium, and the cultural system is given the general function of securing order in action systems by means of consistent value-orientations and norms. On the contrary, Luhmann tends to an outspoken anti-culturalist position. Already in his early writings, he clearly theorizes 'against Parsons' and explicitly rejects the axiom that social order implies a shared social morality (Martens, 1999; Baecker, 2000: 133–60). Moreover, he not only discards the notion of a cultural system but also denies the sociological relevance of the concept of culture altogether. However, one finds in his writings several concepts such as meaning, semantics, self-description and memory that re-articulate insights traditionally associated with that very term. Taken together and placed against the backdrop of his final theoretical edifice, Luhmann's various theoretical manoeuvres to avoid the word 'culture' may even be condensed into a novel conceptualization of that notion.

## THE CULTURAL SYSTEM WITHIN THE AGIL-SCHEME

Parsonian systems theory is in essence an action theory that privileges the cultural system in explaining social order and simultaneously tends to narrow down culture to institutionalized values and norms. Parsons thus claims for both systems theory and the concept of culture a central position in the social sciences, yet at the price of a reductive stance. Nonetheless, his general considerations on the cultural system point to a markedly broader conception actually concurring with the prevailing interpretative approach of culture advocated by for instance Parsons' ex-student Clifford Geertz (1973). Thus Parsons (1961a: 963) asserts that human action precisely differs from sheer behaviour in that it 'is organized through and in terms of the patterning of the "meanings" of objects and of orientations to objects in the world of human experience'. With this loose characterization corresponds a two-dimensional notion of culture (compare the famous statement by Kroeber and Parsons, 1958). On the one hand, culture consists of meanings expressed in symbols that constantly transform reality in a meaningful world; on the other hand, these very meanings also co-direct human action since they imply, for instance, particular cognitive or moral orientations in dealing with the situation at hand. According to this conception, symbolized meanings (or meaningful symbols) are the basic elements of every sort of cultural system. They entertain mutual relations that Parsons again and again typifies as patterned, yet this assertion should not be misread. At stake is not the empirical claim that all cultures are internally consistent and offer congruent meanings, but a general focus on the conditions of equilibrium as the primary vantage point in analysing systems.

Since they are neither context-specific nor only momentarily or subjectively valid, meaningful symbols illustrate the notion of symbolic generalization. They are situationally, temporally and socially generalized, which allows contextual re-specifications or particularizations. 'The linguistic symbol is the prototypical object of generalized meaning', Parsons (1961a: 975) observes. Thanks to their general character, words can be variously combined and deployed with different meaning-accents in specific situations, on a particular moment in time or by an individual language-user. For that matter, Parsons holds a somewhat ambivalent view on the relationship between language and culture. Firm but only sparsely warranted affirmations such as 'language should be treated as a part of culture' (Parsons, 1982: 56) are combined with the acknowledgement of language's role as the basic medium of symbolic communication. As such, language seems crucial for the functioning of social systems and may thus either illustrate the idea of an interchange between the cultural and the social system or be regarded as an example of the notion of (cultural) interpenetration, which Parsons only cursorily uses and refers to one system pervading another one. What complicates matters even more is that he gravitates in his later writings to – but does not really articulate – a generative or structuralist notion of 'culture as language' (Parsons, 1977: 235). This approach puts culture on a par with a linguistic code, or a system of rules relating generalized meanings to symbols and allowing an infinite production of messages.

Meanings or symbols guide human action in or towards the world, including others. Parsons (1953; 1991) initially distinguishes between three main forms of cultural orientation. In relation to the empirical world, culture offers cognition; within modern science this orientation has become autonomous, which has resulted in a particular cultural system. In a comparable way modern art institutionalizes the possibility of using meaningful symbols in an expressive mode, so not in relation to the empirical outside world but the subjective inner world. Moral doctrines in turn highlight the more general evaluative orientation that a culture offers its members, resulting in normatively structured purposive action. Later on Parsons introduces a fourth axis that 'concerns the grounds of the orientations of meaning themselves' or 'the most general worldviews or definitions of the human condition that underlie orientations to more particular problems' (Parsons, 1961a: 970). Religion is an evident example of such 'conceptions of ultimate reality' (1961a: 970) that may justify and frame a particular apprehension of empirical reality, the expression of emotions or other inner states and moral evaluations (see also Parsons (1978) on the orientation to an 'ultimate reality' as co-defining 'the human condition').

Parsons' re-articulation of action in consequently systems-theoretical terms results in a shift in focus from 'the unit act' to 'the action system' and the four functional requisites or basic problems it has to meet (compare Adriaansens, 1980; Alexander, 1983; Travino, 2001; Segre, 2012). First, it must secure in the environment the necessary resources for action or satisfy the imperative of adaption (A). Second, the action needs direction. Purposes have to be formulated and the mobilized resources should subsequently be rearranged as means in view of the realization of the selected aims: this is the double-sided functional requirement of goal-attainment (G). Third, since individual action has to reckon with that of others, a minimum of mutual coordination is demanded. Hence the imperative of integration (I) that is of course crucial in a collective action system such as an organization. The fourth and last requisite concerns latent pattern maintenance (L), or the demand to guarantee over a longer period of time an action system's internal order. Taken together these different functional requisites delineate the famous – and also notorious – four-function paradigm or AGIL-scheme.

The complementary thesis states that they are each satisfied by the contributions of a particular system. Adaption to the environment is secured by the organic or behavioural system and goal-attainment by the personality system. The social system in turn ensures the integration or mutual adjustment of the actions of different actors or, as Parsons often writes, of Ego and Alter. Last but not least, the cultural system takes care of latent pattern maintenance through the preservation of at once generalized and stable meanings.

Parsons' own understanding of the AGIL-paradigm deserves some comment. First, he conceives the organism, personality, sociality and culture as differentiated subsystems of the general action system, yet this is difficult to uphold for the latter (Schmid, 1992). As the expression 'latent pattern maintenance' already suggests, the cultural system foresees the action system with at once symbolized and coherent meanings that particular actions often implicitly realize. Culture indeed orients or informs action and does not immanently involve a specific mode of doing that is comparable to the typical performances of the behavioural or the personality system and the interaction characterizing social systems. Second, Parsons underscores that the notion of an action system is an analytical abstraction but he does not spell out its wider ramifications. Thus the human being actually dissipates as the subject of individual action, in the literal meaning of the Latin word *subiectum* i.e. a bearing surface or ground. 'Rather one must say, thus troubling Westerns hearts: the action system is the subject of the one acting', Luhmann (1980a: 7) observes. According to Parsons' analytical framework, actions ordinarily attributed to an individual subject must indeed be conceived as the emergent effects of the interplay between the contributions of the involved four subsystems. On this account the concept of action system rather accords with the kind of a-humanism commonly associated with French structuralism and post-structuralism.

## CULTURE AS CONTROLLER

Parsons relates the AGIL-scheme to a two-sided cybernetic or control hierarchy (cybernetics is a trans-discipline studying regulatory systems and mechanisms that was intellectually in fashion during the 1950s). The A-G-I-L sequence points to the structured flow of energy in the action system. The organism's energy level conditions the one of the personality system; through their vigour, the participating personalities co-define the vim of the social system, which in turn feeds into a culture's vitality. Of more importance is the reverse sequence of informational control, so L-I-G-A, since it helps to explain why Parsons tends to narrow down culture through the not always substantiated double identification of meanings with values and values with norms (Schmid, 1992). The cultural system is considered the highest in information and therefore defines – rather than determines – the social system precisely through patterned values or morally loaded conceptions of the desirable. Within a social system, rather abstract values such as fairness, competition and the like are translated into more concrete norms that control the interaction among those taking up social positions. The norms thus ensure the function of integration: they imperatively structure and coordinate the various contributions of the different positions. Yet these value-inspired rules also cohere into normative patterns with which correspond roles, or bundles of expectations guiding the involved persons. 'The unit of interpenetration between a personality and a social system is not the individual but a *role* or a complex of *roles*. The *same* personality may participate in *several* social systems in different roles', Parsons observes (1977a: 196, emphasis in original). Social roles thus effectively link the functions of integration and goal-attainment: they offer the participating personality systems predefined tasks and purposes that motivate their individual actions and decision-making. All this in turn obliges a person to control his or her body accordingly: no role-informed individual goal-attainment (I-G) without a vigilant monitoring of the behavioural organism (G-A).

When applying the four-function classification directly to the social system, Parsons (1961) predictably associates the L-prerequisite with values and the I-function with norms. The G-function is observed by the collectivity consisting of all members of a social system: common goals are formulated in relation to this group. Rather tellingly the A-function is connected to roles. The personality system is thus explicitly located in the environment of the social system: the first actually constitutes a set of resources that the second selectively mobilizes. A crucial input, which brings us back to the energetic hierarchy, consists of the motivational drive that persons may bring to role-expectations once they have become individual aims. The chances for effectively motivated social action are heightened by the cultural system's direct grip on both the personality and the social system through two crucial processes of interpenetration that reinforce each other. On the one hand, culture interpenetrates the personality system via the socialization – 'culturalization' would be the more fitting expression – into central values and the corresponding norms. Both become part of a person's need dispositions: they are internalized and will in principle act as lasting motivating forces. On the other hand, the cultural system's interpenetration of the social system results in the institutionalization of value patterns, or their temporal stabilization and social generalization within a collectivity. Institutionalization may also be conceived as a mode of energy spending from the side of the social system, since the process implies that values or norms are socially watched over and sanctioned.

Parsons' sketch of the relationships between the different components of the action system incontestably bears a strong culturalist stamp. The cultural system not only informationally controls the social system by foreseeing it with moral conceptions of the desirable, but also moulds the personality system. Moreover, social order clearly has a normative, indeed moral character. Overall only an institutionalized consensus on a coherent pattern of values and norms can safeguard a social system's equilibrium: 'The most important *single* condition of the integration of an interaction system is a *shared basis of normative order*. ... The concept of a shared basis of normative order is basically the same as that of a common culture or a "symbolic system"' (Parsons, 1977a: 168, emphasis in original). Although a watered-down version of this culturalist view may still be found in many sociological textbooks, often without explicit references to Parsons' work, the vast stress on the ordering role of normative rules and moral consensus became the main target of the surging critique of Parsonianism from the end of the 1950s onwards. We should again take into account that this theoretical paradigm first and foremost analyses conditions of systems-equilibrium without making direct empirical claims. Nevertheless, the combination of a one-sided interest in social order with an outspoken anti-utilitarianism necessarily produces two evident blind spots (compare Alexander, 1983).

First, the model of the action system does not offer much in the way of conceptual handles to get a theoretical grip on material interests, the uneven distribution of scarce goods and related issues. That the cultural system may have a legitimating or ideological function with regard to social inequality is downplayed within Parsons' action frame of reference. In his once widely read *The Coming Crisis of Western Sociology*, Alvin Gouldner (1970) therefore dismisses Parsonianism as a religion-inspired idealism tending towards moralism. Second, the persistent conflation of cultural commonality and social consensus prevents taking into account the possibility of social disagreement on the basis of cultural agreement. Thus Alter may refer to the same value-pattern as Ego but emphasize different elements or invoke the same elements with different interpretative accents. Precisely the interest, partly fuelled by post-structuralism, in divergent readings of a seemingly identical 'cultural text' and in cultural ambiguities or contradictions greatly informs the so-called cultural turn that took off in the 1980s within the social sciences. This did not result in a rehearsal of the 1960s critique of Parsons' work. The 'new cultural sociology' is not anti- but post-Parsonian: both positive and negative references to Parsons' writings are scant, which signals that 'today ... Parsonian theory sets neither the terms of debate, nor the questions to be explored, nor even the tenor of argument' (Smith, 1998: 3–4).

Notwithstanding the overall theoretical repudiation of Parsons' main insights, there continues to exist a rather important branch of latent Parsonianism in quantitative empirical sociology. Countless surveys probe the normative attitudes of the selected respondents in order to detect shared value-patterns and, more generally, a common morality. The observed regularities are related to social background variables, which often results in an at once fragmented and homogenous picture of a population's culture, in the Parsonian sense. Whereas some normative orientations are widely shared, others predominate within for instance particular age cohorts or among those having a high school or university diploma. Underlying this research is not only a notion of culture implicitly reproducing the one advocated by Parsons but also the culturalist idea that the integration of social groups relies on collective values and concomitant norms internalized by their members. Moreover, much quantitative research assumes that the social equilibrium in a nation-state asks for a minimum of value-consensus. Thus the many surveys addressing the multicultural character of contemporary national societies in the West often routinely presuppose that a minimum of overlap is necessary among the normative attitudes of culturally differently socialized individuals. In the background of these studies often looms a political discourse that emphasizes the necessity of a common culture for society's orderly functioning.

## THE SOCIETAL LEVEL: GENERALIZED VALUES AND MEDIA

Although Parsons' general blend of action theory, systems theory and culturalism has distinctive flaws, the current lack of interest in his work perhaps unduly neglects his later work which predominantly addressed the macro-level of society (see especially Parsons, 1971; 1977; 1977a). In these writings the four-function framework is reiterated but also complemented with the concept of exchange media and more germane analyses of the American cultural system. Both give a prominent role to the notion of symbolic generalization in light of the structural differentiation of modern society in four main action subsystems and – according to the AGIL-scheme – 4 × 4 sub-subsystems. On the societal level the economy performs the adaption-function; the political system or polity ensures goal-attainment and the societal community guarantees integration. The function of latent-pattern maintenance is warranted by the so-called fiduciary system, which is the rather awkward neologism Parsons uses when speaking of a society's culture. Besides a common language, it of course comprises institutionalized value-patterns. They condense into a cultural tradition giving a society's members the imperative 'fiduciary responsibility for the maintenance or the development of such a tradition' (Parsons, 1977a: 378)

The differentiated nature of modern society elicits value generalization (e.g., Parsons, 1971: 26; 1977a: 184–95), which is actually a particular instance of symbolic generalization. Widely shared conceptions of the desirable such as fairness or justice are indeed vague, yet this is highly functional since it allows specific normative translations in different social subsystems – or sub-subsystems – such as the economy, the polity, formal education and the family. According to Parsons, two general value-patterns actually inform American society. The first he derives from Weber's famous characterization of Protestantism as a form of inner-worldly asceticism: the Protestant works hard in the profane world in order to save his soul in the hereafter (Weber, 1992). This attitude has been generalized into the value of instrumental activism, which no longer needs a particular religious legitimation and has besides the economy also permeated the spheres of politics, education or science (Parsons, 1991a; compare Lidz, 1991). Instrumental activism appraises performance and achievement in relation to more specific goals such as economic gain, learning or truth, with the proviso that they should be pursued in a cognitively rational way. The second general value-pattern morally cementing American society is institutionalized individualism (Parsons, 2007: 424–510; compare Bourricaud, 1977). In elucidating this tradition Parsons directly builds on Durkheim's scattered considerations on 'moral individualism' and 'the cult of the individual' (e.g., Durkheim, 1973). Like Durkheim he sharply distinguishes between the instrumental individualism reigning within the economy and partly linked to instrumental activism on the one hand, and its moral counterpart that obliges a minimum respect for every human being in whatever social situation, on the other. Institutionalized individualism comprises both but Parsons particularly underlines the cultural importance of the moral variant. Diverse kinds of juridical rules such as those associated with the idea of basic human rights meanwhile ensure the socially binding character of moral individualism. At the same time this value occasions divergent norms in the different societal spheres: the rules trying to ascertain mutual respect and a fair treatment in the relation between teacher and pupils differ from their equivalents in the economic domain.

The integration of a structurally differentiated society cannot only rely on generalized values controlling social and individual action. In addition, specific mechanisms must permit interchanges among culture, the economy, the polity and the societal community. Thus money not only furthers exchange in the economy but also interchanges between this and other social systems. The economy and households for instance interchange labour and goods, yet this activity is mediated by money: it has the form of wages and consumer expenditures. Money can act as a general exchange medium because it is not tied to particular artefacts, persons or situations but has an abstract symbolic meaning allowing re-specifications in order to assess the specific economic value of whatever kind of object or performance. Parsons therefore conceptualizes money as a symbolically generalized medium. He contends that with each of the four main subsystems of modern society correspond such a medium facilitating mutual interchanges. Besides money (the economy), power, influence and value-commitments take up this role in the sphere of politics, the societal community and the fiduciary system respectively (see especially Parsons, 1969: 352–472 and 1977a: 204–28).

In his conceptualization of symbolically generalized media, Parsons actually follows two different tracks (Baum, 1976; Künzler, 1989: 5–42). On the one hand, he considers money as the exemplary interchange medium and consequently tries to find equivalents for phenomena such as banking, inflation and deflation when discussing power, influence and value-commitments. This results in sometimes illuminating comparisons, but overall the monetary model chiefly generates highly metaphorical statements. On the other hand, symbolically generalized media also function as specialized languages that are regulated by a code permitting countless messages. As such, money, power, influence and value-commitments act as a medium of communication within their respective domains. More particularly, they motivate Alter to accept Ego's communicated selections – such as a consumer preference or an order – through inducement (or offering rewards: money), deterrence (threatening with and eventually applying negative sanctions: power), persuasion (giving justifications: influence) or the appeal to implement particular value-commitments. In a word, the four generalized media stand for specific capacities to get something done and to bring about results in the economy, the polity, the societal community and a society's culture. With every generalized medium there corresponds both an associated value-principle and a code, or a normatively obliging framework regulating its actual use. Whereas utility and effectiveness are the predominant value-principles associated with money and power respectively, integrity fulfils this role in relation to value-commitments. Integrity is 'not only a matter of choosing between right and wrong in a particular situation' but 'concerns rather the maintenance of integrity of commitment to the pattern [read: value-pattern] over a wide range of different actual and potential decisions, in differing situations, with differing consequences and levels of predictability of such consequences' (Parsons, 1977a: 445). The value-principle allows assessments, yet in the mundane functioning of a generalized medium its genuine realization is routinely trusted until the contrary is proven. Superiors are, for instance, granted the confidence that they deploy power in an organizationally effective way; comparably, the sincerity of a moral leader's commitment to the principles he professes is trusted, which secures the basis for his authority. Besides the reference to a value-principle, a generalized medium's use implies the existence of a code consisting of a set of institutionalized rules and directions circumscribing the legitimate deployment of money, power, influence and value-commitments. This operative framework modulates the general action-capacity associated with a general medium. Thus, binding property norms and other juridical standards regulating for instance the concluding of contracts define the rightful expenditure of money.

In light of Parsons previous work, the concept of symbolically generalized media clearly involves a shift. The possibility of social order no longer only equals the specification of institutionalized values into normative patterns structuring interaction, but is now also conceived in terms of action-coordinating media whose successful functioning vastly relies on trust. Moreover, the medium of value-commitments allows a more dynamic view on culture since religious or political leaders can put into action the general capacity to appeal to moral principles in order to renew value-patterns. Nevertheless, Parsons' musings on generalized media do not amount to a substantial break with culturalism (for a different view, see Wenzel, 2005). It is indeed striking that he binds their functioning to both an exclusive value-principle and a regulating normative framework or code. In this way, the conceptual couple of values and norms that so vastly permeates Parsons' earlier views remains in a leading position. In sum, a direct or manifest culturalism is supplemented with an indirect, more latent form of the very same approach.

## RE-OBSERVING SOCIAL SYSTEMS

The terms of the debate on the pros and cons of Parsonianism were drastically reset when Luhmann (1995) published around the mid-1980s the definitive outline of his overturn of systems theory that had already been simmering in his writings for quite some years. Several theoretical innovations inform this altogether radical view on the social, which has not yet really rooted in Anglo-Saxon social science and clearly resonates with core ideas of, for instance, Jacques Derrida, Gilles Deleuze and other major figures of French Theory or post-structuralism (for a discussion of these affinities, which I shall not address here, see Moeller (2012) and La Cour and Philippopoulos-Mihalopoulos (2013)). I therefore first briefly introduce the main assumptions underlying Luhmann's later work and will then discuss in more detail its ambiguous relation with cultural theorizing.

A peculiar epistemology combining the 'laws of form' described by polymath George Spencer-Brown (1969) with Heinz von Foerster's (1981) second-order cybernetics underpins Luhmann's later work (e.g., Luhmann, 1990: 31–58; compare Baecker, 1999; Moeller, 2006: 65–78; Borch, 2011: 50–65). A form is a two-sided distinction of whatever nature (e.g., the word-pair 'this/that') allowing observations through its one-sided use: whereas one pole is effectively employed to mark something (e.g., 'it is this'), the other side remains unmarked. Thus a form points to the unity of the difference – a Hegelian-sounding expression frequently used by Luhmann – between a marked 'inside' and an unmarked 'outside'. The notion regularly incites Luhmann to define main concepts in differential terms. A system, for instance, is the unity of the difference between that system and its environment or everything it is not, which implies the existence of a boundary symbolized by the slash separating 'system' from 'environment' in the conceptual distinction 'system/environment' (Luhmann: 1995: 12–58; 2012: 28–39). Moreover, with the idea of forms literally informing observations, there corresponds a thoroughly constructivist, neo-Kantian epistemology that partly resonates with the structuralist stress on the conditioning role of dual categories or binary distinctions in cultural formations of knowledge (Lévi-Strauss, 1963). Observations are indeed invariably form-dependent. When observing the world, one does not see reality as such but 'the reality of the observed reality' framed by the employed distinctions. However, in first-order observations operating in a realistic mode, the one-sidedly used forms per definition escape the observer. An observer for instance perceives 'this' or 'that' but not the difference 'this/that': the form paradoxically acts as the observation's blind spot making observation possible. In order to notice the formative role of forms, one has to switch to the mode of second-order observation, or the observing of first-order observations that amounts to distinguishing distinctions.

Second-order observation has become institutionalized in modernity (Luhmann, 1998). Thus the modern self-conscious subject honoured by Descartes is an individual observing her own observing. Various forms of second-order observation also typify the mundane functioning of societal spheres such as the economy, science or politics. Scientists reading scholarly articles observe how colleagues have observed a particular phenomenon, and merchants keeping track of the fluctuations in the turnover observe how consumers estimate their offer. In his only essay directly addressing the concept of culture, Luhmann (1995a: 31–54) analyses this notion as precisely allowing, even stimulating second-order observation. For instance, one observes that somebody acts unexpectedly because Alter belongs to another culture and therefore 'sees the world differently'. Own ways of doing may as well be re-interpreted as culturally specific: 'Like before, one can cut with a knife, can pray to God, drive to the seaside, sign treaties or embellish objects. But in addition, all this can be observed and described a second time when one conceives it as a cultural phenomenon and exposes it to comparisons' (Luhmann, 1995a: 42). Accordingly, cultural identities are formulated and defended in a frequently essentialist mode. Luhmann (2002; 2013: 167–350) himself prefers to speak of self-observations or, when they have a textual form, of self-descriptions. Every society generates interpretations of itself, which are nowadays primarily diffused through the mass media system (Laermans, 2005). Yet only within modernity are these self-observations once again observed and reflexively processed. Thus our society typifies itself as postmodern, individualized, multicultural or globalized; many social scientists effectively rely on these common identifications in view of more elaborate insights or empirical research, thus also conferring them with academic credibility.

Luhmann firmly sticks to the idea that a truly sociological analysis of society asks for a genuine social theory that distances itself by means of self-devised conceptual distinctions from current societal self-descriptions. At stake is not just the autonomy of theorizing but, more importantly, the possibility of actively constructing a coherent conceptual framework de-familiarizing predominant opinions on the nature of the social world. Luhmann (1995) primarily problematizes the latter on the basis of a systems-notion that focuses on the reproduction of a system's specific elements thanks to a distinctive operation (compare Moeller, 2006: 3–64; Borch, 2011: 19–49). Thus the cells making up organic or living systems continually regenerate themselves by means of bio-chemical interactions; comparably, thinking is the psychic system's or mind's characterizing operation through which it renews its basic components, i.e. thoughts or mental representations. A social system consists of communications referring to each other – hence the notion of self-reference – and therefore reposes on the continual reiteration of the operation called communication. His operation-oriented approach explains Luhmann's clear-cut rejection of the idea of a cultural system. For however defined, it is in fact difficult to formulate a singular operation featuring such a system. At first sight using meaningful symbols may be a plausible candidate, yet this happens both privately and publicly – read: within psychic systems through thinking and within social systems through communication.

Luhmann radicalizes the latent a-humanism in Parsons' work in a twofold way. On the one hand, the link between social systems and action theory is decidedly slit. The second-order observation that it is customary to grasp communication in terms of human action already signals the actual status of this interpretation. Communication indeed routinely observes itself as human-made, but this self-description should not bind social theorizing (Luhmann, 1995: 137–75). On the other hand, Luhmann (1995b) situates psychic and organic systems – and a fortiori human beings, or structural couplings of both kinds of systems – with much more emphasis in the environment of social systems. A clear-cut argument backs this theoretical stance: neither mental representations nor bodily cells can ever directly become part of social systems. Evidently, one may communicate about one's conscious perceptions, thoughts and emotions, or about one's headache or the level of adrenaline in one's blood. More generally, the operational closure of social systems goes hand in hand with a selective communicative openness towards their environment, which of course besides all kinds of artefacts or psychic and organic systems also includes still other social systems (except on the level of global society: this macro-system includes everything social and hence all actually existing social systems). Communicating about something in the environment equals the production of observations. A simple statement such as 'I don't feel well' or 'It's nice weather today' indeed comes down to a communicatively embedded first-order observation of an external state of affairs. Not only psychic systems but social systems as well are observation systems processing forms or distinctions that often have a linguistic nature in order to report on both their own functioning and their environment (Luhmann, 2012: 49–73).

Luhmann (1995: 137–75) combines the observation that communication crosses self-reference and external or other-reference with the conceptual distinction 'utterance/information'. Something is said, or an utterance is made, by pointing implicitly or explicitly to a previous or expected utterance: this is the phenomenon of self-reference, which is ordinarily observed in action-terms within a social system. The utterance is accordingly attributed to a sender who may be held responsible for it. Simultaneously, linguistic or other forms such as visual distinctions are employed to selectively inform about the environment of the communication process: this is the phenomenon of other-reference that amounts to the fabrication of external observations. The self-referential uttering of other-referential information does not yet generate a communication. The effective production of a social system-element demands that the communication is rounded off through the understanding of the uttered information in this or that way. At stake are not the psychic interpretations by the participating minds, which are private and inaccessible to others, but the mostly implicit communicative understanding signalled by an ensuing communication: 'When one communicative action follows another, it tests whether the preceding communication was understood. However surprising the connecting communication may turn out to be, it is also used to indicate and to observe how it rests on an understanding of the preceding communication' (Luhmann, 1995: 143). The phenomenon of lying aptly illustrates the crucial distinction between psychic and communicative understanding. Thus in responding to a lecturer's question a student may say 'Yes, I understand' and simultaneously think 'I do not understand a word of Luhmann's theory…'.

The synthesis of utterance, information and understanding defining communication is not a human performance: 'Humans cannot communicate, only communication can communicate' (Luhmann, 1995c: 31). A social system's functioning of course depends on the involvement of at least two different psychic systems. Oral or written communication requires the attentive perception of sounds or letters respectively, yet only consciousness has the capacity to observe sensorially. Nevertheless, Luhmann maintains that a social system may be theoretically observed as a self-productive or autopoietic process since neither the participating minds nor the bodies sustaining their activity can communicatively confirm that information has been uttered and is selectively understood. Only an ensuing communication is able to do so, thus precisely transforming a previous occurrence such as the production of a series of sounds into a communication. The very same logic of course applies to this next event. In order to exist as a new social system-element calling into life a previous one, a following communication needs a next communication whose status also depends on a succeeding communication, and so on. In other words, the self-production in social systems points to indeterminate events that only acquire retroactively a determinate identity.

## AWAY WITH CULTURE?

As was already noted in the introduction, Luhmann abandons Parsons' theoretical fixation on the conditions furthering social order or systems-equilibrium. Communication is for sure by and large regulated by social structures, which Luhmann (1995: 278–376) does not conceive as normative patterns informed by values but identifies with the expectations pertaining to social positions (or roles) and individual persons. Expectations situationally reduce the range of possible communications, yet without ever ruling out the eventuality of deviations or conflict since at every moment a rebuffing communication can occur: 'The concept of conflict is … related to a precise and empirically comprehensible communicative occurrence: to a communicated "no" that answers the previous communication. … Conflicts serve to continue communication by using one of the possibilities that communication holds open, by saying no', as Luhmann (1995: 389) emphasizes. The eventual subsequent quarrel does not at all threaten a social system's viability since the communication just goes on in the mode of disagreement. It is therefore crucial to distinguish process – or the sheer reproduction of elements in whatever form – from structure when analysing social systems. Furthermore, Luhmann (e.g., 1978; 2012: 396–404) emphatically stresses, 'against Parsons', the so-called polemogenic or conflict-inducing role of moral communication based on values. Such communication commonly assumes without much – if any – justification a social consensus on the invoked conceptions of the desirable. Making this tacit agreement explicit regularly entails the communication of a disagreement augmenting the chances of mutual conflict.

Particular values and the concomitant norms may actually underlie the ordering expectations in interaction systems or face-to-face communication. Yet on the societal level, symbolically generalized communication media act as 'a functional equivalent to the usual normative safeguard of social cohesion ... In a very abstract sense, they are a functional equivalent of morality ...' (Luhmann, 2012: 190–1). This view radicalizes Parsons' diagnosis on the basis of a thorough re-conceptualization of modern society (see especially Luhmann, 1989; 2005; 2013: 65–166). Thus the limiting idea of only four functional prerequisites and concomitant subsystems is rejected in favour of a variety of societal domains each addressing a general problem. Whereas the economy for instance focuses on producing goods and services in a situation of scarcity, politics provides the collectively binding decisions every society demands. Many other societal subsystems can be discerned in relation to an always specific function: education (the socialization into specialized knowledge), the juridical system (upholding the social validity of legal norms against their eventual infringement), the intimate sphere (ensuring the possibility of a genuinely personal communication) or the mass media system (informing about society within society, and in addition procuring entertainment). Each functional subsystem operates autonomously, which logically implies the existence of a distinct form of communication typifying its working. Thus payments and utterances predominantly referring to existing positive law or a transcendent reality make up the basic operations in the economy, the juridical subsystem and the religious sphere respectively.

In most functional subsystems, a symbolically generalized medium furthers both communicative success and their effective reproduction (Luhmann, 2012: 190–238). As Parsons already suggested, such a medium enhances the chances that uttered and already understood information becomes the binding premise for a next communication, action or experience. In the scientific subsystem for example, relevant statements that are empirically proven to be true must be reckoned with in new articles or books (which is indicated by citations, also a directly visible mode of self-reference). In addition, each true communication elicits new true utterances, which ensures the system's autopoiesis. In a comparable way, the use of money routinely guarantees in the economy the acceptance of the communicated desire to buy something, be it sex, illegal substances or weapons. With every monetary transaction, self-(re)production is once again secured: realized payments create the opportunity for future payments. Love functions alike in the subsystem of intimate communication (Luhmann, 2010). This symbolically generalized medium creates the rather implausible constellation that Alter accepts, even takes as the ground for personal experiences, Ego's statements of whatever kind. Although an outsider may observe them as quite boring or utterly idiosyncratic, the medium of love makes communicative success highly probable among those entertaining an intimate relationship.

Luhmann's theory not only disconnects the concepts of functional differentiation and symbolically generalized media from the confining AGIL-scheme. In marked contrast to Parsons' approach, media such as power, money, truth, love or (religious) belief are neither linked to an underlying value-principle nor to an institutionalized normative framework regulating their use (Künzler, 1989: 71–122; Chernilo, 2002). Within their respective domains, these media function in a literally a-moral way and substitute the coordinating function morality once observed on the societal level. Modern society can also do without at once institutionalized and generalized value-patterns or cultural traditions. '[The] most important change in the function of moral communication is likely to have been that morality can no longer integrate society with regard to its optimum state', Luhmann (2012: 243) asserts. Overall contemporary society primarily falls back on moral communication, particularly in the mass media system, when urgent problems have to be faced or a generalized medium is used outside the appropriate sub-systemic context (the bribery of judges or politicians is an evident example). Yet except questioning the theoretical tenability of the idea of cultural systems and their socially stabilizing or integrative function, Luhmann (2012: 374) also provocatively declares – be it in a footnote – that 'the systems-theoretical approach has the advantage of rendering the vague concept of culture superfluous'. The firm dismissal goes together with the coinage of several notions that act as proverbial stand-ins for the repudiated term and the issues commonly associated with it (Burkart, 2004; Laermans, 2007). This partly applies to the already presented notion of societal self-description but the concept of semantics is undoubtedly the most prominent conceptual equivalent.

Put simply, a semantic – Luhmann also sometimes uses the expression 'semantic structure' – is a meaningful form or distinction that is routinely used in communicative observations and often has a linguistic nature (see especially Luhmann, 1980: 9–71). Semantics thus frame both the observations of a social system's environment (e.g., the word-pair 'subject/object' or the distinction 'human/animal') and its self-observations or descriptions (e.g., the form 'traditional/modern' or the distinction 'estate/class'). The genesis and functioning of a semantic involves a two-sided process. On the one hand, a meaningful form transforms into a semantic because this distinction, or one of its two poles, is repeatedly used in the operations of various sorts of social systems. The implicated form or meaning thus becomes evident, yet this familiarity has to be re-affirmed in new future communications. In marked difference to Parsons' idea of latent pattern-maintenance, a semantic therefore does not imperatively steer social systems but is rather the unintended by-product of their autonomous functioning (compare Martens, 1999; Hahn, 2004). A semantic emerges through the reiterative use of, for instance, a word and only retains this status if communications yet to come once again re-employ the concerned term, which is everything but a necessity. On this account, the genesis, reproduction and abandonment of a semantic are directly linked to the memorizing within social systems. Memorizing, thus Luhmann (2012: 348–58) underlines, is not synonymous with recalling, let alone with the selective retrieval of experiences or artefacts from the past. A differential periphrasis is again appropriate: memorizing is the unity of the difference between remembering and forgetting. Communication processes continuously remember or forget meaningful forms, thus either confirming or refuting their structuring capacity as semantics. On the other hand, semantics stabilize meanings over time in a necessarily schematic way, thus offering communication – and also thinking – 'a present stock of types', 'a highly generalized, relatively situation-independent available meaning' (Luhmann, 1980: 19). In reducing the possible meanings of, for instance, a word to an open 'meaning kernel', a semantic allows contextual re-specifications and a plethora of different accentuations. Only in this way can the implicated meaningful form be perpetually re-employed in various sorts of communication. Implied is indeed the process of symbolic generalization already highlighted by Parsons. Luhmann adopts the notion but also vastly re-interprets it on the basis of both Edmund Husserl's phenomenological approach of meaning and Spencer-Brown's 'laws of form'.

## 'THE MEANING OF MEANING'

In speaking of meaning (*Sinn*) Luhmann (1990a: 21–79; 1995: 59–102; 2012: 18–27) actually does not put that term directly on a par with signification in the textual or semiotic sense. Following Husserl he assumes that 'a *difference* is contained in every experience of meaning, namely, the difference between what is *actually given* and what can *possibly* result from it' (Luhmann, 1995: 75, emphasis in original). The concept of meaning thus refers to the unity of the difference between actuality and virtuality, a momentarily realized possibility and possible possibilities. Accordingly, an actual thought or communication is meaningful because it appears against a horizon of possibilities made up of other potential mental representations or communications. Every singular element of a psychic or social system is therefore contingent in the modal-logical sense: neither necessary nor impossible, so just possible. Moreover, a next mental representation or ensuing utterance can be theoretically grasped as an equally non-determined selection out of the horizon of possible possibilities accompanying an actual thought or communication. The novel element of course unavoidably re-articulates the distinction 'actual/possible'. Each new operation in a psychic or social system indeed regenerates meaning and concomitantly refashions the potential for a succeeding one. Since the ever-present horizon of virtual thoughts or communications in light of an actual one is the condition of possibility 'to go on' in social and psychic systems; meaning is the fundamental medium of both. Different from organic systems, they reproduce themselves at once through meaning and in a meaningful way.

When processed in thinking or communication, semantic distinctions are also meaningful in the just elucidated sense (Luhmann, 1980: 9–71). A word or linguistic form, for example, or the unity of the difference between a signifier and a signified, couples a symbol – a fixed series of sounds or letters – to a schematic meaning that is contextually re-specified. The thus produced 'meaning in the use' effectively combines virtuality and actuality. Within a particular strain of thoughts or specific communicative situation, the typified or abstract meaning changes into a peculiar actual signification momentarily opening up a range of other possible significations that the general character of the used form precisely allows. Although at first sight a word's stabilized meaning seems univocal, the reduction of possible significations actually equals a general semantic identity that is again and again made meaningful through the contextual specification into a singular signification pointing to virtual other ones. Seen from the vantage point of the production of an at once determinate and indeterminate meaning-identity, a different and double-sided logic applies that Luhmann (1990: 14–30; 2012: 123–37) clarifies under reference to Spencer-Brown's 'laws of forms'. On the one hand, its genesis logically demands that a situationally realized signification of a meaningful form is taken up again and again in later operations. A once actual specific meaning is thus re-actualized or condensed into a first re-use, which is again condensed into a second one, and so on. With every new condensation, meaning becomes more trans-situational or abstract: as was already pointed out, its stabilization equals generalization. On the other hand, each (re-)condensed meaning is also strictly contextually confirmed: the already produced semantic identity or 'meaning-kernel' fits the situation at hand because it may also be used in a singular way. These circumstantial enrichments are not taken up in a next operation but acquire the status of virtual significations that are only unsystematically re-activated in the particular re-specifications of a condensed or typified meaning.

The notions of semantics, generalized or typified meaning, meaning-identity and condensed meaning are equivalent concepts. The decisive point is that they all refer to forms such as words or visual schemes that do not just convey a delimitable number of significations. Their apparently stable 'meaning-kernel', produced through their iterative and condensing usage in social systems, stands for the potential to be employed meaningfully, or as a combination of an always specific actual signification implying other possible significations. The famous dictum 'meaning is in the use', commonly attributed to Ludwig Wittgenstein and a leading idea within pragmatics, should therefore be taken literally. The implied use is neither a matter of human action (as Parsons and many others assume) nor of more generic social or cultural practices (as for instance Bourdieu, 2010 or Schatzki, 2008 argue), but primarily involves the functioning of either a psychic or a social system. Precisely because both operate in a meaningful way, linguistic and other condensed forms can also secure their structural coupling. This does not imply a merging or an operative overlapping of the connected systems, quite the contrary (Luhmann, 1995b: 37–54). The concept of structural coupling primarily points to a synchronization of operationally closed autonomous systems, resulting in a co-evolution. Thus the participating minds direct their psychic attention to the communication in their environment and think along with it: the uttered information is understood 'thoughtfully'. Luhmann (2012: 49–67) asserts that language and different sorts of schematic distinctions are the two basic forms ensuring the structural coupling between social and psychic systems. Yet in light of his own work, this rather limited view may be substantially broadened in the direction of a novel notion of culture.

## RE-OBSERVING CULTURE

> The combined effect of all communication media – language, dissemination media [like writing and printing], and the symbolically generalized media – is to condense what we might overall call 'culture'. Condensation in this context means that the meaning (*Sinn*) used remains the same through reuse in various situations (otherwise there would be no re-use), but is also confirmed and enriched with implications (*Bedeutungen*) that can no longer be reduced to a simple formula. (Luhmann, 2012: 248)

Thus states a casual aside in *Theory of Society* in which Luhmann exceptionally hints at a possible concept of culture without elaborating this suggestion (given his explicit theoretical aversion for that notion, the digression rather reads as a slip of the pen). The contention actually invites one to regard (a) culture as the momentarily available stock of condensed meanings, symbolic generalizations or typified forms. A still more nuanced conceptualization is possible by also taking into account the notion of medium (Hahn, 2004; Laermans, 2007). Luhmann (2012: 113–20) indeed underpins his considerations on meaning-as-medium and symbolically generalized media with an all-purpose definition of that term (compare Brauns, 2002). Stated abstractly, a medium consists of loosely coupled elements that may be more tightly linked without this having any effect on their status or later re-use as medial components. Language, for instance, is a particular medium in which words are the primary elements; as only loosely connected linguistic forms, words can be selectively combined into a great variety of sentences in which they situationally entertain fixed relationships. Like every medium, language is first and foremost a potential that becomes only partly visible in its temporary actualizations: a medium makes observations possible but is in itself unobservable. Given this abstract concept of medium, culture can be considered as a specific medium within the overall medium of meaning. Condensed meanings are this medium's loosely coupled elements, which are temporarily related in tighter articulations within the context of communicating or thinking. Culture is thus a simultaneously enabling and reproduced resource of both social and psychic systems. Through their functioning, the elements of (a) culture are both contextually re-affirmed (generally re-condensed) and re-interpreted (singularly confirmed).

As the aggregation of all condensed forms or generalized meanings, including for instance visual schemes, (a) culture assures the structural coupling between psychic and cultural systems. Or rather, culture is the medium through which this proverbial link is again and again produced. The coupling's actual effectiveness depends on the communicative use of cultural elements according to the premise that they are always already known by all participating minds. What Luhmann (2012: 61) observes with regard to abstract meaning-schemes has indeed a more general purport: 'In using schemata [or cultural elements], communication presupposes that every participating consciousness understands what is meant, but also that this does not determine how the consciousness systems handle the schema …'. In a word, social systems take for granted that the partaking psychic systems are familiar with the invoked forms of typified meaning. Harold Garfinkel (1984) has demonstrated the crucial role of this assumption in his famous breaching experiments and conceptualized it as one of the ethno-methods implicitly structuring interaction. Given the supposition's double nature I propose to speak of an operative fiction. The notion accentuates both the fictitious or non-verified nature of the presumption of psychic cognizance with communicatively employed meaning-identities on the one hand, and the fact that it is intrinsically connected with the effective operations of a social system on the other. If the operative fiction momentarily proves to be wrong and a participant indicates that she is not acquainted with, for instance, a linguistic expression, the social system does not at all break down. Clarifying communications will follow that once again assume that the employed generalized meanings are known by the partaking minds. The social system just continues and re-affirms the operative fiction that was only a second ago put into question.

The often smooth functioning of the structural coupling between psychic and social systems through the assumed conscious familiarity with the communicatively used meaning-identities creates a peculiar mirage effect. It may indeed look as if the communication works that easily because the participants share a common culture in which they are deeply socialized. This was in essence Parsons' view, but, for instance, Habermas' (1984) notion of a shared life-world conditioning communicative action also tends toward this idea. The continual exposure to condensed meanings that are repeatedly used in communication, not to say anything of their explicit elucidation in education, evidently leaves traces in psychic systems. Nevertheless, it is rather improbable that those participating in joint communication think or understand in unison when hearing a word, seeing a picture or observing whatever kind of meaningful form. Social and psychic systems co-evolve and function synchronically thanks to the medium of culture ensuring their mutual coupling, yet both operate autonomously. At the same time, social systems effectively practice the notion of a common culture shared by all participants as an at once feasible and efficient fiction, thus lending an overall credit to it through their mundane functioning. In addition, the conception of individually shared meanings and an autonomous cultural realm steering personal thinking and action is a prominent societal self-description. The flaws of Parsons' ingenious mix of culturalism and systems theory show that sociology may perhaps better not reflexively re-fashion this semantic configuration or ignore the true status of the impression of cultural commonality when observing social systems.

My double proposal to conceive culture as consisting of condensed meanings on the one hand and as a medium within the general medium of meaning on the other, does not come with the prospect of a thorough renewal of cultural theory or research. Overall the suggestion concords with the meanwhile institutionalized hermeneutic or interpretative approach of culture, yet with the proviso that in light of its medial status a culture is never observable as such. A local subculture, an organizational culture or a however delineated mode of culture – the notion of form or distinction again applies here – is only tentatively reconstructable through the study of its publicly perceivable communicative actualizations. Psychic systems also make use in their operations of generalized schematic meanings but are altogether empirically non-transparent. A culture-oriented second-order observation of communication may eventually also detect coherent patterns, thus subscribing to Clifford Geertz' (1973: 12) well-known assertion – which may have been directly inspired by Parsons since he was a student of his – that culture 'consists of socially established structures of meaning'. A Luhmannian instigated systems-theoretical view will emphasize the observer-dependent nature of the findings resulting from such a structuralist-minded approach and simultaneously offers a theoretically elaborated conceptualization of how meaning is communicatively stabilized or condensed into cultural forms that psychic systems employ autonomously. The social system or, put simply, communication, is indeed the prime medium through which the medium of culture is at once unintentionally and selectively reproduced, and so maintained and reinvigorated. In marked contrast with its Parsonian forerunner, theorizing in the Luhmannian vein thus privileges 'the social' above 'the cultural' and denies that culture is a distinctive sphere or reality that can be the material object of an autonomous brand of theorizing. Cultural sociology just equals a sociology focusing on social systems through the peculiar lens of the symbolic generalization of meaning and the communicative performativity of the thus generated condensed significations.

# REFERENCES

Adriaansens, H.P.M. (1980) *Talcott Parsons and the Conceptual Dilemma*. London: Routledge.

Alexander, J. (1983) *The Modern Reconstruction of Classical Thought: Talcott Parsons (Theoretical Logic in Sociology, Vol. 4)*. London: Routledge.

Alexander, J. (1988) 'The New Theoretical Movement', in N.J. Smelser (ed.), *Handbook of Sociology*. London: Sage. pp. 77–101.

Baecker, D. (ed.) (1999) *Problems of Form*. Stanford, CA: Stanford University Press.

Baecker, D. (2000) *Wozu Kultur?* Berlin: Kadmos.

Baum, R. (1976) 'Introduction to Part IV: Generalized Media in Action', in J. Laubser et al. (eds), *Explorations in the General Theory in Social Science: Essays in Honor of Talcott Parsons*, Vol. Two. New York: Free Press. pp. 448–69.

Borch, C. (2011) *Niklas Luhmann*. Abingdon: Routledge.

Bourdieu, P. (2010) *Distinction*. Abingdon: Routledge.

Bourricaud, F. (1977) *L'individualisme institutionel. Essai sur la sociologie de Talcott Parsons*. Paris: PUF.

Brauns, J. (ed.) (2002) *Form und Medium*. Weimar: VDG.

Burkart, G. (2004) 'Niklas Luhmann: Ein Theoretiker der Kultur?', in G. Burkart and G. Runkel (eds), *Luhmann und die Kulturtheorie*, Frankfurt: Suhrkamp. pp. 11–39.

Chernilo, D. (2002) 'The Theoretization of Social Co-ordinations in Differentiated Societies: The Theory of Generalized Symbolic Media in Parsons, Luhmann and Habermas', *British Journal of Sociology*, 53(3): 431–49.

Durkheim, E. (1973) 'Individualism and the Intellectuals', in R.N. Bellah (ed.), *Emile Durkheim on Morality and Society*. Chicago: Chicago University Press. pp. 43–57.

Garfinkel, H. (1984) *Studies in Ethnomethodology*. Cambridge: Polity.

Geertz, C. (1973) 'Thick Description: Toward an Interpretive Theory of Culture', in C. Geertz, *The Interpretation of Cultures*. New York: Basic Books. pp. 3–32.

Gouldner, A.W. (1970) *The Coming Crisis of Western Sociology*. New York: Basic Books.

Habermas, J. (1984) *The Theory of Communicative Action*. Boston, MA: Beacon Press, 2 vols.

Hahn, A. (2004) 'Ist Kultur ein Medium?', in G. Burkart and G. Runkel (eds), *Luhmann und die Kulturtheorie*, Frankfurt: Suhrkamp. pp. 40–57.

Kroeber, A.L. and Parsons, T. (1958) 'The Concepts of Culture and of Social System', *American Sociological Review*, 23(2): 582–83.

Künzler, J. (1989) *Medien und Gesellschaft. Die Medienkonzepte von Talcott Parsons, Jürgen Habermas und Niklas Luhmann*. Stuttgart: Ferdinand Enke Verlag.

La Cour, A. and Philippopoulos-Mihalapoulos, A. (eds) (2013) *Luhmann Observed: Radical Theoretical Encounters*. London: Palgrave Macmillan.

Laermans, R. (2005) 'Mass Media in Contemporary Society: A Critical Appraisal of Niklas Luhmann's Systems View', *Cybernetics and Human Knowing*, 12(4): 51–70.

Laermans, R. (2007) 'Theorizing Culture, or Reading Luhmann Against Luhmann', *Cybernetics and Human Knowing*, 14(2–3): 67–83.

Lévi-Strauss, C. (1963) *Structuralist Anthropology*. New York: Basic Books.

Lidz, V. (1991) 'The American Value System: A Commentary on Talcott Parsons's Perspective and Understanding', in R. Robertson and B.S. Turner (eds), *Talcott Parsons: Theorist of Modernity*. London: Sage. pp. 22–36.

Luhmann, N. (1970) *Soziologische Aufklärung. Aufsätze zur Theorie sozialer Systeme*. Opladen: Westdeutscher Verlag.

Luhmann, N. (1978) 'Soziologie der Moral', in N. Luhmann and Stephen H. Pfürtner (eds), *Theorietechnik und Moral*. Frankfurt: Suhrkamp. pp. 8–116.

Luhmann, N. (1980) *Gesellschaftsstruktur und Semantik. Studien zur Wissenssoziologie der modernen Gesellschaft (Band 1)*. Frankfurt: Suhrkamp.

Luhmann, N. (1980a) 'Talcott Parsons – Zur Zukunft eines Theorieprogramms', *Zeitschrift gur Soziologie*, 9(1): 5–17.

Luhmann, N. (1989) *Ecological Communication*. Chicago: Chicago University Press.

Luhmann, N. (1990) *Soziologische Aufklärung 5: Konstruktivistische Perspektiven*. Opladen: Westdeutscher Verlag.

Luhmann, N. (1990a) *Essays on Self-Reference*. New York: Columbia University Press.
Luhmann, N. (1995) *Social Systems*. Stanford, CA: Stanford University Press.
Luhmann, N. (1995a) *Gesellschaftsstruktur und Semantik. Studien zur Wissenssoziologie der modernen Gesellschaft (Band 4)*. Frankfurt: Suhrkamp.
Luhmann, N. (1995b) *Soziologische Aufklärung 6: Die Soziologie und der Mensch*. Opladen: Westdeutscher Verlag.
Luhmann, N. (1995c), *Die Wissenschaft der Gesellschaft*. Frankfurt: Suhrkamp.
Luhmann, N. (1998) *Observations on Modernity*. Stanford, CA: Stanford University Press.
Luhmann, N. (2002) *Theories of Distinction: Redescribing the Descriptions of Modernity*. Stanford, CA: Stanford University Press.
Luhmann, N. (2005) *Einführung in die Theorie der Gesellschaft*. Heidelberg: Carl Auer.
Luhmann, N. (2010) *Love: A Sketch*. Cambridge: Polity Press.
Luhmann, N. (2012) *Theory of Society. Volume 1*. Stanford, CA: Stanford University Press.
Luhmann, N. (2013) *Theory of Society. Volume 2*. Stanford, CA: Stanford University Press.
Luhmann, N. (2013a) *Introduction to Systems Theory*. Cambridge: Polity Press.
Martens, W. (1999) 'Die kulturelle und soziale Ordnung des Handelns. Eine Analyse der Beiträge Parsons' und Luhmanns', in R. Greshoff and G. Kneer (eds), *Struktur und Ereignis in theorievergleichender Perspektive*. Opladen: Westdeutscher Verlag. pp. 71–117.
Maturana H.R. and Varela, F.J. (1980) *Autopoiesis and Cognition: The Realization of the Living*. Dordrecht: Reidel.
Mayhew, L.H. (1985) 'Introduction', in L.H. Mayhew (ed.), *Talcott Parsons on Institutions and Social Evolution: Selected Writings*. Chicago: University of Chicago Press. pp. 1–63.
Moeller, H.-G. (2006) *Luhmann Explained: From Souls to Systems*. Peru, IL: Open Court.
Moeller, H.-G. (2012) *The Radical Luhmann*. New York: Columbia University Press.
Parsons, T. (1953) 'The Theory of Symbolism in Relation to Action', in T. Parsons, R.F. Bales and E. Shils (eds), *Working Papers in the Theory of Action*. New York: Free Press. pp. 31–62.
Parsons, T. (1961) 'An Outline of the Social System', in T. Parsons et al. (eds), *Theories of Society*. New York: The Free Press. pp. 30–79.
Parsons, T. (1961a) 'Introduction to Part IV: Culture and the Social System', in T. Parsons et al. (eds), *Theories of Society*. New York: The Free Press. pp. 963–93.
Parsons, T. (1967) *The Structure of Social Action*, 2nd edn. New York: Free Press. Originally published 1937.
Parsons, T. (1969) *Politics and Social Structure*. New York: Free Press.
Parsons, T. (1971) *The System of Modern Societies*. Englewood Cliffs, NJ: Prentice Hall.
Parsons, T. (1977) *The Evolution of Societies*. Englewood Cliffs, NJ: Prentice Hall.
Parsons, T. (1977a) *Social Systems and the Evolution of Action Theory*. New York: Free Press.
Parsons, T. (1978) *Action Theory and the Human Condition*. New York: Free Press.
Parsons, T. (1982) 'Action, Symbols, and Cybernetic Control', in I. Rossi (ed.), *Structural Sociology: Theoretical Perspectives and Substantive Analyses*. New York: Columbia University Press.
Parsons, T. (1991) *The Social System*. London: Routledge. Originally published 1951.
Parsons, T. (1991a) 'A Tentative Outline of American Values', in R. Robertson and B.S. Turner (eds), *Talcott Parsons: Theorist of Modernity*. London: Sage. pp. 37–61.
Parsons, T. (2007) *American Society: A Theory of the Societal Community*. Boulder, CO: Paradigm Publishers.
Parsons, T. and Shils, E.A. (eds) (2001) *Toward a General Theory of Action: Theoretical Foundations for the Social Sciences*. New Brunswick, NJ: Transaction Publishers. Originally published 1951.
Schatzki, T.R. (2008) *Social Practices: A Wittgensteinian Approach to Human Activity and the Social*. Cambridge: Cambridge University Press.
Schmid, M. (1992) 'The Concept of Culture and its Place within a Theory of Social Action: A Critique of Talcott Parsons' Theory of Culture', in R. Münch and N.J. Smelser (eds), *Theory of Culture*. Berkeley: University of California Press. pp. 88–120.
Segre, S. (2012) *Talcott Parsons: An Introduction*. Lanham: University Press of America.
Smith, P. (1998) 'The New American Cultural Sociology: An Introduction', in P. Smith (ed.), *The New American Cultural Sociology*. Cambridge: Cambridge University Press. pp. 1–14.
Spencer-Brown, G. (1969) *Laws of Form*. London: Allen & Unwin.
Travino, A.J. (2001) 'Introduction: The Theory and Legacy of Talcott Parsons', in A.J. Travino (ed.), *Talcott Parsons Today: His Theory and Legacy in Contemporary Sociology*. Oxford: Rowman and Littlefield.
Weber, M. (1992) *The Protestant Ethic and the Spirit of Capitalism*. London: Routledge.
Wenzel, H. (2005), 'Social Order and Communication. Parsons's Theory on the Move from Moral Consensus to Trust', in R.C. Fox, V.M. Lidz and H.J. Bershady (eds), *After Parsons: A Theory of Social Action for the Twenty-First Century*. New York: Russell Sage Foundation. pp. 66–82.
Von Foerster, H. (1981) *Observing Systems*. Seaside, CA: Intersystems Publications.

# 14

# The 'Production of Culture Perspective' in Perspective

Marco Santoro

## INTRODUCTION

With the formula 'production of culture' sociologists may mean two very different albeit intertwined things: a general reference to the world of cultural creation and fabrication, and a more focused intellectual perspective first articulated in the 1970s and developed in the next two decades mainly thanks to sociologist Richard A. Peterson (1932–2010) and his collaborators.[1] A late professor of sociology at Vanderbilt University, in Nashville, Peterson's name has not been among those who sociologists are expected to know or have read, unless they work in those specialties Peterson worked on for almost all his professional life – i.e. the sociology of arts and the sociological analysis of cultural life. Comparatively, his name is much less celebrated – and much less cited – than those of two others who also strongly contributed to the rise of cultural sociology as a legitimate field of the sociological discipline: Howard S. Becker and Pierre Bourdieu. The latter is nowadays the most cited sociologist in the world (according to common wisdom, based on well-established empirical evidence [see e.g. Santoro 2008c]). As for the former, it suffices to say that he is considered by some as 'perhaps the leading U.S. sociologist studying art' (Katz, 2006: xi), while others describe him as 'one of the foremost sociologists of the second half of the twentieth century' (Plummer, 2003: 21). But what has been said for Becker, that he 'reinvigorated the formal study of culture' (Kaufman, 2004: 335), equally applies to Peterson, if not in fact more so.

There are at least two important topics that Richard Peterson's name is particularly associated with today. First, there is the hypothesis of the 'cultural omnivore', a notion that has become central in empirical research on cultural consumption and stratification in the last two decades (e.g. Chan and Goldthorpe, 2007; Warde et al., 2007; see also Peterson, 2005b), and the presence of which in scientific debate is well established and still rising after two decades since its first appearance (Peterson and Kern, 1996; Peterson and Simkus, 1992). Second, there is the production of culture perspective, Peterson's major achievement and for many still his most relevant contribution to sociology as a discipline, independently from the levels of citation it has generated (see Figure 14.1).

Peterson paved the way for the building of what has been in the first instance named 'the sociology of culture' and somewhat later renamed as 'cultural sociology' – two expressions that some take as equivalents while others are eager to strongly distinguish and separate them.[2] His contribution has not always been acknowledged by those

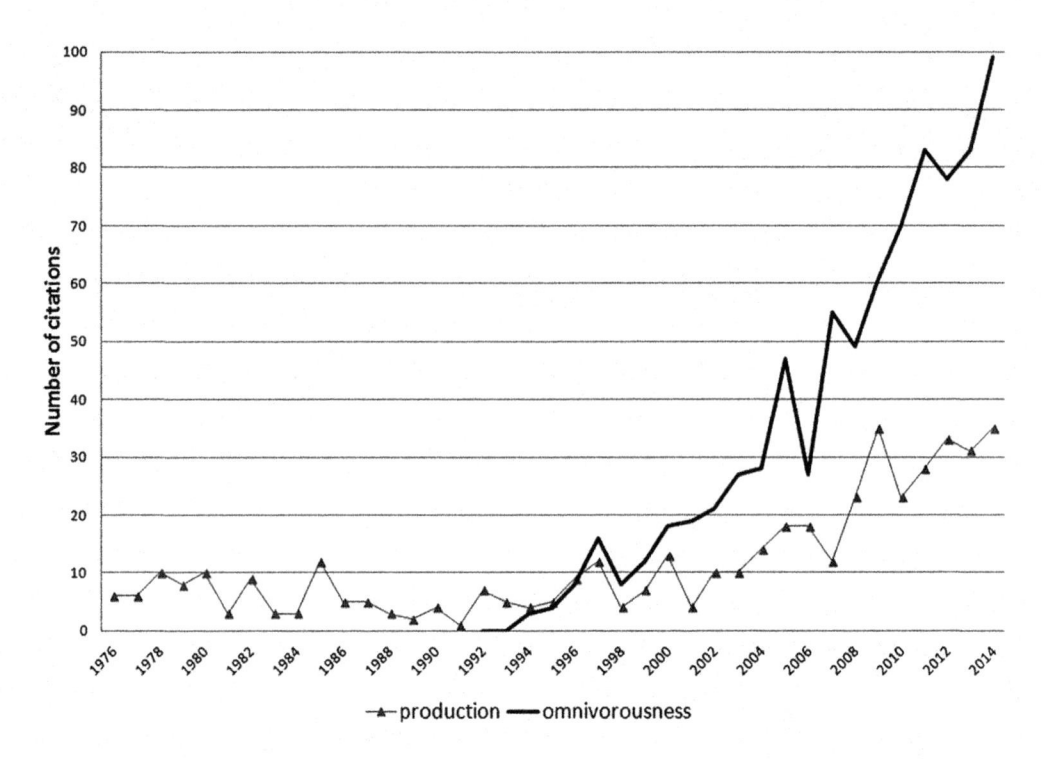

**Figure 14.1 Citations per year of four key works on the production of culture and three key works on omnivorousness, 1976–2014**

Source: DiMaggio (2000) and elaboration from data in Web of Science

Note: Articles/books referenced are Peterson and Berger, 1975; Peterson, 1976 (as both a book and a journal special issue, including Peterson's Introduction); Peterson, 1994; and Peterson and Anand, 2004, for the 'production' stream, and Peterson and Simkus, 1992; Peterson, 1992a and Peterson and Kern, 1996 for the 'omnivorousness' stream.

working in these and adjacent fields – in part for reasons of intentional neglect and in part for what Robert K. Merton once identified as 'obliteration by incorporation'.[3] It is difficult to overestimate the impact of the proposal of a production approach to culture on the development of cultural sociology as a research field.[4] As Paul DiMaggio has noted, 'we are all 'production-of- culture' (POC) theorists now' (2000: 133). In particular, despite the growing array of available sociological perspectives on cultural issues, POC's centrality in the growing field of cultural sociology as the epitome of an empirically focused sociology of culture has been emphasized many times by both its practitioners and its critics (see Alexander and Smith, 2001; Denzin, 1991; Edles, 2002; Eyerman and McCormick, 2006; Smith, 1998; Zaret, 1992).

The POC perspective begins from the idea that cultural items 'do not spring forth full blown' (Peterson, 1979: 152) and that they are not fully made by creative geniuses working alone (Peterson, 1976: 14), as traditionally held in the humanities. But neither do they simply reflect some *Zeitgeist* or national character, as typically held by Marxist or Marxist-oriented sociologists of the arts (e.g. Lukacs, Goldman, Adorno, Hauser, etc.). Peterson insisted in the early 1970s that cultural items, i.e. symbolic elements, are ultimately shaped by the specific contexts in which they are produced, and that a proper account of their existence should focus on these contexts, or infrastructures, as well as on the series of influences these contexts exert on their contents and forms (Peterson, 1976; 1994; Peterson and Anand, 2004). Leaving aside prima facie questions of meaning and reception, the POC perspective started from the observation that in modern societies, cultural and symbolic objects are fabricated by specialists working in particular organizational environments. Simply put, the POC perspective envisioned by Peterson maintain that behind any cultural item there is necessarily a series of contingencies – embodied in concrete social agents – which go well beyond the individual creator with his or her personal inspiration or biography. It is a claim of this perspective that prominent among these contingencies are social arrangements and devices which need to be considered in order to account for the actual content and form of any cultural and symbolic item. In Peterson's (1985, 45) own words:

> The production of culture perspective takes as its point of departure the observation that the nature and content of symbolic products are shaped by the social, legal and economic milieux in which they are produced. The perspective does not contradict the alternative orientations that examine cultural products with respect to each other, as created by inspired artists, as expressing the views of their consumers, or as reflecting the spirit of the society at large (Griswold, 1981). Properly applied, the production of culture perspective complements and reinforces these other perspectives (Peterson, 1976).

Indeed, 'the distinctive characteristic of the production-of-culture perspective' is its focus on the 'infrastructure' that surrounds cultural production (Peterson, 1976: 14). Of course, Peterson was not the first to notice that cultural items exist in socially structured environments and in relation to specific devices. He was well aware, for instance, of the work of scholars like Leo Lowenthal (a German *émigré* in the Nazi period who became professor of sociology at Columbia University and then at Berkeley), and the English literary critic Ian Watt, whose *The Rise of the Novel* (1957) revealed the importance of publishers and of the reading public in literary innovation, as well as of pioneering studies of artistic change such as White and White (1965) on the institutional matrix of French Impressionism. The idea that organizational structures and reward structures have an impact on performances and outcomes was also explored in studies in the sociology of organization and of science, and more generally within the structural form of sociology developed by Robert K. Merton and his students.[5]

What Peterson added to these early works was the packaging of an idea and a programmatic statement – in other words, self-awareness and an agenda. In the 1970s, when it emerged as a self-conscious perspective, POC challenged not only the then-dominant idea that culture and social structure mirror each other, but also the assumption that culture was indeed a legitimate subject for other disciplines – like literary criticism and cultural anthropology – but not for sociology. There was, to be sure, an interest in norms and values as central devices in structural-functionalist theories of society and socialization (as in the case of Parsons' work), as well as specialized endeavours like the already mentioned sociologies of literature and of science, the latter a (sub)field almost literally 'invented' by one scholar, Merton. But culture as such, as the general category to which all these elements belong and refer, was not considered a proper province of sociology as a discipline. Sociology was the study of social structure not of culture, and even socially pervasive popular culture was less a concern for sociologists than for cultural critics (e.g. MacDonald, 1960; Rosenberg and White, 1957). Although certainly not alone in the discovery of popular culture, and cultural industries, as central components of the contemporary social landscape, Peterson played a fundamental role – both intellectually and organizationally – in making these subjects fully 'sociological' topics, catalysing a new intellectual movement around their study.

In this chapter I discuss 'production of culture' as a truly sociological approach to the study of cultural life, reconstructing its intellectual genealogy and the impact this perspective has had on the overall development of sociology in the last quarter of the 20th century and into the 21st. I will thereby briefly consider some of the criticisms addressed to this approach by scholars coming from various circles and schools who have all in their own specific ways made a plea for a more 'interpretivist' and/or more 'critical' approach to the analysis of culture, criticizing POC for its perceived positivistic and uncritical dimensions. I will argue that the heuristic usefulness and epistemological importance of the production of culture approach rests in the fact that it remains attuned to the specificities of cultural objects as symbolic representations and meaning structures, while still being focused on matters to do with social institutions and modes of social organization, which are, after all, what sociology is primarily supposed to study, or are at least what sociology as a discipline cannot escape dealing with unless it were to lose its disciplinary identity altogether. Moreover, the production of culture approach stands as an important, if not in fact necessary, integration of both the more humanistic, literary, textualist and postmodernist strands of cultural analysis on the one hand, and a 'cultural sociology' strongly conceived in structuralist and hermeneutical terms on the other (Alexander, 2003; Alexander and Smith, 2001). Thus the production of culture perspective stands as a crucial resource for a truly multidimensional social science of cultural processes.

This is particularly the case given the fact that Peterson never promoted the production of culture approach as a closed and exclusivist paradigm. He always wanted other analytic perspectives to flourish and for them to enter into dialogue with the approach he was endeavouring to develop. As Paul DiMaggio (2000) once aptly observed, what Peterson has tried to create was not a narrow 'sect' or even a 'school', but rather a broad, open and inclusive intellectual movement. Of course, this openness might be considered as an unintentional by-product of either the relatively untheoretical character of the production of culture approach, or of its general agnosticism towards ontological and epistemological issues. But both the middle-range strategy of research recommended by the production of culture approach, and also its solid empirical orientation towards the grasping of the 'social' and 'institutional' groundings of culture, have clearly worked as assets in the study of cultural matters, an area sometimes perceived as too volatile or merely 'decorative' by some of its critics (Rojek and Turner, 2000). It is these positive features which make the production of culture perspective very important for a cultural sociology respectful of both its identity and its mission qua sociology.[6] In the following sections, I intend to indicate some major grounds to sustain this argument.

## THE 'PRODUCTION OF CULTURE PERSPECTIVE' IN CONTEXT

The notion of a 'production of culture perspective' was launched by Richard Peterson in a presentation at the 1974 American Sociological Association (ASA) meetings. This was followed the year after by a conference at Vanderbilt University, Nashville, where Peterson had been teaching since 1965. The conference was sponsored by the National Science Foundation, and was attended by already well known scholars such as the German *exilé* Leo Lowenthal and the Chicagoan Howard S. Becker, together with younger ones like Paul DiMaggio and Paul Hirsch, at that time in their twenties. From the papers given at the conference was drawn a special issue of the journal *American Behavioral Science*, an influential but not top-level journal. The special issue was also published as a book (Peterson, 1976), a text soon to become, according to one of the authors, a 'foundational work in the new sociology of culture that emerged during the 1970s' (DiMaggio, 2000: 108). The special issue and book functioned as the manifesto of the new intellectual movement that Peterson was seeking to initiate and develop.

The birth of POC can be traced back to some articles on jazz and popular music which Peterson had written in the previous decade (Peterson, 1965; 1967; 1972; Peterson and Berger, 1971; 1972). How to approach the study of music sociologically seems to have been an important question from which the production approach began to take form. Peterson had been trained as an industrial sociologist by Alvin Gouldner, the author of such foundational works as *Patterns of Industrial Bureaucracy* and *Wildcat Strike*, composed some time before the influential and highly polemical *The Coming Crisis of Western Sociology* (Gouldner, 1954a; 1954b; 1970). In these early attempts, Peterson began to apply this brand of organizational sociology to aesthetic materials, dealing not only with their social legitimization, but also with their content, form and variety. The choice of music, albeit initially made for personal and contingent reasons, turned out to be a fortunate one, in part because it was a cultural form that was important in the lives of people in all social strata, and also because music is particularly useful as a means of understanding culture and culture industries more generally (see e.g. DeNora, 2000; Hennion, 1993).[7]

As it was originally conceived, POC can be described as an approach or perspective (but not a formal theory) oriented towards the study of culture, which conceptualizes the latter as a (usually incoherent) set of symbolic elements, whose content and form are understood as functions of the social contexts (or milieux) of their creation, manufacture, marketing, use and evaluation. Culture can therefore be explained sociologically through a detailed analysis of these contexts and the various forms they take. This definition sets out the key characteristics of the POC perspective, namely: (a) a focus on formally produced symbols, that is, symbols explicitly produced and used in organizations specifically devoted to them; and (b) that priority is accorded to structural, organizational, institutional and economic factors, which are external to the creative acts of symbol production. Taken together, these foci helped to differentiate the production approach from both the symbolic interactionist tradition – which at about the same time was developing a specifically sociological perspective on art and cultural objects, through the work of Howard S. Becker[8] – and the critical theory of cultural industries, the focus of which has always been more on general social forces (capitalism, fascism, and so on) than on contingent organizational issues. The critical tradition may be said to encompass, despite all their various differences, both the Frankfurt School and British cultural studies. The POC approach was distinguishable from these analytic orientations in that it possessed a much more neutral position towards (mass) culture and the culture industries, which were understood not as social problems but as social facts. This *depoliticization* of cultural analysis (Hirsch and Fiss, 2000) was deliberate and strategic in two ways: first, because it helped to legitimize the study of culture in the sociological mainstream of the day, and second, because it helped clarify how it was possible to study aesthetic issues sociologically, without slipping into the frame of reference of other disciplines such as aesthetics or art criticism.

## WHERE DID THE 'PRODUCTION OF CULTURE' COME FROM?

Peterson (1976; 1994; see also Santoro 2008b) himself suggested the nature of the intellectual genealogy of his endeavours. One key influence that he noted comes from the so-called 'Columbia school', initiated first by Robert K. Merton and Paul Lazarsfeld, and then further developed in the 1950s and 1960s by such influential figures as Lewis Coser, Alvin Gouldner, James Coleman, Peter Blau, Elihu Katz and various others. The relations between the POC approach and the Columbia school are indeed strong, although they are certainly not the only influences on the former. I will here briefly sketch some of the connections, in order to give some idea of a much richer network of influences and personal ties that characterize the POC genealogy.[9] Columbia was the intellectual training ground for both Peterson's mentor Alvin Gouldner and also Lewis Coser, who authored one of the books Peterson considers a pioneering work of the POC perspective (Coser, 1965), and who edited in 1978 a special issue on POC of the influential journal *Social Research*.[10] Coser then published, with another of Merton's students, Charles Kadushin, one of the first and best exemplars of the production approach (Coser et al., 1982). From Columbia where she gained her PhD also came Diana Crane, whose work on the social production of scientific ideas (Crane, 1972) was credited by Peterson as one of the major early instances of a 'production turn' in the sociological study of culture.[11] Another important Columbia scholar – this time within the context of the Bureau of Applied Social Science, which was founded by Lazarsfeld and managed by both him and Merton – was C. Wright Mills, whom Peterson has indicated as another pioneer in the sociological study of cultural production (which Mills named 'cultural apparatus').[12] It is the Columbia legacy which accounts for both the social-structural focus of the POC approach, and its insistence on methodological soundness and reliability (even if the Wisconsin legacy deserves some mention here too). These latter two features also characterize the work of Harrison C. White, a physicist turned sociologist whose early book on the social conditions lying behind the rise of French impressionist painting (White and White, 1965) was a major influence on Peterson.[13] Likewise, White's teaching at Harvard in the 1970s was a source of inspiration for many young practitioners of POC at that time, such as Paul DiMaggio and Wendy Griswold, who were studying there for their PhDs.

Although perhaps somewhat less powerful than the influences just mentioned, there was also a certain amount of influence on Richard Peterson's thinking which originated from the University of Chicago, in particular from the school of occupational sociology of E.C. Hughes. Out of this school came both Howard S. Becker and, at a later date, another practitioner of the POC approach, albeit a more critically oriented one, namely Gaye Tuchman. Another Chicago influence was the work of David Riesman,[14] whose famous book *The Lonely Crowd* Peterson included among his major formative influences (Riesman 1950; see Santoro 2008b). I should note here briefly the intellectual links that existed between Columbia and Chicago in the mid-20th century. This was in part due to the influence of Florian Znaniecki, the Polish collaborator of W.I. Thomas, on both Merton and Coser.[15] More importantly in this context, Merton himself believed that the macro-level structural analysis fostered by Columbia, and the more micro-oriented symbolic interactionist dispositions of Chicago, were 'like ham and eggs', that is, 'different but mutually enriching' (Merton, 1975: 31).

Peterson, rather like his mentor Gouldner, was always very eclectic in the sources of his intellectual inspiration. Among these were not just Merton and Lazarsfeld and their many students, together with the Chicago heritage, but also critical scholars like Theodor W. Adorno – who was himself an early collaborator of the Columbia Bureau when it was still the Radio Research Project – and Leo Lowenthal, who was also a collaborator of the Bureau in the late 1940s, and a professor at Columbia, before moving to Berkeley.[16] Outside the USA, we can also find influences which have passed not so much through direct academic and personal links, but rather mostly through the medium of the reception of books and articles. A case in point here is the British tradition of cultural studies, with Peterson citing Raymond Williams as one of the main sources for the 'revitalizing of the culture concept' (Peterson, 1979). Similarly, the work of the British scholars Dick Hebdige and Paul Willis has contributed to Peterson's writings on music and cultural consumption. Another great influence on Peterson was Pierre Bourdieu, who had embraced the 'production metaphor' in 1971 in one of his foundational texts in the sociology of culture (Bourdieu, 1971). His distinctive conception of cultural production was further developed in an article of 1977, translated three years later into English by the journal *Media, Culture & Society* (Bourdieu, 1980). Bourdieu's anthropological work on Algeria was known by Peterson well before the successful introduction of his work on education and art to American sociology in the 1980s (Sallaz and Zavisca, 2007). It was from Bourdieu that Peterson (1976) drew in particular both the idea of a *genetic* conception of culture as the matrix of social structure, and also the notion that it is possible to merge different strands of sociological research on cultural processes (e.g. education, religion, science, art, etc.) into a unified research programme.[17]

The impressive range of intellectual influences on Peterson – and through him, on the POC movement per se – might raise some possible suspicions of a spurious intellectual eclecticism lacking strong foundations. One might argue that it is not possible to draw insights from both the 'mainstream' work of Merton and the 'radical' work of Bourdieu without thoroughly transforming – some might say 'perverting' – their respective intellectual projects.[18] But it is here in fact that one of the strengths of Peterson's work lies. Having sought to find and develop intersections between different, even divergent, research programmes, he has given shape to his own distinctive intellectual project through the innovative combination of already existing elements. Given this, Peterson has himself been influential not only on younger sociological scholars who have chosen to focus on cultural topics, but also on consummate practitioners who found his POC ideas 'good to think with' and to work on (for reviews, see Peterson (1994), DiMaggio (2000), Peterson and Anand (2004), Ryan (2007), Dowd (2007)). Evidence of his acknowledged centrality in the sociological study of culture was his election as first President of the newly founded 'Culture' section of the American Sociological Association in 1986 – a section that would become one of the two largest such groupings in the ASH in the next few decades.

The POC approach's great importance in US cultural sociology is nowadays undeniable. Throughout the 1990s, slowly but surely, POC also migrated to Europe, and Peterson played an important role in this process.[19] The journal *Poetics*, which is based in the Netherlands, has probably offered the strongest bridge in the last fifteen years or so between on the one hand the POC movement, and on the other hand European sociologists of culture, at least those devoted to the study of art and media production. In the UK, the impact of POC has probably been slowed by both the strong British tradition of cultural studies and also neo-Marxist political economy approaches, each of which has their own ways of approaching culture as a matter of production (see Barrett et al., 1979; Jones, 2004; Negus, 1999; Williams, 1981; Wolff, 1981). But some POC seeds were scattered in the UK quite early on, through journals like *Media, Culture & Society* – see pieces by DiMaggio (1982) and Schudson (1989) – and then within the sociology of popular music (e.g. Bennett and Peterson, 2004; Frith and Goodwin, 1990; Negus, 1992) and of the arts (Inglis and Hughson, 2005; Wolff, 1981). A growing interest in the workings of cultural industries has recently fuelled the 'domestication' in British cultural sociology of POC ideas (see Hesmondhalgh, 2002; Lash and Urry, 1994; Lury, 1993).

## FROM PRODUCTION TO (CONSUMPTION AS) AUTOPRODUCTION

So far, I have examined Richard Peterson's role in the development of the production approach to cultural analysis. But there is also a second line of thought and research that he is associated with. As this second theme concerns cultural consumption rather than production, it might at first appear as being independent of concerns to do with the latter, but this is not in fact the case. Peterson himself noted that his research on cultural consumption was a sort of expansion of his earlier work on production, involving a movement into the territory of what he has called 'autoproduction' (Peterson, 2000; Peterson and Anand, 2004). He has thus stressed an important issue also focused on by British cultural studies scholars, namely the view that every act of consumption is also an act of meaning creation and therefore of symbolic production (see Willis, 1978; 2000; Hebdige, 1979). Besides the focus on the formal production of culture, which is at the centre of the original approach, Peterson added a focus on the world of informal cultural production in everyday life contexts, opening up the older perspective to new and broader research horizons.

Peterson often retrospectively included the Birmingham School as one of his main sources in this line of work (see Peterson, 1994; Peterson and Anand, 2004). While it is true that Raymond Williams was an important source for Peterson's rethinking of the concept of culture, the British work on youth subcultures seems more to have offered him certain suggestions and insights into carrying out empirical music sociology, rather than giving him particular conceptual tools as such. Indeed if we work in a genealogical fashion, anthropology appears to be the original source of inspiration for Peterson's work on consumption (and of course anthropology was also a source for both Hebdige and Willis). From the work of Ruth Benedict – and thus from the Boasian lineage more generally – he first took the idea of 'pattern of culture' (see Hughes and Peterson, 1983; Peterson, 1983), which then gave way to the notion of 'patterns of cultural choice'. This conception was then further developed – through the analysis of rich empirical materials gathered by the US National Endowment for the Arts, for whom he was acting as a consultant – into a critique of the homology model of cultural stratification theorized by Bourdieu (1984). Peterson thus proposed a new hypothesis about the relationships between cultural taste and social stratification, namely the idea of the cultural omnivore (Peterson, 1992a; Peterson and Kern, 1996; Peterson and Simkus, 1992).

This thesis has been tested so many times since its first exposition – with data from, for example, the USA, the UK, France, Russia, the Netherlands and China, among others – that such testing can now be considered a very important component within the ever growing 'industry' of sociological research on cultural consumption (e.g. Chan, 2010; Lizardo, 2008). This was an area which, only a few years ago, was left either to purely philosophical speculation, or to the abstract empiricism of purely statistical descriptions. Of course, Bourdieu (1984) in the *Distinction* study had drawn attention to the theoretical dimensions and the analytical potentials of the topic. But we may say that Peterson contributed a great deal to the revitalization of the field, first by offering a strong alternative hypothesis to Bourdieu's theory of the social (i.e. class) determinants of cultural taste, and second, by showing that much sociological work could still be done in this area, with the aid of both a large mass of official data (updated since Bourdieu's work in this area), and also of standard multivariate statistical techniques (see Chan and Goldthorpe, 2007; Peterson, 2005b; Sullivan and Katz-Gerro, 2007; Warde et al., 2007; for a critique see Lahire, 2004).

Even if, as Peterson himself has admitted (Santoro, 2008b), this stream of research was generated independently of his production of culture work, it nonetheless has strong and clear conceptual links with it, which the novel category of 'auto-production' brings to light. Indeed, we may consider this line of research as an extension of the POC perspective towards the grasping of informal processes of production of culture in everyday life. The research on taste and taste groups, including that on the (changing) relationships between patterns of consumption and social location, is a complement to the concept of the *product image* (Ryan and Peterson, 1982), originally the means through which POC analysed both the creativity and the preferences of consumers, by means of treating them as endogenous factors within the whole production process (DiMaggio, 2000). Attempts to explain changes in production processes and cultural products through the changing nature of social structures and the sense-making activities of audiences, were integral components of Peterson's life-long work on popular music – including jazz, country music and rock (Peterson, 1972; 1978; 1990; 1997) – and were the special focus of an early episode in the history of the production of culture approach (Peterson and DiMaggio, 1975). DiMaggio (2000: 129) has referred to this sensitivity to 'co-evolving audiences and production systems, which together generate both cultural products and ways of classifying them', as a 'co-evolutionary framework', arguing that it has been central to the POC project 'from the beginning', that is, from Peterson's early works on jazz onwards. This challenges the usual representation of POC, sometimes propagated by its own practitioners as a perspective wholly centred on the effects of institutional and organizational factors on cultural products. Rather than being built on a simple model of unidirectional causality (i.e. from social structure to culture), it emphasizes the underlying presence of a much more complex duality, in which social structure and culture are mutually constructed.[20]

## THE SIX-FACETS MODEL

The production of culture approach is a 'perspective' and not a theory in the strict sense of the word. The closest to the latter it has come is in the so-called 'six-facets model' delineated by Peterson in a series of publications (Peterson, 1985; Peterson and Anand, 2004). Recall that POC moves from the recognition that in modern societies – but in some cases also in traditional societies – cultural objects come into existence through the work of specialists operating in some sort of organized environment. To analyse the interplay of these specialists under a set of interrelated conditions, Peterson devised a framework that proved to be effective in explaining why some particular cultural content comes into existence and becomes widely disseminated at a specific point in time.

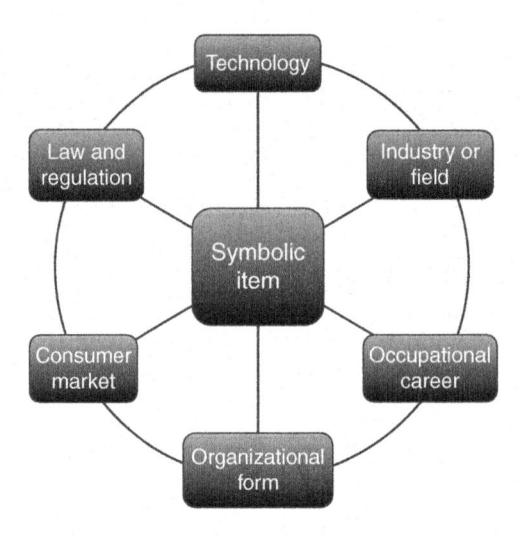

**Figure 14.2 The six-facets model: a graphic representation**

According to this model, a limited series of factors can be identified as being of relevance to the process of cultural creation and diffusion. Initially called 'contingencies' (Peterson, 1979), the earliest formulation included rewards, evaluation, organizational dynamics, market structure and technology (see also Peterson, 1982). Later these became six 'constraints': law and regulation, technology, industry structure, organizational structure or form, consumer market and occupational careers (Peterson, 1985; 1994; Peterson and Anand, 2004). While each constraint is analytically distinct, in practice 'the constraints form an interlocking system in which change in one constraint affects one or more of the others' (Ryan, 2007: 222). In other words, while recognizing the interrelations of these factors in the production process, Peterson proposed this model as a convenient analytical framework for separating out the various factors, so as to allow assessment of their individual impacts (see Figure 14.2).[21] These six constraints – or facets, as Peterson also liked to name them as elements of the model – remain relatively undertheorized in their differential relations and priorities, working more as sensitizing concepts useful for orienting empirical research, and helping to locate historical contingencies that are to be described and assessed locally. The emphasis on contingency is in this sense one of the main features of the POC approach, which distinguishes it from established functionalist approaches, Marxist-oriented cultural theory, and possibly even Bourdieu's sociology of cultural production, while bringing POC closer to narrative and 'eventful' sociologies (Sewell, 2005).[22]

The category of *law and regulation* identifies the general normative framework in which cultural production occurs. What is produced, who is allowed to produce it, and under what conditions, are all affected by legal regulation. For example, copyright laws have often influenced the kinds of fiction and songs that are published, while notions of intellectual property influence the range of cultural expressions, both inhibiting and promoting particular types of production. One of the major institutions here is censorship. This can have a direct impact on cultural content. In addition, regulation of ownership (for example, of media organisations), as well as policies of deregulation, can influence the degree of diversity and variety of cultural products.[23] Copyright law has a prominent position in POC also because of its close ties to changes in technology, which is the second type of constraint to be considered. The category of *technology* identifies the tools and means through which people and institutions communicate and through which cultural content circulates. Changes in technology profoundly affect the culture that can be produced, providing new creative opportunities or making previous ways of producing obsolete. Technology includes innovations in media such as radio, phonograph records, movies, television, electric musical instruments and digitalized communication, as well as pre-modern and modern devices such as writing and printing. To the extent that cultural production occurs in organizations, both *organizational structures* and the larger *organizational fields* (or *industries*)[24] in which production processes are embedded, can influence the cultural product's form and content. For example, there is a difference between the many small firms that compete in producing a diversity of products, and the few vertically integrated oligarchical firms that mass produce relatively few standardized items. Another contrast can be drawn between for-profit organizations, which are typical of cultural industries specializing in large-scale production, and not-for-profit organizations, which are commonly established in high cultural artistic fields to reduce commercial pressures and create a haven from conventional market forces (DiMaggio, 1982). As Becker (1982) also emphasizes, work is a crucial factor in the production of art, and the ways in which work is organized also has an impact on cultural objects. *Occupational careers* can be quite diversified (for example, creative careers, craft-like careers, bureaucratic careers and entrepreneurial careers). Careers tend to be more or less standardized. Less conventional careers tend to generate innovation in so far as they attract creative people likely to challenge conventions and rules. Finally, there are *consumer markets*, typically conceived of by Peterson less as a field of consumer practices than as images, that is, as conceptions constructed by producers in order to organize, understand and predict consumer taste. It is characteristic of this approach that it accounts for consumption from the point of view of production as arrays of 'product images' (see Ryan and Peterson, 1982), and not in terms of consumers' identities and practices – as sociologists of consumption typically do (e.g. Sassatelli, 2007).

Peterson's six-facets model resembles two other models proposed within cultural sociology: Wendy Griswold's 'cultural diamond' – which is said by its author simply to be a heuristic model for pedagogical purposes without any theoretical pretension – and Paul du Gay and Stuart Hall's 'circuit model' (1997). While the cultural diamond shares with Peterson's six-facets model the same genealogy and institutional matrix (US mainstream sociology in the 1970s and 1980s), the latter is a late, and strongly sociologically oriented, outcome of the influential tradition of British cultural studies with its French connections (from Althusser to Foucault) and its Gramscian legacy. A brief comparison with it may be revealing. First, both Peterson's and the circuit model recognize the importance of regulation by law and legal institutions – which is a means to keep the wider social context in the picture. Second, production is, in the circuit model, one of its constitutive elements, while in the six-facets model it is the object itself that is to be analytically decomposed. More importantly, cultural production is conceived in the circuit model as embedded in a larger world of symbolic elements, in a 'cultural environment' which is a key factor for making sense of the production of cultural objects, as of any other kind of production (on this point, see below). Third, consumption figures in the circuit model as a complex sphere in which imagined publics (i.e. segments of markets or niches envisioned by professionals and entrepreneurs) and real consumers' practices overlap, while in POC, the consumer market is seen only from the point of view of producers, that is, as the latter's conceptions and images of what consumers could be and how they could behave. Fourth, prominent in the circuit model are two factors which seem prima facie absent in the six-facets model, that is, 'representation' and 'identity'. Clearly, they are both direct expressions of the more humanistic and philosophically charged tradition of British cultural studies, with its blend of post-Marxism and post-structuralism fused with literary criticism (for a now classic overview, see Turner (2003)). However, it would be unfair to say that Peterson was insensitive to issues of representation and identification, even if it is true that he was not attuned to either Marxism or French post-structuralism. His masterpiece, *Creating Country Music* (Peterson, 1997) is indeed a book about changes in identities (of music and musicians), as well as about representation (of places, of social classes, even of nature). It is a study of how people create meanings – in particular, meanings of that ephemeral thing that is *authenticity* – and how they manage both to create them and use them in their (professional and everyday) lives. Although not explicit as facets in the model, identities and representations figure prominently in POC studies, as both 'contingencies' in cultural productions, and as cultural objects to be explained and accounted for under the rubric of 'autoproduction' (Peterson, 2000).

## FROM THE PRODUCTION OF CULTURE TO CULTURAL SOCIOLOGY

As Figure 14.1 has shown, the amount of attention given by scholars to both the production perspective and its 'autoproduction' (i.e. consumption as meaning production) counterpart has been sustained and on the rise, especially since the turn of the millennium.[25] Now in its fifth decade, the production of culture perspective has consolidated its status as a continually productive research programme, able to raise new questions, to stimulate intellectual debate, and to produce cumulative knowledge.

Paul DiMaggio (2000) has explained POC's success as a function of four factors: first, its 'intrinsic merit in generating compelling explanations'; second, the nature of the sociological environment in which it was originally conceived and proposed, namely the field of the study of arts and the media, which lacked at the time paradigms that were serious competitors to POC; third, Peterson's use of institutions, like the ASA and the National Endowment for the Arts (NEA), to propagate POC ideas while he continued to create a sort of intellectual and academic social movement working on POC's behalf; and fourth, Peterson's framing of the perspective in terms which resonate with much of the (American) sociological tradition, while at the same time facilitating the appropriation of the latter in novel ways. This explanation can be further elaborated by drawing on recent work in the sociology of ideas (see Frickel and Gross, 2005). Building on DiMaggio's definition of POC as an academic social movement, we may consider that it has greatly benefited from the access enjoyed by some of its followers to certain key resources, both endogenous and exogenous, which were provided by some of the most influential and respected sociologists of the day, trained and working in the most prestigious universities and departments in the USA, such as Harvard, Princeton, Northwestern and Yale.

In addition, the success of neo-institutionalism as a theoretical paradigm for sociology (Powell and DiMaggio, 1991) also had some effect on the spread and legitimization of POC as the epitome of an institutional approach to the study of culture. However, processes of 'framing' probably count as the most important factor in the successful development and spread of POC. From the beginning of its history, Peterson was involved in shaping and presenting the perspective's central ideas in ways that could resonate effectively with the concerns and the identities of those who, like him, were working in the new academic field of cultural sociology. The historical narrative that Peterson constructed little by little, and which his followers and students furthered, presents POC as both the authentic heir of a certain very influential sociological tradition (that coming out of Columbia), and as a pluralist interface, acting as the natural mediator for a great variety of alternative intellectual streams, from Frankfurt School critical theory of the media industry, to British cultural studies, Bourdieu's social and cultural theory, and Chicago-influenced sociology of artistic work. The boundaries of POC were always kept loose and mobile, in order both to include various intellectual streams and to expand the POC paradigm. With such a narrative, both 'mainstream' and 'critical' sociologists, and both policy-oriented and 'reflexive' scholars (for this classification, see Burawoy (2005)) could find a place for themselves within POC, and could identify with it, even if at a distance.[26]

POC's influence can also be understood in light of factors internal to the development of cultural sociology and its various specialist subfields. In the last twenty years, music sociology has increased its status and centrality in cultural sociology, as an effect both of the reputation of some of its practitioners (e.g. Howard Becker), and of music's relevance as a powerful symbolic resource and as an important cultural industry. This development has contributed to the expansion of POC, which was developed by Peterson around issues and materials taken from the world of music (for an excellent review, see Dowd (2007)). More broadly, the whole field of cultural sociology has increased in terms both of its demographic size and also of its status and influence inside and outside of sociology (Caves, 2000; Throsby, 2000). Similar considerations may help explain the success of Peterson's work on cultural tastes, and in particular of the omnivore thesis, the study of cultural consumption having been a fast growing area of research where disciplinary boundaries are not well defined (Sassatelli, 2007; Zelizer, 2005). Indeed, as Figure 14.1 still shows, Peterson's work on the omnivore thesis has been even more successful than that of his work on cultural production. The fact that the field of the sociology of taste and consumption was dominated by a very strong intellectual authority, namely Bourdieu, may well have played a part here, in so far as Peterson's thesis could have appeared as a plausible counter-position to Bourdieu's claims as to relatively rigidly socially stratified consumption patterns. The use in the omnivore debates of legitimized and standardized methods of data analysis has helped in attracting to such debates a number of scholars of mainstream persuasion who were dissatisfied both with Bourdieu's theory and his research methods (see, for example, Bennett et al., 2009; Chan and Goldthorpe, 2007; Coulangeon, 2003).

Of course for a position to become very influential involves people debating with it and subjecting it to criticism. Both the POC perspective and the omnivore thesis have attracted a consistent amount of criticism during the last twenty years, within both sociology and cultural studies. In the following I will deal with what appear to be the two major objections to Peterson's work and the writings influenced by it: first, a theoretical-epistemological critique, to the effect that POC neglects cultural meanings and processes of interpretation; second, a political critique, to the effect that POC lacks a critical stance toward culture, the economy and culture industries. The neglect of issues having to do with interpretation – that is to say, the deciphering of meaning and the decoding of texts conceived as culture structures (Reed, 2011) – in favour of a strategy constituted solely of measuring effects on cultural objects from structural and institutional factors, could constitute a very serious limit for sociological analysis, as many critics have rightly pointed out (Alexander and Smith, 2001; Denzin, 1990; 1991; Eyerman and McCormick, 2006; Gottdiener, 1985; Jensen, 1984; Negus, 1997; Wolff, 1981; 1999). This seems especially problematic given that nowadays 'culture' is commonly understood, under the great influence in sociological circles of the ideas of Clifford Geertz, as a complex web of symbols and meanings (see Griswold, 2008; Sewell, 1999; Swidler, 1986). Considerations such as these open up POC to being seen as an instance of a very 'weak' *sociology of culture*, as opposed to a much more conceptually rich *cultural sociology* (Alexander and Smith, 2001; 2010). On this view, culture from a POC angle could only figure as a dependent and abstract variable, with social structure and social organization being left to do all the explanatory work. However, as a rebuttal to such charges, one might say that meaning is a constituent element of every symbol, and it is symbols that are the very objects studied by POC practitioners. Thus in so far as POC tries to explain the how and why of symbolic systems, understood in their detailed local contexts, it cannot ever really abstract itself from identifying the meanings of those symbols in specific contexts. As DiMaggio puts it, 'interpretation would seem to be an inevitable moment in the development of an institutional approach to the sociology of culture, and not a competitive enterprise' (2000: 131; see also Mohr, 1998; Mohr and Ghaziani, 2014).

Measuring meaning has indeed been an integral part of the POC approach ever since Peterson and Berger's (1975) classic article (see Dowd, 2007, for a critical review of the article's impact), and every such act of measurement presumes an effort in interpretation.[27] It is true that up until now in POC studies, a focus on context has been stronger than a focus on text, but this is not a disposition intrinsic to the POC paradigm; it is instead merely a function of historical contingency, and of how the paradigm happens to have been used and applied. Moreover, the production perspective does not preclude studying either the contexts of cultural production in their cultural constitution and symbolic structure, or cultural products themselves in their expressive forms (that is, as instances of 'cultures of production' – see Fine (1992)). Peterson himself worked on a series of interpretative, and indeed ethnographic, research projects on culture-producing organizations and institutions (e.g. Peterson, 1972; 1997; Peterson and Ryan, 1983; Peterson and White, 1979; 1981; Ryan and Peterson, 2001). Indeed this is not really surprising, given that he was a scholar who was familiar with anthropological literature and who was trained in the industrial sociology of Gouldner.[28]

Still it is arguable that the kind of analysis of meaning conducted by Peterson and his colleagues, collaborators and followers is nonetheless substantially different from the kind of hermeneutic and structuralist modes of interpretation promoted by Jeffrey Alexander and his school based at Yale University. Peterson's approach to interpretation is nearer to classical anthropological work than to so-called 'French theory' or German hermeneutics. In other words, there could be a problem here not so much of focus (i.e. on meaning), but of method. Neither (post)structuralism nor hermeneutics entered Peterson's conceptual toolkit, nor those of his close colleagues and students, although this does not mean that they have been unaware of these intellectual developments. Does this mean that POC is essentially positivist in orientation? In a certain way, we might say yes to this question – and this has been explicitly recognized by at least some POC scholars, even if with some qualifications, which made the POC version of positivism merely strategic and temporary (see Griswold, 1990).

The POC paradigm is certainly not a self-proclaimed post-positivist enterprise like the 'strong program' in cultural sociology advanced by Alexander and Smith (2001; 2010), or, for that matter, like (British) cultural studies (even if we have to add that in cultural studies there are also possible some less post-positivist positions than Alexander's: see McLennan (2006)). We can identify the work done under the banner of POC as positivist only in very loose terms, and within the context of an extremely polarized epistemological debate, which nowadays means usually a polarization between positivism on one extreme and postmodernism on the other. POC is positivist in so far as it aims to measure what it takes to be 'social facts'. However, the language of variables does not seem the best way to describe POC, which very often adopts a narrative approach, the very orientation often set up as an alternative to variable-centred methods (Abell, 2004). POC may perhaps be deemed to be inspired more by analytic realism rather than by positivism in a strict sense. This could help to explain why there is so much analytical tension in POC works, and why its practitioners are prone to describe themselves as looking for 'mechanisms' (Hedstrom, 2005). Nonetheless, some weak form of social constructionism is an epistemological posture (almost) intrinsic to an approach overtly aimed at revealing and detailing the production (or fabrication) of culture.[29] Clearly, then, it is not easy to locate POC epistemologically once and for all, and much of what anyone can say about such matters depends more on their position in the scholarly field and their intellectual aims, than on POC's alleged inner and 'fixed' constitution.[30]

Now that we have looked at some epistemological forms of criticism, let us briefly consider the political critique of POC. This involves claims as to its supposed lack of a critical stance towards culture and social relations, and its alleged sociologically orthodox, politically conservative outlook (Denzin, 1990; 1991; Gottdiener, 1985; Tuchman, 1983). Peterson was never close to following the radical turn taken by his mentor Alvin Gouldner. He remained faithful to what he saw as the non-evaluative approach of the classic Columbia school (inspired by the positions of Merton and Lazarsfeld), from which he distanced himself only inasmuch as his attention was devoted to cultural and aesthetic objects rather than to, say, voting patterns or structures of social inequality. It is true that 'production' as a conceptual category has a strong Marxist aura. But 'production' in POC is more a metaphor than an analytic category – and a metaphor asked to do a lot of work. It has come to refer to a whole series of different processes, from cultural creation through to distribution and consumption. Peterson conceived social and cultural matters neither in terms of social class nor in terms of class-based exploitation. His vision of society seemed more functionalist in nature – a system of stratification based on status, not on a class structure. Social groups, strata and status groups are the typical sociological concepts he thought with in his work, both on production and on consumption (see Peterson, 1990; Peterson and Simkus, 1992).[31]

This does not mean that there is no critical tension in POC, or that it is impossible to inject more reflexive components into its practice. Indeed Peterson was very attentive to the political implications of his research, and was very critical towards 'administrative research' (see interview contained in Santoro, 2008b). Depoliticization was more a strategic move, rather than a moral or political choice. It was more a suspension of explicit critical orientations towards the world, in order to grasp its nature in the first place, than a conservative acceptance of the status quo. Indeed, as Abbott (2007) has argued – contra Burawoy (2005) – a pure professional (i.e. instrumental) knowledge, totally detached from a critical (i.e. moral and/or political) posture, is simply impossible because the social world is intrinsically made up of values and value commitments. This suggests a more nuanced reading of the POC literature, whereby what is at stake is not social criticism per se, but rather an evaluation of the different degrees of (political) reflexivity with which its authors have infused their works.

# CONCLUSION

Sociology's master narrative has dramatized cleavages and conflicts as constitutive of its history and identity, forgetting the many connections among scholars and schools of thought through which sociology has developed, and playing down the opportunities for dialogue, if not integration, among different intellectual streams which are inscribed in this disciplinary tradition.[32] An informed perspective on intellectual genealogies suggests that there exists more intellectual space for interchange and dialogue than observation of manifestos and programmatic declarations alone would allow us to see. Historians of the social sciences (Mucchielli, 2004) have made it clear that Max Weber was more akin to Emile Durkheim than either of them would have recognized. Likewise, textbooks often surmise that in the near future we will be able to see that structure-oriented approaches (like POC) are not so very distant from more hermeneutical, interpretive and even critical approaches in the social sciences. Broadly speaking, the new American 'cultural sociology' (Smith, 1998) is mainly the product of meaningful personal ties (patronage, colleagueship, friendship, marriage) among sociologists positioned in influential universities like Harvard, Berkeley and Chicago, as well as, although more distantly, the work done at Columbia in the two decades after World War II, in that extraordinary laboratory of research on mass communication guided by Lazarsfeld and Merton that was the Bureau of Applied Social Research. This dense network cuts across rhetorically constructed intellectual cleavages, whose theoretical foundations have to be assessed not only through official declarations, but also through an inspection of the research practices they are supposed to elicit and guide. If we are ready to leave the standard master narrative aside, we might find unexpected convergences between positions that are apparently very apart. Moreover, the historical existence of 'rival' intellectual positions does not mean that the divisions between them cannot be bridged, with the hope of furthering sociological knowledge. We have to go beyond labels designed more to build schools and promote affiliations than to produce sound knowledge, and to look for possible combinations of apparently contrasting and irreconcilable paradigms. Indeed, this is what usually happens in the cultural life of disciplines, sociology included (Abbott, 2001).[33]

Links between Columbia, Chicago and radical sociologies were never lacking in the 20th century, nor were dialogue and reciprocal fertilization absent. What we have come to call 'mainstream' sociology is less a well-defined research programme and paradigm, and more an eclectic, loose and very contingent array of ideas, methods and authors, the power of which is guaranteed by their occupying some dominant positions in the academic field, by the rhetorical resistance to the complete abandonment of a positivistic image of sociology, and by the creation of certain intellectual myths (see Abbott (1999), for example, on myths to do with the nature of the 'Chicago School'). Richard Peterson worked all his life very close to, if not indeed totally inside, the boundaries of what is usually labelled mainstream (positivist, realist, science-oriented) sociology in the USA. But this did not prevent him from addressing topics (such as the music industry, musical forms, listening practices) and making use of research methods (such as informal qualitative interviews, participant observation and historical document analysis) which were at the time arguably outside those boundaries, and still were almost anathema to most mainstream scholars in his reference group in the 1980s. Although one could argue that the sociology of culture could have been more aggressive and self-confident about its capacity to get inside its object without fear of invading other fields (in the humanities) than Peterson was, our present lack of problems in this regard today nevertheless owes something to his efforts.[34]

Although influential, Peterson was only one of a handful of academic entrepreneurs who in the 1970s 'invented' something which has retrospectively been labelled 'sociology of culture' and then more recently 'cultural sociology'. The field of cultural sociology in the making was always greater and more densely populated than simply involving the production of a production of culture circle centred around Peterson.[35] Yet it would be fair to say that without his work, his entrepreneurship and his plea for a sociological study of culture firmly rooted in the conceptual core of the discipline, the sociology of culture would probably have remained more marginal, or scattered in a plurality of different specialisms, such as the sociologies of art, media, religion and science. His overall contribution to the sociological tradition may be captured by a simple consideration: there was no 'sociology of culture' when Peterson began his production perspective (DiMaggio, 2000: 133). But in order for 'culture' to become 'the dominant trope for discussion of social life' (Abbott, 2001: 20), it was strategic – if not necessary – to package it with a metaphor which could at the same time challenge the mainstream while also being recognizable and legible to it. And we may say that 'production' was really a well-suited metaphor on which to build a research programme on culture, not least because it captures the Latin etymological roots of the culture concept which refer to such 'productive' processes as building and cultivating (Williams, 1983). Thus as an heuristic gambit – that is, as a strategic intellectual move aimed at producing new ideas and research[36] – the 'production of culture' metaphor offered such a package, and the work done under its banner has given it substance, creating an object within articles and books to be discussed, assessed, prized and criticized by the sociological community.[37] What would *cultural sociology* be today – in the sense of a 'strong program' in the sociological study of culture – if there were no *sociology of culture* at all?

## ACKNOWLEDGEMENTS

This chapter draws upon but significantly updates and extends an article published in the journal *Cultural Sociology* (see Santoro, 2008a) which accompanied an interview with Richard Peterson. It was intended as a step in the writing of a book on the same topic which I had planned but that contingencies in life and intellectual work have (for now?) interrupted – possibly a self-exemplification of POC, even if personal contingencies (and troubles) are not fully acknowledged by the POC approach as conditioning factors in cultural production. My thanks and thoughts go to 'Pete' Peterson, even if he is no longer with us. I would like to express my gratitude to Howard S. Becker, Randall Collins, Paul DiMaggio, Timothy Dowd, Gary Alan Fine, Jennifer Lena, John Ryan, Roberta Sassatelli, Philip Smith and Vaughn Schmutz for their knowledge and assistance. Thanks to Andrea Gallelli for help in updating Figure 14.1. I received useful information on the British reception of Peterson's work from conversations with Paul du Gay, Alan Warde and Paul Willis. Last, but not least, thanks to David Inglis for his usual support and patience.

## NOTES

1 Recently a 'production studies' line of research has emerged in the field of media and film studies, only tangentially linked to sociology (and Peterson's work), and mainly grounded on anthropological studies of media production as well as on humanities perspectives: see Mayer, Banks and Caldwell (2009) for an overview, and Caldwell (2008) for a landmark study in this emergent tradition.

2 I will use the two expressions as equivalents, unless otherwise specified. In the latter case, 'cultural sociology' will be understood as the label for the kind of sociological study of culture which is currently associated mostly with Jeffrey Alexander and his school based at Yale University (see e.g. Alexander, 2003; Alexander and Smith, 2001; 2010; see also for a critical assessment, Santoro and Solaroli, 2015).

3 'Obliteration by incorporation' occurs when, at some stage in the development of a science, certain ideas become so accepted and commonly used that their original inventors are no longer cited. Eventually, sources and creators are forgotten ('obliterated') as the concept enters common knowledge ('incorporated').

4 The first book explicitly dedicated to the production of culture was published in 1992, authored by Diana Crane, an early contributor to the approach and a participant at the 1975 conference in Vanderbilt. Crane was also editor, in 1994, of the first systematic overview of this new research field, to which Peterson contributed with a chapter about the POC approach (Crane, 1992; 1994; Peterson, 1994). In that same year, the production of culture approach was the subject of a chapter in what has been arguably the most influential textbook in cultural sociology in the last two decades (Griswold, 2008 [1994]).

5 Peterson acknowledged Merton as a primary source of inspiration not only of the POC approach but more generally of all his sociological work (see Santoro, 2008b). Selznick (1952) showed how the structural form of a party organization affects its cultural effectiveness, while Stinchcombe (1959) argued that the structural organization of work conditions the kinds of products that can be produced.

6 The work of Peterson was the object of a special issue, edited by J. Ryan, of the journal *Poetics* in 2000, with contributions among others by Paul Hirsch, Paul DiMaggio, Vera Zolberg and John R. Hall (cf. Ryan, 2000). This is probably still the best introduction to his work. *Poetics* has been crucial in establishing Peterson's reputation, especially in the later years of his professional career, and pivotal in providing a forum (and a community) for the debating of his ideas and works. For a retrospective assessment of his work on the occasion of his death, see Bennett (2010). For useful reviews of POC – besides those provided by Peterson himself (e.g. Peterson, 1994; Peterson and Anand, 2004) – focused also on its future prospects, see Ryan (2007), Dowd (2007) and Schmutz and Miller (2015). For a comparison of Peterson's perspective with those of Bourdieu (field of cultural production) and Becker (the art world approach), see Santoro (2015).

7 Music has been the empirical focus of at least three crucial developments in the rise of cultural sociology in the past half century: the Frankfurt school (through Adorno), POC and the 'Art World' approach developed by Howard Becker as an extension of his early studies on jazz musicians and jazz culture.

8 This is not the place – if there is one – to discuss the relationships between Peterson and Becker. Suffice to say that Becker has always been very careful, in his writings and pronouncements, not to confound the production of culture perspective (Peterson's own label) with his 'art world' approach – other interpreters notwithstanding (see for instance, Eyerman and McCormick, 2006; Sanders, 1982; Van Rees, 1983). It is true, I have to say, that the 'art worlds' approach (or banner) has been apparently more successful than the POC one, at least according to that simple but also efficacious indicator that is the number of citations in scholarly journals. For a brief comparison, see Santoro (2015).

9 What follows is a simplified description of the whole network of intellectual ties I have been reconstructing through sources like books and articles (including their 'acknowledgments' sections), interviews, correspondence with individual scholars, and historical overviews of American sociology. A graphic rendition of the network is in Santoro (2008a).

10 It seems Coser had been persuaded to do this by his student and collaborator Walter Powell, co-author of Coser's book on *Books* (Coser et al., 1982) and at the time an early follower of POC. Powell would be a future co-author with Paul DiMaggio of one of the most influential research programmes of the 1990s, i.e. organizational institutionalism (see Powell and DiMaggio, 1991), and an influential organizational sociologist in his own right, working especially on the intersections between markets and scientific research.

11 The historical relevance of Crane's book has been acknowledged many times – above all for its last chapter entitled 'Toward a Sociology of Culture', in which is clearly posited the programme of a comparative sociological inquiry of 'the whole

array of cultural products' (Crane, 1972: 129). Crane published a book entitled *The Production of Culture* in 1992, the outcome of her courses at Temple University in Philadelphia, where Peterson's contribution is indeed presented as just one among many.

12  Charles Wright Mills' intellectual career was the object of one of Peterson's early articles (Peterson, 1962). Kadushin was also one of the participants at the 1975 Vanderbilt conference. The Columbia legacy has been carried on into the new millennium through Jennifer C. Lena, a sociologist of music who studied for her PhD at Columbia, started her professional career as an assistant professor at Vanderbilt, and co-authored with Peterson one of his last articles (Lena and Peterson, 2008).

13  On the figure of White – one of the main actors in both the development of network analysis and the rise of the new economic sociology – see Convert and Heilbron (2007). It is worth noting that White left Harvard for Arizona, and then went on to Columbia. His ideas in the sociology of art have been expressed in a relatively recent systematization – see White (1993).

14  See Peterson (1964) for an early expression of interest in Riesman's work. The strong relationships between David Riesman and the Chicago school (and Hughes above all) are discussed by Riesman himself (see Riesman, 1988).

15  According to DiMaggio (2000: 111), Znaniecki's book on *The Social Role of the Man of Knowledge* (1940) was the only *theoretical* antecedent to the production approach he was able to find when as a graduate student he was trying to write an article on this topic. Interestingly, this book has been an important reference for both Merton (who devoted a long review essay to it) and Coser (see in particular, Coser, 1965). On the figure and contribution of Znaniecki to the sociological study of culture (and the thinking of Merton too), see Halas (2006).

16  Lowenthal was not only an important link between Peterson and the Frankfurt tradition, but also an important figure in the birth of American sociology of culture. This was in large part thanks to Ann Swidler, who put this Berkeley-based critical scholar, already in his seventies, in touch with the Harvard cohort of PhD students – among them DiMaggio and Griswold. The latter were contributing to the construction of the new research field, with the help of Swidler, and under the guidance of scholars such as White – at the time at Harvard and already possessor of a 'considerable scientific capital' (Convert and Heilbron, 2007: 34–5) – and Peterson himself.

17  Peterson was an influential, albeit rarely acknowledged, mediator of Bourdieu's work in the American intellectual world, both through his own appropriation and rearrangement of Bourdieu's ideas in the early 1970s, and as mentor of some younger sociologists, including Paul DiMaggio, who had been pivotal in the early reception of Bourdieu's ideas in the US. See, for example, DiMaggio (1979).

18  Indeed, there is evidence on both theoretical and historical grounds that Merton's structuralism (much more influential and central than his alleged functionalism) has strong affinities with Bourdieu's social theory, itself a kind of structuralism. On this point, see Bourdieu (2004: 13) and Santoro (2011: 21).

19  In 1989 he wrote a long review essay on the new American sociology of art and culture for a leading French journal, *L'Année Sociologique* (Peterson, 1989). Even if there is not at present a recognizable production of culture school in France (as there is an 'art world school', for instance), it is certain that its seeds are already well dispersed, thanks to the loose but nonetheless important links with the Bourdieusian approach and with the Chicagoan perspective which has deeply influenced the sociology of art in France (see Becker and Pessin, 2006). This influence also passes through the influential French school of music sociology, and its early research on the recording industry and its production practices: see Hennion (1981; 1993).

20  This makes POC resonate with both Bourdieu's relational epistemology and Giddens' structuration theory, and helps explain the historical links between POC and sociological neo-institutionalism. We can read POC as an instance of that sort of 'new structuralism' which considers cultural schemas as integral features of social structures, aiming to overcome the traditional opposition of material and symbolic factors (see Lounsbury and Ventresca, 2003). This also means that the recent interpretation of Cluley (2012) – rigidly grounded on the assumption of a dualism of structure and agency, with POC totally located in the structure pole – does not do justice to Peterson and the POC perspective.

21  Peterson provided different applications of the model, the most famous of which remains that on the rise of rock music (Peterson, 1990). Particularly insightful is his re-reading of Manuel's *Cassette Culture* (1993) a study of the arrival and effects of recording cassettes in India, as it suggests how POC can work at least *ex post facto* as well as in non-Western social contexts (Peterson and Anand 2004).

22  This acceptance of contingency is what probably explains the recent interest historians have expressed in POC and Peterson's work: see Morris (2012) and Nathaus and Childress (2013).

23 For a now classic study showing the importance of copyright law in shaping cultural contents, in this case plots of novels, see Griswold (1981).
24 The concept of field – which is wider than 'industry' and is also able to capture organizations external to industrial organization, like social and intellectual movements – entered into the POC tradition through the appropriation and reworking of Bourdieu's concept in organizational institutionalism: see Powell and DiMaggio (1991). While not totally missing in earlier studies, social movements have gained increasing centrality in POC-inspired research, as is evident in studies on music mobilization (Danaher and Roscigno 2004) and on literary innovation (Isaac, 2009; 2012).
25 These figures contrast with the idea, popular in some circles, that POC is now in decline: see for instance Berezin (2014).
26 Indeed, POC has always had a very limited impact on the sociology of science and ideas, notwithstanding its apparent potential in this regard. This is probably (as Randall Collins has indicated in personal correspondence to me), because of its contingent focus on popular culture (popular music above all) and cultural industries, instead of philosophical doctrines or academies – a point which casts some doubt on the abilities of sociologists really to move beyond the great divide between 'high' and 'popular' culture, which they are so prone to deconstruct theoretically.
27 The potential relevance of measurement and quantitative methods for mapping the parameters of cultural practices and assessing their autonomy from either texts or social structures has also been claimed from inside the field of cultural studies: see Lewis (1997) and Kim (2004).
28 It is noteworthy that Peterson has slowly transformed his life-long study of the country music industry through research focused on the social fabrication and multiple interpretation of a particular type of meaning, that is, 'authenticity', something apparently distant from his early concerns with markets and organizations, even if strongly dependent on them (see Hughes, 2000). This opened a new research programme on the 'cultural economy of authenticity', currently pursued by management scholars and sociologists (see Peterson, 2005a; Karpik, 2010).
29 Merton also worked and wrote as a constructionist, being an exponent of what Abbott (2001: 63) calls 'ideological constructionism', which is the position underlying most of the sociology of knowledge. We may add that constructionism is not in itself incompatible with measurement (a presumed positivistic feature), as it does not 'necessarily imply that [social symbols] can't be constructed with single, measurable meanings' (2001: 65). Abbott also notes that hermeneutics began as a positivistic technique in German 19th-century historiography (e.g. in the work of Leopold von Ranke).
30 I am thinking here in terms of what Abbott (2001; 2004) has defined as the 'fractal nature' of epistemological debate, that is, the continuous reproduction at different levels of the same apparently stable dichotomies, whose exact meaning is on the contrary totally contingent on the individual contexts in which they are evoked.
31 But see, for an apparent exception which confirms the rule, Peterson (1992b) on class unconsciousness in country music lyrics. And note the following general proposal in Peterson and DiMaggio (1975: 504): 'Rather than begin with social classes, it may prove more fruitful to categorize persons in terms of cultural classes, that is shared patterns of consumption, and then search for the correlates of strata so defined, especially in advanced industrial nations in which most people have a considerable amount of discretionary income'.
32 I find support for this vision again in the fractal theory of disciplines as cultural and social structures developed by Abbott (2001) – itself a tentative attempt to find a bridge, as I read it, between a production of culture variety of cultural analysis on the one hand, and a more hermeneutical one on the other. The neo-institutionalist reworking of the production of culture approach – works by DiMaggio, Powell, Mohr, Dowd, and also by Peterson himself (at least in some sections of his book on country music) – seems to lead in this direction. Furthermore, Eyerman's works on music and social movements (Eyerman and Jamison, 1998) could be cited as evidence of this convergence. Indeed, when Jeffrey Alexander works empirically on a given historical object (e.g. the Holocaust: see Alexander, 2003: 27–84), he seems to be not so very distant from an institutional approach to cultural analysis, a stance which might offer useful tools to a hermeneutic approach to social life: see on this last point Scheinberg and Clemens (2006).
33 Recently I have applied the fractal idea to make sense of the apparent contrast between Bourdieu (elected champion of a supposedly 'weak program') and Alexander ('strong program in cultural sociology'): see Santoro and Solaroli (2015).
34 A comparison with the recent development of economic sociology could be illuminating. It was only when sociologists began to think they could enter into the analysis of economic institutions (i.e. markets, prices, etc.), not leaving these phenomena solely to economists, that a veritable economic sociology was born. But we have to remember that the economy is a much more legitimate topic for sociology than 'culture', at least according to the Marxist tradition.

35 Interestingly, this process of academic entrepreneurship was similar to that from which the 'new economic sociology' emerged: see Swedberg (1997) and Convert and Heilbron (2007). Also, the two processes overlapped at crucial points – thanks to figures like Paul DiMaggio, W.W. Powell, Paul Hirsch, Viviana Zelizer, Roger Friedland and Harrison C. White, the latter being at the same time an accomplished sociologist of art, one of the key actors in the economic sociology movement and an acknowledged source of inspiration for Peterson (and for DiMaggio, who was formally White's PhD student at Harvard). On the 'hidden' cultural dimensions of White's work on the economy and social structure, see Brint (1991).

36 See Abbott (2004) for a discussion of heuristics in the social sciences. A gambit is a chess move in which you lose a pawn to win the game.

37 As Tim Dowd pointed out to me in personal conversation, the strength of this 'productionist' metaphor could also explain the success of Swidler's 'toolkit' concept of culture (see Swidler, 1986).

## REFERENCES

Abbott, A. (1999) *Department and Discipline*. Chicago: University of Chicago Press.

Abbott, A. (2001) *Chaos of Disciplines*. Chicago: University of Chicago Press.

Abbott, A. (2004) *Methods of Discovery: Heuristics for the Social Sciences*. New York: Norton.

Abbott, A. (2007) 'For Humanist Sociology', in D. Clawson et al. (eds), *Public Sociology. Fifteen Eminent Sociologists Debate Politics and the Profession in the Twenty-first Century*. Berkeley: University of California Press. pp. 195–209.

Abell, P. (2004) 'Narrative Explanation: An Alternative to Variable-Centered Explanation?', *Annual Review of Sociology*, 30: 287–310.

Adorno, T.W. (2006) *Current of Music: Elements of a Radio Theory*. Frankfurt: Suhrkamp.

Alexander, J.C. (2003) *The Meanings of Social Life: A Cultural Sociology*. Oxford: Oxford University Press.

Alexander, J.C. and Smith, P. (2001) 'The Strong Program in Cultural Theory: Elements of a Structural Hermeneutics', in J. Turner (ed.), *The Handbook of Sociological Theory*. New York: Kluwer. pp. 135–50.

Alexander, J.C. and Smith, P. (2010) 'The Strong Program: Origins, Achievements and Prospects', in J.R. Hall (ed.), *Handbook of Cultural Sociology*. London: Routledge.

Barrett, M., Corrigan, P., Kuhn, A. and Wolff, J. (eds) (1979) *Ideology and Cultural Production*. London: Croom Helm.

Becker, H.S. (1982) *Art Worlds*. Berkeley: University of California Press.

Becker, H.S. and Pessin, A. (2006) 'A Dialogue on the Ideas of "World" and "Field"', *Sociological Forum*, 21(2): 275–86.

Bennett, A. (2010) 'Commentary: A Tribute to Pete Peterson', *Poetics*, 38(6): 530–3.

Bennett, A. and Peterson, R.A. (eds) (2004) *Music Scenes: Local, Translocal and Virtual*. Nashville: Vanderbilt University Press.

Bennett, T.M., Savage, M. et al. (2009) *Culture, Class, Distinction*. London & New York: Routledge.

Berezin, M. (2014) 'How Do We Know What We Mean? Epistemological. Dilemmas in Cultural Sociology', *Qualitative Sociology*, 37(2): 141–51.

Bourdieu, P. (1971) 'Le marché des biens symboliques', *L'Année Sociologique*, 22: 49–126.

Bourdieu, P. (1980) 'The Production of Belief: Contribution to an Economy of Symbolic Goods', *Media, Culture & Society*, 2(3): 261–93.

Bourdieu, P. (1984) *Distinction*. Cambridge, MA: Harvard University Press.

Bourdieu, P. (2004) *Science of Science and Reflexivity*. Chicago: University of Chicago Press.

Brint, S. (1991) 'Hidden Meanings: Cultural Content and Context in Harrison White's Structural Sociology', *Sociological Theory*, 10(2): 194–208.

Burawoy, M. (2005) 'For Public Sociology', *American Sociological Review*, 70(1): 4–28.

Caldwell, J.T. (2008) *Production Culture: Industrial Reflexivity and Critical Practice in Film and Television*. Durham: Duke University Press.

Caves, R.E. (2000) *Creative Industries*. Cambridge, MA: Harvard University Press.

Chan, T.W. (ed.) (2010) *Social Status and Cultural Consumption*. Cambridge: Cambridge University Press.

Chan, T.W. and Goldthorpe, J.H. (2007) 'Social Stratification and Cultural Consumption: Music in England', *European Sociological Review*, 23(1): 1–19.

Chriss, J.J. (1999) *Alvin W. Gouldner: Sociologist and Outlaw Marxist*. Alderhsot: Ashgate.

Cluley, R. (2012) 'Art Words and Art Worlds: The Methodological Importance of Language Use in Howard S. Becker's Sociology of Art and Cultural Production', *Cultural Sociology*, 6(2): 201–16.

Convert, B. and Heilbron, J. (2007) 'Where Did the New Economic Sociology Come From?', *Theory and Society*, 36(2): 31–54.

Coser, L. (1965) *Men of Ideas: A Sociologist's View*. New York: Free Press.

Coser, L., Kadushin, C. and Powell, W.W. (1982) *Books: The Culture and Commerce of Publishing*. Chicago: University of Chicago Press.

Coulangeon, P. (2003) 'La stratification sociale des gouts musicaux: Le modéle de la légitimité

culturelle en question', *Revue française de sociologie*, 44(1): 3–33.
Crane, D. (1972) *Invisible Colleges*. Chicago: University of Chicago Press.
Crane, D. (1992) *The Production of Culture: Media and Urban Arts*. London: Sage.
Crane, D. (ed.) (1994) *The Sociology of Culture*. Oxford: Blackwell.
Danaher, W.F. and Roscigno, V.J. (2004) 'Cultural Production, Media, and Meaning: Hillbilly Music and the Southern Textile Mills', *Poetics*, 32(1): 51–71.
DeNora, T. (2000) *Music in Everyday Life*. Cambridge: Cambridge University Press.
Denzin, N. (1990) 'Reading Cultural Text', *American Journal of Sociology*, 95(6): 1577–80.
Denzin, N. (1991) 'Empiricist Cultural Studies in America: A Deconstructive Reading', *Current Perspectives in Social Theory*, 11: 17–39.
DiMaggio, P. (1979) 'On Pierre Bourdieu', *American Journal of Sociology*, 84(6): 1460–74.
DiMaggio, P. (1982) 'Cultural Entrepreneurship in Nineteenth-Century Boston, I: The Creation of an Organizational Basis for High Culture in America', *Media, Culture and Society*, 4(1): 33–50.
DiMaggio, P. (2000) 'The Production of Scientific Change: Richard Peterson and the Institutional Turn in Cultural Sociology', *Poetics*, 28(2/3): 107–36.
Dowd, T. (2004) 'Production Perspectives in Music Sociology', *Poetics*, 32(3): 235–46.
Dowd, T. (2007) 'Innovation and Diversity in Cultural Sociology: Notes on Peterson and Berger's Classic Article', *Sociologica: Italian Journal of Sociology*, 1(1), http://www.sociologica.mulino.it/doi/10.2383/24213
Du Gay, P., Hall, S. et al. (1997) *Doing Cultural Studies*. London: Sage.
Eagleton, T. (1976) *The Idea of Culture*. Oxford: Blackwell.
Edles, L.D. (2002) *Cultural Sociology in Practice*. Oxford: Blackwell.
Eyerman, R. and Jamison, A. (1998) *Music and Social Movements*. Cambridge: Cambridge University Press.
Eyerman, R. and McCormick, L. (2006) 'Introduction', in R. Eyerman and L. McCormick (eds), *Myth, Meaning, and Performance*. Boulder: Paradigm. pp. 1–11.
Fine, G.A. (1992) 'The Culture of Production: Aesthetic Choices and Constraints in Culinary Work', *American Journal of Sociology*, 97(5): 1268–94.
Frickel, S. and Gross, N. (2005) 'A General Theory of Scientific/Intellectual Movements', *American Sociological Review*, 70(2): 204–32.
Frith, S. and Goodwin, A. (eds) (1990) *On Record*. London: Routledge.
Gilroy, P. (1993) *The Black Atlantic*. Cambridge, MA: Harvard University Press.
Gottdiener, M. (1985) 'Hegemony and Mass Culture: A Semiotic Approach', *American Journal of Sociology*, 90(5): 979–1001.
Gouldner, A. (1954a) *Patterns of Industrial Bureaucracy*. New York: Free Press.
Gouldner, A. (1954b) *Wildcat Strike*. New York: Antioch Press.
Gouldner, A. (1970) *The Coming Crisis of Western Sociology*. New York: Basic Books.
Griswold W. (1981) 'American Character and the American Novel: An Expansion of Reflection Theory in the Sociology of Literature', *American Journal of Sociology* 86(4): 740–65.
Griswold, W. (1990) 'Provisional, Provincial Positivism: Reply to Denzin', *American Journal of Sociology*, 95(6): 1580–3.
Griswold, W. (2008) *Cultures and Societies in a Changing World*. Third edition. Thousand Oaks: Pine Forge Press. Originally published 1994.
Halas, E. (2006) 'Classical Cultural Sociology: Florian Znaniecki Impact in a New Light', *Journal of Classical Sociology*, 6(3): 256–82.
Hebdige, D. (1979) *Subculture: The Meaning of Style*. London: Methuen.
Hedstrom, P. (2005) *Dissecting the Social: On the Principles of Analytical Sociology*. Cambridge: Cambridge University Press.
Hennion, A. (1981) *Les professionnels du disque*. Paris: Métailié.
Hennion, A. (1993) *La mediation musicale*. Paris: Métailié.
Hesmondhalgh, D. (2002) *The Cultural Industries*. London: Sage.
Hirsch, P.M. and Fiss, P.C. (2000) 'Doing Sociology and Culture: Richard Peterson's Quest and Contribution', *Poetics*, 28(2/3): 97–105.
Hughes, M. (2000) 'Country Music as Impression Management: A Meditation on Fabricating Authenticity', *Poetics*, 28(2/3): 185–205.
Hughes, M. and Peterson, R.A. (1983) 'Isolating Cultural Choice Patterns in the US Population', *American Behavioral Scientist*, 26(4): 459–78.
Inglis, D. and Hughson, J. (eds) (2005) *The Sociology of Art: Ways of Seeing*. Basingstoke: Palgrave.
Isaac, L. (2009) 'Movements, Aesthetics, and Markets in Literary Change: Making the American Labor Problem Novel', *American Sociological Review*, 74(6): 938–65.
Isaac, L. (2012) 'Literary Activists and Battling Books: The Labor Problem Novel as Contentious Movement Medium', *Research in Social Movements, Conflicts and Change*, 33(5): 17–49.
Jensen, J. (1984) 'An Interpretative Approach to Cultural Production', in W. Rowland and B. Watkins (eds), *Interpreting Television*. London: Sage. pp. 98–118.
Jones, P. (2004) *Raymond Williams' Sociology of Culture: A Critical Reconstruction*. Basingstoke: Palgrave.

Karpik, L. (2010) *Valuing the Unique: The Economics of Singularities*. Princeton: Princeton University Press..

Katz, J. (2006) 'Foreword', in H.S. Becker, R.R. Faulkner and B. Kirschenblatt-Gimblett (eds), *Art from Start to Finish: Jazz, Painting, Writing, and Other Improvisations*. Chicago: University of Chicago Press.

Kaufmann, J. (2004) 'Endogenous Explanation in the Sociology of Culture', *Annual Review of Sociology*, 30: 335–57.

Kim, S.J. (2004) 'Rereading David Morley's The 'Nationwide' Audience', *Cultural Studies*, 18(1): 84–108.

Lahire, B. (2004) *La culture des individus*. Paris: La Découverte.

Lash, S. and Urry, J. (1994) *Economies of Signs and Spaces*. London: Sage.

Lena, J.C. and Peterson, R.A. (2008) 'Classification as Culture: Types and Trajectories of Music Genres', *American Sociological Review*, 73(5): 697–718.

Lewis, J. (1997) 'What Counts in Cultural Studies', *Media, Culture & Society*, 19(1): 83–97.

Lizardo, O. (2008) 'The Question of Culture Consumption and Stratification Revisited', *Sociologica* II, 2, doi: 10.2383/27709.

Lounsbury, M. and Ventresca, M. (2003) 'The New Structuralism in Organizational Theory', *Organization*, 10(3): 457–80.

Lury, C. (1993) *Copyright Cultures*. London: Routledge.

MacDonald, D. (1960) 'Masscult and Midcult' *Partisan Review* 27(2): 203-233, 27(4): 589-631.

Manuel, P. (1993) *Cassette Culture: Popular Music and Technology in North India*. Chicago: University of Chicago Press.

Mayer, V., Banks, M.J. and Caldwell, J.T. (2009) *Production Studies: Cultural Studies of Media Industries*. New York and London: Routledge.

McLennan, G. (2006) *Sociological Cultural Studies*. Basingstoke: Palgrave.

Merton, R.K. (1975) 'Structural Analysis in Sociology', in P. Blau (ed.), *Approaches to the Study of Social Structure*. New York: The Free Press. pp. 21–52.

Mohr, J.W. (1998) 'Measuring Meaning Structures', *Annual Review of Sociology*, 24: 345–70.

Mohr, J.M. and Ghaziani, A. (2014) 'Problems and Prospects of Measurement in the Study of Culture', *Theory and Society*, 43(3–4): 225–46.

Morris, J. (2012) 'Why Espresso? Explaining Changes in European Coffee Preferences from a Production of Culture Perspective', *European Review of History*, 2(5): 881–901.

Mucchielli, L. (2004) *Mythes et histoire des sciences humaines*. Paris: La Découverte.

Nathaus, K. and Clayton Childress, C. (2013) 'The Production of Culture Perspective in Historical Research: Integrating the Production, Meaning and Reception of Symbolic Objects', *Zeithistorische Forschungen/Studies in Contemporary History*, 1: 89–100.

Negus, K. (1992) *Producing Pop*. London: Arnold.

Negus, K. (1997) 'The Production of Culture', in P. Du Gay (ed.), *Production of Culture/Cultures of Production*. London: Sage. Pp. 67–118.

Negus, K. (1999) *Corporate Culture and Musical Genres*. London: Sage.

Peterson, R.A. (1962) 'The Intellectual Career of C. Wright Mills: A Case of Sociological Imagination', *Wisconsin Sociologist*, 1(Fall): 17–29.

Peterson, R.A. (1964) 'Dimensions of Social Character: An Empirical Exploration of the Riesman Typology', *Sociometry*, 27(2): 194–207.

Peterson, R.A. (1965) 'Artistic Creativity and Alienation: The Jazz Musician Versus His Audience', *Arts in Society*, 3: 244–48.

Peterson, R.A. (1967) 'Market and Moralist Censors of a Rising Art Form: Jazz', *Arts in Society*, 4: 253–64.

Peterson, R.A. (1971) 'Review' [of Gouldner (1970)], *American Sociological Review*, 36(2): 326–28.

Peterson, R.A. (1972) 'A Process Model of the Folk, Pop, and Fine Art Phase of Jazz', in C. Nanry (ed.), *American Music: From Storyville to Woodstock*. New Brunswick: Transaction. pp. 135–51.

Peterson, R.A. (ed.) (1976) *The Production of Culture*. London: Sage.

Peterson, R.A. (1978) 'The Production of Cultural Change: The Case of Contemporary Country Music', *Social Research*, 45(5): 292–314.

Peterson, R.A. (1979) 'Revitalizing the Culture Concept', *Annual Review of Sociology*, 5: 137–66.

Peterson, R.A. (1982) 'Five Constraints on the Production of Culture: Law, Technology, Market, Organizational Structure and Occupational Careers', *The Journal of Popular Culture*, 16(2): 143–53.

Peterson, R.A. (1983) 'Patterns of Cultural Choice: A Prolegomenon', *American Behavioral Scientist*, 26(4): 422–38.

Peterson, R.A. (1985) 'Six Constraints on the Production of Literary Works', *Poetics*, 14(1–2): 45–67.

Peterson, R.A. (1989) 'La sociologie de l'art et de la culture aux Etats-Unis', *L'Année sociologique*, 39: 153–79.

Peterson, R.A. (1990) 'Why 1955? Explaining the Advent of Rock Music', *Popular Music*, 9(1): 97–116.

Peterson, R.A. (1992a) 'Understanding Audience Segmentation: From Elite and Mass to Omnivore and Univore', *Poetics*, 21(4): 243–58.

Peterson, R.A. (1992b) 'Class Unconsciousness in Country Music', in M.A. McLaurin and R.A. Peterson (eds), *You Wrote My Life: Lyrical Themes in Country Music*. Philadelphia: Gordon and Breach. pp. 35–62.

Peterson, R.A. (1994) 'Culture Studies Through the Production Perspective: Progress and Prospects', in

D. Crane (ed.), *The Sociology of Culture*. Cambridge, MA: Blackwell. pp. 163–90.

Peterson, R.A. (1997) *Creating Country Music: Fabricating Authenticity*. Chicago: University of Chicago Press.

Peterson, R.A. (2000) 'Two Ways Culture is Produced', *Poetics*, 28(2/3): 225–33.

Peterson, R.A. (2005a) 'In Search of Authenticity', *Journal of Management Studies*, 42(5): 1083–98.

Peterson, R.A. (2005b) 'Problems in Comparative Research: The Example of Omnivorousness', *Poetics*, 33(5/6): 257–82.

Peterson, R.A. and Anand, N. (2004) 'The Production of Culture Perspective', *Annual Review of Sociology*, 30: 311–34.

Peterson, R.A. and Berger, D.G. (1971) 'Entrepreneurship in Organizations: Evidence from the Popular Music Industry', *Administrative Science Quarterly*, 16(1): 97–106.

Peterson, R.A. and Berger, D.G. (1972) 'Three Eras in the Manufacture of Popular Music Lyrics', in R.S. Denisoff and R.A. Peterson (eds), *The Sounds of Social Change: Studies in Popular Culture*. Chicago: Rand McNally. pp. 282–303.

Peterson, R.A. and Berger, D.G. (1975) 'Cycles in Symbol Production: The Case of Popular Music', *American Sociological Review*, 40(2): 158–73.

Peterson, R.A. and DiMaggio, P. (1975) 'From Region to Class, The Changing Locus of Country Music: A Test of the Massification Hypothesis', *Social Forces*, 53(3): 497–506.

Peterson, R.A. and Kern, R.M. (1996) 'Changing Highbrow Taste: From Snob to Univore', *American Sociological Review*, 61(5): 900–7.

Peterson, R.A. and Ryan, J. (1983) 'Success, Failure, and Anomie in Arts and Crafts Work', *Research in Sociology of Work*, 2: 301–23.

Peterson, R.A. and Simkus, A. (1992) 'How Musical Taste Groups Mark Occupational Status Groups', in M. Lamont and M. Fournier (eds), *Cultivating Differences: Symbolic Boundaries and the Making of Inequality*. Chicago: University of Chicago Press. pp. 125–68.

Peterson, R.A. and White, H.G. (1979) 'The Simplex Located in Art Worlds', *Urban Life*, 7(4): 411–39.

Peterson, R.A. and White, H.G. (1981) 'Elements of Simplex Structures', *Urban Life*, 10(1): 3–24.

Plummer, K. (2003) 'Continuity and Change in Howard S. Becker's Work: An Interview with Howard S. Becker', *Sociological Perspectives*, 46(1): 21–39.

Powell, W.W. and DiMaggio, P. (eds) (1991) *The New Institutionalism in Organizational Analysis*. Chicago: University of Chicago Press.

Reed, I.A. (2011) *Interpretation and Social Knowledge: On the Use of Theory in the Human Sciences*. Chicago: University of Chicago Press.

Riesman, D. with Denney, R. and Glazer, N. (1950) *The Lonely Crowd: A Study of the Changing American Character*. New Haven, CT: Yale University Press.

Riesman, D. (1988) 'On Discovering and Teaching Sociology: A Memoir', *Annual Review of Sociology*, 14: 1–24.

Rojek, C. and Turner, B. (2000) 'Decorative Sociology: Towards a Critique of the Cultural Turn', *The Sociological Review*, 3(4): 629–48.

Rosenberg, B. and White, D.M. (eds.) (1957) Mass culture: the popular arts in America. Glencoe, Ill.: The Free Press.

Ryan, J.W. (2000) 'The Production and Consumption of Culture. Essays on Richard A. Peterson's Contributions to Cultural Sociology: A Prolegomenon', *Poetics*, 28(2/3): 91–6.

Ryan, J.W. (2007) 'The Production of Culture Perspective', in C.D. Bryant and D.L. Peck (eds), *21st Century Sociology – A Reference Handbook*. Vol. II. Thousand Oaks: Sage.

Ryan, J.W. and Peterson, R.A. (1982) 'The Product Image: The Fate of Creativity in Country Music Songwriting', in J. Ettema and D.C. Whitney (eds), *Individuals in Mass Media Organizations: Creativity and Constraint*. London: Sage. pp. 11–32.

Ryan, J.W. and Peterson, R.A. (2001) 'The Guitar as Artifact and Icon: Identity Formation in the Babyboom Generation', in A. Bennett and K. Dawe (eds), *Guitar Cultures*. Oxford: Berg. pp. 89–116.

Sallaz, J.J. and Zavisca, J. (2007) 'Bourdieu in America, 1980–2004', *Annual Review of Sociology*, 33: 21–41.

Sanders, C.R. (1982) 'Structural and Interactional Features of Popular Culture Production: An Introduction to the Production of Culture Perspective', *Journal of Popular Culture*, 16(2): 66–74.

Santoro, M. (2008a) 'Culture As (and After) Production', *Cultural Sociology*, 2(1): 7–31.

Santoro, M. (2008b) 'Producing Cultural Sociology: An Interview with Richard A. Peterson', *Cultural Sociology*, 2(1): 33–55.

Santoro, M. (2008c) 'Putting Bourdieu in the Global Field', *Sociologica*, 2(2), doi: 10.2383/27719

Santoro, M. (2011) 'From Bourdieu to Cultural Sociology', *Cultural Sociology*, 5(1) 3–23.

Santoro, M. (2015) 'Production Perspectives', in J. Shepherd and K. Devine (eds), *The Routledge Reader of Music Sociology*. London: Routledge.

Santoro, M. and Solaroli, M. (2015) 'Contesting Culture: Bourdieu and the Strong Program in Cultural Sociology', in L. Hanquinet and M. Savage (eds), *Routledge International Handbook of the Sociology of Art and Culture*. London: Routledge.

Sassatelli, R. (2007) *Consumer Culture: History, Theory and Politics*. London: Sage.

Scheinberg, M. and Clemens, E.S. (2006) 'The Typical Tools for the Job: Research Strategies in Institutional Analysis', *Sociological Theory*, 24(3): 195–227.

Schmutz, V. and Miller, C.N. (2015) 'Production of Culture', in R. Scott and S. Kosslyn (eds), *Emerging Trends in the Social and Behavioral Sciences*. Chichester: John Wiley & Sons.

Schudson, M. (1989) 'The Sociology of News Production', *Media, Culture & Society*, 11(3): 263–82.

Selznick, P. (1952) *The Organizational Weapon: A Study of Bolshevik Strategy and Tactics*. New York: McGraw-Hill.

Sewell, W.H. (1999) 'The Concept(s) of Culture', in W.H. Sewell (ed.), *Logics of History*. Chicago: University of Chicago Press. pp. 152–74.

Sewell, W.H. (2005) *Logics of History*, Chicago: University of Chicago Press.

Smith, P. (ed.) (1998) *The New American Cultural Sociology*. Cambridge: Cambridge University Press.

Stinchcombe, A. (1959) 'Bureaucratic and Craft Administration of Production', *Administrative Science Quarterly*, 4: 168–87.

Sullivan, O. and Katz-Gerro, T. (2007) 'The Omnivore Thesis Revisited: Voracious Cultural Consumers', *European Sociological Review*, 23(2): 123–37.

Swedberg, R. (1997) 'New Economic Sociology: What has been Accomplished, What is Ahead?' *Acta Sociologica*, 40(2): 161–82.

Swidler, A. (1986) 'Culture in Action: Symbols and Strategies', *American Sociological Review*, 51(2): 273–86.

Throsby, D. (2000) *Economics and Culture*. Cambridge: Cambridge University Press.

Tuchman, G. (1983) 'Consciousness Industries and the Production of Culture', *Journal of Communication*, 33(3): 330–41.

Turner, G. (2003) *British Cultural Studies: An Introduction*. Third edition. London: Routledge.

Van Rees, C.J. (1983) 'Introduction. Advances in the Empirical Sociology of Literature and the Arts: The Institutional Approach', *Poetics*, 12(4/5): 285–310.

Warde, A., Wright, D. and Gayo-Cal, M. (2007) 'Understanding Cultural Omnivorousness: Or, the Myth of the Omnivore', *Cultural Sociology*, 1(2): 143–64.

Watt, I. (1957) *The Rise of the Novel*. Berkeley: University of California Press.

White, H.C. (1993) *Careers and Creativity: Social Forces in the Arts*. Boulder: Westview Press.

White, H.C. and White, C. (1965) *Canvases and Careers: Institutional Change in the French Painting World*. Chicago: University of Chicago Press.

Williams, R. (1981) *Culture*. London: Fontana.

Williams, R. (1983) *Keywords: A Vocabulary of Culture and Society*. London: Flamingo.

Willis, P. (1978) *Profane Culture*. London: Hutchinson.

Willis, P. (2000) *The Ethnographic Imagination*. Cambridge: Polity.

Wolff, J. (1981) *The Social Production of Art*. Basingstoke: Macmillan.

Wolff, J. (1999) 'Cultural Studies and the Sociology of Culture', *Contemporary Sociology*, 28(5): 499–507.

Zaret, D. (1992) 'Critical Theory and the Sociology of Culture', *Current Perspectives in Social Theory*, 12: 1–28.

Zelizer, V. (2005) 'Culture and Consumption', in N. Smelser and R. Swedberg (eds), *Handbook of Economic Sociology*. Second edition. Princeton: Princeton University Press. pp. 331–54.

Znaniecki, F. (1940) *The Social Role of the Man of Knowledge*. New York: Columbia University Press.

# Cultural Historical Sociology

Chandra Mukerji

## INTRODUCTION

Historical sociology is a particularly lively area of research within cultural sociology in which scholars raise radical questions about fundamental terms and traditions in sociology. Sociology, as a field with foundations in modernism, has traditionally adopted forms of analysis designed to fit the political environment and cultural assumptions of the late 19th and early 20th centuries. As Steinmetz (2013) has argued, early sociologists addressed the historical formation of empires, and European empowerment across the globe. In this context, history was being recast as a history of progress, and the forms of life to know and pursue were Western. Durkheim and Mauss (1969) assumed a progressive view of history, distinguishing between the primitive and modern; so did Simmel (2002 [1903]) when he described modern man in the metropolis in contrast to primitive man in nature. Even though Marx and Engels (1848) were critical of capitalism, they also described history as ultimately progressive. Their politicsfocused on an emancipatory future. Of the founding fathers, only Weber (1947) was truly skeptical of this historical conceit, seeing the rationalization of modern life destroying human qualities while making societies more efficient. In spite of his cautions, sociologists remained tied to these traditions. Norbert Elias (1978), for example, called Western cultural history a civilizing process. He evenexplicitly defended using the term civilizing as an analytic category as a way to understand cultural progress. Learning manners and putting away swords was a move away from a more primitive state. Given the conceptual poverty of this tradition, it should be no surprise that historical cultural sociologists have been trying to find new terms and methods to make sociological sense of cultural history.

Because he eschews progressive history, Foucault (1971; 1977; Foucault and Gordon, 1980) has had a particular importance to historical cultural sociologists. He not only treats culture as politically and socially vital, but also provides ways to engage the past differently, using genealogical and archeological approaches to rethink relations between past and present outside of a directional chronology. For Foucault, history is a struggle over categories and bodies that shifts in form over time, but also bleeds into or is tapped by the present. It has regimes and in some ways became more rational in the Enlightenment, but it is not in principle emancipatory. His vision of the complex meetings of past and present in culture fits better with the conceptions of history shared by most cultural sociologists. It seems more precise, and allows social critique and hopes for emancipation to be detached from historical machinery.

Historical cultural sociologists have adopted terms and analytic approaches from a variety of other authors and fields, too, to try to understand how culture works historically. The debt never properly acknowledged is to the work of cultural historians whose accounts of past ways of life seem close to good ethnographic sociology. The engagements in this work with art history, archeology, material science, and consumer culture have affected the direction of research in sociology. Most self-consciously, cultural sociologists have looked to the humanities for theories of culture and techniques for analyzing it, drawing ideas from semiotics, feminist theory, rhetoric, affect theory, critical geography and cultural studies, among many others, to think more broadly about meaning making or structures of meaning. Others have looked to science and technology studies to understand knowledge practices, metrics and materiality. The result has been a growing sophistication among members of this subfield, and also a sense that sociology can be productively reformed to address history and culture in better ways.

The methodological foundations of historical cultural sociology have been important, too, for example the on-going commitment to empirical practices of social analysis. Many members of the field who have read broadly in culture theory have remained skeptical of losing sight of social practices and institutions in cultural history. William Sewell (2010), for example, has pushed for using methods of social history for studying cultural change. His explanation of the growth of French fashion in the 18th century is a story of capitalism and the design of commodities; of the plant trade and the growth of the Lyonnais silk industry; of labor and the construction of fine clothing; of political dissent and social displacement of workers; and of shopping and the cultivation of taste. In doing layered forms of social history to explain cultural change, he has illustrated how to build a distinctly sociological understanding of culture by connecting meanings to social practices. He has established methods for doing production of culture studies in the past, and turned the production of culture into a historical process with large implications. Others have put forward other methods for doing distinctly sociological versions of genealogical studies, materiality studies, collective memory, and performance studies, taking issues of culture from the humanities and showing how to approach them through social analysis done well by sociological standards.

The search for new ways to conceptualize culture, social theory, and history in addition to a proliferation of empirical research on historical of practices of culture have produced a vibrant area of research. In works of historical cultural sociology, researchers routinely challenge and rework traditional sociological views of power, agency, meaning, materiality, performance, and many other fundamental concepts. I will summarize some of the developments below. What is stunning is how doing research about cultural history forces authors to embrace conceptual changes. Freed from the orthodoxies of the canon in historical sociology, but armed with methodological skills for social analysis, historical cultural sociologists find language to make sense of the social and cultural powers that change history.

## REGIME POWER

Studies of states and regime power started to undergo massive changes when historical sociologists began to consider states as cultural as well as political forms. Many historical sociologists remained committed to studying regime power in terms of structure and agency, but both George Steinmetz and Charles Tilly (1999) tendered the idea that states might be approached as cultural forms, and James Scott (1985; 1998) pointed to the art behind state interventions, and the cultural development of weapons of the weak. Once the stage was set, the work started revealing the startling importance of culture to historical regimes of power.

So, for example, Julia Adams (2005), looking at data on the Dutch Republic, developed a portrait of a patrimonial state very far from a Weberian bureaucracy or Marxist state apparatus. The Dutch state was embedded in a rich cultural fabric of patrimonial relations and cultural traditions that made family life particularly important as a site and model for the exercise of power. The state used patrimonial authority as a mode of governance legitimated by and furthered through families. Mounira Charrad (2001) brought culture squarely into the center of state formation. She examined the history of states in the Maghreb where patrimonial traditions and clan relations entered into the design of states, yielding distinct legal structures that fit extant cultures of power. And Frank Dobbin (1994) demonstrated that national infrastructures were forms of culture, too. Looking at railroads in England, France, and the US, he found local cultural conceptions of modernity entered into the ways railroads were built. English liberal subjectivity, French traditions of stewardship, and American distrust of governments and entrepreneurs helped shape different railways systems that reflected their national identities.

Chandra Mukerji, Patrick Carroll, Patrick, and Sarah Pritchard have all focused on the material formation of states, following Science and Technology Studies (STS. Carroll (2006) focused on the knowledge practices used in the formation of the British state in Ireland, describing the scientific techniques of territorial measurement used to gain control of land and claim sovereignty. Mukerji described how the French state in the 17th century gained power through territorial engineering and demonstrations of engineered power at Versailles (Mukerji, 1997; 2009). These demonstrations of logistical power were legitimated by the king's moral duty as steward of his lands and images of Roman revival embedded in the gardens of Versailles, carrying cultural logics of power that favored a strong state. Patrick Joyce (2003) illustrated how the material forms of liberal cities taught governmentality in 19th-century England, and reflected on how 'little tools of knowledge' (Becker and Clark, 2001) or systems of files were used to build the Raj in India (Joyce, 2013). Arguing that states should be viewed as assemblages of institutions from post offices to schools, Joyce and Mukerji (2014) have highlighted the importance of logistical practices both bureaucratically and territorially. Pritchard makes a similar case looking at the use of infrastructure in France after World War II. The state developed hydroelectric generating facilities on the Rhone River not just to boost the economy, but also to generate feelings of national pride after the humiliation of the occupation by Germany.

All these material approaches to state formation and political practice have pointed to the importance – overlooked in sociology at large – of logistical powers. They point to the role of natural knowledge to territorial development and the importance of paperwork practices to regimes of power/knowledges organized in assemblages rather than rational bureaucracies.

George Steinmetz (2007) and Andreas Glaeser, in quite different way, focus on the representational and interpretive practices of everyday governance within regimes, drawing attention to those who exercise power in the name of the state and the cultural forms that move them. Glaeser's work on the GDR illustrates how the communist ideology of the regime had to be worked through everyday practices so that the reality projected by party leaders was reconciled in some fashion with actions at the local level. People were not directed in their actions by discourse, per se, but rather they thought about what they heard and what they saw. The members of the Stasi or secret police worked hard to make sense of their experiences in relation to regime propaganda, but developed and acted on their own understandings of reality. Steinmetz tells a different kind of story about colonial government in which Orientalist stereotypes enter into the way colonial authorities exercised power. Images of natives as ethnographic subjects and primitives were important to how they governed, not determining the treatment of colonial subjects but affecting how colonists saw their charges and understood how to behave.

The state that emerges from these and comparable studies is far from the Weberian state or the state in Marx. States are culturally complex institutional forms built with multiple social loci and infrastructures, held together with paperwork and acted out around cultural logics and interpretative practices. This kind of state has logistical powers and practices, but is also governed according to cultural understandings of political legitimacy and purpose.

## MEANING AND REPRESENTATION

Much of the work in historical cultural sociology addresses issues of language, classification, representation, and performance, reflecting the growth in the Humanities of myriad tools of cultural analysis based on language and linguistics. For most cultural sociologists, concern about structures of meaning begins with Durkheim (1976 [1912]) and extends to rituals, but concern about methods for studying meaning draws cultural sociologists into a range of forms of semiotic analysis. Those who do historical work then confront the problem of how structures of meaning work dynamically. The point is to specify when and how cultural meanings are evoked or performed.

Robin Wagner-Pacifici's work on political imagery is a good example of the semiotic approach to historical events. In *The Art of Surrender* (2005), she analyzes in detail images of surrender from various historical periods, and explains how these events work. Surrender, she suggests, is a liminal moment between peace and war in which change could go in unanticipated directions. Rituals of surrender help to dispel tensions by maintaining the dignity of those surrendering, even as they give up the tools of war. The result is a historical event – what Braudel (Braudel and Matthews, 1982) describes as the unit of politics in history. Jeffrey Alexander's work on historical political performances is also concerned with structures of meaning and rituals, but calling on both Goffman (1959) and Burke (Burke and Gusfield, 1989), he develops a rich understanding of politics as a form of theater. And he shows the importance of this approach, for example, in analyzing the Arab Spring. Demonstrators played out forms of politics they wanted to make real, but they found that making meaning is not the same as making institutions.

Other sociologists use art history, philosophy, feminist theory, and critical race theory to create critical forms of historical cultural sociology that explain the formation of identities and creation of sociopolitical differences. Mabel Berezin (1997) and Simonetta Falasca-Zamponi (1997), for example, both study Italian fascism, and its uses of spectacle. Berezin is more interested in the political power of spectacle to draw elites to fascism, while Falasca-Zamponi is more concerned about public art and ordinary people. Still, both show how fascism used spectacle as a way to create interest in it as a political ideal. Orlando Patterson (1998), in contrast, has addressed the production and politics of racial differences, drawing more on philosophy to theorize about slavery and subjugated knowledges, and critical cultural studies to study cultures of race. His work on lynching as purification ritual provides a different vision of political theater than the rather innocent one in Alexander's work. In these acts of violence against Black men in the South, structures of meaning from Christianity and ideas of moral purification are not simply evoked and raised, but used to terrorize Blacks. The effective elaboration of moral authority to engage in violent acts of suppression provides chilling lessons about power and the question of who could exercise it. Looking again at the production of difference, but in a different vein, Elizabeth Long (2003) looks at the performative and discursive nature of gender in her work on the history of women's book groups. Women in these groups engage with gendered stories, perform as gendered subjects, and share stories of their lives to create gendered identities between books and experience, both agitating against and sharing in their own subordination. Sociologists confronting political history in all these examples look at social practices of meaning making and social relations of power. The lessons from the cases are different, but in all of them, the cultural forms of these relations are essential to their historical effects.

Historical cultural sociologists have also become increasingly interested in classification and measurement, looking beyond language and discourse to see the formation of meaning in social life through quantification. This trend begins with Viviana Zelizer's work on economic and cultural value, particularly the ground-breaking, *Pricing the Priceless Child* (1985), as well as subsequent work on consumption, money practices, and intimacy (Zelizer, 2005). Money serves as a cultural tool of social life that marks what matters, and has social power, creating and defining bonds among people. Its significance goes well beyond its importance in the market, and is implicated in social relations of even the most intimate kind. Richard Biernacki (1995) looks at value in the economic sphere as cultural too, comparing labor practices between Britain and Germany. The German factories he studies measure work by counting actions on the loom while British factories measure time at work. Both use productivity goals to tie work to output, but make computations differently. Their measures have more to do with traditions of work than with the practical need for computing wages to pay workers. In this sense, they use cultural assumptions to forge contractual terms.

Other scholars focus more on measures and classification, per se. Marion Fourcade (2009; 2015) compares the field of economics in different countries to show that economics is a cultural practice. She also looks at national differences in the social value of nature to make the point that cultures of measurement are connected to local forms of classifications. The question of what to measure and how to do it is a layered historical process to Fourcade. So, the classification of wine in Burgundy and assessments of value derive from classificatory schemes reflecting historical efforts by different groups in different historical moments to gain standing in the region's wine business (Fourcade, 2015). Wendy Espeland (2015) is also interested in assessments of value and commensuration or the quantification of qualitative differences. She looks at different domains, among them, assessment tools for teachers. She follows how questions of similarity and difference are negotiated socially in the development of assessment tools. In developing quantitative measures, what is left out can be just as important as what is measured, according to Anat Leibler (2014). She looks at national demographic studies in the state of Israel, and reflects on the political significance of the categories of the population the government wants use to form policy and make public.

All these historical cultural sociologists are interested in structures of meaning, assessments of value, and the power of representation in social life. They treat measures, rituals, and everyday performances as cultural tools that do social work in marking priorities and shaping attachments. They treat categories and measures as historical phenomena, and look at how and when they are generated or tapped within politics and exercise power through culture.

## COLLECTIVE MEMORY AND GENEALOGY

Cultural sociologists also open up the concept of history itself by writing about collective memory, memorials, genealogies, and memory practices. They treat the past as distinguishable from history, and approach history as a product of cultural interpretation and materialization of the past. Much of the founding research on collective memory is by Barry Schwartz (2000). In his studies of Lincoln, he looks not only at the way Lincoln was memorialized immediately after his death, as his body was taken by train across country to Illinois, but also how permanent monuments define him. Lincoln continues to have a place in popular versions of American history constructed in large part through public events and spaces where his memory is revered. Lynn Spillman (1997) puts this kind of collective memory in comparative perspective, using semiotic analysis to show how national identities are tied to sites of collective memory. Michael Schudson (1993) focuses on the unfinished and emergent character of some collective memories, focusing on Watergate, the significance of which is not settled. The flexibility of memories that are never fully articulated can be important to their cultural endurance as enshrining them in stone. Jeffrey Olick and Joyce Robbins (1998), in turn, place collective memory within a social history of memory practices, connecting to the rich historical literature on how people in different periods try to remember. Olick (1999) reminds us that there are many memory practices, writing history among them. This gives him leave to ask about historical sociology and the forms it should take, arguing for dropping transcendental views of historical forces, and looking at social practices instead.

Wendy Griswold (2013) seems to ground her sociology in a radical localism and empiricism, looking at history as a form of popular writing in her study of the Federal Writer's Project. This program was established during the Depression and employed writers to create travel books about each state of the US. She argues that this project not only helped keep writers off the street, but shaped how Americans would experience their history through travel. The books and accompanying maps focused on local events and points of interest, and, in doing so, drew attention to the beauty of the land and the hardiness of local people, producing a portrait of America as a strong and young country that could bounce back from the Depression. She documents a cultural construction of history for political ends, but also the construction of experiential history for and by tourists visiting sites of collective memory and local beauty.

These studies of culture and memory in historical perspective helped describe the complexities of aligning past and present in cultural practices. They focus on the social activities involved in producing pasts in the present, and document how genealogies of culture are socially formed. They show the flexibility of memory and the efforts to stabilize narratives of greatness. And, reflecting on history, many of these authors question their methods and purposes in doing historical research. They raise questions about what constitutes an object of study, pointing to physical objects as well as cultural imaginaries, and wonder about how to think of them in terms of chronology and their role in the present.

## CULTURAL ATTACHMENT

Historical cultural sociologists have also been rethinking the nature of social subjects and the character of social agency by paying closer attention to forms of attachment. Some of this work has roots in Bourdieu's (1984) discussions of taste, but it has also been a response to the behaviorism of American sociology that denies an inner life to social subjects (Mead and Morris, 1962). Both reading history and holding a behaviorist analytic position is difficult because historians routinely argue that individuals with particular thoughts and feelings make an enormous difference to history. Hitler made a difference and so did Martin Luther King. Eschewing this individualism, sociologists who read a lot of history often feel impelled to describe social actors as thinking, feeling beings with strong motivations, rich inner lives, and strong attachments to people and things. If people have tastes, does it matter if they are passionate about them? How do cultural attachments form? And what are their consequences for culture?

The seminal work on attachments is by Antoine Hennion (2007) in his writings on 'amateurs'. He studies people who love music or wine, learn a great deal about it, and affect the cultural field they love. They change with their preferences how culture producers create the objects of their affection. He illustrates this in the history of music. He makes the case that Baroque music was rediscovered and entered into the classical tradition by amateurs. They became advocates of this period and selected a repertoire to represent the work. The repertoire continues to define Baroque music, and amateurs still affect the history of classical music because of their interest in certain pieces and their drive to hear them. Claudio Benzecry (2011) has used Hennion's ideas and developed the concept of attachment further in his study of the opera house in Argentina. Although much of the work is ethnographic, the historical part deals most directly with the power and limits of cultural attachment. The opera house in Buenos Aires was a major opera center, and its fan base was large and passionate. But it was caught in political currents, and almost shut down. This was prevented by amateurs, but the tradition was broken, the best performers no longer came, and so the patterns of attachment were attenuated in a contest between the power of love and the power of government. This story was in some sense the opposite of the one Victoria Johnson (2008) tells of the Paris Opera, where the passion of patrons that made the Paris Opera famous kept this royal institution alive after the revolution.

Viviana Zelizer's writings have also been important in theorizing attachments. In describing the role of money, objects, and measures in culture, she writes about how attachments are created and assessed (Zelizer, 2005). Cities matter to people too, according to Sharon Zukin (1991; 1995). Urban spaces and architecture are meant to be seductive. It matters less what spaces 'mean' than the attachments people form to them, and to the practices of urban life that spaces make available.

Unlike Bourdieu's taste cultures that classify people, attachments are expressions of agency. They provide motivation to understand and affect social and material environments with money, cafés, food, music, and cultural institutions. They are involved in the formation of taste cultures by the passionate music lovers who affect repertoires, and they are integral to the work of musicians who bring music to life. Attachments are important to how culture is produced, understood, enjoyed, reconfigured, and carried through time. So, seeing cultural attachments at work in history and looking at how they are formed, marked, and enacted is an important step for rethinking human agency in histories of culture.

## OBJECT AGENCY AND INARTICULACY

The material turn in historical sociology and writings about the character of social agency both in cultural sociology and STS provide foundations for the second material turn in historical cultural sociology: the turn to the agency of objects. To treat objects as social actors is a radical change for sociologists, and one repeatedly opposed by some members of the field. But the more sociologists have described the thinking and feeling character of human agents, the more object agency has posed a problem, because in behaviorist sociology human subjects seem a lot like objects, doing what they are designed to do. Mead's social psychology (Mead and Morris, 1962), even though it explained the capacity of social actors to think and form identities, was grounded in an unthinking 'I' whose will seemed to define agency. Since objects often have tendencies to act in certain ways (water flows downhill or cheddar cheese melts when it is heated), why not consider these as agential qualities, narrow ones, but consequential to human cultures. After all, STS researchers have argued that natural knowledge is co-produced by people and things. And critical geographers have highlighted the power of spaces to shape not only social action but also the experience of reality. If objects shape human consciousness, do they have to be conscious to shape history? As Kai Erikson (1976) showed long ago, a flood can change history, politics, collective memory, businesses, and local lives.

All the debates about object agency had resonance with arguments in historical cultural sociology about state power, territorial politics, and logistical governance. They provided language for describing territorial power, monuments as embodiments of collective memory, and the passionate desire for cultural things. Cultural sociology needed some ways to think about all the materiality of the furniture, music, dances, lynchings, books, and dinners that sociologists had been describing in the production of culture school. Object agency discussions posed the question of what they *did* in social life, not just what they *meant*.

Cultural objects, like images of surrender,, do more than simply evoke meanings and document events. They are pedagogical tools for scripting events, and conveying their importance. They demonstrate what needs to be remembered because of their presence in museum collections. Equally, monuments raise questions about object agency, or why it is important that memories are materialized and given spatial presence.. Cultural performances in politics like the Arab Spring are materializations of political passion that are embodied but not well articulated. Social action alone allows people see what is possible to do and what cultural imaginaries people could make real through material action. The embodiment of culture turns representations into demonstrations of agency. Taking over a square is an act of spatial control as well as a tactic for a social movement, and changes the context for everyday life. And little tools of knowledge matter, too. As Steinmetz shows, the journal that is preserved can change how we understand empire, and even sociology. We share social worlds with things. What difference does this make?

Geneviève Zubrzycki's (2006) work on collective memory and Polish nationalism digs into precisely this issue. She studies the struggle over the placement of crosses at Auschwitz to commemorate the death of Christians there. But the site itself is important for memorializing the death of Jews during the Holocaust. The place matters. The crosses matter. The objects are contentious because they tell different stories of what happened, and taking visitors to the heart of the conflict. Zubrzycki does sophisticated semiotic and discursive analysis, but also delves deeply into the place and the material form of Auschwitz. She makes clear that strong affect is attached to things, circulating around the proposed presence of the crosses. Amateurs who care very much about collective memory vie over what Auschwitz is and will be. The physical form stands as witness as well as memorial. The state matters, too. Auschwitz is part of Polish territory and its form matters to the identity of modern Poland, to national and nationalist logics of governance. By pointing to all this, Zubrzycki shows how cultural patterns at the heart of historical cultural sociology are co-produced by people and objects, a cultural order of things defining both a history and a people.

This brilliant piece and other work that treats cultural objects as active parts of social life beg the question of how objects act socially. How are cultural objects endowed with agency in their production? How are the dynamic qualities of things from nature put to work in social life? And how do objects exercise social agency in relation to people? Fernando Dominguez-Rubio (2014) addresses some of these issues as he argues against the reduction of the power of things to the brute materiality of their presence. Looking at art restoration in MoMA, he shows that apparently stable objects like paintings change over time, requiring restoration. And works using new materials and new technologies are more unstable. This means objects are mutable, changing things that have histories, and so, cannot provide unmediated physical evidence of the past or stand for immutable virtues unless they are reconfigured. Objects that have value – economic or emotional – like those in museum collections are actively maintained to try to sustain their value. Museums try to restore, store, and preserve artworks without destroying their essence, but what does that mean? What physical traits are essential or not? Dominguez-Rubio documents how carefully people clean, groom, revitalize, and restore works to maintain their agential properties. Even if the Mona Lisa we see today is not the one people saw in the Renaissance because the paint has undergone chemical change, the painting is still on view so visitors can search for traces of the original. The material matters, but not because it stabilizes the object of attachment. Museums work to sustain their visitors' attachments to things.

Spaces are designed for distinct political effects too. They carry values and logics outside debate into the world of things. So, the garden at Versailles that Mukerji studied was made a dream world of Roman revival, using forms of design and logistical power like Rome to stimulate imperial ambitions. The park at Versailles made no argument about France's future, but placed France in a history that implied a destiny of greatness. It conveyed a political logic without raising controversial arguments about the direction and policies of the French state. The new logic of power was simply seductive because the gardens and parties there seemed to suggest a better life was possible under this administration.

The cultural power invested in the material world is silent. Built environments embody imaginaries and make them seem real, engendering the sense that structures of meaning are 'out there' to call upon and put into action. To the extent that we assume the material order lies outside what we call society, its logics and values can remain naturalized – a product of experience to internalize. Configurations of things and people constitute figured worlds of power that are all the more interesting to reveal because they are so easily overlooked in social histories. This is the mysterious habitus in Bourdieu that turns out, when studied historically and materially, not to be so mysterious at all.

## CONCLUSIONS

Historical cultural sociology, then, uses history to rethink the logics and analytic frameworks of sociology, trying to bring some of the dynamism visible in historical cases into the analytic equipment used to make sense of them. Scholars in this field have moved beyond simple models of structures and agency, looking at the material as well as cultural forms of institutions, and have exploded the concept of agency to reflect a richer understanding of social subjects and objects. Members of this subfield have also questioned the idea of history, and studied the complicated dynamics of interaction between the past and present in cultural life. And cultural sociologists continue to query the character of states and the practice of politics, reworking terms of analysis and revealing the intense desires and wide array of materialized cultural tools at work at all the levels of social action on which history is made.

# REFERENCES

Adams, J. (2005) *The Familial State*. Ithaca, NY: Cornell University Press.

Alexander, J. (2011) *The Performative Revolution in Egypt*. New York: Bloomsbury Academic.

Alexander, J., Bartmanski, D. and Giesen, B. (2011) *Iconic Power: Materiality and Meaning in Social Life*. New York: Palgrave.

Becker, H. and Clark, W. (2001) *Little Tools of Knowledge*. Ann Arbor: University of Michigan Press.

Benzecry, C. (2011) *The Opera Fanatic*. Chicago: University of Chicago Press.

Berezin, M. (1997) *Making the Fascist Self*. Ithaca, NY: Cornell University Press.

Biernacki, R. (1995) *The Fabrication of Labor: Germany and Britain 1640–1914*. Berkeley: University of California Press.

Bourdieu, P. (1984) *Distinction*. Richard Nice, trans. London: Routledge and Kegan Paul.

Braudel, F. and Matthews, S. (1982) *On History*. Chicago: University of Chicago Press.

Burke, K. and Gusfield, J. (1989) *On Symbols and Society*. Chicago: University of Chicago Press.

Carroll, P. (2006) *Science, Culture and Modern State Formation*. Berkeley: University of California Press.

Charrad, M. (2001) *States and Women's Rights: The Making of Postcolonial Tunisia, Algeria, and Morocco*. Berkeley: University of California Press.

Dobbin, F. (1994) Cambridge and New York: Cambridge University Press.

Dominguez-Rubio, F. (2014) 'Preserving the Un-Preservable: Docile and Unruly Objects', *Theory and Society*, 43: 617–45.

Durkheim, E. (1976 [1912]) *Elementary Forms of the Religious Life*. London: Allen and Unwin.

Durkheim, E. and Mauss, M. (1969) *Primitive Classification*. Rodney Needham, trans. London: Cohen and West.

Elias, N. (1978) *The Civilizing Press*. New York: Urizen Books.

Erikson, K. (1976) *Everything in its Path: Destruction of Community in the Buffalo Creek Flood*. New York: Simon and Schuster.

Espeland, W. (2015) 'Narrating Numbers', in R. Rottenberg et al. (eds), *A World of Indicators*. Cambridge: Cambridge University Press.

Falasca-Zamponi, S. (1997) *Fascist Spectacle*. Berkeley: University of California Press.

Foucault, M. (1971) *The Order of Things: An Archeology of the Human Sciences*. New York: Pantheon Books.

Foucault, M. (1977) *Discipline and Punish: The Birth of the Prison*. New York: Pantheon Books.

Foucault, M. and Gordon, C. (1980) *Power/Knowledge: Selected Interviews and Other Writings*. New York: Pantheon.

Fourcade, M. (2009) *Economists and Societies: Discipline and Profession in the United States, Britain, and France, 1890s–1990s*. Princeton: Princeton University Press.

Fourcade, M. (2015) 'The Type and the Grade: On the Institutional Scaffolding of the Judgment of Taste', paper presented in the Science Studies Colloquium Series 2014–15, San Diego.

Glaeser, A. (2011) *Political Epistemics: The Secret Police, the Opposition, and the End of East German Socialism*. Chicago: University of Chicago Press.

Goffman, E. (1959) *Presentation of Self in Everyday Life*. New York: Doubleday Anchor.

Griswold, W. (2013) 'The Federal Writer's Project', paper presented in the Sociology Department Colloquium Series, University of California, San Diego.

Hennion, A. (2007) *La Passion Musicale. Une sociologie de la médiation*. Paris: Editions Métaillier.

Johnson, V. (2008) *Backstage at the Revolution*. Chicago: University of Chicago Press.

Joyce, P. (2003) *Rule of Freedom*. Cambridge and New York: Cambridge University Press.

Joyce, P. (2013) *State of Freedom*. Cambridge and New York: Cambridge University Press.

Joyce, P. and Mukerji, C. (2014) 'Sociomaterial Analysis: Regimes of Impersonal Rule', paper presented at the Annual Meeting of the American Sociological Association.

Leibler, A. (2014) 'Disciplining Ethnicity: Political Demography in Israel's Pre-State Period', *Social Studies of Science*, 44(2): 271–92.

Long, E. (2003) *Book Clubs: Women and the Uses of Reading in Everyday Life*. Chicago: University of Chicago Press.

Marx, K. and Engels, F. (1998 [1848]) *The Communist Manifesto*. Martin Malia, ed. New York: Penguin.

Mead, G.H. and Morris, C. (1962) *Mind, Self, and Society from the Standpoint of a Social Behaviorist*. Chicago: University of Chicago Press.

Mukerji, C. (1997) *Territorial Ambitions and the Gardens of Versailles*. Cambridge: Cambridge University Press.

Mukerji, C. (2009) *Impossible Engineering*. Princeton: Princeton University Press.

Mukerji, C. (2012) 'Space and Political Pedagogy at the Gardens of Versailles', *Public Culture*, 24(3) Issue 68: 509–34.

Olick, J. (1999) 'Collective Memory: The Two Cultures', *Sociological Theory*, 17(3): 333–48.

Olick, J. and Robbins, J. (1998) 'Social Memory Studies: From "Collective Memory" to the Historical Sociology of Mnemonic Practices', *Annual Review of Sociology*, 24: 105–40.

Patterson, O. (1998) *Rituals of Blood*. New York: Basic Civitas.

Porter, T. (1995) *Trust in Numbers*. Princeton: Princeton University Press.

Schudson, M. (1993) *Watergate in American Memory*. New York: Basic Books.

Schudson, M. (1998) *Good Citizen*. New York: The Free Press.

Schwartz, B. (2000) *Abraham Lincoln and the Forge of American Memory*. Chicago: University of Chicago Press.

Scott, J. (1985) *Weapons of the Weak*. New Haven: Yale University Press.

Scott, J. (1998) *Seeing Like a State*. New Haven: Yale University Press.

Sewell, W. (2010) 'The Empire of Fashion and the Rise of Capitalism in Eighteenth-Century France', *Past and Present*, 206(1): 81–120.

Simmel, G. (2002 [1903]) 'The Metropolis and Mental Life', in G. Bridge and S. Watson (eds), *The Blackwell City Reader*. Oxford and Walden, MA: Wiley-Blackwell. http://www.blackwellpublishing.com/content/BPL_Images/Content_store/Sample_chapter/0631225137/Bridge.pdf

Spillman, L. (1997) *Nation and Commemoration*. Cambridge and New York: Cambridge University Press.

Steinmetz, G. (1999) *State/Culture: State Formation after the Cultural Turn*. Ithaca, NY: Cornell University Press.

Steinmetz, G. (2007) *The Devil's Handwriting*. Chicago and London: Chicago University Press.

Steinmetz, G. (ed.) (2013) *Sociology and Empire*. Durham and London: Duke University Press.

Tilly, C. (1999) 'Now Where?', in *State/Culture: State Formation after the Cultural Turn*. Ithaca, NY: Cornell University Press.

Wagner-Pacifici, R. (2005) *Art of Surrender*. Chicago: University of Chicago Press.

Weber, M. (1947) *The Theory of Social and Economic Organization*. New York: Free Press.

Zelizer, V. (1985) *Pricing the Priceless Child*. New York: Basic Books.

Zubrzycki, G. (2006) *The Crosses of Auschwitz*. Chicago: University of Chicago Press.

Zukin, S. (1991) *Landscapes of Power: From Detroit to Disney World*. Berkeley: University of California Press.

Zukin, S. (1995) *The Cultures of Cities*. Cambridge, MA: Blackwell.

# PART II
# Methodological Approaches

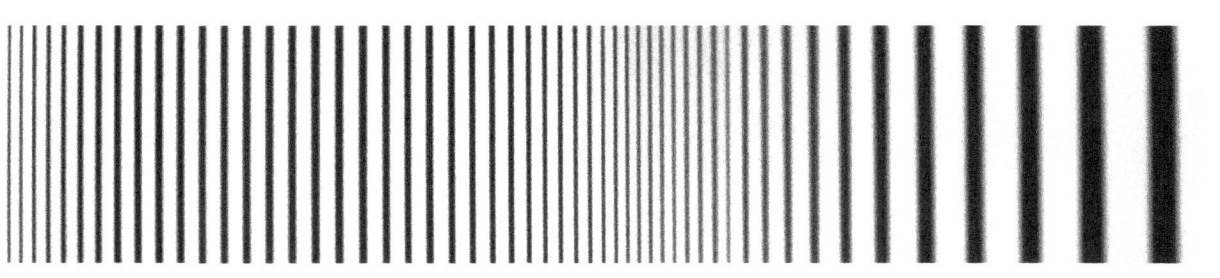

# Quantitative Analysis in Cultural Sociology: Why It Should Be Done, How It Can Be Done

Dick Houtman and Peter Achterberg

## INTRODUCTION: SOCIOLOGY AND CULTURE – AN UNHAPPY MARRIAGE

Sociology took shape in the 19th century as an offshoot of Enlightenment thought, which critiqued religion, tradition, and belief as sources of ignorance and tutelage, conceiving of science, reason, and technology as their superior successors. These Enlightenment roots have had profound and lasting effects on sociology, not least by installing a blind spot for culture (Houtman, 2003). In the hands of sociologists, culture got the connotation of premodern backwardness or even stupidity: it came to be understood as a lack of rational insight into the true nature of things – as the misunderstandings that people needed to be liberated from to enable the light of reason to shine and to make social progress possible (Seidman, 1994: 19–53).

This blind spot for culture still exists today, as can be seen from the notion of 'modernization', which was introduced in the mid-20th century by American sociologists to refer to the social transformations already studied by their classical predecessors. Until the present day, 'modernization' refers hardly, and certainly not in the first place, to processes of cultural change. It is primarily understood as a process of economic and technological change that especially takes place in the realms of work and organization and that is ultimately driven by new scientific knowledge and technological inventions. In their textbook *Sociology: A Global Introduction*, to cite just one example, Macionis and Plummer (1997: 673) define 'modernity' as 'social patterns linked to industrialization' and 'modernization' as 'the process of social change initiated by industrialization'. This example could effortlessly be replaced by many others with the same effect: that industrial (or post-industrial) order is seen as constituting the major characteristic of modernity, from which its cultural features follow more or less logically and automatically.

We understand cultural sociology as a necessary correction to this intellectual marginalization of culture and expand in what follows on the methodological requirements of such a correction. After an elaboration of the sociological habit of relegating culture to the status of something less relevant than economic and technological factors, we argue that for cultural sociology to successfully reconstruct and rejuvenate the discipline as a whole it should not define itself as just another specialization (besides political sociology, sociology of religion, sociology of work and organization, sociology of crime and deviance, etc.) in an already overly fragmented discipline, but rather as a general and substantially non-specialized sociology. Its principal ambition should be to demonstrate to non-cultural sociologists, and indeed to researchers in disciplines beyond sociology and the social sciences, that taking culture more seriously yields increases in explanatory potential.

As we see it, such an endeavor requires a deployment of the quantitative methods that are so strongly emphasized in mainstream sociology and other disciplines. Drawing on examples from our own work of the past ten years, we demonstrate how the classical sociologies of Max Weber and Emile Durkheim can be used to inform quantitative cultural-sociological studies that demonstrate culture's explanatory potential by means of survey research and experimental research respectively.

## THE PROMISE OF CULTURAL SOCIOLOGY

### Sociology's Positivist Legacy and its Blind Spot for Culture

It is telling that most introductory textbooks in sociology do not mention that Auguste Comte, founder of positivism and godfather of sociology, later in his life also founded a pseudo-scientific positivist 'Religion of Humanity', proclaiming himself its pontiff. For later sociologists, this was indeed quite embarrassing, not least because Comte was not just another sociologist – in the United States at the beginning of the 20th century he was even the most often cited sociologist after Herbert Spencer (Hart, 1927). This makes it understandable, as Hadden (1987: 590) and Seidman (1994: 31–2) point out, that later sociologists have often dismissed his shenanigans as an unfortunate accident that had in itself nothing to do with the nature of his positivist sociology. Alvin Gouldner (1970: 88–108), however, gives good reasons to assume that the two were intimately connected so that it is not merely a coincidence that Comte attempted to change sociology into a religion – Comte, who was so convinced that superior 'scientific knowledge' could, would and should replace 'religious belief'.

More important, but also often unacknowledged, is the circumstance that the sociologies of Karl Marx and Emile Durkheim, the discipline's two classical founders besides Max Weber, also share the scientistic pretension of being able to scientifically ground morality. Marx and Durkheim, too, consider it their assignment to evaluate people's beliefs and cultural understandings in the light of rational scientific insight into what social life in modern society 'really' or 'essentially' is, and to reconstruct the former on the basis of the latter if it is found wanting. They both follow the same logic in doing so: they derive their evaluations of what is 'abnormal' and what is not, of what is 'good' and what is 'bad', from an alleged insight in the nature of a 'real' social reality situated 'beyond' or 'underneath' the mystifying and concealing realm of culture (Houtman, 2003: 3–9; 2008). As to the exact nature of that 'real' and 'more fundamental' reality, they both point at the industrial division of labor, even though they imagine the latter quite differently.

For Durkheim, the industrial division of labor under 'normal' circumstances constitutes a realm of shared interests and harmonious cooperation between labor and capital; for Marx, contrariwise, it is under 'normal' circumstances the realm of industrial conflict, struggle, and exploitation, due to irreconcilable class-based economic interests. Whereas for Marx class struggle and exploitation are hence 'normal', and harmonious and peaceful cooperation between labor and capital 'abnormal', Durkheim remarkably enough asserts exactly the reverse. Both Marx and Durkheim thus pretend to be sitting on God's lap, so to say, enabling them to fathom social reality as it 'really' is, in a way inaccessible to ordinary mortals and thus enabling them to distinguish 'normal' from 'pathological' (Durkheim) and 'true' from 'false' (Marx) class consciousness. Because of this scientific and positivist pretension of being able to identify in an intellectually authoritative fashion the degree of rationality of the beliefs, understandings, and behaviors of the participants in social life, and to scientifically ground a morality that can and should replace the latter if they are found wanting, their sociologies have clear traits of secular religions, too. In both cases we are dealing with value judgments disguised as scientific knowledge – value judgments that underscore that the notion that science can and should replace culture and religion remains in no way confined to Auguste Comte (Seidman, 1994: 19–53).

### The Cultural Turn in Sociology

In our understanding, overcoming such a positivist and patronizing understanding of social actors' cultural meanings constitutes the principal promise of cultural sociology. The cultural turn in sociology that has taken shape as a reaction to the crisis of sociology of the 1960s and 1970s aims to accomplish this by giving actors' cultural understandings their full due by placing them at the heart of empirical research. Friedland and Mohr (2004: 4) rightly point out that such a cultural turn augurs nothing less than 'a paradigm shift': 'What we are experiencing ... can be ... understood ... as a recognition of the empirical, theoretical, methodological, and ontological limits of existing intellectual frameworks'.

Such a cultural sociology places the cultural meanings and understandings of those who are studied central stage, while the role of allegedly 'more true' interpretations and evaluations on the part of the researcher is significantly reduced. In the words of Sherwood et al. (1993: 375): 'The question ... should not be how to demystify culture by showing that it 'really' represents something else, but rather how culture allows contemporary actors continually to remystify their social worlds'. Cultural sociology's principal distinguishing feature is hence its recognition that social life cannot have any 'deeper' meanings than those of the participants in social life themselves. Cultural sociology hence refuses to understand culture as merely a '"soft", not really independent variable' and to assume that 'explanatory power lies in the study of the "hard" variables of social structure, such that structured sets of meanings become superstructures and ideologies driven by these more 'real' and tangible social forces' (Alexander and Smith, 2003: 13). It understands culture no longer as something that needs to be understood in terms of something non-cultural, for example as 'the wagging tail of social power, as resistance to hegemony, disguised governmentality, organizational isomorphism, cultural capital, or symbolic politics' (Alexander, 2010: 283).

This type of cultural sociology has become a thriving endeavor since the 1980s, with increasing numbers of university chairs dedicated to it, increasing numbers of researchers joining the bandwagon, and increasingly thriving sections in sociological associations like the American, European and International ones. Yet, as we see it, there are also reasons for concern. Firstly, a disproportionate chunk of cultural-sociological research effort remains confined to the fairly limited and narrowly defined domain of art, popular culture, and media. There is nothing wrong with these research topics in themselves, of course, but more thematic variation is urgently called for, with special attention to research themes that are central to mainstream sociology, like social stratification and politics, to enable cultural sociology to redeem its promise of improving sociology by 'culturalizing' it. A second reason for concern, in actual research practice quite closely related to the former, is cultural sociology's self-imposed restriction to a narrowly defined set of research methods that are conventionally identified with the study of culture, for example ethnography, in-depth interviewing, qualitative content analysis, and discourse analysis. Although we are obviously not 'against' qualitative methodologies like these, and have indeed often relied on them in our own cultural-sociological studies (e.g., Aupers et al., 2012; Harambam et al., 2011; O'Neill et al., 2014), they appear to invite overly descriptive empirical studies that fail to make a clear theoretical contribution and fail to deliver much in terms of sociological explanation. Along related lines, the massive influence in cultural sociology of Clifford Geertz's (1973: 3–30) plea for 'thick description' has been critiqued as stimulating a 'move away from general explanatory theory and towards the fleeting, local and contextual' (Smith, 2008: 171).

This is why we want to stand up for a solid explanatory cultural sociology that addresses the broader social consequences of social actors' cultural meanings and understandings. If sociology's major shortcoming has traditionally been its dismissal of culture as a mere 'side issue' and a necessarily 'dependent' variable, then one has to wonder whether descriptive ethnographic research offers much of a solution. In our opinion, this is not the case, which calls for research that aims to go beyond description, reverses the customary causal order, and explicitly assigns culture an explanatory role as an 'independent' variable. Moreover, if such an intellectual endeavor is to be more than just another sociological sub-field or specialization, two other things are vital as well. Firstly, to convince not only non-cultural sociologists of culture's explanatory potential, but, if possible, researchers in disciplines like cognitive psychology and medicine as well, taking seriously the ('hard') methodologies used in these circles is essential (Perrin, 2004; Steensland, 2009). Secondly, it is also vital to remain in constant critical dialogue with the theoretical tradition of sociology rather than to completely discard the latter and exchange it for more or less fashionable theoretical ideas from the humanities (postmodernism, poststructuralism, semiotics, etc.). In our opinion, such an exchange is not even necessary, because the classical cultural sociologies of Max Weber and Emile Durkheim, largely coinciding with their sociologies of religion (Durkheim, 1965 [1912]; Weber, 1963 [1922]), offer some simple and powerful insights that can, without major difficulties, be adopted to inform quantitative cultural-sociological studies that powerfully demonstrate culture's causal consequences. More specifically, we argue that Weber's cultural sociology can be used to inform survey research that gives social actors' motives their causal due, whereas Durkheim's treatment of culture as a social fact that guides feeling, thinking, and knowing can inform experimental research that demonstrates culture's causal efficacy. In both cases we provide illustrations from our own work of the past ten years.

# SURVEY RESEARCH AND THE WEBERIAN LEGACY: CULTURAL MOTIVES FOR SOCIAL ACTION

## Cultural Sociology's Skepticism about Survey Research: A Weberian Reconstruction

Cultural sociologists tend to be skeptical about survey methodology for two principal reasons. The first is the major influence exerted by the researcher's theoretical preconceptions on the findings that may or may not be attained. The second is the tendency to conceive of people's cultural understandings – measured as 'values', 'attitudes', or 'opinions' – as 'determined by' their 'social status' or 'social position', conceived as an 'objective' variable that determines the aforementioned 'subjective' variables.

The first objection to survey research is in itself valid. It is after all the researcher who decides on the questions to be included in the questionnaire, the response categories to be used for each of these questions, and the variables that are taken to be the 'dependent' and 'independent' ones. This objection assumes, however, that sociological research should always and necessarily be aimed at the intellectual representation of the culturally informed lifeworlds of those who are studied. This aim is, however, not self-evident and can, as indicated above, even be critiqued for producing massively descriptive studies without much theoretical relevance. To the extent that the testing of sociological theories is accepted as a legitimate and worthwhile enterprise, the influence of the researcher's theoretical preconceptions ceases to be a problem. More than that: it becomes the major strength of survey methodology, because it enables researchers to systematically focus on the variables that matter from the perspective of the theory they want to test. Even though such a theory hence defines most of social reality as theoretically irrelevant, this does not mean that the theory is necessarily invalid. All testable theories are after all one-sided reductions of the full complexity of social reality, but the vital question for empirical research is which of them are empirically tenable and which are not.

Cultural sociologists' second reason for skepticism is the tendency in survey research to either leave out people's cultural understandings as 'distortions of real social reality' or to reduce them to the status of 'dependent variables' that as 'values', 'attitudes', or 'opinions' need to be explained from allegedly 'more fundamental' or 'more real' 'objective' variables like 'social class'. Although this does indeed often occur, it is not inherent to survey research. More than that: survey research that purposefully includes cultural variables and liberates them from their status as necessarily 'dependent' ones, constitutes the most promising way of critiquing such tendencies, if only because it uses a methodological language that is understood and accepted as legitimate by those who are the targets of such critiques. Including cultural variables in survey research thus enables cultural sociologists to go beyond descriptive ethnographic analyses by systematically critiquing theories that fail to take culture seriously enough.

Max Weber's classical sociology provides useful guidelines for enriching survey research by taking culture more seriously. This is because his sociology is based on the notion that sociological analysis should address actors' cultural understandings and motives on the one hand, and the broader social consequences of the actions informed by the latter on the other. According to Weber's historical and comparative sociology, after all, all world religions define paths to salvation, and hence define religious interests and motives that encourage particular types of action, while discouraging others. Religiously informed actions by devout believers subsequently have all sorts of broader social consequences, frequently unintended ones, of which Weber singled out the rationalization of the West for special attention. The *Protestant Ethic and the Spirit of Capitalism* (1978 [1904–1905]) addresses just one single causal link in this much more complex and wide-ranging process. Even though virtually all contemporary sociologists underscore the latter's exemplary status, Colin Campbell (2006) points out just how remarkable it is that at a closer and more critical look hardly any of them follow Weber's acclaimed approach in his or her own research (see also Campbell, 1996).

It is clear that survey methodology cannot do justice to the full complexity, richness and subtlety of Max Weber's historical and comparative sociology. Yet, even the mere inclusion of motives for action, so often left out as irrelevant in survey research, can already make a tremendous difference. It enables survey researchers to replace more or less problematic theoretical assumptions about why people do what they do by a systematic analysis of the actual role of motives in driving social action. We provide an example of our own research into the alleged decline in class voting since World War II. It demonstrates how including motives can be used to test and critique sociological theories that downplay the role of culture. In this case this leads to the remarkable conclusion that the often proclaimed decline in class voting has not even occurred. Instead, the West has witnessed a massive increase in non-economic cultural voting, systematically misinterpreted as a decline in class voting due to the neglect of voting motives.

## *Illustration: The Alleged Decline in Class Voting*

Ever since Marx's classical sociology, the relationship between class and politics has been one of sociology's major research interests. After World War II this sparked a research tradition based on the analysis of survey data and aimed at mapping and explaining differences in the degree to which class drives voting behavior across time and between countries. After Robert Alford's pioneering work in the 1960s, the strength of this relation came to be known as the level of 'class voting' and came to be measured by means of a simple index that was subsequently named after him. It is calculated 'by subtracting the percentage of persons in non-manual occupations voting for "Left" parties from the percentage of manual workers voting for such parties' (Alford, 1967: 80). So, the more frequently workers vote for leftist parties and the less frequently non-workers do so, the higher the Alford index, and the higher the level of class voting.

When a quarter of a century later Clark and Lipset affirmatively answered the question posed in the title of their article 'Are Social Classes Dying?' (1991), their claim was critiqued on mostly methodological grounds. This resulted in the so-called 'Death of Class Debate' that raged for more than ten years. Critics maintained that even though calculating the Alford index is in itself simple enough, the study of between-country and over-time variations entails methodological complications that demand more sophisticated statistical procedures (e.g., Hout et al., 1993). Even though this emphasis on statistics is in itself not surprising, because it constitutes one of the defining features of mainstream quantitative sociology, in this case – and doubtlessly in many others, too – it obscured major theoretical shortcomings in most of the empirical studies that the debate evoked, especially the neglect of voting motives.

This neglect of voting motives is in a way surprising, because researchers in this field have of course always had clear ideas about this. Under the heading 'Why Expect Class Voting?', for instance, Alford wrote in the 1960s:

> A relation between class position and voting behavior is a natural and expected association in the Western democracies for a number of reasons: the existence of class interests, the representation of these interests by political parties, and the regular association of certain parties with certain interests. Given the character of the stratification order and the way political parties act as representatives of different class interests, it would be remarkable if such a relation were not found. (1967: 68–69)

Because different classes have different economic interests that are promoted by different parties, people are hence held to vote for the party that best promotes their own economic interests. In the words of Lipset et al. (1954: 1136), 'The lower-income groups will support [the leftist parties] in order to become better off, whereas the higher-income groups will oppose them in order to maintain their economic advantages'. What was assumed, in short, was that the working class voted for leftist parties because it was in favor of economic redistribution, whereas the middle class opposed these parties, because it rejected this political aim.

Research findings by Paul Nieuwbeerta (1995), reprinted in two edited books with the most relevant research findings the debate has sparked – *The End of Class Politics?* (Evans, 1999) and *The Breakdown of Class Politics* (Clark and Lipset, 2001) – have done much to demonstrate that the methodological critiques by Hout et al. (1993) were futile. The use of more advanced statistics and data from more years and more countries, Nieuwbeerta demonstrated, produced basically the same conclusions in terms of differences between countries and the decline in class voting. Much more importantly, but unfortunately also much less acknowledged, is that Nieuwbeerta's attempt to explain these differences and this decline from socio-economic context variables derived from a class-theoretical framework failed miserably: virtually all hypotheses were refuted (Nieuwbeerta, 1995: 57–77).

Our own studies of the alleged decline in class voting have meanwhile demonstrated why Nieuwbeerta's results were so disappointing. The principal cause is that the obsession with statistics in the 'Death of Class Debate' has obscured significant theoretical weaknesses and shortcomings, especially caused by the complete neglect of voting motives. Including these motives in our own research quickly revealed that the newly grown consensus of a decline in class voting in Western countries had in fact been built on quicksand (Achterberg, 2006; Houtman, 2001; 2003; Van der Waal et al., 2007).

Figure 16.1 demonstrates why this is so. It features a conceptualization of voting that gives two voting motives their due. It firstly inserts the voting motive that has always been assumed, i.e., 'economic conservatism'. The type of 'class

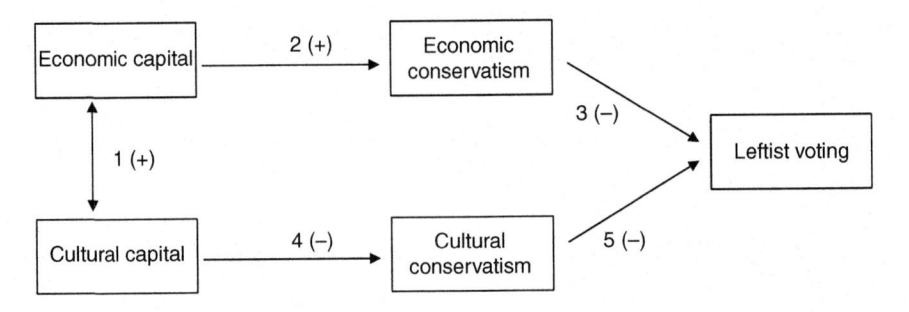

**Figure 16.1 Distinguishing class voting (path 2 × path 3) from cultural voting (path 4 × path 5)**

voting' that the Alford index and its statistically more advanced offspring aim to capture is hence represented by the upper part of Figure 16.1. It can be defined as voting for a leftist or rightist political party on the grounds of economically progressive or conservative political values that are generated by, respectively, a weak or a strong class position. Figure 16.1 also introduces a second voting motive, referred to as 'cultural conservatism'. Among the general public it is basically unrelated to economic conservatism and unlike the latter it is also unrelated to class in an economic sense, i.e., to 'economic capital' in Bourdieu's (1984) sense. Yet, it is closely related to what Bourdieu calls 'cultural capital', measured in our research as high levels of education and participation in highbrow culture, either combined or as two separate variables (Houtman, 2001; 2003). The lower part of Figure 16.1 hence represents what we call 'cultural voting', i.e., voting for a leftist or rightist political party on the grounds of culturally progressive or conservative political values, respectively, grounded not so much in economic capital, but in cultural capital.

Employing this simple model of voting, our research has demonstrated that what has happened in Western countries since World War II is not so much a decline in class voting, but rather a massive increase in cultural voting. Whereas class voting has remained more or less stable during this period, cultural elites (and decidedly not economic ones) have become increasingly likely to vote for leftist or progressive parties for reasons of cultural progressiveness (tolerance, multiculturalism, cosmopolitanism, postmaterialism or however one prefers to call it), whereas those without cultural capital (and decidedly not the poor) have become more and more likely to vote for rightist ones on the basis of culturally conservative motives (authoritarianism, ethnocentrism, nationalism, or however one prefers to call it). Due to the widespread and routine use of the Alford index, which neglects the role of voting motives, political sociologists have hence mistaken a massive increase in cultural voting for a decline in class voting (Houtman and Achterberg, 2010; Van der Waal et al, 2007). Small wonder, then, that Nieuwbeerta's attempt to explain differences in 'class voting' failed: what he recorded were not even differences in class voting in the first place.

## EXPERIMENTAL RESEARCH AND THE DURKHEIMIAN LEGACY: CULTURE AS A SOCIAL FACT

### Cultural Sociology's Skepticism about Experimental Research: A Durkheimian Reconstruction

Consistent with his positivist leanings in *The Division of Labor in Society* (1964 [1893]), *Suicide* (1951 [1897]), and *The Rules of Sociological Method* (1964 [1895]), the early Durkheim has strongly influenced mainstream positivist sociology. The cultural sociology of the late Durkheim of *The Elementary Forms of Religious Life* (1965 [1912]) and (with Mauss) *Primitive Classification* (1963 [1903]), on the other hand, has had much less of an influence on mainstream sociology (apart from the sociology of religion, that is) and much more so on anthropology (Fenton and Hamnett, 1984). *The Elementary Forms of Religious Life* (1965 [1912]) and *Primitive Classification* (Durkheim and Mauss, 1963 [1903]) both trace the fundamental cultural categories that structure a group's thinking and cognition to its social organization. This notion has further been elaborated in Mary Douglas' work (e.g. 1966), which because of that has become a major reference point for cultural sociologists in and of itself.

Douglas' Durkheimian theory of risk, mostly referred to as 'cultural theory', outlines how risk perceptions pertaining to technology and the environment are informed by cultural worldviews that stem from the strictness of definitions of group membership ('group') and the strictness of role definitions ('grid') (Douglas, 1992; Douglas and Wildavsky, 1982). The theory can be critiqued for exaggerating the institutional and social-organizational embeddedness of cultural worldviews (e.g. Kahan, 2012), much like John Fiske (1987) and Stuart Hall (1980 [1973]) in cultural studies can be critiqued for making too strong a priori assumptions about the rootedness of interpretive cultural frames in the structure of capitalist society and the inequalities it engenders. The effect is the same in both cases, i.e., 'pushing 'cultural studies' from the domain of meaning into that of social structure', as Sherwood et al. (1993: 372) observe in the case of cultural studies. Be that as it may, cultural worldviews not only provide social actors with motives for conscious value-rational action, as posited by Weber, but also operate as 'social facts' in a pre-reflexive fashion, 'behind the backs' of those concerned. This Durkheimian notion provides a second powerful classical sociological point of departure for quantitative cultural-sociological research.

Culture plays a role in matters of health and illness, for example, as exemplified by a study that demonstrates that Chinese-Americans, but not whites, tend to die earlier than expected if they feature a combination of disease and birth year that is considered ill-fated in Chinese astrology and medicine. The difference is statistically significant, exists across nearly all major causes of death, amounts to no less than a couple of years, and is larger if those concerned are more firmly embedded in Chinese culture and traditions (Phillips et al., 1993). This is a good example of a powerful consequence of culture that cannot be demonstrated by means of ethnography. The latter is hence not one of the strongest, but one of the weakest methodologies for redeeming cultural sociology's promise of liberating culture from its subordinate position as a side issue and a 'dependent variable'. By far the strongest methodology for doing so is ironically the experiment, a methodology that cultural sociologists tend to be even more skeptical about than survey methodology.

Without doubt, cultural sociology's cold feet about experimental research stem to a large extent from the latter's routine use for wiping out culture as a source of 'distortion' that allegedly prevents researchers from obtaining an 'objective' image of the 'real' and 'undistorted' effect of an independent variable (referred to as an 'experimental condition' or 'treatment variable' in these circles) on a dependent one (referred to as an 'outcome variable' in these circles). Such a positivist treatment of culture as a 'source of distortion' rather than the symbolic universe with which humankind distinguishes itself from other living creatures is obviously hard to swallow for students of culture. Yet, the felt methodological necessity of wiping out culture's distorting influences does of course underscore precisely culture's consequences, conceived in a Durkheimian fashion. 'Placebo effects' in healing processes and in 'double-blind' medical trials, for instance, are effects of culture. More specifically, they are the effects of the trust that patients put in particular types of medical drugs, treatments, or doctors. They are, in Harrington's words (1997: 1), 'the ghosts that haunt our house of biomedical objectivity, the creatures that rise up from the dark and expose the paradoxes and fissures in our own self-created definitions of the real and active factors in treatment'.

The felt necessity of experimentally wiping out culture's allegedly distorting influences even implies that 'culturally enriched' experiments constitute a powerful cultural-sociological tool for demonstrating culture's causal efficacy, even in matters of health and life and death. All that is needed for this is a cultural enrichment of experiments by exposing not one single randomly selected group of test persons to the experimental and control conditions, but two groups that differ from one another in a cultural sense deemed relevant for the experiment at hand. Such experiments enable cultural sociologists to study in a systematic fashion whether different culturally defined groups react differently to, for instance, violent computer games, pornographic movies, leftist or rightist political messages, or 'alternative' medical treatments informed by holistic worldviews, due to culturally mediated differences in interpretation and understanding.

An example would be a research design with two culturally contrasting groups of patients with a particular disease, with one adhering to a holistic worldview and featuring low trust in conventional and high trust in alternative medicine, and another adhering strongly to the rationalist worldview that underlies biomedicine and featuring high trust in conventional and low trust in alternative medicine. One can then give one random half of both groups a conventional medical drug or treatment and the two other halves its 'alternative' counterpart. The resulting research design now no longer addresses the question *whether or not* the two treatments differ in effectiveness, but rather *for which of the two groups either of the two treatments works better or worse*. The subsequent statistical analysis of the resulting data hence no longer focuses on the direct effect of the contrast between the experimental and the control condition, but rather on how this contrast interacts with the patients' worldview in affecting healing processes. As we see it, such culturally enriched experiments are methodologically more powerful for demonstrating culture's causal consequences than either ethnographic research or any other available methodological alternative. We provide an illustration from our own recent research that addresses culture's consequences for cognition.

## Illustration: Culturally Mediated Cognition

One of the mainstays in public opinion research is that that people first need to have some elementary understanding of complicated matters before they can actually learn to appreciate them. This idea applies not only to opinions about issues such as the European Union (Anderson, 1998) or the judicial system (Van Gelder et al., 2015), but also to opinions about emerging technologies (Allum et al., 2008). Following this 'to know it, is to love it' maxim, scholars working on this so-called 'knowledge deficit' question, institutional experts, and policymakers have often claimed that the public needs to be given more information to foster its appreciation and support. Such an alleged undifferentiated and unmediated effect of information provision contrasts sharply with our foregoing argument, which assigns more importance to culturally defined worldviews.

For this reason we recently did a survey experiment on informational provision about hydrogen technology. We deliberately chose hydrogen technology for two reasons. The first, of course, is to inform debates about the 'public uptake of science' (Wynne, 1992: 300). The second is that research has shown, time and again, that the public at large is poorly informed about this complex new type of energy technology (Ricci et al., 2008).

The idea that the uptake of information about such complex technologies as hydrogen technology is culturally mediated closely relates to arguments made in the so-called 'framing' literature (Chong and Druckman, 2007; Scheufele, 1999). The basic argument is that frames – 'principles of selection, emphasis and presentation composed of little tacit theories about what exists, what happens, and what matters' (Gitlin, 1980: 6) – vary across people of different backgrounds. This underlies our expectation that groups of people interpret knowledge made available to them on the basis of their cultural worldviews. More specifically, information is most likely to be accepted and translated into support if it suits one's cultural worldview.

Previous experimental research has shown that technological skepticism does indeed affect (or, technically speaking: 'moderates') the effect of informational provision about hydrogen technology considerably (Achterberg, 2014). Here, following a wider research tradition that addresses the links between religious worldviews on the one hand and public support for science and technology on the other (cf. Nisbet and Mooney, 2007), we study whether three religious worldviews affect the acceptance or rejection of information about hydrogen technology. First, White (1967) has suggested that because of their ideas about *dominion* of nature, Christians are less concerned with the environment (which is confirmed in research by Van Bohemen et al., 2012). Second, Christians are also more inclined to think in terms of *stewardship* – the idea that nature and the environment are to be taken care of (which is also confirmed by Van Bohemen et al., 2012). While a dominion worldview would actually give little or no reason to translate information about sustainable types of energy such as hydrogen into support, the second worldview pertaining to stewardship will do just that. Third, we include a non-Christian worldview pertaining to holistic spirituality. People with this worldview support the idea that mankind and nature are, and should be, strongly related, and that nature is a source of spiritual wisdom (Campbell, 2007; Houtman and Mascini, 2002). As both qualitative (Aupers, 2002) and quantitative (Achterberg et al., 2010) research has shown that people with such an holistic spiritual worldview are not at all dismissive of the use of technology, we expect people embracing such a worldview to be inclined to translate positive information about hydrogen technology into support for this type of technology.

Using a representative sample of the Dutch population (2008, N = 1012), we asked the respondents in our survey several Likert-type items tapping the three worldviews (for details on these measures see Achterberg et al., 2010). Then, drawing from a larger pool of 21 questions, we asked each of the respondents to answer a random selection of seven knowledge questions about hydrogen technology. Some of these questions tapped negative facts (facts that would lead to less support for hydrogen, for instance by focusing on the environmental costs of fabricating hydrogen fuel cells) and some of these questions tapped positive aspects (for instance by focusing on the reduction of polluting emissions from hydrogen-fueled vehicles). Then, respondents were given the correct answers to these seven knowledge questions, so that depending on the questions that were randomly assigned respondents differed in the extent to which they were exposed to either positive or negative information. Finally, we asked the respondents five Likert-type items that measured support for hydrogen technology (see Achterberg et al., 2010).

Our results showed that positive information in fact does lead to more support for hydrogen technology. But this does not mean that this effect is identical for everyone. Two of our three suggested worldviews actually conditioned the effects of informational provision. We found that for people who uphold a dominion worldview, informational provision does not lead to higher or lower support for hydrogen technology. Only for those who do not embrace this worldview does the provision of positive information actually lead to an adjustment in their support for hydrogen technology – a clear demonstration of the conditioning influence of this type of worldview. For the stewardship worldview, the results are depicted in Figure 16.2.

Figure 16.2 shows that people with dissimilar worldviews – those who embrace stewardship and those who do not – react totally differently to information about hydrogen technology. For those who underscore the idea of stewardship, positive information leads to more support for hydrogen technology. For those who do not embrace stewardship, the same type of information leads to *less* support for hydrogen technology. In short, the effect of informational provision varies considerably with the religious frames or worldviews that one adheres to. This survey experiment, hence, clearly demonstrates that cognition is in fact culturally mediated.

## CONCLUSION

As a reaction to the so-called 'crisis of sociology' in the 1960s and 1970s cultural sociology has in the past few decades increasingly got the wind in its sails. It embodies a new intellectual modesty by breaking with the positivist pretension of being able to reveal what social and cultural phenomena 'really' mean. As such, it refuses to marginalize, play down, or retouch out culture as 'really' or 'actually' a reflection of an allegedly 'deeper' or 'more fundamental' and essentially non-cultural social reality. This means that cultural sociology is not a thematically and substantially specialized sociology, aimed at the study of the social aspects of art, popular culture, and media, but rather a general sociology aimed at the study of social reality's cultural layers of meaning and the latter's broader social consequences. Its appeal is hence not so much a matter of taste, but rather of intellectual urgency. Hugely influential rational action theory, for instance, tends to make far-reaching assumptions about instrumental-rational motives allegedly driving peoples' actions. Yet, the resulting empirical studies typically refrain from studying whether this is actually the case. As such, these studies remain more speculative than they could and should be, and they are doubtlessly often beside the mark as far as the actual motives for action are concerned. Cultural-sociological survey research, in short, offers a promising way of revealing shortcomings and misinterpretations in mainstream sociological research.

Cultural sociology's intellectual urgency, moreover, transcends the boundaries of sociology and

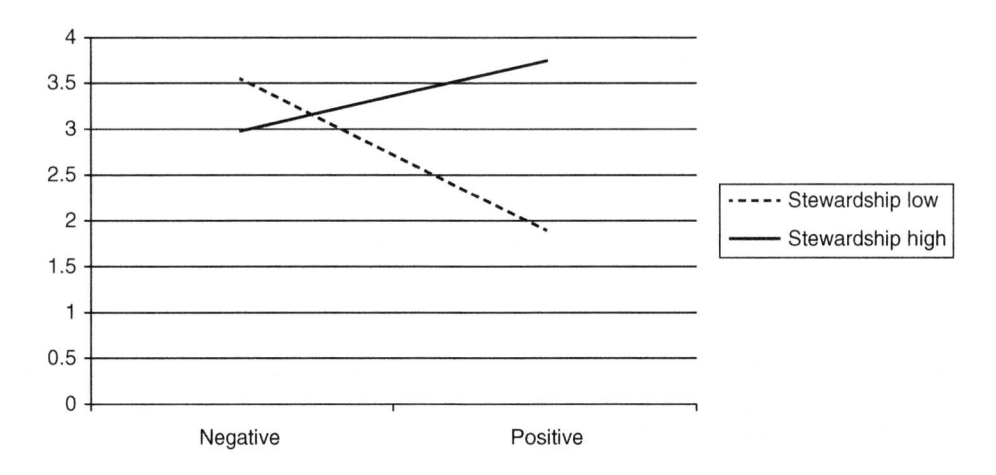

**Figure 16.2 Type of informational provision (x-axis) and predicted support for hydrogen technology (y-axis) for respondents with minimum and maximum levels of stewardship**

extends to other disciplines that have traditionally treated the cultural factor shabbily. In these cases especially, cultural-experimental studies informed by a Durkheimian cultural sociology are called for. An example is the type of psychology that naively assumes that all over the world individuals are in principle identical and hence interchangeable. According to this perspective, it does not really matter whether experimental studies rely on Chinese or European test persons, or whether the latter are well-educated (psychology) students or poorly educated factory workers. A sensational and well-cited article by Henrich et al. (2010), however, demonstrates that all this does make a big difference. In many research areas, ranging from visual perception and spatial reasoning to categorization and inferential induction, psychologists in non-Western parts of the world arrive at very different findings than their Western colleagues. It seems reasonable to assume that this can to a large degree be attributed to cultural differences that cause identical experimental stimuli to evoke very different reactions and consequences. This provides plenty of opportunity and perspective for the type of experimental cultural-sociological research that we have discussed.

Something similar applies to research into the effectiveness of medical treatments. It is quite likely that bio-medical studies that refuse to give cultural differences between patients their due will become increasingly contested in Western multicultural societies that want to recognize these same differences. This may open the gate to medical-cultural-sociological research that no longer aims to study *whether* a particular therapy is effective, but rather *for which culturally defined groups* it works better, worse, or perhaps not at all. Similarly, the circumstance that most of today's alternative medical treatments fail to withstand the test of the double-blind medical trial does not necessarily mean that they do not work for those who believe in them. Conversely, it is also hard to believe that many of the conventional medical treatments are equally effective for those with low trust in Western bio-medicine as for those with high trust in the latter. To the extent that cultural-sociological hypotheses of this type are confirmed in cultural-experimental medical research, we are dealing with powerful causal consequences of culture. Or better: we already know that such effects do exist, because as 'placebo effects' they are responsible for the circumstance that the double-blind medical trial has attained the status of the gold standard in medical research. The only challenge now is to better understand such effects of culture and, if desired, to apply them therapeutically, both of which appear virtually impossible without an input from cultural sociology.

# REFERENCES

Achterberg, P. (2006) *Considering Cultural Conflict: Class Politics and Cultural Politics in Western Societies*. Maastricht: Shaker.

Achterberg, P. (2014) 'Knowing Hydrogen and Loving It Too? Informational Provision, Cultural Predispositions, and Support for Hydrogen Technology Among the Dutch', *Public Understanding of Science*, 23(4): 445–53.

Achterberg, P., Houtman, D., van Bohemen. S. and Manevska, K. (2010) 'Unknowing but Supportive? Predispositions, Knowledge, and Support for Hydrogen Technology in the Netherlands', *International Journal of Hydrogen Energy*, 35: 6075–83.

Alexander, J.C. (2010) *The Performance of Politics: Obama's Victory and the Democratic Struggle for Power*. New York: Oxford University Press.

Alexander, J.C. and Smith, P. (2003) 'The Strong Program in Cultural Sociology: Elements of a Structural Hermeneutics', in J.C. Alexander (ed.), *The Meanings of Social Life: A Cultural Sociology*. Oxford: Oxford University Press. pp. 11–26.

Alford, R.R. (1967) 'Class Voting in the Anglo-American Political Systems', in S.M. Lipset and S. Rokkan (eds), *Party Systems and Voter Alignments: Cross-National Perspectives*. New York: Free Press. pp. 67–93.

Allum, N., Sturgis, P., Tabourazi, D. and Brunton-Smith, I. (2008) 'Science Knowledge and Attitudes across Cultures: A Meta-Analysis', *Public Understanding of Science*, 17: 35–54.

Anderson, C.J. (1998) 'When in Doubt, Use Proxies: Attitudes toward Domestic Politics and Support for European Integration', *Comparative Political Studies*, 31: 367–89.

Aupers, S. (2002) 'The Revenge of the Machines: On Modernity, Digital Technology and Animism', *Asian Journal of Social Science*, 30: 199–221.

Aupers, S., Houtman, D., Achterberg, B., de Koster, W., Mascini, P, Roeland, J. and van der Waal, J. (2012) 'Beyond the Domestication of Nature? Restructuring the Relationship between Nature and Technology in Car Commercials', *European Journal of Cultural Studies*, 15: 3–18.

Bourdieu, P. (1984) *Distinction: A Social Critique of the Judgement of Taste*. London: Routledge and Kegan Paul.

Campbell, C. (1996) *The Myth of Social Action*. Cambridge: Cambridge University Press.

Campbell, C. (2006) 'Do Today's Sociologists Really Appreciate Weber's Essay *The Protestant Ethic and the Spirit of Capitalism?*', *The Sociological Review*, 54: 207–23.

Campbell, C. (2007) *The Easternization of the West: A Thematic Account of Cultural Change in the Modern Era*. Boulder, CO: Paradigm.

Chong, D. and Druckman, J.N. (2007) 'Framing Theory', *Annual Review of Political Science*, 10: 103–26.
Clark, T.M. and Lipset, S.M. (1991) 'Are Social Classes Dying?', *International Sociology*, 6: 397–410.
Clark, T.M. and Lipset, S.M. (eds) (2001) *The Breakdown of Class Politics: A Debate on Post-Industrial Stratification*. Baltimore, MD: Johns Hopkins University Press.
Douglas, M. (1966) *Purity and Danger*. London: Routledge and Kegan Paul.
Douglas, M. (1992) *Risk and Blame: Essays in Cultural Theory*. London: Routledge.
Douglas, M. and Wildavsky, A.B. (1982) *Risk and Culture: An Essay on the Selection of Technical and Environmental Dangers*. Berkeley, CA: University of California Press.
Durkheim, E. (1951 [1897]) *Suicide: A Study in Sociology*. New York: Free Press.
Durkheim, E. (1964 [1893]) *The Division of Labor in Society*. New York: Free Press.
Durkheim, E. (1964 [1895]) *The Rules of Sociological Method*. New York: Free Press.
Durkheim, E. (1965 [1912]) *The Elementary Forms of Religious Life*. New York: Free Press.
Durkheim, E. and Mauss, M. (1963 [1903]) *Primitive Classification*. London: Cohen and West.
Evans, G. (ed.) (1999) *The End of Class Politics? Class Voting in Comparative Context*. Oxford: Oxford University Press.
Fenton, S. and Hamnett, I. (1984) 'Durkheim and the Study of Religion', in S. Fenton (ed.), *Durkheim and Modern Sociology*. Cambridge: Cambridge University Press. pp. 202–18.
Fiske, J. (1987) *Television Culture*. London: Methuen.
Friedland, R. and Mohr, J. (2004) 'The Cultural Turn in American Sociology', in R. Friedland and J. Mohr (eds), *Matters of Culture: Cultural Sociology in Practice*. Cambridge: Cambridge University Press. pp. 1–70.
Geertz, C. (1973) *The Interpretation of Cultures*. New York: Basic Books.
Gitlin, T. (1980) *The Whole World Is Watching: Mass Media in the Making and Unmaking of the New Left*. Berkeley and Los Angeles, CA and London, UK: University of California Press.
Gouldner, A.W. (1970) *The Coming Crisis of Western Sociology*. London: Heinemann.
Hadden, J.K. (1987) 'Toward Desacralizing Secularization Theory', *Social Forces*, 65: 587–611.
Hall, S. (1980 [1973]) 'Encoding/Decoding', in S. Hall, D. Hobson, A. Lowe and P. Willis (eds), *Culture, Media, Language*. London: Hutchinson. pp. 128–39.
Harambam, J., Aupers, S. and Houtman, D. (2011) 'Game Over? Negotiating Modern Capitalism in Online Game Worlds', *European Journal of Cultural Studies*, 14: 299–320.
Harrington, A. (1997) 'Introduction', in A. Harrington (ed.), *The Placebo Effect: An Interdisciplinary Exploration*. Cambridge, MA: Harvard University Press. pp. 1–11.
Hart, H. (1927) 'The History of Social Thought: A Consensus of American Opinion', *Social Forces*, 6: 190–196.
Henrich, J., Heine, S.J. and Norenzayan, A. (2010) 'The Weirdest People in the World?', *Behavioral and Brain Sciences*, 33: 61–83.
Hout, M., Brooks, C. and Manza, J. (1993) 'The Persistence of Classes in Post-Industrial Societies', *International Sociology*, 8: 259–78.
Houtman, D. (2001) 'Class, Culture, and Conservatism: Reassessing Education as a Variable in Political Sociology', in T.N. Clark and S.M. Lipset (eds), *The Breakdown of Class Politics: A Debate on Post-Industrial Stratification*. Baltimore, MD: Johns Hopkins University Press. pp. 161–95.
Houtman, D. (2003) *Class and Politics in Contemporary Social Science: 'Marxism Lite' and Its Blind Spot for Culture*. New York: Aldine de Gruyter.
Houtman, D. (2008) *Op jacht naar de echte werkelijkheid: Dromen over authenticiteit in een wereld zonder fundamenten*. Amsterdam: Pallas.
Houtman, D. and Achterberg, P. (2010) 'Two Lefts and Two Rights: Class Voting and Cultural Voting in the Netherlands, 2002', *Sociologie*, 1: 61–76.
Houtman, D. and Mascini, P. (2002) 'Why Do Churches Become Empty, While New Age Grows? Secularization and Religious Change in the Netherlands', *Journal for the Scientific Study of Religion*, 41: 455–73.
Kahan, D.M. (2012) 'Cultural Cognition as a Conception of the Cultural Theory of Risk', in S. Roeser, R. Hillerbrand, P. Sandin and M. Peterson (eds), *Handbook of Risk Theory: Epistemology, Decision Theory, Ethics, and Social Implications of Risk*. Berlin: Springer. pp. 725–59.
Lipset, S.M., Lazarsfeld, P.F., Barton, A.H. and Linz, J. (1954) 'The Psychology of Voting: An Analysis of Political Behavior', in G. Lindzey (ed.), *Handbook of Social Psychology*. Cambridge, MA: Addison Wesley. pp. 1124–75.
Macionis, J.J. and Plummer, K. (1997) *Sociology: A Global Introduction*. Upper Saddle River, NJ: Prentice Hall.
Nieuwbeerta, P. (1995) *The Democratic Class Struggle in Twenty Countries, 1945–1990*. Amsterdam: Thesis Publishers.
Nisbet, M.C. and Mooney, C. (2007) 'Framing Science', *Science*, 316(5821): 56.
O'Neill, C., Aupers, S. and Houtman, D. (2014) 'Advertising Real Beer: Authenticity Claims beyond

Truth and Falsity', *European Journal of Cultural Studies*, 17(5): 585–601.

Perrin, A.J. (2004) 'Who's Afraid of General Linear Regression?', *Culture*, 18(1): 11–13.

Phillips D.P., Ruth, T.E. and Wagner, L.M. (1993) 'Psychology and Survival', *Lancet*, 342: 1142–5.

Ricci, M., Bellaby, P. and Flynn, R. (2008) 'What Do We Know about Public Perceptions and Acceptance of Hydrogen? A Critical Review and New Case Study Evidence', *International Journal of Hydrogen Energy*, 33: 5868–80.

Scheufele, D.A. (1999) 'Framing as a Theory of Media Effects', *Journal of Communication*, 49: 103–22.

Seidman, S. (1994) *Contested Knowledge: Social Theory in the Postmodern Era*. Cambridge, MA: Blackwell.

Sherwood, S., Smith, P. and Alexander, J.C. (1993) 'The British are Coming ... Again! The Hidden Agenda of "Cultural Studies"', *Contemporary Sociology*, 22: 370–5.

Smith, P. (2008) 'The Balinese Cockfight Decoded: Reflections on Geertz, the Strong Program and Structuralism', *Cultural Sociology*, 2: 169–86.

Steensland, B. (2009) 'Restricted and Elaborated Modes in the Cultural Analysis of Politics', *Sociological Forum*, 24: 926–34.

Van Bohemen, S., Achterberg, P., Houtman, D. and Manevska, K. (2012) 'Spirituality and Environmental Consciousness in the Netherlands: A Comparison of Holistic Spirituality and Christian Dualism', in P. Heelas (ed.), *Spirituality in the Modern World: Within Religious Tradition and Beyond (Volume Four)*. London: Routledge. pp. 164–82.

Van der Waal, J., Achterberg, P. and Houtman, D. (2007) 'Class Is Not Dead – It Has Been Buried Alive: Class Voting and Cultural Voting in Postwar Western Societies (1956–1990)', *Politics and Society*, 35: 403–26.

Van Gelder, J.L., Aarten, P., Lamet, W. and Van der Laan, P. (2015) 'Unknown, Unloved? Public Opinion on and Knowledge of Suspended Sentences in the Netherlands', *Crime and Delinquency*, 61(5): 669–89.

Weber, M. (1963 [1922]) *The Sociology of Religion*. Boston: Beacon Press.

Weber, M. (1978 [1904–1905]) *The Protestant Ethic and the Spirit of Capitalism*. London: Allen and Unwin.

White, L.T. (1967) 'The Historical Roots of Our Ecologic Crisis', *Science*, 155: 1203–7.

Wynne, B. (1992) 'Misunderstood Misunderstanding: Social Identities and Public Uptake of Science', *Public Understanding of Science*, 1: 281–304.

# Qualitative Cultural Sociology

Thomas S. Eberle

## INTRODUCTION

The history of qualitative research has not yet been written, and neither has the history of qualitative cultural sociology. The label *cultural sociology* covers a wide field of theoretical approaches, empirical investigations and applied methods, and it seems daunting to attempt mapping the qualitative research that has been done in this area. Lyn Spillman (2002: 4) suggested that many 'confusions and disputes can be resolved if we consider "culture" as referring to *processes of meaning-making*'. I will follow this suggestion and avoid using an essentialist concept of 'culture'. In line with Max Weber, and with symbolic interactionism and phenomenological sociology, I will primarily focus on how human actors make sense of social actions in the contexts of everyday life situations, and how this can be empirically researched.

Max Weber (1980 [1904]) called his sociological approach explicitly a 'cultural science' (*Kulturwissenschaft*). While Wilhelm Dilthey proclaimed a fundamental distinction between the natural sciences that observe and explain nature, and the human sciences (*Geisteswissenschaften*) that understand human expressions of life, Weber attempted to combine the two methods: Sociology has to understand *and* explain. Following the neo-Kantian Heinrich Rickert, he defined sociology not as a science of the human mind (*Geisteswissenschaft*) but rather of culture (*Kulturwissenschaft*). And culture is whatever human actors endow with meaning. As a cultural science sociology is a *Wirklichkeitswissenschaft*, a science of reality, i.e. a science of cultural, meaningful reality. In other words, sociology is an empirical science that investigates 'real', meaningful social actions.

Sociologists as well as anthropologists studied the meanings of social actions and interactions long before the so-called 'cultural turn.' And as meanings are embedded in concrete contexts and cannot be detached from those without losing essential information, all empirical research on processes of sense-making is 'qualitative' in character or, as I prefer, 'interpretive'. In this chapter I am going to focus on fundamental methodological issues rather than on particular empirical research methods used in cultural sociology. And I attempt to avoid major overlaps with topics that are covered by chapters of this handbook. First, I start with the ascent of qualitative research with the so-called 'Chicago School'. Second, I discuss the resurgence of the interpretive paradigm in the 1960s after a distinct dominance of the positivist, normative paradigm. This includes Symbolic Interactionism, the proclamation of 'grounded theory', and the interactionist, ethnographic studies of the Second and Third Chicago Schools. Third, I discuss Alfred Schutz's attempt to give a philosophical foundation to Max Weber's *Verstehende* Sociology. His phenomenological life-world analysis had a great impact on cultural sociology through its three major offsprings: ethnomethodology, phenomenological sociology, and the new sociology of knowledge by Berger and Luckmann. Fourth, new developments in qualitative cultural sociology are outlined, followed by a conclusion.

## THE ASCENT OF QUALITATIVE SOCIAL RESEARCH: THE 'CHICAGO SCHOOL' OF SOCIOLOGY

From its foundation in 1892, the University of Chicago featured a department of sociology, the first of its kind in the world. Between 1915 and 1940 it dominated sociology in the United States by moving from social philosophy and general theory to first-hand empirical investigation of society. Qualitative social research was born and developed, and programs of collaborative research between teachers and graduate students were carried out, supported by large-scale research grants.

### *Thomas and Znaniecki's The Polish Peasant in Europe and America*

'The significance of the publication of *The Polish Peasant* can hardly be exaggerated' (Bulmer 1984: 45); it signaled the advent of the Chicago School. While the first generation of sociologists was primarily dedicated to sociological theory, it was only William Isaac Thomas (1863–1947) who was wholeheartedly committed to empirical research. After his PhD at the University of Chicago in 1896, he conducted field work in Europe in order to write a comparative study of European nationalities (which was never completed). In the same year he became assistant professor, in 1900 associate professor and in 1910 full professor at the department of sociology. In 1908, he received a substantial grant from the Helen Culver fund to finance research on the lives and culture of immigrants for ten years. He eventually decided to focus his research on Polish immigrants as they represented the largest and most visible immigrant community in Chicago. In addition, their behaviors often appeared incomprehensible to others. Thomas undertook many journeys to Europe, especially to Poland, in order to study the immigrants' country and culture of origin, and he learned the Polish language. In 1913 he met in Warsaw Florian Znaniecki (1882–1958) who had studied philosophy with Henri Bergson. When World War I broke out, Znaniecki moved to Chicago and became Thomas' research assistant and, after a most prolific cooperation, the co-author of *The Polish Peasant*.

The approach was innovative in several respects. First, Thomas moved research out of the library into the field. His main method was collecting personal documents such as letters, diaries and life histories, in Chicago as well as in Poland. The use of such firsthand documentary materials was quite original and constituted the main methodological innovation. Other documents such as materials from agencies and courts, newspaper articles and brochures, were used as complementary data. Thomas was quite critical of using interviews as these are social processes themselves; nevertheless, both authors also relied on middle class informants such as social workers, doctors, teachers and editors.

The second innovative aspect is the theoretical approach: Thomas and Znaniecki developed a biographical approach to researching culture. Personal documents were used as a means to understand the world from the point of view of the immigrant, to explore how s/he perceives the social world, not how the scientist sees it. Social change was conceived as the product of continual interaction between subjective consciousness and objective features of social reality. Thomas attempted to relate the two by the concepts of (subjective) attitude and (objective) social values. An adequate social theory must include the subjective as well as the objective aspects.

*The Polish Peasant in Europe and America* (Thomas and Znaniecki 1918–1920) was published in five volumes between 1918 and 1920 with a total of 2232 pages. The first volume starts with an extensive methodological note and then describes the social and cultural conditions of peasants' lives in Poland. Then the letters are presented in 50 series, one tranche in Volume I and the rest in Volume II. The series contain letters between family members and tell of many aspects of social life, even quite emotional elements, sometimes involving dramatic family conflicts between the emigrated children and their parents who stayed at home. Each series is introduced by a chapter that describes the involved characters and interprets what is going on in the presented series of letters. In Volume III the life record of one immigrant, Władysław Wiśniewski, is presented. In all these empirical forms of evidence of how the writing subjects experienced social change in their traditional as well as in the immigration community, the impacts of industrialization and emigration are manifested. Based on these documents, the disorganization of the traditional Polish peasant families and communities and their partial rational reorganization are analyzed in Volume IV, and in Volume V the disorganization of the Polish immigration community as well as its reorganization is examined. Thus Thomas and Znaniecki present a macrosociological study composed of descriptions of concrete life-worlds. The macrosociological changes are mirrored in the lives of the letter-writers: the decline of the traditional family and local community, immigration, racism, crime and drug abuse, mobility, and the change of gender relations; but also nationalism, social stratification and class structure, democracy and efficiency, even good luck. Furthermore, phenomena such as urbanization, industrialization, and the interdependence of institutions are captured. Similar to Durkheim, social cohesion in the face of increasing individualization and mobility is a central topic; but contrary to Durkheim this is studied in terms of the lives of concrete people, from their subjective viewpoints', and how this is experienced by actors. Consequently, Durkheim's *Rules of Sociological Method* (1982 [1895]) are criticized in Thomas and Znanieski's 'methodological note' (in Vol. I): not the view of the scientist but the view of the actors are said to constitute the relevant data.

Lewis Coser calls *The Polish Peasant* 'the first great classic in American empirical sociology' (1977: 381). Bulmer (1984: 45ff.) writes that it was a landmark in several respects: It employed novel methods, blended theory and data in a way no American study had done before, and, by focusing on immigration as the subject of study, helped to establish sociology as an autonomous academic discipline. In contrast to the moral fervour of the reformist movement and its desire to change society, Thomas's approach was scientific, unemotional and detached, motivated by the desire to understand human behaviour while not morally judging it. Bulmer also emphasizes what is often overlooked – that this study was also path-breaking in two further respects: Thomas got substantial outside funding and pursued research as a collaborative enterprise. In 1918 Thomas was dismissed from the university for non-academic reasons and later taught at the New School of Social Research in New York. He continued to produce seminal research; the famous 'Thomas theorem', 'if men define situations as real, they are real in their consequences', was formulated only later by W.I. Thomas and D.S. Thomas (1928: 553–576) in their study *The Child in America*.

In his review of *The Polish Peasant*, Herbert Blumer (1939) writes that the theoretical and methodological conception was crucial, especially catching human experiences' and subjective factors. The Peasant study was only an application of this scheme. He further points out that there is a problem in regard to the relation between Thomas and Znaniecki's materials and their theoretical analysis; their interpretations often go far beyond the data. Blumer then discusses the validity of interpretations, and argues that interpretations cannot be 'tested' but can be assessed by the criterion that only superior competence and familiarity with the subject can enable critical evaluation.

## Field Research Methods

The field work the Chicago School has become famous for was mainly developed by Park and Burgess in the 1920s and 1930s. While Thomas and Znaniecki primarily relied on personal documents, Park and Burgess used in addition participant observation and informal interviewing. Robert E. Park had studied with John Dewey and later with William James. From 1887 to 1898 he worked as a newspaper reporter; he thereby gained intimate acquaintance with many facets of urban scenes. Park enjoyed 'nosing around' and developed it into an empirical art form, and he saw clear parallels between the work of a newspaper reporter and that of a sociologist: 'One might fairly say that a sociologist is merely a more accurate, responsible, and scientific reporter' (Park 1939, cited by Bulmer 1984: 91). Park had also strong theoretical interests; he studied in Germany with Georg Simmel and got his doctoral degree under Wilhelm Windelband at the University of Heidelberg. He joined the Department of Sociology at the University of Chicago as a lecturer in 1914, and from 1923 to 1933 he was a full professor. He collaborated closely with W.I. Thomas and shared his view that the subjective point of view of the actor is crucial for sociological research, and that one has to investigate the meaning of other people's lives. Real understanding required that a sociologist participated in the lives of others and that he or she had empathy as well as visual acuity. W.I. Thomas made Park familiar with some anthropological writing and he explicitly suggested that the methods that anthropologists like Franz Boas and others had developed for researching indigenous groups could be fruitfully employed for doing urban studies.

Ernest Burgess had studied sociology at the University of Chicago and returned there as a faculty member in 1916. He shared an office with Robert Park and they developed a most fruitful collaboration, which contributed to the intense intellectual climate of Chicago sociology. They published a textbook, *Introduction to the Science of Sociology* (Park and Burgess 1921) that became one of the most influential sociology textbooks ever written. Although Burgess as the younger colleague was much influenced by Park, in regard to research methods he is said to be 'the more involved and original thinker, giving concrete form to Park's general methodological ideas' (Bulmer 1984: 94). Both insisted on gathering data at first hand in natural settings, and their main instrument was their graduate seminar on field studies. The graduate students did the empirical research and Park and Burgess spent a considerable amount of time in close supervision. The research of the Chicago School consisted in a series of monographs, like *The Negro in Chicago, The Hobo, The Ghetto, The Gold Coast and the Slum, The Gang, The Taxi-Dance Hall, The Pilgrims of Russian Town,* and many more (for a list see Bulmer 1984 3–4; for an excellent overview of their significance cf. Faris 1967; cf. also Deegan 2007). None of these research projects relied on a single method; all of them had a multi-method approach, like participant observation, interviewing of various kinds, and the use of personal and public documents. Firsthand contact with the subjects of research was considered essential. At the same time, considerable emphasis was given to theoretical reflections as the underlying purpose of all these studies was scientific generalization.

Neither Park nor Burgess codified their catholic, multimethod approach. The different methods were considered as complementary – each contributed to the mosaic of knowledge. Crucial was openness as well as intellectual curiosity. In 1928 Vivian Palmer, a senior research worker on the programme of urban research, wrote the text *Field Studies in Sociology: A Student's Manual*. This was one of the earliest texts on research methods in American sociology. Each method was presented as having its strengths and weaknesses; Palmer also emphasized their complementarity. The book was inductive and classificatory and suffered from a strong concept of generalization. Bulmer (1984: 122) concludes that the weaknesses of this conception of science are apparent: the impressive case studies lacked a cumulative scientific force, which paved the way for the decline of the Chicago School (cf. also Plummer 1997).

## THE RESURGENCE OF THE 'INTERPRETIVE PARADIGM' IN THE 1960S

While the Chicago School dominated American sociology between 1915 and 1940, it became increasingly challenged and eventually marginalized by two major rivals: the Universities of Harvard and Columbia. Harvard became famous for Talcott Parsons' structural functionalism, a 'grand theory' that would be universally applicable. The main emphasis was given to elaborated theory, and empirical research was designed exclusively within a theoretical framework. The rise of Columbia was due to Robert Merton's middle-range theories and Paul Lazarsfeld's 'modern' survey research and opinion polling. Some call Lazarsfeld 'the founder of modern empirical sociology' (Jeábek 2001). Both strands impressed with their ambitious claims: both had a positivist stance and strived for closing the gap between natural and social sciences. An objective research of objective facts was the goal, subjective contaminations were to be eliminated. Popper's (1935) radical distinction between the 'logic of discovery' and the 'logic of justification' discredited the inductionism of field research and proclaimed a 'strong' conception of science – empirical research had to be framed by preconceived theoretical concepts, propositions deduced from theory and hypotheses put to a 'test'. This version of a 'scientific' sociology as a discipline organized around quantitative methods, became very influential both in research and journals' publication policies as well as on student curricula. It also spread into Europe after World War II as 'the modern American sociology'. 'Data' was increasingly equated with numbers, data analysis with statistics, research methods with survey designs and research papers with mathematical equations.

The field research of the Chicago School proceeded, but in the shadow of quantitative sociology. In the 1960s, however, it became more and more apparent that neither the structural functionalist 'grand theory' nor modern survey methods could fulfill their ambitious promises. The main reason for their failure was that both ignored or downplayed the *problem of meaning* in sociological research. In view of this development, Alvin Gouldner (1970) diagnosed *The Coming Crisis of Western Sociology*. Indeed, there occurred a resurgence of qualitative research and of interpretive methodologies such as symbolic interactionism, phenomenological sociology and hermeneutics. In the following decades we can observe an increasing legitimation and institutionalization of the interpretive paradigm, along with qualitative methods – in European more than in US sociology, where positivism and a quali-quanti-divide still prevail.

### Symbolic Interactionism

A crucial event for the resurgence of the interpretive paradigm was Blumer's programmatic essay

'The Methodological Position of Symbolic Interactionism' (1969), published together with other essays on the topic. Blumer, a student of George Herbert Mead, had coined the term 'Symbolic Interactionism' (SI) in 1937 as 'a somewhat barbaric neologism' (Blumer 1937; cf. Blumer 1969: 1, Fn). Blumer had left Chicago in 1952 to build up the newly formed Sociology Department at the University of Berkeley. With his programmatic statement he attempted to give the Chicago tradition a theoretical identity and an intellectual home. Blumer's essay was very influential, and SI became one of the leading strands of the interpretive paradigm.

Blumer explicates the pragmatist tradition, the process perspective, and the methodological implications of these. While the pragmatist philosophers William James and John Dewey emphasized practical action, they argued with a model of individual action. Charles Cooley and George Herbert Mead both adopted a pragmatist position but considered social processes as more fundamental: Cooley argued that the constitution of individual identity presupposes the other (expressed in the idea of 'looking-glass self') and that primary groups are essential for acting and making experiences. Mead (1934), who had a considerable influence on Chicago students in the 1920s, agreed, and developed a theory of symbol use and socialization. Phylogenetically, humans have developed significant symbols that are determined by convention and allow for 'conscious', 'planned', 'intentional' behaviour, distinct from animals. Ontogenetically, a human actor acquires language that is culturally pre-given in social interaction. In socialization humans learn to take the role of the other, to generalize the expectations of significant others into a 'generalized other', and thereby develop a self with an 'I' and a 'me'. Thinking in this perspective is nothing other than internalized interaction: interacting with oneself. Without society, there is neither a mind nor a self.

On this ground Blumer formulated his famous three premises of SI:

> The first premise is that human beings act toward things on the basis of the meaning that the things have for them. ... The second premise is that the meaning of such things is derived from, or arises out of, the social interaction that one has with one's fellows. The third premise is that these meanings are handled in, and modified through, an interpretative process used by the person in dealing with the things he encounters. (1969: 2)

SI, in other words, investigates how the symbolic order of the world is produced, stabilized and changed. Society and organizations are conceived of as permanent, interrelated processes of producing and changing such orders. Although most interactions have repetitive patterns, there is always a strong creative moment. This can be aptly illustrated by role theory: while in structural functionalism roles consist of institutionalized normative expectations, symbolic interactionists emphasize the interpretive, performative and creative aspect of 'role-making' (Turner 1956). Thomas Wilson (1970) therefore drew a clear distinction between the normative paradigm and the interpretive paradigm. Blumer's methodological statement played a crucial role in defining the interpretive paradigm and became a popular point of reference. However, he offered no concrete advice for how to do empirical research. He distinguished two modes of inquiry: exploration and inspection (Blumer 1969: 40–47). Exploration aims at a comprehensive and accurate picture of what is researched. It is flexible and does not use a particular set of techniques or analytical schemes that were fabricated in advance. It may involve direct observation, interviewing, listening to people's conversations, using letters and diaries, consulting public records, arranging for group discussions – all as means to explore a field in-depth and to elaborate 'sensitizing concepts'. Inspection consists of a meticulous examination by approaching a given analytical element 'in a variety of different ways, viewing it from different angles, asking many different questions' (Blumer 1969: 44).

## Grounded Theory

While Blumer provided the theoretical legitimation of the interpretive paradigm, his colleague Everett Hughes instructed students how to do actual empirical research. The members of the Chicago School have always been convinced that qualitative research methods cannot be taught in class – they have to be learned by practice in the field. This was also the view of Everett Hughes who taught, as previously did Burgess, a graduate seminar in field observation methods that was compulsory for students of sociology and anthropology. Hughes developed participant observation as a distinct methodology, and, criticizing the reduction of survey methods to pure techniques, emphasized 'the inquiring attitude'. He further insisted on the mutual enrichment of the empirical and the theoretical – even the most trivial things allow for analytical insights. In 1967, Anselm Strauss, Blumer's student, and Barney Glaser ventured to codify qualitative research. They feared that the positivist orthodoxy would eliminate qualitative methods from the curriculum. Their

*Discovery of Grounded Theory* (Glaser and Strauss 1967) suggested the opposite to positivist research: not approaching empirical facts by preconceived analytical schemes, but constructing theories through the analysis of data. By reviewing the collected data again and again, asking questions and developing ideas, codes and sensitizing concepts may emerge that guide further data collection and analysis (Glaser 1978). Later on, Corbin and Strauss (2008) went a step further and made grounded theory a systematic procedure that could be taught as rigorously as quantitative methods.

*Grounded Theory* became the bible of qualitative researchers and contributed greatly to legitimatizing qualitative inquiry. For decades grounded theory has been the favourite reference point and procedure of generations of graduate students who, however, often overlooked the fact that formalization cannot replace sociological imagination. Grounded theory has often been combined with other qualitative approaches, and just as often has been criticized. Glaser, who adhered more to the traditional idea that analytic insights emerge from immersion, started a polemical debate against the further formalization advocated by Corbin and Strauss, and reiterated the question of whether qualitative methods can be taught or must be learned in the field (Glaser 1998). Gary Alan Fine states that *The Discovery of Grounded Theory* was 'perhaps the best of the few programmatic statements'; however, the methodology of the Chicago School 'was open to a more artistic, improvised, and situated mode of sociology than implied in the tenets of research design' (Fine 1995: xii–xiii). Another way to learn how qualitative research is profitably done is, therefore, to read concrete studies.

## *Interactionist, Ethnographic Studies*

There are plenty of studies in the Chicago or interactionist tradition that had a great influence in sociology and are still worth reading. There are several readers, reviews and introductions (Charon 2006; Fine 1991; 1993; Plummer 1991a; 1991b; Rose 1962), and many monographs. Most studies combine fieldwork with the creation of new theoretical concepts; some publications are more empirical, others more theoretical. Anselm Strauss and colleagues' *Boys in White* (Becker et al. 1992 [1961]) analyses how a medical school can be understood by examining collective actions, and how medical students learn to become medical doctors in this institution (Becker et al., 1995 [1968]). Strauss became famous for his research in medical institutions, where he tried to link interaction processes with structural properties of the organization. He created many useful concepts such as the negotiated order in organizations (Strauss 1979), the context of awareness (in relation to the dying) (Glaser and Strauss, 2007 [1968]), or the trajectory, defined as '1) the course of any experienced phenomenon as it evolves over time (an engineering project, a chronic illness, dying, a social revolution (…) and 2) the actions and interactions contributing to its evolution' (Strauss 1993: 53f.). Together with Tom Shibutani he developed the 'social world' perspective (Strauss 1991).

Howard S. Becker's book *Outsiders* (1963) 'has had far more influence on the study of deviance than a decade of the *American Sociological Review*' (Fine, 1995: xiv). Himself a jazz piano player, Becker describes the subcultures of jazz and dance musicians, of marihuana smokers, and so on. He (co-)developed the labelling approach, which demonstrated that there is no such thing as deviance *per se*, but that deviance is constructed in interaction, and that deviant behaviour is not the result of individual dispositions, but rather of socialization processes, and that a career model of deviant stages can be identified that results from the interplay of these two processes. Becker explores the whole complex of rule creator, rule enforcer, moral entrepreneur and moral crusade. In this vein, many others investigated suicide, mental diseases, and so on, like Tom Scheff (1975) and Jack Douglas (1973). Likewise, John Gusfield (1986 [1963]; 1996) analyzed the construction of social problems (for instance, of drunk driving) and the making of meaning of moral reformers and social movements.

Many more figures and studies could be cited here, first of all Erving Goffman with his broad array of studies and development of new concepts such as impression management techniques (1959), total organizations (asylums) (1961a), role distance (1961b), stigma (1963), interaction rituals (1967), strategic interaction (1969), frame analysis (1974), the interaction order (1981), and many more. Also worth mentioning are Gary Alan Fines' ethnographic studies of group cultures (2012) in restaurant kitchens (1996) and among meteorologists (2007); or Arlie Hochschild's (1983; 2003) research on emotional labour and new work-life settings; or the work of Norman Denzin (1977) and Adele Clarke (1998) on science and organization studies. Also noteworthy is Strauss' theoretical account (1993) and Tamotsu Shibutani's *Social Processes* (1986). They are all often subsumed under SI, but many of these authors do not identify with this label themselves. Fine, for instance, states that the term 'symbolic interactionism' fails 'to catch the rhythm and sensibilities of the approaches ... What we shared were tacit perspectives without a great deal of concern for rigorous theoretical justifications or deductions. These perspectives reflected a culture of sociological practice which played a part in the dominant sociology of the 1960s and 1970s' (Fine, 1995: xi).

As an alternative, Fine (1995) suggested speaking of a 'Second Chicago School', to praise the eminence of sociological researchers such as Becker, Strauss, Goffman or Gusfield, to name just a few. Meanwhile we could speak of a 'Third Chicago School', with sociologists such as Adele Clarke, Juliette Corbin, Arlie Hochschild, Gary Alan Fine and Norman Denzin, among others. While Diane Crane (1972) speaks of an 'invisible college', Jennifer Platt (1994; 1995) questions such constructs. Institutional places do not suggest a similarity of theoretical development – after all, William Ogburn was appointed at the University of Chicago as early as 1927 in order to establish a 'scientific', quantitative sociology. Meanwhile, it has become more fashionable to label these approaches 'ethnography', based on their use of field work methods. From the point of view of a 'qualitative cultural sociology', one should indeed favour a methodological criterion over other forms of classification.

## PHENOMENOLOGICAL APPROACHES

A considerable contribution to the resurgence of the interpretive paradigm was also made by phenomenology. The key figure who introduced phenomenology to sociology was Alfred Schutz. Schutz aimed at giving Max Weber's *Verstehende Soziologie* a philosophical foundation as early as 1932, and pursued this goal all of his life, which after his emigration from Austria in 1937 was predominantly spent in the United States. With his *Structures of the Life-World*, he provided a substantial contribution to the methodology of the social sciences, and on the basis of these analyses, two influential sociological approaches arose: the *social constructivism* of Berger and Luckmann (1966) and *ethnomethodology* (Garfinkel, 1967). Each of them was essential and influential for cultural sociology.

Only a few scholars have scrutinized the concept of *sense (or meaning)*[1] as thoroughly as Schutz did. If cultural sociology is concerned with processes of meaning-making, an elaborate and sophisticated conception of meaning is obviously a crucial precondition. Schutz was convinced that Max Weber's definition of sociology (1978 [1922]: 1) as *a science that has to understand (verstehen) the subjective sense of social actions* was path-breaking. He praised Weber's methodological individualism: '... it is only by such understanding of individual action that social science can gain access to the meaning of each social relationship and structure, constituted as these are, in the last analysis, by the action of the individual in the social world' (Schutz 1967 [1932]: 6). Although this was the position of a prominent founder of sociology, Max Weber, and although this was formulated as early as 1932, it became more striking after Parsons' structural functionalism, which spoke of emergent properties of social systems, of the society as (collective) actor, and of the logics of institutions. In the 1960s and 1970s, the 'new' methodological credo brought sociological research back to actors' everyday lives and their subjective perspectives. Obviously, it fitted well with the Thomas theorem that sociology should research people's subjective views of reality – that is, how they define their situations.

Schutz recognized that it is not only the theoretical premises that constitute a sociological paradigm but also the pre-theoretical premises. His basic idea was that the methodology of the social sciences has two pillars: first, the logics of scientific explanation; and, second, a constitutive analysis of the social world. The second is much more crucial – and was consistently overlooked by positivist approaches. Schutz therefore contrasted Carnap's *The Logical Structure of the World* (1967 [1928]) with his own book *The Meaningful Structure of the Social World (Der sinnhafte Aufbau der sozialen Welt)* – which is not recognizable anymore in the English translation of the book title, *The Phenomenology of the Social World,* (Schutz 1967 [1932]). As the social world is meaningfully constituted in everyday life *before* any scientific research begins, the social sciences have to take this fact systematically into account. In contrast to natural sciences, social sciences have to understand how their subjects make sense of their actions.

By use of Husserl's phenomenological approach, Schutz attempted to explicate the formal structures of the meaningful life-world. Husserl had diagnosed *The Crisis of European Sciences* [1970 [1936/54]), criticizing them for taking their ideas, their numbers, graphs and formulas for the real world and forgetting that these are rooted in acts of natural apperception in the life-world. Though Husserl meant the natural sciences, there is an obvious parallel to positivist social sciences. Schutz's phenomenological life-world analysis elucidated the point that an adequate methodology of social sciences must investigate how sense (meaning) is constituted at all.

## The Formal Structures of the Life-world

Phenomenology as a philosophical science with an 'autonomous philosophical method' was founded by Edmund Husserl in Germany. It became a broad *Phenomenological Movement* – one of the biggest in the twentieth century – which Herbert Spiegelberg (1982) described in its many ramifications. Husserl's basic idea was that philosophical analysis should turn to *'the things themselves'*. He then analyzed *how we constitute the sense of phenomena*. The core is *apperception*: what is actually perceived? Phenomena are constituted with an outer horizon – against a 'background', within a 'context' – but they have also an inner horizon which is constituted by *appresentation*: we perceive not only what is perceivable but 'appresent' also those' aspects that are not perceivable (e.g. we see a 'house' although we just perceive its front side). Phenomena are constituted in passive syntheses and include sensuous apperception as well as meaning. A crucial difference to many other, especially semiotic and linguistic, approaches is that phenomenology analyses meaning constitution on a *pre-predicative level*. Subjective experience is always more than and different from what is formulated in language. It is therefore crucial to start analysis at the pre-predicative level of subjective experience and not just at the level of its representations on the *predicative level of language* (in definite contrast to all linguistic approaches).

Based on Husserl's insights, Schutz analyzed how meaning is constituted in 'lived' experience, in reflected experience (when people are operating with interpretive schemes), and in action. Sense is always constituted in the here and now, either in regard to present intentional 'objects', or in retrospection to past events, or prospectively in regard to upcoming events. The constitution of sense is always a process in time – which was not explicated in Weber's methodological writings. Schutz investigated carefully what Weber had overlooked: that the modes of givenness of social actions – and therefore their meanings – are different to the actor him- or herself ($S^1$), to an observer in everyday life ($S^2$) and to a social scientist ($S^3$). While the actor perceives his actions in the context of his biographically determined stock of knowledge at hand, and knows about his experiences, his plans and systems of relevances, the observer in everyday life can only perceive observable behaviour and has no direct access to the subjective sense of the other's actions. The *alter ego* is only understandable by means of *appresentative systems*: by indications, marks, signs and symbols. Schutz disapproves of the concept of empathy – Max Scheler's 'inner perception' (2008: 248ff. [1923]) – which implied that another person's lived experiences are as accessible to me as my own. Schutz insists that we can never empathize in the sense that we feel what the other is feeling. *We can only understand the other on the basis of our own subjective experiences*, of our own feelings, of our own reasoning. The other's experiences and subjective constructions are not directly available but 'only available with the help of appresentative systems. For phenomenologists, it is therefore utterly disturbing that many other qualitative approaches do not recognize and acknowledge this basic difference and treat interview data or narrations as direct representations of another person's 'experience'.

The 'structures of the life world' that Schutz elucidates are rich and detailed (cf. Schutz and Luckmann, 1973; 1989). They have a subjective pole as well as a pragmatic, intersubjective pole, with a strong interface with pragmatist and symbolic interactionist theories (Srubar 1988; 2005). Schutz claims that these structures of the life-world are the same for all human beings. The social world is structured in space and time in relation to the experiencing subject: there are those I personally know, and there are contemporaries, predecessors and successors. And every ('normal') actor has a subjective, biographically determined stock of knowledge at hand; uses (linguistic and pre-linguistic) typifications and is guided by systems of relevances; orients in time and space; and relies on systems of appresentation in order to understand others or relate to multiple realities. Such universal formal structures can be phenomenologically described and represent a philosophical anthropology, while the concrete contents of stocks of knowledge, of typifications and systems of relevances, of temporal and spatial orientation, and so on, are historically and culturally contingent and therefore research objects of empirical sciences. As sociological research produces (scientific) second-order constructions that refer to (common-sense) first-order constructions, the most crucial methodological requirement is sense adequacy (or meaning adequacy) (Eberle 2010; Schutz 1962).

## Berger and Luckmann's 'The Social Construction of Reality'

Schutz sees in the constitutive phenomenology of the natural attitude a philosophical anthropology that provides a proper foundation for the empirical social sciences. For Luckmann (1973; 1979), the universal and invariant structures of the life-world represent a proto-sociology in the sense of a *mathesis universalis*, a formal matrix that allows a solution to the problem of measurement in the social sciences. They serve as a *tertium comparationis*, i.e., they allow for translating propositions that are formulated as empirical observations in a certain language into a proper formal language. Luckmann hoped that the *problem of measurement* (Cicourel 1964) in the social sciences could be solved this way. Schutz has, in Luckmann's view, succeeded in providing the scope of this proto-sociological matrix; the details of it may be pondered and modified, and phenomenological analyses must be triangulated by transcultural research and scientific knowledge about the human body (Knoblauch 2011).

If the structures of the life-world serve as a proto-sociology, sociological concepts and theories must refer to these basic structures. This compatibility implies a preference for methodological individualism and a dispreference for holistic constructions (unless they can, as Schutz demanded, be translated into human actions). A well-known example of a clearly compatible sociological theory is Berger and Luckmann's (1966) *The Social Construction of Reality*. It consists of three parts: 'The Foundations of Knowledge in Everyday Life'; 'Society as Objective Reality'; and 'Society as Subjective Reality'. In the first part, they present some key results of Schutz's phenomenological life-world analysis and characterize them explicitly as 'philosophical prolegomena' that are 'pre-sociological' and 'not scientific' (1966: 20). But they treat them as an apt 'starting point for sociological analysis' (1966: 20). In line with these proto-sociological considerations, they design a sociology of knowledge that consists of two perspectives: in 'Society as Objective Reality', they analyze the processes of institutionalization and legitimation; in 'Society as Subjective Reality', the processes of internalization and the evolvement of identity are considered. This book contains ample reflections on how Schutz's findings can be used for sociological analysis and how other sociological theories can be re-interpreted in their light.

In a survey of the International Sociological Association (ISA) among its members at the turn of the 21st century, *The Social Construction of Reality* was elected as the fourth most important sociological book of the twentieth century (after works by Weber and Durkheim). It was undoubtedly ground-breaking in the 1960s as a new synthesis of different sociological theories and as a decisive alternative to structural functionalism. It certainly triggered the social constructivist movement, although both Berger and Luckmann claim that they are no constructivists. And it seems that many have overlooked or misunderstood the systematic architecture of their approach. In Anglo-Saxon sociology, the book appears to be vastly forgotten by now. But in German sociology, due to Luckmann's eminent influence, it is still a prominent sociological framework – phenomenology and the sociology of knowledge have become dominant and very lively approaches in German cultural sociology.

It may be noteworthy here that the term 'cultural sociology' cannot be adequately translated into German. In the German Sociological Association, there is a section 'Kultursoziologie' that was conceived of, since its inception in 1984, as a *general* sociology in Max Weber's sense, and as a counter-movement to structural functionalism and its concept of 'structure.' In fact, Habermas criticized the approach of Berger and Luckmann as a 'culturalist reduction' (1981: 210) that neglects the crucial role of social structures and system rationalities. Dealing with meaning-construction, social constructivists were 'cultural sociologists', but they gathered in the section *Sprachsoziologie* (sociology of language) that Luckmann had founded at the end of the 1970s, together with Hans-Georg Soeffner, Richard Grathoff, Ilja Srubar, and others. In 2000 it was renamed the 'sociology of knowledge'. Most phenomenological sociologists, symbolic interactionists and ethnomethodologists in German-speaking sociology are members of this section. Interestingly, there is still no adequate equivalent in Anglo-Saxon sociology (where 'sociology of knowledge' has not become such a common label and usually means something different than in *The Social Construction of Reality*).

In German sociology, using Berger and Luckmann's *The Social Construction of Reality* as a theoretical framework and referring to Schutz's *Structures of the Life-World* is still widespread. Yet although *The Social Construction* is a programme for an *empirical* sociology of knowledge, it does not give any advice on how to do qualitative research. Empirical sociologists of knowledge therefore adopted the research practices that had been developed by symbolic interactionists, ethnomethodologists and ethnographers. A crucial and influential contribution was made by Hans-Georg Soeffner (2004) who suggested a 'Social Scientific Hermeneutics' approach to *reconstruct* subjective as well as objectified and institutionalized sense, and to reconstruct the meaning of actions as well as the meaning of results of actions. Recently, there have been suggested some newer, compatible approaches in German cultural sociology that are closely related to phenomenology but are hardly known abroad: life-world analytic ethnography, phenomenological hermeneutics and ethnophenomenology (cf. Eberle 2014). *Life-world analytic ethnography* suggests that researchers totally immerse themselves in the field and use their subjective experiences explicitly and reflexively as an 'instrument' of data generation and collection. Most members of a setting are not particularly skilled in verbally describing their subjective experiences, for instance when participating at a techno rave. By participating themselves, life-world analytic ethnographers attempt to describe their own subjective experience as precisely as possible, and thereby complement what they can observe in the field, namely other members' behaviours, by a distinctly subjective perspective (Honer and Hitzler 2015; Pfadenhauer and Grenz 2015). *Phenomenological hermeneutics* attempts to explore person's subjective life-world by scrutinizing verbal accounts in a careful dialogue. It builds on the phenomenological insight that people's verbal accounts do not correspond to their actual subjective experience; first accounts are rather 'glosses' that open the way for more detailed analysis. Phenomenological hermeneutics does not accept interview accounts as 'objective' data – 'objectified' in transcripts – but strives for exploring another's experiences in more depth by repeated dialogical analyses that carefully uncover the different layers of sense (Eberle 2015a). *Ethnophenomenology* uses videography that records all visual and aural aspects of situation and analyses the data sequentially, much as ethnomethodology does. But in addition, the actor's perspective is also explicitly taken into account. Knoblauch and Schnettler (2015) demonstrate this with their analysis of the performance of a Marian vision. The audio-visual data show how the transcendent experience of an apparition is embodied. As the observing researchers do not have direct access to the Marian vision, they explore the descriptions and explanations provided by the actors that actually experienced the vision.

## Ethnomethodology

Another approach directly linked to Schutz was Garfinkel's (1967) *ethnomethodology*. Garfinkel interpreted Schutz's phenomenological life-world analysis not as a philosophical proto-sociology but as an alternative sociological approach. In a careful analysis, Garfinkel (1952) confronted Parsons' structural functionalism with Schutz's phenomenological studies, and interpreted the latter as an alternative approach for explaining the problem of social order. Schutz's conception of the actor, in contrast to Parsons' norm-guided role-player, did not make the actor a 'judgmental dope'. Garfinkel (1967) showed by his incongruity (or breaching) experiments that the social order does not break down when norms get violated but only when people cannot manage to make sense of the situation. Therefore he explained social order not by normative but by constitutive rules and by (ethno-)methods of sense-making.

This view implied a methodological re-orientation: ethnomethodology investigates sense-making, not egologically in the subjective consciousness but in empirical settings that are intersubjectively available. It is not the constitutive acts of consciousness that are the topic of study as in phenomenology, but the empirically observable accounting practices whereby actors make sense recognizable. Garfinkel does not treat Schutz's structures of the life-world as validated insights but seeks the answers himself. He proposed intentional 'misreading' of texts and used Schutz's and other phenomenologists' analyses only as inspiration, starting a new kind of research from scratch. The basic question, however, remains the same: seeking for the *how* and the *know-how*, and investigating the constitution of social phenomena.

Garfinkel's interpretation of phenomenology shaped the understanding of a whole generation of US sociologists. While many phenomenologists engaged in exegeses of texts, ethnomethodologists turned 'to the things themselves' and analyzed what they observed. Garfinkel was quite creative in his empirical studies. In addition, he applied a rare methodological rigour in bracketing knowledge about phenomena. A crucial question became 'what is the phenomenon?' What really is there to be seen? And what is seen but unnoticed? Ethnomethodology, reinforced by conversation analysis, had a ground-breaking influence on qualitative research through its methodological rigour, its attention to detail, its technique of audio- and video-recordings, its careful procedures of transcription, and its meticulous analyses. It advocates a methodological purism that is unique in qualitative research. And although ethnomethodology proclaimed sense-making methods as a research topic in their own right, it has never identified with 'cultural sociology' – on the contrary, most cultural sociologists operate with theoretical concepts that are considered as 'glosses' and hide rather than reveal empirically observable phenomena.

## DEVELOPMENT AND PROSPECTS OF QUALITATIVE CULTURAL RESEARCH

How has the 'cultural turn' in the late 20th century shaped qualitative research? The cultural turn, 'one of the most influential trends in the humanities and social sciences in the last generation' (Jacobs and Spillman 2005: 1), is an amalgam of cultural studies, French poststructuralism and postmodernism and US cultural sociology. The research and current debates (especially in US sociology) are covered in several books and readers (Hall et al. 2010; Jacobs and Weiss Hanrahan 2005; Smith 1998. I stick here with Spillman's definition of 'processes of meaning-making'. No prominent representative of the 'cultural turn' objects that cultural sociology in this sense has had a long tradition since its inception by the classics. Anne Swidler (1986: 273) and Jeffrey C. Alexander (Alexander and Smith 2003: 13–14), for instance, both see Clifford Geertz's 'thick description' as their main starting point. And Geertz, defining culture as 'webs of significance' (1973: 5), explicitly refers to Max Weber's approach (Back et al. 2012: 27). In regard to US cultural sociology, Spillman (2002: 7ff.) identifies three general approaches, each focusing on meaning-making processes at a different analytical level. The first approach investigates 'how interactions constitute meanings and how individuals use them' (2002: 7). Knowledge, or sets of meanings, are not treated as socially shared but are seen as contingently constituted in interaction. In addition to the meaning-making in fluid interactional processes, cultural sociologists also research the wider cultural repertoire social actors use. Typical methods are ethnography and interviews. The second approach 'examines meaning-making processes as they occur within fields of institutions or networks of cultural producers' (2002: 8), e.g. cultural workers in cultural industries and how they can work creatively within organizational constraints. Here a broad set of methodological approaches is used, such as ethnographies, interviews, historical research and quantitative analysis. The third approach investigates meaning-making 'in the text' (2002: 8): 'Cultural repertoires, objects, and texts are analytically distinguished from their social contexts and treated as independent objects of inquiry' (2002: 8). The main method used here is textual analysis (as practiced in the humanities). Spillman suggests that the richest recent developments in the field were provided by combinations of these approaches.

The third approach refers to what Jeffrey Alexander and Philip Smith (2010) describe as 'The Strong Program' of cultural sociology, pioneered at Yale university. They rightly criticize much of US cultural sociology as not empirical at all: 'Too much cultural work is theory of theory, history of theory, "compare and contrast" pseudo-theory, intervention, normative theory, or "readings" of meaning without long-term empirical investigation' (2010: 15) In regard to ethnographic research of the Chicago School type, they contend 'that times have changed', that it does not suffice to study meaning-making only in concrete situations and interpersonal contacts, but that it must be extended to encompass a textual analysis of myth and meaning that might structure situations from above (2010: 14). Their 'Strong Program' has therefore a macrosociological perspective that aims at explanations and the building of middle-range theories, such as, for instance, Alexander's theory of cultural trauma (2004). In regard to their methods, they accept the critique that their work was vastly desk-driven and media focused. And they proudly report that the younger generation of scholars they have trained has taken a different track and generate more ethnographic and interview-based studies, 'tracing the interaction between symbolic structures and interaction at the local level' (Alexander and Smith 2010: 20), and they do this at multiple sites.

Qualitative cultural research studies may illuminate how methods are used in concrete contexts. To be updated about the state of the art of qualitative methods, it is better to turn to a good textbook written by a sociological methodologist (cf. Atkinson et al. 2001; Denzin and Lincoln 2005; Flick 2007; 2014; Flick et al. 2004; Gobo 2008; Gubrium et al. 2012; Seale et al. 2004; Silverman 2010, 2011, 2015; and with a special focus on researching culture, Alasuutari 1995). There is one caveat to this advice: not all qualitative methods are apt to analyze processes of meaning-making. Methods are always linked to *methodologies* and imply epistemological, ontological, theoretical as well as pretheoretical premises. Qualitative research is not always linked to the interpretive paradigm, but is often pursued in a positivist framework, too. And postmodern approaches may favor a looser reference to empirical data and abhor the methodological rigour of, for instance, ethnomethodology.

What are the new strands of qualitative cultural sociology and future ways to go? As much of cultural sociology advocates a semiotic approach, analyzing the meanings of signs, I take a distinctly different approach here. As pointed out earlier, phenomenology uses the term 'sense' instead of 'meaning', and emphasizes the distinction between the prepredicative level of subjective experience and the predicative level of language. Semiotic approaches cannot grasp the sensuousness of the life-world, the sensuality of our bodily senses' worlds, and how sensual experience and meaning are interwoven in the constitution of 'sense'. I am therefore going to organize current and future developments along the (allegedly) five human senses: the visual, the aural, the olfactory, the haptic and taste.

After the linguistic, the interpretive and the cultural turns, there is now a *visual turn* in sociology. The ubiquity of images in modern society made it inevitable to study them systematically. Cultural anthropology used photographs and films from early on, mostly not as a sort of data in their own right, but simply as illustrations to their texts. Documentary photography or the reportages commissioned by the Farm Security Administration (FSA) in the United States produced thousands of photos of people living in poverty and misery. The beginning of visual anthropology in the scientific sense is usually associated with Mead and Bateson's study of the *Balinese Character* (1942), in which they produced about 25,000 photographs and also some short movies about the material culture (houses, tools, etc.), as well as the social rituals and everyday routines and interactions, of the Balinese people. A later ground-breaking work was John Collier Jr.'s book *Visual Anthropology: Photography as a Research Method* (1967, with a new edition in co-authorship with his son: Collier and Collier 1986). A book on *Visual Sociology* appeared as late as 2012 by Douglas Harper, who provides a good overview of the history and development of visual sociology. One of the early pioneers who called for making sociology visual was Howard Becker (1974). He recommended using sociological theory as guidance for taking, sorting and arranging photos. Pierre Bourdieu (1960) did the same even earlier when he documented the culture of the Kabyles in Algeria. Other overviews of visual methods in anthropological qualitative research, as well as of how to analyze images, are given by Marcus Banks (2001; 2007; 2014). He distinguishes two main strands of doing visual sociology: one is the creation of images (photographs, films and videotapes) by the social researcher in the context of doing fieldwork; the other is the sociological study of images that are produced and consumed by the subjects of research – how people watch TV, or how they take photographs or videos in their everyday lives, or how they make and look at photo albums. In fieldwork, photo elicitation techniques proved more seminal in motivating researched subjects to make comments or to tell stories than interviews did. In many studies, the subjects were given cameras and were invited to photograph whatever is important to them – in order to explore their subjective perspectives.

The field of visual methods has developed quickly in recent years. As the relationship between images and texts is quite intricate, rich methodological debates have emerged. The focus has shifted from photos to videos, where we find the same two strands: one is analyzing native video data such as YouTube films or video diaries (e.g. Pink 2007); the other is doing social research by video means. How to pursue workplace studies by video analysis is well demonstrated by Heath et al. (2010), who do research in the tradition of ethnomethodology and conversation analysis. They point to the fact that in modern societies most public spaces are screened by surveillance cameras that produce ample material for the study of social behaviour. This development has recently become a very lively issue in German sociology. Most researchers subscribe to the interpretive paradigm, and a substantial portion are grounded in the phenomenologically inspired sociology of knowledge group. Substantial contributions have been made to a 'visual sociology of knowledge' by Jürgen Raab (2008); to a 'social theory of the image' by Roswitha Breckner (2010); to the methodology and methods of video-analysis by Knoblauch et al. (2006); and to videography, as a merger of video-analysis and ethnographic research, by Knoblauch and colleagues (Knoblauch and Tuma 2011; Knoblauch et al. 2014). A Reader on photography in this tradition was edited by Eberle (2016). Related approaches were conceived by Bohnsack (2011), Reichertz and Englert (2011) and by Corsten et al. (2010), including a sophisticated transcription system and software for video data (Moritz 2010; www.feldpartitur.de).

The second new development is sound studies (cf. the overview by Christoph Maeder, 2014). Cultural sociology, and the sociology of culture, used to consider sounds only insofar as they were speech or music. But the world of sounds is much richer, and sounds are as ubiquitous as images. As our ear has no lid we continuously overhear sounds, and we do this in a 360° spectrum. Murray R. Schafer's 'World Soundscape Project' (1994) so far has been unique in analyzing our acoustic environment: he distinguishes lo-fi and hi-fi environments; keynote sounds (background sounds) against which signals are foreground phenomena such as functional sounds (sirens, warning bells, software sounds, elevator jingles, cashier rings) that we consciously listen to; and there are soundmarks (as landmarks) that refer to a unique community sound. Schafer describes the huge changes that industrial revolution has brought about, such as engines or the mastery of electro-acoustics (radio, telephone, sound recordings, etc.). Why has cultural sociology vastly ignored soundscapes beyond speech and music? Because other kinds of sounds have no meaning? Identifying sounds may be vital, be it the scream of a dangerous animal in the wilderness or the engine noise of an approaching car on the road. However, measuring acoustics does not suffice; soundscapes must be linked to actors' perceptions. Humans obviously have the capacity for selective listening, which implies that they can ignore sounds. As culture shapes the way we hear and evaluate sounds, research must move from sound studies to sound culture studies. Such research must include not only sounds we consciously listen to, but also those sounds that we perceive more as the atmospheric horizon of our activities – such as typing on the computer keyboard, slicing a cucumber, chopping wood – or of the wider acoustic context, such as the humming of engines in urban areas or the buzzing of distant voices in a shopping mall.

Qualitative cultural sociology should also consider the 'lived' experiences provided by the other human senses. Our life-world is not only full of visions and sounds, but also of scents and smells, of tastes and of haptic experiences. Even ethnographers who attempted to describe a local culture in all its aspects often abstained from reporting such kinds of experiences. Paul Stoller (1989) is one of the few who made *The Taste of Ethnographic Things* a topic of its own. He described how he arrived in Niger with sensual openness, hearing all kinds of sounds and noises, smelling the stench of the sewer and the aromatic aromas of roasting meat. But he learned to keep a distanciated, intellectualized research attitude that cleaned his immersion from sensual sentiments. Only upon revisiting the tribe of the Songhay did he become suddenly aware how crucial these sensuous experiences were and how constitutive of their social life. As soundscapes were reduced to speech and music in cultural sociology, the world of smells was usually reduced to the cultural history of fragrant odours, like spices, perfumes, oils or scents. Occidental philosophy has usually regarded smell as a low, animalistic sense that is not worth serious treatment. In German sociology, the world of smells has been recently tackled by phenomenological researchers (Eberle 2015b; Raab 2001). Apartments, shopping malls, railway stations, hospitals, schools or sports stadiums – to name just a few – have not only characteristic sounds and visual appearances, but also characteristic smells. Further fields of research to uncover will be the worlds of taste – not only in the sphere of food or wine-tasting but concerning anything that enters our mouths (including bitter medicine). And finally, the worlds of haptic experience can be researched in much more depth than up to now; human touch is a crucial experience in many realms, whether we touch other humans, plants, fruit, tools or textiles (for the haptic experience of textiles see Kritzmöller 2015). As I have treated research on the (five) senses separately here, let me point out that the more challenging issue is synaesthetics: the multi-modal perception of phenomena in which several senses are combined. (For doing sensory ethnography, see also Pink 2015.)

Finally, new dimensions of qualitative cultural research are created by digital media and virtual data. Two developments have been crucial during the past decade: first, the World Wide Web, in particular the Web 2.0 that allows users to interact and collaborate with each other and create user-generated content in virtual communities; and new cultural forms have emerged such as social media networks, blogs, wikis, photo and video sharing sites, and many more. Second, mobile devices such as smart phones and tablets have intertwined virtual worlds and everyday life so tightly that neither of them can be regarded as separate from the other realm anymore. Face-to-face interactions are increasingly interwoven with phone and skype conversations, video-conferences, e-mails, sms, messages on Twitter and Facebook and Linkedin postings. And people who are geographically widely dispersed can get in contact with each other easily. The cloud services are opening an array of new possibilities, and new business ideas and models are now taking off. Digitalization seems to initiate another industrial revolution that promotes social and cultural changes we currently can hardly guess at. Against this background, Kozinets (2010) coined the term *netnography* to designate a new approach in qualitative research that draws together the terms 'Internet' and 'ethnography'. A netnographer needs to be computer savvy and up-to-date with the current developments in the Web and the state of the art of software. As these research fields change rapidly, any technical advice contained in netnography tends to be outdated soon after publication, and so are many empirical results by the time they are published.

## CONCLUSION

Over the past hundred years qualitative cultural sociology has become, like all the social sciences, more and more sophisticated and specialized. Compared to the early Chicago School scholars who used primarily common-sense methods in their empirical investigations, such as interpreting personal letters, conducting informal interviews and conversations and writing observational field notes, the state of the art of qualitative research has become much more complex: there exist a multiplicity of research approaches with different epistemological and ontological premises, different theoretical and methodological ideas, different methods of data collection, different sorts of data and different strategies for analyzing them. Social sciences cannot produce cumulative knowledge in the same way the natural sciences do. But all in all, the level of *methodological reflexivity* in doing qualitative research has been greatly advanced. This is undoubtedly significant progress. Interestingly enough, the multi-method approach of ethnography has remained dominant, since the early Chicagoans all the way down to the present time and to the Strong Program of the Yale school.

It is my contention that the symbolic interactionist tradition, phenomenological sociology and ethnomethodology have greatly contributed to refining qualitative cultural research, the ethnographic methods as well as their methodological underpinnings. I have also pointed out some new directions to go such as researching the visual, aural, olfactory and haptic aspects of social life as well as its tastes, and the synaesthetics of them. Many of these dimensions have been there all the time but were neglected in cultural research. The new, virtual worlds that emerged from the digital revolution and that will take shape in the future, however, require new approaches of inquiry that the early Chicagoans could not have imagined in their boldest dreams.

# NOTE

1  In their German texts, Schutz as well as Weber used the term *Sinn* (sense), which was usually translated into English as 'meaning'. The phenomenological 'sense' implies not only meaning but also the sensuous aspects of bodily perception and cognition. Phenomenological philosophers translated *Sinn* as sense, and so did Garfinkel (1967) who speaks of 'sense-making' instead of 'meaning-making'. It is a difficult endeavour to scrutinize the differences between the two notions; in this essay, I am using them interchangeably.

# REFERENCES

Alasuutari, P. (1995) *Researching Culture: Qualitative Method and Cultural Studies*. London: Sage.

Alexander, J.C. (1992) 'The Promise of a Cultural Sociology.' In Richard Munch and Neil J. Smelser (eds), *Theory of Culture*. Berkeley: University of California Press. pp. 293–323.

Alexander, J.C. (2004) 'Toward a Theory of Cultural Trauma.' In Jeffrey C. Alexander et al. (eds), *Cultural Trauma and Collective Identity*. Berkeley: University of California Press. pp. 1–30.

Alexander, J.C. and Smith, P. (2003) 'The Strong Program In Cultural Sociology: Elements of a Structural Hermeneutics.' In Jeffrey C. Alexander (ed.), *The Meanings of Social Life*. Oxford: Oxford University Press. pp. 11–26.

Alexander, J.C. and Smith, P. (2010) 'The Strong Program: Origins, Achievements, and Prospects.' In John Hall et al. (eds), *Handbook of Cultural Sociology*. London: Routledge. pp. 13–24.

Atkinson, P. et al. (2001) *Handbook of Ethnography*. London: Sage.

Back, L. et al. (2012) *Cultural Sociology: An introduction*. Oxford: Wiley-Blackwell.

Banks, M. (2001) *Visual Methods in Social Research*. London: Sage.

Banks, M. (2007) *Using Visual Data in Qualitative Research*. London: Sage.

Banks, M. (2014) 'Analysing Images.' In Uwe Flick (ed.), *The SAGE Handbook of Qualitative Data Analysis*. London: Sage. pp. 394–408.

Becker, H. (1963) *Outsiders: Studies in the Sociology of Deviance*. New York: The Free Press.

Becker, H. (1974) 'Photography and Sociology.' *Studies in the Anthropology of Visual Communication* 1(1): 3–16.

Becker, H.S., Geer, B. and Hughes, E.C. (1995 [1968]) *Making the Grade: The Academic Side of College Life*. New Brunswick: Transaction.

Becker, H.S., Geer, B., Hughes, E.C. and Strauss, A.L. (1992 [1961]) *Boys in White: Student Culture in Medical School*. New Brunswick: Transaction.

Berger, P.L. and Luckmann, T. (1966) *The Social Construction of Reality: A Treatise in the Sociology of Knowledge*. Garden City, NY: Anchor Books.

Blumer, H. (1937) 'Social Psychology.' In Emerson P. Schmidt (ed.) *Man and Society: A Substantive Introduction to the Social Sciences*. New York: Prentice Hall. pp. 144–198.

Blumer, H. (1939) 'An Appraisal of Thomas and Znaniecki's *Polish Peasant in Europe and America*.' New York: Social Science Research Council Bulletin 44. (Reprinted in: Blumer 1969: 117–126.)

Blumer, H. (1969) *Symbolic Interactionism: Perspective and Method*. Englewood Cliffs: Prentice-Hall.

Bohnsack, R. (2011) *Qualitative Bild- und Videointerpretation*, 2nd edn. Opladen and Farmington Hills: Budrich (UTB).

Bourdieu, P. (1960) *Algeria: The Disenchantment of the World, the Sense of Honour, the Kabyle House or the World Reversed*. Cambridge: Cambridge University Press.

Breckner, R. (2010) *Sozialtheorie des Bildes. Zur interpretativen Analyse von Bildern und Fotografien*. Bielefeld: transcript.

Bulmer, M. (1984) *The Chicago School of Sociology: Institutionalization, Diversity, and the Rise of Sociological Research*. Chicago: The University of Chicago Press.

Carnap, R. (1967 [1928]) *The Logical Structure of the World: Pseudoproblems in Philosophy*. Berkeley: University of California Press.

Charon, J.M. (2006) *Symbolic Interactionism: An Introduction, an Interpretation, an Integration*, 9th edn. Upper Saddle River: Prentice Hall.

Cicourel, A.V. (1964) *Method and Measurement in Sociology*. New York: Free Press.

Clarke, A.E. (1998) *Disciplining Reproduction: American Life Scientists and the 'Problem of Sex'*. Berkeley: University of California Press.

Collier, J., Jr. (1967) *Visual Anthropology: Photography as a Research Method*. New York: Holt Rinehart and Winston.

Collier, J., Jr. and Collier, M. (1986) *Visual Anthropology: Photography as a Research Method*. Albuquerque: University of New Mexico Press.

Corbin, J. and Strauss, A. (2008) *Basics of Qualitative Research: Grounded Theory Procedures and Techniques*, 3rd edn. Thousand Oaks, CA: Sage.

Corsten, M., Krug, M. and Moritz, C. (eds) (2010) *Videographie praktizieren*. Wiesbaden: VS Verlag (Springer).

Coser, L. (1977) *Masters of Sociological Thought*. New York: Harcourt Brace Jovanovich.

Crane, D. (1972) *Invisible Colleges*. Chicago: University of Chicago Press.

Deegan, M.J. (2007) 'The Chicago School of Ethnography.' In P. Atkinson et al. (eds), *Handbook of Ethnography*. London: Sage. pp. 11–25.

Denzin, N. (1977) 'Notes on the Criminogenic Hypothesis: A Case Study of the American Liquor Industry.' *American Sociological Review* 42: 905–920.

Denzin, N. and Lincoln, Y.S. (eds) (2005) *The SAGE Handbook of Qualitative Research*. Thousand Oaks, CA: Sage.

Douglas, J.D. (1973) *The Social Meanings of Suicide*. Princeton: Princeton University Press.

Durkheim, E. (1982 [1895]) *The Rules of Sociological Method*. Edited and with an introduction by Steven Lukes, translated by E.D. Hall. New York: The Free Press.

Eberle, T.S. (2010) 'Phenomenological Life-world Analysis and the Methodology of the Social Sciences.' *Human Studies* 33(2–3): 123–139.

Eberle, T.S. (2014) 'Phenomenology as a Research Method.' In Uwe Flick (ed.), *The SAGE Handbook of Qualitative Data Analysis*. London: Sage. pp. 184–202.

Eberle, T.S. (2015a) 'Exploring Another's Subjective Life-world: A Phenomenological Approach.' *Journal of Contemporary Ethnography*, 44(5): 563–579.

Eberle, T.S. (2015b) 'Phänomenologie der olfaktorischen Wahrnehmung. Ein Beitrag zur Synästhesie der Sinne', in Ronald Hitzler (ed.), *Hermeneutik als Lebenspraxis. Ein Vorschlag von Hans-Georg Soeffner*. Weinheim und Basel: Beltz Juventa. pp. 22–34.

Eberle, T.S. (ed.) (2016) *Fotografie und Gesellschaft*. Bielefeld: transcript.

Faris, R.E.L. (1967) *Chicago Sociology, 1920–1932*. San Francisco: Chandler.

Fine, G.A. (1991) 'Symbolic Interactionism in the Post-Blumerian Age.' In G. Ritzer (ed.), *Frontiers of Social Theory: The New Syntheses*. New York: Columbia University Press. pp. 117–157.

Fine, G.A. (1993) 'The Sad Demise, Mysterious Disappearance, and Glorious Triumph of Symbolic Interactionism.' *Annual Review of Sociology* 19: 61–87.

Fine, G.A. (1995) *A Second Chicago School? The Development of a Postwar American Sociology*. Chicago: The University of Chicago Press.

Fine, G.A. (1996) *Kitchens: The Culture of Restaurant Work*. Berkeley: University of California Press.

Fine, G.A. (2000) 'Group Cultures and Group Subcultures.' In John Hall, Laura Grindstaff and Ming-Cheng Lo (eds), *Handbook of Cultural Sociology*. London and New York: Routledge. pp. 213–222.

Fine, G.A. (2007) *Authors of the Storm: Meteorologists and the Culture of Prediction*. Chicago: University of Chicago Press.

Fine, G.A. (2012) *Tiny Publics. A Theory of Group Culture and Actions*. New York: Russell Sage Foundation.

Flick, U. (ed.) (2007) *The SAGE Qualitative Research Kit*. 9 vols. London: Sage.

Flick, U. (ed.) (2014) *The SAGE Handbook of Qualitative Data Analysis*. London: Sage.

Flick, U., von Kardorff, E. and Steinke, I. (eds) (2004) *A Companion to Qualitative Research*. Transl. by Bryan Jenner. London: Sage.

Garfinkel, H. (1952) *The Perception of the Other*. Harvard University, unpublished dissertation.

Garfinkel, H. (1967) *Studies in Ethnomethodology*. Englewood Cliffs: Prentice Hall.

Geertz, C. (1973) *The Interpretation of Cultures*. New York: Basic Books.

Glaser, B.G. (1978) *Theoretical Sensitivity: Advances in the Methodology of Grounded Theory*. Mill Valley: The Sociology Press.

Glaser, B.G. (1998) *Doing Grounded Theory – Issues and Discussions*. Mill Valley: The Sociology Press.

Glaser, B. and Strauss, A.L. (1967) *The Discovery of Grounded Theory: Strategies for Qualitative Research*. New York: Aldine de Gruyter.

Glaser, B. and Strauss, A.L. (2007 [1968]) *Time for Dying*. New Brunswick: Transaction.

Gobo, G. (2008) *Doing Ethnography*. London: Sage.

Goffman, E. (1959) *The Presentation of Self in Everyday Life*. University of Edinburgh Social Sciences Research Centre/Anchor Books.

Goffman, E. (1961a) *Asylums: Essays on the Social Situation of Mental Patients and Other Inmates*. New York: Doubleday.

Goffman, E. (1961b) *Encounters: Two Studies in the Sociology of Interaction – Fun in Games & Role Distance*. Indianapolis: Bobbs-Merrill.

Goffman, E. (1963) *Stigma: Notes on the Management of Spoiled Identity*. Englewood Cliffs: Prentice-Hall.

Goffman, E. (1967) *Interaction Ritual: Essays on Face-to-Face Behavior*. New York: Anchor Books.

Goffman, E. (1969) *Strategic Interaction*. Philadelphia: University of Pennsylvania Press.

Goffman, E. (1974) *Frame Analysis: An Essay on the Organization of Experience*. London: Harper and Row.

Goffman, E. (1981) 'The Interaction Order.' *American Sociological Review* 48: 1–17.

Gouldner, A. (1970) *The Coming Crisis of Western Sociology*. New York: Basic Books.

Gubrium, J.F. et al. (eds) (2012) *Handbook of Interview Research: Context and Method*. 2nd edn. London: Sage.

Gusfield, J.R. (1986 [1963]) *Symbolic Crusade: Status Politics and the American Temperance Movement*. Urbana and Chicago: University of Illinois Press.

Gusfield, J.R. (1996) *Contested Meanings: The Construction of Alcohol Problems*. Madison: University of Wisconsin Press.

Habermas, J. (1981) *Theorie des kommunikativen Handelns. Bd. 2: Zur Kritik der funktionalistischen Vernunft*. Frankfurt: Suhrkamp.

Hall, J.R., Grindstaff, L. and Lo, M.-Ch. (eds) (2010) *Handbook of Cultural Sociology*. London and New York: Routledge.

Harper, D. (2012) *Visual Sociology*. New York: Routledge.

Heath, C., Hindmarsh, J. and Luff, P. (2010) *Video in Qualitative Research: Analysing Social Interaction in Everyday Life*. London: Sage.

Hochschild, A.R. (1983) *The Managed Heart: The Commercialization of Human Feeling*. Berkeley: The University of California Press.

Hochschild, A.R. (2003) *The Commercialization of Intimate Life*. Berkeley: University of California Press.

Honer, A. and Hitzler, R. (2015) 'Life-World-Analytical Ethnography: A Phenomenology-Based Research Approach.' *Journal of Contemporary Ethnography*, 44(5): 544–562.

Husserl, Edmund G. [1970 [1936/54]) The Crisis of European Sciences and Transcendental Phenomenology. Translated by David Carr. Evanston, IL: Northwestern University Press.

Jacobs, M. and Spillman, L. (2005) 'Cultural Sociology at the Crossroads of the Discipline.' *Poetics* 33(1): 1–14.

Jacobs, M.D. and Weiss Hanrahan, N. (2005) *The Blackwell Companion to the Sociology of Culture*. Oxford: Blackwell.

Jeábek, H. (2001) 'Paul Lazarsfeld – The Founder of Modern Empirical Sociology: A Research Biography', *International Journal of Public Opinion Research* 13: 229–244.

Knoblauch, H. (2011) 'Relativism, Meaning and the New Sociology of Knowledge'. In R. Schantz and M. Seidel (eds), *The Problem of Relativism in the Sociology of (Scientific) Knowledge*. Frankfurt: Ontos. pp. 131–156.

Knoblauch, H. and Schnettler, B. (2015) Video and Vision: Videography of a Marian Apparition.' *Journal of Contemporary Ethnography*, 44(5): 636–656.

Knoblauch, H. and Tuma, R (2011) 'Videography: An Interpretive Approach to Video-recorded Micro-social Interaction', in E. Margolis and Pauwels, L. (eds), *The SAGE Handbook of Visual Methods*. Thousand Oaks, CA: Sage. pp. 414–430.

Knoblauch, H., Schnettler, B., Soeffner, H.-G. and Raab, J. (2006) *Video Analysis: Methodology and Methods. Qualitative Audiovisual Data Analysis in Sociology*. Frankfurt am Main: Lang.

Knoblauch, H., Tuma, R. and Schnettler, B. (2014) 'Video Analysis and Videography', in U. Flick (ed.) *The SAGE Handbook of Qualitative Data Analysis*. London: Sage. pp. 435–449.

Kozinets, R.V. (2010) *Netnography: Doing Ethnographic Research Online*. London: Sage.

Kritzmöller, M. (2015) *Auf Tuchfühlung. Soziologie der textilen Haptik*. Düsseldorf: Flabelli.

Luckmann, T. (1973) 'Philosophy, Science, and Everyday Life.' In Maurice Natanson (ed.) *Phenomenology and the Social Sciences*. Evanston: Northwestern University Press. pp. 145–185.

Luckmann, T. (1979) 'Phänomenologie und Soziologie.' In Walter M. Sprondel and Richard Grathoff (eds), *Alfred Schütz und die Idee des Alltags in den Sozialwissenschaften*. Stuttgart: Ferdinand Enke. pp. 196–206.

Maeder, C. (2014) 'Analysing Sounds.' In Uwe Flick (ed.), *The SAGE Handbook of Qualitative Data Analysis*. London: Sage. pp. 424–434.

Mead, G.H. (1934) *Mind, Self, and Society*. Edited by Charles W. Morris. Chicago: University of Chicago Press.

Mead, M. and Bateson, G. (1942) *Balinese Character: A Photographic Analysis*. New York: New York Academy of Sciences.

Moritz, C. (2010) 'Die Feldpartitur. Mirkroprozessuale Transkription von Videodaten', in M. Corsten et al. (eds) *Videographie praktizieren*. Wiesbaden: VS Verlag (Springer).

Palmer, V. (1928) *Field Studies in Sociology: A Student's Manual*. Chicago: University of Chicago Press.

Park, R.E. (1939) 'A Note on the Origins of the Society for Social Research.' *Bulletin of the Society for Social Research* August, p. 4.

Park, R.E. and Burgess, E.W. (1921) *Introduction to the Science of Sociology*. Chicago: University of Chicago Press.

Pfadenhauer, M. and Grenz, T. (2015) 'Uncovering the Essence: The Why and How of Supplementing Observation with Participation in Phenomenology-Based Ethnography.' *Journal of Contemporary Ethnography*, 44(5): 598–616.

Pink, S. (2007) *Doing Visual Ethnography: Images, Media and Representation in Research*, 2nd edn. London: Sage.

Pink, S. (2015) *Doing Sensory Ethnography*. 2nd edn. London: Sage.

Platt, J. (1994) 'The Chicago School and First-hand Data.' *History of the Human Sciences* 7: 57-80.

Platt, J. (1995) 'Research Methods and the Second Chicago School', in G.A. Fine, *A Second Chicago School?* Chicago: The Chicago University Press. Pp. 82-107.

Plummer, K. (ed.) (1991a) *Symbolic Interactionism. Vol. I: Foundations and History*. Aldershot: Edward Elgar Publishing Limited.

Plummer, K. (ed.) (1991b) *Symbolic Interactionism. Vol. II: Contemporary Issues*. Aldershot: Edward Elgar Publishing Limited.

Plummer, K. (ed.) (1997) *The Chicago School: Critical Assessments*. London: Routledge.

Popper, K. (1935) *Logik der Forschung*. Wien: Springer. (English edition: *The Logic of Scientific Discovery*. London: Routledge, 1992.)

Raab, J. (2001) *Soziologie des Geruchs*. Konstanz: UVK.

Raab, J. (2008) *Visuelle Wissenssoziologie. Theoretische Konzeption und materiale Analysen*. Konstanz: UVK.

Reichertz, J. and Englert, C.J. (2011) *Einführung in die qualitative Videoanalyse. Eine hermeneutisch-wissenssoziologische Fallanalyse*. Wiesbaden: VS Verlag (Springer).

Rose, A.M. (ed.) (1962) *Human Behavior and Social Process: An Interactionist Approach*. London: Routledge.

Schafer, M.R. (1994) *Soundscapes: Our Sonic Environment and the Tuning of the World*. Rochester, VT: Destiny Books.

Scheff, T. (1975) *Labeling Madness*. Englewood Cliffs, NJ: Spectrum Books.

Scheler, M. (2008 [1923]) The Nature of Sympathy. Translated by Peter Heath. New Brunswick, N.J.: Transaction Publishers.

Schutz, A. (1962) *Collected Papers, Vol. 1*. Edited by M. Natanson. The Hague: Martinus Nijhoff.

Schutz, A. (1967 [1932]) *The Phenomenology of the Social World*. Translated by George Walsh and Frederick Lehnert. Evanston: Northwestern University Press.

Schutz, A. and Luckmann, T. (1973) *The Structures of the Life-World*, Vol. I. Translated by R. Zaner and H Engelhardt. Evanston: Northwestern University Press.

Schutz, A. and Luckmann, T. (1989) *The Structures of the Life-World*, Vol. II. Translated by R. Zaner and D.J. Parent. Evanston: Northwestern University Press.

Seale, C., Gobo, G., Gubrium, J.F. and Silverman, D. (2004) *Qualitative Research Practice*. London: Sage.

Shibutani, T. (1986) *Social Processes: An Introduction to Sociology*. Berkeley and Los Angeles, CA: University of California Press.

Silverman, D. (2010) *Doing Qualitative Research: A Practical Handbook*, 3rd edn. London: Sage.

Silverman, D. (ed.) (2011) *Qualitative Research*, 3rd edn. London: Sage.

Silverman, D. (2015) *Interpreting Qualitative Data*, 4th edn. London: Sage.

Smith, P. (ed.) (1998) *The New American Cultural Sociology*. Cambridge, UK: Cambridge University Press.

Soeffner, H.-G. (2004) 'Social Scientific Hermeneutics', in Flick, U. et al. (eds.). *A Companion to Qualitative Research*. Transl. by Bryan Jenner. London: Sage, 95–100).

Spiegelberg, H. (1982) *The Phenomenological Movement*. The Hague/Boston/London: Martinus Nijhoff.

Spillman, L. (2002) 'Introduction: Culture and Cultural Sociology', in L. Spillman (ed.), *Cultural Sociology*. Malden, MA and Oxford, UK: Blackwell Publishers.

Srubar, I. (1988) *Kosmion. Die Genese der pragmatischen Lebensweltheorie von Alfred Schütz und ihr anthropologischer Hintergrund*. Frankfurt/M.: Suhrkamp.

Srubar, I. (2005) 'The pragmatic theory of the life-world as a basis for intercultural comparison', in M. Endress et al. (eds), *Explorations of the LifeWorld*. Dordrecht: Springer. pp. 235-66.

Stoller, P. (1989) *The Taste of Ethnographic Things*. Philadelphia: The University of Pennsylvania Press.

Strauss, A. (1979) *Negotiations: Varieties, Contexts, Processes and Social Order*. San Francisco: Jossey-Bass.

Strauss, A. (1991) 'A Social World Perspective.' In A. Strauss (ed.), *Creating Sociological Awareness: Collective Images and Symbolic Representations*. New Brunswick: Transaction. pp. 233–244.

Strauss, A. (1993) *Continual Permutations of Action*. New York: Aldine de Gruyter.

Swidler, A. (1986) 'Culture in Action: Symbols and Strategies.' In *American Sociological Review* 51: 273–286.

Thomas, W.I. and Thomas, D.S. (1928) *The Child in America: Behavior Problems and Programs*. New York: Knopf.

Thomas, W.I. and Znaniecki, F. (1918–1920) *The Polish Peasant in Europe and America. Monograph of an Immigrant Group*, 5 Volumes. Boston, MA: Richard Badger.

Turner, R. (1956) 'Role-taking, Role Standpoint, and Reference Group Behavior.' *American Journal of Sociology* 61(4): 316–328.

Weber, M. (1980 [1904]) Die Objektivität sozialwissenschaftlicher und sozialpolitischer Erkenntnis. In Max Weber, *Gesammelte Aufsätze zur Wissenschaftslehre* (7. Aufl.). Tübingen: Mohr. pp. 146–214.

Weber, M. (1978 [1922]) *Economy and Society: An Outline of Interpretive Sociology*. Edited by G. Roth and C. Wittich. Berkeley: University of California Press.

Wilson, T.P. (1970) 'Conceptions and Forms of Sociological Explanation.' *American Sociological Review*, 35(4): 697–710.

# 18

# Multiple Correspondence Analysis

Julien Duval

## INTRODUCTION

Multiple correspondence analysis (MCA) is a statistical method which originated in France, where it was developed in the 1960s and the 1970s. French sociologists and statisticians have used it since the mid-1970s. Pierre Bourdieu used it, notably in *Distinction* (2010 [1979]), which is one of the most influential sociology books, especially in the sociology of culture. However, MCA and its sociological uses were largely ignored outside France for two decades. It is only very recently that MCA began to gain greater attention. For some years now it has been used in the sociology of culture internationally, especially to discuss *Distinction*'s analysis of cultural practices and lifestyles.

In a nutshell, MCA can be seen as 'a data analysis technique which provides a geometric representation of positions by points as a means of summarizing relations between categorized variables' (Meuleman and Savage, 2013: 235), or as 'a descriptive and inductive method for exploring relationships of categorical variables and representing them graphically in a low-dimensional Euclidean space in which closeness of locations indicates similarity of categories and individuals' (Purhonen and Wright, 2013: 258). In fact, MCA is applied to large data tables, in which individuals are characterized by categorical data (sex, level of education, answers given by respondents to a set of closed questions, etc.) MCA enables one to 'sum up' these tables, to unveil the main factors that organize or underlie the data. It is an extension of Correspondence Analysis (CA) which is itself an extension of an old and well-known method, Principle Correspondence Analysis (PCA). In fact, MCA can be seen as an analogue of PCA for numerical variables. CA has been developed in several locations, but MCA is very often attributed to the French mathematician Jean-Paul Benzecri who developed in the 1960s with some of his colleagues what is often called 'French data analysis'. The phrase 'MCA' seems to have been coined in 1975 by Benzecri's student, Ludovic Lebart (Le Roux and Rouanet, 2010).

Bourdieu was one of the first French sociologists to use MCA, in the first drafts of *Distinction* which were published as early as 1976. In *Distinction*, MCA enabled him to lay out the relationships between what he called the social space and the space of lifestyles. In this book, as in later publications (for instance on the economic field, the academic field, the field of the higher education institutions, etc.), he used MCA in a very inventive and fecund way, and in close conjunction with the concept of the field and the relational way of thinking which he promoted. MCA made it possible to explore the structure of the social fields that he studied and Bourdieu sometimes compared the resulting figures of MCA to geographical maps (see for instance Bourdieu, 2010 [1979]: 165). MCA is often seen as 'Bourdieu's statistical method' (Le Roux and Rouanet, 2010: 4). Bourdieu himself explained:

> ... I make extensive use of correspondence analysis, in preference to multivariate regression for instance, ... because correspondence analysis is a relational technique of data analysis whose philosophy corresponds exactly to what, in my view, the reality of the social world is. It is a technique which 'thinks in terms of relation', as I try to do precisely with the notion of field. (Bourdieu and Wacquant, 1992: 96)

The fate of MCA in sociology cannot be disconnected from Bourdieu's legacy. Today the wide influence of Bourdieu's work is one of the major factors leading to the dissemination of MCA. In the sociology of culture, the papers today that use MCA are almost always influenced by Bourdieu: some try to reproduce, on new objects or in new countries, the same empirical operations, while others discuss the Bourdieu's analyses themselves.

This chapter first presents the famous use of MCA by Bourdieu in *Distinction*. Then some mathematical elements are provided in order to allow us better to understand the technique and its peculiarities. The issues that MCA and its sociological uses can raise are then discussed. The last sections of the chapter are devoted to the contemporary uses of MCA in France as well as in other countries, and recent developments of MCA more generally.

## MCA IN *DISTINCTION*

*Distinction* was the first book in which Bourdieu used MCA. Although the famous figure of 'the space of social positions' was not directly produced by MCA (Bourdieu, 2010 [1979]: 120, 122–3), the figures included in the chapter on the dominant class ('The Sense of Distinction') resulted from MCA.[1] These figures help us to understand both the technique itself and how Bourdieu used it in his theoretical framework. MCA enabled Bourdieu to demonstrate two main assumptions of the chapter 'The sense of distinction': (1) the dominant class is 'a relatively autonomous space whose structure is defined by the distribution of economic and cultural capital among its members'; and (2) there is a relationship between lifestyles and positions in the social space (Bourdieu, 2010 [1979]: 257).

The chapter is partly based upon a survey that Bourdieu and his research team carried out in the 1960s. Interviewees had been invited to reply to a questionnaire which included questions on practices and tastes in various areas and some questions on individuals' characteristics (sex, date of birth, occupation, approximate annual income of the family, etc.) For the chapter 'The Sense of Distinction', Bourdieu and his colleagues retained only interviewees who belonged to the dominant class and ten questions that pertained to various cultural domains: the musical knowledge and tastes of the interviewees (they were asked which musical works they knew and liked from within a predetermined list; they were also invited to choose their three favourite singers), their favourite painters, the personal qualities they most appreciated, the kind of shop where they got their furniture, and so on. All the variables were categorical. MCA was applied to a large table that indicated, for the 467 interviewees, what they had replied to each question.

When such a table is subjected to MCA, the statistical software calculates new variables that are, contrary to initial variables, numerical and ordered. The calculations are carried out so that the first new variable expresses the most structuring factor of the data (and the last variable is the least important). The resulting figures of MCA are based upon the coordinates (for these new variables) of the individuals on the one hand, and of the modalities of each variable on the other hand. Figure 18.1 (which is a simplified version of the one to be found in *Distinction*) corresponds to the cloud of modalities (each point representing a modality) according to the first two variables.

As Bourdieu wrote, 'analysis of correspondences makes it possible to isolate ... different sets of preferences' (Bourdieu, 2010: 258). The modalities that correspond to the most distinctive and legitimate tastes tend to be concentrated on the left side of the diagram, whereas the modalities that correspond to the most popular singers or the classical works of bourgeois culture are on the right side. Bourdieu interpreted the axis as an opposition between intellectual taste (on the left) and bourgeois taste (on the right). In the same way, he used the second axis to isolate sets of tastes and preferences. For instance, the modalities on the top of the diagram refer to an old-fashioned lifestyle (inherited furniture, traditional French cuisine, etc.) which characterizes the individuals who originate from the bourgeoisie. Thus MCA is not only used to identify various lifestyles, it also provides

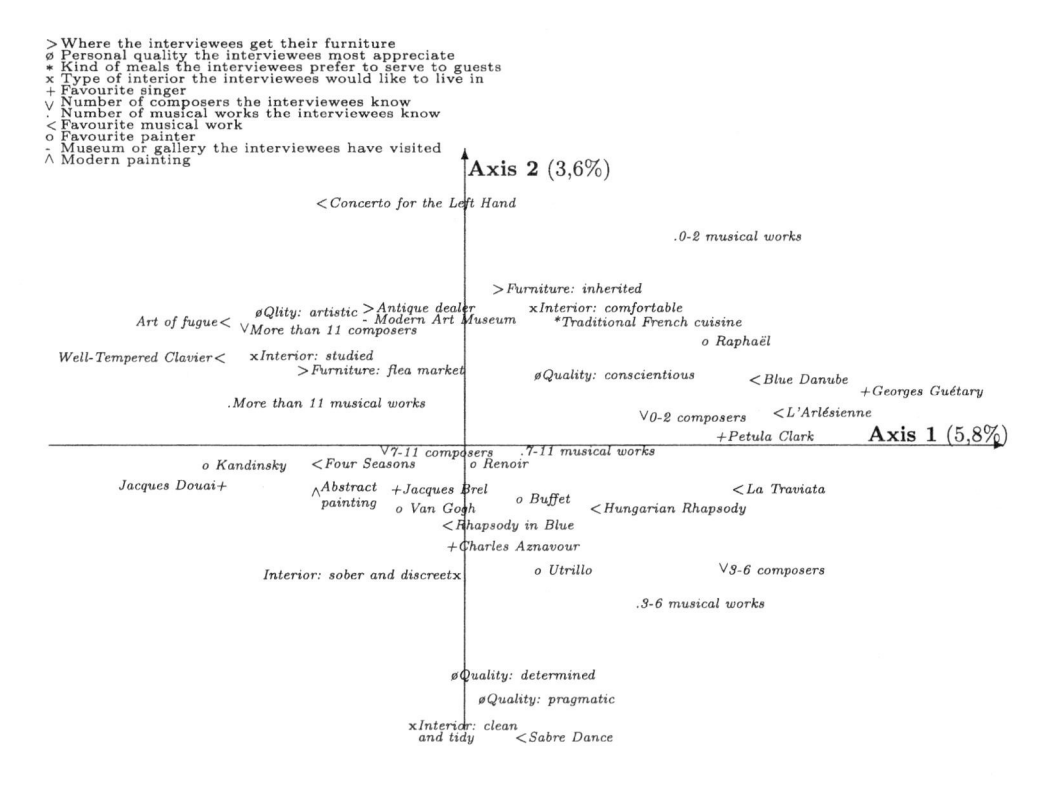

## Figure 18.1 Variants of the dominant taste (a simplified version of Bourdieu (2010 [1979]: 259): only the modalities which most contribute to axes are represented)

Legend:
- &gt; Where the interviewees get their furniture
- ø Personal quality the interviewees most appreciate
- \* Kind of meals the interviewees prefer to serve to guests
- x Type of interior the interviewees would like to live in
- \+ Favourite singer
- ∨ Number of composers the interviewees know
- . Number of musical works the interviewees know
- &lt; Favourite musical work
- o Favourite painter
- \- Museum or gallery the interviewees have visited
- ∧ Modern painting

Modalities positioned on Axis 1 (5,8%) and Axis 2 (3,6%):

- &lt;Concerto for the Left Hand
- .0-2 musical works
- &gt;Furniture: inherited
- xInterior: comfortable
- øQlity: artistic &gt;Antique dealer
- \- Modern Art Museum
- \*Traditional French cuisine
- Art of fugue&lt;   ∨More than 11 composers
- o Raphaël
- Well-Tempered Clavier&lt;   xInterior: studied
- &gt;Furniture: flea market
- øQuality: conscientious
- &lt;Blue Danube
- \+Georges Guétary
- .More than 11 musical works
- ∨0-2 composers   &lt;L'Arlésienne
- \+Petula Clark    Axis 1 (5,8%)
- ∨7-11 composers   .7-11 musical works
- o Kandinsky   &lt;Four Seasons   o Renoir
- Jacques Douai+
- ∧Abstract  +Jacques Brel
- painting   o Van Gogh   o Buffet   &lt;La Traviata
- &lt;Rhapsody in Blue   &lt;Hungarian Rhapsody
- \+Charles Aznavour
- Interior: sober and discreet x   o Utrillo   ∨3-6 composers
- .3-6 musical works
- øQuality: determined
- øQuality: pragmatic
- xInterior: clean and tidy   &lt;Sabre Dance

empirical evidence for some theoretical assumptions. The fact that, in the diagram, two modalities are close to each other when they tend to be chosen by the same individuals, echoes Bourdieu's analyses of the coherence of *habitus*: *habitus* leads a given person to have the same kind of preferences in different domains. Indeed the diagram confirms that those who like the most popular singers – e.g. Petula Clark in France in the 1960s – like generally the most famous musical works, rather than the most distinctive ones. MCA also proves the argument as to the homology between the different fields of cultural production. So the positions of the points on the first axis suggest that the opposition, within the musical domain, between *Well Tempered Clavier* and *Blue Danube* is, in some respects, comparable to the opposition, within the visual arts, between Kandinsky and Raphael. Stressing the strong affinity between the diagrams of MCA and the Bourdieusian relational way of thinking, it is also noteworthy that MCA tends to confirm the relational intuition that taste preferences are always about rejecting certain cultural forms while embracing others, the fact that two modalities that are rarely chosen by the same individuals are distant from each other on the diagram

suggests that those who like the *Art of Fugue* rarely appreciate *The Blue Danube* or *La Traviata*.

Bourdieu used MCA in *Distinction* not only to propose a rich and relational description of lifestyles, but also to develop an explanatory approach. Indeed, he used the technique of 'supplementary variables' which consists in projecting to the diagrams some variables that were not retained, as 'active variables', in the table. To explain this technique, one must realize that, alongside the diagrams of modalities, MCA produces a diagram of individuals, where each interviewee is represented by a point according to his or her coordinate on the new variables. Bourdieu and his colleagues worked on such a diagram, but it was not published in *Distinction*, probably because Bourdieu thought that it would not have been interesting for readers, as the interviewees were anonymous. Bourdieu and colleagues isolated on the diagram the individuals that belong, for instance, to a given class fraction. By repeating this for all the class fractions, they got 'subclouds' that were located very differently in the space of lifestyles (see Figure 18.2). For instance, higher education teachers and artistic producers tended to concentrate on the left side of the diagram, whereas

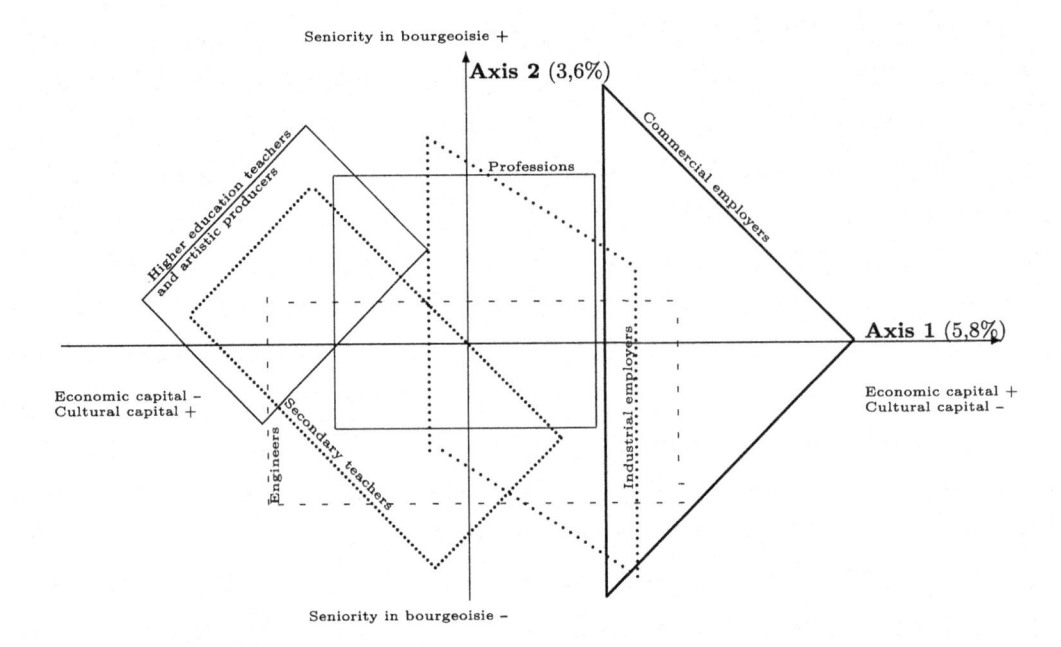

**Figure 18.2 The fractions of the dominant class in the space of lifestyles**

commercial employers were located on the right side. Professionals (physicians, lawyers, etc.) tended to stand in an intermediary position. By also projecting income level and education level as supplementary variables, Bourdieu showed that, as his theory predicted, lifestyles were connected to the position of individuals in the distribution of economic and cultural capital among the members of the dominant class.

Bourdieu used MCA in a very rich way in *Distinction*. Later on, he used MCA in his large-scale study of higher education institutions in France (Bourdieu, 1996 [1989]). The data are taken from a survey that his research team carried out in many institutions throughout the country. Using MCA, he showed that French higher education constituted a field the structure of which was homologous to that of the field of power. The first axes of MCA reveal fundamental oppositions between, on the one hand, the 'royal road' and 'the tradesmen's entrance' and, on the other hand, between the 'academic colleges' and the 'colleges of power', reflecting the opposition, within the field of power, between the academic/artistic pole and the economical/political pole (Bourdieu, 1996 [1989]).

The other papers and books where Bourdieu used MCA were based on prosopographic databases.[2] In 1978, Bourdieu and Monique de Saint-Martin published a study of the presidents of 216 of France's largest companies. MCA showed the opposition between the heads of the big industrial firms, who were closely linked to the State, and the heads of the private companies, who had less educational capital (Bourdieu and Saint-Martin, 1978). Bourdieu also used MCA to analyse the structure of the academic field (Bourdieu, 1988 [1984]) and the actors responsible for a major reform in French housing policy (Bourdieu, 2005 [2000]).

Every time Bourdieu used MCA, he was seeking to unveil the structure of a particular social field. MCA's findings have always supported the idea that the volume of capital was the first structuring factor of social fields, and that the composition of capital was the second factor. From his point of view, there is an opposition, within each (relatively) autonomous field, between the social agents who are endowed with forms of capital which tend to be efficacious in all the fields, and the social agents who are endowed with forms of capital which are specific to the particular field in question. Despite appearances, *Distinction*'s MCA results were not an exception: the first structuring factor was the composition of capital, because the MCA was applied to the members of the 'dominant class' who have approximately the same position in respect of the volume of capital. Another common thread to the uses made by Bourdieu of MCA is the analysis of the relationship between the space of objective positions and the space of stances or 'positions-takings' (*prises de position*). For instance, in *Distinction*, using socio-demographic variables as supplementary variables he looked into the relationship that pertains between lifestyles and positions in the social space. In *Homo Academicus* (1988 [1984]) he considered the relations between the political positions French academics took in May 1968 and the positions they held in the academic field.

The last MCA work that Bourdieu (1999) published, pertained to the field of cultural production. The paper is devoted to the field of publishers of French-language literature in the 1990s. A prosopographic database was constructed from various sources: catalogues, archives, interviews with publishers, databases on the internet, press cuttings, and so on. The 'individuals' – in the statistical sense – were 56 French publishing companies. Sixteen variables were used and groups were divided under five headings in terms of legal and financial status, financial and commercial dependence, market share, symbolic capital, foreign literature (see also Le Roux and Rouanet, 2010: 92–7). By the means of MCA, a first opposition was found. On the one hand, some long-standing, major companies cumulate capital of all varieties – economic, commercial and symbolic. On the other hand, small, recently-formed companies are practically devoid of every kind of capital, even if they have some symbolic capital among avant-garde writers and readers. In other words, this opposition differentiated publishing houses according to the volume of capital each possessed. The second factor pertains to the structure of capital and opposes the major companies which were the richest in financial capital and commercial strength, with the large firms who were the richest in symbolic capital.

## SOME MATHEMATICAL ISSUES

To understand in what sense MCA 'sums up' a table, one can draw a very simple table (see Table 18.1) and adopt a geometrical approach to it (Le Roux and Rouanet, 2004). This table contains for ten French occupational groups (column 1) their average monthly salary in euro (column 2) and their average school leaving age (column 3).

All of the information contained in Table 18.1 can be displayed in a graph, by plotting the monthly salary against the school leaving age. A cloud of ten points representing the occupational groups is produced in this way. However, the shape of the cloud of points depends on the chosen scale (Figure 18.3), which can only be arbitrary. Indeed the two variables are heterogeneous: they are expressed in different units of measurement (euros and years). Their mean value and standard deviation are not comparable. To overcome this difficulty, statisticians often 'standardize' the variables: the initial variables are replaced by new variables, the mean of which is 0 and the standard deviation is 1 (columns 4 and 5). Standardization does not affect the hierarchies between the

**Table 18.1. School leaving age and monthly salary for ten occupational groups**

| | | Observed values | | After standardization | |
|---|---|---|---|---|---|
| Individual | (1) Occupational groups | (2) School leaving age | (3) Monthly salary | (4) School leaving age | (5) Monthly salary |
| i1 | Middle management in the public sector | 20 | 2100 | −0.13 | 0.08 |
| i2 | Supervisors, foremen | 19 | 2000 | −0.56 | −0.06 |
| i3 | Unskilled workers (industry) | 18 | 1200 | −0.99 | −1.17 |
| i4 | Primary School teachers | 22 | 1600 | 0.73 | −0.61 |
| i5 | Skilled workers (industry) | 18 | 1500 | −0.99 | −0.75 |
| i6 | Engineers | 22 | 3100 | 0.73 | 1.48 |
| i7 | Technicians | 20 | 1900 | −0.13 | −0.20 |
| i8 | Company executives | 22 | 3300 | 0.73 | 1.76 |
| i9 | Scientific professions | 25 | 2600 | 2.02 | 0.78 |
| i10 | Agricultural workers | 17 | 1100 | −1.42 | −1.31 |
| | Mean value: | 20.3 | 2040 | 0 | 0 |
| | Standard deviation: | 2.3 | 715.8 | 1 | 1 |

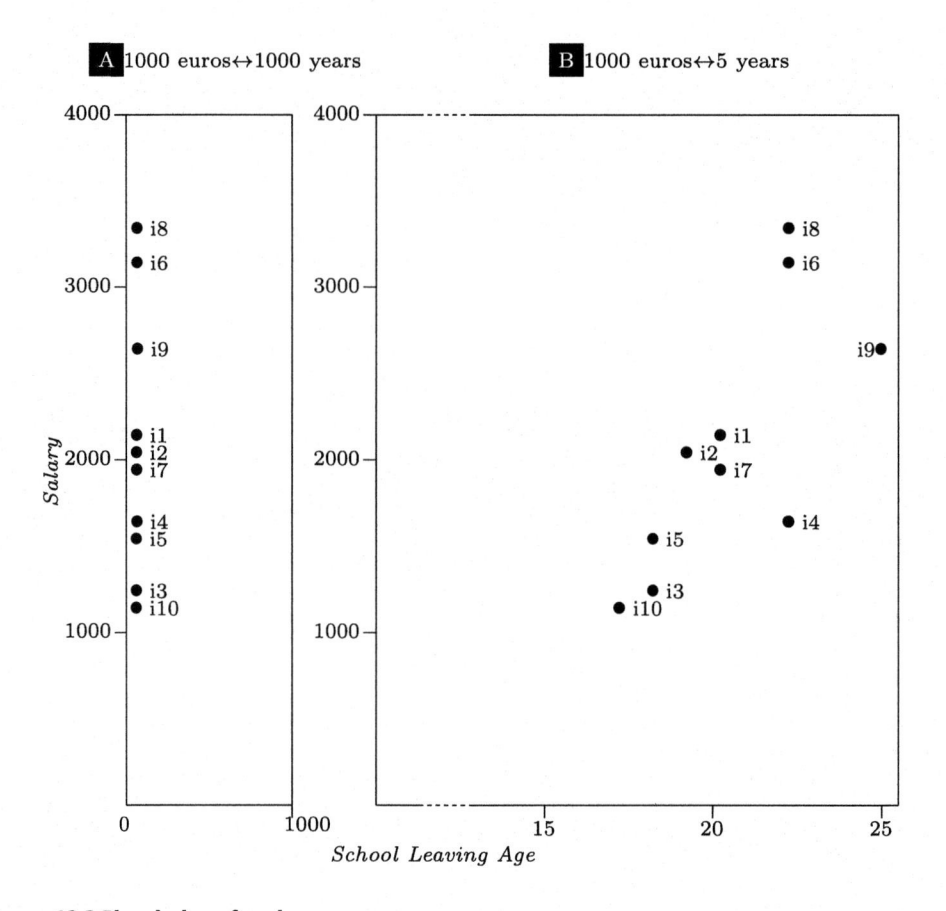

**Figure 18.3 The choice of scale**

statistical individuals. For instance, in Table 18.1, the agricultural workers always have the lowest paid jobs and company executives have the highest paid jobs. After standardization, variables can be represented in a graphic (Figure 18.4). The centre of the axes is also the barycentre of the cloud of points (G). This barycentre – or 'mean point' – can be seen as an eleventh – and fictive – group which would have the average salary (€2040) and would have left formal education at the age of 20.3.

When the table is then subjected to PCA, the calculation made by statistical software amounts to determining first the line through G on which the projection of the cloud of points is most scattered (Figure 18.5). Among the lines going through G, this line is the one which gives the greatest insight into the shape of the two-dimensional cloud. In that sense, this line is the best 'summary' of the cloud. Because of standardization of the variables, this line is here the first bisector. If the cloud is orthogonally projected on this line, one will get a new cloud whose variance is equal to 1.73. There is no other line through G on which the projected cloud has a higher variance. In PCA, this line is the first axis. For the following axes, one has to examine the lines that go through G and that are orthogonal to the first axis. The second axis will be the line on which the projected cloud will have the higher variance. The process is repeated as many times as the initial table has variables. Here, as the table has two variables, only two axes are determined, and the second axis is necessarily the second bisector – it is the only line that goes through G and is orthogonal to the first axis. The diagrams that PCA produces are only the projection of the cloud on the first axis (Figure 18.6) and the projection of the initial variables on the first axis (Figure 18.7).

The axes are easy enough to interpret. The first axis expresses the fundamental correlation between the salary and the school leaving axis (Figure 18.7), and the opposition between those who earn high salaries and left school when they were relatively old, and those who earn

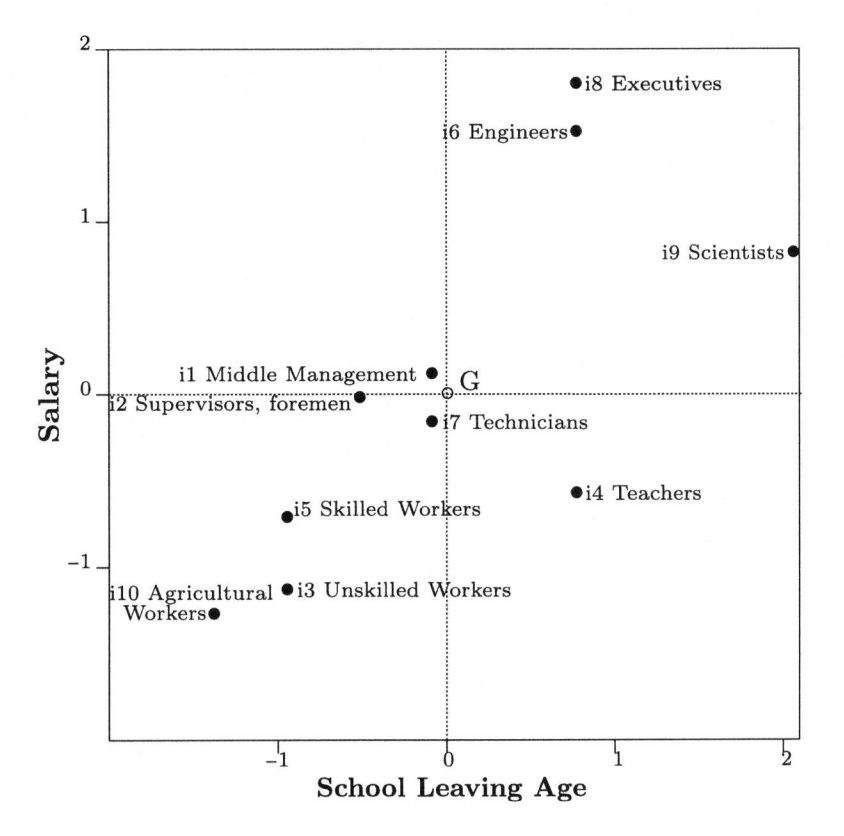

**Figure 18.4 The ten occupational groups (representation after standardization)**

low salaries and who left school relatively early. The second axis expresses a more minor opposition: the correlation between the two variables is not total, and there is an opposition, among the most privileged groups, between those who are highly educated without earning very high salaries – academics, researchers, teachers – and those who earn high salaries but who left school earlier, such as executives in the private sector. It is noteworthy that, in Figure 18.6, a group is positioned further away from the centre of the axes (G), the more different from the eleventh fictive group it is.

This example enables us to understand in which sense PCA produces a 'summary' of a table. It also shows that PCA is only *a change of basis*. Indeed the only difference between the Figures 18.4 and 18.6 is that the cloud has been rotated. MCA that is an extension of PCA could be understood in the same way. It implies a preliminary operation – made by software – in order to transform categorical variables. For each modality of each categorical variable, a dichotomic (or dummy) variable is generated. It takes the value 1 if the individual has the property that corresponds to the modality, otherwise it takes the value 0. Such variables are not genuine numerical variables but, as numerical variables, they have a mean value that expresses the frequency of the modality in the studied population. To subject a table with categorical data to MCA amounts to subjecting a table with these dichotomic variables to PCA.[3]

That is why MCA can be understood as PCA. A new system of axes is determined. The first axis expresses the most structuring factor. The further away from the centre of the axes the individuals tend to be positioned, the more different from the 'mean' – and fictive – individual they are. For instance, in a predominantly male population, the relatively few women present tend to be represented by points which are further away from the centre of the axes. In the cloud of modalities, the modality 'male' is closer to the centre of the axes than the modality 'female'. Two modalities which are close to each other on the first axes are likely to be often associated in the studied population, and two variables which are close to each other in

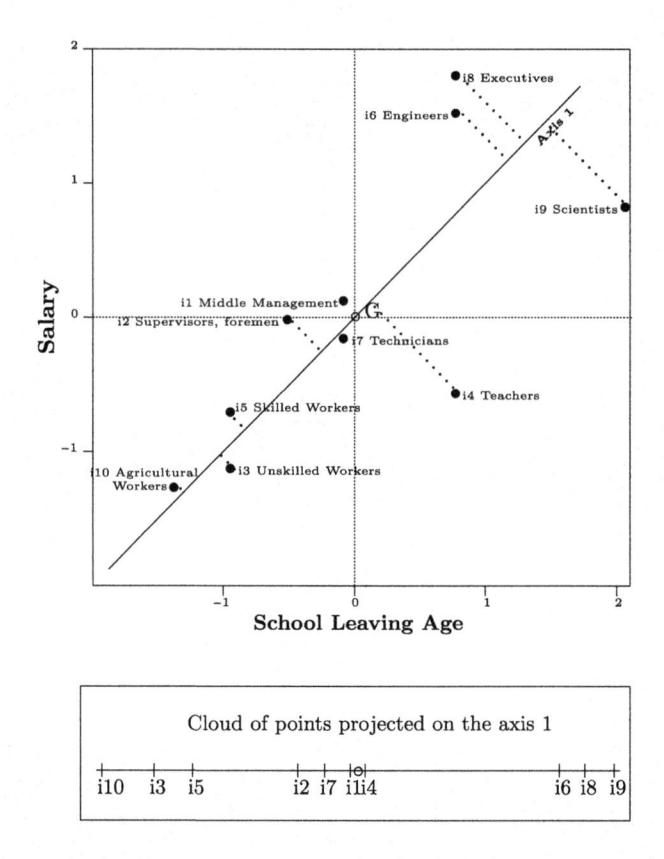

**Figure 18.5 The determination of axis 1**

PCA are likely to be correlated. The role which the modalities play in MCA is comparable in many respects to the role which the variables play in PCA. Furthermore, as already said, supplementary variables or supplementary individuals can be projected on axes and one can isolate individuals which belong to a given category, as Bourdieu did for class fractions in *Distinction*. Contemporary software permits the plotting of ellipses which indicate where individuals of a given category tend to be concentrated.

MCA can be also compared briefly to other statistical methods which are used in sociology. If Table 18.1 had been subjected to a linear regression analysis, based on the hypothesis that school leaving age (X) contributes to the determining of salary (Y), one would have concluded that an additional year of education corresponds to a wage premium of €225. There are many similarities between MCA and regression analysis. First, in both cases, the relationships between variables (or modalities) are studied. Second, the least square line that is drawn in regression analysis aims to sum up the cloud of points, as the first axis does in MCA. The two lines are just constructed in slightly different ways. But a salient difference is that MCA is not used to measure the effect of a variable on other variables, and that its users expect it to give results not only about the variables, but also about the individuals. Another major difference is that regression analysis leads to distinguishing between a dependent variable and independent variables and, more broadly, to stating a model, where hypotheses are made about the relationship between the variables, and the sense and the form of this relationship. Furthermore, regression analysis is very often practised in a probabilistic framework, which involves new hypotheses. By contrast, MCA can be used almost without hypotheses. It was sometimes presented as a 'model-free method'. In fact Benzecri did not like the mainstream statistical approach prominent at the time. He thought that many researchers were idealists and tended to substitute their own a prioris for observations of reality (Van Meter et al., 1994), whereas 'what we need is a rigorous method that extracts structures from the data' (Benzecri et al., 1973: 6).

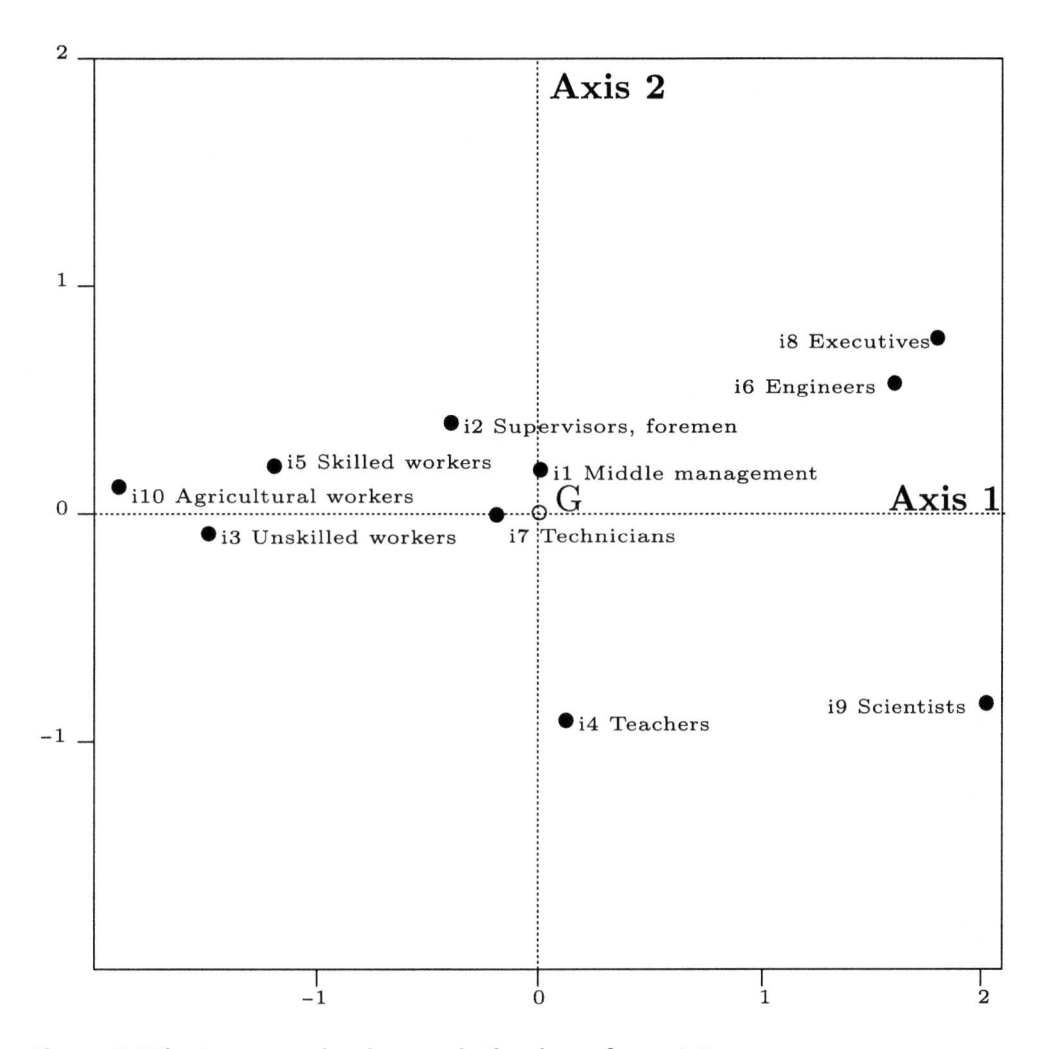

**Figure 18.6 The ten occupational groups in the plane of axes 1–2**

'The model should follow the data, not the reverse' is one of his famous principles. According to him, MCA reverses the mainstream approach in highly productive ways.

MCA can also be compared to classification methods. However, MCA generates spaces, whereas classification methods generate classes. This point is significant in Bourdieusian sociology, in which the concept of the social space aimed to solve some issues raised by the more usual concepts of class or group (Bourdieu, 1985). MCA is sometimes assimilated to latent class analysis which measures a background variable that is not directly measurable. It is true that in some respects axes in MCA can be compared to synthetic and latent variables.

## DEBATES OVER MCA

Although in its history MCA was more often ignored than criticized, it has attracted some critics, at least in France. The French sociologist Philippe Cibois pointed out what he called 'the *distinction* effect' (Cibois, 1997): the users of MCA may be tempted to focus on the atypical combinations of properties located at the extremities of the first axes, whereas these combinations may correspond to very few individuals and be less relevant than the 'mean profile' in describing the whole population. For instance, in the survey used in *Distinction*, there may be very few respondents who simultaneously possess the most distinctive tastes, ranging from *Art*

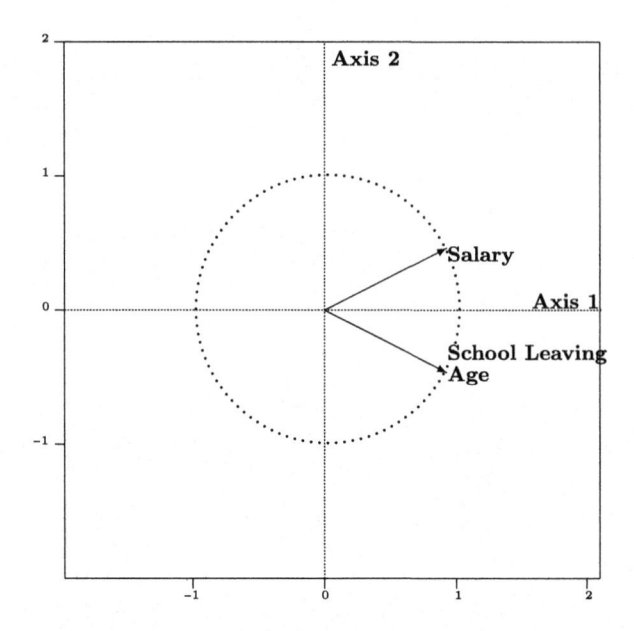

**Figure 18.7 The variables in the plane of axes 1–2**

of *Fugue*, *Well-Tempered Clavier* and studied interiors, through to Kandinsky and the French singer Jacques Douai. No individual might have all of these tastes and preferences. For this very reason, it can be useful to check in the table that had been subjected to MCA how many individuals are involved in the atypical combinations. This point is interesting in the sociology of culture, because Bernard Lahire (2006: 132–41), drawing upon Cibois, argued that MCA could have contributed to leading Bourdieu in *Distinction* to have overestimated the strength of legitimate culture. Whereas Bourdieu stressed the coherence of *habitus*, Lahire developed the concept of 'dissonance' in order to argue that more individuals tend to have practices which are scattered in the space of lifestyles than Bourdieu's use of MCA would have led us to believe.

MCA has also often been criticized from mainstream statistical points of view. The supporters of regression analysis have argued that, contrary to their preferred positions, MCA does not neutralize structural effects and does not enable one to measure the specific effects of variables. This can seem a serious absence, for measuring the effects of variables is often seen as the key objective of statistical sociology. Furthermore, the supporters of modelling approaches have stressed that MCA can be used as 'black box' that prevents social scientists from developing good models of the phenomena they are studying (Van Meter et al., 1994).

For the same reasons, some French statisticians, without rejecting MCA, argued that it can only be a 'descriptive method' that could be implemented as a first step before using other, mainstream methods (Desrosières, 2008). It is clear that Benzecri and the promoters of MCA could not agree with these criticisms. These disadvantages are in fact advantages from their point of view. However, it has been argued that, contrary to Benzecri's thinking, MCA is not entirely a model-free method (Clausen, 1988: 6). For instance, selecting some active variables rather than others implies the presence of hypotheses.

Bourdieu's position on all these points should be noted, because it is much more elaborated than some might think (Duval, 2013). First, Bourdieu would have agreed that MCA does not neutralize structural effects. But even in his early work he criticized what he called the 'sociology of variables'. He was always reluctant to separate the effects of a variable, and he advocated the concept of 'structural causality' (Bourdieu, 2010 [1979]: 96–100) to stress 'the complete system of relationships which constitutes the true principle of the specific strength and form of the effects registered in any particular correlation'. MCA turned out to be a powerful tool to study 'structural causality'. Second, Bourdieu never saw MCA as a model-free method. While doing MCA, he paid very close attention to the selection of the individuals and the variables, knowing that the selection of both implies hypotheses and involves choices that impact upon the results of the MCA. He used MCA neither indiscriminately nor as a 'black box'. On the contrary, he explained several times how the 'square-table of pertinent properties' that is subjected to MCA should be rigorously constructed. To analyse a social space properly, one must address in systematic fashion a set of questions as to both the limits of the universe being studied and the properties and groups of agents that are 'efficient' there (Bourdieu and Wacquant, 1992: 230).

Bourdieu did not see MCA as a preliminary and descriptive method. In one of his last books, he went so far as to claim that MCA was an explanatory method (Bourdieu, 2005 [2000]: 102), a phrase which is usually reserved for modelling approaches. In saying this he meant to challenge mainstream models and methods. Since his earliest research, in Algeria at the end of the 1950s, he was critical of the mainstream uses of statistics by social scientists. He shared many of the views of the American qualitative sociologists who have critiqued Paul Lazarsfeld, who was then at the peak of his career and level of influence (Wright Mills, 1959; Cicourel, 1964). But, unlike the promoters of ethnomethodology, for instance, he refused to leave the statistical field to Lazarsfeld. He belonged to a Durkheimian tradition in which statistics are regarded as very powerful tools for sociology. Bourdieu criticized mainstream uses of statistics. But he searched for an alternative, which he eventually found in the 1970s, by using MCA alongside field theory. The social spaces that he constructed by using MCA can be regarded as explanatory models which aim to account for the nature of social practices and position-takings.

## MCA IN FRENCH SOCIOLOGY OF ART AND CULTURE

Because MCA had been developed in France, it was used earlier on there than in other countries. The use of MCA by sociologists is also a little more disconnected from the influence of Bourdieu than has been the case in other countries, for Bourdieu was not the only French social scientist who used this method. In French sociology, MCA has become one of the most popular statistical methods, alongside the more usual approaches. Its popularity partly comes from the fact that it was used in the 1970s and the 1980s at the INSEE (Institut National des Statistiques et des Études Économiques), and in some applied research offices and private sector opinion polls (Desrosières, 2008). Hence sociological uses of MCA in France are quite diverse. Some sociologists are strongly influenced by Bourdieu and use MCA with field theory. Others have used MCA as a descriptive tool, in order to identify correlations or to explore data tables.

This diversity can partly be seen in the literature which is based upon the French surveys concerning cultural practices. Since 1973, the French *Ministère de la Culture* has carried out a national survey on five occasions, and has published the results in various reports and books. These publications often raised the question as to whether the analyses of Bourdieu were still valid, and themselves often used MCA, but in order to construct typologies rather than to construct spaces. For instance, Donnat (1993) distinguishes between six kinds of readers, on the basis of the results of MCA. Philippe Coulangeon, a sociologist who published several papers based upon French surveys on cultural practices, has also used MCA, but sometimes as a preliminary method. In one of these papers, for example, he showed that in France the ties between aesthetic preference orientation and social status had changed since the era in which Bourdieu wrote *Distinction* (Coulangeon, 2003; see also Coulangeon and Lemel, 2007). He observed increased omnivorousness in upper-class tastes, even if he saw Peterson's (Peterson and Simkus, 1992) influential argument as an extension of Bourdieu's 'cultural legitimacy model'. He used responses to the question of the genres of music most frequently listened to from within the 17 music genres presented to respondents. All the 17 variables are used as active variables in MCA. The first axis arranges individuals hierarchically by degree of musical eclecticism, while the second axis is partly interpretable in terms of cultural legitimacy (as it opposed popular music genres with more 'distinctive' ones). Then he projected as supplementary variables six socio-demographic variables (age, sex, occupational status, educational attainment, income and social origin), and constructed a classification on the basis of MCA results in order to describe five 'preference profiles'. The last section of the paper used a logit model to measure the specific effects on musical preferences of the socio-demographic variables. His approach illustrates a use of MCA in French sociology which is only partly influenced by Bourdieusian methodology. MCA is used as a preliminary step, rather than as a 'core method', before implementing other and more standard statistical methods, involving classification in ascending hierarchical order and logistic regression.

The use of MCA alongside field theory is particularly associated with the journal *Actes de la Recherche en Sciences Sociales*, which Bourdieu founded in 1975 and directed until the time of his death. From 1975 to 2001, alongside the articles written by Bourdieu himself, about ten articles where MCA was used were published. The studied populations were various: MCA was used to construct the space of French farmers (Champagne, 1987), to unveil the relationships between the research topics of students in philosophy and their social and school characteristics (Soulié, 1995), to show that the field of French economists in the 1990s was homologous with the structure of the field of power, while refracting (but to a lesser degree than in most autonomous intellectual universes) external determinations (Lebaron, 1997). Some articles applied MCA to very original data, for instance a corpus of letters of denunciation received by a major newspaper (Boltanski et al., 1984). In a paper entitled 'Responses and respondents: Analysis of a political correspondence', Remi Lenoir (1988) analysed the answers sent by politicians to an association. He used some characteristics of the letters as active variables in MCA.

A few articles pertained to the sociology of culture (or, more precisely, to the sociology of art). Annie Verger (1991) studied the field of the avant-gardes in the 1990s. She worked on a French sample of 50 artists selected on the basis of the consecration given by a certain number of competing institutions (art galleries, cultural centres, etc.), in order to map the terrain of artistic celebrity and to distinguish the different tendencies of the avant-garde. The major structuring factors of the field of the avant-garde turned out to be the degree of internationalization of artists and an opposition between avant-gardes which had emerged in southern France and Paris respectively (Verger, 1991). Gisèle Sapiro (1996; 2002) studied the structure of the literary field during World War II, when France was occupied by the Germans. The first axis of MCA opposed writers according to how renowned they were. The second axis distinguished between two types of consecration – institutional ('heteronomous') and symbolic ('autonomous'). Sapiro paid great attention to the relationship between the political positions of the writers and their position in the literary field, arguing that at the heteronomous pole, most writers supported the newly established powers (the Vichy regime and the Nazis), whereas at the autonomous pole, most writers chose to fight them.

After the death of Bourdieu, other fields of cultural production were analysed by French sociologists who used MCA. Julien Duval (2006) constructed the field of French cinema using MCA for a sample of 250 active film directors. He explained in which measure the general model, developed by Bourdieu about all fields of cultural production (Bourdieu, 1996 [1989]) can be applied to the cinematographic field, and stressed especially that, at least in the French case, there is a continuum between the most autonomous pole and these productions most subject to commercial constraints (Duval, 2006). Sylvia Faure (2008) studied the material conditions of production and diffusion of choreographic works in the early 2000s. Carrying out a survey and using MCA, she showed that cultural policies which support the production and diffusion of 'live' shows contribute very significantly to the structuration of the choreographic field (Faure, 2008). Sophie Noël (2012) studied, within the space of the French publishing field, the small independent presses publishing essays in social science and social critique which have emerged in the past 30 years. She showed that this sub-space is structured by two main principles: the relationship to the market and the logic of political engagement. Her research combined MCA with other research techniques including historical analysis and ethnography, and developed the concept of a 'blurred' social space with no definite frontiers (Noël, 2012). Vincent Dubois constructed (with Jean-Matthieu Méon and Emmanuel Pierru), by means of MCA the 'wind band world' (Dubois et al., 2013: 49) and subjected to MCA the responses to a questionnaire of would-be cultural managers (Dubois, 2013). Sébastien Dubois and Pierre François (2013) used MCA to study the pure pole of the literary field. Their article is based upon a prosopographic database that includes the 150 most highly reputed contemporary Francophone poets in the French contemporary poetry field. They argued that, in contrast to the intuition of Bourdieu, contemporary French poetry is not characterized by anarchy but, instead, is a very structured social space wherein recognition is consensual and hierarchized. In this paper which is inspired by Bourdieu but also by the work of Pierre-Michel Menger (2014: 3), MCA is combined with ascendance hierarchical classification, optimal matching analysis and logit models (Dubois and François, 2013).

## THE DISSEMINATION OF MCA

Outside of France, MCA was not much used by sociologists during the 1980s and the 1990s. However, the first statistical textbooks incorporating MCA were published in English in 1984 (Greenacre, 1984; Lebart et al., 1984; on the international diffusion of MCA, see Le Roux and Rouanet, 2004: 11–14). It was also in 1984 that *La Distinction* was translated into English. Some American sociologists who were interested either in culture or in social stratification challenged the relevance of Bourdieu's analyses to the American context. Michèle Lamont (1992) argued that the social power of culture in France has no equivalence in the United States. Richard Peterson (Peterson and Simkus, 1992) advocated the argument of 'omnivorousness', which has given rise to a large number of empirical analyses. But these works did not use MCA. The question as to whether one can reject Bourdieu's analyses without using MCA was discussed in the journal *Poetics* in 2007 (Chan and Goldthorpe, 2007; Wuggenig, 2007).

It is only during the last decade that MCA really attracted significant attention outside of France. *Poetics* and *Cultural Sociology* have published several articles which discussed the relevance of the analyses of Bourdieu and Peterson by using MCA. Allan Warde, David Wright and Modesto Gayo-Cal studied forms of cultural participation in the UK in order to explore the 'myth of the cultural omnivore' (Warde et al., 2007). In Belgium, Henk Roose, Koen van Eijck and John Lievens used MCA in order to know whether a culture of 'openness' has replaced the culture of 'distinction'. The active variables represent, on the one hand, participation in a number of cultural activities and, on the other hand, dispositional aspects of cultural behaviour (for example, when discussing movies, people are asked whether an original style or special effects are important to them, or are asked whether they like violent scenes). The first axis is an engagement–disengagement axis, and the second one contrasts a preference, which is associated with age, for contemplation and 'legitimate' arts, with a preference for adventure and action (Roose et al., 2012). Mike Savage and Modesto Gayo studied the field of contemporary musical taste in the United Kingdom (Savage and Gayo, 2011). Savage had previously studied cultural values and suggested, by means of MCA, a richer analysis than one that Ronald Inglehart (Inglehart and Welzel, 2005) had proposed by using factor analysis (Majima and Savage, 2007). More recently, with Roza Meuleman, Savage used MCA to analyse cosmopolitan tastes in the Netherlands (Meuleman and Savage, 2013), and to show the complexity of such tastes, which, contrary to what is sometimes assumed, cannot be reduced to a one-dimensional reality. The ability of MCA to explore multidimensional objects is particularly explored by Meuleman and Savage (2013). Other articles could be mentioned, such as the paper by Elizabeth Silva and David Wright which explores the relationship between housing and the position of individuals in social space, mapped out by means of MCA (Silva and Wright, 2009).

Certain British sociologists have undoubtedly contributed to the increasing use of MCA in the sociology of culture. The book *Culture, Class, Distinction* (Bennett et al., 2009) seems to have been the first attempt to replicate, at a national level, the empirical and theoretical template provided by Bourdieu in *Distinction*. Bennett et al. used nationally representative survey data and qualitative interviews. The persons they interviewed had answered a questionnaire, and so could be located on the diagrams generated by MCA. The results of the survey were partially different from Bourdieu's results. Bennett et al. conclude that Bourdieu could have underestimated the role played by gender and age in his analyses of cultural practices. The book *Culture, Class, Distinction* should be seen as a part of a broader trend, with sociologists from different countries attempting to replicate the template provided by *Distinction*. In 2003, Jörg Blasius and Andreas Mühlichen carried out a survey in two German cities, Cologne and Bonn. They had adapted the questionnaire used for *Distinction* and MCA led them to conclude that the German social space was be structured in the same way as the French one, by the volume and structure of capital (Blasius and Mühlichen, 2010). Even earlier, Lennart Roselund (2000; 2009) began to study the city of Stavanger, which is located on the southwest coast of Norway. He carried out two lifestyle surveys with randomly chosen respondents. In his MCA, active variables were indicators of economic capital and of cultural capital, and variables which were related to the working life of respondents. He published several MCA analyses that allowed him to analyse transformations over time of the social space of Stavanger, especially the growing significance of differentiation according to the composition of capital. With Annick Prieur, Rosenlund also studied the Danish city of Aalborg. They constructed the social space and then projected variables related to the cultural practices of the respondents. Their article addressed the character of cultural capital and the role it plays in the formation of social divisions (Prieur et al., 2008). Beyond Scandinavia, José Virgílio Borges Pereira (2005) published a book on the city of Porto, analysed as a social space. Predrag Cvetičanin and Mihaela Popescu (2011) also used MCA in a national survey in Serbia. Their main argument was that to understand the structure of Serbian society, one particularly had to take into account the nature of social capital in that country.

The proliferation of research which uses MCA has made it possible to produce comparative analysis. After using MCA in different contexts, Lennart Roselund (2014) tried to formulate some general postulates. He noticed that in the area of cultural practices some oppositions tend to be found in different locations. Semi Purhonen and David Wright (2013) compared two projects which had developed the methodological model of *Distinction* in the UK and Finland respectively. They argued that MCA, at least when it is used along with field theory, could help to resolve some of the methodological problems inherent in comparative research, involving what Bourdieu called 'the comparison of facts or systems of facts' (Bourdieu et al., 1997: 13).

## CONCLUSION

Undoubtedly in the last decade or so, MCA has become more popular than it has ever been. Certainly, one can notice that, in countries other than France, MCA is more often seen as a tool to map social spaces and lifestyles spaces than as a tool to explore particular fields. For example, in the sociology of the arts, up until now, there has been little research outside of France which has used MCA to explore a particular field of cultural production. The article by Bo G. Ekelund and Mikael Börjesson (2002) on two cohorts of prose fiction writers (1940 and 1955) is an exception to this. In this sense, not all of the methodological innovations which Bourdieu had developed since the middle of the 1970s have yet been disseminated. Meanwhile, it would not be correct to reduce the history of MCA in sociology to the dissemination of innovations which have been developed in France since the 1970s. Since that time, MCA and its uses in sociology have evolved significantly. Improvements in how MCA has been used since then should be mentioned. Certainly, the main improvement is related to the development of what is called 'geometric data analysis' (GDA), by Brigitte Le Roux, a former student of Benzecri, and Henry Rouanet. These two French mathematicians have explicated and formalized what Bourdieu did quite intuitively in the 1970s (Rouanet et al., 2002), and they have done a lot to make MCA better known and easier to use by sociologists (Le Roux and Rouanet, 2004; 2010). They cooperated both with Bourdieu on the last paper using MCA which he published (Bourdieu, 1999) and later on with many researchers in France, Scandinavia and in the UK. One of their guidelines for using MCA involves highlighting the geometrical aspects of MCA, which are much more intuitive than the more usual algebraic approach. They have made many refinements to MCA, for instance in exploring more deeply the cloud of individuals. They also have developed new variants of MCA. Specific MCA permits one to restrict the analysis to the specific modalities of interest to the analyst. Class-specific analysis consists in analysing a sub-cloud of individuals (Chiche and Le Roux, 2010; Le Roux and Rouanet, 2010). These innovations were implemented in new types of statistical software (SPAD).

Developments in MCA have also been more theoretical and experimental in nature. Some researchers have explored how inference statistical analysis on the one hand, and regression analysis on the other, could be integrated within geometric data analysis (Rouanet et al., 2002; Le Roux and Rouanet, 2004: 297–332). Applications are still rare but may prove promising. The same is true of endeavours to integrate MCA and methods associated with network analysis. These attempts raise the broader question as to whether network analysis is compatible with field theory. The two approaches focus on 'social relations', but the term has a different meaning in network analysis and in Bourdieu's works (De Nooy, 2003; Sapiro, 2006), François Denord (2015) has suggested how network analysis might be a part of field analysis, and how network analysis's methods could be implemented within geometric data analysis. His work pertains specifically to the sociology of elites, but could be extended in the next few years to new areas within the sociology of culture. These developments show that MCA promises to be a highly useful tool for sociologists interested in cultural matters for some time to come.

## NOTES

1 These graphs, and the first drafts of parts of the book, were first published in 1976 (Bourdieu and de Saint-Martin, 1976). On the comparison between this article and *Distinction*, see de Saint-Martin (2014).
2 Prosopography (see Stone, 1971; Charle, 2001) was initially developed by historians. It consists in collecting biographical data about a social group.
3 Software also affects a ponderation to each dichotomic variable.

## REFERENCES

Bennett, T., Savage, M., Silva, E., Warde, A., Gayo-Cal, M. and Wright, D. (2009) *Culture, Class, Distinction*. London: Routledge.

Benzecri, J.-P., et al. (1973) *L'analyse des données. Tome 2: L'analyse des correspondances*. Paris: Bordas.

Blasius, J. and Mühlichen, A. (2010) 'Identifying audience segments applying the "social space" approach', *Poetics*, 38(1): 69–89.

Boltanski, L., Darré, Y. and Schiltz, M.-A. (1984) 'La dénonciation', *Actes de la recherche en sciences sociales*, 51: 3–40.

Bourdieu, P. (1985) 'The social space and the genesis of the groups', *Theory and Society*, 14(6): 723–44.

Bourdieu, P. (1988 [1984]) *Homo Academicus*. Trans. P. Collier. Cambridge: Polity Press.

Bourdieu, P. (1992) *The Rules of Art: Genesis and Structure of the Literary Field*. Trans. S. Emanuel. Stanford: Stanford University Press.

Bourdieu, P. (1996 [1989]) *The State Nobility: Elite Schools in the Field of Power*. Trans. L. C. Clough. Stanford: Stanford University Press.

Bourdieu, P. (1999) 'Une révolution conservatrice dans l'édition', *Actes de la recherche en sciences sociales*, 126–7: 3–28.

Bourdieu, P. (2005 [2000]) *The Social Structures of the Economy*. Trans. C. Turner. Cambridge: Polity Press.

Bourdieu, P. (2010 [1979]) *Distinction: A Social Critique of the Judgement of Taste*. Trans. R. Nice. London: Routledge.

Bourdieu, P. and Chartier, R. (2010) *Le sociologue et l'historien*. Paris-Marseille: Raisons d'agir-Agone.

Bourdieu, P. and de Saint Martin, M. (1976) 'Anatomie du goût', *Actes de la Recherche en Sciences Sociales*, 5: 2–112.

Bourdieu, P. and de Saint-Martin, M. (1978) 'Le patronat', *Actes de la recherche en sciences sociales*, 20-1: 3–82.

Bourdieu, P. and Wacquant, L.J.D. (1992) *An Invitation to Reflexive Sociology*. Chicago: University of Chicago Press.

Bourdieu, P. and Darbel, A., with Schnapper, D. (1997) *The Love of Art: European Art Museums and Their Publics*. Trans. C. Beattie and N. Merriman. Cambridge: Polity Press.

Champagne, P. (1987) 'Capital culturel et patrimoine économique. Le cas de l'agriculture bressane', *Actes de la recherche en sciences sociales*, 69: 51–66.

Chan, T.W. and Goldthorpe, J. (2007) 'Data, methods and interpretation in analyses of cultural consumption: A reply to Peterson and Wuggenig', *Poetics*, 35(4–5): 317–29.

Charle, C. (2001) 'Prosopography (collective biography)', in *International Encyclopedia of the Social and Behavioral Sciences, Vol. 18*. Oxford: Elsevier Science Ltd. pp. 12236–41.

Chiche, J. and Le Roux, B. (2010) 'Développements récents en analyse des correspondances multiples', *Modulab*, 42: 110–17.

Cibois, P. (1997) 'Les pièges de l'analyse des correspondances', *Histoire et mesure*, 12(3–4): 299–320.

Cicourel, A. (1964) *Method and Measurement in Sociology*. New York: Free Press.

Clausen, S.-E. (1988) *Applied Correspondence Analysis: An Introduction*. Thousand Oaks: Sage.

Coulangeon, P. (2003) 'Social Stratification of Musical Tastes: Questioning the Cultural Legitimacy Model', *Revue française de sociologie*, 44(1): 3–34.

Coulangeon, P. and Lemel, Y. (2007) 'Is "distinction" really outdated? Questioning the meaning of the omnivorization of musical taste in contemporary France', *Poetics*, 35(2–3): 93–111.

Cvetičanin, P. and Popescu, M. (2011) 'The art of making classes in Serbia: Another particular case of the possible', *Poetics*, 39(6): 444–68.

De Nooy, W. (2003) 'Fields and networks: Correspondence analysis and social network analysis in the framework of field theory', *Poetics*, 31(5–6): 305–27.

Denord F (2015) 'Géométrie des réseaux sociaux', in F. Lebaron and B. Le Roux (eds) *La méthodologie de Pierre Bourdieu en action*. Espace culturel, espace social et analyse des données. Paris: Dunod, 59–79.

De Saint-Martin, M. (2014) 'From "Anatomie du gout" to *La Distinction*: Attempting to construct the social space. Some markers for the history of the research', in P. Coulangeon and J. Duval (eds) *The Routledge Companion to Bourdieu's Distinction*. London: Routledge.

Desrosières, A. (2008) 'Analyse des données et sciences humaines: comment cartographier le monde social ?', *Electronic Journ@l for History of Probability and Statistics* [Electronic], 4(2). Available: http://www.emis.de/journals/JEHPS/Decembre2008/Desrosieres.pdf

Donnat, O. (1994) *Les Français face à la culture. De l'exclusion à l'éclectisme*. Paris: La Découverte.

Dubois, S. and François, P. (2013) 'Career paths and hierarchies in the pure pole of the literary field: The case of contemporary poetry', *Poetics*, 41(5): 501–23.

Dubois, V. (2013) *La culture comme vocation*. Paris: Raisons d'agir.

Dubois, V., Méon, J.-M. and Pierru, E. (2013) *The Sociology of Wind Bands: Amateur Music Between Cultural Domination and Autonomy*. Farnham: Ashgate.

Duval, J. (2006) 'L'art du réalisme. Le champ du cinéma français au début des années 2000', *Actes de la recherche en sciences sociales*, 161-2: 96–115.

Duval, J. (2013) 'L'analyse des correspondances et la construction des champs', *Actes de la recherche en sciences sociales*, 200: 110–23.

Ekelund, B. and Börjesson, M. (2002) 'The shape of the literary career: An analysis of publishing trajectories', *Poetics*, 30(5–6): 341–64.

Faure, S. (2008) 'Les structures du champ chorégraphique français', *Actes de la recherche en sciences sociales*, 175: 82–97.

Greenacre, M. (1984) *Correspondence Analysis in Practice*. London: Academic Press.

Inglehart, R. and Welzel, C. (2005) *Modernization, Cultural Change, and Democracy: The Human Development Sequence*. Cambridge: Cambridge University Press.

Lahire, B. (2006) *La Culture des individus: Dissonances culturelles et distinction de soi*. Paris: La Découverte.

Lamont, M. (1992) *Money, Morals, and Manners: The Culture of the French and the American Upper-middle Class*. Chicago: University of Chicago Press.

Lebaron, F. (1997) 'La dénégation du pouvoir. Le champ des économistes français au milieu des années 1990', *Actes de la recherche en sciences sociales*, 119: 3–26.

Lebart, L., Morineau, A. and Warwick (1984) *Multivariate Descriptive Statistical Analysis. Correspondence Analysis and Related Techniques for Large Matrices*. New York: John Wiley and Sons.

Lenoir, R. (1988) 'Réponses et répondant: analyse d'une correspondance politique', *Actes de la recherche en sciences sociales*, 73: 2–28.

Le Roux, B. and Rouanet, H. (2004) *Geometric Data Analysis*. Dordrecht: Kluwer.

Le Roux, B. and Rouanet, H. (2010) *Multiple Correspondence Analysis*. Thousand Oaks: Sage.

Majima, S. and Savage, M. (2007) 'Have there been culture shifts in Britain? A critical encounter with Ronald Inglehart', *Cultural Sociology*, 1(3): 293–315.

Menger P.-M. (2014) *The Economics of Creativity: Art and Achievement under Uncertainty*. Cambridge: Harvard University Press.

Meuleman, R. and Savage, M. (2013) 'A field analysis of cosmopolitan taste: Lessons from the Netherlands', *Cultural Sociology*, 7(2): 230–56.

Noël, S. (2012) *L'Édition indépendante critique: engagements politiques et intellectuels*. Lyon: Presses de l'Enssib.

Pereira, J.V.B. (2005) *Classes e Culturas de Classe das Famílias Portuenses. Classes sociais e 'modalidades de estilização da vida' na cidade do Porto*. Porto: Afrontamento/Instituto de Sociologia da Faculdade de Letras da Universidade do Porto.

Peterson, R.A. and Simkus, A. (1992) 'How musical tastes mark occupational status groups' in M. Lamont and M. Fournier (eds), *Cultivating Differences: Symbolic Boundaries and the Making of Inequality*. Chicago: The University of Chicago Press. pp. 152–86.

Prieur, A., Rosenlund, L. and Skjott-Larsen, J. (2008) 'Cultural capital today: A case study from Denmark', *Poetics*, 36(1): 45–71.

Purhonen, S. and Wright, D. (2013) 'Research on cultural tastes: The case of cultural capital in the UK and Finland', *Cultural Sociology*, 7(2): 257–73.

Roose, H., van Eijck, K. and Lievens, J. (2012) 'Culture of distinction or culture of openness? Using a social space approach to analyze the social structuring of lifestyles', *Poetics*, 40(6): 491–513.

Rosenlund, L. (2000) 'Cultural change in Norway: Cultural and economic dimensions', *International Journal of Contemporary Sociology*, 37(2): 245–75.

Rosenlund, L. (2009) *Exploring the City with Bourdieu: Applying Pierre Bourdieu's theories and Methods to Study the Community*. Saarbrücken: VDM Verlag.

Roselund, L. (2014) 'Working with *Distinction* – Scandinavian experiences', in P. Coulangeon and J. Duval (eds) *The Routledge Companion to Bourdieu's Distinction*. London: Routledge.

Rouanet, H., Lebaron, F., Le Hay, V., Ackermann, W. and Le Roux, B. (2002) 'Régression et analyse géométrique des données: réflexions et suggestions', *Mathématiques et Sciences Humaines*, 160: 13–45.

Sapiro, G. (1996) 'La raison littéraire. Le champ littéraire français sous l'Occupation (1940–1944)', *Actes de la recherche en sciences sociales*, 111–2: 3–35.

Sapiro, G. (2002) 'The structure of the French literary field during the German Occupation (1940–1944): A multiple correspondence analysis', *Poetics*, 30(5): 387–402.

Sapiro, G. (2006) 'Réseaux, institutions et champ' in D. de Marneff and B. Denis (eds), *Les Réseaux littéraires*. Bruxelles: LE CRI/CIEL-ULB. pp. 44–59.

Savage, M. and Gayo, M. (2011) 'Unravelling the omnivore: A field analysis of contemporary musical taste in the United Kingdom', *Poetics*, 39(5): 337–57.

Silva E. and Wright D. (2009) 'Displaying Desire and Distinction in Housing', *Cultural Sociology*, 3(1): 31–50.

Soulié, C. (1995) 'Anatomie du goût philosophique', *Actes de la recherche en sciences sociales*, 109: 3–28.

Stone, L. (1971) 'Prosopography', *Dædalus*, 100(1): 46–79.

Van Meter K., Schiltz, M.-A., Cibois P. and Mounier, L. (1994) 'History and French Sociological Perspective' in M. Greenacre and J. Blasius (eds),

*Correspondence Analysis in the Social Sciences.* London: Academic Press. pp. 128–37.

Verger, A. (1991) 'Le champ des avant-gardes', *Actes de la recherche en sciences sociales*, 88: 2–40.

Warde, A., Wright, D. and Gayo-Cal, M. (2007) 'Understanding Cultural Omnivorousness: Or, the Myth of the Cultural Omnivore', *Cultural Sociology*, 1(2): 143–64.

Wright Mills, C. (1959) *The Sociological Imagination*. London: Oxford University Press.

Wuggenig, U. (2007) 'Comments on Chan and Goldthorpe: Pitfalls in testing Bourdieu's homology assumptions using mainstream social science methodology: Social stratification and cultural consumption: The visual arts in England', *Poetics*, 35(4–5): 306–16.

# Hermeneutics and Cultural Sociology

Jonathan Roberge

## INTRODUCTION

The questions of what constitutes culture, how to make sense of and interpret it, are anything but new. A long hermeneutic tradition exists, to be sure, which can be traced back to religious readings of sacred texts, early experimentations in the arts, all the way to the emergence of modern philosophy and the very foundations of the humanities and social sciences. Sociology, especially, has never ceased to be deeply challenged by these questions. Of late, 'to take meaning seriously' has in particular become the task of cultural sociology, which may explain at least in part why it has been so successful in North America and beyond. By virtue of its theoretical orientations, cultural sociology deals with old yet fundamental questions regarding the deep structures of collective experience, meaningful social worlds, and the like. The stakes are thus high on multiple fronts, with two issues being particularly salient. On the one hand, raising such matters has forced cultural sociology to interrogate its own conditions of possibility: what is culture – ontologically – as much as how to know and express it from an epistemological point of view. Are meanings truths or realities, and in what sense? Is the discourse of cultural sociology a distinctive 'reading' of the social world? On the other hand, and acutely related to the above, it appears that the questions asked by cultural sociology are increasingly connected to philosophy and the discipline of hermeneutics broadly conceived.[1] Hermeneutics too deals with the deep understanding of cultural forms and how to convey them in a rich and significant way. At stake, in other words, is the possibility of a fruitful dialogue between hermeneutics and cultural sociology. To historically and conceptually reconstruct such a dialogue, and to show in what ways it can be productive for a greater self-understanding of our field, is thus the purpose of this chapter.

For obvious reasons related to spatial constraints, it will not be possible to address all the ramifications that have ever existed between cultural sociology and hermeneutics here. Choices must be made, particular paths and narratives have to be privileged; and in order to do so, the hermeneutical concept of *Wirkungsgeschichte* could prove useful. Hans-Georg Gadamer developed this idea – loosely translated as 'history of influence' or 'reception history' – in *Truth and Method* (1975 [1960]) to elaborate on how any kind of work finds it significance within a complex web of interpretation and re-interpretation. Over time, what remains is only that which has been deemed of particular interest. Following from this, the present chapter wants to focus on a limited set of key moments and figures in the on-going conversation between hermeneutics and cultural sociology. Specific debates and reformulations represent parts that could possibly make sense of the whole; they can be read further as steps towards a more or less unified hermeneutically informed cultural sociology or backwards towards an archaeology of certain concepts. More importantly, I want to argue that the most crucial question of all deals with the connection between a theory of text and a theory of action – or as Paul Ricoeur suggested in 1986, the transition *'from text to action'*. It is this intellectual endeavour that can begin to clarify the *Methodenstreit* and the rise of *Geisteswissenschaften* in Germany in the late 19th century. In the first section I shall demonstrate how authors such as Dilthey and Weber were instrumental in providing the interpretative base for a new kind of science at an equal distance from idealism and romanticism on one side, and from the natural sciences on the other. Another key moment in the dialogue between hermeneutics and cultural sociology was the cultural turn in and around the 1970s. Figures like Ricoeur and Clifford Geertz contributed enormously to situating meaningful actions not only in their local environment, but also within deeper and broader symbolical structures. As this will be the focus of the second section, it will also prove to be one of the major sources of the development of what is known today as the Yale School of Cultural Sociology, in addition to a re-reading of classical social theory in a largely Weberian-Durkheimian light. The Yale School and its leader Jeffrey Alexander have developed an innovative structural hermeneutics by talking about 'text-based societies', while also integrating more and more elements of performativity and performance theory – this is the focus of the third section. Finally, in the fourth section, a discussion of the current and future relevance of a hermeneutically informed cultural sociology will be undertaken in order to demonstrate that any such relevance depends on the capacity of critically expanding on the hermeneutical sensitivity to politics, new media and emerging technologies.

## ESTABLISHING THE *GEISTWISSENSCHAFTEN*

The context of modernity certainly played an important role in defining or redefining what kind of sciences comprised the *Geistwissenshaften*, literally the 'sciences of the spirit', in late-19th-century Germany (the expression *Kulturwissenschaften* was also often used). Specifically, what served as their foundational claims? How did they delimit a space of their own and established themselves on solid epistemological ground? To be sure, different hermeneutical approaches and techniques in the history or philology had by that point matured enough to be influential, but it was the relentless challenge of the natural sciences that proved decisive. From Galileo and Descartes to the rapid development of chemistry and physics at that time, the so-called 'hard' sciences came to rely on facts, laws, causality and falsifiability. According to scholars such as Schleimacher, Dilthey, Rickert, and the like, *Geistwissenshaften* should not attempt to – nor can it, for that matter – resemble this breed of objectivism. Signs are simply not facts, sympathy for others cannot be falsified, and sequences of events cannot be considered from the perspective of pure logic. This is, in a nutshell, how what has been called the *methodenstreit* – literally the 'conflict of methods' – was first established in the 19th century, not only through differences in procedure, but also as a stark different in axiomatic orientations. While the natural sciences would gather under the umbrella of *Erklaren*, or explanation, it was *Verstehen*, or understanding, that came to guarantee the singularity, and thus the autonomy, of the *Geistwissenschaften*.

The work of Wilhelm Dilthey is emblematic in this regard and was recognized as such by subsequent generations of cultural scholars (see, for instance, Dilthey, 1976 [1910]). In the footsteps of Schleimacher, Dilthey posited that the realm of culture is meaningful only in so far as it allows one to interpret and understand the intentions and emotions carried by other subjectivities. Inner experience and its communication are central; they serve as the basis of a shared lifeworld, which can develop into new forms of consciousness. The model used by Dilthey thus largely revolves around the hermeneutical notion of a text – broadly conceived as a work of culture, a monument, painting, piece of music, etc. – but in such a way to give to its author and reader the predominant roles. To understand for the latter is to relive the creative impulse of the former in a sort of pure identification. It might be difficult, in these circumstances, not to see the influence of Romanticism on Dilthey, and many have criticized him for having taken such an idealistic position. In particular, his effort to establish the singularity of a properly human science on a rather empathic notion of understanding led him to coarsen the opposition to the explanatory principle of the natural sciences. This kind of human science might be able to engage in an interesting dialogue with philosophy, though it would cease to interact with more scientific endeavours, thus compromising its ability to evolve as a legitimate science of its own. Such a critique can be found in Ricoeur, for instance (see Ricoeur, 1977b), and we shall return to it in due time.

Another key figure of this foundational period is Max Weber, although for quite different reasons. Weber continues the tradition of *Geistwissenshaften* by significantly repositioning its major tenets towards a new type of empirical, rigorous and systemic research methodology, which came to be known as sociology. The rich and dense definition he gives of the discipline in the early pages of *Economy and Society* (1978 [1947]) deserves periodic re-examination:

> Sociology is a science which attempts the interpretative understanding (*deutend Verstehen*) of social action in order thereby to arrive at a causal explanation (*ursachlich Erklaren*) of its course and effects. In 'action' is included all human behaviour when and in so far as the acting individual attaches a subjective meaning to it. (1978 [1947]: 88)

The first striking thing about this quote is how Weber tries to combine more than oppose the two sides of the *Methodenstreit*, namely explanation and understanding. Epistemologically, the two can contribute to make sense of a world properly inhabited and set in motion by humans. This is something that causal laws alone would be unable to do, and neither can pure subjectivism, as if the sociologist were capable of reading one's mind. This relates to the second element worth underlining in Weber's definition: the undeniable focus on the category of action and how it becomes 'social'. The individual is and remains the bearer of meaning in what has been called Weber's 'methodological individualism'. It is not that nothing emerges later, but rather that everything begins from the individual's action, the ways in which the individual encounters other peoples' actions, and how this opens up to plurality and complex nods of actions. The reason behind this developing gradation in Weber's epistemology is because he fears any kind of conceptual reification or idealistic hypostasis. The State, for instance, is *prima facie* a 'co-action' and the previsibility of a certain course of action based on the continuity of its presence yesterday and today, and the good chance it will be there tomorrow. For Weber, the challenge is thus to bend the elements together – both action and meanings, individuals and interactions, developments and consequences – to show how every single part is linked to the next, as well as connected to the whole of society.

Weber's effort to blend activity (*Handeln*) and meaning, as well as to re-position the notion of scientific objectivity within a paradigm of interpretative understanding, is something that is furthermore visible in the epistemological model of the 'ideal-type'. A 'unified analytical construct', the ideal-type attempts to make sense of certain social patterns, certain meaningful crystallizations of human interaction; it has to be coherent both in and for itself, and must somehow correspond or dialogue with reality. The position is thus anti-realistic, to be sure, as Weber feared materialism as much as pure idealism under the form of Hegelialism. In the best-case scenario, an ideal-type is a heuristic tool, a means of acquiring knowledge that is hermeneutical in its very nature. This is something common with Weber's socio-historical analysis of world religions, for instance, in *Ancient Judaism* (1952 [1920]) and *The Religion of China* (1951). Moreover, it proves to be a central concept in his magnum opus *The Protestant Ethic and the Spirit of Capitalism* (1958 [1905]) and thus influenced generations of cultural sociologists. What could this spirit featured in the title be made of? What kind of economic cultural structure does it represent as an ideal-type? Weber, as always, begins with the individual and his actions, in this case the disciplined asceticism the Protestant applies to his work. Such asceticism spread widely enough throughout Europe to develop its own inner meaning and, from there, influenced the development of the economy and its transformation towards capitalism in the following centuries. Weber thus offers a reconstruction that is logical without being too causal or deterministic; in the end, his attempt is to *understand* complex nodes of correlation.

## THE PIVOTAL PHASE: RICOEUR AND GEERTZ

The period following the Second World War to the early 1980s was a period of intense social and political turmoil, but also in terms of theoretical developments in the broad field of human sciences. It was a period in which structuralism, feminism and neo-Marxism thrived and where multiple schools emerged – Bourdieusian, Birmingham, post-modern, etc. – all helping to shape what would come to be known as 'the cultural turn' (Alexander, 1988b; Jacobs and Spillman, 2005). Neither hermeneutics nor cultural sociology escaped this movement, as they were both instrumental in shaping, and deeply affected by it. The work of Paul Ricoeur is a case in point. A philosopher who specialized in the history and epistemology of hermeneutics, he was convinced of the necessity for the discipline to develop a fruitful 'dialogue with the human sciences' and wrote extensively on the topic (see, for instance, Ricoeur, 1977b). Even more than Gadamer, he rapidly became a key figure in and around these intellectual currents, largely because of his position between France and the United States, where he taught for several years.

To begin with, Ricoeur refused any kind of methodological dualism that would oppose explanation to understanding. Dilthey, according to Ricoeur, promoted such a mutually exclusive option, and this is why Weber's perspective, by contrast, was seen as offering a more viable solution. For Ricoeur, understanding and explanation are relative to each other, in addition to being deeply related to interpretation. On the one hand, the search for further explanation is required while any form of understanding seems blocked. This happens on a daily basis in most, if not all, conversations involving questions and answers, and Ricoeur used it as a model for all the human sciences. On the other hand, it is also true that understanding can still occur after explanation, or that understanding 'envelops' explanation. On this topic, Ricoeur found inspiration in E.D. Hirsch, who argued for the process of validation as something both rigorous and subjective (see Hirsch, 1967). Scientific or juridical facts and data always have to be analysed and weighted, for instance, as well as put into their context. For Ricoeur, this was reminiscent of the hermeneutic circle, where the parts deliver the secret of the whole – and vice versa.

In the long history of hermeneutics, and in the development of Ricoeur's intellectual project in particular, the notion of the text came to occupy centre stage. After the 1960s, Ricoeur would drift from an analysis of the symbol to the text in order to better engage with the main theoretical movement of that time in Western Europe: structuralism. Ferdinand de Saussure, in his *Course in General Linguistics* (1986 [1922]), had established that a language could be analysed as a formal and arbitrary system of differential signs. This discovery allowed for a conception of language – and text, for that matter – as possessing an internal logic that creates an inner structure, which in turn allows for a certain closure or autonomy. At the time, structural semiotics as a scientific explanatory paradigm seemed to have prevailed over philosophy, which can be seen in the influence of Lévi-Strauss and how he attempted to deconstruct large structures of meaning, such as myths (see Lévi-Strauss, 1958). Ricoeur, for his part, was both attracted to the possibilities opened by a semiotics and critical of such an endeavour.[2] The problem for him was that a text is more than just its own cold and rational architecture of signs; rather, it wants to express something, which makes it a semantic object unto itself. A text refers to a projected world and thus to 'understand a text is to follow its movement from sense to reference, ... from what it says, to what it talks about' (Ricoeur, 1986: 87–8). Moreover, the world of the text is our world, i.e. it deals with human experience in such a fashion that it creates something like a *Lebenswelt* – a living world that the reader would be able to relate to.

While Ricoeur's hermeneutics connects semiotics and semantics, explanation and understanding, it also presents itself has an attempt to link textuality with *in situ* human practices. In the 1970s and 1980s, Ricoeur wanted to develop a more 'militant' approach, in particular by being more practical and critical, and engaging more with the human sciences, especially cultural sociology. The move, in a nutshell, is expressed in the title of his 1986 book, *Du texte à l'action (From Text to Action)*, which contains the seminal essay originally published in *Social Research* over a decade earlier, entitled 'The Model of the Text: Meaningful Action Considered as a Text' (1971). In the essay, which can arguably be considered the turning point of Ricoeur's fortune in the United States, he develops four analogies that argue for the objectification of the practical field that are of particular interest. First, as meaning surpasses its occurrence, the significance of an act goes far beyond the simple fact that it happened. Second, the propositional content of an act or text, as much as its illocutionary force, points towards a 'logical status as having such-and-such identifiable meaning or "sense-content"' (Ricoeur, 1981: 205) – saying 'I do' at a wedding, for example. Third, and because of the preceding, the meaning of an act can detach itself from the intentions of its agents and produce its own outcomes. And last but not least, actions or texts can be interpreted by a wide range of readers, present and future, who propose different interpretations and argue for their relative merits. The strength of Ricoeur's model is its adaptability, as it considers meaningful action as a text that opens new ways of understanding the social world – for both sociologists and lay individuals. From then on, Ricoeur applied this model to many fields of inquiry, ranging from the State and ideology to the ideas of justice, memory, etc. (see, for instance, his last opus of 2000).

As it became apparent that Ricoeur was championing a complex interpretative method – and that he himself was a champion of hermeneutical human science – the same could be said of Clifford Geertz. The careers of the two were not only parallel but intertwined: they influenced each another, and were both influenced by the Dilthey-Weberian take on meaning; together they become major source of inspiration for cultural sociologists thereafter. Of course, Geertz was not a philosopher per se, so theorization was never an end in itself for him. Rather, he had a strong commitment to field work, and was interested in textuality and meaning in such a way that they could enhance a more practical and *in-situ* anthropology. The much-discussed 'thick description' in *The Interpretation of Cultures* (1973) is emblematic in this regard. Geertz sees thickness as a sort of ethnographic 'stickiness', the fact of being close to – staying and living with – the people one wants to understand. 'In the study of culture, he notes, 'analysis penetrates into the very body of the object'. The ethnographer describes the experience in which he is embedded with patience, attentiveness and a high degree of sensibility. This rich and 'warm' sense could be associated with Dilthey's perspective. However, it is important to note that the notion of 'thick description' is also (if not more so) Weberian at its core, particularly because it revolves around action and actors' subjective understanding: what is it that moves people, what kind of convictions, feelings, values and sense of urgency do they possess? To answers these questions, the ethnographer proposes tropes and narratives that are quite 'native', yet of a slightly different breed: interpretations are textual reconstructions, 'fictions' of a 'second and third order'. Distance is not a flaw according to Geertz, but rather the very condition of possibility for meaningful descriptions and interpretations.

Another way to grasp Geertz's entrenched and hermeneutical interpretation of culture deals with his notion of 'local knowledge' (1983). Contingent processes are certainly crucial, for what is meaningful here might not be there, or might be for different reasons. Context is thus everything; the problem, however, is how to define it. While a ritual, symbol, or collective representation may very well be concretely situated within a group at a certain time and place, it is also always situated against the backdrop of a larger and deeper cultural structure. Geertz, as a matter of fact, argues for an open notion of the local. Indeed, there is a never-ending dialectic 'between the most local of local detail and the most global of global structures in such a way as to bring them into simultaneous view' (1983: 69). It would be difficult here not to see the similarities with one of the pivotal concepts of hermeneutics, namely the part/whole circle. Geertz follows Ricoeur, and Gadamer before him, and others before them, in saying that it is the smaller occurrences that reveal the broader universe of meaning, while the later makes sense and allows for the interpretation of local understandings. In short, context is everything precisely because it is comprised of a circular dynamic between the local and the global, the part and the whole. To continue with the analogy, it would even be possible to say that this circle represents both the part and the whole of Geertz's core theory of culture. Fundamentally, its aim is to *engage* broad assertions about culture with what he calls 'complex specifics' in a sort of loving struggle that appears to have no end, or for which no end is sought.

Speaking of context in terms of broader cultural structures allows us to talk about another important text, Geertz's 'Ideology as a Cultural System', first published in 1964. Here, he engages with the major theoretical trends of the time, and is particularly suspicious of what he calls 'interest theory'. Marxism, for instance, is for Geertz tautological, as it posits ideology and domination first, to then later 'prove' they strive – the equivalent of postponing the Manheim paradox, rather than finding a proper solution to it. For Geertz, it is instead necessary to propose a deeper, more cultural analysis. Ideologies need to be examined 'as systems of interacting symbols, as patterns of interworking meanings' (1973 [1964]: 207). Ideologies, in other words, possess an inner logic that gives them a significant degree of autonomy. Is it enough to see Geertz as being in line with structuralism? Maybe not, but one thing for certain is that his position is in line with hermeneutics. Ricoeur, for example, talks about the 'symbolic integration' that ideologies offer at a foundational cultural level. In the end, what counts in such hermeneutic readings – both Ricoeurien and Geertzian – is to *understand* how a collectivity exists by virtue of the discourses and images that represent it, a necessary step to be able to engage in a more critical analysis.

## THE YALE SCHOOL OF CULTURAL SOCIOLOGY

The worldwide success that cultural sociology enjoys today can be considered both the cause and effect of an increasingly multifaceted field. As it expands within different national contexts and becomes the object of handbooks like this one, it not only gains substantial legitimacy, but also greater refinement (Lamont and Wuthnow, 1990; Smith, 1998). Alongside David Inglis et al. (2007), it is thus important to note that the specific kind of sociology whose emphasis on the 'cultural' sets it apart from 'normal' sociology should be more appropriately called the

'Alexander paradigm' or the 'Yale School'. Jeffrey C. Alexander is undoubtedly a key figure in contemporary sociology, well known for his theoretical ambitions. Less known, however, is how his approach to cultural sociology is deeply inspired by hermeneutics. For instance, in a piece he co-authored with Isaac Reed in the *European Journal of Social Theory*, he sought 'to crystalize a culturally-based hermeneutic account of rational social science', and further in the text states that his position 'places hermeneutics at the endpoint, as much at the beginning, of the operation of sociological explanation' (Reed and Alexander, 2009: 31). In order to do that, and faithful to what has made his reputation, starting with *Theoretical Logic in Sociology* (1982–1984), Alexander proposes an extensive reading of the classics, from Dilthey, Weber and Durkheim to Ricoeur and Geertz, the latter of whom is said to have 'directly inspired the strong-program approach to cultural sociology' (2015a: 5). The exact nature of such a program will be spelled out below, but it is important first to notice what is really at stake here. More than anything, I want to argue that Alexander's effort is a rare attempt to bend a macrotheory of meaning with a macrotheory of action. In other words, his work could be easily seen as one the most compelling attempts to transition from text to action.

First published in *Sociologie et Société* – a Franco-Canadian journal – in 1998, Alexander and Smith's piece entitled 'The Strong Program in Cultural Theory: Elements of a Structural Hermeneutics' certainly marks a turning point in how cultural sociology is conceived. The tone is rather militant, the authors being particularly hostile towards what they call the 'weak' Bourdieusian or Birmingham programmes. But they also make two positive and interconnected points that would allow them to root their programme in solid epistemological ground. First, since social and cultural realities are so literally infused with meaning, actors and sociologists cannot do otherwise than 'read' such realities. Cultural sociology is an interpretative science to the fullest; it seeks to understand through reconstruction and thick description *à la* Geertz. Second, the object of cultural sociology is or should be both very precise and broad: 'Commitment to a cultural-sociological theory that recognizes *cultural autonomy* is the single-most important quality of a strong program' (Alexander and Smith, 2002: 137, emphasis added). Cultural meanings exist in and for themselves; they are not dependant, and do not have to be 'explained' by other variables. Is the position held by Alexander thus too idealistic? While some seem to think so (see, for instance, McLennan, 2004; 2005), it is especially important to understand the two senses in which this autonomy is said to be 'relative'. On the one hand, culture obviously interacts with other social spheres to the point where it is influenced by them. 'To talk about the relative autonomy of culture', notes Alexander elsewhere, 'we need to have the time to go inside of meaning, find it, and then come back to the question of social structure and change' (2008: 526–7). On the other hand, such relativity echoes the fact that meanings, signs, narratives, and the like mutually condition each other. The subtitle of Alexander and Smith's (2002) piece is 'Elements of a Structural Hermeneutics', and it finds here its decisive justification. Culture has a semiotic 'inside', which is itself a differential system. For instance, in the fifteen or so years since the launch of the strong program in cultural sociology, Alexander and his colleagues have certainly remained true to this idea that culture is made of fundamental binaries, including the classic opposition between the sacred and the profane.[3]

Continuing with what this breed of structural hermeneutics could refer to, and how it situates its practitioners, it would be remiss not to mention the role played by Ricoeur's notion of text. References to the French philosopher are indeed numerous (2002: 137, 140, 146), and probably best summarized by Alexander and Mast in the mid-2000s:

> The strong programs in contemporary cultural sociology ... have followed Ricoeur's philosophical demonstration that meaningful action can be considered as texts, exploring codes and narratives, metaphors, metathemes, values, and rituals in such diverse institutional domains as religion, nation, class, race, family, gender, and sexuality. It has been vital to establish what makes meaning important, what makes some social facts meaningful at all. (2006: 2)

Again, as a text escapes the will of its author, it becomes a whole of its own with its own inner logic that is offered to readers, sociologists, philosophers, and lay individuals. As a concept, the text thus *translates* real, *in-situ* social contexts. It is important here to recognize the influence of Ricoeur's (1971) essay 'The Model of the Text' in the United States in general, and the Yale School of cultural sociology in particular. On many accounts, his ideas serve as the springboard for Alexander and others to effectuate the transition from text to action, or, its near equivalent: from a structural to a more practical hermeneutics.

The development of the strong program in the early 2000s was rapidly coupled with another development in Alexander's theory which took the form of 'cultural pragmatics' (see especially, Alexander, 2004). Here the influences came from closer to home in the United States, particularly salient in and around the performative turn. The work of figures such as Richard Schechner (1977), Victor Turner (1987) and Erving Goffman (1956) were substantial sources of inspiration. But their influence pales in comparison to that of Geertz. His insight into the Balinese cockfight (1973 [1964]), for instance, was very persuasive because he showed how dramatic and intensely choreographed the scripts of masculinity, violence and status are, and also how deeply embedded they are in the event itself. Alexander's aim is to convey this type of powerful theatricality, as when he writes: 'Cultural performance is the social process by which actors, individually or in concert, display for others the meaning of their social situation' (2004: 529). In all social contexts, a *fusion* of many elements is at play –background symbols, means of symbolic production, mise-en-scène, audience, etc. – as if the success of this or that performance depended on such a complex fusion. The objective is to arrive at a certain 'verisimilitude' defined as the capacity to make others believe, to give the appearance of reality, control and authenticity. And this is where it gets so problematic. While pre-modern societies were wholly ritualistic and hence very fusional, contemporary societies are less so and thus more inclined to dispersion.

A more practical hermeneutics means more practical studies, which is certainly reflected in Alexander's more recent work. One example is his studies on what he calls 'political performers' (2010; 2011). While charisma – in the Weberian sense – might be a rare quality nowadays, it nonetheless still manages to create considerable hopes and expectations, that, in turn, generate social change. To be fair, Alexander may have been caught in the ambient enthusiasm surrounding Barack Obama acceding to the White House at the time, which may show a potential limitation of this model. Another example is his latest work on journalism as a key element of democratic culture (see Alexander, 2015a; 2015b), in which he productively rejects the kind of reductionism that identifies the current crisis solely with technological causes. For him, instead, there are sacred values embedded in the profession, which have the potential to be re-invented as citizen journalists increasingly participate in the civil sphere and become important cultural actors. While it might be too early to determine whether this discussion will become a hallmark of Alexander's work, it certainly points towards interesting directions for the bending of hermeneutics and cultural sociology in the near future.

## ACTUAL AND FUTURE RELEVANCE

Properly assessing where the dialogue between hermeneutics and cultural sociology stands after a hundred more years of twists and turns is anything but an easy task. Opting for a militant approach, it would certainly be possible to say that the success of a somewhat unified hermeneutics of culture depends on the capacity to continually and innovatively bend the two sub-fields. If this is the wish, however, it faces some analytical challenges that must be addressed. In particular, it appears important to keep the focus on the transition from text to action, and develop it in a non-reductive, non-instrumental way. One term is not directly equivalent to the other, but rather operates 'as' the other in such a way that it forces a smoother, more refined dialectical interaction. And this, in turn, entails two implications. On the one hand, a hermeneutically informed cultural sociology would always be motivated by the kind of deep sensibility towards meanings that ignited Geertz's writings, for instance. How can we continue to embody such a passionate gaze? How can we engender a sense of urgency for cultural matters in students? These questions will likely remain open for some time to come. On the other hand, and even more problematically, is the fact that this transition from text to action is rather demanding in terms of conceptual and historical knowledge. The dialogue between hermeneutics and cultural sociology plays out epistemologically and ontologically, also mobilizing a multitude of neighbouring social theories. Will this discourage even the most passionate of scholars? Hopefully not. Being aware of the difficulty should rather serve as an encouragement to call for a hermeneutically informed cultural sociology that would be both rigorous and passionate, one that would be 'reflexive' in the best sense of the word. Such a sociology would address and make sense of the pressing issues of today. Two of those that might be evoked here are particularly relevant and intertwined.

The first relates to the capacity of a meaning-centred cultural sociology to deal with politics in a way that more classical and empirical political sociology cannot (see Inglis et al., 2007: 17, for instance). Culture and politics certainly have a lot in common, such as their belonging to the realm of discourse and performance, and their heavy reliance on belief and legitimacy. Of course, this link has been recognized by many over the years, from Weber and Ricoeur, to Geertz and Alexander. Yet, it is possible to argue that these authors have insisted primarily on the *productive* dimension of authority, power and politics, i.e. how these make things and events happen by making them meaningful.

Much less has been done on the receptive side, on how audiences make sense of politics. While there are such things as political texts and interpretations, how are they read and understood? To answer this question inevitably means giving the audience an active role, and positioning understanding as reconstructive, interpretative and critical. In short, the audience is a hermeneutical agent. Alexander has made some incursions in this direction over the last few years, and his current work on citizen journalism can be seen as a significant step to recognizing the full potential of such ideas. Already in 2004 he discussed what he calls 'hermeneutical powers' (2004: 531), and in 2008 he offered this insight: 'We do a great disservice to modern society by underestimating the social role of criticism … in a very wide sense of any interpretative source that is outside of the speaker, such as newspapers, new media, and the sacred and secular-intellectual worlds' (Alexander, 2008: 532; see also Boltanski, 2009). However, much remains to be done. For one thing, the role of hermeneutical agents should be analysed from a perspective that encompasses even the most trivial manifestations of culture and politics (see Roberge, 2011, for instance). In turn, this would radically broaden the way the public sphere is conceived beyond the simple and rather unrealistic exchange of rational arguments *à la* Habermas. Finally, to read the audience as a significant agent, and thus hermeneutically reconstructing the public sphere, would force us to take into consideration the role of new media technologies in forging a participative or convergence culture (see, for instance, Jenkins, 2008). If cultural sociology does not engage with communications scholars in this area, it certainly runs the risk of becoming irrelevant.

Discussing the many ways by which digital and Web 2.0-related technologies have changed the very fabric of culture and politics is not to succumb to technological determinism. On the contrary, it is the instinctive fear of such determinism that constitutes an impasse that has often prevented cultural sociology from properly engaging with technology. Digitalization is not vanishing, to be sure, and the current transformation of computer interfaces to more experiential forms – the Internet of things or virtual reality, for instance – is likely to create new challenges of both a theoretical and practical nature. Lawrence Lessig crafted an expression some years ago that nicely summarizes the situation: 'Code is law' (1999). Networked technologies, either as hardware or software, are far more than just tubes and pipes for content to circulate; they orient, shape and give direction to flows of data. Rather than passive conduits, they thus have to be conceived as active or 'performative' (see Mackenzie, 2005). A hermeneutically informed cultural sociology that is familiar with the deeper performative turn in the social sciences is certainly capable of offering a contribution in this regard. More importantly, such a sociology should at least attempt to make sense of digital culture as exactly that, a significant world (see, for instance, Langlois, 2011). Could code and data be understood *as text*? Further, could networked infrastructures be interpreted as a *complex architext* (Genet, 1979)? The fact of the matter is that they already are thought of this way in everyday practice. Internet searches, for instance, might be geared towards complex algorithms, yet these later rely on the keywords identified by websites to index and make sense of the ambient complexity. In turn, in order to be seen on the Web, these keywords are so compact and so important that they have become the object of intense cultural and economic activity via SEO – Search Engine Optimalization (see Cardon, 2013; Rohle, 2009). Similarly, the current development of the 'Semantic Web' modifies slowly but surely the textual architecture of the network (Halpin, 2013). For example, computer scientists in the field have tried to create clusters of interrelated meanings called 'ontologies' that would go from site to site across the Web, but in order to do so they still must face the very hermeneutical problem of eliminating ambiguity. While they refer to this process as 'disambiguation', it could only with difficulty not be of interest for a hermeneutically informed cultural sociology.

## CONCLUSION

The aim of this chapter was to historically and conceptually reconstruct what could be the fruitful dialogue between hermeneutics and cultural sociology. While it is true that these disciplines come from slightly different backgrounds and see the world from somewhat different lenses, it is also true that they share a powerful commitment to meaning, interpretation and understanding. This essential bond is what has allowed us, increasingly throughout the chapter, to talk of a hermeneutically informed cultural sociology. Indeed, some themes and interrogations have proven recurrent over time; this is the case, for instance, in the tension surrounding the category of explanation as a measurement of scientificity. It was in this way that Dilthey and Weber, and Alexander today, criticized empirical sociology. Explanation is not totally dismissed, but should rather develop *from within* the specificity of the human sciences – which explains in part the success of structuralism in the 1970s and why it was incorporated into both Ricoeur and Alexander's work. Some other inquiries, for their part, have given rise to more original and innovative insights. Such is the case for the transition from text to action and all the theoretical ramifications this implies. Ricoeur, again, was a key figure, but others including Geertz and then Alexander have helped to introduce more performative elements. Today, it is safe to assume that a hermeneutically informed cultural sociology exists in and for itself, that it is self-aware and robust, and that it can count on its own history to thrive in the years to come. Challenges still abound, of course, as the discipline strives to be more practical and more in tune with current social and cultural trends (especially new media technologies), yet this might be seen as the distinctive mark of a tradition and a perspective that is very much alive.

## NOTES

1   Among the works which most helped to clarify this question, one could note those of Bauman (1978), Hekman (1986), Moore (1990) and Outhwaite (2015).
2   The tense debate between the two men in *Esprit* is certainly emblematic of that (see Ricoeur, 1963).
3   Durkheim's influence on Alexander is profound and certainly has multiple ramifications. It is best summarized in Alexander and Smith (2005) and Alexander (1988a).

## REFERENCES

Alexander, J. (1983) *Theoretical Logic in Sociology, Vol. II*. Berkeley/London: University of California Press/Routledge.
Alexander, J. (1988a) *Durkheimian Sociology: Cultural Studies*. Cambridge: Cambridge University Press.
Alexander, J. (1988b) 'The New Theoretical Movement', in N.J. Smelser (ed.), *Handbook of Sociology*. Newbury Park, CA: Sage Publications. pp. 77–101.
Alexander, J. (1990) 'Analytic Debates: Understanding the Relative Autonomy of Culture', in J. Alexander and S. Seidman (eds), *Culture and Society: Contemporary Debates*. Cambridge: Cambridge University Press. pp. 1–27.
Alexander, J. (2004) 'Cultural Pragmatics: Social Performance Between Ritual and Strategy', *Sociological Theory*, 22(4): 527–73.
Alexander, J. (2008) 'Performing Cultural Sociology: A Conversation with Jeffrey Alexander, 0.15 MB Interview by Rodrigo Cordero, Francisco Carballo, and José Ossandón', *European Journal of Social Theory*, 11(4): 523–542.
Alexander, J. (2010) *The Performance of Politics: Obama's Victory and the Democratic Struggle for Power*. Oxford: Oxford University Press.
Alexander, J. (2011) *Performance and Power*. Cambridge: Polity.
Alexander, J. (2015a) 'Introduction to Special Section Cultural Sociology and Journalism', *Fudan Journal of the Humanities and Social Sciences*, 8(1): 1–7.
Alexander, J. (2015b) 'The Crisis of Journalism Reconsidered: Cultural Power', *Fudan Journal of the Humanities and Social Sciences*, 8(1): 9–31.
Alexander, J. C. and Mast, J. (2006) 'Introduction: symbolic action in theory and practice: the cultural pragmatics of symbolic action', in Alexander, J. C., Mast, J. et Giesen, B. (eds), *Social Performance, Symbolic Action, Cultural Pragmatics and Ritual*. Cambridge: Cambridge University Press. pp. 1–28.
Alexander, J. and Smith, P. (1998) 'Sociologie culturelle ou sociologie de la culture? Un programme fort pour donner à la sociologie son second souffle', *Sociologie et sociétés*, 30(1): 107–16.
Alexander, J. and Smith, P. (2002) 'The Strong Program in Cultural Theory: Elements of a Structural Hermeneutics', in J. Turner (ed.), *Handbook of Sociological Theory*. New York: Kluwer Academic/Plenum Publishers. pp. 135–50.
Alexander, J. and Smith, P. (2005) *The Cambridge Companion to Durkheim*. Cambridge: Cambridge University Press.
Bauman, Z. (1978) *Hermeneutics and Social Science*. New York: Columbia University Press.
Boltanski, L. (2009) *De la critique. Précis de sociologie de l'émancipation*. Paris: Gallimard.
Cardon, D. (2013) 'Dans l'esprit du Pagerank', *Réseaux*, 177: 63–95.
de Saussure, F. (1986 [1922]) *Course in General Linguistics*. Chicago and La Salle: Open Court.
Dilthey, W. (1976 [1910]) 'The Construction of the Historical World in the Human Studies', in H.P. Rickman (ed.), *Dilthey: Selected Writings*. Cambridge: Cambridge University Press.
Gadamer, H-G. (1975 [1960]) *Truth and Method*. New York: The Crossroad Publishing Company.
Geertz, C. (1973 [1964]) 'Ideology as a Cultural System', in C. Geertz (ed.), *The Interpretation of Cultures*. New York: Basic Books.
Geertz, C. (1983) *Local Knowledge: Further Essays in Interpretative Anthropology*. New York: Basic Books.

Genet, G. (1979) *Introduction à l'architexte*. Paris: Seuil.

Goffman, E. (1956) *The Presentation of Self in Everyday Life*. Edinburgh: University of Edinburgh, Social Sciences Research Centre.

Halpin, H. (2013) *Social Semantics: The Search for Meaning on the Web*. New York: Springer.

Hekman, S. (1986) *Hermeneutics and the Sociology of Knowledge*. Notre Dame: University of Notre Dame Press.

Hirsch, E. (1967) *Validity in Interpretation*. New Haven and London: Yale University Press.

Inglis, D., Blaikie, A. and Wagner-Pacifici, R. (2007) 'Editorial: Sociology, Culture and the 21st Century', *Cultural Sociology*, 1(1): 5–22.

Jacobs, M. and Spillman, L. (2005) 'Cultural Sociology at the Crossroads of the Discipline', *Poetics*, 33(1): 1–14.

Jenkins, H. (2008) *Convergence Culture: Where Old and New Media Collide*. New York: NYU Press.

Lamont, M. and Wuthnow, R. (1990) 'Betwixt and Between: Recent Cultural Sociology in Europe and the United States', in G. Ritzer (ed.), *Frontiers of Social Theory*. New York: Columbia University Press.

Langlois, G. (2011) 'Meaning, Semiotechnologies and Participatory Media', *Culture Machine*, 12. Available at: www.culturemachine.net/index.php/cm/article/download/437/467

Lessig, L. (1999) *Code and Other Laws of Cyberspace*. New York: Basic Books.

Lévi-Strauss, C. (1958) *Anthropologie structurale*. Paris: Plon.

Mackenzie, A. (2005) 'The Performativity of Code: Software and Cultures of Circulation', *Theory, Culture & Society*, 22(1): 71–92.

McLennan, G. (2004) 'Rationalizing Musicality: A Critique of Alexander's "Strong Program" in Cultural Sociology', *Thesis Eleven*, 79: 75–86.

McLennan, G. (2005) 'The "New American Cultural Sociology": An Appraisal', *Theory, Culture & Society*, 22(6): 1–18.

Moore, H. (1990) 'Paul Ricœur: Action, Meaning and Text', in C. Tilley (ed.), *Reading Material Culture: Structuralism, Hermeneutics and Post-Structuralism*. Oxford: Basil Blackwell.

Outhwaite, W. (2015) 'Hermeneutics and the Social Sciences', in J. Malpas and H-H. Gander (eds), *The Routledge Companion to Hermeneutics*. New York and London: Routledge. pp 486–97.

Reed, I. and Alexander, J. (2009) 'Social Science as Reading and Performance', *European Journal of Social Theory*, 12(1): 21–41.

Ricoeur, P. (1963) 'Réponses à quelques questions', *Esprit*, 322.

Ricoeur, P. (1971) 'The Model of the Text: Meaningful Action Considered as a Text', *Social Research*, 38: 529–62.

Ricoeur, P. (1977a) 'La structure symbolique de l'action', in Coll. *Symbolisme. Conférence Internationale de sociologie religieuse*. Strasbourg: CISR.

Ricoeur, P. (1977b) 'Phenomenology and the Social Sciences', *The Annals of Phenomenological Sociology*, 2: 145–59.

Ricoeur, P. (1981) *Hermeneutics and the Human Sciences*. Cambridge: Cambridge University Press.

Ricoeur, P. (1986) *From Text to Action: Essays in Hermeneutics II*, trans. K. Blamey and J.B. Thompson. Evanston: Northwestern University Press.

Ricoeur, P. (2004 [2000]) *Memory, History, Forgetting*. Chicago: University of Chicago Press.

Roberge, J. (2011) 'The Aesthetic Public Sphere and the Transformation of Criticism', *Social Semiotics*, 21(3): 435–53.

Rohle, T. (2009) 'Dissecting the Gatekeepers: Relational Perspectives on the Power of Search Engines', in F. Becker and F. Stalder (eds), *Deep Search: The Politics of Search Engines Beyond Google*. Vienna: Studien Verlag. pp. 63–95.

Schechner, R. (1977) *Ritual, Play, and Social Drama*. New York: Seabury Press.

Smith, P. (1998) *The New American Cultural Sociology*. Cambridge: Cambridge University Press.

Turner, V. (1987) *The Anthropology of Performance*. New York: PAJ Press.

Weber, M. (1978 [1947]) *Economy and Society*. Berkeley: University of California Press.

Weber, M. (1951) *The Religion of China*. New York: Free Press.

Weber, M. (1952 [1920]) *Ancient Judaism*. New York: Free Press.

Weber, M. (1958 [1905]) *The Protestant Ethic and the Spirit of Capitalism*. New York: Free Press.

# Social Network Analysis

Nick Crossley

## INTRODUCTION

Whether we conceptualise it in the narrow sense of 'art' and specific 'art worlds' (Becker, 1982) or the wider sense of everyday practices and beliefs, culture entails social networks. Everyday cultures are, by definition, shared, and they are shared because they diffuse outwards from a point of origin (itself often a network), through network channels. We speak the language that we do, with the accent that we have, for example, because of our extensive contact with others who do the same. Languages and accents 'travel' through the paths created by interaction. Similarly, the emergence of new and the reproduction of existing art worlds requires a connected critical mass of participants who, because networked, are able to combine their resources and coordinate their activities, jointly performing the various roles required for the (re)production of their art and drawing upon the social capital and related emergent phenomena that specific patterns of connection facilitate (Crossley, 2015a). Beyond individual human actors, moreover, cultural organisations and institutions are connected, and individual cultural units, from words in semantic networks to stylistic markers within artistic schools, each manifest patterns of connection, that is, networks,

which are central to their identity and existence. Furthermore, as DiMaggio (1987; 2011) argues, cultural works and artists often become associated, seeming to form a distinct school or style, where they have ties to a common audience: 'Just as populations of persons can be partitioned into groups on the basis of the works of art they like, so populations of art works can be partitioned into groups, or genres, on the basis of the persons who choose them' (DiMaggio, 1987: 445). The connections of audiences to artists and works define styles, much as styles define audiences (e.g. as subcultures), in complex 'two-mode' networks (see below).

Standard sociological methods, albeit with some tweaking, are usually able to gather data on such networks. Analysis of a network requires a systematic survey of relations, as defined by the researcher, between the members of a specified population of nodes, whether human individuals, texts, organisations, bands, studios, venues, cities, nation states or whatever; but this survey can be conducted in any of a number of ways, including many standard sociological methods of data gathering: e.g. questionnaires, semi-structured interviews, direct observation (participant or non-participant), content analysis, archival analysis or automated net trawls. However, the mainstream social scientific repertoire lacks means of storing and analysing such data in a way which captures the structures (of connection) they involve. This is where social network analysis (SNA) comes in.

A relatively obscure method until recently, SNA is a method for handling, storing and analysing relational data; that is, data regarding connections between various members of a given population of objects ('nodes'). Its origins go back to the 1930s and its development has been truly interdisciplinary, involving sociologists, anthropologists, social psychologists and more recently economists (Scott, 2000). Crucially, however, it has also involved mathematicians, in particular specialists in the field of graph theory. Unlike the graphs most of us are familiar with (e.g. bar charts) the graphs of graph theory comprise a set of objects ('vertices') and a set of links ('edges' or 'arcs') between certain of those vertices. A graph, in other words, is a network, and graph theory is a branch of mathematics devoted to identifying, measuring and analysing the properties of these networks. Not all of this is relevant to social scientific interest in social networks but much of it is and the development of SNA has involved a dialogue between social scientists and graph theorists seeking out their common interests. This is particularly evident in the vocabulary of SNA, which borrows extensively from graph theory.

Lest the mention of maths has struck a chord of fear, scepticism or both it is important to emphasise that the mathematical basis of graph theory is relatively straightforward and resonates directly with sociological observation. The concepts are not difficult to grasp and many students find them much more intuitive than statistical concepts (although, SNA has an emerging statistical wing and many recent advances involve this wing (e.g. Lusher et al., 2013)). The visual aspect of the method (see below) undoubtedly helps in this respect. In addition, a little graph theory goes a long way in SNA, particularly in the contemporary context, where user-friendly software makes computers do the hard work. No less importantly, however, SNA is often case-study focused, such that it fits nicely within an ethnographic or historical-sociological approach. Indeed, network analysts often combine their mathematically based analyses with qualitative analyses in a mixed-method strategy.

This is illustrated by the work of the Manchester School of social anthropologists/sociologists, who were key players in the historical development of SNA (Scott, 2000). Ethnographers by training, they turned to graph theory as a means of trying to capture and analyse complex patterns of connection between social actors which they routinely came across in the course of their work (see especially Mitchell, 1969). This never caused them to abandon the other tools of their trade, however, and I suspect that they would have baulked at the idea that social science might become divided along quantitative/qualitative lines. Some aspects of social life are better captured in numbers, some in words. Most require a bit of both. Networks fall into the latter category and though I will emphasise the mathematical tools in this chapter (because I expect they will be least familiar to the general reader), this is important (on mixing methods see Bellotti, 2014; Crossley, 2010; Edwards, 2009; Edwards and Crossley, 2009).

## WHOLE NETWORKS

Networks can be defined and captured in different ways for the purposes of SNA. In this chapter I will cover the three most common:

1 Whole networks;
2 Ego-nets;
3 Two-mode networks.

My main focus will be on whole networks. Word limits force me to choose and I choose whole networks specifically because most of the methodological work in SNA has been focused upon them –although a lot of empirical work has focused upon ego-nets, and two-mode networks are often used as a means of 'getting' whole networks (see below). In addition, an introduction to whole networks provides a good basis upon which to understand each of the other two types and encompasses much of what would be included in a dedicated introduction to each of them.

A whole network comprises:

1 A set of nodes (also sometimes called 'vertices');
2 A set (or sets) of ties (also sometimes called 'edges' or 'arcs').
3 It may also, optionally, involve:3. A set or sets of node attributes (e.g. age, gender, race, income. etc.).

From a substantive point of view it is vital that the node set is appropriately defined. Analysis is only meaningful if nodes are carefully chosen and criteria for exclusion in the node set, thought through by reference to theory and one's research aims. However, the techniques of SNA will accommodate any type of node, providing that it is capable of engaging in the type(s) of tie being observed in the research. Thus, our node set might be: all of the key participants in a local art world; all of the organisations involved in funding the arts in the UK; all of the music festivals in Germany attracting more than 15,000 attendees between 2008 and 2013; every character in Shakespeare's King Lear; every painting catalogued in France over a specified period, whatever is of interest.

If our interest is an aspect of everyday culture, such as lifestyle choices, patterns of linguistic usage or belief, then our node set might be the entire population of a nation (or more than one nation). Theoretically this is still a node set and networks of personal connection exist on national and international levels, as Stanley Milgram's (1967) famous small world studies illustrate[1] (of course nations are also connected by treaties and interactions between their governments). In practice, however, it is very difficult to conduct whole network analysis on networks involving millions of nodes because of the demands of data gathering and input (web-based SNA sometimes does extend to several million nodes) and, for this reason, an ego-net approach, with appropriate sampling, would be used (see below).

Any type of connection between nodes can count as a tie as long as treating it as such is meaningful in the context of a study. In relation to painters, for example, we might want to know who corresponded by letter to whom. In relation to music venues, we might want to know about any arrangements they have for sharing resources or we might be interested in the flow of artists between them (venues are linked by bands who play in them). Furthermore, it may make sense to survey multiple types of tie within the same study. Thus, within the same set of musicians we may want to know: (1) who has ever played live together; (2) who has ever recorded together; (3) who socialises together outside of their music-making activity; and (4) who was friends with whom before they became involved in making music. As with nodes, however, the freedom which SNA affords us to select and define ties as we wish must be tempered by recourse to theory and careful reflection upon our research aims and hypotheses. A poor choice will result in substantively weak and possibly meaningless findings.

Ties can be directed or undirected. A directed tie points from one actor to another and is not always reciprocated. John may admire Jane's writing (a tie of admiration), for example, without Jane necessarily admiring John's. She may but his admiration for her work does not logically entail hers for his. Similarly, Helen may have influenced Michele (a tie of influence) without Michele influencing Helen. An undirected tie is reciprocal by definition and is not reducible to the attitudes or activities of one party. For example, sharing studio space: if Pete shares with Nick then Nick shares with Pete. Ties can be conceptualised in binary terms, as either existing or not but they might also be weighted. If we ask writers to rate their admiration for other writers in their node set on a scale of 0–5, for example, we will have an ordinal weighting. If we count how many times two artists collaborate then we have an interval weighting.

Our above examples of ties are largely positive but they need not be. A recent survey by the Federation of Entertainment Unions (2013) points to the existence of bullying in the entertainment industry. This might be the basis for a social network analysis. We might look at who bullies whom. In many cases we would do this in exactly the same way that we would study positive ties. As noted above, the analytic routines of SNA are indifferent to the nature of ties and that extends to their positivity or negativity. However, in some cases network analysts want to study negative and positive ties together, exploring issues of 'structural balance' (i.e. are my friend's enemies also my enemies). De Nooy (2008), for example, has explored balance between positive and negative evaluations in a network of literary author-reviewers. Special techniques exist for this type of work.

Node attributes are additional bits of information that we have about nodes. If our nodes are painters, for example, then we might want information about their professed style, training, commissions and exhibitions. In addition, we might want to know their gender, ethnicity, age, annual income, etc. If our nodes are venues we might want to know their capacity, any admission restrictions, whether they sell alcohol, etc.

Network data are gathered, for purposes of SNA, by means of surveys. As noted above, 'survey', in this context, does not necessarily mean 'questionnaire'. Data may be gathered in a variety of ways. For whole network analysis, however, we must survey all nodes in our node set (or as close to that as we can manage) and we need to know about the existence or not of ties between all possible pairings of them. Lack of connection is as important as connection and we need to be as sure as we can about it. Network data are stored in an adjacency matrix, such as Table 20.1, in which each node has both a row and a column. Ties between nodes are represented by numbers in the cells where these rows and columns intersect. Viv's tie to Frank, for example, is indicated by the number 1 in the cell where her row intersects with his column. Because the ties in this matrix are undirected the same relationship is also recorded where Frank's row intersects with Viv's column. There is a 1 in that cell too. If our ties were directed, however, and Frank did not reciprocate a

**Table 20.1. An adjacency matrix**

|       | Viv | Lucy | Sam | Frank | Ollie |
|-------|-----|------|-----|-------|-------|
| Viv   | 1   | 0    | 1   | 1     | 1     |
| Lucy  | 0   | 1    | 0   | 1     | 1     |
| Sam   | 1   | 0    | 1   | 0     | 1     |
| Frank | 1   | 1    | 0   | 1     | 0     |
| Ollie | 1   | 1    | 1   | 0     | 1     |

tie which Viv sent to him then we would find a 0 where his row intersects her column.

Notice that the diagonal of the matrix, from the top left to the bottom right, records each node's relation to itself (a reflexive relation). Reflexive relations are meaningless in relation to many tie types: artists cannot collaborate with themselves, for example, and organisations cannot share resources with themselves. For this reason the default for most routines, in most software packages, is to ignore the diagonal. Reflexive ties might be meaningful, however, and can be included. In a network where musicians are linked if they play one another's songs, for example, we might want to capture musicians who play their own songs.

In Table 20.1 ties are binary. They either exist or they do not. We record this by way of 1s and 0s. If ties were weighted then the numbers in the matrix would reflect the weighting and might have a much wider range. If Viv has covered seven of Lucy's songs, for example, then we would put a 7 where her row intersects with Lucy's column.

Software packages typically allow data to be input in a matrix format, such as Table 20.1. Filling out a spreadsheet can take time, however, and for this reason a number of easier data entry formats are possible, leaving the software to generate the adjacency matrix. The software will also generate a graph, such as the one in Figure 20.1, which maps ties of longstanding friendship and/or musical collaboration between the key participants in Sheffield's post-punk music world between 1976 and 1980 (see Crossley, 2015a; 2015b) (all graphs in this paper are drawn with Ucinet/Netdraw (Borgatti et al., 2002)).

At its simplest a graph represents nodes as small shapes (e.g. squares), all of the same size and colour, connected by lines where they enjoy a tie. Figure 20.1 is a little more elaborate. I have distinguished between those who play some form of support role in this world (e.g. manager or producer), irrespective of other roles played (e.g. musician), representing them as squares, and those who do not (represented as circles). In addition, I have performed a core-periphery analysis (see below) and coloured members of the core grey, whilst members of the periphery are black. Finally, I have measured the number of ties enjoyed by each participant (their 'degree'), as measured in my survey, and sized their node in accordance with this. Big nodes have more connections than smaller notes. This allows me to illustrate a basic observation from my work on punk and post-punk music worlds (Crossley, 2015a; 2015b): namely, that support personnel (squares) tend to be better connected (bigger) and are more likely to belong to the network core (grey) within music world networks.

Graph theory operates with a different conception of space to the one that we ordinarily use when visualising data. In a scatterplot, for example, space is defined by horizontal (x) and vertical (y) axes. The 'position' of a point refers to its location along each of these axes and the distance between points is the difference between their 'score' for each axis and is clear from their location on the plot. In graph theory and SNA, by contrast, space is mapped entirely in connections. The position of a node refers to its pattern of connections and the proximity of any two nodes is measured by reference to the length of the *path* (see below) connecting them. Nodes which are directly connected are closer to one another than nodes which are only indirectly connected via a third party, for example, irrespective of where they are located in the plot. Furthermore, the distance between two nodes which have no path connecting them is undefined and indefinable, irrespective of their co-location within the same plot.

In practice the software packages which network analysts use to draw graphs employ algorithms which locate nodes on the basis of certain principles – usually they are located close to those with which they share a similar profile of ties. However, there are different algorithms, which give different layouts; each can only approximately locate nodes according to its chosen principle, and analysts will often manually alter layouts in any case, either for aesthetic purposes or to illustrate a point which they wish to make (they are perfectly entitled to do this and the software packages make it very easy to do).

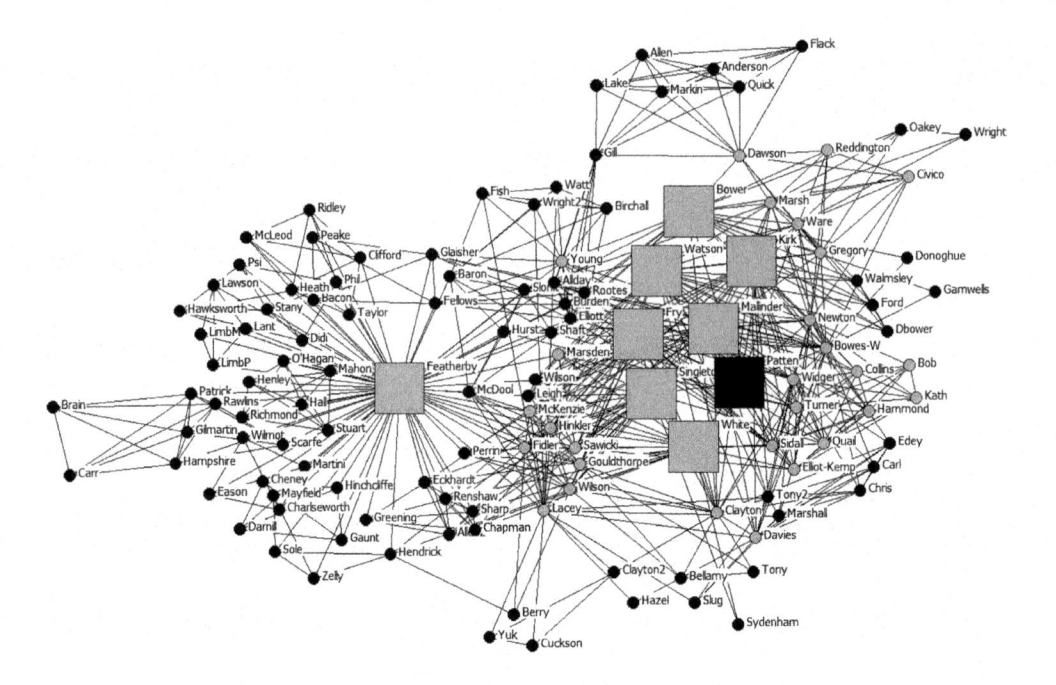

**Figure 20.1 The network structure of Sheffield's post-punk music world, 1976–1980**

## LEVELS OF ANALYSIS

Properties of networks can be identified at five levels: (1) the whole network; (2) sub-sets of nodes; (3) individual nodes; (4) the dyad; and (5) the triad. The latter two levels are particularly important in statistical approaches to SNA and I deal with them separately. Here I briefly summarise the first three.

### Properties of Whole Networks

These include:

1 *Order*. This is the number of nodes in the network.
2 *Density*. This is the number of ties in the network, expressed as a proportion of the total number of ties that are possible given the number of nodes.
3 *Paths* and *path lengths*. A path is a chain of connections which links two nodes. Path lengths are measured by the number of ties (referred to as 'degrees') they involve.
4 *Geodesic distances*. There are often several possible paths between two nodes of differing lengths. Usually it is the shortest path that we are interested in. We call the length of this path, measured in degrees, the geodesic distance.
5 *Average geodesic distance*. If we add up the geodesic distances separating every possible pair of actors in the network and divide by the number of pairs we get the average distance, which gives us a good idea of how far information, innovations and resources typically have to travel in the network before everyone has access to them.
6 *Diameter*. Alternatively, we sometimes measure the width of the network by taking the longest of its geodesic distances. This is called the diameter of a network.
7 *Components*. A component is a sub-set of nodes each of whom is at least indirectly connected to each of the others by a path. There is only one component in Figure 20.1 because each node is indirectly linked to every other by a path.

### Properties of Sub-Networks

Sub-sets of nodes are typically distinguished in one of two ways: (1) *exogenously*, by reference to attributes such as gender or ethnicity; or (2) *endogenously*, by reference to distinctive patterns of connection. A common form of

**Table 20.2. Core–periphery density matrix (derived from the network in Figure 20.1)**

|  | Core | Periphery |
|---|---|---|
| Core (n = 36) | 0.35 | 0.07 |
| Periphery (n = 94) | 0.07 | 0.04 |

endogenous sub-group analysis centres upon the *core–periphery structure*; that is, a common pattern in networks in which we find a subset of nodes who are very densely tied to one another (*the core*) compared to the rest (*the periphery*), whose ties both to one another and to the core are comparatively sparse. In a classic core–periphery structure those at the periphery, though only sparsely connected to it, are better connected to the core than they are to one another. Table 20.2, for example, tells us that the network visualised in Figure 20.1 has a core of 36 members whose density of ties to one another is 0.35 compared to only 0.04 within the periphery and 0.07 between core and periphery. This is a clear core–periphery structure and it is important because the core is most likely an elite within this world and its members' presence will have effects upon it. The next step of our analysis might be to look who is in the core, reflect upon its significance (for its own members, periphery members and the network as a whole), cross-tabulate its membership against other variables (e.g. gender), and identify the mechanisms responsible for its formation.

Endogenously defined subgroups are often of interest because their existence may tell us about conflicts and power structures in a network, or because we might expect different sub-groups to behave differently, either because their members are subject to different influences within the network or because their position in the network enables/constrains them in different ways and to different degrees.

Exogenously defined subgroups, such as different ethnic groups, are often interesting because they allow us to assess how wider inequalities and identities affect the network. For example, we might consider whether women are underrepresented within a network core. In addition, shared attributes or identities often increase the likelihood of connection (homophily). I return to this.

## Properties of Nodes

The key examples of node level properties are the various types of *centrality*. Some nodes are more central than others in a network and this can create both greater opportunities/leverage for them but also greater constraint/resource expenditure. There are many ways of measuring a node's centrality but the three main ones are:

1 *Degree*. A node's degree is the number of ties it has within a network. In a directed network we would distinguish between incoming and outgoing ties (*in-degree* and *out-degree*).
2 *Closeness*. A node's closeness is the sum of the path lengths connecting it to every other node in the network, normalised and inverted so that higher scores indicate shorter distances.
3 *Betweenness*. This is a measure of how often a node falls along the shortest path connecting two other nodes, such that they might 'broker' between these parties.

Though not a measure of centrality, *ego-net density* is also sometimes a useful node level measure. We calculate it by isolating, for each node, the other nodes to which they are connected and the proportion of the potential number of ties between these others which are actually present. A high ego-net density can indicate that a node is highly constrained in the network: most of the others to whom it is connected are connected to one another, affording the node little opportunity for managing the flow of information about herself within the network (a state of affairs which Goffman (1961) found to be very distressing for the inmates of total institutions) or for playing their contacts off against one another. On the other hand, however, social support may be stronger and the node may benefit both from the solidarity of a close knit team and from the control that is exercised over their alters.

## DYADS, TRIADS, HOMOPHILY AND STATISTICAL MODELS

The dyadic level of analysis is seldom focused upon in isolation from the triadic level. However, it was an important first step in early attempts to statistically model networks. Statisticians asked whether ties from one node to another (i to j), in a directed network, were more likely when there was already a tie moving in the other direction (j to i). Of course this will depend upon the type of tie defining the network: if j likes i this will motivate him to do things to make her like him, which will probably increase the likelihood that she will like him (unless he is a pest); if j is bullying i, however, then it is very unlikely that i will be bullying j. The key point, however, is that we are beginning to think about the probability of ties between i and j and therefore moving from description of networks to statistical modelling.

A dyad in a binary, undirected network can only be in one of two states. Either the nodes are connected or they are not. In a directed network that increases to four states, although two are *isomorphic*, such that they reduce to three:

1 Neither node sends a tie to the other.
2 Both nodes send a tie to the other.
3 One node send a tie to the other but this is not reciprocated.

(There are four if we distinguish between a state in which i sends an unreciprocated tie to j and a state in which j sends a unreciprocated tie to i.)

If, as suggested above, there is a tendency towards reciprocation in directed networks then we would expect both state one and state two to occur more often in real world networks than they would purely by chance (in networks with the same density but whose ties are randomly assigned) and we would expect state three to occur less often. Using this thought as our guide we can begin to think about modelling ties statistically and also about testing hypotheses regarding reciprocation.

The next step on from dyadic analysis, within statistical circles, was triadic analysis; that is, analysis of all potential states of connection between every possible combination of three nodes in the network. In an undirected network there are four possible states (excluding isomorphisms):

1 No ties;
2 One tie;
3 Two ties;
4 Three ties.

If we allow for direction there are 64 states but these boil down to 16 when we remove isomorphisms. Most software packages have a 'triad census' function which counts the number and proportion of all possible triads within the network which fall into each of the 16 possibilities. Again the point is usually to identify configurations which occur significantly more often than would be predicted by chance. Reciprocation will be part of this picture but a key addition at the triadic level is *transitivity*. In the simplest (undirected) case this means that if i has a tie to j and j has a tie to k then i is more likely to have a tie to k too: in colloquial terms, and focusing upon friendship for sake of convenience, we are more likely to be connected to our friends' friends than to alters who are unconnected to anybody else that we know.

It is not only factors endogenous to network structure which affect the probability of ties. Exogenous factors may be important too, not least *homophily*, which was introduced above. Focusing upon human nodes, Lazarsfeld and Merton (1964) distinguish between *status homophily*, where nodes link disproportionately to alters with whom they share a social status (e.g. gender, ethnicity, occupational class), and *value homophily*, where they link disproportionately to alters with whom they share values, attitudes or tastes.

Statistical thinking within network analysis has developed hugely in recent years and a new branch of SNA has emerged centred upon 'Exponential Random Graph Models' (ERGMs). The details of these models go beyond our remit here. Suffice it to say, however, that they build upon the considerations regarding reciprocity, transitivity and homophily referred to above, in an attempt to model the factors, both endogenous and exogenous to network structure, which increase (or decrease) the likelihood of a tie (see Lusher et al., 2013).

## NETWORK DYNAMICS

Networks are never static. They are constantly in-process. New ties are formed; established ties are broken; some nodes increase in significance; others decrease; new nodes enter the network; others exit. We can use many of the techniques and measures outlined above, in conjunction with more narrative-focused methods, to explore and explain such changes. Change in networks has also been a key focus within the abovementioned statistical branch of SNA, however, and a number of sophisticated methods for modelling change in networks now exist. These methods allow one to model change in both network ties/structure and node attributes, and allow for the fact that each may causally affect the other. That is to say, nodes may change certain of their attributes (e.g. their tastes) as an effect of *social influence* within relationships, but they may also choose new partners and reject old ones, in a process of *selection*, on the basis of their attributes: for example, forming new ties with alters who share a salient attribute and breaking ties with others who do not (see Snijders, 2011).

## OTHER TYPES OF NETWORK DATA

Our focus hitherto has been upon 'whole network' data. Other types of network data exist, however, and in what follows in this section I will briefly outline two of them: ego-net data and two-mode data. Much of what I have said above applies to these other types of data but there are differences in some cases and I will spell these out as far as I can in the space available.

## Ego-Nets

An ego-net is a network centred upon a particular node (ego). It includes that node, all nodes tied to that node ('*alters*') in the way specified by the researcher, all ties which exist between alters and, optionally, attribute data for both ego and alters. Defined in this way, a whole network is comprised of ego-nets (each of its constitutive nodes has or is an ego-net) and we can extract individual ego-nets from a whole net. In Figure 20.2, for example, I have extracted the ego-net of Paul Shaft from the network in Figure 20.1. Shaft played in seminal Sheffield punk band, 2.3 (to the right of him on the graph), he contributed to the *Gun Rubber* punk zine (run by Paul Bower, at the top right of the graph) and he played in post-punk band, De Tian (to the left of him on the graph).

As with a whole network, an ego-net has a number of measurable properties. We can see from the graph, for example, that Shaft has a degree of 8. His ego-net has a density (0.46). It happens that all of his alters are male, giving him a high score for gender homophily. Perhaps more interesting, however, he appears to be the sole link between the respective members of the two bands he played in. Depending upon context, this could be a very important aspect of his ego-net. Ronald Burt (1992) has argued that nodes which bridge 'structural holes' (i.e. gaps in connection in a network) in this way often achieve considerable advantage as a consequence, and he has introduced a number of ego-net measures which seek to capture the extent to which any node does occupy this position (1992).

In Shaft's case, for example, we might hypothesise that he controls the flow of resources between the left and right hand sides of his ego-net, perhaps imposing a charge (in terms of status if not material rewards) for facilitating this flow. Similarly, in passing ideas and innovations from one side to another he may take credit for them (intentionally or not), seeming to be a source of creativity which, in fact, he is only mediating. I am not saying that he did any of these things. I am merely speculating, for illustrative purposes. He *could have*, given his apparent network position (but see below).

Because a whole network comprises multiple ego-nets we can do everything that we would do in an ego-net analysis in the context of a whole network study by abstracting its ego-nets from the whole network. However, ego-net data is not only gathered in the context of a whole network.

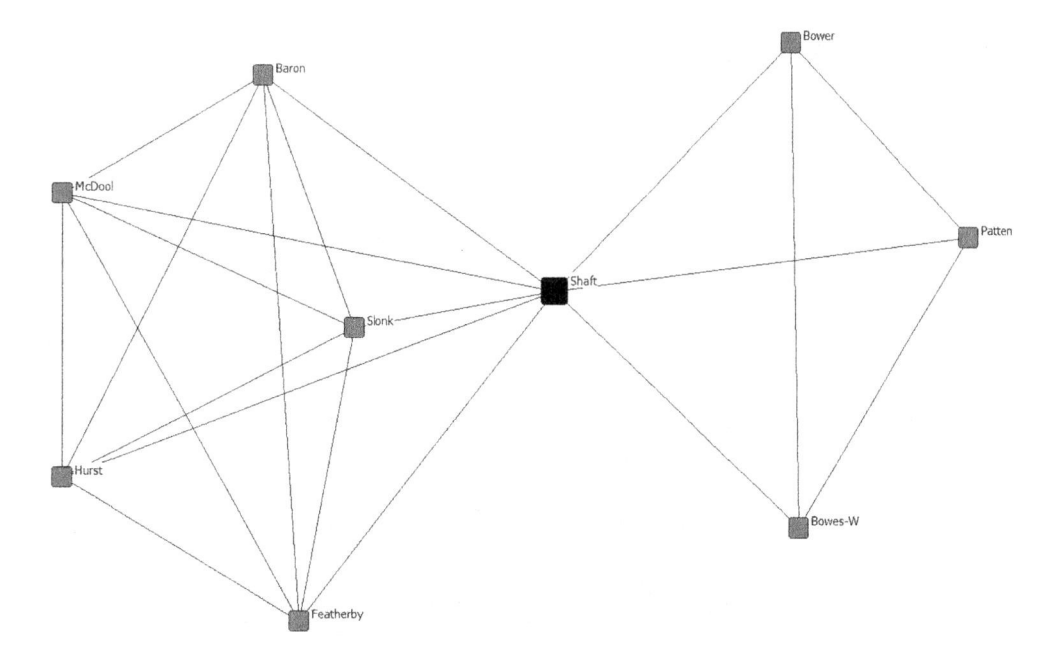

**Figure 20.2 Paul Shaft's ego-net (extracted from the network in Figure 20.1)**

We might gather ego-net data *instead* of whole network data. To do so we would still identify the node set or population of interest to us but rather than attempting a census of all nodes in that population we would take a sample, using one of the recognised sampling strategies typically used in survey research. This would not allow us to reconstruct the whole network, as we would have no information regarding the ties or attributes of the majority of nodes, but we could take ego-net measures and incorporate them within an analysis.

We might conduct a random sample survey of all musicians registered with the Musicians Union, for example, asking them about the other musicians with whom they have collaborated in the last two years. Alternatively, if we were interested in the consumption of music we might gather a random sample of a whole national population, asking people both about their ties and about their musical tastes and consumption. In both cases, with a little information about alter attributes (e.g. their music styles or tastes) we could do interesting and useful network analysis.

There are three advantages to this type of ego-net research. Firstly, it affords a means of analysing big networks. If we are interested in a relatively small population of actors, such as participants in a local music world or orchestra, then it is feasible for us to conduct a census survey of our node set and we can do whole network analysis. If we are interested in bigger populations, however, then a census survey will not be possible, ruling out whole network analysis. Ego-net analysis is still possible, however, because it only requires that we sample the population that is of interest to us.

Secondly, where it has been gathered using one of the sampling strategies more ordinarily used in survey research, ego-net data meets the assumptions of standard techniques of statistical analysis and modelling (whole network data does not).[2] This means both that these techniques can be employed, where desirable, and that ego-net research can be bolted on to projects which have a wider and more varied agenda. Having said that, as noted earlier in the chapter, a whole network study often fits nicely with a historical or ethnographic case study approach, so the choice between a whole and ego-net approach might be influenced by our wider research context.

The final advantage of ego-net research relates to what Simmel (1955) calls 'intersecting social circles' and White (2008) calls network domains or 'net doms'. Both writers observe that in modern societies most people interact and form ties across a number of distinct 'social circles' or 'domains', whose membership, with the exception of them, does not overlap. For example, an amateur actor in a local drama group will have fellow thespians amongst their friends but also a family, neighbours, old friends from school and workmates. They are a point of intersection between these different worlds but they are most likely the only point of intersection. Their fellow actors won't know their work colleagues, for example, and neither will they know their family members. Such intersections, which may be important, are much easier to tap into via ego-net research because the individual is the focus of the research and may identify ties from any and all of the circles/domains in which they are involved. Whole network research tends to define its node population by reference to a single world and must do so to remain manageable.

However, ego-nets can be similarly misleading and involve a considerable loss of information with respect to each of the worlds in which an individual is involved. For example, simply adding Paul Bower's ego-net to Paul Shaft's reveals that the bridge which Shaft seemed to provide between the two bands he played with, and which seemed to be the sole point of contact between them, is actually anything but (see Figure 20.3). Bower actually has several paths of only two degrees through to members of Shaft's other band and Shaft is not in the advantageous position suggested by observation of his ego-net.

This is the effect of adding one more ego-net. If I had added the ego-nets of all of Shaft's alters the picture would have been different again. And the picture in Figure 20.1, which includes all key participants in the Sheffield post-punk world, adds further information still and again alters our perspective.

As these contrasts also suggest, we would glean little about the overall structure of the Sheffield world from Shaft's ego-net. His network position could not be said to be in any way representative. If we are interested in the global structure of a world then there is no substitute for whole network analysis.

## Two-Mode Data

Two-mode data involves two different types of node (two modes) and relations across them. For example, our two types of node might be (1) dancers and (2) dance studios, and the ties we are focusing upon might be 'has trained at during the last six weeks'; that is, for each dancer within our node set we know which of the studios in our node set she has trained at within a six-week period. Note that the ties we are focused on can only exist between a dancer and a studio, not between dancers or between studios.

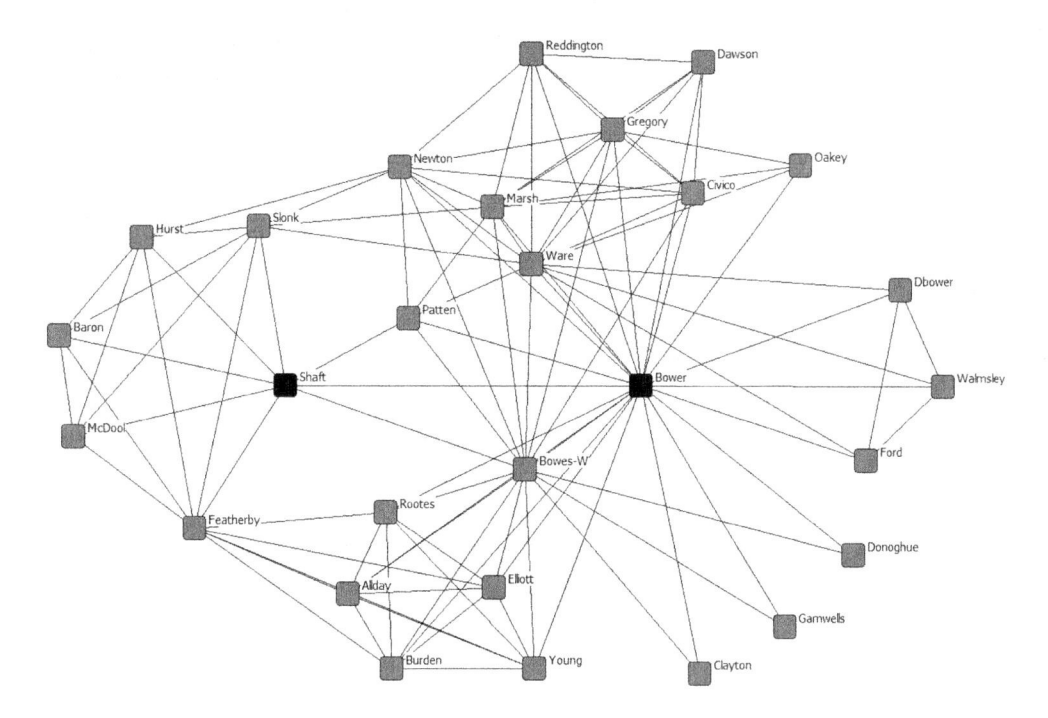

**Figure 20.3 Paul Shaft's ego-net merged with Paul Bower's (extracted from Figure 20.1, egos in black)**

There are two reasons why we might gather this type of data. Firstly, the social networks involved in cultural domains often are two- (or even multi-) mode and it is sometimes important to capture this. The networks of the ballroom world are, amongst other things, networks of dancers and studios, for example. Secondly, two-mode data is often easier to get hold of. It would be very difficult to track down every high-profile dancer in even a small city, to interview and map their friendships and collaborations, for example, but it might be possible to identify the studios at which they train, constructing an *incidence matrix*[3] linking dancers to studios on this basis. Table 20.3 presents a very small hypothetical example of an incidence matrix. As with a single-mode adjacency matrix we may visualise this data in the form of a graph (see Figure 20.4).

In recent years a number of 'two-mode versions' of the measures discussed earlier have been devised: for example, two-mode density and two-mode degree centrality. It is very common when analysing two-mode networks, however, to decompose or 'affiliate' them into two single-mode networks. What this means, in practice, to use our above example, is that we would create a network of dancers tied where they sometimes train at the same studio, and a network of studios, any two of which would be tied if the same dancer had trained at both. In each case the adjacency matrix created would be weighted. Two dancers who had trained at four of the same studios, for example, would

**Table 20.3. A hypothetical incidence matrix: dancers and studios**

|        | Std25 | T-Toes | Kumquat | Rambo | Fame | Dirty |
|--------|-------|--------|---------|-------|------|-------|
| Ola    | 1     | 1      | 1       | 0     | 0    | 0     |
| Pasha  | 0     | 1      | 1       | 1     | 1    | 1     |
| Artem  | 0     | 0      | 1       | 1     | 1    | 1     |
| Aliona | 0     | 1      | 1       | 1     | 0    | 0     |
| Anya   | 1     | 0      | 1       | 0     | 0    | 0     |

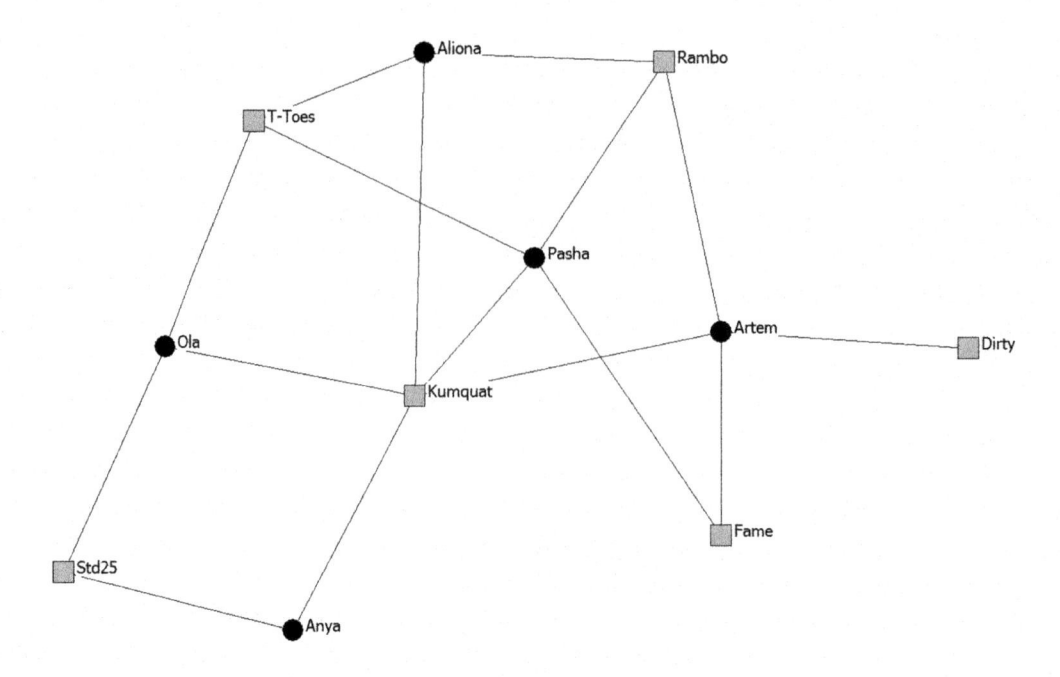

**Figure 20.4 Visualising a two-mode network (based on Table 20.3)**

have a tie strength of 4. We might work with this data as weighted or convert it back to binary format on the basis of a threshold value: for example, any ties stronger that 3 count as present, any equal to or less than 3 count as absent. Having affiliated our two-mode network we may then analyse one or both of the single-mode networks this affords us. Indeed some researchers only gather two-mode data as an indirect way of getting the single-mode data that they are interested in (because the single-mode data is difficult to get).

The sociological logic behind the procedure is spelled out in an important paper by Ronald Breiger (1974). Focusing upon social actors and places (or events), he notes that actors who hang out at the same places or take part in the same events are likely to meet and form ties as a consequence of this (see also Feld, 1981; 1982). Their common use of a space or participation in an event is a proxy measure for their being tied in some way and this is especially so if they co-participate in a number of events. Similarly, spaces and/or events are linked by actors who move between them because those actors effectively transfer ideas, information and other goods (or 'bads') between them. Training and performance techniques might diffuse from one studio to another, for example, by way of dancers who train at both.

The point does not always hold, of course, and we must be cautious in deriving single- from two-mode networks. Audience members at a big music festival will only meet a tiny fraction of their fellow festival goers, for example, because of the sheer number of participants and it would therefore be foolish to link all attendees. In addition, affiliated data is often clumpy because everybody who attends the same event is assumed to be tied to everybody else who attends it (creating a clump of connections). In single-mode data which is gathered in the normal way, such clumpiness (which would be captured by a measure called the clustering coefficient) might be interesting. In single-mode data which is derived from two-mode data, however, it may be no more than an artefact of the way in which the data have been gathered. Finally, it has been argued that studying single modes, when they are derived from two-mode data, involves a loss of important information about network structure. Recent work by Everett and Borgatti (2013) suggests that this can be overcome in relation to some routines by putting the two modes back together. This does not work for all routines but it does for certain key routines, including the core–periphery routine.

In this chapter I have offered a very brief overview of social network analysis. I have tried to introduce some of its key elements and to briefly illustrate some of the ways in which it might be used in cultural sociology. Readers who wish to learn more should consult Borgatti et al. (2012), Scott (2000) or Wasserman and Faust (1994).

## NOTES

1. Milgram is famed, in the context, for his claim that any US citizen is, on average, a mere 'six degrees of separation' from the president: that is, linked by only five intermediaries.
2. Standard tests of statistical significance assume that they are dealing with a sample from a wider population which the researcher is seeking to infer back to, for example. Whole networks are not usually samples of anything else. Furthermore, networks quite explicitly depart from the assumption of case-wise independence, which is crucial to most significance tests.
3. An incidence matrix is like an adjacency matrix except that one mode is represented by the row and the other by the columns.

## REFERENCES

Becker, H. (1982) *Art Worlds*. Berkeley: University of California Press.

Bellotti, E. (2014) *Qualitative Networks*. London: Routledge.

Borgatti, S., Everett, M. and Freeman, L. (2002) *Ucinet for Windows: Software for Social Network Analysis*. Harvard, MA: Analytic Technologies.

Borgatti, S.P, Everett, M.G. and Johnson, J. (2012) *Analysing Social Networks*. London: Sage.

Breiger, R. (1974) 'The Duality of Persons and Groups', *Social Forces*, 53(2): 181–90.

Burt, R. (1992) *Structural Holes*. Cambridge: Harvard University Press.

Crossley, N. (2010) 'The Social World of the Network: Qualitative Aspects of Network analysis', *Sociologica*, 1, http://www.sociologica.mulino.it/main

Crossley, N. (2015a) *Networks of Sound, Style and Subversion: The Punk and Post-Punk Worlds of Liverpool, London, Manchester and Sheffield, 1975–1980*. Manchester: Manchester University Press.

Crossley, N. (2015b) 'Totally Wired: The Network of Structure of the Post-Punk Worlds of Liverpool, Manchester and Sheffield, 1976–1980', in N. Crossley, S. McAndrew and P. Widdop (eds), *Social Networks and Music Worlds*. London: Routledge. pp. 40–60.

De Nooy, W. (2008) 'Signs Over Time', *Journal of Social Structure*, 9(1), http://www.cmu.edu/joss/content/articles/volindex.html

DiMaggio, P. (1987) 'Classification in Art', *American Sociological Review*, 52(4): 440–55.

DiMaggio, P. (2011) 'Cultural Networks', in J. Scott, and P. Carrington (eds), *The Sage Handbook of Social Network Analysis*. London: Sage. Pp. 286–300.

Edwards, G. (2009) 'Mixed Methods Approaches to Social Network Analysis', National Centre for Research Methods (UK) Review Paper.

Edwards, G. and Crossley, N. (2009) 'Measures and Meanings: Exploring the Ego-Net of Helen Kirkpatrick Watts, Militant Suffragette', *Methodological Innovations On-Line*, 3(2).

Everett, M. and Borgatti, S. (2013) 'The Dual-Projection Approach for Two Mode Networks', *Social Networks*, 34(2): 204–10.

Federation of Entertainment Unions (2013) *Creating Without Conflict*, http://www.equity.org.uk/documents/creating-without-conflict-report/

Feld, S. (1981) 'The Focused Organisation of Social Ties', *American Journal of Sociology*, 86: 1015–35.

Feld, S. (1982) 'Social Structural Determinants of Similarity Among Associates', *American Sociological Review*, 47: 797–801.

Goffman, E. (1961) *Asylums*. Harmondsworth: Penguin.

Lazarsfeld, P. and Merton, R. (1964) 'Friendship as Social Process', in M. Berger, T. Abel and C. Page (eds), *Freedom and Control in Modern Society*. New York: Octagon Books. pp. 18–66.

Lusher, D., Koskinen, J. and Robins, G. (2013) *Exponential Random Graph Models for Social Networks*. Cambridge: Cambridge University Press.

Milgram, S. (1967) 'The Small World Problem', in G. Carter (ed.), *Empirical Approaches to Sociology*. Boston: Pearson. pp. 111–18.

Mitchell, J-C. (1969) *Social Networks in Urban Situations*. Manchester: Manchester University Press.

Scott, J. (2000) *Social Network Analysis: A Handbook*. London: Sage.

Simmel, G. (1955) *Conflict and the Web of Group Affiliations*. New York: Free Press.

Snijders, T. (2011) 'Network Dynamics', in J. Scott and P. Carrington (eds), *Sage Handbook of Social Network Analysis*. London: Sage. pp. 501–13.

Wasserman, S and Faust, K. (1994) *Social Network Analysis*. Cambridge: Cambridge University Press.

White, H. (2008) *Identity and Control*. Princeton: Princeton University Press.

# Ethnography and the Sociology of Culture

John Hughson

## INTRODUCTION

This chapter discusses the research method ethnography and looks especially at how ethnography might be considered in relationship to the sociology of culture (or its variant term, cultural sociology). It is pertinent to commence with a brief consideration of how ethnography emerged within the broader disciplinary field of sociology. In short, ethnography came to sociology via the influence of anthropology. Participant fieldwork and observation is usually taken as the hallmark method of the ethnographer. Malinowski's firsthand study of life in the Trobriand Islands, published in the 1920s, is most often cited as a key anthropological study, which inspired sociologists to apply his approach to urban milieus (Atkinson and Hammersley, 1994: 249) in Western cities. Unsurprisingly, the great urban experiment of modernity, Chicago, lent itself to the fascination of scholars assembled within its Department of Sociology. Robert Park, leading professor in what became known as the 'Chicago School', described the city's distinctive neighbourhoods as a 'mosaic of little worlds', each constituted as 'moral regions' characterized by the distinct beliefs and behaviours of their inhabitants (Park, 1952: 51). For Park, Chicago's neighbourhoods provided laboratories on the doorstep of the University, into which he encouraged his colleagues and students to enter and undertake studies in 'human ecology'. The rationale was naturalistic in proposing the need for neighbourhood life to be studied as it occurred, developed and transpired. According to Herbert Blumer, a follower of Park, the researcher's procedures 'must be assessed in terms of whether they respect the nature of the empirical world under study – whether what they signify or imply to be the nature of the empirical world is actually the case' (Blumer, 1954: 28). The ethnographic approach, so understood, is, therefore, anti-positivist and against macro-based theoretical assumptions being transposed onto the world below to explain how people live. Ethnography connected well with symbolic interactionist theory within sociology, which holds that patterns in social behaviour are explainable once we can understand the meanings people give to and take from what they observe to be going on. From such meaning attachments, social action ensues.

Is it possible to speak of a distinctive connection between ethnography and the sociology of culture, apart from the recognisable connection, evinced above, between ethnography and sociology at large? In general terms, the answer is no, because ethnographic research is always concerned with culture understood as a way, or ways, of living, and concerned with how people make sense of and then (re)act upon the social situations within which they find themselves existing. Indeed, 'the *description* of cultures' has been identified as the 'primary goal' of the ethnographer by Hammersley and Atkinson (1995: 10). These writers suggest that the aversion to universalising, characteristic of the type of research encouraged by the 'Chicago School', may limit the analytical ambition of ethnography. So much so, Hammersley and Atkinson (1995: 10) contend, that 'attempts to go beyond this, for instance to *explain* particular cultural forms, are sometimes discouraged'. Such discouragement sits at odds with a primary interest of the cultural sociologist in *cultural forms* and it is this interest that possibly provides the most sensible and meaningful way for us to consider ethnography in specific relationship to cultural sociology. Raymond Williams (1989: 151) contended: 'you cannot understand an intellectual or artistic project without also understanding its formation'. This statement may not appear relevant to all ethnographers or sociologists claiming an interest in ordinary, everyday life, but it will appear relevant to ethnographers with *cultural* sociological sympathies. And, importantly, this is not to suggest a relevance exclusive to sociologists concerned with subjects more conventionally defined as 'intellectual' and 'artistic'. As we will see, some ethnographers researching marginal neighbourhood life of the kind studied by the Chicago School will be prepared to examine aspects of social life within these domains in a way not unrelated to Williams' reference to an 'artistic project'.

## THE UNLIKELY ETHNOGRAPHER: RAYMOND WILLIAMS

The most compelling case for Raymond Williams to be regarded as a scholar of great relevance to ethnography is made by the cultural sociologist, Stanley Aronowitz (1994). Indeed, Aronowitz (1994: 170), unusually, but persuasively, claims Williams to be more an 'ethnographer' than a 'critic'. The claim is made on the basis of what Aronowitz believes to be the most significant intervention of Williams' early, well-known books, *Culture and Society* (1958) and *The Long Revolution* (1961), when read in conjunction with the later book *The Country and the City* (1973). As familiarly observed by other scholars, Aronowitz recognises the lingering legacy of F.R. Leavis' liberal humanism within the critical humanism of Williams' early books. The key difference between the two, according to Aronowitz (1994: 170), is that Williams examines a range of literary works within *Culture and Society* (subtitled in one of its later editions, *Coleridge to Orwell*) without the kind of interest Leavis had in the 'intrinsic merit of the work in terms of criteria of aesthetic value, such as felicitous writing style, formal innovation, or narrative elegance'. Williams was interested in 'whether the novel or poem provides *knowledge* of what he calls the "structure of feeling" of a specific historical moment, and even more concretely of a given *class*' (Aronowitz, 1994: 170). Williams – and like him, Richard Hoggart in *The Uses of Literacy* (1957) – has been credited with challenging the literary canon to the extent that texts from and items of popular culture became regarded as culturally worthy in their own right and, on this basis, suitable matters for intellectual enquiry. *The Long Revolution* rather than *Culture and Society* was the more relevant book for Williams in this regard. For example, it is in this book that he rhetorically asks, 'Can we agree ... that football is indeed a wonderful game (as good as chess), that jazz is a real musical form and that gardening and homemaking are indeed important?' (Williams, 1961: 336).

But Williams did not have an anything goes attitude towards culture. In the subsequent sentence he questions further, 'Can we also agree ... that the horror-film, the rape-novel, the Sunday strip-paper and the latest Tin-Pan drool are not exactly in the same world, and that the nice magazine romance, the manly adventure story ... and the pretty, clever television advertisement are not in it either?' Williams appears to teeter here on the brink of the type of subjective Leavisite evaluation he wants to criticise, but his point is not to overcome distinction making. Not at all. He accepts that people will continue to make distinctions about cultural items on a basis of aesthetic judgement, and that from this basis they will regard some items and cultural forms as being worthy of their interest and others not so. His interest – and this is the point of relevance to the connection with ethnography – is in how these judgements about culture are socially derived. As indicated by Aronowitz, Williams' main interest was in how cultural judgements are class based. But related enquiry is by no means restricted to class. Subsequent ethnographic research relevant to cultural sociology extends the focus on the social derivation of aesthetic judgement to race, ethnicity and gender, as well as to class. The key concern for the ethnographic researcher is to be attuned to the social bearings of particular cultural forms. Williams' own focus on class allowed him to see certain cultural forms in a way that would just not have occurred to Leavis. Football (soccer) is an example. Williams (1961: 337) was able to regard football as part of a 'good living culture' in Britain because he developed an awareness of the sport's cultural traditions around cup finals and seasonal leagues in connection with the 'structure of feeling' pertinent to working-class communities (Hughson, 2013: 286). The historian Richard Holt has written of the aesthetic appreciation of football occurring very much in a collective context: 'Bound together with the sense of community there was the sheer excitement and beauty of the thing – the perfect pass that suddenly switches play from end to end … a centre-forward tearing past the marker …' (Holt, 1989: 165). This insight would have appealed to Williams and he would have agreed with Holt's conclusion that this collective/communal appreciation of football is 'instinctive' and deeply aesthetic.

Williams would also have been sympathetic in regard to the further claim by Holt (1989: 165) that the aesthetic appreciation of footballers' movement is 'beyond social and historical analysis'. Williams (1961: 47) was quite clear in a related comment on the limitations of *cultural history*:

> It is only … our own time and place that we can expect to know, in any substantial way. We can learn a great deal of the life of other places and times, but certain elements, it seems to me, will always be irrecoverable … The most difficult thing to get hold of, in studying any past period is this felt sense of the quality of life at a particular place and time: a sense of the ways in which the particular activities combined into a way of thinking and living.

This passage signposts the importance of cultural historical scholarship to Williams and lends related justification to Aronowitz's categorisation of him as a historical ethnographer (Aronowitz, 1994: 173). It also helps us to comprehend why Williams would be essentially supportive to certain types of ethnographic research being undertaken in contemporary milieus. Although not an active 'field-based' researcher, Williams' particular emphasis on *experience* has been shared by many field-engaged ethnographers. Indeed, his influence in this regard is sometimes explicitly acknowledged, such as in the case of one of the best-known urban ethnographers of all, Paul Willis. Willis (2000: 7–8) refers to Williams' 'double reclamation' of the 'Culture and Society' tradition. The first reclamation is of its 'content', i.e. literature; the second reclamation is of its 'socio-symbolic form and location'. A little further below we look at how Willis saw the second of these reclamations as being most inspirational to his own ethnographic endeavour. Given the nature of Willis' research, his claiming of the second aspect of Williams' achievement is most understandable, but he would surely agree that an awareness of both 'reclamations' is necessary to an understanding of Williams' ethnographic legacy. A good number of academics associated with the area that became known as Cultural Studies would not have made such a recognition, because, as Aronowitz (1994: 178) suggests, they tend to read their own preoccupation with *textual representation* – 'the problematic of correspondence between text and context' – into Williams' critique of the Culture and Society tradition. Although not an irrelevant exercise, such reading risks missing the 'epistemological stance that marks him [Williams] off from traditional criticism' (Aronowitz, 1994: 178). For Williams, the characters in a novel discussed by Leavis – or perhaps a novel not discussed by Leavis – are of interest in the extent to which they are indicative of the constitution of a genuine lifeworld, one which has existed within space and time (Aronowitz, 1994: 179). Again, Williams' endeavour in this regard is a matter of historical ethnography and it was at all times undertaken in mindfulness of the caveat on cultural history, stated from *The Long Revolution* (as quoted above).

*The Country and the City* arguably stands as Williams' finest work of historical ethnography, an attempt to pull together the 'fragments of experience' (Aronowitz, 1994: 171) from a range of literature spanning much the same period as that covered in *Culture and Society*. It is perhaps because Williams believed the past to be ultimately 'irrecoverable', that a reader of *The Country and the City* can sense a certain unstated urgency in the book. Despite his warning, Williams wants to recover from these works a sense of lived experience that is more dedicatedly sociological than that offered by Leavis in his 'great tradition' discourse. The debt to Leavis is undeniable, and one explicitly acknowledged by Williams. Williams (1979: 66) went as far as to refer to the 'cultural radicalism' of Leavis. In practice this meant the antagonism Leavis had developed with the trendy intellectualism of his time, but it also meant a related respect for the latter's understanding of the sociological importance of literature. The key difference arises in regard to Leavis' retention of the notion of a *minority* (derived from Coleridge's idea of *clerisy*) by which the majority of people cannot be expected to understand and therefore engage with the great works of literature. In *Culture and Society* Williams (1958: 300) famously averred:

> There are in fact no masses; there are only ways of seeing people as masses. In an urban industrial society there are many opportunities for such ways

of seeing. The point is not to reiterate the objective conditions but to consider, personally and collectively, what these have done to our thinking.

This viewpoint allows Williams to offer a critical 'reading' of great books in a different way to Leavis. His discussion of Dickens in *The Country and the City* provides an example. Williams notes that in the novel *Hard Times*, Dickens presents a 'uniform view' of the inhabitants of Coketown trudging along to the dreary rhythm of their industrial existence. He notes how this way of describing the city's populace was at odds with Dickens' literary method, which was characteristically concerned with 'seeing people and their actions' (1973: 153). The blurry depiction of a working-class mass would have dissatisfied Williams, all the more given that the fictional Coketown was modelled on Preston, Lancashire, where Dickens had stayed for a period in preparing for the book. To highlight the fallibility of the account, Williams pointed to the difference between the depictions of humanity in *Hard Times* to that in Dickens' novels set in London. London was the city Dickens really knew, a city that, even had he wanted, 'could not easily be described in a rhetorical gesture of repressive uniformity' (Williams, 1973: 153). London provided a more easily observable diversity of human experience in a way suited to easier transference into character development within the literary context. Williams (1973: 154) could thus conclude that Dickens' social focus was 'more penetrating' when his 'central response to the new experience of the city was more various' (as in the case of his writing based on life in London) than when attempting to provide more 'general images of the city' (such as the example of Preston).

The writer Williams comes closest to explicitly discussing as an ethnographer is George Orwell. He commences this account in the chapter preceding the conclusion to *Culture and Society* and develops it more fully in a chapter titled 'Observation and Imagination' in the small book *Orwell*, published in 1971 in Fontana's 'Modern Masters' series. Williams (1971: 41) argues that a consideration of Orwell's early writing exposes the discomfiture caused by a naive insistence, which arose in the 19th century, to delineate between writings dealing with the 'real world' and those dealing with the 'imagination'. For example, drawing a line between the itinerant chronicler, Orwell himself, in the works *Down and Out in Paris and London* and *The Road to Wigan Pier*, and the anxious protagonist, George Bowling, in *Coming Up for Air*, is not as clear-cut as a facile distinction between non-fiction and fiction would demand. Indeed, Williams (1971: 50) contends that Orwell 'began to write literature, in the full sense, when he found ... [the] non-fictional form'. At this point 'he found a form capable of realising his experience directly'. But, herein, lay problems for Orwell the ethnographer; most readily seen in *The Road to Wigan Pier*, a book setting out his travels into the north of England to observe, first hand, and report upon, the difficult living conditions of working-class communities. The key problem recognised by Williams (1971: 51) is Orwell's tendency to slip between two points of ethnographic positioning, which he refers to as 'inside' and 'outside' experience respectively. The diary notes for *The Road to Wigan Pier*, published separately and posthumously, provide an interesting window into Orwell's procedure and a giveaway on how much the account in the book is shaped by the writer's own presence within the narrative. According to Williams (1971: 52): 'What is created in the book is an isolated independent observer and the objects of his observation. Intermediate characters and experiences which do not form part of this world – this structure of feeling – are simply omitted'. Williams claims that in this uncertain territory between fiction and non-fiction Orwell creates his most successful character, 'Orwell'. The character 'Orwell' provides an account of working-class life that Williams (1971: 52) accepts as 'documentary enough', even if the 'process of selection and organisation is a literary act'. The acceptance of Orwell in this particular regard is an example of what Aronowitz (1994: 178) sees as Williams 'straddling the boundary' between 'literary texts' and work more conventionally regarded as 'ethnographic study'.

## 'IN THE DESTRUCTIVE ELEMENT IMMERSE': PAUL WILLIS AND ETHNOGRAPHY

A subsequent writer who evinces a similar straddling, yet coming to it in the opposite direction from Orwell, is the inveterate ethnographer Paul Willis. Willis is best known for the book *Learning to Labour: How Working Class Kids Get Working Class Jobs* (1977). The subtitle gives a clue to the book's project. Based on ethnographic fieldwork done in the mid-1970s, *Learning to Labour* studies a group of male working-class youth – the 'lads' – across their later school to early work years. The specific point of interest to emerge from the study is in how the young men construct what Willis regards as a culture of resistance to social authority in both the school and work environments. They do so to such an extent as to facilitate the reproduction of the subordinate class relations known to their parents' generation. The research was undertaken in an undisclosed industrial town of the West Midlands; not so far from Willis' hometown, Wolverhampton. Familiarity with the locality makes Willis an 'insider', and, we may presume, this status provided an entrée for him into the midst of the young men under study. Had he been from another area of England and had an accent deemed to be 'posh', it is likely that the 'lads' would have ridiculed rather than cooperated with him. Nevertheless, by this time an Oxbridge-educated undergraduate and a postgraduate affiliate to the Centre for Contemporary Cultural Studies (CCCS) at the University of Birmingham, he was hardly in the same class position as the young men. Alikeness in biography is an important consideration. In some cases, it can be essential to the gaining of access and establishment of rapport. But, differences in such factors as education and class (irrespective of the class background of the researcher) remain inevitable between the ethnographer and those within the marginalised communities or subcultures under study and will do so under any circumstances short of ethnography being handed over entirely as an intra-community project.

Willis has remained, over the years, convinced about the ability of the academic ethnographer to be a meaningful producer of knowledge. For Willis (2000: xiii) immersion in participant fieldwork remains the key to knowledge production, and he implores budding ethnographic researchers to 'go and look for yourself', to see 'what's going on' as bound up with 'how they go on'. The undertaking involves a good deal of observation, listening and, then, describing. But the challenge, according to Willis, is to provide not a mere description of what is seen and heard, but, following Clifford Geertz (1973), to provide 'thick description'. Ethnographic reporting on 'how they go on' involves, for Willis, giving a well-informed insight into the cultural meanings of group behaviour and dynamics. The same research philosophy characterised another of Willis' ethnographic research projects, which was undertaken prior to that for *Learning to Labour*. For his doctoral research at the CCCS, Willis conducted a comparative study of the lifeworlds of two rather different, even oppositional, social groupings located in Birmingham, bikers (motorcycle riders) and hippies. The research for this study, which was published as *Profane Culture* (1978), highlighted the 'homologous' relationship between the cultural items and uses of items and the social values of the respective groups. The hippies advocated peace and love and passive non-conformity, and listened to mellow forms of folk and progressive rock music. The bikers, conversely, advocated rebellion and non-conformity, and listened to early rock and roll music. This study contributed to the overall scheme of research at the CCCS into youth (or young adult) subcultures. *Resistance* became the key term of interest to the researchers, as highlighted by the contributions to the volume *Resistance through Rituals: Youth Subcultures in Postwar Britain* (Hall and Jefferson, 1976), which included a chapter by Willis, 'The Cultural Meaning of Drug Use', drawn from his ethnographic study of hippies. None of the other contributions to the book were as ethnographic as Willis' field engagement and none of it involved the type of ethnographic immersion that would be expected by anthropologists. Some of the research, for example, John Clarke's study of skinheads involved a degree of ethnographic type observation, while the work of the scholar most often compared to Willis, Dick Hebdige provided a semiotic analysis of the symbolically resistive meanings of 'mod' culture. In related projects, Hebdige studied a number of youth subcultures, including Teddy Boys, rockers, skinheads and punks. While Hebdige does refer to the ethnographic investigations of subcultures undertaken by Chicago School affiliates in his well-known book *Subculture: the Meaning of Style* (1979), his method is more that of textual analysis undertaken from a distance, without a perception of need for more direct enquiry via immersed participant engagement.

Whether ethnographic or not, the focus of CCCS research into subcultures was on the spectacular rather than the ordinary life of youth. One problem with this focus was that, when connected to the theme of resistance, it seemed to over ambitiously invest a political capacity into symbolism and associated practices of youth subcultures. The examination of these practices tended to blur a distinction between consumption and production, where the young subcultural affiliates were seen to lay claim to items purchased or purloined from the cultural marketplace and then put to symbolic use within their own collective contexts of meaning. Willis (1990: 135) actually went on to name the process as 'production in meaning', whereby the imaginative uses to which products are put involves a process of 'creative consumption into production'. This claim is made in the book *Common Culture*, in which Willis moved beyond the study of youth subcultures to extend a regarding of creative symbolic practice to young people in more individualised settings and non-subcultural gatherings. In doing this, Willis rather upturned Williams' particular understanding of culture as a 'whole way of life' to propose that art itself, in routine uses, occurs as a way of life, because art can be witnessed in everyday activity. Thus understood, art was the preserve of ordinary people within their quotidian undertakings. Willis (1990: 2) recognised 'symbolic creativity' going on all about him in the lives of the young people he (and his research team) observed in Wolverhampton. It was to be seen in the ways people 'humanize, decorate and invest with meanings their common life spaces and social practices'. The recognition and appreciation of such activities as art involved what Willis (1990: 21) referred to as 'grounded aesthetics'; 'the creative element in the process whereby meanings are attributed to symbols and practices … grounded aesthetics are the yeast of common culture'.

Raymond Williams (1958: 43) had claimed 'we need a common culture, not for the sake of abstraction, but because we shall not survive without it'. Willis did not claim that a common culture existed in Britain in the 1990s, but he pointed to how the remnant of such a cultural existence (if it ever had existed) would be constituted in the present time. An understanding of the whole would need to be based on an awareness of the continual, everyday artistic practices of individuals. A critical response by McGuigan (1992) defined Willis' position as 'cultural populism' and far removed from what Williams had meant when declaring the need for a common culture. Particularly at odds with Williams, according to McGuigan, would have been Willis' claim that the capitalistic marketplace readily served up the means of its own subversion. McGuigan was suggesting that the 'symbolic creativity' involved in decorating one's bedroom, with commercially sold items, had no cultural relevance, symbolic or otherwise, beyond the bedroom's walls. Willis certainly did call for a rethinking of how critical cultural scholars should adjudge the possibilities of the marketplace, but he later insisted that this did not make him a foolish optimist. Indeed, Willis (2000: 106) argued that his 'view of creativity embedded in everyday cultural practices is … more troubled, less benevolent than Williams' view of "ordinary", "whole ways of life"'. A related suggestion by Willis was that Williams' long-held belief in the 'cooperative and mutual' spirit of a common culture coming to the fore in modern society sounded, by the turn of the 21st century, more like a forlorn hope. Yet, Willis (2000: 107) maintained Williams' view of 'culture as ordinary' and suggested further that, more than ever, understanding this required an ethnographic lens into the specifics – the mechanisms, contexts and materials – of lived experience. This reflection upon Williams shed a sobering light on Willis' own previous remarks about life as art. The book in which this reflection was made, *The Ethnographic Imagination*, provided a timely reconsideration on the ethnographic approach to cultural study going in the new millennium.

## ETHNOGRAPHY, THEORY AND *PRACTICE*

One of the themes taken up in *The Ethnographic Imagination* was a reiteration of the importance of theoretically informed ethnographic scholarship. This was a matter on which Willis had been less definite in earlier writing dedicated to method, despite the quasi-Marxist theorisation apparent in *Learning to Labour*. Willis (1976: 246) called for an approach that could best reveal the 'richness and authenticity of social phenomena', minus the imposing assumptions of theory-led scholarship. This was not to exclude theory, but to see it coming in later, in an act of 'closure' once the research has been gathered. According to Willis (1976: 246), 'the selectivity and theorization of the final work will reflect the patterning of the real world rather than the patterns of received theory'. In the more recent 'Manifesto for Ethnography', Willis, while declaring a disinterest in theory 'for its own sake', is more circumspect about the relationship between theory and research (Willis and Trondman, 2002: 398). The former does not take a back seat in the reconsidered formulation. Rather, the ethnographic enterprise is now regarded as a matter of 'dialectic surprise', a 'two-way stretch, a continuous process of shifting back and forth between... "induction" and "deduction"' (Willis and Trondman, 2002: 399). No particular theoretical perspective is advanced, but Bourdieu is inspirational to a mindfulness of the need to maintain balance between theory and research (Willis and Trondman, 2002: 398). Bourdieu is a most likely and appropriate theorist to draw upon given that one of his most important concepts, *habitus*, was guided by field research, principally ethnography (Wacquant, 2004). The benefit of Bourdieu to cultural sociology was recognised by Raymond Williams (with Nicholas Garnham) in a discussion of the former's book *La Distinction*. While the subject matter of that, now famous, book might be culture, Garnham and Williams (1980: 211) warn against Bourdieu's appropriation into what they refer to as the 'marginal sub-disciplines' of cultural studies and the sociology of culture. The importance of Bourdieu is more general, they suggest, because of the insight he gives into an understanding of how class relations are maintained via symbolic power, with people finding their place in society on the basis of the 'dispositions' of *habitus* developed from their formative years. *Habitus* may at first glance appear as a concept relevant to explaining individualised social practice, but, for Garnham and Williams (1980: 213) *habitus* is to be regarded as a 'unified phenomenon' because 'it is internalized and operationalized by individuals but not to regulate solitary acts but precisely interaction'.

The sociology of culture developed into more than a 'marginal sub-discipline' by the mid-1980s. By this time, Garnham and Williams' warning about the appropriation of Bourdieu looked decidedly dated. The overwhelming referencing of Bourdieu within the array of scholarship that can be said to constitute the sociology of culture leaves little doubt about his great influence upon its expansion into a major sub-discipline, standing alongside other areas such as the sociology of education, comparative historical sociology, urban sociology, economic sociology and the sociology of organisations (Santoro, 2011: 10). The very fact that Bourdieu did not actually develop a 'concept of culture' (Lizardo, 2011: 27) yet wrote so pertinently about the social relations of culture, has made him irresistible to a good many scholars and students within the sociology of culture. The notion of *habitus* has been a key attraction and it has been put to innovative use by scholars in connection with ethnographic research. For example, Rimmer (2010) refers to a *musical habitus* in his study of the engagement of young people from a deprived residential area in Newcastle (UK) with 'new monkey' music. This music, based in techniques of DJing and MCing, gained its name from the 'New Monkey' club in Sunderland, which was a key gathering point for the youth in Rimmer's study. The importance of this type of music within the lifeworld of these young men could, reasonably enough, have been explained by older sociological positions, such as those offered by symbolic interactionism. However, the *musical habitus* is applied by Rimmer to provide a deeper insight into the significance of this music as a cultural *formation* within that same lifeworld. There is an important socio-historical element to this formation, whereby the liking of the young men in the study for 'new monkey' music and its club-life bears connection to the traditions in sociality of hard drinking in working-class pubs and clubs in Newcastle. As the waterfront bar and club culture of Newcastle was unaffordable to this economically marginalised youth of the new millennium, they sought out 'underground dance clubs' that were not only more affordable, but did not constrain their inclination to dance wildly and without concern of being adjudged unfashionable. The music was felt, embodied in the way suggested by *habitus* when understood as involving cultural embeddedness. The relevance is perhaps best explained when Rimmer (2010: 275) discusses the young men's recognition of an idealised regional identity in the personas of favourite new monkey performers. Accordingly, one respondent spoke of the performer MC Stompin appearing to him as a prototypical 'Geordie hard-man'. This example is presented by Rimmer neither as a means of indicating musical taste complying with or compounding an inescapable class and masculinist positioning, nor as part of a case study of resistance in the manner of the CCCS subcultural research, but to emphasise the centrality of music, a particular type of music, as a cultural form within a particular communal lifeworld.

Some recent ethnographic projects challenge the more established view of *habitus* as a purely deterministic concept, one that rather anchors individuals to a set of outcomes explained by their socio-cultural circumstances and upbringing. A critique of Bourdieu's determinism has been offered by a number of scholars including Alexander (1995). Although Willis did not explicitly use *habitus* in *Learning to Labour*, the book's explanatory aim as expressed in its sub-title, *How Working Class Kids get Working Class Jobs*, speaks to the very idea of the term in a deterministic bent, albeit one sympathetic to the 'lads' in the study. Non-deterministic understandings and uses of habitus within ethnographic work offer a way of going beyond the tendency of the CCCS studies to regard subcultural groupings engaged in forms of resistance that allow them to get on and enjoy their lives according to internally created value systems, but not in a way that challenges external power relations that come to bear on group members' lives outside the symbolic confines of the subcultural domain. An example is the study by Wade (2011) of a community of women who use 'Lindy-hop' dance as a means to challenge the power relations of gender. Wade (2011: 227) describes lindy hop as:

> ... an athletic partner dance invented by African Americans dancing to big bands in 1930's Harlem ... It transitions between an open position (in which the leader's left hand holds the follower's right hand), a closed 'waltz' position, and a return to the open position. The basic move occurs with eight-counts. Despite the 'basic' eight-count move, any two counts can be cut up and rearranged to create unexpected yet co-ordinated movements.

The fast tempo of Lindy hop means the individual must focus on their own bodily movement rather than that of their dance partner. Wade describes her study as being done by way of *embodied ethnography*. As an 'observant participant', she conducted her research over a 14-month period after three years of previous experience as a lindy-hop dancer. There was an element of auto-ethnography to the research – 'my first and most direct source of data was my own body' – although Wade avoided the self-obsessive pitfall of that approach (for a trenchant criticism of auto-ethnography see Delamont (2007)) by concerning herself with 'how it *feels* to do gender as a lindy hopper' from the perspective of other participants. Wade concluded that lindy hop, at least when done at an advanced level, gave female participants the 'ability to embody control, submission, and co-operation' in a way that unsettled a binary power relation evident in other forms of dance whereby feminine subordination and male domination become embodied. Done over time, lindy hop can involve the development of a *bodily habitus*, which, at its core, is about power being challenged instinctively. In contrast to the subcultural perspective discussed above, it is suggested that the 'negotiation of power' learnt through lindy hop can carry over into other areas of the female dancers' lives.

## AESTHETICS, ETHNOGRAPHY AND THE SOCIOLOGY OF CULTURE

Ethnographic studies such as those presented by Rimmer and Wade, although not engaging in explicit discussion of the term, contribute to how we might continue to think about *aesthetics* within the sociology of culture. Towards closing the chapter, it is worth considering how aesthetics might receive more explicit discussion. Willis (2005: 74) actually calls for this, suggesting that sociologists need to take care against fostering a discursive lapse that will allow aesthetics to be re-associated purely with 'high culture'. He seems to admit the 'culture of everyday life' excesses of cultural studies have caused cultural sociologists to shy away from explicit discussion of aesthetics in regard to the cultural activities of the people and groups investigated in their ethnographic research projects. Willis (2005: 74) credits sociologists with having 'cracked the enigma of the social coding of the aesthetic', but this should not be taken to mean the disappearance of the 'aesthetic' from the social domain. If the complexity of the more than simply residual or lingering aesthetic is not dedicatedly examined, Willis (2005: 74) claims sociology is in danger of 'throwing the creative baby out with the aesthetic and artistic water'. This concern impels Willis to demand our attention be directed in search of what he ironically refers to as the *invisible aesthetic* of 'human creativity'. De la Fuente (2007: 415) incorporates this appeal by Willis within what he regards as a 'new sociology of art'. The new direction, notable in a diverse range of sociological work, is taken by scholars that recognize 'the need to grapple with the aesthetic qualities of art' (de la Fuente, 2007: 410) Importantly, this work does not advocate 'un-sociological assumptions' or suggest a return to romantic notions of the gifted artist imbued with the ability to create essential beautiful artworks. Yet, by bringing a consideration of aesthetics back into sociological enquiry, such studies are concerned to overlook the converse vagary of imprecise claims to the 'social determination of art' and the 'artistic representations of reality' (de la Fuente, 2007: 410).

De la Fuente (2007: 423) concludes that the 'new sociology of art' addresses two particular blind spots that have characterised the sociology of art: (1) a blindness to the concrete work that aesthetic factors perform in social life; and (2) a blindness to the artwork itself. Examples of key studies noted in this regard by de la Fuente use ethnographic research to make the advances he advocates. In relation to the first point, Molotch (2003) conducts an ethnography of product design to reveal the consideration invested into the design process with a view to creating consumer goods that are 'aesthetically satisfying' (de la Fuente, 2007: 418). This takes ethnography into the production of culture realm, but in a way that feeds back into the sociology of consumption. Loftier claims about 'grounded aesthetics' occurring post the point of consumption of material items from the commercial marketplace stand to make more sense when aesthetics are brought into consideration across the full processual gamut, i.e. design → production → consumption → use. In regard to the second point, de la Fuente (2007: 420) refers to the work of Howard Becker and associates in the book *Art from Start to Finish*. The contributions to this book go directly to dealing with the artwork itself. The editors of the volume contend, in response to what they see as a deterministic overstating of 'social variables' that 'art is social' for the very reason that 'collective work' goes into its creation (Becker et al., 2006: 3). The sociology of art, they suggest, should be concerned with understanding the *aesthetic* that arises within this process. Following from both of these points, a 'new sociology of art' – which may well be extended to the sociology of culture, given the recognition that the consideration of aesthetics should reach into other fields conventionally regarded as non-artistic (or even antipathetic to the arts) such as sport – would be interested in the communication of aesthetics and the related institutional means of communication. This comes back full circle to the chapter's interest in Raymond Williams and the type of possibility he would have recognised for ethnography within the sociology of culture. To be clear, Williams did not engage in ethnographic research procedures as we understand them within sociology and he would have been disconcerted by some of the uses of ethnographic research, particularly within Cultural Studies (Jones, 2006: 24). However, this did not make him an adversary *per se*. His calls, commencing from the early 1960s, for interventions into policy areas such as media policy (Williams, 1962), were not closed-minded to how meaningful research insights might help facilitate democratic institutional change.

Jones (2007: 88) points out that Williams 'never fully activated' a 'distinctive programme' concerned with aesthetics within 'cultural production'. A way that this might be done is in connection with Habermas' principle of 'communicative democracy', via a reframed version of that theorist's notion of the 'public sphere'. For this purpose, Jones (2007: 88) proposes, via Jacobs, the nomenclature *aesthetic public sphere*. Ethnographic research holds out the potential of giving insight into how 'aesthetic'-related work transpires within relevant institutional contexts. As noted by Jones (2007: 88), Born's ethnographic study of the British Broadcasting Commission (BBC) is exemplary in this regard. Born's research, undertaken over two years in the late 1990s and two follow-up occasions in the early 2000s, was focused on 'two sites in BBC Television' (Born, 2004: 14–15). One site was the 'Drama Group', responsible for drama productions on BBC television channels; the other site was the production floor of BBC's 'flagship' news discussion and analysis programme *Newsnight*. The Drama Group would seemingly lend itself most readily to the observation of an aesthetically creative process and Born does provide related commentary. For example, she regards the 'expansion of docu-soaps' as reflecting an aesthetic connection to the British tradition of documentary filmmaking associated with John Grierson. Importantly, this meant not just paying homage, but moving into new creative territory. According to Born (2004: 442), 'observational documentary' programmes produced during this period 'unleash[ed] aesthetic experimentation', by allowing for 'creative risks' to be taken, which generated forays into 'reflexive filmmaking ... in the manner of *cinema vérité*'. The 'aesthetic public sphere' relevance of Born's study, according to Jones (2007: 88–89) lies not just in relation to her ethnographic observation of the Drama Group, but in the insight her ethnographic closeness is able to provide of the aesthetically driven operation of both the drama and news groupings from their related but different departmental positioning within the BBC as a cultural institution. Born's own overview lends support to this claim:

Television's aesthetic and expressive dimensions cannot be divorced from its informational role, as they tend to be in notions of the aesthetic as a mere delivery mechanism. The informative/cognitive and the cultural/aesthetic are integral to good television, and to the best they co-evolve. Aesthetic vitality is an essential component in the political and cultural value of public service broadcasting. These principles, immanent in the Reithian ethos [John Reith, first Director-General of the BBC and pioneer of public service broadcasting in Britain], have always been subliminally understood by the BBC, as well as Britain's broadcasting industry. (Born, 2004: 381)

For Raymond Williams, the relationship between aesthetics and cultural forms was neither determined nor indeterminate, and this had become more problematic for him by the late 1970s with the increasing theoretical complexity of his work (for example, Williams, 1977). The diversity of scholarship within the sociology of culture need not agree with Williams, but it should acknowledge the 'problem' of how aesthetics is regarded in relation to the range of lived experience addressed within its particular researches. To this purpose, ethnography offers a valuable way of investigating what we might, following Willis (and in the absence of a more appropriate term) refer to as the 'invisible aesthetic'.

# REFERENCES

Alexander, J. (1995) 'The Reality of Reduction: The Failed Synthesis of Pierre Bourdieu', in J. Alexander (ed.), *Fin de Siecle Social Theory: Relativism, Reduction, and the Problem of Reason*. London: Verso. pp. 128–218.

Aronowitz, Stanley (1994) *Dead Artists, Live Theories and Other Cultural Problems*. New York: Routledge.

Atkinson, P. and Hammersley, M. (1994) 'Ethnography and Participant Observation', in N. Denzin and Y. Lincoln (eds), *Handbook of Qualitative Research*. London: Sage. pp. 248–261.

Becker, Howard S., Faulkner, Robert R. and Kirshenblatt-Gimblett, Barbara (2006) 'Editors' Introduction', in H.S. Becker, R.R. Faulkner and B. Kirshenblatt-Gimblett (eds), *Art from Start to Finish: Jazz, Painting, and Other Improvisations*. Chicago: University of Chicago Press. pp. 1–20.

Blumer, Herbert (1954) *Symbolic Interactionism*. Englewood Cliffs, NJ: Prentice-Hall.

Born, Georgina (2004) *Uncertain Vision: Birt, Dyke and the Reinvention of the BBC*. London: Secker and Warburg.

de la Fuente, E. (2007) 'The "New Sociology of Art": Putting Art Back into Social Science Approaches to the Arts', *Cultural Sociology*, 1(3): 409–425.

Delamont, S. (2007) 'Arguments against Auto-Ethnography', *Qualitative Researcher*, 4: 2–4.

Garnham, N. and Williams, R. (1980) 'Pierre Bourdieu and the Sociology of Culture: An Introduction', *Media, Culture & Society*, 2(3): 209–223.

Geertz, Clifford (1973) *The Interpretation of Cultures: Selected Essays*. London: Hutchinson.

Hall, S. and Jefferson, T. (eds) (1976) *Resistance Through Rituals: Youth Subcultures in Postwar Britain*. London: Hutchinson.

Hammersley, Martin and Atkinson, Paul (1995) *Ethnography: Principles in Practice*. London: Tavistock.

Hebdige, Dick (1979) *Subculture: The Meaning of Style*. London: Methuen.

Hoggart, Richard (1957) *The Uses of Literacy: Aspects of Working-class Life with Special Reference to Publications and Entertainment*. London: Chatto and Windus.

Holt, Richard (1989) *Sport and the British: A Modern History*. Oxford: Clarendon Press.

Hughson, J. (2013) 'Watching the Football with Raymond Williams: A Reconsideration of the Global Game as a "Wonderful Game"', in J. Scherer and D. Rowe (eds), *Sport, Public Broadcasting, and Cultural Citizenship: Signal Lost?* New York: Routledge. pp. 283–299.

Jones, Paul (2006) *Raymond Williams's Sociology of Culture: A Critical Reconstruction*. Houndmills, Basingstoke: Palgrave Macmillan.

Jones, P. (2007) 'Beyond the Semantic "Big Bang": Cultural Sociology and an Aesthetic Public Sphere', *Cultural Sociology*, 1(1): 73–95.

Lizardo, O. (2011) 'Pierre Bourdieu as a Post-cultural Theorist', *Cultural Sociology*, 5(1): 25–44.

McGuigan, Jim (1992) *Cultural Populism*. London: Routledge.

Molotch, Harvey (2003) *Where Stuff Comes From: How Toasters, Toilets, Computers, and Many Other Things Come to Be as They Are*. New York: Routledge.

Orwell, George (1937) *The Road to Wigan Pier*. London: Victor Gollancz.

Orwell, G. (1970 [1936]) 'The Road to Wigan Pier Diary', in S. Orwell and I. Angus (eds), *The Collected Essays, Journalism and Letters of George Orwell*, vol. I: *An Age Like This*, 1920–1940. Harmondsworth: Penguin, pp. 194–243.

Park, Robert (1952) *Human Communities*. Glencoe, IL: Free Press.

Rimmer, M. (2010) 'Listening to the Monkey: Class, Youth and the Formation of a *musical habitus*', *Ethnography*, 11(2): 255–283.

Santoro, M. (2011) 'From Bourdieu to Cultural Sociology', *Cultural Sociology*, 5(1): 3–23.

Wacquant, L. (2004) 'Following Pierre Bourdieu into the Field', *Ethnography*, 5(4): 387–414.

Wade, L. (2011) 'The Emancipatory Promise of the Habitus: Lindy Hop, the Body, and Social Change', *Ethnography*, 12(2): 224–246.

Williams, Raymond (1958) *Culture and Society: 1780–1950*. London: Chatto and Windus.

Williams, Raymond (1961) *The Long Revolution*. London: Chatto and Windus.

Williams, Raymond (1962) *Communications (Britain in the Sixties)*. Harmondsworth: Penguin.

Williams, Raymond (1971) *Orwell*. London: Fontana/Collins.

Williams, Raymond (1973) *The Country and the City*. London: Chatto and Windus.

Williams, Raymond (1977) *Marxism and Literature*. Oxford: Oxford University Press.

Williams, Raymond (1979) *Politics and Letters: Interviews with the New Left Review*. London: New Left Books.

Williams, Raymond (1989) *Politics of Modernism: Against the New Conformists*. London: Verso.

Willis, Paul E. (1976) 'Theoretical Confessions and Reflexive Method', in K. Gelder and S. Thornton (ed), *The Subcultures Reader*. London: Routledge. pp. 246–253.

Willis, Paul (1977) *Learning to Labour: How Working Class Kids get Working Class Jobs*. Farnborough, Hants: Saxon House.

Willis, Paul (1978) *Profane Culture*. London: Routledge and Kegan Paul.

Willis, Paul (1990) *Common Culture: Symbolic Work and Play in the Everyday Cultures of the Young*. Milton Keynes: Open University Press.

Willis, Paul (2000) *The Ethnographic Imagination*. Cambridge: Polity Press.

Willis, P. (2005) 'Invisible Aesthetics and the Social Work of Commodity Culture', in D. Inglis and J. Hughson (eds), *The Sociology of Art: Ways of Seeing*. Houndmills, Basingstoke: Palgrave Macmillan. pp. 73–86.

Willis, P. and Trondman, M. (2002) 'Manifesto for Ethnography', *Cultural Studies ↔ Critical Methodologies*, 2(3): 394–402.

# PART III
# Disciplinarity and Interdisciplinarity

# 22

# Sociology and Cultural Studies: A Close and Fraught Relationship

David Inglis

## INTRODUCTION

Cultural studies exists in one of the most ambiguous, and sometimes testy, relationships with sociology of any academic discipline. Indeed, the complicated nature of the relationship is created by the very closeness of the two fields. Sociology and cultural studies are very much alike in many ways, and in some senses identical as far as the gaze of the uninitiated is concerned, but each of them is also very keen to display their own apparently unique features at the expense of the other, and thus their relationship is understandable in part as an ongoing state of ritualized antagonism. That antagonism fundamentally flows not from their ostensible differences – which are superficially responsible for the sometimes fractious nature of their relationship – but in fact from their striking underlying similarities. Their symbiotic relationship both drives, and is hidden by, the rhetorical displays of disciplinary identity in which they have often indulged. And that symbiotic relationship comes to seem even more complex when we consider that the broad domain called 'cultural sociology' not only stands in an ambiguous relationship to cultural studies, but also that some authors describable as cultural sociologists regard cultural studies as an exemplar to be heartily avoided, while others – especially in the US – have hailed cultural studies as possessing a range of intellectual resources with which to distance cultural sociology from what they regard as dull, narrow positivistic 'sociology of culture'. The terrain to be mapped in this chapter is complicated and shifts according to the times and places under consideration, but nonetheless is strongly patterned too.

Seidman (1997: 37, 53) notes that the relationship between sociology and cultural studies 'resists a simple or global description', for given the internal complexity of each of its elements, the sociology/cultural studies 'binary is unstable and perhaps collapses into incoherence if pressed more intently'. There are also some important differences in stress and intonation between particular 'national' sociology and cultural studies 'traditions'. Much depends on how particular national educational systems have organized, and continue to regulate, disciplinary terrains. In some national educational fields, cultural studies is much more of a 'humanities' enterprise than a recognizably social scientific project, because it has grown up in, or close to, departments of language and literature and related areas, rather than in, or close to, social science faculties. In such locales – for instance, many, but not all, cultural studies units in the US – orientations towards 'textualism' are pronounced, both in the sense of cultural studies work not engaging much with 'sociological' knowledges or methods (such as questionnaires or surveys), and in the sense of being very 'academic' in nature, and thus sometimes lacking direct connections to social movements aimed at social transformation, a situation rather less pronounced in, for example, the United Kingdom (Long, 1997; Pfister, 1996; Wolff, 1999).

The concerns and interests of cultural studies scholars, and how they understand what cultural studies 'is', vary depending on what intellectual backgrounds they themselves have and what motivating forces led them to employment in entities designated as cultural studies units, and these factors in turn are shaped by how particular universities and national higher education fields are run and policed by training and tenure systems. For example, for various historical reasons, Australian universities have rather softer barriers between disciplines than those that pertain in other national contexts, hence the greater confusion in the Australian setting in comparison to some other national contexts as to what counts as 'sociology', as 'cultural sociology', and as 'cultural studies' (Seidman, 1997). There is also the issue of *what sorts* of universities facilitate teaching and research in either (cultural) sociology or cultural studies. In the UK, one finds cultural studies units very often in the former polytechnic universities, and less so in the 'old' universities, where sociology since the 1960s gained a fairly strong foothold, and certainly a stronger one than cultural studies has ever been able to achieve.

A complete exposition of the relationships that have pertained and do pertain between sociology, cultural sociology and cultural studies would require a much longer exposition of the specificities of different national education systems, and their organizational particularities, tracing out the morphology of each higher education field and its relations to other social fields (Bourdieu, 1988). In the limited space of this chapter, I will operate more at the level of depicting some of the ways in which (cultural) sociological and cultural studies authors can represent, and have represented, each other discursively, emphasizing how each of them have created and utilized often somewhat negative images of the other, in order to gain a sense of disciplinary identity for themselves. I follow here the important work of McLennan (1998; 2002; 2006). I will generally present ideal-typical modes of such processes of identifying 'self' and 'other', drawing mostly upon the work of British and American authors The approach I adopt hopefully allows us to discern key features of the general relations that have pertained between (cultural) sociology and cultural studies, and to consider that the often fraught relationships between the two antagonists to a significant extent derives more from their actual similarities than their perceived and (self-)constructed differences.

## CULTURAL STUDIES AGAINST SOCIOLOGY

Identifying the recurring features of the discursive relations that have pertained and do pertain between sociology and cultural studies of course involves identifying what each of these terms refers to, in terms of identifiable collections of ideas and activities. But any process of identification cannot simply log 'objective' and uncontested characteristics of each discipline, especially given that each term is open to variant, and often polemical, interpretations, and also given that there is much debate among those who self-identify as 'cultural studies authors' as to whether cultural studies is in fact an academic 'discipline' at all. Moreover, authors positioning themselves within each field often rhetorically construct the nature of their field through the means of saying what the field *is not*, with 'sociological' authors identifying what sociology 'is' by defining cultural studies in a certain manner, often a negative one, then claiming that sociology is not what cultural studies 'is' (McLennan, 2002: 632). Likewise, those viewing themselves as cultural studies authors can carry out the same sort of operation; for example, by stressing the multifarious substantive, theoretical and (to a lesser degree) methodological concerns of cultural studies, which contrast with sociology's allegedly much more monolithic nature.

In one of the first textbooks to attempt to map the field, Graeme Turner (1990: 1) began by stating that cultural studies 'is not a discrete or homogeneous theoretical formation, nor is it easy to define'. The implication here is that although cultural studies is difficult to define, the very heterogeneity that causes this is itself distinctive and in fact something to be welcomed, not least because it differentiates cultural studies from what are taken to be more 'conventional' disciplines such as sociology. Indeed for another textbook author, Barker (2000: 4), 'the term "cultural studies" has no referent to which we can point. Rather, cultural studies is constituted by the language-game of cultural studies. The theoretical terms developed and deployed by persons calling their work "cultural studies" is what cultural studies "is"'. On this account, anything dubbed as cultural studies by a particular intellectual producer is indeed 'in' cultural studies. Yet only a few pages later, Barker has retreated from this complete referential relativism, in the direction of identifying a governing principle which underpins the cultural studies field: the latter is said to be a 'discursive formation ... constituted by a regulated way of speaking about objects (which it brings into view) and [which] coheres around key concepts, ideas and concerns' (2000: 6).

Thus cultural studies is both anything you want it to be, but also a set of recurrent themes and practices. Multiplicity and heterogeneity are presented as 'good' things, fundamentally part of the apparent vibrancy of cultural studies. But total heterogeneity risks being categorized as being equivalent to chaos, and synoptic authors generally want to show that cultural studies is not chaotic, but is rather a broad assemblage of positive and interesting things. A sense of (deliberately relatively weak) disciplinary unity can be gained by depicting cultural studies as being heterogeneous in nature, but not totally so. In this way, a certain sense of unity – of political purpose, and of intellectual practice – is achieved, which does not overpower or undermine the alleged heterogeneity of cultural studies interests and modes of inquiry.

Contrasting cultural studies' alleged virtues of intellectual multiplicity and strong political engagement against what are taken to be sociology's failings in these regards, has been a very useful way for cultural studies authors to define the nature of the intellectual terrain they want to lay claim to. I will now identify four rhetorical methods, each of which allows a construction of a certain dimension of cultural studies which is contrasted positively with a corresponding negative feature of (cultural) sociology.

## 1. Alleged 'Openness' and 'Fluidity'

As McLennan (2002: 633) notes, when many contemporary cultural studies scholars depict what it is that they 'do', they tend to emphasize their subject's 'declared openness to change, its desire to ask questions rather than provide answers, its analytical freedom and pluralism, [and] its self-conscious theoretical instability'. Thus Graeme Turner's textbook from the early 1990s defines cultural studies as 'preeminently a critical field: there is no orthodoxy in this field' (1990: 4), taking this lack of orthodoxy to be what marks out cultural studies from more 'conventional' disciplines such as sociology.

A charge that could be raised against cultural studies is that it is concerned with anything and everything. But many cultural studies scholars can, and do, represent this state of affairs as a beneficial condition. For example, in an influential statement about the nature of the field, Richard Johnson (1986–7), who was the director of the Birmingham Centre for Contemporary Cultural Studies (CCCS) in the mid-1980s, argues that the complexity of cultural studies as a set of research practices in fact mirrors the complexity of 'culture' itself.

For Johnson, the term 'cultural studies' is indeed imprecise, but this is a good thing, as definitional and conceptual rigidity would destroy the complexity of the substantive field to be investigated. For Paul Willis (2000: xx), another English cultural studies scholar associated with the Birmingham CCCS in the 1970s, cultural studies is 'condemned to a kind of eclecticism because of the very eclecticism and indissoluble combinations of the dissimilar in the increasingly complex "real" world around us'. While the use of the word 'condemned' suggests a negative appraisal of cultural studies' apparent unavoidable heterogeneity, Willis like many other writers in this area actually wants to celebrate such diversity, drawing on a left-liberal imaginary's positive connotations of the life-affirming properties of (cultural and other forms of) diversity in the face of the allegedly deadening monolithic characteristics of uniformity. It is but a small step from this kind of presentation of matters towards associating sociology with just such a dull uniformity, in terms of both substantive focus and modes of inquiry.

The presentation of cultural studies' fluidity and openness, as opposed to the presentation of the lack of these qualities in other academic fields, often goes hand-in-hand with an emphasis on the broadness of substantive focus that cultural studies enjoys. Thus the statement of the aims and scope of one of the field's flagship journals, the eponymously titled *Cultural Studies*, has it that scholars in the field explore 'the relation[s] between cultural practices, everyday life, material, economic, political, geographical and historical contexts'[2]. On this definition, cultural studies can look at just about everything in human affairs. The notable exception here is that the definition does not mention the 'social' dimensions of human activities, a focus presumably ceded to sociologists, the owners of the concept of the 'social', the gatekeepers of entry into the realm of analysing this sphere of human endeavours. If that is true, then the implication here is that a key difference between cultural sociology and cultural studies is that, while both aim to be sensitive to the specificities of cultural phenomena and to the meaning-making level of human activities, cultural sociology insists on connecting these matters to the realm of the 'social' (however this may be conceived of, as social actions and forms of agency, or as social structures, patterns and institutions), while cultural studies does not. Whether 'the social' is invoked or not, and defined as a positive resource for thinking or not, would seem to be a key dividing line between cultural studies and cultural sociology for many authors on both sides of this (permeable) dividing line (Inglis and Hughson, 2003). This is complicated, of course, by the fact that how the 'social' is to be defined is a matter of controversy within sociology itself, the contemporary dispute between Bourdieusians and Actor Network Theorists being the most recent version of a debate about what the social is, and whether the term itself is useful or not, that goes back to the founding of the discipline (Inglis with Thorpe, 2012).

## 2. Alleged Troubling of Disciplinary Boundaries

In a typical contemporary textbook definition of cultural studies given by the British authors Baldwin et al. (2004), they state that:

> Cultural studies is a *new way* of engaging in the study of culture. Many academic subjects have long brought *their own disciplinary concerns* to the study of culture; chief among them are anthropology, history, literary studies, human geography and sociology. However, over the past two or three decades there has been *a renewed interest* in the study of culture which has *crossed disciplinary boundaries*. The resulting activity, cultural studies, has emerged as *an intriguing and exciting area of intellectual activity* which has already *shed important new light* on the character of human cultures and which promises to continue so to do. (2004: 3; emphasis added)

There are two points of interest here. First, the emphasis is on both the 'newness' of cultural studies, and the questions – and means of answering them – it brings to bear on cultural matters. Such innovations transcend 'older', possibly 'antiquated', means of conceptualization, like those to be found in sociology. Second, these authors stress the problematizing of existing disciplinary boundaries, which they take to be fundamentally constitutive of cultural studies' distinctive modes of inquiry. Other authors also stress this dimension, but opinion varies as to how best to characterize it. For Graeme Turner (1990: 11), for example, it 'would be a mistake to see cultural studies as a new discipline, or even a discrete constellation of disciplines. Cultural studies is an interdisciplinary field where certain concerns and methods have converged.'

The notion of 'interdisciplinary field', a space where some of the concerns of sociology, anthropology, cultural history, social history, philosophy and so on have been brought together, seems to be a relatively uncontroversial means of defining cultural studies. However, for Grossberg et al. (1992: 4) cultural studies is in fact simultaneously 'an interdisciplinary, trans-disciplinary, and sometimes counterdisciplinary field'. Graeme Turner seems to agree with this characterization when he adds that this field 'defines itself in part through its disruption of the boundaries between disciplines' (1990: 6). Thus the interdisciplinarity of cultural studies is said to allow not just for the conjunction of different disciplines but for the transgression of their boundaries too in the direction of 'trans-disciplinarity'. Thus for Baldwin et al. (2004: 41), cultural studies is best described as an 'interdiscursive space' made up of a number of focuses – problems, themes, theorizations and methods – drawn from the different disciplines, such that 'there are no fixed boundaries and no fortress walls; theories and themes are drawn in from disciplines and may flow back in a transformed state to influence thinking there'. Willis (2000: xx) takes the discussion a step further when he describes cultural studies as 'a field of at times intractable complexity ... perhaps the first great academic experiment in an attempted formulation of a "non-disciplinary" discipline'.

Willis leaves unstated exactly what a 'non-disciplinary discipline' might look like. Adding to the ambiguity, he then goes on to speculate that in fact cultural studies may be more correctly dubbed 'post-disciplinary' rather than 'non-disciplinary' in nature, but he leaves undefined quite what features the paradoxical entity of a 'post-disciplinary discipline' might possess.

Whether cultural studies is labelled by its partisans as inter-, trans- or antidisciplinary in nature, such descriptions connote openness and inclusiveness, the postmodern embracing of all sorts of ideas and approaches, in antithesis to the dry, monolithic dogmatism of 'traditional disciplines'. Some of the more enthusiastic descriptions of cultural studies make it sound like one great ongoing party (e.g. Hays, 2000), a Rabelaisian idyll of unparalleled intellectual fluidity and conceptual suppleness, coupled with, as will be seen below, brave political engagement and sensitivity to the voices of the marginal. But the presentation of cultural studies' beneficent openness is constructed in large part against an imagined monochrome and dogmatic monolith of traditional academic disciplines, including – perhaps especially – sociology.

For example, in his overview of what makes cultural studies 'distinctive' from other approaches to cultural matters, During (1993: 1) argues that *all* sociological investigations of culture involve '"objectively" describing its institutions as if they belonged to a large, regulated system'. Thus what sociologists would take as the broad variety of perspectives on culture possible within sociology (set out in Inglis and Hughson, 2003), is reduced through the assertion that all of these involve regarding culture in terms of its contribution, or otherwise, to 'large, regulated [social] systems', with the latter always given analytic priority over cultural phenomena. On this sort of view, every sociological approach to culture must involve placing particular cultural phenomena in wider 'social systems', imperialistically reducing 'culture' to an apparently more primal and fundamental 'social', and thus robbing culture of its allegedly true nature, i.e. as heterogeneous, ambiguous and fluid. Likewise, other cultural studies authors, such as Stratton and Ang (1996), can argue that sociology is primarily positivistic, objectivistic and politically reactionary in nature. Sociology's monolithic concerns are presented as antithetical to cultural studies' much more vibrant orientations to cultural processes, subjectivities and everyday experiences. But assertions of *our* fluidity versus *their* dogmatism 'generate their own style of sectarianism and exclusiveness' (McLennan, 1998: 7). Thus the self-descriptions of some cultural studies authors can be viewed not just as exercises in wishful thinking, but also as a form of self-aggrandizement, where the constructed other is presented as the essence of conservatism, narrowness and backward-looking dispositions.

## *3. Alleged Broadness of Means of Conceptualization*

Given the issues above, it is not surprising that cultural studies authors' self-descriptions often highlight the apparent conceptual multiplicity of their subject. Thus one of the most influential British writers in the field in the present day, Tony Bennett (1998), concurs with other authors that cultural studies is an interdisciplinary field, which involves drawing upon a very wide range of concepts and procedures historically associated with particular disciplines. But despite the broadness of conceptual possibilities, certain key notions (however more specifically understood by different authors) occur frequently and recurrently in cultural studies authors' descriptions of the conceptual contours of their subject. Thus according to Barker (2000: 8–10), 'key' cultural studies notions include terms such as 'representation', 'materialism and non-reductionism', 'articulation', 'power', 'popular culture', 'texts', 'readers', 'subjectivity' and 'identity'. In the survey by Tony Bennett et al. (2005) of contemporary, state-of-the-art positions in cultural studies, terms like 'citizenship', 'gender', 'sign', 'everyday', 'body', 'celebrity' and 'mobility' are also said to be very important. But given the centrality of these concepts also in contemporary cultural sociology – as anthologised in textbooks like that authored by Back et al. (2012) – it becomes difficult to separate cultural sociology from cultural studies simply by the invoking of key terms like those mentioned by Tony Bennett, not least because there seems to have been a marked 'leakage' from one domain into the other. From cultural studies into cultural sociology over the last fifteen years or so, there has been a movement of terms and themes like 'celebrity', while some other keywords and concerns have travelled the other way, such as 'mobility' and 'body'. In other words, to attempt to define borders between cultural studies and cultural sociology through the invoking of terms taken to be central to the one or the other domain, is increasingly futile. Nonetheless, cultural sociology's insistence on the 'social', not as one important term but as a crucial meta-term, probably continues to point to ongoing and meaningful differences between sociology and cultural studies at a very broad and general level.

Adding to these complexities, cultural studies authors have tended to claim that there is available in cultural studies a very wide range of specific modes of theorizing the central terms that cultural studies works with or is centred around. A strong tendency towards theoretical diversity in the field is thus often asserted, with it being further claimed that no one school of thought occupies a dominant position within the field. Theoretical fracture, multiplicity and innovation are stressed over homogeneity or orthodoxy. Thus in cultural studies readers aimed at undergraduate courses (e.g. Durham and Kellner, 2005; During, 1993; Munns and Rajan, 1995) there are to be found different sets of writers hailing from a diverse range of theoretical – and in fact 'disciplinary' – schools presented as being canonical in cultural studies, with the effect that the cultural studies canon can be depicted as in some senses an 'anti-canon'.

Schools and figures here include: (1) Marxism (key figures: Marx, Lukács, Adorno, Horkheimer, Benjamin, Althusser, Gramsci, Bakhtin); (2) culturalism (key figures: Hoggart, Williams,

E. P. Thompson); (3) linguistic structuralism (key figures: Saussure, Lévi-Strauss, Barthes); (4) post-structuralist literary and philosophical ideas (key figures: Foucault, Derrida, de Certeau); (5) postmodernist philosophy (key figures: Lyotard, Baudrillard); (6) textualist and interpretivist anthropology (key figure: Geertz); (7) post-structuralist psychoanalysis (key figures: Lacan, Irigaray, Kristeva). Writers currently presented as key cultural studies contributors include Edward Said (post-structural literary criticism and cultural history), Judith Butler (post-structuralist feminism); Stuart Hall (Gramscianism and postmodern identity theory), Cornel West (post-colonial theory), Fredric Jameson (neo-Frankfurt School Marxism) and Donna Haraway (post-structuralist philosophy and science studies). The conceptual terrain from which these authors draw is depicted as being profoundly multi-disciplinary, for it encompasses, among other sources, sociology, anthropology, historiography, literary criticism and various branches of philosophy. In recent times, there has been some evidence of a move to include Bruno Latour and Actor Network Theory more generally in the cultural studies canon, partly because the latter is currently fashionable in various fields, sociology included, or is seen to have impeccably French intellectual credentials (a necessary virtue for one to possess if academic stardom in the Anglo-Saxon academy is to be possible), and also because of that position's often strong attack on what it takes to be mainstream sociology and its allegedly erroneous understandings of what 'the social' is.

How did the apparent theoretical heterodoxy in cultural studies come about? A standard 'founding narrative' of the historical emergence of cultural studies has arisen since the 1980s and has become part of the field's understanding of itself. In this account (see, e.g., Tudor, 1999), which draws to a great extent upon a much cited article by Stuart Hall (1981), cultural studies is seen to have been institutionally 'born' at the University of Birmingham in 1964, when the Centre for Contemporary Cultural Studies was formed under the leadership of Richard Hoggart. The first phase of Birmingham Cultural Studies was at the intellectual level 'culturalist' in nature, given Hoggart's position as a doyen of the culturalist position. The emphasis of the latter was on the study – and to some degree, celebration – of 'ordinary' cultures and the creative responses by the English working classes to situations of poverty and underprivilege. The stress on culture both as 'ordinary' and as embodying active and creative human impulses was set out not just in Hoggart's *The Uses of Literacy* (1962 [1957]), but also in Raymond Williams' earlier writing, most notably *The Long Revolution* (1980 [1961]), and in the historian E. P. Thompson's *The Making of the English Working Class* (1976 [1963]). Both Hoggart and Williams were literary scholars, concerned to make a break with the elitist conceptions of 'culture' that the English literary tradition had pursued since the later 18th century, and which encompassed such figures as Burke, Coleridge, Wordsworth, Arnold and Eliot (Williams, 1958). Thus on this account English literary studies and a certain form of leftist, grassroots historiography were at the heart of 'early' cultural studies.

But by the 1970s, this culturalist strain had been seen, in light of analytical importations from France – especially the 'complex Marxism' of Althusser – to be woefully lacking in theoretical substance, being an outdated form of naive humanism. Althusserian Marxism and Saussurean semiotic structuralism arose to take culturalism's place, both being conjoined through the means of a revamped Gramscian analysis of hegemony, with the result that 'subjectivity' and 'identity' became key areas of analytical inquiry over culturalism's concerns with 'ordinary culture' (Hall, 1981). Continuing this standard narration, as cultural studies spread out across the universities of the English speaking world in the 1980s, structuralism gave way to post-structuralism, and Marxism to postmodernism (Grossberg, 1993). Thus by the 1990s, while students were certainly taught the ideas of the likes of Foucault and Derrida, mere lip-service was paid in many 'history of cultural studies' courses to the ideas of the (alleged) 'founders' of the subject (Jones, 1994). Thus the culturalism of Williams and Hoggart was regarded more as a quaint initial staging post of cultural studies than as an ongoing, vibrant research tradition in its own right, the ground having been thoroughly ceded – especially in cultural studies units in North America affiliated to departments of literature – to semiotic post-structuralist 'readings' of 'texts', readings inspired by the work of, among others, Barthes and Derrida.

While this standard narration could be, and indeed has been, challenged from within cultural studies itself (see Wright, 1997), as different factions seek to retell the developmental story to promote their own interests, the Birmingham 'founding myth' remains a powerful form of self-presentation and disciplinary self-understanding in the field. It depicts a historical trajectory the *telos* of which is the apparently self-evident plurality of cultural studies modes of conceptualization, these being presentable in antithesis to the more monolithic concerns of sociology with questions of 'social system' and 'social structure'. This story of the historical evolution of cultural studies can in addition involve emphasis on how the theoretical plurality of cultural studies ways of thinking today was made possible by Birmingham cultural studies breaking in the later 1970s with what is presented (and was presented at the time) as the dead weight of sociological conservatism.

The work of Stuart Hall is very important in this regard, not just for how he has presented and engaged with sociology since the 1970s, but also in terms of how later cultural studies authors, wishing to narrate the history and 'nature' of their subject, have drawn upon and reproduced his views as to the apparently necessary breaks with sociology Birmingham cultural studies was required to enact. An ongoing critique of sociology by Hall was one of the continuing themes in his work from the mid-1970s onwards (Rojek, 2002). We may say that Birmingham cultural studies gained its distinctive sense of self in large part through a distancing of its project(s) from what was presented as 'mainstream sociology'. Thus in the early 1980s Hall (1981: 21–6) criticized the latter's allegedly static sense of social totality and its neglect of the study of ideology.

Cultural studies' epistemological break, involving the move into the 'complex Marxism' of Althusser, was, Hall claimed, necessitated to a large degree by the need to escape from the suffocating constrictions of a largely bankrupt sociology. The Birmingham view of the late 1970s (which draws quite markedly on neo-Marxist critiques of positivist science, such as that of Adorno and Horkheimer) was that 'mainstream sociology' was primarily empiricist and descriptivist, concerned only with surface images of human activities. On that view, actually existing sociology was itself insufficiently 'sociological' if the latter term connoted a critical analysis of the structures of capitalist society.

For Hall (1981: 25) at this period, part of cultural studies' epistemological practice involved 'posing sociological questions against sociology itself'. For Hall in his later work (e.g. 1997), the same theme is continued: 'conventional sociology' has always treated culture as relatively superficial, ephemeral and less important than the 'material' realm, defining 'culture' often in very narrow terms (a critique also mounted, of course, by advocates of a cultural sociology that should break with the deadening assumptions of mainstream 'sociology of culture', which do not attend to the autonomous and complex nature of culture – see Alexander, 2003). For Hall, cultural studies not only gives full due to the importance of culture in human life, it also is highly sensitive to the multiple definitions, and thus multiple dimensions, of 'culture', sensibilities that have for the most part eluded sociology. Other eminent figures working in the cultural studies field, such as Lawrence Grossberg (1993) in his writings of the early 1990s, have followed Hall's arm's-length attitudes towards sociology, urging cultural studies colleagues to transcend the 'sociological pull' of previous modes of cultural studies (ironically, the Birmingham models adumbrated in large part by Hall in the late 1970s and 1980s) in the direction of postmodern narratives of radical cultural alterity and contingency, drawing more on French thinkers such as Lacan, Lyotard and Laclau and Mouffe, than on more apparently 'sociological' luminaries such as Gramsci. The shared element in these sorts of stories is that 'sociology' is first depicted as very epistemologically limited, and then a break (or series of breaks) with it is designated both as a defining feature of cultural studies and as a key means whereby a much more sophisticated epistemic state is reached by the latter. That state in turn is represented as one of 'healthy' conceptual diversity, as opposed to the more limiting orthodoxies of sociology – orthodoxies themselves rhetorically constructed and then rejected by advocates of cultural sociology as opposed to 'sociology of culture', such as Alexander (2003).

## 4. Alleged Strong 'Political' Engagement

The final means we will examine by which 'sociology' can function as a signification of all that cultural studies is not involves the apparent ethical and political superiority of the latter over the former. It is common to find cultural studies authors (e.g. Bennett, 1998) defining their subject as one which, despite all its substantive and conceptual multiplicity, is centrally concerned with the relations that pertain between cultural forms and practices on the one hand, and forms and relations of power on the other. This problematic involves the study of enculturation processes and the rendering by powerful groups of arbitrary cultural relations as 'natural' in the minds of those enculturated. It is also said to encompass the analysis of power in its various and multiple forms, clustering around dynamics of class, gender and ethnicity, among other axes (see also Barker, 2000: 5; Turner, 1990: 5).

Of course some sociologists might think that this description equally well fits as a depiction of contemporary (cultural) sociology. But cultural studies authors can differentiate their subject further from sociology by means of claiming that cultural studies involves much more of a focus on political engagement in intellectual practice, as opposed to apolitical scholarship, than does any other discipline, including (indeed perhaps especially) sociology. Thus the statement of aims of the journal *Cultural Studies* has said that the journal, and by implication the whole field, 'aims to intervene in the processes by which the existing techniques, institutions and structures of power are reproduced, resisted and transformed'[3]. And for Bennett (1998), the politically engaged dimension of cultural studies involving the 'denaturalizing' of those ways of thinking and representing that are presented or taken as 'natural', also involves the dissemination of such critical knowledges, in order both to influence the broader terrain of 'politics' (very broadly defined) and to empower oppressed groups within it. The political programmes expressed in, and developed by, cultural studies work can also be presented as being, like the field itself, very diverse, drawing as they do from political positions within 'a left divided between defenders of neomarxist socialist politics and advocates of a postmarxist identity-based politics' (Seidman, 1997: 41).

Within this manner of representation, while cultural studies is said to be vitally engaged with important contemporaneous matters, sociology drags its heels, burdened both by a tendency towards conservatism in terms of its objects and methods of analysis and by a certain snobbish reserve about what it sees as allegedly ephemeral aspects of culture – rap music lyrics, music videos, fan cultures, and so on – the very cultural forms that cultural studies recognizes as important expressions of contemporary events. While sociology is staid, cultural studies is vibrant, with the result that cultural studies has more truly tapped into contemporary currents than its institutional rival. Yet much contemporary cultural sociology engages with such matters, as a perusal of journals that cater for that field, such as *Cultural Sociology*, the *Journal of Cultural Economy* and the *European Journal of Cultural Studies* attests. Indeed, EJCS is a particularly interesting hybrid case, for although billed as a cultural studies journal, much of its output could easily fit not just into a cultural sociology journal, but in fact into what most people would regard as a 'mainstream sociology' publication. This case should remind us of the increasingly hybrid nature of journal publishing, with various high-profile outlets bridging the (cultural) sociology/cultural studies division in ways that were still relatively rare as recently as the early 2000s.

Cultural studies is also presented by many of its advocates as being strongly politically engaged with the materials it looks at, while sociology adopts a certain form of distance from the objects of its analyses. This is construed in a negative manner, both because sociology is said to be less politically engaged and 'relevant' than cultural studies, and because sociology's posture of distance from its objects of analysis is characterized by a spurious attempt at objectivity. As no form of knowledge is ever objective, runs this argument, sociology's apparent distance from its objects smuggles into its analyses a hidden form of politics, and this politics is reactionary not only because it is undisclosed, but also because it derives from a positivism that falsely presents its findings as the singular 'truth', when in actual fact they are but the reified reflections of hegemonic forces and discourses in the world being investigated. Cultural studies has made a fundamental break with positivist attitudes, seeing them for what they are, while sociology remains stuck behind in what is a 'pre-critical' mindset (During, 1993). We should also note here that an attack on so-called 'mainstream' sociology's positivism, especially in sociology's manifestation in the US higher education field, has frequently been mounted by those, like Alexander (2003), who regard cultural sociology as a post-positivist, hermeneutic exercise that stands in opposition to positivist sociology of culture; but this critique does not usually go hand-in-hand with the cultural studies authors' tendency to align post-positivism with some sort of radical scholarly politics and calls to political engagement. The 'political', 'politicized' and 'transformative' dimension of cultural studies is generally highlighted by programmatic authors, who often turn to sociology to depict what is the antithesis of 'proper' political engagement. Thus when Graeme Turner (1990: 227) contends that cultural studies' 'commitment to understanding the construction of everyday life has the admirable objective of doing so in order to change our lives for the better. Not all academic pursuits have such a practical political objective', he probably has sociology in mind as one, and perhaps as the most exemplary, of the mere 'academic pursuits' that purport to engage with contemporary human life but which are in fact abject in their failure to do so.

## SOCIOLOGY AGAINST CULTURAL STUDIES

If cultural studies can be presented as a (loose, fluid, open) entity by its advocates in contradistinction to the alleged closedness of 'traditional disciplines' like sociology, then so too can partisans of sociology gain a sense of disciplinary identity by presenting cultural studies as a negatively construed 'other'. The disciplinary blurring, the politicization and the concerns with popular culture that cultural studies authors present as the great virtues of their subject, can all be presented as great vices by unconvinced and unsympathetic writers who position themselves as first and foremost 'sociologists'.

One of the more striking examples of negative depictions of cultural studies coming from (those defining themselves as) sociologists in recent years is that issuing from the pens of the British authors Bryan S. Turner and Chris Rojek, both of them notably associated in one way or another with the development of cultural sociological paradigms in British sociology. It is very telling that such a critique of cultural studies has come from authors strongly associated with more cultural sociological dispositions, rather than from more positivist sociology of culture or mainstream sociology that has little interest in cultural matters and debates per se. I suspect that it is Turner and Rojek's relative closeness to cultural studies, as practising cultural sociologists, which propelled them to define with such rhetorical force what they take to be the highly problematic nature of much cultural studies. Scholars in sociology who were less closely positioned to cultural studies would, I think, have been much less perturbed by the alleged failings of the latter, with many mainstream, positivist scholars probably not bothering to develop such a critique in the first place, because in their eyes cultural studies – even if it gets onto their intellectual radar at all – most likely is not even worth mentioning. Being located near a border probably makes one more attentive to the doings of the people on the other side of it, whether these are positively or, as here, negatively construed.

Despite these specificities of orientation, motivation and location, I will use the views of Turner and Rojek to represent some main trends of hostile (British and other) sociological responses to cultural studies. At an institutional and organizational level, Turner and Rojek (2001: vii) lament the alleged fact that 'sociology has, through the so-called cultural turn, been devolved and dissolved into a series of related fields – cultural studies, women's studies, urban studies and media studies'. It is interesting that cultural sociology is not listed here as one of the new sub-fields which are involved in the fragmentation of the sociological discipline. As a concomitant of such processes at the organizational level, at the level of analysis and conceptualization a sort of sociology has arisen that is 'obsessed with the immediacy of commercial and popular cultures'. Rojek and Turner (2000) describe this sort of sociology as 'decorative sociology', and it is clear that they mean by this term a sociology that is all too closely patterned after the nature of (what they take to be) cultural studies. Moreover, they aver that this cultural-studies-derived sociology 'has taken root with such tenacity that it is now the most powerful tendency in … cultural sociology' (2000: 639). The latter, which presumably was free of this taint in the past, has now succumbed to the facile substantive interests and less-than-rigorous methodologies of cultural studies. This is very bad news, as cultural studies 'has no adequate theory or methodology' to grasp cultural processes and artefacts themselves, let alone social relations and institutions, and their relationships to cultural phenomena (Rojek and Turner, 2000: 640).

On this diagnosis, which is a variant on other 'sociological' authors' complaints about cultural studies, cultural sociology has become just like cultural studies, as it has succumbed to an out-and-out textualism, which in its more expansive version regards the human world simply as a series of texts that can be read by the post-Geertzian hermeneutic analyst (but of course with multiple readings possible, because of the 'radical indeterminacy' of meaning), and in its more limited version regards the main foci for analysis as popular cultural texts made available through the mass media. Thus the whole world is reduced to texts and concomitant matters of reading and interpretation, whether those interpretations be the analyst's alone (as in 'critical readings' of films and pop music lyrics) or the analyst's interpretations of other people's interpretations of texts (as in studies of the 'readings' of texts engaged in by particular groups in popular cultural audiences). These readings themselves are often alleged (e.g. Goodwin and Wolff, 1997) to be very arbitrary in nature, claiming to find ideological dimensions or 'resistive' audience readings which are in fact not at all backed up by any sort of systematic evidence. On this view, cultural-studies-style research is content to operate at the level of mere assertions, in the case of readings of media texts, and of the most slipshod quasi-ethnography, in the case of depictions of audience groups.

For sociological critics, cultural studies – and the cultural sociology unfortunately patterned after it – furthermore exhibits little historical sense, being far too concerned with the latest trendy cultural fashions rather than with careful depiction of historically existing life-worlds and the socio-cultural forces that made and transformed them (Rojek and Turner, 2000). When cultural studies does deal with past times, it does so in the most cavalier of fashions. Thus Schudson's (1997) critique of the work of cultural studies star Donna Haraway indicts it for being based on empirically untenable generalizations and uninformed, overly politicized 'readings' of historically existing cultural forms, instead of taking a more properly sociological approach to evidence and the reconstruction of actors' views as to their own activities.

A certain historical irony arises here. Given the Birmingham CCCS scholars' critique of mainstream sociology in the 1970s for being enslaved to 'surface empiricism', by the present day, for many sociological writers, cultural studies and cultural sociology overly influenced by it appear to have succumbed to exactly that sort of vice, because of their highly impressionistic and unsystematic methods of research and findings (McLennan, 1998: 9). On this scenario, while cultural studies 'ought to benefit from its location at the intersection of the humanities and the social sciences, [it] risks falling between the two', because it threatens to become neither good social science nor good literary study (Goodwin and Wolff, 1997).

Sociological authors have also been quick to identify what they take to be the core conceptual failings of cultural studies. The key claim here is that, as we have already noted, cultural studies has no adequate grasp of the 'social' dimensions of human life, the very element that sociology can understand with great sophistication. Nor in fact can it deal with the cultural dimensions of human life as part of a wider assemblage of social relations (Wood, 1998: 410). For Mouzelis (1995), an author wishing to reinstate what he takes to be 'core' problems of sociological thought back into contemporary sociology, from which he believes they threaten to be banished altogether, cultural studies operates conceptually around a unidimensional realm of the 'cultural', rather than viewing human life through the lens of the interplay between 'social structure' and 'social action'. On this view, cultural studies definitions of 'culture' are so broad that they conceptually colonize every aspect of human life, with the effect that the 'social' level is obliterated from view. Thus 'subjectivity', understood (in a postmodernized version of Althusser) as being formed by multiple and contradictory cultural forces, replaces sociological concerns with 'social actors' or agents, and their action and agency. Consequently, cultural studies thinking is presented as being bereft of any adequate notion of action and agency, being stuck within the confines of the analysis of 'subjectivities'.

Although subjectivities are conceived of as the result of the intersection of dynamic cultural forces, nonetheless the overall analytic framework in which these are located is static, because the core sociological problems of *how* social actors act, and *why* they do so, is not properly engaged with. The 'how' question requires sensitive analytic and methodological tools that cultural studies is unaware of; the 'why' question refers one to issues of social institutions and social structures, concepts (and empirically existing entities) that cultural studies has no idea how to engage with. As Bonnell and Hunt (1999: 11–12) put it, 'causal explanation takes a back seat, if it has a seat at all, to the demystification and deconstruction of power'.

When cultural studies work *does* examine agency, it is according to sociological authors only within the conceptually limited, over-politicized and over-interpreted terms of post-Gramscian concerns with 'acts of resistance', as in the work of de Certeau (1984), where 'even walking down the street is a political act' (Rojek and Turner, 2000: 637). The apparent over-interpretation of each and every text and activity as in some senses 'political' testifies to the dramatic over-politicization of cultural studies, according to these critics. The self-description by cultural studies people of themselves as properly politically *engagé*, in juxtaposition to the bad faith of the mainstream (and naively positivist) sociologist, 'bestowed an automatic moral significance upon the cultural studies approach which contrasted with the alleged academicism of established research traditions'. This was an important shaping factor in the 'moral arrogance, intellectual narrowness and over-confidence' that allegedly characterize at least certain wings of cultural studies in the present day (McLennan, 2002: 634). Furthermore, the over-politicization of cultural studies, according to Collini (1994; see also Tester, 1994) threatens to turn the subject away from any kind of proper scholarly endeavour, into an exercise centred around academic expressions of victimhood – with different 'marginalized' groups, especially centred around gender and ethnicity, each expressing their complaints about their oppression, at the expense of any sense of analytic rigour or scholarly detachment.

## BEYOND DIFFERENCES

As we have seen above, those who speak in the name of sociology denounce the perceived inadequacies of cultural studies and cultural-studies-style cultural sociology, just as those who claim to speak 'for' cultural studies allege that sociology is the 'project' that has failed or is failing. However, a number of other modes of representation of the (actual or potential) relations between cultural studies and sociology are possible in the present day. These modes stress points of convergence rather than divergence between the two entities.

The first possibility is for authors positioned within sociology, especially those in the United

States, still to assume that sociology and cultural studies are two separate entities, but in so doing to set cultural studies up as a model of how sociological analysis should be reconfigured so as to overcome its current shortcomings. Very often, these shortcomings are identified as being the very problems that cultural studies scholars have identified as characterizing sociology. Thus the American sociologist Elizabeth Long (1997: 2) echoes cultural studies' allegations as to sociology's long-standing refusal to take 'cultural' matters seriously by arguing that since at least the mid-20th century, (American) sociologists have 'dealt with culture as subsumed to social institutions ... social processes, social groups and their practices'. The superiority of cultural studies to sociology is asserted when it is argued – as, for example, by Friedland and Mohr (2004: 2) – who might well define themselves as cultural sociologists – that while sociology has been very slow to take the cultural features of human life seriously, cultural studies scholars 'made a sociological turn long ago'. Writing in the same vein, Hays (2000) argues that cultural studies threatens to steal ownership of ideas to do with 'culture' away from (American) sociologists. On this view, sociology is compelled to attack cultural studies, partly to attempt to retain control over 'cultural' matters, partly to reassert in public its scientific claims to truth, and, as a corollary of both of these factors, to hold on to funding sources that are necessary for its ongoing survival. For Hays, cultural studies is indeed correct to charge sociology – in the guise of positivist sociology of culture – as being obsessed with methodology, as overly narrow in its substantive foci, and as constitutionally apolitical (2000: 596).

These are opinions shared to some degree by Janet Wolff (1999), herself a cultural sociologist with a British background and training but long resident in the US until her retirement, when she contended in the late 1990s that American sociological studies of culture tend to be narrow, ahistorical and naively empiricist. The residual positivism in the sociology of culture means that 'untheorized and unexamined categories of social analysis' (1999: unpaginated) underpin the research practice. Many sociologists seem to be unaware – or deliberately ignore the fact – that analytic categories, like all social categories, are in fact discursive fabrications, shot through with all sorts of assumptions and power relations.

Cultural studies is very reflexively aware of the constructed nature of all categories, be those concepts used by actors or by analysts, a message that the scientism of the positivist sociology of culture refuses to acknowledge. In response to sociologists who argue that cultural studies lacks the component of systematic empirical data-gathering which sociology is the proud possessor of, the cultural sociologist Steven Seidman (1997: 42) argues that just as much as sociology, cultural studies provides 'systematic analyses of the social that are empirical and analytical and that offer perspectives on whole societies'. Likewise, cultural studies textual analysis is a form of empirical investigation too, but a different sort of empirical investigation from the overly narrow conception of the latter that is hegemonic in sociology. In sum, some American cultural sociologists have used cultural studies as an exemplar to criticise what they see as a moribund tradition of positivist sociology of culture. Cultural studies in these sociologists' hands becomes a rhetorical weapon for attacking, and hopefully refashioning, sociological practice itself.

The second possible way of representing relations between sociology and cultural studies that we will look at here, involves presenting a situation whereby the two are said to have enough overlaps with each other to allow for at least the partial overcoming of disciplinary hostilities, such that each entity can learn useful things from the other. For the British author David Chaney (1994: 43), who would likely define himself as a cultural sociologist, both 'sides' share the view that 'culture in all its forms has to be understood as a mode of social practice'. In a similar vein, Wolff (1999: unpaginated) stresses what she sees as the strong 'sociological' element that existed in Birmingham cultural studies in the 1970s, despite all the rhetoric about making breaks with sociology. Wolff sees much Birmingham work as 'firmly grounded in sociology – in the texts of Weber, Marx, Mannheim, the symbolic interactionists and other sociological and ethnographic traditions', and in the deployment of what could be taken as 'mainstream' sociological vocabularies such as that of labelling theory. Thus, just as cultural studies motions can be deployed to help overhaul the naively empiricist categories of mainstream American sociology, in turn 'sociologists can bring to the project of cultural analysis ... a focus on institutions and social relations, as well as on the broader perspective of structured axes of social differentiation and their historical transformations – axes of class, status, gender, nationality and ethnicity' (Wolff, 1999: unpaginated). On this account the sociology/cultural studies relationship is, or at least could be, mutually enriching rather than antagonistic. This is also the position reached by McLennan (2002; also 2006), who regards cultural studies as primarily involving engaged modes of social description, while sociology tends more towards analytic explanations. For this author, these differing modes are complementary rather than contradictory.

Finally, it is also possible to argue that the ultimate similarity between the two entities is their shared commitments to leftist politics (Long, 1997: 24–5), increasingly of an 'identity-' rather than class-based sort, and their shared purposes vis-à-vis social transformation (Wood, 1998). There have also been a number of attempts by cultural studies scholars to 'return', as they see it, to core 'sociological' concerns, such as developing more sophisticated and diverse methods and methodologies than has hitherto been the case (e.g. Gray, 2003).

While a spirit of co-operation rather than conflict emanates from the pens of these authors, seeking as they do to present cultural studies and sociology as mutually beneficial to, and supportive of, each other, what they miss is in fact the main point of another representational possibility I will examine here. This involves the argument that what all of the above discourses, whether they stress similarities or dissimilarities between the two entities, do not or cannot see, is the fact that sociology and cultural studies are indeed very 'alike', because they both share the same epistemological dispositions. Constraints of space dictate a highly compressed delineation of this argument, which I have pursued at greater length elsewhere (Inglis, 2005). Chaney (1994: 42) in my view is not quite correct when he asserts that cultural studies is one branch of the sociology of knowledge; it would be more accurate to say that both sociology (especially cultural sociology) and cultural studies are hewn from the same conceptual raw materials.

Despite the variations between sociological and cultural studies approaches to matters cultural, and notwithstanding the variety of positions within each discipline, there is nonetheless an identifiable 'meta-discourse' that unites all these strands (Inglis and Hughson, 2003). Both sociology and cultural studies are derivations of a quintessentially 'social scientific' interpretation of Kantian philosophy. Kant saw each object in the world as having two separate manifestations – on the one hand, there is its *noumenal* side, which is its essence and which exists beyond human perception, and on the other hand, its *phenomenal* side, which is the object as it appears in human perception. Kant (1999 [1787]) sees the human mind as playing an active role in organizing the world that the human being sees presented before it. The mind shapes the phenomenal aspect of things, and thus constitutes the world as we perceive it. However, Kant holds that all human minds are alike, and hence the world as perceived by me is found to be the same world as perceived by anyone else because our minds process the world in the same ways. The history of post-Kantian developments in thought, especially as far as the social sciences are concerned, breaks down this position, denying the existence of *noumena* at all, and seeing the world only as a series of *phenomena*. Different groups of people are seen as possessing 'their own' culture, and it is through this cultural gauze that the world not only is perceived, but is *constituted*. This has become *the* central assumption of the modern social sciences (Bergesen, 2004; Inglis, 2005), as filtered through the Kant-inspired work of Marx (ideologies organize experience), Weber and Durkheim (both of whom aver that 'culture' brings order to conceptual chaos), among others.

Out of this way of thinking comes one of the main tenets of contemporary social science, the notion that all forms of 'reality' are social fabrications (Berger and Luckmann, 1967), as in the case of sociology, or cultural constructions, as in the case of anthropology, literary philosophy, semiotics and cultural studies. Moreover, in both Marx and Weber especially, but also in Nietzsche too, the contention that culture constitutes reality is yoked to the assertion that it is powerful social groups who define cultural categories. Thus 'culture' is made almost synonymous with 'power'. The upshot of this is that cultural matters are seen as being thoroughly shot through with social power relations. No cultural form is ever 'innocent', for each is seen to be harbouring some kind of more or less hidden agenda that is itself rooted in forms of power. Mainstream sociological conceptions of culture are thoroughly permeated with these assumptions. So too in fact are cultural studies conceptions, some of which have derived directly or indirectly from the ideas of Marx and Nietzsche, but which have also come down from the constitutional semiotic work of Saussure, itself contemporaneous with, and as a form of relativizing Kantianism conceptually very similar to, the work of the later Durkheim on cultural-cognitive systems. Given that Saussure (1959 [1906–11]: 112) argued that 'without language, thought is a vague, uncharted nebula. There are no pre-existing ideas, and nothing is distinct before the appearance of language', the radical implication of his version of Kantianism is that the 'reality' perceived within a particular linguistic community is solely a product of language, a view developed by such cultural studies star figures as Derrida and Foucault, whose work is also primarily concerned with the conjunction of language/culture and power. Semiotic claims as to the discursively fabricated, power-ridden nature of 'reality' are in the present day as hegemonic in cultural studies as the equation of culture and social power has become in most brands of the sociology of culture. Such ways of thinking, based around the principles of regarding culture as totally arbitrary, and of equating 'culture' and 'power', constitute the disciplinary common sense of both sociology and cultural studies today. It is into these ways of thinking that students are inculcated when they take undergraduate and postgraduate degrees in these subjects. Such forms of conceptualizing are so ingrained, that they are, to use Bourdieu's phrase, 'misrecognized' as representing the 'truth' of things in the world, and are pretty much taken at face value. But it is far from being apparent and incontestable that such 'de-naturalizing' modes of thought are themselves 'natural'. They are but one way of understanding how the world and the human beings within it 'work', and are problematized by recent research in psychology which finds that the human mind is not in fact just a blank slate upon which 'society' or 'culture' writes, for even very young children seem to have certain inbuilt capacities to order the world around them in structured ways (Bergesen, 2004). Just because, as both sociology and cultural studies themselves teach, a way of thinking has become endemic among certain social actors, is not enough to make it 'true'. But an apparently hegemonic truth-regime has arisen in both sociology and cultural studies, and its power is attested to, and reproduced by, its taken-for granted nature in these fields.

McLennan (2006: 41) views the recent rise of the genre called 'social and cultural theory' as a 'shared resource for sociology and cultural studies alike', in that it combines forms of theory that are both produced by, and utilizable by, scholars in each field, as opposed to an earlier situation where 'sociological theory' was purely a possession of sociologists and 'cultural theory' the province of cultural studies people. Thus, for example, the work of Bourdieu has become a key reference point in both sociology and cultural studies – even if sociologists pay more attention to his theory of action and his statistical tables, while in cultural studies he is regarded more as a cultural theorist. The already-noted rise to prominence of Bruno Latour in both fields in recent years is another case in point. But most 'social and cultural theory' is fundamentally based upon the – questionable, unrecognized, historically specific – epistemological assumptions mentioned above, and some of its more problematic assertions, such as claims that there is no such thing as 'nature' or that 'sex' is wholly a cultural fabrication (Butler, 1999), go relatively unquestioned, even despite Latour's critique of mainstream sociology's epistemological foundations.

have often been apparently at war, but their mutual hostility has given each of them a strong sense of themselves. Their ritualised conflict battle has brought certain gains in identity for them both. But beyond rhetorical displays of dissimilarity between them, once one examines their shared epistemological assumptions, one sees that it is actually their likeness that has both allowed and compelled them to engage in the stand-offs they have indulged in. The problem remains that both do not sufficiently acknowledge, or perhaps cannot see at all, the flaws in their joint constitution. For in their strongly shared programme of making culture and power closely related, if not in fact almost synonymous, terms, both sociology and cultural studies treat as 'natural' what are only particular, historically specific ways of thinking and understanding the world. As a result, they have failed to recognize not only their own shared nature, but also the historically constituted and limiting characteristics of that nature.

## NOTES

1 Some elements of this chapter appeared in Inglis, D. (2007) 'The Warring Twins: Sociology, Cultural Studies, Alterity and Sameness', *History of the Human Sciences*, Vol. 20, No. 2, pp. 99–122.
2 www.tandfonline.com/action/journalInformation?show=aimsScope&journalCode=rcus20
3 www.tandfonline.com/action/journalInformation?show=aimsScope&journalCode=rcus20

## REFERENCES

Alexander, J.C. (2003) *The Meanings of Social Life*. Oxford: Oxford University Press.
Back, L, Bennett, A., Edles, L. D., Gibson, M., Inglis, D., Jacobs, R. and Woodward, I. (2012) *Cultural Sociology*. Oxford: Wiley-Blackwell.
Baldwin, E., Longhurst, B. J., Smith, G., McCracken, S. and Ogborn, M. (2004) *Introducing Cultural Studies*, revised 1st edn. Harlow, Essex: Pearson.
Barker, C. (2000) *Cultural Studies: Theory and Practice*. London: Sage.
Bennett, T. (1998) *Culture: A Reformer's Science*. London: Sage.
Bennett, T., Grossberg, L. and Morris, M. (eds) (2005) *New Keywords: A Revised Vocabulary of Culture and Society*. Oxford: Blackwell.

## CONCLUSION

Consideration of the multiple relationships between sociology, including the cultural sociology variant, and cultural studies shows that they

Berger, P. and Luckmann, T. L. (1967) *The Social Construction of Reality: A Treatise in the Sociology of Knowledge*. Harmondsworth: Penguin.

Bergesen, A. J. (2004) 'Durkheim's Theory of Mental Categories: A Review of the Evidence', *Annual Review of Sociology*, 30: 395–408.

Bonnell, V. and Hunt, L. (1999) 'Introduction', in V. Bonnell and L. Hunt (eds), *Beyond the Cultural Turn: New Directions in the Study of Society and Culture*. Berkeley: University of California Press. pp. 1–34.

Bourdieu, P. (1988) *Homo Academicus*. Cambridge: Polity.

Butler, J. (1999) *Gender Trouble – Feminism and the Subversion of Identity*. New York and London: Routledge.

Chaney, D. (1994) *The Cultural Turn: Scene-Setting Essays on Contemporary Cultural History*. London: Routledge.

Collini, S. (1994) 'Escaping from DWEMsville: Is Culture Too Important to be Left to Cultural Studies?', *The Times Literary Supplement*, 27 May.

De Certeau, M. (1984) *The Practice of Everyday Life*, Vol. I. Berkeley: University of California Press.

Durham, M. G. and Kellner, D. (eds) (2005) *Media and Cultural Studies: Key Works*. Oxford: Blackwell.

During, S. (1993) 'Introduction', in S. During (ed.), *The Cultural Studies Reader*. London: Routledge, pp. 1–28.

Friedland, R. and Mohr, J. (2004) 'The Cultural Turn in American Sociology', in R. Friedland, and J. Mohr (eds), *Matters of Culture: Cultural Sociology in Practice*. Cambridge: Cambridge University Press. pp. 1–39.

Goodwin, A. and Wolff, J. (1997) 'Conserving Cultural Studies', in E. Long (ed.) *From Sociology to Cultural Studies: New Perspectives*. Oxford: Blackwell, pp. 123–54.

Gray, A. (2003) *Research Practice for Cultural Studies*. London: Sage.

Grossberg, L. (1993) 'Cultural Studies and/in New Worlds', *Critical Studies in Mass Communication* 10: 1–27.

Grossberg, L., Nelson, C. and Treichler, P. (1992) 'Introduction', in L. Grossberg, C. Nelson and P. Treichler (eds), *Cultural Studies*. London: Routledge.

Hall, Stuart, (1981) 'Cultural Studies: Two Paradigms', in T. Bennett, G. Martin, C. Mercer and J. Woollacott (eds), *Culture, Ideology and Social Process: A Reader*. London: Open University Press, pp. 19–37.

Hall, Stuart (1997) *Representation: Cultural Representations and Signifying Practices*. London: Sage.

Harris, D. (1992) *From Class Struggle to the Politics of Pleasure: The Effects of Gramscianism on Cultural Studies*. London: Routledge.

Hays, S. (2000) 'Constructing the Centrality of Culture – and Deconstructing Sociology?', *Contemporary Sociology*, 29(4): 594–602.

Hoggart, R. (1962 [1957]) *The Uses of Literacy: Aspects of Working-Class Life with Special Reference to Publications and Entertainment*. Harmondsworth: Penguin.

Inglis, D. (2005) 'The Sociology of Art: Between Cynicism and Reflexivity', in D. Inglis and J. Hughson (eds), *The Sociology of Art: Ways of Seeing*. Basingstoke, Hants: Palgrave. pp. 98–112.

Inglis, D. and Hughson, J. (2003) *Confronting Culture: Sociological Vistas*. Cambridge: Polity Press.

Inglis, D. with Thorpe, C. (2012) *An Invitation to Social Theory*. Cambridge: Polity.

Johnson, R. (1986–7) 'What is Cultural Studies Anyway?', *Social Text*, 16: 38–80.

Jones, P. (1994) 'The Myth of "Raymond Hoggart": On "Founding Fathers" and Cultural Policy', *Cultural Studies*, 8(3): 394–416.

Kant, I. (1999 [1787]) *Critique of Pure Reason*. Cambridge: Cambridge University Press.

Long, E. (1997) 'Introduction: Engaging Sociology and Cultural Studies: Disciplinarity and Social Change', in E. Long (ed.), *From Sociology to Cultural Studies: New Perspectives*. Oxford: Blackwell, pp. 1–36.

McGuigan, J. (1992) *Cultural Populism*. London: Routledge.

McLennan, G. (1998) 'Sociology and Cultural Studies: Rhetorics of Disciplinary Identity', *History of the Human Sciences*, 11(3): 1–17.

McLennan, G. (2002) 'Sociological Cultural Studies: The Question of Explanation', *Cultural Studies*, 16(5): 631–49.

McLennan, G. (2006) *Sociological Cultural Studies: Reflexivity and Positivity in the Human Sciences*. Basingstoke, Hants: Palgrave.

Mouzelis, N. (1995) *Sociological Theory: What Went Wrong?* London: Routledge.

Munns, J. and Rajan, G. (eds) (1995) *A Cultural Studies Reader*. Harlow, Essex: Longman.

Pfister, J. (1996) 'The Americanization of Cultural Studies', in J. Storey (ed.), *What Is Cultural Studies?* London: Arnold. pp. 287–99.

Rojek, C. (2002) *Stuart Hall*. Cambridge: Polity.

Rojek, C. and Turner, B. S. (2000) 'Decorative Sociology: Towards a Critique of the Cultural Turn', *The Sociological Review*, 48(4): 629–48.

Saussure, F. (1959 [1906–11]) *Course in General Linguistics*, C. Bally and A. Sechehaye (eds). New York: Philosophical Library.

Schudson, M. (1997) 'Cultural Studies and the Social Construction of "Social Construction": Notes from "Teddy Bear Patriarchy"', in E. Long (ed.), *From Sociology to Cultural Studies: New Perspectives*. Oxford: Blackwell. pp. 379–98.

Seidman, S. (1997) 'Relativizing Sociology: The Challenge of Cultural Studies', in E. Long (ed.), *From Sociology to Cultural Studies: New Perspectives*. Oxford: Blackwell. pp. 37–61.

Stratton, J. and Ang, I. (1996) 'On the Impossibility of a Global Cultural Studies', in D. Morley and K.-H. Chen (eds), *Stuart Hall: Critical Dialogues in Cultural Studies*. London: Routledge. pp. 361–91.

Tester, K. (1994) *Media, Culture and Morality*. London: Routledge.

Thompson, E. P. (1976 [1963]) *The Making of the English Working Class*. Harmondsworth: Penguin.

Tudor, A. (1999) *Decoding Culture*. London: Sage.

Turner, B. S. and Rojek, C. (2001) *Society and Culture: Principles of Scarcity and Solidarity*. London: Sage.

Turner, G. (1990) *British Cultural Studies: An Introduction*. London: Unwin Hyman.

Williams, R. (1958) *Culture and Society 1780–1950*. London: Chatto & Windus.

Williams, R. (1980 [1961]) *The Long Revolution*. Harmondsworth: Penguin.

Willis, P. (2000) 'Foreword', in C. Barker, *Cultural Studies: Theory and Practice*. London: Sage.

Wolff, J. (1999) 'Cultural Studies and the Sociology of Culture', *Invisible Culture: An Electronic Journal for Visual Studies* 1. https://www.rochester.edu/in_visible_culture/issue1/wolff/wolff.html

Wood, B. (1998) 'Stuart Hall's Cultural Studies and the Problem of Hegemony', *British Journal of Sociology*, 49(3): 399–414.

Wright, H. (1997) 'Dare We De-centre Birmingham? Troubling the "Origin" and Trajectories of Cultural Studies', *European Journal of Cultural Studies*, 1(1): 33–56.

# Visual Culture Studies and Cultural Sociology: Extractive Seeing

Janet Stewart

In 1996, the leading modern and contemporary art periodical, *October*, published the results of its 'Visual Culture Questionnaire' (Alpers et al., 1996), which was to become a landmark publication in the construction of visual culture as a field of study. Many of the individual responses to the questionnaire reflect on the boundary line between visual culture and art history, as, more recently, does Whitney Davis (2011) in his comprehensive *General Theory of Visual Culture*. The construction of 'visual culture' as an object of study involves a number of moves, in which visual culture studies seeks to distinguish itself from the range of existing disciplines that engage with visual objects – including Anthropology, Architectural History, English, Film Studies, Geography, History, History of Art, Modern Languages, and Sociology. Visual culture studies steers a sometimes uneasy course of rapprochement with these disciplines, to which, in part at least, it also sets itself up in resistance. A number of programmatic early contributions to the *Journal of Visual Culture* (which was established in 2002) focused on the nature of boundaries between visual culture and other fields of study, discussing the desirability of policing and/or permeating such boundaries and reflecting on disciplinarity, interdisciplinarity and even 'indisciplinarity' (Bal, 2003; Elkins, 2002; Jay, 2002; Mitchell, 2002a; 2002b).

The persistence of such debates notwithstanding, visual culture studies is now an established field, the emergence of which is connected to a series of distinctive shifts in the humanities and social sciences, including the 'linguistic turn', the 'cultural turn' and, finally, the 'pictorial turn' (Mitchell, 1995). There are numerous university programmes in visual culture worldwide, supported by a range of readers (including Evans and Hall, 1999; Mirzoeff, 1998; Schwarz and Pryzbilski, 2004) and textbooks (such as Mirzoeff, 1999; Sturken and Cartwright, 2009; Walker and Chaplin, 1997). As well as the *Journal of Visual Culture*, a number of other dedicated journals have been established, including *Visual Studies*, *Visual Culture in Britain* and *Early Popular Visual Culture*, and a proliferation of scholarly monographs in visual culture has appeared. Visual culture studies, in its contemporary form, is a broad field, encompassing: first, research into the nature of vision; second, the study of visuality, which takes up the question of how images, image-making technologies and 'looking practices' construct social realities; and third, the attentive analysis of visual objects of all kinds, from artworks to scientific images, from vernacular photography to spectacular architecture.

Research into the nature of vision encompasses biology, physics, neuroscience and psychology, as well as drawing upon the study of perception in philosophy. Visual culture studies is a site in which these different fields can combine, as seen, for example, in Donna Haraway's (1997) reflections on 'The Persistence of Vision', in which she draws upon phenomenology and poststructuralism to argue for the importance of a humanities perspective to the study of vision. Poststructuralist thought and, in particular, the work of Michel Foucault also informs the study of visuality, which represents the core of contemporary visual culture studies. This is evident, for example, in Nicholas Mirzoeff's (2011) definition of visuality in terms of 'the right to look' and 'the right to assemble a visualization'.

The study of 'visuality' involves thinking about 'looking relations', drawing upon theories of the gaze, that bring together existentialism (Sartre, 2012 [1943]) phenomenology (Merleau-Ponty, 1962 [1945]), psychoanalysis (Lacan, 1978 [1964]) and others. It also involves investigating the role of technologies of seeing in the formation of subjects and subjectivities (Berger, 1972; Crary, 1990), engaging with the idea of 'attention' (Crary, 2001) and reflecting on the production, consumption and circulation of visual objects of all kinds (Beller, 2006). The study of visuality offers rigorous critical analysis of the role of visual culture in constructing particular ways of seeing, framed in terms of key categories such as race and ethnicity (Jay and Ramaswamy, 2014; Shohat and Stam, 1994) or gender (Burfoot, 2015), or grouped around themes of many different kinds, from violence to environmentalism, from religion to science and technology.

Visual culture studies also draws upon the attentive study of visual objects of different types, recognizing that diverse visual objects demand specific methods of analysis, drawing upon a particular body of work, such as photography theory or film theory, to adequately account for the object under investigation. While visual culture studies has been criticized for its 'presentism' (Starkey, 2005), the field is increasingly witnessing a turn to a longer historical timeframe (Jay, 1994; Kromm and Bakewell, 2010; Mirzoeff, 2011; Starkey, 2005), countering, by doing, the perception that the proper object of visual culture studies is advertising or the internet. The field's increasing awareness of medium specificity and historical specificity is connected to an anthropological perspective that insists on the necessity of studying visual cultures in the plural (Shohat and Stam, 1994). This is tempered, however, by work that draws upon Mitchell's (1995) reflections on the nature of the 'pictorial' to posit a universal theory of the image (Belting, 2011 [2001]; Wiesing, 2014 [2005]). The tension between the particular and the universal underlies recent work that insists on attending to the material nature of visual objects (and their agency) (Latour, 1999 and others), while also recognizing the importance of the non-representative in focusing on the 'immediacy' or 'presence' of an object (Gumbrecht, 2003).

Janet Wolff (2010; 2012), who has consistently charted connections amongst sociology and art history, and, later, cultural sociology and visual culture studies, identifies the 'turn to immediacy', as the most significant point of divergence between visual culture studies and cultural sociology today. She insists that cultural sociology needs to retain critical distance from visual culture's recent focus on immediacy and materiality. This is an interesting point of departure for her, as much of her previous writing has reflected upon what sociology has to learn from art history and/or visual culture studies. In her continuing insistence that sociology needs a theory of the aesthetic (Wolff, 1983; 1999; 2010; 2012), she has kept a line of sociological thinking alive that extends back to Georg Simmel, includes Walter Benjamin (whose innovative sociological work draws on the work of early art historians such as Alois Riegl), Herbert Marcuse, T.W. Adorno and others, and is taken up in the contemporary sociology of art (de la Fuente, 2007; Stewart, 2005; 2013; Tanner, 2010). Wolff (1999: n.p.) has written persuasively on what is missing from much sociological work when it turns to think about the social construction of reality – the 'radical rethinking mandated by poststructuralist and psychoanalytic theory, which exposes the constitutive role of culture and representation in the social world'. She has, however, also always been clear about the influence of the sociological imagination on art history and visual culture studies, which, she maintains, enables these disciplines to offer a rigorous critical analysis of institutions and social relations.

Wolff's (2010) recent critical account of the relationship between cultural sociology and visual culture studies is the point of departure for this chapter's exploration of the nature of the relationship between the two disciplines. In order to trace the interweaving and differentiation of the two fields, the chapter offers a case study of one particular 'boundary object' – the permanent 'Energy Exploration' exhibition, which opened in March 2013 in Aberdeen's Maritime Museum. 'Museology', Janet Wolff (2010: 6) writes, 'is one example of a new area ... which has produced subtle and illuminating studies of the interplay of art object, institution, and social and political processes'. And indeed, museums are objects of interest both to visual culture studies (for example, see Bennett, 1988; Hooper-Greenhill, 2000) and to cultural sociology (for example, see Fyfe, 2006; Marontate, 2005). In line with 'boundary object' theory (Star and Griesemer, 1989), the 'Energy Exploration' exhibition, and the objects around which it is constructed, can be conceived as entities that have different meanings in each discipline, but which are common enough to be recognizable in each. This is the case, both with the form of the museum and with the theme of the particular exhibition under investigation in this chapter; energy is also a theme taken up recently by both visual culture studies (Bozak, 2011; Jolivette, 2014; LeMenager, 2014; O'Brian, 2015; Veder, 2015) and sociology (McKinnon, 2007; Stewart, 2014; Tyfield and Urry, 2014; Urry, 2013). As Boyer and Szeman (2014: n.p.) argue in a programmatic statement on the 'Rise of the Energy Humanities':

> Neither technology nor policy can offer a silver-bullet solution to the environmental effects of an energy-hungry, rapidly modernizing and growing global population. … our energy and environmental dilemmas are fundamentally problems of ethics, habits, values, institutions, beliefs and power – all areas of expertise of the humanities and humanistic social sciences.

Part of the work of the energy humanities is to investigate the narrative strategies and desires that underpin our commitment to fossil fuel and frame our inability to think past this source of energy. Museums, as Latour and Weibel (2005) claim, are important sites for 'making things public'. This being the case, critical analysis of energy exhibitions yields significant insights into the construction of narratives about energy transition. This chapter explores the ways in which visual culture studies and cultural sociology can contribute to this task through engaging in critical analysis of the 'Energy Exploration' exhibition from both disciplinary perspectives. The discussion reveals differences and structural similarities between the two disciplines, and concludes by offering a critical account of these similarities that counters Wolff's critique of the 'turn to immediacy' with a re-evaluation of the concept of 'presence'.

The 'Energy Exploration' exhibition in Aberdeen's Maritime Museum provides the main display space for the history of the North Sea Oil and Gas industry in the UK.[1] The exhibition occupies the central section of the museum, a building that overlooks Aberdeen's busy commercial harbour, with its constant turnover of supply boats and other vessels essential to the offshore oil industry. The display, then, is located in one of the areas of the city in which the visual and material culture of oil and gas is clearly visible, in the shape of objects such as ships, shipping containers, storage tanks, logos and company offices. The exhibition draws explicit attention to its location, making use of the museum's architecture and, in particular, its large picture windows, to connect the assembled museum artefacts to the activities of the harbour area and so, by extension, to the lived experience of the oil industry and its extensive social, political and economic influence in the city and its environs. Aberdeen's Maritime Museum might not boast an exhibit equivalent to the Norwegian Petroleum Museum's oversized digital display, which makes an arresting claim about the contribution of the industry to the Norwegian economy by showing in real time the value of the country's Oil Fund; however, the dominant narrative of the 'Energy Exploration' exhibition, like its Norwegian counterpart, focuses on the positive changes brought to the region after the opening up of the North Sea to oil exploration in the 1970s.

From the perspectives of visual culture studies and cultural sociology, two sets of questions arise in the context of analysing the exhibition's central narrative: the first pertaining to social relations; and the second, relating to the formal presentation of the narrative. Focusing on social relations raises the issue of power and the display of narrative, investigating the ongoing process of the discursive construction of meaning through dialogue amongst museum professionals, external stakeholders, visitors and others. Attending to form, meanwhile, relates to how the exhibition's narrative is presented, taking up questions about practices of display and practices of collecting, and demanding an investigation of the visual processes through which the narrative is constructed and communicated.

The exhibition's central narrative relates the history of North Sea oil exploration as a success story focusing on man's triumph over adversity.[2] In so doing, it follows the logic underlying many accounts of the North Sea oil story, from memoirs such as Brian Page's *Boy's Own Offshore Adventure* (2007) and *Boy's Own Oily Adventure* (2009) to standard histories such as Alex Kemp's *Official History of North Sea Oil and Gas* (2011) and valedictory accounts such as Bill Mackie's *The Oilmen: The North Sea Tigers* (2004). This narrative emphasises the achievements of the oil industry and of the 'ordinary men and women' who were involved in oil exploration. This very particular and limited understanding of social relations in the industry prefigures a particular energy future through the recurrent trope of 'techno-utopianism' that underlies it (Szeman, 2007). That such a narrative line dominates in this exhibition is hardly surprising, given the list of its sponsors, who were drawn almost exclusively from the oil industry.[3] From the perspective of a critical encounter with social relations, both cultural sociology and visual culture studies offer reflection on corporate cultural sponsorship (Bourdieu and Haacke, 1995; Marontate, 2005; Scholette, 2010), showing, for example, how museums are under increasing pressure to tailor exhibitions to the requirements of external funders (Alexander, 1996; 1999; Rectanus, 2002). The particular instance of oil companies engaging in cultural sponsorship is a topic that has been highlighted and investigated in its own right. Mel Evans' (2015) *Artwash*, the publication of which is supported by the NGO Platform London,[4] offers a critical account of oil company sponsorship of the arts, while also showing how activist artists, including Hans Haacke and groups such as BP or not BP, have sought to eliminate corporate sponsorship of the arts by fossil fuel companies, thereby removing one pillar of the industry's 'social licence to operate', a key element of thinking on 'corporate social responsibility'.

While analysis of the dominant narrative and sponsorship arrangements of the permanent exhibition in the Maritime Museum allow us to demonstrate that the 'Energy Exploration' exhibition supports the oil industry's 'social licence to operate', a more detailed engagement with social relations in the museum serves to complicate this picture somewhat. Decisions made by the museum's curatorial team, for example, can offer a counter-narrative within the space of the museum. In 2014, the museum hosted a temporary exhibition of works created as part of an educational project on 'Power Politics'. Supported by the Living Earth Foundation, the project worked with school pupils in Aberdeen City and Shire and Port Harcourt, Nigeria, to encourage them to explore critically questions relating to oil, energy and development in two parts of the world where the dominant industry is oil and gas. The logic of the Power Politics show, located in a small gallery accessed via the central 'Energy Exploration' display, stood in direct contrast to the permanent exhibition. Two video screens showed documentary films discussing aspects of everyday life in Scotland and Nigeria, while a set of wall panels contained a number of large-scale comic strips encouraging critical reflection on the way in which the story of oil is conventionally narrated. The critique of representation offered in the show was extended explicitly to the Maritime Museum itself, and, in particular, to one of the central attractions in the Energy Exploration exhibition: a 3-D cinema showing a corporate documentary film created and donated by TAQA, the Abu Dhabi National Energy Company, which operates in the North Sea as a fully integrated exploration and production company. The achievement of the Power Politics project was to place in question the authority of the story of oil and gas told in the museum. The show made a compelling case for the power of substituting the belief in one authoritative version of the North Sea oil and gas story with the imperative to tell multiple stories, which attend both to local and to global concerns.

This example of the potential for undermining the museum's dominant narrative is a reminder of the importance of taking into account both the intricacy of social relations and the full complexity of the discursive construction of museum meanings in critical encounters with the museum as institution (Fyfe, 2006; Rectanus, 2002). The 'sociology of translation' offers a useful model for thinking through this process. This relational approach, developed by Michel Callon and Bruno Latour, in response to Michel Serres' reflections on the translation of concepts between disciplines, takes as its object the loose structure or 'network' of associations between ideas, things, people and resources around which and through which translation processes are enacted (Callon, 1986; Callon et al., 1986; Latour, 1993). It facilitates an understanding of the creation of narrative and the ongoing production of the museum experience as the result of a network of associations amongst different social actors (as well as sponsors and curators, we might consider visitors in multiple categories, experts of different kinds, and others), different ideas (for example, conceptualizations of the museum as institution or thinking about energy transition) and different things (such as the objects on display and in the collection).

One of the strengths of an approach informed by the 'sociology of translation' is that it brings objects themselves into play, through its insistence on the agency of matter. This approach offers a way of thinking through the agency of collecting and display (Kirshenblatt-Gimblett, 1998), of examining what happens as these images, objects and practices find their way into the space of the museum display. Rubio and Silva have recently employed such an approach in their study of artworks as physical objects in the field of contemporary art, emphasizing the importance for their work of combining 'materiality in field theory' with an 'object-oriented methodology in field analysis' (2013: 161). As a means of exemplifying the potential of such an approach, this chapter turns now to trace the place and function of photographs and photographic images in the Energy Exploration exhibition, considering the different forms of analysis or encounter demanded by this category of object.

Photography is one of the key visual technologies of the 20th century and as such, has a special place in ways of seeing throughout that century and into the 21st century. It can be regarded as a 'boundary object' in its own right, with different meanings and aspirations accorded to it in a variety of disciplinary contexts. In the field of visual sociology, photography figures as a key visual research method, the efficacy of which is due largely to its apparent indexicality. At the same time, as Bourdieu (1991) discusses in his 'Sociology of Photography', it is valued as a form of image-making that is open to many. Visual culture similarly encounters photography in multiple ways, from analysis of art practices through to reflection on the possibilities of documentary and critique of scientific imaging techniques. Recently, the role of photographs in museums has been the subject of a project led by the anthropologist and photography theorist, Elizabeth Edwards, which focuses on photographs and the colonial legacy in European museums (http://photoclec.dmu.ac.uk/content/home).

Edwards' work draws on a seminal article by Gaby Porter (1989) on the use of photography in museums, in which Porter drew attention to the use of photographs as part of an overall design solution in the context of the museum. This can be seen clearly in the 'look' of the Maritime Museum's oil and gas display, which utilizes an aesthetic entirely familiar to those who inhabit the corporate world of the oil industry. Entering the display is not unlike entering a small-scale version of an oil and gas trade fair such as Aberdeen's biannual Offshore Europe, or Houston's annual Oil Technology Conference.[5] That this aesthetic draws heavily on commercial photography is not in itself surprising, when we consider the vast number of photographic images produced by the oil and gas industry. In a presentation given at the 2012 meeting of the European Oil and Gas Archives Network, it was revealed, for example, that the Norwegian Petroleum Museum, has a collection of c. 3.5 million photographic images, of which 60,000 are of corporate provenance.

While photography plays a major role in the archive of the European Oil and Gas industry, this is in stark contrast to its place in museum displays in general. Photographs, as Porter (1989) points out, are often seen as second-class objects in museums, relegated to a contextualizing function that is associated with their presumed indexicality and transparency, their evidentiary power (Tagg, 2009). They might be used, for example, to provide the 'look of the past', to 'authenticate other objects', or to 'fix' their meaning (Edwards, 2001: 186; Edwards and Mead, 2013). In the Energy Exploration exhibition in Aberdeen's Maritime Museum a series of photographic images are reproduced as part of a text panel that describes the way in which the city of Aberdeen changed with the advent of oil extraction in the North Sea in the 1970s. The photographer is named as Fay Godwin, but no further information is provided as to the photographs' provenance. The images are pressed into service in a manner that relies upon their taken-for-granted indexicality, allowing them to be presented as unproblematic evidence of past social change. In neglecting the specificity of these images, the exhibition flattens out their potential to be read critically, both in terms of the conditions of their production and in terms of their aesthetic value. Although no credits are provided for the images, it is likely that they have been taken from a photographic book, *The Oil Rush* (Jones and Godwin, 1976). This is a work of reportage, in which Godwin, a celebrated landscape photographer, reproduced photographs taken in Aberdeen and Peterhead, as well as on the North Sea oil-rigs themselves in the early years of the North Sea boom. Thinking in terms of the conditions of their production, these images offer the possibility of an interesting counterpoint to the dominant masculine narrative of the exhibition. In a prefatory note to the book, Godwin reflects: 'Several times, I was refused permission to make trips to rigs, platforms, pipe-laying barges and other facilities, because I am a woman' (Jones and Godwin, 1976: 5). In the exhibition itself, however, this gendered perspective is absent, as is the critical context of Godwin's important contribution to environmental art, which would have allowed the images to be interpreted differently. The museum's project of 'rendering the visible legible' (Preziosi, 2006), we might argue, remains incomplete without the additional work of the visual and sociological imaginations, which open up and historicize particular visual objects, recognizing the aesthetic and rendering it both discursive and socially grounded (Wolff, 2010: 7).

It might be countered that precisely because of their merely illustrative function in the display, the Godwin photographs cannot properly be classed as museum objects. The same point, however, holds when a photograph is exhibited as an object in its own right. In the 'Energy Exploration' exhibition, only one photograph is encountered in this way. It is to be found in the section devoted to the Piper Alpha disaster, the oilrig blowout of 1988, in which 169 men lost their lives.[6] The curator of the exhibition, Meredith Greiling, suggested in conversation with me in the summer of 2013 that only with the latest refurbishment of the 'Energy Exploration' display, had it been possible to take up the subject matter in the museum – a quarter of a century after the tragedy. Prior to the new display opening, the only public memorial to the Piper Alpha disaster was to be found in Hazlehead Park, on the outskirts of Aberdeen, in the form of a commemorative sculpture largely funded by public money, as the oil companies had been reluctant to contribute.[7] The sculpture was produced by the artist Sue Jane Taylor, who worked extensively in the oil industry before and after the tragedy, having been brought in originally by the Stirling Shipping Company to document its work in the North Sea. Like Godwin before her, Taylor was allowed access to oilrigs to document life at sea; her research included a period of time on the Piper Alpha the year before the explosion (Taylor, 2005).

The solitary photograph on display as photograph in the exhibition is not one of Taylor's works, however, but an object donated by her. Indeed, it is not an original artwork at all, but a commercial postcard: an 'ephemeral object' that, like the museum itself, demands analysis that attends both to the aesthetic and to social relations (Geary and Webb, 1998; Prochaska and Mendelson, 2010; Rogan, 2005; Simpson, 2012). In the context of the Energy Exploration exhibition, this postcard, bearing a photograph of the Piper Alpha taken before the rig assumed its particular historical significance, takes on a secondary commemorative function, the ramifications of which can be explored with recourse to memory studies, an interdisciplinary field that, like museum studies, represents a point of connection between cultural sociology and visual culture studies. Presented in terms of the expected affective response of the viewer, this postcard functions almost as a relic, transported by circumstance from the realm of the profane to that of the sacred – to offer a Durkheimian analysis. Yet the postcard's appearance as museum object masks a host of other questions relating to the status of the object – questions relating to communication and exchange value, to aesthetics and to materiality.

The process of the postcard's translation from commercial photograph to consecrated museum object is captured in its label, which hints at its 'social biography' (Edwards, 2001), inviting reflection upon its journey through multiple communicative networks:

> Postcard of Piper Alpha sent to the medics onboard Piper 'A' by Gareth Watkinson.
> Artist Sue Jane Taylor donated this postcard. 'It was given to me by the medic on Piper A during my stay on the platform. He had it displayed on the front check-in desk.'

This text raises two sets of questions: the first relates to the singular journey of this postcard, asking who Gareth Watkinson was and why he sent a postcard of the Piper Alpha to the medics onboard. The second is connected to the general history of the postcard, asking about its place in postcard culture: Where was the postcard produced? Who was the photographer? Which company sold them? In what numbers were they sold? None of this information is provided in the exhibition.

These questions as to the postcard's provenance lead to another set of questions pertaining to the photograph reproduced on the card; postcards also demand iconographic analysis, as Mark Simpson (2012: 170–1) argues. Alongside these questions about the object's 'social biography', aesthetic questions are also raised about the photograph's status as a representation of oil exploration. The postcard shows an image of an oilrig on a calm North Sea taken at sunset. In terms of its 'look', it is typical of the hyper-vivid glossy postcard prints of the era, which Ben Highmore (2007), in his foreword to a collection of John Hinde popular postcards, memorably describes as 'technicolor daydreams'. Similarly, the motif is ubiquitous; in corporate publications, postcards, advertisements and fine art prints, the calm seascape featuring an oilrig at sunset is a recurrent trope.[8] Like so many images that form the canon of stock images in the photography of exploration (Ryan 2013), this aerial shot signifies the idea of human endurance and perseverance to triumph over a hostile environment. It is an image that does so by drawing upon the 'technological sublime', which David Nye (1996 23) glosses as an 'amalgamation of natural, technological, classical and religious elements into a single aesthetic'.[9] Nye here is writing of a uniquely American form of the sublime. In images of North Sea platforms such as the Piper Alpha, we see the natural, in the shape of the seascape, and the technological, but the classical and religious are superseded by the Futurist and utopian, which Justin Beale shows to be typical of the architecture of the North Sea oil industry (2006).

Visual culture studies of postcard imagery often focus on its importance in constructing and consolidating social power (Simpson, 2012: 171). Writing about views of Paris reproduced in early postcards, Naomi Schor (1992: 216) draws upon a Foucauldian framework to argue that: 'the ontology of the postcard is totalizing'. While her concern is with the troubling stereotypes characteristic of early Parisian postcard culture, her claim is pertinent for the Piper Alpha postcard under consideration here. The image constructs a particular narrative of control, familiar in imagery of the oil industry – even if that control is, as Beale (2006) argues, always tempered by the possibility of impending disaster. This narrative is produced not only through the image's reliance on the 'technological sublime', but also in the very process of its production, for this is an image that was expensive to produce. To take the aerial shot of the oilrig at sunset required significant investment, both in image-making technology and in transport technology. Postcards depend upon the ability to reproduce images cheaply, and yet in this case, the condition of production of the image, both in terms of technology (the camera, the helicopter) and of nature (the sunset, the calm sea), is not easily reproducible. It is the kind of imagery with which canonical oilscape photographers such as Edward Burtynsky (2009) are associated.[10] His practice, it might be argued, draws not only upon the technological sublime, but also on the 'reification of the visible', which the photography theorist, Ariella Azoulay, argues: 'is carried out either as a result of reliance on the photographer as someone with the authority to manage the photographic act or as the result of the instrument's apparent neutrality, which assumes an absence of human involvement' (Azoulay, 2008: 328).

In the case of Burtynsky's photographs, these elements merge in the assumed authority of the photographer and the studied neutrality of his detached view. In other unattributed stock photographs of the oilscape, it is the apparent neutrality of the camera that provides the images with their force. The trope of the oilrig at sunset is part of a particular 'scopic regime' that is predicated on the reification of the visible, which, Azoulay (2008: 328) claims, functions to absolve the spectator of responsibility for the visible and for the 'commitment to the civil contract of photography' (by which she means a new form of deterritorialized citizenship that emerges in the encounter between the photographed person, the photographer and the spectator (2008: 24–5)). The photographic process of making visible North Sea oil exploration, which also lies at the heart of the Energy Exploration exhibition in Aberdeen's Maritime Museum,[11] serves to normalize extractive activities, rendering critique unnecessary by absolving the visitor of the responsibility of forming a critical response to issues relating to fossil fuel production and consumption.

The process that underpins the Energy Exploration exhibition – of making the invisible visible through strategies that rely upon the 'reification of the visible' – is also part of the central logic of the oil industry itself. Seen in this light, the postcard is one of a series of visual technologies on display in the museum that support the process of oil exploration, extraction, production and consumption. Other examples of technologized ways of seeing on show include geological diagrams donated by Marathon Oil. As Latour (1986: 14) has argued, drawing on Martin Rudwick's (1976) ground-breaking work in the History of Science, the significance of geological imagery lies in its presumed 'optical consistency'. This aspect contributes to the 'reification of the visible' in its reliance on the apparent neutrality of the image-making technology employed to survey and map the earth, and on the authority of the geologist as someone with the power to manage the photographic act. Yet such maps are not neutral, as critical geography reminds us. Geological maps serve to imagine the seabed as the site of extractive spaces that provide access to the mineral resources that lie beneath it. Mapping such spaces provides the basis for their capitalization (Harvey, 2001), the results of which are represented, amongst other places, in the sector maps that show the location of oil and gas concessions in the North Sea.[12] As well as the visual appropriation of space, geological image-making practices also provide the basis for a visual appropriation of time as the drill bit (and camera) navigates, collects and maps the layers of sediment and rock that bear material testament to different geological eras. The Energy Exploration exhibition seeks to make sense of these technical images by juxtaposing them with reproductions of photographs of the subsea environment and with images and material examples of the forms of technology (from diving suits to unmanned submarines) that enabled such images to be captured. These images and visual technologies are further contextualized in the architecture of the exhibition, which is dominated by a three-storey tall scale model of the Murchison oil platform. The spatial order of the exhibition is arranged around the principle of drilling down from the surface into the seabed, and the model serves to render the photographic images and visual technologies on display legible as part of an argument that values and supports the logic of the oil industry. Visual technologies, in other words, enable particular technological practices and construct the specific ways of seeing that support such practices.

More than merely supporting the logic of the oil industry, photographic images and technologies are also material objects dependent on fossil fuels and oil derivatives in terms of both production and consumption. The photographs in the museum (no matter whether they are presented as contextual material or as objects in their own right) are not, then, merely abstractions that function as representations of oil sites, technologies and infrastructure, but are also physical objects that form part of the complex that we might call the 'oil assemblage' (Stewart, 2013). As Nadia Bozak (2011: 8) argues in respect both of analogue and of digital photography, 'images, however intangible or immaterial they might ... appear to be, come bearing a physical and biophysical make-up'. It is a relatively simple matter to show how the history of photography is entwined with the history of the oil and gas industry: the first permanent photographic print was made by the French inventor Joseph Nicephore Niepce on a pewter plate covered with bitumen of Judea (a petroleum derivative), while George Eastman of Kodak popularized photography by developing photographic film made from the petrochemical ethylene. While the apparent immateriality of digital images might appear to signal a shift away from fossil fuel dependency, they do still of course require fuel to provide the energy upon which their production, transmission, storage and consumption is predicated. Moreover, they depend on the extractive industries more broadly for the production of essential minerals such as coltan (Bozak, 2011: 59), while plastic is a significant component in the production of the hardware that enables digital photography. All this goes to show that not only does visual technology play a central role in the day-to-day operations of the oil industry, but the industry is also essential for the production of the visual technology upon which the industry relies and upon which the displays in the petroleum museum depend.

Investigating the use of photography in the petroleum museum, then, reveals the central role that photographic image-making technologies play in knowledge-making practices around the excavation of fossil fuels. This enables us to understand that oil fuels the dominant scopic regime upon which the Energy Exploration exhibition depends, a regime that inscribes a narrative of control over the natural environment and supports the extraction of value from 'natural resources' through processes of visualization, while removing from spectators any responsibility for offering a critical response to these ideas. In relation to exhibition form, of practices of display and collecting, and in terms of social relations, these insights have been obtained through engaging with a range of theoretical sources, spanning visual culture studies and cultural sociology to investigate the interplay amongst social relations, aesthetics and materiality. The results of this encounter with the petroleum museum, however, also have wider ramifications for the way in which we understand these disciplines themselves.

The architecture of the Energy Exploration exhibition, as we have seen, is predicated upon the idea of 'drilling down' from the surface to the subsea level and into the Earth's crust. This design choice functions both literally, as a way of modelling the process of oil extraction in the North Sea, and metaphorically, standing in for the process of 'drilling down' in pursuit of knowledge. The latter is not merely the central structuring device for the 'Energy Exploration' exhibition at Aberdeen's Maritime Museum; it also accurately describes the epistemological stance of cultural sociology and visual culture studies, both of which, as David Inglis (2007: 116) argues in relation to cultural sociology and cultural studies, 'are derivations of a quintessentially "social scientific" interpretation of Kantian philosophy'. Inglis advances his argument by showing how these disciplines are connected through their belief in the social construction of reality that underpins the argument that '"culture" is made almost synonymous with power' (2007: 117). I argue that it is possible to identify a further point of connection between the two disciplines, which lies in their mutual belief in the fundamental importance of setting out to render visible the invisible. This belief underpins both visual research methods and the documentary form. It is also the fundamental methodological assumption that lies at the heart of textual and visual analysis in the humanities, which seeks to employ close reading to reveal that which remains hidden in the text or visual object. This form of thinking can be found in the post-Kantian writings of classical sociologists – in Marx's (2002 [1848]: xxii) memorable description of ideology in terms of the 'sentimental veil' being 'torn away from the family' by the bourgeoisie, for instance, or in Simmel's use of the metaphor of dropping a 'plumb line' from surface-level manifestations of all kinds to reveal their underlying metaphysical realities, which he does in his much-cited essay 'The Metropolis and Mental Life' (Simmel, 1997 [1903]: 177) and again in the preface to his later study of Rembrandt (Simmel, 2005 [1916]: 3). In relation to this project of making visible the invisible, both cultural sociology and visual culture studies often have recourse to the metaphor of 'drilling down' to access the 'deep knowledge' that exists beneath the surface of the object under investigation. What we might call 'extractive seeing' is the dominant logic upon which both disciplines are predicated.

If fossil fuel culture is implicated in the belief in the value of 'making visible' that lies at the core of both visual culture studies and cultural sociology, is there any way of eluding this way of seeing? To answer this question, I would like to return to Janet Wolff's critique of the 'turn to immediacy', in which she expresses her anxiety about the denigration of the sociological imagination in 'the turn to affect, the return to phenomenology, the discussion of "presence" in aesthetic experience, new theories of materiality and of the agency of objects and ... the emergence of neuroaesthetics' (2010: 3). The 'turn to immediacy', as she describes it, 'by-passes, or even rejects, critical theory' (2010: 3). I would like to suggest here a different reading of the 'turn to immediacy', one that proposes the critical potential of the idea of 'presence', in particular. In the *Future of the Image*, Jacques Ranciere (2007: 121) seeks to differentiate art from other forms of discourse by claiming that critical art 'does not make visible; it imposes presence'.[13] Ranciere's implied critique of the project of 'making visible' is akin to the critical account of the logic of 'extractive seeing' offered in this article, the indexical relationship between object and image upon which both cultural sociology and visual culture studies are predicated. To 'impose presence' is a rather more ambivalent undertaking. On the one hand, it indicates a process of appropriation or objectification which sociology would seek to criticize. On the other hand, however, for Ranciere, the act of 'imposing presence' also allows the preservation of illegibility that allows a subject to avoid objectification by resisting the imperative to be fully knowable, to be fully visible. Despite Ranciere's (2003: 165–202) dismissive account of sociology in general, and his polemical critique of Bourdieu and the sociology of art in particular, and despite Wolff's misgivings about the 'turn to immediacy', thinking about 'presence' in this way is not fundamentally anti-sociological. Indeed, the concept has already found its way into sociological thought. It plays, for example, a key role in Saskia Sassen's (2006; 2008) critical analysis of globalization. Meanwhile, the contemporary 'turn to immediacy' identified by Wolff has its sociological precursors. In his *Aesthetic Theory*, Adorno (1999 [1972]) posits a primacy of experience that exists before discursive language, drawing on Walter Benjamin's (1979 [1916]; 1991 [1935]) insistence on understanding the mimetic dimension of language, the primordial sensuous source of language (Wolin, 1994: 245). In his writing on language, Benjamin makes a similar connection between 'immediacy' and 'materialism' to that which lies at the core of Wolff's diagnosis of early 21st-century cultural theory. What is at stake when sociologists such as Adorno, Benjamin and Sassen insist on the importance of retaining the illegible, the unknowable at the centre of their thinking and demand that attention is paid to that which eludes discursive language, which is pre-cognitive and unmediated? They set out to question the dominance of the scientific worldview and the particular understanding of social relations upon which it is predicated. This worldview, as has been argued in this article, is underpinned by a logic of 'extractive seeing'. Since 'extractive seeing' is tied to the promise of 'making visible', then the only way to counter it is to challenge that promise. Given their common focus on understanding the power of seeing and being seen, and the mechanisms that underpin this power, cultural sociology and visual culture studies need to draw upon and develop theoretical language that encompasses not only the visible, but also that which eludes visibility. This insight, in turn, yields new challenges for museums, to think their remit not only in terms of making visible and then making the visible legible (Preziosi, 2006), but also in terms of challenging that logic by retaining a central illegibility as a way of countering the totalization of 'extractive seeing'. This is a vitally important project, given the dominance of 'extractive seeing' and the urgent injunctive, in the face of compelling evidence of destructive climate change, to offer alternatives to this way of seeing,

## NOTES

1 However, there are a number of museums in the UK devoted to aspects of the history of the oil and gas industry (such as the Scottish Shale Oil Museum in Livingstone and the Dukes Wood Oil Museum in Nottinghamshire) or with significant holdings in this area (notably the Science Museum in London). The Science Museum's Petroleum Exhibition was in existence from 1983 until the early 1990s. It was replaced, according to its curator, Robert Bud, when London 'lost its interest in industry'. The Museum holds a large collection of materials relating to the industry in storage. There are also a number of projects under way to collect and archive materials pertaining to the history of the offshore oil and gas industry in the UK, such as 'Lives in the Oil Industry' and 'Capturing the Energy'.

2 I use 'man' here advisedly. Although there are attempts in the exhibition to provide space for other perspectives, the dominant narrative is that of the adventure story, a genre that serves to construct a particular form of masculinity.

3 A full list of sponsors is listed in an Aberdeen City Council press release of 21/12/2012: Talisman Energy (UK); Marathon International Petroleum (GB); Serica Energy (UK); BP Exploration Operating Company; ConocoPhillips (UK); AMEC Group; TOTAL E&P UK; Chevron Upstream Europe; AGR Petroleum Services; Nexen Petroleum UK; Schlumberger Oilfield UK; Centrica Energy; Statoil (UK); Offshore Design Engineering; GDF SUEZ EandP UK; PSN; Apache North Sea; BG Group; Subsea 7 (UK Service Company); Shell UK; Suncor Energy; KCA DEUTAG Drilling; Wood Group Management Services; Peterson SBS; Petrofac (http://www.aberdeencity.gov.uk/CouncilNews/ci_cns/pr_maritimeupgrade_211212.asp)

4 For details, see http://platformlondon.org/about-us/

5 It is remarkable that cultural sociology has devoted itself so little to an analysis of the trade

exhibition, particularly as Georg Simmel (1997 [1896]) devoted an essay to the form, which has been taken up extensively in cultural history and also visual culture studies in relation to trade exhibitions. For a critical encounter with Houston's Oil Technology Conference, see the following blog post: http://culturesofenergy.com/deeper-water-a-report-from-houstons-offshore-technology-conference/

6 For a journalistic account of the tragedy, see McGinty (2009). For a sociological account of the consequences of the event, see Woolfson, Foster and Beck (2013).

7 For discussion of the controversy around the erection of a memorial to those lost in the Piper Alpha tragedy, see O'Byrne (2011).

8 In 2005, Peter Scholle gave a paper at a conference on 'Oil Industry History' in which he argued that today images of oil infrastructure are seldom found on postcards. When they are, he maintained, then they are 'stylized, miniaturized or shown in the colors of flaming sunsets'.

9 It should be noted that Nye is attempting to define a specifically American version of the 'technological sublime'.

10 Burtynsky's oil photography can also be viewed on his website: http://www.edwardburtynsky.com/site_contents/Photographs/Oil.html

11 Typical of reactions to the new display is this comment by Malcolm Webb taken from a press release relating to the exhibition, in which he emphasized the importance of the exhibition in making visible the largely invisible activities in the North Sea: 'Oil and gas is a fascinating, high-tech industry which has impacts on all our lives to a greater or lesser degree. I'm very pleased to see Aberdeen now has a museum which tells the story of oil and gas and will allow visitors a 'hands on' experience of an offshore life which, to many, would seem remote and difficult to imagine or understand' (http://www.aberdeencity.gov.uk/CouncilNews/ci_cns/pr_maritimeupgrade_270313.asp).

12 For further details of relations amongst space, oil and capital, see Labban (2008).

13 Perhaps surprisingly, Wolff does not mention Ranciere in her discussion of the 'turn to immediacy'.

## REFERENCES

Adorno, T.W. (1999 [1972]) *Aesthetic Theory*, trans. R. Hullot-Kentor. London: Continuum.

Alexander, V.D. (1996) 'Pictures at an Exhibition: Conflicting Pressures in Museums and the Display of Art', *American Journal of Sociology*, 101(4): 797–839.

Alexander, V.D. (1999) 'A Delicate Balance: Museums and the Market-place', *Museum International*, 51(2): 29–34.

Alpers, S. et al. (1996) 'Visual Culture Questionnaire', *October*, 77: 25–70.

Azoulay, A. (2008) *The Civil Contract of Photography*. Cambridge, MA: MIT Press.

Bal, M. (2003) 'Visual Essentialism and the Object of Visual Culture', *Journal of Visual Culture*, 2: 5–32.

Beale, J. (2006) 'Oil and Water: Offshore Architecture', in R. Kronenburg and F. Klassen (eds), *Transportable Environments 3*. London: Taylor and Francis. pp. 30–9.

Beller, J. (2006) *The Cinematic Mode of Production*. Dartmouth: Dartmouth College Press.

Belting, H. (2011 [2001]) *An Anthropology of Images: Picture, Medium, Body*, trans. T. Dunlap. Princeton, NJ: Princeton University Press.

Benjamin, W. (1979 [1916]) 'On Language as Such and on the Language of Man', in *One-Way Street, and Other Writings*, trans. E. Jephcott. London: NLB. pp. 107–23.

Benjamin, W. (1991 [1935]) 'Probleme der Sprachsoziologie', in H. Tiedemann-Bartels (ed.), *Walter Benjamin. Gesammelte Schriften*, Vol. III. Frankfurt a.M.: Suhrkamp. pp. 452–79.

Bennett, T. (1988) 'The Exhibitionary Complex', *New Formations*, 4: 73–102.

Berger, J. (1972) *Ways of Seeing*. London: Penguin.

Bourdieu, P. (1991) 'Towards a Sociology of Photography', *Visual Anthropology Review*, 7(1): 129–33.

Bourdieu, P. and Haacke, H. (1995) *Free Exchange*. Redwood, CA: Stanford University Press.

Boyer, D. and Szeman, I. (2014) 'The Rise of the Energy Humanities', *University Affairs*, 12 February. Available at: http://www.universityaffairs.ca/opinion/in-my-opinion/the-rise-of-energy-humanities/ (accessed 20 April 2015).

Bozak, N. (2011) *The Cinematic Footprint*. New Brunswick, NJ: Rutgers University Press.

Burfoot, A. (ed.) (2015) *Visual Culture and Gender*. London: Routledge.

Burtynsky, E. (2009) *Oil*. Göttingen: Steidl.

Callon, M. (1986) 'Some Elements of a Sociology of Translation: Domestication of the Scallops and the Fishermen of St Brieuc Bay', in J. Law (ed), *Power, Action and Belief: A New Sociology of Knowledge?*. London, New York: Routledge, 196–233.

Callon, M., Law, J., & Rip, A. (eds.). (1986) *Mapping the Dynamics of Science and Technology*. London: Macmillan.

Crary, J. (1990) *Techniques of the Observer*. Cambridge, MA: MIT Press.

Crary, J. (2001) *Suspensions of Perception*. Cambridge, MA: MIT Press.

Davis, W. (2011) *A General Theory of Visual Culture*. Princeton, NJ: Princeton University Press.

de la Fuente, E. (2007) 'The "New Sociology of Art": Putting Art Back into Social Science Approaches to the Arts', *Cultural Sociology*, 1: 409–25.

Edwards, E. (2001) *Raw Histories: Anthropology, Photography and Museums*. Oxford: Berg.

Edwards, E. and Mead, M. (2013) 'Absent Histories and Absent Images: Photographs, Images and the Colonial Past', *Museum Studies*, 11(1): 19–37.

Elkins, J. (2002) 'Preface to the Book A Skeptical Introduction to Visual Culture', *Journal of Visual Culture*, 1: 93–9.

Evans, J. and Hall, S. (eds) (1999) *Visual Culture: The Reader*. London: Sage.

Evans, M. (2015) *Artwash: Big Oil and the Arts*. London: Pluto.

Fyfe, G. (2006) 'Sociology and the Social Aspects of Museums', in S. MacDonald (ed.), *A Companion to Museum Studies*. Oxford: Blackwell.

Geary, C. and Webb, V-L. (eds) (1998) *Delivering Views: Distant Cultures in Early Postcards*. Washington DC: Smithsonian Institution Scholarly Press.

Gumbrecht, H.U. (2003) *Production of Presence: What Meaning Cannot Convey*. Redwood, CA: Stanford University Press.

Haraway, D. (1997) 'The Persistence of Vision', in K. Conboy, N. Medina and S. Stanbury (eds), *Writing on the Body: Female Embodiment and Feminist Theory*. New York: Columbia University Press. pp. 283–95.

Harvey, D. (2001) *Spaces of Capital: Towards a Critical Geography*. Edinburgh: Edinburgh University Press.

Highmore, B. (2007) 'Foreword', in M. Abadie and S. Beale (eds), *Nothing to Write Home About*. The Friday Project Limited. Available at: http://www.johnhindecollection.com/contact_benhighmore.html (accessed 1 January 2015).

Hooper-Greenhill, E. (2000) *Museums and the Interpretation of Visual Culture*. London: Routledge.

Inglis, D. (2007) 'The Warring Twins: Sociology, Cultural Studies, Alterity and Sameness', *History of the Human Sciences*, 20: 99–122.

Jay, M. (1994) *Downcast Eyes: The Denigration of Vision in French Thought*. Berkeley: University of California Press.

Jay, M. (2002) 'Cultural Relativism and the Visual Turn', *Journal of Visual Culture*, 1: 267–78.

Jay, M. and Ramaswamy, S. (eds) (2014) *Empires of Vision: A Reader*. Durham, NC: Duke University Press.

Jolivette, C. (ed.) (2014) *British Art in the Nuclear Age*. Farnham: Ashgate.

Jones, M. and Godwin, F. (1976) *The Oil Rush*. London: Quartet Books.

Kemp, A. (2011) *Official History of North Sea Oil and Gas*. London: Routledge.

Kirshenblatt-Gimblett, B. (1998) *Destination Culture: Tourism, Museums and Heritage*. Berkeley: University of California Press.

Krauss, R. (1979) 'Sculpture in the Expanded Field', *October*, 8: 30–44.

Krom, J. and Bakewell, S.B. (2009) *A History of Visual Culture: Western Civilization from the 18th to the 21st Century*. London: Berg.

Kromm, J. and Bakewell, S. (eds) (2010) *A History of Visual Culture: Western Civilization from the 18th to the 21st Century*. New York: Bloomsbury Academic.

Labban, M. (2008) *Space, Oil and Capital*. London: Routledge.

Lacan, J. (1978 [1964]) 'The Split between the Eye and the Gaze', in *The Four Fundamental Concepts of Psychoanalysis*, trans. A. Sheridan. New York: Norton. pp. 67–78.

Latour, B. (1986) 'Visualisation and Cognition: Drawing Things Together', in H. Kuklick (ed.), *Knowledge and Society: Studies in the Sociology of Culture Past and Present*. London: Jai Press. pp. 1–40.

Latour, B. (1993) *We Have Never Been Modern*, trans. C. Porter. Cambridge, MA: Harvard University Press.

Latour, B. (1999) *Pandora's Hope: Essays on the Reality of Science Studies*. Cambridge: Harvard University Press.

Latour, B. (2005) *Reassembling the Social: An Introduction to Actor-Network Theory*. Oxford: OUP.

Latour, B. and Weibel, P. (eds) (2005) *Making Things Public: Atmospheres of Democracy*. Cambridge, MA: MIT Press.

LeMenager, S. (2014) *Living Oil*. Oxford: Oxford University Press.

MacDonald, S. (2008) 'Museum Europe: Negotiating Heritage', *Anthropological Journal of European Cultures*, 17: 47–65.

Mackie, B. (2004) *The Oilmen: The North Sea Tigers*. Edinburgh: Birlinn.

Marontate, J. (2005) 'Museums and the Constitution of Culture', in M. Jacobs and N.W. Hanrahan (eds), *The Blackwell Companion to the Sociology of Culture*. Oxford: Blackwell. pp. 286–301.

Marx, K. (2002 [1848]) *The Communist Manifesto*. London: Penguin.

McGinty, S. (2009) *Fire in the Night: The Piper Alpha Disaster*. London: Pan.

McKinnon, A. (2007) 'For an "Energetic" Sociology, or Why Coal, Gas and Electricity Should Matter for Sociological Theory', *Critical Sociology*, 33: 345–56.

Merleau-Ponty, M. (1962 [1945]) *Phenomenology of Perception*, trans. C. Smith. New York: Humanities Press.

Mirzoeff, N. (ed.) (1998) *The Visual Culture Reader*. London: Routledge.

Mirzoeff, N. (1999) *An Introduction to Visual Culture*. London: Routledge.

Mirzoeff, N. (2011) *The Right to Look: A Counter-History of Visuality*. Durham, NC: Duke University Press.

Mitchell, W.J.T. (1995) *Picture Theory*. Chicago: University of Chicago Press.

Mitchell, W.J.T. (2002a) 'Showing Seeing: a Critique of Visual Culture', *Journal of Visual Culture*, 1: 165–81.

Mitchell, W.J.T. (2002b) 'That Visual Turn', *Journal of Visual Culture*, 1: 87–92.

Nye, D. (1996) *The American Technological Sublime*. Cambridge, MA: MIT Press.

O'Brian, J. (ed.) (2015) *Camera Atomica*. London: Black Dog Publishing.

O'Byrne (2011) 'Remembering the Piper Alpha Disaster', *Historical Reflections* 37/2: 90–104.

Page, B. (2007) *A Boy's Own Offshore Adventure*. Friockheim: PlashMill Press.

Page, B. (2009) *A Boy's Own Oily Adventure*. Friockheim: PlashMill Press.

Porter, G. (1989) 'The Economy of Truth: Photography in the Museum', *Ten-8*, 34: 20–33.

Preziosi, D. (2006) 'Art History and Museology: Rendering the Visible Legible', in S. Macdonald (ed.), *A Companion to Museum Studies*. Malden, MA: Wiley-Blackwell. pp. 50–63

Prochaska, C. and Mendelson, J. (eds) (2010) *Postcards: Ephemeral Histories of Modernity*. University Park: Penn State University Press.

Ranciere, J. (2003) *The Philosopher and his Poor*, trans. J. Drury, C. Oster and A. Parker, ed. A. Parker. Durham and London: Duke University Press.

Ranciere, J. (2007) *The Future of the Image*, trans. G. Elliot. London: Verso.

Rectanus, M. (2002) *Culture Incorporated: Museums, Artists and Corporate Sponsorships*. Minneapolis: University of Minnesota Press.

Rogan, B. (2005) 'An Entangled Object: The Picture Postcard as Souvenir and Collectible, Exchange and Ritual Communication', *Cultural Analysis*, 4: 1–27.

Rubio, F.D. and Silva, E.B. (2013) 'Materials in the Field: Object-trajectories and Object-positions in the Field of Contemporary Art', *Cultural Sociology*, 7(2): 161–78.

Rudwick, M. (1976) 'The Emergence of a Visual Language for Geological Science, 1760–1940', *History of Science*, 14: 148–95.

Ryan. J. (2013) *Photography and Exploration*. London: Reaktion.

Sartre, J.P. (2012 [1943]) *Being and Nothingness*. New York: Open Road Media.

Sassen, S. (2006) *Territory, Authority, Rights: From Medieval to Global Assemblages*. Princeton: Princeton University Press.

Sassen, S. (2008) 'Narrating Unsettlement', *Ctrl+P Journal of Contemporary Art*, 11: 10–12.

Scholette, G. (2010) *Dark Matter: Art and Politics in the Age of Enterprise Culture*. London: Pluto.

Scholle, P. (2005) 'The Changing Image of the Oil Industry as Reflected in Postcards of the 19th and 20th Centuries', in Aston, K.C, John, P. J. and Woodfork, L. (eds), *Abstracts of International Symposium on Oil Industry History*. Available at: http://archives.datapages.com/data/phi/v6_2005/scholle.html (accessed 17 March 2015).

Schor, N. (1992) '"Cartes Postales": Representing Paris 1900', *Critical Inquiry*, 18(2): 188–244.

Schwarz, V. and Pryzbilski, J. (eds) (2004) *The Nineteenth-Century Visual Culture Reader*. New York: Routledge.

Shohat, E. and Stam, R. (1994) *Unthinking Eurocentrism: Multiculturalism and the Media*. London: Routledge.

Simmel, G. (1997 [1896]) 'The Berlin Trade Exhibition', in D. Frisby and M. Featherstone (eds), *Simmel on Culture*. London: Sage. pp. 255–8.

Simmel, G. (1997 [1903]) 'The Metropolis and Mental Life', in D. Frisby and M. Featherstone (eds), *Simmel on Culture*. London: Sage. pp. 174–86.

Simmel, G. (2005 [1916]) *Rembrandt: An Essay in the Philosophy of Art*, trans. A. Scott and H. Staubmann. London: Routledge.

Simpson, M. (2012) 'Postcard Culture in America: The Traffic in Traffic', in C. Bold (ed.), *US Popular Print Culture, 1860–1920*. Oxford and New York: Oxford University Press. pp. 169–89.

Star, S.L. and Griesemer, J. (1989) 'Institutional Ecology, "Translations" and Boundary Objects: Amateurs and Professionals in Berkeley's Museum of Vertebrate Zoology, 1907–39', *Social Studies of Science*, 19(3): 387–420.

Starkey, K. (2005) *Visual Culture and the German Middle Ages*. Basingstoke: Palgrave Macmillan.

Stewart, J. (2005) 'Reconstructing the Centre: Sociological Approaches to the Rebuilding of Berlin', in D. Inglis and J. Hughson (eds), *The Sociology of Art: Ways of Seeing*. Basingstoke: Palgrave Macmillan. pp. 183–95.

Stewart, J. (2013) 'Making Globalization Visible? The Oil Assemblage, the Work of Sociology and the Work of Art', *Cultural Sociology*, 7: 368–84.

Stewart, J. (2014) 'Sociology, Culture and Energy: The Case of Wilhelm Ostwald's "Sociological Energetics" – A Translation and Exposition of a Classic Text', *Cultural Sociology*, 8: 333–50.

Sturken, M. and Cartwright. L. (2009) *Practices of Looking: An Introduction to Visual Culture*, 2nd edn. Oxford: Oxford University Press.

Szeman, I. (2007) 'System Failure: Oil, Futurity and the Anticipation of Disaster', *South Atlantic Quarterly*, 106(4): 805–23.

Tagg, J. (2009) *The Disciplinary Frame: Photographic Truths and the Capture of Meaning*. Minneapolis: University of Minnesota Press.

Tanner, J. (2010) 'Karl Mannheim and Alois Riegl: From Art History to the Sociology of Culture', in D. Arnold (ed.), *Art History: Contemporary Perspectives on Method*, Oxford: Wiley Blackwell. pp. 99–128.

Taylor, S.J. (2005) *Oilwork: North Sea Diaries*. Edinburgh: Birlinn.

Tyfield, D. and Urry, J. (eds) (2014) *Special Issue: Energy & Society. Theory, Culture and Society* 31/5.

Urry, J. (2013) *Societies Beyond Oil: Oil Dregs and Social Futures*. London: Zed Books.

Veder, R. (2015) *The Living Line: Modern Art and the Economy of Energy*. Dartmouth: Dartmouth College Press.

Walker, J. and Chaplin, S. (1997) *Visual Culture: An Introduction*. Manchester: Manchester University Press.

Wiesing, L. (2014 [2005]) *Artificial Presence: Philosophical Studies in Image Theory*, trans. N.F. Shott, Redwood, CA: Stanford University Press.

Wolff, J. (1983) *Aesthetics and the Sociology of Art*. London: George Allen and Unwin.

Wolff, J. (1999) 'Cultural Studies and the Sociology of Culture', *In[]Visible Culture*, 1. Available at: https://www.rochester.edu/in_visible_culture/issue1/wolff/wolff.html (accessed 20 April 2015).

Wolff, J. (2010) 'In Defence of Sociology: Aesthetics in the Age of Uncertainty', in O. Dadejik and J. Stejskal (eds), *The Aesthetic Dimension of Visual Culture*. Newcastle: Cambridge Scholars Publishing. pp. 2–16.

Wolff, J. (2012) 'After Cultural Theory: The Power of Images, the Lure of Immediacy', *Journal of Visual Culture*, 11(1): 3–19.

Wolin, R. (1994) *Walter Benjamin: An Aesthetic of Redemption*. Berkeley: University of California Press.

Woolfson, C., Foster, J. and Beck, M. (2013) *Paying for the Piper: Capital and Labour in Britain's Offshore Oil Industry*. Oxford: Routledge.

# Queering Gender, Art and Culture in the Age of Media Convergence

Mary Kosut

The veneration of 'Art' and 'Culture' – besides leading many women into boring, passive, activity that distracts from more important and rewarding activities, from cultivating active abilities – leads to the constant intrusion on our own sensibilities of pompous dissertations on the deep beauty of this and that turn. (Solanas, 2004: 59)

## INTRODUCTION

In the mid-1980s, the feminist performance art collective Guerilla Girls asked a rhetorical question that still continues to reverberate 'Do women have to be naked to get into the Metropolitan Museum of Art?' The question illuminated the fact that venerated arts institutions are stocked with paintings and sculptures depicting nude women, disproportionately painted by 'great male artists' (Nochlin, 1972). At the time, less than 5% of artists in the modern art section were women, but 85% of the nude art objects were representations of women. Calling attention to the chokehold that patriarchy has on cultural arts institutions, the Guerilla Girls made stickers, posters, books and billboards in addition to their in situ performance interventions at key exhibition openings wearing guerilla masks. The material objects and ephemera amassed over the last three decades are now recognized as art and exhibited in museums and galleries internationally. The Guerilla Girls have achieved representation in art worlds through critical, radical (dis)engagement with dominant modes of representation and discourse. In a sea of 'inoffensive tchotchkes for billionaires' this kind of art work does not blend in seamlessly with the institutional furniture.[1] But it is now part of the permanent collection.

Thirty years later, not much has changed with regards to the gender representation gap in Western art worlds. In the fall of 2013, artist, writer and feminist activist Micol Hebron launched the Gallery Tally project – an international, collaborative, crowd-sourced endeavour to tally and visualize statistical data pertaining to the numbers of male and female artists who were represented by top contemporary art galleries.[2] Hebron culled statistics showing how grossly underrepresented women are in the arts and then placed an open call for artists to design posters that visually and aesthetically communicated the imbalance. The first posters focused on galleries in Los Angeles, but the project has become an international one including artists and galleries in New York, Berlin, London, Paris and other cities. The project reflects cultural critique and reproduction in the digital age as a multimedia and multinational hybrid. In raising a simple question about male/female ratios, other inequities in art world representation fall like dominos. What about queer or trans artists? Or artists of color? ... and so on and so forth.

This chapter begins with a discussion of the Guerilla Girls and the Gallery Tally Project – two cultural locales more towards the far reaches of the sociological fringes than anywhere near the disciplinary centre – because they are examples of the impact of oppositional meaning-making within the confines of hegemonic cultural landscapes. Both projects morph and continue and mutate. They expand time and space (as in a fixed physical location), they engage with history but are of the moment, and future-oriented in their respective aims. They speak to how culture is fluid, permeable and rhizomatic. As I explore the relationship between gender and cultural sociology, or the sociology of culture, I purposefully begin outside of the academy before I make my way in.[3] I deploy micro subversive tactics at this textual site as a way to de-centre cultural knowledge and the production of knowledge, drawing from feminist standpoint epistemologies, especially the work of Nancy Hartsock (1983; 1997), Dorothy Smith (1987) and Sandra Harding (1991; 1995). The writing style is conversational, not really for anything, but against the stilted rhetoric often found in academic journals aimed at specialists. Standard protocol and procedure are not being followed.

As a cultural sociologist and a feminist, I seek to collaborate, or at least to converse, with works that rattle the discipline. I am interested in experimenting with new forms in a response to 'negative data', as described in this statement from the Gallery Tally Project call for artist participation that was posted on their Facebook page in 2013:

> A collaboration among artists results in the creation of a horizontal or rhizomatic labor structure, rather than a hierarchical (and patriarchal) one. We have engaged in a positive, creative response to this very negative data. The data has provided an opportunity to build a new community of concerned and engaged citizens in the art world, and to showcase each individual artist's creative voice within the group collaboration. It is a response and alternative to the hegemonic, hierarchical, patriarchal, heteronormative 'standard' that has unjustly dominated the art world for far too long.

With this in mind, I will locate where gender is and where it is not within sociological studies of culture, emphasizing the absence of women, and by extension other marginalized groups and identities, focusing on queer and transgender identities. I will explore where women and the 'women question' show up in cultural sociology, cultural studies and gender studies. My focus is on visual cultures and media forms – from Fine Art (high culture) to the realm of popular culture, keeping in mind that the distinction between the two has been eroded for quite some time (see Zolberg, Peterson, DiMaggio amongst others). After a tour of the 'big house' (museums and culture industries, also known as old media forms and institutions), I end with a discussion of feminist zines, self-published, inexpensive do-it-yourself media. Zines, as both material artefacts and digital networking and distribution sites, echo and bounce across transnational networks of cultural production and consumption. With Zobl (2009) in mind, I assert that zines function as a heterogeneous, 'culturally productive, politicized counterpublic' (Nguyen, 2000) for feminist networking and critical reflection by young women in different parts of the world, and, as such, are a productive place to start updating how sociologists think about culture in a mediated, queer world. How do those constrained and marginalized by gender create meaning and new forms of culture in a dynamic media terrain?

## HISTORICAL AND CONTEMPORARY BACKGROUND: THE NATURE/CULTURE DIVIDE

To paraphrase sociologist Judith Lorber (1994), gender and culture share much in common. Both are created and revised through social interaction and fused in everyday routines, yet their social production is taken for granted, veiled. Gender and culture provide order and meaning and are dependent upon our constant participation in their making (Butler, 2000). Just as everyone is 'constantly doing gender', we are all engaging in the human production of culture (Lorber, 1994: 13). Even outside of academic discourse, it is commonly understood that human societies are gendered and cultured. And by extension, women have historically been linked to the natural realm as creative, nurturing and inherently (re)productive due to their physiological make-up ('mother earth'), and men to culture as scholars, scientists, and builders of civilization and cultural institutions. Nature and culture are powerful constructs, and their bifurcated gendering is linked to the devaluation of women in all societies (Ortner, 1974). Gender – the cultural inscription of distinctions between the sexes – profoundly defines human existence and has far-reaching implications for the course of our lives. Clearly, gender has shaped the larger discipline of sociology and the subfield of culture in immeasurable ways.

Women's participation in realms of institutionalized culture – science, art, academia, work, religion – or lack thereof, has been anchored by essentialist notions between genders with respect to social power, as in the truism that 'women's and men's bodies are just different'. These presumed biological variations are offered as evidence for why culture is organized in certain ways. Importantly, feminist scholars of the body have worked to reveal how these 'self-evident' differences are actually culturally produced (Grosz, 1994; Rich, 1976).

Just as the Western art world is a history of great male painters, great male thinkers – Weber, Durkheim, White, Parsons, Bourdieu, Foucault – dominate the field of cultural sociology. There is a historical absence of women in the discipline as architects of theory. It is only in the last fifty years or so that gender has been welcomed into sociology as a legitimate subfield (currently the American Sociological Association (ASA) has a section called Sex and Gender). Gender roles and the standpoint of women were critically investigated as subjects of cultural significance beginning with sociologist Alice Rossi's work on the status of women and work, familial structures and sexuality (1983). One of her most influential feminist articles, 'Equality Between the Sexes: An Immodest Proposal', was first presented in 1963 at a meeting of the American Academy of Arts and Sciences. Rossi and others were instrumental in establishing the ASA section 'Sex Roles' in 1972. Rossi's scholarship also helped to build the foundations of the early feminist movement. In Europe and the United States, political protest and the civil rights movements of the 1960s propelled what is commonly referred to as second wave feminism.

Importantly, the second wave feminist movement encompasses both liberal and radical feminisms, both with differing foci as to the cause of women's oppression and the abolition of it. Radical feminists broke away from liberal feminist ideology, advocating systemic change rather than an inclusion of women in economic, political and cultural arenas. Alternative sexualities, ethnic diversity and the inclusion of experiential knowledge were a few of the many issues radical feminists called attention to as a breach from middle-class, white and more privileged discourses, as exemplified in Betty Friedan's (1963) *The Feminine Mystique*, a liberal feminist classic. Regardless of the theoretical, substantive and methodological distinctions that fracture the second wave, gender studies, as a legitimate area of study within the academy began to solidify, as did the sociology of gender as a subfield.

Within the academy, the emergence of feminism and development of feminist theory in the 1970s problematized sex, sexuality and gender, assiduously questioning the conservative and functionalist views of female embodiment advanced by Parsons and many others. Much of the strongest work in this area aims to focus on how the socialization process transforms the biologically defined categories of male and female into the cultural designations masculine and feminine, directly leading to the subjugation of women in various spheres (de Beauvoir, 1972; Smith, 1987). Sociobiology developed simultaneously with the rise of the women's movement, particularly radical feminism.

E.O. Wilson maintained that women's social subordination was natural because 'women as a group were less assertive and physical aggressive' due to their genetic makeup (Wilson, 1978: 128). Sociobiology quickly became a useful way to undermine the increase in feminist discourse and the call for gender equality in both lay and academic communities. Notwithstanding, social theorists studying culture have attributed female inequality to biology, as in the case of Parson's AGIL system that posits women (expressive role) as different than men (instrumental role) due to their childbearing capacity. For Parsons, woman is an inherently natural creature (best suited for reproductive work), while man, the more cultured being, belongs in the public sphere (the world of production). Parsons maintains that female discrimination in the workplace is functional to society because occupational equality is 'incompatible with any positive solidarity in the family' (Parsons, 1940: 852). For Wilson and Parsons, women's oppression is conveniently answered in one word – biology. Again, they cement the essentialist concept that women are less suited for participation in public cultural spheres as the makers of great art and great sociological theory, in addition to other prestigious occupational identities.

In the past few decades, theoretical and everyday notions of gender and sexuality have undergone dramatic changes, influenced by transformations in both the organization of society, and technological and medical advancements. The field of gender studies has expanded beyond women's studies to include men and masculinity studies, beginning with sociologist R.W. Connell's influential *Masculinities* (1995). Emerging in the 1990s, men and masculinity studies confronts the notion of a hegemonic singular masculinity, and asks key questions such as 'do all men have or want cultural power?' (see Kimmel, 1987; 2005; 2008; 2010; Messner, 1992; 1997).

Most recently, the interdisciplinary field of queer studies which gelled in the early 2000s, has been radically questions gender studies scholarship for a sometimes naive, heterosexist and dualistic approach to sexuality and gender identities. Purposefully playing with the word queer as a synonym for odd and peculiar, as well as the use of queer as a pejorative homophobic slur, queer studies focuses on (LGBTI) issues (lesbian, gay, bisexual, trans and intersexed) as well as on the social production and regulation of sexualities and genders. In the words of Lee Edelman, 'queerness can never define an identity; it can only ever disturb one' (2004: 17). Queer studies is especially driven by intersectional, social-constructionist, and transnational understandings of gender, sexuality, social norms and power (see Berlant and Warner, 1995; Edelman, 2006; de Lauretis, 1991; Halberstam, 2003; Halperin, 1990; Huffer, 2010; Muñoz, 1997; 1999; 2009; Sedgwick, 1985; 1990; 1993; and others). Finally, transgender studies is another emergent field in conversation with both LGBTI research and queer studies. The academic journal *Transgender Studies Quarterly* was launched in May 2014, anchoring the field.

It is apparent that our knowledge and conceptualization of gender has gotten more complex and critical, especially in the last twenty years. As gay, gender queer and trans people are visible in mass media, new medical technologies allow for more complicated forms of embodiment, and gay marriage is politicized and legalized, lived experiences of gender and sexuality are also transforming. Scholars are beginning to listen for the odd sounds and dissonant noises that are necessary in order to break the rhythms of customary conversation. Queer studies, in particular, is an antidote to outmoded dualisms like male/female, gay/straight, human/animal and nature/culture. It is the messy bleed between these binaries that is the most fertile space in which to explore how gender is learned, negotiated, performed and transgressed in a range of cultural contexts. Cultural sociologists can benefit from assiduously, creatively, playfully queering their approach to the study of gender and culture.

## BECOMING CULTURED: LOCATING GENDER IN FINE ART AND POPULAR MEDIA

Contemporary cultural sociologists have given consideration to how powerful institutions shape meanings and constrain access and participation across cultural fields. Social stratification, in particular class and status, rather than an explicit focus on gender has driven much analysis (Bourdieu, 1984; Willis, 1977). With respect to art, cultural sociologists have historically begun with the premise that a network of cultural specialists and institutional organizations shape the nature and development of art (Peterson, 1997; Zolberg, 1990), or looked at art-making from an occupational perspective and as a collective activity (Becker, 1982). Moving away from humanistic art talk – form, content, style – sociologists have conceptually removed art objects from hallowed venues and relocated them within a world of actors, markets and publics, in order to understand the social processes that transform cultural products and their meanings (Inglis and Hughson, 2005; Zolberg, 1990). This perspective, which is often characterized as the production of culture approach, is an important subfield that emphasizes how procedures, rules, gatekeepers and dominant status groups influence the institutionalization of what is referred to as art or high culture through the formation of various fields and forms of symbolic capital (Becker, 1982; Bauman, 2001; DiMaggio, 1982; Ferguson, 1998; 2004; Levine, 1988; Peterson, 1997).

With respect to how gender intersects institutional art cultures, sociologists have not had as much to say. Not surprisingly, gender analysis has emphasized the work and culture of women within the confines of the family and private sphere of the home, and how family as a cultural institution constrains public life (Glenn et al., 1994; Hochschild, 1989). As men made history, most women (save for a few rare exceptions such as Gertrude Stein, Charlotte Brontë, Rosa Bonheur, Hannah Arendt, etc.) were making beds, or, if affluent, taking up so-called feminine hobbies such as needlepoint, quilt-making and other crafts that could easily be executed within the home without formal educational training. Women were not admitted into art academies in the United States until the early 20th century. Men dominated art worlds, especially the mediums of painting and sculpture, and the art studio was a rarefied masculine sphere where women primarily gained entry as models, wives or lovers.

One of the most important institutional critiques of the effect of patriarchy on art worlds is feminist art historian Linda Nochlin's 'Why Have There Been No Great Women Artists?', originally published in 1972. This seminal essay opened the gates for feminist art history by employing a sociological analysis in answering the question. Nochlin argued that it was not due to biology – that women painted in a feminine style, or women were inherently incapable of artistic genius – but in the structural and cultural constraints in place at any given historical period. Women were not nurtured or socialized to become painters (they were steered towards domestic hobbies), and when they were admitted to academies they did not have access to nude models, either male or female, which limited their technical training, as historically painting and drawing were taught in a strict linear fashion. Nochlin (1972) points out that the few women who did achieve artistic greatness to become included into the Western art historical canon all had ties to influential male artists. For example, Frida Kahlo was married to Diego Rivera, Marie Cassatt was friends with Edgar Degas, and Georgia O'Keefe was married to Lee Friedlander. One of the strengths of this piece is that it offered an institutional and historical analysis, but at the same time also focused on the content of the art objects themselves. Recent sociological studies of the arts champion the need to push the field further and towards a multi-disciplinary lens (Becker, 2006; de la Fuente, 2007; Inglis and Hughson, 2005). A 'new sociology of the arts' has emerged that is in dialogue with art history and cultural studies projects that see art as a social construct and acknowledge the socio-cultural character of its production and consumption (de la Fuente, 2007). With this in mind, Nochlin's work should serve as classic example in the development of a new sociology of the arts.

While gender-driven studies of institutionalized Fine Art worlds have mainly come from the field of feminist art history, sociologists and culture studies and media studies scholars have assiduously explored popular cultural forms, especially advertising, television, film, print media and digital culture. Poststructuralist and postmodern feminist theorists argue that woman, or man, as a category does not exist outside the symbolic communication that produces it. Images and narratives, especially mediated ones, play a significant role in constructing gendered meanings, sexualities and embodied lived experiences. The social constructionist view of gender as fertilized, performed and represented in cultural contexts is in direct opposition to biologically based gendered analysis that tether gender to science. Rather than chromosomes, researchers examine visual culture and media platforms to explore how dominant and oppositional gender representations and 'ways of seeing' circulate (Berger, 1974).

To paraphrase cultural critic and artist John Berger, even a cursory look at the Western art historical canon and contemporary advertising reveals how men are often portrayed as actors while women appear (as docile objects) (1974). In *Ways of Seeing* Berger's Marxist and semiotic analysis centres on media, from oil paintings to advertisements, to illustrate how women are objectified, shamed, displayed and judged. For Berger, the nude female body is reduced to an aesthetic convention, the classic supine figure that has dominated art history from the Renaissance to today. Berger emphasizes certain types of gazes in his analysis, the gaze of the spectator, the gaze of the owner of the object, and the awareness that women have of being watched (and by extension, the self-objectifying gaze). *Ways of Seeing* has been influential in media studies, but is more stylistic than substantive.

A more nuanced theory of the male gaze was developed by feminist film theorist Laura Mulvey in the influential essay 'Visual Pleasure and Narrative Cinema' (1975). Drawing from conventional Hollywood films of the 1950s, Mulvey describes cinematic viewership and how subject positions are constructed. Mulvey's study draws from Freudian and Lacanian psychoanalysis, especially the Freudian concept of scopophilia and the pleasure involved in looking, asserting that women on the screen are objectified and stereotyped in three different ways. First, because most film directors are male, the camera represents a voyeuristic framing of the position of women on the screen. Secondly, the gaze exists within the dynamics of relationships within the narrative of the film itself, as the male protagonist is usually active as distinct from the female object of his gaze. The third gaze is that of the viewer, who is assumed to be male within the context of a patriarchy. Like Berger, Mulvey has garnered criticism for being essentialist and using the binary frames of masculinity and femininity as evidenced in stereotypical traits, as well as for a lack of empirical evidence or methodological framework to support her assertions. Nonetheless, these works remain in circulation as essential film and media texts, and the concept of a male gaze is part of gender and cultural studies vocabulary.

Goffman's *Gender Advertisements* (1979) was the first sociological study to use found images – advertisements from magazines – as a basis to explore the cultural construction of masculinity and femininity. *Gender Advertisements* was ground-breaking as an early example of visual sociology, a relatively new subfield within the discipline that solidified at the end of the 20th century. It is arguably one of the most systematic and detailed analyses of gender representation in mass media to date. Rather than text, Goffman concentrated on the positioning of bodies (hands, knees, eyes) and their juxtaposition to other bodies and things. What he found is that there are clear visual norms that regulate how a male or female body should be displayed, and these gendered codes are so taken for granted that they appear natural. We should see them as odd, but they are normalized as part of other gender cues that we absorb. Unsurprisingly, Goffman concluded that advertisements usually depict women as mothers, as children themselves, as smaller in size than men, or as sexual objects. Femininity was also communicated in ritualized subordination (flirtatiousness), distraction, or through self-touching or in the caressing and stroking of objects. Goffman's methodology establishes this work as a standard in visual social analyses and in the subfield of visual sociology.

*Gender Advertisements* has had an enormous impact on media studies and gender studies scholarship, and in documentaries produced by the Media Education Foundation such as Jean Killborne's *Killing Us Softly 4* (2010) and Sut Jhally's *Dreamworlds* (1991) that describe how gender binaries are reproduced in media texts, negatively effecting the bodies and subjectivities of men and women. Susan Bordo's *Unbearable Weight* (1997) employs a visual social analysis of media in this same tradition. An idealized female body, one that is unattainably thin, beautiful and typically white, has become a normative standard by which women judge themselves and in turn are evaluated by others. Bordo makes an explicit connection between low self-esteem, distorted body image, and eating disorders such as anorexia and bulimia, and media representations that reify an unreachable standard of what constitutes an attractive feminine body. According to Bordo, gendered embodiment materializes in 'complex crystallizations of culture' (1997: 35).

Media effects are hard to tease out empirically, and there is debate over to what extent media influences the ideological construction of gender and hegemonic understandings of masculinity, femininity, heterosexuality and homosexuality. Media consumption studies examine the process of how audiences interpret texts, attempting to assess the degree to which individuals critically and reflexively engage with media. Reception theories assert that all consumers are not simply passive vessels when it comes to encountering media content. For example, Janice Radway's (1984) study of women's interpretation of romance novels that typically perpetuate traditional gender roles vis-à-vis plotlines based on heteronormative readings of romance, marriage and sexuality, suggests alternative meaning-making. Radway states that readers of such novels re-interpreted the narratives, viewing female characters as empowered and independent. Studies in this vein reject a naive injection model approach to media consumption as unidirectional. Notwithstanding, even if individuals reflexively revise and reinterpret media content, these alternative readings do not challenge dominant social structures and cultural institutions that reproduce media that is gender-biased, heteronormative and racist.

Mass communication research has expanded our understandings of how media forms play a role in perpetuating not only gender inequalities, but those based on race, class and sexuality. Cultural studies scholars, such as bell hooks (1992), underscore the powerful dynamic of intersectionality and how sexism, racism and heterocentrism pulse through a variety of popular media, especially advertisements, film and rap music. Birmingham School founder Stuart Hall's encoding/decoding model of communication targets how media perpetuates dominant ideologies and how audiences engage in semiotic interpretations of content. Hall's theory of reception focuses on how the viewer (or decoder) can engage in one of three positions – dominant-hegemonic (agree), negotiated (neutral) and oppositional (rejection) while interpreting media signs and messages. Hall's (1977) work on black representation in media has been influential in the field of media studies, much in the same way as Bordo's (2004) *Unbearable Weight* took everyday media seriously as a conduit of cultural meanings. Notwithstanding, reception studies have been criticized for an absence of methodological rigour.

Work on gender in art and popular media in the fields of sociology, gender studies and cultural studies has focused on the lack of women's participation in making culture, or on how men and women are represented in stereotypical ways that are often essentialist and heteronormative. What is missing here is how women and other marginalized people construct meanings and make media as agentic participants in cultural production. In the following section, I explore how alternative media forms, particularly zines, have been produced by girls, young women and those who identify as gender queer as an antidote to mainstream hegemonic media narratives and images. Rather than being made by media, grrrls have responded by making their own.

## GRRRLS MAKING MEANING: ZINES AND DIGITAL NETWORKS

Thus far, the discussion has centred on gender and pre-digital media forms – print, television, film, paintings, photography – that emerged prior to the development of the internet and the omnipresence of digital culture. Importantly, we must be careful to avoid naive binary distinctions between so-called new media (Web 2.0 and beyond) and forms before it. At this stage, media convergence is part of the fabric of cultural production, communication and social networking. The merging of video, audio and text into one platform is technologically significant, but from a cultural perspective media convergence has facilitated more active participation in individual cultural production than at any time in history. Media convergence complicates previous reception studies and presents quite a challenge in disentangling production and consumption. We are in an era where such categories are consistently blurred, as technological advancements are coupled with creative user adaptation to new media platforms.

While the term convergence was popularized in de Sola Pool's *Technologies of Freedom* (1983) and later in Negroponte's *Being Digital* (1995), the most influential work on media convergence and participatory culture is Henry Jenkins' *Convergence Culture* (2006). According to Jenkins, convergence allows us to participate in cultural production via user-generated content in blogging platforms like Tumblr, video file-sharing sites like YouTube, and popular photo-based platforms such as Flickr and Instagram. User-generated content can presumably allow for multiple perspectives and meanings and the remixing of mass media narrative and images. Audiences also participate in cultural production through commentary, cross-platform linking, and creating multi-media responses to current events in real time. For example, mobile media and social media, particularly Facebook and Twitter, are believed to have played a significant role in the Arab Spring and Global Occupy Movement, both in 2011. Levy (1997) argues that cultural convergence can lead to 'collective intelligence', in which audiences collaboratively produce information through social bookmarking (user-created organizational systems for online resources) and crowdsourcing.

Regardless of the potential for user-generated content, historic unprecedented media consolidation has resulted from media convergence. Multimedia conglomerates that own websites, televisual content, music, and so forth, charge a premium for accessing content. Additionally, Google and other search engines determine how users access content. Media convergence has extensive social, economic and political ramifications. Concerns over how to protect private information, an individual's digital footprint and surveillance have arisen. Gender studies scholars have found that the increasingly complex media-scape has had positive and negative effects on historically marginalized groups. Convergence has provided a forum for the perspectives of the previously silenced – girls, women and LGBTQI communities – to be articulated. For example, blogs centred on motherhood, gay parenting, and feminism have created a wealth of personal and political cultural content that is in direct resistance to hegemonic gender norms. However, feminists are concerned that there has been an increase in bullying in the form of slut shaming, objectification of women and sexist representations within a ubiquitous porn culture.

Within the convergence and flow of media forms and content, zines are a medium that straddle the material, digital, local and transnational. Traditionally, zines were defined as self-published magazines that circulated outside of mainstream media production and discourse. Zines came of age in the 1970s, within the context of new technology (photocopying machines) and punk music scenes (Duncombe, 1997; Zobl, 2009). Zines, similar to pamphlets, are folded sheets of paper in booklet form that are made to be cheap and easily reproducible, and were originally distributed by hand or through the post. A zine is a complicated medium to categorize because they can take different forms and cover a range of issues, from the banal (my cat) to indie music scenes, public health and transnational politics. Zines can be one issue only, or a series of issues that spans years. Zines can be different sizes, lengths and formats – both material and digital, or both. For these reasons zines are queer media *par excellence*. They escape and elude one cohesive definition; their identity is mutable.

The content and aesthetic of zines, like traditional mediums such as painting and sculpture, are shaped by both zine history and the maker's subjective hand. There are no formal rules or education; however, informal zine making 'how-to's' and instructional books have been published on- and offline. The process of zine construction has yet to be formally institutionalized, and that keeps the medium in reach of anyone who is interested. You do not need an MFA in zine-making to create one, or to distribute or exhibit one. Zines are a uniquely affordable, democratic and accessible medium.

Zobl (2009), frames zines in relationship to artistic movements like surrealism, Dadaism and situationism, and social and political movements such as anarchism and lesbian, queer, and transgender liberation. According to Zobl (2009), zine history has three historical periods in the United States: 1930s sci-fi fan zines; 1970s punk zines; and zines produced out of the riot grrrl movement in the 1990s. Riot grrrl was a third-wave feminist cultural movement that crystallized in punk music scenes in the US and England as a do-it-yourself critique against the misogyny in mainstream and alternative music. Young women formed bands (such as Bikini Kill, Heavens to Betsy, and others) that questioned heteronormativity, issues of violence against women, and the music industry itself. Zines became a large part of riot grrrl, and no doubt helped in promoting feminist musicians and feminist ideas to a new generation of mainly white college-educated women in their teens and early twenties. Although riot grrrl has been critiqued for its lack of attention to intersectionality, it did help to define and create an oppositional media history that questioned mainstream representation of women and their absence in the production of culture.

The age of zine producers, evidenced in the merging of the word girl and riot, is significant in studying the formation of zine cultures. Zine scenes are often populated by younger people – from teens to thirty-somethings. Young people, especially teenagers, are rarely considered as agentic and critical subjects and tend to be the subject of mass media effects. As a mode of personal expression and politic resistance, girls and adolescent gender queers are the *producers* of media and constructive community building and engagement. Zines are a form of subcultural entrepreneurship where alternative values, support and participation amongst young creators and readers is fertilized (Chidgey, 2009). Frequently, the potential harmful nature of media usage by younger populations (eating disorders, the media cocoon, social anxiety, etc.) overshadows any promise of criticality and creativity in media production/consumption (Guzzetti and Gamboa, 2011). In zines we find the opposite. Increasingly, youth are a key demographic in cultural production in an era of media convergence. Cultural sociologists working outside of youth studies should not count the kids out, as it were.

As riot grrrl was gaining momentum, the homocore (later queercore) movement had already come into being, due in large part to the zines it produced. The first official homocore zine was G.B. Jones and Bruce LaBruce's ground-breaking 'J.D.s' (juvenile delinquents) (1985) which created a radical experimental space for queer-identified artists to question the boundaries of sexuality and gender. Just like the term grrrl, homocore is a neologism based on mixing the terms homosexual and hardcore. Also influenced by punk subcultural activity, the homo/queercore scene was comprised of culturally disenfranchised queer, lesbian, bisexual and transgender punks. A key issue in queercore zines was the rejection of the more mainstream gay and lesbian community, which many saw as too conservative and built on heteronormative assimilation and values. Arguably, the most queer and complex critique came from Vaginal Crème Davis (or Vaginal Davis, Prof. Vaginal Davis), a self-described genderqueer, black, intersexed Chicana, multi-media artist and drag queen. In her zines, drag performances, and videos she calls out the assumed notion that queer always means white. Davis also plays with other stereotypes and slurs – embracing the foul, freak and useless. Muñoz (1999) refers to this as 'disidentification', a process wherein damaging stereotypes are recycled to create powerful and seductive sites of self-creation. Queercore zines by Davis and others were revolutionary because they welcomed tensions and ambiguities in identities.

By the mid-1990s, the Internet had given rise to engaged transnational networks and virtual international communities of queer and feminist zine-makers (Comstock, 2001; Harris, 2003; Schilt and Zobl, 2008). Although zines are mainly produced and distributed in North America, there are feminist zine-makers all over the word – in Israel, Argentina, Malaysia, Australia, Japan and many other countries.[4] The cultivation of zine networks has created a transnational dialogue around oppression, power, privilege and how patriarchy affects individuals within their local communities and beyond. Websites such as grrrlzines.net and grassrootsfeminism.net are transnational archives and digital communities that preserve and fertilize zine culture. Such databases are crucial in documenting the amount of zines and their diversity, but, just as important, they help solidify zines as a legitimate medium – one that cultural scholars, particularly cultural sociologists and gender theorists, should assiduously be studying as a site of media resistance, cultural production and consumption. On- and offline zine networks are an alternative public sphere where new meanings are made and oppositional meanings converge.

Like the Guerilla Girls work, part of zine history is being archived and institutionally assimilated. As of 2010, New York University has a zine archive in their library collection and Barnard College has a zine library, with 'zine librarians' that oversee it. Scholars have official archival material vetted by zine experts to study. Produced from within the feminist queer margins, zines are beginning to occupy insider/outsider status. To date, cultural sociologists have not given much attention to zines. As a complex and rather queer medium that defies and complicates boundaries – material/digital, local/transnational, personal/political – they are a rich site to conceptualize culture in the early 21st century. Vaginal Davis critiques the institutional award system that disproportionately favours the work of heterosexual, white, privileged men by nominating herself for the *Nobel Prize for Afro-American-Militant-Drag-Queen-Babylonian-Thrash-Gargantutues-Award-Winning-Blacktress* in literature. I hope sociologists acknowledge her perverted achievements and take them very seriously.

## CONCLUSION

Born out of the political zeitgeist that fuelled the radical cultural transformations of the 1970s, both feminist theory and gender studies are now an integral part of the academic curriculum and key areas of specialization within the field of sociology. Feminism has effectively challenged the roles, identities, functions and categories that have longed buttressed the supposed inherent divide between nature and culture; tethering all things female to the natural world and at the same time positioning men as architects of culture, and male identity as culturally dominant. Feminist sociology explores how the social construction of gender and sexuality relates to the production, consumption and institutionalization of cultural forms. The terms *human* and *history* have been rightfully problematized, as this language reflects the structural subjugation of women within all realms of cultural life – political, economic, scientific and aesthetic.

Cultural examinations focusing on the spheres of the Fine Arts and popular media forms – within sociology, gender studies and cultural studies – have primarily emphasized on how gender roles affect the ability to fully participate in all aspects of culture, or how media representations have promoted essentialist and heteronormative narratives and visual imagery. Much of the scholarship thus far has looked at culture and gender from a traditional binary perspective (high/low, male/female, production/reception). However, the recent emergence of the interdisciplinary field of queer studies (within the last decade) and the study of post-internet participatory media culture(s) offer new conceptual and empirical terrain to explore gender and sexuality. Radical feminist and queer media forms challenge us to reconsider the creation, distribution and reception of culture, and present opportunities to resist, and in some cases pervert, dominant narratives, policies and ways of seeing.

## NOTES

1 http://davidbyrne.com/i-dont-care-about-contemporary-art-anymore
2 According to the US Census, 50.15% of the population in Los Angeles is female. Undergraduate BA and BFA programmes in studio are approximately 80% female, and 20% male. On average, MFA programmes in the US are approximately 60% female, 40% male. In Los Angeles, over 70% of the artists represented in the top 100 galleries are male. From Hebron's Facebook page and call for participation (https://www.facebook.com/notes/micol-hebron/the-gallery-tally-project-summary/10151821151261987).
3 See 'The Strong Program in Cultural Sociology' by Jeffery Alexander and Phillip Smith for an overview of current debates in the sociology of culture. Available online at: http://ccs.research.yale.edu/about/strong-program/
4 See the website http://grrrlzines.net/about.htm for more examples of the range of international zine activity.

## REFERENCES

Bauman, S. (2001) 'Intellectualization and Art World Development: Film in the United States', *American Sociological Review*, 66(3): 404–26.

Becker, H. (1974) 'Art as Collective Action', *American Sociological Review*, 39(6): 767–76.

Becker, H. (1982) *Artworlds*. Berkeley: University of California Press.

Becker, H. (2006) 'The Work Itself', in H. Becker, R. Faulkner R. and B. Kirshenblatt-Gimblett (eds), *Art From Start to Finish: Jazz, Painting, Writing and Other Improvisations*. Chicago: The University of Chicago Press, pp. 21–30.

Berger, J. (1974) *Ways of Seeing*. New York: Penguin Books.

Berlant, L. and Warner, M. (1995) 'What Does Queer Theory Teach Us About X?', *PMLA*, 110(2): 343–9.

Bordo, S. (2004) *Unbearable Weight: Feminism, Western Culture, and the Body, Tenth Anniversary Edition*, 2nd edn. Berkeley: University of California Press.

Bourdieu, P. (1984) *Distinction: A Social Critique of the Judgment of Taste*. Cambridge: Harvard University Press.

Butler, J. (2000) *Gender Trouble: Feminism and the Subversion of Identity*. New York: Routledge.

Chidgey, R. (2009) 'Free, Trade: Distribution Economies in Feminist Zine Networks', *Signs: Journal of Women in Culture and Society*, 35(1): 28–36.

Comstock, M. (2001) 'Grrrl Zine Networks: Re-composing Spaces of Authority, Gender, and Culture', *JAC: A Journal of Composition Theory*, 21(2): 383–409.

Connell, R.W. (1995) *Masculinities*. Los Angeles: University of California Press.

de Beauvoir, S. (1972) *The Second Sex*. Harmondsworth: Penguin.

de la Fuente, E. (2007) 'The "New Sociology of Art": Putting Art Back into Social Science Approaches to the Arts', *Cultural Sociology*, 1: 409–25.

de Lauretis, T. (1991) 'Queer Theory: Lesbian and Gay Sexualities: An Introduction', *Differences: A Journal of Feminist Cultural Studies*, 3(2): iii–xviii.

DiMaggio, P. (1982) 'Cultural Entrepreneurship in Nineteenth-Century Boston', *Media, Culture and Society*, 4(1): 195–209.

DiMaggio, P. (1987) 'Classification in Art', *American Sociological Review*, 52(4): 440–55.

Duncombe, S. (1997) *Notes from Underground: Zines and the Politics of Alternative Culture*. Verso.

Edelman, L. (1995) 'Queer Theory: Unstating Desire', *GLQ: A Journal of Lesbian and Gay Studies*, 2(4): 343–6.

Edelman, L. (2004) *No Future: Queer Theory and the Death Drive*.

Edelman, L. (2006) 'Antagonism, Negativity and the Subject of Queer Theory', *PMLA*, 121(3): 821–2.

Fausto-Sterling, A. (1992) *Myths of Gender: Biological Theories about Men and Women*. New York: Basic Books.

Ferguson, P. (1998) 'A Cultural Field in the Making: Gastronomy in 19th-Century France', *American Journal of Sociology*, 104(3): 597–641.

Ferguson, P. (2004) *Accounting for Taste: The Triumph of French Cuisine*. Chicago: University of Chicago Press.

Friedan, B. (1963) *The Feminine Mystique*. New York: W.W. Norton & Company.

Glenn, E.N., Chang, G. and Forcey, L. (eds) (1994) *Mothering: Ideology, Experience and Agency*. New York: Routledge.

Goffman, E. (1979) *Gender Advertisements*. New York: Harper and Row.

Grosz, E. (1994) *Volatile Bodies: Toward a Corporeal Feminism*. Bloomington: Indiana University Press.

Grosz, E. (1995) *Space, Time and Perversion: Essays on the Politics of Bodies*. New York: Routledge.

Guzzetti, B.J. and Gamboa, M. (2011) 'Zines for Social Justice: Adolescent Girls Writing on their Own', *Reading Research Quarterly*, 39(4): 408–36.

Halberstam, J. (2003) 'Reflections on Queer Studies and Queer Pedagogy', *Journal of Homosexuality*, 45(2–4): 361–4.

Hall, S. (1977) *Representation: Cultural Representations and Signifying Practices*. London: The Open University Press/Sage Publications.

Halperin, D. (1990) *One Hundred Years of Homosexuality*. London: Routledge.

Haraway, D. (1991) *Simians, Cyborgs and Women: The Reinvention of Nature*. New York: Routledge.

Haraway, D. (1997) *Modest_Witness@Second_Millennium. FemaleMan_Meets_OncoMouse: Feminism and Technoscience*. New York: Routledge.

Harding, S, (1991) *Whose Science? Whose Knowledge? Thinking from Women's Lives*. Milton Keynes: Open University Press.

Harding, S. (1995) 'Starting from Marginalised Lives', *JAC: A Journal of Composition Theory*, 15(2): 193–225.

Harris, A. (1999) 'Is DIY DOA? Zines and the Revolution Grrrl Style', in R. White (ed.), *Australian Youth Subcultures: On the Margins and in the Mainstream*. Hobart, Tasmania: Australian Clearinghouse for Youth Studies, pp. 84–93.

Harris, A. (2003) 'gURL Scenes and Grrrl Zines: The Regulation and Resistance of Girls in Late Modernity', *Feminist Review*, 75: 38–56.

Hartsock, N.C.M. (1983) *Money, Sex, and Power: Toward a Feminist Historical Materialism*. New York: Longman.

Hartsock, N.C.M. (1997) 'Standpoint Theories for Next Century', in S.J. Kenney and H. Kinsella (eds), *Politics and Feminist Standpoint Theories*. New York: Haworth Press.

Hochschild, A. (1989) *The Second Shift: Working Parents and the Revolution at Home* (with Anne Machung). New York: Viking.

hooks, b. (1992) *Black Looks: Race and Representation*. Boston: South End Press.

Huffer, L. (2010) *Mad for Foucault: Rethinking the Foundations of Queer Theory*. New York: Columbia University Press.

Inglis, D. and Hughson, J. (eds) (2005) *The Sociology of Art: Ways of Seeing*. New York: Palgrave Macmillan.

Jenkins, H. (2006) *Convergence Culture: Where Old and New Media Collide*. New York: New York University Press.

Kimmel, M. (1996) *Manhood in America: A Cultural History*. New York: Free Press.

Kimmel, M. (1987) *Changing Men: New Directions in the Study of Men and Masculinity*. Newbury Park, CA: Sage Publications.

Kimmel, M. (2005) *The Gender of Desire: Essays on Masculinity and Sexuality*. New York: SUNY Press.

Kimmel, M. (2008) *Guyland: The Perilous World Where Boys Become Men*. New York: HarperCollins.

Kimmel, M. (2010) *Misframing Men: Essays on the Politics of Contemporary Masculinities*. New Brunswick: Rutgers University Press.

Lawson-Borders, G. (2006) *Media Organizations and Convergence: Case Studies of Media Convergence Pioneers*. Mahwah, NJ: Lawrence Erlbaum Associates.

Levine, L.W. (1988) *Highbrow, Lowbrow: The Emergence of Cultural Hierarchy in America*. Cambridge MA: Harvard University Press.

Levy, P. (1997) *Collective Intelligence: Mankind's Emerging World in Cyberspace*. Cambridge, MA: Perseus Books.

Lorber, J. (1994) *Paradoxes of Gender*. New Haven, CT: Yale University Press.

Messner, M. (1992) *Power at Play: Sports and the Problem of Masculinity*. Boston, MA: Beacon Press.

Messner, M. (1997) *Politics of Masculinities: Men in Movements*. Lanham, MD: Alta Mira Press.

Muñoz, J.E. (1997) '"The White to Be Angry": Vaginal Davis's Terrorist Drag', *Social Text*, 53(1): 80–103.

Muñoz, J.E. (1999) *Disidentifications: Queers of Color and the Performance of Politics*. Minneapolis: University of Minnesota Press.

Muñoz, J.E. (2009) *Cruising Utopia: The Then and There of Queer Futurity*. New York University Press.

Mulvey, L. (1975) 'Visual Pleasure and Narrative Cinema', *Screen*, 16: 8–18.

Negroponte, N. (1995) *Being Digital*. New York: Vintage Books.

Nguyen, M (2000) Untitled column, *Punk Planet*, 40 (November/December).

Nochlin, L. (1972) 'Why Have There Been No Great Women Artists?', *ARTnews*, January: 22–39, 67–71.

Ortner, S. (1974) 'Is Female to Male as Nature is to Culture?', in M.Z. Rosaldo and L. Lamphere (eds), *Woman, Culture and Society*. Stanford, CA: Stanford University Press, pp. 67–87.

Parsons, T. (1940) *Essays in Sociological Theory*. New York: The Free Press.

Peterson, R. (1997) *Creating Country Music: Fabricating Authenticity*. Chicago: University of Chicago Press.

Pool, I. de Sola (1983) *Technologies of Freedom*. Cambridge, MA: Belknap Press.

Radway, J. (1984) *Reading the Romance*. North Carolina: The University of North Carolina Press.

Rich, A. (1976) *Of Woman Born: Motherhood as Experience and Institution*. New York: Norton and Company.

Rossi, A. (1983) *Seasons of a Woman's Life: A Self-Reflective Essay on Love and Work in Family, Profession, and Politics*. Amherst: University of Massachusetts, Social and Demographic Research Institute.

Schilt, K. and Zobl, E. (2008) 'Connecting the Dots: Riot Grrris, Ladyfests, 12 I Symposium: Feminist Zines and the International Grrrl Zine Network', in A. Harris (ed.), *Next Wave Cultures: Feminism, Subcultures, Activism*. New York: Routledge. pp. 171–92.

Sedgwick, E.K. (1985) *Between Men: English Literature and Male Homosexual Desire*. New York: Columbia University Press.

Sedgwick, E.K. (1990) *Epistemology of the Closet*. Oakland: University of California Press.

Sedgwick, E.K. (1993) *Tendencies*. Durham NC and London: Duke University Press Books.

Smith, D. (1987) *The Everyday World as Problematic: A Feminist Sociology*. Boston: Northeastern University Press.

Smith, D.E. (1990) *The Conceptual Practices of Power*. Grand Rapids, MI: Northeastern University Press.

Solanas, V. (2004) *SCUM Manifesto*. New York: Verso.

Willis, P. (1977) *Learning to Labour*. Farnborough: Saxon House.

Wilson, E.O. (1975) *Sociobiology: The New Synthesis*. Cambridge: Harvard University Press.

Wilson, E.O. (1978) *On Human Nature*. London: Tavistock.

Zobl, E. (2004) 'Persephone Is Pissed! Grrrl Zine Reading, Making, and Distributing Across the Globe', *Hecate*, 30(2): 156–75.

Zobl, E. (2009) 'Comparative perspectives symposium: feminist zines, cultural production, transnational networking, and critical reflection in feminist zines. (Critical essay)', *Signs*, 35(1): 1–12.

Zolberg, V. (1990) *Constructing a Sociology of the Arts*. New York: Cambridge University Press.

PART IV
# Culture and Society

# Symbolic Boundaries

Bethany Bryson

Symbolic boundaries are cultural delineations of some sort that are understood to constitute the limit or perimeter of an entity or idea or the distinction between two such entities/ideas. A symbolic boundary may be symbolic itself, or it could be marked by symbols (such as status symbols). Symbolic boundaries can also be produced by social actions for cultural reasons; they can take their shape from organizations or institutional patterns, or they can even be bound with physical markers, such as a river, a wall, or a fence. Physical and even natural contours can be symbolic when imbued with meaning. In addition, our understanding of symbolic boundaries includes more than the simple circle but also the multiple 'internal distinctions of classification systems and even complex temporal, spatial, and visual cognitive distinctions' (Lamont, Pendergrass, and Pachucki, 2015: 850).

## INTRODUCTION

The definition above is based on a 'big tent' approach to symbolic boundaries, which has been my experience with the term since the early 1990s. My analysis of the field-building work that Michèle Lamont has devoted to symbolic boundaries over the years shows that she has often done the hard work for us of thinking creatively about how the many threads of research on symbolic boundaries are connected to one another.[1] It was a process of reaching out, connecting, and adding fuel. As Lamont would eventually say, 'I would suggest that from the start there was a major tension in the importation of Bourdieu to the United States, between what we could term the "orthodox" and the "heterodox" take on his work. From the onset, I located myself firmly in the heterodox camp' (Lamont, 2012: 230). Heterodoxy would inform much of what became of symbolic boundaries in the next two decades: growth and creativity.

There are always challenges to imposing heterodoxy in any field, however. Trying to build cumulative knowledge without a core foundation on which to build is never easy (Bryson, 2005). This is one reason that some scholars draw *clear* distinctions between, for example, symbolic boundaries and classification structures or between symbolic boundaries and performativity (in producing gender differences), excising pieces from the term symbolic boundaries as much as possible so that the thing remaining will have a smaller definition. I am still a fan of heterodoxy, however. It is the state of the field, and the field is healthy, vibrant and growing.

What I plan to offer, then, is a description of the field, organized by a heterodox list of boundary characteristics. It will be a list that I cannot claim to be exhaustive, and so it is a list to which I hope future scholars will add. At least, that is my challenge. In offering this list of boundary characteristics, I hope to provide some of the theoretical foundation upon which more general claims might be made or tested. At the same time, it might serve as one view of the mechanistic terrain that one might take into account in the early stages of research design, for example. Finally, I am hoping that this perspective on mapping the terrain is at least useful in that it is a view not readily available from the research databases and search engines, so while the number of works I am able to reference is limited, at least the classification system might be of some use.

## HISTORY

In classical theory, Durkheim's influence on symbolic boundaries is felt most strongly both through direct inspiration and by way of the scholars he inspired. In the symbolic boundaries literature, he is generally cited for his work in *The Elementary Forms of Religious Life* (2008 [1912]), where a single social and religious boundary marks the difference between the sacred and the profane – between members of society and outcasts. In this book, Durkheim discusses the moral order, which is more a common system of meaning than a religious leader with a stick, but being on the wrong side of a moral boundary can still imply grave power issues. Nevertheless, this book has led symbolic boundaries scholars to see Durkheim as a theorist of collective effervescence, rather than someone who could help us think about inequality. But Durkheim did theorize larger chunks of inequality in *The Division of Labour* both as binaries and as classification systems. Again, our memories tend to focus on the role of divided labour on social cohesion, but Durkheim did not forget the classification system below and he made clear symbolic claims about the relationship between occupational categories and social groups within.

> The division of labor ... determines the relations of friendship ... [T]he moral effect that it produces, and its true function is to create two or more persons feeling a solidarity ... its aim is to cause coherence among friends *and to stamp them with its seal.*' (1933 [1983]: 56, emphasis mine)

Durkheim had a direct influence on some of the precursors to symbolic boundaries research in sociology – people who, like Durkheim, studied binary boundaries around social groups, largely based on moral order and issues of crime and deviance. Kai Erickson, most famously published *Wayward Puritans* (1966), a study of the symbolic boundary drawn by the Puritan witch trials in the 17th-century Massachusetts Bay Colony. Erickson, spent most of his career studying symbolic boundaries and even used the term several times in a paper he co-authored with Robert Dentler (1959). Although the term 'symbolic boundaries' did not catch on, the idea certainly did and thrived in the deviance literature, where books like Howard Becker's *Outsiders* and Goffman's *Stigma* (1986 [1963]) are still hot commodities with the booksellers.

The anthropologist Mary Douglas might be our most significant conduit of Durkheimian boundary theory at the moment, however. She lures us in by explicitly using the term 'symbolic boundaries' (1972) and by swiftly advancing Durkheim's work in her 1966 book, *Purity and Danger*. There, she asks what happens when a person or object is unclassified in a given boundary system or doesn't fit with any of the options. She argues that this is the definition of dirt (matter out of place). For example, rice on a plate is food, but rice on the floor is dirt. And to highlight failures to classify in social situations, people who are difficult to classify by race or gender pose difficulties for their conversation partners. Depending on the nation and the situation, the difficulties may be socially awkward, legally challenging, or even life threatening (see e.g. Meadow, 2010; Spade, 2011; Zylan, 2011). Douglas goes on to discuss the likely responses to classification problems, such as eliminating the problematic matter by death or banishment, correcting them so that they fit within a category, stigmatizing them, marking them as dangerous, or deifying their difference. Finally, Douglas published a short collection of essays in 1986 called *How Institutions Think*. That book, especially the introduction, laid much groundwork for the methods that connect organizational boundaries (and research) to symbolic and even social boundaries.

Weber also gave us some very clear, if not lengthy, writing on social class and on the way group boundaries can preserve resources in a small section of *Economy and Society* (1978 [1922]) devoted to the relationship between class and status, where he simply argues that people are born into social locations that determine their life chances. We then work to preserve them through 'social closure' to exclude outsiders gaining access to our resources. This fits nicely with Durkheim's view above. Weber also offers endless pages of analysis on ethnic group contact, but that has been less influential outside his important role in helping to define ethnicity (and to some extent race) for the discipline (Morning, 2005). Weber's work has, however, been influential in studies that draw on the importance of bureaucracies (see 'Classification Systems' below) and rationalization processes. For example, Espeland and Stevens (1998) demonstrate that the commensuration process is not merely rationalization, but also a delineation of things that can be compared to each other and excluded things that cannot be compared, evaluated, or included. In a later work, Espeland and Sauder (2007) demonstrate how ranking systems construct symbolic boundaries and affect social behaviour through self-fulfilling prophecies and commensuration.

Historically it is Weber and Marx (more so, and especially through other theorists such as Veblen, Gramsci, Bourdieu, and Foucault) who played the larger role in sealing our ability to fuse cultural analyses of social inequality through the study of symbolic boundaries; but for the next few decades, the scholars who used boundaries or neighbouring ideas would not be making the boundaries themselves the stars of the show.

Moreover, the influences of Marx and Weber on symbolic boundaries (not to mention several theoretical issues) come to us primarily through the work of Pierre Bourdieu. Bourdieu's *Distinction* (1984 [1979]) is probably the most important theoretical piece for contemporary scholars of symbolic boundaries, as well as those who study social inequality. He synthesizes Marx and Weber, includes micro–macro links, and gives the reader a fairly complete picture of how things work in his model; but, following the title, one will see that there is a special emphasis on social class differentiation. But underneath all this grand theorizing is a survey of the people of Paris.

The empirical piece running through this book adds a level of richness to the text that has contributed to its rapid adoption as a source of research hypotheses among empirical scholars (Lamont, 2012). Moreover, the US audience had already been primed for the arrival of the translation of *Distinction* by a very popular review of two previous books of Bourdieu's by DiMaggio (1979). From here, a crescendo of events put Bourdieu on the path to fame in the United States. DiMaggio got to work testing several of Bourdieu's claims in orderly succession. In 1982 he demonstrated an empirical effect of cultural capital on school grades, laying a red carpet for the translation of *Distinction* to be released in 1984 (DiMaggio, 1982). One year later, DiMaggio and Mohr (1985) upped the ante, showing a positive effect of cultural capital on educational attainment and marital selection.

Drawing on the rich treasure trove of theoretical claims about culture, power, social class, and other forms of inequality to be found in *Distinction*, an initial bloom of research grounded in *Distinction* was devoted almost exclusively to questions of class and culture. In 1988, Lamont and Lareau published a paper that critically engaged Bourdieu's concept of cultural capital in *Sociological Theory*, giving us all more strings to pull on, as did Lamont's first big empirical study of symbolic boundaries among upper-class men in the US and France, *Money, Morals, and Manners* (1992).

By this point the bug had begun to spread and Lamont was elected chair of the American Sociological Association Culture Section in the 1994–1995 academic year. Her primary legacy from that term was the institution of a set of research networks that concentrate the interests of cultural sociologist and help make face-to-face network ties. In a section that was rapidly expanding from an intimate group of scholars with shared interests to what would become the largest section in the ASA with over 1000 members, Lamont devised a plan to create 'research networks' of free association within the section. There is no particular expectation for them, but most maintain email lists, a few host a roundtable event of some sort at ASA, and there is an occasional mini-conference. The Symbolic Boundaries Research Network, which I have co-ordinated since inception, meets regularly at an ASA roundtable, and maintains an email list (brysonbp@jmu.edu). The network sponsored an online conference in 2003, and we have published two online working papers series editions. But of most historical importance was the conscious development of the field that occurred during a 1995 Symbolic Boundaries Research Network mini conference hosted by Mark Jacobs at George Mason University (near Washington, DC, USA) and organized in tandem with Ann Swidler and the Meaning and Measurement Network. Of particular note are efforts to identify and develop theoretical and methodological interests, and organizational strategies intended to encourage a 'ground-up' production of ideas: in keeping with the heterodoxy principle, workshop topics for the conference were determined by participants, not organizers.

After this point the primary challenge for symbolic boundaries research was structural. Most of the people first involved in symbolic boundaries research – whose work would later be considered foundational – were all located inside the culture section, and so largely studied cultural objects and meanings. As a result, our first flourishes centred around the relationship between music, art, fashion, and social class (e.g. Bryson, 1996; Crane, 1987; Erickson, 1996; Peterson, 1992; Peterson and Kern, 1996). By the time we turn the corner into the 21st century, however, research on race and gender has become more cultural, and a greater number of scholars are beginning to articulate their questions as matters of social construction and cultural processes. In 2002, Lamont and Molnár (2002) published an influential Annual Review paper that demonstrates how symbolic boundaries are central to the study of society by pointing to similarities between the boundaries found in a variety of institutions, topics, and realms of activity. They also provide directions for the study of those boundaries and their properties. As a result, more new research is making connections between the (constantly developing) symbolic boundaries literature and other literatures that have been with us all along.

An important example, especially for scholars of race and ethnicity is Frederick Douglass (1881), who spent most of his career studying 'the color line', and made important contributions to the sociological corpus in so doing. W.E.B. DuBois (1903) took his analysis of that line to a new level with his ideas of the 'veil' and 'double consciousness'. The idea that boundaries do not look (or operate) the same way from the inside as they do from the outside is an important concept (possibly related to inclusion and exclusion, above) that can and should be extended to other fields. In addition, Edward Said's Orientalism (2003 [1994]) has also been influential in describing post-colonial cultural representations as a series of binary boundaries experienced differently from each side: east vs. west, familiar vs. exotic, insiders vs. outsiders/others, etc.

We also had a quantitative bloom around 2000. Although Pierre Bourdieu, Richard Peterson, Paul DiMaggio, John Mohr, and myself, just to name a few, had already begun testing cultural questions with quantitative data, the idea was slow to catch on, mostly because of the placement of people training students in culture and methods. That is, programmes specializing in culture did not invest in quantitative methods and vice versa. Happily, scholarly generations are short, and that is about how long it took for a new generation of students to start proving us all wrong.

The study of gender, likewise started out with pioneering work both in the theory of gender boundaries (Gerson and Peiss, 1985) and insightful ethnographic studies from prolific, generous and inspirational scholars like Cynthia Fuchs Epstein (e.g. 1989; 1992) and Kathleen Gerson (e.g. Gerson, 1993; Jacobs and Gerson, 2004). *Gender Play*, Barrie Thorne's (1993) ground-breaking ethnography of children doing gender, provides strong evidence that many of the sex characteristics that had previously been attributed to genetics, because they influenced children at such a young age, were, in fact, imposed by school practices or even produced by children themselves. The book served as a turning point in gender studies and sociology, and it is an inspiring study in boundaries as well.

The idea that biological gender is a social production, and thus a social and symbolic boundary in need of study, slowly gained popularity through the years under the guises of sex/gender and queer theory. In 1990, Joan Acker showed how the boundaries of gender are institutionalized in organizations, Gamson expressed his fear of the movement in 1995, and Lorber (e.g. 1999) has been explaining the concept for some time. Rene Almeling's (2011) book *Sex Cells*, which uncovers the way egg and sperm donation organizations assign gender characteristics to reproductive cells and the people who produce them, is another empirical feather in the hat for how we socially construct biological sex (Fausto-Sterling, 2012; Martin, 1991). In all, the impressive and expansive cross-disciplinary scholarship I describe above (and will highlight below) is great news for the body of symbolic boundaries research. It shows that the field is strong and flourishing.

## BOUNDARY CHARACTERISTICS

Below I will discuss nine characteristics of symbolic boundaries evident in the research, and the many different ways that scholars have used and meant the term symbolic boundary. This is only a first step in providing a theoretical description of the field, however, as I do not have the space to analyse the entirety of the vast and impressive symbolic boundaries literature. This list is admittedly not exhaustive, nor are the categories mutually exclusive, but I hope it will be an exciting beginning in thinking about some of the areas of cumulative work we have amassed as well as our breadth and our opportunities for creativity and growth.

It is important to note, at the outset, that there is a fair amount of research that only uses the term boundary or 'symbolic boundary' once or twice, descriptively, without giving much thought to the theoretical or methodological power that they *could* be harnessing to analyse the phenomenon they just described as bounded. That is fine, of course. I only hope that the following analysis helps to make some of the literature more accessible if desired. What follows is divided into three main groups: 'System Issues', 'Symbols', and 'Social Action' (social boundaries). 'System Issues' cover large-scale boundary characteristics including: binaries, systems, and the question of symbolic versus social boundaries. Under 'Symbols', I cover 'symbols on boundaries', such as boundary and status markers, 'bounded meanings', and the 'meaning of concrete boundaries'. Finally under Social Action, I cover three different topics. The first is boundary work. The second is performance, ritual, and dramaturgy, while the third is inclusive versus exclusive boundaries. Finally, I end with some promising misfits that take us in new directions for the future. The end is a good place to start.

## System Issues

### Binaries

Binary boundaries are the quintessential form of symbolic boundary, such as a circle, doughnut, or dividing line. Alone, a binary boundary would take the form of Durkheim's (2008 [1912]): sacred-profane dichotomy, or the fairy tale divide between: masculine and feminine. Jeffrey Swindle (2014), for example, catalogues the terms that have been used to place societies into binary categories such as 'developing' and 'developed' or even 'savage' and 'civilized'. The words have changed a bit over time, as have the allocation of specific nations to one side or the other, but the binary division remains the same.

The study of binaries assumes that there will be two sides, but not that they will be equal. At the very least, there is likely to be an inside and an outside or a high road and a low. In fact, Tilly (1998) has argued that a vast network of binary processes of inequality lie beneath all the power structures we are accustomed to observing. And Mario Small wrote, in collaboration with David Harding and Michèle Lamont (Small et al., 2010: 17) that together multiple 'symbolic boundaries constitute a system of classification that defines a hierarchy of groups and the similarities and difference between them'. Likewise, Wagner-Pacifici's (2000) definition of symbolic boundaries included in the opening of this piece, argued that individual boundaries mark the divisions in classification systems – a whole host of simple decisions added together.

Even in contemporary gender theory, there is a sense in which gender is considered one big binary thing, but there are also calls to complicate the way we describe that image. To the extent that gender is a dividing line for societies, cultural sociologists have moved from cataloguing gender differences to recognizing the ways in which this boundary is also an organizing principle for social systems and organizations (Acker, 1988; Bourdieu, 1979; Lorber, 2006; Salzinger, 2003).

But while gender scholars are abandoning the binary approach, whiteness studies scholars have found some use for the binary model because it allows them to highlight the boundary work that whites do relative to other races and to highlight whites' confusion about their own racial identity (Hale, 1998; Hughey, 2012; Shirley, 2010; Warren and Twine, 1997). The whiteness perspective also allows for a certain amount of traction on the power dynamic, which no one could argue is equivalent across racial groups in any nation, but race is a classification system, and so re-coding the categories of analysis comes at some cost in the form of gathering critics who worry that a group of people studying themselves might wander away with the research question (and the TV remote – as a chunk of this literature is devoted to documenting the unbearable taste-culture of whiteness), which is why we have the critics. The more angles we have on these problems, the better.

### Classification Systems

Questions of classification were central to Bourdieu's discussion of boundary work, but have also been addressed by Schwartz (1981) and DiMaggio (1987). These studies have been foundational in our field, and were especially important for demonstrating the relationship between cultural systems and other social and organizational systems – connections that made the sociology of culture relevant and interesting to the rest of the discipline. This foundation in grounded classification informs work such as Reyes' (2015) ethnographic study of two universities, and connects the organizational boundaries of the schools to the cultural boundaries and activities of Latino student organizations, therein. Similarly, Saperstein and Penner (2010) studied racial classification inside prisons. This fascinating paper uses classification to demonstrate that *crime commits race*. Lena and Peterson (2008) tracked the classification of music over time, a question that Roy (2014) is currently taking up, asking why we organize music into genres instead of some other classification system.

Biologists have also generated an entire classification system for plants and animals with fascinating boundaries, and these have been fruitful targets of study for social theorists as well. The class that separates mammals from reptiles, for example, draws on the presence of mammary glands, and the reason for that choice, according to

Marks (2000) is that a political battle was brewing in the 1750s over the importance of breastfeeding. If not for that, we might think of ourselves as special for having hair or not laying eggs.

Scientific taxonomies also ripped Pluto from our planetary system (Jenness, 2008), while economic classifications silently lump and sort us into categories that deem us more and less worthy to fully participate in the economy (Fourcade and Healy, 2013; Zelizer, 1994). But the former scholars are not the only ones who noticed the market's role in generating boundaries, even Parsons devoted much of *Economy and Society* (Parsons and Smelser, 1956) and *The Structure of Social Action* (1968) to analysing the boundaries of economic activity.

Classification methods that show careful attention to the symbolic boundaries in effect between each category are especially applicable to rapidly shifting categorical identities, as is the case for racial classification in the United States today. This literature is rich and vast. It reaches from macro-level studies of unexpected shifts in census categories such as the whitening of Puerto Ricans in the first half of the 20th century (Loveman and Muniz, 2007). While Puerto Ricans were seeking whiteness, however, whites seemed to be fleeing that category, as whiteness studies would predict. The number of Native Americans tripled in the latter half of the 20th century (Nagel, 1995), and, using ethnographic research, Hughey (2007; 2012) found that both white supremacists and white antiracists seek 'meaningful' racial identities, usually accomplished by generating a classification system grounded in essentialist (i.e. racist) distinctions.

At the organizational level, Hannan et al. (2007) even have a theory for predicting the emergence of organizational categories and the forms they contain, such as 'hospital' or 'electrician'. In addition, Hsu (2006) addresses a classification problem involving simultaneous membership in two groups. Her data (film genres) are not all that different from human racial identities: in theory, it should be easy and perhaps even beneficial to claim dual membership, but the real-world experience is far less accepting. Hsu's movie audiences are not delighted by the double-voiced abilities of dual-classified films. Instead, they went seeking one genre (say romance) and were confused if not annoyed by the material intended to lure fans of the other genre (action-adventure material, for example). In both cases, the audience is key in conveying legitimacy to new categories or for the classification of products.

## Symbolic Versus Social

Lamont's 2002 definition of symbolic boundaries is quite broad, whereas social boundaries are much narrower: '*Symbolic* boundaries are conceptual distinctions made by social actors to categorize objects, people, practices, and even time and space … *Social* boundaries are objectified forms of social differences manifested in unequal access to and unequal distribution of resources (material and nonmaterial) and social opportunities' (Lamont and Molnár, 2002: 169, emphasis mine). We will not limit ourselves to this definition, of course, but it is theoretically and conceptually rich. There is much worth exploring therein.

There is a large contingent of symbolic boundaries researchers who examine symbols that serve as boundary markers. These can range from the esoteric 'self-actualization' (Lamont, 1992) to very specific status markers, involving, not just music genres, but artists, pieces, brands, choices, and fit. One way to study symbols is to study the way they are used to mark the boundaries of other social categories, such as race (Appelrouth and Kelly, 2013; Schwartzman, 2007) or social class (Bryson, 1996; Coulangeon, 2005).

Finally, I would like to point out that boundaries scholars do not often consciously theorize the relationship between their boundaries system and other systems of meaning that might be in play at the same time. In many cases, there are likely to be multiple reinforcing systems (see e.g. Bryson, 2005; Davis, 2014; Spade, 2011), other systems of meaning might meet resistance and contradiction from their environment. Bourdieu was especially good at connecting the various layers in a system, and Bourdeusian research focusing on culture and inequality such as Lamont (1992), and the work in Lamont and Fournier (1992) laid important groundwork for rich multi-system analysis. When considering the relationship among various systems of meaning, this is also a good place to theorize institutionalization (Zucker, 1977) and intersectionality, that is, interlocking systems of oppression (Collins, 2000; Dill, 1994).

In sum, then, the quest for the symbolic might be a search for specific boundary markers, or a whole classification system built on as few as two symbols, but no upper limit is known for the number of such boundary markers or the complexity classification systems. In fact a simple society's meaning system might even revolve around a single sacred symbol, such as Durkheim's purity. Lamont and Molnár (2002) suggested more leeway in this category than this list would imply. I hope to see some great new additions to this in the future, but here is a starter for conversation, theory and research design.

## Symbols

### Symbols on Boundaries

Lamont's seminal work *Money Morals and Manners* (1992), which is best consumed with significant foreshadowing from Lamont and Lareau (1988), launched the initial salvo in symbolic boundaries research in the current era. Taken-for-granted today, the method and overall research design for the book was considered revolutionary at the time. Elegant in its ability to leverage qualitative and comparative methods to address issues that had been long-held assumptions in the social sciences, it 'merely' involved asking respondents (in four cities and two countries) how they judged people above and below them, thus eliciting the specific criteria and symbols that guard each boundary. Coding and analysis were more onerous, of course, not that the long interview is a simple task. At any rate, this book, and the cultural-capital-style theories that hang around as its awkward cousins, are the reasons we often default to searching for symbols that mark boundaries.

Since that time, symbolic boundaries scholars have offered several variations on this theme. For example, Abigail Saguy's (2013) book, *What's Wrong with Fat?* chronicles the way that debates over the meaning of fat bodies have moved the relevant boundary away from the symbol of individual bodies. Instead, the various claims-makers appeal to different *master frames and analogies* (health vs. civil rights, illness, racial group, etc.) that flip the symbolic field, shifting focus from bodies onto these new symbols of political debate (e.g., health vs. civil rights) and use different analogies to argue that fatness is akin to, say cancer (an illness), or, in contrast, to race, gender, disability or sexual orientation (a trait against which people discriminate). It is a way of drawing symbolic boundaries around groups of issues, as opposed to between individual people.

In race and gender studies, it's not unusual for theorists to conceptualize people (usually women's bodies and/or the bodies of people of colour) as the symbols that mark key boundaries, which are also important sites of power and likely intersections between both boundaries and power (Collins, 2000; Dill, 1994). For example, Pei-Chia Lan (2003) shows how the sexual control of women's bodies marks the boundary between colonizer and colonized for migrant women in Taiwan that, of course, simultaneously intersects with gender and gender domination. The meaning and value of all related categories, such as reproductive labour, are also multiplied outward for all related groups. Central to these critical and feminist approaches such as Lan's are the simultaneous actions of human boundaries as social and symbolic because bodies have shapes, colours, and sexual and labour re/productive possibilities, all of which might be controlled and/or imbued with meanings.

In another variation, Gretchen Purser (2009) shows how two competing groups of Latino day labourers, who are all-male, nevertheless use gender (masculinity) as the primary boundary marker that they draw against each other. This is a common finding of our usually binary gender system. Single-gender groups often use specific boundary markers to guard their own gender boundaries without requiring the presence of people from a relational category (Pascoe, 2011).

### Bounded Meanings

Eviatar Zerubavel's (1991) *The Fine Line* directly addresses the boundaries of meaning and conceptualizes meaning in such a way that a whole meaning system could be a very complex classification system. Zerubavel and his methods are exceptionally skilful at illuminating unexpected elements of our meanings system, and for that reason, his work continues to delight and influence generations of scholars, many of whom also incorporate a traditional symbolic boundaries approach, which, in this case, would mostly imply making connections between the observed meaning system and some other social system or portion thereof (see e.g. Aneesh, 2010; Cherry, 2010; Friese, 2010).

Drawing inspiration from Zerubavel, I applied Lamont's (1992) methods to meaning, rather than people and interviewed English professors about their definition of a word (multiculturalism) for my 2005 book, *Making Multiculturalism* (Bryson, 2005). I was then able to make connections between localized meanings and the governance structures inside English departments. This approach of applying the social method to meaning has become increasingly popular (e.g. Ajrouch, 2004; DeSoucey, 2010; Hughey, 2012; Ollivier, 2006; Saguy, 2013), and also follows a call from Lamont (2000) to do just that.

### The Meaning of Concrete Boundaries

I hope to open some space here for something that does not have an identity of its own, but we all trip over to some extent. That is the cultural problem of physical boundaries. I am hoping for some recognition that no wall or mountain can successfully contain its human contents unless there is a system of meaning in place that tells us we never want to go mounting hiking or we'd rather die in a flood than scale the wall, or whatever is necessary to keep us inside. In most of our research, I think this chunk of culture goes unexamined, and sometimes leaves our cultural analysis disconnected from the material world.

One beautiful example of how to study concrete barriers successfully is the work of Christina Nippert-Eng (1996). For her 1996 book, she studied how people separate their work and home lives. Work and home are already separated, physically speaking, and yet we know that, especially for engaged parents, the question of the work–home divide is an enormous problem. When Nippert-Eng interviewed her respondents, she asked to see their calendars, telephone books, and key chains to see whether home and work were separated or merged. She used similar tricks for her 2010 study of privacy to discover which boundaries provide privacy and which do not (Nippert-Eng, 2010). Similarly, Hila Lifshitz-Assaf (2015) studies the boundaries of innovation in a NASA experiment in which Research and Development professionals posted their innovations on an open platform. Although they quickly generated an important scientific breakthrough, participants reported problems such as professional identity where existing boundaries did not fit the new structure.

In another example of structures working right under our noses, Alexander Davis (2014) explores the paradox of a quintessentially concrete phenomenon in the paradox of gender-segregated restrooms. As gender-neutral facilities have become more common he asks why gender segregation in the washroom remains so persistent, even as our other social spaces become more integrated, and if there is really a compelling reason to keep them separate, then why is there now such a strong trend in the other direction? Gender-segregated bathrooms are not mountains, but they might be the closest thing to universal concrete boundaries in our workplaces and public spaces. The upheaval there is no small thing.

## Social Action

### Boundary Work

Gieryn's research on boundary work began on a separate track from the symbolic boundaries line of study (as did many relevant inspirations), but the intersection of these two lines of research has been especially beneficial and inspirational for thinking about how social actors make boundaries happen in the real world. His description of the boundary-work process is most succinctly summarized in a 1983 paper (Gieryn, 1983), but it is evident in a wide range of interesting applications throughout his work. Much of Gieryn's research was already cultural, and symbolic boundaries researchers found it useful for helping devise research on Weber's (1978 [1922]) social closure and to fill in some of the details on the function of Bourdieu's (1984 [1979]) cultural capital and social exclusion.

In some fields, boundary work is called identity work, and can operate on an individual or a group level. For example, Matthew Ezzell (2012) studied a group of men facing a masculinity problem in that they had been assigned to a drug treatment programme and had to take orders from all manner of staff and join in with whatever group activity was assigned. Ezzell found that the men responded through a strategy of 'compensatory manhood acts' (based on Schrock and Schwalbe, 2009) that involved masculine aggression, female subordination, challenging other men, and control of emotions. Most seriously, this form of identity work manages to further female subordination, even from within the confines of their captivity.

### Performance, Ritual, and Dramaturgy

Ritual and dramaturgical forms of boundary work can be quite different things, but I can at least put them in the same fuzzy category. For example, some rituals literally happen on stage, as when religious performances, such as Christmas pageants, occur every year in schools. These are examples of ritual dramaturgy, but we expect other performances to be spontaneously rendered, especially on surprise occasions and most seriously when they are public, such as surprise wedding proposals. Davis et al. (2014), studied gender 'performances' on reality makeover television shows. Given the scripted nature of reality television, combined with the heightened importance of gender performances on such programmes (not to mention generally), they show that this kind of performance is more exaggerated than an everyday gender performance.

Performances tend to clear out space between what Zerubavel (1991) called 'islands of meaning', or bounded categories, rather than walking or marking boundaries. One might also think of these as 'fat boundaries'. Having a handbag will not make anyone a girl (and two X chromosomes are not really enough, either). One must perform far from the masculine boundary in order to be convincing as a girl or woman, and performance does not just mean walking with (or without) a swish. It includes all the clothing, hair, colour, body sculpting, diets, steroids, and surgical methods of hyper-gendering the body that many people engage in (Pitts, 2005), adding up to the message that biological sex is *real*. That universal gender boundary is commonly called 'the gender binary' (see e.g. Gagné and Tewksbury, 1999).

## Inclusive and Exclusive

Although we are strongly influenced by Weber's sense of social closure (that is, exclusive boundaries), inclusive boundaries are also possible (DiTomaso, 2014). For example, boundaries could work in a more Durkheimian manner where the primary idea is to bring a community together under a unifying sense of itself. Even Weberian-style boundaries would tilt towards inclusion if they operated in a more life-like manner. That is, the most elite clubs do not spend a lot of time excluding the working class. They handle that problem by being invisible to most outsiders. The boundaries are hidden, and the entrance would be even more elusive.

The strategies that the super-rich use to prevent others from trying to join them also include cultivating a genuine affection for otherwise distasteful status markers (like Kelly Green Pants). Bourdieu (1984 [1979]) discussed the process and Diana Crane furthered the discussion in *The Transformation of the Avant-Garde* (1987). But simply stated, it is the reason soaring sopranos make opera the quintessential status marker of highbrow music, regardless of how many omnivore genres are required to go with it. One might argue that such strategies still constitute methods of exclusion, and they do, but they centre on methods of drawing members to the centre and hiding boundaries, rather than hosting skirmishes at the boundary.

The condition of drawing members to the centre brings attention to the fact that boundaries can occur when things *are not* happening, when there is a gap in human interaction, for example, network theorists might draw a dot for each person and a line for each relationship between two people. A mass of dots and lines is a network, but the space around them is often theorized as a boundary (see e.g. McPherson et al.'s (1992) use of the boundary concept). In addition, while those of us whose main interest was in social status studied the boundaries of memberships that basically amounted to identities, social network researchers noticed important changes in our real-world memberships, finding that our networks are smaller than they were in the mid-1980s – we especially have fewer non-kin confidants, and fewer friends made through voluntary associations. Our friends are more likely to share our level of education, indicating some social closure there, but today's social networks are more racially diverse. The sad story, however, is happening in the land outside the boundaries of social networks in a space that much of symbolic boundaries theorizing forgets to follow. McPherson et al. (2006) found that the number of people with no friends had increased from 10 to 25 per cent between 1985 and 2004.

Although there are studies of single exclusions in the form of excommunication or (more seriously) shunning (Gingrich and Lightman, 2006), sociologists are uniquely positioned to answer questions about why single people find themselves catapulted from any type of boundary, en masse. One possibility suggested by the authors is that families are forgoing external ties because they are buried in housework, and this might especially account for men's declining social networks (Sigle-Rushton, 2010). Lizardo (2006) also used network analysis to identify boundaries and found that highbrow cultural taste contributes to strong ties and network closure (and boundaries in the form of empty space, or no social ties) compared to popular culture, which is associated with weak ties and more disperse networks.

Bourdieu used yet another visual quantitative method called Multi-Dimensional Scaling to plot cultural products in a space described by status, looking for clusters of products, gaps (boundaries) between them, and patterns according to status. Michèle Ollivier (2006) has done this with popular music genres, and Kim and White (2010) used the method to test the 'Panethnicity Hypothesis' on residential segregation and found some affinity among Black, White (white ethnic), and Latino residents, while Asian neighbourhoods had firmer boundaries. Edgell and Tranby (2010) used a variation of this technique called Cluster Analysis to address questions of moral order, asking 2000 US respondents whether (and which) other people shared their views of 'America'. Using a related method, Bail (2008) applied fuzzy set analysis to compare the configurations of symbolic boundaries against immigrants in 21 European countries.

Finally, another variation on this theme is the question of whether a given population is polarized on one or various moral issues or opinion questions. Researchers, beginning with DiMaggio et al. (1996) have approached the question using a variety of methods, all looking for a gap in the data to indicate polarization. The latest dispatch from the field (as of this writing) comes from Mäs et al. (2013), who report that having possible fault lines between demographic groups in, for example, a workplace atmosphere might increase polarization at first, but over time 'crisscrossing actors' who could bridge the gap, ultimately build stronger connections over the weak structure than a group that did not have such a gap in the first place. This is a great example of a place where attending to boundary processes leads naturally to questions of social change.

## NEW DIRECTIONS

One question we might address is when and under what conditions do people break out of boundaries. Laura Rogers (2014) demonstrates that people with breast cancer often break out of the very powerful pink ribbon support-group movement in order to salvage a sense of self from illness and grief by constructing themselves as lucky compared to the people in the support groups from whom they withdraw – on the grounds that contact with so much illness would make them feel worse. McCoy and Scarborough's (2014) study of ironic consumption is especially useful here because it can help us study (methodologically) cases that might have a certain amount of empirical similarity and also understand or theorize that behaviour. That is one person might have an upper-middle-class consumption profile with the exception of one or two 'guilty pleasure' items or 'tacky' items, carefully displayed with irony. We are much better analysts today than we were two decades ago.

Another question lies in the modelling of boundaries. We have a sense of how to conceptualize the centre and even the spaces between bounded regions, thanks to Mary Douglas (1966) and Zerubavel (1991). But, in some cases, it might be useful to model the width of the boundary. Is there a razor-sharp edge between members and outcasts, for example? Or, is there a wider area, perhaps a collection of status markers or a loose network of boundary work? This kind of question could also apply to the bounded area or the ocean between them, as well (the size of which would matter if it were theorized *à la* Douglas (1966) or otherwise). In addition, the various boundaries in a single study might be compared to each other according to factors such as permeability, fluidity, rigidity, and size, especially width. All these characteristics have been addressed at one time or another, but they have not significantly influenced our images or dominant metaphors. Perhaps that is because of the rich variation in our literature.

The last example I will describe should not be an end, but a beginning, so I have aptly chosen to focus on the movement of boundaries. There are, of course, many ways that boundaries can change, and moving symbolic boundaries research further into the social change literature should certainly be one of our many goals, but it is also possible that boundaries or bounded groups have movement as part of their fundamental condition. Anthony Jack (2014), for example, compares two groups of economically disadvantaged black undergraduates at an elite private college. One group arrives on campus with extensive exposure to and experiences developing meaningful relationships with wealthy whites by way of private high school scholarships and the accompanying immersion experiences and enrichment. The other group got their first scholarship and introduction to elite academic life at the college level. The two groups are different, but Jack's analysis is not static. For these young students the boundary that they struggle with is not race but social class, and the question of its salience in the college context depends on their dissimilar experiences before college. Therefore, Jack (2014) offers a trajectory analysis that allows us to compare the two groups as they move through time, given the sorts of experiences they were likely to encounter, adding up to – not changes in boundary formation – but different expressions of what we generally understand as the same boundary.

## NOTE

1 For review articles see Lamont (2001; 2012), Lamont and Molnár (2002), and Lamont, Pendergrass, and Pachucki (2015). For collected volumes devoted to symbolic boundaries, see Lamont (1992; 1999), and for theoretical and empirical work (in that order) see Lamont and Lareau (1988) and Lamont (1992; 2000; 2009).

## REFERENCES

Abbott, A. (1988) *The System of Professions: An Essay on the Division of Expert Labor*. Chicago: University of Chicago Press.

Acker, J. (1988) 'Class, Gender, and the Relations of Distribution', *Signs*, 13: 473–97.

Acker, J. (1990) 'Hierarchies, Jobs, Bodies: A Theory of Gendered Organizations', *Gender and Society*, 4: 139–58.

Ajrouch, K.J. (2004) 'Gender, Race, and Symbolic Boundaries: Contested Spaces of Identity among Arab American Adolescents', *Sociological Perspectives*, 47: 371–91.

Almeling, R. and Ebrary Academic Complete Subscription Collection (2011) 'Sex Cells'.

Aneesh, A. (2010) 'Bloody Language: Clashes and Constructions of Linguistic Nationalism in India', *Sociological Forum*, 25: 86–109.

Kim, A.H. and White, M.J. (2010) 'Panethnicity, Ethnic Diversity, and Residential Segregation', *American Journal of Sociology*, 115: 1558–96.

Appelrouth, S. and Kelly, C. (2013) 'Rap, Race and the (Re)Production of Boundaries', *Sociological Perspectives*, 56: 301–26.

Bail, C. (2008) 'The Configuration of Symbolic Boundaries against Immigrants in Europe', *American Sociological Review*, 73(1): 37–59.

Becker, H.S. (1963) *Outsiders: Studies in the Sociology of Deviance*. London: Free Press of Glencoe.

Bourdieu, P. (1979) *Algeria 1960: The Disenchantment of the World: The Sense of Honour: The Kabyle House Or the World Reversed: Essays*. Cambridge and New York: Cambridge University Press.

Bourdieu, P. (1984 [1979]) *Distinction: A Social Critique of the Judgement of Taste*. Cambridge, MA: Harvard University Press.

Bryson, B. (1996) '"Anything but Heavy Metal": Symbolic Exclusion and Musical Dislikes', *American Sociological Review*, 61: 884–99.

Bryson, B. (2005) *Making Multiculturalism: Boundaries and Meaning in U.S. English Departments*. Stanford, CA: Stanford University Press.

Butler, J. (1990) *Gender Trouble: Feminism and the Subversion of Identity*. New York: Routledge.

Cherry, E. (2010) 'Shifting Symbolic Boundaries: Cultural Strategies of the Animal Rights Movement', *Sociological Forum*, 25: 450–75.

Collins, P.H. (2000) *Black Feminist Thought: Knowledge, Consciousness, and the Politics of Empowerment*. New York: Routledge.

Coulangeon, P. (2005) 'Social Stratification of Musical Tastes: Questioning the Cultural Legitimacy Model', *Revue Française De Sociologie*, 46: 123–54.

Crane, D. (1987) *The Transformation of the Avant-Garde: The New York Art World, 1940–1985*. Chicago: University of Chicago Press.

Crane, D. (2000) *Fashion and its Social Agendas: Class, Gender, and Identity in Clothing*. Chicago: University of Chicago Press.

Davis, A.K. (2014) 'Equal but Separate? Gender, Culture, and the Social Organization of Public Space', Meeting of American Sociological Association, San Francisco, CA.

Davis, A.K., Rogers, L.E., and Bryson, B. (2014) 'Own it! Constructions of Masculinity and Heterosexuality on Reality Makeover Television', *Cultural Sociology*, 8(3): 258–74.

Dentler, R.A. and Erikson, K.T. (1959) 'The Functions of Deviance in Groups', *Social Problems*, 7: 98–107.

DeSoucey, M. (2010) 'Gastronationalism: Food Traditions and Authenticity Politics in the European Union', *American Sociological Review*, 75: 432–55.

Dill, B.T. (1994) *Across the Boundaries of Race and Class: An Exploration of Work and Family among Black Female Domestic Servants*. New York: Garland.

DiMaggio, P. (1979) 'On Pierre Bourdieu', *American Journal of Sociology*, 84: 1460–74.

DiMaggio, P. (1982) 'Cultural Capital and School Success: The Impact of Status Culture Participation on the Grades of U.S. High School Students', *American Sociological Review*, 47: 189–201.

DiMaggio, P. (1987) 'Classification in Art', *American Sociological Review*, 52: 440–55.

DiMaggio, P. and Mohr, J. (1985) 'Cultural Capital, Educational Attainment, and Marital Selection', *American Journal of Sociology*, 90: 1231–61.

DiMaggio, P., Evans, J., and Bryson, B. (1996) 'Have Americans' Social Attitudes Become More Polarized?', *American Journal of Sociology*, 102: 690–755.

DiTomaso, N. (2014) 'Are Boundaries to Keep People Out Or In?', Meeting of the American Sociological Association, San Francisco, CA.

Douglas, M. (1966) *Purity and Danger: An Analysis of Concepts of Pollution and Taboo*. New York: Praeger.

Douglas, M. (1972) 'Deciphering a Meal', *Daedalus*, 101: 61–81.

Douglas, M. (1986) *How Institutions Think*. Syracuse, NY: Syracuse University Press.

Douglass, F. (1881) 'The Color Line', *The North American Review*, 567.

DuBois, W.E.B. and Bartleby Library (1903) 'The Souls of Black Folk'.

Durkheim, É. (1933 [1893]) *The Division of Labor in Society*. New York: Free Press.

Durkheim, É. (2008 [1912]) *The Elementary Forms of Religious Life*. Oxford: Oxford University Press.

Edgell, P. and Tranby, E. (2010) 'Shared Visions? Diversity and Cultural Membership in American Life', *Social Problems*, 57: 175–204.

Epstein, C.F. (1989) 'Workplace Boundaries: Conceptions and Creations', *Social Research*, 56: 571–90.

Epstein, C.F. (1992) 'Tinkerbells and Pinups: The Construction and Reconstruction of Gender Boundaries at Work', in M. Lamont and M. Fournier (eds), *Cultivating Differences: Symbolic Boundaries and the Making of Inequality*. Chicago: University of Chicago Press. pp. 232–56.

Erickson, B.H. (1996) 'Culture, Class, and Connections', *American Journal of Sociology*, 102: 217–51.

Erikson, K. (1966) *Wayward Puritans: A Study in the Sociology of Deviance*. New York: Wiley.

Espeland, W. and Sauder, M. (2007) 'Rankings and Reactivity: How Public Measures Re-create Social Worlds', *American Journal of Sociology*, 24: 313–43.

Espeland, W. and Stevens, M. (1998) 'Commensuration as a Social Process', *Annual Review of Sociology*, 113: 1–40.

Ezzell, M. (2012) 'I'm in Control, Compensatory Manhood in a Therapeutic Community', *Gender & Society*, 26(2):190–215.

Fausto-Sterling, A. (2012) *Sexgender: Biology in a Social World*. New York: Routledge.

Fourcade, M. and Healy, K. (2013) 'Classification Situations: Life-Chances in the Neoliberal Era', *Accounting, Organizations and Society*, 38: 559–72.

Friese, C. (2010) 'Classification Conundrums: Categorizing Chimeras and Enacting Species Preservation', *Theory and Society*, 39: 145–72.

Gagné, P. and Tewksbury, R. (1999) 'Knowledge and Power, Body and Self: An Analysis of Knowledge Systems and the Transgendered Self', *The Sociological Quarterly*, 40: 59–83.

Gamson, J. (1995) 'Must Identity Movements Self-Destruct? A Queer Dilemma', *Social Problems*, 42: 390–407.

Gerson, J.M. and Peiss, K. (1985) 'Boundaries, Negotiation, Consciousness: Reconceptualizing Gender Relations', *Social Problems*, 317–31.

Gerson, K. (1993) *No Man's Land: Men's Changing Commitments to Family and Work*. New York, NY: Basic Books.

Gieryn, T.F. (1983) 'Boundary-Work and the Demarcation of Science from Non-Science: Strains and Interests in Professional Ideologies of Scientists', *American Sociological Review*, 48: 781–95.

Gingrich, L.G. and Lightman, E. (2006) 'Striving Toward Self-Sufficiency: A Qualitative Study of Mutual Aid in an Old Order Mennonite Community', *Family Relations*, 55: 175–89.

Goffman, E. (1986 [1963]) *Stigma: Notes on the Management of Spoiled Identity*. New York: Simon and Schuster.

Hale, G.E. (1998) *Making Whiteness: The Culture of Segregation in the South, 1890–1940*. New York: Pantheon Books.

Hannan, M.T., Pólos, L., and Carroll, L.R. (2007) *Logics of Organization Theory: Audiences, Codes, and Ecologies*. Princeton, NJ: Princeton University Press.

Hsu, G. (2006) 'Jacks of all Trades and Masters of None: Audiences' Reactions to Spanning Genres in Feature Film Production', *Administrative Science Quarterly*, 51: 420–50.

Hughey, M.W. (2007) 'Racism with Antiracists: Color-Conscious Racism and the Unintentional Persistence of Inequality', *Social Thought and Research*, 28: 67–108.

Hughey, M.W. (2012) *White Bound: Nationalists, Antiracists, and the Shared Meanings of Race*. Stanford, CA: Stanford University Press.

Jack, A.A. (2014) 'Culture Shock Revisited: The Social and Cultural Contingencies to Class Marginality', *Sociological Forum*, 29: 453–75.

Jacobs, J.A. and Gerson, K. (2004) *The Time Divide: Work, Family, And Gender Inequality*. Cambridge, MA: Harvard University Press.

Jenness, V. (2008) 'Pluto, Prisons, and Plaintiffs: Notes on Systematic Back-Translation from an Embedded Researcher', *Social Problems*, 55: 1–22.

Lamont, M. (1992) *Money, Morals, and Manners: The Culture of the French and American Upper-Middle Class*. Chicago, IL: University of Chicago Press.

Lamont, M. (1999) *The Cultural Territories of Race: Black and White Boundaries*. Chicago: University of Chicago Press and New York: Russell Sage Foundation.

Lamont, M. (2000) 'Meaning-Making in Cultural Sociology: Broadening our Agenda', *Contemporary Sociology*, 29: 602–7.

Lamont, M. (2001) 'Symbolic Boundaries', in N.J. Smelser and P.B. Baltes (eds) *International Encyclopedia of the Social and Behavioral Sciences*, pp. 15341–15347. London: Pergamon Press.

Lamont, M. (2009) *How Professors Think: Inside the Curious World of Academic Judgment*. Cambridge, MA: Harvard University Press.

Lamont, M. (2012) 'How has Bourdieu been Good to Think With? The Case of the United States', *Sociological Forum*, 27: 228–37.

Lamont, M. and Fournier, M. (1992) *Cultivating Differences: Symbolic Boundaries and the Making of Inequality*. Chicago: University of Chicago Press.

Lamont, M. and Lareau, A. (1988) 'Cultural Capital: Allusions, Gaps and Glissandos in Recent Theoretical Developments', *Sociological Theory*, 6: 153–68.

Lamont, M. and Molnár, V. (2002) 'The Study of Boundaries in the Social Sciences', *Annual Review of Sociology*, 28: 167–95.

Lamont, M., Pendergrass, S., and Pachucki, M. (2015) 'Symbolic Boundaries', in J. Wright (ed.), *International Encyclopedia of Social and Behavioral Sciences*, pp. 850–55. Oxford: Elsevier.

Lan, P-C. (2003) 'Negotiating Social Boundaries and Private Zones: The Micropolitics of Employing Migrant Domestic Workers', *Social Problems*, 50: 525–49.

Lena, J.C. and Peterson, R.A. (2008) 'Classification as Culture: Types and Trajectories of Music Genres', *American Sociological Review*, 73: 697–718.

Lifshitz-Assaf, H. (2015) 'From Problem Solvers to Solution Seekers: The Permeation of Knowledge Boundaries at NASA', *Social Science Research Network*. New York and Cambridge, MA: New York University Leonard N. Stern School of Business and Harvard Business School, January 4, 2015. http://papers.ssrn.com/sol3/papers.cfm?abstract_id=2431717

Lizardo, O. (2006) 'How Cultural Tastes Shape Personal Networks', *American Sociological Review*, 71: 778–807.

Lorber, J. (1999) 'Crossing Borders and Erasing Boundaries: Paradoxes of Identity Politics', *Sociological Focus*, 32: 355–70.

Lorber, J. (2006) 'Shifting Paradigms and Challenging Categories', *Social Problems,* 53: 448–53.

Loveman, M. and Muniz, J.O. (2007) 'How Puerto Rico Became White: Boundary Dynamics and Intercensus Racial Reclassification', *American Sociological Review,* 72: 915–39.

Marks, J. (2000) 'Scientific and Folk Ideas about Heredity', in R.A. Zilinskas and P.J. Balint (eds), *the Human Genome Project and Minority Communities: Ethical, Social and Political Dilemmas.* Westport, CT: Greenwood. pp. 53–66.

Martin, E. (1991) 'The Egg and the Sperm: How Science has Constructed a Romance Based on Stereotypical Male-Female Roles', *Signs,* 16: 485–501.

Mäs, M., Flache, A., Takács, K., and Jehn, K.A. (2013) 'In the Short Term we Divide, in the Long Term we Unite: Demographic Crisscrossing and the Effects of Faultlines on Subgroup Polarization', *Organization Science,* 24: 716–36.

McCoy, C. and Scarborough, R.C. (2014) 'Watching "Bad" Television: Ironic Consumption, Camp, and Guilty Pleasures', *Poetics,* 47: 41–59.

McPherson, J.M., Popielarz, P.A. and Drobnic, S. (1992) 'Social Networks and Organizational Dynamics', *American Sociological Review,* 57: 153–70.

McPherson, M., Smith-Lovin, L. and Brashears, M.E. (2006) 'Social Isolation in America: Changes in Core Discussion Networks over Two Decades', *American Sociological Review,* 71: 353–75.

Meadow, T. (2010) 'A Rose is a Rose: On Producing Legal Gender Classifications', *Gender and Society,* 24: 814–37.

Meadow, T. (2011) '"Deep Down Where the Music Plays": How Parents Account for Childhood Gender Variance', *Sexualities,* 14: 725–47.

Morning, A. (2005) 'Keywords: Race', *Contexts,* 4: 44–6.

Morrison, T. (1992) *Playing in the Dark: Whiteness and the Literary Imagination.* Cambridge, MA: Harvard University Press.

Nagel, J. (1995) 'American Indian Ethnic Renewal: Politics and the Resurgence of Identity', *American Sociological Review,* 60: 947–65.

Nippert-Eng, C. (1996) 'Calendars and Keys: The Classification of "Home" and "Work"', *Sociological Forum,* 11: 563–82.

Nippert-Eng, C. (2010) *Islands of Privacy.* Chicago: University of Chicago Press.

Ollivier, M. (2006) 'Snobs and Quétaines: Prestige and Boundaries in Popular Music in Quebec', *Popular Music,* 25: 97–116.

Parsons, T. (1968) *The Structure of Social Action.* New York: Free Press.

Parsons, T. and Smelser, N.J. (1956) *Economy and Society: A Study in the Integration of Economic and Social Theory.* Glencoe, IL: Free Press.

Pascoe, C.J. (2011) *Dude, You're a Fag: Masculinity and Sexuality in High School.* Berkeley: University of California Press.

Peterson, R.A. (1992) 'Understanding Audience Segmentation: From Elite and Mass to Omnivore and Univore', *Poetics,* 21: 243–58.

Peterson, R.A. and Kern, R.M. (1996) 'Changing Highbrow Taste: From Snob to Omnivore', *American Sociological Review,* 61: 900–7.

Phillips, D.T. (2013) 'Moving with the Women: Tracing Racialization, Migration, and Domestic Workers in the Archive', *Signs,* 38: 379–404.

Pitts, V. (2005) 'Feminism, Technology and Body Projects', *Women's Studies,* 34: 229–47.

Pitts-Taylor, V. (2007) *Surgery Junkies: Wellness and Pathology in Cosmetic Culture.* New Brunswick, NJ: Rutgers University Press.

Purser, G. (2009) 'The Dignity of Job-Seeking Men: Boundary Work among Immigrant Day Laborers', *Journal of Contemporary Ethnography,* 38: 117–39.

Reyes, D. (2015) 'Inhabiting Latino Politics: How Colleges Shape Students' Political Styles', *Sociology of Education,* 88: 302–19.

Rogers, L.E. (2014) '"In Comparison, I'm Really Lucky": How Breast Cancer Patients Utilize Symbolic Boundaries as a Coping Mechanism' presented to the American Sociological Association, San Francisco, CA.

Roy, W.G. (2014) 'Musical Genres', unpublished manuscript.

Saguy, A. (2013) *What's Wrong with Fat?* Oxford: Oxford University Press.

Said, E.W. (2003 [1994]) *Orientalism.* New York: Vintage Books.

Saperstein, A. and Penner, A.M. (2010) 'The Race of a Criminal Record: How Incarceration Colors Racial Perceptions', *Social Problems,* 57: 92–113.

Salzinger, L. (2003) *Genders in Production: Making Workers in Mexico's Global Factories.* Berkeley, CA: University of California Press.

Schrock, D. and Schwalbe, M. (2009) 'Men, Masculinity, and Manhood Acts', *Annual Review of Sociology,* 35: 277–295.

Schwartz, B. (1981) *Vertical Classification: A Study in Structuralism and the Sociology of Knowledge.* Chicago: University of Chicago Press.

Schwartzman, L.F. (2007) 'Does Money Whiten? Intergenerational Changes in Racial Classification in Brazil', *American Sociological Review,* 72: 940–63.

Sedgwick, E.K. (1990) *Epistemology of the Closet.* Berkeley: University of California Press.

Shirley, C.D. (2010) '"You might be a Redneck if …": Boundary Work among Rural, Southern Whites', *Social Forces,* 89: 35–61.

Sigle-Rushton, W. (2010) 'Men's Unpaid Work and Divorce: Reassessing Specialization and Trade in British Families', *Feminist Economics,* 16: 1–26.

Small, M.L., Harding, D.J. and Lamont, M. (2010) 'Introduction: Reconsidering Culture and Poverty', *Annals of the American Academy of Political and Social Science*, 629: 6–27.

Spade, D. (2011) *Normal Life: Administrative Violence, Critical Trans Politics and the Limits of Law*. New York: South End Press.

Swartz, B. (1981) *Vertical Classification: A Study in Structuralism and the Sociology of Knowledge*. Chicago: University of Chicago Press.

Swindle, J. (2014) 'The Cultural Model of a Developmental Hierarchy of Societies', Center for Cultural Sociology Working Paper Series.

Tilly, C. (1998) *Durable Inequality*. Berkeley: University of California Press.

Thorne, B. (1993) *Gender Play: Girls and Boys in School*. New Brunswick, NJ: Rutgers University Press.

Wagner-Pacifici, R.E. (2000) *Theorizing the Standoff: Contingency in Action*. Cambridge and New York: Cambridge University Press.

Warren, J.W. and Twine, F.W. (1997) 'White Americans, the New Minority? Non-Blacks and the Ever-Expanding Boundaries of Whiteness', *Journal of Black Studies*, 28: 200–18.

Weber, M. (1978 [1922]) *Economy and Society: An Outline of Interpretive Sociology*. Edited by Guenther, R. and Wittich, C. Berkeley: University of California Press.

Zelizer, V. (1994) *Pricing the Priceless Child: The Changing Social Value of Children*. Princeton: Princeton University Press.

Zerubavel, E. (1991) *The Fine Line: Making Distinctions in Everyday Life*. New York: Free Press.

Zucker, L.G. (1977) 'The Role of Institutionalization in Cultural Persistence', *American Sociological Review*, 42(5): 726–43.

Zylan, Y. (2011) *States of Passion: Law, Identity, and the Social Construction of Desire*. Oxford and New York: Oxford University Press.

# 26

# Cultural Sociology of Religion and Beliefs

Laura D. Edles

## INTRODUCTION

The primary issue at the heart of both the sociology of religion and the cultural sociology of religion is: What is the role of religion in our contemporary world? Cultural sociologists and sociologists of religion approach this question in a variety of ways, but they are rooted above all in the broad, 'functionalist' conceptualization of religion of Émile Durkheim and the narrower, more 'substantive' one of Max Weber. This is not to say that the question as to the role of religion in our contemporary world cannot be answered in a variety of 'non-cultural' ways too, for instance by focusing on institutional matters (e.g. the political clout of the Catholic Church) or psychological issues (e.g., the power of meditation, prayer or guilt). But cultural sociologists emphasize that whether one examines religion as a dominant, authoritative structure, or a deeply personal world-view, religion is indisputably and above all, a powerful system of meaning; religion is a *cultural* system and therefore positioned at the interface between the institutional and psychological realms. As Geertz (1973: 5) famously states, 'man is an animal suspended in webs of significance he himself has spun', and clearly a fundamental web of significance is religion.

## DURKHEIM AND DURKHEIMIAN APPROACHES TO RELIGION

This broad conceptualization of religion as a transcendent web of significance is firmly rooted in the work of Émile Durkheim. For Durkheim, religion does not just mean 'churchly' things, but rather, systems of symbols and rituals about the sacred and practiced by a community of believers. From a Durkheimian perspective, there is no significant difference between the opening moment of a religious service in which congregants are called to prayer ('Let us pray'), and the opening moment of a baseball game, in which congregants are called to 'stand for the national anthem'. Both are sacred ritual moments, imbued with sacred symbols that tie the community together. This is called a 'functionalist' rather than 'substantive' definition of religion because it emphasizes not the substantive content of religion (e.g. specific doctrines) but the social *function* of religion. As Durkheim (1965 [1912]: 253) states, 'religious force is nothing other than the collective and anonymous force' of society. The worship of transcendent gods or spirits and the respect and awe accorded to their power is in actuality the worship of the social group and the force it exerts over the individual, according to Durkheim. Religion is:

a system of ideas with which the individuals represent to themselves the society of which they are members, and the obscure but intimate relationship which they have with it ... for it is an eternal truth that outside of us there exists something greater than us, with which we enter into communion. (1965 [1912]: 257)

Religious ceremonials are celebrations of social life, and the notion that religion can be entirely 'private' is fallacious. Social life is inherently 'religious'; so long as there are societies, there will be religion.

Durkheim maintains that this social and communal function of religion is carried out through the dual processes of ritualization and symbolization. Whereas the former refer to acts or practices (e.g. such as taking communion), the latter refer to relatively intangible 'states of opinion', 'representations', 'symbols', and 'thought', though clearly these two processes are intimately intertwined. As Durkheim (1965 [1912]: 474–5) famously states:

> There can be no society which does not feel the need of upholding and reaffirming at regular intervals the collective sentiments and the collective ideas which makes its unity and its personality. Now this moral remaking cannot be achieved except by the means of reunions, assemblies and meetings where the individuals, being closely united to one another, reaffirm in common their common sentiments.

Durkheim classifies symbols and rites into two categories: the sacred and the profane. The sacred refers to that which is set apart from, above and beyond, the everyday world. The symbolic opposite of the sacred is the emotionally uncharged realm of the profane or mundane. A major part of Durkheim's work involved showing how mundane objects, such as lizards and plants, could take on the sacredness of the 'totem' or symbol of the tribe. His point was that there is nothing intrinsically sacred about these objects, but that they are invested with sacrality through social processes. The function of symbolic classification is that it creates symbolic order. It imposes system on the 'inherently untidy experience' of living (Douglas, 1966: 4; Gamson, 1998: 141).

Whereas Durkheim ambiguously used 'profane' to refer to both the emotionally charged realm of evil and the uncharged realm of the everyday world, followers of Durkheim such as Hertz (2009) and Callois (1959) resolved this ambiguity by turning the sacred/profane dichotomy into a threefold classification. Hertz proposed a trichotomy of the pure, the impure (or the transgressive sacred), and the profane. According to Hertz (2009: 92):

in the classification that, from the beginning and increasingly more so as time has passed, has dominated religious consciousness, there is a natural affinity and nearly an equivalence between the profane and the impure; the two notions combine and form, in opposition to the sacred, the negative pole of the spiritual world.

Similarly, Callois (1959) resolved this ambiguity by utilizing the term 'profane' to refer to what Hertz called the transgressive sacred or impure, and the term mundane to refer to the emotionally uncharged realm. For Callois the sacred and the profane are effervescent, charged categories which contrast with routine, mundane signs, which do not carry such profound symbolic weight.

As indicated previously, Durkheim underscored the mutually reinforcing character of 'beliefs' (collective sentiments and collective ideas) and 'rites' (reunions, assemblies). Yet, the analytical separation 'beliefs' and 'rites' is important, for it distinguishes the communal (social) from the moral (cultural) function of religion. For instance, acts and practices have the capability of uniting disparate individuals regardless of individual differences in beliefs, strength of belief, etc. Mere participation in ritual acts can bind participants together.

Put in another way, many animals – including human animals – are highly social, that is, they like to be with one another. However, human animals are unique in terms of the extent to which their lives involve developing and maintaining intricate, nuanced symbolic systems. Moreover, unlike rites, symbols have the capability of calling up and reaffirming collective sentiments, even if people are not physically together. Symbols can invoke an *imagined* community, in Benedict Anderson's terms. Thus, for instance, wearing a religious symbol on a necklace might fortify one's bonds with one's religious community, even if one does not practice his/her religion.

In *Primitive Classification* (1963 [1903]), Durkheim and his nephew and collaborator Marcel Mauss [1872–1950] further show that the function of classificatory schemes is not merely (or even mainly) intellectual, but rather moral and normative. This is also the central theme of Mauss' most well-known work, translated into English as *The Gift*. Mauss turns the universal assumption of free market enthusiasts – that what essentially drives human beings is a desire to maximize their pleasures, comforts and material possessions – upside down by arguing that gift exchange is imbued with ceremonial and communal functions. Stressing that 'gifts carry with them a kind of magical force and a strong sense of obligation': namely, the obligation: (1) to give; (2) to receive; (3) to repay gifts received; (4) to return a gift different from the original gift; and (5) to delay the return gift (Smith, 2001: 75), Mauss questions the idea of gift giving, as discussed by Graeber:

> Why is it that, when one receives a gift from a friend (a drink, a dinner invitation, a compliment), one feels somehow obliged to reciprocate in kind? Why is it that a recipient of generosity often somehow feels reduced if he or she cannot? Are these not examples of universal human feelings, which are somehow discounted in our own society – but in others were the very basis of the economic system? (Graeber, 2000: n.p.)

This Durkheimian notion that social life is fundamentally symbolic and expressive rather than instrumental was taken up by a variety of Durkheim's followers, most importantly, Robert Hertz [1881–1915], Claude Lévi-Strauss [1908–2009], Mary Douglas [1921–2007], Peter Berger [1929–] and Victor Turner [1920–1983]. Specifically, in his most famous essay, 'The Pre-eminence of the Right Hand: A Study in Religious Polarity', Hertz (2009) examines how the dualisms found in the natural environment (e.g. between night and day, sky and earth, etc.) provide the conceptual schema for the construction of social order (Back et al., 2012: 94). Hertz (2009) points out that the right's moral superiority over the left is embodied in language (for instance 'right' means 'correct'), and it is symbolized in rituals (for instance, the right hand takes the oath in court, and in two right hands creating a handshake). So too, in *The Savage Mind* (1966 [1962]) Lévi-Strauss argues that classification systems and knowledge are built up by locating differences and resemblance in things. Focusing on the 'unconscious attitudes' of primitive societies as evident in kinship systems, myths and art, Lévi-Strauss demonstrates that social life is 'language-like', symbolic and expressive rather than instrumental.

In her now classic book *Purity and Danger* (1966), Mary Douglas offers further insights into resemblances and differences. Extending Durkheim's central argument in *The Elementary Forms of Religious Life* (that religious systems are the guardians of symbolic order), Douglas shows that the central task of religion and culture is 'separating, purifying, demarcating, and punishing transgressions' and defending classifications against the ambiguities and anomalies to which they give rise. For instance, concentrating on the food taboos in Leviticus 11, Douglas maintains that biblical taboos are not necessarily health-related; rather they have to do with protecting the distinction between the sacred and profane. The function of food taboos – and religious rules in general – is to protect symbolic order. Anomalies are abominations. As Douglas (1966: 55) states:

> In the firmament two legged fowls fly with wings. In the water scaly fish swim with fins. On the earth four-legged animals hop, jump, or walk. Any class of creatures which is not equipped for the right kind of locomotion in its element is contrary to holiness. Contact with it disqualifies a person from approaching the Temple. Thus anything in the water which has not fins and scales is unclean.

That the primary function of religion and culture is to provide symbolic and moral order is also the major premise of Peter Berger's now classic book *The Sacred Canopy*. Indeed, Berger maintains that the primary distinction between human and non-human animals is that the former are 'congenitally' compelled to impose a meaningful order (or *nomos*) upon reality. Unlike non-human animals, which are endowed biologically with highly developed ordering mechanisms (instincts), human animals are 'unfinished' at birth. Hence they must create their own world. As Berger (1967: 22–4) states:

> The socially established nomos may thus be understood, perhaps in its most important aspect, as a shield against terror ... The most important function of society is nomization ... Every *nomos* is an area of meaning carved out of a vast mass of meaninglessness, a small clearing of lucidity in a formless, dark, always ominous jungle ... every *nomos* is an edifice erected in the face of the potent and alien forces of chaos. This chaos must be kept at bay at all cost.

However, in contrast to Durkheim, anthropologists such as Douglas (1966) and Turner (1969) emphasize that the creation and maintenance of order is not all-pervasive. Douglas points out that the possibility of seeing a sculpture equally as well as a landscape or as a reclining nude enriches the viewers' interest the work; aesthetic pleasure often arises from the perceiving of inarticulate forms. Ambiguity and anomaly are stimulating. Expanding on the work of Arnold van Gennep, Turner maintains that all rites of passage (birth, initiation, marriage, etc.) contain a moment of ambiguity. Specifically, Turner argues that there are three phases in the ritual process: in the first phase, separation, the individual symbolically detaches from an earlier fixed point in the social structure or state. During the second, intervening 'liminal' period, the characteristics of the ritual subject are an ambiguous blend of lowliness and sacrality, or homogeneity and comradeship. In the third phase, reaggregation, the passage is consummated, and the ritual subject is expected to behave in accordance with the norms and ethical standards of the new social state. In the liminal phase the ritual subject is literally 'betwixt and between' the old and new social states; Turner points out that societies also fluctuate between periods of order and disorder (such as Carnival). Social life requires periods of 'structure' and 'anti-structure', and liminal moments are 'moments in and out of time' in which social classifications and codes can be reworked as well as reaffirmed.

## RATIONALIZATION AND SECULARIZATION

Thus far we have seen that the cultural sociology of religion is rooted above all in the work of Émile Durkheim and his followers. However, the cultural sociology of religion is also anchored in the seminal writings of Max Weber, who, in stark contrast to Durkheim, set his sights on demonstrating the impact and historical consequences of a variety of religious and cultural constructs. Weber sought to sort out the 'practical impulses for action which are found in the psychological and pragmatic contexts of religion', that is, how a specific religious or cultural perspective ('world-view') shapes action.

Also in stark contrast to Durkheim, Weber was most intrigued by the process of the *rationalization* of society, i.e. the increasing reliance on methodical procedures and calculable rules rather than tradition and emotion in not only attitudes, but interactions and institutions in human society. Weber (1958 [1919]: 130) maintained that while the rationalization of society would result in greater efficiency in obtaining designated ends, it would also lead to the 'disenchantment of the world' where 'there are no mysterious incalculable forces that come into play, but rather that one can, in principle, master all things by calculation'. Weber perceived the process of rationalization and secularization as inescapable as the empirical world became increasingly complex; the growing dominance of an instrumental and scientific orientation to life would necessarily result in the disenchantment of the world, that is, a loss of ultimate meaning.

Weber's notion of a purely secular, disenchanted world clearly reflects that Weber's definition of religion is radically different from that of Durkheim. Though he never set out a single, explicit definition of religion, in practice Weber conceived of religion as dealing with three substantive issues: (1) *soteriology* – a 'right' relationship with a higher power; (2) *theology* – an explanation for evil; and (3) *ethics*, notions of right and wrong. Yet, despite their distinct conceptual frameworks, Durkheimian and Weberian approaches to religion reflect a similar symbolic dichotomy. Weber's concepts of 'enchantment' and 'disenchantment' parallel Durkheim's concepts of 'sacred' and the 'profane'. Weber conceptualized a disenchanted world as lacking in ultimate transcendence, that is, one in which 'nothing' is held 'sacred' in Durkheim's terms.

Consider, for instance, the scientific method as an ideal type of disenchantment. From both a Durkheimian and Weberian perspective, one of the pivotal differences between "science" and "religion" is that whereas religion is rooted in explicitly sacred ideas (i.e. that are not to be 'touched', that are symbolically set apart and revered for all eternity); scientific data is absolutely mutable (rather than immutable), and in that regard science is 'profane'. New data can and should upend old theories and 'facts' without consternation, and scientific objectivity means that scientists must be 'unattached' to their theories. Continually open to testing, if disproven, theories are intended to be thrown out and replaced with new ideas. However, here is where Weber and Durkheim diverge: For Durkheim, the scientific community can still be considered a Church, in which the scientific method is the 'ultimate truth' that it holds most dear since it sets the *boundaries* of science. To be a scientist, one must 'believe' in the scientific method as the ultimate means for attaining the 'truth'; one must not forsake it (the scientific method), for it defines what it is to be a scientist and to take a scientific approach to the world.

Secularization theory was the dominant paradigm in the early 20th century for good reason: evidence of secularization abounds. Since the start of the Enlightenment, more and more people have turned to science rather than religion to explain both expected and unexpected, and natural and human-induced events (e.g. weather, earthquakes, disease, plane crashes, poverty); and Western Europe has witnessed a particularly sharp decline in religiosity. For instance, France officially separated itself from the Catholic Church in 1905, and since then has vigorously sought to keep religion out of the public sphere. In the last decade, the French have defended the tradition of secularism (instigated most famously by French Enlightenment figures such as Voltaire, Diderot and Montesquieu) by banning head-scarves in state schools in 2004, and outlawing full face veils in public in 2010.

Yet, one of the most startling global developments of the late 20th and early 21st centuries has been the rise of religious fundamentalisms. While, at the dawn of the 20th century, Weber pessimistically imagined that rational and bureaucratic structures would render the religious spirit obsolete, what we have seen throughout the 20th century and now in the 21st is that the human search for meaning and community cannot be so easily eradicated. That French secularism would be met by an intense Muslim backlash was not at all anticipated.

Market theorists (e.g. Stark and Finke, 2000) explain the failure of the secularization thesis by pointing to the expansion of 'choices' and products in the religious marketplace. But sociologists of religion (e.g. Edgell, 2006; Smilde, 2007) criticize this 'religious market model' for its acultural and asocial assumptions, that is, for implying that the 'selling of religion' is not *really* about religion at all. For culturalists, the point is that, regardless of the tactics and nuances of religious marketing, *something* is being marketed here. The question is: What is the appeal of religion in our increasingly modernized, industrialized and rationalized, 'secular' world?

From a cultural perspective, it should come as no surprise that the human need for emotional sustenance, social solidarity and meaning has not waned – but may well be increasing (rather than decreasing) in this post-industrial age. Divorce and remarriage; the geographical dispersion of families in search of employment and sustenance; war; poverty; drug and alcohol addictions; domestic and global violence, to name a few rampant postmodern social conditions, mean that finding and maintaining emotional, psychological and communal sustenance and stability may be even more difficult than in 'pre-modern' days. Regardless of the monumental changes in our global world, our basic psychological and communal needs are no different than those of our pre-modern forbearers.

This is precisely the point of religion scholars such as Karen Armstrong (2000: ix) who argue that religious fundamentalism is not an archaic throwback to an earlier era, but part and parcel of modern and postmodern society. The relationship between modernity and fundamentalism is symbiotic, not paradoxical. As Armstrong (2000: xiii) states, 'there have always been people, in every age and in each tradition, who have fought the modernity of their day'. Wherever they are found, religious fundamentalisms are rooted in a sense of moral decadence, and 'it's not a trivial backlash', says history professor Scott Appleby (Patterson 2004). Fundamentalists see the world dualistically and perceive themselves to be in a clash of good against evil (Patterson 2004). Of course, this is precisely the clash that came to a tragic head in Paris in January 2015, when a terrorist attack on the offices of the French satirical magazine *Charlie Hebdo* (*Charlie Weekly*) resulted in the deaths of 12 people; and again in November 2015, when three suicide bombers engaged in a series of coordinated terrorist attacks, killing 130 people and injuring hundreds of others, many of them seriously.

In addition, it is not only frustration and angst in regards to liberalizing trends in society as a whole – but within their own faith – that helps explain why religious fundamentalisms are continual and thriving. Whether European counter-reformers in the 16th century, American Christian fundamentalists in the 1920s, or Islamic fundamentalists in the Middle East in the 1980s, in all the major religions throughout history, fundamentalists have been propelled into action by what they perceive as intolerable internal as well as external change. The plea 'back to the well-springs!' is one and the same (Armstrong, 2000: 5). Thus, for instance, today protracted battles over gender and sexual orientation are dividing churches and temples right and left (pun intended). In 2008 conservative Anglicans and Episcopalians split off from the worldwide Anglican Communion and formed a new body, called the Fellowship of Confessing Anglicans, in direct response to the appointment of Gene Robinson, an openly gay man, as bishop. Similarly, 'irreconcilable differences concerning the roles and rights of men and women in the synagogue' led to a split in one Jewish temple sociologist Phil Zuckerman studied (2003: 88). Paralleling the conservative Episcopalians who could not tolerate a gay man as bishop, the more Orthodox group left the Synagogue because they could not stomach the inclusion of women in every aspect of the synagogue rituals. Both conservative groups found refuge in traditional patriarchal religion. Both progressive camps found strength in a revitalized 'living' religion (rather than archaic forms).

In short, from a Durkheimian point of view, religion is 'alive and well' today because as individuals and social groups attempt to navigate modern and postmodern realities, religion is more fundamental than ever. Not only does it provide beliefs and practices at the level of the individual and membership in specific social groups, it provides a meaningful order (or *nomos*) that shields human beings against *terror*. For while science and engineering can provide technological advances that enable us to address more efficiently how to do things, it cannot provide us with answers as to the more fundamental philosophical and existential questions.

Moreover, from a Durkheimian point of view despite their obvious substantive differences, the social and communal function of religion is evident in both traditional religious and 'secular' groups. For instance, in January 2009, 800 buses rolled out of depots across Britain plastered with advertisements informing people that 'There's probably no God. Now stop worrying and enjoy your life'. The ad campaign, sponsored by the British Humanist Association, was a direct response to the Christian messages on buses and websites that warn nonbelievers that they are destined to go to hell (*New York Times*, 1/06/09). The British Humanist Association is a 'Church' (in

Durkheim's terms) that performs the vital social function of bringing 'like-minded' souls together under the same 'sacred canopy'. Akin to their religious counterparts, secular humanists provide concrete directives concerning the proverbial (religious) question: How shall we act and live? That secularism and fundamentalism are both 'religious' in Durkheimian terms also explains the collective response to tragedies such as the 2015 terrorist attack on the offices of the French satirical magazine *Charlie Hebdo* (*Charlie Weekly*). As UCLA Professor of English and Comparative Literature Saree Makdisi points out, the mantra 'Je suis Charlie' ('I am Charlie'), chanted by marchers in the Place de la Republique and repeated on Hollywood stages, is a gesture of solidarity that 'has the appeal of hashtag simplicity and bumper sticker righteousness'. And yet:

> It hardens the 'us'/'them' opposition between a supposedly tolerant and liberal West and its supposedly intolerant and violent antagonist, the Muslim East. The rush to identify with Charlie Hebdo is not just about commemorating massacred journalists, but also about celebrating Western culture, especially freedom of expression. The weekly – whose main claim to fame in recent years has been the relentless lampooning of Islam – has all too hastily been made a symbol of that principle. To 'be Charlie' means to affiliate yourself with freedom of speech in absolute terms, as a core element of Western civilization. (http://www.latimes.com/opinion/op-ed/la-oe-0118-makdisi-je-suis-charlie-makes-things-worse-20150118-story.html)

But what we are witnessing today is not simply a bipartisan clash between religious fundamentalists and secularists, but rather, the complexity of belief and 'unbelief'. Ironically, despite a plethora of research indicating that religious ideas and practices are 'fragmented and situational rather and congruent', scholars and laypeople alike nevertheless erroneously presume religious congruence, i.e. that 'religious ideas hang together, that religious beliefs and actions hang together, or that religious beliefs and values indicate stable and chronically accessible dispositions in people' (Chaves, 2010: 2) Evidence of religious incongruence is apparent, for instance, in that in the most 'religious' of all post-industrial nations – the United States – the number of folks who profess 'no religion' is rising; but a majority of these folks still profess that they *do* believe in God or a Higher Power, and that they *do* believe in life after death (Hout and Fischer, 2002; Zuckerman, 2003). The numbers and sales of religious and spiritual books and media is on the rise, and there is a renewed interest not only in religious fundamentalisms, but also 'new age' and pre-modern spiritual symbols and practices, for example yoga, Kabbalah, paganism, crystals, angels, walking meditation and pilgrimages. While in the 1980s only a few pilgrims arrived at the Cathedral of Santiago de Compostela in Spain annually, the route now attracts millions of pilgrims from around the world – many of whom profess that are not 'religious' at all. At the same time, more than 90% of people born Jewish, stay Jewish, and more than 90% born Protestant stay Protestant (Greeley, 1991, cited by Zuckerman, 2003: 45). Even when individuals do convert, they are most likely to do so in order to align themselves with the religion of significant others, most commonly their spouse (Stark and Finke, 2000).

## POSTMODERNITY AND RELIGION

From a postmodern perspective, the pastiche quality of religion in contemporary society makes sense. As the American religious historian Leigh Eric Schmidt (2005: 1) states, 'In a mix and match world, why not create your own religion? Eclectic devotions, creedal crossings, consumer sampling, and individualistic expression are widely seen as the religious order of the day'. The feminist spiritual writer Carol Lee Flinders (1998: 24–5, as cited by Schmidt, 2005: 1) adroitly encapsulates the 'pastiche spirituality' of the postmodern religious seeker when she states:

> I cannot describe my spiritual practice as Buddhist, or ... as Hindu or Catholic or Sufi, though I feel that in a sense it is all of these ... I meditate as best I can on Native American prayers and Taoist verses, on passages drawn from the Bible or the Upanishads, on passionate love songs composed for the One Beloved by a Spanish monk or an Indian princess-turned minstrel.

To be sure, Flinders' comment may reflect that so-called 'spiritual but not religious' beliefs and ideas are often simply religious ideas in a more narcissistic and disembodied form. Our world may be more 'bric-a-brac' and hyper-mediated than ever before, but religious experience is necessarily a complex blend of 'first-hand' (individual and experiential) and 'second-hand' (cultural, corporate) realms (in William James' terms). American Protestants in particular have long been not only Bible readers, but 'practitioners of rigorous self-examination and introspective journaling' (Schmidt, 2005). '"My own mind is my own church", the revolutionary pamphleteer Thomas Paine insisted with plenty of bravado, but little overstatement'

(Schmidt, 2005: 5). But the Protestant right of private judgment goes back at least to the Protestant Reformation (Schmidt, 2005: 3).

Sociologist of religion Robert Wuthnow (1998: 3–9) distinguishes between two distinct types of religious experience: 'dwelling' and 'seeking'. Whereas a spirituality of dwelling emphasizes 'habitation' and 'requires sharp symbolic boundaries to protect sacred space from its surrounding'; a spirituality of seeking emphasizes 'negotiation' and 'draws fewer distinctions of such magnitude'. Dwelling-oriented spirituality emphasizes order, formal liturgy, and tightly bound and formalized sets of rules: 'individuals are expected to conform to these rules, indeed to internalize them'; while seeker-oriented spirituality emphasizes the individual search for sacrality, which may well be found in everyday experience, rather than formal institutional settings (Wuthnow, 1998).

While Wuthnow (1998: 6) points out that 'the wisdom of Saint Benedict is that dwelling and seeking are both part of what it means to be human', he also argues that some folks are 'dwellers' (e.g. religious fundamentalists) and others are 'seekers' (e.g. spiritual progressives, such as Flinders), and that historical eras too tend to be 'dweller' or 'seeker' based (e.g. the United States in the 1950s and 1960s, as opposed to the 1960s and 1970s). Were he alive, Durkheim might emphasize that both ardent atheists and religious fundamentalists can be considered 'dwellers', sharing as they do, a firm emphasis on a fixed set of standards (whether 'positivistic' or 'religious'). Just as the scientist must adhere to the scientific method in order to *be* a (practicing) scientist, so too the Orthodox Jew must adhere to the Mishnah (the compiled rabbinical interpretations of scriptural ordinances), in order to be a (practicing) Jew at all.

Wuthnow's juxtaposition between 'dwellers' and 'seekers' also recalls a pivotal symbolic dichotomy in the sociology of religion coined by Max Weber: 'this-worldly' and 'other-worldly'. For Weber was not simply interested in documenting the substantive differences between various religions, but also in assessing the psychological and social consequences of these distinct world-views. Toward that end, he developed an ideal typical symbolic dichotomy between '*other-worldly*' orientations that encourage the individual to transcend or escape 'this-world', and '*this-worldly*' orientations that steer the individual toward enacting spiritual and religious teachings here on earth, thereby changing this world. For instance, in other-worldly Buddhist practices of meditation, change occurs internally, rather than externally. The idea is not to rebel against the external causes of suffering, but to accept that life is suffering. Enlightenment is achieved not by 'meeting' desires, but by abandoning them. By contrast, this-worldly evangelical Protestants, for instance, are compelled to proselytize to and convert unbelievers in order that they might be saved to, or to engage in social action such as sheltering the homeless, feeding the poor, visiting the sick and comforting the dying. Weber maintained that Christians began to dominate the globe because of their 'this-worldly' approach. Theirs was an activist religion, and the social consequences of this orientation were both weighty and manifold. In *The Revolution of the Saints* (1965), Michael Walzer extended Weber's thesis and argued that the Puritan movement forged a disciplined self, capable of the extraordinary feat of world-transformation.

Most interestingly, today we seem to be witnessing a resurgence of both 'this-worldly' and 'other-worldly' religion, or both 'dwelling' and 'seeking' in Wuthnow's terms. On one hand, as indicated previously, one of the fastest growing religions today is Islam, which is renowned for its orthodoxy and activism. The world's Muslim population is expected to increase by about 35% in the next twenty years, rising from 1.6 billion in 2010 to 2.2 billion by 2030, a growth rate about twice that of the non-Muslim population; and some analysts contend that Islam will overtake Christianity as the most popular world religion sometime in the mid-21st century (Lipka and Hackett 2015). Yet, it is not only traditional Islam that is thriving today. In Latin America and sub-Saharan Africa, especially, Pentecostalism and other renewalist forms of Christianity are flourishing, and since the collapse of the Soviet Union, we have seen a resurgence in Christianity in the former communist states as well. Pentecostals believe that God, acting through the Holy Spirit, continues to play a direct, active role in everyday life, as evident in spiritually renewing 'gifts of the Spirit' such as speaking in tongues and divine healing (Pew Research Center, 2006).

On the other hand, in the last few decades we have also been witnessing the 'Easternization of the West' (Campbell, 2007). Not only are large numbers of Westerners increasingly fascinated by the wisdom of the East and turning enthusiastically to Eastern religions and spiritual techniques (what Campbell calls the 'yogaization of the West'); Westerners are increasingly becoming disillusioned with the wisdom of the West, that is, with 'rationalistic' approaches to the world. Specifically, in stark contrast to the Western notion of the divine as both personal and transcendent (i.e. 'a perfect person') as well as the secular version that there *is* no divine being; we are seeing Eastern conceptualizations of the divine as an *immanent* divine presence that pervades all things. Now the divine is being conceived of not in personal terms, but as a form of *energy*. So too we are seeing an increasing fascination with nature, animal rights and vegetarianism, all of which reflect a shift away from the dualistic assumption that humans and animals are entirely different forms of being, in favor of the notion that all life is in some measure divine; and instead of the (Western) notion that there is a single overriding principle guiding human history, a more cyclical notion of time or a belief in reincarnation and cosmic or spiritual evolution is taking hold. In point of fact, one of the fastest growing religions today is said to be the Earth-based neo-pagan religion Wicca, which is reportedly doubling in size every thirty months (Barrett, Kurian and Johnson 2001). And while the numbers of folks claiming 'no religious denomination' is, as we have seen, rapidly rising (especially among the youth; see Putnam and Campbell, 2011), it is important to remember that this category includes not only agnostics and atheists, but neo-pagans and other 'Easternized' religionists as well.

This brings us to another important contemporary trend: the infiltration of religion into popular culture. Today religion is not only an explicit topic of choice in films such as Mel Gibson's infamous *The Passion of the Christ*; issues of religion and spirituality proliferate in books and films such as J.K. Rowling's Harry Potter series, the *Matrix* trilogy, and the current vampire craze. 'Apocalyptic' themes have long been rampant on the silver screen (e.g. *Dr. Strangelove*, *Soylent Green*, *Logan's Run*, *Terminator 2*, *Mad Max*, *Waterworld*), providing a compelling way to address technological, environmental, and nuclear fears and concerns (see Stone, 2011). Moreover, an entire sociology of religion course can be found in *The Simpsons*, which not only lampoons but edifies the audience in religion and spiritual matters in relatively sophisticated ways. Because regular characters include a Hindu convenience store manager, a Jewish entertainer and an evangelical neighbor, there is oftentimes somewhat detailed dialogue and discussion about these religions, and entire episodes have been devoted to Islam, Buddhism, Scientology and well-known Biblical stories as well (Dalton et al., 2011).

## CONTEMPORARY CULTURAL SOCIOLOGICAL APPROACHES TO RELIGION

Contemporary cultural sociological research on religion can be categorized into two overlapping types of research: one body of research conceptualizes religion as an organized field of activity and explains how institutions shape religious belief, practice and mobilization; and a second body of research focuses on lived religion, that is, the wide range of religious expression and experience in everyday life (Edgell, 2012: 251–3). Interestingly, both types of research reflect cultural sociology's dual Durkheimian and Weberian heritage.

Institutional field perspectives, grounded in Bourdieu's (1977) discussion of a field as a body of elites who marshal resources and whose positions are sustained by credentials, focus on the symbolic struggles of elites in the field of religion to determine orthodoxy and orthopraxy (Bourdieu, 1977). For instance, in her extraordinary analysis of Vatican II (which, as Wilde notes, is perhaps the most significant example of institutional religious change since the Protestant Reformation), Wilde (2004; 2007) demonstrates that progressive Roman Catholic bishops had a more effective organizational structure than their conservative counterparts. Firmly rooted in consensus and collegiality, progressive bishops built a flexible organization which enabled them not only to compromise, but to experience a collective effervescence that they attributed to the Holy Spirit leading them toward renewal of the Roman Catholic Church. By contrast, anti-change conservative bishops, hampered by their belief in hierarchy rather than consensus and collegiality, were unable to pull off a successful counter-attack to progressives.

Exemplars of research in the 'lived religion' category include Smilde's (2007) exploration of the reasons that the Evangelical men he spent time with in Caracas, Venezuela 'believe'. Directly contradicting the neo-Marxist contention that religion is merely an illusionary tool, Smilde (2007: 13) argues that these Evangelical men 'use Evangelical meanings to address issues of personal development and social life such as unemployment, family, and conjugal conflict' and to 'conceptualize problems of substance abuse, crime and violence in such a way that they can overcome or at least address their pernicious effects'. Thus, 'Evangelical conversion is not a reactive response to identities lost but a forward-looking, intentional project of self or family reform' (Smilde (2007: 13).

Significantly, both exemplars in contemporary cultural sociological religious analysis confirm the phenomena of 'multiple modernities' (Taylor, 2000). That is, rather than imagine a single, uniform process of global modernization, and the necessary and inevitable abandonment of religion, spirituality and metaphysics, etc., the multiple modernities thesis sees that 'modernity and its features and forces can actually be received, developed and expressed in significantly different ways in different parts of the world' (Smith, 2008: 1571). In addition, both exemplars in cultural sociological religious analysis affirm Chaves' (2010) point that sociologists of religion would do well to assume religious incongruence rather than congruence. Among the most intriguing topics for contemporary cultural sociologists of religion to explore, in my view, are the unique, incongruent paths to modernity being taken in Islamic and quasi-Islamic and post-communist states and societies today (Moaddel, 2005; Yang and Tamney, 2005).

# REFERENCES

Armstrong, K. (2000) *The Battle for God*. Knopf.
Barrett, D., G. Kurian and T. Johnson (eds.) (2001) *World Christian Encyclopedia: A Comparative Survey of Churches and Religions in the Modern Word*, 2nd ed. Oxford University Press.
Back, L. et al. (2012) *Cultural Sociology: An Introduction*. Wiley-Blackwell.
Berger, P. (1967) *The Sacred Canopy*. Anchor Books.
Bourdieu, P. (1977) *Outline of a Theory of Practice*. Cambridge University Press.
Campbell, C. (2007) *The Easternization of the West*. Paradigm Publishers.
Callois, R. (1959) *Man and the Sacred*. Free Press.
Chaves, M. (2010) 'SSSR Presidential Address Rain Dances in the Dry Season: Overcoming the Religious Congruence Fallacy', *Journal for the Scientific Study of Religion*, 49 (1): 1–14.
Dalton, L. et al. (2011) 'Homer the Heretic and Charlie Church', in E.M. Mazur and K. McCarthy (eds), *God in the Details*. Routledge. pp. 231–47.
Douglas, M. (1966) *Purity and Danger*. Routledge.
Durkheim, E. (1965 [1912]) *The Elementary Forms of Religious Life*. Free Press.
Durkheim, E. and Mauss, M. (1963 [1902]) *Primitive Classification*. University of Chicago Press.
Edgell, P. (2012) 'A Cultural Sociology of Religion: New Directions', *Annual Review of Sociology*, 38: 247–65.
Edgell, P. (2006) *Religion and Family in a Changing Society*. Princeton University Press.
Flinders, C.L. (1998) *At the Root of this Longing*. Harper Books.
Gamson, J. (1998) *Freaks Talk Back*. University of Chicago Press.
Geertz, C. (1973) *Interpretation of Cultures*. Basic Books.
Graeber, D. (2000) 'Give It Away', *In These Times* 8(21) (http://inthesetimes.com/issue/24/19/graeber2419.html).
Greeley, M. (1991) 'American Exceptionalism: The Religious Phenomenon', in B. Shafer (ed), *Is America Different? A New Look at American Exceptionalism*. Clarendon Press.
Hertz, R. (2009) 'The Pre-eminence of the Right Hand: A Study in Religious Polarity', in M. Mauss, H. Hubert and R. Hertz (eds), *Saints, Heroes, Myths, and Rites*. Paradigm.

Hout, M. and Fischer, C. (2002) 'Why More Americans Have No Religious Preference', *American Sociological Review*, 67(2): 165–90.
James, W. (1902/1936) *The Varieties of Religious Experience*. Modern Library.
Lévi-Strauss, C. (1966 [1962]) *The Savage Mind*. Weidenfield and Nicolson.
Lipka, M. and Hackett, C (2015) 'Why Muslims are the Fastest-Growing Religious Group'. (http://www.pewresearch.org/fact-tank/2015/04/23/why-muslims-are-the-worlds-fastest-growing-religious-group/)
Lyall, Sarah (2009) "Atheists Send a Message, on 800 British Buses". *New York Times* (http://www.nytimes.com/2009/01/07/world/europe/07london.html)
Mauss, M. (1954) *The Gift: Forms and Functions of Exchange in Archaic Societies*. Cohen and West.
Moaddel, M. (2005) *Islamic Modernism, Nationalism, and Fundamentalism*. University of Chicago Press.
Patterson, M. (2004) 'The Rise of Global Fundamentalism', *National Catholic Reporter*, 5 July.
Pew Research Center (2006) 'Spirit and Power: A Ten Country Survey of Pentecostals'. (http://www.pewforum.org/2006/10/05/spirit-and-power/)
Putnam, R. and Campbell, D. (2010) *American Grace*. Simon and Schuster.
Schmidt, L.E. (2005) *Restless Souls: The Making of American Spirituality*. Harper.
Smilde, D. (2007) *Reason to Believe: Cultural Agency in Latin American Evangelicalism*. University of California Press.
Smith, C. (2008) 'Future Directions in the Sociology of Religion', *Social Forces*, 86(4): 1561–89.
Smith, P. (2001) *Cultural Theory*. Blackwell.
Stark, R. and Finke, R. (2000) *Acts of Faith*. University of California Press.
Stone, J. (2011) 'A Fire in the Sky', in E.M. Mazur and K. McCarthy (eds), *God in the Details*. Routledge. pp. 62–79.
Taylor, C. (2000) 'Modernity and Difference', in P. Gilroy, L. Grossberg and A. McRobbie (eds), *Without Guarantees: In Honor of Stuart Hall*. Verso. pp. 364–74.
Turner, V. (1969) *The Ritual Process*. Aldine.
Walzer, M. (1965) *The Revolution of the Saints*. Harvard University Press.
Weber, M. (1958 [1919]) *The Protestant Ethic and the Spirit of Capitalism*. Scribner.
Wilde, M. (2004) 'How Culture Mattered at Vatican II', *American Sociological Review*, 69(4): 576–602.
Wilde, M. (2007) *Vatican II: A Sociological Analysis of Religious Change*. Princeton University Press.
Wuthnow, R. (1998) *After Heaven: Spirituality in America since the 1950s*. University of California Press.
Yang, F. and Tamney, J. (eds) (2005) *State, Market, and Religions in Chinese Societies*. Brill.
Zuckerman, P. (2003) *Invitation to the Sociology of Religion*. Routledge.

# Everyday Life: The Making of a Sociological Topic, Then Making it 'Cultural Sociology'

Rachel Hurdley

## INTRODUCTION

What on earth is 'everyday life'? How can studying everyday life, rather than just living it, become 'sociological'? How can its representation ever be held neatly in a book, let alone a chapter? Why does it matter as a sociological enterprise, rather than a subject for chat, fiction, documentary, poetry or drama? What, specifically, is the cultural sociology of everyday life? Questioning the commonplace, the mundane, the taken-for-granted dullness of the everyday is one reason for examining 'it', making the familiar strange, even sensational, including sociology and academia. Pierre Bourdieu, seen by many as the grandpère of cultural analysis for the last fifty years or so, paid close attention to scholarly cultures (1988; 1990). In this case, then, *who* is producing 'the cultural sociology of everyday life'? Therefore, *his* mid-20th-century French approach is itself the subject of ongoing debates about the purpose, meaning and focus of cultural sociology (Heinich, 2010; Atkinson, 2012). *When* and *where* scholarship is produced are also important questions.

Such squabbles are common in academia, but have particular salience in the cultural sociology of everyday life. If culture is understood as meaning-making (Douglas, 2002 [1966]; Chaney, 1994), then defining cultural sociology's everyday cultural processes is imperative for its future not only as an academic pursuit, but also as relevant to the everyday 'everyday'. For although 'the everyday' sounds and looks solid, 'it' is not a thing, but always happening, even now. some scholars have made this process – drama, situated accomplishment, interaction, practice, complexity, mess – the focus of data collection, analysis and representation. Early urban ethnography (Riis, 1890; Zorbaugh, 1983 [1929]; Whyte, 1934), ethnomethodology and dramaturgy (Goffman, 1959; Garfinkel, 1967), micro-sociological interviews (Oakley, 1974; Kaufmann, 1998), autoethnography and interwoven narratives (Law, 1994; Ellis, 2004) vivify social worlds through modes of writing. Others have gone further, using ethnodrama and/or ethnotheatre in the 'performative turn' within social sciences (Denzin, 2001; Saldaña, 2005). Even the 'things' of everyday life like food, rubbish, clothes and houses, are processes, contingent upon multiple interactions, social relations and cultural practices (Murcott, 1983; Appadurai, 1986; Miller and Woodward, 2012; Hurdley, 2013; Evans, 2014).

Before going on, I will address the 'trouble' that arises when 'sociology' and 'culture' are brought together (Inglis et al., 2007), because it is precisely the study of 'everyday life' that brings 'cultural sociology' and 'sociology of culture' into happy union. At least, this is the case if attention is paid to the complexity of the cultural forms and social action that constitute the organization of everyday life (Atkinson et al., 2007). Atkinson and his co-authors undertake ethnographies of what might be viewed as elite or minority cultural forms – opera, art and capoeira – to elicit how these are accomplished as everyday social processes.

As a parallel, 'ethnographic imagination' as articulated by Willis (2000: ix), is 'the bringing together of everyday life and aesthetic questions … what happens if we understand the raw materials of lived cultures as if they were living art forms?' Both approaches practise reflexivity regarding modes of organization – sense-making practices – in fieldwork, theory, analysis and representation. In other words, to develop acute sensibility towards *how* meaning is made by research participants, researchers and their audiences/readers. This aesthetic is not, then, only about surfaces, but also about processes; cultural artefacts, forms of talk, embodied movement, types of data, analytic methods, theoretical frames or developments and choices of representation are all transformative. Everyday life is always emergent, rooted in many soils, flourishing in countless fields.

While an article, book, picture or film might seem to capture only a moment or snapshot 'about' everyday life, the principle task of a cultural sociologist is to interpret and articulate those depths and pluralities. 'Everyday life' sociology is not the same as 'real life', as in the multitude of TV shows that endlessly repeat the same plot of self-improvement through weight loss, better dressing, decluttering, becoming a farmer, singer or good mother, although a sociological study of such phenomena and their audiences is possible (Skeggs and Wood, 2012). Interpreting naturally occurring situated practices can articulate 'the interaction order' in ways that emphasize the staging of everyday life (Goffman, 1983), as 'actors' are also 'audiences' for each other, accomplishing social organization moment by moment. This dramaturgical approach is taken from the theatre, where, as that master director Alfred Hitchcock said, 'Drama is life with the dull bits cut out' (British Broadcasting Corporation, 1960), to outline the jagged tragedy and comic harmonies in every social setting. Theatre, like all cultural forms, relies on shared understandings, values and common histories, because it needs an audience. It frames and distances what otherwise might be too close to see:

> Let us imagine a theatre; the curtain goes up and we see a man alone in a room … we should be observing something more wonderful than a playwright could arrange to be acted or spoken on the stage: life itself. But then we do see this every day without its making the slightest impression on us! True enough, but we do not see it from *that* point of view. (Wittgenstein, 1998 [1977]: 4)

Thinking about cultural forms, such as plays, theatres, novels, books, images and paintings accentuates how everyday life has been constructed through diverse cultural modes since, possibly, Palaeolithic times (Snow, 2013). Apart from the value of looking at the 'here and now' from a cultural historical distance (for which, see Weber, 2008 [1891]; Arendt, 1958; McCarthy, 2012), it is helpful to remember that life is strange, even when wrapped up as 'everyday'. Second, this clarifies the distinction between everyday life, and its representations (Atkinson, 1990; Strathern, 2004). Third, we can recall that identity is an everyday embodied practice, yet with complex histories, caught up in relations with people, places, things and times. Finally, everyday life is not just the concern of sociology (of any sort), nor should sociology limit itself to 'modernity', however that might be defined. Bourdieu was critical of sociologists' 'genesis amnesia' (1979) towards both sociology and cultural practices. Social anthropology, somehow the rival and companion of sociology, throws this forgetfulness into sharp relief (for example, Douglas, 2002 [1966]), as does social history (Genovese, 1974). And, as an addendum (because sociology is never finished), I assert that studies and stories of everyday life follow two patterns (or cultural forms): comedy and tragedy. This last point is central, since both the form and tone of cultural sociology matter for its future. There has been a tendency in some classic and contemporary social science towards the tragic, involving a three-part drama with a flawed hero and conforming to a conventional pattern (see Hurdley, 2014 for discussion). Moreover, there is the 'failure' of Marx's revolution, haunting European sociology, and the long shadow of the Holocaust. Myriad discriminative practices against people who deviate from the heterosexual, able-bodied, mentally 'well', trouser-wearing, salaried white male, characterize humans as disposed to cruelty and/or suffering. This chapter's conclusion will envision future cultural sociology as an exercise in hope.

To be clear, this is not a review or discussion of all the literature which may count as cultural sociology of everyday life, either past or current. There are excellent handbooks and articles available that encompass this and more (Douglas, 1970; Douglas et al., 1980; Smith, 1987; Adler and Adler, 1987; Crane, 1994b; Ludtke, 1995; Bennett et al., 1999; Bennett and Watson, 2002; Chaney, 2002; Tiryakian, 2002; Inglis, 2005; Hviid Jacobsen, 2008; Scott, 2009; Shove et al., 2009; 2012; Alabarces, 2012; Alexander et al., 2012; Back et al., 2012). Nor is it global in its reach, although the topic is increasingly receiving academic attention across the world (McMichael, 2002; Guo, 2009; Sztompka, 2009; Pysnakova and Hohnova, 2010; Jenkins, 2010; Eglitis, 2011; Kalekin-Fishman, 2013; Ts'ai, 2013; Nielsen and Waldrop, 2014). Surrealist, existential and psychoanalytic approaches to being and doing in the world are deeply connected with everyday life studies and cultural sociology (for example, Kierkegaard, 1980 [1844]; Freud, 1901; 1913 [1901]; Jung, 1961 [1913]; Heidegger, 1927; 2003 [1927]; Kafka, 1994 [1935]; Sartre, 1965 [1938]; Beckett, 1952; Pinter, 1960; Fromm, 1961; Camus, 1971 [1961]; Perec, 1990 [1967]; 2010 [1982]; Lyman, 1970; Douglas and Johnson, 1977). However, these cannot be dealt with here. This chapter focuses on how 'the everyday' has garnered such cultural legitimacy that it is possible to treat it as an academic topic. And to focus on such matters, a certain narrowing of vision is required. Therefore, the US, Britain and northern Europe in the early 19th century form the horizon of discussion.

## CULTURES AND CONTEXTS: SOCIOLOGY AND MODERNITY

Whereas the city invites sociological explanation, as the hard material of modernity, alienation and individualism, the countryside is too easily opened up to nostalgic, primitivist interpretations (Williams, 1973). Conversely, Thoreau's canonical work on simple rural American life centres more on an ideal of individual freedom versus authority than ideas of collective tradition:

> How womankind, who are confined to the house still more than men, stand it I do not know; but I have ground to suspect that they do not STAND it at all ... the walking of which I speak has nothing in it akin to taking exercise ... (Thoreau, 2007 [1862]: 2)

Thoreau's wanderer might find his European urban match in Balzac's *flaneur*, the detached, masculine observer who surfaces repeatedly as a cultural figure (Benjamin, 1999; Simmel, 1971; Sontag, 1977; Wolff, 1985; Harvey, 2003). It is strange how such a sociologically dominant trope of the alienated modern individual mirrors this pastoral hero. Yet the interpretive power of a cultural perspective is in its attention to collectivity and historicity, for '... many personal troubles cannot be solved merely as troubles, but must be understood in terms of public issues — and in terms of the problems of history making' (Mills, 1959: appendix). It is not therefore not merely 'decorative' (Rojek and Turner, 2000) to articulate 'structures of feeling' nor to explicate 'knowable communities' in Victorian novels (Williams, 1973) but instead involves sociological imaginations in practice (Mills, 1959). Rurality in later fiction by Steinbeck (2001 [1939]) is materialized in the bitter dustbowl of the Great Depression, with a long history and far-reaching consequences. Realist fiction and classic social analyses share common ground:

> You cannot imagine how many ruined hopes, how many unknown dramas in that city of sorrow! ... these amazing scenes, tragic and comic, masterpieces born of chance. (Balzac, 2014 [1845]: 4–5)

Both Marx and Engels admired Balzac's fiction, from which, Engels wrote, 'I have learned more than from all the professed historians, economists, and statisticians of the period together' (Engels, 1888). Classic analyses of everyday life are explicitly political, addressing social inequalities and oppression from a Marxist, socialist or leftist perspective (Marx, 1844; Engels, 1892 [1844]; Lefebvre, 1991 [1974]; de Certeau, 1984; Williams, 1961; Willis, 1977; Hall et al., 2013 [1978]). The 'cultural turn' in sociology has long been a contested topic in itself (Barrett et al., 1979; Chaney, 1994; 2012; Crane, 1994 a; Woolf, 1999; Rojek and Turner, 2000; Alexander, 2003; 2008; Alexander and Smith, 2005; Gartman, 2007; Inglis, 2014). Chaney (2012), like Inglis (2014), considers presentism a problem in sociology, and believes that in order to understand change, any sociological interpretation of modernity must be historically situated. Marx, Durkheim and Weber were all historians, with Weber's (1897) sociology of agriculture in ancient civilizations supplying a long history for capitalism. However, 'when we look closely at the construction of past time, we find the process has very little to do with the past at all, and everything to do with the present. Institutions create shadowed places where nothing can be seen, and no questions asked' (Douglas, 1986: 69). Marx, Durkheim and Weber are sociological institutions themselves, using history as a resource to support their specific interpretations of modernity. Historiography – writings of history, rather than history – is what they produce. Critical awareness of such written interpretations is central in cultural sociology, since representation is its key concern.

For example, Chaney argues that the purpose of cultural sociology of the everyday is to demonstrate how social ordering, repression and inequality are accomplished as seemingly mundane practices that may otherwise pass unseen, for being seemingly trivial 'cultural matters' (1994). Social entities such as class are cultural matters in that they are talked about and represented and therefore constructed through interaction, rather than existing purely as external structures. Chaney has argued persuasively that 'in important ways, culture has become the basis for, rather than the reflection of social life' (Chaney, 2012: 11). The challenge of doing cultural sociologies of everyday life is to produce understandable representations whilst keeping some kind of integrity with our sources. Bourdieu's work on the Kabyle agrarian calendar noted the

> great temptation to amass and collate these different productions in order to construct a lacuna-free, contradiction-free whole, a sort of unwritten score of which all the calendars derived from informants are then regarded as imperfect, impoverished performances. The problem is that the calendar cannot be understood unless it is set down on paper, and that it is impossible to understand how it works unless one fully realises that it exists only on paper. (1977: 98)

Bourdieu's (1986) cultural analysis relied on an external, privileged observer and an assumed structure (Buchli, 1999), yet, as a rigorous exercise of systematic interpretation, it has been foundational for studies of social inequalities that extend well beyond late 20th century France (Skeggs, 2004; Adkins and Skeggs, 2005; Lawler, 2008; Bennett et al., 2009; Fernandez Rodriguez and Heikkila, 2011; Coulangeon and Duval, 2013; Taylor, 2013).

A digression towards the 'cultural turn' in criminology is helpful at this point, since representations of crime, deviance and criminal justice are central to understanding how culture, power and identity work in the practice of everyday life (Simon, 2002–8). In Garland's (2006) incisive critique of the concept of 'culture' in the sociology of punishment, the 'problem' of culture and cultural is clarified. Whereas cultural sociology has found various places and paths either beside, within or throughout contemporary sociology, there is a definite schism in criminology created by cultural criminologists (Ferrell et al., 2004; Ferrell and Websdale, 1999) separating off 'culture/cultural' as style, symbol, ritual, text, image and spectacle, with 'sub' cultures as the defiant domain of culture opposed to multiple forms of power (see also Jones, 2012). As Garland argues,

> [the scholar] must show *how* the meanings in question come to relate to action ... Cultural forms ... can be isolated for the purposes of study ... But it ought not to mark the limits of our ambition ... For the discipline, if not necessarily for the researcher, cultural explication ought to be the preliminary to the social explanation of the phenomenon in question. (2006: 438–9; see Garland, 2010 for a demonstration of this)

The 'strong program' (Alexander and Smith, 2005; Alexander, 2008) of cultural sociology may indeed foment debate within the field (Gartman, 2008), and seeking distinction from other disciplines and sub-fields (Chaney, 1994; 2002; Crane, 1994a; Woolf, 1999; Heinich, 2010; Neto, 2014) is important for stopping to think about what it is we are doing. Yet to make sense, cultural sociology ought to be collective, if not always friendly, making connections with other studies and fields, both synchronically and historically (Inglis, 2014). The 'classic' texts of sociology are useful for producing these dialogues and working with common purpose towards explanation and, if necessary, change. Even single books of astounding reach and impact, such as the recent ethnography on everyday life in a poor black Philadelphia neighbourhood by Alice Goffman (2014), are produced within a complex of cultural, economic and social phenomena.

Marx's (1844) concept of cultural materialism, in which culture is always dependent on structure, has provided the stamping ground for many of cultural sociology's debates, particularly with the turn from production to consumption as the contemporary, though similarly disputed, paradigm (Slater, 1997; Lury, 2011). In fact, these twin concerns are brought to the fore in studies of everyday life, as are Durkheim's (2008 [1912]) distinction between the sacred and profane, and Weber's (1968 [1922]) theory of rationality. Arnold's (1869) division between 'high' and 'low' culture looks old-fashioned now, blurred by Williams' (1989 [1958]) assertion that *Culture is Ordinary* and seemingly wiped out by the rise of cultural 'omnivores' (Peterson and Simkus, 1992; Bennett et al., 2009; Chan, 2013). Technology allowing proliferation of cheap mass-produced 'popular' culture products such as tabloid newspapers and illustrated magazines, books, photographs, movies, television shows, and now social media, make many cultural products available globally through multiple media platforms. Anyone with a tablet, computer or smartphone (and in some cases, a sophisticated printer) can produce news, videos, books, houses, teeth or guns, with knowledge gleaned online, while sitting on the toilet or walking the dog. A global, diverse crowd may find communality in the online presence of an Oxford-educated fifty-something shepherd, blogging his solitary everyday life on Northern English hills (Rebanks, 2015).

Inglis' (2005) introductory discussion of culture and everyday life is a comprehensive survey of multiple historical roots, emphasizing the importance of the Kantian notion of culture as a set of collective representations (Kant, 2007 [1787]; see also Durkheim, 1915). Consumption, production and representation are converging, the spectacular is too-often commonplace, and collectivities no longer depend on 'neighbourliness' (Williams, 1989 [1958]) or shared *habitus* (Bourdieu, 1986). However, just as cultural sociology focuses on the everyday, rather than 'anyday' (Douglas, 1967), it focuses on everyone, rather than 'anyone' who can clasp a smartphone in their hands. Although the mediaeval morality play *Everyman* has been updated to represent the common existential crises of a secular audience, rather than one which inhabited a Christian cosmos (Duffy, 2015), it keeps faith with the trope of the original drama. The materials which pass through our hands may be different from those which our ancestors held a century ago, and everyday life in a small Welsh village may seem extraordinary to a New York commuter. However, all groups have a notion of what is ordinary (Gouldner, 1975, cited in Inglis, 2005: 6). This is not the same as 'popular' culture (Storey, 2014), such as circuses (Juvenal, 1992 [c.100]), public executions (Elias, 1978; Garland, 2010) or pop concerts (Lashua et al., 2007), which are out of the ordinary.

The three principal challenges in cultural sociological everyday life studies are interlinked. The first is an old one: to make the familiar everyday, strange, and the strange everyday, familiar. The second task is to challenge the refusal by mainstream 'social scientists' (as many still persist in calling themselves) to treat representation as problematic. Citing Benjamin's search for a 'possibly incompletable' 'profane illumination', Chaney explicates the 'threat' that everyday methodology poses to social theory based on clear divisions, rationality, causes and effects (2002: 30). Its third task is the hardest: to establish clearly how *this* 'particular case of the possible' (Bachelard, 1994 [1957]: 16) related through *this* account of 'immortal ordinary society' (Garfinkel, 2002: 65) matters. Bryson distinguished between *rhopography* – studies of trivia – and *megalography* – studies of great things (1990: 61). Our task, collectively, is to demonstrate how minute, unnoticed and taken-for-granted everyday actions, talk, silences and inactions constitute processes of social organization. As Berger and Luckmann (1967) explained so clearly, reality is a social construction. There is no grand structure 'out there', except as a sociological imaginary, in the way an architectural drawing relates to the daily sweat of building a house, which is then lived in, cleaned, repainted, extended, and sold on. Houses are relevant here, since domesticity, private life, and their meanings and representations are one of the topics of everyday life studies. Bryson (1990) draws parallels between the perceived triviality of everyday life and of still life paintings, since both are seen as feminine. The house is an archaic feminine private space, its interiority equivalent to irrationality and/or pre-modernity (see also Bourdieu, 1977). Everyday concerns are women's business, in contrast to the public world of work, which is masculine, rational modernity (Wolff, 2000; Chaney, 2002; Hurdley, 2013).

Such binaries are crass, yet social theory is built on such an imaginary, since patriarchy has systematically side-lined, hidden or deleted women's accounts from history. Similarly invisible are the histories and practices of vanquished first peoples, captive or otherwise oppressed 'minorities', poor communities and, in fact, the majority of those who practise everyday life. These are difficult to recover, precisely because they were rarely documented, their artefacts destroyed or just not designed to last, and although practices continued, they changed over time. As Chaney points out, irrationality (in social theory) is seen as such from the 'perspective of economic and social exploitation' (2002: 181). This is why the third challenge, to elicit the pattern, the social order, from everyday life, is so hard: it does not fit dominant social theory; its histories are lost or negligible, and practices disguised or detached from their origins. However, our companions are archaeologists and social and cultural historians ancient and modern, whose recent and growing work in recovering or reviewing everyday neglected histories is vital for cultural sociology. For example, the sedimentary rock of Western democracy and social relations lies in ancient Athens, but revisionist histories and new archaeological work in Crete question taken for granted assumptions regarding social and gender relations in antiquity (Westgate, 2010). Cooking, a hidden female kitchen practice, its tools often lost, is brought centre-stage (Pennell, 1999) and native American meals are analysed (Fitzgerald, 2007). Thus oral history (Charlton et al., 2007) and social and cultural history and archaeology (Shanks and Tilley, 1992; Hodder, 2012) are close relations of cultural sociology. This also demonstrates why exhaustive, careful historiography, and the use of any and all sources that are available, are so important to cultural sociology.

## CULTURAL COMMONS: SHARED MEMORIES AND COLLECTIVE PURSUITS

Sociology of everyday life is 'less a form of analysis than a specific perspective on things' (Maffesoli, 1989: 1). In Berger and Luckmann's seminal book, they argued that 'reality *sui generis* of society requires an inquiry into the manner in which this is constructed' (1967: 30). How is everyday life possible? How do members sustain the ordinary, the usual, the routine? And how is change possible? From the late 1950s, the New Left movement developed in Britain, the US, continental Europe and in different forms elsewhere (Dworkin, 1997).

The New Left in Britain was strongly connected with cultural Marxism and new forms of theatre, such as 'kitchen-sink drama' (for example, Wesker, 1959; Osborne, 1993 [1956]; for a full discussion see Rebellato, 2002). Stuart Hall viewed the New Left as a decision by people to 'choose to live' (1959: 113); Raymond Williams saw it as making a 'claim to life', in re-appropriating culture and civilization as belonging to ordinary people (1965: 23; see also 1989 [1958]). Just as the New Leftist C. Wright Mills' view that private ills had to be understood as public and historically situated issues was published in the US, British historian E. P. Thompson was writing that '... what is peculiar to the apathetic decade is that people have, increasingly, looked to *private* solutions to *public* evils' (1960: 5). Life, neighbourliness, collectivity and structures of feeling are themes throughout their writings:

> It was always a limited inquiry: the country and the city within a single tradition. But it has brought me to the point where I can offer its meanings, its implications and its connections to others: for discussion and amendment; for many kinds of possible cooperative work; but above all for an emphasis – the sense of an experience and of ways of changing it – in the many countries and cities where we live. (Williams, 1973: 306)

The New Left's continuing legacy in Britain is the field of cultural studies, originating at the university of Birmingham in 1974, which was also, in part, a reaction to sociology, seen as an instrument of the state (Hoggart, 1957; Hall et al., 2013 [1978]; Cashmore and Troyna, 1981; Centre for Contemporary Cultural Studies, 1982) Yet Cultural Studies' contribution to sociologies of everyday life is unmistakable, with a strong connection to ethnography (Willis, 1977; Hall et al., 2013 [1978]; McRobbie, 1991). At the same time, English translations of some continental sociologists appeared for the first time, together with expanded works in translation (for example, Durkheim, 1964 [1895]; Schutz, 1967 [1932]; Weber, 1968 [1922]). The US dominance over sociology was tempered by these translations and a 'cultural turn' in British sociology (Chaney, 1994; Barrett et al., 1979). This is the commonly accepted starting point of 'cultural sociology' in Britain. However, there are earlier lost roots, which are more strongly connected to the Chicago School, to continental Europe, and to local, regional, rather than state-oriented perspectives, to which we now turn.

An English businessman, Victor Branford, and Scottish academic, Patrick Geddes, with their wide network of friends and collaborators, pursued numerous multidisciplinary projects in the early 20th century, including founding the Sociological Society and the first British sociology journal, *The Sociological Review* (Keele University, 2010). These 'amateurs' (Evans, 1986) were marginalized by the London-focused emergent institutional sociology, which as a result lost their peculiar combination of regionalism and cosmopolitanism, with strong links to the US as well as continental Europe. Their links with the first Chicago ethnographers and Branford's coining of 'the third way' 'between liberal individualism and state centralism' (Scott and Bromley, 2013: 191) demonstrate the international and innovative vision of their approach. Civic engagement was key. Grounded in journalistic, proto-ethnographies of social inequality by, for example, Mayhew (2009 [1851]) and Engels (1892 [1844]), they pursued an applied sociology that both appealed to ordinary people and was based on local observation, with a view to practical change (Geddes, 1905). Basing their studies upon French sociologist/engineer Le Play's (1935 [1855]) 'Folk, Work, Place' regionalism, their ecological urban social science clearly relates to the Chicago School approach, rooted in the same traditions of journalism, observation and participation (Riis, 1890; Anderson, 1961 [1923]; Park et al., 1925; Whyte, 1934). Riis, like his near-contemporary Jack London (1903; 1907), was fully aware of the power that photographic representations of poverty held over his readers, as were the group around Geddes and Branford. Their methodology was as eclectic as Geddes', although this, combined with Anderson's journalistic background and popularity with public audiences led to his Masters examiners telling him, 'You know your sociology out there better than we do, but you don't know your sociology in here' (Anderson, 1961 [1923]: 12, cited in Prus, 1996: 121). Park similarly referred to the influence of his 'muckraker' journalist past (Odum, 1951: 132), urging his students to '... go get the seat of your pants dirty in real research' (cited in Bulmer, 1984: 97–8), rather than sitting in the library.

Geddes and his companions failed to institutionalize their wide-ranging and pragmatic approach to society's problems, but their foresight can be seen in contemporary ecological sociology, glocalism and 'third way' political philosophies (for example Giddens, 1998). Similarly conceived to counter elite, institutional versions of social science and history, the Mass Observation project, started in 1937, asked 'ordinary' people to participate in an 'anthropology of ourselves', to make 'museums ... of domestic objects' (Madge and Harrisson, 1939: 35). Set up by poet Charles Madge, anthropologist Tom Harrisson and painter/ documentary film-maker Humphrey Jennings, Mass Observation was to counter government ignorance about the feelings and attitudes of the British 'masses' (see Mass Observation, 2015). The tension between the three founders' approaches was never resolved: was it to be a social document, data collection, or a surrealist technique to 'shock' new knowledge from the mass 'unconscious' through written collages in which a 'day in the life of' slum poverty, and leisurely wealth sat side by side (Jennings et al., 1937), or something else again? What Mass Observation was, and why it was, and who was involved, remain closely contested questions (Hubble, 2006; Savage, 2010; Hinton, 2013), yet its latest incarnation is an increasingly popular resource for social historians, sociologists and cultural studies scholars (Kynaston, 2007; Clarke, 2009; Charles, 2014). Although entirely unrepresentative of the British population, Mass Observation was (and is) a unique resource of people's diaries, observations, day surveys, responses to twice-yearly Directives, as well as studies on 'Worktown' (Bolton, an industrial town in northern England), including photographs (Mass Observation, 1987; Bolton Council, 2015). Contemporaneous observations of the London Blitz, leisure pursuits (not altogether wholesome) in the English seaside town Blackpool and reports of overheard street conversations led to accusations of spying and voyeurism in the national press (Madge and Harrisson, 1938). The sheer volume of material generated in, for example, the Worktown studies, very nearly rotted in a cellar (Sheridan, 1987). Both these problems, together with the tensions and ambiguities of the Mass Observation endeavour, are emblematic of any exploration of everyday life. This aesthetically charged, mundane 'anthropology of ourselves', with its methodological pluralism (Pollen, 2013) and contested aims, is not only an ancestor of cultural sociology and everyday life studies; it is their flamboyant companion.

## ACTION, INTERACTION AND INTERPRETATION

Without going into a lengthy discussion of their complexities, this section will first focus on the influence of ethnography and symbolic interactionism that characterize the 'second Chicago School'. Influenced by Simmel's ideas on interaction and 'sociation' (Wolff, 1950), as well as G. H. Mead's pragmatism (2009 [1934]; 1982), symbolic interactionist perspectives focus on the microsociological dynamics of cultural change. Herbert Blumer's notion of 'sensitising concepts' is helpful for understanding everyday life rather than trying to fit it into prescriptive categories:

> ... the empirical world of our discipline is the natural social world of every-day experience ... we ... cannot meaningfully, confine our consideration of it strictly to what is covered by the abstract reference of the concept. (Blumer, 1954: 7–8)

Everett Hughes, a contemporary of Blumer, undertook wide-ranging interpretive sociologies of institutions (1937; 1958), whom his students credited with teaching them 'to think comparatively across situations' (Becker et al., 2009 [1968]: 272). In contrast, conventional social science sought to describe and explain social organization through formal analytic methods developed by Talcott Parsons (1937). Such a functionalist approach seemingly assumed a sociological 'grand theory' (although Parsons never claimed this), in which the irrationalities and contingencies of everyday life would disappear into an objective explanatory framework or model. The problem with this conventional social science was that there was no acknowledgement of everyday actors' perspectives, or the situatedness of their accounts of social relationships. Demographic information became codable, measurable variables, which could be subjected to scientific tests of validity and reliability (vom Lehn, 2014: 102). It was also 'trans-historical' (Wilson and Zimmerman, 1979: 63–7). Although Parsons' work has undergone thorough re-examination and recuperation (Fox et al., 2005), this representation of functionalism persists, against which other theorizations of society have been built.

Garfinkel, a student of Parsons, was initially opposed to the key symbolic interactionist concept that in becoming a 'member' there was any possibility of 'taking the role of the other' (Garfinkel, 2006 [1948]: 176), maintaining Schutz's view that there could be no empathy between observer and social actor. Schutz's phenomenology (1967 [1932]; 1962) interpreted Husserl's concept of *Lebenswelt* (lifeworld) in dialogue with Weber's central notion of *verstehen* (understanding). In everyday life, actors use *verstehen* to interpret the meanings of other actors, a process which relies on intersubjective or shared meanings. This depends upon a social world that can be taken for granted, a common-sense, typified lifeworld. As a second order of understanding, social scientists then seek to understand actors' meanings. This involves creating 'typical course-of-action patterns models' to ascribe to ideal actors with 'fictitious consciousness' who inter-acted with other 'puppets' or 'homunculi' to populate a 'model of the social world of everyday life ... in such a way as the scientific problems under scrutiny require' (Schutz, 1962: 63–4). The problem dictated the model. The relation between this objective model, the subjective meaning of an individual actor and 'common-sense' shared understandings was not explained by Schutz, who relied upon a 'postulate of adequacy' (1962: 44) to maintain consistency between the sociological model, subjective meaning and the lifeworld (vom Lehn, 2014). Garfinkel was grounded in Schutz's phenomenology but moved on to examine locally situated embodied practices (1967). Ethnomethodology involved looking at *how* members 'construct and sustain those meaningful accounts out of which sociological phenomena are constituted, rather than sociological phenomena themselves' (Wilson and Zimmerman, 1979: 75). So, for example, Weber's bureaucracy was not an 'ideal type' but a model for comparing historically and culturally specific instances of concrete social order.

Garfinkel (2002) cites Durkheim (1964 [1895]): '"The objective reality of social facts is sociology's fundamental principle". Sociology's fundamental principle? There's the rub'. Returning to Durkheim's revision of 'principle' to 'phenomenon', Garfinkel takes this as a starting point for his critique of the 'good work' of formal analytic social science, which treats everyday life as 'empty of order' until 'respecified in ... generic representational theories' (2002: 65). Focusing on Durkheim's notion of 'immortal ordinary society', he argues that 'immortal is a metaphor for the great recurrences of ordinary society ... just *thisness* ... [but] doable and done again' (2002: 92 footnote). In other words, ethnomethodology was seeking order in the everyday, not the anyday, as Douglas (1967) emphasizes. The error of formal analytic social sciences was in ignoring the orderliness of 'local actual concretely detailed circumstantial workings of immortal ordinary society' (Garfinkel, 2002: 65). Garfinkel and Sacks (1986 [1970]) emphasised the 'fleetingness ... of social order' (vom Lehn, 2014: 148) to investigate 'the general question of how any such commonsense world is possible' (Garfinkel, 1967: 36) as 'a contingent accomplishment of socially organized common practices' (Garfinkel, 1967: 33). Thus, the focus changed from organization to the processes of organizing (Garfinkel, 1956; 2002; Bittner, 1965), through interaction. Ethnomethodology's influence on 'organization studies' of workplaces, which developed from the 1980s, is clear (Button, 1993; Fine, 1993; Boden, 1994; Harper, 1997; Roucefield and Tolmie, 2011). The move towards ordering as process, to examining taken-for-granted interactions and events, continued into studies of 'the everyday' as 'naturally occurring interaction' (Adler and Adler, 1987: 219).

Goffman's use of *'unofficial methodology'* (Baldamus, 1972: 281, original emphasis) was an ongoing development of Blumer's 'sensitizing concepts'. A student of Hughes, Goffman created a dramaturgical idiom, bringing with it his 'metaphorical cornucopia' of 'drama, ritual, game and frame' to avoid falling into the trap of taken-for-grantedness (Smith and Hviid Jacobsen, 2010: 130–2). It is worth noting that in a rare instance of explicit attribution, he named Durkheim as an influence (Verhoeven, 1993: 343). Also recalling the early Chicago studies of Park and his students, working with 'the benefit of an absence of methodological training' (Hobbs, 2001: 205), Goffman had a clear commitment to observing the situated, concrete organization of everyday life.

## METHODOLOGY: FIELDWORK, INTERPRETATION, REPRESENTATION AND REFLECTION

As C. Wright Mills argued, 'the requirements of one's problem, rather than the limitations of any one rigid method, should be and have been the classic social analyst's paramount consideration' (1959: 146). As methods and methodology textbooks proliferate, *doing* research looks ever more complicated, especially since options for collecting, storing, analysing, disseminating and representing data – whatever 'data' are – constantly increase. The temptation is often to rely on the familiar – literature review, questionnaires, interviews – or plunge into the latest fashionable technique, using a range of new instruments. There are also a number of recent innovations which have become the norm, such as using CAQDAS to store and analyse qualitative data, or online survey packages for quantitative studies. Without going into the many excellent debates around conventional and ever-novel approaches (Atkinson and Silverman, 1997; Gubrium and Holstein, 2002; Alasuutari et al., 2008; Fielding et al., 2008; Denzin and Lincoln, 2011; Brannen, 2013), it is impossible to do these justice. Achieving pragmatism and imagination in perfect measure is difficult, yet Mills' suggestion is an excellent guide. Above all, space and time to think are the most vital, and least available, components of a research project.

Bourdieu (1977) demonstrated that the practice of representing social life, and everyday practices of living those lives, are quite different (see also Strathern, 2004). Employing auto-ethnography, (constructed) stream-of-consciousness and/or inter-textuality are some methods for researching and representing everyday life. However, these can fall too easily into mistaking everyday life as resource for everyday life as topic (Silverman, 2013), or poor editing for authorial honesty (see Richardson, 1990; Delamont, 2009). When the substantive topic is mess, background, trivia, detail and marginalia, it discomfits those practices of tidying it all up into neat tables, with a few quotes 'cherry-picked' (Savage, 2010) from interviews for the journal article, a short film for the conference, yet legitimated by Durkheim and a catalogue of more-or-less relevant empirical studies. But, for research to matter, it must balance the close-ups with distancing analysis, the 'hermeneutic circle' that Dilthey developed from Schleiermacher (1998 [1838]; Rickman, 2011 [1976]). This practice of understanding parts of a text through its whole and its whole through its parts, from particularities to the general, always in a specific cultural historical setting, originates in the mediaeval scholastic practice of Biblical exegesis. While difficult to accomplish neatly when interpreting the Bible, it is impossible on encountering the complexities of everyday life.

A single research project cannot encompass the whole, yet it can leave threads untied, endings open, and margins messy, so as to avoid the elaborate pretence of mainstream social science. Walter Benjamin never published his influential *Arcades Project*, now edited, translated and published by other people (1999). Sociologists will never know fully what *really* happens inside people's homes (Jackson and Moores, 1995; Cieraad, 1999; Morgan, 2011), or hospitals (Goffman, 1961) or on the fields of Algeria (Bourdieu, 1977), nor, it is hoped, will a sociologist's readers ever know the unanswered emails, lost books, discarded ideas and unwashed hair that contributed to the 'product'. It is not enough to record the 'doings' of everyday life (Chaney, 2002: 35), or throw our hands in the air, claiming it is all an unknowable chaos (Atkinson, 2014). Even 'mess' depends upon assumed modes of organizing space, time and action. Mess is important, because it highlights the edges of taken-for-granted values and practices (Douglas, 2002 [1966]). Mary Douglas conveys this with reference to the ordinary activity of using someone else's bathroom:

> I am personally rather tolerant of disorder. But I always remember how unrelaxed I felt in a particular bathroom ... in an old house in a space created by the simple expedient of setting a door at each end of a corridor between two staircases. The décor remained unchanged ... It all made good sense as the scene of a back corridor, but as a bathroom – the impression destroyed repose. I began to understand the activities of more sensitive friends. In chasing dirt ... [and] tidying, we are not governed by anxiety to escape disease, but are positively re-ordering our environment, making it conform to an idea. (Douglas, 2002 [1966]: 2)

Wherever possible, researchers read, hold, hear, smell or see their sources, rather than accepting only reports or second-hand accounts, although these are also crucial for understanding how other people make sense of everyday life. For example, ethnographies and documentary research focusing on smell, hearing or touch emphasize how temporal worlds change when church bells stop ringing, how the construction of the 'smelly immigrant' contributes to discriminatory practices, and how touch is degraded in a sense hierarchy (for discussion, see Hurdley and Dicks, 2011). Since 'everyday life' is the 'taken-for-granted', common-sense, authentic, experienced realm of sociologists, it is critical that as many sources and pathways as possible, however seemingly irrelevant, are explored and followed. We are not the only experts at 'doing' everyday life. Although 'an overfocused and obsessional vision that ends by making everyday life seem unreal and hyper-real at the same time' is risky, developing that acuity to 'render the everydayness of the everyday' (Bryson, 1990: 90), requires us to open our minds. *Data* is Latin for 'the given things' or 'givens', and until those ordinary things are held up to critical sociological gaze, or conventional social life interpreted through fieldwork, and furnished with histories revised through exhaustive research, we can never explain how everyday life is accomplished.

Throughout a project, it is important to keep a journal, whether in the form of a diary, annotated photographs or sketches, scrapbooks, emails to self, notes on a CAQDAS package, through social media (public or limited view) or whatever works. How and to what extent these reflexive writings make it into a published article or monograph depends on one's approach to researcher 'presence'.

Scholarly rigour and reflexivity are mutually constitutive, and cultural sociologists, like many other academics, will engage readers, situate the research within wider settings, and also make plain that this is *their* analysis through occasional use of 'we', referring to broad literatures rather than a narrow field, first-person accounts of experiences in the field and authorial decisions. Atkinson states that our purpose is to be 'profoundly ethical', 'profoundly social' and 'humane' in our investigations into 'common humanity' (2014: 5). This involves not only the ability to step back from the everyday, to avoid such proximity to our informants' perspectives that 'co-construction of knowledge' means losing critical distance, but also to draw near to things, to look closely.

[The ethnographic] gaze captures and calls into question the tensions between the self and the other, between the near and the distant, between the familiar and the strange. It is not new, it is as old, in general terms, as human curiosity and the encounter between the writer and an 'other' ... we can detect the ethnographic imagination at work from Antiquity onwards. (Atkinson, 2014: 5)

## REPRESENTATION

Although Cultural Studies was most influential in the early development of British cultural sociology – in its focus on discourse, signs and symbols, the mutual constitution of meaning and representation, and of societies and their texts – the two fields continue to share some boundaries. In particular, they both attend to representation and rhetoric – modes of writing, talking, picturing and other forms of communicating ideas. While 'literariness' in sociological writing and oratorical skills at conferences and public events may seem tangential to the business at hand, it is central (Hurdley, 2014). What is the point of excelling at researching 'the everyday', only to publish dull jargon in an obscure journal, or present thirty unreadable charts to peers? The very reason advertising is so fruitful to analysis (Goffman, 1979), photographs were used in the earliest forms of social science and journalists became public sociologists, is because these forms of communication work. Following Abbott's (2007) declaration 'against narrative', Wagner-Pacifici (2012) argues for lyrical writing, singularity rather than generalizations, and a shift back to interpretive, rather than explanatory cultural sociology, with an awareness of modes of representation, and the roles and practices of the spectator. Goffman's essayist form, involving pragmatic use of miscellaneous sources, and the way in which he built a special relationship with the reader, means that when the reader fills in the gaps, she somehow follows Goffman's line of thought (Smith and Hviid Jacobsen, 2010). He draws us in, so that his habitual 'we' seems like an invitation rather than a trap. Paradoxically, his uneven, contradictory intimacy, also allows the reader the option of telling him he is talking nonsense. Conventional forms of scholarly representation perform the same arts of persuasion, but the reader is too accustomed to accepting their authorial authority to hold a dialogue (Dicks and Hurdley, 2009). Thinking about cultures of representation, and consciously working at these arts, is therefore more honest than forcing the reader to digest a monologue. Representation matters greatly when studying the everyday. First, because 'the everyday' is by definition ephemeral and mundane – sometimes quiet, even dull, but always a complex accomplishment, contingent on so many histories, backgrounds, taking so much for granted – and, second, because everyday forms of talk, action, text and things are similarly astonishing artefacts.

Balancing the poetics of research projects and texts, the politics of meaning, and sharing knowledge is difficult to do gracefully. Forms of representation, their aesthetics, and the gaps left for readers' interpretations, are all constitutive of meaning. In writing up research projects, or reaching for that next concept that seems tantalizingly just beyond words, we can give readers and audiences space to think through aesthetic, representational choices that may not conform to an assumed academic gold standard. In naturally occurring talk, one of the topics of everyday sociology, people use figurative language and complex syntax, contradicting and amending as they go along, often in conversation. Academic writers can employ similar techniques in a conscious metaphysics of meaning, with no need for jargon or pseudo-scientific logic to support their theses. Moving between ephemera and eternity, 'immortal ordinary society' is both made and expressed. Representation is everything, yet not in that floating, postmodernist sense, where there is nothing else. Representation is bound up with rights and responsibilities; its inversions are invisibility, unaccountability, silence, misrecognition and lack of legitimacy. Its varying modes frame meanings and values in ways that benefit some and discount others. Who contributes, who seemingly does not or cannot contribute to dominant representations of everyday life, is ultimately about value. In the politics of knowledge, who and what is valued? How have value and meaning been created, and by whom? Representations have histories, so without enquiry into the processes that made them, it is too easy to view 'culture' and 'society' as discrete spheres (Becker, 2007). Bennett (2007) examines how treating culture as meaning-making practice without scrutinizing *how* specific meanings are made, can result in the elision of the social and cultural. Through tracing how 'Aboriginal culture' was created, he demonstrates how culture relates to the social, thence to governmentality and social policy.

## CONCLUSION – THERE'S THE RUB

The familiar and the strange, the comic and the tragic, light and shadow everyday life, and it is too easy to view all as ambiguous, crepuscular gloom. Yet this is precisely what cultural sociology can and must challenge, by bringing what Hitchcock (BBC, 1960) called 'the dull bits' of life into the spotlight, breaking up conceptually neat narrative lines and dramatic structures. Blumer's 'sensitizing concepts' seem more theoretically sympathetic to our endeavour, than does the raw, untried rationality of normative sociology:

> Some say that sociology is a normative science. If they mean that social norms are one of its main objects of study, I agree. If they mean anything else, I do not agree. Many branches of human learning have suffered from taking norms too seriously. (Hughes, 1984 [1971]: xviii–xix)

As an ending, let us turn to our own mortality, which gives everyday life its particular brilliance, since we know it will continue even after we have disappeared. Durkheim's 'social fact' of suicide (2006 [1897]), is not a fact, but rather made up of historically, culturally specific ways of thinking about death and its representations (Fincham et al., 2011). Conceived as a rational act in some ancient philosophies (Marcus Aurelius, 2005 [167]) and currently at the centre of euthanasia policy debates, suicide is both symbol and situated practice embedded in complex social relations (Scourfield, 2005). Ideas about death and modes of death which are culturally legitimate are always in dialogue with ideas of how to live a 'good life', thus what kinds of people are culturally valuable – a central philosophical concern since Plato (see also Habermas, 1991). While legislation regarding suicide and assisted dying might make such practices legitimate, the relation between 'fact' and cultural value is 'the rub', since it is in the frictions between these worlds where change happens. Unconfined by bureaucratic temporality, *post mortem* reports and juridical process, scholars can pace their interpretations of identities and actions differently, with care and social justice as their organizing tropes. Cultural sociology's work is to explore, explain and represent the place of culture within these forms, relations and practices.

Mary Douglas' discomfort on seeing a corridor redefined as a bathroom was caused by the disruption to her meaning-making pattern, which, unknown to her until that moment, gave clarity and definition even to 'dull bits' such as bathrooms and corridors. It made them. Goffman's (1961) ethnography of a psychiatric facility demonstrated how patients used corridors and, indeed, urination, as settings and actions in the performance of their identities and everyday lives. His study of this 'total institution', like those of other institutions and settings, shows how 'social facts' are cultural matters (Chaney, 1994). The here and now is not a 'social fact' made by a rational, public Western white male preaching modernity, as some filthy peasant woman lurks in the kitchen nursing a baby and peeling carrots. The only way in which grand social theories of modernity are made, be it late, fluid, post, globular, atomic, liquid, fractal or hyper, is by excluding the dirty, messy, bloody bodies that tramp through everyday life, somehow getting along. Such smooth rendering of modernity is decorative. In contrast, the *somehow* of everyday life and its representations is cultural sociology's focus. This requires scepticism, yet without pessimism. For it is only through stubborn reluctance to accept that modernity is a *fait accompli*, through examining the ephemera of change, and its trailing dust, that the future becomes hope.

## REFERENCES

Abbott, A. (2007) 'Against Narrative: Preface to Lyrical Sociology', *Sociological Theory*, 25(1): 67–99.

Adkins, L. and Skeggs, B. (2005) *Feminism After Bourdieu*. Oxford: Wiley-Blackwell.

Adler, P. and Adler, P. (1987) 'Everyday Life Sociology', *Annual Review of Sociology*, 13: 217–35.

Alabarces, P. (2012) 'Culture and the Periphery: Nomadic Wanderings in the Argentine Sociology of Culture', *Current Sociology*, 60(5): 705–18.

Alasuutari, P., Bickman L. and Brannen J. (eds) (2008) *The SAGE Handbook of Social Research Methods*. London: Sage.

Alexander, J.C. (2003) *The Meanings of Social Life: A Cultural Sociology*. New York: Oxford University Press.

Alexander, J.C. (2008) 'Clifford Geertz and the Strong Program: The Human Sciences and Cultural Sociology', *Cultural Sociology*, 2: 157.

Alexander, J.C. and Smith, P. (2005) 'The Strong Program in Cultural Sociology: Elements of a Structural Hermeneutic', in J. Alexander (ed.), *The*

*Meanings of Social Life: A Cultural Sociology.* New York: Oxford University Press. pp. 11–26.

Alexander, J.C., Jacobs, R. and Smith, P. (2012) *The Oxford Handbook of Cultural Sociology.* Oxford: Oxford University Press.

Anderson, N. (1961 [1923]) *The American Hobo: An Autobiography.* Chicago: University of Chicago Press.

Appadurai, A. (1986) *The Social Life of Things.* Cambridge: Cambridge University Press.

Arendt, H. (1958) *The Human Condition.* Chicago: University of Chicago Press.

Atkinson, P. (1990) *The ethnographic imagination: Textual constructions of reality.* London: Routledge.

Atkinson, P. (2014) *For Ethnography.* London: Sage.

Atkinson, P. and Silverman, D. (1997) 'Kundera's *Immortality*: The Interview Society and the Invention of Self', *Qualitative Inquiry*, 3: 304–25.

Atkinson, P., Delamont, S. and Housley, W. (2007) *Contours of Culture: Complex Ethnography and the Ethnography of Complexity.* Walnut Creek, CA: AltaMira Press.

Atkinson, W. (2012) 'Where Now for Bourdieu-inspired Sociology?', *Sociology*, 46: 167–73.

Bachelard, G. (1994 [1957]) *Hommage à Gaston Bachelard. Études de philosophie et d'histoire des sciences par G. Bouligand, G. Canguilhem [and others].* Paris: Presses Universitaires de France.

Back, L., Bennett, A., Edles, L.D., Gibson, M., Inglis, D., Jacobs, R. and Woodward, I. (2012) *Cultural Sociology: An Introduction.* Oxford: Wiley-Blackwell.

Baldamus, W. (1972) 'The Role of Discoveries in Social Science', in T. Shannin (ed.), *The Rules of the Game: Cross-disciplinary Models in Scholarly Thought.* London: Tavistock. pp. 280–301.

Balzac, H. de (2014 [1845]) *The Human Comedy: Selected Stories*, ed. P. Brooks, trans. L. Asher, C. Cosman and J. Stump. Harmondsworth: Penguin.

Barrett, M., Corrigan, P., Kuhn, A. and Wolff, J. (1979) *Ideology and Cultural Production.* London: Croom Helm/BSA.

Bastida-Rodriguez, P. (2014) 'The Invisible Flâneuse: European Cities and the African Sex Worker in Chika Unigwe's On Black Sisters' Street', *The Journal of Commonwealth Literature*, 49: 203–14.

Becker, H. (2007) *Telling About Society.* Chicago: University of Chicago Press.

Becker, H., Geer, B., Weiss, R. and Riesman, D. (2009 [1968]) *Institutions and the Person: Festschrift in Honor of Everett C. Hughes.* Chicago: Aldine Publishers.

Beckett, S. (1949 [2006]) *Waiting for Godot.* London: Faber and Faber.

Benjamin, W. (2006) *Berlin Childhood around 1900.* Cambridge, MA: Harvard University Press.

Benjamin, W. and Tiedemann, R. (1999) *The Arcades Project.* Cambridge, MA and London: Belknap Press.

Bennett, T. (2002) 'Home and Everyday Life', in T. Bennett and D. Watson (eds), *Understanding Everyday Life.* Oxford: Blackwell. pp. 1–50.

Bennett, T. (2007) 'The Work of Culture', *Cultural Sociology*, 1(1): 31–47.

Bennett, T. and Watson, D. (eds) (2002) *Understanding Everyday Life.* Milton Keynes: Open University.

Bennett, T., Emmison, M. and Frow, J. (1999) *Accounting for Tastes: Australian Everyday Cultures.* Melbourne: Cambridge University Press.

Bennett, T., Savage, M., Silva, E., Warde, A., Gayo-Cal, M. and Wright, D. (2009) *Culture, Class, Distinction.* London: Routledge.

Berger, P. and Luckmann, T. (1967) *The Social Construction of Reality: A Treatise in the Sociology of Knowledge.* London: Penguin.

Bittner, E. (1965) 'The Concept of Organization', *Social Research*, 32(3): 239–55.

Blumer, H. (1954) 'What is Wrong with Social Theory', *American Sociological Review*, 18: 3–10. https://www.brocku.ca/MeadProject/Blumer/Blumer_1954.html [accessed 15 November 2014].

Blumer, H. (1969) *Symbolic Interactionism: Perspective and Method.* Englewood Cliffs, NJ: Prentice Hall.

Boden, D. (1994) *The Business of Talk: Organizations in Action.* Cambridge: Polity Press.

Bolton Council (2015) Worktown Project (Website): http://boltonworktown.co.uk [accessed 7 July 2015].

Bourdieu, P. (1977) *Algeria 1960: The Disenchantment of the World: The Sense of Honour: The Kabyle House or the World Reversed: Essays.* Cambridge: Cambridge University Press.

Bourdieu, P. (1979) *Outline of a Theory of Practice.* Cambridge: Cambridge University Press.

Bourdieu, P. (1986) *Distinction: A Social Critique of the Judgment of Taste.* London: Routledge.

Bourdieu, P. (1988) *Homo Academicus.* Cambridge: Polity Press.

Bourdieu, P. (1990) *In Other Words: Essays Towards a Reflexive Sociology.* Cambridge: Polity.

British Broadcasting Corporation [BBC] (5 July 1960) 'Picture Parade': http://the.hitchcock.zone/wiki/Picture_Parade_(BBC,_05/Jul/1960) [accessed 25 November 2014].

Bryson, N. (1990) *Looking at the Overlooked: Four Essays on Still Life Painting.* Cambridge, MA: Harvard University Press.

Buchli, V. (1999) *An Archaeology of Socialism.* Oxford: Berg.

Bulmer, M. (1984) *The Chicago School of Sociology: Institutionalization, Diversity and the Rise of Sociological Research.* Chicago: University of Chicago Press.

Button, G. (1993) *Technology in Working Order: Studies of Work, Interaction, and Technology.* London: Routledge.

Camus, A. (1971 [1961]) *The Outsider*. Harmondsworth: Penguin.
Cashmore, E. and Troyna, B. (1981) 'Just for White Boys? Elitism, Racism and Research', *Multi-Racial Education*, 10: 43–8.
Centre for Contemporary Cultural Studies (1982) *The Empire Strikes Back – Race and Racism in '70s Britain*. London: Hutchinson/Centre for Contemporary Cultural Studies.
Chaney, D. (1994) *The Cultural Turn: Scene-setting Essays on Contemporary Cultural History*. London: Routledge.
Chaney, D. (2002) *Cultural Change and Everyday Life*. London: Palgrave Macmillan.
Chaney, D. (2012) 'Starting to Write a History of the Present Day: Culture and Sociology', in L. Back, A. Bennett et al. (eds), *Cultural Sociology: An Introduction*. Oxford: Wiley-Blackwell. pp. 3–18.
Charles, N. (2014) '"Animals Just Love You as You Are": Experiencing Kinship across the Species Barrier', *Sociology*, 48(4): 715–30.
Charlton, T., Myers, L. and Sharpless, R. (eds) (2007) *History of Oral History: Foundations and Methodology*. Walnut Creek, CA: Altamira Press.
Cieraad, I. (ed.) (1999) *At Home: An Anthropology of Domestic Space*. Syracuse: Syracuse University Press.
Coser, L.A. and Merton, R.K. (1975) *The Idea of Social Structure: Papers in Honor of Robert K. Merton*. New York: Harcourt Brace Jovanovich.
Coulangeon, P. and Duval, J. (eds) (2013) *Trente ans après La Distinction de Pierre Bourdieu*. Paris: La Découverte.
Crane, D. (1994a) 'Introduction: The Challenge of the Sociology of Culture to Sociology as a Discipline', in D. Crane (ed.), *The Sociology of Culture*. Oxford: Blackwell. pp. 1–19.
Crane, D. (ed.) (1994b) *The Sociology of Culture*. Oxford: Blackwell.
De Certeau, M. (1984) *The Practice of Everyday Life*, trans. S. Rendall. Berkeley: University of California Press.
Delamont, S. (2009) 'The Only Honest Thing: Autoethnography, Reflexivity and Small Crises in Fieldwork', *Ethnography and Education*, 4(1): 51–63.
Denzin, N. (2001) 'The Reflexive Interview and a Performative Social Science', in *Qualitative Research*, 1(1): 23–46.
Denzin, N. and Lincoln, Y. (eds) (2011) *The SAGE Handbook of Qualitative Research*. London: Sage.
Dicks, B. and Hurdley, R. (2009) Using Unconventional Media to Disseminate Qualitative Research, *Qualitative Researcher*, 10: 2–6.
Douglas, J. (1967) *The Social Meanings of Suicide*. Princeton, NJ: Princeton University Press.
Douglas, J. (ed.) (1970) *Understanding Everyday Life: Toward the Reconstruction of Sociological Knowledge*. London: Routledge.
Douglas J. A., Adler, P.A., Adler, P., Fontana, A., Freeman, C.R. and Kotarba, J.A. (eds) (1980) *Introduction to the Sociologies of Everyday Life*. Boston: Allyn & Bacon.
Douglas, J. and Johnson, J.M. (eds) (1977) *Existential Sociology*. Cambridge: Cambridge University Press.
Douglas, M. (1986) *How Institutions Think*. Syracuse, NY: Syracuse University Press.
Douglas, M. (2002 [1966]) *Purity and Danger: An Analysis of the Concepts of Pollution and Taboo*. London: Routledge.
Duffy, C. (2015) *Everyman* [adaptation of 15th century original, author unknown]. London: Faber and Faber.
Durkheim, E. (1905) 'On the Relations of Sociology to the Social Sciences and to Philosophy', *The Sociological Papers I*, 197–216.
Durkheim, E. (1915), *The elementary forms of the religious life, a study in religious sociology*. New York, Macmillan.
Durkheim, E. (2008 [1912]) *The Elementary Forms of Religious Life*. Oxford: Oxford Classics.
Durkheim, E. (1964 [1895]) *The Rules of Sociological Method: And Selected Texts on Sociology and Its Method*. New York: Free Press.
Durkheim, E. (2006 [1897]) *On Suicide*. Harmondsworth: Penguin.
Dworkin, D. (1997) *Cultural Marxism in Postwar Britain: History, the New Left, and the Origins of Cultural Studies*. Durham and London: Duke University Press.
Eglitis, D. (2011) 'Class, Culture, and Consumption: Representations of Stratification in Post-communist Latvia', *Cultural Sociology*, 5(3): 423–46.
Elias, N. (1978) *The Civilizing Process: The History of Manners*. Oxford: Blackwell.
Ellis (2004) The ethnographic I: A methodological novel about autoethnography. Walnut Creek, CA: AltaMira Press.
Engels (1976 [1888]) 'Engels to Margaret Harkness', in Marx Engels On Literature and Art. Moscow: Progress Publishers.
Engels, F. (1892 [1844]) *The Condition of the Working Class in England in 1844*. London: George Allen and Unwin Ltd. http://www.gutenberg.org/files/17306-h/17306-h.htm.
Evans, D.F.T. (1986) 'Le Play House and the Regional Survey Movement in British Sociology, 1920–1955', unpublished MPhil thesis, City of Birmingham Polytechnic/CNAA. http://www.dfte.co.uk/ios [accessed 3 June 2015].
Evans, D. (2014) *Food Waste: Home Consumption, Material Culture and Everyday Life*. London: Bloomsbury.
Fernandez Rodriguez, C.J. and Heikkila, R. (2011) 'The Debate on Cultural Omnivorousness: New Trends in Sociology of Consumption', *Revista Internacional De Sociologia*, 69(3): 585–606.

Ferrell, J. and Websdale, N. (1999) *Making Trouble: Cultural Constructions of Crime, Deviance, and Control*. New York: Aldine de Gruyter.

Ferrell, J. et al. (2004) *Cultural Criminology Unleashed*. London: The GlassHouse Press.

Fielding, N., Lee, R. and Blank, G. (2008) *The SAGE Handbook of Online Research Methods*. London: Sage.

Fincham, B., Langer, S., Scourfield, J. and Shiner, M. (2011) *Understanding Suicide: A Social Autopsy*. Basingstoke: Palgrave Macmillan.

Fine, G.A. (1993) 'The Sad Demise, Mysterious Disappearance, and Glorious Triumph of Symbolic Interactionism', *Annual Review of Sociology*, 19: 61–87.

Fitzgerald, K. (2007) *Beyond White Ethnicity: Developing a Sociological Understanding of Native American Identity Reclamation*. New York: Lexington Books.

Fox, R., Lidz, V. and Vershady, H. (2005) *After Parsons: A Theory of Social Action for the Twenty-First Century*. New York: Russell Sage Foundation Publications.

Freud, S. (1901) *The Psychopathology of Everyday Life*.

Freud, S. (1913 [1901]) *The Interpretation of Dreams*. New York: Macmillan.

Fromm, E. (1961) *Marx's Concept of Man*. New York: F. Ungar Pub. Co.

Garfinkel, H. (1956) 'Conditions of Successful Degradation Ceremonies', *American Journal of Sociology*, 61: 420–24.

Garfinkel, H. (1967) *Studies in Ethnomethodology*. Englewood Cliffs, NJ: Prentice-Hall.

Garfinkel, H. (2002) *Ethnomethodology's Program: Working out Durkheim's Aphorism*. New York: Rowman and Littlefield.

Garfinkel, H. (2006 [1948]) *Seeing Sociologically: The Routine Grounds of Social Action*. Boulder, CO: Paradigm.

Garfinkel, H. and Sacks, H. (1986 [1970]) 'On Formal Structures of Practical Actions', in H. Garfinkel (ed.), *Ethnomethodological Studies of Work*. London: Routledge and Kegan Paul. pp. 160–93.

Garland, D. (2006) 'Concepts of Culture in the Sociology of Punishment', *Theoretical Criminology*, 10(4): 419–47.

Garland, D. (2010) *Peculiar Institution: America's Death Penalty in an Age of Abolition*. Cambridge, MA: Harvard University Press.

Gartman, D. (2007) 'The Strength of Weak Programs in Cultural Sociology: A Critique of Alexander's Critique of Bourdieu', *Theory and Society*, 36: 381–413.

Geddes, P. (1905) 'Civics: As Applied Sociology', in *Sociological Society: Sociological Papers 1904*. London: Macmillan. pp. 103–18.

Genovese, E. (1974) *Roll, Jordan, Roll: The World the Slaves Made*. New York: Pantheon Books.

Giddens, A. (1998) *The Third Way: The Renewal of Social Democracy*. Cambridge: Polity.

Goffman, A. (2014) *On the Run: Fugitive Life in an American City*. Chicago: Chicago University Press.

Goffman, E. (1959) *The Presentation of Self in Everyday Life*. Harmondsworth: Penguin.

Goffman, E. (1961) *Asylums: Essays on the Social Situation of Mental Patients and Other Inmates*. New York: Anchor Books.

Goffman, E. (1971) *Relations in Public*. New York: Harper and Row.

Goffman, E. (1979) *Gender Advertisements*. London: Macmillan.

Goffman, E. (1983) 'The Interaction Order', *American Sociological Review*, 48: 1–17.

Gouldner, A.W. (1975) 'Sociology and the Everyday Life', in L. Coser (ed.), *The Idea of Social Structure*. New York: Harcourt Brace Jovanovich. pp. 417–32.

Gubrium, J. and Holstein, J. (2002) 'From the Individual Interview to the Interview Society', in J. Gubrium and J. Holstein (eds), *Handbook of Interview Research: Context and Method*. London: Sage. pp. 3–32.

Guo, Y. (2009) 'Making History from Everyday Life of Common People: The Oral History Studies in a Chinese Village', *Polish Sociological Review*, 167: 399–413.

Hall, J., Grindstaff, L. and Lo, M-C. (2007) *Handbook of Cultural Sociology*. London: Routledge.

Hall, S. (1959) 'Something to Live For', in C. Marowitz, T. Milne and O. Hale (eds), *The Encore Reader: A Chronicle of the New Drama*. London: Methuen. pp. 110–15.

Hall, S., Critcher, C., Jefferson, T., Clarke, J. and Roberts, B. (2013 [1978]) *Policing the Crisis*. London: Macmillan.

Harper, D. (1997), Visualizing Structure: Reading surfaces of Social Life, *Qualitative Sociology*, 20: 57–77.

Harvey, D. (2003) *Paris, Capital of Modernity*. New York: Routledge.

Heidegger, M. (1962) *Being and Time*. London: S.C.M. Press.

Heidegger, M (2003 [1927]) *Being and Nothingness: An Essay on Phenomenological Ontology*. London: Routledge.

Heinich, N. (2010) 'What Does "Sociology of Culture" Mean? Notes on a Few Trans-Cultural Misunderstandings', *Cultural Sociology*, 4(2): 257–65.

Hinton, J. (2013) *The Mass Observers: A History, 1937–1949*. Oxford: Oxford University Press.

Hobbs, D. (2001) 'Ethnography and the Study of Deviance', in P. Atkinson, A. Coffey, S. Delamont and J. Lofland (eds), *Handbook of Ethnography*. London: Sage. pp. 204–19.

Hodder, I. (2012) *Entangled: An Archaeology of the Relationships between Humans and Things*. Oxford: Wiley Blackwell.

Hoggart, R. (1957) *The Uses of Literacy*. Piscataway, NJ: Transaction Publishers.

Hubble, N. (2006) *Mass Observation and Everyday Life: Culture, History, Theory*. Basingstoke: Palgrave.

Hughes, E.C. (1937) 'Institutional Office and the Person', *American Journal of Sociology*, 43: 404–13.

Hughes, E.C. (1958) *Men and their Work*. New York: Free Press.

Hughes, E.C. (1984 [1971]) *The Sociological Eye*. New Brunswick, NJ: Transaction Publishers.

Hurdley, R. (2013) *Home, Materiality, Memory and Belonging: Keeping Culture*. Basingstoke: Palgrave Macmillan.

Hurdley, R. (2014) 'Synthetic Sociology and the "Long Workshop": How Mass Observation Ruined Meta-methodology', *Sociological Research Online*, 19(3) http://www.socresonline.org.uk/19/3/contents.htm [accessed 12 July 2015]

Hurdley, R. and Dicks, B. (2011) 'In-between Practice: Working in the "Third Space" of Sensory and Multimodal Ethnography', *Qualitative Research*, 11(3): 277–92.

Hviid Jacobsen, M. (ed.) (2008) *Encountering the Everyday: An Introduction to the Sociologies of the Unnoticed*. London: Palgrave Macmillan.

Inglis, D. (2005) *Culture and Everyday Life*. New York: Psychology Press.

Inglis, D. (2014) 'What is Worth Defending in Sociology Today? Presentism, Historical Vision and the Uses of Sociology', *Cultural Sociology*, 8: 99–118.

Inglis, D., Blaikie, A. and Wagner-Pacifici, R. (2007) 'Editorial: Sociology, Culture and the 21st Century', *Cultural Sociology*, 1(1): 5–22.

Jackson, S. and Moores, S. (eds) (1995) *The Politics of Domestic Consumption: Critical Readings*. Hemel Hempstead: Prentice Hall/Harvester Wheatsheaf.

Jenkins, R. (2010) *Being Danish: Paradoxes of Identity in Everyday Life*. Copenhagen: Museum Tusculanum Press.

Jennings, H. and Madge, C., with Beachcroft, T.O., Blackburn, J., Empson, W., Legg, S. and Raine, K. (1937) *May the Twelfth: Mass Observation Day Surveys*. London: Faber and Faber.

Jung, C. (1961 [1913]) 'The Theory of Psychoanalysis', in *Carl Gustav Jung, Collected Works. Volume 4: Freud and Psychoanalysis*. New York: Pantheon. pp. 83–226.

Juvenal (1992 [c.100]) *The Satires*. Oxford: Oxford University Press.

Kafka, F. (1994 [1935]) *The Trial*. London: Compact.

Kalekin-Fishman, D. (2013) 'Sociology of Everyday Life', *Current Sociology*, 61(5–6): 714–32.

Kant, I. (2007 [1787]) *Critique of Pure Reason*. Basingstoke: Palgrave Macmillan.

Kaufmann, J-C. (1998) *Dirty Linen: Couples and Their Laundry*. Middlesex: Middlesex University Press.

Kierkegaard, S. (1980 [1844]) *The Concept of Anxiety: A Simple Psychologically Orienting Deliberation on the Dogmatic Issue of Hereditary Sin*. Princeton, NJ: Princeton University Press.

Keele University (2010) 'Foundations of Sociology/The Sociological Review', webpage: https://calmview.keele.ac.uk/CalmView/Aboutcatalogue.aspx [accessed 26/11/14].

Kynaston, D. (2007) *Austerity Britain*. London: Bloomsbury.

Lashua, B., Spracklen, K. and Wagg, S. (2014) *Sounds and the City: Popular Music, Place and Globalization*. Basingstoke: Palgrave Macmillan.

Law, J. (1994) *Organizing Modernity*. Oxford: Blackwell.

Lawler, S. (2008) *Identity; Sociological Perspectives*. Cambridge: Polity.

Lefebvre, H. (1991 [1974]) *The Production of Space*. Oxford: Blackwell.

Le Play, F. (1935 [1855]) 'Les Ouvriers Europeens', in C. Zimmerman (ed.), *Family and Society*. New York: D. Van Nostrand.

London, J. (1903) *The People of the Abyss*. New York: Macmillan. http://london.sonoma.edu/Writings/PeopleOfTheAbyss/ [accessed 1 May 2015].

London, J. (1907) *The Road*. New York: Macmillan. http://london.sonoma.edu/Writings/TheRoad/ [accessed 1 May 2015].

Lüdtke, A. (ed) (1995) *The History of Everyday Life: Reconstructing Historical Experiences and Ways of Life*. Princeton: Princeton University Press.

Lury, C. (2011) *Consumer Culture* (2nd edn). New Brunswick, NJ: Rutgers University Press.

Lyman, S.M. (1970) *A Sociology of the Absurd*. New York: Appleton Century Croft.

McCarthy, G. (2012) *Classical Horizons: The Origins of Sociology in Ancient Greece*. New York: SUNY Press.

McMichael, C. (2002) 'Everywhere is Allah's Place: Islam and the Everyday Life of Somali Women in Melbourne, Australia', *Journal of Refugee Studies*, 15(2): 171–88.

McRobbie, A. (1991) *Feminism and Youth Culture: from Jackie to Just Seventeen*. Basingstoke: Macmillan Education.

Madge, C. and Harrisson, T.H. (1938) *Mass Observation: First Year's Work 1937–1938*. London: Frederick Muller Ltd.

Madge, C. and Harrisson, T.H. (1939) *Mass Observation: Britain*. London: Frederick Muller Ltd.

Maffesoli, M. (1989) 'The Sociology of Everyday Life (Epistemological Elements)', *Current Sociology-Sociologie Contemporaine*, 37(1): 1–16.

Marcus Aurelius (2005 [167]) *Meditations*. Charleston, SC: Bibliobazaar. Ebook: http://classics.mit.edu/Antoninus/meditations.html [accessed 10 May 2015].

Marx, K. (1867 [1990]) *Capital Vols. I–III*. Harmondsworth: Penguin Classics.

Marx, K. (2011 [1844]) *Economic and Philosophic Manuscripts of 1844*. New York: Wilder.

Mass Observation (1987) *The Pub and the People: A Worktown Study*. London: Hutchinson.
Mass Observation (2015) Website: http://www.massobs.org.uk/ [accessed 3 July 2015].
Mayhew, H. (2009 [1851]) *London Labour and the London Poor*. Oxford: Oxford University Press.
Mead, G.H. (1982) *The Individual and the Social Self: Unpublished Essays by G.H. Mead*, ed. D.L. Miller. Chicago: University of Chicago Press.
Mead, G.H. (2009 [1934]) *Mind, Self and Society: From the Standpoint of a Social Behaviorist*. Chicago: The University of Chicago Press.
Miller, D. and Woodward, S. (2012) *Blue Jeans: The Art of the Ordinary*. Berkeley, CA: University of California Press.
Mills, C.W. (1959) *The Sociological Imagination*. New York: Oxford University Press.
Morgan, D. (2011) *Rethinking Family Practices*. Basingstoke: Palgrave Macmillan.
Murcott, A. (1983) *The Sociology of Food and Eating: Essays on the Sociological Significance of Food*. Aldershot: Gower.
Neto, F. (2014) 'Cultural Sociology in Perspective: Linking Culture and Power', *Current Sociology*, 62(6): 928–46.
Nielsen, K.B. and Waldrop, A. (2014) *Women, Gender and Everyday Social Transformation in India*. London: Anthem Press.
Oakley, A. (1974) *The Sociology of Housework*. London: Robertson.
Odum, H. (1951) *American Sociology: The Story of Sociology in the United States through 1950*. New York: Longmans, Green and Co.
Osborne, J. (1993 [1956]) *Look Back in Anger and Other Plays*. London: Faber and Faber.
Park, R.E., Burgess, E.W. and McKenzie, R.D. (1925) *The City*. Chicago: The University of Chicago Press.
Parsons, T. (1937) *The Structure of Social Action: A Study in Social Theory with Special Reference to a Group of Recent European writers, Volume 1*. New York: Free Press.
Pennell, S. (1999) 'The Material Culture of Food in Early Modern England', in S. Tarlow and S. West (eds), *The Familiar Past? Archaeologies of Later Historical Britain*. London: Routledge. pp. 35–50.
Perec, G. (1990 [1967]) *A Man Asleep [in Things: A Story of the Sixties with a Man Asleep]*. London: Vintage.
Perec, G. (2010 [1982]) *An Attempt at Exhausting a Place in Paris*. Wakefield: Wakefield Press.
Peterson, R.A. and Simkus, A. (1992) 'How musical tastes mark occupational status groups', in M. Lamont and M. Fournier (eds), *Cultivating Differences*. Chicago: University of Chicago Press. pp. 152–86.
Pinter, H. (1960) *The Caretaker. A Play*. London: Methuen and Co.
Pollen, A. (2013) 'Research Methodology in Mass Observation Past and Present: "Scientifically, about as Valuable as a Chimpanzee's Tea Party at the Zoo"?', *History Workshop Journal*, 75: 213–35.
Prus, R. (1996) *Symbolic Interaction and Ethnographic Research: Intersubjectivity and the Study of Human Lived Experience*. New York: SUNY Press.
Pysnakova, M. and Hohnova, B. (2010) 'From a Monolithic Mass to Unbridled Individualism? The Meaning of Consumption in the Everyday Lives of "Mainstream Youth"', *Sociologicky Casopis-Czech Sociological Review*, 46(2): 257–80.
Rebanks, J. (2015) *The Shepherd's Life: Modern Dispatches from an Ancient Landscape*. Canada: Doubleday.
Rebellato, D. (2002) *1956 and All That: The Making of Modern British Drama*. London: Routledge.
Richardson, L. (1990) *Writing Strategies: Reaching Diverse Audiences*. Newbury Park, CA: Sage.
Rickman, H. (ed.) (2011 [1976]) *Dilthey: Selected Writings*. Cambridge: Cambridge University Press.
Riis, J. (1890) *How the Other Half Lives: Studies among the Tenements of New York*. New York: Charles Scribner's Sons. Online text: http://www.authentichistory.com/1898-1913/2-progressivism/2-riis/index.html [accessed 10 April 2015].
Rojek, C. and Turner, B. (2000) 'Decorative Sociology: Towards a Critique of the Cultural Turn', *The Sociological Review*, 48: 629–48.
Rouncefield M. and Peter T. (eds.) (2011), *Ethnomethodology at Work*. Farnham-Burlington: Ashgate.
Rouncefield, M. and Tolmie, P. (eds) (2013) *Ethnomethodology at Play*. London: Ashgate.
Saldaña, J. (2005) *Ethnodrama: An Anthology of Reality Theatre*. Walnut Creek, CA: AltaMira Press.
Sanger, T. and Taylor, Y. (2013) *Mapping Intimacies: Relations, Exchanges, Affects*. Basingstoke: Palgrave Macmillan. http://www.qualitative-research.net/index.php/fqs/article/view/429/928
Sartre, J-P. (1965 [1938]) *Nausea*. Harmondsworth: Penguin.
Savage, M. (2010) *Identities and Social Change in Britain Since 1940: The Politics of Method*. Oxford: Oxford University Press.
Schleiermacher, F. (1998 [1838]) *Hermeneutics and Criticism and Other Writings*. Cambridge: Cambridge University Press.
Schutz, A. (1962): *The Problem of Social Reality: Collected Papers I*. The Hague: Martinus Nijhoff.
Schutz, A. (1967 [1932]) *The Phenomenology of the Social World*. Evanston, IL: Northwestern University Press.
Scott, S. (2009) *Making Sense of Everyday Life*. Cambridge: Polity.
Scott, J. and Bromley, R. (2013) *Envisioning Sociology: Victor Branford, Patrick Geddes, and the Quest for Social Reconstruction*. New York: State University of New York Press.

Scourfield, J. (2005) 'Suicidal Masculinities', *Sociological Research Online*, 10(2). http://www.socresonline.org.uk/10/2/.html [accessed 11 May 2015].

Shanks, M. and Tilley, C. (1992) *Re-constructing Archaeology: Theory and Practice*. New York: Psychology Press.

Sheridan, D. (1987) 'Appendix', in Mass Observation, *The Pub and the People: A Worktown Study*. London: Cresset Library.

Shove, E., Pantzar, M. and Watson, M. (2012) *The Dynamics of Social Practice: Everyday Life and How it Changes*. London: Sage.

Shove, E., Trentmann, F. and Wilk, R. (eds) (2009) *Time, Consumption and Everyday Life: Practice, Materiality and Culture*. Oxford: Berg.

Simmel, G. (1971) *On Individuality and Social Forms: Selected Writings*. Chicago: University of Chicago Press.

Simon, D. (2002–8) *The Wire*. Television series. HBO.

Skeggs, B. (2004) *Class, Self, Culture*. London: Routledge.

Skeggs, B. and Wood, H. (2012) *Reacting to Reality Television: Performance, Audience and Value*. London: Routledge.

Slater, D. (1997) *Consumer Culture and Modernity*. Cambridge, UK: Polity Press.

Smith, D. (1987) 'Women's Perspective as a Radical Critique of Sociology', in S. Harding (ed.), *Feminism and Methodology*. Bloomington: Indiana University Press.

Smith, G. and Hviid Jacobsen, M. (2010) 'Goffman's Textuality: Literary Sensibilities and Sociological Rhetorics', in M. Hviid Jacobsen (ed.), *The Contemporary Goffman*. London: Routledge. pp. 119–46.

Snow, D. (2013) 'Sexual Dimorphism in European Upper Paleolithic Cave Art', *American Antiquity*, 78(4): 746.

Sontag, S. (1977) *Susan Sontag on Photography*. London: Allen Lane.

Steinbeck, J. (2001 [1939]) *The Grapes of Wrath*. Harmondsworth: Penguin.

Storey, J. (2014) *From Popular Culture to Everyday Life*. London: Routledge.

Strathern, M. (2004) *Partial Connections*. Walnut Creek, CA: AltaMira Press.

Sztompka, P. (2009) 'The Focus on Everyday Life: A New Turn in Sociology', *Sotsiologicheskie Issledovaniya*, 8: 3–13.

Taylor, Y. (2013) *Fitting into Place? Class and Gender Geographies and Temporalities*. London: Ashgate.

Thompson, E.P. (1960) 'At the Point of Decay', in E.P. Thompson (ed.), *Out of Apathy*. London: New Left Books. pp. 3–18.

Thoreau, H. (2007 [1862]) *Walking*. Rockville, MD: Arc Manor.

Tiryakian, E.A. (2002) 'Rethinking Comparative Cultural Sociology: Repertoires of Evaluation in France and the United States', *International Sociology*, 17(2): 323–28.

Ts'ai, H.C. (2013) 'Diaries and Everyday Life in Colonial Taiwan', *Japan Review*, 145–68.

Turner, J. (1988) *A Theory of Social Interaction*. Redwood City, CA: Stanford University Press.

Verhoeven, J. (1993) 'An Interview with Erving Goffman', *Research in Language and Social Interaction*, 26(3): 417–38.

vom Lehn, D. (2014) *Harold Garfinkel: The Creation and Development of Ethnomethodology*. Walnut Creek, CA: Left Coast Press.

Wagner-Pacifici, R. (2012) 'From Moral Sentiments to Civic Engagement: Sociological Analysis as Responsible Spectatorship', in J. Alexander, R. Jacobs and P. Smith (eds), *The Oxford Handbook of Cultural Sociology*. Oxford: Oxford University Press. pp. 193–206.

Weber, M. (1968 [1922]) *Economy and Society*. Berkeley, CA: University of California Press.

Weber, M. (2008 [1891]) *Roman Agrarian History in its Relation to Roman Public and Civil Law*. Claremont, CA: Regina Books.

Weber, M. (2013 [1897]) *The Agrarian Sociology of Ancient Civilizations*. London: Verso.

Wesker, A. (1959) *The Wesker Trilogy: Chicken Soup with Barley; Roots; I'm Talking about Jerusalem*. London: Jonathan Cape.

Westgate, R. (2015) 'Space and Social Complexity in Greece from the Early Iron Age to the Classical Period', *Hesperia*, 84: 47–95.

Whyte, W. (1934) *Street Corner Society: The Social Structure of an Italian Slum*. Chicago: University of Chicago Press.

Williams, R. (1989 [1958]) 'Culture is Ordinary', in R. Williams (ed.), *Resources of Hope: Culture, Democracy, Socialism*. London: Verso. pp. 3–14.

Williams, R. (1961) *The long revolution*. London: Chatto & Windus.

Williams, R. (1965) *The Long Revolution*. Harmondsworth: Penguin.

Williams, R. (1973) *The Country and The City*. London: Chatto and Windus.

Willis, P. (1977) *Learning to Labour*. Farnborough: Saxon House.

Willis, P. (2000) *The Ethnographic Imagination*. Cambridge, UK: Polity Press.

Wilson, T. and Zimmerman, D. (1979) 'Ethnomethodology, Sociology and Theory', *Humboldt Journal of Social Relations*, 1: 52–88.

Wittgenstein, L. (1998 [1977]) *Culture and Value*. Oxford: Blackwell.

Witz, A. (2007) 'Georg Simmel and the Masculinity of Modernity', *Journal of Classical Sociology*, 1(3): 353–70.

Wolff, K. (1950) *The Sociology of Georg Simmel*. Glencoe, IL: The Free Press.

Wolff, J. (1985) 'The Invisible Flâneuse: Women and the Literature of Modernity', *Theory, Culture & Society*, 2(3): 37–46.

Wolff, J. (1999) 'Sociology and Border Disciplines: Opportunities and Barriers to Intellectual Growth – Cultural Studies and the Sociology of Culture', *Contemporary Sociology*, 28(5): 499–507.

Zorbaugh, H. (1983 [1929]) *The Gold Coast and the Slum: A Sociological Study of Chicago's Near North Side*. Chicago: Chicago University Press.

# 'Turn, Turn, Turn!' Musicalizing Cultural Sociology with the 'in Action' Perspective

Tia DeNora

## INTRODUCTION

Insofar as sociology's 'cultural turn' (Alexander and Smith, 2003; Jacobs and Spillman, 2005) has dealt with questions of meaning, feeling and (shared) experience, it has also returned sociology to a focus on action and the culture–agency nexus. In this chapter I suggest these matters dovetail with, but are extended by, perspectives in arts sociology, especially music sociology, and the work within these areas devoted to culture 'in action' (Acord and DeNora, 2008; Witkin and DeNora, 1997).

The 'in action' focus is addressed to the question of how culture 'gets into' action and vice versa and how this process can be observed and explained. The impetus is ethnographic, focused upon actual social interaction, the real stuff that people do in, with, because of culture. At the same time, this chapter will describe the idea that ethnographic intent is not an affiliate only of 'micro' sociology, nor would it be fair to portray the 'in action' focus as one that emphasizes agency at the expense of structure, constraint or, more broadly, the stuff outside of individuals. On the contrary, a focus on culture 'in action' is devoted to the interaction order, ecologies of action (DeNora, 2011; 2013), worlds (Becker, 1982; 1986; 2015) and local or immediate spheres of collaborative action (Fine, 1979; 2010; 2012) wherein both individuals and social structures can be seen to take shape *simultaneously*.

This devotion marks the 'in action' focus as located in *meso* structures, that is, organizations, groups, circles, scenes and institutional settings and their furnishings. It is a focus on what actors do and on how they confront and interact with objects, how they act and react in order to exist, pass, feel and do. It is also a focus on how actors make do with circumstances that exceed their control and how they become embroiled in these circumstances in ways that provide capacities for action. In this regard, the 'in action' perspective can reveal potentially much about what 'large' social forces such as modes of distribution and production, institutions, standardized technologies, laws, networked power and discrimination look and feel like on the ground, in terms of their effects and impact upon real people. And so, if, as they say, the 'devil is in the detail', then perhaps sociology's various demons may be better documented and explained through the high resolution lens directed to action's specific circumstances, contingencies and patterns. An additional benefit is that the attention to detail tempers impulses toward theoretical grandiosity and over-generalization (DeNora, 2003: 40).

To think about culture 'in action' then is to think about and document how we (social actors) inhabit various realms and worlds and situations in which there are many forms of sensuous, meaningful media. That project includes questions about how we mobilize, come to be interpolated between, or otherwise confront and appropriate those media in real time. Thus the cultural turn, insofar as it is interested in 'the conditions of sensuous perception', as Kant defined aesthetics (Williams, 1976: 31), is also a turn to the concern with consciousness, affect, embodiment and embodied experience, and – crucially, as this chapter will describe in some detail – *time and the temporal*.

That turn toward temporality in its turn aligns cultural sociology with a concern for 'histories of the present' and 'historically oriented sociology' (Inglis, 2014), by which here I here mean interest in the temporally unfolding matter of how things get put together in ways that draw together what came before with what happens now and what will or may happen later on. This temporal focus downplays the distinction between 'historical' and 'current' forms of sociological investigation (for what is not, ultimately, historical? And how can what happened 'before' not possibly be drawn in and appropriated for what happens 'now'?). So too, it eschews simplistic periodization and 'before and after' casuistries in favor of emergent investigations of history in the making (DeNora, 1995a; 1995b). This explicitly temporal 'in action' approach is perhaps nowhere better introduced than through examples from the 'new' music sociology (Prior, 2011), perhaps unsurprisingly since music is, nearly always, a temporal medium (though see also work on the 'new' arts sociology in general, e.g., Acord, 2010; Farkhatdinov, 2014).

It therefore seems appropriate to use as this chapter's point of departure the famous Pete Seeger song with its description of temporality and – more specifically for the purposes of cultural sociology – timeliness ('to everything there is a season').[1] There is a time for all things – but how do we tell that time and drawn into temporally scripted and plotted scenarios? How are our social 'seasonings' discovered and, indeed, concocted such that we as social actors feel a sense that the time 'is ripe to/for …'? In what follows I suggest that thinking about these questions helps us to see how culture comes, as it were, in to play and in ways that produce what ethnomethodologists refer to as scenic specificity, the fine-grained details of action scenes that furnish conditions of/for action in time and space and so shape the contours of action over time and space. This consideration of 'live' or 'real time' cultural action is one, as I shall suggest, that 'musicalizes' sociology and refigures action as a kind of 'making music together' (Schutz, 1964).

## MUSICALIZING ACTION – SIX FEATURES

Within music sociology – as opposed to the sociology *of* music – music and action are understood symmetrically (Hennion, 2007; 2015), that is, they are seen to be co-productive and mutually performed. The one is the other such that sonic engagement and so-called more 'reflective' or cognitively-based forms of action such as talk or writing are mutually referencing; they are simply different-but-related *modalities* of being together in time. Such a perspective is attentive simultaneously to music as it gets into action, and action as it gets into music, understanding these as not quite simultaneous moments but so intricately connected that the differences are often undetectable. Music sociology's particular devil therefore can be found in questions about music's (and by extension, culture's) ontology: what music is and what its, specifically, musical properties are, and can be made to be. What, for example, is specifically *musical* about music as a condition of action and, conversely, about action as a condition of music? To develop this discussion, consider the following six interrelated features.

First, along with theatre, dance, poetry and literature, music unfolds over time, even when it is created in ways that seek to effect a sense of stasis.[2] To a greater and perhaps less subtle and more forceful degree than in poetry or prose, music can entrain through rhythm and pulse and thus structure embodiment (as made explicit when people move to music, whether as dance or more mundane forms of choreography [DeNora, 2003: 136; Korczynski, 2011: 92, 97]). Because it is rhythmically organized, music can also align individual and potentially inchoate or unruly bodies into shared time. Music thus involves communicative synchrony such that 'making music together' requires and facilitates intimate and precise forms of attunement. In this sense, music, though it is by no means the only cultural medium to do so, provides a means and qualitative format for literally being together in time. How music manages to achieve this end may occur pre-cognitively, pre-verbally and proto-symbolically, and thus thinking about music helps us to think about how culture operates at a very 'deep' level and in ways that come to organize bodies, hearts and (sometimes only later) minds.

Second, music is materially flexible. It can be highly portable and thus easily introduced into action's settings through user-friendly technologies such as harmonicas, guitars, portable music devices like radios and televisions, iPods and MP3 players[3] and loudspeaker systems. The fact that music has the capacity to be a highly unobtrusive medium (invisible, potentially accessible with the flick of a switch, the turn of a dial) means – as has been shown in research on music in the retail sector, in clubs and exercise classes – that music can be a stealthy art, potentially insidious. Conversely, music has the capacity to be imposing, to fill a space with conspicuous objects and literally vibrate bodies – giant pipe organs, grand pianos, harps, bass viols, tubas, bagpipes and drum kits, for example.

Third, music is most often experienced and described in physical terms. It is a medium that, in Western cultures but also elsewhere (though by no means always in the same ways), is often associated with embodied practice, spatial relations and the sense of touch. Music also fills space, or projects outwards and thus permeates the entirety of a space. At the level of production, music often requires physical action (acoustic/embodied technique); it is rendered through physical handling (think of Barthes' 'grain of voice' and beyond to the bowing arm, tongue, fingers, feet in some cases, forearms, lungs and lips, which are integral to so much of musical production) and these handlings are responsible for the shape of the sound envelope, musical timbre, volume, and pitch (e.g., singing a low note involves relaxed vocal chords, playing the acoustic guitar loudly involves plucking the strings with more force, fading out on a note on the violin involves a gradual decrease of pressure on the bow). Because of these physical associations and physical practices, music is often understood and experienced as a simulacrum for movement and for touch (e.g., up, down, across, one on top/under another, far apart, crowded together, all occupying the same place [e.g., singing in unison], pressing hard or lightly, attacking, grabbing, releasing, going up high, down low, further away). The embodied experience of music can in turn afford embodied response – pace, energy, physiological processes – and linked to this capacity music can act and be used as a prosthetic technology (I can use it to 'push' me up a hill, or to 'press on' with an exercise routine, or as a way of making it easier to complete a course of physical therapy). I am or can become a human-music cyborg.

Fourth, and most familiarly to sociologists, music is often recognized in generic, conventional, ways that are often associated with historical (long-term and shorter-term) trends and with meaning and connotation. Some of these connotations arise from the ways that musical forms, styles, motifs and other features are connected to and used for social functions, ways of life, types of consumers and situations. These uses and the craft and collaborative conventions that give rise to music across the world thus also give music 'a history' which can be invoked, recognized, and otherwise drawn in to spheres where musicking (Small, 1998) is occurring.

Fifth, and following from music's capacity for connotation, and linked to the fact that music is rarely denotative, music can be severed from words and visual images, and because it is a flexible and highly mobile medium, music is highly amenable, indeed, susceptible, as Tota (2001) argues, to 'contamination'. Music's connotations can be, sometimes, irrevocably transformed, as musical scores and snippets of musical works transmigrate from their initial pairings and contexts to new contexts of presentation and use (e.g., as Tota describes, the use of a Mahler symphony in Visconti's *Death in Venice*, but also the delineated meanings [Green, 1997] that arise when music is performed [McCormick, 2009] and as its performance is framed).

Finally, sixth, and as a function of music's pairings, or transmigrations, music is closely associated with memory and forms of emotion experience ('my/our music, my/our memories'). Music thus can and is called upon to refresh memory, to occasion social action and to calibrate feeling parameters and feeling styles, at the individual level as a technology of self (DeNora, 2000), and at the collective level as a matrix for public memory, commemoration and emotion.

## SONGS WITH AND WITHOUT WORDS, 'IN ACTION'

So music is a diachronic, rhythmic (rhythm need not involve pulse per se) medium of organized sound. It is un-denotative, flexible, mobile, a virtual-physical repository of embodied practice. It is a trans-migratory, temporal, mnemonic, symbolic and sensory medium. It is a historical product. How, then, does such a medium 'get into' action, how can we understand social action to be musical? Addressing these questions highlights, as I have said, how music gets into action and experience. It also highlights how the arts are no mere frivolity, but – at times quite literally – life and lifeworld making. For example:

> Pam hits the xylophone hard with the beaters and throws them towards the piano, which they hit, causing the piano strings to vibrate. She shouts 'This fucking life!' and becomes very upset. (The therapist [Gary Ansdell] later finds out that the

outburst was caused by her seeing the letter names on the xylophone spelling out abusive messages to her from an internal voice.) Immediately after the blow-up the therapist encourages Pam to come to the piano, to sit beside him, and encourages her back into musical engagement again. She begins playing a few notes on the top of the piano, which leads into a short piano duet and then into shared singing with the therapist. Pam takes over the singing herself after a short time (accompanied by the therapist on the piano), becoming involved and expressive. The music seems to take her somewhere else. After the music cadences she sighs and says 'That's better!' The entire episode has lasted just over four minutes. (Ansdell et al., 2010)

In the seemingly brief interval of four minutes as described here, a mental health client dis-engages abruptly (and somewhat violently) from music, and becomes musically re-engaged in ways that (in her own words) made a change for the 'better'. This transformation or 'turn' can be closely documented. That documentation suggests that the 'change' was music-led, social and collaboratively achieved, and that it mobilized environmental materials and music-historical conventions so as to effect 'change'. As Ansdell et al. put it, that change resulted from the real time manifestation of 'communicative musicality':

> Trevarthen (2002: 21) defines communicative musicality as '… the dynamic sympathetic state of a human person that allows co-ordinated companionship to arise'. Such active musical communication happens through the largely non-conscious mutual negotiation between interacting partners, using three music-like dimensions: (i) shared timing (through pulse), (ii) shared shaping of the melodic contour, texture and intensity, and (iii) shared overall narrative form. (Ansdell et al., 2010)

It is worth considering in more detail here just how musical culture (existing conventions, meanings, associations and musical codes) came to be invoked in ways that made a change for Pam (and Gary). In the four-minute episode just described:

1 Music's *instruments* were changed (Pam 'drops' the insidious xylophone[4] and its beaters, distancing herself from the latter by actually throwing them away from her – they hit the piano and cause it to sound). After this and as part of a (literal and symbolic) re-orchestration, Ansdell encourages Pam to sit beside him at the piano which requires and affects …

2 a physical *repositioning* (sitting together at the piano and facing the piano rather than each other). This new positioning has historical resonances back to the 18th century (note the historical resonance and its mobilization here, with or without Pam's acknowledgement of it) – the classic 'four hands at piano' format in which, conventionally and as happened here, the male partner sits on the left side of the keyboard (thus playing the lower pitched notes and, in music therapeutic terms, being the one to provide both rhythm and bass, thus in the musical 'driving seat'). This format change in turn also enabled …

3 the musical and institutional *relationship* between therapist and client to be both literally and figuratively re-positioned as music-instrumental 'equals' (both seated at the biggest, most expensive and most 'high status' instrument in the room), as collaborators and as companions who become engaged in, as Ansdell puts it, 'a short piano duet' and 'shared singing'/playing and eventually moving into Pam's solo, with Ansdell's accompaniment. Thus, in four minutes of musical time, moment-by-moment, Pam and Ansdell move away from the crisis of the xylophone and toward increased possibilities of musical companionship (both facing the keyboard and performing a duet together, both piano and vocal). This transformed relationship in turn leads to …

4 a narrative account or definition of the situation: When the music comes to a close (and Ansdell remains silent) Pam sighs and then describes what has happened and where they are 'now'. ('That's better!') Her words offer an abbreviated narrative cap for, or frame around, what went before (the beaters of the xylophone). Those two words ('that's better') project both backward and forward to collect events into a before-and-after account of what has happened, and what has been achieved, prioritizing events and interpretations. It also takes precedence over her earlier utterance ('this f*****g world').

Thus, in the space of four minutes Pam has offered two definitions of the situation, at Time A and at Time B, from one place and set of stances (laden with psychiatric implications and roles – Pam's psychosis, Ansdell's role as a representative of the mental hospital) to another 'better', and noticeably calmer stance (Pam sighs before she speaks, they are now in the role of co-musicians). Her second spoken contribution is explicitly oriented to her first and intended to modify the former. The situation has been turned around, from a, 'f*****g world' to 'better', officially marked by her words, but her words have taken shape, been afforded by, the shape of music that came before. The point being that music, then, in this case embodied, shared communicative musicking, can cue or elicit alternate narrative or discursive registers and thus offer prerequisites for forms of agency.

By prerequisites I mean that the real-time musicking brought into the scene of action a range of affordances and possibilities for aesthetic relating, for emotional condition and energy levels, for situation definition, and thus for identity and role relationship. This 'new place' and set of stances in turn offered potential action trajectories and resources for the future – albeit with no guarantee that the newly turned features of interaction and identity will be replicable. Nonetheless, in the moment, Pam has managed to do new things, and that new experience and new capacity might be brought off again in other scenes at later times. The point is that *in this moment*, a new feature of Pam and Gary's *history* has been crafted, and it is one that has important potential for Pam and her future action opportunities (such as when she will be released from the mental health unit, when she will no longer require medication linked to unpleasant side-effects [to which she refers elsewhere]).

Thus, the music (its instrumentalities, its embodied relational stances and forms of comportment, its format) has 'acted'. It has acted *in concert* with other practices (not least Ansdell's considerable craft, his long experience working with mental health clients and his great familiarity with this client in particular). The practices by which this musical craft is mobilized and has cleared a space for situation re-definition are not achieved, and could not have been achieved by Pam all on her own. Indeed, in this case she could not plausibly be deemed an 'equal' partner in the crafting of cultural agency and cultural situation. On the contrary, as should be clear, the materials she was given to work with were structured and managed by the musically knowing and 'crafty' Gary. In this case that structuring was arguably benignant; it was oriented to helping Pam develop musically, to recover from the outburst, and to find a 'better' way of being there, in the real-time moments, and of course, through that tiny change, potentially later in other moments.

Historically, within these four minutes, musical engagement (mobilizing prior conventions, positioning, ways of relating and roles, verbal contributions) resulted in a 'better' situation, musically defined (playing entrained, mutually oriented to conventions, achieving a shared sense of musical closure), and in ways that 'made history'. They created a shared history of what (musically and beyond) these two may achieve and what other things (psychotic moments, words spelled out by the xylophone) can or might be put behind them. In so doing, the musical interaction and its history offered the premise for the narrative cap, the turned definition of the situation ('that's better'). Here, then, it is possible to see a small example of how musical materials *in tandem with* musical practices thus come to afford new situations in ways that direct the course of history – for participants in these meso structures.[5] This musical-verbal-practical spiral can continue and be 'repeated' at the time and later at other times. Through repetition, role relationships can continue to be redirected and elaborated. The social is or can be enacted through and in relation to music.

## MUSICALIZING ACTION STYLE AT TIME B, AFTER THE MUSIC STOPS

At times, music's parameters can be seen to leave their imprint upon actors after the music stops. In this sense music not only offers resources for action (metaphors or props), but music, understood as communicative musicality, is a modus operandi for action, as the following example shows.

We are in a group music therapy session, in a community centre adjacent to the hospital where Pam and Ansdell made their music in example one (and where Pam is a regular attendee). About thirty mental health clients, some hospital residents, some not, meet here each week to sing and perform. There are solos, ensemble songs, instrumental interludes and group singing. While Gary works as a strategic 'accompanist' (musical shepherd might be a more appropriate term) he is not entirely in charge of the musical doings, sometimes others take the piano, and sometimes the group who have formed a band take over.

In this case, Robbie goes up to the microphone and mentions in an off-hand way as he prepares to sing (*If I Loved You*) that he *is* Billy Holiday ('I am Billy Holiday').[6] This affiliation is evident in Robbie's manner of performing jazz ballads where he channels some of Holiday's delivery as 'his way' of doing the song – and beyond, his way of being in and with this group, his speech style, postures and gestures, all of which can be seen to take shape from and be exemplified by what he does musically. Music is a medium, in other words, for capturing, holding (Witkin, 1974) and projecting self to others.

Robbie's musical and para-musical performance has been given a promissory character. His words offer a cue of what we can expect from him in future. By the term, promissory, I mean that

Robbie's statement, before he sings, of, 'I am Billy Holiday' calls his and our attention to a musical/extra-musical style and associated allusion to forms of action. It is part of how he builds, between himself and others, for himself and others, a persona, and with that persona, a sensibility, one that he invites us to witness, sanction and share. It is promissory in its expectations and its claims upon that world, a kind of 'this is my way' or 'my stylistic bandwidth'. Finding, tuning in to that bandwidth, involves a musical-spatial location, a 'this is where you will find me', I inhabit this part/this kind of space, form of declaration. Music thus can be seen here to offer a potential form of agency in the world.

The elements of performance style, in other words, become proxies for identity, signs of embodied and tacit dispositions that shoot through and structure social action. Perhaps it is not, therefore, surprising that the question of how a song is to be rendered is potentially contentious (see Hennion, 2007): it is after all the way that we instantiate social relations (e.g., 'I don't like your tone of voice'). In this sense, musical activity can be understood to be an active ingredient of community formation; as McCormick (2009: 7) puts it, 'the context of musical performance is itself the result of an on-going process of cultural construction'.

Insofar as music is part of wider cultural construction, it is also an arena of conflict and a mode of doing that can serve as a proxy for conflict. It can, as various studies of conflicts over musical value have shown, be a resource over which conflicts occur. For example, on one occasion, another participant (Jane) had initiated a performance of *The Way You Look Tonight* which she began as a lyrical ballad, and Ansdell's musical introduction announced it in this way. On hearing the opening notes, Robbie hurried up to the microphone to join Jane because, as he put it, 'this is my song, I've got to sing this song'. Robbie's rendition was musically different, however – it was more of a swing version ('I am Billie Holiday'). A musical 'struggle' then ensued, with each participant seeking to pull the music in stylistically different directions in what was tantamount to a musical-stylistic tug-of-war. While (in the dual role of music therapist and accompanist) Ansdell functioned as the rope (not un-stressful for him), the 'audience' (the rest of us in the role of listeners and chorus) were enlisted as further 'musical muscle' by each of the vying parties. At stake were territorial rights, not to the song per se, but to the musical resources within this environment through which persona is routinely produced and sustained. In this case, this corner of the repertoire was not big enough for the both of them, hence the struggle over song ownership as marked by the struggle over style.

This struggle is vital because the ownership of a song and a style comes with what I would like to speak of as musical fringe benefits after the music stops, at Time B. So, when Robbie performs himself musically, in the persona of Billy Holiday, and when, after the performance ends, he remains partially in role, employing verbally an echo of Holiday's musical manner, he has found a modus operandi that transfers from making music to performing self (getting by, or 'passing' in Garfinkel's [1967] sense) through the medium of spoken interaction. He has found a musical-social vehicle for self-presentation and thus for getting into and through a situation. Indeed, the very point of the community music therapy project that Robbie is part of is to offer a medium (one that is relatively 'safe') within which self may be projected and – outside and after the musical action – sustained as ways of being in the world which will seem 'OK' to others, plausible and doable. Here then, we can see how music may, subtly and, in variously mediated, partial and morphologically altered ways, 'get into' para-musical action. For example, if I can acquire the knack of presenting myself musically (through a two- or three-minute song), and if I can forge a musical identity indexed by some form of stylistic regularity, repertoire and persona, I have developed a more general skill of sustaining a self through the mastery of competences in a communicative medium. In both musical and social realms performance involves playing with conventions and mastering certain, at least basic, communicative competences.

In this sense, musical performance is a means for resource generation, a kind of modus operandi for gathering steam for other actions and other action modalities. This 'gathering' considerably exceeds the ways that music offers a technology of self (DeNora, 2000). Musical engagement also offers what Procter describes as proto-social capital (Procter, 2012), aesthetic orientations, energy styles, mnemonic devices, and non-verbal forms of scaffolding for present/future action including collective action.

To take a hypothetical example, after my performance or listening experience, I can talk about that music (I have a topic of conversation, something to say) and, if only to myself, recall that I did well there yesterday (confidence, the beginning of 'form' in the sense of being known, having some kind of social career). I can tap my developing skills at interpersonal performance, of rendering myself to others in ways that allow them to relate (recognize, attune) to me. In doing these things, I am turning my musical activity into something else – a topic of conversation and in my conversation I may resort to some of the musical manners that I have absorbed by, to take Robbie's case, 'being' Billie Holiday. I am, in other words, made by things I just did, things I do, and things that came before me such as recognizable stylistic features, conventions, famous vocal mannerisms (things that existed at Time A), and those things got drawn into my musicking (at Time B), mediated through my attempts to appropriate them. Then, later (at Time C), my actions, thoughts, conversation may tap and partake of musicking (Times A and B) and in ways that may retain traces of those features. To the extent that those traces exist we may speak of the (partial) transmission of culture (always understanding that any transmission is a fresh act and potentially transformative or distortional of what it transmits).

So, for example, when I speak at Time C, there may still be a kind of split-second hesitance before the 'downbeat', my voice may be redolent of the Holiday timbre or, more broadly, the Holiday 'grain of voice', as Barthes termed the embodied features of the singing voice such as the sound of breath and other idiosyncratic features of an individual voice (Barthes, 1991 [1979]). I may, in other words, be 'speaking/portraying the blues' – perhaps even in the ways I introduce conversational topics, but more subtly through the paralinguistic features of how I speak, for example, when my vocal timbre is made by a resonance in my chest rather than in my head. In all of this activity, I am offering up myself as a bundle of aesthetic (sensory) cues (of what, it will depend upon how others read me and respond) and in ways that may help to anchor action, situation and action trajectory. (Conversely, I may adapt these aesthetic features according to where I think/feel I 'am', and at the time when I adapt, perhaps suppress the voice I find most familiar or most comfortable, we can see power at work in interaction and at the frequently tacit level of aesthetic media and aesthetic ecology.) In these examples, it is possible to see how meanings about my presence are cast out in time and in ways that may affect how I and others come to enter into a relationship here and now, and now, here, as I am speaking with you. A key by-product of this self-expansion is that I have been able to construct new resources that might connect me to others and I have been musically remediated in ways that, perhaps, enhance or diminish the perception of my 'difference' from you, to my detriment or my credit (as perceived by you and others). I can turn away from some things and (begin to) turn toward others.

## MUSIC INTO ACTION AND ORIENTATION

I have employed examples so far from music therapy because I believe that area offers a natural laboratory for documenting how music and action are mutually constitutive, and how music 'gets into' (enables/constrains) para-musical activities (Ansdell, 2014; Ansdell and DeNora, forthcoming). This is the 'how does culture get into action' question. But there are many other kinds of examples.

In relation to music, using music or through music, actors' stances, orientations and sensibilities shift, opening up and closing down possibilities for future engagement and also for consciousness, understood as selective orientation (DeNora, 2013: 97–120). A rich range of studies describe how music is used and how it works to structure agency in many realms, including leisure and work but also including social movement activity and conflict transformation. For example, in real time, consumers can be seen (albeit not necessarily with reflexive awareness) to 'fit' their shopping conduct and purchase behavior to perceived ambience and ambient cues (Areni and Kim, 1993; DeNora, 2000; North and Hargreaves, 1997). In the world of war and soldiering, music has been shown to be a part of how soldiers gear up for battle (Pieslack, 2009). As part of the culture of social movements, music has been shown to be part of what animates and sustains motivation within movement activity and in conflict resolution, working at times as an exemplar or holding form that sustains collaborative, concerted, coordinated action in real time and in terms of 'vision' or keeping 'eyes on the prize', to quote another famous folk song (Bergh, 2007; Eyerman and Jamison, 1998; Robertson, 2010). Music has also been described as part of what it takes to remain 'immune' to repressive cultural and/or political regimes, and thus as a part of urban 'underground' well-being (Hagen, 2012; Hagen with DeNora, 2012). Linked to what music may be able to 'do' for conflict/conflict transformation, on-going work devoted to music, understanding and empathy, suggests that music can be seen to encourage affiliation with different social groups though the ways that (in those who are susceptible to music's inducements) it induces motor and affective resonance with its rhythmic and emotional elements (Vuoskoski et al., n.d.).

In all of these cases, and in relation to the practices of its deployment and invocation, music is a medium that can draw people together, inflect space and 'turn' people in ways that both shapes and can alter action's course. This musical organization can affect individuals (personal listening, care of self) and collectives (organizational action, movements, scenes and worlds). Indeed, because music's effects in and on action are always linked to social/physical/emotional realignment, the individual/social distinction is misleading – what, that music might do, is not being done on the social plane, involving meaning and culturally constituted perception?

## MUSICALIZING SOCIOLOGY? SOUND ECOLOGIES AND HUMAN/ NON-HUMAN BEING

In his study of Kaluli musicking, ethnomusicologist Steven Feld (1983) describes the supra-individual character of aesthetic environments and the ways humans and other animals co-create aesthetic environments and habitats so as to build niches for action forms. He points to the 'co-evolutionary tendencies for ecology and aesthetics' (1983: 395) by which the Kaluli people not only take pleasure from the sounds of the rain forest, but become a part of the forest through their/its soundings in a virtuous spiral. In that spiral, sounding and sentiment are mutually enhancing and sounding can be understood to be an active ingredient of – Durkheim's term – collective effervescence, those features of collective life that emerge or bubble up to create collective phenomena that are more than, and different in kind from, the sum of its parts. A key question that arises from this perspective is how is soundscape more than a backdrop, and how does sound/music/culture offer action affordances in real time? That has been the question I have attempted to address in this chapter.

The issue of music's functionality (but without reductionist behaviorist accounts) has been considered at length by Dissanayake (2006), who, in a discussion of the adaptive features of music, points to similarities between human musicking and the role of sonic culture across animal species. In highlighting music as a means of conveying and shaping emotion, Dissanayake points to 'suggestive similarities' between evolutionary processes in animal communication and the ritual uses of music in human societies. She considers the rhythmic scratching and pecking of pheasants in terms of how these soundings can be understood as ritualized display (2006: 36–7) or, as she puts it elsewhere, 'making special' (later re-termed 'artifying' [2008]), the hallmark for Dissanayake of what art is. While there is tremendous risk here of projecting desirable stories and visions upon animal kingdoms who are unlikely to reply in writing (cf. Haraway, 1990), Dissanayake would seem to have a point. That point is that rhythmic action is a medium through which pheasants (not unlike people) achieve focus, meaning and coordination, and through which they signal intent and inclination so as to pave the way for collaborative action. Here, musicking or sounding would appear to be part of a general strategy for calling up and conducting behavior, and for accomplishing tasks in concert through the organization of action's aesthetic-sensory features.

Conceptualized in this way, music is much more than a form of communication and much more than the sonic representation of meaning; it is a constitutive ingredient of association. From simplistic statements about shared situation (sonic warnings such as alarm calls, whether made by birds or ambulance sirens) to ambient tones (music for meditation, music for dining) to music that inspires activities in common such as protest, war and worship, humans, and it would seem other animals, seem to musick not as part of but *as* the social condition, as a means of being social and being affected (in specific ways) and for continuing to produce sociality situated in real time.

Finally, while music sociology has arguably led the way in helping to articulate an 'in action' perspective for sociology concerned with how culture 'gets into' action, it is by no means the only area in which such studies can be pursued. There is untapped potential for studies of how other aesthetic media (images, poetic ways of speaking and writing, forms of movement and dance, and the various crafts) enter into action and prepare us for action, and in ways that give social life structure and texture. Such investigations have begun and cross disciplinary divides, with notable earlier work on the plastic arts, decor and the visual (Witkin, 1994), on organizational aesthetics (Strati, 1999; Witz et al., 2003), and more recent work concerned with aesthetics and embodiment (Colombetti, 2013; Thomas, 2013). Tapping this work but turning to how these matters can be investigated 'in action' may advance cultural sociology, as I have tried to indicate. It may enrich our understanding of the mediated processes and meso-level ways in which culture works, and it may allow for much greater exploration of aesthetic media 'live', as they enter into all that we do here, now, there and then, in time and place. Is it time for the 'in action' perspective in cultural sociology? To be sure, time will tell.

## NOTES

1  'To every thing there is a season, and a time to every purpose under the heaven: A time to be born, and a time to die; a time to plant, a time to reap that which is planted; A time to kill, and a time to heal; a time to break down, and a time to build up; A time to weep, and a time to laugh;

a time to mourn, and a time to dance; A time to cast away stones, and a time to gather stones together; A time to embrace, and a time to refrain from embracing; A time to get, and a time to lose; a time to keep, and a time to cast away; A time to rend, and a time to sew; a time to keep silence, and a time to speak; A time to love, and a time to hate; a time of war, and a time of peace' (Holy Bible, Ecclesiastes 3:1–8).

2   This point can be overstated since the idea that by contrast the visual arts – painting, sculpture – are synchronic, static, 'paints' perhaps too simple a picture: a picture is never actually static in terms of its perception. For example, Rothko's paintings 'move' after a certain time elapses. A Rembrandt also 'unfolds' over time as research on eye-tracking suggests (Quiroga and Pedreira, 2011). Viewers look first at one part of the picture, then another, from different angles, sometimes retracing their steps and gathering up the 'whole' work gradually.

3   Mobile music practices are by no means new: well before the personal stereo, MP3 player or iPod, music and sound were used to inflect space and organize human beings. The military drum, sirens, bells, foghorns, whistles and – that most portable of all musical instruments, the human voice – have all been used for centuries and across cultures to warn, incite, occasion, remind and comfort.

4   The xylophone's broader cultural and historical connotations include images and meanings associated with death and the supernatural. Musically, its 'hollow' timbre is often exploited to create macabre effects, the sound of bones in particular, in for example, Saint-Saëns' *Danse Macabre*, but also Walt Disney's 1929 cartoon, 'Skeleton Dance' where the xylophone being played is the backbone of a 'live' skeleton.

5   The music therapy research literature offers many examples of how key or heightened musical 'moments' or events may instigate 'turning points' in clients' medical, psychiatric and general well-being trajectories. These 'turning points' are marked by such things as 'the first good sleep' or 'the first time the pain did not result in screaming' (for a striking example of music and change in pain management, see Edwards [1995]).

6   Clients' names and identifying details have been changed. Here, Robbie's musical affiliation has also been changed to protect his anonymity.

## REFERENCES

Acord, S.K. (2010) 'Beyond the Head: The Practical Work of Curating art', *Qualitative Sociology*, 33: 447–67.

Acord, S.K and DeNora, T. (2008) 'Culture and the Arts: From Art Worlds to Arts-in-Action', *The Annals of the American Academy of Political and Social Science*, 619: 223–37.

Adorno, T. (1973) *Philosophy of Modern Music*. London: Sheed and Ward.

Aggeler, W. (1954) *The Flowers of Evil*. Fresno, CA: Academy Library Guild.

Alexander, J. and Smith, P. (2003) 'The Strong Program in Cultural Sociology: Elements of a Structural Hermeneutics', in J. Alexander (ed.), *The Meanings of Social Life: A Cultural Sociology*. Oxford: Oxford University Press. pp. 11–26.

Ansdell, G. (2014) *How Music Helps*. Farnham: Ashgate.

Ansdell, G. and DeNora, T. (forthcoming) *Musical Pathways in Recovery*. Farnham: Ashgate.

Ansdell, G., Davidson, J., Magee, W., Meehan, J. and Procter, S. (2010), "From "This F***ing life" to "that's better" … in four minutes: an interdisciplinary study of music therapy's "present moments" and their potential for affect modulation. *Nordic Journal of Music Therapy*. Taylor & Francis Ltd. Retrieved March 27, 2016 from www.highbeam.com/doc/1G1-252115637.html.

Areni, C.S. and Kim, D. (1993) 'The Influence of Background Music on Shopping Behaviour: Classical Versus Top-Forty Music in a Wine Store', *Advances in Consumer Research*, 20: 336–40.

Barthes, R. (1991 [1979]) 'The Grain of Voice', in S. Frith and A. Goodwin (eds), *On Record: Pop, Rock and the Written Word*. London: Routledge. pp. 250–4.

Becker, H.S. (1982) *Art Worlds*. Berkeley, Los Angeles and London: University of California Press.

Becker, H.S. (1986) *Doing Things Together: Selected Papers*. Chicago: Northwestern University Press.

Becker, H.S. (2015) *What About Mozart? What About Murder? Reasoning from Cases*. Chicago: University of Chicago Press.

Bergh, A. (2007) 'I'd Like to Teach the World to Sing: Music and Conflict Transformation', *Musicae Scientiae*, 141–57.

De la Fuente, E. (2007) 'The "New Sociology of Art": Putting Art Back into Social Science Approaches to the Arts', *Cultural Sociology*, 1(3): 409–25.

DeNora, T. (1995a) *Beethoven and the Construction of Genius: Musical Politics in Vienna, 1792–1803*. Berkeley, Los Angeles and London: University of California Press.

DeNora, T. (1995b) 'Deconstructing Periodization: Sociological Methods and Historical Ethnography', *Beethoven Forum*, 4: 1–15.

DeNora, T. (2000) *Music in Everyday Life*. Cambridge: Cambridge University Press.

DeNora, T. (2003) *After Adorno: Rethinking Music Sociology*. Cambridge: Cambridge University Press.

DeNora, T. (2011) *Music in Action: Selected Essays in Sonic Ecology*. Farnham: Ashgate.

DeNora, T. (2013) *Music Asylums: Wellbeing Through Music in Everyday Life*. Farnham: Ashgate.

DeNora, T. and Witkin, R. (2001) 'Configuring the Classics: Musical Experience and Musical Consciousness', *Poetics*, 29(2): 71–4.

Dissanayake, E. (2008) 'The Arts After Darwin: Does Art Have an Origin and Adaptive Function?', in K. Zijlmans and W. van Damme (eds), *World Art Studies: Exploring Concepts and Approaches*. Amsterdam: Valiz. pp. 241–63.

Edwards, J. (1995) '"You Are Singing Beautifully": Music Therapy and the Debridement Bath', *The Arts in Psychotherapy*, 22(1): 53–5.

Eyerman, R. and Jamison, A. (1998) *Music and Social Movements*. Cambridge: Cambridge University Press.

Farkhatdinov, N. (2014) 'Beyond Decoding: Art Installations and Mediation of Audiences', *Music and Arts in Action*, 4(2). Available at: http://www.musicandartsinaction.net/index.php/maia/article/view/artinstallationmediation/94 (accessed 19 June 2015).

Feld, S. (1983) 'Sound Structure as Social Structure', *Ethnomusicology*, 28(3): 383–409.

Fine, G.A. (1979) 'Small Groups and Cultural Creation: The Idioculture of Little League Baseball Teams', *American Sociological Review*, 44: 733–45.

Fine, G.A. (2010) 'The Sociology of the Local: Action and its Publics', *Sociological Theory*, 28(4): 356–76.

Fine, G.A. (2012) *Tiny Publics: A Theory of Group Action and Culture*. New York: Russel Sage Foundation.

Garfinkel, H. (1967) *Studies in Ethnomethodology*. Englewood Cliffs: Prentice Hall.

Green, L. (1997) *Music, Gender, Education*. Cambridge: Cambridge University Press.

Hagen, T. (2012) 'From Inhibition to Commitment: Politics in the Czech Underground', *EastBound: Special Issue 'Popular Music in Eastern Europe'*. Available at http://www.eastbound.eu/treverhagen

Hagen, T. with DeNora, T. (2012) 'From Listening to Distribution: Nonofficial Music Practices in Hungary and Czechoslovakia from the 1960s to the 1980s', in T. Pinch and K. Bijsterveld (eds), *Oxford Handbook of Sound Studies*. Oxford: Oxford University Press. pp. 440–58.

Hara, M. (2011) 'Expanding a Care Network for People with Dementia and their Carers Through Musicking', *Voices: A World Forum for Music Therapy*, 11(2). Available at: https://normt.uib.no/index.php/voices/article/viewArticle/570

Haraway, D. (1990) *Primate Visions: Gender, Race, and Nature in the World of Modern Science*. London: Routledge.

Hartshorne, C. (1992 [1973]) *Born to Sing: Interpretation and World Survey of Bird Song*. Chichester: Wiley.

Hennion, A. (2007) 'Those Things that Hold Us Together: Taset and Sociology', *Cultural Sociology*, 1(1): 97–114.

Hennion, A. (2015) *The Passion for Music*. Farnham: Ashgate.

Inglis, D. (2014) 'What is Worth Defending in Sociology Today? Presentism, Historical Vision and the Uses of Sociology', *Cultural Sociology*, 8(1): 99–118.

Jacobs, M. and Spillman, L. (2005) 'Cultural Sociology at the Crossroads of the Discipline', *Poetics*, 33(1): 1–14.

Korczynski, M. (2011) 'Stayin' Alive on the Factory Floor: An Ethnography of the Dialectics of Music Use in the Routinized Workplace', *Poetics*, 39: 87–106.

McCormick, L. (2009) 'Higher, Faster, Louder: Representations of the International Music Competition', *Cultural Sociology*, 3(1): 5–30.

North, A. and Hargreaves, D. (1997) 'Music and Consumer Behaviour', in D. Hargreaves and A. North (eds), *The Social Psychology of Music*. Oxford: Oxford University Press. pp. 268–89.

Pieslak, J. (2009) *Sound Targets: American Soldiers and Music in the Iraq War*. Bloomington: Indiana University Press.

Prior, N. (2011) 'Critique and Renewal in the Sociology of Music: Bourdieu and Beyond', *Cultural Sociology*, 5(1): 121–38.

Procter, S. (2011) 'Reparative Musicing: Thinking on the Usefulness of Social Capital Theory within Music Therapy', *Nordic Journal of Music Therapy*, 2(3) 242–62.

Quiroga, R.Q. and Pedreira, C. (2011) How Do We See Art: An Eye-Tracker Study', *Frontiers of Human Neuroscience*, 5: 98. Available at: http://www.ncbi.nlm.nih.gov/pmc/articles/PMC3170918/

Robertson, C. (2011) 'Music and Conflict Transformation in Bosnia: Constructing and Reconstructing the Normal', *Music and Arts in Action*, 2(2): 38–55.

Schutz, A. (1964) 'Making Music Together', in *Collected Papers II*. The Hague: Martinus Njhoff. pp. 159–79.

Small, C. (1998) *Musicking: The Meanings of Performing and Listening*. Middletown, CT: Wesleyan University Press.

Strati, A. (1999) *Organization and Aesthetics*. London: Sage.

Tota, A.L. (2001) 'When Orff Meets Guinness: Music in Advertising as a Form of Cultural Hybrid', *Poetics*, 29(1): 109–23.

Vuoskoski, J., Clarke, E.F. and DeNora, D. (n.d.) 'Music Listening Evokes Implicit Affiliation. AHRC Project on Music, Empathy and Understanding'.

Williams, R. (1976) *Keywords*. London: Croom Helm.

Witkin, R. (1974) *The Intelligence of Feeling*. London: Heinemann Educational.

Witkin, R. and DeNora, T. (1997) 'Aesthetic Materials and Aesthetic Agency', *Newsletter of the ASA Culture* Section 12:1. Availble at: http://www.ibiblio.org/culture/newsletter-archive/1997cFall.pdf

Witz, A., Warhurst, C. and Nicholson, D. (2003) 'The Labour of Aesthetics and the Aesthetics of Organization', *Organization*, 10(1): 33–54.

# PART V
# Culture and Politics

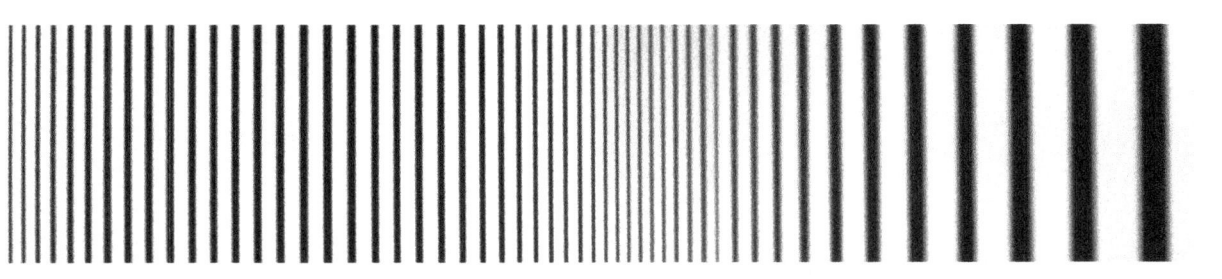

# Cultural Citizenship

Nick Stevenson

## INTRODUCTION

The idea of cultural citizenship has a strong connection to classical sociological theory (especially, although not exclusively, to the work of W.E.B. Du Bois) but it needs to be reinvented for our own times. Here I shall argue against those who have presumed that the concept is either purely descriptive or indeed that it could be subsumed under postmodern pluralism. On the contrary, cultural citizenship is the struggle for the educative and communications-based society that prioritizes the possibility of human rights, democracy and social justice. In this respect, it is not merely concerned with cultural rights (although these are important), but rather concerns the future possibility of a more emancipated society. Questions of cultural citizenship should not be understood separately from the demand for civil, political and social rights. At the heart of cultural citizenship is the search for a meaningful and dignified life where we each find answers to the question as to what it means to be human. However, this is a life lived in common with other human beings and is currently threatened by indignity, privatization and acts of enclosure. Cultural citizenship then requires a commons where people are able to meet, interact and exchange different ideas and perspectives. Historically, this has been undermined by both the economic system and the state, which often seek to promote more instrumental uses of culture. The struggle for cultural citizenship has been transformed historically due to the arrival of different social movements, technologies and identities, but retains at its heart the attempt to preserve a meaningful democratic life in common. As Raymond Williams (1989: 38) argues, a genuine culture in common (or cultural citizenship) is best preserved by 'keeping the channels and institutions of communication clear, so that all may contribute, and be helped to contribute'. However, if cultural citizenship requires an active and democratically organized civil society we also need to attend to the ways in which different codes and understandings construct the civic order. All civil campaigns seek to construct the civic order in terms of qualities that deserve to be included and excluded (Alexander, 2013). In this respect, the struggle for a genuinely civil and inclusive society is likely to be on-going and without end, full of stories of defiance, defeat, exclusion and occasionally success. Before returning to these questions we need to investigate how the idea of cultural citizenship has emerged historically.

## CULTURAL CITIZENSHIP AND THE ROMANTICS

The idea of cultural citizenship has a long historical lineage in respect of the political and cultural traditions of European societies. Cornelius Castoriadis (1997) has long associated the struggle for a meaningful and democratic life as opposed to a common life ruled by heteronomy back to the Ancient Greeks. Democracy, in this understanding, is a cultural invention that requires a critical and imaginative life in common with other citizens. The Enlightenment and the Romantic age were also crucial periods in seeking to define modern ideas of freedom being connected to the need to authentically become the person you were meant to be within a democratic context (Berman, 1970). The radical move made by Rousseau (1991 [1762]) was in seeking to devise an education system where citizens could think for themselves so that they could authentically become themselves. This was an assault on the idea that citizens were educated to occupy particular occupational ranks. Education was called upon to develop self-expression and exploration, not just conformity to the needs of more traditional forms of order. If the liberal society was to emerge it could only do so if it was able to radically reform the surrounding society in order to combat progressive inequality and poverty, and by encouraging independent thought and ideas.

If the Enlightenment had helped raise questions related to human rights, democracy and freedom, then the Romantics would push these questions even further. Raymond Williams (1958) has argued how historically the idea of culture is caught up with questions of judgement about the quality of common life under industrialism. This rich and politically varied heritage sought to make sense of the arrival of capitalism, spread of democracy, and the role of art and culture in the wider society. Mathew Arnold (1987 [1869]) and John Ruskin (1985 [1862]) both argued that the instrumentalism of Victorian capitalism was having a corrupting effect on notions of meaning, value and worth. For Arnold, whereas 'culture' aimed at the perfection of the citizenry, the economic system sought to persuade people to only think of profit and gain. Questions of culture raised ideas about human sympathy and the meaningfulness of human life. Similarly for Ruskin, modern political economy showed very little interest in ideas of community, human relationships and the role of art more generally. Of course, as Williams (1958) reminds us, the way these questions were raised trades upon a host of anti-democratic and elitist sentiments about the barbarism of the masses, but they at least raised concerns beyond the purely instrumental. Edward Said (1993) takes these arguments further, arguing that for the Romantic movement 'their' culture was the superior culture in the context of colonial and imperial domination. However, as Said also recognizes, such a view does not silence some of the considerable intellectual resources and complexities to be found among different artists and writers within this tradition.

Under the rule of utilitarianism, human beings lose their complexity and meaningfulness as life is increasingly assessed in terms of statistics and the balance sheet (Nussbaum, 1995). Indeed, if we only have instrumental ways of understanding at our disposal then it is likely we will see human beings as being motivated by either economic instincts or other more easily calculable criteria. Jonathan Rutherford (2005) argues that the conservative idea of culture offered by Arnold and other Romantic writers like Ruskin was central to the growth of the idea of the humanities. The so-called 'men of culture' set themselves up against the dominant logic of the market society during the Victorian period. More recently, however, others like Tony Bennett (1998) have been critical of the dominance of the Romantic approach to aesthetics still evident within cultural studies. For Bennett, many Romantic intellectuals fail to recognize that 'the aesthetic disposition forms merely a particular market segment' and that there are other equally valid interests and agencies involved in the governance of culture (Bennett, 1998: 199). Bennett seemingly wishes to replace some of the self-importance of 'cultural theory' with a more pragmatically orientated set of concerns necessary for the functioning of a democratic society. While this view offers a number of insights, I would agree with Jonathan Rutherford (2005: 313), who suggests that arguments of this type give up on the idea of the value and meaningfulness of our shared cultural lives altogether. The historian E.P. Thompson (1997) argues that the critique of the idea of rank and hierarchy only began to emerge with the emergence of the Romantic movement after the French Revolution. It was the Romantics who raised questions of human potential and notions of equal worth, and argued that ideas needed to be tested out through experience. These concerns alone suggest that the impact of the Romantics upon ideas of cultural value cannot simply be confined to an elitist sensibility. Further, there is an explicit recognition of the value of culture in terms of shaping questions of identity, experience and meaning that continues to have a resonance in our own times.

## CLASSICAL SOCIOLOGY AND THE IMPORTANCE OF W.E.B. DU BOIS

As I indicated in the introduction, questions of culture were also important for classical sociology. Both Weber and Simmel were concerned with the impact of the rise of modernity upon subjective experience, and the role that art might play in a rationalized world (Scaff, 1989). However, for all their complexity, neither Weber nor Simmel perceived within the cultural domain a more specifically emancipatory role. More recently there has been a considerable amount of interest in Durkheim's work on the construction of social solidarities (Alexander, 1998). However, like Weber and Simmel, it could be argued that Durkheim is more concerned with the moral order than he is with questions of human freedom. Missing from some of this sociological work is a deeper concern with the radical culture of the Enlightenment. Stephen Eric Bronner (2004) argues that the culture of critical liberalism can be said to have emerged from Enlightenment-based concerns. The Enlightenment was an attempt to criticize dogma of all kinds, including overt nationalism, instrumentalism and religious traditions. While the Enlightenment was a complex philosophical and cultural movement, it largely sought to critique the established traditions in favour of tolerance, freedom and democracy, and for this reason remains central to our argument. If Marx was one inheritor of this tradition then so was liberalism and social democracy. The problem in terms of questions of citizenship and civility being that Marxism has a long history of both reducing the civil domain to the class struggle and of neglecting the importance and continued vibrancy of the public sphere. As Jeffrey Alexander (2010) argues, despite claims to the contrary, the public is not wholly controlled by either the economy or the state, although these are powerful agencies seeking to shape the quality of civic life. More significant in this respect remains the power of moral ideas like human rights and citizenship. Further, if 'official' Marxism over the course of the 20th century became converted into an authoritarian set of political concerns, then more 'humanistic' versions of Marxism, liberalism and liberal socialism maintained traditions of critique. These traditions were to prove particularly important in the context of the development of totalitarianism, given the attack on ideas of autonomy and freedom evident in state-dominated societies. Further, the worker's movement, feminism, black politics and other social movements all sought to make liberalism their own, extending the idea of liberty and freedom beyond elite concerns. However, as we shall also see, the culture of liberalism often has a poor understanding of wider questions of cultural domination.

The idea of equality, human rights and democracy could not be maintained as elite concerns. The border-crossing culture of the French and American Revolutions would become transformed as it entered into new intellectual and social and cultural contexts. Here we should consider the Haitian Revolution, where slaves fought for their own liberation thereby revealing the contradictoriness of modernity (Hardt and Negri, 2009). The racist contours of both the Enlightenment and the Romantic movement are important to appreciate in this context. The economic and cultural legacy of European imperialism and colonialism has done much to shape the modern world and remains largely under-appreciated by some writing in the sociological tradition. Here we need to be careful of moves simply to brand the Enlightenment or the Romantic movement as inherently racist, given the role that both intellectual and cultural movements would play in questioning domination in the modern world.

Arguably it is the American sociologist W.E.B. Du Bois, rather than Marx, Weber, Simmel or Durkheim, who has made the most important contribution to our understanding of cultural citizenship. This was because Du Bois was aware that full citizenship was not merely a question of having formal legal access to certain rights, but that the cultural meanings of a particular society could permanently injure the self-understandings of the citizen. If cultural citizenship is concerned with how issues related to morality and the imagination enter into the everyday lives of ordinary people, it is equally concerned with the injury that might be done to the self through the promotion of harmful stereotypes and damaging cultural assumptions. Du Bois remains historically important through the way he sought to radically transform the histories of the Enlightenment and the Romantic period in order to tackle the degraded status of black people in America. Further, Du Bois did this with a strong recognition that the world was still dealing with the consequences of what with hindsight we can call the first wave of globalization.

David Theo Goldberg (2009) has described this phase of globalization as the world transforming power of Europeans that made race a central category of modernity. Despite ideas of European civility, this did not prevent them from occupying much of the globe. As Cornel West (1993) argues, by the beginning of the First World War Europeans had control over about one-third of the globe's population. This system was held in place through the unashamed promotion of white superiority and the inferiority of the black Other. What is significant here is the lack of cultural power available to black people (and the same argument could also be made for other subordinate groups) to promote more complex and less reductive understandings. In this setting Du Bois sought to both combat the problems of invisibility and the rule of a degrading culture, not simply by promoting other cultural frameworks, but also by seeking to address critical problems related to emancipation and educated understanding.

W.E.B. Du Bois (2007 [1903]: 8) introduced the idea of 'double-consciousness' as a means of making sense of black Americans' struggle for citizenship. This was necessary in the context of a racist white society where the recognition of the self as both black and American was a difficult if not impossible achievement. Du Bois wished to see black people attain an emancipatory citizenship that would only come about once they had learned to educate themselves and gain a level of cultural respect. He argued that, up until this point, sociologists had been content to count and quantify the problems of 'black folk'. Alternatively, what was necessary was 'the freedom to work and think, the freedom to love and aspire' (Du Bois, 2007 [1903]: 13). This would only be possible if the ideals of the American republic (life, liberty and the pursuit of happiness) became ideals not exclusively reserved for white Americans but the property of the world's people. Here we have the emergence of a new national and global citizenship beyond the confines of a racist society. If, as Du Bois argued (2007 [1903]: 15), 'the problem of the twentieth century is the problem of the color line' then one of the most significant struggles was to recognize the humanity of everyone. This meant the achievement of civic equality that required political equality, equal legal rights and the development of educated forms of critical understanding. This was not only a demand for resources, but, in our terms, for cultural citizenship. Like the Romantic movement before him, Du Bois was suspicious of those who were mainly interested in material wealth or economic profit. The education that interested Du Bois (2007 [1903]: 57) concerned questions of critique and self-realization. Du Bois was deeply committed to the idea that black people not only concern themselves with the pursuit of wealth, but with a life of learning. What, he asks, is the point of living if only to pursue material possessions? A more meaningful life involved the 'love of knowing' (Du Bois, 2007 [1903]: 57).

However, what 'counts' as knowledge and culture is also deeply influenced by the wider structures of society. What Mathew Arnold and others took as the relatively self-evident cultural 'jewels' of civilization required further interrogation. With Du Bois we have the beginning of a critical questioning as to whose culture counts as 'the culture'. Within a society built upon domination we need to ask complex questions about whose history is remembered, whose voices are heard and, of course, which stories and narratives are preserved when it comes to addressing matters of culture. Here Du Bois (2007 [1903]: 168) takes a special interest in what he calls 'Negro folk songs' or 'the sorrow songs'. These songs, if looked at closely, are complex cultural achievements conceived under the conditions of an oppressive society, and are significant as they articulate a sense of hope for a more just future. As Paul Gilroy (1993: 40) has argued, in the black American tradition if work signifies oppression, freedom emerges within aesthetic and public expression. The institution of slavery and the histories of European barbarism suggest that faith in rationalism and progress are in this setting misplaced. Such views offer difficult questions for mainstream liberalism caught up in philosophical fictions of political neutrality. As Gilroy (1993: 74) reminds us, slaves were indeed barred from literacy in such a way that gives an obvious power to music as a symbolic means to communicate ideas and feelings with broader publics. Music then communicates not only partially repressed memories but also 'a lived blackness' (Gilroy, 1993: 82). Different cultural practices (like musical expression) potentially enable the carving out of different public spaces with alternative meanings not often found in more official versions of the public sphere. This also suggests that cultural development is not a linear process. If Du Bois identifies the coerced illiteracy of the slave and the battle for full civic citizenship and education, then these ideas were transformed by later social movements.

## CULTURAL CITIZENSHIP IN THE SOCIAL DEMOCRATIC ERA

If the first phase of globalization was centrally concerned with the politics of imperial conquest, the second can be related to the rise of global corporations and consumer culture. The development of the global flows of capitalism facilitated by computer networks has altered the main means of domination. However, before the rise of networked capitalism we need to consider the rethinking of cultural citizenship evident within the social democratic era. At the end of the Second World War, in the wake of the Holocaust, there was a concerted attempt to tackle the dominance of racialized thinking in the West. This was also the age of national anti-colonial struggle against the rule of the West throughout the world. Popular revolts and resistance began to move into a post-colonial period, although the transformation here was far from neat. There is considerable evidence that much of the cultural power and ideological assumptions that were used to legitimate the dominance of the West continued to linger in the cultural sphere. As Goldberg (2009) argues, the end of empire meant the birth of a considerable amount of anxiety in respect of race, including increased competition for jobs and employment, the loss of Western ascendancy and the fragmentation of national cultures. Further, there was also a considerable nostalgia evident in many European nations, along with a refusal to mourn the loss of dominance more generally (Gilroy, 2004). In addition, the rise of totalitarian societies was widely recognized to have been influenced by social and economic collapse. This was a period marked by an increasing concern with the politics of national citizenship, with the establishment of the welfare state and social rights (Marshall 1992). There was a fusion of questions of social class, poverty and the politics of inequality. This had implications for the different ways more emancipatory questions might be spread to the cultural sphere more generally. Geoff Mulgan and Ken Worpole (1986) argued that the dominant liberal culture during this period had been adopted after a model that sought to bring 'civilized' culture to the masses. This civic impetus meant that the arts, libraries, education and broadcasting all had a specifically civic character that was mostly top down in orientation. The public provision of culture reflected the broader class hierarchies that dominated modern society. Culture was mostly thought to signify class distinctions and different socially stratified taste communities. There was widespread concern about the impact of a largely Americanized popular culture and the development of popular entertainment more generally. Liberal elites presumed that the public provision of 'serious' art and 'thoughtful' culture was necessary to provide a bulwark against the spread of commercialism. So-called 'high culture', as it was established within Victorian society, was called upon to civilize the barbarian.

If these powerful sentiments played an important role in the governance of culture then the idea of being a 'cultured' citizen was given a different set of meanings by a new generation of critics who were especially concerned to combat class elitism. Richard Hoggart (1957), like Du Bois before him, was especially concerned with the educated development of subordinated economic groups and argued that their own lives already exhibited a considerable degree of imagination and creativity.

Hoggart was particularly keen to dispel what he saw to be the 'myth' of the classless society in the context of a complex portrait of Northern English working-class life in the 1960s. The traditions, social attitudes and popular leisure activities of the working class are all outlined by Hoggart. While many have accused Hoggart of reproducing a warm nostalgia about the working class during this period, he does not seek to disguise some of the intense personal difficulties experienced by working-class children who sought to become educated. For Hoggart, many working-class children enter into education with a deep sense of personal inadequacy, and the few who do indeed wish to go on into further study are often caught somewhat anxiously between the markers of class. In other parts of the book Hoggart revisits many of Matthew Arnold's concerns in respect of the value of culture and how this is being eroded by the market. However, he transforms this argument somewhat by suggesting that not only should value be attached to complex works of art, but also to more collective forms of life evident in the lives of ordinary working-class people. Again like Du Bois, Hoggart pays a considerable amount of attention to the production of music through popular song, but this time in terms of communal singing in public houses. If, unlike those caught up in the slave system, the lower orders are no longer barred from more complex forms of cultural literacy, there are nonetheless more subtle forms of oppression at work. Partially this is the continuation of class hierarchy and distinction, but also because the culture of the market insists upon a form of relativism. Hoggart devotes a considerable amount of time to exploring the complex seductions of consumerism, with its mostly empty promises of quick-fix happiness. However, what mostly concerns him is the effect that a capitalist consumer culture has on our appreciation of the value of things. Cultural critics and experts are too quickly dismissed as elitist in a world where the market seeks to insist that all tastes have equal validity. It is generally assumed that only the very snobbish wish to make cultural distinctions. Such a view led Hoggart to defend the liberalism of the dominant cultural institutions, but this time in the context of an education system and social welfare society where major class distinctions had been somewhat reduced.

Hoggart's social democratic concerns could be contrasted to the more radical democratic preoccupations of Raymond Williams. Williams (1962) argued more forcibly than Hoggart that questions of culture need to be radically democratized in the context of a hierarchical class society. Like Hoggart, Williams shares a concern about the effects of living in an emergent consumer society built upon class domination, but argues that a genuinely cultural citizenship (or as he preferred to call it 'the long revolution') could only emerge if societies' dominant institutions are all democratized. The problem of class hierarchy was not simply about questions of taste and the division between high and low culture, but the imposition of a deeply undemocratic culture. The increasingly market-based society of the 1960s had sought to undermine the practice of democracy through the universal spread of consumer culture. Williams hoped that the labour movement would press for change, seeking to develop new means of communication, education and political organization based upon principles beyond the need to circulate commodities. By the 1970s and 1980s Williams would perceive that the democratic moment had passed and that a more aggressive kind of capitalism was beginning to emerge. This had led to 'the actual defeat of major sections of the working class, in prolonged mass unemployment and in the restoration of the absolute prerogatives of capital' (Williams, 2005 [1980]: 250).

The social democratic era was beginning to fade, and as it did so there emerged a much stronger need to expand ideas related to citizenship and culture beyond those of social class. Many radical social movements had sought to develop a new cultural citizenship that interrupted the dominant norms and assumptions of society. These groups pressed questions of gender, sexuality, race and other features. Especially significant here was Michel Foucault's (1984) radical questioning of the culture of the Enlightenment. For Foucault, the language of emancipation and freedom that usually accompanied Enlightenment-based concerns depended upon an overly simplistic opposition between tradition and autonomy. Indeed what it offers is a 'programme' for a new kind of human being, instructing them as to how they should live. Alternatively, Foucault argues, we should develop an ethics of Otherness and difference. Here we should aim less for liberation and more for the recognition of difference beyond liberal concerns of tolerance. These aspects gave rise to a considerable amount of postmodern debate in the area of identity politics. Steve Seidman (1995) argues that from the 1950s up until the 1970s there was a sense that the 'homosexual' experienced similar kinds of oppression and exclusion across a number of cultural contexts; then later this position was undermined by a more social constructivist position. An ethics of Otherness, following some of Foucault's seminal work, opened out questions related to different kinds of heterosexist domination and the way the 'gay community' might also play a disciplining role. The emergence of gay, black, feminist and other liberation movements have been significant in both providing alternative sources of knowledge and in resisting pathologizing stereotypes and understandings. However, new concerns developed around the ways in which a more complex understanding of identity might become shut down by movements that often sought to impose ideas of identity upon its followers. While these concerns raised a number of complex issues for others, a politics of this kind was in danger of reaching a narcissistic dead-end. The main problems these questions raised are related to broader issues of social solidarity. The concern was that postmodernism had simply led to the fragmentation of civil society, with different groups engaged within their own questions related to identity. Here the argument was not to return to a position where these would be silenced, but to find ways to link them to more broadly understood normative criteria. Renato Rosaldo (1999) makes an important contribution in this respect by seeking to talk about the idea of 'second-class' citizenship. If we follow legalistic criteria, then someone is either included or excluded from the basic norms of citizenship and legal criteria. However a 'second-class' citizen concerns groups who have been denied adequate economic and cultural resources and have either experienced disrespect or have been considered inferior. Cultural citizenship is centrally concerned with 'who needs to be visible, to be heard, and to belong' (Rosaldo, 1999: 260). Cultural citizenship becomes the struggle to respect and recognize those who have been placed in a subordinate position by society. This would not presume a politics that was only dominated by class or one that simply reproduced a fragmented society, but would instead base a critical politics upon different experiences of exclusion and marginalization.

More recently, Nira Yuval-Davis (2011) has argued that a politics of belonging needs to move beyond the confines of identity politics to recognize the multiple ways in which we might imagine our shared and personal sense of identity. Especially significant here is the need to recognise the role that power and authority play in the regulation of identity. Here we might also remember Edward Said's (2004: 40) critique of academic work not rooted in social and cultural struggle. Said argues that rather than retreating into a politics centred around questions of identity, we need to be able to relate our writing to more worldly concerns. In other words, questions of cultural citizenship need to be alive to the ways in which historical and social transformation directly impinge upon the lived and imagined dimensions of citizenship. For all of its analytical power I remain unconvinced that questions related to identity politics do much to help us understand the main frames through which questions of citizenship are being repositioned in our own times. Here I am especially concerned with how questions of identity potentially lose their connection to the more broadly located questions in respect of the struggle for an educated and democratic society that can be found in the work of earlier figures such as Du Bois, Hoggart and Williams.

## CULTURAL CITIZENSHIP IN THE NEOLIBERAL AND GLOBAL ERA

If during the social democratic era more multicultural concerns could be seen as an extension of the language of citizenship to include subordinate groups, then currently these assumptions need to be radically rethought. The arrival of a more aggressive politics of capitalism since the end of the 1980s has radically reshaped the politics of cultural citizenship. Toby Miller (2007) argues that despite the sophistication of the previous models of cultural citizenship, they have all failed to deal with questions of capitalism and consumerism. As David Harvey (2001) argues, a new politics of imperialism re-emerges through the guise of globalization mark II, but this time through the imposition of a political doctrine that is concerned to cut the social state, promote entrepreneurialism, privatize public assets, lower taxation and introduce the culture of market calculation. The central fault line for a politics of culture changes in these terms from social democratic questions concerned with access to 'quality' culture and more multicultural questions concerned with 'Otherness', to issues related to privatization and cultural enclosure.

In this setting, Hardt and Negri (2000) have argued that previous modes of cultural analysis need to be radically rethought. If the politics of difference made sense in opposition to the homogenous claims of nationalism and imperialism, what happens to these argumentative strategies in the current age of capitalistic Empire? Ultimately there is a new regime of sovereignty in the age of globalization that works through the somewhat restricted capacities of states to manage the global flow of money, information and bodies. Empire is a specifically political project that seeks to impose capitalism from above using force and sometimes the normative claims of human rights to create the global space necessary for the free mobility of capital. In this respect, postmodernism loses its focus as ideas of national sovereignty and racial superiority lose their importance. The ideology of the global market is perfectly comfortable with certain versions of multiculturalism that seek to use ideas of diversity to legitimate their rule and of course sell consumer products. What postmodernism fails to grasp is that the new capitalist world order imposes new hierarchies and requires the international flow of labour and cultural intermixing. Further, it can be seen that the informational economy has changed the basis of cultural and economic production within society. The decline of industrialism and Fordism has enhanced the amount of labour that is required to be computer literate. Workers today are increasingly invited to 'think like computers' and endure conditions of work that are increasingly insecure, part-time and determined by the needs of capital rather than labour (Hardt and Negri, 2000: 297).

While the complexity of Hardt and Negri's analysis cannot be fully grasped here, this offers a number of possibilities in respect of the organization of resistance across national boundaries through new technology. While these are indeed important features, however, missing from the argument is a more complex understanding of different cultural mediations, like nationalism, and of the continuing power of states to negotiate different relationships with the dominant neoliberal discourse. Further, Hardt and Negri radically underestimate the extent to which the subjectivities of the population can be structured by the dominant hegemony, and perhaps overstate the possibilities for global resistance and revolt. However, their analysis is at its most powerful in seeking to capture some of the major structural transformations that have come about since the ending of the social democratic order, such as the global nature of capitalism and the arrival of the post-industrial economy. Significantly, Hardt and Negri (2009: 137) recognize that in the virtual post-industrial economy capitalism is increasingly involved in the 'expropriation of the common'. This proceeds by transforming public goods into private property, and through the exploitation of 'biopolitical labor' (Hardt and Negri, 2009: 139) which is linked to the progressive privatization of culture. If for example, our schools and universities were mostly run as public institutions in the past, what happens when they are increasingly turned over to private providers, charge fees to customers, spend increasing amounts of capital on advertising and at some point in the future aim to deliver a profit? Similarly, the ideal of public broadcasting is increasingly being replaced by subscription channels, advertising and commodification. If the idea of the commons aims to preserve the notion of shared democratic and public space for the people, then privatization initiatives attack these ideas and practices in the interests of capital and accumulation.

Henry Giroux (2011) has argued that neoliberalism, rather than seeking to develop a critical and informed citizenry, has orchestrated an assault on a number of public spaces, including education and the media, in order to promote the identities necessary for the consumer economy rather than critical citizenship. Giroux argues that we learn to view contested sites like the media and education as places of public pedagogy where a narrow range of identities are made available in our increasingly market-driven times. If the effort to secure critical public places where citizens can meet together and discuss the nature of the good society are increasingly diminished in the neoliberal age, then the same might also be said about more creative forms of learning. Education in this setting is increasingly being converted into a commodity and viewed as a form of job training, which in itself closes the possibility of more experimental and less instrumental objectives. Further, the rise of an overtly positivist agenda within education has marginalized more critical and indeed historical forms of analysis. Here Giroux recognizes the extent to which more critical forms of knowledge often require deeper, more historical forms of analysis in order to both ask questions of the present, and seek to unravel alternative futures beyond the confines of the present. The doctrine of neoliberalism imposes certain categories that seek to 'naturalize' competitive individualism, speaking of personal rather than collective responsibility and disabling any critical thinking in relation to the dominant consumer society.

Here we perhaps need to consider whether neoliberalism, despite its inevitably multiple forms, is itself a form of totalitarianism that seeks to cancel more plural and critical modes of understanding? Tzvetan Todorov (2011) argues that if totalitarian ideologies sought to replace the idea of plural dissenting citizens with a state imposed view of the collective good, then neoliberalism seeks to outlaw any sense of collective solidarity with the more vulnerable sections of society. However, it is worth remembering that, unlike totalitarianism, neoliberalism can only go so far in curbing civil and intellectual freedoms. This is because it remains formally connected to the idea of equal rights, although it does tend to focus upon civil rather than social rights in this respect.

If this is indeed the age of the market, it is also the time of global human rights. The more cosmopolitan features of living in an increasingly interconnected world make themselves felt through the global rise in the popularity of human rights, especially at the end of the Cold War. Human rights, originally associated with the European Enlightenment, have become part of a genuinely global modernity, providing a thin universalism that crosses the world today. The cultural implications of the idea of human rights in our more global times mean that, despite attempts on behalf of states to impose market-led solutions, issues of 'what it means to be human' are very much part of our world today. If human rights after the signing of the 1948 Declaration meant a set of shared freedoms that states may fail to live up to, then today they perhaps mean something else. The United States has been widely criticized by social movements and citizens across the world for its part in the war on terror and for undermining rather than promoting human rights. Indeed, human rights are often dismissed by critics as meaningless documents that states have the power to ignore if they wish. Another argument is that ideas of human rights have gained widespread popularity in a context where more authentic forms of emancipatory politics have been erased (Badiou, 2001). What these arguments neglect to analyse is the normative power of human rights in the 21st century and their emancipatory potential. Considerable moral outrage and embarrassment can be caused if states are seen to be abusing the human rights of their own citizens or indeed those of other states.

What we mean by human rights is also changing in the context of the 21st century. Georgio Agamben (1995) has introduced the idea of the 'bare life' into debates about human rights. This means that increasingly states are creating the conditions for a new category of personhood beneath that of the legally enfranchised citizen we might call the disposable citizen. This can be done by stripping citizens of welfare rights, legitimating torture and human rights abuse or failing to respect the rights of migrants and asylum seekers. The 'bare life' is a status beneath that of the second-class citizen where populations have their rights removed and are treated in ways that are undignified. Yet Axel Honneth (2007) argues that the spread of human rights globally offers the normative potential of the world coming to see itself not just as governed by nation-states, but also as a moral community based upon the idea of human dignity. The idea of a dignified life then becomes a matter of global concern. This aspect is likely to create a number of contradictions as some citizens are labelled disposable and unwanted while others seek to press a new language of global compassion and concern. Questions as to how we imagine our responsibilities to other human beings who should be able to share a dignified life in common become increasingly central. Human rights have a utopian dimension asking us to imagine a different world where global humanity lives together in dignity and peace. Despite attempts by many to dismiss human rights as simply the discourse of the powerful, this remains an area fraught with ambiguity and tension. If democratic societies partially legitimate their rule through ideas of human rights, this does not necessarily close down other meanings and more radical possibilities. John Holloway (2010) asks in this context whether ideas of human dignity are actually compatible with the rule of capitalism. Many people are drawn together globally as they search for a life of meaning beyond the cash nexus and ideas of hierarchy and brute instrumentality. Such cultural activities could include working on a garden, reading a novel or indeed starting a political group, all of which potentially contain values in opposition to the increasingly brutal nature of the economic sphere. Hardt and Negri (2009) argue that groups across global civil society could find a common platform through the claim that all humanity should enjoy the material means to a dignified life, access to education (and therefore the possibility of acting as a citizen) and open access to the common wealth of knowledge. Of course the global ruling elite has no intention of meeting these demands, preferring to legitimate free market capitalism through ideas of competition, economic growth and philanthropy.

More meaningful understandings of human rights and dignity have been taken up by anti-globalization movements that seek to recapture ideas of the commons from privatization initiatives and the rule of consumer brands (Klein, 2001). The big shift here from the social democratic era is both the invitation to view these political dimensions as operating globally beyond the nation-state and to understand the organization of resistance as operating through a kind of global anti-politics. As the state increasingly becomes captured by competing versions of neoliberalism, then meaningful forms of resistance like the Occupy movement operate less through political parties and more through grassroots initiatives. If it was a distinctive feature of a range of movements to introduce questions of difference into public life during the social democratic era, then in the neoliberal age the aim is similarly to disrupt homogeneity, but this time less in terms of the categories of identity and more connected to the rule of capital and the state. This does not mean that states are no longer capable of being 'progressive' to a greater or lesser extent, but more that critical and engaged forms of citizenship are less clearly located. As Lewis Hyde (2010) argues, the rule of private property and enclosure in the neoliberal era opens up new questions for cultural citizenship. The rights of the community to produce, criticize and engage in cultural production and reception become reopened again in the age of the shrinking social state and the privatizing imperatives of capital. Here the argument needs to return to Williams' (1989) ideas of a democratic culture that is threatened by a social structure which rules through private property and control over the production of knowledge and information in education, media and the culture industries. The task of emancipatory movements in new times remains the same (under altered conditions) as the one originally recognized by Du Bois and later developed by Williams and others. How to struggle for 'an educated and participatory democracy' in a world that is dominated and controlled by the rule of capital and an increasingly security-focused state (Williams, 1989: 37)? It is to these questions that those scholars who are concerned with questions of cultural citizenship are urged to return.

## CULTURAL CITIZENSHIP TODAY

The arrival of the global and internet-based society has been accompanied by the eclipse of social democracy and the emergence of neoliberalism. In this context cultural citizenship becomes increasingly defined through an attempt to construct genuinely meaningful public spaces. After the end of national social democracy that sought to create liberal institutions to educate the population in the neoliberal era, culture becomes increasingly a matter of choice and consumerism. What becomes more pressing is the search for relatively democratic spaces and the creation of cultural forms that seek to question the dominance of capitalism and the security state. On one level, this becomes increasingly possible for growing numbers of people, given the mass availability of computers and the requirement that most people achieve a basic literacy. However, more radical and democratic ideas have been increasingly removed from the civil sphere as the economic system has sought to promote ideas of competition, entrepreneurialism and upward mobility.

There remain considerable possibilities, however, given the widespread enthusiasm for human rights in the world today and the redefinition of human dignity by social movements. As we have seen, the idea of human rights has a range of meanings that can become attached to its practice and significance. However, if cultural citizenship has long been associated with the practice of artistic and social movements rather than political parties, capitalism or the state this is even more the case in the neoliberal age. As critical ideas find it increasingly difficult to find a way into mainstream society, then one of the most pressing questions for cultural citizenship becomes the ability to open up new spaces and places that attract the attention of citizens. The availability of the internet is clearly important in this respect, but as the Occupy movement demonstrated so dramatically, actual physical place is still centrally important. Critical forms of cultural citizenship increasingly work as a form of anti-politics (in a way that they did not during the social democratic era), finding expression outside of the rituals of increasingly post-democratic societies. Yet the struggle for an educated and dignified life is far from over and shows no sign of dying away in the turbulent 21st century. Despite attempts by capital to spread the normalizing logic of consumer goods and pro-market identities, there is good reason to think that this will not go unquestioned now or in the future. It will be the struggle for a common cultural citizenship that resists the enclosures of profit and commerce in favour of genuinely public art, expression, dissent and critical engagement which will become increasingly important in the future. As the historian Peter Linebaugh (2007: 11) argues, the global rule of 'unrestricted profiteering' has resulted in an attack on hard-won liberties that includes the law and more social and cultural dimensions that are unlikely to go unopposed despite appeals to security and economic efficiency. The human cruelty evident in torture, the war on terror and economic liberalism, the take-over of education, urban places and the media by conglomerates, and the hollowing out of the state are unlikely to be met by mass political and cultural complicity. However, the diverse and precise forms that cultural citizenship will take in the 21st century remain a matter of open debate.

## REFERENCES

Agamben, G. (1995) *Homo Sacer*. Stanford: Stanford University Press.
Alexander, J.C. (1998) 'Introduction: Durkheimian Sociology and Cultural Studies Today', in J.C. Alexander (ed.), *Durkheimian Sociology: Cultural Studies*. Cambridge: Cambridge University Press. pp. 1–22.
Alexander, J.C. (2010) 'Power, Politics, and the Civil Sphere', in K.T. Leicht and J.C. Jenkins (eds), *Handbook of Politics: State and Society in Global Perspective*. New York: Springer Science+Business Media.
Alexander, J.C. (2013) *The Dark Side of Modernity*. Cambridge: Polity Press.
Arnold, M. (1987 [1869]) 'Culture and Anarchy', in *Selected Prose*. London: Penguin. pp. 202–300.
Badiou, A. (2001) *Ethics*. London: Verso.
Bennett, T. (1998) *Culture: A Reformer's Science*. London: Sage.
Berman, M. (1970) *The Politics of Authenticity*. London: Verso.
Bronner, S.E. (2004) *Reclaiming the Enlightenment*. New York: Columbia University Press.
Castells, M. (2012) *Networks of Outrage and Hope*. Cambridge: Polity Press.
Castoriadis, C. (1997) 'Culture in a Democratic Society', in D.A. Curtis (ed.), *The Castoriadis Reader*. Oxford, Blackwell. pp. 338–48.
Du Bois, W.E.B. (2007 [1903]) *The Souls of Black Folk*. Oxford: Oxford University Press.
Foucault, M. (1984) 'What is Enlightenment?', in P. Rabinow (ed.), *The Foucault Reader*. London: Penguin.
Gilroy, P. (1993) *The Black Atlantic: Modernity and Double Consciousness*. London: Verso.
Gilroy, P. (2004) *After Empire*. London: Routledge.
Giroux, H. (2011) *On Critical Pedagogy*. London: Continuum.
Goldberg, D.T. (2009) *The Threat of Race*. Oxford: Blackwell.
Hardt, M. and Negri, A. (2000) *Empire*. Cambridge, MA: Harvard University Press.
Hardt, M. and Negri, A. (2009) *Commonwealth*. Cambridge, MA: Harvard University Press.
Harvey, D. (2001) The New Imperialism, Oxford, Oxford University Press.
Hoggart, R. (1957) *The Uses of Literacy*. London: Penguin.
Honneth, A. (2007) *Disrespect: The Normative Foundations of Critical Theory*. Cambridge: Polity Press.
Holloway, J. (2010) Crack Capitalism, London, Pluto Press.
Hyde, L. (2010) *Common as Air*. New York: Straus and Giroux.
Klein, N. (2001) 'Reclaiming the Commons', *New Left Review*, 9: 81–89.
Linebaugh, P. (2007) *Liberties and Commons for All*. Berkeley: University of California Press.
Marshall, T.H. (1992) *Citizenship and Social Class*. London: Pluto Press.
Miller, T. (2007) Cultural Citizenship: Cosmopolitanism, Consumerism and Television in a Neoliberal Age, Temple University Press.
Mulgan, G. and Warpole, K. (1986) *Saturday Night or Sunday Morning: From Arts to Industry-New Forms of Cultural Policy*. London: Comedia.
Nussbaum, M. (1995) *Poetic Justice: The Literary Imagination and Public Life*. Boston: Beacon Press.
Nussbaum, M. (2010) *Not For Profit: Why Democracy Needs the Humanities*. Princeton: Princeton University Press.
Rosaldo, R. (1999) 'Cultural Citizenship, Inequality and Multiculturalism', in R.D. Torres (ed.), *Race, Identity and Citizenship: A Reader*. Oxford: Blackwell.

Rousseau, J. (1991 [1762]) *Émile or On Education*. London: Penguin.

Ruskin, J. (1985 [1862]) *Unto This Last and Other Writings*. London: Penguin.

Rutherford, J. (2005) 'Cultural Studies in the Corporate University', *Cultural Studies*, 19(3): 297–317.

Said, E. (1993) *Culture and Imperialism*. London: Chatto and Windus.

Said, E. (2004) *Power, Politics and Culture*. London: Blackwell.

Scaff, L.A. (1989) *Fleeing the Iron Cage: Culture, Politics and Modernity in the Thought of Max Weber*. Berkeley and Los Angeles: California Press.

Seidman, S. (1995) 'Deconstructing Queer Theory or the Under-theorization of the Social and the Ethical', in L. Nicholson and S. Seidman (ed.), *Social Postmodernism: Beyond Identity Politics*. Cambridge: Cambridge University Press.

Thompson, E.P. (1997) *The Romantics*. Suffolk: Merlin Press.

Todorov, T. (2011) *The Totalitarian Experience*. Calcutta: Seagull Books.

West, C. (1993) 'The New Cultural Politics of Difference', in S. During (ed.), *The Cultural Studies Reader*, 2nd edn. London: Routledge. pp. 256–70.

Williams, R. (1958) *Culture and Society 1780–1950*. London: Pelican.

Williams, R. (1962) *The Long Revolution*. London: Pelican.

Williams, R. (2005, 1980) Culture and Materialism, London, Verso.

Williams, R. (1989) 'The Idea of a Common Culture', in *Resources of Hope*. London: Verso. pp. 32–38.

Young, T. (2007) *Cultural Citizenship: Cosmopolitanism, Consumerism and Television in a Neoliberal Age*. Philadelphia: Temple University Press.

Yuval-Davis, N. (2011) *The Politics of Belonging: Intersectional Contestations*. London: Sage.

# 30
# Dimensions of Culture in Social Movement Research

Hank Johnston

## INTRODUCTION

This chapter reviews the field of social movement research from a contemporary culturalist perspective, taking the position that the entry point of the research enterprise is everything. It is axiomatic that social movements are cultural phenomena, but the main threads of theory and research in the social movements field have for a long time mostly missed this fact. The result has been a fragmentation and division of labor among researchers that often de-emphasizes the cultural dimensions of social movements. This chapter argues that a performative approach to social movement analysis accords culture its proper place and provides a lens through which the main approaches to social movement research can be seen anew.

Part of this fragmentation derives from the way that the study of social movements has developed, straddling sociology and political science. As the field evolved over the past half-century into an important sub-discipline in the social sciences, its prominence came with a shift in focus. From a sociology of ideational and cultural factors stressing the extraordinary character of collective action, researchers began to focus on the role of structural and material variables characteristic of political science approaches. It was a shift that began in the late 1970s in North American sociology. It situated social movements squarely amidst the normal play of political contention and built a bridge between sociologists and political scientists that continues to bear a lot of traffic to this day. The narrative is well known to practitioners in the field: as part of the resource mobilization perspective, researchers noticed the increasing relevance of organized groups and formal campaigns in the civil society sector. A focus on material resources, organizational capacity and relations introduced variables that were measurable and conducive to quantitative analysis, but shifted the field's focus away from conceptual and methodological approaches conducive to analyzing the role of cultural influences. Later, institutional and political-structural factors of opportunity and threat were added to the mix to produce a synthetic approach called political process theory, which, it is fair to say, remained paradigmatic into the first decade of the new millennium.

Yet an analytical focus on ideational and interpretative processes – a focus more in sync with traditional cultural approaches – was never fully eclipsed on the sociology side. Several studies stressed the influence, diversity, and variation in culture (Fine, 1985; Lofland, 1985). Swidler's tool box metaphor (1986), which suggested culture can be thought of as a complex and varied resource for making sense of the world, offering a felicitous

**IDEATIONAL:**
Ideologies, frames, interests, collective identities, values, beliefs

**PERFORMATIVE:**
Protests, marches, demonstrations, strikes, meetings, speeches, narrations

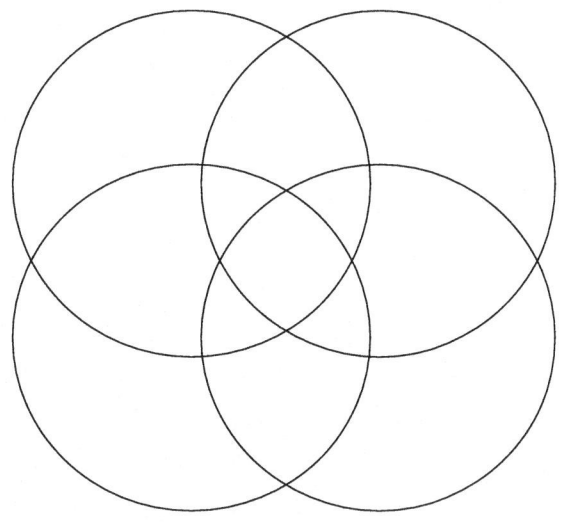

**STRUCTURAL:**
Institutions, organizations, networks, informal groups, associations

**ARTIFACTUAL:**
Material productions: songs, art, texts, clothing, blogs

**Figure 30.1 Analytical dimensions of social movement research**

synergy with the organizational-strategic elements of the resource mobilization perspective. An early benchmark of cultural research in the field was the publication of Johnston and Klandermans' *Social Movements and Culture* (1995), which brought together European and North American perspectives. Since that time, there have been important additions to the cultural study of protest mobilization: Jasper (on moral protests, 1997), Rochon (on cultural elites, 1998), Steinberg (on discourse, 1999); Stryker, Owens, and White (on collective identity, 2000); Davis (on narratives 2002); Young (on religious morality 2002); Goodwin and Jasper (a critique of structuralism 2004), Polletta (on storytelling, 2006a), and Johnston (on methodological approaches 2009), to name a few. This ongoing work has developed into clear streams of cultural analysis in the protest studies field: narratives and stories, cultural resistance, social movement cultures, collective identity, and cultural performance.

## ANALYTICAL DIMENSIONS

I approach the contemporary cultural analysis of social movements guided by Tilly's observation (1978: 8–9) that researchers approach the phenomena from three basic analytical perspectives. Tilly specifies: (1) the ideas that unify the groups and guide their protests; (2) the events – or performances – that are part of the action repertoire, most notably the modern protest repertoire that distinguishes what social movements do from other forms of collective ritual; and (3) the continuities of association – commonly labeled the structural and organizational elements of a movement and its environment. These perspectives are represented by the three intersecting circles at the upper left of Figure 30.1.

This structural sphere does not typically fall into the realm of cultural analysis. Indeed, it often invokes analytical approaches that cast collectivities in pursuit of interests, and relegates the other two dimensions to secondary status. That is not the approach that we take here. Organizations, associations, institutions, and how they perceive and define their interests are important but they are always accomplished through the vehicles of cultural creation, which brings concepts such as frames, discourse, and narratives into the equation. There is a large literature that has recently developed which stresses organizational cultures and networks of interaction, especially the discursive elements that give relative permanence to these relations.

Ideations are the traditional stuff of cultural analysis such as values, beliefs, *mentalités*, social representations, discourse, habitus, ideologies, or more specific norms of behavior, including normative forms of speech, action, and protest. We can also include here recent cognitive reformulations of these concepts, such as collective action frames, schemata, algorithms, mental models, and grammars that are collectively shared (DiMaggio, 1997; Johnston, 1995; 2010). These ideational elements are central components of what a social movement is. The key theme of contemporary cultural analysis, however, is that there is always diversity, conflict, and opposition in these ideas, rather than their being seen mainly as an integrating and coordinating force.

To Tilly's trinity, I add a dimension that, in the past, has been secondary in social movement analysis: cultural artifacts (see Figure 30.1). These are productions that activists and non-aligned publics can feel, touch, hear, and read – multiple times – that are made by movement adherents acting individually – perhaps as cultural entrepreneurs (Rochon, 1998) – or collectively. Although artifacts are often the 'stepchildren' of cultural analysis, I argue that they enjoy a central role when social movements are seen through a performative lens. They can serve as foci of collective interpretations. Their materiality means they can do this many times in different ways, depending on the situation, and their presence is often woven through collective performances in ways that shape them significantly. These roles seem to increase significantly via contemporary social media and digital technology (Tavera and Johnston, 2014).

When the analyst looks at a social movement, the tendency is to focus on just one of these analytical dimensions, which, in turn, situates the study in a place that offers a limited perspective of the other dimensions. For example, if we are interested in studying a protest performance, say an anti-war mobilization in a large city, we are invariably drawn to the organizing groups (the structural dimension) that mobilize participants to action, and then directed to their ideologies and frames (ideational dimension) that motivate their claims, which are, in turn, manifested by the flyers, press releases, signs and songs that they produce (the artifacts). Speeches might be posted on YouTube. So too might smartphone pictures of police brutality. In both cases, performances are artifactualized in ways that were impossible fifty years ago, opening new horizons for both research (digital data) and theory (performance–artifact synergy).

Applied to the analysis of social movements and political protest, and drawing on recent cultural theory, the performance dimension – as the locus of meaning making – is a more than equal partner in Tilly's analytical dimensions. Following Alexander, Giesen, and Mast (2006), I accord the performance dimension status of *primus inter pares* among the analytical foci of social movement research. Such a shift in perspective raises the question, what are the implications of a performance-oriented perspective on social movements theory and research? A useful approach is to consider the full quartet of analytical dimensions, starting with the main signature of almost all social movements: the modern repertoire of marches, demonstrations, strikes, rallies, sit-ins, and so on – which we take as big cultural performances *par excellence*.

## SOCIAL MOVEMENTS AS PERFORMANCE

Alexander has observed that highly complex, diverse, and differentiated societies create the conditions for the transformation of rituals into performances (2004: 540). In less developed societies, rituals are acted out according to well-defined scripts, and their interpretations tend to be constrained and closed to debate and contention. Contemporary public performances, on the other hand, are more contingent processes of symbolic communication, where actors have greater flexibility, and various audiences take greater liberty in interpretation. In cultural theory, performances are everywhere: in politics, religion, economic transactions, finances, and international relations (Alexander et al., 2006). They comprise the web of meaning creation and the basis of contemporary cultural analysis via the narratives and discourse they produce. In the field of protest studies, it is not surprising that Tilly's classic (1995) work on repertoires traces the transformation of well-defined ritualistic collective actions of rural villagers and urban *sans culottes* characteristic of traditional societies, to more flexible, diverse, and audience-conscious contentious actions characteristic of modern society – the modern social movement repertoire. Protest events in the modern repertoire are fundamentally complex performances as well. They have diverse actors, audiences – of which the mass media play a central role – and multifaceted interpretations based on perspective and context (Johnston, 2014).

Performances in the modern repertoire are one way that social movement actions create meanings at a macroscopic level, meaning that they are performances that include and affect many people and embrace a variety of interpretations under the general umbrella of collective action.

At the meso- and micro-levels several researchers working in the new social movement perspective brought a focus on the process-oriented, performance-based construction of new meanings that occur in multiple and overlapping networks (Melucci, 1989; 1995; Castells, 1996; 1997). Like the grand-scale protest events, numerous small-scale encounters at meetings, planning sessions, recruitment forays, and socializing – the actions of everyday life that also constitute a movement – have a performance dimensions at the interactional level and at the level of self-identity. Individuals come together and discuss, debate, assert, narrate, and affirm their positions in everyday social contexts, making meaning, testing it, and remaking it. A key insight of the new social movement perspective was that profound social change occurs, especially in postmodern societies, at these levels too. The network basis of these encounters also means that some performative situations will have more participants than others, and/or will be more significant and central in meaning production for the movement.

Obviously the big marches and demonstrations that mobilize thousands are critical in defining the movement for its participants as well as for their audiences. But what the movement means to its participants is crucial for mobilizing these large protests, and small organizational meetings and coffee shop gatherings where movement ideas are discussed, elaborated, and 'performed' are locales where rationales and motivations for action are grounded. In any given moment, a social movement is composed of a vast matrix of big and small performances. To put it another way, a social movement is sustained by a dense network of performances, macro and micro, by which both the structural-organizational dimension and the ideational-interpretative spheres are acted out in real time. When the analyst focuses on the actions of these various parties and how they are connected, the theatrical metaphor is not only apt, but, more importantly, locates culture where it is actually taking place, in the interaction among participants, firmly grounding culture in its collective enactment.

As a consequence, from a contemporary culturalist perspective, it is best to consider a social movement as a matrix of performances – a *web of meaning making* – big and small, located both in the extraordinary events of movement mobilization and in the numerous interactional performances distributed throughout the social patterns of daily life (Norton, 2004; Johnston, 2010). This is a perspective that shifts the view of culture from how it is available to individuals as a set of received ideations to how it is created as an ongoing process through performances (Alexander and Mast, 2006; Eyerman, 2006; Alexander, 2012). The vehicle by which this occurs is talk, and one genre that becomes central to culture creation is the narrative performance. Fine (1995; 2001; 2009) and Polletta (1998a; 1998b; 2006a; 2009) have been instrumental in showing how narratives play a role in recruitment and the articulation of grievances.

Narratives are often recapitulations of past experiences and events that are sequenced according to general principles of 'story grammars' (Abbott, 1995). Events are presented teleologically in that a narrative's ending clarifies its sequencing and selection of events. Up until that point, understanding is tentative without the story's ending (White, 1981). Successful narratives of social movement participation presume a degree of identification between the teller and the audience, and their moral point assumes shared normative orientations, as Klimova (2009) has shown in her research on Russian protests. Also, they build upon presuppositions held by the audience that allows the teller to lead them to intended conclusions. These grammatical and functional elements of narratives help the social movement analysis determine what makes a compelling story, but formal structure alone does not capture the performative aspects of narratives – on the part of both the speaker and hearer.

An important insight that has developed from the literary analysis of stories is the narrativity of the audience. Benford (2002) points out that ambiguity and conflict are often present in what he calls the 'controlling myths' of social movements, stories that attract participants and maintain solidarity. Not only do these stories seek to cast a wide net of adherence, but also ambiguity and tension allow members to construct their own interpretations, in effect, making them participants in the narrative too. Narrativity refers to the ways that the audience is allowed to make connections that are left out of the story's telling, allowing space for the hearers' participation and creativity (Leitch, 1986).

Polletta (2009) draws on these insights in her analysis of stories in the battered women's groups. She shows how the narrator creates a tension at the story's climax created by a gap in the reasoning that the auditors of the story must fill. This gap requires that those hearing the story make the meaningful connections themselves, which, as narrativity theory holds, is central to what makes a good tale. In one instance, Polletta describes a narrator who had been in an abusive relationship and contemplated suicide. Her story tells of a beating at the hands of her boyfriend, and at a climactic point, 'choosing life instead of death', which, in this tale, led to her seizing a knife and attacking him. While the story itself is dramatic, the central tension comes from how her critical decision is simply offered up without explanation or analysis, necessitating that the auditor make the connections, in a sense, making the story his or her own. Such narrative tropes allow listeners to cognitively appropriate the story as their own, which seems to ride on their own agentic imputation of meaning. This insight merges narrative performance concepts of identity, as Somers (1994) has pointed out. She states, 'People construct identities (however multiple and changing) by locating themselves or being located within a repertoire of emplotted stories' (1994: 614). From a stock of available stories, people construct their identities by drawing others into its unfolding future (Polletta, 2006a). A recent current of research anchors these activities in organizations and networks.

## CULTURE AND MOBILIZING STRUCTURES

A propos my four-path approach to social movement phenomena, the relevant question becomes, if the analyst studies social movement organizations (SMOs) and/or their networked relations (both within those organizations and within a movement broadly defined), where does narrative performance, agency, contingency enter in? The answer is that there is a rising tide of scholarship in the social movement field that, while looking at movements through the lens of structural-organizational relations, considers them as a playing field of interaction where organizational cultures are works in progress and social relations are sustained by narrative constructions of identity and linguistic markers. These elements guide mobilizing actions but do not preordain outcomes.

Social movement organizations (SMOs) have been a primary focus in the social movement field since the 1970s, when John McCarthy and Mayer Zald began to define the resource mobilization perspective (hereafter RM). To quickly gloss a huge and productive literature, organizations are social actors defined by their resources, efficiencies of structure and lines of authority, strategic choices (including strategic framing, which in this context is more akin to marketing), and ties with political elites and/or other networked groups (a reflection of RM's later iteration into political process theory). As such, their actions as unified actors can be taken as variables associated with policy outcomes, protest activities and campaigns, levels of collective action, strategic and tactical adjustments, and relations with other organizations. Subsequent theoretical developments of political process approaches brought RM concepts into the institutional-political context of modern states, introducing elite ties and divisions, and state agencies as actors in the mix. A parallel theoretical development on the structural-organizational dimension is the network perspective (Diani, 1992; della Porta and Diani, 2006). Few social movements are solely composed of one large organization, but rather are collections of numerous groups and organizations united by general goals, and, more importantly, by network linkages that bind individual and associational actors together into a broad web. Network analysis captures the relatively permanent ties among organizations, informal groups, and individuals that make up the movement. Its focus is often on the nature of the ties, their mathematical modeling, and especially how they concentrate in nodes that affect movement processes such as protest levels, information diffusion, strategic choices, and so on.

The basic culturalist critique is that counting ties and mapping the structure of contacts are exercises that altogether miss the symbolic content that takes place in those interactions and which is the *raison d'être* of the ties in the first place. In fact, the relational quality and interactional and linguistic plays that sustain what appears to be a network constitute the real work that occurs there (Emirmayer and Goodwin, 1994). Mische (2008) has shown that the networks of social movements are complex, overlapping in actions, meanings, and memberships. This forces the analyst to consider networks as symbolic constructs just as much as they are structural features – namely, relatively fixed and recurring – of a movement. Her ethnography of various Brazilian youth groups is intensely microsociological, linguistically informed, and relational. By tracing the overlapping networks of members in religious, political, and civic groups, the analysis plots how actors manage multiple identities and discursive settings as they move forward in their civic activism. It is an analysis of multiple intersecting networks that is at the forefront of an emergent relational-culturalist perspective on organizations and their network structures. This is a perspective that promises to bring agency, diversity, conflict, and meaning-making back in.

Much of this research seeks 'to recover the insights of symbolic interactionism' (Clemens and Minkoff, 2004: 156), and recast them in light of the linguistic turn in the social sciences. Two themes are recurrent in this literature: (1) that complex organizations are spheres of interaction where identities are constructed and reconciled, sometimes with other identities in related spheres or 'publics'; and (2) that organizations and networks are discursive settings whereby the questions of 'what to do', 'how to organize', and 'what to speak' are constructed, yielding what might be called 'organizational repertoire' (Clemens, 1996). The first develops the constructionist focus on the self and its performance, and links it with social movement theory's preoccupation with collective identities, especially as inspired by new social movement perspectives (Melucci, 1989; Taylor and Whittier, 1992). It also links with the interactionist emphasis on interpersonal performances whereby the self is defined by ongoing monitoring of the rules of interaction. Lichterman (1996) has shown that much of the talk in civic engagement is 'self-talk' and that recognition of the personalistic basis of organizational participation glosses differences that may interrupt activism. Eliasoph (1998) similarly speaks of understood organizational etiquettes that shape discursive behavior by closing off topics within organizations. She also shows how new etiquettes open possibilities for strategic innovation as members enter new organizations.

This research points to how developing interorganizational networks are interactional accomplishments in which actors bring discursive resources from other spheres of interaction and creatively transpose them to social movement contexts. While there is a tendency to congeal organizational form into relatively fixed structural relations, this strand of research might be characterized as a type of meso-level interactionism that looks at how organizational forms are diverse, often dynamic and highly debated among members, sometimes yielding novel adaptations that impart advantages to groups and SMOs. Ganz (2000) demonstrated this regarding resource-poor mobilization in his analysis of the United Farm Workers. New models of action were often passed through members' network ties that reached far beyond movement groups. This is a relational network element of the organizational sphere derived from the fact that members are not members of social movement organizations alone. In tracing the development of the home school movement in the US, Stevens (2001) demonstrated the role of evangelical Protestant networks among homeschooler groups and how their stronger interactional rules and identities conflicted with homeschooling parents of progressive leanings. In the long run, it was the cultural density and richness of the former's culture that eventually predominated in the movement. Research strategies in both these interactionist foci are typically organizational ethnographies, sometimes with comparisons between different groups.

Another stream of research applies insights that are fundamentally interactionist, yet with a strong linguistic turn, to the network quality of movement structure, stressing the 'relational sociology' of the interaction that sustains these networks. Mische describes this stream as a broad theoretical project that insists that 'what sociologists call 'structure' is intrinsically relational ... [and] that relational thinking is a way to overcome stale antinomies between structure and agency through a focus on the dynamics of social interactions (Mische 2011: 80). Relational sociology was mostly articulated by a gathering of scholars located in New York City and its environs – especially Columbia University and the Graduate Faculty at the New School – many of whom were researchers in social movements and protest processes, and among whom Charles Tilly was a key figure. Tilly's early work carried the strong structuralist stamp of historical sociology, but he later developed an interest in discursive processes and identity formation in contentious politics (Tilly, 2004), in part via engagement with members of the New York study groups, and notably the linguistic approaches to networks taken by Harrison White, also at Columbia. This was a turn that took him and his students to closer examination of how collective identities are constructed through recognition of similarities. This is a process not widely stressed by symbolic-interactionist approaches to the self, but which reaffirms a holy trinity in the relational perspective of identity, talk, and performance. Tilly called the project of identifying such processes of meaning-making in contentious politics and – more broadly – in social relations, *relational realism*, 'The doctrine that transactions, interactions, social ties, and conversations constitute the central stuff of social life' (Tilly, 2004: 72).

Tilly's emphasis on networks is mostly implied, especially in his joint project with McAdam and Tarrow, *Dynamics of Contention* (McAdam et al., 1996; 2001), which had a persistent leitmotiv of social constructionism and culture (as reflected in the 'robust processes' of boundary maintenance, brokerage, and identity formation, for example). This book had a significant impact on the social movements field (McAdam and Tarrow, 2011), yet remained aloof from the micro-processes of conversational understandings, setting, discursive moves, and interaction performances that move these higher-level processes along. Regretfully, the meaning-making elements of *Dynamics of Contention* have been mostly unappreciated by the field of social movement research, but there is a rising tide of network-sensitive research that draws upon linguistic and discursive insights in various ways that span the old structure–agency hiatus. Plotting the strategic and performative speech and interactive moves by culturally pragmatic actors shows how social structures are maintained by ties that are essentially talked into existence (Mische, 2003).

## IDEATIONS

So far, this chapter has been mostly mute on the traditional focus of cultural analysis: the determining effects of ideational and interpretative factors in social behavior. In the broader sweep of the social sciences, the lexicon of this focus is varied and often overlapping: social representations, discourse, *mentalités*, habitus, discursive fields, values, beliefs, norms, attitudes, morality, ideologies, and frames. There is a huge literature in social movements, political sociology and political science that assumes that values, beliefs, attitudes, and other mental predispositions shape social behaviors in significant ways (Inglehart, 1990; 1997; Jasper, 1997; Rochon, 1998; Wildavsky, 2006). The presumption is that taking measures of how these meanings are distributed in a population gives insight into its cultural fabric. Also, because all social action is preceded by an ideation, knowing how these meanings cluster gives insights into patterns of behaviors, both as explanations of the past and predictions of the future. Values, beliefs, identities, and attitudes, all elements of culture, have commonly been measured this way, with presumptions about their relation to social action.

In addition to these recognized approaches, it is fair to say that, for the past twenty-five years, the main vehicle of ideational factors in social movement research has been the framing perspective. Twenty years ago, the concept of collective action frames was undoubtedly an idea whose time had come. On the one hand, it offered a way that researchers could reintroduce interpretative elements that had been closed out by the field's paradigmatic shift to resource mobilization concepts. On the other, that organizations could strategically frame their messages provided a felicitous connection between mobilizing ideas and mobilizing structures. The result was a huge and important literature (e.g., Snow and Benford, 1988; Benford, 1993; McCaffrey and Keys, 2000; Ferree et al., 2002; Snow, 2004; Hewitt and McCammon, 2005; McCammon et al., 2007; Snow and Byrd, 2007; see Snow et al., 2014 for an assessment). From a 30,000 foot view, it embraces two general streams that course through this diverse body of research and divide it fundamentally.

The first might be characterized as a cognitive iteration of the traditional approach to the influence of ideations mentioned above. It includes empirical research that records the content of frames and links it with mobilization and organizational processes. Frames are clusters of ideas – some analysts refer to them as schemata – that, as collective representations, guide participants' interpretations of what needs to be changed, how to do it, and why. This stream draws on the commonly accepted definition of frames as 'interpretative schemata that signify and condense 'the world out there' by selectively punctuating and encoding objects, situations, events, experiences and sequences of actions ... (Snow and Benford, 1992: 137). Frames direct attention to some aspects of a situation and away from others. Used in this sense, collective action frames can be specific to movements, such as an 'environmental justice frame', a 'global justice frame', or an 'anti-Wall Street frame'. They give individual participants ways of seeing the world, through a 'global-justice lens' for example, that highlights unfair practices, such as sweatshop production. A common theme here is to link frame content with the strategic considerations and actions of social movement organizations and with general cultural patterns. Frame alignment considerations for strategic advantage are one of the most common research foci in this stream.

The empirical task of documenting frame content is typically based on the analysis of movement documents such as tracts, manifestos, statements, minutes, printed speeches, or, in other cases, surveys and recorded interviews, talks, and presentations. Just where patterns in these texts come from raises the question of the relation of frames to the venerable concept of ideology. Ideologies are important sources for the content in collective action frames, and, in practice, the two concepts often overlap. An articulated ideology does many of the things that frames do. It gives guidelines for perceiving injustice, supplies motivation, and specifies strategies of action – the basis of diagnostic, motivational, and prognostic frames. But there are important differences, most significantly that ideologies are often 'artifactualized' in that they are codified textually – the writings of Marx and Lenin for communists, or those of Hassan al-Banna for the Muslim Brotherhood, for example. This means that some movements have 'holy scriptures' that provide foci for discussion and debate (Oliver and Johnston, 2005: 192), sites where meaning is made and remade, but mostly within the contours of the texts. This kind of talk is precisely the sort of micro-performance that sustains movement networks, as mentioned earlier, and it does this in ways that frames do not. Frames work behind the scenes as cognitive structures, guiding how participants interpret what is going on and how to act. While the analysis of ideologies often focuses on the systematic relation among the ideas, values, and interests that constitute them, this cannot be said of frames. Except for when movement leaders consciously strategize how to frame a protest theme, frames are usually not talked about.

Nevertheless, a culturalist perspective points out that there is an inherent conflictual diversity and oppositional nature to all ideologies in practice. This occurs as they are talked about, reworked, and renegotiated as contextual situations change. This brings me to the second stream of frame analysis that lays stress upon the ongoing interactional processes of interpretation and meaning-production dynamism. This is a perspective that remains true to the symbolic interactionist roots of the framing perspective *à la* Erving Goffman, and more in line with contemporary culturalist approaches. Here, researchers are interested in how frames are constructed, how they are negotiated in the heat of social movement contention, and how framing battles are waged and resolved among different social actors. The distinction between the two streams has been recognized by the framing perspective's key proponents and remains a recurring theme in approaches to social movement framing to this day. Leading researchers on the topic have criticized tendencies to reify frames and to conceptualize them as 'things', rather than focusing on ongoing and iterative processes of frame construction (Benford, 1997; Snow and Benford, 2000; Snow, 2004). Their critiques emphasize how meaning is never fixed but rather is in the continual flux of ongoing definition and redefinition. A similar view was also developed by Steinberg, who applied it to frame analysis (1999) and in his 'dialogic analysis' of 19th-century political contention.

Numerous studies approach the emergent and iterative nature of framing processes by describing frames at different points in time (e.g., McCaffery and Keys, 2000; Hewitt and McCammon, 2005; Johnston, 2005; Rothman and Oliver, 1999; McCammon, 2009; Miethe, 2009; Steensland, 2008). By sampling frames longitudinally, framing processes can be linked with different actors, changes in organizational strategy, and with changing political opportunities as perceived by activists and leaders who construct frames. For example, linking frames with organizational actors and analyzing how distributions of frames change over time was Steensland's analytical strategy for changing policy frames (2008).

These two streams are not necessarily mutually exclusive. Ontologically, frames may be in constant flux, but methodologically the researcher must embrace the artifice of 'freezing frames' at different points in time in order to reconstruct their content and trace how they change. At the same time, the researcher must describe in depth the contextual influences on social actors as they negotiate and shape the contents of their frames. A third research task is that the analyst must grapple with the diversity that resides in the nature of frames as cognitive structures that are generalized to collective levels – requiring another methodological artifice that the researcher can only deal with by sampling relevant groups to know whose texts to analyze. A culturalist emphasis on ongoing meaning-making does not mean that these interpretative and narrative processes are randomly distributed. A research interest in frames must also capture their ongoing creation by relevant groups. In social movements, this means a three-fold analytical strategy of (1) identifying the key social actors in the broad movement matrix to know (2) where to take 'frame snapshots' and (3) when to do it to gauge the major framing shifts.

This is the strategy followed by Johnston and Alimi's (2013) analysis of framing processes in the Palestinian Intifada. Stressing the dynamism of framing, the study selects two central actors, the PLO and the Muslim Brotherhood-Hamas, and traces changes in their framing of the Palestinian struggle by close textual analysis of press releases and informational bulletins. The temporal dynamic was captured by identifying key before-and-after junctures in the movement's development. Significant events, such as King Hussein's speech recognizing the PLO as the sole legitimate authority of Palestinians, are points when assessments of changing political contexts would be reflected in changes in the organizations' frames, as measured by the bulletins' narratives of events. 'Snapshots' of frame content (through analysis of their textual production) are taken at two critical points in time for two critical organizations. Obviously, methodological choices concerning excluding data about framing in other groups and at other times had to be made, but this strategy offers a boiled-down dynamism for the analyst to consider.

Another element of frame dynamism is recognizing that its various elements change in relation to each other. As frames shape interpretation for collective action, Johnston and Alimi's (2013) study also sought to trace changing textual content in terms of the grammatical elements of subject, verb, and object. The assumption is that frames contain guidance for defining 'Who we are', 'What we do', and 'To whom we do it', and that all three are in a dynamic relationship. In the past, framing theory has focused on S-V-O elements in isolation. Hunt, Benford, and Snow's (1994) identified 'collective identity frames' regarding the subject. Snow and Benford (1988) theorized 'prognostic and motivational frames' regarding the verb. What is missed by these separate formulations is how the independent actions of the object – the target – shape definitions of 'who we are' and 'what we must do'. Also, for each of the S-V-O elements, changing definitions of one affects the range of possibilities that can be talked about for the others. Thus, we have a picture of framing akin to wheels rotating within wheels: (1) frames change through time, and (2) they change among different players, and (3) all the time, their internal structures, reduced to the sentential formula of S-V-O, are changing in relation to each other.

As Tilly recognized in his relational approach, among the three S-V-O elements of framing, the most important is the actor's identity, or the subject. For the individual, performances are accomplished from the perspective of the self, and statements are made that reflect upon the audience's reaction to the self. For social movement performances, they are in part defined by the imputation of a sense of shared belongingness accomplished through collective performances of 'what to do'. About the same time that the framing perspective began to gain purchase in North America, a parallel theoretical shift in Europe emphasized the centrality of collective identity in contemporary movements: the new social movement perspective. Researchers noticed a new trend: increasingly, movements were focused less on class interests and more on actions linked with lifestyle and identity, such as feminism and environmentalism (Melucci, 1989; 1985; 1989; Kitschelt, 1985; Kriesi, 1989; Kriesi et al., 1995). These new identities were a product of postindustrial society in which low-level survival needs are more easily fulfilled, and higher-level needs, such as identity and self-actualization are given prominence.

In North America, a focus on identity had been a consistent thread in symbolic interactionist theory in which the relationship between the individual and society is fundamental. Concepts of the social self, the performance of social roles, and the ongoing confirmation of identity by others' reactions, based on the theories of Mead and Goffman, underscore the strongly social nature of who we are. The symbolic-interactionist perspective emphasizes that personal identity cannot be separated from its ongoing social construction and confirmation. This is a view that, as applied to social movements: (1) stresses the merger of collective identity with personal identity; (2) focuses on the realization that collective identity, like self-identity, is emergent – defined and confirmed in performances occurring at least in part in the context of movement activities; and (3) involves various audiences or publics, both internal and external to the movement. Identity-affirming performances can range from mundane activities, such as staff meetings, grabbing lunch together, or stuffing envelopes with other members, to the highly dramatic, such as protest marches, building occupations, strikes, and experiencing police repression and even imprisonment.

Social movement research has confirmed the ongoing social construction of collective identity on these two planes: internal to the movement among members, and external to the movement, among opponents, politicians, potential adherents, and bystander publics. Regarding the internal dynamics among movement members, Taylor and Whittier (1992) analyze the use of identity narratives among lesbian feminists to impart value to the collective identity and to politicize it. Young (2002) demonstrates that the 19th-century abolitionist movement used revival-meeting narratives among young Christians to build collective identities. Others have noted that participation in protests, risk taking, and shared fears work to foster collective identity over time (Pfaff, 1996). In contrast, Robnett's (2002) study of the SNCC (Student Nonviolent Coordinating Committee) wing of the civil rights movement chronicled how the bitterly fought rejection of their platform by the Democratic Party at its national convention was a significant event in radicalizing members' collective identity. Here the boundary was partly imposed by movement opponents. Boundary maintenance occurs both ways – internally and externally. Because a positive group identity is central, the external efforts by opponents to stigmatize a movement group give rise to internal processes of valorization and affirmation.

While it is tempting to speak of collective identity as something that a group has, ultimately it is based on the ongoing relationships among the members of a movement. While a social scientist might compose a questionnaire to measure it among movement adherents, collective identity arises from the density and the frequency of relations that can be conceptualized as multiple microperformances of identity. If a movement is defined as a network of relations, a strong collective identity means that members are highly interconnected and their interactions are frequent. They are based on shared vocabularies, songs and music, common experiences that are talked and reminisced about, as well as ways of dressing and hair styles that present a self-image as a group member (Taylor and Whittier, 1992; Meyer and Whittier, 1994; Whittier, 1995). In line with the approach to culture developed in this chapter, collective identity is an ideational dimension of movement culture whereby belongingness is defined in part by identity artifacts or markers, and affirmed continually and densely by small performances of who members are.

## CULTURAL ARTIFACTS

To close this chapter, I discuss the centrality of cultural artifacts in a performance-oriented approach to social movements, and suggest that their relevance may increase even more in a digitized world. Like ancient shards of pottery or funerary relics, the traditional assumption was that cultural artifacts can inform the analyst about social patterns because they are embedded in the culture's web-of-meaning. Applied to social and political movements, this assumption has meant that artifacts such as music, art, literature, speeches, narratives, videos, recruitment tracts and other movement texts can be taken as data to enlighten and deepen one's interpretative understanding of a movement, but are mostly reflective rather than determinative. In contrast, a performative approach to culture brings artifacts center stage to see how they often have a focal role in the other three dimensions of social movement research. Social actors produce artifacts; others encounter them, perhaps modifying them to enhance their mobilizing role. Always, actors interpret them, and, above all, discuss them and tell stories about them. This means that the analyst can consider cultural artifacts in ways that go beyond thinking of them as vaguely attributed 'powerful symbols' that reflect larger processes.

Whether a product of one person's creativity – the artwork of Ai Wei Wei in China's democracy movement – or a collective endeavor – the Zapatista websites – artifacts take on significance because their materiality brings them to the center of a movement's matrix-based meaning-making. Their materiality allows them to 'stand firm' amidst the swirling of speech acts that form the discursive foundations of network construction. Widely shared, they can invoke common interpretations and help bridge the inevitable diversity of a movement. They also can foster collective identity around the meanings that are made and talked about so that coordinated movement activities can occur. Importantly, when used as data, their materiality means the analyst can point to them as evidence of his or her interpretations, to be judged by others.

There are 'high cultural' artifacts of protest, such as the plastic arts, poetry, literature, theater, music, even opera. Then, there are counterparts in popular culture such as rhymes, jokes, styles, fashions, graffiti, masks (Guy Fawkes), and iconic symbols, to name a few, but among popular artifacts, music is probably the most widely studied as part of mobilization processes. It has been a factor in many major movements, such as the labor movement, the civil rights movement, socialism (Denisoff and Peterson, 1973; Halker, 1991; Eyerman and Jamison, 1998; Roscigno and Danaher, 2004), and, of course, the aggressive, anarchist punk scene (Moore and Roberts, 2009; Haenfler, 2006). Johnston (2009) chronicles music's role in various ethno-nationalist movements and in Eastern Europe's democracy movements twenty-five years ago. There are cases where music and/or the symbolic stature of a musician or a musical group, become important players in the trajectory of a movement, such that seeing music as *just* an artifact of the movement, that is, once removed from the real forces of change, or *just* a resource to build solidarity, misses the point. Following Rosenthal and Flacks (2012), music not only can function as a resource to build collective identity, or to pass information, or preserve a tradition, but also can be integral in the unfolding performance of the movement itself, constituting it by the way songs bring people to participation, by the meaning the songs come to assume, and by the meaning the opponents attribute to them.

Like music, the linguistic production of a movement – its printed texts – can include powerful artifacts that have long lives after their initial production. Where music can tug at emotions, textual artifacts appeal to the intellect. A key tract or manifesto, say Lenin's *What is to be Done?* regarding the Bolsheviks, or the Port Huron Statement of the North American New Left, often becomes the focus of ideological discussion in which collective identity is shaped and confirmed, from which collective action emerges, and by which interpretation evolves over time in the movement. In practice, the texts of a movement can include pamphlets, signs, slogans, minutes or recollections of meetings and strategy sessions, speeches, media coverage, public statements of leaders, and organizational records. When a movement is structured according to different SMOs (unlike the Bolsheviks but quite like the New Left), their textual production forms part of the polyphonous voice of a movement's discourse, typically reflecting the conflicts, struggles, and political cleavages of the broader social and cultural environment. Analysts often use the plural form, *discourses and texts*, to emphasize that what is being discussed and acted upon is never unanimous, but frequently challenged and negated by opposing groups, a focus that reflects the overlapping and intersecting of numerous cultural submatrices. Contemporary perspectives also stress the emergent and agentic character of textual production, variably called the discursive/rhetorical approach (Billig, 1992; 1995), the rhetorical turn (Simon, 1990), or the dialogic perspective (Steinberg, 1999), such that all meaning is context-specific, multifaceted, ever-evolving, and contested.

The textual artifacts of a movement not only are the foci of movement micro-performances, but, for the analyst, they also become data. Textual artifacts can often assume this dual quality in that they are meaningful both for social actors and to researchers (who are, of course, social actors in their own networks of meaning-making). Also, the research act can produce a different kind of text and a different form of performance when interviews with activists and leaders are audio/video recorded, to which linguistically schooled analysts have been long sensitive. The effects on the data produced may be significant (Johnston, 1995), but the effects on the movement may be significant as well. Some researchers have embraced their involvement in movement meaning-making; for example, Touraine and his associates have elaborated their method of research intervention (Touraine, 1981; Dubet and Wieviorka, 1996; see also Polletta, 2006b), but it is fair to say that this view has had little impact on the field as a whole.

When narrative performances are recorded they are artifactualized for both the participants and the analyst. Cassettes and VHS tapes of Salifist Imans in the 1980s and 1990s, as well as the first forays of movement groups into the internet and email lists, offered the researcher new data sources enmeshed in the cultural submatrix of movement participants. In the 21st century, when images are caught on a cell phone camera and uploaded to YouTube, MySpace, or Facebook, we encounter the artifactualization of performances that in the past would have been fleeting. Their impact as foci of talk and eventually action would have been limited to immediate observers and their word-of-mouth networks. Today, the dispersion of recorded events reaches far beyond the immediate audience of their creation. Consider the images of the slain body of Neda Agah-Soltan, shot by Iranian security forces on June 22, 2009, during street protests as part of the Green mobilizations against fraudulent elections. The poignant image went viral worldwide, becoming an artifact representing the regime's brutality and unresponsiveness. Consider too the creative images of the YouTube upload of #YoSoy132 (I am number 132), the largest student movement in Mexico since 1968, which shaped the presidential elections in 2012 (Figueiras, 2012; Tavera and Johnston, 2014).

This suggests, first, that digital media create new artifactualized forms distinguished by their diffusion to millions, which create vast opportunities for micro-performances of talk, identity construction, and activism – not necessarily via traditional street protests and demonstrations exclusively, but through digital forums – and, second, that internet-based social media open creative avenues for new performance forms and merge them with the process of artifactualization. Together, these two effects hold the potential for new forms of internet-2.0 collective action that, third, offer the researcher new methodologies to take soundings through digital dredging of metadata. I close with the observation that several recent mass movements merge identity creation, creative activism, social media, and standard party politics via web-based actions. They are often leaderless, horizontal movements for democratic reform, and predominately youth-based movements, such as in Spain (M-15 or *los indignados*), in the US (Occupy Wall Street), in Turkey (Taksim Square), and in Mexico (#YoSoy132). All relied on heavy use of the internet's networking functions via social media.

## REFERENCES

Abbott, A. (1995) 'Sequence Analysis: New Methods for Old Ideas', *Annual Review of Sociology*, 21: 93–113.

Alexander, J. (2004) 'Cultural Pragmatics: Social Performance between Ritual and Strategy', *Sociological Theory*, 22(4): 527–73.

Alexander, J. (2006) 'Cultural Pragmatics: Social Performance between Ritual and Strategy', in J. Alexander, B. Giesen, and J. L. Mast (eds), *Social Performance: Symbolic Action, Cultural Pragmatics and Ritual*. New York: Cambridge University Press. pp. 29–90.

Alexander, J. (2012) *Performative Revolution in Egypt*. London: Bloomsbury Academic.

Alexander, J., Giesen, B., and Mast, J. L. (2006) *Social Performance: Symbolic Action, Cultural Pragmatics and Ritual*. New York: Cambridge University Press.

Alexander, J. and Mast, J. L. (2006) 'Introduction: Symbolic Action in Theory and in Practice – The Cultural Pragmatics of Symbolic Action', in J. Alexander, B. Giesen, and J. L. Mast (eds), *Social Performance: Symbolic Action, Cultural Pragmatics and Ritual*. New York: Cambridge University Press. pp. 1–28.

Archer, M. S. (1996) *Culture and Agency: The Place of Culture in Social Theory*. New York: Cambridge University Press.

Benford, R. (1993) 'Frame Disputes within the Nuclear Disarmament Movement', *Social Forces*, 71: 677–701.

Benford, R. (1997) 'An Insider's Critique of the Social Movement Framing Perspective', *Sociological Inquiry*, 67: 409–30.

Benford, R. (2002) 'Controlling Narratives and narratives as Control within Social Movements', in J. Holstein and G. Miller (eds), *Challenges and Choices: Constructionist Prspectives on Social Problems*. Hawthorne, NY: Aldine de Gruyter. pp. 53–75.

Benford, R. D. and Snow, D. A. (2000) 'Framing Processes and Social Movements: An Overview and Assessment', *Annual Review of Sociology*, 26: 611–39.

Billig, M. (1992) *Talking of the Royal Family*. London: Routledge.

Billig, M. (1995) 'Rhetorical Psychology, Ideological Thinking, and Imaging Nationhood', in H. Johnston and B. Klandermans (eds), *Social Movements and Culture*. Minneapolis: University of Minnesota Press. pp. 64–81.

Castells, M. (1996) *The Rise of the Networked Society*. Malden, MA: Blackwell.

Castells, M. (1997) *The Power of Identity*. Malden, MA: Blackwell.

Clemens, E. S. (1996) 'Organizational Form as Frame: Collective Identity and Political Strategy in the American Labor Movement', in D. McAdam, J. D. McCarthy, and M. N. Zald (eds), *Comparative Perspectives on Social Movements: Political Opportunities, Mobilizing Structures, and Cultural Framings*. New York: Cambridge University Press. pp. 205–25.

Clemens, E. S. and Minkoff, D. C. (2004) 'Beyond the Iron Law: Rethinking the Place of Organizations in Social Movement Research', in *The Blackwell Companion to Social Movements*. Malden, MA: Blackwell. pp. 155–70.

Davis, J. E. (2002) *Stories of Change: Narrative and Social Movements*. Albany: SUNY Press.

Della Porta, D. and Diani, M. (2006) *Social Movements: An Introduction*, 2nd edition. Malden, MA: Blackwell Publishing.

Denisoff, R. S. and Peterson, R. (1973) *The Sounds of Social Change*. New York: Rand McNally.

Diani, M. (1992) 'The Concept of Social Movement', *Sociological Review*, 40: 1–25.

Diani, M. (1996) 'Social Movements and Social Capital: A Network Perspective on Movement Outcomes', *Mobilization*, 1: 129–47.

DiMaggio, P. (1997) 'Culture and Cognition', *Annual Review of Sociology*, 23: 263–87.

DiMaggio, P. (2002) 'Why Cognitive (and Cultural) Sociology Needs Cognitive Psychology', in K. Cerulo (ed.), *Culture in Mind*. New York: Routledge. pp. 274–81.

Dubet, F. and Wieviorka, M. (1996) 'Touraine and the Method of Sociological Intervention', in J. Clark and M. Diani (eds), *Social Movements in a Comparative Perspective: Situating Alain Touraine*. London: Falmer Press. pp. 55–75.

Eliasoph, N. (1998) *Avoiding Politics: How Americans Produce Apathy in Everyday Life*. New York: Cambridge University Press.

Emirbayer, M. and Goodwin, J. (1994) 'Network Analysis, Culture, and the Problem of Agency', *American Journal of Sociology*, 99: 1411.

Eyerman, R. (2006) 'Performing Opposition, or How Social Movements Move', in J. Alexander, B. Giesen, and J. L. Mast (eds), *Social Performance: Symbolic Action, Cultural Pragmatics and Ritual*. New York: Cambridge University Press. pp. 193–217.

Eyerman, R. and Jamison, A. (1998) *Music and Social Movements*. New York: Cambridge University Press.

Ewick, P. and Silbey, S. (2003) 'Narrating Social Structure: Stories of Resistance to Legal Authority', *American Journal of Sociology*, 108: 1328–72.

Ferree, M. M., Gerhards, J., Gamson, W., and Rucht, D. (2002) *Shaping Abortion Discourse: Parties, Movements and Media in Germany and the United States, 1970–1994*. New York: Cambridge University Press.

Fine, G. A. (1985) 'Can the Circle be Unbroken? Small Groups and Social Movements', in E. Lawler (ed.), *Advances in Group Processes. Vol. 2*. Greenwich, CT: JAI Press.

Fine, G. A. (1995) 'Public Narration and Group Culture: Discerning Discourse in Social Movements', in H. Johnston and B. Klandermans (eds), *Social Movements and Culture*. Minneapolis, MN: University of Minnesota Press. pp. 127–43.

Fine, G. A. (2001) *Difficult Reputations: Collective Memories of the Evil, Inept and Controversial*. Chicago: University of Chicago Press.

Fine, G. A. (2009) 'Notorious Support: The America First Committee and the Personalization of Policy', in H. Johnston (ed.), *Culture, Social Movements, and Protest*. Farnham, UK: Ashgate. pp. 77–102.

Figueiras, T. L. (2012) *Del 131 al #YoSoy132. Elección 2012*. México DF: Comunicación y Política Editores.

Ganz, M. (2000) 'Resources and Resourcefulness: Strategic Capacity in the Unionization of California Agriculture 1959–1966', *American Journal of Sociology*, 105: 1003–63.

Goffman, E. (1974) *Frame Analysis*. Cambridge: Harvard University Press.

Goodwin, J. and Jasper, J. M. (2004) *Rethinking Social Movements*. Lanham, MD: Rowman and Littlefield.

Haenfler, R. (2006) *Straight Edge: Clean-Living Youth, Hardcore Punk, and Social Change*. New Brunswick, NJ: Rutgers University Press.

Halker, C. D. (1991) *For Democracy, Workers, and God: Labor Song-Poems and Labor Protest 1865–95*. Urbana: University of Illinois Press.

Hewitt, L. and McCammon, H. J. (2005) 'Explaining Suffrage Mobilization: Balance, Neutralization and Range in Collective Action Frames', in H. Johnston and J. A. Noakes (eds), *Frames of Protest: Social Movements and the Framing Perspective*. Lanham, MD: Rowman and Littlefield. pp. 33–52.

Hunt, S., Benford, R. D., and Snow, D. A. (1994) 'Identity Fields: Framing Processes and the Social Construction of Movement Identities', in

H. Johnston, E. Larana and J. R. Gusfield (eds), *New Social Movements*. Philadelphia: Temple. pp. 185–208.

Inglehart, R. (1990) *Culture Shift in Advanced Industrial Society*. Princeton, NJ: Princeton University Press.

Inglehart, R. (1997) *Modernization and Postmodernization: Cultural, Economic, and Political Change in 43 Societies*. Princeton, NJ: Princeton University Press.

Jasper, J. M. (1997) *The Art of Moral Protest*. Chicago: University of Chicago Press.

Johnston, H. (1995) 'A Methodology for Frame Analysis: From Discourse to Cognitive Schemata', in H. Johnston and B. Klandermans (eds), *Social Movements and Culture*. Minneapolis: University of Minnesota Press. pp. 217–46.

Johnston, H. (2005) 'Comparative Frame Analysis', in H. Johnston and J. A. Noakes (eds), *Frames of Protest*. Lanham, MD: Rowman and Littlefield. pp. 237–60.

Johnston, H. (2009) *Culture, Social Movements, and Protest*. Aldershot, UK: Ashgate.

Johnston, H. (2010) 'Cultural Analysis of Political Protest', in K. T. Leicht and J. C. Jenkins (eds), *Handbook of Politics*. New York: Springer. pp. 327–48.

Johnston, H. (2014) *What is a Social Movement?* Cambridge, UK: Polity Press.

Johnston, H. and Alimi, E. Y. (2013) 'A Methodology for Analyzing Frame Dynamics: The Grammar of Keying Battles in Palestinian Nationalism', *Mobilization: An International Quarterly*, 18: 453–74.

Johnston, H. and Klandermans, B. (1995) *Social Movements and Culture*. Minneapolis: University of Minnesota Press.

Kitschelt, H. (1985) 'New Social Movements in West Germany and the United States', *Political Power and Social Theory*, 5: 273–342.

Klimova, S. (2009) 'Speech Act Theory and Protest Discourse: Normative Claims in the Communicative Repertoire of Three Russian Movements', in H. Johnston (ed.), *Culture, Social Movements, and Protest*. Farnham, UK: Ashgate. pp. 105–33.

Kriesi, H. (1989) 'New Social Movements and the New Class in the Netherlands', *American Journal of Sociology*, 94: 1078–116.

Kriesi, H., Koopmans, R., Duvendak, J-W. and Giugni, M. (1995) *New Social Movements in Western Europe*. Minneapolis: University of Minnesota Press.

Leitch, T. M. (1986) *What Stories Are: Narrative Theory and Interpretation*. University Park: Pennsylvania State University Press.

Lichterman, P. (1996) *The Search for Political Community: American Activists Reinventing Commitment*. New York: Cambridge University Press.

Lofland, J. (1985) *Protest*, New Brunswick, NJ: Transaction

McAdam, D., Tarrow, S., and Tilly, C. (1996) 'To Map Contentious Politics', *Mobilization*, 1: 17–34.

McAdam, D., Tarrow, S., and Tilly, C. (2001) *Dynamics of Contention*. Cambridge: Cambridge University Press.

McAdam, D. and Tarrow, S. (2011) 'Dynamics of Contention Ten Years On', *Mobilization*, 11: 1–10.

McCaffrey, D. and Keys, J. (2000) 'Competitive Framing Processes in the Abortion Debate: Polarization-Vilification, Frame Saving, and Frame Debunking', *Sociological Quarterly*, 41: 41–61.

McCammon, H. J. (2009) 'Beyond Frame Resonance: The Argumentative Structure and Persuasive Capacity of Twentieth-century U.S. Women's Jury-Rights Frames', *Mobilization*, 14: 45–64.

McCammon, H. J., Muse, C. S, Newman, H. D., and Terrell. T. M. (2007) 'Movement Framing and Discursive Opportunity Structures: The Political Successes of the U.S. Women's Jury Movements', *American Sociological Review*, 72(5): 725–49.

McLean, P. (2007) 'A Frame Analysis of Favor Seeking in the Renaissance: Agency, Networks, and Political Culture', *American Journal of Sociology*, 104: 51–91.

Melucci, A. (1985) 'The Symbolic Challenge of Contemporary Movements', *Social Research* 52: 789–816.

Melucci, A. (1989) *Nomads of the Present*. Philadelphia: Temple University Press.

Melucci, A. (1995) 'The Process of Collective Identity', in H. Johnston and B. Klandermans (eds), *Social Movements and Culture*. Minneapolis: University of Minnesota Press. pp. 41–63.

Meyer, D. S. and Whittier, N. (1994) 'Social Movement Spillover', *Social Problems*, 41: 277–98.

Miethe, I. (2009) 'Frames, Framing, and Keying: Biographical Perspectives on Social Movement Participation', in H. Johnston (ed.), *Culture, Social Movements, and Protest*. Farnham, UK: Ashgate. pp. 135–56.

Mische, A. (2003) 'Cross-Talk in Movements: Reconceiving the Culture-Network Link', in M. Diani and D. McAdam (eds), *Social Movements and Networks*. New York: Oxford University Press. pp. 258–80.

Mische, A. (2008) *Partisan Publics*. Princeton, NJ: Princeton University Press.

Mische, A. (2011) 'Relational Sociology, Culture, and Agency', in J. Scott and P. J. Carrington (eds), *The SAGE Handbook of Social Network Analysis*. London: Sage. pp. 80–97.

Moore, R. and Roberts, M. (2009) 'Do-It-Yourself Mobilization: Punk and Social Movements', *Mobilization: An International Quarterly*, 14: 273–92.

Norton, A. (2004) *Ninety-Five Theses on Politics, Culture, and Method*. New Haven, CT: Yale University Press.

Oliver, P. E. and Johnston, H. (2005) 'What a Good Idea! Ideologies and Frames in Social Movement Research', in H. Johnston and J. A. Noakes (eds), *Frames of Protest*. Lanham, MD: Rowman and Littlefield. pp. 185–203.

Pfaff, S. (1996) 'Collective Identity and Informal Groups in Revolutionary Mobilization: East Germany in 1989', *Social Forces*, 75: 91–118.

Polletta, F. (1998a) '"It Was Like a Fever": Narrative and Identity in Social Protest', *Social Problems*, 45: 137–59.

Polletta, F. (1998b) 'Legacies and Liabilities of an Insurgent Past: Remembering Martin Luther King on the House and Senate Floor', *Social Science History*, 22(4): 479–512.

Polletta, F. (2006a) *It Was Like a Fever: Storytelling in Protest and Politics*. Chicago: University Chicago Press.

Polletta, F. (2006b) 'Mobilization Forum: Awkward Movements', *Mobilization: An International Quarterly*, 11: 475–8.

Polletta, F. (2009). 'Storytelling in Social Movements', in H. Johnston (ed), *Culture, Social Movements, and Protest*. Farnham: Ashgate. pp. 33–54.

Robnett, B. (1997) *How Long? How Long? African-American Women in the Struggle for Civil Rights*. New York: Oxford University Press.

Robnett, B. (2002) 'External Political Change, Collective Identities, and Participation in Social Movement Organizations', in D. S, Meyer, N. Whittier, and B. Robnett (eds), *Social Movements*. New York: Oxford University Press. pp. 266–85.

Rochon, T. R. (1998) *Culture Moves: Ideas, Activism, and Changing Values*. Princeton, NJ: Princeton University Press.

Rosenthal, B. and Flacks, R. (2012) *Playing for Change: Music and Musicians in the Service of Social Movements*. Boulder, CO: Paradigm Publishers.

Roscigno, V. J. and Danaher, W. F. (2004) *The Voice of Southern Labor*. Minneapolis: University of Minnesota Press.

Rothman, F. D. and Oliver, P. (1999) 'From Local to Global: The Anti-Dam Movement in Southern Brazil, 1979–1992', *Mobilization*, 4: 41–58.

Schneider, A. and Ingram, H. (1993) 'Social Construction of Target Populations: Implications for Politics and Policy', *American Political Science Review*, 87(2): 334–47.

Simon, H. W. (1990) *The Rhetorical Turn: Invention and Persuasion in the Conduct of Inquiry*. Chicago: University of Chicago Press.

Snow, D. (2004) 'Framing Processes, Ideology, and Discursive Fields', in D. A. Snow, S. A. Soule, and H. Kriesi (eds), *The Blackwell Companion to Social Movements*. Malden, MA: Blackwell. pp. 380–412.

Snow, D. A. (2013) 'Framing and Social Movements', in D. A. Snow, D. della Porta, B. Klandermans, and D. McAdam (eds), *Encyclopedia of Social and Political Movements*. Malden, MA: Wiley-Blackwell. pp. 470–5.

Snow, D. A. and Benford, R. D. (1988) 'Ideology, Frame Resonance, and Participant Mobilization', in B. Klandermans, H. Kriesi, and S. Tarrow (eds), *International Social Movement Research*. Greenwich, CT: JAI Press. pp. 197–217.

Snow, D. A. and Benford, R. D. (2000) 'Clarifying the Relationship between Framing and Ideology: Comment on Oliver and Johnston', *Mobilization*, 5(1): 55–60.

Snow, D. A. and Byrd, S. C. (2007) 'Ideology, Framing Processes, and Islamic Terrorist Movements', *Mobilization*, 12(2): 119–36.

Snow, D. A., Benford, R. D., McCammon, H., Hewitt, L. and Fitzgerald, S. (2014) 'The Emergence and Development of Framing Perspective: Twenty-Five Years Since the Publication of Frame Alignment and What Lies Ahead', *Mobilization*, 19(1): 227–46.

Snow, D. A., Rochford Jr., E. B., Worden, S. K., and Benford, R. D. (1986) 'Frame Alignment Processes, Micromobilization, and Movement Participation', *American Sociological Review*, 51: 464–81.

Somers, M. (1992) 'Narrativity, Narrative Identity and Social Action: Rethinking English Working-Class Formation', *Social Science History*, 16: 591–630.

Somers, M. (1994) 'The Narrative Constitution of Identity: A Relational and Network Approach', *Theory and Society*, 23: 605–49.

Steensland, B. (2008) 'Why Do Policy Frames Change? Actor-Idea Coevolution in Debates over Welfare Reform', *Social Forces*, 86: 1027–53.

Steinberg, M. W. (1999) *Fighting Words: Working-Class Formation, Collective Action, and Discourse in Early Nineteenth Century England*. Ithaca NY: Cornell University Press.

Stevens, M. L. (2001) *Kingdom of Children: Culture and Controversy in the Homeschooling Movement*. Princeton, NJ: Princeton University Press.

Stryker, S., Owens, T. K., and White, R. W. (eds) (2000) *Self, Identity, and Social Movements*. Minneapolis: University of Minnesota Press.

Swidler, A. (1986) 'Culture in Action: Symbols and Strategies', *American Sociological Review*, 51: 273–86.

Tavera, L. and Johnston, H. (2014) 'Protest Artifacts in the Mexican Social Movement Sector: Reflections on the "Stepchild" of Cultural Analysis', in P. Almeida (ed.), *The SAGE Handbook of Latin American Social Movements*. Thousand Oaks, CA: Sage.

Taylor, V. and Whittier, N. (1992) 'Collective Identity in Social Movement Communities: Lesbian Feminist Mobilization', in A. Morris and C. McClurg Mueller (eds), *Frontiers in Social*

*Movement Theory*. New Haven: Yale University Press. pp. 104–32.

Tilly, C. (1978) *From Mobilization to Revolution*. Reading, MA: Addison-Wesley.

Tilly, C. (1995) *Popular Contention in Great Britain, 1758–1834*. Cambridge, MA: Harvard University Press.

Tilly, C. (2004) *Stories, Identities and Political Change*. Lanham, MD: Rowman and Littlefield.

Touraine, A. (1981) *The Voice and the Eye: An Analysis of Social Movements*. Cambridge: Cambridge University Press.

White, H. (1981) 'The Nature of Narrativity in the Representation of Reality', in W. J. T. Mitchell (ed.), *On Narrative*. Chicago: University of Chicago Press. pp. 1–23.

Whittier, N. (1995) *Feminist Generations*. Philadelphia: Temple University Press.

Wildavsky, A. (2006) *Cultural Analysis*, edited by Brendon Swedlow. New Brunswick, NJ: Transaction Publishers.

Young, M. (2002) 'Confessional Protest: The Religious Birth of U.S. National Social Movements', *American Sociological Review*, 67: 660–88.

# 31

# Cultural Nationalism

Eric Taylor Woods

## INTRODUCTION

Nationalism may involve the combination of culture and politics, but for many of its most prominent students, the former is subordinate to the latter. In this view, nationalist appeals to culture are a means to a political end; that is, the achievement of statehood. Hence, for Ernest Gellner (2006 [1983]: 124), culture is but an epiphenomenon, a 'false-consciousness ... hardly worth analyzing'. For their part, Eric Hobsbawm and Terence Ranger (1983) suggest that national traditions are 'invented' by elites concerned with the legitimization of state power. Similarly, John Breuilly (2006 [1982]: 11) defines national movements as 'political movements ... which seek to gain or exercise state power and justify their objectives in terms of nationalist doctrine'. A broadly similar characterization of nationalism can be found in the writings of many other esteemed scholars (Giddens, 1985; Laitin, 2007; Mann, 1995; Tilly, 1975).

The privileging of politics over culture remains the dominant approach to understanding nationalism, but it is not without criticism. There is now a vast and rapidly growing body of literature insisting that the role of culture should be made more prominent. In opposition to the argument that nationalist appeals to culture are but an exercise in legitimation, this body of literature suggests that they can be ends unto themselves. This latter phenomenon, generally referred to as cultural nationalism, is the subject of this chapter. The chapter proceeds as follows. I begin with the definition and history of cultural nationalism before discussing several key themes in its study. To conclude, I briefly outline several lines of research that I believe hold particular potential for developing the field. In the light of the huge array of literature on cultural nationalism, the review is focused on seminal contributions.

## DEFINITION AND HISTORY

In much of the scholarly literature, cultural nationalism has become a stretched concept, encompassing the full gamut of cultural practices and texts. Inspired by Benedict Anderson's (1983) *Imagined Communities*, researchers have gone in search of all those elements of culture that factor in the construction of national identity, from the extraordinary to the everyday, and everything in between. In this review, I employ a more limited definition of the term, which is largely in agreement with the work of John Hutchinson (2013). In short, I am focused on reflexive practices and texts where it is the national community that provides the chief inspiration. This definition shares much with Joep Leerssen's (2014) definition of Romantic nationalism. However, whereas Leerssen is focused on Romantic nationalism as a historically and spatially specific phenomenon in Europe, I approach cultural nationalism more as an ideal-typical concept, which finds its origins in the Romanticism of Europe, but has since migrated throughout the world, and can now be applied in a wide variety of contexts.

Because I am focused on practices and texts that are oriented to the national community, I do not include in this chapter literature that relates to 'official' cultural nationalism, whose form and content is tightly controlled by the state. My reasoning is that it is often unclear in these instances whether they are oriented to the state or the nation. For example, the many ceremonies around the world that annually commemorate the founding of states tend to more closely fit the interpretation of the uses of culture I suggested could be found in the work of John Breuilly and the others mentioned in the opening paragraph. However, I do acknowledge that the distinction I have adopted here is a fuzzy one; even when cultural activities and texts are imposed by the state, the actors involved can find ways of inserting their own interpretation. Indeed, I am aware that the idea that there exists a class of state bureaucrats who are somehow inured against culture is surely in need of revision. Nevertheless, I make the distinction in the hopes that it will result in a more coherent chapter.

In sum, if political nationalism is focused on the achievement of political autonomy, cultural nationalism is focused on the cultivation of a nation. Here the vision of the nation is not a political organization, but a moral community. As such, cultural nationalism sets out to provide a vision of the nation's identity, history and destiny. The key agents of cultural nationalism are intellectuals and artists, who seek to convey their vision of the nation to the wider community. The need to articulate and express this vision tends to be felt most acutely during times of social, cultural and political upheaval resulting from an encounter with modernity. Cultural nationalism often occurs in the early phase of a national movement, sometimes before an explicitly political nationalism has appeared. But it can also periodically recur in long-established national states (for an excellent summary of this phenomenon, see Hutchinson, 2013).

The history of cultural nationalism begins in 18th-century Europe. A variety of developments in the realms of ideas, culture and politics converge at this time to produce what Leerssen refers to as a 'tipping point' leading the explosion of cultural nationalism in the 19th century. These developments include: the emergence of historicism and Indo-European linguistics; the rise of Romanticism in literature and the arts; and a growing commitment to constitutional politics and the idea of 'rule by the people' (Leerssen, 2014: 11). From this period of change, John Hutchinson writes,

> emerged a polycentric *Weltanschauung* that presented a pantheistic conception of the universe, in which all natural entities were animated by a force that individualized them and endowed them with a drive for realization. The nation was one such life-force, a primordial, cultural, and territorial people through which individuals developed their authenticity as moral and rational beings. (2013: 76)

As part of this heady new world-view, Gregory Jusdanis (2001) argues that the rise of a historicist belief in the possibility of progress was a crucial ingredient in the emergence of cultural nationalism. According to Jusdanis, intellectuals in central and northern Europe became aware of their 'backwardness' in the face of French dominance and simultaneously sought prestige in their own cultures, while also embarking upon a programme of progress.

The writings of Johann Gottfried Herder (1744–1803), a key figure of this period who I describe in greater depth below, encapsulate the new programme of cultural nationalism that emerged from these developments. In sum, Herder edified the nation as the primordial scene from which the best of human endeavour owed its provenance, and which therefore obliged its cultivation through the recovery and celebration of its history and culture. Interestingly, Herder was as much practitioner as he was intellectual. In his search for the true character of the nation among the rural peasantry of central Europe, he played an influential role in the development of several practices that became associated with the cultural nationalism of the 19th century, including: philology; the writing of history; and the collection of folk songs, myths, and other practices.

In the wake of Herder's elucidation of a doctrine and program for cultural nationalism, Europe became the site of a massive efflorescence of intellectual and cultural activities devoted to national 'revival'. Poets, historians, philologists, painters and architects, among many other professions, arose from, or were rapidly transformed by, the new spirit of the era. Across Europe, they formed cultural societies, pressed for the institutionalization of their pursuits in universities, and demanded sponsorship from governments. Critical to the rapid spread of their ideas and practices was the increasing density of communication in the 19th century triggered by the '"second print revolution", which hugely increases the availability of printed matter: cheap woodpulp paper, stereotype and rotary printing, mechanized binding, improved distribution services' (Leerssen, 2014: 13). To this, we can add the growing numbers of the educated middle classes, who encounter the new spirit of cultural nationalism in the recently reformed universities, and then go on to consume its products (Leerssen, 2014: 13). From its European origins, cultural nationalism spread outwards, enjoying a renewed efflorescence in the decolonizing efforts of the 20th century. It is now a recurring phenomenon throughout much of the world.

Returning now to Herder, a German-speaking Lutheran minister, poet, philosopher, historian and all-around celebrity-intellectual of his day. Herder is often attributed the greatest individual responsibility for elucidating the ideology and practice of cultural nationalism. His writings on nationhood became renowned in his own lifetime, giving succour not only to German pan-nationalism, but also providing a chief inspiration for the Slavic national revival. So lasting has been Herder's impact that it is now possible to find traces of his thought and practice in national movements throughout the world. In the light of Herder's enduring influence, I will elaborate on some basic elements of his thought as both a historical and ideal-typical illustration of the doctrine and practice of cultural nationalism.

According to Herder, humanity, with its distinct capacity for culture, is naturally divided into cultural groups referred to as nations (*volk*), each of which has a unique character (*geist*). Nations have a quasi-sacred status, for it is only through their languages, traditions and practices that individual creativity can be fully realized. Yet, here Herder betrays the paradox common to nationalists everywhere. On the one hand, nations have naturally existed since time immemorial, yet, on the other hand, they also need constant cultivation lest they fade away. Thus, even as he suggests that nations are a natural component of human existence, Herder suggests that they can decline. Given the importance of the nation for human expression, it therefore behoves intellectuals to revive or 'awaken' nations from their 'slumber', as Herder beseeched of the various Slavic nations (see Barnard, 2003: 14).

While Herder wrote extensively on folk song and dance, he accords to language primacy of place as the chief expression of the nation. In *Treatise on the Origin of Language*, Herder writes, 'no greater harm can befall a nation than to be robbed of its character by being deprived of its language, for without its language it loses its own mode of thinking' (cited in Barnard, 2003: 12). Territory is also emphasized as the crucible for the emergence of nations. For Herder, nations are historically constituted through interaction with territory and environment. In *Reflections on the Philosophy and History of Mankind*, Herder remarks,

> it is obvious why all sensual people, fashioned to their country, are so much attached to the soil, and so inseparable from it. The constitution of their body, their way of life, the pleasures and occupations to which they have become accustomed from their infancy, and the whole circle of their ideas, are climatic. Deprive them of their country, you deprive them of everything. (cited in Penrose, 2002: 286)

Herder's writings often reflect a kind of national egalitarianism, suggesting that all nations are equally endowed with a unique character which should therefore be allowed to flourish in the 'garden of humanity'. As Barnard (2003: 11) writes, 'even though Herder's own conception of nationhood as the essential foundation for the complex fabric of social and political entities *was* the alpha and omega of his nationalism, this nationalism by no means ruled out international fellowship, for it was not tantamount to an exclusionary chauvinism ...'. It is this genre of national thinking that Barnard suggests provides inspiration for the cosmopolitan nationalists of the 19th century, such as Giuseppe Mazzini. And yet, against Barnard's assertion, I would suggest that just as Herder endorses a degree of relativism, he also frequently betrays a degree of ethnic chauvinism. For example, when Herder writes on behalf of the nation with which he identifies, it is often to lament the status of the Germans vis-à-vis the more dominant French. And when Herder enjoins Germans to replace the use of the French language with their mother tongue, and to rediscover their national myths, traditions and practices, he descends into xenophobia. In *Treatise*, Herder infamously writes in a poem,

> Look at other nationalities
> Do they wander about
> So that nowhere in the whole world they are strangers
> Except to themselves?
> They regard foreign countries with proud disdain.
> And you German alone, returning from abroad,
> Wouldst thou greet your mother in French?
> O spew it out before your door
> Spew out the ugly slime of the Seine. Speak German, O You German
> (cited in Kedourie, 1961: 9)

In this stanza, not only do we find the links between Herder and the more ethnocentric philosophy of his disciple Johann Gotlieb Fichte, but more generally we also see an early expression of the widespread obsession with national and ethnic authenticity that now afflicts much of the modern world.

## RESEARCH THEMES

### Cultural and Political Nationalism

Much ink has been spilled debating the character of cultural nationalism and its relationship to political nationalism. The most influential author in these debates is Hans Kohn. In his magisterial history of the idea of nationalism, Kohn (1960 [1944]) distinguishes between the political forms of nationalism that are ostensibly associated with the United States, France, the Netherlands and Britain, and the cultural nationalisms that he suggests are representative of central and eastern Europe and the former European colonies. Kohn's dichotomy is similar to the distinction that Friedrich Meinecke made in 1907 between the *Staatsnation* and the *Kulturnation*, but it is Kohn's writings that have had the most enduring influence. In sum, in Kohn's view, 'western nationalism' derives its solidarity from adherence to Rousseau's notion of a social contract between rulers and ruled. Membership in the national community is voluntary, and hence potentially open to all individuals, irrespective of their cultural background. By contrast, 'eastern nationalism', which derives its solidarity from an organic view of the national community based on shared origins and culture, has a closed membership (Kohn, 1960 [1944]: 391).

Kohn's dichotomy is the most enduring heuristic device in the study of nationalism, informing a number of related dichotomies, most notably the civic–ethnic dichotomy. Yet, if the dichotomy has endured, it has not been without criticism. Several prominent critics claim that it should be abandoned on the basis that all national movements, whether originating in the West or elsewhere, tend to contain political and cultural elements (e.g. Kuzio, 2002; Yack, 1996). As an alternative to the dichotomy, Oliver Zimmer (2003: 178) proposes a process-oriented approach that distinguishes between 'the mechanisms which social actors use as they reconstruct the boundaries of national identity at a particular point in time; and, on the other hand, the symbolic resources upon which they draw when they reconstruct these boundaries'. While Zimmer's model seeks to move away from the essentialist tendencies in Kohn's and others' work, the fact that he distinguishes between resources that are 'voluntary' or 'organic', suggests that he still sees some value in Kohn's dichotomy.

Kohn's suggestion that there are western and eastern forms of nationalism is not the only source of debate. His valuation of these two types of nationalism has also had great impact. While Meinecke previously deplored the ostensible vacuity of the French *Staatsnation* in favour of the poetry of the German *Kulturnation*, Kohn takes the opposite view. Kohn approvingly characterizes the political nationalism of the West as a liberal ideology deeply marked by the enlightenment and particularly by Rousseau's idea that political communities are actively willed into being. In contrast, he characterizes the cultural nationalism of central and eastern Europe as a reactionary ideology, fatally influenced by Herder's obsession with a nation's unique character. While he stresses that Herder himself was a committed liberal, Kohn nonetheless traces how his ideas planted the seed leading to the growth of the racist nationalism of the 20th century. This assessment of 'cultural' nationalism as the 'bad' form of nationalism has coloured much academic and popular thinking about the phenomenon ever since.

There have recently been efforts to rehabilitate cultural nationalism. In the realm of political theory, writers have questioned Kohn's characterization of cultural nationalism as a specifically ethnic ideology, arguing, to the contrary, that it is defensible from a liberal perspective (e.g. Gans, 2000). Indeed, some analysts have taken to distinguishing cultural nationalism from both ethnic *and* civic nationalism, suggesting that a focus on language and culture is distinct from adherence to citizenship rights, as well as a belief in common ancestry (e.g. Nielsen, 1996). Several historical sociologists, whose work on cultural nationalism I will discuss in greater depth in the succeeding section, have also taken issue with the view of cultural nationalism as anti-modern (e.g. Chatterjee, 1993; Hutchinson, 2013; Jusdanis, 2001; Smith, 1995). These authors suggest is that when cultural nationalists turn to the past, it is above all to find ways of *accommodating* their purported communities with modernity.

### Ethno-Symbolism

Notwithstanding the long-running theoretical debates on the concept and character of cultural nationalism, it has proven to be a fruitful concept among researchers who employ it as an ideal type, while acknowledging that in reality it can take many forms. The most heavily trodden of the various themes in cultural nationalism is associated with the ethno-symbolist school of inquiry devised by doyen of nationalism studies Anthony D. Smith. The research in this area is most often concerned with the historicity of cultural nationalism and the relationship between cultural nationalism and the wider society, especially the process by which it is institutionalized and disseminated, and also its relationship to political nationalism.

An early exemplar is provided by Miroslav Hroch (2000 [1985]). Of course, at the time of the publication of Hroch's book, Smith had not yet fully elaborated the elements of ethno-symbolism. And even if Smith had already done so, it is not clear that Hroch would have aligned his work with Smith, writing as he did from a Marxist perspective. Nevertheless, I discuss Hroch's landmark study here because of the influence that it has had on subsequent iterations of ethno-symbolism. Indeed, in subsequent years, Hroch himself also implies a degree of complementarity between his approach and that of ethno-symbolism, contributing to a special issue on ethno-symbolism in the journal *Nations and Nationalism* in 2004. Hroch embeds cultural nationalism within a processual model describing the route by which national movements among several 'small nations' of Europe became institutionalized. The concept of small nations refers to non-dominant nations that are not already in possession of a state – now more commonly referred to as stateless nations. According to Hroch, cultural nationalism typifies the first phase (Phase A) of the process of nation-formation, when the ideas and practices associated with the national community are conceived and disseminated by artists and intellectuals. Although Hroch concentrates much of his analysis on the second phase (Phase B), when the national idea becomes political, his analysis is nevertheless notable for putting cultural nationalism at the very heart of nation-formation. In Hroch's analysis, it is the artists and intellectuals who lay the foundation for those with political ambitions.

If not specifically interested in cultural nationalism, at least in his earlier work, Smith has had great influence on scholarship in this area. For Smith, all nationalism has a cultural dimension; hence his insistence that it is an ideological movement rather than merely a political movement, as John Breuilly and others would have it. In Smith's hands, nationalism appears as a Durkheimian political religion aimed at ensuring the solidarity of national community, rather than as a secular ideology seeking to bind it to the state (e.g. Smith, 2000). Across his lengthy career, Smith (e.g. 1986; 1991; 2003) has sought to demonstrate the trans-generational 'stickiness' of the culture of nations. According to Smith, this pattern of myths, symbols, memories and values often extends backwards into the pre-modern era, as well as structuring a nation's particular path towards modernization.

While Smith stresses the capacity for cultural patterns to endure in the face of social change, he also acknowledges that they can undergo rapid change. Here Smith attempts to carve out a middle ground between those who view nationalism as a Herderian expression of an innate collective spirit stretching back into time immemorial, and those who view it as a wholly modern ideology conjured up by enterprising elites and imposed upon the masses. For Smith (1995), national cultures take shape through a process of reinterpretation and rediscovery rather than mere invention – a process that is aimed at the regeneration of communities. Smith's interpretation of nationalism as having a progressive thrust provides the inspiration for a line of scholarship on cultural nationalism that stands in stark contrast to Kohn's characterization of cultural nationalism as a regressive force.

Smith has lately begun to focus more explicitly on cultural nationalism. In doing so, he has made a welcome foray into the visual arts. His most recent book seeks to uncover the significance of visual art in the making of national identity in France and Britain, which presents an original typology of the different kinds of national art, including didactic, evocative, and commemorative (Smith, 2013b). The book is presented as an implied critique of the line of scholarship inspired by Anderson's (1983) *Imagined Communities*, in which written texts take centre stage in the construction of national identity. By contrast, Smith's study explores how the abstract ideas associated with nationalism and national identity are rendered as visual objects. This book provides an exemplar of how the analysis of non-written texts can contribute to the traditional concerns associated with the sociology of cultural nationalism.

John Hutchinson has done much to enrich understanding of cultural nationalism. He was Smith's first PhD student and his work remains aligned with his approach. Hutchinson's (1987) lauded case-study of Gaelic revivalism and the establishment of the Irish national state greatly extends Hroch's approach to cultural nationalism. While Hroch's linear model suggests that the importance of cultural nationalism will diminish once the political movement takes off, Hutchinson presents cultural nationalism as an episodic phenomenon, which can recur even after a national state is established. Observing that the Irish national movement was often split amongst protagonists favouring cultural or political aims, Hutchinson's study implies that cultural nationalism proceeds dialectically with political nationalism, with the former periodically reinforcing the latter, and vice versa. To bring to light how cultural nationalism is institutionalized and disseminated, the book distinguishes between two kinds of cultural nationalists: intellectuals and artists on the one hand, and the intelligentsia on the other hand. The intellectuals and artists furnish the symbols and vision of the nation. The intelligentsia, a vocational and occupational group including the professions and tertiary education instructors, communicate this vision to the 'masses'.

Over the course of his career, Hutchinson has continued to refine understanding of cultural nationalism. In a wide-ranging comparative book, he includes an extended theoretical chapter on the history of cultural nationalism and its relationship to pre-modern ethnic revivals. Emphasizing the modernity of cultural nationalism, Hutchinson nevertheless stresses its many similarities with earlier ethnic revivals, observing that pre-modern myths, symbols and practices are often incorporated into modern national movements (1994). As such, cultural nationalism appears to have a much longer genealogy than has been conventionally presented. In a more recent analysis, Hutchinson (2005) focuses on the role of contestation in the endurance of national communities. Here he suggests that the often intense struggles among cultural nationalists over national identity can paradoxically serve to reify the nation. By drawing on a common pool of symbols and orienting themselves to a common referent, Hutchinson finds that competing nationalists actually have the effect of bolstering national solidarity.

Hutchinson (2013) has also recently disavowed the commonly-held view that cultural nationalists will invariably turn to organic myths and symbols of common descent. By contrast, he suggests that in their struggle to define the nation, cultural nationalists may be just as predisposed to characterize the nation as a voluntary community grounded in civic principles. This important revision of cultural nationalism aligns well with recent conceptual debates on the phenomenon, particularly Zimmer's (2003) processual model. As a result of Hutchinson's work, it is now possible to analyse cultural nationalism as an ongoing struggle over the definition and character of the nation, with the proponents seeking to convey competing visions to the wider community. In Hutchinson's various analyses, this struggle is expressed as a series of binary visions of the 'true' character of the nation, whether it is progressive or regressive, organic or voluntary, religious or secular, monocultural or multi-cultural, etc.

Kosaku Yoshino's (1992) highly cited study of cultural nationalism in Japan not only takes Hutchinson and Smith beyond Europe, but also takes their work in a new research direction. Yoshino applies the distinction between intellectuals and intelligentsia put forward by Hutchinson and Smith to investigate how the ideas of intellectuals are diffused among two separate groups of 'intelligentsia' – businessmen and educators. Interestingly, Yoshino finds that it is the businessmen who are the more committed carriers of the ideas of the intellectuals. This finding provides a further rationale for the recent turn towards corporate nationalism (e.g. Olins, 2002).

More recently, Yingjie Guo (2004) has applied the ethno-symbolist approach to cultural nationalism in a fascinating study of China, where he suggests that a group of intellectuals have become increasingly emboldened to assert an ethnic vision of a Chinese national community against the long-standing rationalist and Marxist representations of China. Taken together, both the studies by Yoshino and Guo serve to confirm Hutchinson's argument that the occurrence of cultural nationalism is as much a feature of long-established national states as it is of national movements that seek to establish a state. As such, they pave the way for closer analysis of when and why the members of 'dominant nations' find it necessary to turn to symbols of the communities rather than the state. This would conjoin nicely with Eric Kaufmann's (2004; Kaufmann and Haklai, 2008) research agenda on 'dominant ethnicity', in which he suggests that a perception that state elites are not adequately representing the interests of the dominant group can provoke the rise of national sentiment against 'their' state.

## *Postcolonialism*

The study of nationalism in Asia and Africa has contributed much to the understanding of cultural nationalism. Against the tendency to read the spread of nationalism among indigenous elites as wholly imitative of existing patterns in the Americas and Europe, several scholars have uncovered long-standing efforts to define the character and destiny of the colonized communities. As with the national movements of Europe, these efforts have notably tended to precede the emergence of their political counterparts. Also, the progressive element to cultural nationalism that Smith, Hutchinson and others have found to have been so central to the European movements is re-confirmed in the literature on Asia and Africa. Time and again, the finding is that the turn to indigenous culture and history arises as an attempt to find ways of authentically embarking on a path of modernization.

An earlier study uncovering this phenomenon, which presages the body of literature that might generally be labelled postcolonial studies, was conducted by David Kopf (1969). Kopf's history of the intellectual ferment of the College of Fort William of Bengal sheds light on the challenge of fusing (foreign) modernity with (indigenous) culture. With the emergence of postcolonial studies proper, this dynamic has taken on particular importance. Homi Bhabha's (2013 [1990]) suggestion that what emerges is an unstable 'hybrid' identity that is neither European nor Indigenous has triggered a massive outpouring of research. This research has even impacted the study of nationalism in the former metropole, where several scholars associated with 'British cultural studies' have focused on the cultural politics of the formerly colonized who now make their home in Britain (e.g. Gilroy, 2013; Hall, 1993).

A central figure in the study of postcolonial nationalism is Partha Chatterjee. In his first major study, Chatterjee (1986) takes aim at Elie Kedourie's assertion that the rise of postcolonial nationalism in Asia and Africa is merely a derivative discourse imported from Europe. By contrast, Chatterjee suggests that nationalism arises out of a dialogue between European and Indigenous ideas and practices. The agents of these novel ideologies are the educated indigenous elite. Much like the cultural nationalists in Hutchinson's work, who concern themselves above all with the moral dimensions of the national community, Chatterjee suggests that these elites are concerned with its 'spiritual realm'. While the colonial administrations may have dominated the 'material realm', in Chatterjee's view, they never really fully penetrated the spiritual realm, where indigenous intellectuals were involved in the elaboration of the moral community from the middle of the 19th century onwards. In a subsequent book, Chatterjee (1993) applies his approach to a study of the emergence of a national ideology in Bengal through attention to a wide variety of cultural practices, from drama to art and from education to religion, among others. In the process, Chatterjee focuses on efforts by marginalized groups within India to draw on the emergent national discourse to make claims for their inclusion. John Peel (2003 [1989]) makes comparable findings in an interesting study of the emergence of Yoruban identity in south-western Nigeria. Focusing on the impact of 19th-century Christian missionaries, Peel, like Chatterjee in the case of India, finds a modern identity emerging out of a dialogue of western and Indigenous ideas and practices.

The challenge of constructing novel national identities is also a key characteristic of settler nationalism. Settler societies are faced with the peculiar challenge of distinguishing themselves from a metropole that shares a similar culture, while also not being able to lay claim to an authentic culture rooted in a particular territory 'from time immemorial'. In this context, Bhabha's notion of 'hybridity' has again been put to good effect (e.g. McDonald, 2013; Proudfoot and Roche, 2005). As Christopher McDonald puts it, 'the concept of hybridity includes not just Bhabha's "third space" between European and "Native", but also the cultural "ambivalence" experienced by Europeans in a colonial setting' (2013: 174). To overcome this ambivalence, settler nationalists in Mexico, for example, sought to construct a 'mestizo' national identity, which through the mixing of settler and indigenous, can claim rootedness in the territory and also embrace the prestige of European modernity (Doremus, 2001). Others have sought a solution by turning to the future. In the former British settler societies, cultural nationalists proclaim their national communities to be at the vanguard in the construction of a new kind of 'rainbow' or 'multicultural' community whose strength is its diversity (Hutchinson, 1994: Chapter 6).

## *Globalization*

An important area of research asks questions about the persistence of cultural nationalism in an era characterized by the increasing globalization of culture and the rise of new forms of cultural expression. For many scholars, globalization undermines nationalism. In the decades following the Second World War, the view that American cultural dominance was leading to the cultural homogenization of the world was widespread. More recently, others, such as Anthony Giddens (1991) have suggested that globalization produces a paradoxical simultaneous movement away from the nation towards large-scale continental identities and much smaller, local identities. Pointing to the proliferation of new imagined worlds that do not readily fit within a national schema, Arjun Appadurai (1990) provides a fascinating analysis suggesting that global flows of 'ethnoscapes', 'mediascapes', 'financescapes' and 'technoscapes' are leading to new forms of identification in the era of globalization. In all these readings of the impact of globalization, cultural nationalism appears as a throwback to another era, enduring as a quaint anachronism, or as a mere reaction to its inevitable decline, like Katsushika Hokusai's famous woodcut of the *Great Wave of Kanagawa* crashing down upon the fishing boats below.

Against the arguments that globalization and nationalism are inimical, ethno-symbolists Smith (1995) and Hutchinson (1994: Chapter 5; 2013) have mounted an impressive alternative reading of the impact of globalization. Finding that most analyses of the impact of globalization are too short-sighted, Hutchinson (2005) suggests that the long-range historical perspective associated with 'world history' provides a better approach. For Hutchinson (2005: 160), globalization is not the recent phenomenon associated with global capitalism and new developments in information technology that it is often supposed to be, but rather it is a 'recurring and evolutionary process' whose story begins in central Asia in the 13th century. It is in adopting such a perspective that Hutchinson argues that the causal relationship between globalization, ethnicity and nationalism should be reconsidered, and suggests the possibility that nationalism is actually engendered by globalization. Here we find agreement with Anne-Marie Thiesse (2001: 11), who writes that 'there is nothing more international than the formation of national identities' (*'Rien de plus international que la formation des identités nationales'* [my translation]).

For his part, Smith (2010: 149) also suggests that the global era could arguably be considered a period of 'internationalising nationalism'. According to Smith, nationalism can be seen to have a 'demonstration effect', whereby 'wave after wave of nationalisms have engulfed successive regions, engendering new claims and making equivalent demands'. In this view, ongoing developments in information technology, capitalism and politics can only serve to 'amplify the nationalist message'. Turning more specifically to the realm of culture, Smith (2010: 50) suggests that we are now witnessing an increasing role for cultural nationalism. For if the criteria for entry into the global community of national states were initially political sovereignty and territorial jurisdiction, they now also include a demonstration of 'cultural unity and solidarity, and preferably some degree of cultural "uniqueness"'.

To bring these debates out of the world of grand theory towards a more concrete expression of culture, we can see similar lines of argumentation being drawn in the study of film and cinema. As relatively new forms of culture that are highly mobile, television and film are inevitably a key area of concern in debates over the impact of globalization and the future of cultural nationalism. Large-scale Hollywood feature films and American television programmes, for example, are ubiquitous throughout the world, except in those places where there is a concerted effort to prevent their dissemination. In response, in almost all regions there have arisen efforts to produce a 'national cinema', often with the support of the state. Yet does this indicate the ongoing vitality of the nation as a source of inspiration, or is it a last gasp indication of its decline – a lament rather than a celebration?

In a highly cited essay, Andrew Higson (1989) raises doubts about the possibility of a 'national' cinema, observing that the production teams and the audiences of even the seemingly most nationalist of films are often transnational. Yet, the fact that films continue to draw heavily on national narratives and imagery seems to suggest nationalism's ongoing grip on our imaginations. For example, in an analysis of the film *Braveheart*, Tim Edensor (2002: Chapter 5) shows how a film made in Hollywood, whose largest audience was American, nevertheless had significant impact on Scottish nationalism. Edensor's analysis points to the possibility of an international 'normalization' of national myths and symbols through Hollywood. However, we should also be aware that there is nothing new in this process. Even in 19th-century Europe, Leerssen (2014: 15) suggests that national art had wide appeal among international audiences, 'owing to their reliance on an established, transnational and European-wide repertoire of forms and expression'. Of course, the overwhelming dominance of Hollywood in the case of cinema also suggests the possibility of conflict, as audiences see themselves refracted through American stereotypes. Indeed, in the case of *Braveheart*, which depicts the English in an unsavoury light, Edensor observes that cinemagoers in England largely chose to stay home on this occasion.

## *Gender*

The significance of gender for cultural nationalism has begun to attract increasing attention from scholars. According to Glenda Sluga (1998), the rise of nationalism in Europe coincided with the widespread acceptance out of the patriarchal family. As such, nationalism came to be seen as a masculine project. Sluga writes: 'Mazzini, like Michelet and Fichte, drew on the image of the patriarchal family (with the father at its head) as a natural unit to shore up the legitimacy of the fraternal nation-state and determine its preference for the male citizen as the active and military patriot' (cited in Smith, 1998: 209).

From the metaphor of the nation as a family flow specific symbolic roles for men and women. Masculinity is associated with the public sphere, and above all with the nation's relations with other nations. Men are thereby given an 'active' status, as the defenders of the national community, periodically called upon to the sacrifice themselves for the 'motherland.' In 19th-century central Europe, George Mosse (1985) shows how men were therefore expected to embody the best of the bourgeois ideals of heterosexual masculinity (see also Parker et al., 1992). As Smith (1998: 208) writes, 'such neo-classic images as David's painting of the *Oath of the Horatii* (1784), West's *The Death of Wolfe* (1770) and Fuseli's *Oath of the Rutli* (1779) focus explicitly on the traditional masculine attributes of energy, force and duty'. Sculptors also took up the cause, depicting the national community as a neoclassical muscular, male body (see Leoussi, 1997).

The nation's private sphere, its ostensibly 'untainted' inner essence, tends to be represented by femininity. Nira Yuval-Davis writes, 'A figure of a woman, often a mother, symbolises in many cultures the spirit of the collectivity, whether it is Mother Russia, Mother Ireland or Mother India' (Yuval-Davis, 1997: 45). In defending the nation, men are therefore by definition defending the women. In this sense, although women have a role as reproducers, they are subordinate to the men. Eley and Suny (1996: 26) observe wryly that '*woman* is at least a positive term of the national good, albeit in some disempowering and subordinating sense'. The 'active' role that is assigned to women is above all as reproducers, by giving birth to the next generation and by transferring to it the community's core cultural characteristics and values (Yuval-Davis, 1997: 43).

A woman's body, and how she adorns it, is of particular symbolic importance, given the status that women occupy as the essence and reproducer of the national community. In the confrontation with modernity, women's bodies frequently become the object of a cultural struggle; whether they are enjoined to maintain the link with tradition by wearing ethnic and religious adornments or whether they are exhorted to lead the nation into modernity by adopting new kinds of fashions. For example, women's fashion has been a key site of struggle in postcolonial India, where nationalists sought to reform the treatment of women in line with Western expectations, but also sought to retain authenticity (Chatterjee, 1989). Of course, this dynamic also lies at the heart of struggles over the wearing of the veil in Turkey and, indeed, throughout much of the Muslim world (Kandiyoti, 1991; Timmerman, 2000).

The symbolic status occupied by women as the 'pure' essence of the nation means that they have also been the target of horrific sexual violence in times of war and crisis. These crimes tend to be represented as an attack on the whole nation, which ultimately ostensibly calls into question its masculinity. Hence, Wendy Bracewell (2000: 563) shows how reports in Serbia of the rape of women by Albanians were linked to 'perceptions of national victimisation and a crisis of masculinity'. Rape can also lead to national anxieties over the potential birth of 'mongrel' children, who bear the 'blood' of the enemy. The rape of French women by German soldiers, for example, triggered a debate in France over what to do about the potential *enfants du barbare*, and the threat that they posed (Harris, 1993).

## Cultural History

It is true that all the themes I have covered so far in this review could be defined as studies in cultural history. Peter Burke (2008) suggests that the relationship of culture and society has long been integral to cultural history. And as we have seen, this relationship is a core concern of research on cultural nationalism. However, in this section I am more concerned with the genre of cultural history that primarily addresses developments within culture, rather than its relationship to society. But even with this slightly more circumscribed approach, the number of studies is truly enormous, and I would be performing a disservice to even begin to pretend to summarize the field here. Instead, I will take the opposite approach by discussing the work of one scholar in particular, whose work in cultural history I believe shows particular promise in deepening our understanding of cultural nationalism.

Joep Leerssen (2006a; 2006b; 2014) has recently sought to carve out a unique approach to the study of cultural nationalism. Leerssen enjoins his fellow researchers to move away from a concern with the significance of cultural nationalism in the progression of particular national movements, towards uncovering how the ideas and practices of cultural nationalists are shared across transnational networks. As such, Leerssen advocates greater attention to intellectual and artistic developments, whereby new practices and cultural forms emerge and are disseminated among its practitioners in a process of creation and sharing. Leerssen is now spearheading a large-scale research project that seeks to shed light on the dissemination of cultural nationalism through time and space in 19th-century Europe. The preliminary results of this project have been mapped on to the project's interactive website (see http://www.spinnct.cu).

Leerssen's approach to cultural nationalism sheds light on the two sides of cultural nationalism, whereby a concern for authenticity ensures that the *content* is national, but the sharing of ideas and practices among a transnational body of practitioners ensures that the *form* is international. For example, Leerssen (2006b) details how Sir Walter Scott's approach to the historical novel, as exemplified by *Ivanhoe*, was adapted by authors working in other social settings, to become an important mechanism in the construction of national myths and symbols throughout 19th-century Europe. Thus the historical novel as a cultural form becomes associated with several different national movements, but the content of each novel is unique to that particular movement. Leerssen's approach also holds much promise in shedding light on the dynamics of cultural nationalism from a transnational perspective, as new modes of nationalist expression sweep across the globe, whether it is, for example, a renewed focus on blood and belonging or the celebration of hybridity. Such a research direction might take a leaf from the quantitative approach to literature associated with Franco Moretti (2007). Rather than focus on the particularities of the literary canon, Moretti charts the rise and fall of whole genres. The combination of Moretti and Leerssen could surely add to our understanding of the rise and fall of various forms of cultural nationalism.

## CONCLUSION

Recent research has done much to refine our understanding of the concept and character of cultural nationalism, uncovering a practice that is distinct from political nationalism and which is now a recurring phenomenon throughout the modern world. The significance of cultural nationalism is in the construction and dissemination of the ideas, myths and symbols of national communities. Not only does this cultural repertoire help to construct a sense of shared subjectivity, but it also provides the symbolic content which political nationalists draw upon in their struggles for political and territorial autonomy. In this short conclusion, I return to several lines of research that I believe show particular promise. Several of the most promising lines of research ask processual questions related to cultural nationalism's contestation, dissemination and recurrence. Research on the transnational interactions of cultural producers is also a highly innovative area of research.

We have seen that John Hutchinson (2005) has been critical in moving the study of cultural nationalism towards processual questions. His view of cultural nationalism as a field of contestation in particular helps to ensure that its study remains at the vanguard of the study of culture, in which other fields have long foregrounded the role of contestation. What is needed now is for scholars of cultural nationalism to reach across to developments in these other fields. For example, the increasing use of a dramaturgical metaphor in the study of cultural politics could do much to uncover the process related to why certain visions of the nation become established over others. For example, in a recent special issue of *Nations and Nationalism* several colleagues explored the ways in which Jeffrey Alexander's 'strong program' in cultural sociology, which has recently undergone a 'performative turn', might be used in the study of cultural nationalism (Woods and Debs, 2013).

Yoshino's (1992) study of cultural nationalism in Japan was a major intervention in the field for focusing on the process of how the ideas, symbols and practices of intellectuals and artists are disseminated among the intelligentsia. There is much work that remains to be done in this area. In particular, there needs to be more research on how cultural nationalism is received by ordinary members of the national community, not only the intelligentsia. How do the ideas and symbols of our national communities enter into our everyday lives, to become, in Michael Billig's (1995) terms, a part of our 'banal' social ecology, in our homes, places of work and leisure, and in our behaviours and hopes and dreams? Here a fascinating recent book by Kristin Surak (2013) points in a promising direction. Surak's study draws on research on 'everyday nationalism' to uncover the role of the tea ceremony in constructing 'ideal' Japanese citizens. Surak shows how teachers of the popular practice are involved in continually reiterating a particular vision of the national community. Gender plays an especially important role in the ceremony, as students learn how to perform ideals of Japanese masculinity and femininity.

In addition to uncovering how cultural nationalism enters our collective consciousness to become a part of our everyday ideas and practices, there is scope for uncovering how and when it returns to the fore as a reflexive struggle among artists and intellectuals. In Hutchinson's (2006) terms, how does cultural nationalism move from 'hot' to 'banal', and back again? Here again, work in the area of performance studies might be useful. In particular, the revival of Victor Turner's (1986) dramaturgical model of the process of symbolic conflicts could be of particular use here. Turner's model seeks to uncover the phases related to how a cultural struggle is triggered, how it is transformed into a full-blown societal contest, and how it is concluded. The model is especially useful for shedding light on why these kinds of struggles tend to align with familiar axes of tension within a particular group, even if those axes have been long-submerged. This could lead to important insights in the study of cultural nationalism, where its historicity is a key point of debate among scholars.

Perhaps the most innovative area of research on cultural nationalism focuses on the creation, dissemination and transformation of culture among its producers. Joep Leerssen, whom I discussed in depth, is a key scholar pushing this agenda. Leerssen reminds scholars that cultural nationalists are not merely agents of nationalism, but they are also agents of culture, whose ideas and practices reflect developments within their respective disciplines. This element of cultural nationalism has for too long been ignored. While Leerssen shows how the construction of the culture of nations was a European-wide phenomenon involving the sharing of ideas and practices, it would be fascinating to connect this to processes outside of Europe. Focusing more explicitly on processes related to developments within culture should also greatly add to debates on nationalism's future. If we are to take cultural nationalism seriously, then it should be in the field of culture where we look for clues as to its future.

# REFERENCES

Anderson, B. (1983) *Imagined Communities: Reflections on the Origin and Spread of Nationalism*. London: Verso.

Appadurai, A. (1990) 'Disjuncture and Difference in the Global Cultural Economy', *Theory, Culture & Society*, 7(2): 295–310.

Barnard, F. M. (2003) *Herder on Nationality, Humanity and History*. Montreal and Kingston: McGill-Queen's University Press.

Bhabha, H. K. (ed.) (2013 [1990]) *Nation and Narration*. London: Routledge.

Billig, M. (1995) *Banal Nationalism*. London: Sage.

Bracewell, W. (2000) 'Rape in Kosovo: Masculinity and Serbian Nationalism', *Nations and Nationalism*, 6(4): 563–590.

Breuilly, J. (2006 [1982]) *Nationalism and the State*. University of Chicago Press

Burke, P. (2008) *What Is Cultural History?* 2nd Edition. Cambridge: Polity.

Chatterjee, P. (1986) *Nationalist Thought and the Colonial World: A Derivative Discourse*. London: Zed Books.

Chatterjee, P. (1989) 'Colonialism, Nationalism, and Colonialized Women: The Contest in India', *American Ethnologist*, 16(4): 622–633.

Chatterjee, P. (1993) *The Nation and its Fragments: Colonial and Postcolonial Histories*. Princeton, NJ: Princeton University Press.

Doremus, A. (2001) 'Indigenism, Mestizaje, and National Identity in Mexico during the 1940s and the 1950s', *Mexican Studies*, 17(2): 375–402.

Edensor, T. (2002) *National Identity, Popular Culture and Everyday Life*. Oxford and New York: Berg.

Eley, G. and Suny, R. (eds) (1996) *Becoming National: A Reader*. Oxford: Oxford University Press.

Featherstone, M. (ed.) (1990) *Global Culture: Nationalism, Globalization and Modernity*. London: Sage, in association with *Theory, Culture & Society*.

Gans, C. (2000) 'The Liberal Foundations of Cultural Nationalism', *Canadian Journal of Philosophy* 30(3): 441–466.

Gellner, E. (2006 [1983]) *Nations and Nationalism*. Hoboken: Wiley-Blackwell.

Giddens, A. (1985) *The Nation-State and Violence*. Los Angeles and Berkeley: University of California Press.

Giddens, A. (1991) *Modernity and Self-identity: Self and Society in the Late Modern Age*. Stanford: Stanford University Press.

Gilroy, P. (2013) *Between Camps: Nations, Cultures and the Allure of Race*. London: Routledge.

Guibernau, M. and Hutchinson, J. (eds) (2004) *History and National Destiny: Ethnosymbolism and its Critics*. London: Wiley-Blackwell.

Guo, Y. (2004) *Cultural Nationalism in Contemporary China: The Search for National Identity under Reform*. London: Routledge.

Hall, S. (1993) 'Culture, Community, Nation', *Cultural Studies*, 7(3): 349–363.

Harris, R. (1993) 'The "Child of the Barbarian": Rape, Race and Nationalism in France During the First World War', *Past and Present*, 141: 170–206.

Higson, A. (1989) 'The Concept of National Cinema', *Screen*, 30(4): 36–47.

Hobsbawm, E. and Ranger, T. (eds) (1983) *The Invention of Tradition*. Cambridge: Cambridge University Press.

Hroch, M. (2000 [1985]) *Social Preconditions of National Revival in Europe: A Comparative Analysis of the Social Composition of Patriotic Groups among the Smaller European Nations*. New York: Columbia University Press.

Hutchinson, J. (1987) *The Dynamics of Cultural Nationalism: The Gaelic Revival and the Creation of the Irish Nation-State*. London: Allen and Unwin.

Hutchinson, J. (1994) *Modern Nationalism*. London: Fontana Press.

Hutchinson, J. (2003) 'Nationalism, Globalism and the Conflict of Civilizations', in Umut Özkirimli (ed.) *Nationalism and its Futures*. London: Palgrave Macmillan.

Hutchinson, J. (2005) *Nations as Zones of Conflict*. London: Sage.

Hutchinson, J. (2006) 'Hot and Banal Nationalism: The Nationalization of the "Masses"', in G. Delanty and K. Kumar (eds), *The SAGE Handbook of Nations and Nationalism*. London: Sage, pp. 295–306.

Hutchinson, J. (2013) 'Cultural Nationalism', in J. Breuilly (ed.), *The Oxford Handbook of the History of Nationalism*. Oxford: Oxford University Press, pp. 75–96.

Jusdanis, G. (2001) *The Necessary Nation*. Princeton, NJ: Princeton University Press.

Kandiyoti, D. (1991) 'Identity and its Discontents: Women and the Nation', *Millennium: Journal of International Studies*, 20(3): 126–149.

Kaufmann, E. (ed.) (2004) *Rethinking Ethnicity: Majority Groups and Dominant Minorities*. London: Routledge.

Kaufmann, E. and Haklai, O. (2008) 'Dominant Ethnicity: From Minority to Majority', *Nations and Nationalism*, 14(4): 743–767.

Kedourie, E. (1961) *Nationalism*, rev. edn. London: Hutchinson & Co.

Kohn, H. (1960 [1944]) *The Idea of Nationalism: A Study in its Origins and Background*, 5th edn. New York: Macmillan.

Kopf, D. (1969) *British Orientalism and the Bengal Renaissance: The Dynamics of Indian Modernization 1773–1835*. Berkeley, CA: University of California Press.

Kuzio, T. (2002) 'The Myth of the Civic State: A Critical Survey of Hans Kohn's Framework for Understanding Nationalism', *Ethnic and Racial Studies*, 25(1): 20–39.

Laitin, D. (2007) *Nations, States, and Violence*. Oxford: Oxford University Press.

Leerssen, J. (2006a) *National Thought in Europe: A Cultural History*. Amsterdam: University of Amsterdam Press.

Leerssen, J. (2006b) 'Nationalism and the Cultivation of Culture', *Nations and Nationalism*, 12(4): 559–578.

Leerssen, J. (2014) *When was Romantic Nationalism? The Onset, The Long Tail, The Banal*. Antwerp: NISE.

Leoussi, A. S. (1997) 'Nationalism and Racial Hellenism in Nineteenth-Century England and France', *Ethnic and Racial Studies*, 20(1): 42–68.

Mann, M. (1995) 'A Political Theory of Nationalism and its Excesses', in S. Periwal (ed.), *Notions of Nationalism*. Budapest: Central European Press, pp. 44–64.

McDonald, C. (2013) 'Britons in Maoriland', in R. Tsang and E. T. Woods (eds), *The Cultural Politics of Nationalism and Nation-Building: Ritual and Performance in the Forging of Nations*. London: Routledge, pp. 171–196.

Meinecke, F. (1970 [1907]) *Cosmopolitanism and the National State*, trans. R. B. Kimber. Princeton, NJ: Princeton University Press.

Mosse, G. (1985) *Nationalism and Sexuality: Middle-class Morality and Sexual Norms in Modern Europe*. Madison: University of Wisconsin Press.

Moretti, F. (2007) *Graphs, Maps, Trees*. London: Verso.

Nielsen, K. (1996) 'Cultural Nationalism, Neither Ethnic Nor Civic', *The Philosophical Forum*, 28(4): 2–51.

Olins, W. (2002) 'Branding the Nation – the Historical Context', *The Journal of Brand Management*, 9: 1–9.

Parker, A., Russo, M., Sommer, D. and Yaeger, P. (eds) (1992) *Nationalisms and Sexualities*. New York: Routledge.

Peel, J. (2003 [1989]) *Religious Encounter and the Making of the Yoruba*. Bloomington: Indiana University Press.

Penrose, J. (2002) 'Nations, States and Homelands: Territory and Territoriality in Nationalist Thought', *Nations and Nationalism*, 8(3): 277–297.

Proudfoot, L. J. and Roche, M. M. (2005) *(Dis) Placing Empire: Renegotiating British Colonial Geographies*. Aldershot, UK: Ashgate.

Sluga, G. (1998) 'Identity, Gender, and the History of European Nationalisms', *Nations and Nationalism*, 4: 87–111.

Smith, A. D. (1986) *The Ethnic Origins of Nations*. Oxford: Blackwell Publishers.

Smith, A.D. (1991) *National Identity*. Harmondsworth: Penguin.

Smith, A. D. (1995) 'Gastronomy or Geology? The Role of Nationalism in the Reconstruction of Nations', *Nations and Nationalism*, 1(1): 3–23.

Smith, A.D. (1998) *Nationalism and Modernism*. London: Routledge.

Smith, A. D. (2000) 'The "Sacred" Dimension of Nationalism', *Millennium – Journal of International Studies*, 29(3): 791–814.

Smith, A. D. (2003) *Chosen Peoples: Sacred Sources of National Identity*. Oxford: Oxford University Press.

Smith, A. D. (2010) *Nationalism: Theory, Ideology, History*, 2nd edn. Cambridge: Polity Press.

Smith, A. D. (2013a) *Nations and Nationalism in a Global Era*. Cambridge: Polity Press.

Smith, A. D. (2013b) *The Nation Made Real: Art and National Identity in Western Europe, 1600–1850*. Oxford: Oxford University Press.

Surak, K. (2013) *Making Tea, Making Japan: Cultural Nationalism in Practice*. Stanford: Stanford University Press.

Thiesse, A-M. (2001) *La création des identités nationales. Europe XVIIIe–XXe siècle*. Paris: Seuil.

Tilly, C (1975) 'Western State-making and Theories of Political Transformation', in C. Tilly (ed), *The Formation of National States in Western Europe*. Princeton, NJ: Princeton University Press. pp. 601–638.

Timmerman, C. (2000) 'Muslim Women and Nationalism: The Power of the Image', *Current Sociology*, 48(4): 15–27.

Turner, V. (1974) *Dramas, Fields and Metaphors: Symbolic Action in Human Society*. Ithaca: Cornell University Press.

Turner, V. (1986) *The Anthropology of Performance*. New York: PAJ Publishers.

Woods, E. T. and Debs, M. (2013) 'Towards a Cultural Sociology of Nations and Nationalism', *Nations and Nationalism*, 19(4): 607–614.

Yack, B. (1996) 'The Myth of the Civic Nation', *Critical Review*, 10(2): 193–211.

Yoshino, K. (1992) *Cultural Nationalism in Contemporary Japan: a Sociological Enquiry*. London: Routledge.

Yuval-Davis, N. (1997) *Gender and Nation*. London: Sage.

Zimmer, O. (2003) 'Boundary Mechanisms and Symbolic Resources: Towards a Process-oriented Approach to National Identity', *Nations and Nationalism*, 9(2): 173–193.

# Cultural Sociology of News Media

Ronald N. Jacobs

## INTRODUCTION

Media sociology appears to be making a comeback. New edited volumes assessing the field are appearing (e.g. Alexander et al., forthcoming; Waisbord, 2014), and media-focused articles are beginning to appear with slightly more regularity in the general-interest sociology journals (e.g. Bail, 2012; Brym et al., 2014; Couldry, 2014). A big reason for this resurgence is the growth and institutionalization of cultural sociology, whose practitioners have consistently recognized the central role that media play in people's lives. The British journal *Cultural Sociology* has regularly published work on media, as has the more recent *American Journal of Cultural Sociology*.

It is not surprising that cultural sociologists would be interested in the worlds of media and journalism. At the institutional level, the products that are produced by media organizations are centrally connected to a vast, interconnected, and global cultural industry. Today, virtually all cultural products are shaped by media institutions. Furthermore, because of the mediatization of social life, the Geertzian 'webs of significance' within which actors find themselves suspended are always already mediated webs. Contemporary society is a deeply intertextual space of linguistic, sonic, and iconic bricolage, in which people construct meanings about their world by combining and adapting scripts that they get from media texts, and in which those meanings frequently get posted in the various environments of user-generated media.

News media and journalism are not the only parts of the media world worth studying, but they remain one of the most important empirical sites of interest for cultural sociologists and media scholars alike. Journalists continue to act as key gatekeepers of the public sphere, even as their legitimacy is challenged by new arenas and styles of public debate, and even as the distinction between news and entertainment grows ever more porous (delli Carpini and Williams, 2011; Jacobs and Townsley, 2011). Audiences continue to turn to the products of journalism, even if they find those products in new ways, and even if they find them jumbled together with the other media content that streams in front of them in a nearly continuous scroll.

News media and journalism also remain important sites of research for cultural sociologists because they are connected to a long tradition of empirical research and social theory, which dates back to the very origins of disciplinary sociology. Because of this long history, news media and journalism offer key sites for assessing the past, present, and future contributions of cultural sociology. In what follows, I tell the story of media sociology, viewed through the lens of cultural sociology. It is a story of early promise, followed by neglect, and finally a hopeful and promising renaissance. In the process of telling this story, I also hope to show: (a) how media sociology is strongest when it is closely aligned with the project of cultural sociology; and (b) how media sociology can make important contributions and interventions into current cultural sociological debates.

## THE EARLY HISTORY: MEDIA SOCIOLOGY AS CULTURAL SOCIOLOGY

Media sociology can trace its origins back to two giants in the history of sociology, Max Weber and Robert Park. Max Weber planned a comprehensive empirical study of journalism, which he never completed (Hardt, 2001: 135–7). He did, however, give a lecture to the German Sociological Society on the sociology of the press in 1910, in which he argued that research on the press was perhaps the most important topic for a scientific sociology to pursue (Weber, 1976: 96). The questions Weber posed for a yet-to-be-formed media sociology are questions that are of continuing relevance for cultural sociology and media sociology alike.

For Weber's media sociology, there were three general topics of pressing importance. First, Weber wanted sociologists to explore the organization of publicity, focusing on what contemporary publicity looks like as well as what it was likely to look like in the future (Weber, 1976: 97). Recognizing the important gatekeeping function of the press, Weber (1976: 97) suggested that answering this question would involve a comparison of the kinds of topics that were most likely to be publicized by the newspaper.

Furthermore, because access to the press was such an important resource for generating publicity, Weber wanted to know how much of the media space was dominated by journalists, and what kinds of people besides journalists had the kind of access that allowed them to write regularly for the newspaper (Weber, 1976: 100).

The second topic of media research Weber identified was an examination of journalists and professional autonomy. Weber recognized that the modern newspaper was a business enterprise, and its practices were shaped in part by the pursuit of profit in the form of advertising. Weber wanted to understand how the economic incentives of media organizations influenced the process of public opinion formation, in the selection of newsworthy stories as well as the specific ways stories were written (Weber, 1976: 99–100). More generally, Weber (1976: 98) wanted to explore the balance of power that existed between the press, the business world, the political world, and the various collective interests coming from civil society.

Weber's third area of focus was the relationship between journalism and deliberation. In particular, Weber wanted to understand the difference between mediated and direct deliberation. He wanted to know whether social problems were discussed in the same way on the pages of the newspaper as they were outside of the newspaper (Weber, 1976: 101). Ultimately, Weber (1976: 100–1) argued, sociologists need to understand how media contribute to the making of the modern person; Weber argued that the existence of the press allowed the reader to become acquainted with an astonishing variety of public issues before ever leaving the house in the morning, but he was concerned that this might lead people to float over the surface of issues rather than exploring them in depth.

It is striking how closely the research agenda that Weber identified foreshadowed key concerns that cultural sociologists have today. Autonomy, deliberation, and the public sphere continue to be three of the most important theoretical concepts that cultural sociologists use to think about journalism. Like Weber, today's cultural sociologists remain interested in how the rise of mediated communication is connected to specific organizational and institutional systems. They are also interested in how different groups jockey to narrate the social, in an agonistic process of claims-making and discursive contestation.

Like Weber, Robert Park's media sociology was equally engaged with questions that would be seen, by today's standards, as cultural sociological issues. While Park is probably best known as a scholar of race, urban ecology, and collective behavior, he maintained a serious and sustained interest in mass media. This is not surprising, perhaps, given that Park spent ten years as a newspaper journalist before entering graduate school in 1898. Park's scholarly writing on the press began shortly after he joined the faculty of the University of Chicago's sociology department in 1914, and continued even after his formal retirement from the university.

Park's media sociology covered two related themes. Initially, the focus was on news and the power of the press. While the conceptual vocabulary was different, this work was clearly engaged with questions that today would invoke the language of media and public sphere. By the time he published 'News and the Power of the Press' in 1941, Park had a fully-developed theory of media and the public sphere. In essence, Park distinguished between an elite public sphere and a popular public sphere, and linked each to a specific part of the newspaper. The elite public sphere consisted of politicians, party leaders, and intellectuals, all of whom argued about how the events of the day supported or challenged specific policy proposals. For these elites, the editorial page was the most important part of the paper; having its origins in the letter to the editor – 'in which men interested in political matters sought to express their opinion in regard to debatable measures proposed or undertaken by the government' (Park, 1941a: 8) – the editorial was designed to interpret the news through a consistent and coherent political philosophy. Park thought that the editorial page and the elite public sphere could maintain significant influence and control over political society, particularly during periods of political stability, when there was more likely to be party discipline and when it was much easier for editorial columnists 'to maintain contact with events as recorded in the news' (Park, 1941a: 9).

On the other hand, during periods of change and social transformation, Park's theory of press and public sphere pointed to the importance of the news column and the way that it organized political discussion among ordinary citizens. Park argued that the news editor was not constrained by the demands of philosophical consistency, but rather by the goal of expanding the circle of readers. By publishing news items that would be of interest to the widest range of readers, the news editor helped to increase the number of people who were aware of what was going on in their society. And this allowed for the development of public opinion formation.

The second component of Park's media sociology was a focus on the different cultural forms of newspaper discourse. As early as his 1923 'Natural History of the Newspaper', Park argued that newspapers of the time were developing their own distinctive literary forms, which borrowed from fiction and other dramatic forms, in a way that made the cultural structure of the news story and the fiction story very similar (Park, 1923: 283–4). In fact, Park (1938: 204) argued that a good deal of what was printed in the newspaper – most notably, the human-interest story – was read by its audience as if it was literature, in the sense that it was read to stir the imagination rather than to focus public discussion or public action. The same was true of many breaking news stories, particularly when they were reported as a series of stories and updates:

> As a story it becomes more enthralling just because it is published in installments which give opportunity for readers to reflect, speculate, or brood over the significance of each successive installment. Under the circumstances readers of the news interpret these instances and all the details in terms of memories and of similar tragic episodes with which they are familiar. In this way the news ceases to be mere news and acquires the significance of literature, but of realistic literature like the 'true stories' of the popular magazines and of the earlier ballads that preceded them in the history of the newspaper. (Park, 1941b: 374–5)

Just as news frequently resembles literature, so too does literature follow the news, in its choice of subject matter as well as its use of specific poetic techniques. As Park (1940: 686) observed, 'Emile Zola's novels were essentially reports upon contemporary manners in France just as Steinbeck's *The Grapes of Wrath* has been described as an epoch-making report on the share-cropper in the United States'. Recognizing the deeply intertextual relationship between news and fiction, Park's reflections on journalism were surprisingly similar to arguments that cultural sociologists continue to make today (e.g. Alexander, 2006; Alexander and Jacobs, 1998; Jacobs, 2005; 2007).

## THE MOVEMENT AWAY FROM CULTURE

While Weber's and Park's media sociology was deeply cultural, and offered excellent resources for developing a cultural sociology, this possibility was undercut by a sharp turn away from culture in the sociology of media that developed in the 1960s and 1970s. As Gitlin (1978) has suggested, the 'dominant paradigm' of media sociology that developed in the 1960s and 1970s moved away from a concern with the cultural power of media texts. There were two parts to this. The first, which was part of a larger debate about mass society, challenged claims about the ideological power of media, and suggested an alternative argument about limited effects. The second part involved a close examination of news workers, and an emphasis on practical problem-solving and news routines as the key determinant of newsworthiness. Both were important conceptual moves for media sociology because they revealed important facts about the organizational and social embedding of media texts and media practices. Unfortunately for the purposes of moving forward a cultural sociology of media, both were dead ends.

## Debates about Mass Society, and the Idea of Limited Effects

If anything, developments in sociology during the 1940s suggested a rapid movement toward a media sociology that was predominantly cultural in its orientation. Concerns about media, ideology, and the cultural industries were central to the Frankfurt School's critical sociology (e.g. Adorno and Horkheimer, 1993; Lowenthal, 1984). Mass society theorists wrote about media's strong cultural effects, suggesting that media encouraged passivity, disengagement, and a retreat from public life (Kornhauser, 1959; Mills, 1956). Ultimately, these theories were undermined by their own hyperbole and overstatement. As sociologists sought to develop more empirically precise accounts of the relationship between media and their audiences (e.g. Freidson, 1953), they turned their attention toward social networks and away from social meanings.

By the end of the 1950s, the model of the socially connected media audience had largely come to replace the model of social isolation in mass society. As Katz and Lazarsfeld (1955) wrote in their path-breaking study, *Personal Influence*, the effects of mass culture are relatively small and limited, because they are mediated through: (1) the different uses they make of the media text; and (2) the specific networks to which they belong, as well as the dynamics of influence that operate within those networks. Rather than exploring meanings, Katz and Lazarsfeld's model of influence emphasized the interaction between audience uses, social networks, and the natural history of a news story. During earlier periods of a news story, the early adopters and informational elite who constitute the 'opinion leaders' of many social networks rely heavily on the press, but they use it primarily for information. As a story moved more generally into public focus, the opinion leaders took over, shaping deliberation and decision making within their social networks.[1] While they did not focus on meanings directly, the assumption in this model was that the cultural work was being done by opinion leaders. The press provided information, but the opinion leaders turned that raw information into meaningful narratives. This assumption was closely aligned with the dominant model of deliberation from that time, the model of the 'rational information-seeking citizen' (Jacobs and Townsley, 2011).

In more recent reflections, Katz has lamented the unintended consequences of the 'limited effects' paradigm (Pooley and Katz, 2008). With the discovery that the media were not as powerful as people had thought, sociologists lost interest in media and media sociology. From the perspective of cultural sociology, though, the lament is slightly different. By assuming that meaning construction existed somewhere outside the media, isolated in individual minds and small-group discussions, the limited effects paradigm led sociologists of media away from the more cultural questions that concerned Weber and Park. Forgetting about this earlier work, the sociology of news became part of organizational sociology. This movement was clearly ascendant in the newsroom studies of the 1970s, which came to define media sociology for nearly twenty years.

## The Newsroom Studies: Toward a Thin Model of Culture

The sociology of news that developed during the 1970s offers a good example of what Alexander and Smith (2003) have called a 'weak program' of cultural sociology. In other words, while media sociologists during this period insisted that news was a product of significant cultural consequence, their primary goal was to show how news outcomes could be explained without referring to larger social meanings. Specifically, the general argument of the newsroom studies was that news was a social accomplishment, which resulted from the attempt by news workers to solve the organizational problems that emerged from their work. Tuchman (1972), for example, argued that news workers defined 'objective facts' in a way that allowed them to protect themselves from internal and external critics. Most elements of news objectivity were designed to separate journalists from the risky demand of having to make truth claims, for example: presenting conflicting interpretations of a 'fact'; presenting supplementary evidence to support a fact; using quotation marks to signal that the reporter is not making a truth claim, but simply reporting the 'fact' of a truth claim; and carefully separating 'fact' and 'analysis' with clear labels attached to the latter. In a similar way, news workers relied upon typifications in order to force 'unexpected events' into normal news routines, and thereby to control the variability and contingency of news work.

Molotch and Lester (1974; 1975) also argued that media ideology could be explained as a reflection of organizational processes. Studying news coverage of an oil spill, for example, they found that federal officials and business spokesman had better access to news workers than conservationists or local officials. Like Tuchman, however, Molotch and Lester wanted to move beyond an explanation of this access as the result of conspiracy or coercion, and wanted to explain the finding as the result of routinized news gathering practices. Because federal executives and large corporations are routinely part of the news gathering process, it is easier and more natural to journalists to turn to these sources, even during non-routine news. This explains why non-routine news stories increase the privilege given to these sources as they continue to develop in time; as the story gets typified into a particular category of news story, the normal routines of news work come to exert an ever-greater influence over the news-making process (Molotch and Lester, 1975: 255–7).

Gans' (1979) ethnography of network television news in the US focused more attention on meanings, but like the other studies of the period he provided an account in which those meanings could be explained by social status and organizational considerations. Gans argued that journalists' 'values' shape their decisions about the news, and he pointed to key values such as ethnocentrism, responsible capitalism, and social order. But the origin of these values, according to Gans, was to be found in the professional and upper-middle-class social origins of the journalists themselves. For Gans, journalists' values have nothing to do with the cultural logic of professional journalism. Instead, they are connected to the status-seeking behavior of journalists, the organizational requirements of getting 'good sources', and power dynamics. Taken together, these three social processes explain the preference for 'important' and powerful sources: government leaders, business leaders, and the affluent.

While the newsroom studies were important and influential, they moved media sociology away from the more strongly cultural approach that was evident in the earlier work of Park and Weber. The interest in autonomy, deliberation, and the public sphere faded from view, and the model of journalism as meaningful action was replaced by a new model of journalists as status-seeking, practical, pragmatic actors enmeshed within deeply institutionalized organizational routines. The analytical focus was on news workers and news promoters, who were viewed as active participants in media production, participating in purposive behavior that was enmeshed within complex social networks. The people who consumed the news were rarely discussed, and when they were an object of consideration they were described as undiscriminating individuals who accepted the 'reality' of the news without recognizing its socially constructed nature.

# RECOVERING A CULTURAL SOCIOLOGY OF MEDIA: AUDIENCES, PUBLICS, AND JOURNALISTS AS MEANING-CENTERED ACTORS

Since the 1990s, we have seen the development of a renewed cultural sociology of media. Research on media audiences has documented the ways that readers and viewers use media texts to creatively and actively construct a meaningful set of narratives about themselves and the world around them. Research on journalists has explored the different ways that journalists struggle and compete to define what counts as good journalism. Research on the public sphere has reminded us that media spaces are not so much arenas for large debates as they are stages for large performances, on which powerful public actors compete to tell the most compelling narratives about matters of common concern.

## A Cultural Sociology of Media Audiences

While scholars from the field of Communications developed an entire paradigm of 'uses and gratifications' research during the 1960s and 1970s, their work was largely uninterested in the different meanings that audiences derived from their media consumption. A cultural sociology of media audiences began to develop in the late 1980s, and by the end of the 20th century it had become a well-established field of research.

The initial interest in meaning and media audiences came from British Cultural Studies, and was characterized by a strong focus on meaning and resistance. Stuart Hall's (2006 [1973]) iconic 'Encoding/Decoding' article provided the central question about audience meanings, which highlighted the extent to which people could resist hegemonically encoded texts by producing oppositional interpretations of the media products they were consuming. For example, while romance novels may be based on an underlying text that reinforces patriarchy, Radway (1983: 60–1) argued that women who read these novels see through the underlying message of the text, and reinterpret their act of reading as a temporary 'declaration of independence' from their regular social roles as wife and mother. For Morley and Brundson's study of television, the focus on audience resistance was even more explicit; showing a television news program to different kinds of people, they found that managers were more likely to make preferred (i.e., ideological) readings of the news text, while people who belonged to unions were more likely to make oppositional readings of those texts (Morley, 1980).

While these early studies were useful in pointing to the way that audiences actively engaged with the meanings of a media text, they were limited in two important respects. First, there was a tendency to decide in advance which audience characteristics mattered for interpretation. Second, the concern for resistant or oppositional interpretations was too constraining. In short, by deciding in advance which audience characteristics and which interpretive processes mattered, they were unable to capture the full complexity of audience meaning-making.

An important move toward a more nuanced cultural sociology of audiences was Press' (1991) research, which examined the meanings that working-class and middle-class women generated from their consumption of popular television programs. While Press found interesting class-based differences in interpretation, she emphasized the fact that most audience meanings were hybrid, multivalent, and referential. Middle-class viewers had a more playful and imaginative relationship with their television programs. They maintained a clearer awareness that they were watching fictional and exaggerated characters, but they enjoyed the process of identifying with (and fantasizing about) their favorite characters. Working-class viewers were more likely to accept the television settings as realistic, but they were also more likely to criticize the television characters for using their sexuality to gain power. In other words, the most critical readings were made by the people least likely to recognize the constructed nature of the text, in a way that was much more complicated than the model of encoding and decoding had suggested.

Perhaps the most important work in the cultural sociology of audiences was Liebes and Katz's (1990) *The Export of Meaning*. Rather than deciding in advance the criteria that mattered for audience interpretation, Liebes and Katz instead created focus groups composed of family members and friends, and let those groups view and discuss the global television hit *Dallas*. What they discovered was that viewers used the show as a forum to reflect upon their identities. Sometimes their discussions involved the kind of ideological deconstruction that Hall called 'oppositional readings'. But there were many other types of interpretations that emerged from the discussions. Groups used the television show to draw boundaries between their own ethnic group and other groups. They used characters on the program as a springboard for discussing current events. They discussed the aesthetic qualities of the programs, and the way those qualities helped to make the program successful (or not). And they had more playful and imaginative interpretations, trying to think, about why they identified with characters who were so different from themselves. In general, Liebes and Katz argued, audiences made referential readings of media texts, using them as a springboard for discussing matters of common concern.

Another important line of audience research was Grindstaff's (2002; 2014) work on reality television. Most of the early studies of reality television focused on the material factors that helped to explain its success, essentially arguing that programmers were attracted to the new genre because of its cost advantages, particularly in an industry environment characterized by shrinking niche audiences. Following this, research focused on the technological innovations produced by the new genre, in the way that it encouraged a synergistic mode of engagement across a variety of different media platforms. Similar to the earlier work, the presumed cause of this heightened engagement was material. By capturing the attention of the increasingly fickle and distracted audience, synergistic media platforms could increase advertising revenue for programmers.

Grindstaff's work was important because it focused on the world of meaning that is created in and around reality television. The shows may indeed be less expensive to produce, but this does not explain why people like them. What is powerful about this new genre is the way it allows for text and audience to co-produce a narrative that privileges emotion over information, confrontation over deliberation, and performance over expertise. These shows, together with the websites and coaching services that offer guidance on how to successfully get on a reality program, elevate the pursuit of celebrity as the signal aspiration for the postmodern age (Grindstaff, 2014). But attractions to these programs are also shaped by the larger public meanings about the genre. Producers and audiences of these shows are bound together by a sense of gnawing guilt, clearly aware that the larger public narrative denounces the genre as worthless trash. In this sense, as Liebes and Katz showed in their study of *Dallas*, audience meanings are always connected to public sphere discourses (see also Livingstone, 2005).

While there is a good deal of porousness between entertainment media and news media, there is still a good deal of work to be done to see if the kinds of interpretive practices that audiences use for entertainment programming also exist for news content. As Grindstaff's work suggests, and as I argue below, public meanings about news and entertainment are shaped by a clear cultural hierarchy that privileges news and aligns it with 'seriousness'. These issues have been taken up in the cultural sociology of media publics, but they have not yet been fully explored in the cultural sociology of media audiences.

## A Cultural Sociology of Media Publics

For cultural sociologists studying media and journalism, the concept of the public sphere has probably been the central axis around which research and debate have revolved. Referring to a particular type of communicative practice – the practice of open discussion about matters of common public concern – the concept owes much of its academic popularity to Jürgen Habermas, and the publication of his now-classic *The Structural Transformation of the Public Sphere*. Habermas argued that the creation of the public sphere was a crucial event in the history of democracy, because it led for the first time to the 'people's public use of their reason'. Claiming the space of public discourse from state regulation, and demanding that the state engage them in debate about matters of common concern, private citizens successfully campaigned to replace the dominant political practice of parliamentary secrecy with a new principle of open public discussion. Newspapers were at the center of this battle, as journalists fought for an official place in the Houses of Parliament, and as opposition parties realized that they could use political journalism to mobilize public opinion.

Habermas' theory of the public sphere has come under criticism from a number of different angles, most of which are relevant for developing a more cultural sociological approach. First, Habermas failed to appreciate how collective life is organized into a variety of different interpretive communities, each of which forms its own distinctive public sphere. Second, Habermas over-emphasized the importance of rational discourse, failing to appreciate how deliberation involves a variety of different cultural forms and formats. Finally, Habermas failed to recognize the ways that his preferred styles of communication could reinforce existing privileges while undermining the possibility for new forms of critique and discursive innovation.

My early work (Jacobs, 1996; 2000) was an empirical test of one of the most important criticisms of Habermas: namely, that his idealized vision of a single public sphere understated the historical importance played by alternative publics. Tracing the history of African-American newspapers in New York, Chicago, and Los Angeles, I compared African-American and 'mainstream' media coverage of the 1965 Watts riot, the 1991 Rodney King beating, the 1992 Los Angeles uprisings, and the 1995 O.J. Simpson verdict, and found that African-American newspapers continued to provide a distinct perspective on public issues that is missing in the majority media. Importantly, African-American news publics supported different kinds of stories than the mainstream media publics. The African-American press was more likely to rely on tragic and ironic narratives. They were also much more likely to narrate racial crisis as part of a long and ongoing historical sequence, rather than the first event in a putatively new narrative. These different narrative strategies allowed for much more complicated and reflexive meanings than the kinds of stories which circulated in the mainstream press.

For cultural sociologists, the biggest problem with Habermas' focus on rational-critical discourse was that it presented an overly narrow understanding of what actually happens in the public sphere. Rational deliberation is a rare presence in mediated public discussions. More commonly, people tell stories and they enact performances. They engage in symbolic communication, attempting to purify themselves and their allies while polluting their enemies. In other words, rational deliberation is one strategy among many. It is a normatively preferred strategy, occupying the sacred side of the 'discourse of civil society' (Alexander and Smith, 1993), but it is a discursive strategy rather than an unquestioned good. In other words, because rational-critical discourse is part of a larger semiotic system, it can be used either to open or close public debate (Jacobs, 2012). Rationality can be deployed as an ideal to be strived for, or it can be used as a symbolic weapon to exclude those who are considered to lack sufficiently rational qualities (Alexander, 2006). Trust can be used to create solidarity, or it can be used to pollute and exclude those who are seen as cynical, self-interested, and distrustful.

The normative preference for rational deliberation has influenced media research by encouraging scholars only to study 'objective journalism', and to denounce the presence of non-objective journalism wherever they see it. This is unfortunate, because media offer a much wider array of communicative forms which have been largely ignored by the research community. While the newspaper op-ed page, the political talk shows on television, and the more tabloid-influenced cable-news television lineup have an obvious and growing influence in politics and political communication, they have not been subject to close empirical analysis. As I argued in *The Space of Opinion* (Jacobs and Townsley, 2011), and as Park recognized nearly a century earlier, opinion media exist as a distinct social space with a unique history and an autonomous cultural logic. In the US, it is populated by journalists, politicians, academics, and the new sector of think tanks. Our research reveals a proliferation of genres and forms of opinion; not only have the people who speak within the space of opinion become more diverse over time, but the formats of opinion – claims to authority, styles of speech, and modes of addressing publics – have also become more varied.

Despite the climate of denunciation that typically surrounds opinion media, *The Space of Opinion* tells a more complicated story about the kinds of discourse that circulates in different media genres. Each opinion format has developed its own distinctive relationship to the wider journalistic field and its own understanding of the journalistic values regarding critique, autonomy, and complexity. Importantly, the proliferation of formats has produced discursive innovation and new forms of media reflexivity, in the sense that they generate a greater awareness about the mediated nature of all public sphere communication. To be sure, the growth of opinion media has developed alongside a more polarized civil society, in a manner that calls for careful scrutiny. But it has also encouraged a recognition that the ideal of rational deliberation is one position among many. Those who are committed to this ideal can no longer simply assume the hegemony of their principles. Rather, they are now forced to produce their own media meta-critique, criticizing the communicative styles they view as dangerous, and offering their own clear vision of what media intellectuals should be offering to the public and its citizens.

Recognizing that the mediated public sphere is a complicated cultural environment that includes a variety of aesthetic and performative structures, a number of cultural sociologists are beginning to think more seriously about the relationship between entertainment media and 'serious journalism'. Just as the sacred discourse of journalism and democracy privileges objective journalism over other types of journalistic discourse (Breese, 2012), so too does it draw a sharp normative distinction that privileges 'serious news' over a putatively trivial and diversionary world of entertainment (Jacobs, 2012). These normative preferences may create hierarchies that favor certain communicative styles and media formats, but the preferred and non-preferred styles are part of a common and densely intertextual cultural environment.

The relationship between entertainment media and serious journalism is the focus of a number of cultural sociologists who are doing research about the aesthetic public sphere. First introduced by Jones (2007) and Jacobs (2007; 2012), the concept of the aesthetic public sphere refers to 'all forms of aesthetico-cultural production – and their critical discussion – whose conditions of composition are sufficient to permit articulated dissent and advocacy (Jones, 2007: 88). The concept of the aesthetic public sphere recognizes that, for most people, their engagement with the creative industries is deeply meaningful, important, and a matter of common concern. It is part of their civic consciousness. As I have written elsewhere (Jacobs, 2012: 322), readers and viewers do not join a serious, civic, interpretive community when dealing with factual news media, or a trivializing, escapist one when they are interacting with fictional entertainment. These different styles of communication are mingled together in public discourse, rather than being separated by sharply defined boundaries.

At one level, aesthetic publics operate at the level of the social imaginary, providing important meaning structures and cultural scripts that people use to make sense of themselves and the world around them. As Alexander (2006: 76) has argued, fictional media organize characters and plots in a dichotomous manner, in which purity and pollution map quite easily and powerfully onto larger discourses about civil and uncivil motivations. This is clear enough with Balzac's Rastignac or Jane Austen's Elizabeth Bennett. But the same kinds of civically meaningful cultural scripts are available in more putatively debased forms of entertainment, such as television or video games. For example, Wu's (2013) research on the Chinese reality television program *Supergirl* showed how fans on Internet forums talked about the show and its contestants in terms of fairness, inequality, politics, and democracy. McKernan's (2013; 2015) research on video games suggests that self-consciously artistic video games challenge the social imaginary of their audiences, and that, while occurrences are somewhat uncommon, it is possible to design video games in a manner that encourages the cultivation of deliberative practices. In research on youth and political engagement, Inthorn, Street and Scott (2013) suggest that television, video games, and popular music help young people to learn about social issues and explore moral questions that are relevant for civic identities.

Because aesthetic texts are so frequently effective at engaging the social imaginary of their audience, they often help to organize and motivate public sphere debates taking place in the 'real world'. On the one, hand, we can think about the 'Arts' section of the newspaper as an important part of the public sphere, in which articles not only consider the aesthetic properties of entertainment but also engage in extended commentary about important social issues.[2] On the other hand, we can also identify instances when entertainers and entertainment products get inserted into the 'official' public sphere, as people who have something to say about a particular political issue or the larger climate of political discourse; this is particularly true for comedians and ironists, who are often highlighted for their ability to critically expose and deconstruct the strategic communication and 'spin' of professional politicians (Guhin, 2013; Jacobs and Wild, 2013).

Aesthetic publics are also important because they bring cultural policy discussions onto the public agenda in a way that encourages the idea that cultural citizenship is an important part of civil society. Within the field of Cultural Studies, where the questions of cultural policy and cultural citizenship have been central for a long time, debate seems to have foundered on the question of whether it is possible to maintain the spirit of critique while also providing 'useful knowledge' that can have an influence on cultural policymaking (e.g. Bennett, 1992; 2007; Cunningham, 2003; McGuigan, 2003). For cultural sociologists, however, the interest in cultural policy is more empirical, focusing on the actual public discourses that develop about the kinds of culture that ought to be available in order to make a 'better' society.

A cultural sociology of cultural policy has not fully emerged yet, though I have outlined some key issues that such a research program might consider (Jacobs, 2012). First, the research on cultural policy should be comparative in its orientation. For example, cultural policy debates in the US are quite unusual – not only because they assume American media hegemony, but also because they naturalize a market discourse in which audiences and advertisers will decide what will be available. In this model, debates about cultural policy are often connected to social movements, whose campaigns are targeted at convincing audiences and advertisers to boycott specific products. Outside of the US, foreign media has a much more visible presence, and the question of American cultural influence is a central topic of public debate (e.g. Jacobs, 2012).

## A Cultural Sociology of Journalists

Cultural sociology has also returned to the study of journalists themselves, by combining insights from two disparate sources: the cultural sociology of the public sphere, and the Bourdieuian theory of cultural fields. Challenging the central assumptions of the newsroom ethnographies, this work demonstrates clearly how journalists work to tell compelling stories and to make important distinctions about what counts as good journalism.

Schudson provided the first and the most significant intervention in what has become a cultural re-imagining of journalistic practice. In his classic work *Discovering the News*, Schudson (1978) examined how the ideal of objectivity came to define journalism. The rise of the penny press was an important part of the story, because the shift to advertising as their source of revenue meant that newspapers needed to emphasize impartiality as a way of increasing audience size. In time, these urban papers came to articulate egalitarianism in politics and social life, in a way that transformed who journalists thought they were (Schudson, 1978: 60). These new journalists waged a moral campaign against the sensationalist 'yellow journalism' of Pulitzer and Hearst, developing an alternative vision that privileged informational journalism and reasoned opinion. By the end of the 1960s, an adversarial culture had developed in which (1) journalists aggressively asserted their autonomy against attempts at government control, and where (2) journalists actively debated the best way to ensure that journalism would remain an autonomous institution that served democracy (Schudson, 1978: 176–93).

As journalists rediscovered and updated the literary traditions of their past in the 'new journalism' of the 1970s (see Schudson, 1978: 186–7), so too have cultural sociologists thought about the connection between narrative and newswork. Schudson (1978) argued that the modern news story displayed a clear narrative structure, organized around reporting conventions such as the summary lead and the inverted pyramid. Campbell (1991) showed how storytelling was the central feature of the influential television program *60 Minutes*, and argued that it was effective storytelling that established the legitimacy of the television magazine program. In an ethnographic study of a local television news station, I argued that narrative was at the center of most news routines (Jacobs, 1996). During each step of news production, journalists transformed events into potential stories. Events were perceived as newsworthy when they were recognized as plot elements in a news story, and they were legitimated as newsworthy by 'pitching the story' to news editors. News anchors did not merely read the stories, they performed them as scripts that fell into clearly defined genres. The work of journalism is more than an instrumental task of 'filling the news hole'; it is an interpretive practice that is deeply meaningful to its practitioners (Jacobs, 1996: 392).

Journalism is also meaningful because it is organized as a cultural field, shaped by distinctions and debates about what counts as good journalism.

As Bourdieu (1993) has argued, there are two competing principles that can be used to claim distinction within a cultural field. On the one hand, it is possible to achieve success according to structural logics operating outside the cultural field itself: for example, market success, proximity to economic or political elites, or alignment with the values or the rhetoric of a specific cultural or social movement.[3] On the other hand, cultural producers can achieve distinction by appealing to principles of classification that are internal to that specific cultural field. This involves considerations about what constitutes good art, literature, journalism, or science, as well as a consideration of the history of debates about these matters within the field.[4] For Bourdieu (1993: 661, 664), internalist principles of distinction define the 'privileged social universes' constructed by specific cultural groups who have established both the right to control the 'means of cultural production and diffusion' and also 'the power of evaluating themselves according to their own criteria'. It is these internalist principles of distinction that are related to the demand for autonomy.

If a normative theory of the public sphere asserts that the intellectual autonomy of speakers is always desirable and important, then a theory of cultural fields contributes the insight that the demand for autonomy will always be asserted against a range of alternative positions. Within the journalistic field, there are extremely powerful alternative positions that compete with high-end professional understandings of journalistic autonomy. Such alternative positions rely on external sources of distinction such as circulation size, audience ratings, and advertising revenue. In addition, because the journalistic field overlaps the political field, there is an important alternative position that comes from a journalist's proximity to political elites or to official representatives of the state (Bourdieu, 2005 [1994]; Darras, 2005). In fact, Bourdieu argues that journalism is a 'weakly autonomous' field, precisely because it is more easily steered by external sources of distinction than are other cultural fields like the academy or literature (Bourdieu, 2005 [1994]: 33). What this means is that journalism, at least in its dominant tendency (i.e., general-interest media), is more susceptible to the influence of money and power than are many other fields of cultural production (Benson and Neveu, 2005: 5). To be sure, the internalist principles of distinction are important too, and they are associated with the exercise of autonomy in the form of quality in-depth reporting and incisive commentaries on the op-ed page. Such marks of distinction are also usually sanctified through prestigious journalism awards such as the Pulitzer Prize or the Peabody Award (Benson and Neveu, 2005: 4; Revers, 2014a). But the point is that the commitment to these principles of distinction is a contested one.

Recent work by Revers (2014a; 2014b) reveals the insights that cultural sociologists can contribute when they examine journalists and their work as a contested terrain of meaning rather than an instrumental space of organizational routines. For example, while sources are clearly an important resource for journalists, Revers demonstrates that they are also an object of interpretation. Committed to the principle of autonomy, and recognizing that (government) sources are trying to use them strategically, journalists define themselves in terms of how they maintain professional boundaries with their sources, and they talk about other journalists through a cultural binary that demarcates pure and impure forms of boundary relationships. The same is true of their relationship with Twitter; while there were certainly economic motives that encouraged journalists to adopt this new media technology, the most important reasons for why they embraced the technology were largely cultural. The extent to which journalists adopted Twitter was closely related to how they defined good journalism. The most enthusiastic adopters were committed to a model of journalism that emphasized the sharing of information, mutual recognition of other journalists, and an ethic of transparency. Less enthusiastic adopters defined effective journalism through the language of objectivity, gatekeeping, and authoritative distance.

## CONCLUSION: THE FUTURE OF MEDIA SOCIOLOGY AS CULTURAL SOCIOLOGY

As I have tried to demonstrate, the new cultural sociology of the news represents a promising return to the original questions posed by Weber and Park. While others (e.g. Benson, 2009) suggest that media sociology should focus on social structure and social critique, my own position is that is should focus on the three meaning-centered issues that were first identified by Weber (if, perhaps, using different language): autonomy, deliberation, and the public sphere.

The new cultural sociology of media is also connected in significant ways to some of the key debates and insights that are of interest to cultural sociologists. Research on audiences has highlighted the different resources or scripts that people use to create meaning, and the hybrid ways that they combine media texts and everyday experience. Research on media and the public sphere has identified the important ways that intertextuality operates in public life, as part of a binary distinction between news and entertainment that is simultaneously porous and hierarchical. Research on journalists has shown how meanings about autonomy are connected to journalists' identities as well as the cultural fields in which they find themselves situated. And all of this research demonstrates an awareness of the importance of cultural performance in public life. Cultural sociologists have clear contributions to make to a resurgent media sociology, in the past as well as the future.

## NOTES

1. Media still had a strong (though more indirect) influence during this second phase of interpersonal influence, because the most influential members of many social networks were those early adopters and informational elites who were most involved with media products. Gitlin (1978) made a big point of this fact in a critique of the Katz and Lazarsfeld paradigm, arguing that the two-step flow model actually demonstrated the great power of media, even if it posited a more indirect model of media power. A closer reading of Katz and Lazarsfeld, however, shows that Gitlin probably overstated this critique, and that Katz and Lazarsfeld did in fact account for the continued relevance of media power during both phases of social influence (see e.g. Katz, 1960: 440).
2. See Jacobs and Townsley (2011) on television criticism, McKernan (2015) on video game criticism, and Debs (2013) on art criticism.
3. As Benson (2008; 2009) has argued, Bourdieu tends to focus on market principles as the primary source of heteronomous principles of classification; for a more useful theory of the journalistic field, Benson suggests that greater attention needs to be paid to how a wider range of political and cultural forces can act as 'external' classification principles available to actors within the journalistic field.
4. One of Bourdieu's primary interests is to try to connect the range of cultural distinctions that are deployed in a cultural field to the social-structural resources and backgrounds of the different participants. This interest is not necessary in order to leverage the analytical usefulness of the theory of cultural fields. Indeed, if one is interested in cultural actions that take place at the intersection of multiple fields, the focus on class habitus becomes increasingly difficult to sustain, as is evidenced by its relative absence in Bourdieu's work on television (Bourdieu, 1998) and journalism (Bourdieu, 2005 [1994]).

## REFERENCES

Adorno, T. and Horkheimer, M. (1993) *Dialectic of Enlightenment*. New York: Continuum Books.

Alexander, J. C. (2003) 'The Strong Program in Cultural Sociology: Elements of a Structural Hermeneutics', in J. Alexander (ed.), *The Meanings of Social Life*. Oxford: Oxford University Press. pp. 11–26.

Alexander, J. C. (2006) *The Civil Sphere*. Oxford: Oxford University Press.

Alexander, J. C. and Jacobs, R. N. (1998) 'Mass Communication, Ritual, and Civil Society', in T. Liebes and J. Curran (eds), *Media, Ritual, and Identity*. London: Routledge. pp. 23–41.

Alexander, J. C. and Smith, P. (1993) 'The Discourse of American Civil Society: A New Proposal for Cultural Studies', *Theory and Society*, 22(2): 151–207.

Alexander, J. C., Breese, E. and Luengo, M. (eds) (forthcoming) *The Crisis of Journalism Reconsidered*. Cambridge: Cambridge University Press.

Bail, C. A. (2012) 'The Fringe Effect: Civil Society Organizations and the Evolution of Media Discourse about Islam since the September 11th Attacks', *American Sociological Review*, 77: 855–79.

Bennett, T. (1992) 'Putting the Policy into Cultural Studies', in L. Grossberg, C. Nelson, and P. Treichler (eds), *Cultural Studies*. New York: Routledge. pp. 23–34.

Bennett, T. (2007) *Critical Trajectories: Culture, Society, Intellectuals*. Oxford: Blackwell.

Benson, R. (2008) *Framing Immigration: How the French and American Media Shape Public Debate*. Cambridge: Cambridge University Press.

Benson, R. (2009) 'Shaping the Public Sphere: Habermas and Beyond', *American Sociologist* 40: 175–92.

Benson, R. and Neveu, E. (eds) (2005) *Bourdieu and the Journalistic Field*. Cambridge: Polity Press.

Bourdieu, P. (1993) *The Field of Cultural Production*. New York Columbia University Press.

Bourdieu, P. (1998) *On Television*. NY: New Press.

Bourdieu, P. (2005 [1994]) 'Political, Social Science, and Journalistic Fields', in R. Benson and E. Neveu (eds), *Bourdieu and the Journalistic Field*. Cambridge: Polity. pp. 29–47.

Breese, E. (2012) *Interpreting the News: A Cultural Sociology of Journalistic Discourse in the United States*. PhD Dissertation, Yale University.

Brym, R., Godbout, M., Hoffbauer, A., Menard, G. and Huiquan, T. (2014) 'Social Media in the 2011 Egyptian Uprising', *British Journal of Sociology*, 65: 266–92.

Campbell, R. (1991) *60 Minutes and the News*. Urbana, IL: University of Illinois Press.

Couldry, N. (2014) 'A Necessary Disenchantment: Myth, Agency, and Injustice in a Digital World', *Sociological Review*, 62: 880–97.

Cunningham, S. (2003) 'Cultural Studies from the Viewpoint of Cultural Policy', in J. Lewis and T. Miller (eds), *Critical Cultural Policy Studies*. Oxford: Blackwell. pp. 13–22.

Darras, E. (2005) 'Media Consecration of the Political Order', in R. Benson and E. Neveu (eds), *Bourdieu and the Journalistic Field*. Cambridge: Polity Press. pp. 156–73.

Debs, M. (2013) 'The Suffering of Symbols: Giotto Frescoes and the Cultural Trauma of Objects', *Cultural Sociology*, 7: 479–94.

delli Carpini, M. and Williams, B. (2011) *After Broadcast News*. Cambridge: Cambridge University Press.

Debs, M. (2013) 'The Suffering of Symbols: Giotto Frescoes and the Cultural Trauma of Objects', *Cultural Sociology* 7: 479–494.

Freidson, E. (1953) 'Communications Research and the Concept of the Mass', *American Sociological Review*, 18(3): 313–17.

Gans, H. (1979) *Deciding What's News*. New York: Vintage.

Gitlin, T. (1978) 'Media Sociology: The Dominant Paradigm', *Theory and Society*, 6: 205–53.

Grindstaff, L. (2002) *The Money Shot: Trash, Class, and the Making of TV Talk Shows*. Chicago: University of Chicago Press.

Grindstaff, L. (2014) 'The Importance of Being Ordinary: Celebrity in the Age of Reality TV', paper presented at the Annual Meeting of the American Sociological Association, San Francisco, California.

Guhin, J. (2013) 'Is Irony Good for America: The Threat of Nihilism, the Importance of Romance, and the Power of Cultural Forms', *Cultural Sociology*, 7: 23–38.

Habermas, J. (1989) *The Structural Transformation of the Public Sphere*. Cambridge, MA: MIT Press.

Hall, S. (2006) 'Encoding/Decoding', in M. Durham and D. Kellner (eds), *Media and Cultural Studies*. Oxford: Blackwell. pp. 163–73.

Hardt, H. (2001) *Social Theories of the Press*. Lanham, MD: Rowman and Littlefield.

Inthorn, S., Street, J., and Scott, M. (2013) 'Popular Culture as a Resource for Political Engagement', *Cultural Sociology*, 7: 336–51.

Jacobs, R. N. (1996) 'Producing the News, Producing the Crisis: Narrativity, Television, and News Work', *Media, Culture & Society*, 18(3): 373–97.

Jacobs, R. N. (2000) *Race, Media, and the Crisis of Civil Society: From Watts to Rodney King*. Cambridge: Cambridge University Press.

Jacobs, R. N. (2005) 'Media Culture(s) and Public Life', in M. Jacobs and N. Hanrahan (eds), *Blackwell Companion to the Sociology of Culture*. Cambridge, MA: Blackwell. pp. 80–96.

Jacobs, R. N. (2007) 'From Mass to Public: Rethinking the Value of the Culture Industry', in J. Alexander and I. Reed (eds), *Culture in the World, Vol. 1: Cultural Sociology and the Democratic Imperative*. Boulder, CO: Paradigm Press. pp. 101–28.

Jacobs, R. N. (2012) 'Entertainment Media and the Aesthetic Public Sphere', in J. Alexander, R. Jacobs, and P. Smith (eds), *Oxford Handbook of Cultural Sociology*. Oxford: Oxford University Press. pp. 318–42.

Jacobs, R. N. and Townsley, E. (2011) *The Space of Opinion*. Oxford: Oxford University Press.

Jacobs, R. N. and Wild, N. M. (2013) 'A Cultural Sociology of *The Colbert Report* and *The Daily Show*', *American Journal of Cultural Sociology*, 1: 69–95.

Jones, P. (2007) 'Beyond the Semantic "Big Bang": Cultural Sociology and an Aesthetic Public Sphere', *Cultural Sociology*, 1: 73–95.

Katz, E. (1960) 'Communication Research and the Image of Society: Covergence of Two Traditions', *American Journal of Sociology*, 65: 435–440.

Katz, E. and Lazarsfeld, P. F. (1955) *Personal Influence: The Part Played by People in the Flow of Mass Communications*. Glencoe, IL: Free Press.

Kornhauser, W. (1959) *The Politics of Mass Society*. New York: Free Press.

Liebes, T. and Katz, E. (1990) *The Export of Meaning: Cross-Cultural Readings of Dallas*. Cambridge: Polity Press.

Livingstone, S. (2005) 'On the Relation Between Audiences and Publics', in S. Livingstone (ed), *Audiences and Publics*. Bristol: Intellect Books. pp. 17–42.

Lowenthal, Leo (1984) *Literature and Mass Culture*. New Brunswick and London: Transaction Books.

McGuigan, J. (2003) 'Cultural Policy Studies', in J. Lewis and T. Miller (eds), *Critical Cultural Policy Studies*. Oxford: Blackwell. pp. 23–42.

McKernan, B. (2013) 'The Morality of Play: Video Game Coverage in the New York Times from 1980 to 2010', *Games and Culture*, 8: 307–29.

McKernan, B. (2015) 'The Meaning of a Game: Stereotypes, Video Game Commentary, and Color-Blind Racism', *American Journal of Cultural Sociology*, 3: 224–53.

Mills, C. Wright (1956) *The Power Elite*. Oxford: Oxford University Press.

Molotch, H. and Lester, M. (1974) 'News as Purposive Behavior: On the Strategic Use of Routine Events, Accidents, and Scandals', *American Sociological Review*, 39: 101–12.

Molotch, H. and Lester, M. (1975) 'Accidental News: The Great Oil Spill as Local Occurrence and National Event', *American Journal of Sociology*, 81: 235–60.

Morley, D. (1980) *The Nationwide Audience*. London: British Film Institute.

Park, R. (1923) 'Natural History of the Newspaper', *American Journal of Sociology*, 29: 273–89.

Park, R. (1938) 'Reflections on Communication and Culture', *American Journal of Sociology*, 44: 187–205.

Park, R. (1940) 'News as a Form of Knowledge: A Chapter in the Sociology of Knowledge', *American Journal of Sociology*, 45: 669–86.

Park, R. (1941a) 'News and the Power of the Press', *American Journal of Sociology*, 47: 1–11.

Park, R. (1941b) 'Morale and the News', *American Journal of Sociology*, 47: 360–77.

Pooley, J. and Katz, E. (2008) 'Further Notes on Why American Sociology Abandoned Mass Communication Research', *Journal of Communication*, 58: 767–86.

Press, A. (1991) *Women Watching Television*. Philadelphia: University of Pennsylvania Press.

Radway, J. (1983) 'Women Read the Romance: The Interaction of Text and Context', *Feminist Studies*, 9: 53–78.

Revers, M. (2014a) 'Journalistic Professionalism as Performance and Boundary Work', *Journalism*, 15: 37–52.

Revers, M. (2014b) 'The Twitterization of Newsmaking: Transparency and Journalistic Professionalism', *Journal of Communication*, 64: 806–26.

Schudson, M. (1978) *Discovering the News*. New York: Basic Books.

Tuchman, G. (1972) 'Objectivity as Strategic Ritual: An Examination of Newsmen's Notions of Objectivity', *American Journal of Sociology*, 77(4): 660–79.

Waisbord, S. (ed.) (2014) *Media Sociology: A Reappraisal*. Cambridge: Polity Press.

Weber, M. (1976) 'Toward a Sociology of the Press', *Journal of Communication*, 26: 96–101.

Wu, J. (2013) 'Cultural Citizenship at the Intersection of Television and New Media', *Television and New Media*, 14: 402–20.

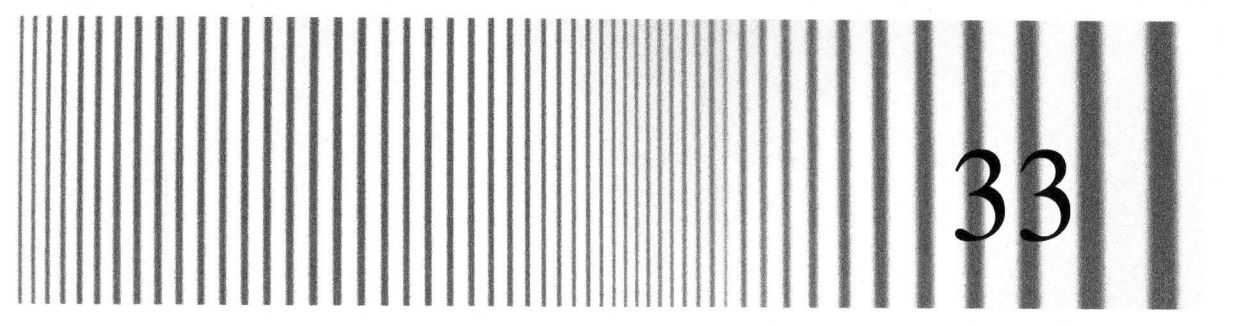

# Cultural Memory

Brad West

## INTRODUCTION

In this chapter the notion of 'cultural memory' is used broadly to refer to the ways in which people make sense of the present by recalling and engaging with the past. While ultimately it is individuals that remember history, cultural memory research is concerned with how this is influenced by public attitudes, beliefs, commemorations, emotions, ideologies and power structures of the current age. The dynamics of cultural memory are of sociological interest as they reflect and influence social order. This occurs by either allowing key historical events or figures to remain culturally relevant in the face of rapid social changes or by providing contemporary social identities, beliefs and practices with a primordial guise.

## MEMORY, SOCIOLOGY AND CULTURAL STUDIES

Like most subject matter studied by sociology, cultural memory is of interest to scholars in cognate areas. These include the disciplines of anthropology, geography, history and psychology.

In recent years there have also been attempts to form a new intellectual field of social memory studies, something that is currently being spearheaded by the journal *Memory Studies* (Roediger and Wertsch, 2008). While social memory studies is typically thought of as an interdisciplinary project that works at the intersection of the above disciplines, much of its core derives from the interdisciplinary field of British cultural studies (Radstone, 2008). The differences between the cultural sociology of memory and social memory studies then are like those between cultural sociology and British cultural studies. As outlined in other chapters of this Handbook, to the extent that it is possible or desirable to distinguish between the two areas (McLennan, 2006; Seidman, 1991), they differ in relation to cultural sociology's greater concern for issues of measurement, an emphasis on culture having a causal significance, and an analytic and methodological concern beyond cultural representations to empirically analyse how the symbolic maps onto attitudes and social action (Alexander and Smith, 2010; Inglis, 2007; Jacobs and Spillman, 2005; Schudson, 1997; Smith and West, 2003).

Memory research though holds somewhat of a liminal position within cultural sociology, in various ways being both core and peripheral to the sub-discipline. It has been a core focus of much foundational work in the area (Bellah, 1967; Shils and Young, 1956; Warner, 1959). Studies of cultural memory are also amongst the most prominent and influential within cultural sociology today (Alexander, 2009; Bennett, 2013; Eyerman, 2002;Fine, 2001; Schudson, 1992; Schuman and Rogers, 2004; Schwartz, 2008; Spillman, 1997; Wagner-Pacifici and Schwartz, 1991; Zelizer, 1998; Zerubavel, 2003). The intellectual significance of memory research also looks set to continue with the emergence of a younger generation of scholars analysing memory in order to advance theoretical and methodological debates in the discipline as a whole (Conway, 2010; Edkins, 2003; Levy and Sznaider, 2010; Olick, 2007; West, 2008).

In other ways, however, cultural memory research is situated as quite marginal to the burgeoning field of cultural sociology and sociology more broadly. It is a theme relatively absent in classical sociology. While classical scholars occasionally note that a consciousness of the past is a key characteristic of modernity (e.g. Durkheim, 1968 [1912]: 427; Mannheim, 1936: 84; Marx, 1962 [1852]: 247; Mead, 1929: 130), no classical scholar engages in a sustained analysis of memory or outlines 'rules' for studying it. While today cultural memory certainly attracts a vast amount of scholarly attention in sociology, it is typically missing or marginal within recent accounts of cultural sociology (Alexander and Smith, 2010; Jacobs and Spillman, 2005). A large proportion of this research done on memory also comes from scholars not primarily interested in cultural memory, with memory being an avenue to better understand other spheres and dynamics of social life. Traditionally this memory scholarship derived from the analysis of state power and concentrated on institutional contexts for remembering the past. For example, there is a great deal of analysis of memory as it relates to museums (Bennett, 2013; Macdonald, 2009), political response to crisis periods (Berezin, 1997; Collins, 2004; Edkins, 2003) and educational curriculums (FitzGerald, 1979; Goodson et al., 2006; McKiernan, 1993). Today cultural memory research is just as likely to emerge from investigations focused upon popular culture (Lipsitz, 1990), illuminating the role of informal mnemonic devices in our perceptions of the past. For example, we have seen a proliferation of memory studies into online and digital media (Garde-Hansen et al., 2009; Neiger et al., 2011; van Dijck, 2007); television and film (Grainge, 2003; Leavy, 2005); genealogy (Erbin, 1991); music (Keightley and Pickering, 2006); literature (Griswold, 2000); and recreational and tourist activities (Crang, 1996; Edensor, 2001; Urry and Larson, 2012). While both intellectual traditions provide important insights into the dynamics of memory, the derivative nature of such scholarship has meant that the cultural sociology of memory has been a fragmented field.

## TRADITIONS OF MEMORY

In recent decades there have been important attempts made in establishing greater coherence in the cultural sociology of memory and in developing a comprehensive theory of cultural memory (Middleton and Edwards, 1990; Olick, 1999). This has been facilitated by the field's creation of a European foundation story for itself (Connell, 1997) concentrating on the work of Maurice Halbwachs (1952 [1925]; 1941; 1950; 1992). As a colleague of the classical sociologist Émile Durkheim and an editorial board member of *L'Année Sociologique*, Halbwachs was writing about the reshaping of memory at the turn of the 20th century. However, his canonical status is principally retrospective as he was largely unknown in English-speaking sociology until Coser's (1991) translation of his collected works in 1991 (Schwartz, 1996a: 276). Halbwachs though now plays a pedagogical defining role, both by informing the intellectual scope of memory research in cultural sociology as well as in providing a focus of critique in debates about the limitations of established approaches to studying memory.

Halbwachs' analysis revolved around the concept of collective memory which he defined as 'essentially a reconstruction of the past [which] adapts the image of ancient facts to the beliefs and spiritual needs of the present' (1941: 7). According to Halbwachs, history begins only when the social memory of individual witnesses to the past starts to fade (Halbwachs, 1950: 78). As those who give personal testament to events die off, memory begins to manifest itself in qualitatively new ways. Often motivated by the loss of witnesses, historians and other entrepreneurs of the past seek to record what is known, to preserve it for future generations. In writing it down, however, they not only mark it as something worth remembering but frame it within a public narrative (Halbwachs, 1950: 79) which requires a minimal coherence of facts and consistency of genre. Once in this (re) collective form, interpretations of the past are more strongly influenced by present concerns and spiritual needs (Halbwachs, 1941: 7).

This focus on memory is significant within cultural sociology as it addresses the limitations of Durkheim's theories about symbolic classification systems and ritual, in particular by addressing how symbols endure outside ritual times of 'collective effervescence' (Coser, 1991: 25). Halbwachs' work also addresses the issue of historical variability in relation to ritual, something Durkheim did not systematically cover in his classical work *The Elementary Forms of Religious Life* (1968 [1912]). While Halbwachs primarily sought to distinguish between individual and collective memory, he saw the latter as essentially a product of modernity, arising as a consequence of a severing of organic connections to the past. For Halbwachs, collective memory becomes established with the breakdown of accepted history being passed along generationally, initiating a process by which the past becomes a site of preservation, narrative revision and reproduction in new forms of symbolic representation and engagement.

An emphasis on the qualitative differences of memory in pre-modern and modern eras is also a characteristic of the writings of a number of cultural historians of memory whose works have become influential within cultural sociology. Eric Hobsbawm, for example, has argued that pre-modern Europe engaged with the past in terms of custom, involving a loose and broadly local transmission of convention in rather uncontroversial ways (Hobsbawm, 1983: 2). Associating historical engagement with the formation of the nation, Hobsbawm argues that only in the modern era does history become the basis of grand narratives with historical interpretation open to 'invention' and political manipulation. Pierre Nora (1996) argues something similar in contrasting engagement with the past in pre-literate and literate societies. While Nora (1996) argues the former involved a 'real memory' that was embedded within the routines of daily life, such as within song and ceremony, in the present age the past becomes an object we feel impelled to capture, archive and recall.

Hobsbawn and Nora, however, also signify two intellectual trajectories in cultural memory scholarship, including within cultural sociology, that diverge from that of Halwbachs. Following Halbwachs, various cultural sociologists have focused on generational differences in comprehending historical events and figures and how the meaning of history has come to reflect the cultural ethos of the era (Larson and Lizardo, 2007; Schuman and Corning, 2012; Schwartz and Schuman, 2005). While this work emphasises the constructed nature of the past, it tends to de-emphasise political power and elite interests. An alternative critical perspective emerged within cultural sociology, largely drawing on Eric Hobsbawm's influential conceptualisation of the invention of tradition (1983). For Hobsbawm (1983) an invented tradition is a set of practices which inculcates certain values and norms by repetition. As the term is used, it refers to two phenomena. Firstly 'traditions' that can be shown to have been actually invented by elites. Secondly, traditions whose origins are more difficult to establish, but which have been seized upon to symbolise membership and social cohesion. Trevor-Roper (1983) provides a famous illustration of the invention of tradition. He argues that the Scottish kilt is not the product of antiquity it is believed to be. The modern form was designed by an English Quaker and developed after the union with England. Furthermore, it was created to facilitate industrial work and enhance productivity, not to emblematise Highland culture. During the 18th century, however, the Highland tradition was re-written as the authentic Scottish tradition, and the invented form of kilt was adopted as a key national symbol.

The critical tradition in memory research places a greater emphasis on the fabricated nature of history, however; like the generational research into cultural memory, it assumes that the past is a constant resource for legitimising the present. In contrast, Nora (1996) adopts the postmodern paradigm to argue that the grand narratives of modernity have been replaced with a new present-focused social world lacking a sense of continuity (Baudrillard, 1983) and bereft of emotional affect (Jameson, 1991: xv). As Nora argues, rather than our present engagement with the past reflecting a continuation of modern forms of meaning-making, 'memory is constantly on our lips because it no longer exists' (1996: 1). For postmodern scholars it is a detachment from the past which ironically explains the contemporary 'memory boom' (Huyssen, 1995), in which we have seen an unprecedented widespread interest in history, ranging from increased sales of popular history books, to the production of Hollywood period films, new documentary forms and television 'history reality' genres. Consistent with this theoretical approach Nora's (1996) analysis of French social memory focuses upon the cultural significance of the everyday *lieux de memoire* (sites of memory), such as texts, objects and themes of popular culture, rather than official state-sanctioned commemorative forms which were the focus of early sociological studies that emphasised the role of ritual for socially integrating societies (Lukes, 1975).While traditional commemorative forms continue, for Nora these are simply 'fleeting incursions of the sacred ... vestiges of parochial loyalties ...' (1996: 7), 'rituals of a ritual-less society' that is 'busily effacing all parochialisms' (1996: 7).

Other scholars working from the postmodern paradigm have focused upon the contestation and social conflict which now surrounds history, inferring that it illustrates that the past is no longer able to provide a basis for social consensus. Sturken (2007), for example, has argued that historical discontinuity and a postmodern sensibility are reflected in the debate and controversies surrounding selecting appropriate forms of mourning and commemoration at New York's 'Ground Zero' following the September 11 terrorist attacks. The validity of theories about postmodernity and culture, of course, have been widely debated in sociology (Lemert, 2005; Mirchandani, 2005; Seidman, 1991; Woodward et al., 2000). However, as postmodern theory relates to historical abandonment and social conflict, it is important to note that it is broadly consistent with contemporary social theory's emphasis on societal transformation and fragmentation. For example, Anthony Giddens' influential theorising of de-traditionalisation (1994) argues that globalisation and late capitalism have made cultural patterns no longer influential in individual identity construction and decision-making. To the extent that such scholarship sees the past as a site of cultural engagement it is one that is associated with regressive ideologies, history being a fundamentalist refuge from the complexities of the contemporary world.

## MEMORY PRACTICES, AGENCY AND PERFORMANCE

Despite accounting for variability in levels and depth of engagement with the past, like generational and critical perspectives on memory, the postmodern paradigm contends that understandings and engagements with the past reflect contemporary social structures. The structural emphasis of this approach can be problematic in comprehending the contingent and dynamic dimensions of mnemonic practices and meaning-making. Cultural sociologists in recent years have increasingly looked to address this limitation by better accounting for agency and performance. One way agency has been accounted for in the study of memory is through a greater interactionist focus on the role of individuals in advancing particular understandings of the past (Fine and Beim, 2007). For example, Gary Alan Fine uses the term reputational entrepreneurs (2001) to document the role of influential individuals in establishing popular and formal understandings of history. While the original application of such concepts has been on institutional and cultural elites, more recently the term has been utilised to identify individuals and groups that are closer to the periphery of society but play a key role in the production of culture. For example, in his studies of commemoration and travel by Australians to the World War I Gallipoli battlefields, West (2008) emphasises the role of young Australian tourists and local tour guides in providing new historical narratives that are subsequently taken up within formal political discourse.

Cultural sociologists have also been increasingly attentive to performative social action, particularly its role in challenging dominant historical narratives. While symbolic action has always been a core part of the study of memory, this has typically been considered in relation to mass ritual forms. In contrast, performance studies examine less institutional forms of politics as they relate to new social movements. An important part of this analytic shift has been reconceptualising Habermas' (1989) notion of the public sphere to account for diversity and counter-narratives within domestic and international public debate (Conway, 2010; Olick, 1999). For example, the contested nature of memories surrounding the state repression and human rights abuses in Argentina, Chile and Uruguay during the 1970s and 1980s has been a fertile ground for thinking about the multiple ways in which counter-narratives attain cultural resonance in the public sphere. Studies in this area have particularly pointed to the ritual protests of women and the way they use domestic identities to provide an affective resistance to state sanctioned silences, such as that surrounding the children who 'disappeared' as a consequence of state terrorism (Bell and Di Paolantonio, 2009; Fried, 2006; Lessa and Druliolle, 2011).

This performative turn in memory studies has resulted in a declining influence of the binary classifications that align memory practices with historical eras, for example in relation to analytic distinctions made between the concepts of history, memory, tradition and custom. Instead we have seen new typologies emerge focused on the multitude of mnemonic populations and practices (Conway, 2010), with an appreciation of the enduring relevance of oral traditions and everyday experiences for remembering the past (Assman, 1992; Bodnar, 1992; Connerton, 1989; Zerubavel, 1997). As well as the term cultural memory, which elsewhere has been used to specifically refer to memory being informed by civil society and popular culture (Assman, 1992; Sturken, 1997), the proliferation of terms used in regards to the process of remembering include: communicative memory (Assmann, 1992); cosmopolitan memory (Levy and Sznaider, 2006); diasporic memory (Baronian et al., 2007); generational memory (Schman and Scott, 1989); historical memory; social memory (Burke, 1989); postmemory (Hirch, 1997); prosthetic memory (Landsberg, 2004); and witnessing (Wagner-Pacifici, 2006; Zelizer, 2002).

## TRADITIONAL AND COSMOPOLITAN MEMORY

This chapter will conclude by arguing that the study of cultural memory should not only examine the malleability of history but how meaning endures over time. As Schudson (1989) argues, while it is true that the present shapes the past, the opposite is equally the case. Possible strategies for studying memory from this perspective can be seen in the way cultural sociologists currently utilise the work of two key theorists in the field: Edward Shils and Clifford Geertz. Edward Shils' theorising of societies as having a centre and periphery and his work on charisma (1975) have been widely used by cultural sociologists, including in the study of cultural memory (Smith, 2000; Spillman, 1997). However, the essays that appear in Shils' published collection *Tradition* (1981) have been far less cited in cultural sociology. For Shils, tradition is not simply that which is framed as traditional but the persistence of cultural forms at multiple levels. Shils most notably defined tradition as anything 'handed down from one generation to the next' (1981: 12). This included 'material objects, beliefs about all sorts of things, images of persons and events, practices and institutions' as well as 'buildings, monuments, landscapes, sculptures, paintings, books, tools, machines' (Shils, 1981: 12). Indeed, Shils notes that an anti-traditionalist impulse is an important tradition in modern society.

The anthropologist Clifford Geertz has been an even more influential figure in cultural sociology (Alexander et al., 2011). Cultural sociologists though typically focus on his ethnographical approaches and analytic insights that emphasise social life being based on social encounters and ritual engagements that have contingent outcomes. However, little attention is given to how Geertz has argued that these fit within cultural systems which allow for cultural meaning to endure through cultural patterns (Geertz, 1983; 1993 [1964]; 1993 [1967]. Barry Schwartz is one of the few scholars of cultural memory to adopt this cultural systems approach. He argues that the key issue for cultural sociologists should not be whether history has been continuous or discontinuous over a period of time, but to what extent we comprehend history as a dependent variable that simply reflects other social and material variables (Schwartz, 1996b: 909). In adopting a cultural systems approach to memory Schwartz argues it is possible to appreciate how cultural memory itself is a resource for reinterpreting and making history.

Other cultural sociologists have emphasised the endurance of memory by focusing on the role of historical events and narratives in the formation of new post-national identities, countering the belief within certain globalisation theories that the nation and its history will be replaced by a subscription to a new present-focused cosmopolitan ethics. Refuting the postmodern argument that history has lost its affect, various cultural sociologists have pointed to the ability of existing cultural memories to adapt to new global complexities. Levy and Sznaider (2006), for example, argue that there is a growth of transnational cosmopolitan memories around the Holocaust, ones that emphasise a humanist and universalist sense of citizenship. There has also been a proliferation of studies into the significance of shared memories for sustaining more specific transnational identities, for example those related to ethnic diasporas (Conway, 2010) and new supranational political institutions such as the European Union (Delanty, 2009). West (2008) argues that an unintended consequence of providing history with a cosmopolitan cultural relevance can actually be the reinvigoration of national identity. Others question the extent to which cosmopolitan memories can be sustained across national boundaries. Margalit (2002), for example, argues that it is the global north rather than the south which forms the basis of so-called global and cosmopolitan memories, signifying an enduring ethnocentric bias in the academy. Such work also tends to make generalisations about the dynamics of cultural memory from particular cultural contexts. Zhang and Schwartz in their study of cultural memory in China, for example, have argued that while sociologists of cultural memory deem that the reconstruction of the past is a cultural universal, it differs significantly in relation to subscription to the cultural values of innovation, libertarianism and moral relativism (1997: 191). To address these issues it will be important for cultural sociologists in the future to incorporate more of a comparative dimension in their analysis of cultural memory.

## REFERENCES

Alexander, J.C. (ed.) (2009) *Remembering the Holocaust: A Debate*. Oxford: Oxford University Press.

Alexander, J.C. and Smith, P. (2010) 'The Strong Program: Origins, Achievements and Prospects', in J. Hall (ed.), *Handbook of Cultural Sociology*. London: Routledge.

Alexander, J.C., Smith, P. and Norton, M. (2011) *Interpreting Clifford Geertz: Cultural Investigation in the Social Sciences*. New York: Palgrave.

Assman, J. (1992) *Das kulturelle Gedächtnis*. Munich: Beck.
Baronian, M., Besser, S. and Jansen, Y. (eds) (2007) *Diaspora and Memory: Figures of Displacement in Contemporary Literature, Arts and Politics*. Amsterdam: Rodopi.
Baudrillard, J. (1983) *Simulations*. New York: Semiotext(e).
Bell, V. and Di Paolantonio, M. (2009) 'The Haunted Nomos: Activist-Artists and the (Im)possible Politics of Memory in Transitional Argentina', *Cultural Politics*, 5(2): 149–78.
Bellah, R. (1967) Civil Religion in America', *Daedalus*, 96: 1–21.
Bennett, T. (2013) *Making Culture, Changing Society*. London: Routledge.
Berezin, M. (1997) *Making the Fascist Self: The Political Culture of Inter-war Italy*. Ithaca: Cornell University Press.
Bodnar, J. (1992) *Remaking America: Public Memory, Commemoration, and Patriotism in the Twentieth Century*. Princeton: Princeton University Press.
Burke, P. (1989) 'History as Social Memory', in T. Butler (ed.), *Memory: History, Culture and the Mind*. New York: Blackwell. pp. 97–113.
Collins, R. (2004) 'Rituals of Solidarity and Security in the Wake of Terrorist Attack', *Sociological Theory*, 22(1): 53–87.
Connell, R.W. (1997) 'Why is Classical Theory Classical?', *American Journal of Sociology*, 102(6): 1511–57.
Connerton, P. (1989) *How Societies Remember*. Cambridge: Cambridge University Press.
Conway, B. (2010) *Commemoration and Bloody Sunday: Pathways of Memory*. New York: Palgrave Macmillan.
Coser, L. (ed.) (1991) *Maurice Halbwachs on Collective Memory*. Chicago: University of Chicago Press.
Crang, M. (1996) 'Magic Kingdom or a Quixotic Quest for Authenticity?', *Annals of Tourism Research*, 23(2): 415–31.
Delanty, G. (2009) 'The European Heritage: History, Memory and Time', in *The SAGE Handbook of European Studies*. London: Sage. pp. 36–51.
Durkheim, E. (1968 [1912]) *The Elementary Forms of Religious Life*. New York: The Free Press.
Edensor, T. (2001) 'Performing Tourism, Staging Tourism: (Re)producing Tourist Space and Practice', *Tourist Studies*, 1(1): 59–81.
Edkins, J. (2003) *Trauma and the Memory of Politics*. New York: Cambridge University Press.
Erbin, M. (1991) 'Genealogy and Sociology: A Preliminary Set of Statements and Speculation', *Sociology*, 25(2): 275–92.
Eyerman, R. (2002) *Cultural Trauma: Slavery and the Formation of African American Identity*. Cambridge: Cambridge University Press.
Featherstone, M. (2000) 'Archiving Cultures', *British Journal of Sociology*, 51(1): 161–84.
Fine, G.A. (2001) *Difficult Reputations: Collective Memories of the Evil, Inept, and Controversial*. Chicago: University of Chicago Press.
Fine, G.A. and Beim, A. (2007) 'Introduction: Interactionist Approaches to Collective Memory', *Symbolic Interaction*, 30(1): 1–5.
FitzGerald, F. (1979) *America Revised: History Schoolbooks in the Twentieth Century*. Boston: Little Brown.
Fried, G. (2006) 'Piecing Memories Together after State Terror and Policies of Oblivion in Uruguay: The Female Political Prisioner's Testimonial Project (1997–2004)', *Social Identities*, 12(5): 543–62.
Garde-Hansen, J., Hoskins, A. and Reading, A. (2009) *Save As… Digital Memories*. Palgrave Macmillan.
Geertz, C. (1983) 'Art as a Cultural System', in *Local Knowledge: Further Essays in Interpretative Anthropology*. New York: Basic Books. pp. 94–120.
Geertz, C. (1993 [1964]) 'Ideology as a Cultural System', in *Interpretation of Cultures*. London: Fontana Press. pp. 193–233.
Geertz, C. (1993 [1967]) 'Religion as a Cultural System', in *Interpretation of Cultures*. London: Fontana Press. pp. 87–125.
Giddens, A. (1994) 'Living in a Post-traditional Society', in U. Beck, A. Giddens and S. Lash (eds), *Reflexive Modernization – Politics, Tradition and Aesthetics in the Modern Social Order*. Stanford, CA: Stanford University Press. pp. 56–110.
Giddens, A. (1999) 'Tradition', Third of the Reith Lectures for 1999, downloaded from the BBC Online Network (http://www.bbc.co.uk/radio4/reith1999/lecture3.shtml).
Goodson, I., Moore, S. and Hargreaves, A. (2006) 'Teacher Nostalgia and the Sustainability of Reform: The Generation and Degeneration of Teachers' Missions, Memory and Meanings', *Educational Administration Quarterly*, February, 42(1): 42–61.
Grainge, P. (ed.) (2003) *Memory and Popular Film*. Manchester: Manchester University Press.
Griswold, W. (2000) *Bearing Witness: Readers, Writers, and the Novel in Nigeria*. Chicago: University of Chicago Press.
Habermas, J. (1989) *The Structural Transformations of the Public Sphere*. Cambridge, MA: MIT Press.
Halbwachs, M. (1941) *La Topographie Legendaire des Evangiles* Paris: Presses Universitaires de France.
Halbwachs, M. (1950) *The Collective Memory*. New York: Harper and Row.
Halbwachs, M. (1992) *On Collective Memory*. Chicago: University of Chicago Press.
Halbwachs, M. (1952 [1925]) *Les Cadres sociaux de la mémoire*. Paris: Presses Universitaires de France.

Hirch, M. (1997) *Family Frames: Photography, Narrative and Postmemory*. Cambridge, MA: Harvard University Press.

Hobsbawm, E. (1983) 'Introduction: Inventing Traditions', in E. Hobsbawm and T. Ranger (eds), *The Invention of Tradition*. Cambridge: Cambridge University Press. pp. 1–14.

Huyssen, A. (1995) *Twilight Memories: Marking Time in a Culture of Amnesia*. New York: Routledge.

Inglis, D. (2007) 'The Warring Twins: Sociology, Cultural Studies, Alterity and Sameness', *History of the Human Sciences*, 20(2): 99–122.

Jacobs, M. and Spillman, L. (2005) 'Cultural Sociology at the Crossroads of the Discipline', *Poetics*, 33: 1–14.

Jameson, F. (1991) *Postmodernism, or, the Cultural Logic of Late Capitalism*. Durham: Duke University Press.

Keightley, E. and Pickering, M. (2006) 'For the Record: Popular Music and Photography as Techniques of Memory', *European Journal of Cultural Studies*, 9(2): 149–65.

Landsberg, A. (2004) *Prosthetic Memory: The Transformation of American Remembrance in the Age of Mass Culture*. New York: Columbia University Press.

Larson, J. and Lizardo, O. (2007) 'Generations, Identities and the Collective Memory of Che Guevara', *Sociological Forum*, 22: 425–51.

Leavy, P. (2005) 'The Memory-History-Popular Culture Nexus: Pearl Harbor as a Case Study in Consumer-Driven Collective Memory', *Sociological Research Online*, 10(1).

Lemert, C. (2005) *Postmodernism Is Not What You Thought: Why Globalization Threatens Modernity*, 2nd edition. Boulder: Paradigm Publishers.

Lessa, F. and Druliolle, V. (eds) (2011) *The Memory of State Terrorism in the Southern Cone: Argentina, Chile and Uruguay*. New York: Palgrave Macmillan.

Levy, D. and Sznaider, N. (2006) *The Holocaust and Memory in the Global Age*. Philadelphia: Temple University Press.

Levy, D. and Sznaider, N. (2010) *Human Rights and Memory*. University Park, PA: Pennsylvania State University Press.

Lipsitz, G. (1990) *Time Passages: Collective Memory and American Popular Culture*. Minneapolis and London: University of Minnesota Press.

Lukes, S. (1975) 'Political Ritual and Social Integration', *Sociology*, 9: 289–308.

Macdonald, S. (2009) *Difficult Heritage*. Oxford and New York: Routledge.

Mannheim, K. (1936) *Ideology and Utopia*. New York: Harcourt, Brace and World.

Margalit, A. (2002) *The Ethics of Memory*. Cambridge, MA: Harvard University Press.

Marx, K. (1962 [1852]) 'The Eighteenth Brumaire of Louis Bonaparte', in K. Marx and F. Engels, *Selected Works*, Vol. 1. Moscow: Foreign Languages Publishing House. pp. 246–360.

McKiernan, D. (1993) 'History in a National Curriculum: Imagining the Nation at the 20th Century', *Journal of Curriculum Studies*, 25: 33–51.

McLennan, G. (2006) *Sociological Cultural Studies: Reflexivity and Positivity in the Human Sciences*. New York: Palgrave Macmillan.

Mead, G.H. (1929) 'The Nature of the Past', in J. Coss (ed.), *Essays in Honor of John Dewey*. New York: Henry Holt.

Middleton, D. and Edwards, E. (eds) (1990) *Collective Remembering*. London: Sage.

Mirchandani, R. (2005) 'Postmodernism and Sociology: From Epistemology to the Empirical', *Sociological Theory*, 23(1): 86–115.

Neiger, M., Meyers, O. and Zandberg, E. (eds) (2011) *On Media Memory: Collective Memory in a New Media Age*. Houndmills: Palgrave Macmillan.

Nora, P. (1996) 'Between Memory and History', in P. Nora (ed.), *Realms of Memory: Rethinking the French Past*. New York: Columbia University Press. pp. 1–20.

Olick, J.K. (1999) 'Collective Memory: The Two Cultures', *Sociological Theory*, 17(3): 333–48.

Olick, J.K. (2007) *The Politics of Regret: On Collective Memory and Historical Responsibility*. New York: Routledge.

Radstone, S. (2008) 'Memory Studies: For or Against?', *Memory Studies*, 1(1): 31–3.

Roediger, H.L. and Wertsch, J.V. (2008) 'Creating a New Discipline of Memory Studies', *Memory Studies*, 1: 9–22.

Schudson, M. (1989) 'The Present in the Past Versus the Past in the Present', *Communication*, 11: 105–13.

Schudson, M. (1992) *Watergate in American Memory: How We Remember, Forget and Reconstruct the Past*. New York: Basic Books.

Schudson, M. (1997) 'Cultural Studies and the Social Construction of "Social Construction": Notes on "Teddy Bear Patriarchy"', in E. Long (ed.), *From Sociology to Cultural Studies: New Perspectives*. Oxford: Blackwell. pp. 379–98.

Schuman, H. and Corning, A. (2012) 'Generational memory and the Critical Period: Evidence for National and World Events', *Public Opinion Quarterly*, 76(1): 1–31.

Schuman, H. and Rogers, W.L. (2004) 'Cohorts, Chronology, and Collective Memories', *Public Opinion Quarterly*, 68: 217–54.

Schuman, H. and Scott, J. (1989) 'Generations and Collective Memory', *American Sociological Review*, 54: 359–81.

Schwartz, B. (1996a) 'Introduction: The Expanding Past', *Qualitative Sociology*, 19(3): 275–82.

Schwartz, B. (1996b) 'Memory as a Cultural System: Abraham Lincoln in World War II', *American Sociological Review*, 61: 908–27.

Schwartz, B. (2008) *Abraham Lincoln in the Post-Heroic Era: History and Memory in Late-Twentieth Century America*. Chicago: University of Chicago Press.

Schwartz, B. and Schuman, H. (2005) 'History, Commemoration and Belief: Abraham Lincoln in American memory, 1945-2001', *American Sociological* Review, 70: 183-203.

Seidman, S. (1991) 'The End of Sociological Theory: The Postmodern Hope', *Sociological Theory*, 9(2): 131–46.

Shils, E. (1975) *Center and Periphery: Essays in Macrosociology*. Chicago: University of Chicago Press.

Shils, E. (1981) *Tradition*. Chicago: University of Chicago Press.

Shils, E. and Young, M. (1956) 'The Meaning of the Coronation', *Sociological Review*, 1: 63–81.

Smith, P. (2000) 'Culture and Charisma: Outline of a Theory', *Acta Sociologica*, 43(2): 101–11.

Smith, P. and West, B. (2003) 'Cultural Studies, Australian Studies and Cultural Sociology', in I. McAllister, S. Dowrick and R. Hassan (eds), *Cambridge Handbook of the Social Sciences in Australia*. Melbourne: Cambridge University Press. pp. 638–53.

Spillman, L. (1997) *Nation and Commemoration: Creating National Identities in the United States and Australia*. Cambridge: Cambridge University Press.

Sturken, M. (1997) *Tangled Memories: The Vietnam War, the AIDS Epidemic, and the Politics of Remembering*. Berkeley: University of California Press.

Sturken, M. (2007) *Tourists of History: Memory, Kitsch, and Consumerism from Oklahoma City to Ground Zero*. Durham, NC: Duke University Press.

Trevor-Roper, H. (1983) 'The Invention of Tradition: The Highland Tradition of Scotland', in E. Hobsbawm and T. Ranger (eds), *The Invention of Tradition*. Cambridge: Cambridge University Press. pp. 15–42.

Urry, J. and Larsen, J. (2012) *The Tourist Gaze: 3.0*. London: Sage.

van Dijck, J. (2007) *Mediated Memories in the Digital Age*. Stanford, CA: Stanford University Press.

Wagner-Pacifici, R. (2006) *The Art of Surrender*. Chicago: University of Chicago Press.

Wagner-Pacifici, R. and Schwartz, B. (1991) 'The Vietnam Veterans Memorial: Commemorating a Difficult Past', *American Journal of Sociology*, 97: 376–420.

Warner, L. (1959) *The Living and the Dead*. New Haven: Yale University Press.

West, B. (2008) 'Enchanting Pasts: The Role of International Civil Religious Pilgrimage in Reimagining National Collective Memory', *Sociological Theory*, 26(3): 258–70.

Woodward, I., Emmison, M. and Smith, P. (2000) 'Consumerism, Disorientation and Postmodern Space: A Modest Test of an Immodest Theory', *British Journal of Sociology*, 51(2): 339–54.

Zelizer, B. (1998) *Remembering to Forget: Holocaust Memory through the Camera's Eye*. Chicago: University of Chicago Press.

Zelizer, B. (2002) 'Finding Aids to the Past: Bearing Personal Witness to Traumatic Public Events', *Media, Culture and Society*, 24: 697–714.

Zerubavel, E. (1997) *Social Mindscapes: An Invitation to Cognitive Sociology*. Cambridge, MA: Harvard University Press.

Zerubavel, E. (2003) *Time Maps: Collective Memory and the Social Shape of the Past*. Chicago: University of Chicago Press.

Zhang, T. and Schwartz, B. (1997) 'Confucius and the Cultural Revolution: A Study in Collective Memory', *International Journal of Politics, Culture and Society*, 11(2): 189–212.

# PART VI
# Arts and Aesthetics

# (Cultural) Sociologies of Architecture?

Paul Jones

## INTRODUCTION

In 2011 I published *The Sociology of Architecture*, since which time I have come to regret somewhat the book's title. In place of the definitive article – the *The* – I increasingly feel that an indefinite 'A' would have been more appropriate, or perhaps that the plural Sociologies should have featured somewhere, in place of the singular *Sociology*. Although this issue does not exactly keep me awake at night, it is fair to say that should I be writing this book now, the title would be different, and quite possibly less assuredly disciplinary.

This rather self-indulgent opening is intended to hint at the relatively wide scope of what can meaningfully be considered cultural sociological analyses of architecture, which by now is a growing, and intellectually vibrant, field of inquiry. Throughout this chapter I hope to communicate the insights that have emerged as a result of what broadly could be understood as sociological engagements with architecture.[1] Thanks to the socially meaningful nature of architecture's material form – not to mention the production and reception of such – and its associated entanglements with both 'everyday' and out-of-the-ordinary practices alike, architecture presents a beguiling area of study for those interested in social order and sense-making social action. Additionally it would seem that sociologists are well equipped to research the specific ways in which buildings and the spaces between them are, to coin a phrase, socially produced. However, this is a deceptively challenging terrain of study, replete with a number of pitfalls, some of which are also considered here.

So, there is polemic intent in this chapter. On the one hand, I hope to encourage sociologists to contribute more research insights about architecture, and, on the other, am keen to share the recently widened scope of resources available to sharpen such inquiry. In general I make a case for the necessity of theoretically sophisticated and empirically grounded studies, attentive to the specificity of architecture as a form of cultural production, and the social contexts in which it is embedded/ from which it emerges. The chapter is organised in such a way so as to provide those who may be interested in pursuing this research agenda with the major reference points (at least as I see them). By surveying a hundred or so of the key academic contributions to the debate, the chapter aims to allow for the emergence of some generalities of sociological approaches to the study of architecture and the built environment.

Following this Introduction, the first section of the chapter briefly unpacks the assumptions that underpin the subsequent organisation of the research literature. Highlighting some of the perils associated with such exercises in 'canon-formation', sociology – and, to a lesser extent, cultural sociology and architecture – are frames that inform the rest of the chapter. The remaining sections are concerned with an analytical review of the rapidly expanding sociological research literature addressing architecture. This amounts to a necessarily fleeting overview of some of the key academic research contributions – primarily published books, articles, and chapters – that constitute landmarks in a (cultural) sociology of architecture. Three subsections act as a rough-and-ready typology that divide[3] these circa one hundred pieces into: (i) those sociological contributions that have positioned architecture as reflective of major political, economic, and cultural shifts; (ii) ethnographic studies of architecture as a profession/practice; and (iii) analysis of human-built environment interactions (inspired, to a greater or lesser extent, by Science and Technology Studies). This division of the research literature is proposed for present purposes only, and to organise the wide and varied existing research on architecture that is sociological in character.

## A LOADED CANON?

Garry Stevens has suggested it would take just one day to read sociological research contributions focused on architecture (1998: 12). This was probably more or less true when he wrote his ground-breaking architectural-sociological book *The Favored Circle* – on which much more later – but the intervening fifteen or so years have seen this research landscape significantly expanded. While not presenting as small a sub-field of knowledge production as mainstream sociological activity (understood for example relative to the numbers of scholars working on the topic, national association study groups, publications, major funding bids, or taught courses), there is a vibrant community of academic sociologists addressing architecture either directly or in more *en passant* ways. Significant insights have, been garnered from this research; before discussing what I consider to be some of the landmark classic and contemporary sociological theories and studies in this tradition, I want to make some initial observations concerning the task of representing such.

When seeking to articulate the range of sociological studies of architecture that have been carried out to date, one quickly becomes entangled in a series of thorny issues pertaining to disciplinary boundaries and canonisation. As the aim here is to sketch out the contours of sociological engagements with architecture, there is a need to say at least a few words about the rationales that guide the inclusion of some contributions (and, by extension, saw the exclusion of some others).

If we start from the perspective that disciplines, including, but not limited to, sociology, act primarily as 'flags of convenience' under which we sail when researching, teaching, and studying, then the problem of defining precisely what a *sociological* approach to the study of architecture is recedes to a secondary concern, with what research is called or who is doing it having less significance than what is being done. If adopting this pluralistic understanding of sociology as a discipline, we are in danger of tilting at a windmill, inasmuch as we are using an ill-defined approach to address an amorphous topic. Under these circumstances such an extremely broad range of things can be understood as 'sociologies of architecture', and one could question the clarity added by the label, such a, critique of disciplinary frontiers also makes writing a chapter like this almost impossible …).

If, on the other hand, if we start from the perspective that disciplines remain intellectually meaningful, either because they define a systematic set of theories and methods that underpin inquiry, standing proxy for a particular 'way of seeing', then the question of what a *sociology* of architecture adds to our understanding of architecture takes on some import.[2] However, while operating with stricter threshold criteria for 'sociology' – perhaps defined by a particular set of theories, methods, or combinations thereof – may promise clarification, it also necessarily contains so many arbitrary factors as to be inherently contestable: is sociology to be defined as research carried out by those working in sociology departments? Or perhaps research produced by those working outside of these institutional settings but drawing more or less significantly on sociologists' frameworks or approaches? Should discussion be limited to articles published in sociology journals, or open to the rather more numerous interdisciplinary engagements, addressing, for example, cities and urban form? Et cetera, et cetera.

My approach here tends towards the former, more permissive, alternative in most counts; in terms of this chapter, such a stance makes more possible the inclusion of a wide range of published contributions and discussions that have added much to – or drawn meaningfully from – sociological understandings of architecture and the built environment. Still, canon-forming exercises like the one you are reading now must proceed with much care in ensuring that representations are reflective of the fact that the academic sociological community is a disparate and diverse one.[3]

Also reflective of a rather lenient approach to disciplinary boundaries, I have understood cultural sociology in just one sense of the term, that is, to mean encompassing sociological analysis of architecture as an inherently 'cultural' form (so bound up with meaning-making in its social production and use). While this approach – associated less with a 'strong programme' of cultural sociology – ostensibly gives latitude, in what follows, I embark on the research-landscaping task fully aware that such a fuzzy approach to disciplinary boundaries will not be to everyone's liking and that my approach remains contingent on some relatively arbitrary lines of demarcation, while being safe in the knowledge that any single chapter like this will not do justice to the depth of insights contained in the contributions I discuss. With these initial caveats in place, what are some of the landmark contributions that sociologists have made to our understanding of architecture?

## ARCHITECTURE, MEANING, AND SOCIAL CHANGE

Robert Gutman, for much of his career a Professor of Sociology working in the Architecture School at Princeton, is a key figure in architectural-sociology, who developed systematic sociological inquiry into the ways in which architects and their buildings are implicated in the design of buildings that are often positioned so as to symbolise major civilisational shifts (1968; 1972; 1988; 1992; 2007). Gutman's long-standing interest was in structural accounts of the architectural profession's relationship to broader social relations, and his path-breaking research led him to observe that:

> Rare is the building not designed by an architect that represents the supreme values of a civilization. This has been true for temples, palaces, libraries, and city halls in Greece, Rome, and Europe during the Renaissance, and for museums, university buildings, and corporate headquarters more recently. The design of great seminal monumental buildings is the unique province of architecture, its 'natural market' which he observed. (1992: 40)

Gutman's starting point was to position architecture vis-à-vis the culturally, politically, and economically powerful and to understand buildings as reflective of the broader sets of social arrangements from which they emerge. It is this general approach that informs the contributions of the first group of sociologists, who in their varied analyses have approached 'famous' landmark buildings as cultural reflections of broader cultural and/or political-economic trends. Much of this type of research has emerged as a result of sociologists seeking to engage with architectural forms as materialisations of social dynamics or phenomena that they have elsewhere pursued analysis of. Accordingly, much of this research is theoretically motivated and tends towards generalised accounts of the built environment rather than close empirical engagement.

In this tradition of inquiry could be mentioned Jürgen Habermas' (1989) engagement with architecture, which formed a chapter-length contribution to his wider analysis of the 'philosophical discourse of modernity'. Habermas situates architecture relative to this theory of modernity and postmodernity, exploring the potential of a recovery of the potential of a less rationalised and technocratic modern architecture movement (and in the process critiquing the 'conservatism' he sees as inherent in ostensibly radical architectural moves associated with postmodernism). Similarly, Ulrich Beck's analysis of the 'City of Or' (in *Democracy Without Enemies*) interrogates what he sees as the increasing reflexivity of architects relative to identity politics and public representations of culture (1999). Another major figure of European social theory, Göran Therbon, has published on the built environment, with particular reference to the 19th-century state-led projects that saw major cities and capitals become sites of political celebration and expression (2002). In this important article Therbon draws particular attention to the proliferation of statues and other designed elements in the European urban built environment in the 19th century. Also perhaps worthy of mention in the context of theoretically motivated analyses of architecture vis-à-vis major political shifts is an article that Gerard Delanty and I published that sought to tease out the ways in which the political project of European identity-building was implicating and imbricating architectural production and the built environment more widely (Delanty and Jones, 2002).

While these theoretical accounts of architecture have illuminated much, it is fair to say that such research tends towards broad-sweep analysis of the ways in which architects and their built productions get drawn into cultural and political claims regarding the definition of the situation.

Arguably, the type of work addressed above is less than attentive to the embedded practices through which architecture becomes culturally meaningful in a specific context. And, to generalise the formulation that architectural theorist and urbanist Anthony Vidler (1991) develops in his discussion of the French Revolution, cultural sociologists should arguably be concerned less with finding a definitive, essential, style of a given social context and more with studying the practical roles of architects and the uses of architecture during a given socio-cultural period.

Next, a group of scholars have done just this, namely studied empirically the specificities of the ways in which states have deployed architects and architecture in periods of political change. Evgeny Dobrenko is a representative if this group; his book *The Political Economy of Socialist Realism* (2007) is an exemplar of research sensitised to the nuances of architectural production that takes place under the auspices of state-led cultural projects. Dobrenko, a Professor of Russian Studies at the University of Sheffield, addresses architecture's practical deployment – which can of course be symbolic – at the interface of culture, economy and politics.[4] Dobrenko argues that socialist realist architecture was not simply a way of aestheticising an economic movement, and so a case where architectural meaning could be 'read off' economic organisation, but rather that architectural production – alongside literature, films, photography, and other forms – was a key site of the practical production of the socialist project itself. By pursing this analysis Dobrenko understands architecture as a culturally distinctive form of representational politics with a reality-making quality. Similarly, *Architecture, Power and National Identity* ([1992] 2000), Lawrence J. Vale's definitive study of parliament buildings (capitols) in post-colonial contexts, is particularly interested in those architectural sites that are mobilised as part of broader political attempts to reposition states relative to internal and external publics. For Vale, crucial political questions in the design of parliaments often centre on which architectural style should be chosen and what buildings mean; in his analysis these controversies often serve as proxies for struggles concerning whose identity should be represented publicly. Vale traces a number of disputes in post-colonial contexts – including Papua New Guinea, Brazil, India, and Sri Lanka – where the formal architecture of government is bound up with cultural representations of social pasts and futures, collective identities, and the role of the nation in the world; in Vale's account parliament architecture is inextricably bound up with the question of the nation.

Similarly, in her research on the uses of modernist architecture in the Turkish Republic (published as an illuminating book entitled *Modernism and Nation Building: Turkish Architectural Culture in the Early Republic*) Sibel Bozdoğan has explored the ways in which the commission of highly rationalised architectural form saw the coterminous rejection of a vernacular Ottoman revivalism. Rather than reducing the state commission of European modernist architects to a colonial cultural politics, Bozdoğan skilfully draws together the political contingencies and aesthetic struggles internal to architecture that were articulated into political meanings (also see Bozdoğan's more recent co-authored book – 2012, with Esra Akcan – *Turkey: Modern Architectures in History*, which provides a definitive architectural-historical treatment of modernism in Turkey). Anthony D. King is a prominent sociologist who also addresses colonialism and architecture, associated with the colonial period when the built environment of capital cities reflected much of their status as quasi-global administrative, political, and economic centres (1976). King artfully addresses the ways in which negotiations between pasts and futures, the mobility and incorporation of 'foreign' architectural patterns, and the cultural inter-relationship and influences centre on the built environment (King also edited the classic volume entitled *Buildings and Society* (1984), which drew together essays focused on the relationship between 19th-century disciplinary institutions – such as the school, the prison, and the factory – and architectural development).

Looming large in all these accounts is the question of how and what architecture comes to mean. In my opinion, an under-read and under-cited book on this question is *Architecture and Its Interpretation* by Juan Pablo Bonta (1979), which provides a masterful empirically grounded illustration of the contested social processes through which buildings come to acquire social meanings. In this study Bonta shows the ways in which a 'collective plagiarism' – or perhaps collusion? – between architects, theorists, critics, and students underpins agreement on meanings and values within the architectural field; he argues that powerful critics have the capacity to define meanings and values therein. Foreshadowing the Bourdieu-inspired engagements discussed below, Bonta analyses how 'the meaning of architecture can be removed – and sometimes even dissociated – from what architecture actually *is*' (1979: 14, emphasis in original). Researching empirically how architectural styles come to be attributed with social meanings over and above the actual built form, Bonta shows how the development of symbolic associations is contingent on collectivised judgements that architects – and others in the field – attach to buildings and styles and disseminate via review, critique, and teaching.

Approaches such as Bonta's examine the social judgements that exist around the built object itself, critiquing the tendency for the judgement of the critic to be obscured at the very point that they make arbitrary pronouncements of architectural value. The arbitrary, judgements of critics are made clearly visible in Bonta's analysis of the initially muted reception and subsequent celebration of Ludwig Mies van der Rohe's German Pavilion at the Barcelona Expo in 1929, a case study that illustrates his wider point about the relative power of voices within the architectural field. Focusing on the reviews of critics published in the international architectural press, Bonta shows how influential critics' retrospective judgements contributed to this initially unremarked-upon structure becoming widely considered a modernist masterpiece. Through studying the creation of 'architectural orthodoxy', Bonta shows how 'collective plagiarism' is effectively responsible for the collective aesthetic judgements that 'originate and disappear with time' (1979: 138).

The anti-foundationalist approach adopted by Bonta is in general characteristic of cultural sociological engagements with architectural form, for example such as can be found in the excellent study published in *The American Journal of Sociology* by Virag Molnár (2005), a sociologist at The New School, New York. In this paper Molnár engages with a controversy surrounding the use of tulips on Hungarian modernist architecture. Her analysis unpacks the ways in which the decoration of modernist architecture with these national folk symbols became a touchstone for a whole set of wider, and deeply political, struggles (Molnar has also very recently published a monograph on state architecture in post-war central Europe). In some sense the controversy over the tulip decorations on buildings has resonances with the 'Battle of the Styles' in Victorian Britain, which was a highly politicized struggle centring on the quest for an 'appropriate' architectural style in which to design major public buildings. In this context architecture became politicized objects whose meaning and import was interpreted by political and cultural elites and citizens engaged in highly abstracted readings of architectural styles and claims concerning British national identity. It was in this context that gothic revivalism and neo-classicism became imbued with questions of the cultural representation of the civilizational aspirations of the British nation state; the 'Battle of the Styles' is a historical illustration both of the ways in which architects and their work can get drawn into state projects at particular junctures, and that social values come to be 'read off' architectural styles (Jones, 2011: 54–64).

The clutch of studies discussed in this section all help to illustrate the relational and contingent ways in which social judgements of built objects become operative, with meaning residing in the architectural community rather than in essentialised characteristics of the objects or spaces themselves (Wolff, 1981). It is this characteristic – if not only this (Löw and Steets [2010] for a critique of the over-extension of this perspective) – that makes architectural production and consumption both ripe for sociological analysis, and for mobilisation in all sorts of political contests. In other words it is precisely 'the essential arbitrariness of [architectural] symbols … [that] allows them to be the object of struggles, in which groups try to convince others to value their capital more than that of their rivals' (Stevens, 1998: 69). The studies carried out by Bonta (1979), Lipstadt (2003), Molnár (2005), and myself (2006; 2011) provide reminders that when it comes to pronouncements on/judgements of architectural value, cultural statements are never objective nor natural, nor do they capture some underlying essence of the design; rather, the observation that there is an arbitrary foundation to the architectural field leads us to ask far-reaching sociological questions of the claims made by architects and others operating therein (Stevens, 1998).

Against this backdrop I published a piece on the Ground Zero reconstruction in *Sociology*, in which I wanted to give some analysis of the public pronouncements of an internationally-leading architect, Daniel Libeskind, vis-à-vis the symbolic component of his masterplanning design. I argued that as well as lending their house style to the design of buildings, leading architects such as Libeskind – sometimes referred to as 'starchitects' (Sklair, 2005; McNeill, 2009 for critiques) – are prolific generators of social and political interpretations of their own design work. I argued that architectural meaning-making is not limited to built form alone, and that an important facet of the commissioned work of leading architects is in talk about their designs (and accordingly that sociologists should pay attention to how these ostensibly 'non-architectural' interventions are deployed in context). In the case of the New York rebuilding I argued that 'it is often against a mistakenly assumed backdrop of political autonomy and neutrality that high-profile architects are engaged in the creation and reproduction of cultural identities' (Jones, 2006: 550).

In an important book on discourse and architecture entitled *Buildings and Power* (1993), Thomas Markus analyses the mid-18th to mid-19th centuries, managing to balance technical analyses of architectural drawings and plans with semiotic engagement about building types. His analysis covers the disciplinary function of buildings housing galleries, museums, expos, libraries, etc. Markus' approach can also be read as a withering critique of those architectural histories that position buildings as neutral objects somehow set outside social relations – including capitalist ones (for critiques see also Wolff, 1981; and for Marxist readings of architectural aesthetics, Tafuri, [1976] 1999; Bentmann and Muller, 1992; Dutton and Mann, 1996; Jones, 2009). This critical approach is echoed in *Space and Power*, a book in which Birkbeck sociologist Paul Hirst addresses the ways in which 'architecture is configured by power ... and becomes a resource for power' (2005: 3), with particular respect to military architecture. Hirst's contribution is perhaps less architecturally expert than is Markus' – which demonstrates a sophisticated grasp of the nuances of architectural style and its meaning (albeit from a critical perspective) – but nonetheless draws on a range of social theorists of space to excellent effect (see also Löw and Steets [2010], who surveyed in detail these types of 'spatial-architectural' contributions).

Another major concern of sociologists analysing architecture as a manifestation of broader social change has been to situate architecture within broader capitalist relations. In a series of articles LSE sociologist Leslie Sklair has drawn attention to the links between capitalist globalisation, internationally high-profile architectural practices and architecture (his analysis grows out of his long-standing analysis of a transnational capitalist class and global-political-economy) (2005; 2006; 2010; 2013). Sklair positions the emergence of contemporary iconic architecture as an expression of the long-standing desire of economic elites to materialize their power, contending that 'in the era of capitalist globalization the dominant force driving iconic architecture is the transnational capitalist class' (2010: 138). Sklair's research is primarily addressed towards those buildings that are recognisable, widely disseminated and celebrated within and outwith the architectural community.

Understanding those eye-catching, distinctive forms designed by high-profile architects as 'resource[s] in struggles for meaning and, by implication, for power' (Sklair, 2006: 21), Sklair's approach is one of the most distinctively 'sociological' assessed here. In foregrounding the temporal, spatial, and aesthetic components of major architectural schemes – asking: 'iconic for where, iconic for whom and iconic for when?' (2005; 2006) – Sklair goes to the heart of issues pertaining to how the built environment contributes to the global capitalist imagination, both via the aesthetic consolidation of a transnational corporate class (Sklair, 2005) and more prosaically through providing material structures in which surplus value – and meaning concerning such – is generated (Sklair, 2010). Like Sklair, I have also sought to investigate architecture as one space in which capitalism is culturally narrated/becomes socially meaningful (Jones, 2009; 2011). Sklair's forthcoming book *The Icon Project: Architecture, Cities, and Capitalist Globalization* promises to extend this approach; other studies that have sought to draw critical sociological theories to bear on the study of architecture include Monika Grubbauer (2014), who has recently utilised Marxist theory to address the development and surplus value associated with the architecture of office towers, and Monika Kaika and Korinna Thielen, who – in an excellent article in the journal *City* (2006) – analyse parallels between contemporary urban capitalist 'shrines' and traditional religious architecture that dominated 'landscape' and 'imagination'. Recent analysis of the huge scope and scale of architectural development in urban China (for example Jianfei, 2009; Ren, 2011; Bracken, 2012) has included sociological critique in a variety of guises, with much drawn from classical urban sociology in this general debate.

## CULTURAL SOCIOLOGIES OF ARCHITECTURAL PRACTICE

If one tradition of the sociological study of architecture has been to position built form as reflective of major social and political-economic shifts, another approach has been to study empirically the practical things that architects do in studios, firms, and on building sites. These by-and-large ethnographic studies have the longest lineage of the sociological studies of architecture, and in general have drawn much from the sociology of the professions literature; latterly the considerable influence of Pierre Bourdieu is highly visible in engagements in this tradition.[5]

One of the by-now classic accounts of architectural practice is Dana Cuff's study *Architecture: The Story of Practice* (1991). In this landmark study, Cuff positions architects as cultural intermediaries closely connected to capital – especially property interests – and political elites. While retaining a critical approach, Cuff manages to develop an uncluttered and analytic ethnography, drawing our attention to the situated rationalities and practices of architects working in specific firms. Through careful empirically evidenced research, Cuff avoids a reductionism that would understand architects' motivations as driven primarily by economically accumulative motives; on the contrary, despite their close linkages with and reliance on the corporate class who commission much of their work – in fact often because of them – the architects that Cuff studies emerge as a highly reflexive group, whose own political and cultural positions are oftentimes at odds with those of their clients. Similarly, Judith Blau (1984) also studied constraints on architects' action from a sociological perspective, and in particular the ways in which disagreements between various interests in design and building are managed – typically skilfully – by architects in situ. Blau and Cuff's monographs were path-breaking ethnographies of architectural practice.[6] For a good example of a contemporary ethnography of architecture, which draws a great deal from ethnomethodology and conversation analysis, see the work of Jörg Fuhrmann (2015). Magali Safuri Larson's *Behind the Post-Modern Facade: Architectural Change in Late-Twentieth Century America* (1993) also contains sharp sociological analysis of professional practice, with particular attention paid to the key role of prize-giving in the architectural hierarchy. Larson interrogates the speeches of the judges of the prestigious annual American Progressive Architecture Award 1965–1985, revealing how radically different conceptions of the architect's social role were both reflected and constructed therein. In a recent reflective piece, Larson has suggested that her key study gives a 'microhistory of [an aesthetic] shift, seen from inside the profession by individuals constituted as gatekeepers, [identifying] the "anointing" function that elites have' (1993: 327); the book certainly demonstrates convincingly how architectural meaning is contested and consecrated as a key part of professional architectural practice. In Larson's account power operates as a taken-for-granted element of the architectural field, crucially capturing the specificity of architecture as a symbolic – as well as material – production. Getting close to the often niche nature and self-referentiality of architectural 'insiders'' aesthetic claims, Larson's – like Cuff and Blau's work – is a study of design professionals contingent on a depth of research engagement.

Other studies of architectural practice that are sociological in nature are to be found, for example, in the work of Hélène Lipstadt, who works in architecture at MIT, but who has a background in cultural theory and anthropology. Lipstadt has interrogated the architectural competition as a key component of elite architectural practice (2003). While Lipstadt's inclusion illustrates my somewhat elastic conception of 'sociology' – at least institutionally speaking – she is one of the thinkers to have drawn extensively on Bourdieu in assessing architecture. Lipstadt has researched the competition stage, during which architects compete for the award of commissions, and from her perspective accordingly become embroiled in conflicts over symbolic and material capital. By interrogating this stage of a broader process of cultural production, Lipstadt shows how the competition represents a site of struggle to define the social parameters of architecture itself. Similarly, Garry Stevens (1998: 97), also operationalising Bourdieu, suggests that the competition allows participating architects

> to make a ritual demonstration of allegiance to the elites, … if the competition obliges the economically and politically dominant to aver in the most public manner their symbolic dependence on architects, the architects always re-avow the covenant by affirming their material dependence on the wealthy and powerful.

Studying in depth some of the 'tournaments of value' (Appadurai, 1986) – for example, the competition, prize-giving, and other struggles over status – allows Cuff, Stevens, Lipstadt, Larson, and Blau to reveal the practical dynamics of consecration crucial to the field of architecture.

Approaches from historical sociology have added much to our understanding of the emergence of the architect as a distinctive occupational and social role. For example, David Brain, a Professor of Sociology & Environmental Studies (New College of Florida), has published on the emergence and consolidation of the architectural profession in the United States and Europe. While having antecedents in ancient Egypt, Rome, Renaissance Florence, etc., Brain argues that it was significantly in the period of 1820–40 that a fertile cultural and institutional context saw the emergence of the modern professional architectural class in these places. During the early–mid-19th century, Europe and the US witnessed a growing stock of clients/patrons – crucially including the state – that saw architects being engaged specifically as designers (as distinct from the less specifically design-focused 'gentleman-architects' and 'builder-architects' predominant in the 18th century). For Brain, architectural design in and of itself became conceived as a professional practice only when '[t]he work of producing drawings provided architects with the practical foundation for a discipline of design, and its anchoring point in a division of labor' (Brain, 1991: 244). Drawings became in effect intellectual properties, but this was certainly not a linear or uncontested process, and Brain shows how the emergent practice of professional architecture was highly iterative, developing in conjunction and contradistinction with other building professions such as engineering, construction and surveying (also see Cohen et al. [2005] for a contemporary study of such professional demarcations).

Accordingly, and via a critique of the limitations of a rational choice/market monopoly model of professions, Brain focuses our attention on the contingencies and opportunistic dynamics of the architectural profession. Rather than taking for granted the emergence of the profession as inevitable, he unpacks the production of architectural knowledge, understanding such as a practical and ongoing achievement (1991: 240). This is especially the case given the scarcity within the market for buildings symbolising major civilisational achievements in 'great, monumental' buildings (Gutman, 1992), outside of which the vast majority of architects operate (also see Stevens, 1996; 1998). In his accounts, Brain draws attention to the circulation of a stock of cultural knowledge derived from the 'Grand Tours' of Europe, which allowed for the reproduction of Roman and Greek styles in Anglo-US contexts.[7] Similarly, but addressing a more modern history, the sociologist Florent Champy – who in fact also wrote a monograph entitled *Sociologie de L'Architecture* (2001), which addresses architectural production from a sociology of the professions perspective – analyses the ways in which the self-generated repositioning of the architectural profession in France post-May 1968 rested in some part on an 'old', stable, and protected status of the professional architect vis-à-vis cognate practices, such as for example those associated with landscape design or engineering (2006).

A point of encouragement for sociologists researching architectural practice can be found in the myriad ways in which their analysis has been imported into architects' conceptualisation and practice. In fact, the exporting of sociological ideas into architectural practice was one of the explicit aims of the early sociologists of architecture, as was expressed by luminaries such as Robert Gutman (1968; 1988) and Herbert Gans (1977), both of whom would doubtless be delighted to see Jeremy Till – an architect and leading architectural theorist – engaging so explicitly with sociological theory to make sense of the 'mess' and 'contingency' of architectural practice and training (2009). Also cause for optimism about sociology's capacity as an 'exporter' is to be found in the publications of Robert Adam, a practising architect and partner in ADAM Architecture (a major London firm). For example, in his book *The Globalization of Modern Architecture* (2012), which draws extensively on recent sociological theory (in addition to being enriched by reflection on his own experience as a well-established international architect), Adam uses the work of Giddens, Beck, Bourdieu and many of those discussed in this chapter to frame and make sense of the political-economic currents shaping the internationalisation of architectural practice and its client base. Other notable attempts to 'translate' sociology for architects can be found in the 'Thinkers for Architects' series, which aims to introduce the ideas of major social thinkers – such as Bourdieu (Webster, 2010), Lefebvre (Coleman, 2015), Foucault (Fontina-Giusti, 2013), and Deleuze and Guattari (Ballantyne, 2007) – to architects.

Another vibrant area of sociological engagement can be found in sociological studies of architects' training/socialisation and the broader social reproduction function of the profession more generally. The major figure in this area is the architect-cum-architectural-sociologist, Garry Stevens. His perceptive analyses of architectural production (1995; 1996; 1998) are reflective of both a depth of understanding concerning architectural pedagogy and a sharp 'sociological imagination', which draws extensively on concepts from Bourdieu. Stevens (1998) convincingly demonstrates how the demography of architects is inextricably linked to the (symbolic and material) markets for architecture; by connecting the structural conditions of architectural action to the waxes and wanes of numbers of architects, Stevens reveals the relation between the socialisation of architects and the parameters of the field itself. Master–pupil chains, understood from Stevens' perspective as the sites of aesthetic socialisation and class reproduction, are a crucial mechanism for this consolidation. Against the backdrop of the broader structure of the profession, which at any one time has so much symbolic capital to compete over (1995), Stevens is interested in the disjunct between those leading architects who set the aesthetic and practice tone – in effect coming to dictate the architectural terms of engagement – and others in the field, whose day-to-day work is not understood by others (or themselves) as serving a high aesthetic purpose.

Also drawing on critical sociological tradition to interrogate the social reproduction function of architecture, Thomas Dutton, a Marxist architectural theorist who for many years has worked in Miami University, has also focused attention on the 'hidden curriculum' in architectural pedagogy; that is, those sets of implicit but unarticulated values and assumptions that shape the ways in which architects are trained and subsequently practice. As does Stevens' research, Dutton's evidences the key point that architectural schools are far from being neutral sites of education, but rather that studio and classroom pedagogies 'reinforce certain ideologies, values, and assumptions about social reality so as to sustain the interests of some groups at the expense of others' (Dutton, 1987: 17). Dutton's and Stevens' analyses both have much to tell us concerning the classed nature of architecture as pedagogical and professional practice.

Sociologists engaging with architectural practice have also made very important interventions in both revealing and critiquing the social divisions that characterise architectural practice. For example, in their article 'Women Architects and their Discontents' (2004), sociologists Bridget Fowler and Fiona Wilson report on a study that unpacked the gendered assumptions implicitly and explicitly at play in the socialisation of architects, with a key conclusion of their study – which is based on interviews with 72 architects – that the partial and arbitrary nature of judgements in the field have a masculinist character, and underpin the highly unequal and gendered nature of architectural reward and practice. Addressed to similar sets of issues, although drawing less extensively on Bourdieu and sociological theory than do Fowler and Wilson, Annmarie Adams and Petra Tancred (2000) reveal the ways in which Canadian women architects are positioned in major journals by powerful critics (typically men); they also explore the range of resistances that followed. Adams and Tancred reflect on the space of possibilities for more equitable practice that are opened up – if not always realised – by the emergence of modernism and associated 'new' practices in the Canadian architectural community. Taken in the round, sociologically grounded studies of architectural firms clearly reflect the insights that can be derived from ethnographic engagement and, relatedly, from problematizing the taken-for-granted nature of the practice. Researching the ways in which social inequalities play out and are sustained in the architectural field requires an approach sensitised to the nuances of practice and the associated motivations of architects, which of course cannot be reduced to economic extrinsic reward, and that in fact are often highly aestheticised (Blau, 1984; Crawford, 1991; Cuff, 1991; 2014; Stevens, 1995; 1996; 1998; Jones, 2009; 2011; 2015).

Importantly, there are also notable attempts from within architecture to challenge the constraints associated with professional practice and sociologists who have sought to make sense of such. Noting that the vast majority of the world's buildings and spaces between them are not designed by architects,[8] as did Rudofsky in his seminal *Architecture Without Architects* (1972 [1964]), opens up a series of pertinent questions about: (i) user-designed architecture; and (ii) the reward structures and working assumptions of professional architects in contexts where to a greater or lesser extent there is an architectural monopoly on building design. Still, by-and-large, sociological analysis has focused on elite architectural practice and the built outcomes of such, although there is emerging interest in those design-build programmes – where architecture students engage in design in communities – such as the one at the Rural Studio that myself and Kenton Card have published on (2011), or the work of the humanitarian networks such as Architecture for Humanity (Sinclair and Stor, 2006).

## ARCHITECTURE, HUMAN–OBJECT INTERACTIONS, AND STUDYING MATERIAL CULTURE

A major catalyst for the recent growth of interest in sociologies of architecture has emerged thanks to a group of scholars pursuing analysis drawing from Science and Technology Studies (STS) and Actor-Network Theory (ANT) (see Fallan [2008] for a lucid and comprehensive summary of ANT approaches to architectural analysis, and Latour and Yaneva [2008] for an operationalization of the approach). Although the studies that I have grouped together in this section are extremely disparate in terms of topic focus and their conclusions concerning material culture, they do share an overarching general aim to assess empirically the ways in which human–object interactions – of course including elements of the built environment – are made and become normalised.

Albana Yaneva, a Professor in Architectural Theory and now Director of Manchester Architecture Research Centre, has been path-breaking in pushing forward these distinct but related approaches. In fact, Yaneva's work draws extensively on perspectives derived from STS, showcasing the insights that can emerge when bringing together some of the carefully observed traditional studies of architectural firms with sociological currents emerging from material cultures and Actor-Network Theory. For example, in her monograph reporting on an ethnographic study of the major Dutch firm OMA (2009), and her the article with Bruno Latour on analytical approaches to capturing the dynamic nature of architecture-in-use (2008), or the more recently published book *Mapping Controversies in Architecture*, Yaneva is concerned to unpack the interactions between human and non-human actants. In her studies Yaneva adopts a pragmatist approach to explore architectural production, and as a result is concerned with the practical ways in which architecture as a situated practice and material production is contingent on, and constitutive of, a whole range of human–object relations.

Yaneva's studies are underpinned by a concern to reveal the ways in which architectural production is fundamentally entangled with a series of materialities, which extend far beyond the building itself (her discussion of the role of models and presentations in her study of OMA is an illuminating example of this broader concern). Similarly, Michael Guggenheim – a sociologist at Goldsmiths, University of London – has also published widely on architecture, using theory and methods derived from STS, broadly understood. Some of Guggenheim's research makes sense of the ways in which architecture becomes bound up with temporalities (2009), or how changes in buildings' uses to/from sacred ones reflect something of architecture's status as a 'mutable immobile' (2013), in other words the ways in which meanings and practices in and around buildings become more or less stable contingent on the efficacy of certain key material interventions.

The work of Thomas Gieryn (2000; 2002; 2006) also provides a useful lens through which to view the implication of architecture within broader cultural projects. In a series of articles, Gieryn, a sociologist working within the STS research tradition, has sought to reveal entanglements between architectural materiality and the stabilisation/credibility of knowledge claims. More widely, Gieryn's analysis has directed attention towards the 'provenance' of knowledge claims, reflecting the ways in which origins at a specific place and time both leave their 'hallmarks' on the production, and – most distinctively – form the basis for representations of place to themselves, mobilised as a resource that adds authority to truth claims. Gieryn's work on the concept of the 'truth spot' (2006: 6–29) – that is a 'geographic, architectural and rhetorical construction [of] "place" [that] is mobilised as a resource to allow claims to gain believability and persuasiveness' – has much potential to sharpen understanding of the scientific and cultural claims that derive and draw from the built environment. Gieryn himself (2000; 2002; 2006) directs attention towards the ways in which cultural representations of place are themselves mobilised as a resource that adds authority to truth claims (2006: 28–9), allowing them to cohere and to 'gain believability and persuasiveness' (Gieryn, 2006: 6; also see Jones, 2015).

This process fundamentally implicates architecture, as Gieryn demonstrates in 'What Buildings Do', an article that is underpinned by a pragmatist analysis of the built environment and that does much to bring together a social constructivists programme of sociological research on the built environment. Questioning how architecture is mobilised to 'do' things in specific contexts – such as '[stabilising] social life [, giving] structure to social institutions, durability to social networks, persistence to behavior patterns' (Gieryn, 2002: 35) – Gieryn analyses the development of a new science building and lab at Cornell.

Another significant line of inquiry that can be understood within this general category, but that does not always draw explicitly on STS or ANT, is research exploring the ways in which the built environment is experienced by many as hostile to their capabilities and bodies. A number of very important studies have drawn out the disabling nature of many buildings and the spaces between them; see for example Rob Imrie's analyses of disability and architecture which have made a very significant contribution here (he worked for many years in a Geography Department but has relatively recently joined Goldsmiths as a Professor of Sociology). Imrie's research has been extremely significant in raising questions about the right to the city, and the key role in relation to access and facilitation played by architect-designed urban spaces (see for example Imrie and Kumar, 1998). Imrie's critical approach to these questions is one sensitised to the practice of architects as well as the built 'products' that are the outcome of such; see for example his analysis of architects' conceptualisations of the human body (2003), housing (2006), or the relationship between architectural regulation and practice (2011, with Emma Street). Imrie has recently been developing these set of concerns to address the Universal Design movement, which implicates architecture as part of attempts to make the built environment less hostile to users' bodies and capabilities (also see Jones [2014] on the same topic, or related studies revealing the normate assumptions that underpin urban design and architecture vis-à-vis ageing and architecture from Galčanová and Sýkorová [2014] and Jarmin Yeh [2015] or gendered embodiment assumptions [Grosz, 2001; Evans, 2006]).

There are also many studies of the 'social life' of buildings that draw less ostensibly on STS, but that are still fundamentally concerned with architectural-material culture. For example, see the museum studies scholar Suzanne MacLeod, whose 'new social biography' of the Walker Art Gallery in Liverpool – although not situated explicitly within the STS tradition – demonstrates clearly the ways in which careful empirical study of the materiality of a building, particularly focused on periods of experimentation in architectural fabric, can illuminate broader competing cultural visions concerning the social role of art. In particular, through careful archival and visual analysis, MacLeod charts the shifts in the self-conception of those governing the gallery alongside the various forms of architectural interventions commissioned by them. Or, in a similar vein, see for example the work of Linda Mulcahy, a socio-legal academic working in the Law Department at King's College London, who pursues analysis of the positioning of publics in court architecture. In her carefully argued and scholarly book *Legal Architecture* Mulcahy draws attention to the ways in which conceptualisation of 'the public' through history has been reflected in the positioning of publics in trials.

As is reflected by the work of both MacLeod and Mulcahy, it is fair to say that many extremely successful sociological engagements with architecture have come from outside the discipline formally considered. See for example the analysis of the major transformation of architectural practice afforded by computer aided design (CAD) by the architect and theorist Paolo Tombesi (2001), or the analysis of the architect and urbanist Simon Guy – in collaboration with Lancaster University sociologist Elisabeth Shove – on architectural technology, engineering, and green policy and practice. *The Glass State* (2006) by architectural theorist Annette Fierro is another significant contribution that engages in analysis of a technology popular in contemporary political architecture; addressing the Parisian Grand Projects with particular reference to the ways in which glass is positioned in political and architectural discourse, Fierro understands glass as a building material with significant symbolic associations vis-à-vis the discourses of transparency so common in European political discourse (also see Delanty and Jones, 2002; Jones, 2011).

In general a major strength of STS perspectives has been to add significant descriptive depth to sociological engagement with materiality. Recent accounts of parliament buildings (Danyi, 2012), ageing and the built environment (Yeh, 2015), gender and space (Bartram, 2011), and urban planning (Herberg, 2015), have all yielded much sociological insight about the built environment (see also the edited collection focused on STS-inspired sociological accounts of architecture edited by Anna-Lisa Müller and Werner Reichmann (2015), in which some of these chapters appear). While such STS-inspired analysis has been responsible for adding much momentum to sociological analyses of architecture and the built environment, a potential limitation of this approach is that a deep description of a particular site, material or building can sometimes miss the connections between architecture and the broader contextual relations in which buildings are commissioned, designed, and used.[9] Of course, from the perspective of this tradition, 'contexts' such as capitalism, democracy, or the social itself, may be considered false stabilities and artefacts of disciplinary knowledge production. Regardless, recent dynamic currents in 'sociological' STS studies of architecture have provided a useful corrective to the over-generalised accounts that can risk missing the nuance and specificity of both architectural production and product, and have doubtless added much to our understanding of human interactions with architecture and the built environment.

## CONCLUSION

While some sociologists have explicitly sought to articulate what a programmatic sociology of architecture may look like or include (Gutman, 1968; Zeisel, 1975; Gans, 1977; Ankerl, 1981; Champy, 2006; Delitz, 2006; 2009; Löw and Steets, 2010; Jones, 2011), the contributions assessed above were generally not addressed to such a task but rather to studying architecture as a profession or as a set of meaningful spaces (and interactions therein). I hope that this chapter serves as an encouragement to sociologists to give consideration to the social production of the built environment, even if this is understood quite minimally. For the sake of space, ironically, I have included those contributions quite tightly focused on architectural practice and the built outcomes of such, and have neglected to include related discussions of sociologies of space (see Löw and Steets, 2010), or those numerous analyses of social action that include more *en passant* engagement with the built environment (for an extension of this argument see Gieryn [2006]). One thing I would note is that as architect-designed buildings and spaces provide the contexts in which a great deal of social practice takes place, and against this backdrop there is much potential for more *en passant* sociological accounts of architecture (a point also made by Gieryn [2002] and Löw and Steets [2010] on architecture, space, and sociality). The rich and varied contributions surveyed have been brought together as a result of the latitude I have taken with respect to definitions of 'sociology' in general and 'cultural sociology' in particular, and it is notable that the research literature addressed above is so varied in theoretical and methodological approach.

My somewhat rough-and-ready typology, reflective of my own readings and interpretations – and in a number of cases limited by my linguistic limitations – has hopefully organised this literature in a legible and sensible way. Writing this chapter has strengthened my sense that this is an intellectually fruitful moment for 'sociologists of architecture'; as a community, even such a disparate and eclectic one, we find ourselves in the enviable position of exporting many analytical resources with respect to the built environment. Developments in STS-inspired research studies have attracted a group of career-young sociologists whom I feel have enlivened and sharpened thinking in this field. Well established questions of power, inequality, and space persist and are given specificity by engagement with buildings and the spaces between them. In conclusion I would echo the important points made with such precision and eloquence by many of those discussed above: architecture is entangled in projects of reproduction and celebrations of power, while also simultaneously providing a space for social experimentation and radical critique of the prevailing order. It is the tension that exists between these competing possibles and their realisation that provides such a rich context for sociological research.

## ACKNOWLEDGEMENTS

I am extremely grateful to a number of people for their perceptive and intellectually generous comments on this chapter. Colleagues themselves engaged in this research field – Robin Bartram, Rob Imrie, Anthony D. King, Suzanne MacLeod, and Leslie Sklair – all offered extremely valuable comments, as did my colleague Michael Mair. As ever, the usual disclaimers apply.

## NOTES

1 There are some exceptions though, with a number of taught programmes organised around sociologically oriented studies of the built environment. For example, there is a Sociology of Architecture postgraduate module in the Faculty of Social Sciences at Masaryk University, and a module that I co-ordinate as part of the Sociology undergraduate programme at the University of Liverpool. Manchester School of Architecture's MA in Architecture and Urbanism also draws in much of the STS research that characterises the work of colleagues working there. There is also a vibrant Sociology of Architecture study group of the German Sociological Association, which includes, amongst others, Heike Delitz, Monika Grubbaeur, Silke Steets, Anna-Lisa Müller and Werner Reichmann, all of whose work is discussed in this chapter (also see http://www.heike-delitz.de/Index%20archsoz.html). Another excellent online resource is Garry Stevens' www.archsoc.com, where he both 'lightens up' sociology and illuminates architecture. Further, there has recently been an international symposium on so-called 'starchitecture' hosted at Paris-Sorbonne, and organised by Maria Gravari-Barbas and Cécile Renard-Delautre.

2 A cursory glance at the literature reminds us that social research on architecture is not solely the domain of sociologists; many other cognate disciplines have explicitly sought to clarify positions on the built environment. For example, from cognate disciplines there have been self-defined geographies (Lees, 2001) and anthropologies (Buchli, 2013) of architecture.

3 One further thing that is noticeable here is that I have limited my discussion to relatively recent contributions, with the bulk of articles and books discussed having been published in the last thirty years or so; for a comprehensive engagement with the classical sociological tradition vis-à-vis architecture, see Heike Delitz's *Architektursoziologie* (2006) or the review chapter by Martina Löw and Silke Steets (2010). One of Delitz's other key contributions to the debate is a book, the title of which translates as *Built Society. Architecture as Medium of the Social*. This is a furthering of sociological engagement with the built environment, that draws out the socially-constitutive dynamics – both symbolic and non-representational – of designed spaces (I am grateful to Heike for discussing this book at length with me, and for Uta Karstein's review, 2011, the combination of which I hope have helped me understand the key claims of the book and help me bridge a language gap that has doubtless still limited my engagement with this research).

4 Since 1989, commemoration in many former Soviet states has become tied to new definitions of architectural spaces broadly understood, such as the oft-evident renaming of streets, squares, and monuments (Leach 1999; Young and Kaczmarek, 2008).

5 Garry Stevens, along with Lipstadt (2003), was one of the first to exploit the rich analytic potential of Pierre Bourdieu's perspective for analysis of architecture, although others have followed (for example Fowler and Wilson, 2004; Jones, 2009; 2011; Webster, 2010; Sahin-Dikmen, 2013), with particular reference to 'struggles in the [architectural] studio' and the ways in which architectural training is underpinned by social – and aesthetic – reproduction.

6   Blau also published a short reflection on the collaborative potential between architecture and sociology, although this call for inter-disciplinary collaboration perhaps strikes a more pessimistic tone than the one I am sounding here, I think Blau's analysis is contingent on a rather hermetic conception of sociology, with academic sociological research 'not very relevant or useful' (1991: 37) to architects in particular and in need of reformulation before connecting to the 'real world' [sic] (1991: 39) in general. The tone of this short commentary is puzzling, not least as Blau has been responsible for some of the most important sociological insights into the profession. Furthermore, and as reflected here, the intervening years suggest a highly fertile collaboration between sociology and architecture.
7   In fact, architectural libraries whose holdings contained such opened in this period, as architects consolidated an emergent aesthetic conception of their roles, reflected in expertise on styles and form (albeit allied to some practical skills in building that were learnt in apprenticeship) (Brain, 1991: 245).
8   Despite using the term 'architecture' in a somewhat portmanteau way, it is understood throughout as both a professional practice and the built outcomes of such. There are swingeing critiques the professionalisation of architecture, for example see the movement of Critical Regionalism, which amounts to an architectural critique of the standardising tendencies of modernism (Frampton, 1983). My discussion here, as arguably the field of research is generally understood, has an elite bias inasmuch as it is focused primarily on famous buildings designed by high-profile architects. Still, the chapter by Martina Löw and Silke Steets (2010) comes closest to my intentions here, albeit their analysis sits against a broader backdrop, taking account as it does of key sociological analyses of space and spatiality as well as studies of architecture, more tightly conscribed.
9   See, for example, critic Nikolas Pevsner, whose authoritative, sweeping accounts of architectural movements and buildings are notable for both their careful descriptive quality and their generalising tendency.

## REFERENCES

Adam, R. (2012) *The Globalization of Modern Architecture: The Impact of Politics, Economics, and Social Change on Architecture and Urban Design since 1990*. Cambridge: Cambridge Scholars Press.

Adams, A. and Tancred, P. (2000) *Designing Women: Gender and the Architectural Profession*. London: University of Toronto Press.

Ankerl, G. (1981) *Experimental Sociology of Architecture: A Guide to Theory, Research and Literature*. New York: Basic Books.

Appaduri, A. (1986) *The Social Life of Things*. Cambridge, MA: Cambridge University Press.

Ballantyne, A. (2007) *Deleuze and Guattari for Architects*. London: Routledge.

Bartram, R. (2011) 'Emplacing Ideologies of Risk and the Use of the Built Environment in Two Women's Residential Clubs in Turn of the 20th Century Chicago', MA thesis, Paper 545, at http://ecommons.luc.edu/luc_theses/545

Beck, U. (1999) 'The Open City: Architecture and Reflexive Modernity', in *Democracy Without Enemies*. Cambridge: Polity Press.

Bentmann, R. and Muller, M. (1992) *The Villa as Hegemonic Architecture*. New Jersey: Humanities Press.

Blau, J. (1984) *Architects and Firms: A Sociological Perspective on Architectural Practice*. Cambridge, MA: MIT Press.

Blau, J. (1991) 'The Context and Content of Collaboration: Architecture and Sociology', *Journal of Architectural Education*, 45(1): 36–40

Bonta, J. P. (1979) *Architecture and its Interpretation*. London: Lund Humphries.

Bozdoğan, S. (2001) *Modernism and Nation Building: Turkish Architectural Culture in the Early Republic*. Seattle and London: University of Washington Press.

Bozdoğan, S. and Akcan, E. (2012) *Turkey: Modern Architectures in History*. London: Reaktion Books.

Bracken, G. (ed.) (2012) *Aspects of Urbanization in China: Shanghai, Hong Kong, Guangzhou*. Amsterdam, Amsterdam University Press.

Brain, D. (1991) 'Practical Knowledge and Occupational Control: The Professionalization of Architecture in the United States', *Sociological Forum*, 6(2): 239–68.

Buchli, V. (2013) *An Anthropology of Architecture*. Bloomsbury: London.

Champy, F. (2001) *Sociologie de L'Architecture*. Paris: La Découverte.

Champy, F. (2006) 'Professional Discourses Under the Pressure of Economic Values: The Case of French Architects, Landscape Designers and Industrial Designers', *Current Sociology*, 54(4): 649–61.

Cohen, L., Wilkinson, A. and Arnold, J. (2005) '"Remember I'm the Bloody Architect!" Architects, Organizations and Discourses of Profession', *Work, Employment & Society*, 19(4): 775–96.

Coleman, N. (2015) *Lefebvre for Architects (Thinkers for Architects)*. London: Routledge.

Coutard, O. and Guy, S. (2007) 'STS and the City: Politics and Practices of Hope', *Science, Technology & Human Values*, 20(10): 1–22.

Crawford, M. (1991) 'Can Architects Be Socially Responsible?', in D. Ghirardo (ed.), *Out of Site: A Social Criticism of Architecture*. Seattle: Bay Press.

Cuff, D. (1991) *Architecture: The Story of Practice*. Cambridge, MA: MIT Press.

Cuff, D. (2014) 'Architecture's Undisciplined Urban Desire', *Architectural Theory Review*, 19(1): 92–7.

Danyi, E. (2012) 'The Architecture of Democracy', Center for Global Communication Studies, at https://cgcsblog.wordpress.com/2012/07/13/the-architecture-of-democracy-by-endre-danyi/ [last accessed 15 January 2015].

Delanty, G. and Jones, P. (2002) 'European Identity and Architecture', *European Journal of Social Theory*, 5(4): 449–63.

Delitz, H. (2006) *Architektursoziologie*. Bielefeld: Reihe Einsichten.

Delitz, H. (2009) *Gebaute Gesellschaft. Architektur als Medium des Sozialen*. Frankfurt: Verlag.

Dobrenko, E. (2007) *The Political Economy of Socialist Realism*. London: Yale University Press.

Dovey, K. (2000) 'The Silent Complicity of Architecture', in J. Hillier and E. Rooksby (eds), *Habitus 2000: A Sense of Place*. Aldershot: Ashgate.

Dutton, T. A. (1987) 'Design and Studio Pedagogy', *Journal of Architectural Education*, 41(1): 16–25.

Dutton, T. and Mann, L. (1996) *Reconstructing Architecture: Critical Discourses and Social Practices*. Minneapolis: University of Minnesota Press.

Dutton, T. and Mann, L. (2000) 'Problems in Theorizing "The Political" in Architectural Discourse', *Rethinking Marxism*, 12(4): 117–29.

Evans, B. (2006) '"Gluttony or Sloth": Critical Geographies of Bodies and Morality in (Anti) Obesity Policy', *Area*, 38(3): 259–67.

Fallan, K. (2008) 'Architecture in Action: Travelling with Actor-Network Theory in the Land of Architectural Research', *Architectural Theory Review*, 13(1): 80–96.

Fierro, A. (2006) *The Glass State: The Technology of the Spectacle, Paris 1981–1998*. Cambridge, MA: MIT Press.

Fontina-Giusti, G. (2013) *Foucault for Architects*. Routledge: London.

Fowler, B. and Wilson, F. (2004) 'Women Architects and their Discontents', *Sociology*, 38(1): 101–19.

Frampton, K. (1983) 'Towards a Critical Regionalism: Six Points for an Architecture of Resistance', in H. Foster (ed.), *Postmodern Culture: The Anti-Aesthetic*. London: Pluto.

Fuhrmann, J. (2015) 'Building "Objects of Desire": Workplace Studies and Reflections in the World of Architects'. Manuscript.

Galčanová, L. and Sýkorová, D. (2014) 'Socio-Spatial Aspects of Ageing in an Urban Context: An Example from Three Czech Republic Cities', *Ageing & Society*, 1–21.

Gans, H. (1977) 'Toward a Human Architecture: A Sociologist's View of the Profession', *Journal of Architectural Education*, 31(2): 26–31.

Gieryn, T. F. (2000) 'A Space for Place in Sociology', *Annual Review of Sociology*, 26: 462–93.

Gieryn, T. F. (2002) 'What Buildings Do', *Theory and Society*, 31: 35–74.

Gieryn, T. F. (2006) 'City as Truth-Spot: Laboratories and Field-Sites in Urban Studies', *Social Studies of Science* 36(1): 5–38.

Grosz, E. (2001) *Architecture from the Outside: Essays on Virtual and Real Space*. Foreword by Peter Eisenman. Cambridge, MA: MIT Press.

Grubbauer, M. (2014) 'Architecture, Economic Imaginaries and Urban Politics: The Office Tower as Socially-Classifying Device', *International Journal of Urban and Regional Research*, 38(1): 336–59.

Guggenheim, M. (2009) 'Building Memory: Architecture, Networks and Users', *Memory Studies*, 2(1): 39–53.

Guggenheim, M. (2013) 'Unifying and Decomposing Building Types: How to Analyse the Change of Use of Sacred Buildings', *Qualitative Sociology*, 36(4): 445–64.

Gutman, R. (1968) 'What Architectural Schools Expect from Sociology', *Journal of Architectural Education*, 22(2/3): 13–20.

Gutman, R. (1972) *People and Buildings*. New York: Basic Books.

Gutman, R. (1988) *Architectural Practice: A Critical View*. Princeton, NJ: Architectural Press.

Gutman, R. (1992) 'Architects and Power: The Natural Market for Architecture', *Progressive Architecture*, 73(12): 39–41.

Gutman, R. (2007) *Architecture from the Outside*. Princeton, NJ: Princeton University Press.

Guy, S. and Shove, E. (2000) *A Sociology of Energy, Buildings and the Environment*. London: Routledge.

Habermas, J. (1989) 'Modern and Postmodern Architecture', in *The New Conservatism: Cultural Criticism and the Historians' Debate*. Cambridge, MA: MIT Press.

Herberg, J. (2015) 'Putting Architecture in its Social Space: The Fields and Skills of Planning Maastricht', in A-M. Müller and W. Reichmann (eds), *Architecture, Materiality and Society: Connecting Sociology of Architecture with Science and Technology Studies*. Basingstoke: Palgrave.

Hirst, P. (2005) *Space and Power: Politics, War and Architecture*. Cambridge: Polity Press.

Imrie, R. (2003) 'Architects' Conceptions of the Human Body', *Environment and Planning D*, 21(1): 47–66.

Imrie, R. (2006) *Accessible Housing: Quality, Disability and Design*. London: Routledge.

Imrie, R. and Kumar, M. (1998) 'Focusing on Disability and Access in the Built Environment', *Disability & Society*, 13(3): 357–74.

Imrie, R. and Street, E. (2011) *Architectural Design and Regulation*. Oxford: Wiley-Blackwell.

Jianfei, Z. (2009) *Architecture of Modern China: A Historical Critique*. London, Routledge.

Jenson, M. (2014) *Mapping the Global Architect of Alterity: Practice, Education and Representation*. London: Routledge.

Jones, P. (2006) 'The Sociology of Architecture and the Politics of Building: The Discursive Construction of Ground Zero', *Sociology*, 40(3): 549–65.

Jones, P. (2009) 'Putting Architecture in its Social Place: A Cultural Political Economy of Architecture', *Urban Studies*, 46(12): 2519–36.

Jones, P. (2011) *The Sociology of Architecture*. Liverpool: Liverpool University Press.

Jones, P. (2014) 'Situating Universal Design Architecture: Designing With Whom?', *Disability & Rehabilitation*, 36(16): 1369–74.

Jones, P. (2015) 'Modelling Urban Futures: A Study of Architectural Models of Liverpool Waters', *City*, 19(4): 456–72.

Jones, P. and Card, K. (2011) 'Constructing "Social Architecture": The Politics of Representing Practice', *Architectural Theory Review*, 16(3): 228–44.

Kaika, M. and Thielen, K. (2006) 'Form Follows Power', *City*, 10(1): 59–69.

Karstein, U. (2011) 'Architecture As A Symbolic Medium: Heike Delitz, *Gebaute Gesellschaft. Architektur als Medium des Sozialen*', *European Journal of Sociology* (52)3: 570–572.

Kennedy, P. (2004) 'Linking the Local and the Global: Transnational Architects in a Globalizing World', in F. Eckhard and D. Hassenpflug (eds), *Urbanism and Globalization*. Frankfurt: Peter Lang.

King, A. D. (1976) *Colonial Urban Development: Culture, Social Power and Development*. London: Routledge Kegan & Paul.

King, A. D. (ed.) (1984) *Buildings and Society: Essays on the Social Development of the Built Environment*. London: Routledge, Kegan & Paul.

King, A. D. (2010) 'Notes Towards a Global Historical Sociology of Building Types', in M. Guggenheim and O. Soderstrom (eds) (2010) *How Global Mobility Transforms Architecture and Urban Form*. London: Routledge.

Knox, P. L. (1998) *Design Professionals and the Built Environment*. London: Nichols.

Knox, P. L. (1987) 'The Social Production of the Built Environment: Architects, Architecture and the Postmodern City', *Progress in Human Geography*, 11(3): 354–77.

Latour, B. and Yaneva, A. (2008) 'Give Me a Gun and I Will Make All Buildings Move: An ANT's View of Architecture', *Explorations in Architecture: Teaching, Design, Research*, 80–9.

Larson, M. S. (1993) *Behind the Postmodern Facade: Architectural Change in Late-Twentieth Century America*. Berkeley: University of California Press.

Larson, M. S. (1994) 'Architectural Competitions as Discursive Events', *Theory and Society*, 23(4): 469–504.

Leach, N. (ed.) (1999) *Architecture and Revolution*. London: Routledge.

Lees, L. (2001) 'Towards a Critical Geography of Architecture: The Case of the Ersatz Coliseum', *Cultural Geography*, 8(1): 51–86.

Lipstadt, H. (2003) 'Can "Art Professions" be Bourdieuean Fields of Cultural Production? The Case of the Architecture Competition', *Cultural Studies*, 30(3–4): 319–40.

Löw, M. and Steets, S. (2010) 'The Spatial Turn and the Sociology of the Built Environment', in K. Koniordos and S. Kyrtsis (eds), *Routledge Handbook of European Societies*. London: Routledge.

MacLeod, S. (2013) *Museum Architecture: A New Biography*. London: Routledge.

Markus, T. (1993) *Buildings and Power: Freedom and Control in the Origin of Modern Building Types*. London: Routledge.

Markus, T. and Cameron, D. (2003) *The Words Between the Spaces: Buildings and Language*. London: Routledge.

McNeill, D. (2009) *The Global Architect: Firms, Fame, and Urban Form*. London: Routledge.

Molnár, V. (2005) 'Cultural Politics and Modernist Architecture: The Tulip Debate in Postwar Hungary', *American Sociological Review*, 70(1): 111–35.

Molnár, V. (2013) *Building the State: Architecture, Politics, and State Formation in Post-war Central Europe*. London: Routledge.

Mulcahy, L. (2007) 'Architects of Justice: The Politics of Courtroom Design', *Social & Legal Studies*, 16(3): 383–403.

Mulcahy, L. (2011) *Legal Architecture: Justice, Due Process, and the Place of Law*. New York: Routledge.

Müller, A-M; and Reichmann, W. (eds) *Architecture, Materiality and Society: Connecting Sociology of Architecture with Science and Technology Studies*. Basingstoke: Palgrave

Pløger, J. (2010) 'Foucault's Dispotif and the City', *Planning Theory*, 7(1): 51–70.

Ren, X. (2011) *Building Globalization: Transnational Architecture Production in Urban China*. Chicago: University of Chicago Press.

Rudofsky, B. (1972 [1964]) *Architecture Without Architects: A Short Introduction to Non-Pedigreed Architecture*. New York: Academy Editions.

Sahin-Dikmen, M. (2013) *A Bourdieusian Lens onto Professions: A Case Study of Architecture*. PhD thesis, University of York, at http://etheses.whiterose.ac.uk/5616/

Saint, A. (1983) *The Image of the Architect*. New Haven and London: Yale University Press.

Saint, A. (1987) *Towards a Social Architecture*. New Haven and London: Yale University Press.

Schön, D. A. (1984) 'The Architectural Studio as an Exemplar of Education for Reflection-in-Action', *Journal of Architectural Education*, 38(1): 2–9.

Scott, J. C. (1998) *Seeing Like a State: How Certain Schemes to Improve the Human Condition have Failed*. New Haven, CT and London: Yale University Press.

Sinclair, C. and Stor, K. (2006) *Architecture for Humanity: Design Like You Give A Damn: Architectural Responses to Humanitarian Crises*. New York: Metropolis Books.

Sklair, L. (2005) 'The Transnational Capitalist Class and Contemporary Architecture in Globalizing Cities', *International Journal of Urban and Regional Research*, 29: 485–500.

Sklair, L. (2006) 'Iconic Architecture and Capitalist Globalization', *City*, 10(1): 21–47.

Sklair, L. (2010) 'Iconic Architecture and the Culture-Ideology of Consumerism', *Theory, Culture & Society*, 27(5): 135–59.

Sklair, L. (2013) 'Postcolonialisms, Globalization and Iconic Architecture', in O. P. Dwivedi and M. Kich (eds), *Postcolonial Theory in the Global Age: Interdisciplinary Essays*. North Carolina, USA: MacFarlane & Co. pp. 156–73.

Steets, S. (2015) Taking Berger and Luckmann into the realm of materiality: Architect as social construction. *Cultural Sociology*, 10(1) 93–108.

Steets, S. and Grubbaeur, M. (eds) (2014) 'Special Edition: The Making of Architects: Knowledge Production and Legitimation in Education and Professional Practice', *Architectural Theory Review*, 19(1).

Stevens, G. (1995) 'Struggle in the Studio: A Bourdivin Look at Architectural Pedagogy', *Journal of Architectural Education*, 49(2): 105–22.

Stevens, G. (1996) 'The Historical Demography of Architects', *Journal of the Society of Architectural Historians*, 55(4): 435–53.

Stevens, G. (1998) *The Favored Circle: The Social Foundations of Architectural Distinction*. Cambridge, MA: MIT Press.

Tafuri, M. ([1976] 1999) *Architecture and Utopia*. Cambridge, MA: MIT Press.

Therbon, G. (2002) 'Monumental Europe: The National Years. On the Iconography of European Capital Cities', *Housing, Theory and Society*, 19: 26–47.

Till, J. (2009) *Architecture Depends*. Cambridge, MA: MIT Press.

Tombesi, P. (2001) 'A True South for Design? The New International Division of Labour in Architecture', *Architectural Research Quarterly*, 5(2): 171–80.

Vale, L. J. (1992) *Architecture, Power, and National Identity*. New Haven, CT: Yale University Press.

Vidler, A. (1991) 'Researching Revolutionary Architecture', *Journal of Architectural Education*, 44(4): 206–10.

Webster, H. (2010) *Bourdieu for Architects*. London: Routledge.

Wolff, J. (1981) *The Social Production of Art*. London: Macmillan.

Yaneva, A. (2005) 'Scaling Up and Down: Extraction Trials in Architectural Design', *Social Studies of Science*, 35(6): 867–94.

Yaneva, A. (2009) *Made by the Office of Metropolitan Architecture: An Ethnography of Design*. Rotterdam: Uitgeverij.

Yaneva, A. (2012) *Mapping Controversies in Architecture*. Farnham, UK: Ashgate.

Yeh, J. C. (2015) 'The Lure of Restoration: Transforming Buildings and Bodies for Ever-Longer Life', in A-M. Müller and W. Reichmann (eds), *Architecture, Materiality and Society: Connecting Sociology of Architecture with Science and Technology Studies*. Basingstoke: Palgrave.

Young, C. and Kaczmarek, S. (2008) 'The Socialist and Postsocialist Urban Identity in Central and Eastern Europe: The Case of Łódź, Poland', *European Urban and Regional Studies*, 15(1): 53–70.

Zeisel, J. (1975) *Sociology and Architectural Design*. New York: Russell Sage Foundation.

# 35

# For a Sociology of the Cinema

Tatiana Signorelli Heise and Andrew Tudor

## INTRODUCTION

On December 28th 1895, in the Grand Café in Paris, the Lumière brothers screened the first ten short films that they had made with their recently patented *cinématographe* machine, an occasion customarily, if debatably, identified as the birth of the cinema. Earlier that year, also in Paris, Émile Durkheim had published his manifesto for the newly legitimate discipline of sociology, *Les Règles de la Méthode Sociologique*, and, in 1896, as the Lumières toured the world with their show, he became the founding director of *L'Année Sociologique*, a journal which continues publication to this day. In Germany, also in 1896, Max Weber took up a chair in sociology at the University of Heidelberg and, by the time that the new medium was beginning to develop its narrative potential in *The Great Train Robbery* of 1903, he was in the process of writing what would become his best known work: *Die protestantische Ethik und der 'Geist' des Kapitalismus* (1905). Two decades later in the USA, Hollywood had become the centre of a rampantly capitalist, world-wide film industry, while the American variant of the discipline of sociology was attaining professional and academic respectability in the likes of the Chicago School in the 1920s, and, in the following decade, the influential Harvard sociology department. So, although it is the case that Comte's initial prescription for a scientific discipline of sociology far predates the founding moments of cinema, there is a real sense in which the cinema and sociology grew to maturity together.

It is therefore all the more striking that there has been so little systematic sociology of the cinema. Sociology, *the* discipline born of a desire to properly comprehend the rise of modern society, might well have been expected to seek out the new medium which was seen by many as one of the most distinctive products of modernity itself. Yet, by and large, it has never done so in a sustained way, making only intermittent contributions to our understanding of the social role and cultural significance of film. As we shall seek to show here, there are discernible theoretical and empirical reasons for this puzzling omission, as well as problems arising from the kind of inter-disciplinary boundary disputes that have so often dogged those focusing in areas where the social sciences rub up against the humanities. One of us (Tudor, 1998) has previously explored some of these questions, primarily in the context of sociology's troubled relationship with film studies. Here, however, we shall focus principally on the history of sociological approaches to the cinema – especially during the early era of movie dominance when more of a contribution might have been expected – as well as on the conceptual reasons for their comparative rarity.

## BEGINNINGS

That history is probably best begun in 1914 with the appearance of Emilie Altenloh's pioneering study (Altenloh, 1914). Though there are other early texts which purport to examine the new medium's social role, they are essentially moralising works – and negative ones at that – rather than sociological reflections founded on systematic evidence. Altenloh's dissertation, however, is quite distinctive. Conducted under the supervision of Alfred Weber at the University of Heidelberg, it runs to 102 pages in the original German, of which some eighty pages are available in translation (Altenloh, 2001; 2004). In Part I she examines film production, its economic organisation, the national source of exhibited films, and the film genres which dominated the industry at the time. Sections 3 and 4 of this discussion form the translation in Altenloh (2004). Part II examines the contemporary audience, its social composition, its tastes and its cinema-going practices. The entirety of this Part, plus some elements from the dissertation's overall introduction, are translated in Altenloh (2001).

The study is based primarily on survey research conducted in the city of Mannheim during the course of 1912/13, some of the data derived from brief self-completed questionnaires and some from verbal responses.[1] One way or another, 2400 responses were obtained, and, while by modern standards no clear sampling frame is elucidated, Altenloh evidently sought to cover as wide a range of respondents as possible across the familiar face-sheet dimensions of age, gender and (occupational) class. In pursuing the systematic collection of empirical materials in this way she was leaning on a tradition of survey research that had developed in Germany in the second half of the 19th century (Oberschall, 1965), and she was no doubt much influenced in this respect by Alfred Weber's concerns with political economics, the urban environment and social geography.

We have no need here to summarise her findings in any detail. More interesting for present purposes are the kinds of presuppositions implicit in her presentation and analysis of the survey data. While there is no systematic theorising as such in her study – hardly surprising given the intellectual context in which she was working – certain general assumptions are apparent. Throughout the analysis there is both a presumption of, and an attempt to demonstrate empirically, the central significance of class in forming cinema-going behaviour. Embedded in this discussion is a relatively elaborate model of occupational class segmentation. So, for example, when considering 'young male workers' she distinguishes three sub-categories whose cinema-going tastes differ: a 'bottom group consisting of those not tied to any particular occupational group'; a 'characteristically proletarian' group of metalworkers; and 'a petit-bourgeois group' of clerical assistants, technicians and the like (Altenloh, 2001: 264). The adult audience is even further sub-classified, distinguishing among artisans (urban and rural), trade unionists, rural labourers, working-class women, male clerical workers, female clerical assistants, and 'women of the higher social classes' (Altenloh, 2001: 285). Along with the fact that her data enables her to demonstrate different patterns of cinema-going and film taste among and between these groups, the systematic concern with class segments serves to problematise the well-entrenched conventional view that early cinema-going was largely a homogenous lower-class pursuit. While it is clear from her study that upper echelons of the class system are not frequent cinema-goers, the audience from the lower and middle sectors vary significantly in patterns of taste and attendance. As Loiperdinger (1996: 44) observes, Altenloh's work suggests that 'the most significant feature of the cinema-going public before World War I was not its proletarian origins (however significant a proportion this represented) but its class and gender diversity'.

And Altenloh does indeed pay close attention to the role of gender in cinema-going behaviour. She examines gendered differences in preferences for particular genres and narratives as well as considering the greater frequency of attendance by women even of the otherwise absent higher social classes. Occasionally she speculates on why this gender specificity is apparent.

> Cinema brings representations of a wider world to small towns, it shows women the new Paris fashions, and the kinds of hats that are being worn. With sensations large and small, cinema helps them to while away those dreary daytime hours that are these days increasing as domestic chores become progressively simpler. Films must be especially accessible to women, and indeed it is said that women tend to absorb cinematic impressions on a purely emotional level, as a unified whole. (Altenloh, 2001: 285)

The implicit theorisation here evidently takes for granted prevailing social attitudes to the sexual division of labour, though the very fact of her close attention to gender differences remains a significant distinguishing feature of the study.

Also apparent among the more general reflections occasioned by the data is a characteristic view of the impact industrial modernity is having on the lifestyles of her survey subjects. Distinguishing between a small elite and the much larger social groupings created by the industrial economy, she argues in familiar terms that '[m]ost people are integrated into the overall economic system like a small cog in a machine, and this system not only dominates people's working lives but also constrains the totality of the individual' (Altenloh, 2001: 251). As it did for so many other observers of early industrialism, this view leads her towards an often negative assessment of the quality of the culture consumed by those thus constrained, an evaluation which finds expression in an incipient elitism.

> The fact that erotic films and films about criminals attract such large audiences is utterly explicable: surely these films are the only ones that can strike a chord among the mass of people whose intellectual life is often in deep slumber and who have nothing in common with each other, at least as far as more elevated matters are concerned. (Altenloh, 2001: 258)

Such judgements are familiar enough, of course, and Altenloh is rather less determined in making them than many of her contemporaries. Partly because her data leads her to recognise the heterogeneity of the growing cinema audience, the elitism which she derives from her own cultural and educational background is more qualified than was then often the norm. Indeed, at times she adopts a position which assumes considerable analytic distance from such value judgements, leading her towards consideration of the processes through which people establish cultural distinction for themselves and thereby anticipating analyses found so many years later in Bourdieu (1986). In discussing male clerical workers, for example, she observes that '… the younger ones will emphasise rather strongly – often unnecessarily so – that they go to a better kind of movie theatre, while for the older ones this becomes a quite natural expression of their distinct group identity' (Altenloh, 2001: 278). And more generally, of older adult workers she notes that '[w]anting to 'have a share' in the intellectual property of society motivates them to go to the theatre, to concerts and to museums' (Altenloh, 2001: 270), an observation which carries her quite close to the Bourdieusian concept of cultural capital.

There is, then, a certain ambivalence in Altenloh's work which stems from the tension between, on the one hand, her desire to pay neutral, analytic attention to her extensive body of data and thus follow where it leads, and, on the other, the negative and elitist views of the new medium which were in currency at the time. Accordingly, mixed in with often perceptive observations sensitive to the nuances of audience behaviour we find phrases which reveal firm moral judgements: 'a group as weak, as morally wayward and as irresponsible as this' (Altenloh, 2001: 265); 'one cannot fail to recognize the moral threat that the cinema poses to the city's young people' (266); 'the average person needs something that will occupy his senses but requires no effort' (288). Oberschall (1965: 87), in a somewhat dismissive summary of her study, goes so far as to suggest that '[s]he used her data to illustrate the preconceived notions she entertained on the effects of seeing blood and violence upon an audience bent on cheap entertainment'. This allegation, though colourful, is unduly harsh, but there is certainly some truth to it, and her preconceptions are particularly apparent where the presumed negative impact of film on children is concerned, an area in which she suggests state intervention might be appropriate (Altenloh, 2001: 263). In that, of course, she was not alone, and the later Payne Fund Studies, to which we shall shortly turn, were significantly driven by such concerns. Nevertheless, Altenloh's research is distinguished by an admirable commitment to systematic data collection and by her willingness to take seriously the new medium and its audience on its, and their, own terms. As a piece of early work on the sociology of the cinema it remains exemplary.

The next major attempt to formulate a sociological, indeed a social science approach to the cinema, does not arrive until the late 1920s and early 1930s with a series of research projects conducted in the United States and subsequently known as the Payne Fund Studies. These projects were initiated by William Harrison Short, a Congregationalist minister much concerned about the potential impact the movies might have on children's behaviour and moral perceptions, and founding director in 1927 of the National Committee for the Study of Social Values in Motion Pictures. Short saw the products of the by now extensive film industry as a moral and practical threat to the youth of America, and in search of concrete evidence to support his views he recruited W.W. Charters, then Professor of Education at the University of Chicago, as overall research director for the project. The studies that they initiated were mostly conducted between 1928 and 1932 in a variety of disciplinary contexts, though clearly much influenced by what is now seen as the Chicago School approach to social science. Seven volumes reporting the research were published in 1933, ranging across such topics as film content, effects on children's attitudes, the social conduct of fans, the cinema's relation with juvenile delinquency, and so on. A notional popularization of the research by Henry James Forman was also published ahead of the studies themselves under the somewhat tendentious title *Our Movie Made Children* (1933), evidently directed at influencing social policy and 'giving the false impression that the researchers had lent themselves to a moralizing crusade' (Jowett et al., 1996: 7). A more sober summarizing volume was produced by Charters himself and given the neutral title which provided the rubric for the whole series: *Motion Pictures and Youth* (1933).

As the contrast between those two titles might suggest, there is a marked tension apparent in the studies between social scientific rigour and morally concerned commitment. Given Short's motives for initiating the research this is hardly surprising. Jowett et al. (1996: 58) in their excellent examination of the history and character of the studies observe that 'Short labored incessantly to shape the researchers' questions and results to forward his imperatives'. Initially, at least, some of the researchers themselves (including, notably, Herbert Blumer) were also inclined to presuppose that the cinema's social and psychological role was deeply problematic, and while for the most part the reported findings did not offer unqualified support to such a view, public perception was significantly formed by Short's beliefs and Forman's volume. This bending of the research findings was a matter of concern for the researchers and for Charters, and throughout the enterprise they were disagreeing among themselves as to what constituted an acceptable social science methodology and, therefore, on what conclusions might validly be drawn from their work.

A detailed account of all this can be found in Jowett et al.'s (1996) indispensable volume, which provides fascinating insights into the history of the studies, thereby correcting many of the mistaken comments made about them by later observers. We have neither need nor space to enter into this detail here so will confine ourselves to some observations about the theoretical and methodological presumptions which informed the Payne Fund research. On the theoretical front it is probably safe to say that coming, as they did, from different disciplines within the broad social science rubric, the researchers did not share a conceptual framework – either in general terms or in specifically focusing on the cinema. These differences crossed various conceptual dimensions, though on the matter of conducting value-neutral research they by and large concurred, if with different emphases. As Jowett et al. (1996: 58) note:

The PFS were undertaken during a period of methodological and ideological conflicts in the social sciences. Debates over whether academic reaction to social problems should favor value-oriented social policy or value-neutral objective study led Charters and most of the sociologists and psychologists involved in the Payne Fund program to stress objectivity over advocacy.

But although they could agree on the broad need for evidence-based conclusions – a position which led to considerable tensions with Short – the concepts to be deployed and the frameworks within which data were to be interpreted were far from settled. Part of that, of course, arose from disciplinary differences; sociology and psychology have often made uneasy bedfellows. In this context it is significant that even five years after the publication of the Studies, Paul G. Cressey, who had himself been one of the researchers,[2] still felt it necessary to propose that '[w]hat is most needed today is an adequate frame of reference for studying the motion picture which is acceptable to all the special disciplines involved in such research' (Cressey, 1938: 518). By the late thirties, of course, the necessity for such systematic sociological theorising had become more widely accepted. The kind of empirical research harnessed to a pragmatic policy orientation that informed Chicago School sociology was being supplanted by a growing theoretical emphasis and, in the case of the increasingly significant Harvard department, by a commitment to developing a general theory that would draw together the social sciences as Cressey desired. While Cressey was hardly a follower of Talcott Parsons, the main inspiration for this 'general theory of action', his analysis of the motion picture experience does emphasise its systemic character, the need to fully comprehend the nature of the social situation in which cinema is viewed, the role of identification in that experience, and the interactive importance of social background and personality. 'The cinema's role in general conduct', he argues 'is found for the most part to be *reflexive*, to take its specific character from the social configuration, the social-psychological "frame" in which the motion picture is experienced and in which responses to it arise' (Cressey, 1938: 523). Unfortunately, as we shall see, the distinctive approach to 'mass communication' which would subsequently come to dominate research in the forties and fifties resorted to rather cruder models of the communication process than that proposed here by Cressey.

So, what kind of contribution did the Payne Fund Studies make to sociological understanding of the cinema? Clearly they provide an extraordinary range of empirical materials about the consumption of film in the late twenties and early thirties. Where they equally clearly fail is in drawing together that material into a systematic analysis. This is partly because their research methodologies are diverse in nature, ranging from experimental studies to ethnographic portraits. It was always going to be difficult to synthesise such diverse types of evidence, let alone in the absence of an overarching conceptual scheme within which to make them make sense. Indeed, the researchers themselves were increasingly at odds with each other as to what could be inferred from their work: '[t]heir growing antipathies blended personal animosity, departmental and disciplinary rivalries and ideological disagreements over how the Payne Fund research should be interpreted' (Jowett et al., 1996: 89). In the absence of agreement, the field was left clear for the likes of Forman to present an account emphasising the (undesirable) influence of the movies, and, in consequence, for a general perception to develop that the Studies supported some kind of 'strong effects' model. This is not entirely unjustified. The driving force for the whole Payne Fund enterprise was to find evidence for the presumed negative impact of the cinema on young people, even if not all the researchers felt that they had found such evidence. Furthermore – Cressey's significant qualifications notwithstanding – the lack of a theoretical, as opposed to a policy-oriented, focus meant that the central methodological concern to find ways of measuring such presumed effects would be their major legacy to later media research. And, of course, if research always begins by asking about effects, then, in the absence of appropriate contextual theorisation, it is unlikely to come up with an account which addresses the interactive complexity of people's responses to a medium as rich as film. So although, as Jowett et al. (1996: 11) claim, the Payne Fund researchers 'were not all naïve adherents to what has been caricatured as the 'hypodermic' or 'magic bullet' theory of mass communications', the policy-driven focus of the studies and their lack of a shared theoretical frame of reference meant that they lent considerable weight to such a perspective. As the first large-scale body of empirical work on a mass medium, they unwittingly provided the foundations on which that hypodermic model could come to dominate later mass communications research.

## MASS SOCIETY AND MASS CULTURE

Even though Altenloh's work and the Payne Fund Studies constitute promising beginnings for sociological research into film, theirs was a promise which was not fulfilled. The period from the 1940s to the 1960s saw an enormous expansion in sociology generally and, more specifically, in studies of the various mass media. However, relatively little of this research attended directly to the cinema, surprisingly given that film remained the dominant mass medium in audience terms until the growth of television precipitated the first of several crises for the industry. Two factors are central to this somewhat puzzling neglect. One derives from the widespread influence of 'mass society' ideas in the post-war period, with their far-reaching presumptions about the problematic and simplistic nature of the cultural products of such a society. The second, not unrelated of course, is to be found in the constant focus on measuring the direct effects of mass communications, with its attendant paucity of theoretical contextualisation, its mechanistic reliance on reductive forms of 'content analysis', and its consequent failure to grapple with the specifics of cinematic 'language'.

This idea that capitalist modernity was generating a 'mass society' and a concomitant 'mass culture' was not new in the 1940s and 1950s; indeed, its origins can be traced in 19th-century thought (Swingewood, 1977). But it found its most forceful articulation in the mid-20th century and in a variety of forms. Conventionally, mass society and mass culture arguments are divided into those of the left and right, with the former often exemplified in the Marxist-inflected critical sociology of the Frankfurt School, and the latter associated with conservative cultural criticism of the kind espoused by the likes of Eliot and Leavis. Whatever their differing analyses of the underlying causes, however, their diagnosis of the crassness of popular culture remains broadly the same. As early as 1930 Leavis (1930: 11) is bemoaning 'that deliberate exploitation of the cheap response which characterises our civilisation', a phenomenon which he saw as becoming all pervasive in 20th-century popular culture. And in 1940 Horkheimer and Adorno (2004: 170), starting from a radically different socio-political analysis, bluntly conclude that '[u]nder monopoly all mass culture is identical'. As that unlikely consensus between left and right suggests, while there are certainly diverse explanations for the alleged emergence of mass society and mass culture, a number of which find expression in the media sociology of the period, they all tend to converge on the view that mass culture is simplistic and all too often meretricious. Aside from their unreflective elitism, such views have the unfortunate consequence of precluding detailed and sensitive analyses of the media, since, in this conception, popular cultural forms self-evidently neither merit nor require such attention. Mass media products, then, are *presumed* to be homogenous and straightforward, rather than demonstrated to be thus, and the methodologies developed for their examination under the general rubric of 'content analysis' are insensitive to the distinctive specificities of different forms and to the potential complexity of meanings to which they may give rise. From this perspective, therefore, it is impossible to grasp the remarkable variation and depth created in the first half-century of film history, and the cinema comes to be seen as just another pernicious purveyor of trivial entertainment; a 'conclusion' which simply echoes the mass culture presumptions from which analysis begins.

Implicit in mass society theories, furthermore, is a belief in the remarkable strength of media effects and their role in creating this undesirable and lowest common denominator mass culture. This is well captured in a famous rhetorical passage from C. Wright Mills' *The Power Elite*:

> (1) The media tell the man in the mass who he is – they give him identity; (2) they tell him what he wants to be – they give him aspirations; (3) they tell him how to get that way – they give him technique; and (4) they tell him how to feel that he is that way even when he is not – they give him escape. (Mills, 1959: 314)

In this account the 'man in the mass' is a victim, always on the receiving end of all-powerful media messages. Here, of course, we encounter the discourse of the so-called 'hypodermic model' of mass communication wherein the media metaphorically inject a powerful drug into the receptive vein of the body politic. Quite how pervasive was this model has been a matter for some debate (Bineham, 1988; Lubken, 2008), but here it suffices only to recognise that part and parcel of the mass society perspective was the assumption that the media were powerful sources of largely one-way influence, and that the primary task of research was to measure those effects. Any suggestion, therefore, that film was a rich, meaning-making artefact that would only properly be intelligible as a complex interaction between medium and spectator proved to be anathema to the prevailing modes of mass communications research.[3] The methodologies of content analysis – themselves a product of an overly scientific epistemology – were simply inadequate to the task of capturing the modes of meaning construction that the cinema and its audiences had created (Tudor, 1995; 1999: 22–33).

In consequence of the ontological and epistemological assumptions embedded in the mass society perspective, and its offshoot in effects research, film, as a by then highly developed 'language' and an extensive cultural resource, was largely ignored in the sociology of mass communications. There is a scattering of interesting work, particularly from the late 1930s to the early 1950s, some of it developing a kind of mass social psychology of film in which the cinema is seen as a domain in which particular kinds of collective fantasies are played out. In their different ways, Kracauer (1947) and Wolfenstein and Leites (1950) exemplify this approach. A more socially oriented perspective informs Margaret Farrand Thorp's 1939 *America at the Movies*, though the book itself, for all its perceptive concern with the significance of the movies for American culture, shows little sign of a specifically sociological sensibility.[4] In that same year, however, Rosten (1939) published the first report from his more than two years of systematic empirical research into Hollywood, funded by both Carnegie and Rockefeller Foundations, and employing several research staff. Like so many of the earlier Payne Fund Researchers, Rosten was a graduate of the Chicago School and had been a PhD student under Harold Lasswell, though he also worked as a journalist and briefly as a screenwriter. The research was heavily influenced by the Lynd's famous 'Middletown' studies (Lynd and Lynd, 1929; 1937) with Rosten aiming to examine Hollywood in detail from a similar objective, social science viewpoint. Only one volume was published (Rosten, 1941), though a second was projected but became a casualty of the onset of war and Rosten's consequent deployment elsewhere.

Like so many of his contemporaries, Rosten was convinced both of the general cultural inferiority of the products of the movie industry and of their far-reaching influence on individuals and society at large. He also stressed the centrality of the tension between creativity and commercialism in Hollywood, as would Powdermaker (1947; 1950) in her later anthropological study, and he proposes a model of Hollywood society as a hierarchical social system comprised of three concentric circles differentiated from each other by status and financial reward. In support of his analysis Rosten provides a good deal of factual and statistical information derived from extensive survey and interview work, government and industry statistics, and an array of less formal sources consequent upon his having, to some degree, an insider perspective. There is therefore also much anecdotal material in his study, and the style is journalistic rather than academic. More significantly, and hardly surprising at that time, the research lacks the kind of integrating perspective that, as we have seen, Cressey (1938) thought necessary if social science studies of the cinema were to progress. Nevertheless, as Sullivan (2009) suggests, Rosten's work merits more attention than it has received.

Powdermaker (1950) is also concerned to provide a portrait of Hollywood society, in her case based on a year of interviewing and participant observation in 1946/47. It is her background in social anthropology that principally distinguishes her approach – she did graduate work at the LSE with Malinowski. Her aim in the Hollywood study was 'to explain in nontechnical language how the social system underlying the production of movies influences them' (Powdermaker, 1950: 9) and in this she partially succeeds. She offers some vivid accounts of the mores of Hollywood society, and is at her most interesting in documenting what might be described as the crisis culture which pervades Hollywood life – a feature to which Rosten also draws attention. At the time her study received a mixed reception. Predictably, it drew negative comments from industry sources like *Variety*, and, more surprisingly, an extraordinarily aggressive review from Robert Bierstedt (1951) in the *American Sociological Review*. Although she did respond with some justice to Bierstedt's attack, looking back on the study in the 1960s, Powdermaker (1967: 11) professed herself unhappy with various aspects of it. Nevertheless, it remains a significant and rare attempt to apply the concepts and methods of anthropology to the workings of film production.

Perhaps the oddest of these sporadic 1940s attempts to foster a sociology of film are the two related volumes produced by J.P. Mayer (1946b; 1948). This research was initially supported by British studio and cinema owner J. Arthur Rank, an arrangement which came to an end after a year, and although Mayer observes that they did not 'quarrel', he does stress the importance of his developing an *independent* piece of research (1946b: 11); certainly, his subsequent negative evaluations of the growing commercial monopoly in production and distribution would not have enamoured him to Rank. Much of both volumes consists of essay-like responses to Mayer's questionnaires from Rank cinema audience members (including children) and, later, readers of the popular film magazine *Picturegoer*. This material does cast interesting light on the views of keen cinemagoers of the period, but very little is added to it in the way of significant sociological analysis. Even allowing for the disciplinary heterogeneity of British sociology at the time, Mayer's sociological observations are limited and somewhat eccentric. Drawing on Lévy-Bruhl and Malinowski he suggests that 'myth' is key to a sociological approach to film. Cinema audiences are seeking a '*participation mystique* in the events on the screen' (1946b: 19), through which they achieve a form of self-identification. This, in his view, is not a positive development. Though many of his respondents claim that films had helped them to discover their 'real' personalities, Mayer refuses to take that at face value, arguing instead that what they have established is themselves as 'types' derived from films. Accordingly, '... the majority of films we see are pernicious to our nervous system. They are a mere drug which undermines our health, physical and spiritual' (1946b: 278–9). Lurking behind this observation, of course, are the familiar mass culture/strong effects assumptions which in Mayer's case lead him to argue for state intervention, not simply to prevent economic monopoly, but also to exert 'spiritual' control over the 'value patterns' of films. In a revealing exception to this requirement, he adds: '... the artistic and cultural standard of a cinema like *The Academy* in London must under all circumstances be maintained. Here "control" would appear to be quite unnecessary or purely formal' (1946b: 324). As always in negative evaluations of mass culture, the educated elite (Academy audiences in this case) remains immune. Indeed, in his second volume he expands on this theme in terms of the need for 'cultural leadership' from 'a leading and responsible *élite* not only in the sphere of politics but also in the realm of culture' (Mayer, 1948: 244). Clearly the ordinary cinema audience could not be trusted.

The cinema audience was also the focus of Leo A. Handel's *Hollywood Looks at its Audience* (1950), but from a rather different point of view. Another writer sometimes (mis)described as a sociologist, Handel had a background in economics and for most of the 1940s ran the Motion Picture Research Bureau at MGM, which, along with Gallup's Audience Research Inc., was responsible for modernising the somewhat crude methodologies of market research which had hitherto prevailed in the movie business (Handel, 1953). While providing a profusion of data derived from studio-sponsored research into audience preferences, some of which is of considerable interest for historians of 1940s Hollywood, the research on which his book reports is inevitably driven by the commercial imperatives of the film producers rather than by any more analytical social science concerns. As Paul F. Lazarsfeld observes in the book's foreword: 'The reader will not find in this text any attempt to connect film research with the broader social and political problems of our time' (Handel, 1950: xiii), adding, with some regret, 'but he would probably find it nowhere'.

It is significant that the handful of aspiring contributions to a sociology of film examined above have so little to say about film content.

Powdermaker and Rosten offer illuminating accounts of the social structures of production, Handel and Mayer quantitatively and qualitatively explore audience responses, Thorp provides general cultural reflections, but no one asks *systematically* about the distinctive language of film and the associated construction of meaning on the part of film spectators. In part that is a consequence of the blinkers imposed by mass culture presuppositions about the simplicity, even crudity, of media messages. In part also it derives from the dominance of particular kinds of content analysis techniques which were not well suited to dealing with relatively complex narratives, as opposed to, for example, news reports or propaganda pieces. This failure to address how film language worked was shortly to change, but in the newly emergent field of film studies rather than in sociology.

## THE RISE (AND RISE) OF FILM STUDIES

The 1960s and 1970s saw a remarkable growth in scholarly work on the cinema and a concomitant expansion of film studies departments in institutions of higher education, a development which proved to be a mixed blessing for the (still) nascent sociology of film. The growth of interest was welcome enough and for a while it appeared as if a useful alliance might be forged between sociology and the newly emergent discipline (Wollen, 1969). However, in the event, film studies moved in a different direction, developing a body of theory which effectively precluded such an alliance. This is not the place to examine the considerable intricacies of post-1970 film theory; its relation to sociology has been explored elsewhere (Tudor, 1998: 192–3). Other than tensions arising from the long-standing mistrust of sociology by those in traditional literary studies (from which film studies significantly emerged), the fundamental assumptions of the new film theory were at odds with more sociological approaches. Not, it should be noted, because sociology of film was trapped in the unacceptable empiricism of earlier mass communications research, although that claim was frequently made. It was, rather, a consequence of the conceptual emphases that entered film studies from structuralism and semiotics. These newly arrived perspectives generated a timely concern with the systematic analysis of film language, and one which, furthermore, logically necessitated examination of the social construction of these language-like processes in filmic communication. Here was an opportunity for an appropriately formulated sociology. But, as a result of the particular structuralist ideas that emerged after the first wave of Saussurian influence, the dominant tradition in film theory came to depend on concepts derived from Althusser's theories of ideology and Lacan's distinctive psychoanalytic approach to subject formation, rather than on a more thoroughgoing social (or even sociological) perspective. This remarkable combination of structuralist *enfants terribles* gave rise to a theory of filmic communication which was as deterministic in its way as was the earlier mass society/hypodermic model. The very structure of film language was conceived as imbued with ideology and, in what came to be known as subject-positioning theory, the film spectator was conceived as constructed by the film text primarily through that ideological positioning. The most influential variation of these ideas was found in 'Screen theory', so called because its main locus was in the journal *Screen* (Jancovich, 1995; Tudor, 1999: 81–108), which, together with its conceptual offshoots, was to occupy a dominant position in film theorising for the next two decades.

Meanwhile there remained sporadic attempts at developing a more thoroughgoing sociology of film. In the early years some were entirely independent of the burgeoning field of film studies where popular cinema had increasingly become the focus. Huaco (1965), for example, offers a study of 'film art' as found in three 'film movements': German expressionism; Soviet expressive realism; and Italian neorealism. He proposes a macroscopic model which utilises a somewhat uneasy combination of Marxian base/superstructure imagery with 'categories borrowed from the work of Neil J. Smelser' (1965: 18). He assumes that some films can validly be seen as 'art' and, in marked contrast with popular cinema, therefore merit close attention in a mode similar to the then approaches of the sociologies of art and literature. Quite what distinguished this 'film art' is not made clear. He utilises what he describes as 'content analysis of film plots' (1965: 20) to establish the 'ideology' of the film movement, though the details of this methodology are also unclear. In assuming a traditional view of the aesthetic distinctiveness of 'art cinema' his is the last ostensibly sociological study conducted without reference to popular cinema, which was rapidly becoming a key focus in modern film theorising.

But before the divergent paths of film theory and film sociology became fully apparent, there remained sufficient, perhaps naive, optimism about future possibilities to encourage sociologists in programmatic explorations of the field. Both Jarvie (1970) and Tudor (1974) offer field-mapping enterprises, if from somewhat different theoretical starting points. But as film studies colonised the field through into the 1980s and 1990s, specifically sociological contributions became increasingly rare. To be sure, writers with sociological backgrounds continued to contribute significant work, but not with the objective of constituting a distinctive sociology *of* the cinema. They might in part utilise perspectives drawn from sociology, and they certainly attended to social dimensions of the cinematic institutions and products which concerned them, but in a piecemeal way. The diversity of such material can be seen in, for example, Denzin (1991; 1995) and Orr (1993; 1998; 2000) who, in their different ways, address general issues of the social theorisation of modernism and postmodernism by reference to the cinema, or in more specific studies such as those by Wright (1975) on the Western, Hill (1986; 1999) on British cinema, or Tudor (1989) on horror movies, which are sociologically inflected but without in any way constituting a sociology of film as such. During this period there also developed a substantial literature, particularly in the journal *Teaching Sociology*, focusing upon the use of film as a teaching resource for sociology, but sometimes also exploring more general issues (e.g. among many others, Demerath, 1981; Prendergast, 1986; Burton, 1988; Pescosolido, 1990; Leblanc, 1998; Dowd, 1999). In addition there were always organizational studies of the film industry, some of which, such as Baker and Faulkner (1991), have a strong sociological component.

This somewhat erratic pattern continued even as the centre of gravity of film studies and film theory once more began to shift. By the 1990s the deterministic certainties of *Screen* Theory were in some retreat, faced by an increasingly influential counter-view utilising cognitive psychology and developed primarily by Bordwell (1985; 1989), which in turn precipitated much rethinking of the field (Bordwell and Carroll, 1996). These years also saw a growing emphasis on cultural studies and, in particular, the increasing prominence of so-called 'ethnographic' work on media audiences (especially television), and the turn towards 'reception studies'. Some sense of the stimulating range of this work can be found by consulting the material collected in Brooker and Jermyn (2003), Jancovich, Faire and Stubbings (2003) and Christie (2012), among others. In film studies, film history and in cultural studies, then, aspects of the 'social' became of greater significance in consequence of these changes and the research areas that they opened up. But substantive sociological contributions were rare and remain so still.

Let us briefly take some examples which illustrate this continuing pattern. Dudrah (2006), for instance, draws on a variety of perspectives to explore aspects of Bollywood cinema. He is clear on the conceptual and methodological pluralism of his preferred approach:

> The sociology that has been advocated and demonstrated throughout this book has been one that has little to do with following the canonical figures and classical theories of the discipline in a systemic and exhaustive manner, and more to do with demonstrating a practicing of the sociological imagination as it is brought into dialogue with studies of the cinema, namely from the related disciplines of film, media and cultural studies. (Dudrah, 2006: 167)

In adopting this position, of course, he continues the long-standing tradition of combinatorial strategies for the study of film. In that sense, his book is not so much a case of, as his subtitle suggests, 'sociology goes to the movies'; rather, aspects of sociology meet up with aspects of a number of other disciplines to collectively seek fresh understanding of cinema. To misappropriate some terminology that originated in the sociology of science,[5] this might be described as the 'weak programme' for a sociology of film wherein the sociology is one tool among many with no special demands on explanatory priority. To describe such an approach as 'weak' is not a judgement of worth. Indeed, the present authors in their own work have often adopted such a pluralist approach (Heise, 2012; Heise and Tudor, 2013; 2014) and continue to do so.

Heise, for example, is developing research in the context of recent scholarly attention paid to the construction of social memory in 'post-dictatorship' Latin American films, films addressing the rise and consequences of the military dictatorships that swept the continent from the 1960s to the 1980s. Research in this area, such as some of that reported in the 'Political Documentary Film and Video in the Southern Cone' issue of *Latin American Perspectives* (2013), adopts tools drawn from a range of disciplines to understand the strategies that these films employ to rewrite and recuperate a past that has been obliterated in hegemonic historical discourse. In her current work Heise (forthcoming) examines Brazilian post-dictatorship films in the light of recent social-historical shifts in the ways in which Brazilians deal with the memory of their dictatorial past. Her pluralistic approach incorporates elements from memory studies and trauma theory to examine the uses of personal testimony and re-enactments as means of bearing witness to history. In this approach, psychoanalytical concepts borrowed from trauma theory add a further dimension to more familiar social and political analyses, the latter including elements of gender theory employed to examine the representation on screen of women's role in historic political resistance. This is then conjoined with the methods of film studies to closely analyse specific films and to explore what some have understood as a tendency in trauma texts to favour a modernist aesthetic over 'realism' (Craps, 2014).

In contrast to that pluralist strategy, a 'strong programme' for the sociology of film would aim to prioritise sociological theories and methodologies in comprehending the workings of the system of cinema, including those aspects of the cinematic institution which are part of its own self-understanding. The latter, of course, would include film criticism and, indeed, products of the discipline of film studies. A recent example of this stronger use of sociology, though not one that reflexively examines film studies itself, is Hughey (2014) which marshals an array of carefully elucidated methods in examining white saviour films and their contribution to a 'post-racial racial ideology' in American society. As well as content analysis of 50 films and detailed examination of 2799 critics' reviews of those films, he also researched 83 screening audience members using ten carefully constructed focus groups plus pre- and post-group interviews (Hughey, 2014: 175–92). His research is systematically analytic and empirical, and it places those methodological commitments in the service of a distinctively sociological approach. While it may not provide the overarching frame of reference that Cressey was seeking back in 1938, Hughey's study does underline its strongly sociological character in terms of scale and methodological rigour, features which serve to distinguish it both from many examples of the 'weak programme' and from film studies traditions more generally.

## TOWARDS A BOURDIEUSIAN STRONG PROGRAMME

What is to be done, then, to further the historically neglected sociology of cinema? There is no simple answer, but, in seeking a framework in modern sociology within which to develop a strong programme, Bourdieu's work is of immediate relevance. Of course, his ideas have already had some isolated influence in film studies and, more often, cultural studies. At one point his expression 'cultural capital' gained a good deal of general currency, particularly in the later 1980s when *La Distinction* was first translated (Bourdieu, 1986). Many would argue however – not least Bourdieu himself – that in being torn from its context in the rest of his theory, that concept (along with others, such as habitus, field and strategy) was systematically misread (Bourdieu and Wacquant, 1992: 79). But taken as a whole, rather than in this piecemeal fashion, Bourdieu's is the most extensive and stimulating examination of cultural reproduction to be found in modern sociology. In particular, it is in his focus on the relation between structure and agency that his work can be used as a foundation here. Now some might argue against that claim, suggesting that the resolution that Bourdieu offers to the traditional sociological 'problem' of structure and agency – if resolution it is – is too much inclined to focus upon the constraining features of structure at the expense of the creative activities of agents. His appears to be a strong socialisation model in which internalised dispositions play a key role in forming the terms within which agents constitute their practices. What we want to suggest here, however, is that the basic thrust of Bourdieu's thinking still retains considerable potential for a sociology of cinema – especially in suggesting lines of inquiry which might rectify the recent drift towards over-voluntarism in audience 'ethnography' and reception studies. The interaction between the structuring capacities of cultural forms and social worlds, on the one hand, and the meaning-making practices of audiences, on the other, requires examination as a process, not by emphasising one or another side of the duality. It is this complex feedback system that is central to any understanding of the workings of cinema in society.

Let us examine this aspect of Bourdieu's work a little more closely. It is clear that his central *habitus* concept does envision agents as powerfully constrained. Consider just one of his typically roundabout attempts at definition:

> The conditionings associated with a particular class of conditions of existence produce *habitus*, systems of durable, transposable dispositions, structured structures predisposed to function as structuring structures, that is, as principles which generate and organize practices and representations that can be objectively adapted to their outcomes without presupposing a conscious aiming at ends or an express mastery of the operations necessary to attain them. (Bourdieu, 1990: 53)

The language is tangled but illuminating. 'Conditionings', 'durable', 'structured', 'structuring', all reflect the power of these acquired, non-conscious dispositions to mould our social practice. Nevertheless, active agency survives:

> There is action, and history, and conservation or transformation of structures only because there

are agents, but agents who are acting and efficacious only because they are not reduced to what is ordinarily put under the notion of individual and who, as socialised organisms, are endowed with an ensemble of dispositions ... (Bourdieu and Wacquant, 1992: 19)

Bourdieu's agent, then, is not mechanistically controlled by internalised norms and values – rules to *govern* social activity. Habitus, rather, *disposes* us to act in certain ways, to prefer this way of being to that, to comprehend the world after a particular fashion. Only to that degree does Bourdieu present us as creatures of our socialisation and of the dispositions, those 'structuring structures', given to us through the medium of habitus. The latter, he writes (1990: 56), is 'embodied history, internalized as a second nature and so forgotten as history'. But, as he also observes (2000: 180), 'habitus is not destiny'. We are practical *users* of the principles our habitus provides, not marionettes whose strings are pulled by some dispositional puppet master.

It is here that the key concept of 'fields', as well as Bourdieu's account of positions and position-taking within fields, takes on a central role. As bearers of the dispositions of our habitus, themselves significantly derived from our consumption of cultural forms such as the cinema, we take up specific locations within the relational structure of social positions offered by the field. In so doing we are indeed agents making choices, but agents who are constrained by the habitus that we bring to bear and by the positions pre-given in the logic of the field. Bourdieu is always careful to deny inevitability or finality in this habitus/field/positions/position-taking nexus. 'There is nothing mechanical about the relationship between the field and the habitus', he insists (Bourdieu, 1993: 65), and 'the correspondence that is observed between positions and position-taking never has a mechanical or inevitable character' (Bourdieu, 2000: 151). Nevertheless, this formulation does suggest a social ontology in which agents are caught up in a network of (almost) self-fulfilling constraints. This is at its clearest in his later formulations of the general theory, in the essay on 'Bodily Knowledge', for example, in *Pascalian Meditations*. Here he writes of social space in terms of a juxtaposition of positions, the social topology of which can be mapped, and of agents acquiring habitus from past experience: 'systems of schemes of perception, appreciation and action [which] enable them to perform acts of practical knowledge' (Bourdieu, 2000: 138). Although particular dispositions do not determine our actions, habitus does lead us to have 'a feel for the game' in specific fields. The positions we adopt, then, are the positions to which we are fitted by virtue of our habitus and the capital at our disposal. Thus is social order reproduced. The agent 'feels at home in the world because the world is also in him, in the form of habitus' (Bourdieu, 2000: 143). How is this so? Because 'the instruments of construction that he uses to know the world are constructed by the world' (Bourdieu, 2000: 136). The circle completes itself.

Elsewhere we have sought to utilise elements of this field model in application to the historical construction of film 'art' (Tudor, 2005; Heise and Tudor, 2007). This involves a further distinction that Bourdieu makes between two 'principles of hierarchisation' at work in the field of art. One – the 'heteronomous principle' – is 'favourable to those who dominate the field economically and politically (e.g. bourgeois art)', while the 'autonomous principle' (often exemplified by Bourdieu in 'art for art's sake') is identified by its advocates 'with degree of independence from the economy, seeing temporal failure as a sign of election and success as a sign of compromise' (Bourdieu, 1993: 40). The world of art, then, is an 'economic world reversed' (Bourdieu, 1983) in two senses: its proponents negatively evaluate economic success, rejecting it in favour of what they see as the necessary autonomy of art; and, more profoundly, the very possibility of this 'anti-"economic" economy of pure art' (Bourdieu, 1996: 142) is predicated upon the existence of a social and political system dominated by the rational calculation of the market and the interests of those thus engaged. For Bourdieu, then, the opposition between art and commerce is fundamentally constitutive of the fields of artistic production and consumption within capitalist modernity.

It is important to note that this model is historically specific (it depends on the widespread diffusion of the market orientation of capitalism) and that, strictly speaking, it applies only to those sub-fields of cultural production in the modern era which aspire to, or are widely consecrated as, art. Thus, while it may be illuminating when applied to Flaubert and to 19th-century French literature and painting more generally (Bourdieu, 1993; 1996), at first sight it appears to be of less obvious value in application to what we now tend to think of as the 'popular arts' of film, television, and the like, except in those periods when their artistic status is particularly at issue. Indeed, it is striking how silent is the later Bourdieu on processes of cultural production in 'popular culture', other than in advancing a broad socio-political critique such as the one he makes of journalism and television (Bourdieu, 1998a). Does this seriously limit the applicability of Bourdieu's field model only to those areas where the concept of 'art' is central, and therefore confound its use as the basis for a more general sociology of cinema? We think not. Although his analysis has been developed in the classic art/commerce context, the tension caught in the heteronomy/autonomy distinction is one that finds expression in all areas of culture, albeit without necessarily invoking 'art' by name. As the early studies of Hollywood by Rosten (1941) and Powdermaker (1950) made clear, commerce versus creativity was a significant structuring feature of the Hollywood system, even though few, if any, of the participants would have been remotely concerned about 'art'. And as we have argued elsewhere (Heise and Tudor, 2007), heteronomy/autonomy anyway takes on a rather different character when its primary reference point is to the political field rather than the economic, as was the case in the era of dictatorship in Brazil.

We would propose, then, that Bourdieu's analysis of the field of art can be extended and elaborated in relation to other notionally non-art fields of cultural production and consumption (cf Fowler, 2016). The two dimensions that Bourdieu uses to map the positions offered by the logic of the field, and which are variously occupied by agents who bring to the process the dispositions of their habitus, are more general than his particular application to art might suggest. Thus, the first dimension, Bourdieu's 'degree of consecration', is a specific case of a more general parameter along which are distributed differing evaluations made of agents, cultural artefacts and processes, evaluations which are the subject of struggle between dominant and subordinate groups. Such processes have been the focus of some recent cultural sociology: Cattani et al. (2014) have empirically explored the struggle for consecration in the context of differing evaluations expressed in awards by 'peers' and 'critics' in the Hollywood context; Allen and Lincoln (2004) consider processes of 'retrospective consecration' of Hollywood films; and Kersten and Bielby (2012) examine the function of film reviewing. Bourdieu's second dimension, heteronomy/autonomy, refers to degrees of dependence or independence in relation to prior existing structures of social division. In his analysis of art that is construed in relation to the economic field, but it could of course relate to other fields such as the political, military, religious or ethnic. In addition, these various fields may overlap or, indeed, be nested one within another. Drawing on this kind of multi-field perspective it becomes possible, for example, to examine a particular film genre, or a national cinema, or a distinctive thematic pattern in relation to a range of constraining structures, thus mapping the field as it changes over time and examining the ways in which other fields impinge upon it. The resulting sequence of 'maps' provides a systematization of the positions made available in the logic of the field, which, in conjunction with an account of the habituses and cultural capital of the agents who choose to occupy those positions, allows examination of the various conjunctions of agency and structure in cinematic fields. This is not an analysis to which we can give empirical substance here; that remains a task for the future. But we nevertheless contend that such a framework offers considerable promise for the development of a strong programme in the sociology of the cinema.

## NOTES

1  The *Screen* editorial in the issue in which this material is published suggests that it 'offers a methodological template for the sort of ethnographic study of media audiences which is being reinvented today' (*Screen* Editors, 2001: 248). It should be noted, however, that Altenloh's study is not an ethnography in any sense that would be recognised by an anthropologist or sociologist. The use of the term 'ethnographic' here is a product of its systematic misappropriation by modern film studies and cultural studies to describe almost any audience-focused methodology (cf. Tudor, 1999: 165–94). Altenloh's work is in fact a piece of early survey research, and all the more useful for that. However, given advances in survey research techniques over the past 100 years, it could hardly serve as a 'methodological template'.

2  Jowett et al. (1996) make a good case for Cressey as a particularly interesting and neglected contributor to the Payne Fund research. They have recovered various unpublished drafts of his work which they include as Chapters 4 and 5 of their volume. As his 1938 *American Sociological Review* article cited here makes clear, he had a subtle appreciation of the theoretical issues involved in understanding the social significance of cinema. That article is also included in their volume as an appendix.

3  An honourable exception to this was the sociologist Herbert J. Gans who sought to develop more sensitive ways of addressing the 'creator–audience relationship' (Gans, 1957) and who refused to accept the standard opposition between 'high' and 'mass' culture (Gans, 1974).

4  This book is sometimes described as 'sociological' and as written by a sociologist. Neither is the case; Thorp's academic field was English. Describing it in this way seems to originate from J.P. Mayer's (1946a) insistence on its sociological credentials

in the Editors' Preface and Introduction to the UK edition, perhaps reflecting his own determination to develop sociological study of film at that time.

5   The key element in the weak/strong programme distinction in the sociology of scientific knowledge was that the strong programme treated 'true' scientific knowledge to be as much socially determined as 'false' knowledge, including the claims of SSK itself. In the sociology of film (and culture more generally) we are clearly not dealing with truth claims but rather with the degree to which sociological factors are seen as powerful determinants. But in both cases, of course, sociology is treated as the primary theoretical and methodological resource for providing explanations. It is in that sense that we employ the distinction here.

## REFERENCES

Allen, M.P. and Lincoln, A.E. (2004) 'Critical Discourse and the Cultural Consecration of American Films', *Social Forces*, 82(3): 871–94.

Altenloh, E. (1914) *Zur Soziologie des Kino: Die Kino-Unternehmung und die sozialen Schichten ihrer Besucher*. Jena: Diederichs (text available at http://www.massenmedien.de/allg/altenloh/index.htm).

Altenloh, E. (2001) 'A Sociology of the Cinema: The Audience', *Screen*, 42(3): 249–93. (reprinted in P. Simpson, A. Utterson and K.J. Shepherdson (eds), (2003) *Film Theory: Critical Concepts in Media and Cultural Studies*, Volume III. London and New York: Routledge. pp. 9–55).

Altenloh, E. (2004) 'From On the Sociology of the Cinema: The Cinema Business and the Social Strata of Its Audience (1914)', in R.W. McCormick and A. Guenther-Pal (eds), *German Essays on Film*. New York and London: Continuum. pp. 29–47.

Baker, W.E. and Faulkner, R.R. (1991) 'Role as Resource in the Hollywood Film Industry', *American Journal of Sociology*, 97(2): 279–309.

Bierstedt, R. (1951) 'Review of *Hollywood, the Dream Factory*', *American Sociological Review*, 16(1): 124–5.

Bineham, J.L. (1988) 'A Historical Account of the Hypodermic Model in Mass Communication', *Communication Monographs*, 55(3): 230–46.

Bordwell, D. (1985) *Narration in the Fiction Film*. London: Methuen.

Bordwell, D. (1989) *Making Meaning: Inference and Rhetoric in the Interpretation of Cinema*. Cambridge, MA and London: Harvard University Press.

Bordwell, D. and Carroll, N. (eds) (1996) *Post-Theory: Reconstructing Film Studies*. Madison: University of Wisconsin Press.

Bourdieu, P. (1983) 'The Field of Cultural Production, or: The Economic World Reversed', *Poetics*, 12(4–5): 311–56.

Bourdieu, P. (1986) *Distinction: A Social Critique of the Judgement of Taste*. London: Routledge.

Bourdieu, P. (1990) *The Logic of Practice*. Cambridge: Polity Press.

Bourdieu, P. (1993) *The Field of Cultural Production*. Cambridge: Polity Press.

Bourdieu, P. (1996) *The Rules of Art: Genesis and Structure of the Literary Field*. Cambridge: Polity Press.

Bourdieu, P. (1998a) *On Television and Journalism*. London: Pluto Press.

Bourdieu, P. (1998b) *Practical Reason: On the Theory of Action*. Cambridge: Polity Press.

Bourdieu, P. (2000) *Pascalian Meditations*. Cambridge: Polity Press.

Bourdieu, P. and Wacquant, L. (1992) *An Invitation to Reflexive Sociology*. Cambridge: Polity Press.

Brooker, W. and Jermyn, D. (eds) (2003) *The Audience Studies Reader*. London and New York: Routledge.

Burton, C.E. (1988) 'Sociology and the Feature Film', *Teaching Sociology*, 16(3): 263–71.

Cattani, G., Ferriani, S. and Allison, P.D. (2014) 'Insiders, Outsiders, and the Struggle for Consecration in Cultural Fields: A Core-Periphery Perspective', *American Sociological Review*, 79(2): 258–81.

Charters, W.W. (1933) *Motion Pictures and Youth*. New York: Macmillan.

Christie, I. (ed) (2012) *Audiences: Defining and Researching Screen Entertainment Reception*. Amsterdam: Amsterdam University Press.

Craps, S. (2014) 'Beyond Eurocentrism: Trauma Theory in the Global Age', in G. Buelens, S. Durrant and R. Eaglestone (eds), *The Future of Trauma Theory: Contemporary Literary and Cultural Criticism*. London and New York: Routledge. pp. 45–61.

Cressey, P.G. (1938) 'The Motion Picture Experience as Modified by Social Background and Personality', *American Sociological Review*, 3(4): 516–25 (reprinted in G.S. Jowett, I.C. Jarvie and K. H. Fuller (1996) *Children and the Movies: Media Influence and the Payne Fund Controversy*. Cambridge, New York, Melbourne: Cambridge University Press. Appendix B, pp. 336–45).

Demerath, N.J. (1981) 'Through a Double-Crossed Eye: Sociology and the Movies', *Teaching Sociology*, 9(1): 69–82.

Denzin, N.K. (1991) *Images of Postmodern Society: Social Theory and Contemporary Cinema*. London: Sage.

Denzin, N.K. (1995) *The Cinematic Society: The Voyeur's Gaze*. London: Sage.

Dowd, J.T. (1999) 'Waiting for Louis Prima: On the Possibility of a Sociology of Film', *Teaching Sociology*, 27(4): 324–42.

Dudrah, R.K. (2006) *Bollywood: Sociology Goes to the Movies*. New Delhi: Sage.

Durkheim, E. (1895) *Les Règles de la Méthode Sociologique*. Paris: Ancienne Librairie Germer Baillière.

Forman, H.J. (1933) *Our Movie Made Children*. New York: Macmillan.

Fowler, B. (2016) 'Bourdieu, Field of Cultural Production and Cinema: Illumination and Blindspots', in Austin, G. (ed) *New Uses of Bourdieu in Film and Media Studies*. New York, Oxford: Berghahn. Forthcoming.

Gans, H.J. (1957) 'The Creator–Audience Relationship in the Mass Media: An Analysis of Movie Making', in B. Rosenberg and D.M. White (eds), *Mass Culture: The Popular Arts in America*. Glencoe, IL: Free Press. pp. 315–24.

Gans, H.J. (1974) *Popular Culture and High Culture: An Analysis and Evaluation of Taste*. New York: Basic Books.

Handel, L.A. (1950) *Hollywood Looks at its Audience: A Report of Film Audience Research*. Urbana: University of Illinois Press.

Handel, L.A. (1953) 'Hollywood Market Research', *The Quarterly of Film, Radio and Television*, 7(3): 304–10.

Heise, T.S. (2012) *Remaking Brazil: Contested National Identities in Contemporary Brazilian Cinema*. Cardiff: University of Wales Press.

Heise, T.S. (forthcoming) 'The Weight of the Past: Memory and Trauma in Lúcia Murat's *Que Bom Te Ver Viva*', New Cinemas.

Heise, T. and Tudor, A. (2007) 'Constructing (Film) Art: Bourdieu's Field Model in a Comparative Context', *Cultural Sociology*, 1(2): 165–87.

Heise, T.S. and Tudor, A. (2013) 'Dangerous, Divine, and Marvellous? The Legacy of the 1960s in the Political Cinema of Europe and Brazil', *The Sixties: A Journal of History, Politics and Culture*, 6(1): 82–100.

Heise, T.S. and Tudor, A. (2014) 'Shooting for a Cause: Cyberactivism and Genre Hybridization in *The Cove*', in L. Nagib and A. Jerslev (eds), *Impure Cinema: Intermedial and Intercultural Approaches to Film*. London and New York: I.B. Tauris. pp. 268–81.

Hill, J. (1986) *Sex, Class and Realism: British Cinema 1956–63*. London: BFI Publishing.

Hill, J. (1999) *British Cinema in the 1980s: Issues and Themes*. Oxford: Clarendon Press.

Horkheimer, M. and Adorno, T.W. (2004) 'The Culture Industry: Enlightenment as Mass Deception', in R.W. McCormick and A. Guenther-Pal (eds), *German Essays on Film*. New York and London: Continuum. pp. 170–80.

Huaco, G.A. (1965) *The Sociology of Film Art*. New York and London: Basic Books.

Hughey, M.W. (2014) *The White Savior Film: Content, Critics, and Consumption*. Philadelphia: Temple University Press.

Jancovich, M. (1995) 'Screen Theory', in J. Hollows and M. Jancovich (eds), *Approaches to Popular Film*. Manchester and New York: Manchester University Press. pp. 123–50.

Jancovich, M., Faire, L. and Stubbings, S. (eds) (2003) *The Place of the Audience: Cultural Geographies of Film Consumption*. London: BFI Publishing.

Jarvie, I.C. (1970) *Towards a Sociology of the Cinema: A Comparative Essay on the Structure and Functioning of a Major Entertainment Industry*. London: Routledge and Kegan Paul.

Jowett, G.S., Jarvie, I.C. and Fuller, K.H. (1996) *Children and the Movies: Media Influence and the Payne Fund Controversy*. New York: Cambridge University Press.

Kersten, A. and Bielby, D.D. (2012) 'Film Discourse on the Praised and Acclaimed: Reviewing Criteria in the United States and the United Kingdom', *Popular Communication: The International Journal of Media and Culture*, 10(3): 183–200.

Kracauer, S. (1947) *From Caligari to Hitler: A Psychological History of the German Film*. Princeton, NJ: Princeton University Press.

*Latin American Perspectives* (2013) Issue 188, 40(1).

Leavis, F.R. (1930) *Mass Civilisation and Minority Culture*. Cambridge: The Minority Press.

Leblanc, L. (1998) 'Observing Reel Life: Using Feature Films to Teach Ethnographic Methods', *Teaching Sociology*, 26(1): 62–68.

Loiperdinger, M. (1996) 'The Kaiser's Cinema: An Archeology of Attitudes and Audiences', in T. Elsaesser and M. Wedel (eds), *A Second Life: German Cinema's First Decades*. Amsterdam: Amsterdam University Press. pp. 41–50.

Lubken, D. (2008) 'Remembering the Straw Man: The Travels and Adventures of *Hypodermic*', in D.W. Park and J. Pooley (eds), *The History of Media and Communication Research: Contested Memories*. New York: Peter Lang. pp. 19–42.

Lynd, R.S. and Lynd, H.M. (1929) *Middletown: A Study in Contemporary American Culture*. New York: Harcourt Brace.

Lynd, R.S. and Lynd, H.M. (1937) *Middletown in Transition: A Study in Cultural Conflicts*. New York: Harcourt Brace.

Mayer, J.P. (1946a) 'Introduction', in M.F. Thorp (ed.), *America at the Movies*. London: Faber and Faber. pp. 10–12.

Mayer, J.P. (1946b) *Sociology of Film: Studies and Documents*. London: Faber and Faber.

Mayer, J.P. (1948) *British Cinemas and their Audiences: Sociological Studies*. London: Dennis Dobson.

Mills, C.W. (1959) *The Power Elite*. New York: Oxford University Press.

Oberschall, A. (1965) *Empirical Social Research in Germany 1848-1914*. Paris and The Hague: Mouton.

Orr, J. (1993) *Cinema and Modernity*. Cambridge: Polity Press.

Orr, J. (1998) *Contemporary Cinema*. Edinburgh: Edinburgh University Press.

Orr, J. (2000) *The Art and Politics of Film*. Edinburgh: Edinburgh University Press.

Pescosolido, B.A. (1990) 'Teaching Medical Sociology through Film: Theoretical Perspectives and Practical Tools', *Teaching Sociology*, 18(3): 337–46.

Powdermaker, H. (1947) 'An Anthropologist Looks at the Movies', *Annals of the American Academy of Political and Social Science*, 254: 80–7.

Powdermaker, H. (1950) *Hollywood, the Dream Factory: An Anthropologist Looks at the Movie-Makers*. Boston: Little Brown.

Powdermaker, H. (1967) *Stranger and Friend: The Way of an Anthropologist*. New York: W.W. Norton and Company.

Prendergast, C. (1986) 'Cinema Sociology: Cultivating the Sociological Imagination through Popular Film', *Teaching Sociology*, 14(4): 243–48.

Rosten, L.C. (1939) 'A "Middletown" Study of Hollywood', *Public Opinion Quarterly*, 3(2): 314–20.

Rosten, L.C. (1941) *Hollywood: The Movie Colony, the Movie Makers*. New York: Harcourt Brace.

*Screen* Editors (2001) 'Editorial', *Screen*, 42(3): 245–48.

Sullivan, J.L. (2009) 'Leo C. Rosten's Hollywood: Power, Status, and the Primacy of Economic and Social Networks in Cultural Production', in V. Mayer, M.J. Banks and J.T. Caldwell (eds), *Production Studies: Cultural Studies of Media Industries*. New York: Routledge. pp. 39–53.

Swingewood, A. (1977) *The Myth of Mass Culture*. London: Macmillan.

Thorp, M.F. (1939) *America at the Movies*. New Haven: Yale University Press.

Tudor, A. (1974) *Image and Influence: Studies in the Sociology of Film*. London: George Allen and Unwin.

Tudor, A. (1989) *Monsters and Mad Scientists: A Cultural History of the Horror Movie*. Oxford: Basil Blackwell.

Tudor, A. (1995) 'Culture, Mass Communication and Social Agency', *Theory Culture & Society*, 12(1): 83–107.

Tudor, A. (1998) 'Sociology and film', in J. Hill and P.C. Gibson (eds), *The Oxford Guide to Film Studies*. Oxford and New York: Oxford University Press. pp. 190–94.

Tudor, A. (1999) *Decoding Culture: Theory and Method in Cultural Studies*. London: Sage.

Tudor, A. (2005) 'The Rise and Fall of the Art (House) Movie', in D. Inglis and J. Hughson (eds), *The Sociology of Art: Ways of Seeing*. Basingstoke and New York: Palgrave Macmillan. pp. 125–38.

Weber, M. (1905) *Die protestantische Ethik und der 'Geist' des Kapitalismus*. Tubingen: Verlag von 1905. J.C.B. Mohr (Paul Siebeck).

Wolfenstein, M. and Leites, N. (1950) *Movies: A Psychological Study*. Glencoe, IL: Free Press.

Wollen, P. (ed.) (1969) *Working Papers on the Cinema: Sociology and Semiology*. London: British Film Institute.

Wright, W. (1975) *Sixguns and Society: A Structural Study of the Western*. Berkeley: University of California Press.

# Witnessing Culture: Museums, Exhibitions and the Artistic Encounter

Nail Farkhatdinov and Sophia Krzys Acord

## INTRODUCTION

As public institutions that serve society by conserving and communicating the tangible and intangible heritage of humanity, museums aim to provide opportunities for social groups to engage with their unique collections and gain 'unforgettable' experiences (López-Sintas et al., 2012). As with many other cultural institutions, museums are highly dependent on national histories, traditions and funding, and vary widely by organizational structure, audiences and exhibits. Conventionally, in academic and professional literature, museums are classified according to the types of the objects they contain (e.g., ethnographic museums, art galleries, science museums, etc.), the purpose they are expected to serve, the type of management, the scale of their operation, or the nature of their audiences (e.g. Ambrose and Paine, 2006: 6–8; Goode, 1896).

Despite these differences in form and mission, museums seem to be exceptional among all sociological topics for several reasons. First, they are not simply neutral stages that bear witness to the struggles to define culture, as seen in the controversies over the display of images from Robert Mapplethorpe's *X Portfolio* in Cincinnati or the 'Elgin marbles' at London's British Museum (Hamilakis, 1999). Museums also *participate in* the controversies and introduce new stakes in these 'culture wars'. Through the work of exhibition-making, they shape public perception of social and political events, and thus '*solidify* culture, science, history, identity, and world-views' (Dubin, 2006: 479).

Second, museums are able to bring new political, cultural and aesthetic meanings to material objects by putting them into the specific context of exhibitions. As many have observed, museums provide the highest kind of institutional approval available in the art world (Heinich, 1998a; Moulin, 1992; Zolberg, 1992). This sorting is more critical in the case of contemporary art because it has not been preceded by a history of eliminations, but actually participates in the creation of art history (Bernier, 2002; Moulin, 1992). Museums, galleries and other public exhibition spaces are also important institutions that provide resources for artistic recognition in art markets. As culturally-loaded environments, museums convey their own meanings and mediate social relations in particular ways. They actively contribute to social processes of legitimation and consecration by providing social, political and institutional resources (e.g., Moulin, 1986). For example, in the case of Marcel Duchamp's renowned *Fontaine* (1917), a functional and mass-produced object – a porcelain urinal – was consecrated as an art object by many actors and institutions, including public museums and commercial art galleries.[1] Museums, as well as other institutions, continue to participate in the maintenance of the legitimate status of this artwork by constructing cultural and material biographies of its replicas. Put another way, museums are cultural institutions that are themselves culture-producing.

Third, being active in culture production processes, museums are made up of people who carry out the routine work of constructing meanings and experiences. As Becker (1982) observes, the personnel of art worlds, including museums, is composed of individuals and groups who do everything from insuring artworks to purchasing the exhibition catalogue. When sociologists examine precisely how these individuals go about doing their work, it reveals much about the relationship of individual agency and affect to the more structural variables of power and expertise as exerted through formal museum organizations. In this way, the cultural study of museums reveals the enormous *work* required for culture to be produced, reproduced and changed. Therefore, museums offer a tangible space to examine the intersection of human action and structural systems in the creation and perpetuation of culture.

Finally, the creation of culture in museums involves interactions between social meanings, individuals and exhibits as material objects. Interpretations of exhibits are social, but interaction with them is always materially and physically grounded: the way visitors move, stand and respond to objects impacts upon what they consider to be meaningful. In scholarly literature museums are often described as heterogeneous spaces (e.g., Hetherington, 1999) where actors are confronted with an uncertainty of physical space and meanings. So while museums are social organizations concerned with representations of culture, they also serve as places to see culture as continuously recreated and enacted in different models of action and experience (learning, entertainment, aesthetic comprehension, political and social engagement, etc.) which involve social and material components.

Museums are sites where cultural sociology can examine the link between our theoretical ideas of how culture operates and the material processes of cultural production and consumption, in the sense of physical artworks as 'explicit' culture (Wuthnow and Witten, 1988). As we will argue in this chapter, the sociological study of museums thus requires sociology to be precise about the robust role played by culture in our social lives.

In this chapter, we will explore three overarching approaches to the sociological study of museums, and discuss the varying contributions of these perspectives for the development of cultural sociology. First, we will look at theoretical approaches within sociology, and critical theory more broadly, that have sought to define the role of museums in structuring the social world. While work in this area has been foundational in describing the role of cultural systems vis-à-vis other sociological processes and institutions, it does not examine the museum as a mediated entity in and of itself. Second, we turn to studies of museum professionals to examine the museum itself as a site of ongoing cultural work. While these studies demonstrate how social systems shape cultural production, they are largely human-centered in their focus, involving the risk of overlooking the very cultural products that make museum settings so unique. Third, we look to contemporary sociological research on museums that examines exhibition encounters as sites of socio-material assemblage. These micro-level ethnographic studies examine closely the work of culture in action, as humans, artworks and mediating texts and spaces combine to showcase the intricate ways in which cultural and social systems are constantly co-mediating and reconstructed in finite moments. We conclude with a discussion of the necessary interrelatedness of these approaches in the future of cultural sociology.

In 2006, Gordon Fyfe wrote that museums were 'rarely mentioned by sociologists' (Fyfe, 2006: 33). By this, he meant that sociology generally considers the museum as a context or site where social interactions and cultural encounters take place, rather than an object of study in its own right. Indeed, sociological studies of museums have been primarily a part of broader sociological disciplines, such as the sociology of art (examining, for example, institutional aspects of museum organizations), the sociology of cultural consumption or education (looking at, for example, museum attendance and reproduction of class inequality), the sociology of occupations (analyzing the work of museum professionals) and so on. The interdisciplinary field of museum studies spans a wide area, ranging from professional manuals to critical theory. Though it is hard to claim that there is a specific sociology of museums, it is reasonable to argue that a variety of sociological approaches have been applied to museums in many different contexts.[2] We draw liberally across this literature in our discussions below, though this chapter focuses most specifically on the exhibition of visual art.

## THEORIZING MUSEUMS: THE PRODUCTION OF CULTURAL CIVILITY

Contemporary museums are the outgrowth of the social transformations and revolutions that took place in Europe and North America in the 18th century.[3] In this Enlightenment period, increased levels of education and wealth saw '[an] expansion of the public for art, as reflected in the growth of the art market and the advent of public exhibitions and museums' (McClellan, 2003: 4). As specifically Western inventions, museums gained a particular sociological relevance when they became public social institutions performing specific social functions. Consequently, functionalist and theoretical approaches in historical sociology generally emphasize the specific roles that museums played in creating and maintaining a general sense of order in Western society, by organizing the consecration and performance of material culture, and also by organizing the audiences who perpetuate processes of cultural sanctification and consume museum products.

Theoretical approaches to understanding these roles for museums vary from critical perspectives that view museums as tools to govern and discipline populations (e.g., Duncan, 1995), to more positive perspectives that consider museums as places for sharing and creating collective identity (e.g., Falk and Dierking, 2000). Museum studies scholars (e.g., Crimp, 1993) have been largely inspired by the former position and have viewed museums as social institutions 'in which citizens ... have met, conversed, been instructed, or otherwise engaged in rituals through which their rights and duties as citizens have been enacted' (Bennett, 2006: 263). Another positive view of museums is provided by Romanticism. In the essay 'Museum', Hetherington (2006) draws on Walter Benjamin's work to consider museums as institutions which are able to fabricate *Erfahrung*, a form of pre-modern experience. By constructing shared historical time and bringing meanings to various objects, museums aim 'to provide people with a sense that they are living in a world where our uncertain and complex set of experiences make sense' (Hetherington, 2006: 600). These two negative and positive viewpoints represent the research continuum, and the following discussion of empirical and historical studies shows that there is evidence to support both of the claims.

Before the advent of modern museums, the majority of art collections, curiosities and other valuable objects were unavailable for viewing by the general public. Most individuals could only encounter these objects during sacred rituals such as religious ceremonies. Museums were storehouses presenting miscellaneous collections of curiosities to learned scholars and collectors. The emergence of the new, modern form of museum reshaped these encounters to a significant extent and established a new social practice: museum-going. This dramatically extended potential audiences for particular collections. Consequently, the social institutions of artistic display, conservation and curation became standardized in the 19th century, going hand in hand with the advent of the modern museum form. As Bourdieu (1993: 260) explains, the 'emergence of the entire set of the specific institutions' (including the museum) and an array of 'specialized agents' (e.g., curators, critics, dealers and collectors) shaped the 'necessary conditions for the functioning of the economy of cultural goods'. As museums became sites which people visited with the purpose of seeing specifically selected and arranged objects of various kinds, the new mission for museums focused on display practices which 'framed' collections appropriately, to help visitors interpret the meanings of the objects which they beheld (Holt, 1979).

On this front, the museum studies and cultural theory literatures have contributed important perspectives to cultural sociology. Studies of the mass media have long embraced the notion of framing in order to describe how, after McLuhan (2003), the medium through which a text or object is presented has concrete implications for shaping its message. In this case, the museum forms the interaction between the creator of the aesthetic experience and the person who experiences it (Gumpert, 1987). Work in cultural and museum studies demonstrates, similarly, that the physical expanse of the museum organizes and gives meaning to artworks in a performative way, as visitors enact the 'ritual' of going through the museum (Duncan, 1995). While this has always been true in ethnographic and historical museums (Clifford, 1988; MacDonald, 1998), contemporary conditions have brought this to the fore in art museums as well, because in contemporary art the museum is the context of the origin of the artwork (Barker, 1999; Buskirk, 2005; Crimp, 1993). The result is what Bernier (2002: 97) terms 'the culture of exhibition', because it is the physical exhibition of the artistic work (its packaging by the museum) which produces its value.

The creation of culture by museums is not simply an exercise of social representations and performance of expert power. It also involves aesthetic manipulation which consists of conceptual and practical work. Artistic objects are, as Raymond Williams (1981: 131) points out, signaled by occasion and place. In particular, the white cube – a gallery space characterized by blank, white walls – is a 'technology of aesthetics', wherein the gallery space 'quotes things' and 'makes them art' in the same manner as the technology of the picture frame indicates the value of the image contained within (O'Doherty, 1999). The main defining element of the institutionalization of high art is the isolation of different artworks from each other, what DiMaggio (1982b) and Bourdieu (1993) note subliminally indicates the 'pure aesthetic'. Museums contribute to what Inglis (2010: 217) describes as 'highly reflexive games as to what counts as "art" and what does not'. Just as the museum establishes its own historical accounts of canonized artworks, the museological space is also a framework through which to control and enact particular types of cultural readings and understandings; it establishes viewing conditions with an invisible regime of control. These modern display conventions limit the nature and media of artworks that can be effectively exhibited; and, as Leahy (2012) argues, the display mechanisms and guided tours at different museums literally created a 'social body' that knows how to stand, where to look and how to comport itself in particular museums. The literature in museum studies reminds the sociologist that spaces carry meaning as much as do accounts, objects and actions.

Once objects are placed within exhibition displays, they are framed as aesthetic objects for demonstration, not function (such as Duchamp's *Fontaine* or indigenous artefacts), through the use of white walls, labels and other technologies of the gallery space. In this way, museums reveal the aesthetic dimensions of displayed objects. Museum exhibits can be understood as objects which Alexander, Bartmanski and Giesen (2012) describe as iconic, i.e., objects that condense meanings through the interplay of aesthetic surface and discursive depth. To a certain extent, museums are unique in the way they organize encounters with iconic objects, and at the same time they provide insights into how iconicity is routinely constructed through professional practices and in visitor experiences. Museums are open laboratories where everyone is able to observe how culture is fabricated.

The museum, of course, is not a neutral body in relation to its culture-producing function, but is itself a social institution involved in the cultural politics of differentiation (Bennett, 1995; Bourdieu, 1984; DiMaggio, 1982a; 1982b). Within the domain of museum studies, scholars often refer to the works of Michel Foucault, who conceptualized museums as heterotopias: spaces of otherness that invert our normal standards of reference (Foucault and Miskowiec, 1986). As Bennett (1995) argues, this process of inversion is fundamental to how museums have framed the development of power/knowledge relations in society; he argues that museums were organized on the basis of an 'exhibitionary complex'. Through submitting objects to the disciplinary regimes of museum display, museums constitute new spaces where the general public can view objects that were previously available only to restricted social groups. Seen in this way, museums discipline populations through the material settings of exhibitions and the articulation of power/knowledge relations between those who are behind the scenes of museums (Hooper-Greenhill, 1992: 188–90), and those who attend exhibitions and are subject to education and instruction (Bennett, 2006: 263–81).

Over the course of the 20th century, the museum was transformed from a private collection to the site of nationally sponsored education, the source of aesthetic pleasure for a broad public, and the symbol of a virtuous State (Bennett, 1995). From the very beginning, modern museum professionals were concerned not only with the ways to represent events and objects and to organize exhibitions, but also with the people who were expected to come to museums. And sociologists have noted an ongoing tension in the social function of museums in relation to the general public. On the one hand, lofty ideals about mass education presumed that museums should attract all social groups in order to provide equal access to their collections and thus to contribute to broader civilizing and educating processes. However, in practice museums have contributed to processes of social differentiation by strengthening the social position of elites through sanctifying their cultural preferences and discriminating against the tastes and habits of lower social classes (Bennett, 1995: 28; DiMaggio, 1982a; Zolberg, 1992).

This tension between elite valorization and democratization in museums has grown alongside broader social changes. In his reconstruction of the history of museum publics, McClellan (2003) describes the transformation that the ideas of a museum have undergone, from the 'innocence' of museum education as a tool of democratization, to museums playing an active role in addressing 'relevant' social issues and shaping current political agendas. These transformations are also reflected in the way museums built relations with their publics. While the belief in the power of a museum to provide education in arts and crafts was typical for 'modern' museums, in so-called post-modern times 'post-modern' museums are expected to contribute to the politics of representation and identity in a much more reflexive way. As a result, their educational aspirations to provide universal knowledge are challenged in a world where the organization of knowledge and culture has itself become fragmented. The educational function of museums is still at the centre of relations between organizations and audiences, but its meaning has changed, and now museums are expected to address contemporary public issues and to be as flexible as possible by referring to various segments of audiences, including those who are under-represented in the public sphere (McClellan, 2003: 39–40).

Overall, one could say that modern museums became part of a broader worldview of the 18th and 19th centuries, and consequently reflected the social structuring of knowledge of that period. They became a part of the broader *episteme* at that time, and contributed to emerging modernity by differentiating between those who had expertise to curate collections and those who were only allowed to see objects under the surveillance of professionals. Museums became one more instrument of power in the modern world, as part of a burgeoning civilizing process which involved establishing and controlling cultural meanings. Research that theorizes museums from historical and functionalist perspectives demonstrates how this form of cultural production intersects with other significant sociological phenomena such as social class and inequality, power and governance and the establishment of group identity. In their more macro-level focus, however, these studies are not able to fully examine the details by which this mediation of museums and wider social forces takes place.

In the 21st century, museums have seen their authority challenged and their universalistic claims to truth criticized. Museums are now considered to be one of the many routes through which individuals can know about and experience the world. Similarly, for a cultural sociology of museums, it is important to go beyond an understanding of culture as only 'high' or 'legitimate', and to extend the notion of culture into the realm of individual actions. This involves asking what happens inside museums. We turn now to interview-based and ethnographic research that examines the actions and roles of individuals in museum worlds.

## INVESTIGATING MUSEUMS: INSTITUTIONS, PROFESSIONALS AND THE WORK OF CULTURE

The bulk of work on museums coming out of the sociology of the arts emerged from the 1960s onwards, and focused less on museums per se than on their staff and audiences, groups who were engaged in particular processes of cultural production. For example, the pioneering 1969 work of Bourdieu and his colleagues examining European museums and their audiences discusses museums as places where social class profoundly shapes cultural practices (Bourdieu et al., 1969). The development of empirical sociology of art, along with the application of approaches from industrial, organization and occupational sociologies to the realm of culture (e.g. Peterson, 1976), brought a slightly different focus on museums. Following analytical frameworks of institutional analysis, sociologists began looking at museums as organizational structures that shape cultural practices, involving production, consumption, market, recognition and so on.

Historically, there are three distinct institutions that have shaped the visual arts, all with their roots in 18th- and 19th-century Europe: public art museums, the world of visual arts discourse and the art market. The relative prominence of these three institutions has changed over time, as different 'institutional systems' (White and White, 1993) have emerged to give value to art and to project value into artworks. Rather than having become obsolete, recently the work of artistic mediators in attributing value and shaping classification schemes has become particularly integral to processes of consecration and meaning-making in contemporary art, where assertions of value and judgments of taste are increasingly open to challenge by publics, governments, funding bodies and the media (Zolberg, 1990). And the contemporary art world is now composed of an increasing plurality of local and international mediators (Foster and Blau, 1989; Moulin, 1992; Mulkay and Chaplin, 1982; Zolberg, 2005). The work of such constituencies is particularly important in the case of objects newly consecrated as 'art', such as aboriginal art forms (Myers, 2002), popular cultural artefacts (Heinich and Shapiro, 2012) and so-called outsider art (Zolberg, 2001; Zolberg and Cherbo, 1997), as well as in periods of artistic controversy (Dubin, 1994). The influence of the mediator in purchasing or exhibiting an artwork is an important signaling device as to the quality of the artist or the work, which sends ripples through the art world, which in turn acts to confirm these choices in an act of auto-realization.

Empirical work has also examined in depth the individual work practices involved in artistic encounters inside the museum. Particular individuals in museums, such as curators, museum educators and invigilators, play significant roles as intermediaries that shape the nature of cultural reproduction and audience experience in the museum. As mentioned earlier, in contrast to the taxonomical or art historical approach to exhibiting fine art, the exhibition process in modern and contemporary art is integral to the meaning of the artwork (Ducret et al., 1990). Significantly, its role of mediation is one of communication: the exhibition communicates the object by contributing another layer of meaning or interpretation to the artist's original intentions, which may have been hazy to begin with (Becker et al., 2006). The exhibition is a way to validate the originality of the curator's point of view, his or her aptitude for discovering new talents, and the artworks themselves, by exhibiting them in dialogue with each other, the dialogue being understood by an initiated public (Heinich and Pollack, 1989; Octobre, 1996: 231). Once the exhibition is open to the public, mediation processes are guided by invigilators who often assist visitors in dealing with artworks. Their role has become of particular importance for contemporary art, which often aims to challenge visitors' expectations and as a result can puzzle them. Consequently, the institution of contemporary art is no longer the single ground from which the understandings of visual culture are made, but rather is a site involving the display of shifting cultural, artistic, social and power relations (Greenberg et al., 1996; Luke, 2002).

While it is important to understand the role of museums in culture-producing institutional systems (Blau, 1988), sociological studies which only aim to discern the 'peopled arrangements' that govern the production of art leave much unexplored territory in the arena of meanings and their connection to wider social orders. To understand the work involved in producing culture, we turn now to consider more focused studies of mediation, so as to examine how culture operates in a highly mediated environment.

For Bourdieu (1984), artistic mediation is quite literally a cultural battlefield of 'position takings'. The mediator's position in a field in the social space – as defined largely through shared understandings of values, and experienced through personal habitus – plays an important, structuring role in his or her work, by giving it legitimacy, as well as by suggesting the cognitive 'strategies' by which the mediator goes about making meanings. Bourdieu's greatest contribution to the organizational study of mediation described above is his specification of the practical cognitive mechanisms by which an organizational consensus is achieved, namely through inherited cultural codes which render certain artworks perceivable (Bourdieu, 1968).

Developing a less explicitly critical approach, Becker (1982) shows that an artwork takes the form it does at a particular moment because of the choices, both small and large, made by artists, mediators and others up to that point – choices between multiple possibilities of subject, format, stylistic treatment, material, assembly, techniques and so on. Curatorial and other professionals engage in 'editing' processes that bring works of art into line with the conventions of the museum, gallery or exhibition space. For Becker, there is a tremendous amount of collective coordinated work that goes into the making and operation of a museum exhibition, which is organized through adherence to common, tacit conventions.

These important studies of mediation focus largely on the accomplishment of ongoing action, and see culture operating as 'imaginary feedback loops' and 'internal logics' organized through systems of social reproduction and coordination. Meaning making in art, then, involves a 'mediate deciphering operation' of these codes or conventions (Bourdieu, 1968), as museum actors 'apply' tacit knowledge to shape artworks for their expected publics. As Greenfeld (1989: 105) notes:

> The quality of the work of art ... is determined by its ability to arouse a reaction of this special kind among this special public, while the public is defined by its ability to react in this specific fashion to a work of art of the kind defined above, namely defined by the reaction it is capable to arouse among this public.

There is thus a mutually-constituting circle involving art, artists, museum professionals and publics.

Some studies of mediation, however, reveal the perhaps subversive contradictions going on behind the scenes of museum spaces. Research that resonates with recent historical work hailing the 'new organizational analysis' school of thought reveals tensions between the goals and beliefs of cultural mediators and the institutions or fields in which they act (Alexander, 1996; Powell and DiMaggio, 1991; Zolberg, 1981). As DiMaggio (1991) observes, the action of curators in the contemporary art world is itself shaped and regulated on a variety of levels, including their organizational identity as a profession and the type of institution in which they work. Contemporary work on cultural industries also examines the negotiations made between creative managers and institutional demands (Banks, 2007; Bilton, 2006; Montebello et al., 2006). These studies, particularly Alexander (1996), demonstrate the personal dilemmas curators face between curating for their peers and curating for broader publics.

The lived nature of these conflicts and contradictions is evidenced by further research that has examined mediation in contemporary art in a detailed, qualitative manner, often through participant observation or interviews. This includes examinations of the evolving nature of curatorial expertise (Heinich, 1995; Moulin and Quemin, 2001; 1993), the work of building museum collections (Herrero, 2006), curatorial decision-making (Gielen, 2005), and changing notions of museum curatorship which have to accommodate the challenges involved in presenting contemporary art (Jouvenet, 2001; Michaud, 1987; Octobre, 1998; Tobelem, 2005).

In particular, studies of conservation dilemmas in modern and contemporary art (e.g., Henaut, 2008; Irvin, 2006; Marontate, 2006) illuminate the outcomes of these conflicts as they impact upon the physical editing, display and interpretation of particular artworks. The studies cited here make important contributions to the sociological study of mediation in the visual arts by demonstrating how the specific and dynamic nature of contemporary art poses striking problems for older systems of producing culture in museums. To take an important example, in her various studies of curators and other artistic mediators in action – in an art commission (Heinich, 1997a; 1997b), in planning an exhibition (Heinich and Pollack, 1989), and in museum work (Heinich, 1998b; 2009) – Nathalie Heinich focuses on discussions between curators and other intermediaries as they carry out their work of framing. In doing so, she reveals their personal value orientations, beliefs and the discursive word games they engage in to bring their framing work into line with the conventions of the art world, whether it be convincing fellow commission members to buy a particular artwork, or writing an exhibition catalogue. As Heinich (1998b: 41) observes, 'interpretation is a fundamental instrument of artistic integration: interpreting, or giving something a value, involves justifying the interest paid to the object'. This dilemma faced by art and museum professionals is at the heart of Heinich's work, which connects the 'sociology of domination' (a more critical type of sociology associated with Bourdieu) with a broader 'sociology of values'.

Visual ethnographic studies by Yaneva (2003a; 2003b) and Acord (2010; 2014) of contemporary art installations reveal that mediation processes do not merely conform to existing limitations and museum codes, but actually create opportunities for the unexpected usage and new functional possibilities of artworks and other objects in the gallery space. These opportunities arise in the course of the decision-making processes described by Becker (1982), but are born specifically from the fact that every ecological arrangement of artworks, actors and environments presents a unique possibility for meaning-making (Becker, 2006; Heath and Hindmarsh, 2002). As Benzecry (2007) notes in a study of opera mediators, the work of the interpretive sociologist is to complement analysis of institutional networks with an appreciation of the self-understandings of the practitioners themselves, rather than reducing agents' 'experience' to participation in a collective form of deception or delusion. Such studies reveal that culture does not simply govern how mediation takes place, but rather that culture is put to work by individuals engaged in processes of cultural production, and is sometimes transformed in the process.

As demonstrated by much literature in the sociology of the visual arts, mediators play an important role not only in the material creation of culture, but also in the production of symbolic worth and the value of art in general. Their role is not simply economic, but also involves the creation and maintenance of social relations. This production of belief in artworks takes the form of 'creating and maintaining the rationale according to which all these other activities make sense and are worth doing' (Becker, 1982: 4). Mediators, therefore, produce two things in art worlds: the artworks themselves and the institutional structure in which these circulate, in what Bourdieu (1996) terms the 'two-step social construction of events'. They produce culture, as well as the systems required for the ongoing production of culture.

Sociological work in this area fleshes out some of the broad theoretical discussions of museums presented above. It demonstrates that individual museum professionals are active cultural actors who shape and mediate cultural processes. A common limitation ascribed to work in this vein, however, is that it risks focusing on the human and social-relational elements of art worlds at the expense of their aesthetic elements. In the process, actual encounters between artworks and audiences become merely 'black boxes to explain intergroup relationships' (Alexander, 2003: 241). The irony here, as pointed out by Heinich and Ténédos (2007), is that this position both reduces culture to the mere reflection of a social group or network, while simultaneously endowing artworks as cultural objects with the extraordinary capacity to transmit the essence of a society. To understand how culture really works, it is important to bridge theoretical and empirical perspectives with aesthetic research that can examine in detail the nature of visitor interactions with artworks inside museums.

## ENCOUNTERING MUSEUMS: VISITOR INTERACTION AND CULTURAL AGENCY

Museums are spaces where one can witness civilizing processes, human and group relations and social systems involving hierarchy, power and cultural inequality. But museums are also spaces where one can observe the production and consumption of specifically *aesthetic* goods. In any exhibition, the materiality of space and objects informs professional practices, while space itself is a matter of social design where each object and its place within the overall display are meaningful. Indeed, the previously cited theoretical perspectives offered by DiMaggio (1982a; 1982b) and O'Doherty (1999) demonstrate that museums are not neutral spaces, for framing processes provide certain spatial-aesthetic cues to individuals. Moreover, some of the visual and interpretive studies of museum professionals cited in the previous section reveal that mediators may themselves have unanticipated reactions to the cultural forms and processes they mediate. For Latour (2005: 39), mediators of all varieties, including artworks, 'transform, translate, distort, and modify the meaning or the elements they are supposed to carry'. In this final section, we turn to consider studies that use museums as opportunities to examine the uniquely aesthetic, embodied, spatial and temporal character of cultural experience through considering visitor interactions with artworks. These studies understand museums as socio-material assemblages whose use by visitors reveals the extensive work of culture in and through social action.

As mentioned earlier, museum professionals have been concerned with visitor experiences from the time of the beginnings of their profession.[4] Over time, museums have elaborated various policies aiming to control and regulate visitor behavior in relation to exhibits (McClellan, 2003). Since museums have more recently been recognized as learning environments (Falk and Dierking, 2000), museum professionals and scholars from anthropology, psychology, education and sociology have begun studying interaction at exhibitions in order to discover audience reactions to exhibits. Understanding visitor behavior is a way to enhance the museum experience and to increase the educational significance of exhibitions. It is not surprising therefore that many visitor behavior studies are focused on providing practical recommendations to improve the design of exhibits and environments. Using experimental research design, observational techniques and interviewing, scholars have explored the impact of many factors on museum experience, including time spent with particular exhibits and within exhibitions, the presence of, and interaction with, other visitors, and various other factors (e.g., Cone and Kendall, 1978; Falk, 1991).

While applied museum research has been focused on visitor behavior for some decades, academic sociology has long neglected the interactional, real-time aspects of museum experience. Rather, following Bourdieu (1984), sociologists have considered museums as vehicles of social distinction and as sites that reveal how art perception is predetermined by the social and economic status of visitors (Bourdieu, 1968; for review of relevant literature, see Katz-Gerro, 2004; Lizardo and Skiles, 2008). Consequently the sociological study of art perception shifts towards the analysis of how tastes (i.e., aesthetic codes) correspond to social positions, and does not leave any room for the analysis of what visitors actually do at exhibitions. Another academic discipline, museum studies, as Kirchberg and Tröndle note, also primarily disregards visitor experiences in favor of focusing on 'cultural, historical, or critical analyses of the museum as an institution' (Kirchberg and Tröndle, 2012: 436). Consequently, one can argue that visitor experience research is predominantly an applied research field that has been influenced by explanatory models from psychology and educational studies.

Yet there are several recent examples of studies that aim to offer an interdisciplinary space for the study of visitor experience using sociological data from surveys and questionnaires. For example, integrating physiological (heart rate and skin conductance) and time-tracking data with sociological and psychological self-reports, a group of German scholars elaborated a complex methodology to test various theories from empirical aesthetics, visitor experience research and the sociology of art (Tröndle et al., 2014a; Tschacher et al., 2012). The results of this study challenge the reductionist perspectives in the sociology of the arts (Tröndle et al., 2014b), by calling sociologists' attention to other factors beyond social class that influence artistic experience. These include age, appreciation of new art forms, the display of artwork, and the nature of the artwork itself, among many other factors that are mostly neglected in types of sociology interested primarily in socio-economic factors and social class determinants. These studies show that museums and their professional mediators are not the only ones involved in the construction of art objects, since museum visitors also actively participate in processes by bringing their own meanings and expectations to the encounter. As with studies of 'audiencing' (Hall, 1980), audiences may decode artworks in many different ways, partly based on their social position and forms of previous cultural knowledge acquisition, but not simply reducible to these. For this perspective, culture and cultural production are therefore not merely cognitive phenomena, for they are inseparable from the situated character of museum experience as this is laid out in multiple ways by particular museum visitors.

The situated character of museum experience can also be addressed from micro-sociological perspectives. Ethnomethodologists, ethnographers and other qualitative analysts have carried out systematic observations in museums, in order to explore how visitors make sense of exhibits in interaction with each other. The collaborative dimension of museum experiences is crucial for this domain of research, since it is in interaction with others that visitors organize their aesthetic activities. Often curators and exhibition designers are not aware of what visitors actually do at exhibitions. Close and detailed observation of such practices, as exemplified in the studies of Christian Heath, Dirk vom Lehn and others (e.g. Heath et al., 2002; vom Lehn et al., 2001), sheds light on what actually happens at an exhibition site. Though it seems to be obvious that museum experience is a collaborative activity, as Heath and vom Lehn put it, 'theories of the perception and experience of art and artefacts largely rely upon an imaginary situation in which an individual views a single artwork alone, independently of the circumstances of viewing' (Heath and vom Lehn, 2004: 46). Neither a Bourdieusian sociology of art perception, nor applied studies of visitor behavior trace the course of art perception as a situated activity. But ethnographic studies can show how visitors create and articulate various contexts for their action, depending on what other visitors do. Individuals are engaged in flows of interaction and conversations with many other actors who are usually ignored by more conventional sociological analysis.

These micro-level studies also show how visitors obtain 'aesthetic' competencies which allow them to interact with exhibits and perform particular emotions (e.g., Scott et al., 2013). Authors writing in this vein argue that the perception of artworks is a situational activity continuously redefined in interaction with artefacts and other people, and this activity is 'hardly reducible to cognitive abilities and dispositions of the participants', as it is in Bourdieu-inspired forms of analysis (Heath and vom Lehn, 2004: 60). One of the examples that Heath and vom Lehn discuss concerns visitors' experience of *The Flagellation of Christ* by Caravaggio in the Musée des Beaux Arts in Rouen. They analyzed the interactions between family members in detail and show how, for example, a son shapes the way his father moves his body in order to discover incisions used typically by Caravaggio in his work. They summarize the interaction as follows: 'The talk and bodily conduct of the son figure how the father examines the picture and responds. The son's actions not only show the incisions, but also establish, through the ways in which they are revealed, the relevant ways in which the father should respond, with awe and appreciation' (Heath and vom Lehn, 2004: 52). This example, among many others, is a detailed description of what happened when a particular family unit stood in front of a specific artwork.

Actor-network theoretical vocabulary is also useful for studying museum experiences and visitors' interactions with artworks, understood not simply as texts to be decoded but as material objects endowed with certain capacities. Contemporary interactive art installations are a good example of how artworks can organize and shape the activities of visitors. Acord and DeNora (2008) describe these processes in terms of the 'affordances' that artworks provide. Griswold et al. (2013) show that these affordances act in both material and cognitive ways to de-stabilize planned routines in museum spaces. They propose a formula to study the relation of cognitive (including meaning-making processes) and material (including physical movements) experiences: 'position [in a physical space] guides [cognitive] location, and location guides meaning-making' (2013: 360). Observing how people approach artworks, they show how the ways objects are arranged impact on what visitors expect to experience and understand. Farkhatdinov (2014) supports these arguments empirically by revealing how visitors collaborate in various ways in order to make sense of and resolve their sense of puzzlement when visiting contemporary art exhibitions. Actor-network theory describes this process as the 'stabilization' of objects (Law, 2002). In other words, the museum experience is a continuous process of reducing one's uncertainty of action and meaning by stabilizing the relations that exist between the materialities of artworks, the exhibition environment, visitors and other participating actors. Just as Becker et al. (2006) argued that artworks are always in a state of flux, in the different stages of visitor encounter, there is no singular artwork. Artworks are always multiple in the sense that their meaning is never pre-ordained and fixed, and that meanings arise contingently in and through encounters between a variety of actors and objects.

In methodological terms, ethnographic studies emphasize the details of interaction in museums and galleries. Using observational techniques and conversation analysis in order to transcribe visitor behaviors, scholars seek to grasp tiny movements, the direction of gazes, fleeting conversations and passing sounds. Everything, no matter how apparently small or trivial, becomes an important element of the analysis. All these elements constitute the situational order of museum experience. To grasp all these sorts of details, scholars have adapted video-based ethnographic methods

(Heath et al., 2010), and this has equipped sociologists and other scholars with a method that can be used in almost any museum context. As Heath and others note, 'museums provide an opportunity to explore how the "affordances" and experience of objects and artifacts emerge within and are constituted through interaction, interaction that inextricably relies on a social organization which informs the very ways in which things are seen and experienced' (vom Lehn et al., 2001: 209). For cultural sociology the significance of such ethnographic studies is that they can discover how forms of interaction emerge at the micro-level within museum exhibitions. They reveal a multiplication of meanings through a context specific situation.

The micro-case study of museums demonstrates that cultural communication is mediated on many levels through the course of its production and reception. In this way, these studies show the multiple negotiations between cultural and social systems that artistic users and other mediators enter into in the course of experiencing an exhibition. Museum experience has its own specific dynamics, and forms of materiality and sociality. Cultural sociology benefits from analyses of these processes by being able to comprehend how objects come into social being both materially and meaningfully. As research objects, museums enable cultural sociology to follow culture in action. This approach does not stand alone, however, but necessarily must enter into dialogue with the earlier approaches to studying museums which we have already outlined. We must consider how cultural repertoires of power are intertwined with both human mediators and forms of micro-interactions, for all of these shape culture in profound ways.

## CONCLUSION: TOWARDS CULTURE AS A THEORY OF ACTION

In this chapter, we have discussed how the sociological study of museums reveals much about the specific workings of culture in social life. Theoretical and historical approaches from museum studies have demonstrated that culture is produced by framing mechanisms which produce and are produced by regimes of power and distinction. Empirical research on museum professionals demonstrates that culture shapes the nature of social interactions in museum spaces. And micro-level research on museum audiences shows that culture is also put to work by individuals in the process of meaning-making. Museums may produce culture, but when one looks more closely, culture is not a passive script that is produced and reproduced but rather it is a resource for action that is drawn on and applied in myriad aesthetic circumstances. Consequently, all of these approaches must work together to understand how regimes of culture can be created, perpetuated and, most importantly, changed. In particular, further work should seek to examine how the micro-level uses of culture evident in visitor interactions affect larger, codified processes of mediation and cultural production.

The material, aesthetic and physical dimensions of social actions and interactions are central to the sociological interest in museums. While for the majority of cultural sociological approaches, bringing materiality into the forefront of research is a conceptual and methodological challenge, for cultural sociological studies of museums it is a crucial part of analysis. Museums are always material. The ways museum professionals and audiences organize their expertise and experiences include the arrangement of, and interactions with, material art objects in meaningful settings. General cultural sociology can benefit significantly from the ways that empirical studies of museums have addressed issues of materiality.

As Heinich (1998a) notes in 'What Art Does to Sociology', art is a particularly rich heuristic device for showing sociology its presuppositions and permitting its practitioners to rethink, and sometimes to abandon or to reverse, mental habits that are entrenched within the sociological tradition. Museums also can 'do things to sociology'. The different sociological approaches to studying museums that have been outlined here are themselves profoundly shaped by the nature of museums and art. Modern museums exhibiting major oil canvases in gilded frames certainly afford a different level of analysis than installation artworks that require touch or other visitor actions to 'activate' them according to the artist's intent (or not). Artworks and museums themselves produce and affect the kind of sociology that we can do with them. And the classification of museums reflects the organization of knowledge in a particular society. In a society where museums try to bring art and science, the everyday and the extraordinary, and culture and nature together, sociology can expect to encounter even more opportunities for cultural theorizing. Thus museums above all show that sociology in general, and cultural sociology in particular, must maintain an open-ended dialogue with changing practices of art and culture, and the museums and curatorial models that evolve to 'cope' with them. Future research in the cultural sociology of museums should focus on the place that museums occupy in the networks of institutions which shape cultural production and aesthetic experience. As this chapter shows, there are many empirical studies in the sociology of the arts and cultural sociology that address this question, yet these fields still lack a unified theoretical framework which can integrate a number of approaches and provide a solid and robust understanding of culture(s) in action. The pursuit of such a framework constitutes a major task for sociologists to undertake in the near future.

## NOTES

1  For a pragmatist interpretation of *Fontaine* (1917)'s artistic consecration, see Heinich (2012).
2  Attempts to establish a sociology of museums go back to the 1970s (e.g. Eisenbeis, 1972).
3  See the discussion of the etymology and intellectual history of the term 'museum' in Findlen (1989).
4  See, for example, Elliott and Loomis (1975) for the annotated bibliography of visitor studies which clearly represents a research field that dates back to the end of the 19th century. Some scholars also refer to Robinson's (1928) work on tracking visitors in museums. Earlier attempts to study and design museum experience are discussed by historians (Bennett, 1995; Duncan, 1995). Nowadays the field of visitor behavior studies is a legitimate field of applied research with its own journal (*Visitor Studies*) and a professional association (the Visitor Studies Association).

## REFERENCES

Acord, S.K. (2010) 'Beyond the Head: The Practical Work of Curating Contemporary Art', *Qualitative Sociology*, 33(4): 447–67.
Acord, S.K. (2014) 'Art Installation as Knowledge Assembly: Curating Contemporary Art', in T. Zembylas (ed.), *Artistic Practices: Social Interactions and Cultural Dynamics*. London: Routledge. pp. 151–65.
Acord, S.K. and DeNora, T. (2008) 'Culture and the Arts: From Art Worlds to Arts-in-Action', *The Annals of the American Academy of Political and Social Science*, 619(1): 223–37.
Alexander, J., Bartmanski, D. and Giesen, B. (eds) (2012) *Iconic Power:Materiality and Meaning in Social Life*. New York: Palgrave Macmillan.
Alexander, V.D. (1996) 'Pictures at an Exhibition: Conflicting Pressures in Museums and the Display of Art', *American Journal of Sociology*, 101(4), 797–839.
Alexander, V.D. (2003) *Sociology of the Arts: Exploring Fine and Popular Forms*. Malden, MA: Wiley-Blackwell.
Ambrose, T. and Paine, C. (2006) *Museum Basics*. London: Routledge.
Banks, M. (2007) *The Politics of Cultural Work*. Basingstoke: Palgrave.
Barker, E. (1999) *Contemporary Cultures of Display*. New Haven, CT: Yale University Press.
Becker, H.S. (1982) *Art Worlds*. Berkeley and Los Angeles, CA: University of California Press.
Becker, H.S. (2006) 'The Work Itself', in H.S. Becker, R. Faulkner, and B. Kirshenblatt-Gimblett (eds), *Art from Start to Finish: Jazz, Painting, Writing, and Other Improvisations*. Chicago: University of Chicago Press. pp. 21–30.
Becker, H.S., Faulkner, R.R. and Kirshenblatt-Gimblett, B. (eds) (2006) *Art from Start to Finish: Jazz, Painting, Writing, and Other Improvisations*. Chicago and London: University of Chicago Press.
Bennett, T. (1995) *The Birth of the Museum: History, Theory, Politics*. London: Routledge.
Bennett, T. (2006) 'Civic Seeing: Museums and the Organization of Vision', in S. MacDonald (ed.), *A Companion to Museum Studies*. Oxford: Blackwell.
Benzecry, C. (2007) 'Beauty at the Gallery: Sentimental Education and Operatic Community in Contemporary Buenos Aires', in C. Calhoun and R. Sennett (eds), *Practicing Culture*. London and New York: Routledge. pp. 171–92.
Bernier, C. (2002) *L'Art au Musée: De l'Oeuvre à l'Institution*. Paris: L'Harmattan.
Bilton, C. (2006) *Management and Creativity: From Creative Industries to Creative Management*. Malden, MA: Wiley-Blackwell.
Blau, J.R. (1988) 'Study of the Arts: A Reappraisal', *Annual Review of Sociology*, 14(1), 269–92.
Bourdieu, P. (1968) 'Outline of a Sociological Theory of Art Perception', *International Social Science Journal*, 20(4): 589–612.
Bourdieu, P. (1984) *Distinction: A Social Critique of Judgement of Taste*. London: Routledge and Kegan Paul.
Bourdieu, P. (1993) 'The Historical Genesis of a Pure Aesthetic', in R. Johnson (ed.), *The Field of Cultural Production: Essays on Art and Literature*. New York: Columbia University Press. pp. 254–66.
Bourdieu, P. (1996) *On Television*. New York: The New Press.
Bourdieu, P., Darbel, A. and Schnapper, D. (1969) *The Love of Art: European Museums and their Public*. Stanford: Stanford University Press.
Buskirk, M. (2005) *The Contingent Object of Contemporary Art*. Cambridge, MA: MIT Press.

Clifford, J. (1988) *The Predicament of Culture: Twentieth-Century Ethnography, Literature, and Art*. Cambridge, MA: Harvard University Press.

Cone, C.A. and Kendall, K. (1978) 'Space, Time, and Family Interaction: Visitor Behavior at the Science Museum of Minnesota', *Curator: The Museum Journal*, 21(3): 245–58.

Crimp, D. (1993) *On the Museum's Ruins*. Cambridge, MA: MIT Press.

DiMaggio, P. (1982a) 'Cultural Entrepreneurship in Nineteenth-century Boston, Part I: The Creation of an Organizational Base for High Culture in America', *Media, Culture & Society*, 4(1): 33–50.

DiMaggio, P. (1982b) 'Cultural Entrepreneurship in Nineteenth-century Boston, Part II: The Classification and Framing of American Art', *Media, Culture & Society*, 4: 303–322.

DiMaggio, P. (1991) 'Constructing an Organizational Field as a Professional Project: U.S. Art Museums, 1920–1940', in W.W. Powell and P. DiMaggio (eds), *The New Institutionalism in Organizational Analysis*. Chicago: Chicago University Press.

Dubin, S.C. (1994) *Arresting Images: Impolitic Art and Uncivil Actions*, New Edition. London and New York: Routledge.

Dubin, S.C. (2006) 'Incivilities in Civil(-ized) Places: "Culture Wars" in Comparative Perspective', in S. MacDonald (ed.), *A Companion to Museum Studies*. Oxford: Blackwell Publishers. pp. 477–93.

Ducret, A., Heinich, N. and Vander Gucht, D. (1990) *La mise en scène de l'art contemporain*. Bruxelles: Les Éperonniers.

Duncan, C. (1995) *Civilizing Rituals: Inside Public Art Museums*. London: Routledge.

Eisenbeis, M. (1972) 'Elements for a Sociology of Museums', *Museum International*, 24(2): 110–17.

Elliott, P. and Loomis, R.J. (1975) *Studies of Visitor Behavior in Museums and Exhibitions: An Annotated Bibliography of Sources Primarily in the English Language*. Washington DC: Office of Museum Programs, Smithsonian Institute.

Falk, J.H. (1991) 'Analysis of the Behavior of Family Visitors in Natural History Museums: The National Museum of Natural History', *Curator: The Museum Journal*, 34(1): 44–50.

Falk, J.H. and Dierking, L.D. (2000) *Learning from Museums: Visitor Experiences and the Making of Meaning*. Walnut Creek, CA: AltaMira Press.

Farkhatdinov, N. (2014) ' Beyond Decoding: Art Installations and Mediation of Audiences', *Music and Arts in Action*, 4(2): 52-73.

Findlen, P. (1989) 'The Museum: Its Classical Etymology and Renaissance Genealogy', *Journal of the History of Collections*, 1(1): 59–78.

Foster, A.W. and Blau, J.R. (1989) *Art and Society: Readings in the Sociology of the Arts*. New York: SUNY Press.

Foucault, M. and Miskowiec, J. (1986) 'Of Other Spaces', *Diacritics*, 16(1): 22.

Fyfe, G. (2006) 'Sociology and Social Aspects of Museums', in S. MacDonald (ed.), *A Companion to Museum Studies*. Oxford: Blackwell Publishers. pp. 33–49.

Gielen, P. (2005) 'Art and Social Value Regimes', *Current Sociology*, 53(5): 789–806.

Goode, G.B. (1896) 'On the Classification of Museums', *Science*, 3(57): 154–61.

Greenberg, R., Ferguson, B.W. and Nairne, S. (1996) *Thinking About Exhibitions*. New York and London: Routledge.

Greenfeld, L. (1989) *Different Worlds: A Sociological Study of Taste, Choice and Success in Art*. Cambridge and New York: Cambridge University Press.

Griswold, W., Mangione, G. and McDonnell, T.E. (2013) 'Objects, Words, and Bodies in Space: Bringing Materiality into Cultural Analysis', *Qualitative Sociology*, 36(4): 343–64.

Gumpert, G. (1987) *Talking Tombstones and Other Tales of the Media Age*. New York and Oxford: Oxford University Press.

Hall, S. (1980) 'Encoding/Decoding', in S. Hall, D. Hobson, A. Lowe and P. Willis (eds.), *Culture, Media, Language: Working Papers in Cultural Studies, 1972-79*. London: Routledge. pp. 128-38.

Hamilakis, Y. (1999) 'Stories from Exile: Fragments from the Cultural Biography of the Parthenon (or "Elgin") Marbles', *World Archaeology*, 31(2): 303–20.

Heath, C. and Hindmarsh, J. (2002) 'Analysing Interaction: Video, Ethnography and Situated Conduct', in T. May (ed.), *Qualitative Research in Action*. London: Sage.

Heath, C. and vom Lehn, D. (2004) 'Configuring Reception (Dis-)Regarding the "Spectator" in Museums and Galleries', *Theory, Culture & Society*, 21(6): 43–65.

Heath, C., Hindmarsh, J. and Luff, P. (2010) *Video in Qualitative Research: Analysing Social Interaction in Everyday Life*. London: Sage Publications.

Heath, C., Luff, P., vom Lehn, D., Hindmarsh, J. and Cleverly, J. (2002) 'Crafting Participation: Designing Ecologies, Configuring Experience', *Visual Communication*, 1(1): 9–33.

Heinich, N. (1995) *Harald Szeemann, un cas singulier*. Paris: L' Echoppe.

Heinich, N. (1997a) 'Expertise et politique publique de l'art contemporain: les critères d'achat dans un FRAC', *Sociologie du travail*, 189–209.

Heinich, N. (1997b) 'Les frontières de l'art à l'épreuve de l'expertise. Politique de la décision dans une commission municipale', *Politix*, 10(38): 111–35.

Heinich, N. (1998a) *Ce que l'art fait à la sociologie*. Paris: Les Éditions de Minuit.

Heinich, N. (1998b) *Le Triple Jeu de l'Art Contemporain. Sociologie des arts plastiques*. Paris: Editions de Minuit.

Heinich, N. (2009) *Faire voir: l'art à l'épreuve de ses médiations*. Bruxelles: Impressions nouvelles.

Heinich, N. (2012) 'Mapping Intermediaries in Contemporary Art According to Pragmatic Sociology', *European Journal of Cultural Studies*, 15(6): 695–702.

Heinich, N. and Pollack, M. (1989) 'Du conservateur de musée à l'auteur d'expositions: l'invention d'une position singulière', *Sociologie Du Travail*, 31(1): 29–50.

Heinich, N. and Shapiro, R. (2012) 'When is Artification?', *Contemporary Aesthetics*, 10(4). http://www.contempaesthetics.org/newvolume/pages/article.php?articleID=639

Heinich, N. and Ténédos, J. (2007) *La sociologie à l'épreuve de l'art: Duexieme partie*. La Courneuve: Aux Lieux d'être.

Henaut, L. (2008) *La restauration des oeuvres de musées: Transformation d'une activité et dynamique professionnelle*. PhD dissertation. Université Paris 8, Paris.

Herrero, M. (2006) *Irish Intellectuals and Aesthetics: The Making of a Modern Art Collection*. Dublin and Portland: Irish Academic Press.

Hetherington, K. (1999) 'From Blindness to Blindness: Museums, Heterogeneity and the Subject', in J. Law and J. Hassard (eds), *Actor Network Theory and After*. Blackwell Publishers. pp. 51–73.

Hetherington, K. (2006) 'Museum', *Theory, Culture & Society*, 23(2–3): 597–603.

Holt, E.G. (1979) *The Triumph of Art for the Public: The Emerging Role of Exhibitions and Critics*. Garden City, NY: Anchor Books.

Hooper-Greenhill, E. (1992) *Museums and the Shaping of Knowledge*. London and New York: Routledge.

Inglis, D. (2010) 'Politics and Reflexivity in the Sociology of Art', *Sociologie de l'Art – OpuS*, 15(1): 115–36.

Irvin, S. (2006) 'Museums and the Shaping of Contemporary Artworks', *Museum Management and Curatorship*, 21(2): 143–56.

Jouvenet, M. (2001) 'Le style du commissaire. Aperçus sur la construction des expositions d'art contemporain', *Sociétés and Représentations*, 11(1): 325–48.

Katz-Gerro, T. (2004) 'Cultural Consumption Research: Review of Methodology, Theory, and Consequence', *International Review of Sociology*, 14(1): 11–29.

Kirchberg, V. and Tröndle, M. (2012) 'Experiencing Exhibitions: A Review of Studies on Visitor Experiences in Museums', *Curator: The Museum Journal*, 55(4): 435–52.

Latour, B. (2005) *Reassembling the Social: An Introduction to Actor-Network-Theory*. Oxford and New York: Oxford University Press.

Law, J. (2002) 'Objects and Spaces', *Theory, Culture & Society*, 19(5–6): 91–105.

Leahy, H.R. (2012) *Museum Bodies: The Politics and Practices of Visiting and Viewing*. Surrey, UK: Ashgate.

Lizardo, O. and Skiles, S. (2008) 'Cultural Consumption in the Fine and Popular Arts Realms', *Sociology Compass*, 2(2): 485–502.

López-Sintas, J., García-Álvarez, E. and Pérez-Rubiales, E. (2012) 'The Unforgettable Aesthetic Experience: The Relationship between the Originality of Artworks and Local Culture', *Poetics*, 40(4): 337–58.

Luke, T.W. (2002) *Museum Politics: Power Plays at the Exhibition*. Minneapolis: University of Minnesota Press.

MacDonald, S. (ed.) (1998) *The Politics of Display: Museums, Science, Culture*. London and New York: Routledge.

Marontate, J. (2006) 'Trans-disciplinary Communication and the Field of Contemporary Art Conservation: Questions of Mission and Constraint', *Techne. Revue Scientifique Du Service de La Recherche et de La Restauration Des Musées de France*, 26: 11–18.

McClellan, A. (2003) 'A Brief History of the Art Museum Public', in A. McClellan (ed.), *Art and its Public: Museum Studies at the Millennium*. Oxford: Blackwell Publishing. pp. 1–50.

McLuhan, M. (2003) *Understanding Media: The Extensions of Man*. ed. W.T. Gordon. Vol. 2. Corte Medara, CA: Gingko Press.

Michaud, Y. (1987) 'L'art contemporain et le musée: Un bilan', *Les Cahiers Du Musée National d'Art Moderne*, 76–82.

Montebello, P. de, Lowry, G.D., MacGregor, N., Walsh, J. and Wood, J.N. (2006) *Whose Muse? Art Museums and the Public Trust*. Princeton, NJ: Princeton University Press.

Moulin, R. (1986) 'Le marché et le musée La constitution des valeurs artistiques contemporaines', *Revue Française de Sociologie*, 27(3): 369–95.

Moulin, R. (1992) *L'Artiste, l'institution et le marché*. eds P.-M. Menger and A. Mérot. Paris: Flammarion.

Moulin, R. and Quemin, A. (2001) 'L'expertise artistique', in F. Aubert and J.-P. Sylvestre (eds), *Confiance et rationalité*. Paris: INRA. pp. 185–200.

Mulkay, M. and Chaplin, E. (1982) 'Aesthetics and the Artistic Career: A Study of Anomie in Fine-Art Painting', *Sociological Quarterly*, 23(1): 117–38.

Myers, F.R. (2002) *Painting Culture: The Making of an Aboriginal High Art*. Durham and London: Duke University Press.

Octobre, S. (1996) *Conservateur de musée: Entre profession et métier*. PhD dissertation. École des Hautes Études en Sciences Sociales, Paris.

Octobre, S. (1998) 'Rhétoriques de conservation, rhétoriques de conservateurs: au sujet de quelques paradoxes de la médiation en art contemporain', *Publics et Musées*, 14(1): 89–111.

O'Doherty, B. (1999) *Inside the White Cube: The Ideology of the Gallery Space*. Expanded edition. Berkeley: University of California Press.

Peterson, R.A. (1976) 'The Production of Culture: A Prolegomenon', *American Behavioral Scientist*, 19(6): 669–84.

Powell, W.W. and DiMaggio, P.J. (eds) (1991) *The New Institutionalism in Organizational Analysis*. Chicago: University of Chicago Press.

Prior, N. (2006) 'Postmodern Restructurings', in S. MacDonald (ed.), *A Companion to Museum Studies*. Oxford: Blackwell Publishers. pp. 509–24.

Quemin, A. and Moulin, R. (1993) 'La certification de la valeur de l'art. Experts et expertises', *Annales Économies, Sociétés, Civilisations*, 48(6): 1421–45.

Robinson, E.S. (1928) *The Behavior of the Museum Visitor*. Washington, DC: American Association of Museums.

Scott, S., Hinton-Smith, T., Härmä, V. and Broome, K. (2013) 'Goffman in the Gallery: Interactive Art and Visitor Shyness', *Symbolic Interaction*, 36(4): 417–38.

Tobelem, J.-M. (2005) *Le nouvel âge des musées: Les institutions culturelles au défi de la gestion*. Paris: Armand Colin.

Tröndle, M., Greenwood, S., Kirchberg, V. and Tschacher, W. (2014a) 'An Integrative and Comprehensive Methodology for Studying Aesthetic Experience in the Field Merging Movement Tracking, Physiology, and Psychological Data', *Environment and Behavior*, 46(1): 102–35.

Tröndle, M., Kirchberg, V. and Tschacher, W. (2014b) 'Is This Art? An Experimental Study on Visitors' Judgement of Contemporary Art', *Cultural Sociology*, 8 (3): 310-32.

Tschacher, W., Greenwood, S., Kirchberg, V., Wintzerith, S., van den Berg, K. and Tröndle, M. (2012) 'Physiological Correlates of Aesthetic Perception of Artworks in a Museum', *Psychology of Aesthetics, Creativity, and the Arts*, 6(1): 96–103.

Vom Lehn, D., Heath, C. and Hindmarsh, J. (2001) 'Exhibiting Interaction: Conduct and Collaboration in Museums and Galleries', *Symbolic Interaction*, 24(2): 189–216.

White, H.C. and White, C.A. (1993) *Canvases and Careers: Institutional Change in the French Painting World*. Chicago: University of Chicago Press.

Williams, R. (1981) *The Sociology of Culture*. Chicago: University of Chicago Press.

Wuthnow, R. and Witten, M. (1988) 'New Directions in the Study of Culture', *Annual Review of Sociology*, 14: 49–67.

Yaneva, A. (2003a) 'Chalk Steps on the Museum Floor: The "Pulses" of Objects in an Art Installation', *Journal of Material Culture*, 8(2): 169–88.

Yaneva, A. (2003b) 'When a Bus Met a Museum: Following Artists, Curators and Workers in Art Installation', *Museum and Society*, 1(3): 116–31.

Zolberg, V.L. (1981) 'Conflicting Visions in American Art Museums', *Theory and Society*, 10(1): 103–25.

Zolberg, V.L. (1990) *Constructing a Sociology of the Arts*. Cambridge: Cambridge University Press.

Zolberg, V.L. (1992) 'Barrier or Leveler? The Case of the Art Museum', in M. Lamont and M. Fournier (eds), *Cultivating Differences: Symbolic Boundaries and the Making of Inequality*. Chicago and London: University of Chicago Press. pp. 187–209.

Zolberg, V.L. (2001) 'Cultural Policy: Outsider Art', in N. Smelser and P. Baltes (eds), *International Encyclopedia of Social and Behavioral Sciences*. Oxford and Amsterdam: Elsevier. pp. 3097–102.

Zolberg, V.L. (2005) 'Aesthetic Uncertainty: The New Canon?', in M.D. Jacobs and N.W. Hanrahan (eds), *The Blackwell Companion to the Sociology of Culture*. Malden: Blackwell Publishers. pp. 114–30.

Zolberg, V.L. and Cherbo, J.M. (eds) (1997) *Outsider Art: Contesting Boundaries in Contemporary Culture*. Cambridge University Press.

# Cultural Sociology of Fashion: On the Sartorial, Symbolic and Social

Anna-Mari Almila

> If you're a fashion journalist, it is not advisable to have a sociological view of the world. (Pierre Bourdieu, 'Haute Couture and Haute Culture', in *Sociology in Question* 1993 [1984]: 138)

## INTRODUCTION – DOES SOCIOLOGY IGNORE FASHION?

Sociologists of fashion have for a long time claimed that fashion is underexplored, or outright ignored, by 'mainstream' sociology (e.g. Aspers and Godart, 2013; Blumer, 1969; Crane and Bovone, 2006; Entwistle and Wilson, 2001). While this may be true to some extent, the significance of sociology and sociological theories to fashion studies is great. In the quickly growing field of fashion scholarship, the conceptual tools provided by sociology are of utmost importance. This chapter seeks to offer an overview of the uses of sociology when exploring fashion phenomena.

Fashions appear in many shapes and forms: names, restaurants, interior design, architecture, academic practices – all have their fashions. In this chapter I focus specifically on sartorial fashion. This is an area where fashion is, in addition to being *worn* and thus 'created' by individuals expressing and constructing their social locations, also elaborately *produced* in a way that is unique. It is also this specific area of fashion that the field of Fashion Studies has as its primary focus. While I draw from a variety of disciplinary sources – Cultural Studies, Consumption Studies, Anthropology, Social Psychology – in essence, this chapter is a defence of sociology, and sociological thinking, in fashion studies. As indicated by Bourdieu (see above), the strength of sociology when studying fashion is its critical stance in respect to myth-creation.

This chapter is divided into three parts. In the first, I discuss theories and empirical studies about the *nature* of fashion. The definition of fashion is a long-standing battle among scholars contributing to the field, and I trace some of the elements in this debate. The second part focuses on what is today the most sociological arena of fashion studies, that is, the *creation* of fashion. I explore here three relevant areas: production, mediation, and consumption of fashion. In the third section, I turn to the forms of *wearing* fashion. From 'master statuses' – class, gender, age, race, nation – to more ambiguous and reflexive forms of self, identity and the body, I outline some important developments in the scholarly understandings of the everyday wearing of fashion and dress.

## THE NATURE OF FASHION – TRICKLE-EVERYWHERE?

Scholars of fashion have presented several lists of conditions which need to be fulfilled in order for fashion to appear in a society. The major conditions that everyone seems to agree upon are: (1) a comparatively large number of people living in a relatively limited area; (2) some possibilities of social mobility among social sectors; and (3) economic conditions that allow 'excess' spending for at least some people. While these conditions are often associated with 'modernity', fashion phenomena are not about 'modernity' per se, but rather about social hierarchies and, often, about aspirational attempts to move within such hierarchies. It is important to stress here the difference between *fashion* and *fashion system* – while there are essentially 'modern' fashion systems (see e.g. Lipovetsky, 1994 [1987] on *haute couture* as modern bureaucratisation of fashion), fashion phenomena go back in time to much earlier eras. In this section I briefly review the hundred-year-old sociologically-informed debate as to what fashion is and how it functions.

### Classical Theories

Probably the best known and most cited sociological analysis of fashion is that of Georg Simmel (1904). His short essay called 'Fashion' has been a recurrent reference point to sociologists and other scholars of fashion. Simmel discusses fashion as a social process which functions within class hierarchies but is based on fundamental psychological desires of individuals. He argues that the two characteristics of fashion – imitation and differentiation – are based on two individual psychological desires. Each individual desires to be independent, but at the same time is overwhelmed by the sense of responsibility brought along with independence. Uniformity and belonging to a group bring with them a removal of the constant responsibility of independence. The third crucial characteristic of fashion, namely change, is also, according to Simmel, based on a psychological desire; Simmel considers 'cultured' people as constantly desiring change and alterity.

Fashion, for Simmel, is a social structure, a product of class distinction. Fashion is necessarily different for different classes, for it is born out of desires to either blur or protect class boundaries. Lower classes imitate upper classes who seek to re-establish class distinction by donning new fashions. These processes happen not only between high and low classes, but also within upper and middle classes. But Simmel goes further than to suggest that changes in upper-class fashion are prompted by the desire to protect class borders; he argues that the upper classes, due to being more 'cultured' and educated, are more open to novelty and change and therefore have a 'natural' desire for change. In a certain way, only the upper class wears 'fashion', since the lower classes only imitate the dress practices of their social superiors. Similar thoughts about fashions trickling down the social hierarchy were expressed by Herbert Spencer (1898), but it is Simmel's work which has been widely cited and applied within the sociology of fashion and fashion studies.

A variety of criticisms have been voiced against Simmel's analysis, and many of these have made the point that Simmel's arguments are not fully empirically supported. First, it is the case that particularly since the later 20th century, fashion also trickles *up* (Field, 1970) and *across* social strata (King, 1973), and there is nothing to support the claim that the upper classes would be more keen on novelty than other classes (Blumberg, 1974). Today, youth is a more likely factor to keep an individual at the frontline of fashion (Crane, 1999). Further arguments against Simmel include the fact that there is no one 'upper class' today, but different elites, which may compete with each other. Also, many acts of imitation are 'unsuccessful' in both material and status terms, and therefore cannot be expected to 'threaten' the fashions and status of the elites (Campbell, 1992).

Another important figure, particularly for studies of economy and consumption, is Thorstein Veblen (1899). According to him, one important reason for fashion consumption's significance in 'modern' life is that in an urban environment, consumption is a visible, widely 'available' means of socially locating others, particularly when other means, such as specific knowledge of the individual's social status and position, are not available.

Veblen's theory of conspicuous consumption can be summarised as follows. Exemption from productive labour is a sign of status and power, and a privilege of powerful individuals. Such exemption puts an individual in possession of *leisure* time, which they can use in non-productive labour, such as cultivating *manners* and forms of unprofitable knowledge. Because leisure time is associated with refined manners, it also comes to be seen as *civilised* (although it was initially based on violence over other individuals who were forced to participate in profitable labour). Manners, made possible through leisure, come to be seen as proof of civilisation and thus embedded in *morality*.

Wealth enables the employment of others for the benefit of the wealthy individual. Some of these servants engage in profitable labour and thus directly contribute to the wealth of the master, but others are performers of unprofitable labour. One of the most important of these is the wife of the master. The ownership of unprofitable subservient others is a sign of even greater wealth, and these others contribute to the *reputation* of the master. The particular role of the wife in this context is to demonstrate the master's wealth by being 'wasteful'. Therefore she engages in acts of *conspicuous consumption*. In these acts of 'wasting' wealth, both *quantity* and *quality* matter: the wife's acts of consumption are worthless unless she can demonstrate to others the 'right' kind of *taste* in her acts of consumption. Also, the wife does not consume for her own comfort but for the *benefit of her master*. In a 'modern' household, argues Veblen, the members of the household engage *together* in social performances of reputability, for the sake of *decency*, *honour* and *reputability* rather than comfort.

Veblen's account is rather more useful for understanding cultured consumption than fashion. This may be because he is focused on a household as a unit of consumption rather than individuals' class struggles (Bell, 1976). The concept of change is the weak point in Veblen, and that is what Simmel engages with. Therefore these two social analyses are sometimes used as a combined 'model', particularly within consumption studies. They complement each other due to their different approaches, but there is also an important difference between them: while Veblen's theory presents conspicuous consumption as an act of *creating* and *gaining* status, Simmel considers fashionable dress as *expression* and *protection* of status (Campbell, 1992). Simmel's view in particular is problematic, since if it was true, elites could wear anything and it would be embraced as fashionable. Yet we know this not to be the case.

## *Later Developments*

Within the Symbolic Interactionist tradition, Herbert Blumer (1969) and Fred Davis (1991) have drawn upon and critiqued Simmel. Blumer took Parisian fashion buyers and designers as his empirical focus, and argued for 'collective selection' as a more empirically grounded model than class distinction. He stresses that fashion is followed in both willing, unwilling and unwitting ways, and that fashion is largely about unconscious, socially shared transformations of taste. While fashion has collective elements, such as respectability and social distinction, it is also about individuals' 'free selection' from a range of choices. Rather than blindly following elite fashions, individuals seek to present themselves as timely. It is worth bearing in mind that Blumer's focus on fashion buyers, rather than individuals wearing fashion, is as much a product of his time as Simmel's focus is of the time when he was writing. In fashion systems which developed particularly after World War II, manufacturers, buyers and consumers participate in filtering processes through which fashions come into existence (King, 1973).

Davis (1991) developed Blumer's ideas further, using the concept of 'social world'. He argued that fashion is a segmented social world, meaning that it is formed of the interpreted tastes of the masses, filtered through the 'values and interests of the fashion industry's subworlds' (1991: 17). In other words, both Blumer and Davis argue that the fashion industry and the people working for it, rather than abstract systems of social distinction, formulate fashions today. Since the late 1980s, arguments about the importance of individuals' identity in fashion have also become more common. Lipovetsky (1994 [1987]) argued that fashion is about the breakdown of old laws and a search for 'authenticity'. Fashion is not due to conspicuous consumption and class distinction, but is about the establishment of differences between the self and others. Such a view can be seen as a 'democratisation' thesis of fashion, according to which access to fashion for all social groups has removed the significance of class in fashion consumption (Crane, 2000). Such developments have brought along so-called mass fashions, which are slower, more widely spread, and specifically designed for middle-class consumers.

So where do we stand today? Is fashion about class, individual, or masses? Ragone (1996) has argued that it may be about all of this. According to him, different kinds of fashions – consumption-driven middle-class mass fashions, life-style based fashions, and quick-spreading fads – exist simultaneously. Thus fashion is both about conflict between groups in terms of social stratification and 'trickle-down phenomena, about integration in terms of mass fashion, and also about individual enjoyment' (1996: 312). In the fashion process, it may well be that 'innovators' are less important in something becoming truly fashionable than are 'influentials' whose taste is considered superior (King, 1973). In other words, fashion leaders are not the ones who pick up new fashions first, but those who popularise them.

Crane (2000) has argued, based on empirical data, that neither 'diffusion theory' – class difference maintained through new styles – nor the 'democratisation thesis' – class differences eliminated through standardised clothing – are fully convincing. Instead, she suggests that Bourdieu's (2010 [1979]) more sophisticated analysis of *taste* as classed may be an empirically sounder theoretical framework. She argues that, for instance, contacts between particular groups of the lower and middle classes create opportunities for acquiring and cultivating cultural capital, and that the working classes adopt upper- and middle-class fashions in a selective manner, depending on their acquired tastes, the physical demands of their work, and their social aspirations.

As is clear from all of this, there is no agreement among scholars of fashion as to what exactly fashion is and how it functions. Aspers and Godart (2013) have recognised the lack of a clear definition of fashion as one of the key failures of the field. In their search for a comprehensive definition, they focus on fashion as *change*, but not just any kind of change. They stress that fashion changes are not random, but happen in ways that are ordered in some ways, unlike, for example, fads which need not be related to previous fads. They conclude that fashion is 'an unplanned process of recurrent change against a backdrop of order in the public realm' (2013: 185). This definition has the benefit of being a *sociological* definition of fashion. It is also applicable to societies which are not usually seen as 'modern', and therefore as locales where fashion could happen. Therefore this is a definition which has potential for breaking down Eurocentric understandings of fashion, to which I return towards the end of this chapter.

As already indicated above, 'fashion' and 'fashion system', while sometimes confused, are two different concepts (see also Entwistle, 2015 [2000]). Fashion systems are systems of production and consumption wherein symbolic value is created, interpreted, and used. In the next section I discuss how such systems function.

## THE CREATION OF FASHION – SYMBOLIC VALUE

The production of symbolic value, and the system of fashion creation, are typical foci of the sociology of fashion (e.g. Aspers, 2010a; 2010b; Bourdieu, 1993 [1984]; Entwistle, 2009; Kawamura, 2004; Mora, 2006; Rocamora, 2002). Crane and Bovone (2006) have argued that cultural sociology of fashion should study the meaning-making processes, cultural production and cultural industries centred on fashion production and consumption. Since the invention of a 'designer' in Paris in the mid-19th century, the myth of the 'creative individual' has been central to fashion production (Lipovetsky, 1994 [1987]). An essential part of this myth-creation has been the (more or less successful) institutionalisation of fashion in several 'world cities' (Breward and Gilbert, 2006). The production of symbolic value is deeply dependent on systems of belief where individual designers and certain cities are created as prestigious and superior to others. It has also been argued that such beliefs have profoundly shaped the field of fashion studies, where more attention has been paid to high fashion and its makers rather than to 'everyday fashion' (Craik, 1994).

Studies of fashion production as a *field* owe much to Bourdieu (1993 [1984]). He considers *haute couture* as one form of producing luxury goods, similar to other such forms. He argues that *haute couture* as a field seeks to create itself as prestigious, and this is achieved through various systems of beliefs, in which the status of the designer matters far more than her designs themselves. Top designers with the highest capital in the field have the power to define objects as rare (and therefore as pricier). New people entering the field seek to challenge the top designers, while the established designers seek to defend their position. The high-up players in the field create power by consecrating each other, which can be done either by praise or by attack. This struggle ensures that the field keeps functioning, and that people keep believing in the 'creativity' of the creators of fashion.

What Bourdieu wrote about *haute couture* is very similar to what he also said about fields of cultural production more generally (Bourdieu, 1993). Rocamora (2002) has critiqued Bourdieu's work on fashion on these grounds. She points out that Bourdieu talks about fields of 'high' culture as directly comparable, and considers mass fashion as fundamentally different from high fashion. In reality, however, the high and mass-produced fashion fields overlap, and individuals often participate in more than one field. Despite this justified critique, Bourdieu's work has been fundamental for research which examines fashion as a cultural industry.

I will now review empirical research on three areas of the fashion system: production, mediation, and consumption. It is worth remembering here that the creation of symbolic value often happens at the cost of some people in the system: those with less relevant capitals, those who produce the physical fashion objects, and those who live in areas that suffer ecologically from the activities of the fashion industries. The global inequalities embedded in fashion systems are also gendered: the freedom to consume for middle-class women has been made possible by large numbers of low-paid working women (McRobbie, 1997).

### *Fashion Production: Manufacture and Design*

The difference between the production of garments and the production of value is a significant element in understanding the functioning of fashion systems. Aspers' (2010a; 2010b) work on fashion production is ground-breaking, for it seeks to understand the different logics according to which fashion manufacture and fashion marketing function. While garment production is located in numerous countries around the world, the production of *value* is not global. This creates an uneven field of power between manufacturers and producers of value: power is located where value is created. Manufacturers are interchangeable, but producers of value (designers) are considered 'unique'. Therefore, manufacturers and designers operate within two different markets, using different forms of contextual knowledge. By using design value – involving a design label – a company can charge more for their products; therefore the creation of value corresponds with increased economic capital.

Manufacturers can try to 'upgrade' by using different kinds of knowledge. This means, first, making themselves less interchangeable by offering a highly competitive service and thus moving upwards in the commodity chain. This involves the manufacturer offering design services to their buyers. The next step is to develop one's own brand – but this is very hard and rarely successful. While the manufacturers have knowledge about design, they lack knowledge about the value market. That is, they have *design* knowledge (how to design a garment) but no *designer* knowledge about the market, clientele, and branding. They can seek to overcome this problem by hiring a designer who possesses such knowledge, by targeting limited local markets, or by using personal networks of knowledgeable individuals, such as local designers trained in London (Aspers, 2010b).

But such attempts to upgrade the business may not benefit the workers who manufacture the garments. One acknowledged problem in garment production is the central importance of the hand-controlled sewing machine and the failure to fully automatise the production chain. By its very nature, the fashion industry has a huge demand for a relatively unskilled workforce, and under a globalised production system, this workforce is largely female, and located in countries where workers' rights are weak and the organisation of the labour force is restricted (Hoskins, 2014).

At the other end of the production hierarchy are designers, some of them celebrated as 'creative geniuses', others an anonymous workforce in less prestigious fashion companies. Kawamura (2004) has analysed in detail how in Paris, for example, a complicated political-economic system keeps creating fashion brands and designers, while also recreating Paris as a fashion city. Through the collective, hierarchical activities of fashion world participants, the entire Parisian fashion system is legitimised, and certain individuals are consecrated. Everyone needs everyone else to create the myth of fashion.

According to Mora (2006), various roles within the fashion industry help to create 'creativity'. While workers in various different roles participate in creative labour, only some are attributed with 'creativity'. Innovation is in reality a result of co-operation, which does not come simply from those defined as the 'creative' members of the team, but to keep up the myth of fashion, 'creativity' and 'taste' are perceived as 'inborn' characteristics of certain individuals. These 'creative' individuals lend prestige to products, without which marketing garments as fashionable items would be impossible.

A 'creative designer' does not spring from nowhere, but is the product of a particular type of education system. McRobbie (1997) has argued that because 'art' – as opposed to commercial production – functions as a form of legitimation and added value, the fashion education system tends to ignore fashion production. Considering the history of British fashion education, the placement of fashion education in art schools, rather than craft schools, eventually helped to establish a higher status for fashion design and designers (McRobbie, 1998). Such an education system, which separates the 'image makers' from material labourers, serves to institutionalise the 'creative individual', and thus recreates inequality between 'creative' and other types of labour within the field of fashion production.

Mystification and glamour, argues McRobbie (1997), are therefore conditions for exploitation. But she also argues that fashion education engages in a process of 'individualising' and disciplining the design student. This is done through the regulation of emotions, particularly 'passion', as well as through surveillance of the student's 'fit' with the department's ethos. Such a system ensures that the 'creative individuals' the fashion school produces will fit the existing fashion system, and therefore are capable of reproducing the system on their own part (McRobbie, 1998). In all these ways, the 'creative' fashion system keeps reproducing itself, but it also keeps separating itself from the world of low-paid, unglamorous manufacturing labour.

## Fashion Mediation: Modelling, Photography and Media

Fashion mediation is a huge business, of which only a minor part is directly visible to the public. As in any field, there are hierarchies and subfields, and actors in these include models, model scouts, model agencies, photographers and magazine editors. In terms of value, a central logic of the field makes a division between high-end fashion mediation – e.g. catwalks, magazine editorials – and low-end fashion mediation – e.g. mass market catalogues. The former subfield is considered more 'artistic' and less commercial (and often pays the various workers involved very little or nothing), while the latter has very low symbolic value but more immediate monetary benefits, money that comes with the risk of decreasing the actor's symbolic value. Only through symbolic value gained through participation on low-paying, high-value jobs, can an individual win the chance of enormously high economic gains, but the chances of this are extremely low. Models, scouts, agencies, and photographers negotiate between these subfields, often being acutely aware that this economic-cultural system defines their symbolic and commercial value (Mears, 2011). As Bourdieu (1993) would have it, it is fundamental that all these actors in the field have a belief in the field. What keeps the field functioning is a shared *illusio*, the unquestioned belief that the game is worth playing.

The field of 'creative' (as opposed to 'commercial') fashion can be seen in its most dramatic form during the Fashion Weeks in the various cities which are defined as major fashion locations. Entwistle and Rocamora (2006) argue that the London Fashion Week (LFW) is a concrete representation of the fashion world and its hierarchies. Hierarchies and belonging in the field are demonstrated through controlling entry to various events, seating maps in catwalk shows, time management (arriving late is the privilege of the powerful players), displaying invitation cards as proof of capital, and through the demonstration of cultural and social capital in the form of dress, posture, bodily ease, gestures, and greeting ceremonies. Gatekeeping processes are massive, and presence and visibility in LFW functions as an indication of power in the field. But the extraordinary amount of unpaid or low-paid labour needed to run the fashion week is all hidden from the public eye.

Fashion models play an important role in fashion mediation. From a stigmatised occupation in 19th-century Paris, to an increasingly appealing opportunity for social mobility among young women since the 1920s, the hype surrounding fashion models reached its high point in the 1970s and 1980s with supermodels whose earnings were extraordinarily high. But since the 1990s, competition has become increasingly hard and salaries have been decreasing. The vast majority of models struggle with low and unpredictable incomes, and with no health or pension coverage. In a field where a model's symbolic value can change extremely quickly, there are no guarantees whatsoever. Yet thousands of young women worldwide live this insecure life in a casualised workforce. They believe the game is worth playing (Mears, 2011). However, fashion models can also be seen as privileged, and part of an elite, as do Entwistle and Wissinger (2012), who question the 'victimisation' of models, and argue that there is more agency involved than many accounts – including journalistic ones – of passive victimhood would have it.

Fashion modelling is not only about an exploited (or not) labour force, it is also a form of cultural imagery that is gendered, classed, and racialised. This highly idealised imagery is often accused by feminist activists, journalists, and others of presenting female bodies in a highly exclusive, and often unhealthy, manner. The bodily and aesthetic labour involved in producing these images places different demands, and offers different opportunities, depending on the individual's bodily characteristics and perceived bodily capital (Entwistle and Mears, 2013; Haidarli, 2012; Wissinger, 2011).

When in the post-World-War-II US black women tried to enter the modelling profession, they met extreme difficulties when faced with all-white standards of beauty. Yet there was a growing black middle class with significant consumption power, which could not be ignored in marketing terms. An alternative culture industry – including all-black model agencies and 'black' magazines – soon emerged. Such cultural production was not only about commerce, but also about racial pride, and about challenging mainstream, white ideals of beauty, as well as ideas of black women as inferior to whites. But the new magazines also served to establish standards for 'ideal black beauty' (Haidarali, 2012). Today's fashion modelling world remains a hard one for black women to penetrate. Wissinger (2011) argues that due to the people choosing models being largely white, and a lack of formal selection criteria, the criteria for black models becomes more restrictive than for white models. Therefore, black models struggle more to fit in, and face stricter aesthetic standards. Wissinger argues that racialised relations in the fashion field construct a specific form of aesthetic labour in terms of black models, who simply must try harder to 'make it'.

While fashion modelling is one of the few careers where top women earn far more than men, the gender' difference is not only about different earnings, but also about different ways of performing idealised genders. Entwistle and Mears (2013) have used Butler's (1990) ideas about gender as constructed through performances to analyse gender differences in female and male modelling. They argue that while women perform heteronormativity, male models engage in both homosexual and heterosexual gender performances, depending on their audience. Since many powerful actors in the fashion world are gay, straight male models often engage in flirting and consciously 'queered' performances in order to secure employment. Yet male models also 'do' gender in heteronormative ways, that is, they avoid paying 'too much' attention to their adornment and dress, and use their 'normal', 'male' walk on the catwalks. This is in striking contrast to female models who are trained in a completely different manner of walking, which happens only on catwalks.

Fashion photographers are another important, and sometimes glamorised and celebrated, group of actors in the field of fashion. Their professional prominence started in the 1920s when the technical quality of photographs improved and printing costs decreased. Aspers (2006 [2001]) finds the world of fashion photography to be strictly hierarchical, from the photo-shoot situation where a rigid hierarchy structures the relations between all participants, to professional hierarches where photographers have different levels of status in relation to each other, and their assistants are evaluated according to whose assistants they are. In this game, it is essential for the photographer to control not only her/his perceived 'style' – involving aesthetic differentiation between particular photographers – but also the types of jobs s/he accepts. While 'commercial' work provides income for the photographer, accepting 'too many' such jobs decreases her/his symbolic value. These actors must constantly negotiate between economic and symbolic value systems.

Fashion magazines appeared first in 17th-century France. These magazines did more than just describe and illustrate tastes: they formulated taste, and in effect told readers what to wear. The fashion magazine spread elsewhere in Europe by the late 18th century (Miller, 2013). In the quest of establishing Paris as the fashion capital of the world, and *la Parisienne* as the embodiment of stylishness, fashion magazines have played a central role for several centuries (Rocamora, 2006).

Fashion magazines today, according to Moeran (2006), are both cultural products and commodities, and it is generally understood that they operate with two audiences: readers and advertisers. While advertisements make up the magazine's income (and restrict its content, because editors do not dare print anything that could antagonise advertisers), reader records are necessary to tempt advertisers: 'magazine publishers sell their readerships to (potential) advertisers, while editors sell advertised products to their readers' (Moeran, 2006: 728). Fashion magazines also function to consecrate the fashion system itself, and powerful actors within it. Particular fashion editorial pieces, typically presenting garments from the brands that advertise in the magazine, can hold high significance in the estimation of a brand's and a designer's symbolic value. Therefore, fashion magazines have a third audience: the world of fashion insiders. Magazines are 'classed' in the estimation of fashion industry insiders, and those perceived to be 'creative' in the accepted manner are seen to be in the 'highest class'.

While the established fashion media is very rigid and hierarchical, new forms of media, such as blogging, often appear more democratic and less hegemonic. However, as blogging has become increasingly professionalised, its structural characteristics have also become more rigid (Pedroni, 2015). The first fashion blogs appeared in 2001, but only around 2004–6 can we talk of the appearance of significant blogging phenomena, in the form of independent, amateur personal style blogs. The commercial potential of these was quickly realised by the fashion industry, and by 2010 fashion bloggers had become a part of the fashion industry itself, being invited to catwalk shows, or designing collections under established brand names. Some bloggers had achieved a status of authority (and considerable income) in the fashion world (Findlay, 2015).

Such celebrity and authority status does not come to everyone. The game here is very much dependent on forms of existing capital, such as the initial opportunity of investing time on blogging and inherited cultural capital, such as knowledge about fashion trends and confidence with making fashion statements. Bloggers often make claims as to their 'innate capacity' to judge good and bad design. This blurs the actual structural conditions behind success in bloggers being recognised by the fashion world, and further contributes to the myths that keep the field of fashion functioning. A blogger's success is also dependent on her ability to cultivate social capital which will secure her access to venues and events closed from the less well connected (Pedroni, 2015).

I have discussed fashion mediation at length, for this is the realm where 'fashion' is in fact created. Barthes (1990 [1983]) has argued that fashion media 'creates' fashion through various semiotic means. The fashion system is not about making garments, but rather is about creating glamour and myths, and through them creating value. This is the fundamental sociological truth of the fashion system, and therefore the methods and practices through which such myths are created deserve an extended exploration when discussing the sociology of fashion.

## Fashion Consumption: Retail and Shopping

Several significant changes contributed to the change in availability of clothing fashions for increasingly diverse groups of consumers in the 19th century. The invention of standard measurements resulted in an increasing amount of ready-made clothing. Access to ready-made patterns and sewing machines aided consumers in their search for fashionable styles (Crane, 2000). At the same time, a new form of retail in dress fabric and accessories started in London. Sourcing cheap goods across Europe in large quantities, and selling quickly with small profits, James Morrison revolutionised the trade (Dakers, 2005). All this made it possible for a new form of fashion, namely consumer fashion, to appear in the post-World-War-I period.

Consumption cannot be spoken of separately from production. Indeed, Fine and Leopold's (1993) landmark work *The World of Consumption* discusses production more than consumption, as demand cannot be considered without supply. Therefore, the segmentation of consumers, which increasingly developed during the 20th and early 21st centuries, must be understood as going together with the segmentation of producers.

In the fashion system, argues Kawamura (2004), consumers must believe in the system as much as the insiders of the game believe in it. This belief takes many forms. Aspers (2010a) has argued that in the garment market, 'quality' is not about quality per se, but rather involves a contract between the brand and the customer, where the customer and the brand have agreed as to what 'quality' means. There must be a 'fit' between the brand identity and the customer's identity. Like the producers of garments, customers also attribute symbolic value to material goods (Crane and Bovone, 2006). Yet it is not only the garments that matter in such processes of creating symbolic value. Increasingly, it is important what kinds of shopping environments are created. For example in Tokyo, the salesgirls of commercialised street fashions are considered important trendsetters whose influence goes beyond their immediate environment, reaching out to other locations, such as Hong Kong, a locale where Tokyo street fashion is held in high regard (Kawamura, 2006). Yet retail staff are often on low-paid, insecure contracts, and in a worse financial position in relation to the consumers they serve (McRobbie, 1997).

Fashion consumption studies are typically studies of specific groups of consumers in specific geographical locations. They often seek to produce knowledge useful for fashion managers. So, for example, studies of mature women's clothing consumption introduce several elements that are important for the increasingly large group of ageing consumers, and similarities can be seen in different locations such as the UK, Brazil and China (Rocha et al., 2005), and Finland (Holmlund et al., 2011). The growing Chinese market has a huge significance for the world economy, and therefore it is no surprise that it is the subject of much interest in consumption studies. New department stores and shopping centres, and consumption based on credit, have changed the Chinese fashion consumption market in profound ways, creating new forms of conspicuous consumption (Ma et al., 2012). Especially when considering locations outside Europe and North America, cultural differences come to matter. Power distances in societies, and whether the culture in question is collectivist or individualist, are important factors in consumption behaviour (Souiden et al., 2011).

Another increasingly interesting form of consumption is ethical consumption. It has been argued that most consumers tend to opt for cheap rather than ethically produced clothing, and that even those interested in ethical consumption tend to assume that a high price or a highly regarded brand guarantees ethical production, rather than trying to find out whether the garments actually were produced in ethically and ecologically sustainable conditions (Ritch and Schröder, 2012). Yet a sector of ethically aware consumers committed to 'slow fashion' – a lifestyle movement stressing sustainability and social responsibility in fashion consumption and production – has emerged and grown recently (Pookulangara and Shephard, 2013). Given the rapidly changing global economic, political and environmental conditions, understanding ethical fashion consumption behaviour must be of great importance in the future. Within design studies, ways of creating sustainable fashion have been of interest for some time already (Fletcher, 2014; Gwuilt and Rissanen, 2011). At the same time, a growing scholarship on ethical consumption has appeared, focusing largely on the production and consumption of foodstuffs (see Varul, this volume). Bringing these scholarships together in the future may offer new ways of both understanding and furthering sustainable, ethical fashion consumption.

## THE WEARING OF FASHION – DRESS AND SOCIAL LOCATION

In this section, I focus on 'everyday fashion' (Craik, 1994). The wearing of fashion is not often researched empirically by sociologists of fashion, who tend to be more focused on the production of symbolic value. There are some notable exceptions (e.g. Crane, 2000; Entwistle, 2000), but among studies of everyday fashion, approaches coming from the disciplines of cultural studies and anthropology are more prominent. Among fashion scholars, there is a general consensus that fashion has two sides: production and consumption. Yet everyday fashion practices involve much more than consumption practices. For example, street fashions have been linked to social conditions, social change, and class politics outside of commercialised consumption processes. While studies as to whether fashions are related to macro-level socio-political changes in societies (e.g. Robenstine and Kelley, 1981) have sometimes been rather simplifying, dress's potential for political commitment, resistance, solidarity and respect still matters (Miller, 2005). These factors cannot be reduced to consumption alone. In the following part of the chapter, I often draw from sources outside sociology, in order to highlight what the cultural sociology of fashion can draw upon and learn from other fields, such as cultural studies, social psychology, and anthropology.

## *Is Class Dead? From Subcultural Studies to Postmodernity and Beyond*

From Simmel onwards, class has been recognised as one crucial element in the existence of fashion. It took a long time, however, before sociological studies interested in class started to take dress or fashion into account. The Birmingham Centre of Contemporary Cultural Studies (CCCS) in the 1970s was one of the first schools of analysis to take 'style' seriously. They drew upon Chicago School studies of deviance and resistance, and worked upon the assumption that working-class deviant 'subcultures' were constructed as forms of resistance to modes of class-based oppression to which the young male members of these subcultures were subjected. Their influence is particularly important for the cultural sociology of fashion, for they were the first to consider dress and style as *cultural* phenomena, as opposed to purely socio-economic phenomena. Their focus on youth cultures, life experiences, and culture as practices which make forms of group existence meaningful (Clarke et al., 2004 [1976]), meant that dress styles came to be analysed as culturally meaningful. The landmark work analysing working-class resistance and style is that of Hebdige (1979). Drawing from Barthes (1990 [1983]; 2006 [2004]) and Gramsci (1971), Hebdige frames subcultural resistance as a challenge to the dominant, hegemonic symbolic order, particularly through processes of resisting 'noise'. Through 'noisy' visual styles, such as punk, symbols of stigmatisation are turned into forms of self-validation through self-imposed exile from the mainstream society and its symbolic values. In this process of 'translations', signifiers are made to point to different signifieds than they initially did, so that an everyday domestic object becomes a sign of deviance and resistance. Hebdige's most famous example of this is the domestic, mundane safety pin used by punks in 'offensive' ways. These processes of translation involve the borrowing (or stealing) of cultural and racial signifiers, particularly white working-class youth making use of signifiers (i.e. garments and styles) drawn from white middle-class and black working-class cultures. Thus the subculture of resistance comes to be expressed in and through style, by the means of a variety of 'taken over' and re-defined signifiers.

Later analysts of youth cultures and style criticised the CCCS approach for imposing meanings on the members of subcultures and their practices. Bennett (1999) argued that for youth culture styles, lifestyle matters more than class. According to him, lifestyle-based styles are more constructed than given, more fluid than fixed. This he attributed primarily to increased consumer choice. Thus a person may dress to stress her/his class background (or desired class background), but this is a conscious choice of style rather than something that happened automatically through socialisation. Muggleton (2000) followed Schutz (1972 [1932]) in saying that analytical second-degree constructions of the life-worlds of 'subculturalists' should be based on actors' own interpretations rather than on 'imposed' economic-political assumptions held by analysts. He insisted on not 'reading' styles, as Hebdige had done, but rather letting people explain for themselves what the styles mean to them. Continuing in a similar vein, Hodkinson (2002) argued that class and politics matter less today than they did in the 1970s, while media and commerce are increasingly important for the formation of subcultural styles. Instead of class identities, today's styles are based on consumer identities, which are largely framed by communication technologies and commercial processes, while the processes involved consist of both fluidity and forms of rigid commitment.

All these studies tend to focus on male members of spectacular subcultures. Already in the CCCS hallmark publication, *Resistance through Rituals*, McRobbie and Garber (1991 [1976]) critiqued such a focus. They argued that girls' absence from scholarly narratives was only partly due to girls not being empirically present within youth groups, and more due to male scholars ignoring them, or accepting their male research subjects' views on the girls and their allegedly marginal position within such groups uncritically. Although girls' participation in subcultures on the streets was limited through parental control, this did not mean that girls were not there, and that when they were not on the streets, they would have no subcultural activities for themselves. While these activities were much less spectacular and deviant than those of their male counterparts, they still existed, and often took the form of clothes consumption and consumerism. McRobbie (1991 [1977]) found that working-class girls expressed their cultural affiliations through subtle dress strategies, including modifications to their school uniforms and subtle resistance to make-up restrictions imposed by parents and teachers. Female working-class distinction strategies were also subtle elsewhere. In the US in the 1950s, working-class women wore fashions in 'improper' manners, as far as mainstream social norms were concerned. They did not imitate upper- and middle-class fashions, but consumed and combined styles in a 'segmented' way. Therefore class relations were reproduced through dress, not by means of imitation (as Simmel would have it), but by means of these women's own strategies of distinction (Partington, 1992).

The studies discussed so far considered class, style and fashion in terms of working-class experience. Diana Crane (2000), however, took a different focus. Her remarkably extensive analyses of male and female fashions from the 19th century to today in the US, UK, and France gives a valuable picture of class relations and their subtleties which goes beyond the small-scale studies of particular subcultures discussed previously. Her theoretical contributions have already been discussed; here I draw attention to her analysis of the subtleties within and between classes, and the change from a class-based society towards more 'democratised', lifestyle- and identity-based forms of consumption and modes of wearing fashion. Crane demonstrates that while fashion became more 'democratic' in some ways throughout the 20th century, class differences have never fully disappeared. Some styles and garments were adopted by aspirational classes, while some others (particularly etiquette-related hats and gloves) were not. Occupational status, particularly through contact with higher classes, was more significant a factor than economic capital for the adoption of fashionable forms of dress, and this was also visible in the male–female divide: if the female members of a family stayed at home while the men went about their business, the men were more aspirational in their dress. Ethnic background and migrant status also played a part – new migrants tended to be highly aspirational in their dress choices, often spending proportionally more on clothes than other groups.

In all of this literature, there has been a clear trend away from consideration of social class towards analyses of lifestyle and consumer processes. So where does research on class and fashion stand today? The concept of resistance very much survives within fashion studies today, particularly in studies of 'anti-fashion'. Whether this is understood as counter-hegemonic, religiously-driven styles (Almila, 2015; Heath, 1992) or in analysis of working-class fashions (Partington, 1992; Rafferty, 2011), individuals responding to social pressures in non-conformist ways remain an important focus for the sociology of fashion, and fashion studies more generally. There have also been recent indicators that class in the study of fashion may not be as moribund as it may seem at first glance. In addition to recent sociological work (Almila, 2015; Appleford, 2013), a number of symposium and conference presentations by fashion scholars have recently considered class-based forms of style and fashion. Such a trend promises an increasing attention towards social class and dress in the future.

## *Gender, Age, Race, and Nation*

In terms of social locations, the 'master statuses' – class, gender, race, and age – are undeniably important as regards the wearing of fashions. Gender, race, and age are all socially constructed in multiple ways. They all also have bodily dimensions: sex and ethnicity take certain bodily forms and characteristics, aging changes bodies in certain ways, and class influences body height, weight, appearance, and health.

Gender and, relatedly, sexuality are fundamental aspects of fashion research. Fashion has for a long time been associated with femininity, and female dress has been the focus of much fashion scholarship. But as gender constructions have been challenged, and an increasing number of (often male) researchers have started focusing on male dress, this imbalance has started to shift (Breward, 2001; Edwards, 2006; Hollander, 1994). Butler's (1990) radical claims about the social construction of heteronormative gender identities and behaviours have been influential for research on queer dress and fashion, in particular when the ambiguity of gender construction is discussed (Cole, 2000; Fillin-Yeh, 2001). Social and physical control of the female body is a recurring theme in sociology of the body (Turner, 2008 [1984]; Young, 2005) and fashion studies alike (Ribeiro,

2003 [1986]; Eco, 1998). In such processes, dress both communicates and creates gender (Barnes and Eicher, 1993).

Age is in certain ways under-researched in terms of dress and fashion. Since the young became the fashion leaders in the post-World-War-II era (Field, 1970), the vast majority of fashion studies focus either on youth cultures or young adults. A notable exception is the work of Twigg (2013), who has taken the fashion practices of elderly and ageing women seriously, and has also demonstrated that the complete exclusion of elderly women from the world of fashion is actually more recent a phenomenon than one would assume. Today there are signs that this trend is coming to its end, as women in their later life are actively claiming rights to be fashion leaders and 'fashionistas'.

Analyses of race and ethnicity in fashion studies have taken several different paths. While many scholars recognise the importance of these to the wearing of dress and fashion (e.g. Crane, 2000; Hebdige, 1979), others downplay this element as a relatively minor part of identity (Woodward, 2007), and others still make it the focus of their research (Eicher, 1999 [1995]; Miller, 2009). Race is a politically charged realm of dress and fashion. Although the concept of race is itself socially constructed (Eicher, 2012), it was used as a category more or less uncritically for a long time. From early researcher statements – such as Field (1970) arguing that 'negro culture' has become an important part of cultural life and fashion consumption in the US – to more recent views of 'blackness' being performed through fashion (Miller, 2009), the links between race and fashion have been explored by scholars. Already in the US in the 1940s, the zoot suit was a highly significant element of black and Mexican-American resistance to the white social establishment and its characteristic forms of identity-seeking (Cosgrove, 1984). In the 1960s, Afro hairstyles became the emblem of resistance and identity-construction among those self-identifying as black (Giddings, 1990). While black fashions have been tools of resistance for a long time (Miller, 2009), a more recent phenomenon of mainstream-resistant fashions is Islamic veiling. It is often embedded in politics of racial othering (Almila, 2015; Franks, 2000), but Islamic fashions are also consumerist and aesthetic-driven (Al-Qasimi, 2010; Sandıkcı and Ger, 2005).

The nation's meaning for dress has also been significant. 'National costumes' have played a part in nation-building in many parts of the world. From the kilt in Scotland, invented in the 18th century (Myuhtar-May, 2014), to several other European national-romantic costume projects in the 19th century (Earle, 2007), nation has been constructed, imagined, and created by various sartorial means. This is not only a European phenomenon. In Asia and South America, post-colonial projects of identity-construction have made use of 'national' forms of dress (Earle, 2007; Peleggi, 2007; Roces, 2007). One interesting aspect of such phenomena is that while they typically function as a rejection of 'Westernisation', they often are partly created for the benefit of local tourist industries seeking to attract global tourism (Earle, 2007).

## Self, Identity, the Body and Materiality

When theorising and thinking about the self, the Symbolic Interactionist approach has to be involved. Cooley's (1998 [1908]) and, more famously, Mead's (1967) arguments as to how the individual self is constructed as a response to, and in dialogue with, others, form a basis for how many subsequent scholars have understood human interaction and the creation of senses of self. Stone (1962) argued that Cooley and Mead were biased towards discourse and verbal communication, when in fact physical appearance – including what one wears – was an important part of such interactions and consequential senses of self. He argued that the role-taking processes and identification *with* others described by Mead crucially require identification *of* others. This identification is facilitated and made possible by physical appearance, which establishes certain guiding social factors (e.g. gender) before any verbal conversation takes place, and thereby fundamentally influences the nature of the interaction that will ensue.

Goffman (1990 [1959]) considered appearance one important factor in the management of self-image in terms of different audiences. His ideas were later taken up by Barker (2001), who considered dress as an implicit presentation of the self in terms of group belonging. She argues that an individual's sartorial adaptation to, for example, a religious group happens through implicit clues, such as experienced difference (and consequential discomfort) in a group meeting. When changing one's appearance as a result of affiliation with a group, an individual becomes a normative member of the group, but also the new, visually constructed 'self' becomes part of the individual's new self-understanding.

In her social-psychological account of fashion, Kaiser (1985) draws attention to appearance management and appearance perception. She argues that appearance is comprised of both actions and ideas. Consumers actively shape realities through selective purchases (thus fashions cannot be 'forced' upon consumers), and so appearances create realities, partly through shared symbolic meanings. The symbolic meanings of appearance emerge in and through social interaction, and are constantly interpreted, re-interpreted, reframed, and transformed. But there is always a certain amount of continuity in such meanings. With the emergence of the 'postmodern condition', Kaiser et al. (1991) argue, symbolic meanings become more ambiguous. The construction of self through appearance management becomes a process of negotiation, which happens partly through the observation and borrowing of sartorial styles, and partly through visual-verbal negotiations within a group. What makes this ambiguity possible is the wide variety of garments available for each consumer within a postmodern social order.

Davis (1994 [1992]) considers fashion as a system of aesthetic codes, which do not emerge randomly, but through conscious and semi-conscious activities of both producers and consumers. Codes and meanings are not clear-cut, but can be contradictory, alternative, and obscure. Such ambiguous processes of meaning-construction and interpretation play a part in the formulation of social identities and construction of the self. While he recognises the importance of the master statuses, he argues that they are elements of constructing a flexible social identity, rather than determining social locations.

Entwistle (2015 [2000]) sees dress as fundamental for micro-social order and for a stable sense of self. This is particularly expressed and experienced when socially inappropriate dress is donned by individuals. Feelings of vulnerability in such situations evoke the fear of disruption of moral order. Dress, both subjectively and intersubjectively, makes the individual inevitably a part of particular social and moral orders. As Woodward (2007) argues, the choice (and rejection) of clothes when dressing is variously guided by memories of social interaction, the imagining of social interaction, norms and contemporary fashion. Dress choices derive from the desire to 'fit in', in terms of one's reference group and specific occasions, personal aesthetic preferences, and the continuity of, and fit with, self and identity. Her analysis of women's everyday dress choices makes the point that not everything that is bought gets worn, while some garments get worn rarely and some constantly. The ambivalences that Davis (1994 [1992]) considers central for macro-level fashion phenomena driven by producers' and consumers' interests, also appear in micro-level, everyday dress choices.

While it is obvious that the wearing of fashions has much to do with the body, and while this is increasingly recognised by fashion scholars, sociology of fashion (and sociology of the body) are very much still in the state they were fifteen years ago when Entwistle (2000; Entwistle and Wilson, 2001) criticised both fields for mostly ignoring each other. Drawing from Mauss (1973) and Douglas (1973), along with phenomenological (Merleau-Ponty, 1996 [1962]) and post-structuralist ideas (Foucault, 1980), Entwistle argued that the dressed body is both discursive and lived, both social and physical, both subject and object. It is culturally constructed, and socially controlled and surveilled. She argued that different spaces allocate particular bodies with different meanings, and therefore require different management strategies, including the management of the gaze of others. According to Falk (1995), there is not any one 'natural' body, for the body is always differentially socially and culturally constructed. Garments shape, modify, and alter the body and its postures, and each of these modifications always carries particular form of social and cultural value, whether negative or positive.

Garments are also material as well as symbolic. While material culture scholars have attempted to introduce more considerations of materiality into clothing and fashion studies (e.g. Küchler and Miller, 2005; Miller and Woodward, 2011), often such considerations are still discourse-focused rather than exploring the materiality and material characteristics of garments (exceptions include Blaszczyk, 2006; O'Connor, 2005; Olesen, 2010). But the dressed body cannot be considered without considering the materiality of what dresses it. Getting habituated with certain sorts of clothing constructs not only bodily gestures and postures (Falk, 1995), but also how the individual understands bodily comfort and discomfort (Blaszczyk, 2006). Sociologists of fashion could learn more from sociologists of art, who have for some time taken seriously artworks' roles as actants and mediators in art practices (de la Fuente, 2007; Dominguez Rubio and Silva, 2013; Strandvad, 2012). Using Actor-Network-Theory-influenced methods and concepts, and particularly integrating more technology-oriented approaches into analysis of dress and fashion, would offer new possibilities for analyses of the dressed body.

## Globalisation

Fashion systems today are no more wholly or mostly national or local, but instead increasingly globalised and hybridised. The globalisation of fashion takes many forms. For example, Asian fashions have appeared in the 'West' at the same time as many Asians have had to negotiate between more 'Asian' and 'Western' styles. Such processes have also been complicated by many Asian states promoting 'local modernities', which are often embedded in 'traditional' values, particularly as regards female dress (Jones and Leshkowich, 2003). While in the 1990s, 'world fashions' or 'cosmopolitan fashions' were definitely seen as European or 'Western' derived (Eicher and Sumberg, 1999 [1995]), today locations elsewhere, such as Dubai and Istanbul, have become leaders in global 'Islamic' fashions (Moors, 2009). The migration of people, goods, and ideas has created more cosmopolitan identities, and new types of cosmopolitan fashions and styles. For example, African Americans' historically low social status in the US has encouraged the development of more cosmopolitan identities expressed through fashions (Miller, 2009). In large cities such as London, many Muslim women create their sartorial styles in a highly cosmopolitan manner (Tarlo, 2007). It seems clear that the importance of globalisation and cosmopolitanism for the sociology of fashion can only be increasing.

Yet it remains the case that globalisation and cosmopolitanism very rarely appear as important and meaningful categories in fashion studies. In many ways, fashion scholars are still often researching a world divided into historically constructed geographical categories. This 'Eurocentrism' in fashion scholarship has been criticised extensively (Baizerman et al., 1993; Craik, 1994; Moors, 2009; Niessen, 2010). One reason why fashion has for such a long time been associated with Europe and 'the West' is that a distinctive fashion system developed in Europe from the 14th century onwards. This development has been taken as proof that fashion appeared only in Europe in that time. But this is not the case, for historians and archaeologists have found potential indicators of the presence of sartorial fashions in ancient Egypt (Brewer and Teeter, 1999), Maya and Aztec cultures (Beckert, 2014: 8), and Imperial China (Finnane, 2007). I stressed above the importance of not confusing fashion in general with particular empirically existing fashion system(s). Fashion systems are many, but fashion as social phenomenon is not the property of any particular empirical system. As sociology of fashion, and fashion studies more generally, become more global and globalised, we must approach fashion phenomena with no prior assumptions as to their forms and geographical locations. While there have been European and 'Western' fashions and fashion systems, fashion itself was never solely European or 'Western', a lesson that historians have known for a long time but sociologists and fashion studies scholars have been much more reluctant to embrace.

## CONCLUSION

In this chapter, I have outlined some important questions that the sociology of fashion must attend to in future. These include questions about the nature and functioning of fashion, its meaning and applications in everyday social interactions, the materiality of garments, and increasing global inter-connectedness. I have suggested that globalisation and cosmopolitanism as categories of analysis should become more prominent in the sociology of fashion. I have also argued that in terms of the materiality of fashion, we could learn much from ANT-inspired sociology of art. I have also argued that we must abandon Eurocentric assumptions as to how and where fashions have appeared historically and can appear today.

While there has been a general trend within research on everyday forms of fashion to move away from the collective and structural levels towards the individual and reflexive levels of analysis, the importance of the former cannot be denied. It is in fact possible that today the wearers of sartorial fashions are more than ever controlled by global economic, cultural, political, and material forces. Sociology of fashion's role in understanding these developments continues to be the de-mystification of fashion processes and dress-related social processes. Analyses will increasingly need to include considerations of trans-national, global and cosmopolitan factors in the shaping of everyday forms of sartorial fashion, but they should also go beyond the cultural level alone, and more fully acknowledge the importance of technology and material forms of production. For as long as we focus on the production, circulation, and evaluation of symbolic value alone, rather than on connecting these to material forms of production, we keep ignoring those in globalised fashion systems who are in the weakest socio-economic position, namely those workers – usually located in the developing world – who make our clothes. And surely it is sociology's job to defend those who are weak rather than to ignore them.

## REFERENCES

Almila, A. (2015) 'Fashion, Anti-Fashion, Non-Fashion and Symbolic Capital: The Uses of Dress among Muslim Minorities in Finland', *Fashion Theory*. DOI :10.1080/1362704X.2015.1078136

Al-Qasimi, N. (2010) 'Immodest Modesty: Accommodating Dissent and the 'Abaya-as-Fashion in the Arab Gulf States', *Journal of Middle East Women's Studies*, 6(1): 46–74.

Appleford, K. (2013) 'Fashion and Class Evaluations', in S. Black, A. de la Haye, J. Entwistle, R. Root, H. Thomas and A. Rocamora (eds), *The Handbook of Fashion Studies*. London: Bloomsbury. pp. 102–20.

Aspers, P. (2006 [2001]) *Markets in Fashion*. London: Psychology Press.

Aspers, P. (2010a) 'Using Design for Upgrading in the Fashion Industry', *Journal of Economic Geography*, 10: 189–207.

Aspers, P. (2010b) *Orderly Fashion: A Sociology of Markets*. Princeton: Princeton University Press.

Aspers, P. and Godart, F. (2013) 'Sociology of Fashion: Order and Change', *Annual Review of Sociology*, 39: 171–92.

Baizerman, S., Eicher, J.B. and Cerny, C. (1993) 'Eurocentrism in the Study of Ethnic Dress', *Dress*, 20: 19–32.

Barker, E. (2001) 'A Comparative Exploration of Dress and the Presentation of Self as Implicit Religion', in W.J.F. Keenan (ed.), *Dressed to Impress: Looking the Part*. Oxford: Berg. pp. 51–68.

Barnes, R. and Eicher, J.B. (1993) 'Introduction', in R. Barnes and J.B. Eicher (eds), *Dress and Gender: Making and Meaning*. London: Bloomsbury. pp. 1–7.

Barthes, R. (1990 [1983]) *The Fashion System*. Berkeley: University of California Press.

Barthes, R. (2006 [2004]) *The Language of Fashion*. Oxford: Berg.

Beckert, S. (2014) *Empire of Cotton: A New History of Global Capitalism*. New York: Knopf Doubleday.

Bell, Q. (1976) *On Human Finery*, 2nd edition. London: Hogarth Press.

Bennett, A. (1999) 'Subcultures or Neo-Tribes? Rethinking the Relationship between Youth, Style and Musical Taste', *Sociology*, 33(3): 599–617.

Blaszczyk, R.L. (2006) 'Styling Synthetics: DuPont's Marketing of Fabrics and Fashions in Postwar America', *The Business History Review*, 80(3): 485–528.

Blumberg, P. (1974) 'The Decline and Fall of the Status Symbol: Some Thoughts on Status in a Post-Industrial Society', *Social Problems*, 21(4): 480–98.

Blumer, H. (1969) 'Fashion: From Class Differentiation to Collective Selection', *The Sociological Quarterly*, 10: 275–91.

Bourdieu, P. (1993) *The Field of Cultural Production: Essays on Art and Literature*. New York: Columbia University Press.

Bourdieu, P. (1993 [1984]) *Sociology in Question*. London: Sage.

Bourdieu, P. (2010 [1979]) *Distinction: A Social Critique of the Judgement of Taste*. London: Routledge.

Breward, C. (2001) 'Manliness, Modernity and the Shaping of Male Clothing', in J. Entwistle and E. Wilson (eds), *Body Dressing*. Oxford: Berg. pp. 165–82.

Breward, C. and Gilbert, D. (eds) (2006) *Fashion's World Cities*. Oxford, Berg.

Brewer, D.J. and Teeter, E. (1999) *Egypt and Egyptians*. Cambridge: Cambridge University Press.

Butler, J. (1990) *Gender Trouble*. London: Routledge.

Campbell, C. (1992) 'The Desire for the New: Its Nature and Social Location as Presented in Theories of Fashion and Modern Consumerism', in R. Silverstone and E. Hirsch (eds), *Consuming Technologies: Media and Information in Domestic Spaces*. London: Routledge. pp. 44–58.

Clarke, J., Hall, S., Jefferson, T. and Roberts, B. (2004 [1976]) 'Subcultures, Cultures and Class', in S. Hall and T. Jefferson (eds), *Resistance through Rituals: Youth Subcultures in Post-War Britain*. London: Routledge. pp. 9–73.

Cole, S. (2000) *Don We Now Our Gay Apparel: Gay Men's Dress in the Twentieth Century*. Oxford: Berg.

Cooley, C.H. (1998 [1908]) *On Self and Social Organization*. Chicago: University of Chicago Press.

Cosgrove, S. (1984) 'The Zoot-Suit and Style Warfare', *History Workshop*, 18: 77–91.

Craik, J. (1994) *The Face of Fashion*. London: Routledge.

Crane, D. (1999) 'Diffusion Models and Fashion: A Reassessment', *Annals of the American Academy of Political and Social Science*, 566: 13–24.

Crane, D. (2000) *Fashion and its Social Agendas: Class, Gender, and Identity in Clothing*. Chicago: University of Chicago Press.

Crane, D. and Bovone, L. (2006) 'Approaches to Material Culture: The Sociology of Fashion and Clothing', *Poetics*, 34: 319–33.

Dakers, C. (2005) 'James Morrison (1789–1857), "Napoleon of Shopkeepers", Millionaire Haberdasher, Modern Entrepreneur', in C. Breward and C. Evans (eds), *Fashion and Modernity*. Oxford: Berg. pp. 17–32.

Davis, F. (1991) 'Herbert Blumer and the Study of Fashion: A Reminiscence and a Critique', *Symbolic Interactionism*, 14: 1–21.

Davis, F. (1994 [1992]) *Fashion, Culture, and Identity*. Chicago: University of Chicago Press.

de la Fuente, E. (2007) 'The "New Sociology of Art": Putting Art Back into Social Science Approaches to the Arts', *Cultural Sociology*, 1(3): 409–425.

Dominguez Rubio, F. and Silva, E.B. (2013) 'Materials in the Field: Object-trajectories and Object-positions in the Field of Contemporary Art', *Cultural Sociology*, 7(2): 161–78.

Douglas, M. (1973) *Natural Symbols*. Harmondsworth: Pelican Books.

Earle, R. (2007) 'Nationalism and National Dress in Spanish America', in M. Roces and L. Edwards (eds), *The Politics of Dress in Asia and the Americas*. Eastbourne: Sussex Academic Press. pp. 162–81.

Eco, U. (1998) 'Lumbar Thought', in *Faith in Fakes: Travels in Hyperreality*. London: Vintage. pp. 191–6.

Edwards, T. (2006) *Cultures of Masculinity*. Abingdon: Routledge.

Eicher, J.B. (1999 [1995]) 'Introduction: Dress as Expression of Ethnic Identity', in J.B. Eicher (ed.) *Dress and Ethnicity: Change Across Space and Time*. Oxford: Berg. pp. 1–5.

Eicher, J.B. (2012) 'Body: The Dressed Body in Fashion and Art', in A. Geczy and V. Karaminas (eds), *Fashion and Art*. London: Berg. pp. 77–86.

Eicher, J.B. and Sumberg, B. (1999 [1995]) 'World Fashion, Ethnic, and National Dress', in J.B. Eicher (ed.), *Dress and Ethnicity: Change Across Space and Time*. Oxford: Berg. pp 295–306.

Entwistle, J. (2000) 'Fashion and the Fleshy Body: Dress as Embodied Practice', *Fashion Theory*, 4(3): 323–47.

Entwistle, J. (2009) *Aesthetic Economy of Fashion: Markets and Value in Clothing and Modelling*. Oxford: Berg.

Entwistle, J. (2015 [2000]) *The Fashioned Body: Fashion, Dress and Modern Social Theory*, 2nd edition. Cambridge: Polity.

Entwistle, J. and Mears, A. (2013) 'Gender on Display: Performativity in Fashion Modelling', *Cultural Sociology*, 7(3): 320–35.

Entwistle, J. and Rocamora, A. (2006) 'The Field of Fashion Materialized: A Study of London Fashion Week', *Sociology*, 40(4): 735–51.

Entwistle, J. and Wilson, E. (2001) 'Introduction: Body Dressing', in J. Entwistle and E. Wilson (eds), *Body Dressing*. Oxford: Berg. pp. 1–9.

Entwistle, J. and Wissinger, E. (2012) 'Introduction', in J. Entwistle and E. Wissinger (eds), *Fashioning Models: Image, Text and Industry*. London: Berg. pp. 1–14.

Falk, P. (1995) 'Written in the Flesh', *Body & Society*, 1(1): 95–105.

Field, G.A. (1970) 'The Status Float Phenomenon: The Upward Diffusion of Innovation', *Business Horizons*, August 1970: 45–52.

Fillin-Yeh, S. (2001) *Dandies: Fashion and Finesse in Art and Culture*. New York: New York University Press.

Fine, B. and Leopold, E. (1993) *The World of Consumption*. London: Routledge.

Findlay, R. (2015) 'The Short, Passionate, and Close-Knit History of Personal Style Blogs', *Fashion Theory*, 19(2): 157–78.

Finnane, A. (2007) *Changing Clothes in China: Fashion, History, Nation*. London: Hurst & Company.

Fletcher, K. (2014) *Sustainable Fashion and Textiles: Design Journeys*, 2nd edition. Abingdon: Routledge.

Foucault, M. (1980) 'Body/Power', in C. Gordon (ed.), *Power/Knowledge: Selected Interviews and Other Writings 1972–77*. New York: Pantheon Books. pp. 55–62.

Franks, M. (2000) 'Crossing the Borders of Whiteness? White Muslim Women Who Wear the Hijab in Britain Today', *Ethnic and Racial Studies*, 23(5): 917–29.

Giddings, V.L. (1990) 'African American Dress in the 1960s', in B.M. Starke, L.O. Holloman, and B.K. Nordquist (eds), *African American Dress and Adornment: A Cultural Perspective*. Dubuque, IA: Kendall/Hunt. pp. 152–5.

Goffman, E. (1990 [1959]) *The Presentation of Self in Everyday Life*. London: Penguin.

Gramsci, A. (1971) *Selections from the Prison Notebooks*. Q. Hoare and G.N. Smith (ed and trans). London: Lawrence and Wishart.

Gwuilt, A. and Rissanen, T. (eds) (2011) *Shaping Sustainable Fashion: Changing the Way We Make and Use Clothes*. London: Earthscan.

Haidarali, L. (2012) '"Giving Coloured Sisters a Superficial Equality": Re-Modelling African American Womanhood in Early Postwar America', in J. Entwistle and E. Wissinger (eds), *Fashioning Models: Image, Text and Industry*. London: Berg. pp. 56–79.

Heath, D. (1992) 'Fashion, Anti-Fashion, and Heteroglossia in Urban Senegal', *American Ethnologist*, 19(1): 19–33.

Hebdige, D. (1979) *Subculture: The Meaning of Style*. London: Routledge.

Hodkinson, P. (2002) *Goth: Identity, Style and Subculture*. Oxford: Berg.

Hollander, A. (1994) *Sex and Suits*. New York: Knopf.

Holmlund, M., Hagman, A. and Polsa, P. (2011) 'An Exploration of How Mature Women Buy Clothing: Empirical Insights and a Model', *Journal of Fashion Marketing and Management*, 15(1): 108–22.

Hoskins, T. (2014) *Stitched Up: The Anti-Capitalist Book of Fashion*. London: Pluto Press.

Jones, C. and Leshkowich, A.M. (2003) 'Introduction: The Globalization of Asian Dress: Re-Orienting Fashion or Re-Orientalizing Asia?', in S. Niessen, A.M. Leshkowich, and C. Jones (eds), *Re-Orienting Fashion: The Globalization of Asian Dress*. London: Berg. pp. 1–48.

Kaiser, S.B. (1985) *The Social Psychology of Clothing and Personal Adornment*. London: Macmillan.

Kaiser, S.B., Nagasawa, R.H. and Hutton, S.S. (1991) 'Fashion, Postmodernity and Personal Appearance: A Symbolic Interactionist Formulation', *Symbolic Interaction*, 14(2): 165–85.

Kawamura, Y. (2004) *Japanese Revolution in Paris Fashion*. Oxford: Berg.

Kawamura, Y. (2006) 'Japanese Teens as Producers of Street Fashion', *Current Sociology*, 54(5): 784–801.

King, C.W. (1973) 'A Rebuttal of the "Trickle Down" Theory', in G. Wills and D. Midgley (eds), *Fashion Marketing: An Anthology of Viewpoints and Perspectives*. London: George Allen. pp. 215–27.

Küchler, S. and Miller, D. (eds) (2005) *Clothing as Material Culture*. Oxford: Berg.

Lipovetsky, G. (1994 [1987]) *The Empire of Fashion: Dressing Modern Democracy*. Princeton: Princeton University Press.

Ma, F., Shi, H., Chen, L. and Luo, Y. (2012) 'A Theory on Fashion Consumption', *Journal of Management and Strategy*, 3(4): 84–92.

Mauss, M. (1973) 'Techniques of the Body', *Economy and Society*, 2(1): 70–88.

McRobbie, A. (1991 [1977]) 'The Culture of Working-Class Girls', in *Feminism and Youth Culture*. Basingstoke: Macmillan. pp. 35–60.

McRobbie, A. (1997) 'Bridging the Gap: Feminism, Fashion and Consumption', *Feminist Review*, 55: 73–89.

McRobbie, A. (1998) *British Fashion Design: Rag Trade or Image Industry?* London: Routledge.

McRobbie, A. and Garber, J. (1991 [1976]) 'Girls and Subcultures', in *Feminism and Youth Culture*. Basingstoke: Macmillan. pp. 1–15.

Mead, G.H. (1967) *Mind, Self and Society – From the Standpoint of a Behavioural Social Scientist*. W. Morris (ed.). Chicago: Chicago University Press.

Mears, A. (2011) *Pricing Beauty: The Making of a Fashion Model*. Berkeley: University of California Press.

Merleau-Ponty, M. (1996 [1962]) *Phenomenology of Perception*. London: Routledge.

Miller, D. and Woodward, S. (eds) (2011) *Global Denim*. Oxford: Berg.

Miller, J.I. (2005) 'Fashion and Democratic Relationships', *Polity*, 37(1): 3–23.

Miller, M.L. (2009) *Slaves to Fashion: Black Dandyism and the Styling of Black Diasporic Identity*. Durham: Duke University Press.

Miller, S. (2013) 'Taste, Fashion and the French Fashion Magazine', in D. Bartlett, S. Cole and A. Rocamora (eds), *Fashion Media: Past and Present*. London: Bloomsbury. pp 13–21.

Moeran, B. (2006) 'More than Just a Fashion Magazine', *Current Sociology*, 54(5): 725–44.

Moors, A. (2009) '"Islamic Fashion" in Europe: Religious Conviction, Aesthetic Style and Creative Consumption', *Encounters*, 1: 175–201.

Mora, E. (2006) 'Collective Production of Creativity in the Italian Fashion System', *Poetics*, 34: 334–53.

Muggleton, D. (2000) *Inside Subculture: The Postmodern Meaning of Style*. Oxford: Berg.

Myuhtar-May, F. (2014) *Identity, Nationalism, and Cultural Heritage under Siege: Five Narratives of Pomak Heritage*. Leiden: Brill.

Niessen, S. (2010) 'Interpreting "Civilization" through Dress', in L. Skov (ed.), *Berg Encyclopedia of World Dress and Fashion, Volume 8: West Europe*. Oxford: Berg. pp 39–43.

O'Connor, K. (2005) 'The Other Half: The Material Culture of New Fibres', in S. Küchler, and D. Miller (eds), *Clothing as Material Culture*. Oxford: Berg. pp. 41–60.

Olesen, B.B. (2010) 'How Blue Jeans Went Green: The Materiality of an American Icon', in D. Miller and S. Woodward (eds), *Global Denim*. Oxford: Berg. pp. 69–86.

Partington, A. (1992) 'Popular Fashion and Working-Class Affluence', in J. Ash and E. Wilson (eds), *Chic Thrills*. London: Pandora. pp. 145–61.

Pedroni, M. (2015) '"Stumbling on the Heels of my Blog": Career, Forms of Capital, and Strategies in the (Sub)Field of Fashion Blogging', *Fashion Theory*, 19(2): 179–200.

Peleggi, M. (2007) 'Refashioning Civilization: Dress and Bodily Practice in Thai Nation-Building', in M. Roces and L. Edwards (eds), *The Politics of Dress in Asia and the Americas*. Eastbourne: Sussex Academic Press. pp. 65–80.

Pookulangara, S. and Shephard, A. (2013) 'Slow Fashion Movement: Understanding Consumer Perceptions – An Exploratory Study', *Journal of Retailing and Consumer Services*, 20: 200–6.

Rafferty, K. (2011) 'Class-Based Emotions and the Allure of Fashion Consumption', *Journal of Consumer Culture*, 11(2): 239–60.

Ragone, G. (1996) 'Consumption Diffusion: Elite Phenomena and Mass Processes', *International Sociology*, 11: 309–15.

Ribeiro, A. (2003 [1986]) *Dress and Morality*. Oxford: Berg.

Ritch, E.L. and Schröder, M.J. (2012) 'Accessing and Affording Sustainability: The Experience of Fashion Consumption within Young Families', *International Journal of Consumer Studies*, 36: 203–10.

Robenstine, C. and Kelley, E. (1981) 'Relating Fashion Change to Social Change: A Methodological Approach', *Family & Consumption Science Research*, 10: 78–87.

Rocamora, A. (2002) 'Fields of Fashion: Critical Insights into Bourdieu's Sociology of Culture', *Journal of Consumer Culture*, 2(3): 341–62.

Rocamora, A. (2006) 'Paris, Capitale de la Mode: Representing the Fashion City in the Media', in C. Breward and D. Gilbert (eds), *Fashion's World Cities*. Oxford, Berg. pp. 43–54.

Roces, M. (2007) 'Gender, Nation and the Politics of Dress in Twentieth-Century Philippines', in M. Roces and L. Edwards (eds), *The Politics of Dress* in Asia and the Americas. Eastbourne: Sussex Academic Press. pp. 19–41.

Rocha, M.A.V., Hammond, L., and Hawkins, D. (2005) 'Age, Gender and National Factors in Fashion Consumption', Journal of Fashion Marketing and Management, 9(4): 380–90.

Sandıkcı, Ö. and Ger, G. (2005) 'Aesthetics, Ethics and Politics of the Turkish Headscarf', in S. Küchler and D. Miller (eds), Clothing as Material Culture. Oxford: Berg. pp. 61–82.

Schutz, A. (1972 [1932]) The Phenomenology of the Social World. Evanston, IL: Northwestern University Press.

Simmel, G. (1904) 'Fashion', International Quarterly, 10: 130–55.

Souiden, N., M'Saad, B. and Pons, F. (2011) 'A Cross-Cultural Analysis of Consumers' Conspicuous Consumption of Branded Fashion Accessories', Journal of International Consumer Marketing, 23(5): 329–43.

Spencer, H. (1898) Principles of Sociology, Volume II. New York: Appleton.

Stone, G.P. (1962) 'Appearance and the Self', in A. Rose (ed.), Human Behavior and Social Processes. Boston: Houghton-Mifflin Company. pp. 86–118.

Strandvad, S.M. (2012) 'Attached by the Product: A Socio-Material Direction in the Sociology of Art', Cultural Sociology, 6(2): 163–76.

Tarlo, E. (2007) 'Islamic Cosmopolitanism: The Sartorial Biographies of Three Muslim Women in London', Fashion Theory, 11(2/3): 143–72.

Turner, B. (2008 [1984]) The Body and Society, 2nd edition. London: Sage.

Twigg, J. (2013) Fashion and Old Age. London: Bloomsbury.

Veblen, T. (1899) The Theory of the Leisure Class. London: Macmillan.

Wissinger, E. (2011) 'Managing the Semiotics of Skin Tone: Race and Aesthetic Labor in the Fashion Modeling Industry', Economic and Industrial Democracy, 33(1): 125–43.

Woodward, S. (2007) Why Women Wear What They Wear. Oxford: Berg.

Young, I. (2005) On Female Body Experience: "Throwing like a Girl" and Other Essays. Oxford: Oxford University Press.

# Popular Music and Cultural Sociology

Andy Bennett

## INTRODUCTION

Popular music has been a focus for academic researchers since at least the middle of the 20th century when Theodor Adorno (1941) published his highly influential work on the role and significance of pop as a form of industrially produced, mass disseminated music. The first monograph-length, sociological study of popular music appeared nearly four decades later with the publication of Simon Frith's (1978) *The Sociology of Rock*. As this lineage suggests, the socio-cultural significance of popular music has been a long-standing theme for focus and debate. That said, it is equally the case that the proliferation of popular music genres, particularly since the mid-1960s, and their close proximity to forms of youth cultural expression, has engendered a particularly close interest from sociologists regarding the connections between popular music and society. Likewise, focus on the apparent tensions between popular music's status as a product of consumer capitalism and its importance as a cultural resource in the hands of audiences also continues to be a critical focus for sociological research. With the emergence of cultural sociology, the volume of sociological work focusing on popular music has grown exponentially, including a marked increase in ethnographic work focusing on the relationship between popular music and everyday life, and the role and significance of popular music in particular scenes and subcultures. Similarly, in the wake of the so-called 'digital revolution', work by cultural sociologists has made an important contribution to our understanding of new forms of de-centralised music production and dissemination, and the emergence of what could be regarded as a DIY cultural economy of popular music.

The purpose of this chapter is twofold. First, to provide a broad overview of the contributions that cultural sociology has thus far made to our understanding of popular music as a contemporary form of cultural practice. Second, to consider how cultural sociological approaches to popular music might develop over the next fifteen to twenty years in response to the increasingly diverse ways in which popular music intersects with everyday life. The chapter begins by examining the origins of the sociology of popular music, with particular reference to the work of key scholars such as Simon Frith, Richard A. Peterson, and Paul Willis. These and other scholars were among the first to take poplar music seriously as an object of sociological study. Through their in-depth examination of the social significance of pop, rock, and associated genres, such scholars offered an important new dimension to popular music scholarship which, up until that point, had been primarily considered in terms of its musical content (see, for example, Mellers, 1973). The next section of the chapter examines how sociological approaches to popular music have been influenced by the 'cultural turn'. The cultural turn has been a pivotal element in the emergence and development of cultural sociology. In the field of popular music research, a particularly important influence of the cultural turn has been to engender a closer focus on the microsocial and localised importance of popular music, in relation to issues of production, performance, and consumption. As noted above, this focus has also extended to the impact of digital media on popular music and its significance as a cultural resource in everyday life.

## POPULAR MUSIC AND SOCIOLOGY

As noted above, an important foundation for the sociological study of popular music was Adorno's highly influential, if simultaneously controversial, work of the mid-20th century. Situated firmly within the critical theory of the Frankfurt School, Adorno considered that the mass produced aspect of popular music exerted a controlling influence on its audience. For Adorno, this quality of popular music was embedded in the standardisation of both its composition and performance. In contrast to art music, whose complex musical structures required a more intense and acquired form of listening on the part of the audience, popular music, according to Adorno, was an entirely predictable form which resulted in a type of lazy listening that exerted a controlling influence over its audience:

> The composition hears for the listener ... Not only does it not require effort to follow its concrete stream; it actually gives him models under which anything concrete still remaining may be subsumed. The schematic build up dictates the way in which he must listen while, at the same time, it makes any effort in listening unnecessary. Popular music is 'pre-digested' in a way strongly resembling the fad of 'digests' of printed material. (1941: 306)

This interpretation of popular music held sway for several decades becoming a powerful steer for the way in which successive generations of popular music artists were received. Thus, for example, in an article on The Beatles published in the *New Statesman* in 1964, Paul Johnson describes the band as an exemplar of the pre-packaged 'pop' described by Adorno:

> If the Beatles and their like were in fact what the youth of Britain wanted, one might well despair. I refuse to believe it – and so will any other intelligent person who casts his or her mind back far enough. What were we doing at 16? I remember reading the whole of Shakespeare and Marlowe, writing poems and plays and stories. At 16, I and my friends heard our first performance of Beethoven's Ninth Symphony; I can remember the excitement even today. We would not have wasted 30 seconds of our precious time on the Beatles and their ilk. (1964: 327)

As Johnson's depiction suggests, a critical element in such concern about popular music was its perceived impact on youth. From the point of view of the establishment, and to a lesser extent the mass media of the time, popular music icons such as Elvis Presley and the Beatles were serving to undermine the moral values of youth and also damaging their capacity for intellectual growth. This perception was graphically illustrated in the attempts to censor Elvis Presley's early television performances (see Shumway, 1992), and was also seen several years later in the British media's reporting of minor clashes between mods and rockers at seaside towns on the south-east coast of England (Cohen, 1987). Such negative representations of popular music and its youth audience only began to be challenged during the late 1960s, when the work of cultural theorists such as Hall (1968) and Laing (1969) began to offer new accounts of the ways in which youth audiences interacted with music. Against a backdrop of the rapid cultural changes taking place in the 1960s, Hall, Laing and others (see, for example, Melley, 1970) argued that rather than producing cultural dupes, popular music and its associated assemblage of cultural resources was offering audiences alternative, and in some cases, potentially subversive expressions of identity and lifestyle. This period also saw the publication of books such as Gillett's (1983) *Sounds of the City* and Reich's (1971) *The Greening of America*. Each of these books established important new parameters for the way that popular music would come to be conceptualised, including in the emergent sociology of popular music. Gillett, in exploring the relationship between popular music production, consumption and the city opened up a new space for the exploration of popular music as a soundtrack for everyday life, a form of urban cool that became imprinted on city life and the forms of cultural sensibilities that evolve there. Reich's main focus was on the importance of popular music, looking at the hippie counter-culture and its capacity to offer new forms of consciousness that attempted to subvert the technocratic basis (Clecak, 1983) of contemporary social life.

The early indications of an emerging sociology of popular music were evident in studies such as Denisoff and Peterson's (1972) *The Sounds of Social Change*. Although published in the early 1970s, this edited collection brought together a series of studies that in some cases had been published some years earlier, notably Howard Becker's (1972 [1951]) highly instructive work on the socio-cultural milieu of the jazz musician, as well as new essays on genres such as country (DiMaggio et al., 1972), soul (Larkin, 1972) and the politically charged rock of the late 1960s and early 1970s (Gleason, 1972; Marcus, 1972). The book thus presents an in-depth study of popular music's historical significance as a medium for social awareness and change, while at the same time looking at more micro-social dimensions such as the relationship between music and place, the significance of music scenes, and the relevance of song lyrics for audiences. Each of these topics were to become further developed as the sociology of popular music gathered momentum during the 1970s.

Another important development during the early to mid-1970s was the emergence of cultural studies, and in particular the focus among some cultural studies on youth and youth subcultures. Although this work was in some ways tangential to the academic study of popular music (for accounts of this see, among others, Laing, 1985), the fact that it attempted to offer new explanations of music-centred youth cultures was of significance. Taking issue with the pessimistic reading of popular culture offered by critical theorists such as Adorno and Horkheimer (1969), the Birmingham Centre for Contemporary Cultural Studies (CCCS) represented stylised post-war British youth (sub) cultures such as the Teddy Boys, mods, and skinheads as subversive cultural forms (see Hall and Jefferson, 1976). The CCCS's work on youth subcultures has been criticised on various grounds, including its lack of attention to gender (McRobbie, 1980), the predominant use of textual analysis (with the results that little empirical evidence exists to support the CCCS's claims) (Cohen, 1987), and the predominant emphasis on class as an explanation for the subversive tendencies of post-war youth (Bennett, 1999; Muggleton, 2000). Nevertheless, the concepts used by the CCCS and their argument that mass produced popular cultural forms such as style (and by definition popular music) could become resources for use in forms of anti-hegemonic action and thought was to become a critical underpinning for the way that popular music would be studied from a sociological perspective in subsequent years.

Simon Frith's (1978) *The Sociology of Rock* (republished in 1983 as *Sound Affects*) was the first book-length attempt to study popular music from a sociological perspective. Taking stock of the critical perspectives weighed against popular music as a mass-produced, largely effete and throw-away form of leisure, Frith was among the first to consider the contradictions of rock, pop, and other genres of popular music (notably punk which had recently emerged on the popular music landscape), as industrially produced music became embedded in national and localised scenes where performers and audiences were positioned in discourses of authenticity relating to lifestyle, politics, space, and place. Challenging the previously held dichotomy between high and low culture, Frith suggested that, in the world of popular music, such categories became largely a matter of aesthetic preference. This is a topic that Frith would return to periodically over the course of the next twenty years, notably in his essay 'Towards an Aesthetic of Popular Music' where he observed:

> There is no doubt that sociologists have tended to explain away pop music. In my own academic work I have examined how rock is produced and consumed, and have tried to place it ideologically, but there is no way that a reading of my books (or those of other sociologists) could be used to explain why some pop songs are good and others bad … how is it that people (myself included) can say, quite confidently, that some popular music is better than others? (1987: 133–4, 144)

A further important study in the initial development of the sociology of popular music was Paul Willis' (1978) *Profane Culture*. Although this study is often associated with the work of the CCCS, it is, nevertheless, different in several respects. First, Willis does not apply the term subculture in his work, assuming instead that practices of resistance pertain in a cross-class situation, something that had not been fully investigated in the work of the CCCS, whose focus was primarily on working-class youth. Second, Willis moves beyond textual analysis and makes extensive use of ethnographic methods in his work, the basis of *Profane Culture* being two case studies comprising observation of and interviews with two distinct youth cultural groups – the 'bike boys' and 'hippies'. Using a conceptual framework referred to as 'homology', Willis suggests that the cultural meanings embedded by the working-class bike boys and middle-class hippies are homologically related to their class backgrounds. According to

Willis, homology denotes a process whereby structurally derived interpretations of meanings inscribed in cultural objects become over a period of time taken-for-granted and 'natural' to the social actors concerned. Thus, for Willis, homology represents 'the continuous play between the group and a particular item which produces specific styles, meanings, contents and forms of consciousness' (1978: 191). This contention is then explored, for example, in relation to the bike boys' collective representation of the brashness and straightforward nature of rock and roll music as symbolic of the tough and independent nature of the working-class male, and the hippies' understanding of LSD as a means through which more fully to appreciate the complex and multi-layered structures of progressive rock music while simultaneously acquiring an altered and higher level of perception. Willis' work has been criticised for attempting to explain away the meaning of music as a facet of class background (Bennett, 2008), while the concept of homology is considered by some theorists as reducing the individual back to the level of cultural dupe, unable to make reflexive choices beyond those structured by a predetermined digest of taste possibilities (Harris, 1992).

A study that attempts to move beyond a class-based explanation of musical taste is George H. Lewis's 'Who Do You Love? The Dimensions of Musical Taste'. According to Lewis:

> ... the relationship between [musical preferences and social class] is not the clean and neat one that some, perhaps naively, have assumed it to be – especially in our modern, mass-mediated technological society. In such a society, under conditions of relatively high social mobility, greater discretionary income, easy credit, efficient distribution of goods, a high diffusion rate of cultural products, conspicuous consumption, and a greater amount of leisure time, the link between social and cultural structures becomes a question, not a given. Rather than assume it to be simply correlative, it is perhaps better to view it as contingent, problematic, variable, and – to a higher degree than we might imagine – subjectively determined. (1992: 141)

In exploring this contention, Lewis applies the concept of taste cultures, originally introduced in the work by Herbert Gans (1967), in an attempt better to understand and explain the ways in which the musical tastes of individuals are acquired and used as a basis through which to form bonds with others. In certain respects, there are similarities here with Straw's (1991) work on scenes in as much as both Lewis and Straw consider the collective expression of musical tastes to extend beyond a simple question of shared class background, and engage with aspects of lifestyle and aesthetics as these relate to and become inscribed within specific forms of cultural consumption. Lewis identifies three main factors relevant to the creation of taste cultures – *demographics*, *aesthetics*, and *politics*. According to Lewis, *demographics* relates to factors including age, gender, race, and locality. These factors, argues Lewis, can be seen to dramatically cut across class in the ways that they supply a basis for individual and collective investments in a particular style, or styles, of music. *Aesthetics*, relates to personal outlook, which may be the result of growing up in a particular place but may also result from, for example, reading a particular kind of literature, spiritual beliefs, attitudes towards health and well-being, and so on. According to Lewis, such factors can also be important triggers for determining a preference for particular kinds of music. In this sense, a specific genre of music may be more aesthetically fulfilling, because of its resonance with other acquired sensibilities, than other musical genres. The final category explored by Lewis is *politics*, connoting a perceived connection for an individual between a particular style of music and the dominant power structure. Thus, for example, whereas a genre such as country may be understood to support and be bound up with the dominant hegemony, punk and rap may be perceived as assuming a more subversive and oppositional stance. Therefore, argues Lewis, in adopting a preference for a particular kind of music, individuals are able both to assert their own political values and to assert themselves in opposition to other musical taste groups.

Lewis' study is of significant importance due to the way that it breaks with the then relatively established tradition in academic work of looking for underlying structures as a means of explaining particular expressions of individual and collective taste in popular music. Taking issue with this approach, Lewis regards individuals as more agentive and reflexive in choosing a particular kind of music, and regards such choice as part of a broader assemblage of objects, images, and texts that inform a lifestyle aesthetic. Furthermore, in Lewis' view, even as certain pre-determined and external factors, such as gender, race, and locality, play a role in the acquisition of musical taste, the latter do not act like dead weights on the individual. Rather, they act on individuals at different levels and in different ways, thus producing a plurality of responses to musical genres rather than a monolithic response.

## POPULAR MUSIC SOCIOLOGY AND THE CULTURAL TURN

As discussed elsewhere in this Handbook, the cultural turn had a profound influence on sociology in a broad sense (see Chaney, 1994). The principle tenet of the cultural turn is a need for a focus on culture as central to the co-production of society rather than merely a by-product of the existing social structure. Within this an emphasis on the everyday cultural sphere is also paramount in understanding the impact of the cultural turn on the new directions that emerged in sociology:

> ... rather than existing as a site of exploitation and oppression, everyday life is a site of contestation and struggles; a site on which a plurality of cultural values give rise to competing sensibilities through which individuals reflexively define themselves, their relationship to others and their place in the physical and symbolic order of things. (Bennett, 2005: 54)

In the field of popular music sociology, the specific importance of the cultural turn was most keenly apparent in the emergence of a new sub-genre of literature that was more locally specific in its focus and more empirically informed in its approach. Tia DeNora's (2000) *Music in Everyday Life*, although not strictly a popular-music-focused study, saw participants citing various songs from different eras of pop in a study that instructively investigates the connections between music, memory, and emotion in mundane, everyday contexts. A key departure in DeNora's work, and something that aligns it with the critical vision of cultural sociology, is the way it positions the individual as a co-producer of the musical text. Although such co-production had been intimated in earlier work (see Frith, 1987), DeNora brings a more fully-fledged conceptual basis to this debate through her theorisation of music as a resource used by individuals in what she refers to as a 'technology of the self':

> Reliving experience through music ..., in so far as it is experienced as an identification with or of 'the past', is part of the work of producing oneself as a coherent being over time, part of producing a retrospection that is in turn a projection into the future, a cuing in how to proceed. (2000: 66)

Certainly DeNora's perspective on the relationship between text and agency opens up new questions in the sociology of music. Although it does not discount the role of structure in this equation, the work positions this in a more fluid relationship to how individuals respond to and use music in their everyday lives. This is in marked contrast to the work of earlier sociologists such as Willis (1978) (see above), for whom music, among other cultural texts and objects, serves primarily to reinforce the bond between structure and agency. For DeNora, music's role is not one of structural reinforcement. Rather it serves to provide the individual with resources for the reflexive (re) production of the self over time.

A further important contribution in this regard is Antoine Hennion's (2007) work on musical taste. In a study that takes to task Bourdieu's (1984) concepts of habitus and cultural capital, Hennion suggests that patterns of taste in music, as with other forms of cultural consumption, cannot be regarded as pre-formed and pre-digested. That common patterns of musical taste exist between individuals, argues Hennion, has more to do with the ways that individuals seek to belong to 'communities' and articulate modes of belonging in a contemporary social context where more traditional modes of community no longer exist or are more weakly formulated than in previous times. In this context, suggests Hennion, taste becomes a credible indicator of belonging and can enunciate an authentic feeling of community for individuals. In this sense there are connections between Hennion's work and that of Chaney (1996) whose concept of lifestyle also reflects the ways that late modern individuals connect as aesthetically informed communities through the collective inscription of common meanings in images, objects, and texts produced by the cultural industries.

Andy Bennett's (2000) work on youth, popular music and locality offers a different perspective on the relevance of popular music as a cultural resource through considering its role in the reflexive production of collective narratives of space and place. Again, for Bennett, the role of music is not one of serving to highlight the fixity of the individual within a set of rigidly determined structural circumstances; instead, popular music genres such as rap and dance provide a means through which individuals are able to negotiate the everyday socio-cultural circumstances they find themselves in through the creation of spatial narratives that offer agency and power. Key to this kind of situating strategy is the way that individuals are able to use music in the production of what Bennett refers to as multiple narratives of the local. In other words, through their absorption of specific musical texts, individuals produce a narrative synthesis of local knowledges and the aesthetic sensibilities they acquire through particular genres, and then use these to symbolically mark themselves out as distinctive in given urban spaces. For example, in identifying a dominant local night-time economy as driven by over-regulation and a profit motive, fans of rap, dance and alternative forms of music may not only seek out alternative spaces for the performance and consumption of their preferred musics, but will also regard themselves as the collective embodiment (see Driver and Bennett, 2015) of those spaces. Narratives of the local thus become an important means through which music is imbricated in discourses of belonging and collective identity. As Bennett observes, such narratives can often criss-cross physical city spaces in a highly complex fashion:

> ... in referring to the 'local', we are in effect speaking about a space which is crossed by a variety of different collective sensibilities each of which imposes a different set of expectations and cultural needs upon that space. In doing so, such sensibilities also construct the local in particular ways, a process which ensures that terms such as *locality* and *local identity* are always, in part at least, subjective elements which begin by utilising the same basic knowledges about the local, its social and spatial organisation, but supplement such knowledges with their own collectively held values to create particular narratives of locality. (2000: 66)

If cultural sociology has been important in terms of throwing light on popular music's role in the narrative construction of space and place, its insights regarding the role of digital media in the ways that individuals actively use music in the co-production of cultural life have also been fruitful and highly instructive. Writers outside the field of cultural sociology, notably Bull (2000), had already begun to consider how mobile music technologies such as the personal stereo were creating new sensorial experiences for individuals in their everyday interface with urban and rural landscapes. Peterson and Bennett's (2004) introduction of the concept of the *virtual* music scene represents an early sociological foray into the new possibilities offered by digital technology for the reflexive production and articulation of collective identities in ways that may not necessarily rely on the appropriation of physical space but can still engender important feelings of belonging in an increasingly fragmented late modern landscape (Chaney, 2002). Thus, according to Peterson and Bennett:

> Whereas a conventional local scene is kept in motion by a series of gigs, club nights, fairs, and similar events, where fans converge, communicate and reinforce their sense of belonging to a particular scene, the virtual scene involves direct net-mediated person-to-person communication between fans ... This may, involve, for example, the creation of chat-rooms or list-serves dedicated to the scene and may involve the trading of music and images on-line. (2004: 11)

Since the publication of Peterson and Bennett's work, the emergence of social media sites such as Facebook has significantly expanded the horizons for such forms of virtual connectivity. Instructive in this respect is David Beer's (2008) study of social networking sites as a means though which individuals connect and form associations based around shared musical tastes, knowledge, and a desire both to discover new music and learn more about their existing musical tastes and preferred music icons. According to Beer, Web 2.0 in general, and social networking sites in particular, have become a significant new landscape for musical life in the early 21st century. In addition to offering technological platforms for the acquisition and sharing of music (see also Nowak and Bennett, 2014), Web 2.0 has become a new sociocultural universe for a collective aesthetic investment in music, which, although it existed in a mediated context prior to the arrival of the internet and social media, was experienced more at the level of the affective rather than the interactive. Additional credence is given to Beer's arguments when one considers the sheer amount of work that invokes the digital domain, for example in work on scenes and (post)subcultures (Bennett, 2002; 2004; Hodkinson, 2003; Williams, 2006), festivals (Cummings, 2006; Dowd et al., 2004), and what are increasingly referred to as 'prosumers' – those who both produce music (in both a practical and aesthetic/discursive sense) and consume it (Jung, 2014).

As the above survey of key works in the cultural sociology of popular music reveals, this area of work has opened up an important series of new opportunities for sociologists to examine the cultural importance of popular music as a textual and material resource. Importantly, the field is still in a critical stage of development and, as such, is set to rapidly evolve. The following section of this chapter offers some reflections and suggestions as to areas that the cultural sociology of popular music might productively focus on over the course of the next fifteen to twenty years. What follows is by no means an exhaustive account but is rather intended to provide some inspiration and guidance for cultural sociologists engaged in the study of popular music.

## NEW PATHWAYS FOR THE CULTURAL SOCIOLOGY OF POPULAR MUSIC

At the time of writing there are a number of interesting developments occurring in the sphere of popular music, notably in relation to production and consumption, history, memory, and representation, and also the shifting demographic of popular music audiences. Similarly, the extent to which popular music impacts on the everyday soundscape has shifted dramatically. Certainly, cultural sociologists of popular music have not been ignorant of such developments. That said, each of these themes has significant potential for further exploration in relation to the intersections between popular music, everyday life, and individual agency.

It is certainly no secret that developments in digital media since the 1990s have significantly impacted on how popular music is produced, accessed, and consumed. Whereas popular music, in its recorded form, was once tightly controlled by the music industry, this is no longer the case. The development of the MP3 enabled the easy uploading and download of digital sound-files and thus became an important new way for individuals to access music (Nowak, 2014). Although original file-sharing sites such as Napster incurred legal sanctions (Rojek, 2005), the digital files and supporting software have become a standard means through which music is now disseminated – both legally and illegally – and this is something which is supported by a plethora of devices such as the laptop, smartphone, and iPad (all of which can support MP3 playback) and the iPod, which is purpose-built for this use. Existing cultural sociological work on this theme has begun to map the contours of this new music acquisition and listening landscape. Raphaël Nowak (2015) draws on Gibson's (1979) concept or affordances and Martin's (1995) notion of the sound environment to examine how digital music technologies form part of a continuum of technologically enabled listening experiences that cohere closely with taste, mood, activity, and time of day (see also Nowak and Bennett, 2014). Ben Green (2015) extends this premise to examine the technological dimension of music and experience – rooting this in what he refers to as 'peak music experiences', that is to say, the memorised moments of when deep personal connections with particular music and/or artists are made. Such recent developments in the cultural sociology of popular music are important, not least of all in how they continue to build on and finesse in important ways the ground-breaking work of writers such as DeNora (2000) and Hennion (2007). If digital technologies are delivering new ways in which music can be accessed, at the same time they are offering sociologists new ways of studying and understanding how music is experienced at an everyday level and, thus, offering important new insights as to why music 'matters' as a textual and material resource both in the everyday soundscape and in the lifestyle assemblages of late modern individuals.

If the ways in which popular music is being accessed and listened to by audiences is changing, then the changing nature of the audience itself is something that also warrants closer attention in sociological research. Andy Bennett (2006; 2013) has observed that the once taken for granted relationship between youth culture and popular music is increasingly problematised by the multi-generational audiences and scenes that characterise a range of music genres, including metal, punk rap and dance. As Bennett observes:

> One might reasonably expect then, that where investment in a musical style has been particularly intensive during one's teenage to twenty-something years such investment may well continue well into middle age and beyond. The fact that an individual becomes a follower of a style of music as a 'young' person may matter far less than what that music continues to mean to them as they grow older. (2013: 20)

In a further study, Bennett and Hodkinson (2012) assemble a range of studies that examine in depth how, for example, straight-edge scene, urban dance music clubs, breakdancing events, mosh pits and festivals are all sites of multi-generational interaction and exchange. This body of work also throws light on how a number of other central aspects of social life are becoming interwoven with the musical tastes and activities of the ageing music fan. For example, their work provides evidence of how ageing punk and dance fans have found ways of combining their musical and cultural tastes with work in the form of DiY music careers, while others involve their families in particular music-based activities or have provided their children with a point of reference to follow in their musical footsteps (see also Smith's (2012) work on the children of Northern Soul fans). The findings of the emergent research on popular music and ageing connote the shifting significance of popular music in society. At the level of the music consumer, it is no longer possible to see music merely as a form of leisure that may also extend to, for example, the acquisition of political sensibilities and lifestyle. Rather, for many ageing fans, music strongly informs a narrative of self. At this stage, although the work is informative, it is also quite limited in scope and range. For example, there is little work that looks at the relationship between music, ageing and ethnic identity, or between music, ageing and gender (for an exception here, see Vroomen, 2004). These are clearly areas where further research will need to be done in order to gain a more comprehensive understanding of how popular music shapes ageing identities.

The connections that are becoming apparent between popular music and ageing are also giving rise to questions regarding popular music, memory, and heritage. Strong's (2011) study of grunge and memory marks an early and important contribution in this newly emerging direction. Through interviews with fans of grunge some fifteen years after the global rise of grunge due to the commercial success of bands such as Nirvana and Pearl Jam, Strong depicts the importance of popular music in the articulation of a cultural memory (Huyssen, 2003). Thus, for the individual grunge fans, while their individual accounts of grunge and its cultural significance are insightful, what is of perhaps more importance is the way in which their views cohere to preserve a particulate collective memory of grunge as a music that supplied a particular series of sensibilities and a worldview. What is also important to note here is the way that such collective, cultural memory is also held together and articulated through particular assemblages of artefacts. This may take the form of a personal collection of, for example, albums, photographs, ticket stubs, and so on, or may take a more official or semi-official form in the shape of an archive (Bennett and Rogers, forthcoming). As Baker and Huber (2015) observe, the drive among fans and other interested individuals actively to preserve a popular music heritage that they personally feel a connection with has given rise to a variety of what could be called DiY music archives around the world.

At the other end of the spectrum, notions of popular music as heritage are shaping a number of official responses that have become the backbone of what could be termed a popular music heritage industry. There has been an increasing push, primarily in the UK and USA, but also in other European countries, to archive and celebrate the history of popular music and to re-present it as a pivotal aspect of contemporary cultural heritage (Bennett, 2009; Brandellero and Janssen, 2014). This has been facilitated through a range of initiatives that include organised tours of music-related sites and spaces, one of the more established and well-known examples being the Magical Mystery Tour of various sites of interest in Liverpool connected with the Beatles (Cohen, 2007). Such tours are supplemented by permanent museums or temporary exhibitions focusing on aspects of contemporary popular music history (Leonard, 2010; Leonard and Knifton, 2012; Van der Hoeven, 2014). A further important dimension of the popular music heritage industry is the consecration of buildings with significant connections to the history of popular music, for example, the childhood homes of John Lennon and Paul McCartney in Liverpool, or Sun Studio in Memphis (where Elvis Presley made his early recordings) (Gibson, 2005). The importance of acknowledging popular music as an aspect of cultural heritage is also borne out in the way that connections are made between music and understandings of local and national identity, including music's relevance for regional and urban regeneration through, for example, the promotion of cultural tourism (Baker et al., 2009; Brandellero and Janssen, 2014; Connell and Gibson, 2003).

Although not all of the work being conducted on the theme of music and heritage is sociological in nature, much of it is nevertheless concerned with the more cultural dimensions of music heritage initiatives and the ways that the latter are received by audiences and other key stakeholders. At present, though, the field is still quite thinly mapped. In this context, a key deficit is arguably a more refined knowledge of the connections between the local and global, and centre and periphery in the ongoing roll-out of the popular music heritage industry. Bennett (2015) has warned that at present much of the music heritage work in progress is either situated in Anglo-American contexts and/or showcases music that is predominantly Anglo-American influenced. This 'problem' in the current envisaging of popular music heritage is something that necessitates close attention, particularly given the disjuncture here between heritage discourses and the increasingly localised nature of popular music scenes throughout the world. Or, to put this another way, the cultural imperialism that has often been cited as a threat to local cultures (Tomlinson, 1991) figures also in the current canons of popular music deemed worthy of preservation as bona fide aspects of late 20th-century and early 21st-century cultural heritage.

As noted earlier in this chapter, the status of popular music as a 'cultural' object of study has, by necessity, been cast against the backdrop of its industrial production. Since the late 1990s, however, it has become increasingly clear that popular music production, dissemination and consumption are also being shaped by patterns and trends that are distinctly post-industrial in nature. The most obvious, and aforementioned, dimension of this is the increasing role played by the internet in the way that popular music is now sourced by audiences. But digital technology has had a more wholesale effect on popular music, offering musicians the opportunity to compose, produce, and market their music, by-passing the need for a conventional recording and/or management deal (see Rogers, 2008). Although the latter avenues still exist for musicians, the fact that digital technology has opened up significant pathways for professional and semi-professional music-making without the need for support from the mainstream music industry has given rise to what could be termed a DiY music industry on a global scale. That said, however, there is currently a dearth of literature that systematically addresses such new developments in the way that, for example, Negus (1992) provided an in-depth analysis of the more traditional music industry in the pre-digital age. As such, there is an important role to be played here by cultural sociologists in providing frameworks for understanding both the political economy of the 'new music industry' and the micro-social components that hold it together. Preliminary research (see, for example, Tarassi, 2012) illustrates how current music industry practitioners typically manage a wide ranging portfolio that may include not only musical composition and performance, but also music production, management, journalism, and so on. Similarly, there is a critical need for more research on the types of bonds that exist between local DiY music scenes and global flows of production, performance, and consumption that intersect such scenes.

## CONCLUSION

This chapter has focused on the evolution of the cultural sociology of popular music. The chapter began by considering how popular music originally became a focus for sociological enquiry, examining important antecedents in this respect, notably the critical theory of the Frankfurt School during the early part of the 20th century and the emergence of cultural studies during the late 1960s and early 1970s. The following section of the chapter examined and evaluated the contribution of some early examples of sociological work to our understanding of the socio-cultural significance of popular music. Such work, it was observed, was of critical importance in establishing many of the foundations for subsequent sociological work on aspects of popular music production and performance, and on music audiences. In the next section of the chapter, the importance of the cultural turn on sociological approaches to popular music was considered. It was shown how the resulting cultural sociological approaches to the study of popular music offered an important range of new insights regarding the relationship between music and memory, music and taste, and music and identity. Core to cultural sociological approaches was a move away from discussions of music as a reflection of pre-existing social structures and a focus instead on the individual as a reflexive agent whose engagement with music involves a co-production of musical meaning and significance. The final part of the chapter offered a series of reflections on how the cultural sociology of music might fruitfully develop over the next ten to fifteen years. As discussed in this section of the chapter, emerging new bodies of work in the fields of music taste, technology, ageing, memory, and heritage provide important indicators of where the new foci for cultural sociologists interested in popular music are located. Likewise, at the level of music production there is an urgent need for new work that maps and analyses new patterns and trends in what could be termed the DiY music industry.

## REFERENCES

Adorno, T.W. (1941) 'On Popular Music', in S. Frith and A. Goodwin (eds) (1990) *On Record: Rock, Pop and the Written Word*. London: Routledge.

Adorno, T. and Horkheimer, M. (1969) *The Dialectic of Enlightenment*. London: Allen Lane.

Baker, S. and Huber, A. (2015) 'Saving "Rubbish": Preserving Popular Music's Material Culture in Amateur Archives and Museums', in S. Cohen, R. Knifton, M. Leonard and L. Roberts (eds), *Sites of Popular Music Heritage: Memories, Histories, Places*. London: Routledge.

Baker, S., Bennett, A. and Homan, S. (2009) 'Cultural Precincts, Creative Spaces: Giving the Local a Musical Spin', *Space and Culture*, 12(2): 148–65.

Becker, H.S. (1972 [1951]) 'The Professional Jazz Musician and his Audience', in R.S. Denisoff and R.A. Peterson (eds), *The Sounds of Social Change*. Chicago: Rand McNally and Company.

Beer, D. (2008) 'Making Friends with Jarvis Cocker: Music Culture in the Context of Web 2.0', *Cultural Sociology*, 2(2): 222–41.

Bennett, A. (1999) 'Subcultures or Neo-Tribes? Rethinking the Relationship between Youth, Style and Musical Taste', *Sociology*, 33(3): 599–617.

Bennett, A. (2000) *Popular Music and Youth Culture: Music, Identity and Place*. London: Macmillan.

Bennett, A. (2002) 'Researching Youth Culture and Popular Music: A Methodological Critique', *British Journal of Sociology*, 53(3): 451–66.

Bennett, A. (2004) 'New Tales from Canterbury: The Making of a Virtual Music Scene', in A. Bennett, and R.A. Peterson (eds), *Music Scenes: Local, Trans-Local and Virtual*. Nashville, TN: Vanderbilt University Press.

Bennett, A. (2005) *Culture and Everyday Life*. London: Sage.

Bennett, A. (2006) 'Punks Not Dead: The Significance of Punk Rock for an Older Generation of Fans', *Sociology*, 40(1): 219–35.

Bennett, A. (2008) 'Towards a Cultural Sociology of Popular Music', *Journal of Sociology*, 4(4): 419–32.
Bennett, A. (2009) '"Heritage Rock": Rock Music, Re-presentation and Heritage Discourse', *Poetics*, 37(5–6): 474–89.
Bennett, A. (2013) *Music, Style and Aging: Growing Old Disgracefully?* Philadelphia: Temple University Press.
Bennett, A. (2015) 'Popular Music and the "Problem" of Heritage', in S. Cohen, R. Knifton, M. Leonard, and L. Roberts (eds), *Sites of Popular Music Heritage*. London: Routledge.
Bennett, A. and Hodkinson, P. (eds) (2012) *Ageing and Youth Cultures: Music, Style and Identity*. Oxford: Berg.
Bennett, A. and Peterson, R.A. (eds) (2004) *Music Scenes: Local, Trans-Local and Virtual*. Nashville, TN: Vanderbilt University Press.
Bennett, A. and Rogers, I. (forthcoming) 'Popular Music and Materiality: Memorabilia, Archives and Memory Traces', *Popular Music and Society*.
Bourdieu, P. (1984) *Distinction: A Social Critique of the Judgement of Taste*. London: Routledge.
Brandellero, A. and Janssen, S. (2014) 'Popular Music as Cultural Heritage: Scoping Out the Field of Practice', *International Journal of Heritage Studies*, 20(3): 223–40.
Bull, M. (2000) *Sounding Out the City: Personal Stereos and the Management of Everyday Life*. Oxford: Berg.
Chaney, D. (1994) *The Cultural Turn: Scene Setting Essays on Contemporary Cultural History*. London: Routledge.
Chaney, D. (1996) *Lifestyles*. London: Routledge.
Chaney, D. (2002) *Cultural Change and Everyday Life*. Basingstoke: Palgrave.
Clecak, P. (1983) *America's Quest for the Ideal Self: Dissent and Fulfilment in the 60s and 70s*. Oxford: Oxford University Press.
Cohen, S. (1987) *Folk Devils and Moral Panics: The Creation of the Mods and Rockers*, 3rd edn. Oxford: Basil Blackwell.
Cohen, S. (2007) *Decline, Renewal and the City in Popular Music Culture: Beyond the Beatles*. Aldershot: Ashgate.
Connell, J. and Gibson, C. (2003) *Sound Tracks: Popular Music, Identity, and Place*. London: Routledge.
Cummings, J. (2006) 'It's More than a T-Shirt: Neo-tribal Sociality and Linking Images at Australian Indie Music Festivals', *Perfect Beat*, 8(1): 65–84.
Denisoff, R.S. and Peterson, R.A. (1972) *The Sounds of Social Change: Studies in Popular Culture*. Chicago: Rand McNally.
DeNora, T. (2000) *Music in Everyday Life*. Cambridge. Cambridge University Press.
DiMaggio, P. Peterson, R.A. and Esco Jr, J. (1972) 'Country Music: Ballad of the Silent Majority', in R.S. Denisoff and R.A. Peterson (eds), *The Sounds of Social Change*. Chicago: Rand McNally and Company.
Dowd, T.J., Liddle, K. and Nelson, J. (2004) 'Music Festivals as Scenes: Examples from Serious Music, Womyn's Music and SkatePunk', in A. Bennett and R.A. Peterson (eds), *Music Scenes: Local, Translocal and Virtual*. Nashville, TN: Vanderbilt University Press.
Driver, C. and Bennett, A. (2015) 'Music Scenes, Space and the Body', *Cultural Sociology*, 9(1): 99–115.
Frith, S. (1978) *The Sociology of Rock*. London: Constable.
Frith, S. (1983) *Sound Effects: Youth, Leisure and the Politics of Rock*. London: Constable.
Frith, S. (1987) 'Towards an Aesthetic of Popular Music', in R. Leppert and S. McClary (eds), *Music and Society: The Politics of Composition, Performance and Reception*. Cambridge: Cambridge University Press.
Gans, H.J. (1967) 'Popular Culture in America', in H.S. Becker (ed.), *Social Problems: A Modern Approach*. New York: John Wiley.
Gibson, J. (1979) *The Ecological Approach to Visual Perception*. Boston, MA: Houghton Mifflin.
Gibson, C. (2005) 'Recording Studios: Relational Spaces of Creativity in the City', *Built Environment*, 31(3): 192–207.
Gillett, C. (1983) *The Sound of the City: The Rise of Rock and Roll*, 2nd edn. London: Souvenir Press.
Gleason, R.J. (1972) 'A Cultural Revolution', in R.S. Denisoff and R.A. Peterson (eds), *The Sounds of Social Change: Studies in Popular Culture*. Chicago: Rand McNally.
Green, B. (2015) '"I Always Remember That Moment": Peak Music Experiences as Epiphanies', *Sociology*. DOI: 0038038514565835, first published on February 19, 2015.
Hall, S. (1968) *The Hippies: An American 'Moment'*. Birmingham Centre for Contemporary Cultural Studies, University of Birmingham.
Hall, S. and Jefferson, T. (1976) (eds) *Resistance Through Rituals: Youth Subcultures in Post-War Britain*. London: Hutchinson.
Harris, D. (1992) *From Class Struggle to the Politics of Pleasure: The Effects of Gramscianism on Cultural Studies*. London: Routledge.
Hennion, A. (2007) 'Those Things That Hold Us Together: Taste and Sociology', *Cultural Sociology*, 1(1): 97–114.
Hodkinson, P. (2003) '"Net. Goth": Internet Communication and (Sub)Cultural Boundaries', in D. Muggleton and R. Weinzierl (eds), *The Post-subcultures Reader*. Oxford: Berg.

Huyssen, A. (2003) *Present Pasts: Urban Palimpsests and the Politics of Memory*. Stanford: Stanford University Press.

Johnson, P. (1964) 'The Menace of Beatlism', *The New Statesman*, 28 February: 326–7.

Jung, S. (2014) 'Youth, Social Media and Transnational Cultural Distribution: The Case of Online K-pop Circulation', in A. Bennett and B. Robards (eds), *Mediated Youth Culture: The Internet, Belonging and New Cultural Configurations*. Basingstoke: Palgrave Macmillan.

Laing, D. (1969) *The Sound of Our Time*. London: Sheed and Ward.

Laing, D. (1985) *One Chord Wonders: Power and Meaning in Punk Rock*. Milton Keynes: Open University Press.

Larkin, R. (1972) 'The Soul Message', in R.S. Denisoff and R.A. Peterson (eds), *The Sounds of Social Change: Studies in Popular Culture*. Chicago: Rand McNally.

Leonard, M. (2010) 'Exhibiting Popular Music: Museum Audiences, Inclusion and Social History', *Journal of New Music Research*, 39(2): 171–81.

Leonard, M. and Knifton, R. (2012) '"Museums of Sound": Collecting and Curating Everyday Popular Music Experiences', in R. Snape, H. Pussard and M. Constantine (eds), *Recording Leisure Lives: Everyday Leisure in 20th Century Britain*. Eastbourne: LSA.

Lewis, G.H. (1992) 'Who Do You Love? The Dimensions of Musical Taste', in J. Lull (ed.), *Popular Music and Communication*, 2nd edn. London: Sage.

Marcus, G. (1972) 'A New Awakening', in R.S. Denisoff and R.A. Peterson (eds), *The Sounds of Social Change*. Chicago: Rand McNally and Company.

Martin, P. (1995) *Sounds and Society: Themes in the Sociology of Music*. Manchester: Manchester University Press.

McRobbie, A. (1980) Settling Accounts with Subcultures: A Feminist Critique', *Screen Education*, 34: 37–49.

Melley, G. (1970) *Revolt Into Style: The Pop Arts in Britain*. London: Faber and Faber.

Mellers, W. (1973) *Twilight of the Gods: The Beatles in Retrospect*. London: Faber and Faber.

Muggleton, D. (2000) *Inside Subculture: The Postmodern Meaning of Style*. Oxford: Berg.

Negus, K. (1992) *Producing Pop: Culture and Conflict in the Popular Music Industry*. London: Edward Arnold.

Nowak, J. (2014) 'Understanding Everyday Uses of Music Technologies in the Digital Age', in A. Bennett and B. Robards (eds), *Mediated Youth Culture: The Internet, Belonging and New Cultural Configurations*. Basingstoke: Palgrave Macmillan.

Nowak, R. (2015) *Consuming Music in the Digital Age. Technologies, Roles and Everyday Life*. Basingstoke: Palgrave Macmillan.

Nowak, R. and Bennett, A. (2014) 'Analyzing Everyday Sound Environments: The Space, Time and Corporality of Musical Listening', *Cultural Sociology*, 8(4): 426–42.

Peterson, R.A. and Bennett, A. (2004) 'Introducing Music Scenes', in A. Bennett, and R.A. Peterson (eds), *Music Scenes: Local, Trans-local and Virtual*. Nashville, TN. Vanderbilt University Press.

Reich, C.A. (1971) *The Greening of America*. London: Allen Lane.

Rogers, I. (2008) '"You've Got to Go to Gigs to Get Gigs": Indie Musicians, Eclecticism and the Brisbane Scene', *Continuum: Journal of Media and Cultural Studies*, 22(5): 639–49.

Rojek, C. (2005) 'PP2 Leisure Exchange: Net Banditry and the Policing of Intellectual Property', *Leisure Studies*, 24(4): 357–69.

Shumway, D. (1992) 'Rock and Roll as a Cultural Practice', in A. DeCurtis (ed.), *Present Tense: Rock and Roll and Culture*. Durham, NC: Duke University Press.

Smith, N. (2012) 'Parenthood and the Transfer of Capital in the Northern Soul Scene', in A. Bennett and P. Hodkinson (eds), *Ageing and Youth Cultures: Music, Style and Identity*. Berg: Oxford.Straw, W. (1991) 'Systems of Articulation, Logics of Change: Communities and Scenes in Popular Music', *Cultural Studies*, 5(3): 368–88.

Strong, C. (2011) *Grunge: Music and Memory*. Farnham: Ashgate.

Tarassi, S. (2012) *Independent to What? An Analysis of the Live Music Scene in Milan*. Unpublished PhD thesis. The Catholic University of Milan.

Tomlinson, J. (1991) *Cultural Imperialism: A Critical Introduction*. London: Pinter.

Van der Hoeven, A. (2014) *Popular Music Memories: Places and Practices of Popular Music Heritage, Memory and Cultural Identity*. Doctoral Dissertation. Erasmus University Rotterdam.

Vroomen, L. (2004) 'Kate Bush: Teen Pop and Older Female Fans', in A. Bennett and R.A. Peterson (eds), *Music Scenes: Local, Translocal and Virtual*. Nashville, TN: Vanderbilt University Press.

Williams, J.P. (2006) 'Authentic Identities Straightedge Subculture, Music, and the Internet', *Journal of Contemporary Ethnography*, 35(2): 173–200.

Willis, P. (1978) *Profane Culture*. London: Routledge and Kegan Paul.

# Iconicity

Dominik Bartmanski

## INTRODUCTION

Iconicity has been thematized in sociology in part because of its usefulness in studying cultural icons and their heightened public visibility occasioned by the digitalization of culture. While it is certainly true that cultural icons of all kinds 'dominate our world' (Holt, 2004: 1), a distinctly conceptual need also inspired the process of appropriating iconicity for sociological purposes. After all, if we define icons as 'exemplary symbols that people accept as shorthand to represent important ideas' (Holt, 2004: 1), or more generally as aesthetically powerful condensations of experiential meanings (Alexander, 2008b), then one can hardly deny that cultural icons have densely populated the world for quite some time. Sociology had plenty of opportunities to recognize iconicity in the phenomena it had traditionally studied, from charisma and fetish to aura and totem. And yet it has not thematized it until very recently. Despite taking on board such categories like symbol and sign, cultural sociology kept icons either outside of its systematic theories, or subsumed them under the generic rubric of arbitrary symbolic signification. Iconicity was barely recognized. This situation has now changed because iconicity can offer a series of uniquely pragmatic, rather than purely semantic, insights concerning meaning-making. These are the insights that the dominant linguistic and structuralist theories of symbolic communication and culture could hardly generate on their own. The sensuous and aesthetic experiences that iconicity foregrounds were secondary to the abstract, structuralist conception of meaning-making based on language in Saussure-inspired semiotics. Iconicity reclaims these pragmatic material categories, emphasizing how meaning-making is *sense*-making, with all the rich webs of connotations this term implies: embodied faculties of perception, sensation, feeling, emotion, comprehensibility, significance, import, and so on.

After decades of explorations inspired by the dominant French intellectuals from Saussure and to Lévi-Strauss and the influence of the 'empire of meaning' they devised (Lamont, 1987; Dosse, 1999), our sociological knowledge of symbolic action as text has been deepened. However, our understanding of cultural sense-making has not been commensurately widened. Cultural sociology became epistemologically refined but ontologically agnostic. Meaning was mostly about communication, not experience. Sociologists now have a series of answers to the Austinian question of 'how to do things with words', but comparatively fewer about how things impact upon words, let alone how things make things. Despite incorporating so-called 'thick' description as a rich analytic technique that prevents materialistic reduction, for a long time cultural sociology has been rather 'thin' in aesthetic, sensory and phenomenological terms. If the modern sociological mainstream was prone to reduce society to its economic and institutional bases, then the standard cultural sociological practice has been inclined to couch culture in structuralist/ linguistic terms, which tend to translate cultural complexity to discursive complexity. This was a useful move at the time of its inception, but one that circumscribed the sociological imagination. Importantly, the problems of diffuse idealism and cultural determinism have not been conclusively solved (see Lizardo, 2010: 684; McLennan, 2005) Nowadays, the models of culture as discursive structure that permeated the discipline in the second half of the 20th century are 'threatening to reach a level of saturation and predictability' (Marcus, 1993). A part of the problem is that *culture* in the constructivist view was narrowly modelled after language. Language was the master metaphor and key object of inquiry, that is, culture has been claimed to be *like* language and to work in similar ways to its constitutive modes of operation, i.e. speech and text based on a series of systemic rules. A realization that cultural complexity cannot be exhaustively modelled on the basis of language made it possible to call the sociological usefulness of linguistic paradigms into question. Conceiving of cultural complexity as the social organization of meaning, the Swedish anthropologist Ulf Hannerz (1992: 3) argued that 'to study culture is to study ideas, experiences, feelings, as well as the external forms that such internalities take as they are made public, available to the senses and thus truly social'.

In this context, the introduction of iconicity to cultural sociological scholarship is about making it receptive to materiality and sensuality as irreducible dimensions of sociation and meaning. It is about a decisive recalibration of systemic semiotic understandings of culture as text, an agenda that reclaims phenomenological and emotive aspects of sense-making, whereby the manifold meanings of 'sense' are joined together. Including a series of materially mediated and embodied elements also means adding diachronic context to the synchronic focus of structuralist paradigms. Our bodies change over time, and so do things. Thus iconicity is part of an agenda that 'aims to shake off what has been described as 'one of [Saussure's] most durable legacies', the radical separation of the sign from the material world. The result can be a better understanding of the historicity *inherent* to signs *in their very materiality*'

(Keane, 2005: 183, emphasis in original). Such an agenda insists on taking 'external forms' and 'the senses' seriously, recognizing their own structuring impact on the traditional 'internalities' by which culture was conceptualized in sociology, from Znaniecki and Parsons to Swidler and Vaisey. Iconicity as a new sociological category thematizes social symbolization as an inevitably and irrefutably material phenomenon, a powerful even if sometimes imperceptible and taken-for-granted intersubjective fact whose 'construction' rarely, if ever, stems solely from linguistic acts. Sense-making is a nested social practice dependent on material context, not just playing by or against the rules of a text. The entwinement of material, corporeal and discursive dimensions is postulated as a key condition of sense-making. Iconic effects depend on the occurrence of such entwinements and the possibility of their sustained social existence, which includes the means of symbolic production and what Hannerz called the 'social distribution' of meanings. If cultural sociology is a sociology that treats *meaning* as its central category, and asks how things do or do not *make sense*, then engaging both the abstract and the concrete aspects of sense is not only advisable but indispensable. However mundane they may be, the 'externalities' of human social signification partake in making sense effective.

In this respect, iconicity is compatible with Simmel's seminal understanding that 'every event – however restricted to the superficial level it may appear – comes immediately into contact with the depths of the soul … [and] most banal externalities are – in the last analysis – bound up with the final decisions concerning the meaning and the style of life' (Simmel, 2002 [1903]). In short, by emphasizing the meaningful capacity of the material and the sensuous, iconicity has gradually helped revisit the conceptions of meaning-making and social construction, two fundamental notions in the modern theory of culture. Let us look at this process in greater detail.

## RETHINKING 'THE CULTURAL' AND ITS 'CONSTRUCTEDNESS'

Standard articulations of the master notions of cultural meaning and social construction say that it is *symbols* that are crucial to understanding both domains. It is said that symbolic structures – signs, concepts and their referents – 'are at the heart of cultural systems and the constitution and reproduction of meaning' (Elliott, 2006: 618). However, these accounts largely subsume symbolization to textuality, whereby discursive acts and the referentiality they feature are considered the backbone of culture. The pertinent models developed by philosophers (e.g. Wittgenstein and Austin), and canonically applied by symbolic anthropologists and semiologists (e.g. Geertz and Barthes), marginalized notions such as icon and did not treat them as distinct topics in need of special theorization, as in fact had earlier been proposed by Charles Peirce (1998 [1894]). If some conceptual bridges were made, then often it was to 'the internally' oriented theories, for example the psychoanalytical ideas of Lacan, whose notorious character was more compatible with philosophical abstraction than rigorous empirical sociology. Inspired by those intellectual traditions, one of the main tasks of cultural sociology may have seemed to involve 'unearth[ing] the functioning of the linguistic field in the symbolic determination of the subject … through examination of the intricate connections between Oedipal identifications and projections on the one hand, and the productivities of the signifier on the other' (Elliott, 2006: 618). In principle, the icon as powerful symbolic structure laden with a variety of social identifications could enter 'the heart' of cultural sociology's analytical apparatus. However, due to its indexical specificity and phenomenological dimension, it posed what may be called the 'materiality problem'. Iconicity as modality of signification points to concrete circumstances that contribute to meaningfulness. It points to culturally potent alignment of material and mental factors. In icons the signifier itself matters. Insofar as the icon can be characterized as 'representation', it does not merely *refer to* something else but it *is* itself a part of meaning-making, dependent as much on the concrete impact of its existence, as on any abstract formulation about its functioning in the linguistic field. Here the 'Oedipal identifications' and other psychoanalytical postulates may be interesting, but certainly are not privileged in any interpretive or explanatory sense. Most importantly, textuality is not the master *explanans* but a frame or dimension of cultural action, or is indeed an *explanandum* itself (Keane, 2005).

To use commonplace words, the icon is a visual, often tangible form that affects through the senses as much as intellectually. It is reductive to presume that meaning is an information effortlessly traveling from mind to mind. Meanings are lived and experienced, not just thought of or communicated. Iconic meaning is an illustration of this phenomenon. It is typically instantiated as artifact, tool, person, event, or place, whose cultural efficacy requires material mediation and contextualization. If the word 'structure' is to be used here too, the icon is reducible neither to the elements of its thingness nor to the elements of its textuality. Rather, it is a matrix of the alighment of, or entwinement between, these spheres. *What* icon is thought to *articulate* is deeply influenced by *how* it is *felt* to work, and by the experiential conditions that afford particular kinds of encounter and plausible interpretations. Therefore to study icons is to study iconic processes, their forms and effects, launched and sustained by a set of affordances of given performative constellations, including people, objects, places, and so on.

Needless to say, neither materialist nor idealist paradigms available within the sociological tradition found this complex set of dynamics tractable. Even in the relatively new sub-discipline of visual sociology the term has not been common until very recently. Apart from the sociological work of Bruno Latour, few social theorists thematized iconicity, and more systematic attempts to understand the 'impure' character of iconic mediation were proposed mostly in the humanities, notably by W.J.T. Mitchell's 'iconology' and Gottfried Boehm's agenda of the 'iconic turn.' Social scientists focusing on photographic icons noted that 'no theory we know of can account adequately for the generation, circulation, and uses of the full range of visual icons' (Hariman and Lucaites, 2007: 27). Of course, from the classic cases of cultural studies to the new ones developed within material culture studies, materiality of signification has been present as something crucial rather than secondary. Looking at a wide range of pop cultural phenomena, from the Walkman to the iPod to the vinyl record (du Gay et al., 1997; Bull, 2007; Bartmanski and Woodward, 2013), sociologists connect materiality with iconicity. They discover that effective cultural meaning inescapably relies on material mediation and spatially constituted sensory instantiation, and that therefore the social power of many symbols and mythologies cannot be related solely to textual coherence and the felicitous enactment of the illocutionary force of a given 'message' or 'narrative'. There is a distinct kind of material 'iconic power' (Bartmanski and Alexander, 2012) or 'iconic effect' (Boehm, 2012). Last but not least, in linguistics itself there is evidence that alongside arbitrariness, iconicity is the 'fundamental property' of language and learning, and that it grounds knowledge in experience (Campisi and Özyürek, 2013: 25).

In this sense, the agenda of iconicity outlines a series of specific limits to the foundational semiological culturalism of Roland Barthes (2009: 132), which influenced much of cultural sociology by arguing that such key phenomena as the sociocultural myth 'can be defined neither by its object nor by its material'. The social lives of the contemporary icons that Barthes studied indicate, however, that under certain conditions some symbols are at least partly defined by their very materiality, and by the nexus of object-place-person that unfolds in space and time (Woodward, 2007: 29). The precise extent to which this happens in various circumstances is debated, but nowadays cultural objects are not seen just as passive screens of arbitrary or conventional discursive 'projection', or what Barthes deemed merely 'supporting' acts in the cultural performance of society. Such a unilateral model of the social 'attribution' or ascription' of meaning is substantially revisited and revised by the iconic understanding.

In other words, iconicity indicates that 'material medium' is often in reciprocal relation with the 'discursive message'. Indeed, it is merely a matter of analytic convenience to distinguish the two. Iconic effects stem from the practical blending of these dimensions. It is the patterns of the relationships between them that are important, not just the patterns of discursive formations that give rise to meaningfulness, that is, to something that *makes sense*. The *experience* that a medium affords significantly informs and shapes the *communication* of the message, often to the point of blurring the line that supposedly sets the two apart. In iconic effects human experience can recognize the object itself as partaking in meaning-making, not just a sign pointing to other, actual or ideal referents. It is instructive to note here that even Claude Lévi-Strauss (1962: 20) realized this kind of iconic principle when he wrote that in the case of images that have acquired significance, their 'extension' and 'intension' – their content and form – 'are not two distinct and complementary aspects but one and the same thing'. Icons *present* meaning as much as they *represent* it. In his theory of iconicity, Gottfried Boehm (2012: 21) develops this point, arguing that in certain situations 'the signified serves simultaneously as a signifier. This irritates our common expectations, which assumes a difference between the reality of the piece and its subject'. Thus iconicity alters the sociological view of the construction of social reality. It indicates that there is a non-representational component to meaning-making, closely related to the indexical and experiential character of much of human signification.

The iconological perspective insists that most socially significant meanings operate not only according to conventional semiotics and systematic reasons, but also in accordance with how articulations of these domains are inflected by somatics and feelings in the here and now (Schusterman, 2000; Pugh, 2014). Consequently, contemporary cultural sociologists began to approach the 'construction' of social groups such as nations and their foundational events not only as mythically told and narratively 'imagined', but as visually instantiated and framed, embodied and collectively felt (i.e. in terms of 'national sensorium'), involving aesthetic imaginaries and the iconic fusion of means and effects of symbolic action (Bartmanski, 2011; 2012; Zubrzycki, 2011; 2013; Hodder, 2012: 113). These aspects must be taken into account in order to understand why certain forms have social resonance and others do not. This is important because there is evidence that specific images, and their distribution and transformation, can provide a decisive iconic impetus for powerful political processes, so that we can credit them with changing the course of history, that is, to see them as iconic 'switchmen', to paraphrase Weber, or simply as 'iconic turning points' (Binder, 2013).

If we are to speak in this context of 'iconic agency', this can be seen as a focused signification based on specific affordances of objects (McDonnell, 2010; Hodder, 2012), as well as a form of practical bricolage, not just as an ideal typical sign or sign-user. As Lévi-Strauss notes, the bricoleur '"speaks" not only with things but also *through* the medium of things' (1962: 21, emphasis mine). Materiality matters far beyond simply playing the role of a prop in social performance. It is more than a 'container' or 'carrier' of meaning. Rather, it is a part of meaning, because social meanings are pragmatic experiential phenomena. Considered in relation to the human sensorium and external contexts, iconicity brings back the intensive phenomenological valences and extensive materialities of life to the study of culture. Icons as material symbols of high social impact indicate that 'social construction' cannot be reduced to codes and ideas, as these hardly ever work simply in and through abstraction and the mind alone. The cultural is always concretely embodied, emplaced and felt, and these circumstances are particularly relevant in sociology. Sociologists can hardly fathom how meanings are 'constructed' and how things human 'make sense' without having a systematic grasp of the shared sensuous, experiential and material dimensions of life. If such ontological and phenomenological assumptions are often implicit, then iconicity is a conception that indicates the benefits of making them explicit and thus much more systematically re-inscribed within cultural sociological theory than previously was the case.

## BETWEEN TOTEMIC SIGN AND ICONIC FORM

Insofar as iconicity is implicated in the processes of mobilization of collective feelings and emotional identifications (or repulsions), it might be seen as an actualization of the old principle of totemism as theorized by Émile Durkheim. According to the neo-Durkheimian conception of Alexander (2008a; 2008b), 'iconic condensation' of meaning is attained through performative fusion of aesthetic *surface* and discursive *depth*. When accomplished, this fusion offers a totemic kind of typification, so that the specific material sign can function as what Douglas Holt (2004) calls the effective shorthand for whole social values or cultural myths. Durkheim himself argued that 'to express our own ideas even to ourselves we need to attach those ideas to material things that symbolize them' (Durkheim, 1995: 229). The problem here was that Durkheim never convincingly explained why people seemed to have this need, and what it tells us about the significance of materiality itself. He conjectured that it was the case 'probably because collective feelings become conscious of themselves only by settling upon external objects', and because moral forces 'could not organize themselves without taking some of their traits from things' (Durkheim, 1995: 421). This can count as a useful starting insight or presupposition. Yet being inspired by the then-emerging structuralist mind-set, Durkheim did not provide any theory as to how certain patterns of 'material traits' could 'organize' the meanings of social life and thus make collective feelings 'fully conscious of themselves'. These are crucial issues that were simply left under-theorized. There is no developed aesthetic sensibility in his theory of signification either, for in the end totemic objects are arbitrarily selected, their material qualities secondary and subordinated to collective ideas.

Developing his own agenda, Barthes mentioned that the very material of objects such as toys introduces one to 'coenaesthesis', i.e. the sensual awareness of one's own body. Barthes (1977: 45) suggested that a different type of consciousness needs to be presupposed in order for analysts to adequately account for the effects of the surface – this was the 'spectatorial' consciousness. But these are residual rather than systematic categories in his work. Alexander introduces 'iconic consciousness' more systematically, and elaborates it in aesthetic and experiential terms that are lacking in Durkheim. Ultimately, however, he remains Durkheimian when he states that 'the discursive and moral meaning of material objects comes not from aesthetic surface but from society' (Alexander, 2012: 26). Here the icon has the potential of being what Alexander sees as a 'bridge concept' between the aesthetic and the moral, the singular and the collective, the thing and the idea, the material and the meaningful. But because he maintains that the meaning travels one way through the bridge of iconicity, 'coming from society' and 'attaching itself' to signs, he invests the surface neither with agency nor with the capacity to co-constitute meaning, for example in phenomenological, experiential ways. Perhaps most importantly, this somewhat unequal surface/depth analytical distinction prevents one from complexifying and unpacking the generic concept of the *surface*.

In other intellectual traditions, for example those more influenced by Peirce's pragmatic conception of signs, there is an opportunity to elaborate and differentiate the generic 'surface', and recognize that it comes in plural forms, as different kinds or modalities of 'surfaces', each of which is amenable to different modalities of signification. It is this very possibility of recognizing the culturally consequential variability of 'surfaces' that makes the iconicity conceptually distinct and thus sociologically attractive. If we are to keep the surface/depth distinction, then it is in order to notice that meaning does not 'come' from a specific 'location of culture', but rather emerges through the *interaction* between, or *entwinement* of, the surface and depth, and that the way it emerges and works depends partly on the kind of surface and experiential situation at hand.

As cultural icons feature certain effects of semblance and indexicality, they predicate particular experiences, not just discursive references. Such effects are experientially rather than arbitrarily or conventionally bound to the world around us. The kind of signifier at work has a bearing on how its meaningfulness is or can be (dis)assembled in a given context for particular kinds of purposes. An iconic technological object like the iPod or iPhone derives its power from the material affordances of its design, the spatial body-related mobility, and the sensual interface it provides, not just through the top-down linguistic instructions of its functionality. It is a social icon in far more ways than any structuralist theory would allow. This is a moment when sociologists can recognize that the materiality and aesthetics of the object are not merely *reflective* but profoundly *co-productive* of the context in which certain meanings can be created and cultural narratives made plausible. It also enables sociologists to understand the constitutive effects of icons as elements of social and cultural change.

Although there seems to be something especially iconically potent in the sheer mechanical reproduction and multidimensional materiality of contemporary mobile smart phones, the argument about the power of materiality and its variable effects is not entirely novel and has been in the making for quite some time now, especially in cultural anthropology. For example, in his conception of symbolic action, Victor Turner (1974: 269) noted that:

> a major stumbling block in the development of sociological and anthropological theory has been

the almost total identification of the social with the social structural. Even informal relations are considered structural. Many of them are, of course, but not all ... This has created enormous difficulties with regard to many problems such as social change.

Webb Keane (2005: 195, 193) further pushes this point when he points out that 'not all social life in all domains is tightly controlled and totalized' by conventional systems of signification, and that therefore we need to treat the materiality of signifying things 'in their own right'. Turner (1974: 270) considered it a 'vain task' to try to find out in what precise ways certain symbols found in the rituals 'or iconography of a given society "reflect" or "express" its social or political structure ... Symbols may well reflect not structure but anti-structure, and not only reflect but contribute to creating it'. Similarly, Hariman and Lucaites (2007: 5) conclude that different aspects of cultural action such as sensory formations and discursive formations, 'hard' politics and 'soft' symbolism, 'are not so neatly separated in practice, so there is good reason to move beyond the question of which mode is dominant and consider more complicated relationships between communication technology and culture'. This is a re-articulation of cultural complexity thematised by Hannerz in his aforementioned work.

In other words, there is more to iconicity than Durkheimian structuralism would presume. Indeed, the expanded pragmatic definition of iconicity indicates that when it comes to cultural icons, the principles of arbitrary and conventional attribution may be the exception rather than the rule. Objects are not perfectly equal when it comes to effective iconic symbolization. In a given material-historical context, certain 'surfaces' are more amenable to certain significatory uses than others. Of course, things do not simply comprise a physical world as such, but they are also 'definitely more than the content of cultural "representations": they are used and have effects in their materiality' (Reckwitz, 2002: 209). This realization occasions a shift in cultural theory that Andreas Reckwitz sees as proceeding from 'structure to artefacts', from a structuralist cultural 'logics' to social pragmatics of cultural 'forms'.

In his discussion of this momentous transformation in cultural theorizing, Reckwitz draws on the materialism of Latour and the philosophical conception of social practices offered by Theodore Schatzki. But useful prefigurations of materially and aesthetically conscious cultural sociology can be found within the foundational works of the discipline itself too, notably in Simmel. In his classic discussion of the meaningfulness of art and fashion, he intuited the existence of non-structuralist principles operative in social meaning-making, by describing how the 'deeper nature' of material forms, and especially the relations between them, create limits to immaterial (mental) structures of signification. While today such notions as 'nature' have been complexified, they remain present as a series of related ontological categories. Importantly, Simmel (2008: 384) reported that even in the highly socially conventional phenomena of fashion and art, one could discern the variability of 'suitable' material forms that circumscribe the seemingly free-floating process of meaning-attribution:

> It is a very enticing opinion, but one that cannot hold water, that every real object is equally suited to become the object of the work of art. The forms of art, as they have developed historically, by no means occupy a neutral height above all world objects ... The sovereignty of art over reality by no means implies the ability to draw all the contents of existence uniformly into its sphere.

In sum, iconicity is not only a totemic structure, but a material form whose social effects can be traced back to a set of definitive aesthetic qualities and practical affordances, which in turn occasion certain meaningful experiences rather than others. Iconicity as significatory power emerges out of specific interdependencies of materially articulated form and discursively articulated content, not simply from the autonomous force of the latter. In this sense it exemplifies Simmel's notion of *Wechselwirkung* in practice. Icons worth their name can emerge only at rather precisely calibrated sociomaterial conjunctions, not just through any arbitrary ascription of value. As cultural forms, they are dense *crystallizations* of such fitting conjunctions, instantiating what Simmel would call *Verdichtung*. In the two following sections I will elaborate first the idea that material 'surface' deserves deeper sociological inquiry, and then a corresponding plea for a 'thicker' description, one able to do justice to iconic condensations of meaning.

## THE DEPTH OF THE SURFACE ITSELF

Different kinds of material signifiers can be presumed to feature different types of socially consequential 'surfaces' and thus different types of plausible cultural effects. As Jane Bennett (2010: 9) observes, 'agentic capacity is now seen as differentially distributed across a wider range of ontological types'. Pictures, objects, places, events and bodies can all act as iconic 'surfaces', often jointly, but their relation to discursive construction is not the same in each case. One can say that there is a considerable 'material depth' to each such 'surface', both in terms of complexity of qualities and affordances at hand, and in terms of sets of relationships and interdependencies between a given sign-object and other objects that jointly create a situation or a place. The specific surface never stands in isolation from other surfaces. Just as the meaningfulness of concepts depends on contrast and similarities with other concepts and background representations, so does the sensuous experience depend on a series of material entanglements that render reality phenomenologically discernable.

There are different ways theoretically to elaborate this set of observations. One can lead simply to distinguishing between pictorial (2D) and objectual (3D) icons. Focusing on the former, W.J.T. Mitchell (1995: 418) developed 'picture theory', advocating a 'pictorial turn' in the cultural sciences and underscoring the hybrid nature of signifiers that mediate social meanings and the 'inescapable heterogeneity of representation'. Gottfried Boehm (2012) outlines the concept of *homo pictor* in his version of the 'iconic turn'. The entire new sub-discipline of visual sociology has been based on the recognition of the growing role of pictures in contemporary culture (Mirzoeff, 2013). The surface/depth divide may be even further transcended when we consider the highly vibrant materiality of the body in social construction. In this respect Judith Butler proposes to 'return to the notion of matter, not as site or surface, but as a process of materialization that stabilizes over time to produce effects of boundary, fixity, and surface we call matter' (Butler, 2011: xviii).

Many of these influential theorizations often start and end at a high level of abstraction, informed by literary and philosophical conceptions more than by social research. They may need a great deal of translation and operationalization to be useful as descriptive and explanatory tools in sociology. Iconicity as a sociological concept that reclaims materiality provides such a translation, and thus allows us more clearly to delineate how the material and the ideal *jointly* produce meaning. Such a robust synthetic view is hard to find in constructivist descriptions that tend to incorporate materiality on constructivist terms. Yet the social persistence and vehemence of iconic identifications suggest that an alternative view of construction needs to be considered, one that takes materiality seriously, or as Webb Keane writes, 'on its own terms'. Martha Nussbaum's (1999) criticism of Judith Butler is instructive in this respect: 'Culture can shape and reshape some aspects of our bodily existence but it doesn't shape all the aspects of it. "In the man burdened by hunger and thirst," as Sextus Empiricus observed long ago, "it is impossible to produce by argument the conviction that he is not so burdened"'. What is needed, Nussbaum (1999) argues, is a 'subtle study of the interplay' between materially constituted aspects and cultural construction.

A more concrete and iconicity-related template for incorporating the bodily and the material to cultural sociological analysis can be found in disciplines intimately connected to images and objects, for example in art history and archaeology. The German art historian Hans Belting (2012: 188) points out that excessively reifying structuralist binaries by 'opposing internal (mental) and external (media) images obstructs access to the process of perception and imagination … "Internal" representations have fluid boundaries with "external representations" because internal representations are products of our bodies, while our bodies themselves are shaped by the external representations of visual media'. Moreover, he argues that 'we need to find our way back to an *integral* understanding of the body as a medium', because we perceive with our whole bodies, connecting the senses and blurring the impressions for an experience to produce its meanings (Belting, 2012: 190). Of course, 'each generation establishes a new balance between mental and physical images. The imaginary of a given society develops in the 'symbiosis' between what Marc Augé called 'official icons' and private dreams' (Belting, 2012: 188). The historicity of signification thematized by iconology of Webb Keane covers this issue. Nevertheless, this balance, although always re-established anew, is hardly achieved in any arbitrarily chosen way. The iconic meaning-making is jointly bounded by material affordances, bodily dispositions and social contingencies. Iconicity is a category that enables one to specify, or at least approximate, these boundaries, not to return to any naive notion of either materialism or linguistic constructivism.

In order systematically to study the interplay between materiality and immateriality, sociologists need to recognize the multiplicity of material types of iconic surfaces. This in turn implies the multiplicity of distinct mechanisms of meaning-making. Studying icons sheds light on this plurality, and suggests the existence of different 'orders of semiosis' rather than the single independent significatory logic. Webb Keane (2005: 199–200), echoing some of the points evoked by Simmel, emphasizes this point:

> Different orders of semiosis are differently subject to determination or autonomous logics. Thus the more indexical aspects of any configuration of

signs will be more subject to direct transformation in response to material circumstances, whereas a system of conventions is subject to quite distinct modes of determination and transformation ... Each of these processes involves very different temporalities, social logics, and consequentialities. But since even the most conventional signs are instantiated in material forms, they are, at least to that extent, subject to material causality.

Iconicity points to such a differentiation of semiosis. It takes a multidimensional category such as iconicity in order to enable cultural sociologists to defend their work against the critics who demand that we must 'recognize the reciprocal influence' of different spheres of social life, and who insist that 'some way of relating and measuring factors is needed, and not just the claim that they are co-present' (Goldman, 2014: 126). By recognizing the variety of surfaces and their influence on how representations make sense, cultural sociologists gain a vantage point from which to weigh the material and immaterial factors against each other. Different signifiers can be expected to feature different levels of material impact on cultural signification and its potential transformations. For example, machines and various functional objects have more constrained forms of cultural existence than everyday signs do (Miller, 1987: 116). It is exceedingly hard radically to resignify physiological experiences, such as hunger, mentioned by Nussbaum, many of which – as noticed already by Simmel (2008: 149) – ground knowledge and produce, rather than merely raise, social value, giving rise to deep meanings of sacrifice and suffering, and so on.

Regardless of the specific path the sociologist takes, and how far one is prepared to push the respective arguments, a series of methodological and theoretical consequences inevitably ensue. Signification is not based on the immutable logics but on contextualized experiential references. Meaning varies over time and according to the socio-material matrix within which it functions. In icons the material and discursive aspects are reciprocally conditioned. As the iconic surface gets operationalized by ever more specific terms such as mediation, materialization, material affordance, and so on, its meaningful role appears to be less of a 'vehicle' of meaning – the traditional culturalist metaphor – and more of a 'soil' needed for an iconic entity not only to take root but also grow and blossom. The connections implied by such a metaphor form not a loose contingent correspondence, but a tight entwinement, a kind of meaning ecology, or what archaeologist Ian Hodder (2012) calls 'sticky entrapment.'

In short, the 'surface' itself is variegated. It has its own 'depth'. It can have multiple effects traceable to specific material properties and phenomenological relationships. Frequently, it is not just the simple 'screen' on which our discourses 'project' meanings. It is also a means of 'projection' itself, if we are to stick to this term. It inflects our projections. Therefore, in addition to standard discursive methodology, whether media-based or archival, a whole range of intensive ethnographic techniques and observational studies must be employed, each of which involves attention to at least three elements: (1) relevant objectifications, (2) involved temporalities and (3) actual emplacements. This in turn enables one to take the cultural sociological postulate of thick description to a whole new level.

## A 'THICKER' DESCRIPTION: MATERIALITY, THE SENSES AND INTERPRETATION

In order to establish the parameters of the interplay between materiality and cultural construction, iconic research in cultural sociology involves the standard procedures of 'thick description' developed by Clifford Geertz. However, it goes beyond classic studies of *symbolic* anthropology by accounting for the whole spectrum of *sensory* formations and describing how exactly sensual experiences, often minute and seemingly trivial, figure in the practical ways people put symbols into action. As Ann Swidler (2001: 20, 22) explains, 'for Geertz, there is no need to describe how symbols are brought to bear on social life' and to recognize 'the variable ways people hold or use culture'. The aforementioned variability of material signifiers and their practical entanglements can be linked to the ways of sense-making Swidler talks about. The pragmatic senses-oriented iconic analysis has troubled semiotically-minded cultural scholars, partly because they feared – like Barthes – that in order to describe sensual domains of life, for example sound, we have to rely 'on the poorest of linguistic categories: the adjective' (Barthes cited in Back and Bull, 2005: 12).

There is, however, much more to human *parole* than adjectives (e.g. timbre, tone, intensity, etc.), just as there is more to *langue* than arbitrariness. While experiences are not fully assimilable to language, it does not follow that we cannot understand the cultural role of experiences and their variability. In their *Auditory Culture Reader*, Les Back and Michael Bull (2005: 12) find that 'it is important to reach for a way of representing the qualities of sound without merely resorting to adjectives following Barthes' warning'. One way underscored by Swidler is by employing new metaphors. Some critics of constructivist cultural sociology point out that 'a metaphor should be deployed, if ever, only after reconstructive, empirical work, not before, so that one can determine whether the metaphor "makes sense" and is applicable to the problem or case at hand, and, if so, to what extent' (Goldman, 2014: 128). The problem is that all kinds of metaphors are always already there, in social life and science. We live by them (Lakoff and Johnson, 2003).

Therefore, among the key procedures of new iconicity research are: (1) to observe what people do (and shun doing) in relation to what they say (and shun saying); and (2) to extend the description of material-sensuous experiences, via embracing the manifold ways in which people metaphorically make sense of their lives, not just testing the preconceived master metaphors. This is partly based on the observation that everyday linguistic metaphors – just like objectual icons – are indexical and rooted in lived experiences, and are not merely conventional. Here metaphors in language are like icons in reality – they tend to be experiential, rather than arbitrary signifiers. Systematically linking language, materiality and experience in this way enables cultural sociologists to offer a new, 'thicker' engagement with discourses and objectual surroundings. Finding out what makes its way into metaphorical language, and how these tropes are in turn used in relation to specific practical circumstances, will offer deeper insights into the problem of signification and meaning-making.

Such an enhanced thick description is about attempts to 'examine the relationship between what people *say* and what they actually *do*. For this reason, ethnographers must come to grips with the subject's understandings of his or her situation but also go beyond simple reportage in his or her own analysis' (Duneier et al., 2014: 3, emphasis in original). Interpreting meanings derived from participant observation is not inherently more vulnerable than performing a linguistic interpretation of fixed texts. A degree of ambiguity and indeterminacy is part and parcel of any interpretive qualitative procedure. Cultural texts in the strict sense of the term remain as relevant as ever, but ethnographic interpretive interviews may well be more important when we ask certain kinds of interpretive questions, for example those related to experience, affect and aesthetics. This is the case because unlike other, more formal or regimented channels of communication, 'interviews can excavate the visceral emotional layer elusive for many other methods' (Pugh, 2014: 160).

This 'archaeological' approach is hugely important for understanding layered iconic symbolization whose social power stems from a tight bundling of various materials, emotions and ideas. Iconicity problematizes the very distinction of feeling *vs.* thought. Icons splice the two in practical situations. The iconic effects attest to the observation that there is hardly any socially significant idea or concept devoid of collective feeling, and hardly any feeling unconnected to materially mediated and/or embodied experiences. As Allison Pugh (2014: 161) has pointed out:

> [our cultural and cognitive] schemas are inflected with emotion as we incorporate them, and layered with even more feeling as we use or encounter them in other situations. I would even go so far as to say there is no such thing as an emotionally neutral narrative. We can think of that emotional inflection as giving some bits of culture a more powerful resonance than others, with consequences for action … We are more emotionally attached to, and thus more invested in, certain kinds of narratives than others.

To sum up, what changes in relation to language is the degree of reflexivity about its assets and drawbacks, its entanglements with materiality and affect. David Howes (2005: 4) identified the crux of this issue when he observed that 'the limitations of language are unavoidable so long as language is the medium of communication. What it is possible to avoid, however, is the expansion of language into a structural model that dictates all cultural and personal experience and expression'. As the observational spectrum widens and as immersion into the fullness of the research field yields new knowledge, our descriptive vocabularies expand too. Unlike in the case of more traditional discursively grounded description (e.g. Reed, 2009: 3), it is precisely the multisensory constellations and associated social practices, not just textuality, where the 'messy' descriptive work of cultural sociology offers not only the greatest challenges but also considerably 'thicker' insights. One of the key challenges posed by the conception of iconicity is to capture the sequences and pathways within the interplay of material *affordances* and discursive *articulations* that icons both encapsulate and galvanize.

Iconicity is a social phenomenon that *makes sense* in a double, tightly intertwined way: (1) as a message that can be narratively decoded, socially communicated and understood; and (2) as an experiential signifier or medium that engages the senses and inspires intersubjectively shared feelings. Thus, for example, discussing a contemporary political campaign only through discursive data without a simultaneous account of visual projections and spatial orchestration, can only produce partial results. There are serious reasons why modern advertising is unthinkable without image work, and why the immemorial human quest for spirituality, transcendence and non-material values often ends up relying on multisensory performances of belief (e.g. celebration, training) and specific bodily practices (e.g. meditation, diet). Daniel Miller (2005: 42) observes that 'in many cases the way this immateriality has had to be expressed is precisely through the efflorescence of the material'. Both the letter and the spirit of a belief or a law need specific iconic materializations to be symbolically effective, especially in the longer run.

Comprehensive description is thus a vital condition of adequate empirical research, not only directed to specific icons, but about meaning-making more generally. It includes visual analysis of different integuments of social life, or what Nigel Thrift (2005) calls different 'material registers of mediation' (e.g. screens, clothes, building facades, etc.). One needs also to reconstruct the relationally constituted situatedness of entities and their emplacement, and the traces of time and use that they bear. Taking a series of such 'unobtrusive measures' that comprise observational studies, is invaluable for any social iconology (Emmison and Smith 2000: 110). This kind of qualitative sociological practice enables researchers to *see* what people actually do on the ground, and to begin to appreciate 'cultural objects as objects' (McDonnell, 2010), that is, as inescapable bundles of sensory qualities and material entanglements that actively partake in the social construction of reality. Again, this is not to forego discourses or to postulate the independent agency of things. Instead, it is about adding a dense description of social pragmatics, accompanied by an understanding of how we do things with things, and how materiality creates and inflects meanings of social narratives.

Because materiality is endowed with agency relative to human subjects, systematic description of iconic *affordances* becomes a major task. Terrence McDonnell (2010: 1806) defines affordance as 'the latent set of possible actions that environments and objects enable ... these actions, while attributed to an object, are relationally tied to the capabilities of the person interacting with that object'. He specifies that affordances 'are made manifest through interactions between audiences, objects, and contexts', and it is these interactions on which iconic effects depend and therefore require new kinds of thick 'sensuous description' (Classen, 2012: xii). To reveal the 'deep play' of iconic surfaces, sociologists need to integrate the depth of feeling and sensation, expanding visual and acoustic sensitivity, as well as including the touch that Constance Classen (2012) tellingly calls 'the deepest sense'. As she explains:

> [the] intention is ... to explore how the corporeal practices of any particular period relate to the cultural context of the time, and how this relationship changes under the influence of new factors ... touch does not simply recede from cultural life in modernity, it is reeducated, and while it retreats from some domains, it expands into others. (Classen, 2012: xiv)

If the meanings of social symbols 'have to be understood in a holistic manner, which is to say that any given sign or symbol takes its meaning in relation to those with which it is contrasted and figuratively related' (Reed and Alexander, 2006: 112), then cultural sociologists need to extend this procedure to the complex material constitution of signifiers and their relation to human bodies. The principles of difference, contrast and juxtaposition remain important, but are not restricted to descriptions of texts and discourses treated as privileged interfaces to social reality. Such privileging unduly disembodies subjectivities, over-intellectualizes culture, and threatens to de-historicize meaning-making. As Webb Keane (2005: 193) observes:

> surfaces are not just the tangible garments draped on otherwise invisible and immaterial ideas ... if things mediate our historicity, we cannot be content to ask only what meanings people attribute to them now. And even of those meanings, we must be attentive to the ways in which they are regimented and brought into relation to other things'.

Cultural sociologists can take at least one step further when it comes to thick description. In addition to the synchronic and diachronic dimensions, there is an aspect to the materiality of some icons that resists description in terms of relationality and unilinear time. Perhaps the most uniquely qualified scholars to realize this are archaeologists, who often must reconstruct meanings and social structures and practices not from texts but from things and material remnants, and from an assessment of what time has or has not done to them. Here multiple temporalities and long-term durations, rather than the hitherto dominant uniform notion of time, prove helpful. Ian Hodder (2012: 94), critiquing Bruno Latour, made a relevant point when he wrote that 'everything is relational and this insight is important but it is also the case that materials and objects have affordances that are continuous from context to context'. For example, the 'mundane' or 'obvious' phenomena that materially define a *longue durée* may have eluded the attention of sociologists in the past, but contemporary cultural sociology can hardly afford to treat these elements as if they were capable of being bracketed out or sequestered as the subject matter of a separate discipline, like archaeology or history. The multiplicity of temporalities should be taken into account, especially when different objects with manifold connotations come into play. Drawing on Siegfried Kracauer, Christopher Pinney (2005: 264) develops a metaphor to understand that socially relevant time is 'not a single river or a mighty cascade. It is a series of cataracts, each pursuing their own uncontemporaneousness in incoherent trajectories'. What this means in practice is, for instance, that a given object, like a picture, does not simply 'reflect' the moment of its creation or its ostensible reference. Another effect worth considering is that seemingly banal, short- and long-lasting material conditions frame meaning-making at multiple time-points. 'There is more to history than a linear account of sequences of events; there is also the material history, the heritage of past acts, the detritus of past millennia that bumps up against us in a non-linear way. It is this material history that continues to play a role in the present' (Hodder, 2012: 100).

This dynamic becomes particularly visible when sociologists reflect on material mediums of art and information, urban culture or environmental issues of pollution and sustainability, each of which features specific material entanglements and human–object relations. The iconic framework can be particularly helpful in understanding, for example, that historically changing *city-scapes* always feature partially overlapping *media-scapes* and palimpsest-like complexity. The iconicity of the city is an unevenly additive unfolding of forms, not just a successive progression or development. Architectural landmarks can gain social salience by sheer persistence through time and vagaries of history at a given place, enabled by the material of their building blocks. They can also become cultural icons because of their uniqueness or grandeur, outstanding in the context of a given time, likewise owing to their specific materials. The Eiffel Tower in Paris is an example of a structure – both symbolic and physical – that is unthinkable without steel, technologically cutting-edge at the time of its creation, and metonymically evocative of a whole modern social formation. Icons can epitomize various temporal contexts, their being highly dependent on the material and experiential contexts in which they are ensconced. Urban space is an experiential space in which shared experiences co-produce salient intensive social meanings (Löw, 2013). This kind of understanding helps to explain apparent paradoxes, such as counter-intuitive nostalgias or revivals that *make sense* from an experiential, phenomenological point of view (Bartmanski, 2011; Bartmanski and Woodward, 2015).

In sum, multi-sensory, relational, embodied and layered time- and space-sensitive analysis comprises the thick iconic description being advocated here. It is such a description that is a key precondition for an interpretive explanation of cultural change (or lack thereof). It has been observed that in structuralist conceptions of signification and cultural construction, the principle of 'independence of culture' can be tenable only in 'relative' or purely analytical terms, and that therefore 'interdependence' is a more fitting description of culture and society (Kurasawa, 2004). Hodder proposes the term co-dependence of objects and humans: 'most material symbols in particular tend to be iconic and indexical; there tends to be some relationship between sign and referent. Notions of contiguity and association abound' (Hodder, 2012: 97). What cultural sociologists have traditionally called 'webs of meaning' are in fact layered and lasting heterogeneous configurations rather than simply chains of signifiers. 'It is these multiple, co-dependent strands that create the webs in which societies are formed, endure and fall apart. The determination is produced not by an idealism or by a materialism but by the contingent ways in which the multiple strands of entanglement are tied together' (Hodder, 2012: 97). Consequently, in order for cultural sociology to provide detailed adequate descriptions that yield robust interpretive explanations, a series of descriptors more robust than 'relative' or 'social' are needed (Olick, 2010: 98). The emergence of iconicity as an interpretive and descriptive category responds precisely to these calls for the enhancement of cultural research.

## SOCIAL CRITIQUE AFTER THE ICONIC TURN

Iconicity as a new way of thinking about cultural signification and social construction implies a series of potential revisions that go far enough to offer new critical perspectives, not just new modes of interpretation. A concise way to emphasize this boils down to the realization that, in itself, discourse can hardly exhaust the phenomena that critical sociology traditionally thematized as its key concerns: (false) consciousness, (symbolic) violence, (capitalist) hegemony, (deliberative) politics, and ideology. Thematizing the difference between 'the politics of the word' and 'the politics of the eye', Stephen Turner (2003: 67) pointed out that:

> it is reasonable to wonder whether our perception of the centrality of ideology in the period from 1848 to 1956 is to a greater extent than usually

acknowledged an illusion of perspective, and that as intellectuals we tend to ascribe a greater significance to the words of the intellectuals of the past than they had at the time.

Thinking iconically creates a sociological context in which a kind of re-evaluation suggested by Turner is not only thinkable but desirable.

Hariman and Lucaites (2007: 5) explicitly state that 'it is becoming evident that Western culture has always been more dependent on visual materials than had been thought … that cities and nations have been organized visually'. As far as cultural sociology is concerned, iconicity may be of prime importance for renewing the critical vocabulary, especially in the intensively mediated society of an increasingly digitalized era. The transformative effects of the 'medium' on the 'message' seem strong enough to alter the very way we look at this distinction. Moreover, digitalization accelerates the changes of media to the extent that the different iconic effects and shifts in meaning they produce are being critically juxtaposed more than ever before.

While iconicity is a novel perspective rather than a specific critical agenda, it does call into question the assumption that both power and resistance occur mainly through the linguistic effects of epistemic control. An undeniable asset of various strands of the 20th-century critical social theory was that they have sensitized social scientists to the issue of the insidious power of all kinds in linguistic performances. This showed that conventional signifiers carry meanings of considerable social clout. Despite revealing the power of language, and thus exposing the naivety of essentialist conceptions, critical theorists of the twentieth century did comparatively little to reform materialistic stances and systematically lay bare the dense entanglements of subjects and objects, consciousness and body, thoughts and feelings, signs and things, and so on. As critics, sociologists tended to be iconoclastic rather than iconically conscious. Regis Debray (2000: 84) symptomatically noted that in 'wanting to demystify the fetishism of tools and equipment, we lose sight of their very reality'.

In sociology, the standard kinds of cultural criticism tend to be *counter-cultural* and *anti-hegemonic*, revealing the ongoing materialistic and symbolic domination associated with capitalism and (neo) colonial practices. This historically understandable approach has meant that while sociological criticism has been growing ever more progressive politically, it has advanced less in the conceptual sense. Bruno Latour (2010: 57) detected one of the resulting paradoxes when he argued that 'the progressives commit an error as flagrant as that of their ostensive opponents', because, not unlike the reactionaries and conservatives, they cling to their key concepts as 'ideals' rather than 'a heritage to be sorted out'. The new concepts of iconicity and iconic power equip sociologists with complex tools of criticism. 'The perspective provided by entanglement is that such power relations are not just about control of the means of production, or the control of social relations or social ideologies, since those mechanisms of control are themselves set within wider human-thing entanglements' (Hodder, 2012: 214). These wider contexts include visuality, haptics, acoustics and all pragmatic vicissitudes of meaning-making which generate, sustain and transform collective feelings and social desires, not only social mindsets. Social critique can and should systematically account for these wider entanglements in shaping social motivations and mobilizations. Sociology as a discipline grew up 'visually illiterate'. While it still derives much critical vitality from its core foundational canons, those resources are characterized by what David Howes (2005: 1) called the 'sensorial poverty' of theory. To redress this problem, cultural sociology was reaching out to other disciplines to re-establish what counts as 'sociology', but it also needs to transform its critical capacity from within, for example by juxtaposing its classical thinkers (e.g. Simmel vs Durkheim) and bringing back marginalized ones (e.g. Du Bois), rather than just relying on any particular one.

Iconicity as cultural form helps to reinvigorate the sociological heritage without inventing neologisms. It is about looking at what is happening 'on the ground' and 'in-between' humans and things. It introduces an element of self-criticism that involves a recognition that the entanglements between materiality and meaning run so deep in contemporary society that by itself no particular tradition of old style 'materialistic' or 'linguistic' critique will suffice in the task of reconceptualizing and thus altering problematic power dynamics. This affects not only the kind of critical arguments involved, but also what kinds of social advocacy should accompany them, and what human and non-human subjects deserve special attention. Regarding the former, it has become clearer that 'the path of criticism can no longer be imagined, as it once was, to be the high road toward a utopian realm of truth or toward a conservation of a secure cultural legacy. Criticism has no choice but to work through the conditions it is given' (Mitchell, 1995: 416). 'Intellectuals' no longer occupy a special position of social criticism, if they ever truly did at all. As Hodder (2012: 220) points out:

> we cannot reduce things solely to the relational, to a semiotics of things. To do so undermines the power of things to entrap, and particularly to trap the more vulnerable … In the modern world, we have to come to see that we need to use things sustainably and responsibly, to care for things.

If icons as heterogeneous, complex entanglements can be at once objects of critique and tools of cultural change, then we need to take seriously their manifold socio-material entwinements and dependencies. Implications for criticism can be manifold, and include expanding the standard sociological repertoire of critically examined tropes. For one thing,

> [such a perspective] allows a more nuanced approach to colonial and post-colonial processes since it is less absorbed by domination and resistance; similarly it incorporates agency while at the same time de-centering the human in social life; it allows an emphasis on the immediate and short term but embedded within long-term evolutionary trajectories; it allows directionality without teleology. (Hodder, 2012: 222)

At the same time, and for the same purpose of refining the sociological critique of empire, this perspective points out that deconstructive antilogocentrism directed against imperial power 'derives from precisely that same Enlightenment whose insistence on reason was attacked as the cause of imperial domination' (Berman, 1998: 7).

Critical sociology has often boiled down to denunciation of deeply unjust acts of oppression, to accounts and criticisms of ruthless powerful structures, forms and systems. This is partly why Marxism and structuralism held sway over the sociological imagination for such a long time. Such agendas efficiently reduced the messy complexity of life to manageable toolkits capable of drawing distinctions and distributing responsibilities. But in this way they grew susceptible to serving social science and its increasingly insular debates more than social life itself and its practical tasks. The trick is to work with formal categories that retain a series of immediate conduits to, and palpable resonance with, those 'messy' imperatives of the social. Acknowledging concrete entanglements themselves, without reducing them to analytically distinct components, is one way of starting the new interpretive process. Iconicity is a kind of active entanglement, an emergent quality that is greater than the simple sum of its elements. Icons are complex signifiers that do not just reflect but crucially inflect human culture.

## REFERENCES

Alexander, J.C. (2008a) 'Iconic Consciousness: The Material Feeling of Meaning', *Environment and Planning D: Society and Space*, 26: 782–94.

Alexander, J.C. (2008b) 'Iconic Experience in Art and Life: Surface/Depth Beginning with Giacometti's "Standing Woman"', *Theory, Culture & Society*, 25: 1–19.

Alexander, J.C. (2012) 'Iconic Power and Performance: The Role of the Critic', in J.C. Alexander et al. (eds), *Iconic Power: Materiality and Meaning in Social Life*. New York: Palgrave Macmillan. pp. 25–35.

Back, L. and Bull, M. (eds.) (2005) *The Auditory Culture Reader*. Oxford and New York: Berg.

Back, L., Bennett A., Edles, L., Gibson, M., Inglis, D., Jacobs R. and Woodward, I. (2012) *Cultural Sociology: An Introduction*. Malden, MA: Wiley-Blackwell.

Barthes, R. (1977) *Image, Music, Text*. New York: Hill and Wang.

Barthes, R. (2009) *Mythologies*. New York: Vintage.

Bartmanski, D. (2011) 'Successful Icons of Failed Time: Rethinking Post-Communist Nostalgia', *Acta Sociologica*, 54(3): 213–33.

Bartmanski, D. (2012) 'How to Become an Iconic Social Thinker: The Intellectual Pursuits of Malinowski and Foucault', *European Journal of Social Theory*, 15(4): 427–53.

Bartmanski, D. (2014) 'The Word/Image Dualism Revisited: Towards an Iconic Conception of Visual Culture', *Journal of Sociology*, 50(2): 164–81.

Bartmanski, D. and Alexander, J.C. (2012) 'Materiality and Meaning in Social Life: Toward an Iconic Turn in Cultural Sociology', in J.C. Alexander, D. Bartmanski, and B. Giesen (eds), *Iconic Power: Materiality and Meaning in Social Life*. New York: Palgrave.

Bartmanski, D. and Woodward, I. (2014) *Vinyl: The Analogue Record in the Digital Age*. London: Bloomsbury.

Bartmanski, D. and Woodward, I. (2015) 'The Vinyl: The Analogue Medium in the Age of Digital Reproduction', *Journal of Consumer Culture*, 15(1): 3–27.

Belting, H. (2012) 'Body and Image', in J.C. Alexander, D. Bartmanski and B. Giesen (eds), *Iconic Power: Materiality and Meaning in Social Life*. New York: Palgrave.

Bennett, J. (2010) *Vibrant Matter: A Political Ecology of Things*. Durham and London: Duke University Press.

Berman, R.A. (1998) *Enlightenment or Empire: Colonial Discourse in German Culture*. Lincoln and London: University of Nebraska Press.

Binder, W. (2013) *Abu Ghraib und die Folgen: Ein Skandal als Ikonische Wende im Krieg gegen den Terror*. Bielefeld: Verlag.

Boehm, G. (2012) 'Representation, Presentation, Presence: Tracing the Homo Pictor', in J.C. Alexander, D. Bartmanski, and B. Giesen (eds), *Iconic Power: Materiality and Meaning in Social Life*. New York: Palgrave.

Bull, M. (2007) *Sound Moves: iPod Culture and Urban Experience*. London and New York: Routledge.

Butler, J. (2011) *Bodies That Matter*. London: Routledge.

Campisi, E. and Özyürek, A. (2013) 'Iconicity as a Communicative Strategy: Recipient Design in Multimodal Demonstrations for Adults and Children', *Journal of Pragmatics*, 47: 14–27.

Classen, C. (2012) *The Deepest Sense: A Cultural History of Touch*. Urbana, Chicago and Springfield: University of Illinois Press.

Debray, R. (2000) *Transmitting Culture*. New York: Columbia University Press.

Dosse, F. (1999) *Empire of Meaning: The Humanization of the Social Sciences*. Minneapolis and London: University of Minnesota Press.

du Gay, P. et al. (1997) *Doing Cultural Studies: The Story of the Sony Walkman*. London: Sage.

Duneier, M. et al. (2014) *The Urban Ethnography Reader*. Oxford: Oxford University Press.

Durkheim, E. (1995) *Elementary Forms of Religious Life*. New York: Free Press.

Elliott, A. (2006) 'Symbol', in B. Turner (ed.), *The Cambridge Dictionary of Sociology*. Cambridge: Cambridge University Press. pp. 618–19.

Emmison, M. and Smith, P. (2000) *Researching the Visual: Images, Objects, Contexts and Interactions in Social and Cultural Inquiry*. Sage: London.

Goldman, H. (2014) 'Interpretation and Explanation in Cultural Sociology', *History and Theory*, 53: 119–29.

Hannerz, U. (1992) *Cultural Complexity: Studies in the Social Organization of Meaning*. New York: Columbia University Press.

Hariman, R. and Lucaites, J.L. (2007) *No Caption Needed*. Chicago: University of Chicago Press.

Hodder, I. (2012) *Entangled: An Archaeology of the relationships between Humans and Things*. Malden, MA: Wiley and Sons.

Holt, D.B. (2004) *How Brands Become Icons: The Principles of Cultural Branding*. Cambridge, MA: Harvard Business School Press.

Howes, D. (ed.) (2005) *Empire of the Senses: The Sensual Culture Reader*. Oxford: Berg.

Keane, W. (2005) 'Signs are Not the Garb of Meaning: On the Social Analysis of Material Things', in Daniel Miller (ed.), *Materiality*. Durham: Duke University Press.

Kurasawa, F. (2004) 'Alexander and the Cultural Refounding of American Sociology', *Thesis Eleven*, 79: 53–64.

Lakoff, G. and Johnson, M. (2003) *Metaphors We Live By*. Chicago: University of Chicago Press.

Lamont, M. (1987) 'How to Become a Dominant French Philosopher: The Case of Jacques Derrida', *The American Journal of Sociology*, 93(3): 584–622.

Latour, B. (2010) *On the Modern Cult of the Factish Gods*. Durham and London: Duke University Press.

Levi-Strauss, C. (1962) *The Savage Mind*. Chicago: The University of Chicago Press.

Lizardo, O. (2010) 'Beyond the Antinomies of Structure: Levi-Strauss, Giddens, Bourdieu and Sewell', *Theory and Society*, 39: 651–88.

Löw, M. (2013) 'The City as Experiential Space: The Reproduction of Shared Meaning', *International Journal of Urban and Regional Research*, 37(3): 894–908.

Marcus, G.E. in Taussig, M. (1993) *Mimesis and Alterity. A Particular History of the Senses*. London: Routledge. (this is from the blurb on the back cover of Taussig's book)

McDonnell, T. (2010) 'Cultural Objects as Objects: Materiality, Urban Space, and the Interpretation of AIDS Campaigns in Accra, Ghana', *American Journal of Sociology*, 115(6): 1800–52.

McLennan, G. (2005) 'The "New American Cultural Sociology": An Appraisal', *Theory Culture & Society*, 22(6): 1–18.

Miller, D. (1987) *Material Culture and Mass Consumption*. Oxford: Blackwell.

Miller, D. (ed.) (2005) *Materiality*. Durham: Duke University Press.

Miller, D. (2010) *Stuff*. Cambridge: Polity.

Mirzoeff, N. (ed.) (2013) *The Visual Culture Reader*, 3rd edition. London: Routledge.

Mitchell, W.J.T. (1995) *Picture Theory: Essays on Verbal and Visual Representation*. Chicago: University of Chicago Press.

Nussbaum, M. (1999) 'The Professor of Parody', *The New Republic* 22 Feb. 1999: 37–45.

Olick, J.K. (2010) "What is 'the Relative Autonomy of Culture?'" In *Sociology of Culture: A Handbook*, edited by J.R. Hall, L. Grindstaff and M-C. Lo. New York: Routledge.

Peirce, C.S. (1998 [1894]) 'What is a Sign?', in *The Essential Peirce: Selected Philosophical Writings (1893–1913)*. Bloomington: Indiana University Press. pp. 4–10.

Pinney, C. (2005) 'Things Happen: Or, from which Moment Does that Object Come?', in D. Miller (ed.), *Materiality*. Durham: Duke University Press. pp. 256–70.

Pugh, A. (2014) 'The Divining Rod of Talk: Emotions, Contradictions, and the Limits of Research', *American Journal of Cultural Sociology*, 2(1): 159–63.

Reckwitz, A. (2002) 'The Status of the Material in Theories of Culture', *From Social Structure to Artefacts, Journal for the Theory of Social Behavior*, 32(2): 195–217.

Reed, I. (2009) 'Culture as Object and Approach in Sociology', in J.C. Alexander and I. Reed (eds), *Meaning and Method: The Cultural Approach to Sociology*. Boulder, CO: Paradigm Publishers.

Reed, I. and Alexander, J.C. (2006) 'Culture' In: Turner, B.S. (ed.) The Cambridge Dictionary of Sociology. Cambridge: Cambridge University Press.

Shusterman, R. (2000) *Pragmatist Aesthetics: Living Beauty, Rethinking Art*. New York: Rowman and Littlefield.

Simmel, G. (2002 [1903]) 'The Metropolis and Mental Life', in G. Bridge and S. Watson (eds), *The Blackwell City Reader*. Oxford and Malden, MA: Wiley-Blackwell. pp. 11–19.

Simmel, G. (2008) *Englischsprachige Veröffentlichungen 1893–1910*. Frankfurt: Suhrkamp.

Swidler, A. (2001) *Talk of Love: How Culture Matters*. Chicago, IL and London: University of Chicago Press.

Taussig, M. (1993) *Mimesis and Alterity: A Particular History of the Senses*. New York and London: Routledge.

Thrift, N. (2005) 'Beyond Mediation: Three New Material Registers and their Consequences', in D. Miller (ed.), *Materiality*. Durham and London: Duke University Press.

Turner, S. (2003) 'The Politics of the Word and the Politics of the Eye', *Thesis Eleven*, 73: 51–70.

Turner, V. (1974) *Dramas, Fields and Metaphors. Symbolic Action in Human Society*. Ithaca and London: Cornell University Press.

Woodward, I. (2007) *Understanding Material Culture*. London: Sage.

Zubrzycki, G. (2011) 'History and the National Sensorium: Making Sense of Polish Mythology' Qualitative Sociology, 34(1): 21–57.

# The Cultural Sociology of Markets

Frederick F. Wherry

## INTRODUCTION

As people contemplate their bottom-line issues – how the job market will punish or reward, how to increase or maintain happiness through consumption and investment decisions, or whether to sustain a human life – they turn almost exclusively to professional economists for definitive answers. Economic analysis draws on pure mathematics, sanctioned equations, and universal methods that deliver clean answers. These answers operate as an unveiling of boundedly rational practices long in operation but invisible to the non-economic eye. Books such as *Freakonomics* (Levitt and Dubner, 2005) gained popularity by offering up one surprise after another. If only we treat people as if they are rational actors with utility functions to maximize, we can discover the previously unexamined dynamics and consequences of drug dealing, abortions, and gambling, to name but a few of the socially contentious topics. What we thought were norms, values, or shared beliefs seemed better explained by economic theories amenable to mathematical representation.

By contrast, cultural sociologists have demonstrated that the utility functions that economists take for granted come from the meaningful practices of life. People are not walking calculators engaged in a series of maximization problems, nor do they act as if they are. By bringing blurry symbols into focus and taking seriously the enacted histrionics of market encounters, cultural sociologists have developed a strong program led by meanings. These meanings do not operate at the level of the individuals but impinge on different types of situations (Norton, 2014). Without mathematics as its guide, the strong cultural program rejects theoretical parsimony in favor of the thickly described and the theoretically interpreted case. This does not mean that mathematical modeling is impossible or that demographic processes and resource constraints do not enter the analysis. It does mean that collective meanings structure and transform the assemblage of social relations, the emergence of goals, and the legitimate pathways for goal achievement.

## THE FAULT LINES

At the center of cultural economic sociology stands a commitment to consequential meanings. Such meanings exist prior to action, operate externally to the individuals in question, and operate as causes rather than outcomes (independent rather than dependent variables). We are not faced with a buyer and seller who discover through their negotiations a single, shared understanding of value, expressed as price. The meanings of the negotiation, the object, and the roles of the individuals negotiating over the terms of the exchange exist prior to the encounter and across a wide set of similar encounters (trans-situational). No matter how straightforward the economic goal or how lucrative the monetary incentives for action, individuals try to understand whether their course of action is legitimate, who the beneficiaries and victims of their actions might be, and what the goal's achievement will communicate to socially significant others. The individual may not fully understand or coherently articulate what those meanings are, yet those overarching meanings will be relatively stable and will provide a refracting device for interpretation and a configured set of signifiers against which the individual may act.

Rather than dismiss weak cultural programs in economic sociology, this chapter advocates building strength from them. Weak programs display empirical adequacy at the expense of hermeneutic interpretation. The observable patterns of social relations and the empirically verifiable meaning patterns they privilege preclude what Granovetter (1985) called 'over-socialized approaches' where individuals seemed to be programmed to act robotically without needing to take account of their social histories or their political realities. Zelizer (1988; 2010) has demonstrated how economic sociologists can navigate between under- and over-socialized views, offering thick historical accounts of market transformations while asking how demographic shifts, urbanization patterns, and other macro-economic and political factors might explain (or not) the transformations she analyzes. This avoidance of the over-socialized notion of the individual takes on a view of individual action that concurs with that of the strong program:

> [E]very action, no matter how instrumental, reflexive or coerced vis-à-vis its external environments (Alexander, 1988), is embedded to some extent in a horizon of affect and meaning. This internal environment is one towards which the actor can never be fully instrumental or reflexive. It is, rather, an ideal resource that partially enables and partially constrains action, providing for both routine and creativity, and allowing for the reproduction and transformation of structure (Sewell, 1992). (Alexander and Smith, 2001: 136)

In practical terms this means identifying moments in the transaction sequence when emotions and attention run high (Collins, 2004), where passion mixes with interests (Hirschman, 1977), and where the outcomes of the transaction vary. Wherry (2014: 429) has updated this under- and over-socialized concern to promote a cultural analysis of economic life.

From the over-culturalized perspective, the economic culture sets into motion a set of scripts. Economic culture cannot autonomously re-shape itself; it becomes a weapon for those who understand that society is subordinate to it and who know how to manipulate the symbolic conditions of their cultural subordination to gain symbolic and material advantages. The under- versus over-socialized views of human behavior that Mark Granovetter (1985: 486) critiques parallel the under- and over-culturalized views of economic activities and markets I sketch here. In the over-culturalized view, once we know the meaningful intentions of society and the sequence of transactions that those meanings dictate, economic transactions become automatic reflexes because the individuals in question are so thoroughly acculturated – societal values having been introjected through and through.

While values are introjected in individuals, these individuals nonetheless can disagree with, struggle against, or transform those values. In these struggles, the core set of implicit beliefs against which the individual reacts becomes manifest. And the variations in how strongly held or how coherent those values are provide the analyst with opportunities to practice a cultural sociology piqued by hermeneutic and positivist skepticism. Following Vaisey and Lizardo (2010), I leave open the possibility that culture may be a cause or a consequence of any particular outcome. They write: 'The issue of the structural determination of culture and the cultural formation of structure cannot be solved by appealing to a single, general formula (Sewell, 2005); they must be reopened and subject to empirical specification and theoretical reformulation in concrete social contexts' (1595).

Nina Bandelj (2008) distills economic culture from public debates about foreign direct investment in national newspapers. She argues that much of the public sphere debates are either led or enacted by known or knowable public figures. These public figures are generally viewed as embodying the collective representations of a sizable portion of the population or of a socially significant group (of whatever size). These public figures need not represent a majority opinion or be concerned that their depictions of majority opinion diverge from available polling data. And the selected dialogues that appear in national newspapers and other public forums need not capture the full range of what these public figures have said. Indeed, these snippets of dialogue or selected statements illustrate opposing views, symbolic oppositions illuminating the fault-lines in public debate:

> [B]ecause of their cultural significance, or meaning potentiality, economic actions can be mobilized as sites of public debates, where the social meaning of economic actions is 'put into words' most explicitly. Hence, investor attempts to acquire assets in another country initiate interpretations of these actions by the business actors directly involved in the transactions as well as by the broader public who attributes significance to these actions because it perceives that it has some stake in the activity. (Bandelj, 2008: 5)

These debates in the public sphere help actors navigate uncertainty, providing encouragement to make risky moves or reassurances to play it safe. She and others understand the challenge in understanding the relationship between societal-wide debates about markets and the state (Krippner, 2001; Somers and Block, 2005) religion, and other cultural (discursive) structures that shape expectations and goals, that make resonant various action strategies, and that modulate the pace and potentialities of economic transactions.

Lyn Spillman's (2012) study of trade associations takes aim at standard economic organizations that sociologists have largely ignored. She examines a national census of over four thousand business associations in the United States, and engages in more in-depth analysis of over two hundred businesses (her focal sample), in order to show how much these associations rely on and generate a solidaristic ethos that pure calculations for gain cannot explain. Although she does not include an analysis of meeting situations or thick descriptions of actors enacting the associations' goals, she provides a systematic approach to surveying a population with the concerns of cultural sociology at the fore.

Frank Dobbin (2004) has tried to bridge some of the approaches in cultural and economic sociology by focusing on conventions. As he introduces the 'Sociological View of the Economy', Dobbin offers a direct, vivid comparison between Yonamamo people in the jungles of Brazil and frenetic bond traders Salomon Brothers. He writes:

> Both cosmologies tie social customs and physical objects to something bigger than society itself, in one case to a spirit world, in the other to a corpus of natural laws. ... The bond traders envision a roster of social and physical laws that transcend time and space, and trace conventions (arbitrage) and objects (blowfish sushi) to specific laws. In each tribe, the average man on the street may not know everything about the ancestor spirits or scientific laws that govern the world, but he trusts that the experts know. (2004: 1)

Dobbin brings together institutions, networks, and individual-level cognition to ask what generates roles in economic situations, how network structures facilitate the spread of myths, how myths and meaningful practices are consequential for economic action, and how the sense of one's choice set emerges. While customs and conventions play key roles in the economy, the existing literature in economic sociology has not spent a great deal of analytic power in specifying the cultural origins and structures of these conventions.

## WEAK PROGRAMS IN ECONOMIC SOCIOLOGY

When Mark Granovetter promoted the idea of the economy as embedded in society, he did so with an empirical agenda meant to clarify the theoretical concept. Rather than talking about a diffuse set of values or pretending that values did not matter at all, Granovetter (1985) looked to actual, ongoing relationships (behaviors) apparent in economic transactions and consequential for market outcomes. Interpersonal relationships affected whether individuals were able to get a job (Granovetter, 1983; 1995), all other things begin equal. And these relationships also affected how new industries were structured. Culture seemed to be bracketed or at least rendered analytically distinct, but cultural meanings showed up in the historical accounts of people trying to make sense of what to call things and which choices to make among a set of technically feasible options. Gone was material determinism, or so it seemed, because these relational ties had a demonstrable effect.

To rescue embeddedness from becoming a mere sensitizing concept, a number of scholars privileged its network manifestations. The way people were linked together determined their constraints relative to closely situated others. This allowed individuals occupying structural holes in a network to operate with less constraint and thereby advance more quickly in pay and promotion (Burt, 1998). It also determined whose ideas would be perceived to be creative or innovative: the same thing being expressed from the wrong network position would not be perceived as carrying the same weight (Burt, 2004). It seemed that culture was an outcome of network structures, and that culture (in the form of status) only modified the operations of networked actors (Smith et al., 2012). Paul DiMaggio (1992) called this Nadel's paradox, meaning that the cultural and relational aspects of networks is crucial for understanding behavior, yet analysts engaged in a 'purely tactical' move of ignoring this in order to measure and operationalize the consequential network structures. Some of the earlier work seemed to assume that a well-measured network structure offered a 'self-sufficient means of analyzing social systems without recourse to meaning systems and culturally embedded categories' (DiMaggio, 1992: 121). Emirbayer and Goodwin (1994: 1413) write: 'Network analysis neglects or inadequately conceptualizes the crucial dimension of subjective meaning and motivation – including the normative commitments of actors – and thereby fails to show exactly how it is that intentional, creative human action serves in part to constitute those very social networks that so powerfully constrain actors'. (For a review of critiques of network theory, see Vaisey and Lizardo, 2010: 1597–9.)

Even Harrison White (1992) failed to take culture seriously, though his attention to story-sets and identity would suggest otherwise. In their discussion of White, Vaisey and Lizardo (2010: 1598) note that, 'for White (1997: 64): talk of persons, internal motivations and value-orientations is not relevant, because "interactions, ties in sociocultural context, are coming to supplant persons as building blocks – and a person may come to be seen as a knotted vortex among social networks"'. Thus, even though White reconsiders the importance of culture in social networks, his structuralist sociology continues to conceive of culture as a post hoc commentary on ongoing projects of control in concrete social contexts (Emirbayer and Goodwin, 1994; White, 1992). The actors in White's model are strategic actors engaged in control projects, deploying identities and stories strategically to maintain and extend control. The more control, the better.

Likewise, Randall Collins (2004) studies the standard operating procedures evident in face-to-face encounters as Goffmanian interaction orders. The actors recognize the rituals they are in and the corresponding playbook for how to behave in them. As actors follow the playbook, they individually generate emotional energy but collectively re-create group symbols, a sense of the sacred (the singular/the authentic), and righteous anger at the violation of the sacred. In the Interaction Ritual Chain (IRC), the actors consume and re-generate emotional energy (EE), itself a strong and steady feeling that the actor stores psychically, allowing her to act with resolve. Collins does not ask where the ritual playbooks come from beyond the interaction itself; moreover, his reliance on the concept of emotional energy is too compatible with rational choice theory. Collins conjures up an image of the social animal on the perpetual hunt for more hits of EE (like a drug addict or a hyper capitalist). Because more of it is always better and because it operates like utiles in utility theory, Collins evacuates culture from these linked network exchanges (Alexander, 2004; Emirbayer, 1996) and does not explain why people may make moves from one network position to another, especially for moves that cause them pain (emotional drainage). Ritual theory itself includes acts of privation that may be energy draining as well as acts of piety that are energy generating (Durkheim, 1995 [1912]; Radcliffe-Brown, 2014 [1939]). People not only manage their own roles while being carried along by the ritual, but they also find themselves carried away by cognitive forces beyond their command (Vaisey, 2009). Emirbayer and Goodwin (1994: 1413) write: 'Network analysis neglects or inadequately conceptualizes the crucial dimension of subjective meaning and motivation – including the normative commitments of actors – and thereby fails to show exactly how it is that intentional, creative human action serves in part to constitute those very social networks that so powerfully constrain actors'. (For a review of critiques of network theory, see Vaisey and Lizardo, 2010: 1597–9.)

Countering imagined instances where IRCs might contradict notions of rational action, Collins (2004: 170) writes: 'Altruistic behavior is not an anomaly for rational action. It is predictable from the distribution of interactional situations from which individuals derive their EE'. The market for IRCs maximizes the benefits of EE (the numerator) in proportion to the costs of EE plus the materials used to generate it (the denominator). There is no moral deliberation needed, nor is the equation conditioned on existing cultural structures (discourse regarding legitimate courses of action). Rational choice is merely extended into encounters whose outcomes are conditioned on prior encounters (and the results of EE generation or depletion).

Likewise, field theorists such as Pierre Bourdieu (1984; 2005) have tied themselves to the metaphor of capital. People use capital to create more capital, whether that capital be symbolic, cultural, economic, or social. George Steinmetz (2008) goes so far as to introduce 'ethnographic capital', the legitimate authority to render a strange people and its practices as real and as well understood. These forms of capital can be represented by mathematical equations or as factors in a fuzzy set Qualitative Comparative Analysis. Where are surplus capitals to be found and who captures the surplus? These field theorists provide a more parsimonious framework for analyzing markets by reducing the meanings of economic life to different forms of capital. And while these forms of capital can be related to one another by way of equations, this approach privileges parsimony over meanings. Meanings are typecast quickly so that the real event of material struggles for capital can take center stage.

## STRONG CULTURAL PROGRAMS IN ECONOMIC SOCIOLOGY

There are opportunities to build a strong cultural program of economics by analyzing the social imaginaries of markets. Such landscapes include collective representations constituting genres, populated by narrative characters – some, protagonists; a few, stock; others, foil (Alexander, 2011; Beckert, 2013; Spillman, 2011; Wherry, 2012). Economic policymakers along with people running businesses, Beckert writes, rely on 'mental representations of future states [he] calls[s] "fictional expectations." Fictional expectations in the economy take narrative form as stories, theories, and discourses' (Beckert, 2013: 220). Therefore, it stands to reason that when actors try to make big decisions about whom to promote, whom to hire, or what to market, they will 'attempt to find "proof" of the soundness of the imaginaries constituting their decisions' (Beckert, 2013: 237). They are imagining scenarios, plots with danger, eventful outcomes, in order to decide on the best course of action. Beckert does not insist on the autonomy of these fictional expectations, but he offers a reasonable explanation for why these expectations can drive economic action.

For the actors involved, the stories 'proving' the soundness of their claims do not feel fictional but natural, in the sense that a religious ritual evoking an emotional response feels natural, real, and sound. The market stories provide simplifying assumptions that help individuals categorize their situations and evaluate their attitudes and reactions towards them; and there is often an explicit evaluation of right and wrong that carries moral as well as practical weight. These stories function as folk algorithms, inducing the behaviors they describe.

The performance of these stories is not as freshly accomplished as Bruno Latour's (2005) actor-network theory posits because story systems lie outside of the observed relations among humans, nonhumans, and objects and these story systems impinge on how actors assemble their dramaturgical demonstrations of sound rationality while they attempt to move across network boundaries. (Again, ANT has no first-order conceptual place for culture.) Koray Caliskan and Michel Callon (2009) explain that the 'universal instrumental rationality ... induces "economic" behaviors' and that 'the notion of culture [accounts] for the diversity of the concrete actions observed'. This economizing approach generates what it claims to reveal, 'by uncovering instrumental rationality in numerous locations, the formalist program produces an effect (of surprise) that is parallel to the role that economics plays in the construction of economic reality' (2009: 374). Just as economization begins to offer an approach amenable to a strong cultural program, it abandons culture and turns, instead, to science and technology studies where there are devices and meanings generated in specific locales as individuals interact with those devices and one another to make 'economic' things happen.

Market stories, like the societal ones Durkheim studied, allow analysts to use public opinion (collective representations) to predict 'changes in taste and in wage levels' as well as 'changes in the mode of production itself' (Alexander, 1982: 290). In Durkheim's analysis, the different wages people earn do not derive from a material domination of one class over another, as argued by Marx, but rather from a categorical evaluation of the stories that define different types of workers, the character of production, and the roles that different characters play in production. In short, shared stories mediate human responses to materiality by arraying categories of roles along with the candidate responses and conditions expected to constitute those roles. These stories and the roles populating them uphold sacred (off-limits) objects and depict sequentially prescribed processes. The story's assumptions usually fall along a symbolic, oppositional binary mirroring the sacred/profane split: clear-cut versus messy transactions; smooth negotiations versus rough ones; morally sound versus morally unsound practices; high quality versus low; and niche versus mass.

Setting aside their commitment to methodological individualism, behavioral economists, psychologists, and legal scholars seem to offer support for building a strong cultural program in economic sociology and behavioral economics. Christine Jolls, Cass Sunstein, and Richard Thaler (2000) list the three parsimonious principles outlined by Gary Becker in order to show the shortcomings of each. For Becker, 'all human behavior can be viewed as involving participants who (1) maximize their utility (2) from a stable set of preferences and (3) accumulate an optimal amount of information and other inputs in a variety of markets' (Becker cited in Jolls et al., 2000: 14). These principles do not depict what actual individuals do in competitive market environments or why.

To say that people act 'as if' they are following these principles is to ignore the observed patterns of behavior in specific situational contexts. Jolls and her colleagues ask that 'bounded rationality, bounded willpower, and bounded self-interest' (14) be used as more accurate and useful characterizations of economic actors.

These bounded concepts of rationality, willpower, and self-interest present a problem for cultural economic sociologists. These qualities inhere at the level of the individual, while cultural qualities exist outside of individuals. Culture is a structured set of understandings largely shared within a group that affects what makes sense, what is desirable, what seems right or wrong, what alluring or abhorrent, and why something feels satisfying. To say that these understandings are shared is not to say that the individuals affected by a set of cultural understandings know what those understandings are. They act as if they know by the justifications they make, the strategies of action that are feasible but seldom openly verbalized, and the paradigmatic stories and images they are exposed to. Culture is both explicit and implicit: explicit texts and symbolic objects; implicit orientations towards norms, values, and the social ecology (Griswold, 2012). These texts, images, and orientations constitute the environments that enable and constrain action, while their justifications and non-verbalizations indicate how moral considerations, emotional salience, and concerns for socially significant others guide their actions.

## *Moral Deliberations*

Instead of thinking about individuals as suffering from bounded rationality (too much information to process efficiently) or weak willpower, cultural sociologists tend to their moral concerns. People are not always acting as if more is better. And possibilities for material gain do not often overwhelm their self-control. If that were the case, recent experiments would not have such puzzling findings: as rewards increase for greater work output, work effort does not rise as expected. People reach a moment where they worry that doing much more might be wrong, harmful to others, or perhaps unfair.

These concerns with justice and fairness do not simply 'linger' from previous stages of economic evolution but constitute how we think about and respond to work opportunities. In *The Moral Economy of the Peasant* (1976), James Scott noted that the villagers he studied had their own 'notion of economic justice and their working definition of exploitation – their view of which claims on their product were tolerable and which intolerable' (3). Scott moves us away from a mechanical analysis of capital–labor relations to the realm of how people are categorized and what rights and obligations are attached to what categories of persons. Scott's conclusions accord with Émile Durkheim's (2005 [1900]) earlier explanation that work, compensation, and inviolable property rights depend on compelling moral content that emerged from sacred rituals.

A well-known example of moral deliberation comes from the insurance market. Zelizer (2010) has documented how potential consumers of life insurance were not swayed by actuarial arguments given for its utility. These people could process the information and understood that when their loved one died, the surviving spouse would have fewer monetary resources for survival, yet some consumers engaged in moral deliberations first and foremost: would buying insurance be equivalent to betting on and profiting from death? Consumers also felt the sway of superstition: would preparing for death bring it about sooner? The advocates of insurance soon learned that these understandings about death, afterlife, and its preparation required more than a boundedly rational rationale. The purchasers of insurance would need to be assured of its moral legitimacy and its magical consequences.

## *Ritual Commitments*

Rather than showing a lack of resolve, people are resolute in their ritual commitments. Ritual commitments refer to the sense of obligation to the sacred, often collectively displayed during a festival, a religious holiday, or a significant rite of passage. Individuals often weight their obligation to honor these events as more important than their routine obligations or mundane needs. Most families find high school and college graduations to be momentous events requiring gatherings and gifts, even when those families cannot afford such things. Likewise, gifts for Christmas, bar/bat mitzvahs, and quinciñeras cannot be resisted, even when the family's budget constraints caution savings or consumption. As with moral concerns, many businesses take into account what people's ritual commitments are and structure their sales and marketing around those commitments. There are Christmas Savings Clubs, holiday lay-away-plans, and small shops with specialty sections for young Latino girls coming of age in their quinciñeras. The entire family budget may be structured all year around these rituals, and the thought of ignoring such commitments may be rejected outright as mean, nasty, and cruel. The head of household who rejects ritual commitments in favor of a cold mathematical calculation (can we afford it?) may find the family unit soon dissolved or the decision widely scorned. And businesses that dishonor or take advantage of these ritual commitments through price gouging or disrespectful advertising campaigns find themselves beset by consumers expressing righteous indignation. Therefore, supply and demand depends on ritual meanings, as producers, advertisers, and consumers borrow from and respond to intersubjectively shared understandings about the rituals, their sacred elements and obligations, and what constitutes defilement. They cross red lines on occasion and are quickly pushed back, but often they look toward the light of the sacred and attempt fusion.

## Relational Interests

Rather than thinking about interests as bounded, we consider them tied to socially significant others. Zelizer has called this relational accounting: 'Mental accounting ... represents the individual counterpart of relational earmarking. ... One sees monetary variations as cognitive or emotional computations leading to often-unexpected budgetary choices. The other sees monetary differentiation as emerging from interactions among persons and marking distinctive social relations and meaning systems' (Zelizer, 2012: 159). By linking the types of relationships with meaning systems, Zelizer goes beyond the concerns that individuals have for close relations versus unknown persons and the varying notions of fairness that apply to these dichotomous categories. She takes us into a world of messy negotiations, effortful relationship building, and the incessant matching and mismatching of money (or other media of exchange) with the right bundle of meaningful social ties. Similarly, Jane Guyer (2004) presents creative actors, who make some things commensurate with money-value while simultaneously insisting on their disjuncture in valuation regimes.

Zelizer's relational work resembles the pragmatics of valuation. Caliskan and Callon (2009: 389) note: 'Zelizer's concept of earmarking is crucial if we wish to understand the singularity and specificity of a mode of valuation capable of transforming circulating things into gifts. She calls this "earmarking"'. To arrive at the earmark, however, one engages in relational work, a dynamic process in people align the various media of exchange and the objects gifted, sold, exchanged, or consumed by virtue of their concerns with the type of relationship they are in and the messages they wish to convey to socially significant others. What allows relational interests to withstand strong material pressures? And what types of exchange objects carry inherent versus imbued qualities that affect their probable earmarks?

Ironically, the a-cultural prescription offered by Çaliskan and Callon (2009) may offer the second of a three-step process for building strength in a weak cultural program of economic analysis. They call for 'analysing socio-technical assemblages and things that circulate from hand to hand? What would an economy be without commodities and their physical properties and materialities' (2009: 384)? If the analysis of textual sets and binary fault lines preceded the identification and analysis of socio-technical ensembles, we would be more firmly rooted in the strong program. We would find ourselves thickly describing these assemblages, the devices used, and the dramaturgical performance of their deployment. This leaves open the possibility that things embody innate values within their own materials. The qualities of the components are both projected onto the objects from without but may also emanate from within the object. A similar approach is emerging in socio-biology, where genetic configuration and hard-wired bodily responses are studied alongside demographic process and cultural practices. In the case of commodities, one could argue that silver, gold, and bronze may appeal to human beings by virtue of their feel, their color, and attributes inherent in their materiality, while also having those attributes amplified and re-constructed based on existing social texts and ongoing struggles over meanings. In other words, just as culture is analytically distinct from these objects, these objects and their character may be distinguished by their physics, their chemistry, and/or their biology. A strong cultural program facilitates the concomitant rise of other strong analytic distinctions and new research vistas.

## THE THEORETICAL ANTECEDENTS

A number of economic sociologists, including the paradigm's founder (Granovetter, 1985), have challenged the umbrella concept of embeddedness as elusive, and requiring more precise conceptual tools that complement the well-developed network analyses that gave embeddedness such empirical traction. These challenges have resulted in disagreements about the essence of and the relationships among social tics, transactions, exchange media, culture, and the state (Krippner, 2001; Krippner and Alvarez, 2007; Zelizer, 1988;

2010). The most common response to these disagreements articulates how a return to Karl Polanyi's texts on the economy as an instituted process and to his analysis in *The Great Transformation* (2001 [1944]) more clearly defines what markets are and how they work, but these theoretical reconciliations have been unsatisfying, even for the reconcilers.

In her critique of embeddedness as elusive, Krippner (2001) argues that Granovetter does not fully theorize the political struggles that shape markets along with the various institutions and ideations (Somers and Block, 2005) that give sense to market exchange and to economic interventions; this renders the markets elusive, cloaking the powerful agents and institutions shaping them. She turns to Polanyi's claim that 'religion and government may be as important for the structure and functioning of the economy as monetary institutions' (Polanyi quoted in Krippner, 2001: 779), but she largely eschews religion for the institutions of government, examining only one of the two factors that she and Polanyi deem as structuring structures. She comes close to examining religion as she argues that cultural templates and political processes are co-constituting markets, but never addresses religion per se. Although Krippner and Alvarez (2007) acknowledge the (religious-like) entanglements and disentanglements in the marketplace (Callon, 1998; Callon et al., 2002), where the sacred presumably invigorates the former, and the profane the latter, the authors do not address the role of religion and its ritual manifestations that undergird market institutions and economic action.

Sociologists have also acknowledged the role of religious elements (including rituals) in economic life. Writing in 2003, Swedberg avers that the full implications of Durkheim's work remain '*largely unexplored* in light of economic sociology' (Swedberg, 2003: 18, emphasis added), with the notable exception of Philippe Steiner (2010). Earlier Jeffrey Alexander (1982) outlined Durkheim's economic program and its unexamined contributions to sociology in Volume 2 of *Theoretical Logic in Sociology* where he compares the thought of Marx with that of Durkheim. Likewise, in *Economic Sociology: State, Market, and Society in Modern Capitalism* (2002 [1998]), Carlo Trigilia addressed the importance of Durkheim, asserting that economic facts come from society not from the individuals comprising it, but these arguments did not offer a pathway to study the ritual-like processes operating across a range of phenomena, especially in the domains of household budgeting, consumer demand, and marketing. While the introduction to the second edition of the *Handbook of Economic Sociology* refers to the role of religion for the constitution of private property (Smelser and Swedberg, 2005), the *Handbook* does not go on to include chapters on the religious foundations of commodification or its role in the attraction that people have to specific objects.

Cultural sociologists take from *The Elementary Forms* a ritual framework for examining encounters and discerning the function of the sacred/profane boundary in social life. For specific applications to market life, cultural analysts turn to Durkheim's *Professional Ethics and Civic Morals* (2005 [1900]) where he outlines how ancient beliefs as well as ritual practices undergird markets, property rights, and work/occupations. Private property, for example, rests on 'the right of a given individual to exclude other individual and collective entities from the usage of a given thing' (2005 [1900]: 143). Such rights have religious (sacred) origins, because the capacity to distinguish private from common property is a feature of religious and sacred things:

> [T]he sacred entities ... are withdrawn from general circulation; they are separate and set apart. The common people cannot enjoy them. They cannot even touch them. Those who have kinship, as it were, with sacred things of this kind, can alone have access to them – that is, those who are sacred as they are: the priests, the great, and the magistrates, especially where these latter have a sacred character. It is these prohibitions that lie at the foundation of what is called taboo, as an institution ... Taboo is the setting apart of an object as something consecrated. ... By virtue of this setting apart, it is forbidden to appropriate the object of taboo under pain of sacrilege ... (2005 [1900]: 143)

One has to have the proper qualifications to approach, touch, and use a sacred object. Declarations of taboo were used to protect a diamond mine near Honolulu and fishing yields during fishing season. So long as a sacred character could be imbued in an object, it would be set apart and protected from violation. These justifications simultaneously could serve as cover for economic interests, could structure the interests of economic actors, and could firm up the categorical identities of supra- and subordinate actors in a historically specific symbolic environment; some of these outcomes may not be recognized or easily recognizable for the actors involved in the transaction focused on their own goals, inattentive to latent goals in the symbolic environment or to emergent goals that are culturally particular; moreover, the emphasis of religious beliefs on the inalienability and inviolability of sacred objects gets interwoven into legal beliefs about private property ownership.

Ritual practices function to make beliefs and notions of inviolability publicly visible. In agricultural societies, some landed properties were held in common and the rights of individuals to such commonly held properties were vague; however, clans possessed clearly defined property rights on pieces of land that they could inhabit permanently. The land was inalienable in that it belonged to the same family in perpetuity. The property was inalienable due to its sacred nature, and this sacred nature was generated and affirmed through the agricultural rituals observed among the Romans, the Greeks, and the Indians (of India). Singing hymns, the head of the household would walk along the boundaries of the property on certain days of the month and offer sacrifices: 'What amounts to a magic circle is drawn about the field, which shields it from trespass or encroachment, because such intrusions, in these circumstances, become sacrilege' (Durkheim, 2005 [1900]: 152). Boundary stones would mark the limits of the owners claimed land and would serve as 'so many altars' (2005 [1900]: 151). In Rome, for example, myths about Jupiter and the Capitoline Hill affirmed the property's inviolable nature. And burial places remained off the market, incapable of being sold to the highest bidder or to anyone else, for that matter. The contracts that indicate property ownership derive their power from 'illusory beliefs and ancient notions which are held to have no objective foundation' (2005 [1900]: 160). The ritual-like pronouncement of the oath marks the violation of the contract as taboo.

The importance of rituals (whether they are tightly or loosely scripted; positive or negative) and the identification of the sacred totem a tribe must protect, present a contrast with the networks metaphor of differently positioned actors within a field acting strategically to increase their own, individual-level utility. Granovetter (1985) and the network-based studies of embeddedness he inspired rejected the over-socialized, highly scripted conceptions of humans and the functionalist paradigms steeped in societal evolutionary theory. The objects of study, he points out, should be observable relationships so that the social sciences could engage in empirical, substantive studies of markets rather than continue in an a-empirical, formal understanding of the economy. Taking Granovetter's concerns seriously, cultural economic sociologists bring specificity to their analyses of relationships, myth, shared stories, materials, feelings, and their movements as *a meaningful, observable, and contingently unfolding process.*

The embeddedness approach largely left religion out of the analysis of how markets operate; relationships affect economic action, not magic, spirits, or ritual-like ceremonies. Although Max Weber's (2002 [1905]) thesis on the Protestant ethic gave a nod to the religious motivations for capital accumulation at a specific historical moment under specific institutional conditions, Weber (1978 [1922]) himself argued that religion and charisma precluded modern, rational markets. More recent studies of religion's impact on economic action have found correlations between religious beliefs and the propensity to save (Keister, 2003), affirming Weber's understanding that the religious ethos and associated practices can facilitate or hinder capital accumulation, but these studies do not investigate the cultural structures leading to different saving propensities, nor do they thickly describe the meanings, settings, and enactments that render these correlations. There are market rituals, symbols of membership, and totems tying together the members of a tribe. In such circumstances emotions intensify and feelings of righteous indignation resonate with the violation of the sacred; collectivities struggle for equilibrium and for protection from defilement; and economic strategies and outcomes shift in their course.

## MOVING INTO CONSUMPTION

Consumer culture theorists in marketing departments have studied Jeep as a brand community, dependent on ritual and traditions, infused with a sense of moral obligation towards the brand, and characterized by a consciousness of kind among its consumers (Muniz and O'Guinn, 2001). One can see Jeep adherents gathering for the weekend (at their own expense) to participate in Jeep Jubilees; they rally along a rugged route, on a pilgrimage to affirm the group's values. 'Real' Jeep drivers abhor imposters but are quick to lend a hand to others who really care about the vehicle and what it represents. Perfect strangers flash their lights at one another as they encounter other users of the same brand. The most zealous know the Jeep's history and are eager to share it.

What would consumer culture theorists gain from a ritualized markets perspective? Consumer culture theorists emphasize practices but de-emphasize their ritual character:

> Practices link behaviors, performances, and representations through (1) procedures – explicit rules, principles, precepts, and instructions – (2) knowledge of what to say and do, skills and projects, or know-how (i.e., tacit cultural templates for understanding and actions); and (3) engagements – ends

and purposes that are emotionally charged insofar as people are committed to them. (Schau et al., 2009: :31)

The tacit cultural templates are not specified, nor are these cultural templates rendered autonomous, operating within a system of templates, influencing and being influenced by those who re-combine the templates in innovative ways (Stark, 2011). In the ritualized markets paradigm, the procedures function as unfolding rituals that generate emotional energy; and the procedures as well as the know-how in enacting them generate, reinforce, or challenge the barriers to entering the ritual. This results in what Schau, Muniz, and Arnould (2009) recognize as '(1) evangelizing and (2) justifying':

> Members of [the Star Trek and the Apple Newton brand communities] engaged in impression management, evangelizing and justifying 'their devotion to manage stigmas associated with overt sci-fi fandom and reliance on an obsolete and abandoned technology, respectively'. (Stark, 2011: 34)

The symbolic environment pits Star Trek believers and Apple Newton devotees against respective unbelievers. These consumers identify their totems, express their devotions to it, and act to protect the values they hold sacred. At the same time, they tend to spread the good news, offering stories of salvation where harrowing events were brought to heel, and stories of transformations, where a filthy, exhausted person became transformed into a new creature through her exposure to a sacred object (the brand).

The birth of the new person (a well-known religious trope) finds itself applied to the arrival of new products. For the BMW Mini, the production week for the new model unfolds through a highly ritualized process. The customers name their cars, anticipate its arrival, and 'create commemorative "baby books" to document the new arrival' (Schau et al., 2009: 36). As the process unfolds, the emotional engagement of the customers increases and 'a special dialect to speak about the impending arrival' (2009: 36) functions as a symbol of membership in an exclusive community. While the authors specify this process as one of social networking, they would benefit from an explicit theorizing of these processes through a ritualized market perspective. Rituals, unlike networks, include collective enactments of practices, demonstrations of beliefs, and the generation of emotional energy along with symbols of membership. Social networks are not theoretically tied to symbolic environments; ritualized markets are. And theories of brand communities are not attentive to the (implicit, often unseen) bundle of relationships relevant to the purchases and use of a good; the ritualized markets paradigm would bring this relational work to the fore. Klaus Weber and Tina Dacin (2011) ask: 'How do actors with variable social resources and degrees of cohesion manage the performativity requirements of their roles? What are the mechanisms invoked to shape and hold the attention of diverse and fragmented audiences? What is the temporal and spatial portability of ritual performances across contexts?'

## CONCLUSION

In the embeddedness perspective, markets are socially constructed phenomena in which social networks and the structure of social relations explain exchange outcomes. In cultural sociology, markets are arenas where rituals unfold that make objects desirable and that attract people to worship, appraise, and protect those objects. Rather than networks, the object of study is the set of meanings and the corresponding social performances or ritual-like processes that sometimes lead to sacralization. For many Granovetterians, the objects of study are networks and the structure of relationships along with the direction of transfers in the marketplace. In the second, the models are not so clean. For cultural sociologists, there are collective representations (especially symbolic binaries), negotiated (ritual-like) processes that resemble what Zelizer (2010; 2012) calls relational work, relational packages of exchange media, and dramaturgical enactments in dynamic/unfolding situations. Actors are interactively assessing the meanings of their situations, weighing the morality of their actions, appealing to imperatives greater than their own sense of self-gain. They do so while accomplishing social performances in the service of production and consumption (Alexander, 2011, Wherry, 2014). As cultural sociologists examine these meaningful activities and the environments in which they unfold, and as culture is rendered analytically distinct and prior to the situation at hand, old assumptions give way to meaningful interpretations infused with scientific discovery.

## REFERENCES

Alexander, J.C. (1982) *Theoretical Logic in Sociology: The Antinomies of Classical Thought: Marx and*

Durkheim, Volume 2. Berkeley: University of California Press.
Alexander, J.C. (1988) Action and its Environments: Toward a New Synthesis. New York: Columbia University Press.
Alexander, J.C. (2004) 'Cultural Pragmatics: Social Performance between Ritual and Strategy', Sociological Theory, 22: 527–73.
Alexander, J.C. (2011) 'Market as Narrative and Character', Journal of Cultural Economy, 4: 477–88.
Alexander, J. and Smith, P. (2001) 'The Strong Program in Cultural Theory: Elements of a Structural Hermeneutics', in J.H. Turner (ed.), The Handbook of Sociological Theory. New York: Springer.
Bandelj, N. (2008) 'Economic Objects as Cultural Objects: Discourse on Foreign Investment in Post-socialist Europe', Socio-Economic Review, 6: 671–702.
Beckert, J. (2013) 'Imagined Futures: Fictional Expectations in the Economy', Theory and Society, 42: 219–40.
Bourdieu, P. (1984) Distinction: A Social Critique of the Judgement of Taste. Cambridge, MA: Harvard University Press.
Bourdieu, P. (2005) The Social Structures of the Economy. Malden, MA: Polity.
Burt, R.S. (1998) 'The Gender of Social Capital', Rationality and Society, 10: 5–46.
Burt, R. (2004) 'Structural Holes and Good Ideas', American Journal of Sociology, 110: 349–99.
Caliskan, K. and Callon M. (2009) 'Economization, Part 1: Shifting Attention from the Economy Towards Processes of Economization', Economy and Society, 38: 369–98.
Callon, M. (1998) 'The Embeddedness of Economic Markets in Economics', in M. Callon (ed), The Laws of the Market. Malden, MA: Blackwell. pp. 1–57.
Callon, M., Méadel, C. and Rabeharisoa, V. (2002) 'The Economy of Qualities', Economy and Society, 31: 194–217.
Collins, R. (2004) Interaction Ritual Chains, Princeton, NJ: Princeton University Press.
DiMaggio, P. (1992) 'Nadel's Paradox Revisited: Relational and Cultural Aspects of Organizational Structure', in N. Nohria and R.G. Eccles (eds), Networks and Organizations: Structure, Form, and Action. Boston. MA: Harvard Business School Press.
Dobbin, F. (2004) 'The Sociological View of the Economy', in F. Dobbin (ed.), The New Economic Sociology: A Reader. Princeton: Princeton University Press.
Durkheim, É. (1995 [1912]) The Elementary Forms of Religious Life. New York: The Free Press.
Durkheim, É. (2005 [1900]) Professional Ethics and Civic Morals. New York: Routledge.
Emirbayer, M. (1996) 'Useful Durkheim', Sociological Theory, 14: 109–30.
Emirbayer, M. and Goodwin, J. (1994) 'Network Analysis, Culture, and the Problem of Agency', American Journal of Sociology, 99: 1411–54.
Granovetter, M. (1983) 'The Strength of Weak Ties: A Network Theory Revisited', Sociological Theory, 1: 201–33.
Granovetter, M. (1985) 'Economic Action and Social Structure: The Problem of Embeddedness', American Journal of Sociology, 91: 481–510.
Granovetter, M. (1995) Getting a Job: A Study of Contacts and Careers. Chicago: University of Chicago Press.
Griswold, W. (2012) Cultures and Societies in a Changing World. Thousand Oaks, CA: Sage.
Guyer, J.I., (2004) Marginal Gains: Monetary Transactions in Atlantic Africa. Chicago: University of Chicago Press.
Hirschman, A.O. (1977) The Passions and the Interests: Political Arguments for Capitalism before Its Triumph. Princeton: Princeton University Press.
Jolls, C., Sunstein, C.R. and Thaler, R.H. (2000) 'A Behavioral Approach to Law and Economics', in C.R. Sunstein (ed.), Behavioral Law and Economics. New York: Cambridge University Press.
Keister, L.A. (2003) 'Religion and Wealth: The Role of Religious Affiliation and Participation in Early Adult Asset Accumulation', Social Forces, 82: 175–207.
Krippner, G.R. (2001) 'The Elusive Market: Embeddedness and the Paradigm of Economic Sociology', Theory and Society, 30: 775–810.
Krippner, G.R. and Alvarez, A.S. (2007) 'Embeddedness and the Intellectual Projects of Economic Sociology', Annual Review of Sociology, 33: 219–240.
Latour, B. (2005) Reassembling the Social: An Introduction to Actor-Network-Theory. New York: Oxford University Press.
Levitt, S.D. and Dubner, S.J. (2005) Freakonomics: A Rogue Economist Explores the Hidden Side of Everything. New York: William Morrow.
Muniz Jr., A.M. and O'Guinn, T.C. (2001) 'Brand Community', Journal of Consumer Research, 27: 412–32.
Norton, M. (2014) 'Mechanisms and Meaning Structures', Sociological Theory, 32: 162–87.
Polanyi, K. (2001 [1944]) The Great Transformation: The Political and Economic Origins of Our Time. Boston: Beacon Press.
Radcliffe-Brown, A.R. (2014 [1939]) Taboo. New York: Cambridge University Press.
Schau, H.J., Muñiz Jr., A.M. and Arnould, E.J. (2009) 'How Brand Community Practices Create Value', Journal of Marketing, 73: 30–51.
Scott, J. C. (1977) The Moral Economy of the Peasant: Rebellion and Subsistence in Southeast Asia. New Haven: Yale University Press.

Sewell Jr., W.H. (1992) 'A Theory of Structure: Duality, Agency, and Transformation', *American Journal of Sociology*, 98: 1–29.

Sewell Jr, W.H. (2005) 'The concept (s) of culture.' in G.M. Spiegel (ed), *Practicing history: New Directions in Historical Writing After the Linguistic Turn.* New York: Routledge.

Smelser, N.J. and Swedberg, R. (2005). 'Introducing Economic Sociology', in N.J. Smelser & R. Swedberg (eds.), *The Handbook of Economic Sociology.* New York and Princeton: Russell Sage Foundation Press and Princeton University Press.

Smith, E.B., Menon, T. and Thompson, L. (2012) 'Status Differences in the Cognitive Activation of Social Networks', *Organization Science*, 23: 67–82.

Somers, M.R. and Block, F. (2005) 'From Poverty to Perversity: Ideas, Markets and Institutions over 200 Years of Welfare Debate', *American Sociological Review*, 70: 260–87.

Spillman, L. (2011) 'Culture and Economic Life', in J. Alexander, P. Smith, and R. Jacobs (eds), *The Oxford Handbook of Cultural Sociology.* New York: Oxford University Press.

Spillman, L. (2012) *Solidarity in Strategy: Making Business Meaningful in American Trade Associations.* Chicago: University of Chicago Press.

Stark, D. (2011) *The Sense of Dissonance: Accounts of Worth in Economic Life.* Princeton: Princeton University Press.

Steiner, P. (2010) *Durkheim and the Birth of Economic Sociology.* Princeton: Princeton University Press.

Steinmetz, G. (2008) 'The Colonial State as a Social Field: Ethnographic Capital and Native Policy in the German Overseas Empire before 1914', *American Sociological Review*, 73: 589–612.

Swedberg, R. (2003) *The Principles of Economic Sociology.* Princeton: Princeton University Press.

Triglia, C. (2002 [1998]) *Economic Sociology: State, Market, and Society in Modern Capitalism.* Malden, MA: Wiley-Blackwell.

Vaisey, S. (2009) 'Motivation and Justification: A Dual-Process Model of Culture in Action', *American Journal of Sociology*, 114: 1675–715.

Vaisey, S. and Lizardo, O. (2010) 'Can Cultural Worldviews Influence Network Composition?', *Social Forces*, 88: 1595–618.

Weber, K. and Dacin, M.T. (2011) 'The Cultural Construction of Organizational Life: Introduction to the Special Issue', *Organization Science*, 22: 287–98.

Weber, M. (1978 [1922]) *Economy and Society: An Outline of Interpretive Sociology.* Berkeley and Los Angeles: University of California Press.

Weber, M. (2002 [1905]) *The Protestant Ethic and the Spirit of Capitalism.* Los Angeles: Roxbury.

Wherry, F.F. (2012) *The Culture of Markets.* Malden, MA: Polity.

Wherry, F.F. (2014) 'Analyzing the Culture of Markets', *Thory and Society*, 421–36.

White, H.C. (1992) *Identity and Control: A Structural Theory of Social Action.* Princeton: Princeton University Press.

White, H.C. (1997) 'Can Mathematics be Social? Flexible Representations for Interaction Process and its Sociocultural Constructions', *Sociological Forum*, 12: 53–71.

Zelizer, V.A. (1988) 'Beyond the Polemics of the Market: Establishing a Theoretical and Empirical Agenda', *Sociological Forum*, 3: 614–34.

Zelizer V.A. (2010) *Economic Lives: How Culture Shapes the Economy.* Princeton: Princeton University Press.

Zelizer, V.A. (2012). 'How I Became a Relational Economic Sociologist and What Does That Mean?', *Politics & Society*, 40: 145–174.

# PART VII
# Culture and Consumption

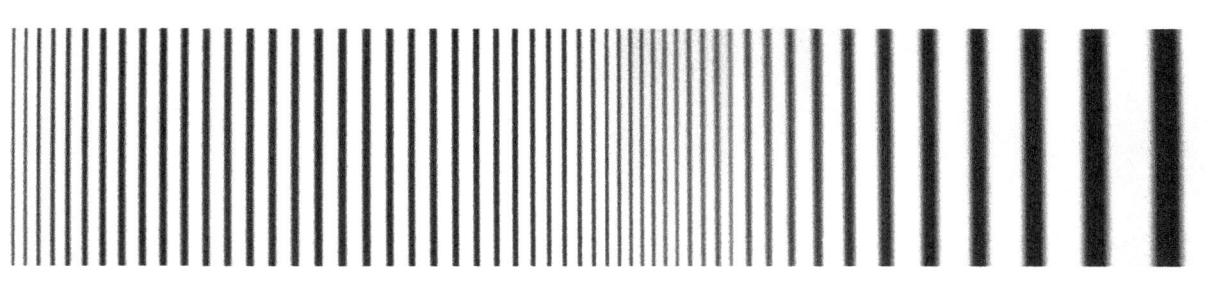

# 41

# Cultural Consumption and Cultural Omnivorousness

David Wright

## INTRODUCING THE 'OMNIVORE'

This chapter uses debates about the figure of the cultural omnivore to reflect on how scholars within the sociology of culture have approached the problem of cultural consumption. Cultural consumption here is defined as a subset of the broader forms of consumer culture, the analysis of which has been central to sociology's contribution to the understanding of late-modern societies (Lury, 1996; Sassatelli, 2007; Slater, 1997). Its distinct characteristics include the goods which are being *consumed*, i.e. the visual arts, literature and other print media, film, television and music of various forms – and the manner in which they are consumed, i.e. not only through the market exchange of money for commodities but also through the forms of disinterested contemplation, scholarly reflection and personal exploration and enthusiasm which characterise culture as a set of special symbolic things distinct from the material needs of life. As such, concern with cultural consumption can be seen to exemplify the emergence of this more restricted definition of culture as an object for sociological analysis.

Debates about the 'cultural omnivore', a particular kind of cultural consumer, have proliferated, in the late 20th and early 21st centuries, inspired, as the discussion below will explore, by two key scholars in this tradition – Richard A. Peterson and his various collaborators (Peterson, 1992; Peterson and Kern, 1996; Peterson and Rossman, 2008; Peterson and Simkus, 1992) responding to the earlier insights of Pierre Bourdieu (1984). Both these important contributions are themselves part of a broader and older conversation in the sociology of culture about, to use a recurring motif in this debate, the form and the function of cultural consumption in and for complex societies. This has its most obvious manifestation in the anxieties of Adorno and the Frankfurt School (Adorno and Horkheimer, 1997 [1947]) about the assumed effect of the *industrial* production of culture on its aesthetic qualities and on its audience. Interrogating the influence of the pejoratively titled *mass* consumption, already bound up with longer historical anxieties about the appetites of the masses themselves, gained a particular urgency in the mid-20th century as the products of the cultural industries – the *mass* media: film, popular music and later TV – challenged an assumed monopoly of cultural and intellectual elites over the ready access to cultural or symbolic life and questioned the belief, evident in intellectual culture of the early to mid-20th century (see Arendt, 1960; Ortega y Gasset, 1932, that special kinds of culture were perhaps best suited to and preserved for special kinds of people. Sociology, then contributed both to cementing these anxieties (Lazarsfeld and Merton, 1948) and later to challenging them, through such scholars as Gans (1999 [1974]) and, in the UK at least, through the broadening out of the conversation about the meaningfulness of everyday forms of cultural life wrought by the Cultural Studies tradition of inquiry (e.g. Hall and Jefferson, 1975).

The 'omnivore debate' has largely been carried out in parallel to, rather than in direct engagement with, these kinds of developments. This may be a result of the geographical location of its 'genesis' in the US and the relative reluctance of US sociology to take the more restricted definition of culture, and especially its commercial variants, seriously as objects of analysis in their own right. It is notable, for example, that the instigator of the omnivore debate was also a founding figure in establishment of the 'Culture section' of the America Sociological Association as late as 1982 (Santoro, 2008). It may also be because of the location of research into the omnivore in the methodological tradition of large-scale survey research – a mode which lends itself more to a specialist and technically attuned journal audience than to ready translation for teaching purposes. In this context this chapter argues that the strengths of the omnivore debate lie precisely in its focus on the *empirical* identification of patterns of cultural consumption. Such patterns are always a cause for controversy and discussion in the field of academic life, but observing and establishing these patterns, rather than assuming them, remains important to any theorising in the sociology of culture. At the same time, the chapter will conclude, whilst the last twenty to thirty years have been marked by the inexorable *rise* of the omnivore, it may be an increasingly less remarkable figure in the present and near future.

The meaning of the term 'omnivore' has morphed and developed in the years since its discovery in the early 90s, as we will see. Originally it can be summarised by the revelation that, in the US of the late 20th century, elite or high-status individuals were the most voracious consumers of culture and moreover that their tastes were not exclusive. That was in stark contrast to the dominant sociological narratives of the earlier 20th century about the relationship between consumption and status (emerging for example from the work of Max Weber (1980) or Thorstein Veblen (1994 [1899]) and specifically in contrast to Bourdieu's (1984) influential thesis about the specific role that tastes for cultural goods played in the struggle for social position in France. There are effectively two objects of empirical analysis in the debate about the omnivore. First are the people who are doing the consuming and their relative position in class or status hierarchies. Peterson, with his various collaborators, and Bourdieu empirically identify that there are specific characteristics to the cultural consumption patterns of more privileged groups, i.e. those higher up income and occupational class structures who possess higher levels of educational attainment, although they disagree on the nature of these characteristics. The consumption activities of these people are judged in relation to the second object, the hierarchies of the things they consume. Again, both Bourdieu and Peterson draw on an apparently settled and solid hierarchy of genres, objects or practices which can be readily recognised as moving from 'high' (or legitimate) cultural forms through 'middle' and down to 'low' (or popular, or commercial) forms. The former, Bourdieusian position, based on a wide-ranging empirical inquiry into the France of the 1960s, with the statistical analysis of survey responses at its centre, identifies this relationship as being broadly homologous, i.e. that people higher up the social hierarchy consume higher up the cultural hierarchy. The latter position is similarly based on empirical data gathered in the early 1980s in the US, and subsequently in the next two decades as part of a large-scale public survey of cultural participation, although in its early iterations the question of omnivorousness is exclusively concerned with the consumption of music. The more elite members of these samples are not just consuming elite or high cultural genres (here classical music and opera) but are also exhibiting preferences for the middle-brow (easy-listening, Broadway musicals and big-band) and popular forms (country, gospel, blue-grass, rock and blues). Thus the *omnivore* of the late 20th-century US is contrasted with the *snob* of mid to late 20th-century France.

The nuances of the differences and similarities of these positions will be explored in more depth below. Readers returning to the original contributions may be surprised, given both the relative modesty of the claims and the reasonableness of the tone in which they are made that they have generated such controversy. The review of the field by Peterson (2005) and a subsequent special edition of the journal *Poetics* in 2008, along with a wide range of other contributions, indicate, though, that the omnivore has emerged as a significant figure in the more empirical end of the contemporary sociology of culture, either identified, looked for or deconstructed and critiqued in most of North America and Europe, if less so elsewhere.

Part of the explanation for the spread of the phenomenon might well lie in the spread of the means to identify it and reflects the increased availability of nationally produced data on cultural participation as part of emerging policy priorities. The formal identification and measurement of people's leisure activities has become a focus of policy energy in the US and Western Europe, and indeed Peterson himself was involved in the development of the indicators for cultural participation that underpinned the Survey of Public Participation in the Arts (SPPA) as part of a role in the research division of the National Endowment for the Arts (Santoro, 2008) in the early 1980s. Although he himself expresses some caution about the relation between large-scale survey work, the state or commercial interests and a critical sociology of culture, in the years since the establishment of the SPPA, organisations such as UNESCO and the OECD have continued to make explicit or implicit links between the cultural life of a nation or region and its relative development of 'human capital', and equivalent publicly funded surveys in other countries have provided the resources for much of the sociological discussion in the field. We might speculate that evidence that contemporary cultural consuming practices amongst relatively privileged groups are *not* exclusionary is attractive to policymakers in the context of national, regional and local political debates about the public funding of the arts and their democratic accountability to a whole population. More recently this exclusive quantitative focus has been complemented by more *qualitative* approaches, resulting in the complication of the meanings and significance of the figure of the omnivore. These developments will be discussed in more detail below, beginning with an examination of the claims made for the 'omnivore'.

## CLAIMS OF 'THE OMNIVORE THESIS'

The empirical basis of the original identification of the omnivore are three observations, initially seen in data about preferences for music from the SPPA in 1982 (Peterson, 1992; Peterson and Simkus, 1992) and repeated and developed in relation to data from 1992 (Peterson and Kern, 1996) and 2002 (Peterson and Rossman, 2008). The first of these claims is that a distinct group can be identified, labelled as 'highbrow', through their ranking of a list of musical genres. This group chooses both classical and opera as genres they like and chooses one of these as the genre they liked best. The choice of music as the basis for this investigation, as Peterson and Kern (1996) explain, is partly strategic as it is the only topic covered in the SPPA survey which provided the appropriate range of options to allow the identification of the range of taste positions which could be ranked in relation to a cultural hierarchy. Musical taste was also chosen as an indicator of aesthetic taste because it was assumed to be relatively accessible to all participants, regardless of their income, their geographical location (e.g. rural or urban) or their time constraints (Peterson, 1992). Music was similarly considered significant to debates about cultural taste for Bourdieu, who famously characterised the expression, or 'flaunting', of musical culture as a particular kind of cultural display. 'Music', he suggests, 'represents the most radical and absolute negation of the world ... which the bourgeois ethos tends to demand of all forms of art' (Bourdieu, 1984: 19).

This highbrow group of classical and opera enthusiasts is also found to be, as might be predicted by earlier insights into relations between social and cultural hierarchies, more likely to frequent theatrical performances, ballet and art galleries than other groups in the SPPA sample and – perhaps more significantly – they were found to be generally better educated (in terms of years spent in education) and wealthier (in terms of annual income) than other groups. Following the identification of the highbrow group, the second significant observation is that they were not *exclusive* in their tastes for music. In addition to their choices of opera and classical music they were also found to choose an average of 1.74 of the five low brow genres in 1982 and 2.74 in 1992 and around 2 (1.98, then 2.12) of the three middlebrow genres. The final significant finding is that this highbrow group, with its tendency to like a wider variety of musical genres than might have been anticipated by an elite-mass model of cultural hierarchy, can be contrasted with a group found on the lower end of the occupational structure identified in the sample who only identify *one* genre of music as their favourite. Peterson deliberately avoids labelling this group as indicative of the *mass* taste of earlier critiques as both misleading and empirically inaccurate, not least perhaps because the SPPA also shows that the activity more associated with the label *mass* in the critical imaginary, watching television, was as likely to be associated with workers in the middle occupational and service categories, and, interestingly, artists, as with lower occupational groups alone. Instead the omnivorous highbrow group is contrasted, in what is characterised as an inverted pyramid rather than a linear structure of tastes, with a base made up of 'univores'.

In the game of scholarly cultural analysis, the invention of a label is also an invitation to critique or unpick or re-define it, and subsequent scholarship has attempted to do so. Peterson himself suggests both 'dilettante' (1992) and 'cosmopolitan' (2005) were considered as labels for the category of people he identified, before the 'omnivore' was finally settled upon as best capturing an appetite for activities that crossed real or perceived boundaries. Amongst subsequent scholarship these labels have included 'voraciousness' (Katz-Gerro and Sullivan, 2006), where an emphasis has been on the *volume* as well as the *breadth* of forms of cultural consumption. Other significant labels include the 'eclectic' (Ollivier, 2008) which places omnivorousness both within an older tradition of the taste profiles of the relatively privileged, such as the bohemians, but also conceptualises an openness to cultural variety as resonating with other theoretical tropes about the forms of diversity and re-formulated hierarchies which are assumed to typify late-modernity. It is important in re-visiting these original accounts to emphasise that, for Peterson and his collaborators, the discovery and labelling of the omnivore does not necessarily entail the *end* of the kinds distinctions proposed by Bourdieu so much as their re-formulation. They might perhaps be claiming an end of simplistic notions of snobbishness that preclude any possibility of elite people liking any popular culture. Such a possibility is not entirely absent from Bourdieu's account either, where, for example, younger educated groups, especially those close to the cultural or symbolic industries, attempt to assert their presence in the cultural field by consecrating popular items as part of inter-generational struggles. What these foundational contributions *are* revealing is a more widespread openness to popular and commercial cultural forms which might have broader social significance and which certainly troubles the mass culture critique. Peterson and Kern (1996) also suggest some linked factors which are speculatively proposed to explain this. These include social changes wrought by the expansion of liberal forms of education which involve the spread of tolerance towards the values of others to broader populations and the role of popular culture in inter-generational politics in the mid-20th century. They also include factors which might be characterised as endogenous to the field of culture, namely the role of the mass media in *democratising* access both to the legitimate arts and to the very possibility of a symbolic life and the challenge, from within the art world itself, to the notion of a single standard of aesthetic value which can be exclusively policed by expert academics and critics.

Twenty years on, these explanations remain plausible. Subsequent research has also focused on music (e.g. Atkinson, 2011; Bryson,1996; Chan and Goldthorpe, 2007; Rimmer, 2012; Savage and Gayo, 2011), but also broadened out the conversation about omnivorousness to include food (Warde et al., 1999), reading (Zavisca, 2005), television (Lizardo and Skiles, 2008), tastes for comedy (Friedman, 2012), and more holistic attempts to capture omnivorousness 'in the round' by exploring preferences for and attitudes to a wider range of distinct genres and activities at once (Ollivier, 2008; Warde et al., 2007; 2008). Much of this scholarship is also critical of the omnivore as an archetype, but for those scholars who see value in the omnivore as a useful figure in explaining aspects of contemporary experience, there is some agreement that there are a variety of *types* of omnivorousness which the original statistically identified relationship might have failed to capture. These include those omnivores who appear to empirically embody broader sociological narratives of late-modern consumer culture, characterised by an inquisitive, self-developmental quest for a variety of experiences and freed from the constraints of class. These freedoms are more accessible to some groups than others – and such omnivores tend to be located within the professional groups most closely associated with the production and circulation of culture. Peterson and Rossman (2008) point out the 'elective affinity' between omnivores and the contemporary business and administrative elite, whilst Bellevance (2008) points out the relations between urban, educated cultural consumers and Florida's (2002) 'creative class', with eclectic attitudes to cultural consumption being almost a precursor to membership of this group. Whilst omnivorousness appears as a disposition synonymous with the liberal and professional middle classes, research has also discovered other types of 'omnivores', including those who are self-consciously and politically antithetical to hierarchies of culture in their consuming practices (Warde et al., 2007) and those whose expressions of preference for a wide range of types of culture can be interpreted as reflecting a rather weak investment in and indifference to cultural preference at all (Ollivier, 2008), or indeed a reluctance to be seen to make judgements in the socially awkward survey-interview encounter.

Some of these more critical reflections focus on the limitations of extrapolating from survey questions and quite marginal statistical differences to broader processes of social and cultural change. We'll consider the methodological critique in more depth below, but particular critical attention has been focused on the notion that more general forms of social, ethical or civic tolerance can be read into the empirical identification of openness to a variety of forms of music. Ollivier (2008) has warned, for example, of the dangers of a binary division between omnivore and univore standing alongside other divisive binaries of contemporary cultural life (mobility and stasis, openness and closure, heterogeneity and homogeneity) that valorise the middle class as in the vanguard of social progress and condemn other groups as its other. Doing so would, of course, undermine Peterson's careful framing of the omnivore as a more nuanced contribution to the sociological conversation about culture than the elite-mass culture theorists which preceded him. A key contribution to this debate is provided by the work of Bethany Bryson (1996) whose analysis is again based on a large-scale survey in which a stratified random sample of 1606 people are asked questions about their preferences for 18 genres of music. This survey importantly draws on a Likert scale in its questions, so *intensity* of liking and, importantly, *dis*liking can be identified. Whilst Bryson's work broadly confirms the omnivore hypothesis by revealing that higher levels of education increase the range of preferences for musical genres amongst her sample, there are also significant patterns to this apparent tolerance. Certain genres which are outside of an obvious 'highbrow' categorisation, such as latin, jazz and blues, are incorporated into more educated tastes, whilst others such as rap, heavy metal, country and gospel music are not. These final four also happen to be the genres most preferred by those with lower levels of education in Bryson's sample (though not, as we'll see, necessarily so elsewhere). The implication here is that if, as Bryson contends, cultural tolerance and civic tolerance are associated with one another, judgements of these genres might also be judgements of the people who like them. A similar finding emerges from Warde et al. (2008) who identify a general social value attributed to liking a wide variety of culture amongst more educated groups in their survey of British tastes, but also identify some items as genres – in their case fast food, reality television and electronic pop music – as beyond the pale of omnivorous taste. From this they conclude that omnivorousness might precisely be a strategy for distinction in the specific conditions of early 21st-century Britain.

Such findings resonate with Lizardo and Skiles' (2012) more recent attempt to reconnect the proliferation of empirical studies of omnivorousness with some theoretical explanations about the types of experience that it appears to identify. They point out the good reasons to be sceptical about the *novelty* of the omnivore. If culture has a role in the reproduction of class privilege in Western societies, it is likely to have been developed over a significant time period, and unlikely to be transformed substantively in the few generations between Bourdieu's *Distinction* and the 'discovery' of the omnivore in North America and beyond. The concentration on the comparative surveying of tastes and preferences, albeit that these collectively provide substantive evidence for the existence of a phenomenon 'on the surface', is, they argue, at the expense of any sustained theoretical consideration of the mechanisms that might be at play in producing that phenomenon. The speculative explanations from Peterson and Kern's contribution – about inter-generational struggle, the levelling effect of the mass media, and the decline of single authoritative notions of artistic or aesthetic value, remain plausible but relatively unproven and have generally not been taken up by scholars in the omnivore debate, at least compared to the energetic pursuit and analysis of patterns of cultural preference.

For Lizardo and Skiles, Bourdieu's notion of the 'aesthetic disposition', evident in those versed from an early age in the language of form over function in relation to their cultural choices, remains crucial to interpreting the significance of the omnivore. Its recurrent identification as a position within or even synonymous with the taste profiles of the more educated middle classes suggest it is less a break with Bourdieu and more 'an empirical manifestation of the operation of the aesthetic disposition under contemporary macro-level conditions' (Lizardo and Skiles, 2012: 269). The disposition itself might be spread more broadly (if it is learned from higher education as well as from the family, then this is likely to be so, given levels of access to higher education in the last thirty years have increased), but it is also likely to be applied more widely, i.e. in the conditions of the proliferation of cultural production of the late 20th and early 21st centuries (Wright, 2011). Such an insight shifts the significance away from the apparent intrinsic, aesthetic qualities of *what* is being consumed and moves them towards *how* it is being consumed. The following section will explore this and consider how scholars have attempted to go beyond the identification of the existence of the omnivore to consider what, if anything, this existence *means*.

## CRITIQUING THE OMNIVORE THESIS

As outlined above, the key positions in debates about cultural consumption have been established through the analysis of large-scale surveys, albeit that the surveys are differently constructed and analysed. In the case of Bourdieu, the survey that underpins *Distinction* is also complemented with additional empirical material, statistical data, a sample of qualitative interviews, and textual analysis of a range of media, which help to illustrate how the established relationships between cultural tastes and social positions are visible and experienced in the world. This additional material is largely absent from the discussion of the omnivore in Peterson's account, and it is perhaps partly a scholarly desire to fill that gap which accounts for the energy and urgency of the omnivore debate. The reception and discussion of the omnivore can also be understood in the context of grand and on-going methodological skirmishes between the great warring tribes of quantitative and qualitative sociological work. Within British sociology, as Halsey (2004) describes, there has been a distinct shift away from the quantitative in recent decades with the smaller scale, semi-structured interview or ethnographic approach to generating knowledge becoming increasingly dominant. Survey analysis of questions of cultural taste and preference might have a significant place in this debate given the more general inclination within the various traditions of cultural analysis, from literary studies to anthropology to Cultural Studies, to disavow the perceived empiricism or, worse, positivism of quantitative approaches (Deacon, 2008; Murdock, 1997).

There are a range of critiques from both an epistemological and practical point of view which assume that survey questions about cultural preference are unable to capture the complexity of the experience of culture. These critiques can be related to the two objects of the omnivore debate – the relative solidity of categories of people and the relative solidity of genres of activity. Both appear concrete on a survey questionnaire but might become less solid the further away from the survey encounter that one travels. One substantive critique in this direction comes from the philosopher Jacques Rancière who decried the survey method of *Distinction* as the equivalent to an exam in which 'students from the university get the best grades' (Rancière, 2003: 187) and expressed specific disquiet with the strategy of judging people's tastes for music without actually giving them music to listen and respond to. Without that, he implies, the affective, emotional or spiritual elements of listening to music –all of which are elements of a conception of *aesthetic* qualities that is not necessarily captured in a pre-ordained cultural hierarchy of high and low – are lost in a survey encounter which becomes merely a test of knowledge and a recursive performance of status. Bourdieu himself acknowledges the survey encounter as a 'legitimacy-imposing situation' (Bourdieu, 1984: 318) in which those lacking in the skills, knowledge or confidence to discriminate between cultural forms choose those they think they identify as the 'right' ones. In his own review of the spread of the omnivore concept, Peterson (2005) acknowledges the tendency, evident in the SPPA, for publicly funded surveys of cultural activity, which might be explicitly concerned with providing evidence to underpin or justify public funding of the arts, to be weighted towards legitimate forms of culture and therefore be effectively blind to the forms of variety which might be at play in the everyday lives of the population in which they are conducted. Patterns of cultural consumption as they are revealed by such surveys are always patterns within and between the items, practices and preferences which were asked about – and few surveys, for reasons of cost and time can be comprehensive enough to capture cultural life in the all its variety and complexity.

Such is the lot of *any* empirical work, which attempts to tidy up the complex *mess* of the social world through the objective categorisation of people and things. Scholars who are sceptical of the value of that endeavour at all are unlikely to be persuaded by its application in this context, but debates about the performative nature of social science methods in creating the phenomenon they purport to measure are especially apposite to the questions of cultural consumption (Law, 2009; Osborne and Rose, 1999), given the ways in which survey instruments are constructed. Ollivier (2008) speculates, for example, about the existence of a archetypical cultural consumer without the experiences or networks to develop substantive knowledge of the kinds of musical genres or legitimate arts practices that feature in such surveys but who is curious – indeed, *open*, to exploring them. Such a participant might emerge as a 'univore' on a scalar measure of cultural participation, erroneously reproducing and cementing the imaginary of openness as a reflection of expressed cultural preference. As Peterson (2005) reveals in his commendably frank account of the fragile processes of data gathering in the various iterations of the SPPA, survey encounters can be performative in other ways. In the first two runs, in 1982 and 1992, participants who answered 'all of the above' in relation to the choice of genre were discounted, partly because of an assumption of interviewer/interviewee fatigue as the SPPA questions came after a long survey of other matters – specifically the experience of crime – and partly because the social and educational characteristics of these 'alls' did not seem to chime with the characteristics of other omnivores. This group increased significantly in 2002, though, and so their continued exclusion was likely to *underestimate* the number of omnivores and specifically *overestimate* the degree to which the characteristic of omnivorousness was associated with a particular group. Specifically, it would underestimate the number of 'lowbrow' consumers who might have been exhibiting tendencies associated with omnivorousness.

More recent interventions into the omnivore debate often take these assumed methodological limitations on board in proposing alternative methods – principally that of qualitative interviewing. These more ethnographic techniques have been used productively within the sociological exploration of cultural consumption (see Halle, 1993 on tastes for visual art) and are certainly more common in the examination of the *uses* of popular culture in the Cultural Studies tradition on genre fiction (e.g. Radway, 1984), or the influential studies of viewers of soap opera (e.g. Hobson, 1982). Such qualitative approaches are assumed to provide a more immediate sense of what tastes and preferences *mean* to the people who express them, rather than having that meaning read into the relationships between statistical variables, which are, necessarily, removed from the immediate experiences of the people who 'produce' them. In the context of the omnivore debate, one recent contribution goes so far as to take this qualitative turn as something of an 'counter-insurgency' (Atkinson, 2011: 170) in the context of a dominant quantitative mode of inquiry, in this case imagined as giving empirical succour to narratives of individualisation that characterise the theorising of late-modernity.

Perhaps the key problem for research taking this direction is the *identification* of omnivores that allows the exploration of the nature of their dispositions. The publications emerging from the recent British empirical inquiries into tastes (Bennett et al., 2009) and regarding the question of omnivorousness (Savage and Gayo, 2011; Warde et al. 2007; 2008) achieve this through some combination of the quantitative and the qualitative, i.e. there is an a priori process of the identification of a range of cultural preferences and interests through a scale of activities, and then a separate exploration of semi-structured interviews with identified individuals as examples of omnivores on these scales. Ollivier (2008) takes a slightly different approach in identifying individuals through a survey of a range of preferences and practices submitted alongside an interview with a pre-identified sample of people in the categories she was interested in, in combination with a discourse analysis of their interview transcripts. This enables her to both identify *quantitative* forms of omnivore due to their relative position on scales of practice and preference, but also to identify as omnivores those people who express omnivorous tendencies in their interviews – with participants whose contributions could be understood in relation to a discourse of 'discovery' also being explored as omnivores. This latter category, though, includes almost everyone interviewed. Atkinson (2011) similarly draws on a broad sample, slightly skewed towards the more affluent, and then analyses interviews which included some discussion of music. Here, though, the aim is less to objectively identify omnivores *per se* and more to explore omnivorousness 'in action' through identifying the various adjectives that participants use to describe their musical preferences. So liking a 'mish-mash', avoiding being 'put in a pigeon-hole' or listening to 'pretty much anything' are here interpreted as indicating the ready presence of at least the rhetoric of cultural tolerance – including that being expressed by participants who might otherwise be in the univorous group. These declarations of openness to variety are conceived of as 'specious' (Atkinson, 2011: 174) in the light of fuller interrogation of the musical tastes of these research participants, which indicates dispositions more readily recognised as Bourdieusian – relating in particular to educational and family experiences of music. Rimmer (2012) similarly focuses on foundational family or educational experiences in the formation of a 'musical habitus', in keeping with Lahire's conception of the cultural tastes gathered in survey work as reflective of the 'visible – and signposted part of an enormous iceberg' (Lahire, 2008) Here again the focus is not so much 'omnivores' as identified in relation to the tastes and practices of relatively elite groups, but 'omnivorousness' as one disposition amongst others expressed this time by 36 young people, aged 12–20 in urban and rural contexts of relative affluence or deprivation.

These accounts do commendable work in *complicating* the notion of omnivorousness as it emerges from quantitative accounts alone – and might also, in the cases of Rimmer and Atkinson, provide more evidence to support the argument that the omnivore debate reflects an empirical discovery that extends, rather than breaks with the more nuanced and methodologically sophisticated insight of Bourdieu's *Distinction*. It is not clear, though, that such methods are in themselves any less *performative* than survey methods. Conceptualising omnivorousness in relation to discursive expressions of tolerance for diversity, for example, assumes a shared understanding of the range of genres, activities or preferences between interviewed and interviewer. A preference for 'a bit of everything' expressed in an interview setting has a different ontological status than the selection of a range of items in a questionnaire distributed to a representative sample of a population. Without some a priori exploration of the scale and range of variety – which are, necessarily *quantitative* in nature – relying on qualitative data alone runs the risk of, as Lizardo and Skiles point out, confusing 'a superficial empirical manifestation of a phenomenon for the mechanism that produces that manifestation in the first place' (2012: 264).

One complication which has been usefully provided by qualitative studies relates to what was identified earlier as the second empirical object of the omnivore debate, the hierarchy of genres which omnivores are assumed to ignore or traverse. The relative positions of genres within these hierarchies are not matters of empirical categorisation as they might be in relation to social or occupational hierarchies. Instead they more often reflect a tacit understanding of the cultural world which is also performative. The original interventions relates to a list of some ten genres, Bryson explores patterns in relation to 18, subsequent analysis has been based on as few as four and as many as eight The construction of such a list is partly a practical problem, pertaining to both the length of a survey instrument, the legibility of categories to a broader population and the requirement to produce categories with enough answers to allow meaningful statistical work. It is also a conceptual one, requiring that genres are solid categories which mean the same to survey participants as they do to survey analysts. Silva and Wright's (2008) account of the differing interpretations of 'film noir' in a survey of British tastes indicates that reading and understanding these categories requires a priori levels of cultural experience and competence. More significantly perhaps, debates within Cultural Studies and the sociology of culture have focused attention on genres, not as identifiable aesthetic characteristics of things, but as themselves a reflection of social processes incorporating the practices and priorities of musicians, the industries in which they work, the audiences for whom they perform and the technologies through which they are managed (Beer, 2013; Frow, 2006; Lena and Peterson, 2008). Peterson's work in the 'production of culture' tradition exemplifies this, identifying how jazz music was subject to 'aesthetic mobility' – emerging as emblematic of a racialised and diminished popular music culture, but being subsequently accredited and institutionalised to also become a kind of avant-garde for US and European sophisticates (Peterson, 1972). Such movements of individual genres or practices up cultural hierarchies have also been revealed in relation to film. Baumann (2007), for example, explores the processes by which the Hollywood film moves, across the late 20th century, from exemplifying a diminished mass culture to being a recognised and revered art form. Such processes included demographic and technological changes to broader US society (the expansion of higher education, the invention of TV) and changes within the film industry itself, including shifting conceptions of the authorial role of the director and the institutionalisation of awards and festivals as strategies of evaluation that mirrored other parts of the art world. In all these movements, genres move *up* the hierarchy; it is difficult indeed to conceptualise a genre or practice that has moved in the opposite direction, albeit that internal genre differentiation allows experts and connoisseurs to mark and police their territories.

These kinds of mobility are difficult to capture within survey work – and here perhaps Bourdieu's relational approach to questions of genre hierarchy is more methodologically robust. *Distinction* does not simply reveal that classical music is the music of the upper classes, for example, but distinguishes within the genre to the extent that Strauss' *Blue Danube* can be diametrically opposed to Bach's *Well-Tempered Clavier* in the analysis of the tastes of the petit-bourgeoisie (Bourdieu, 1984: 340), in that those relatively rich in cultural capital prefer the latter and those relatively poor in cultural capital the former. Similarly, in their 'unravelling' of the omnivore, Savage and Gayo (2011), drawing on a similar analytic strategy to Bourdieu, identify the relative proximity and distance of likes and dislikes of genres with likes and dislikes of pieces of music. They find that preferences for some forms of classical music are closer to preferences for what they identify as mainstream 'easy listening' music, such as Frank Sinatra, than to the classical avant-garde such as Mahler. Importantly they, and Chan and Goldthorpe (2007) who make a similar point, partly attribute this transformation to the circulation of classical music texts through commercial radio. This might indeed be evidence of the democratising potential of the mass media, which might arguably be extended and intensified through TV and latterly digital means for the rapid and hard-to-police circulation of texts, practices and genres which were once the preserve of cultured elites.

Such divisions within groups and within genres are of course crucial to the story of the omnivore where, for good empirical reasons, both groups and genres are required to be coherent. Recognising these complexities though is important to any understanding of the omnivore as emblematic of broader social and cultural changes which are legible and accessible to the methods of empirical inquiry. The example of Heavy Metal is illustrative of this. In itself it is a complex and multi-faceted genre with a distinct history. This might be summarised as emerging from the live blues 'scene' of the industrial and manufacturing heartlands of the British West Midlands in the late 1960s, and drawing from the kitsch theatricality of glam rock, the artistic sensibilities of progressive rock in the 1970s, and, latterly, the nihilism and challenging aural aesthetics of punk. It has contained within it a significant variety of sub-genres (death-, thrash-, glam-, even *post-*), distinctions between which are hugely significant for enthusiasts, as well as a 'canon' of great works, established through interrelations between fans and specialist music journalism, which a neophyte might need to familiarise themselves with in order to enter this field. Enthusiasts might also point to the overlaps between heavy-metal and the European avant-garde tradition, identifying for example, the 2009 collaboration between Lou Reed and Metallica, inspired by the German expressionist playwright Frank Wedekind. Moreover, the genre has itself become, along with commercial pop music more generally, an object of academic inquiry in its own right, with, as Brown's (2011) review of the field suggests, its own key texts, such as Weinstein (1991). Bryson's survey analysis revealed that the genre was outside the realm of omnivorous taste in the US of the early 1990s, and moreover that it was a genre especially preferred by, and associated with the least educated groups. In the analysis of Bennett et al. (2009) and Warde et al. (2007) in the UK of the early 21st century, though, the picture was different. Here expressing a preference for heavy metal was far more likely amongst *highly* educated groups. More recent research still reveals that the popularity of heavy metal, as measured by number of bands performing, is greater in more prosperous and educated countries and regions (Florida, 2014). It would perhaps be too much of a leap to conclude from this that heavy metal has transformed itself into a form of high culture, a preference for which, in the Bourdieusian tradition, is likely to be translated into a form of cultural capital which can convey social advantages. It is, though an important indicator that genres and genre hierarchies are fluid things in which positions are liable to be contested and struggled over – and should certainly make researchers in this field cautious of re-creating any genres as new forms of 'mass' culture against which a similarly simple elite or legitimate culture can be empirically opposed. Research instruments which do not take the possibilities of these kinds of transformations into account are only ever likely to be able to give a partial insight into the relationships between cultural consumption and social organisation. This point is especially significant in contemporary versions of the omnivore debate, as the perennial empirical difficulty of placing *people* into researchable categories is matched by a proliferation of *genres* and *activities* which themselves require simplification and categorisation, and all at a time when the established sociological technologies of classification are themselves in flux. I conclude with some reflections on the implications of these changes for future discussions of cultural consumption.

## THE 'END' OF THE OMNIVORE?

This chapter has explored some methodological and conceptual limitations of research into cultural consumption, with a focus on more recent work into the cultural omnivore. In doing so my aim is not simply to critique as much as to reveal the difficulties of conducting empirical work in this field. The great contribution of work in this tradition is to provide the kinds of empirical snapshots which can be creatively debated in the light of more abstract theoretical considerations. Researchers in this tradition have established, at the very least, a powerful range of empirical evidence of the enduring relationships between cultural consumption and the organisation of social life – including evidence which troubles powerful narratives of contemporary consumer culture as free from the influence of abiding social structures. Work in this tradition also contributes to the continued complication of popular culture as 'other' to the legitimate arts. Such evidence remains useful in exploring and explaining the changes, to late-modern societies in general and to the production and circulation of culture in particular. Whilst research into the patterns of cultural consumption is likely to continue to make these contributions, the figure of the omnivore itself might become an increasingly less remarkable and distinguishable figure for two overlapping reasons.

As suggested above, the empirical objects of research in this tradition have been cultural consumers, arraigned in relation to cultural hierarchies through the operation of survey analysis, albeit more recently supplemented with ethnographic approaches. The chapter has illustrated how both the survey technique and the cultural hierarchies are rather fragile and imperfect, and these characteristics are accentuated in a contemporary context in which the authority of both are under scrutiny. Savage and Burrow's (2007) construction of an empirical crisis in contemporary sociology, brought about by the ways of knowing the social world produced by commercial interests is particularly relevant to debates about cultural consumption, where transactional data about tastes, likes and preferences are increasingly significant ways of knowing the contemporary social world. Moreover, the digital context of cultural production and circulation allows, even depends on, a proliferation of genres, with their internal differentiation, their processes of 'canonisation' and their rise and fall providing some circulating energy to cultural production and to the pleasures of cultural consumption (see Sandywell and Beer, 2005). Such techniques and practices are able to imagine and capture a much more complex figure of the cultural consumer than established methods.

Whilst surveys of cultural participation require categories to be legible enough to participants which stand for whole populations and take their findings from inferences evident in the patterns, the methods available to, say, Amazon or Spotify, allow for a data-rich picture of the person as he/she is, without his/her preferences being forced into artificially constructed categories that reflect a survey designers best approximation of the cultural world. The cultural industries themselves are more attuned to the possibilities of the former techniques of knowing their cultural consumer, making the consumer who ranges across various types of genres and practices an idealised but ordinary figure rather than an interesting and noteworthy exception. For all the historical strength of survey methods in identifying macro-level social trends, they appear increasingly slow-moving in comparison to these techniques, and are likely even to lose the authority with policymakers that was so crucial to the instigation of the omnivore debate in the first place. The actual figure of the omnivore is likely, in this process, to become less theoretically remarkable as the relations between tastes, cultural hierarchies and social life move in new directions. The energy and impetus of the omnivore debate, and the range of techniques and insights it has generated into cultural consumption, can still provide the inspiration for contemporary and future sociologists of culture as they continue to attempt to identify and analyse these relationships empirically.

# REFERENCES

Adorno, T. and Horkheimer, M. (1997 [1947]) 'The culture industry: enlightenment as mass deception', in S. During (ed.), *The Cultural Studies Reader*. London: Routledge. pp. 29–43.
Arendt, H. (1960) 'Society and Culture', *Daedalus*, 89(2): 278–87.
Atkinson, W. (2011) 'The context and genesis of musical taste: omnivorousness debunked, Bourdieu buttressed', *Poetics*, 39: 169–86.
Baumann, S. (2007) *Hollywood Highbrow: From Entertainment to Art*. Princeton: Princeton UP.
Beer, D. (2013) 'Genre, boundary drawing and the classificatory imagination', *Cultural Sociology*, 7(2): 145–60.
Bellevance, G. (2008) 'Where's high? Who's low? What's new? Classification and stratification inside cultural "repertoires"', *Poetics*, 36: 189–216.

Bennett, T. et al. (2009) *Culture, Class, Distinction*. London: Routledge.
Bourdieu, P. (1984) *Distinction: a Social Critique of the Judgment of Taste*. London: Routledge.
Brown, A.R. (2011) 'Heavy genealogy: mapping the currents, contraflows and conflicts of the emergent field of Metal Studies, 1978–2010', *Journal of Cultural Research*, 15(3): 213–42.
Bryson, B. (1996) '"Anything but heavy metal": symbolic exclusion and musical dislikes', *American Journal of Sociology*, 102(3): 884–99.
Chan, T.W. and Goldthorpe, J. (2007) 'Social stratification and cultural consumption: music in England', *European Sociological Review*, 23(1): 1–19.
Deacon, D. (2008) 'Why counting counts', in M. Pickering (ed.), *Research Methods for Cultural Studies*. Edinburgh: Edinburgh University Press. pp. 89–104.
Florida, R. (2002) *The Rise of the Creative Class*. New York: Basic Books.
Florida, R. (2014) 'How heavy metal tracks the wealth of nations', CityLab, May 24th: http://www.citylab.com/politics/2014/05/how-heavy-metal-tracks-the-wealth-of-nations/371473/
Friedman, S. (2012) 'Cultural omnivores or culturally homeless? Exploring the shifting cultural identities of the upwardly mobile', *Poetics*, 40: 467–89.
Frow, J. (2006) *Genre: The New Critical Idiom*. London: Routledge.
Gans, H. (1999 [1974]) *Popular Culture and High Culture: An Analysis and Evaluation of Taste* (revised edn.). New York: Basic.
Hall, S. and Jefferson, T. (1975) *Resistance Through Rituals*. London: Hutchinson.
Halle, D. (1993) *Inside Culture: Art and Class in the American Home*. Chicago: University of Chicago Press.
Halsey, A.H. (2004) *A History of Sociology in Britain*. Oxford: Clarendon.
Hobson, D. (1982) *Crossroads: The Drama of a Soap Opera*. London: Methuen.
Katz-Gerro, T. and Sullivan, O. (2006) 'The omnivore thesis revisited: voracious cultural consumers', *European Sociological Review*, 23(2): 123–37.
Lahire, B. (2008) 'The individual and the mixing of genres: cultural dissonance and self-distinction', *Poetics*, 36(2–3): 166–88.
Law, J. (2009) 'Seeing like a survey', *Cultural Sociology*, 3(2): 239–56.
Lazarsfeld, P.F. and Merton, R.K. (1948) 'Mass communication, popular taste, and organized social action' in L. Bryson (1948) (ed.) *The Communication of Ideas: A Series of Addresses*. New York: The Institute for Religious and Social Studies. pp. 95–118.
Lena, J. and Peterson R.A. (2008) 'Classification as culture: types and trajectories of music genres', *American Sociological Review*, 73: 697–718.

Lizardo, O. and Skiles, S. (2008) 'Highbrow omnivorousness on the small screen? Cultural industry systems and patterns of cultural choice in Europe', *Poetics*, 37(1): 1–23.

Lizardo, O. and Skiles, S. (2012) Reconceptualising and theorising "omnivorousness": genetic and relational mechanisms', *Sociological Theory*, 30(4): 263–82.

Lury, C. (1996) *Consumer Culture*. Cambridge: Polity.

Murdock, G. (1997) 'Thin descriptions: questions of method in cultural analysis', in J. McGuigan (ed.), *Cultural Methodologies*. London: Sage. pp. 178–91.

Ollivier, M. (2008) 'Modes of openness to cultural diversity: humanist, populist, practical and indifferent', *Poetics*, 36: 120–47.

Ortega y Gasett, J. (1932) *The Revolt of the Masses*. New York: W.W. Norton.

Osborne, T. and Rose, N. (1999) 'Do the social sciences create phenomena? The example of public opinion research', *British Journal of Sociology*, 50(3): 367–96.

Peterson, R.A. (1972) 'A process model of the folk, pop and fine art phases of Jazz', in C. Nanry (ed.), *American Music*. New Brunswick: Transaction Books. pp. 135–51.

Peterson, R.A. (1992) 'Understanding audience segmentation: from elite and mass to omnivore and univore', *Poetics*, 21: 243–58.

Peterson, R.A. (2005) 'Problems in comparative research: the example of omnivorousness', *Poetics*, 33: 257–82.

Peterson, R.A. and Kern, R.M. (1996) 'Changing highbrow taste: from snob to omnivore', *American Sociological Review*, 61: 900–9.

Peterson, R.A. and Rossman, G. (2008) 'Changing arts audiences: capitalizing on omnivorousness', in S. Tepper and B. Ivey (eds), *Engaging Art: The Next Great Transformation in American Life*. London: Routledge. pp. 307–42.

Peterson, R.A. and Simkus, A. (1992) 'How musical tastes mark occupational status groups', in M. Lamont and M. Fournier (eds), *Cultivating Differences*. Chicago: University of Chicago Press. pp. 152–86.

Radway, J. (1984) *Reading the Romance: Women Patriarchy and Popular Literature*. Chapel Hill: University of North Carolina Press.

Rancière, J. (2003) *The Philosopher and his Poor*. Durham: Duke University Press.

Rimmer, M. (2012) 'Beyond omnivores and univores: the promise of a concept of musical habitus', *Cultural Sociology*, 6(3): 299–318.

Sandywell, B. and Beer, D. (2005) 'Stylistic morphing: notes on the digitisation of contemporary music culture', *Convergence*, 11: 106–21.

Santoro, M. (2008) 'Producing cultural sociology: an interview with Richard A. Peterson', *Cultural Sociology*, 2(1): 33–55.

Sassatelli, R. (2007) *Consumer Culture: History, Theory, Politics*. London: Sage.

Savage, M. and Burrows, R. (2007) 'The coming crisis of empirical sociology', *Sociology*, 4(5): 885–99.

Savage, M. and Gayo, M. (2011) 'Unravelling the omnivore: a field analysis of contemporary musical taste in the United Kingdom', *Poetics*, 39: 337–57.

Silva, E.B and Wright, D. (2008) 'Researching cultural capital: complexities in mixing methods', *Methodological Innovations Online*, 2(3): 50–62.

Slater, D. (1997) *Consumer Culture and Modernity*. Cambridge: Polity.

Veblen, T. (1994 [1899]) *The Theory of the Leisure Class*. London: Macmillan.

Warde, A., Martens, L. and Olsen, W. (1999) 'Consumption and the problem of variety: cultural omnivorousness, social distinction, and dining out', *Sociology*, 33(1): 105–27.

Warde, A., Wright, D. and Gayo-Cal, M. (2007) 'Understanding cultural omnivorousness or the myth of the cultural omnivore', *Cultural Sociology*, 1(2): 143–64.

Warde, A., Wright, D. and Gayo-Cal, M. (2008) 'The omnivorous orientation in the UK', *Poetics*, 36: 148–65.

Weber, M. (1980) *General Economic History*. New Brunswick: Transaction Books.

Weinstein, D. (1991) *Heavy Metal: A Cultural Sociology*. New York: Macmillan.

Wright, D. (2011) 'Making Tastes for Everything: Omnivorousness and Cultural Abundance' *Journal for Cultural Research*, 15(4): 355–71.

Zavisca, J. (2005) 'The status of cultural omnivorism: a case study of reading in Russia', *Social Forces*, 84(2): 1233–55.

# Cultural Sociology: Brands

Sonia Bookman

## INTRODUCTION

Brands are ubiquitous elements of contemporary social and economic life. Multi-faceted market cultural forms, brands are important cultural resources for the expression of taste, the performance of identities, and the construction of common social worlds (Arvidsson, 2006; Holt, 2004). At the same time, they are sites for the management of employees, the coordination of markets, and the creation of economic value (Lury, 2004; Moor, 2007). Brands are mundane components of everyday life, integrated into shopping routines, neighbourhood streetscapes, and ordinary practices of consumption (Holt, 2006a). Yet, they also feature as spectacular elements of the 'fantasy city' (Hannigan, 1998) and in some cases, perform as tourist destinations (Evans, 2003; Miles, 2010). Not limited in their application to consumer goods, brands and branding have been adapted to an ever-widening range of commercial and non-commercial services, organizations, and locations, including urban districts (Wherry, 2011), sports teams (Rein, Kotler, and Shields 2006), universities (Hearn, 2010), health care (Ebeling, 2010) and charities (Moor, 2007). Although brands have a long history as elements of industrial capitalism (Moor, 2007), their current logic and form took shape in the 1980s (Arvidsson, 2006). As Klein (1999: 3) notes in her influential account, *No Logo*, it was during this period that management theorists promoted the idea 'that successful corporations must primarily produce brands, as opposed to products'. In addition to shifts in management theory, however, the rise of brands and branding is associated with a complex of factors, including but not limited to: developments in, and expanded roles for, marketing, design, and media in consumer culture; the shift towards flexible, globalized systems of production; the advancement of corporate systems of brand valorization; and developments in legal regimes (intellectual property, trademark) that serve to protect and promote the brand (Arvidsson, 2006; Lury, 2004; Moor, 2007).

Academic attention to brands and branding has grown, especially since the 1990s (Pike, 2011). However, as Holt (2006a) argues in the introduction to a special issue on brands in the *Journal of Consumer Culture*, much of this attention has been confined to business schools: 'While marketing gurus assign to brands near-religious powers, academics and critics have largely ignored brands except to shake their heads in disgust' (2006a: 300). Nonetheless, there is a growing literature on brands outside of marketing, with important contributions from fields as diverse as geography (Catungal and Leslie, 2009; Harris, 2011; Pike, 2009), architecture and urban design (Evans, 2003; Jensen, 2007; Julier, 2005, 2011; Klingmann, 2007), cultural studies (Gibson, 2005; Gutzmer, 2014), communications (Aronczyk and Powers, 2010), and sociology (Arvidsson, 2006; Holt, 2004; Lury, 2004; Miles, 2010; Moor, 2007).

In this chapter, I will outline the contours of an emerging sociology of brands, and discuss the significance of this scholarship for cultural sociology. I begin by identifying key theoretical developments and sociological perspectives on brands. This is followed by a discussion of some of the ways in which sociological accounts of brands and branding contribute to developments and debates in cultural sociology, focusing on the areas of cultural economy, cultural work and intermediaries, as well as cultural consumption and global cultural flows. I then outline some recent developments in the field, featuring work that examines issues of corporate social responsibility (CSR) and urban branding. Finally, the chapter concludes with a discussion of possible directions for future research in the ongoing development of a sociology of brands and branding.

## KEY LINES OF THOUGHT

An emerging sociology of brands and branding has mainly taken shape over the past decade or so. It is characterized by at least two key perspectives, each of which posits a different view of brands and their relationships to production, consumption, and culture. These perspectives can be broadly categorized as symbolic approaches on the one hand, and new media perspectives on the other. Here, I briefly summarize the main elements and variations within each perspective, noting important points of divergence between them.

### *Symbolic Approaches*

Symbolic approaches to brands and branding proffer a view of the brand as a symbolic device – an idea, image, or story – constituted through processes of visual imaging, narration, and association. The brand as form of symbolic culture is harnessed as a resource by corporations and consumers alike. For companies, the brand is a key site of value creation and source of advantage in a globalized neoliberal economy where manufacturing is increasingly outsourced, liberalized markets create opportunities for brand-led expansion, and the trade in culture and experience is foregrounded (Holt, 2006a; Klein, 1999). For consumers, brands are cultural resources used in processes of self-fashioning and expression. They operate as aesthetic markers of taste and are bound up with the performance of lifestyles and distinction (Featherstone, 1991; Holt, 2004; 2006a).

There are at least two main theoretical strands within symbolic approaches to brands. One consists of a critical political economy perspective that is associated with the work of Naomi Klein (1999), and is especially prominent in sociological accounts of urban brands and branding (i.e. Greenberg, 2008; Hannigan, 2003; also see Zukin, 1995). This perspective maintains a dual concern with the growing role of brands in the neoliberal economy, on the one hand, and the impact of manufactured culture on society, on the other. According to this view, companies such as Nike have turned their attention to the construction of brand images in virtual 'brand factories' where value is created through design and innovation, marketing, and display. No longer in the business of selling goods (which are interchangeable) and free from the 'weight' of production, brand-led companies now sell ideas, values, and lifestyles (Klein, 1999).

Inspired by Marxist thought, brands are understood to extend the process of commodity fetishism. As Greenberg (2008: 31) asserts: 'branding not only makes the "mystical veil" which hides the social origins of the commodity that much thicker, but creates a veritable industry for the production and circulation of mystical veils and devises methods for knitting these together to give the illusion of totality'. Branding thus deepens the disarticulation of branded goods from their circumstances of production and contributes to the devaluing of production. At the same time it creates new, manufactured meanings for goods and services, which consumers are invited to identify with. For writers in this vein, brands are understood to have a degenerative effect on culture since they manipulate meanings for profit and 'colonize' otherwise authentic or non-commercial cultures (such as cultures of sport in the case of Nike) as well as the spaces in which brands are staged (i.e. Burkitt, 1998; Goldman and Papson, 1998; Greenberg, 2008; Klein, 1999).

A second variation of the symbolic approach suggests a more complex view of the culture of brands. Moving beyond 'old formulations of false consciousness', this perspective maintains that brands and their meanings are not simply foisted on consumers (Holt, 2006a: 301). Rather, brands as symbolic culture are cultivated over time through collective, even conflictual processes of narration, performance, and use

(Holt, 2004; Jackson, Russell, and Ward, 2011; Wherry, 2011). Holt (2004: 3), for instance, asserts that brands are narrated by a host of 'authors' with varying degrees of influence, including 'companies, the culture industries, intermediaries (such as critics and retail salespeople), and customers (particularly when they form communities)'. Brands emerge when the stories told about them converge and crystallize; in other words, when 'collective understandings become firmly established' (Holt, 2004: 3).

For Holt (2004), there are distinctive types of brand, which require different strategies for the creation of brand value. Only some brands have significant cultural influence in society due to their symbolism. These are what he refers to as 'iconic brands', defined as 'consensus expressions of particular values held dear by some members of a society' (Holt, 2004: 4). Iconic brands encompass brands that have significant 'identity value' for consumers who use them as a means of self-expression. Identity brands that become iconic are those whose 'identity myths' most resonate with the imaginations, aspirations, and anxieties of a public in a particular moment (Holt, 2004: 8). Such myths – which are ideological – are not invented by brands; instead, they tap into and promote existing culture (Holt, 2006b). Holt points to the example of Budweiser, whose success can be attributed to the brand's ability to address the 1980s crisis of masculinity in the United States (wherein historical masculine ideals were increasingly brought under question) (Holt, 2004). In this sense, brands are seen to have a parasitic relationship to culture: rather than reworking present symbolism and denigrating culture, iconic brands 'typically enjoin and embellish existing myth markets', contributing to their diffusion in everyday life (Holt, 2006b: 372).

## New Media Perspectives

New media perspectives propose a notion of the brand as a kind of frame that carries out an 'orchestration of information' (Lash, 2002: 148) and that operates as 'a platform for the patterning of activity, a mode of organizing activities in time and space' (Lury, 2004: 1). Brands are moreover considered to be complex market forms that manage and articulate production and consumption, contributing to the organization and shaping of markets (Lury, 2011). In this view, brands are not only symbolic; rather, they are multidimensional, informational objects comprised of various material and immaterial elements, layers, and processes (Lury, 2011; Lash and Lury, 2007; Moor, 2007).

New media approaches to the brand are especially associated with Celia Lury's extensive work on branding. In her book, *Brands: The Logos of the Global Economy* (2004), Lury discusses several reasons as to why the brand can be considered a new media object. Chief among these are: the operation of the brand as an interface; the informational nature of the brand and its power; and the incorporation of programming techniques associated with computing.

For Lury (2004), the brand is an interface of communication that, like a frame, serves to connect and separate inner environments of production and outer environments of consumption and everyday life across disparate times and spaces. It acts as a communicative meeting point, organizing a two-way, though asymmetrical 'exchange of information', which is 'a matter not merely of qualitative calculation, but also of affect, intensivity, and the re-introduction of qualities' (2004: 7). Such information is conveyed through the functioning of the interface; the mobilization of a patterning of activity which involves the organization and ordering of relations between products and services, producers and consumers. Accordingly, the production of brands is not distinct from the configuration of goods and services, as suggested by symbolic approaches. Rather, brands are intricately bound up with various aspects of production, from the design of products and servicescapes to the work of employees, all of which help to establish the qualities, values, and emotion associated to the brand.

The informational nature and power of brands relates to their operation as devices for capital accumulation in a postindustrial, informational economy. Brands establish boundaries around information that they claim as their own. The information inside the frame – which makes the brand marketable *as* a brand – is protected in law as private, intellectual property. This allows companies to valorize such information and its uses, while excluding others (Lash, 2002; Lury, 2004). Moreover, branding activity and innovation involves the incorporation of information about competitors and consumption, for instance, through marketing practices that Lury describes as 'looping devices' (similar to computer programming) (2011: 151). These include online feedback mechanisms and other forms of data collection such as loyalty cards, which offer a constant source of information about consumer tastes, preferences, and behaviour. Such information, Lury maintains, enables brands to adapt to consumer activity and develop products based on consumption trends.

Building on Lury's work, Arvidsson forwards a critical variation of the new media perspective, arguing that the brand is 'a paradigmatic embodiment of the logic of informational capitalism' due to its ability to harness the immaterial labour of consumers – their autonomous communicative capacity – which is appropriated and made into brand value (2006: 7). In his book, *Brands: Meaning and Value in Media Culture* (2006), Arvidsson forwards a notion of the brand as a 'frame of action' that offers consumers mediated contexts for being, feeling, or acting in a particular way with the brand (2006: 8). Individuals are encouraged use brands as a means to construct meanings, express identities, and create common worlds. Such productive activity is central to the realization of brand identity and the achievement of brand 'value-in-use' (Zwick, Bonsu, and Darmody, 2008) wherein 'brand identity – the context of action that the brand represents – becomes a real use-value that people are prepared to pay extra for' (Arvidsson, 2006: 82).

Brand management plays a key role in this view, since it works to assemble contexts of consumption with the aim of guiding consumer activity and attention in ways that will add to rather than detract from desired brand image. This involves the use of immersive marketing strategies such as event marketing and themed environments, alongside advertising and the cultivation of online media settings designed to enable constructive brand-consumer performances. In this way, branding operates according to a model of 'advanced liberal' governance (Barry, 2001; also see Rose, 1999) that does not impose ideas or a structure of tastes, but rather 'works *with* the freedom of consumers' whose consumption activity is supported via the brand (Arvidsson, 2006: 8, emphasis in original).

Central to new media perspectives are three key aspects that serve to distinguish them from symbolic approaches – especially critical variations. First, the brand is based on an interactive new media model, in which information flows are not simply one-way but are multi-directional, if uneven. Second, the brand is conceptualized as open-ended; while it is programmed and managed to operate in a certain manner, as Lury (2004: 51) suggests, brands are also 'complex, indeterminate or open' objects. In particular, they are entangled in various relations in which brands are used, related to, and transformed, and through which they are spun into everyday life (Arvidsson, 2006; Lury, 2004). Third, the brand is performative; more than the sum of its parts, the brand emerges through the mobilization of a pattern of activity and a process of relationality among the products and/or services it organizes and with its broader environment, which includes consumption and everyday life (Lury, 2004; Moor, 2007). The performative nature of the brand not only generates brand image and value, it also shapes broader facets of social and cultural life.

Taken together, these aspects imply a greater role for consumers in the co-creation of brands than proposed by symbolic approaches; moreover, their role is not limited to mainly symbolic forms of engagement (such as interpretation or narration) but is also informational and involves embodied practices, or is a matter of what consumers 'do' with the brand. In addition, they suggest that such entanglements of consumers and brands are co-generative of cultures and social life. In this sense brands do not straightforwardly 'colonize' culture or parasitically ride on its coattails, but are involved in a dynamic interplay with consumers through which brands, cultures, and identities surface and take form.

## BRANDS AND CULTURAL SOCIOLOGY

As market cultural forms and salient aspect of everyday life, brands are at once economic, social, and cultural entities. Addressing the multi-faceted dimensions of brands, sociological accounts contribute to a wide range of discussion and debate within the field of cultural sociology. In this section, I chart some key contributions in the areas of cultural economy and work, cultural consumption, and the impact of global cultural flows. In the following section, I consider how the recent focus on urban branding offers further insights regarding configurations of urban cultures.

### *Cultural Economy*

Numerous accounts have examined the relationship of brands to the cultural economy, which is variably referred to as postmodern (Holt, 2006a), postindustrial (Lury, 2011; Miles, 2010), experience-oriented (Hannigan, 2003), informational (Arvidsson, 2006; Lash, 2002); and entrepreneurial (Cronin and Hetherington, 2008; Greenberg, 2008). In general, and despite significant conceptual differences, these accounts suggest that the rise of brands goes hand-in-hand with the rise of an economy based on information, signs, and symbols rather than manufacturing.

For some analysts, this marks a shift whereby the economy and culture have merged. Brands, in this view, provide insight into the fusion of the economic and cultural realms. For those writing in the postmodern tradition, brands reflect a culturalization of the economy, which is increasingly driven by the production of signs. The rise of brands is understood as part of the broader aestheticization of everyday life, including the economy (Featherstone, 1991; Lash and Urry, 1994). Those writing in the critical political economy tradition, on the other hand, suggest that brands represent a commodification of culture, which is flattened out and condensed into image form in order to invest goods with symbolic significance (Greenberg, 2008; Klein, 1999; Zukin, 1995). One variation suggests that the commodification of culture is bound up with the process of mediatization, whereby a commercialized Media Culture has 'expanded to infuse virtually all walks of life' (Arvidsson, 2006: 12; also see Hjarvard, 2013). The media, in this view, provide an 'ambiance' for everyday life; they are platforms for the performance of daily activities and 'places' where people have experiences. As such, the brand (as new media object) is seen as 'but one aspect of a general movement towards the commodification and capitalist appropriation of the bio-political framework in which life unfolds' (Arvidsson, 2006: 13). Another strand, however, maintains that brands operate as a form of promotional culture in a context where promotionalism – an outcome of creeping commercialization - has affected all aspects of social life (Aronczyk and Powers, 2010; Wernick, 1991). In each of these versions, however, the rise of brands is ultimately related to the expansion of capital and the economy into the realm of culture and everyday life.

Parallel to arguments about advertising and the economy, accounts focusing on the fusion of culture and economy, whether in the postmodern or critical political economy traditions, nonetheless tend to problematically assume a (previous) separation of culture and economy (McFall, 2004). Alternatively, various scholars maintain that the rise of brands reflects particular (re)configurations of economy and culture, based on an assumption that these are not separate spheres, but are mutually constitutive and interdependent (Lury, 2004; Moor, 2007). Writers in this vein point to the insights brands offer into specific, symbiotic economic and cultural shifts. For example, Lury and Moor (2010) show how the significance of brands has grown alongside new methods of valuation designed to capture 'intangibles' such as brand reputation or the impact of a company's corporate social responsibility initiatives, otherwise known as 'triple bottom-line' accounting. These methods, which aim to translate a range of qualitative features into financial values and other kinds of quantitative calculation, not only measure brand value, but help to create the value of brands and guide their ongoing development (Lury and Moor, 2010). For Lury and Moor (2010), brand valuation techniques reflect both a change in the 'economic value form' as well as a shift towards a 'topological culture' which provides a new logic for economic systems.

In this vein, analysts have explored a range of cultural and economic developments related to the rise of brands and branding, such as: the establishment of intellectual property rights through which brands can accrue rents (Lury, 2004); the expanded role of design in late modern economies and its growing entanglement with production (Julier and Moor, 2009; Moor, 2007); and the rise of entrepreneurial urban governance and its link to urban branding (Cronin and Hetherington, 2008). Overall, such accounts provide more nuanced understanding of the complex yet specific array of economic, institutional, technical, social, and cultural arrangements involved in the ongoing development of brands and the cultural economies in which they operate.

## Cultural Intermediaries, Cultural Work

Since Bourdieu's (1984) discussion of new cultural intermediaries in *Distinction*, there has been considerable debate regarding who counts as a cultural intermediary and why (Hesmondhalgh, 2002; Nixon and du Gay, 2002; Smith Maguire and Matthews, 2012). The term, cultural intermediary, is used to describe groups of workers involved in the production of cultural goods and services. Such workers construct value for goods by framing their meanings and use, and shaping notions of legitimate culture. Since this can potentially include 'any creative or cultural occupation or institution' (Smith Maguire and Matthews, 2012: 552), not to mention a whole gamut of creative 'prosumers' (Ritzer, Dean, and Jurgenson, 2012), concerted effort has been made to delineate the notion in order to maintain its conceptual utility (Nixon and du Gay, 2002; Smith Maguire and Matthews, 2012.).

Sociological accounts of brands and branding have contributed to this effort. Specifically, Moor (2008) has proposed that branding consultants be considered cultural intermediaries. The argument is that branding consultants are involved in cultural production by engaging in processes of translation – the communication of a set of values and qualities associated with the brand via a wide range of visual and material media. This work is carried out by trained designers who understand the relationship between various media and their cultural associations, and who claim the capacity to 'connect' with targeted audiences in terms of their expertise on trends and tastes. However, while branding consultants are understood to have significant influence on material culture – the design of goods and services as well as the spaces in which they are consumed – Moor cautions against attributing them too much power in the shaping of consumer tastes and dispositions. Moor's work thus advances the notion of cultural intermediary (also see Moor [2012], in which she argues for a recognition of various devices as intermediaries) and differentiates such intermediaries in terms of their practices, dispositions, and impacts.

In addition to debates about cultural intermediaries, sociological accounts have reflected on cultural work more broadly as it relates to brands and branding. For the most part, analysts have focused on the work of employees who, for example, deliver services as part of the brand. Contributing to discussions regarding the 'aesthetics of labour' (Witz, Warhurst, and Nickerson, 2003) and the configuration of employees as enterprising subjects (du Gay, 1996), such accounts have shown that the nature of work in brand regimes is increasingly aesthetic, on the one hand, and entrepreneurial, on the other.

Within contemporary processes of branding, employees are considered an important element of the material and visual environment designed to communicate brand qualities, comprising a key point of contact with consumers. Expected to embody the brand and convey brand values to consumers, employees are increasingly subject to a process of 'performatting', wherein 'workers are trained in the stylistics of performance and moreover a particular performance or consumer interface is attributed to specific brands' (Adkins, 2005: 123). The work performed by brand employees in this context is not only functional, but is primarily affective and aesthetic, and is oriented towards consumers as part of the brand experience. For example, Starbucks baristas are not only trained to provide high quality customized coffee beverages, but also to extend hospitality and co-construct a sense of community with patrons through smalltalk and other types of 'third place' (Oldenburg, 1989) social interaction (Bookman, 2014b). As Lury argues, this has important implications for 'the incorporation, marginalisation and exclusion of particular social groups *as producers or workers*' (2004: 34) since it privileges those who most closely conform to the aesthetics of a service organization or consumer interface.

At the same time, the labour of brand employees is configured as entrepreneurial. This is related in part to a growing emphasis on internal marketing (Lury, 2004) or 'internal branding' premised on the idea that 'if employees fully understand and appreciate their brand they will be better able to provide the desired brand experience to consumers' (Fan, 2005: 345; also see Knude and Cunningham, 2002). In other words, employees are encouraged to 'live the brand' by adapting brand philosophies and values to their own lifestyles. This involves employees voluntarily cultivating cultural capital and conducting performances that reflect brand principles, and requires that they 'consider their work as a means of adding value to themselves' (Lury, 2004: 35). Through its involvement in the organization of work, the brand can thus be seen to operate as a device of employee management: it 'performats' (aesthetic) labour, yet makes employees responsible for their own performances and work trajectories in brand regimes (Lury, 2004; also see Bookman and Martens, 2013; Shamir, 2008).

## *Cultural Consumption*

Brand theorists have considered the relationship between brands and consumption, arguing that the rise of brands is closely related to the emergence and expansion of contemporary consumer culture (Arvidsson, 2006; Aronczyk and Powers, 2011; Lury, 2011). A growing body of work in this area has contributed to debates regarding the nature of consumption in relation to brands, as well as the social and cultural effects of brand-consumer engagement, particularly the impact of 'global' brands on 'local' cultures.

Accounts of brands and cultural consumption offer significantly different conceptualizations of consumers and the ways in which they engage with brands. Scholars who take a symbolic approach to brands tend to view consumers as 'readers' or 'story tellers' who reflexively consume brands as part of a process of self-expression or identification and 'to enact the basic status and affiliation processes that are the bread-and-butter functions of all symbols' (Holt, 2006b: 357). In this view, consumers encounter brands as media texts whose meanings they either accept, reject, or more commonly negotiate based on differentiated social positions and situated preferences, following Hall's (1980) encoding/decoding model of communication.

Analysts in the new media tradition, however, consider consumers as 'users' or 'prosumers' involved in the very co-production of the brands they consume through the incorporation of information about consumers (Lury, 2004), or the adaption of consumer activity in the realization of brand identity and value (Arvidsson, 2006). In this view, consumers encounter brands as open-ended objects or frames that implicate and enable a broad range of consumer activity (beyond symbolic communication) and involvement with brands. Instead of focusing on consumer preferences, writers in this vein place more emphasis on consumer practices (Warde, 2005) – or what consumers *do* with brands and the frames they afford. At the same time, the structuring nature of brands suggests that brands are not straightforwardly integrated into existing consumer practices, but actively shape these in a dynamic interplay. Drawing on practice theory, brands can be understood as elements of an 'infrastructure of particular practices' that organize practices and influence consumption patterns, which are more than the outcome of individual choice and a matter of self- expression (Warde, 2012: 414; also see Arsel and Bean, 2013).

An expanding range of studies have examined just what is it consumers do with brands, and the various social and cultural implications of their involvement. Scholars have explored the role of brands in the formation and expression of social identities and lifestyles (Cormack, 2008; Holt, 2004; Lury, 2011), as well as brand communities (Muñiz and O'Guinn, 2001; Schau, Muñiz, and Arnould, 2009) or socialities (Arvidsson, 2006; Bookman, 2014b). For example, Cormack (2008) examines how the Canadian coffee brand, Tim Hortons, has become an important source and site of Canadian identity. An 'iconic brand' (Holt, 2004), Tim Hortons is closely associated with Canadian culture through a range of marketing strategies (advertising, sponsorship, and social responsibility initiatives) designed to align the brand with the stories and activities of 'ordinary Canadians'. Such accounts illustrate how brands have become increasingly important cultural resources for the expression of social identities such as national, class-based, or gender identities, as well as articulations of social belonging. At the same time, they operate as sites for cultural capital accumulation and constitute a source of social differentiation, marking and shaping differences in tastes and values in multi-layered processes of distinction.

Analysts have also considered some of the ways in which brand consumption shapes or gives rise to specific local, urban, and global cultures. Studies have examined how brands are spun into popular cultural discourses (Holt, 2006b), shape everyday practices and ways of life (Arsel and Bean, 2013; Arvidsson, 2006; Holt, 2006b); configure spaces of consumption (Hannigan, 2003; Jayne, 2006; Miles, 2010) and structure leisure cultures (Chatterton and Hollands, 2003; Hannigan, 1998). One strand of work in this arena has been concerned with the social and cultural impact of 'global' brands. While the term 'global' is often used to refer to brands of multinational companies that are circulated on an international scale (such as McDonalds, which has restaurants in more than a hundred countries around the world), it is important to note that brands can also be 'global' with regard to their image (for example, The Body Shop, which features ingredients and beauty rituals from around the world in its products, communications, and branded environments) (see Lury, 2000).

Various accounts suggest that global brands are de-territorialized, and constitute a homogenizing global cultural force (Klein, 1999; Klingmann, 2007; Lash, 2002). Yet many scholars recognize the interplay between global brands and local cultures, arguing for more nuanced understandings of the heterogeneous ways in which global brands are adapted by individuals to express aspects of 'local' culture and identity (Jackson, 2004; Luna-Garcia, 2008; Miles, 2010). Scholars who draw on new media approaches to brands, moreover, suggest that the consumption of global brands is co-generative of both 'local' cultures and brands themselves (Bookman, 2013; 2014a), including the spaces in which they operate (Yakhlef, 2004). For example, Bookman (2013) argues that the dynamic interplay between urban Canadian consumers, their everyday coffee consumption practices, and Starbucks' global café brandscape (featuring multilingual menu boards and coffees from around the world) generates a situated, cosmopolitan 'cool' as a source of middle-class sentiment, identity, and distinction in localized class relations and coffee markets.

## RECENT DIRECTIONS

As the sociology of brands and branding has expanded, scholars have pursued many, diverse lines of inquiry. Here I focus on two recent directions in the field: urban branding and corporate social responsibility.

### *Urban Branding, Urban Cultures*

Urban branding has garnered considerable attention among academics in a variety of disciplinary traditions. The issue of urban branding was raised in early sociological accounts of the rise of the symbolic economy of cities and the reconfiguration of postindustrial cities as 'fantasy cities' – sites of consumption, culture, and entertainment (Hannigan, 1998; Zukin, 1995). Still, branding was not the main focus of these studies. With the publication of a special symposium on branding, entertainment, and place-making by Hannigan (2003), and Greenberg's (2008) award-winning book, *Branding New York*, however, urban branding has begun to receive more sustained sociological attention.

Urban branding involves the application of commercial branding techniques to urban spaces or the city as a whole. It is increasingly widespread in entrepreneurial cities characterized by an emphasis on image promotion as a key strategy for local economic development (Hall and Hubbard, 1998; Hannigan, 2003; Zukin, 2008). In this context, branding practices have been deployed by urban governments and private-public assemblages seeking to 're-image perceptions of urban space and transform the way it is consumed' (Harris, 2011: 188). Bound up with culture-led redevelopment and revitalization (Jayne, 2006; Miles and Paddison, 2005), urban branding involves an emphasis on the cultivation of cities' consumer cultures (Cronin and Hetherington, 2008), tourist geographies (Bell and Jayne, 2004), and, more recently, 'creativity' (Arvidsson, 2011; Peck, 2005), with the aim of attracting businesses, tourists, and so-called 'creative' workers.

Sociological accounts have focused on different aspects of urban brands and branding. Scholars have drawn attention to the linkages between urban branding and neoliberal governance (Greenberg, 2008; Zukin, 1995). For example, Greenberg (2008: 10) outlines a dual role for urban branding, which is to reimage the city via place marketing, on the one hand, and restructure the city with a series of pro-business reforms, on the other. Some analysts have examined how urban brands afford opportunities to 'enlist' various populations in the performance of a particular image (Arvidsson, 2011; Bookman and Woolford, 2013; Moor, 2007). In these accounts, urban branding can be understood as 'an *extension* of an entrepreneurial model of governance' (Rantisi and Leslie, 2006: 364), whereby responsibility for revitalization, for instance, is downloaded to urban residents, tourists, or business owners. Still others have been concerned with the way brands create new spaces of consumption and the paradoxical effects of these, which both structure space and activity, on the one hand, and enable new experiences, identities, and pleasures, on the other (Hannigan, 1998; 2003; Miles, 2010; Young, Diep, and Drabble, 2006).

A central theme of this literature, and source of debate, concerns the effect of brands on the cultures of cities (Chatterton and Hollands, 2003; Cronin and Hetherington, 2008; Greenberg, 2008; Hannigan, 2003; Miles, 2010; Zukin, 1995; 1998). Some writers, especially in the critical political economy tradition, address issues regarding commodification and the privatization of urban space. As Greenberg maintains, the branded city is 'increasingly transformed from a real place of value and meaning for residents and workers to an abstract space for capital investment and profit-making, and a commodity for broader consumption' (2008: 36). Such commodification, it is argued, involves a shift in control over urban space, which is increasingly in the preserve of corporations and private-public coalitions of elites who overhaul the image of an urban district or city and impose a dominant vision. This raises concerns with regard to the definition of urban culture. As Zukin (1995: 3) indicates, those with the power to produce a vision of public culture also define it: 'those who create images stamp a collective identity'. Related to this concern, some accounts further emphasize the decline of cultural diversity. The argument is that city branding, intended to differentiate cities and their consumer cultures, involves familiar strategies – branded museums and entertainment districts anchored by global media and retail brands – that render cities less rather than more distinct (Chatterton and Hollands, 2003; Evans, 2003; Hannigan, 2003). Still others concentrate on the surfacing of particular urban cultures through entanglements of urban brands in geographically and historically situated social and cultural worlds (Bookman, 2014a; Harris, 2011; Wherry, 2011).

Throughout this literature, and despite differences in theoretical orientation, there is a shared concern with the implications of urban branding for for social and cultural divisions and inequalities. Indeed, many scholars argue that urban branding serves to highlight and deepen existing socio-spatial divisions in cities through its relation to gentrification, as well as uneven urban development (Bell and Jayne, 2004; Catungal and Leslie, 2009; Greenberg, 2008; Hannigan, 1998; Young, Diep, and Drabble, 2006). Nonetheless, some scholars point to the possibilities of counter-branding as a mode of resistance or reclaiming urban space (Greenberg, 2008; Julier, 2011). Julier (2011: 214), for example, forwards a notion of counter-branding as an instance of 'design activism'. In this view, counter-branding involves the development of platforms that enable a range of 'alternative actions' (Julier, 2011: 214) and aim to mobilize 'local enthusiasms', which are oriented toward enacting 'a more equal and inclusive practice of urban life' (2011: 214). The potential of counter-branding in terms of its application and effectiveness, however, requires further study.

## Corporate Social Responsibility

The growth of CSR from the 1980s and 1990s has been met by a proliferation of work on CSR programs, especially in the fields of marketing and business. Some attention has also been directed to CSR in recent sociological accounts of brands and branding. CSR is an important area of investigation since brands are increasingly involved in aspects of environmental and social responsibility, reflecting a movement towards the 'moralization of markets' (Shamir, 2008; Stehr, 2008). Many companies have adapted CSR as part of their core values and philosophies, establishing CSR departments and board committees, engaging in cause-related marketing, and featuring socially responsible initiatives in brand communications. Moreover, 'global' brands such as MTV and Starbucks have been increasingly involved with non-governmental organizations and international political institutions such as the UN as part of an effort to 'advance responsible corporate citizenship so that business can be part of the solution to the challenges of globalisation' (United Nations, 2005).

Within the sociological work on brands and CSR, some accounts have shown how CSR is deeply inscribed into brands, arguing that brands have become a key site for the communication of values and ethics of responsibility. For example, Moor and Littler (2008) critically analyse how American Apparel conveys an anti-sweatshop ethos through the coordination of 'neo-Fordist' production in the United States instead of outsourcing manufacturing to places where workers rights are at risk. The company communicates its ethics via the use of advertising and design (such as the implementation of a minimalist aesthetic in its retail stores) in order to achieve a 'transparency effect' (Moor and Littler, 2008: 703). Moor and Littler demonstrate how CSR is patterned as part of the brand interface in ways that extend far beyond cause-related marketing, illustrating how morals are conveyed through a range of brand elements such as architecture and space.

Another strand of work considers how CSR is integrated into processes of brand management as a tool for the organization of cultural work and consumption activity. Accounts have shown how CSR contributes to the responsibilization of employees and consumers by offering specific frames through which responsibility can be enacted (Bookman and Martens, 2013; Caruana and Crane, 2008; Shamir, 2008). Employees are called on to volunteer in brand-led socially responsible initiatives such as Earth Day events, where ethical performances form another dimension of entrepreneurial, aesthetic labour. Consumers too, are invited to engage in brand-sponsored fundraisers or simply to purchase 'ethical' products. Such brand-led practices, it is argued, not only contribute to the emergence of a socially responsible brand image, they also co-produce particular discourses of responsibility – what it means to be, act, and feel responsible towards the environment and others in society (Bookman and Martens, 2013).

Overall, these accounts illustrate the growing significance of CSR for brands and the shaping of moral markets. In addition, they raise concerns regarding the involvement of myriad actors and auspices in the performance of particular notions of social responsibility.

## CONCLUSION: POSSIBLE FUTURE DIRECTIONS

Almost a decade has passed since Holt (2006a) aimed to jumpstart a sociology of brands in the special issue on brands in the *Journal of Consumer Culture*. While this period has seen important theoretical developments and growth in empirical studies, a sociology of brands and branding is still emerging and there is much scope for further work. Many aspects of brands and branding remain underexplored, while new developments call for renewed investigation.

It is important to consider how branding evolves in relation to new developments in media. In recent years, the rise of mobile and social media, for instance, have generated new forms of mobile marketing and consumption (as well as a whole host of new brands) that not only influence brand configurations but have significant implications for the ways in which consumers relate to and use brands. For example, 'brand in the hand' mobile marketing (Rohm et al., 2012) allows brands to forge connections with consumers 'on the go', shaping new kinds of urban mobility, sociality, and cultures. Platforms such as Foursquare and Facebook Places are used by consumer brands to generate location-based advertising and encourage loyalty by offering awards for frequent check-ins. At the same time, they allow users to share their location with friends, offering new possibilities for 'spontaneous' social interactions whilst 'on the move' (de Souza e Silva and Firth, 2012). The social and cultural implications of such 'brand mobilities' are still emerging, however, and mobile strategies continue to evolve, suggesting the need for further, ongoing empirical research to grasp their unfolding effects.

In addition, as urban branding continues to expand throughout entrepreneurial cities, it is important to conduct more empirical work regarding the impact of urban brands on urban space and cultures. In particular, there remains a lack of empirical examination of the ways in which urban brands are encountered and used by urban dwellers, which is important for developing insight into the role of brands in shaping metropolitan cultures and everyday life. Moreover, avenues for, and cases of, urban counter-branding could be further explored. Such work can move beyond symbolic perspectives, which focus on visual and representational modes of resistance, by drawing on Juliers' (2011) notion of counter-branding as a matter of alternative design. Investigations along these lines could consider how different populations might engage counter-branding for the purposes of reclaiming or reworking urban space and forwarding agendas such as the 'right to the city' (Harvey, 2012).

Finally, while there has been growth in the empirical examination of brands, including some detailed brand genealogies (Greenberg, 2008; Holt, 2004; 2006b), much of the empirical work concentrates on aspects of brand production in terms of brand management, design, valuation, and marketing strategies, for example. Less attention has been paid to the involvement of cultural workers and employees in branding, especially those working the 'front lines' in retail and services. Moreover, there continues to be a paucity of sociological research on the ways that the variety of brands are used, consumed, and transformed in everyday life, as well as the kinds of practices brands support. Such empirical work is crucial for ongoing theoretical developments in the field, as well as the development of new and further research agendas.

## REFERENCES

Adkins, L. (2005) 'The new economy, property and personhood', *Theory, Culture & Society*, 22(1): 111–30.

Aronczyk, M. and Powers, D. (2010) 'Introduction: Blowing up the brand', in M. Aronczyk and D. Power (eds), *Blowing Up the Brand*. New York: Peter Lang Publishing, Inc. pp. 1–26.

Arsel, Z. and Bean, J. (2013) 'Taste Regimes and Market-Mediated Practice', *Journal of Consumer Research*, 39(5): 899–917.

Arvidsson, A. (2006) *Brands: Meaning and Value in Media Culture*. London: Routledge.

Arvidsson, A. (2011) 'Creativity, brands, finance and beyond: Notes towards a theoretical perspective on city branding', in A. Pike (ed.), *Brands and Branding Geographies*. Cheltenham, UK: Edward Elgar. pp. 305–23.

Barry, A. (2001) *Political Machines: Governing a Technological Society*. London: Athlone Press.

Bell, D. and Jayne, M. (2004) 'Conceptualizing the city of quarters', in D. Bell and M. Jayne (eds), *City of Quarters: Urban Villages in the Contemporary City*. Aldershot, UK: Ashgate. pp. 1–14.

Bookman, S. (2013) 'Branded cosmopolitanisms: "Global" coffee brands and the co-creation of "cosmopolitan cool"', *Cultural Sociology*, 7(1): 56–72.

Bookman, S. (2014a) 'Urban brands, culture and social division: Creativity, tension and differentiation among middle class consumers', *Journal of Consumer Culture*, 14(3): 324–42.

Bookman, S. (2014b) 'Brands and urban life: Specialty coffee, consumers and the co-creation of urban café sociality', *Space and Culture*, 17(1): 85–99.

Bookman, S. and Martens, C. (2013) 'Responsibilization and governmentality in social partnerships', in M. Seitanidi and A. Crane (eds), *Social Partnerships and Responsible Business: A Research Handbook*. Oxford: Routledge. pp. 288–305.

Bookman, S. and Woolford, A. (2013) 'Policing (by) the brand: Urban branding, private police and social exclusion', *Social and Cultural Geography*, 14(3): 300–17.

Bourdieu, P. (1984) *Distinction: A Social Critique of the Judgment of Taste*. Translated by R. Nice. London: Routledge.

Burkett, I. (1998) 'Coca-community: Corporately imagined communities and the colonization of place', *Development*, (41): 59–64.

Caruana, R. and Crane, A. (2008) 'Constructing consumer responsibility: Exploring the role of corporate communications', *Organization Studies*, 29(12): 1495–519.

Catungal, J. and Leslie, D. (2009) 'Placing power in the creative city: Governmentalities and subjectivities in Liberty Village, Toronto', *Environment and Planning A*, 41(11): 2576–94.

Chatterton, P. and Hollands, R. (2003) 'Producing nightlife in the new urban entertainment economy: Corporatization, branding and market segmentation', *International Journal of Urban and Regional Research*, 27(2): 361–84.

Cormack, P. (2008) 'True stories' of Canada: Tim Hortons and the branding of national identity', *Cultural Sociology*, 2(3): 369–84.

Cronin, A. and Hetherington, K. (2008) 'Introduction', in A. Cronin and K. Hetherington (eds), *Consuming the Entrepreneurial City: Image, Memory, Spectacle*. London: Routledge. pp. 1–19.

de Souza e Silva, A. and Firth, J. (2012) *Mobile Interfaces in Public Spaces: Locational Privacy, Control, and Urban Sociability*. New York: Routledge.

du Gay, P. (1996) *Consumption and Identity at Work*. London: Sage.

Ebeling, M. (2010) 'Marketing chimeras: The bio-value of branded medical devices', in M. Aronczyk and D. Power (eds), *Blowing Up the Brand*. New York: Peter Lang Publishing, Inc. pp. 241–59.

Evans, G. (2003) 'Hard-branding the cultural city – from Prado to Prada', *International Journal of Urban and Regional Research*, 27(2): 417–41.

Fan, Y. (2005) 'Ethical branding and corporate reputation', *Corporate Communications: An International Journal*, 10(4): 341–50.

Featherstone, M. (1991) *Consumer Culture and Postmodernism*. London: Sage.

Gibson, T. (2005) 'Selling city living: Urban branding campaigns, class power and the civic good', *International Journal of Cultural Studies*, 8(3): 259–80.

Goldman, R. and Papson, S. (1998) *Nike Culture*. London: Sage.

Greenberg, M. (2008) *Branding New York: How a City in Crisis was Sold to the World*. London: Routledge.

Gutzmer, A. (2014) *Brand-Driven City Building and the Virtualizing of Space*. London: Routledge.

Hall, S. (1980) 'Encoding/Decoding', in S. Hall, D. Hobson, A. Love and P. Willis (eds), *Culture, Media, Language*. London: Hutchinson. pp. 128–38.

Hall, T. and Hubbard, P. (1998) *The Entrepreneurial City: Geographies of Politics, Regime and Representation*. New York: John Wiley and Sons.

Hannigan, J. (1998) *Fantasy City: Pleasure and Profit in the Postmodern Metropolis*. London: Routledge.

Hannigan, J. (2003) 'Symposium on branding, the entertainment economy and urban place building: Introduction', *International Journal of Urban and Regional Research*, 27(2): 352–60.

Harris, A. (2011) 'Branding Hoxton: Cultural landscapes of post-industrial London', in A. Pike (ed.), *Brands and Branding Geographies*. Cheltenham, UK: Edward Elgar. pp. 187–99.

Harvey, D. (2012) *Rebel Cities: From the Right to the City to the Urban Revolution*. London: Verso.

Hearn, A. (2010) '"Through the looking glass": The promotional university 2.0', in M. Aronczyk and D. Power (eds), *Blowing Up the Brand*. New York: Peter Lang Publishing, Inc. pp. 195–218.

Hesmondhalgh, D. (2002) *The Cultural Industries*. London: Sage.

Hjarvard, S. (2013) *The Mediatization of Culture and Society*. New York: Routledge.

Holt, D. (2004) *How Brands Become Icons*. Boston: Harvard Business School Press.

Holt, D. (2006a) 'Toward a sociology of branding', *Journal of Consumer Culture*, 6(3): 299–302.

Holt, D. (2006b) 'Jack Daniel's America: Iconic brands as ideological parasites and proselytizers', *Journal of Consumer Culture*, 6(3): 355–77.

Jackson, P. (2004) 'Local consumption cultures in a globalizing world', *Transactions of the Institute of British Geographers*, NS 29: 165–78.

Jackson, P., Russel, P., and Ward, N. (2011) 'Brands in the making: A life history approach', in A. Pike (ed.), *Brands and Branding Geographies*. Cheltenham, UK: Edward Elgar. pp. 59–74.

Jayne, M. (2006) *Cities and Consumption*. London and New York: Routledge.

Jensen, O. (2007) 'Culture stories: Understanding cultural urban branding', *Planning Theory*, 6(3): 211–36.

Julier, G. (2011) 'Design activism meets place-branding: Reconfiguring urban representation and everyday life', in A. Pike (ed.), *Brands and Branding Geographies*. Cheltenham, UK: Edward Elgar. pp. 213–29.

Julier, G. and Moor, L. (2009) 'Introduction: Design and creativity', in G. Julier and L. Moor (eds), *Design and Creativity: Policy, Management and Practice*. Oxford: Berg. pp. 1–20.

Klein, N. (1999) *No Logo*. Toronto: Knopf Canada.

Klingmann, A. (2007) *Brandscapes: Architecture in the Experience Economy*. Cambridge: MIT Press.

Kunde, J. and Cunningham, B.J. (2002) *Corporate Religion*. London: FT Management.

Lash, S. (2002) *Critique of Information*. London: Sage Publications.

Lash, S. and Lury, C. (2007) *Global Culture Industry*. Cambridge: Polity Press.

Lash, S. and Urry, J. (1994) *Economies of Signs and Space*. London: Sage.

Luna-Garcia, A. (2008) 'Just another coffee! Milking the Barcelona model, marketing a global image, and the resistance of local identities', in A. Cronin and K. Hetherington (eds), *Consuming the Entrepreneurial City: Image, Memory, Spectacle*. London: Routledge. pp. 143–60.

Lury, C. (2000) 'The united colours of diversity', in S. Franklin, C. Lury, and J. Stacey (eds), *Global Nature, Global Culture*. London: Sage. pp. 146–87.

Lury, C. (2004) *Brands: The Logos of the Global Economy*. London: Routledge.

Lury, C. (2011) *Consumer Culture*, 2nd edition. New Brunswick, NJ: Rutgers University Press.

Lury, C. and Moor, L. (2010) 'Brand valuation and topological culture', in M. Aronczyk and D. Powers (eds), *Blowing Up the Brand*. New York: Peter Lang. pp. 29–52.

McFall, L. (2004) *Advertising: A Cultural Economy*. London: Sage.

Miles, S. (2010) *Spaces for Consumption*. Sage: London.

Miles, S. and Paddison, R. (2005) 'Introduction: The rise and rise of culture-led urban regeneration', *Urban Studies*, 42(5/6): 833–9.

Moor, L. (2007) *The Rise of Brands*. Oxford: Berg.

Moor, L. (2008) 'Branding consultants and cultural intermediaries', *The Sociological Review*, 56(3): 408–28.

Moor, L. (2012) 'beyond cultural intermediaries? A socio-technical perspective on the market for

social interventions', *European Journal of Cultural Studies*, 15(5): 563–80.
Moor, L. and Littler, J. (2008) 'Fourth worlds and neo-Fordism', *Cultural Studies*, 22(5): 700–23.
Muñiz, A. and O'Guinn, T. (2001) 'Brand community', *Journal of Consumer Research*, 27(4): 412–32.
Nixon, S. and du Gay, P. (2002) 'Who needs cultural intermediaries?', *Cultural Studies*, 16(4): 495–500.
Oldenburg, R. (1989). *The great good place*. New York: Marlowe & Company.
Peck, J. (2005) 'Struggling with the creative class', *International Journal of Urban and Regional Research*, 29(4): 740–70.
Pike, A. (2009) 'Geographies of brands and branding', *Progress in Human Geography*, 33(5): 619–45.
Pike, A. (2011) 'Introduction: Brands and branding geographies', in A. Pike (ed.), *Brands and Branding Geographies*. Cheltenham, UK: Edward Elgar. pp. 3–24.
Rantisi, N. and Leslie, D. (2006) 'Branding the design metropole: The case of Montréal, Canada', *Area*, 38(4): 364–76.
Rein, I., Kotler, P., and Shields, B. (2006) *The Elusive Fan: Reinventing Sports in a Crowded Marketplace*. New York: McGraw-Hill.
Ritzer, G., Dean, P., and Jurgenson, N. (2012) 'The Coming of Age of the Prosumer', *American Behavioral Scientist*, 56(4): 379–98.
Rohm, A., Gao, T., Sultan, F., and Pagani, M. (2012) 'Brand in the hand: A cross-market investigation of consumer acceptance of mobile marketing', *Business Horizons*, 55(5): 485–93.
Rose, N. (1999) *Powers of Freedom: Reframing Political Thought*. Cambridge, UK: Cambridge University Press.
Schau, H. J., Muniz, A., and Arnould, E. (2009) 'How Brand Community Practices Create Value', *Journal of Marketing*, 73(5): 30–51.
Shamir, R. (2008) 'The age of responsiblization: On market-embedded morality', *Economy and Society*, 37(1): 1–19.
Smith Maguire, J. and Matthews, J. (2012) 'Are we all cultural intermediaries now? An introduction to cultural intermediaries in context', *European Journal of Cultural Studies*, 15(5): 551–62.
Stehr, N. (2008) *Moral Markets: How Knowledge and Affluence Change Consumers and Products*. London: Paradigm Publishers.
United Nations (2005) 'What is the global compact?', (http://www.unglobalcompact.org/Portal/Default.asp?) [accessed September 24, 2005].
Warde, A. (2005) 'Consumption and Theories of Practice', *Journal of Consumer Culture*, 5(2): 131–53.
Warde, A. (2012) 'Consumption and Critique', in J. Hall, L. Grindstaff and M. Lo (eds.), *Handbook of Cultural Sociology*. London: Routledge. pp. 408–416.
Wernick, A. (1991) *Promotional Culture: Advertising, Ideology, and Symbolic Expression*. London: Sage.
Wherry, F. (2011) *The Philadelphia Barrio: The Arts, Branding, and Neighbourhood Transformation*. Chicago: The University of Chicago Press.
Witz, A., Warhurst, C., and Nickson, D. (2003) 'The labour of aesthetics and the aesthetics of organization', *Organization*, 10(1): 33–54.
Yakhlef, A. (2004) 'Global brands as embodied "generic spaces"', *Space and Culture*, 7(2): 237–48.
Young, C., Diep, M., and Drabble, S. (2006) 'Living with difference? The "cosmopolitan city" and urban reimagining in Manchester, UK', *Urban Studies*, 43(10): 1687–714.
Zukin, S. (1995) *The Cultures of Cities*. Oxford: Blackwell Publishing.
Zukin, S. (1998) 'Urban lifestyles: Diversity and standardisation in spaces of consumption', *Urban Studies*, 35(5–6): 825–39.
Zukin, S. (2008) 'Forward', in A. Cronin and K. Hetherington (eds), *Consuming the Entrepreneurial City: Image, Memory, Spectacle*. London: Routledge. pp. xi–xiii.
Zwick, D., Bonsu, S.K., and Darmody, A. (2008) 'Putting consumers to work: "Co-creation" and new marketing govern-mentality', *Journal of Consumer Culture*, 8(2): 163–96.

# Cultural Sociology of Ethical Consumption

Matthias Varul

## INTRODUCTION

Ethical consumption – the infusion of consumer practices with moral and political considerations and purpose – has been a growing phenomenon over three decades in Europe and North America, with the most rapid increase taking place in around the middle of the last decade (Stolle and Micheletti, 2013: 54–5). In the UK a report commissioned by the Co-Operative Group puts the total spent in ethical consumer practices in 2012 at over £54 billion, a figure that includes spending on a wide variety of ethical products from food to financial services, which is linked to a wide variety of causes from human rights to green energy and animal welfare (Ethical Consumer Research Association, 2013). The report puts the value of the sector most commonly associated with ethical consumerism, fair-trade, at over one and a half billion pounds. According to the Fairtrade Foundation (2014) the flagship products, roast-and-ground coffee and bananas, have reached UK market shares of 27% and 35% respectively. Beyond its basic economic significance, the social and cultural significance of ethical consumerism has been underpinned by institutional and political commitments (Fisher, 2012) as well as underlined by widespread celebrity endorsement (Goodman, 2010).

The explicit association of consumer practices with moral and political concerns is a phenomenon which highlights the necessity of cultural approaches to understanding economic practices. Such approaches have always been at the heart of sociological reflections on 'the economy', from Durkheim and Weber onwards into the more assertive 'cultural turn' in the late 20th-century social sciences (Slater and Tonkiss, 2001: 149–96). The role of cultural norms in economic action (e.g. Storper and Salais, 1997), the institutional embeddedness of markets (Granovetter, 1985), the symbolic nature of the economic (e.g. Lash and Urry, 1994) and the centrality of work, trade and consumption in the social construction of identities (e.g. du Gay, 1996), are all prominent in ethical consumption and maybe even more pronounced there than they are in the economy generally. From the 1980s onwards, consumer culture in particular has been identified not only as field where the economic has a cultural impact, but where the economy itself is a cultural process, meriting intense study from various theoretical perspectives, from the late-Marxist (Haug, 1986) to the neo-Weberian (Campbell, 1987). Ethical consumerism is not only, as are all forms of consumerism, analysed using concepts like inequality, alienation and self-expression, but practices of ethical consumption themselves try to address and redress inequality and alienation, and they do so with a strong emphasis on authentic self-expression.[1]

However, cultural sociology has been a latecomer to the theme of ethical consumption, the study of which was from the late 1990s into the first decade of the new millennium dominated by adjacent disciplines and sub-disciplines in the social sciences, such as human geography and political sociology, and by more practically oriented disciplines such as critical marketing and management studies, and development studies. All these disciplines have emphasised aspects that are cultural-sociologically relevant and, in the relative absence of contributions from cultural sociology, they have begun to incorporate elements of cultural-sociological reflection,[2] thereby pointing to a role for cultural sociology as a connecting approach in an interdisciplinary field. Since around 2005 there have been a number examples of cultural-sociological and anthropological theorisations and empirical research, but in 2008 Adams and Raisborough's question 'What can sociology say about fair-trade?' was still justified (and to an extent remains so even after their own empirical contributions, e.g. Adams and Raisborough, 2010).

The main themes for study have been set by scholars in other disciplines, however. Critical marketing and management studies have used ethical consumption to challenge taken-for-granted assumptions in the mainstream of their disciplines, namely the still prevalent fiction of the *homo economicus*, i.e. the idea of the rationally calculating and informed consumer. Human geographers have been fascinated by the reflective establishment of cross-border relations through ethical trade. Both the human geographical and the marketing/management interest in ethical consumption may help to explain why fair-trade has become the paradigmatic case. The former is generated by the way that fair-trade connects (or seems to connect) places globally, the latter because not only is the utilitarian paradigm undermined by seemingly altruistic motives, but, more importantly, the moral concern is about trade and commerce themselves (rather than, as in the case of, for example, ecological consumption, about the consequences of trade and commerce). This focus has been productive in many ways, but it has, as we shall see, also led to some limitations that need to be overcome.

## FAIR-TRADE AS REFLEXIVE/ ALTERNATIVE GLOBALISATION

Human geographers and political sociologists have conceptualised fair-trade using a range of spatio-social metaphors, such as that of the commodity chain (Talbot, 1997) and – often inspired by Actor-Network Theory – of alternative food networks (Whatmore and Thorne, 1997). Such studies emphasised the fact that in fair-trade and other forms of alternative trade what is normally hidden in capitalist market economies – the conditions of production and the terms of trade – are laid open. Some have gone so far as to diagnose an end to commodity fetishism (Hudson and Hudson, 2003). But early on there were also questions as to how realistic the 'unveiled' picture of alternative trading relations really was. In most cases, 'following the commodities' meant accepting the reported flow and the self-reported rules of alternative trading organisations, while direct empirical involvement, if any, was sought mainly with retailers and consumers (e.g. Levi and Linton, 2003). Research within such organisations was rare since, despite the claim to greater transparency, until recently access remained difficult to obtain. An early exception was the study by Davies and Crane (2003) on decision-making processes in an alternative trading organisation, which showed up a rather pragmatic and business-oriented approach that sometimes was inconsistent with the image projected.

There are now a number of, mainly anthropological, studies (Lyon, 2006; Jaffee, 2007; Berlan, 2008), but also at least one sociological one (Wright and Madrid, 2007). These studies highlight the fact that the impact of fair-trade is more complex and less straightforward than was presented by alternative trading organisations. Particularly the financial benefits tended not to meet the expectations created by fair-trade campaigning, mainly because most fair-trade co-operatives still had to sell into the conventional market since the demand for fair-trade produce was not high enough to do otherwise. They also emphasise that the image often evoked of the victimised farmer in dire need of external help tends to deny the role of producers as strategic actors. But in this regard, however, major benefits were also identified. Berlan (2008), for example, points out that while financially there was not much of a difference between the fair-trade and the conventional cocoa-buying organisations in Ghana, many farming communities chose the fair-trade co-operative Kuapa Kokoo because they valued their democratic structure and empowering procedures. Central to this was the fact that Kuapa Kokoo, uniquely at the time, held part ownership of one of the ethical chocolate brands in the UK, the Day Chocolate Company (now Divine Chocolate). Ownership gave the producers more of a say in the trade of their produce. One narrative that anthropological research tends to disconfirm, however, is the notion of de-fetishisation and its value to producers. Lyon (2006: 458) found that very few of the Guatemalan coffee farmers she spoke to named relationships to coffee roasters and coffee consumers as a benefit of being members of fair-trade networks. Lyon also reports producers' amazement when they learned about the high price of a cup of coffee in the USA, which still stood in stark contrast to the price that they received for their beans.

The notion of de-fetishisation was also questioned at a theoretical level. Wright (2010) examines the transparency and adequacy of various stated connectivities (economic, political, cultural), finding that with regards to commodity fetishism, fair-trade produce is not much different from conventional goods. This is not surprising given that the only way fair-trade could increase sales to make bigger economic impact than hitherto, was through conventional capitalist markets. In particular, she attests that the use of accounts and images regarding communities of producers as marketing devices counter-acts claims to de-fetishisation.

## THE IMAGE OF THE PRODUCER

As indicated, there were questions as to how realistic the images presented of the producers and the conditions of production really are. But for cultural sociology it is not only interesting to ask whether and if so how these images are distorted, but also what kind of projections are invested in them. Bryant and Goodman (2004) diagnosed a commodification of people and nature in an 'edenic discourse', and Wright (2004) showed how fair-trade coffee is sold as a package where the consumption of an exotic, pristine and people-free landscape blanks out the ethical motive of solidarity. Varul (2008) suggests that images of producers are romanticised in a way that unintentionally plays on problematic colonialist registers. Such imagery symbolically condemns fair-trade producers to an idyllic but austere rustic and ethnically-defined existence. Furthermore, the de-fetishisation thesis is undermined not only because the presentation of Developing World farmers' lives is distorted, but also because the un-veiling is only partial. Fair-trade producers carry the burden of proof for their conformity to standards of production and are aesthetically exposed on producer vignettes, but the consumers are not under any similar pressure to justify the income out of which they pay for ethical produce. Their authenticity remains unquestioned, while they can draw, in their identity constructions, on the documented authenticity of product and producer. Indicative as the relatively few available analyses of fair-trade imageries may be, a full iconography of fair-trade remains to be written; an iconography, that is, which fully links the employed visualities and also the products themselves to their colonial historical references, to the material practices they are part of in consumers' everyday lives, and to the political and personal meanings the various actors attach to fair-trade producer companies. Such iconographic analysis would also entail an intensive engagement with the practices of ethical consumption, reflecting on the experience of ethical consumers since 'the iconic is about experience, not communication. To be iconically conscious is to understand without knowing, or at least without knowing that one knows. It is to understand by feeling, by contact, by the "evidence of our senses" rather than the mind' (Alexander, 2008: 782).

Only a few studies, however, examine the way consumers receive and process such imagery empirically and in greater depth. Varul (2009b: 378) highlights the tension between the positioning of consumers and producers in fair-trade advertising and some consumers' discomfort with such imagery. But so far the only study that considers how the producer is constructed in consumers' discourses remains that of Diaz Pedregal (2005). She observes a tendency to construct the producer as a distant other within an essentialised and monolithic culture, and one whose existence is entirely linked to the 'ethical object' that is the fair-trade commodity. She also remarks upon the fact that, against her expectations, the appreciation of ethical goods did not go together with a further personal investment in cultural diversity. Interrogating fair-trade advertisers, Golding (2009) shows that fair-trade marketers do reflect on the implications of ads – for example, by infusing them with hitherto hidden geographies, in this case with Africanicity – but can only achieve this at the price of their commodification along the lines analysed by Wright (2004).

That iconographies and ideologies do matter in informing the practices of both fair-trade consumers and the whole fair-trade system itself is demonstrated by Leclair's (2002: 957) assertion that the romanticism of fair-trade marketing is a factor in confining the offered product range to handicraft and agricultural produce only. Wright and Madrid (2007), in their study of the Kenyan cut-flower industry, show that cultural representations of ethical trade do indeed impact on how power and resources are allocated. In an examination of the Vietnamese coffee trade, Fridell (2014) comes to similar conclusion.

While in human geography there are critical examinations of the representations involved in fair-trade consumerism, they are partly held back by methodological and epistemological limitations. Semiotics has been shown to be too limited an approach to the study of images, while the broadly non-representational (often outright Heideggerian) approach that is now prevalent in both human geography and anthropology limits researchers' capacities to develop such an iconography. This suggests the pressing need for cultural sociologists to embark on such a project.

## THE ETHICS OF ETHICAL CONSUMPTION

The way the imagery of fair-trade is ethically contested throws up the question of where the morality of ethical consumption is derived from. Initial approaches looked to linking Aristotelian, utilitarian and Kantian philosophical ideas to possible justifications for engaging in ethical consumption (e.g. Barnett et al., 2005).

This leaves open two lines of investigation, both of which are promising and have been partly followed up in productive ways. The first follows from Foucault's (e.g. 1991) rejection of the (Sartrean) search for an authentic core to constructed identity and morality. Here the construction of an ethical self becomes an *aesthetic* endeavour in which the inner consistency of the ethical subject is a way of dealing with the problem of freedom as it first emerged in the Greek polis and now is radicalised in liberal market societies (Rose, 1990: 227). In this perspective, imageries as discussed above become elements of stylisations of selfhood whose ethical content no longer has a material moral reference point. But even where this is the case (and there is evidence of very low levels of awareness for the moral discourses behind ethical produce, as Davies et al. [2012] show), from a cultural-sociological point of view aesthetics must be understood as intrinsically social. With reference to Bourdieu's (1979) conceptualisation of taste as a powerful visceralisation of forms of sociocultural distinction, Varul (2009a) tried to capture this in the twin notions of ethical tastes and tastes for ethics – the former denoting the choice of ethical products out of an aesthetic intuition (typically found in the mainstream ethical consumer) and the latter a predilection for reflection and searching (typically found in the reflective ethical consumer). Such notions can become functional in social positioning (see below).

Furthermore – and this leads to the second line of investigation – ethical consumption clearly is not just (and not even mainly) communicated as an aesthetic choice. And this makes it difficult to think of the ethics involved as a construction of selfhood that is mainly committed to inner consistency. Having started from a Foucauldian notion of ethics, Barnett et al. (2005: 29) slide back into talking of 'ethical dispositions', and thereby return to something closer to the expression of the authentic self to which Foucault thought he had dealt a fatal blow. This slippage is not so much due to theoretical inconsistency, but to an accommodation of empirical evidence encountered in observing and interrogating ethical consumers. So this line of investigation therefore would take the fact seriously that the expressed authentic core is felt to be valid, even if it is known to be 'constructed'. There appears to be a genuine desire to 'be good' rather than just to 'do good', let alone only appear to be good, which shows in a search for both internal and external consistency (demonstrated early on by Shaw and Clarke [1999], and more recently by Papaoikonomou et al. [2014]). This resonates with the major Weberian approach to consumption, which emphatically insists on the centrality of subjective motive (Campbell, 2006), and in relation to consumer behaviour suggests an 'approach from character' in which it is assumed that 'if it is possible for an individual to represent a potential action as indicative of an admirable or virtuous character then it is likely to be undertaken' (Campbell, 1990: 44–5). Again, we have here the inner self as an ultimate reference point. If not tied into the full classical sociological approach from which this suggestion emerges, this would only replicate those Aristotelian assumptions of a not-further-determinable sense of moral rightness and flourishing (as introduced into sociological debate by Sayer (2005) through a consideration of Adam Smith's notion of 'moral sentiment'). That a discourse of authenticity is omnipresent in consumer culture (Arnould and Price, 2000), not only with respect to the expressive aspect of the act of consuming but also in what is sought in products themselves (Scrase, 2003), does not mean that it is to be taken as proof of an ontological truth which then is to be dealt with by philosophical imports. Instead it may be expedient to take a Weberian lead in a broader sense and, with Fraser (1993: 17ff.), try to mend the neglect of the notion of legitimacy in Foucault himself and subsequently in the governmentality school (Rose, 1990). Useful as it is in drawing attention to the role of organisations and discourses, the governmentality perspective which looks at governing ethical consumption by intermediate agency, edited choices, and constructed responsibilities, has its limits. Crucially it leaves out the role of individual actors in prioritising what is important to them, in seeking legitimacy in interaction with significant others and in maintaining a continuous sense of self (Barnett et al., 2008), which means that the power-technological perspective of governmentality neglects that which power is exerted on, its raw material so to speak (Varul, 2004: 112–20). As with its aesthetics, the morality of ethical consumption then needed to be re-socialised and also re-centred.

One way of doing this is to insist, as do Stolle and Micheletti (2013), on the political nature of what they refuse to call 'ethical consumption'. Here intentionality is re-emphasised, and at the same time an active relation to nationally and regionally specific political discourses and structures is established. It has also been noted that national political cultures play a role as to which discourses of ethical consumption are linked to political movements (and also the extent to which internal conflicts within ethical consumer movements are politicised). The rifts within French *commerce equitable* point to a particular politicisation of ethical consumption in that context (e.g. Gateau, 2007). The strong Marxist and *altermondialiste* tendencies in French fair-trade can be read through some of its more militant micromyths (Robert-Demontrond, 2011), whereas the mainly Christian roots of British fair-trade show in the fact that the biggest importing organisation, Traidcraft, operates on a theological justification (Sugden, 1999), and in that the imagery often used reverberates with colonial traditions of missionary charity (Varul, 2008: 644ff.). But generally it can be said that clear references to either source of original fair-trade legitimacy (Marxist or Christian) tend to be limited to organisers and campaigners, while the receptivity of less politically motivated consumers needs to be accounted for in other terms, especially where fair-trade and other forms of ethical consumption have undergone a process of 'mainstreaming'. Moving from more politically driven to more mass-market oriented modes of distribution leads to a de-politicisation (Dolan, 2009), after which what remains is shopping for a vaguely better world. Buying things becomes both a means of 'doing good' and evidence of 'being good' (e.g. Low and Davenport, 2006).

Le Velly (2006) suggests that fair-trade constitutes, in Weberian terms, an attempt to revert from a prevalent formal rationality of bureaucracy and the market to a substantive rationality that is more attentive to the effects of processes and decisions on individuals' lives. This approach resonates with the aforementioned neo-Aristotelian emphasis on flourishing, as substantive rationality, like Aristotelian justice, relies on a functioning moral intuition. Varul (2009a; 2009b) proposes understanding such a moral intuition as informed by rules implicit in routine everyday practices along the lines suggested by practice theorists from various traditions (e.g. along Wittgensteinian lines, see Pitkin, 1972). This would include intuitive ideas about equitable exchange reinforced by the experience of being citizens within a capitalist commodity society (Varul, 2010), by institutional frameworks of welfare (Mau, 2003), and by common representations of imperial pasts (e.g. Ramamurthy, 2003; Mergner, 2000). Such linkages into everyday experience suggest that closer attention to the ordinary practices of ethical consumption is required, and studies supplying such accounts are beginning to be available (see next section). Self-reported deviations from ethical commitments can be understood, in this framework, not just as evidence for an intriguing 'attitude–behaviour gap' (Boulstridge and Carrigan, 2000) but as ways of affirming authentic self-identity as documented in individual tastes (Grauel, 2014) whose slight inconsistencies testify to the sincerity of ethical commitment (Varul, 2009b).

Adams and Raisborough (2011) are less concerned with contextualising the concrete values promoted by campaign organisations and 'bought into' by consumers, and more with what such ethics entail. By highlighting how fair-trade is linked to a 'self-control ethos' they bring together (without being explicit about it) Foucauldian ideas about modernity and discipline/self-discipline, and Weberian ideas about bourgeois rationality as informed by a Protestant tradition. Diaz Pedregal (2008) argues that the presentation of the fair-trade producer is indeed informed by a displacement of a quasi-Protestant ethic which the virtuous consumer can identify with. Similarly, Gould (2003: 343) emphasises the identificational value of the abstention from consumption that he sees in the representation of producers on fair-trade packaging. Such fictitious alliances with the distant deprived who are framed as the 'deserving poor' can play a role in the affirmation of class position vis-à-vis domestic 'underclasses' which are experienced as threatening (e.g. Raisborough and Adams, 2009). Here, too, the ethics of ethical consumption is understood against its sociocultural background. This task has, repeatedly, been highlighted by the marketing literature (e.g. recently by Valor and Carrero, 2014: 1119) and it is, of course, a job for cultural sociology to tackle. This is of particular importance as earlier literature on fair-trade was unconcerned about fairness in relation to workers in the importing countries. Fridell (2003: 6), for example, points out that Waridel (2002: 105f.) brushes off any concern about fair treatment of less distant workers, citing allegedly sufficient protection through labour laws and unionisation.

## ETHICAL CONSUMPTION AS EMBEDDED

As previously mentioned, ethical consumption is embedded in everyday practices, social contexts, dominant moral discourses, and economic structures. In a way this is not surprising, given that the concept of ethical consumption aims at 're-embedding' trade (e.g. Raynolds, 2000). But by positing ethical consumption as contrasting case of embeddedness, such an approach accepts the general validity the neo-liberal paradigm of a deregulated market unaffected by institutional arrangements. Cultural sociology, however, will look at *any* economic phenomenon as always already embedded (Granovetter, 1985). Institutional and cultural embeddedness is thrown into particularly sharp relief when internationally comparative perspectives are applied (Krier, 2005; Varul, 2009a). Comparative studies, however, are still rare (for a recent exception see Aritzía et al., 2014). Another way of uncovering the complexities of ethical consumption as negotiating individual self-identities in dense social contexts, is to address the question through a pronounced practice approach – such as suggested by Warde (2005) – which is prevalent in more recent sociological and anthropological studies (e.g. Wheeler, 2012; Lyon et al., 2014)

One of the issues that a practice approach has shed light on is the classed nature of fair-trade. The relative absence of working-class ethical consumption – which given the history of international solidarity in labour movements is striking (Frank, 2003) – and the prevalence of certain segments of the middle classes, particularly in fair-trade consumerism and activism, was noted early on (e.g. Cowe and Williams, 2001). *Why* that might be had been left to speculation until practices were examined more closely and, importantly, in cultural context. Here the relevance of the above-mentioned (and so far still missing) iconographies of fair-trade is seen: given the way that fair-trade has been, from the beginning, symbolically organised around coffee, and given the role of coffee culture as a focal point of new middle-class sociabilities at work and in leisure (Gaudio, 2003), the middle-class dominance in this particular field should not come as a surprise. A practice-centred approach is able to highlight barriers to participation of this and also of more trivial kinds (Lyon et al., 2014).

Further, it has been shown that distancing can be an ambivalent and ambiguous aspect of the class character of fair-trade. The object of solidarity is spatially removed from the subject and thus less threatening (Johnston, 2002). By romanticising the Developing World producer as heroic worker and patient sufferer, a counter-image to the less distant poor at home is created (Raisborough and Adams, 2009), so that the association with the distant poor affords a morally charged class distinction from the less distant and allegedly less deserving deprived groups closer to home. The crucial role of distancing in classing ethical consumption becomes tangible when the pattern is broken and the fair-trade model is transplanted to deprived areas spatially and socially closer to consumers. Then categories are challenged and consumer anxieties return, as in the case of American Apparel analysed by Moor and Littler (2008). The use of sexualised images of employees in advertising campaigns by American Apparel has proven to be far more controversial than the equally sexualising (and racialising) use of Kuapa Kokoo employees for Divine Chocolate (Varul, 2008; Golding, 2009).

However, the issue of class is more complex than ethical consumption just being a marker of middle-class practices of distinction. Adams and Raisborough (2008: 1176) point out that engaging in practices like fair-trade always also implies an egalitarian aspiration that counter-acts and holds at bay discourses of social distinction. The role of the Co-Operative movement in British fair-trade and its affiliation to the labour movement also makes matters more complex here (see e.g. Wheeler, 2012: 131ff.).

Accessing the classed nature of ethical consumption from a practice-oriented sociological perspective has not only led to a developing understanding of what exclusionary mechanisms are at work, but has also shown that in less prominent practices of ethical consumption there is more access for working-class and minority participation (Sassatelli, 2006: 224). Broadening the scope, as for example Adams and Raisborough (2010) and Grauel (2014) have done, brings to light less socially exclusive forms of ethical consumption that have hitherto been largely under the scholarly radar. In his anthropology of shopping in North London, Miller (1998) uncovered that most ordinary practices of consumption have a moral dimension which is informed by a care for others (in most cases here, family members). Barnett et al. (2005) have pointed out that there may not be such a great qualitative difference between such taken-for-granted forms of care and the more explicitly ethicised care for *distant* others as is exhibited in fair-trade practices.

## CONCLUSION

If more fully developed as an approach, the cultural sociology of ethical consumption may be well positioned to link everyday moral intuitions that seem to govern consumption, and the wide variety of attempts to govern consumers by activating those intuitions, to the socio-cultural sources of such intuitions and their formation, affirmation and manifestation in everyday practices. The task of cultural sociology with regards to ethical consumption is to situate it within the broader moralities and aesthetics which such everyday practices refer to. The study of ethical consumption needs to make connections, not only in terms of relating diverse socio-economic positionings, but also in terms of juxtaposing and conjugating seemingly unrelated cultural practices and experiences. For example, much can be learned by referring the valuations, self-images and anxieties of fair-trade and ecological consumers to representations of class, authenticity and knowledge as played out in films such as *Avatar* and other forms of popular culture.

## NOTES

1 In a play on Campbell's (1987) notion of modern consumers' 'autonomous imaginative hedonism', Soper (2007) suggests understanding ethical consumers as 'alternative hedonists'.
2 See Andorfer and Liebe (2012) and Shaw and Newholm's (2002) research on voluntary simplicity.

## REFERENCES

Adams, M. and Raisborough, J. (2008) 'What Can Sociology Say About Fair-trade? Class, Reflexivity and Ethical Consumption', *Sociology*, 42(6): 1165–82.
Adams, M. and Raisborough, J. (2010) 'Making a Difference: Ethical Consumption and the Everyday', *British Journal of Sociology*, 61(2): 256–74.
Adams, M. and Raisbourough, J. (2011) 'Encountering the Fair-trade Farmer: Solidarity, Stereotypes and the Self-Control Ethos', *Papers on Social Representations*, 20: 8.1–8.21.
Alexander, J.C. (2008) 'Iconic Consciousness: The Material Feeling of Meaning', *Environment and Planning D: Society and Space*, 28: 782–94.
Ariztía, T., Kleine, D., das Graças, M., Brightwell, S. L., Agloni, N., Afonso, R. and Bartholo, R. (2014) 'Ethical consumption in Brazil and Chile: institutional contexts and development trajectories', *Journal of Cleaner Production* 63: 84–92.
Andorfer, V.A. and Liebe, U. (2012) 'Research on Fair-trade Consumption: A Review', *Journal of Business Ethics*, 106: 415–35.
Arnould, E.J. and Price, L.L. (2000) 'Authenticating Acts and Authoritative Performances' in S. Ratneshwar, D.G. Mick and S. Huffman (eds), *The Why of Consumption*. London: Routledge.
Barnett, C., Cafaro, P. and Newholm, T. (2005) 'Philosophy and Ethical Consumption', in R. Harrison, T. Newholm and D. Shaw (eds), *The Ethical Consumer*. London: Sage. pp. 11–24.
Barnett, C., Clarke, N., Cloke, P. and Malpass, A. (2008) 'The Elusive Subjects of Neo-Liberalism: Beyond the Analytics of Governmentality', *Cultural Studies*, 22(5): 624–53.
Barnett, C., Cloke, P., Clarke, N., Malpass, A. (2005) 'Consuming Ethics: Articulating the Subjects and Spaces of Ethical Consumption', *Antipode*, 37(1): 24–45.
Berlan, A. (2008) 'Making or Marketing a Difference? An Anthropological Examination of the Marketing of Fair-trade Cocoa form Ghana', *Research in Economic Anthropology*, 28: 171–94.
Boulstridge, E. and Carrigan, M. (2000) 'Do Consumers Really Care About Corporate Responsibility? Highlighting the Attitude–Behaviour Gap', *Journal of Communication Management*, 4(4): 355–68.
Bourdieu, P. (1979) *La Distinction*. Paris: Minuit.
Bryant, R.L. and Goodman, M.K. (2004) 'Consuming Narratives: The Political Ecology of "Alternative" Consumption', *Transactions of the Institute of British Geographers*, New Series, 29: 344–66.
Campbell, C. (1987) *The Romantic Ethic and the Spirit of Modern Consumerism*. Oxford: Blackwell.
Campbell, C. (1990) 'Character and Consumption', *Culture and History*, 7(1): 37–48.
Campbell, C. (2006) 'Do Today's Sociologists Really Appreciate Weber's Essay *The Protestant Ethic and the Spirit of Capitalism?*', *Sociological Review*, 54(2): 207–23.
Cowe, R. and Williams, S. (2001) *Who Are the Ethical Consumers?* Manchester: Co-operative Bank.
Davies, I.A. and Crane, A. (2003) 'Ethical Decision Making in Fair-trade Companies', *Journal of Business Ethics*, 45: 79–92.
Davies, I., Doherty, R. and Gutsche, S. (2012) 'Where is the Ethics in Fair-trade Consumption?', presentation at the 4th Fair-trade International Symposium, Liverpool, [http://marketing.conference-services.net/resources/327/2958/pdf/AM2012_0072_paper.pdf].
Diaz Pedregal, V. (2005) 'Éthique et objets ethniques. Pratiques et représentations des consommateurs', *Consommations and Sociétés*, 5.
Diaz Pedregal, V. (2008) 'La morale de l'histoire … du commerce équitable', paper presented at the 3rd Fair-trade International Symposium, Montpellier.
Dolan, C.S. (2009) 'Virtual Moralities: The Mainstreaming of Fair-trade in Kenyan Tea Fields', *Geoforum*, 41(1): 33–43.

Du Gay, P. (1996) *Consumption and Identity at Work*. London: Sage.

Ethical Consumer Research Association (2013) *Ethical Consumer Markets Report* http://www.ethicalconsumer.org/portals/0/downloads/ethical_consumer_markets_report_2013.pdf [last accessed 7 December 2015]

Fisher, E. (2012) 'The "Fair-trade Nation": Market-Oriented Development in Devolved European Regions', *Human Organization*, 71(3): 255–67.

Foucault, M. (1991) 'On the Genealogy of Ethics: An Overview of Work in Progress', in P. Rabinow (ed.), *The Foucault Reader*. London: Penguin. pp. 340–72.

Fairtrade Foundation (2014): *Annual Report and Financial Statements for the Year Ended 31 December 2013*, London.

Frank, D. (2003) 'Where Are the Workers in Consumer-Worker Alliances? Class Dynamics and the History of Consumer-Labor Campaigns', *Politics and Society*, 31(3): 363–79.

Fraser, N. (1993) *Unruly Practices*. Cambridge: Polity Press.

Fridell, G. (2003) 'Fair-trade and the International Moral Economy: Within and Against the Market', *CERLAC Working Paper Series*. Toronto: York University.

Fridell, G. (2014) 'Fair-trade Slippages and Vietnam Gaps: The Ideological Fantasies of Fair-trade Coffee', *Third World Quarterly*, 35(7): 1179–94.

Gateau, M. (2007) 'Militer pour Artisans du Monde et Max Havelaar. Étude de cas des acteurs associatifs et militants du commerce équitable dijonnais', *Revue ¿Interrogations?* No.4: Formes et figures de la précarité. [http://www.revue-interrogations.org/Militer-pour-Artisans-du-Monde-et] accessed 5th March 2015.

Gaudio, R.P. (2003) 'Coffeetalk: Starbucks™ and the Commercialization of Casual Conversation', *Language and Society*, 32(5): 659–91.

Golding, K.M. (2009) 'Fair-trade's Dual Aspect: The Communications Challenge of Fair-trade Marketing', *Journal of Macromarketing*, 29(2): 160–71.

Goodman, M.K. (2010) 'The Mirror of Consumption: Celebritization, Developmental Consumption and the Shifting Politics of Fair-trade', *Geoforum*, 41(1): 104–16.

Gould, N.J. (2003) 'Fair-trade and the Consumer Interest: A Personal Account', *International Journal of Consumer Studies*, 27(4): 341–5.

Granovetter, M. (1985) 'Economic Action and Social Structure: The Problem of Embeddedness', *American Journal of Sociology*, 91(3): 481–510.

Grauel, J. (2014) 'Being Authentic or Being Responsible? Food Consumption, Morality and the Presentation of Self', *Journal of Consumer Culture*, online first [http://joc.sagepub.com/content/early/2014/07/07/1469540514541880.full.pdf+html] accessed 5th March 2015.

Haug, W.F. (1986) *Critique of Commodity Æsthetics: Appearance, Sexuality, and Advertising in Capitalist Society*. Minneapolis: University of Minnesota Press.

Hudson, I. and Hudson, M. (2003): 'Removing the Veil? Commodity Fetishism, Fair-trade, and the Environment', *Organization and Environment*, 16(4): 413–30.

Jaffee, D. (2007) *Brewing Justice: Fair-trade Coffee, Sustainability and Survival*. Berkeley: University of California Press.

Johnston, J. (2002) 'Consuming Global Justice', in J. Goodman (ed.), *Protest and Globalisation*. Annandale, NSW: Pluto Press. pp. 38–56.

Krier, J.-M. (2005) *Fair-trade in Europe 2005*. Brussels: Fair-trade Advocacy Office.

Lash, S. and Urry, J. (1994) *Economies of Signs and Spaces*. London: SAGE.

Leclair, M.S. (2002) 'Fighting the Tide: Alternative Trade Organizations in the Era of Global Free Trade', *World Development*, 30(6): 949–58.

Le Velly, R. (2006) 'Le commerce équitable: des échanges marchands contre et dans le marché', *Revue Française de Sociologie*, 47(2): 319–40.

Levi, M. and Linton, A. (2003) 'Fair-trade: A Cup at a Time?', *Politics and Society*, 31(3): 407–32.

Low, W. and Davenport, E. (2006) 'Mainstreaming Fair-trade: Adoption, Assimilation, Appropriation', *Journal of Strategic Marketing*, 14(4): 315–27.

Lyon, S. (2006) 'Evaluating Fair-trade Consumption: Politics, Defetishization and Producer Participation', *International Journal of Consumer Studies*, 30: 452–64.

Lyon, S., Ailshire, S. and Sehon, A. (2014) 'Fair-trade Consumption and the Limits to Solidarity', *Human Organization*, 73(2): 141–52.

Mau, S. (2003) *The Moral Economy of Welfare States: Britain and Germany Compared*. London: Routledge.

Mergner, G. (2000) '"Unser Nationales Erbe" des deutschen Kolonialismus: Rassistische Bilder – Mitleid mit den Opfern – die Unschuld der Erben', in A. Foitzik, R. Leiprecht, A. Marvakis and U. Seid (eds), *Ein Herrenvolk von Untertanen: Rassismus – Nationalismus – Sexismus*. Duisburg: DISS.

Miller, D. (1998) *A Theory of Shopping*. Cambridge: Polity Press.

Moor, L. and Littler, J. (2008) 'Fourth Worlds and Neo-Fordism: American Apparel and the Cultural Economy of Consumer Anxiety', *Cultural Studies*, 22(5): 700–23.

Papaoikonomou, E., Cascon-Pereira, R. and Ryan, G. (2014) 'Constructing and Communicating an Ethical Consumer Identity: A Social Identity Approach', *Journal of Consumer Culture*, online first [http://joc.sagepub.com/content/early/2014/02/03/1469540514521080.full.pdf+html].

Pitkin, H.F. (1972) *Wittgenstein and Justice*. Berkeley: University of California Press.

Raisborough, J. and Adams, M. (2009) 'Departing from Denigration: Mediations of Desert and Fairness in Ethical Consumption', paper presented at The British Sociological Association Annual Conference 2009: The Challenge of Global Social Inquiry, Cardiff City Hall, Cardiff [http://about.brighton.ac.uk/sass/publications/Raisborough Adams_denigration.pdf] accessed 4th March 2015.

Ramamurthy, A. (2003) *Imperial Persuaders: Images of Africa and Asia in British Advertising*. Manchester: Manchester University Press.

Raynolds, L.T. (2000) 'Re-embedding Global Agriculture: The International Organic and Fair-trade Movements', *Agriculture and Human Values*, 17: 297–309.

Robert-Demontrond, P. (2011) 'Les ambiguïtés sémantiques du commerce équitable: micro-mythanalyse des imaginaires de consommation', *Recherche et Application en Marketing*, 26(4): 54–70.

Rose, N. (1990) *Governing the Soul: The Shaping of the Private Self*. London: Routledge.

Sassatelli, R. (2006) 'Virtue, Responsibility and Consumer Choice', in J. Brewer and F. Trentmann (eds), *Consuming Cultures, Global Perspectives: Historical Trajectories, Transnational Exchanges*. Oxford: Berg. pp. 219–50.

Sayer, A. (2005) 'Class, Moral Worth, and Recognition', *Sociology*, 39(5): 947–63.

Scrase, T.J. (2003) 'Precarious Production: Globalisation and Artisan Labour in the Third World', *Third World Quarterly*, 24(3): 449–61.

Shaw, D. and Clarke, I. (1999) 'Belief Formation in Ethical Consumer Groups: An Exploratory Study', *Marketing Intelligence and Planning*, 17(2): 109–19.

Shaw, D. and Newholm, T. (2002) 'Voluntary Simplicity and the Ethics of Consumption', *Psychology and Marketing*, 19(2): 167–85.

Slater, D. and Tonkiss, F. (2001) *Market Society*. Cambridge: Polity Press.

Smith, A.M. (2013) 'Continuing the Legacy of David Livingstone: The Contribution of Fair-trade to International Development', *Expository Times*, 125(2): 53–66.

Soper, K. (2007) 'Re-thinking the "Good Life": The Citizenship Dimension of Consumer Disaffection with Consumerism', *Journal of Consumer Culture*, 7(2): 205–29.

Stolle, D. and Micheletti, M. (2013) *Political Consumption: Global Responsibility in Action*. Cambridge: Cambridge University Press.

Storper, M. and Salais, R. (1997) *Worlds of Production: The Action Frameworks of the Economy*. Cambridge: Harvard University Press.

Sugden, C. (1999) *Fair-trade as Christian Mission*. Bramcote: Grove.

Talbot, J.M. (1997) 'Where Does Your Coffee Dollar Go? The Division of Income and Surplus along the Coffee Commodity Chain', *Studies in Comparative International Development*, 32(1): 56–91.

Valor, C. and Carrero, I. (2014) 'Viewing Responsible Consumption as a Personal Project', *Psychology and Marketing*, 31(12): 1110–21.

Varul, M.Z. (2004) *Geld und Gesundheit: Konsum als Transform von Geld in Moral*. Berlin: Logos.

Varul, M.Z. (2008) 'Consuming the Campesino: Fair-trade Marketing Between Recognition and Romantic Commodification', *Cultural Studies*, 22(5): 654–79.

Varul, M.Z. (2009a) 'Ethical Selving in Cultural Contexts: Fair-trade Consumption as an Everyday Ethical Practice in the UK and in Germany', *International Journal of Consumer Studies*, 33(2): 183–9.

Varul, M.Z. (2009b) 'Ethical Consumption: The Case of Fair-trade', *Kölner Zeitschrift für Soziologie und Sozialpsychologie*, 49: 366–85.

Varul, M.Z. (2010) 'Reciprocity, Recognition and Labor Value: Marx's Incidental Moral Anthropology of Capitalist Market Exchange', *Journal of Social Philosophy*, 41(1): 50–72.

Warde, A. (2005) 'Consumption and Theories of Practice', *Journal of Consumer Culture*, 5(2): 131–55.

Waridel, L. (2002) *Coffee With Pleasure: Just Java and World Trade*. Montreal: Black Rose Books.

Whatmore, S. and Thorne, L. (1997) 'Nourishing Networks: Alternative Geographies of Food', in D. Goodman and M. Watts (eds), *Globalising Food: Agrarian Questions and Global Restructuring*. London: Routledge. pp. 287–304.

Wheeler, K. (2012) 'The Practice of Fair-trade Support', *Sociology*, 46(1): 126–41.

Wright, C. (2004) 'Consuming Lives, Consuming Landscapes: Interpreting Advertisements for Cafédirect Coffees', *Journal of International Development*, 16(5): 665–80.

Wright, C. (2010) 'Fair-trade Food: Connecting Producers and Consumers', in D. Inglis and D. Gimlin (eds), *The Globalization of Food*. Oxford: Berg. pp. 139–60.

Wright, C. and Madrid, G. (2007) 'Contesting Ethical Trade in Colombia's Cut-Flower Industry: A Case of Cultural and Economic Injustice', *Cultural Sociology*, 1(2): 255–75.

# Index

Abbott, A. 204, 205
Achterberg, Peter 225–36
Acker, Joan 352
Acord, Sophia Krzys 496–509
action theory 6, 178–9, 181–2
  museums 505–6
activism 109, 110
Actor Network Theory (ANT) 6, 43, 44, 310, 312
  architecture 473
  cultural uses 131–43
  economic sociology 557
  fair-trade 591
  fashion 521, 522
  museums 504
Adam, Robert 472
Adams, Annemarie 473
Adams, Julia 215
Adams, M. 591, 594, 595
adjacency matrix 284, 285, 291
Adorno, Theodor 12, 15, 16, 43, 197, 330, 485, 527, 528, 567
advertisements, gender 339–40
aesthetic disposition 571
aesthetic ecology 85–7
aesthetic public sphere 302, 449–50
aesthetic sociology 82, 85–6, 98
aesthetics 391, 463–564
  architecture 465–80
  and ecology 397
  ethnography 301–2
  fashion 510–26
  iconicity 538–52
  of labour 583
  museums and exhibitions 496–509
  music 530
  omnivorousness 572
  symbolic interactionism 108–9, 112–13
affordances 86, 504, 533, 547
Agamben, Georgio 410
age, fashion 520
agency
  in action perspective 390
  ANT 133, 135, 136, 139
  historical sociology 219–20
  memory 458
  museums 502–5
AGIL-scheme 180–1, 187, 337
agnosticism 132, 135
Alasuutari, Pertti 144–58
Alexander, Jeffrey C. 3, 17, 19–20, 21, 32, 36, 60, 68, 69, 71–5, 165–6, 203, 247, 311, 314, 445, 448, 449, 499

citizenship 405
everyday life 375
hermeneutics 273, 277–80
historical sociology 216–17
iconicity 542
markets 560
media 449
performance 416
Alexander, V. D. 501, 502
Alford, Robert 229
alienation 13, 53
Almeling, Rene 352
Almila, Anna-Mari 131–43, 510–26
Altenloh, Emilie 482–3, 485
Althusser, Louis 14, 16, 18, 312
Althusserian scientism 13–14, 17
Alvarez, A. S. 559, 560
Amsterdamska, O. 136–7
Anderson, Benedict 364, 429, 433
anomie 62
Ansdell, G. 393–5, 396
anti-globalization movements 411
apologies 124–5
Appadurai, Arjun 435
appresentative systems 244
Arato, A. 19
'archaeological' approach 546
architecture 465–80, 548
Armstrong, Karen 367
Arnold, Mathew 404, 406
Aron, Raymond 28
Aronowitz, Stanley 295, 296
art 463–564
  in action perspective 397
  cinema 481–95
  ethnography 301–2
  films 488
  media convergence 335–45
  museums and exhibitions 496–509
  nationalism 436–7
  sociology of 301
  see also music
art history 323
artifacts 416, 423–4
Arvidsson, A. 578, 580–2, 583, 584, 585
Aspers, P. 513, 514, 516, 517
Atkinson, Paul 294, 295, 373, 380, 381
Atkinson, W. 573
attachment 121–2
attention 118–21
audiences, media 446–8

Austin, J. L. 134
authenticity 40, 201, 512, 592, 593
auto-ethnography 300–1
autonomy of culture 277
autopoiesis 179
autoproduction 198–9, 201
Azoulay, Ariella 328

baby schema 121
Back, Les 545
Baehr, P. 39–40
Bakhtin Circle 14, 15, 17
Bakhtin, M. 14
Baldwin, E. 310
Balzac, H. de 96, 374
Bandelj, Nina 554–5
Banks, Marcus 248
Barbalet, J. M. 29, 41
'bare life' 410
Barker, C. 308–9, 311, 313
Barker, E. 520
Barnard, F. M. 431
Barnett, C. 595
Barthes, Roland 14, 392, 396, 516, 540–2, 545
Bartmanski, Dominik 499, 538–52
Bateson, G. 248
'Battle of the Styles' 469
Baudelaire, Charles 81
Baumann, S. 574
Beale, Justin 327
The Beatles 528, 534
Beck, Ulrich 467
Becker, Gary 94, 557
Becker, Howard S. 6, 31, 193, 196, 201, 242
    artworks 497, 501, 502, 504
    sociology of art 301
    visual sociology 248
Beckert, J. 557
Beer, David 532
Bell, Daniel 62
Bellah, Robert 70–1
'below-the-public' level of analysis 164
Belting, Hans 544
Bendix, R. 28
Benedict, Ruth 199
Benford, R. 417, 420, 421–2
Benjamin, Walter 12, 16, 81, 330, 380, 498
Bennett, Andy 527–37, 530, 531–4
Bennett, Jane 543
Bennett, Tony 267, 311, 314, 381–2, 404, 498, 499, 518, 575
Benzecri, Jean-Paul 255, 262–3, 264
Benzecry, Claudio 218–19, 502
Berezin, Mabel 217
Berger, John 339
Berger, Peter 117, 163, 203, 244–6, 318, 365, 376, 377
Bergesen, Albert 126
Berlan, A. 591

Bernier, C. 496, 498
*Beruf* 29
Bhabha, Homi 435
Biernacki, Richard 217
Bierstedt, Robert 487
Billig, Michael 438
binary boundaries 353
biographical approach 238
Birmingham Centre 2, 17–19, 21, 198–9, 298, 309, 312–13, 316, 317, 377
    fashion 518
    music 529
Black Arts Movement 109–10
Blasius, Jörg 267
Blau, Judith 471
Bloch, Marc 66
blogs, fashion 516
Bloor, D. 136
Blumer, Herbert 239, 240–1, 294, 378, 379, 382, 512
bodily habitus 301
Boehm, Gottfried 540, 541, 544
Boltanski, Luc 159, 160, 161, 163–5, 166–7
Bonnell, V. 316
Bonta, Juan Pablo 468–9
Bookman, Sonia 578–89
Bordo, Susan 340
Borgatti, S. 285, 292
Börjesson, Mikael 268
Born Georgina 302
boundaries
    binary 353
    concrete 355–6
    modelling 358
    symbolic 349–62
boundary object theory 323–4, 326
Bourdieu, Pierre 2, 3, 5–6, 20, 27, 31, 32, 62, 67, 72, 91–104, 193, 230
    ANT 138, 139
    cinema 490–2
    cultural fields 451
    ethnography 299–300
    everyday life 373, 375, 380
    fashion 510, 512–13, 515
    mind-body 117
    Multiple Correspondence Analysis 255–9, 262–8
    museums 498–9, 500, 501, 502, 503
    omnivorousness 567, 568–75
    photography 326
    production of culture 197–8, 199, 202
    religion 370
    symbolic boundaries 351, 353, 354, 357
    taste 593
    visual sociology 248
    Weber's work 27, 31, 32, 37, 38, 42–3, 44
Boyer, D. 324
Bozak, Nadia 328–9
Bracewell, Wendy 437
Brain, David 471–2

brands 578–89
  in the hand 586
  *see also* fair-trade
Branford, Victor 377
Breckner, Roswitha 248
Breiger, Ronald 292
Breuilly, John 429, 430, 433
British Humanist Association 367–8
Bromley, P. 154
Bronner, S. 13, 405
Brundson, C. 446–7
Bruner, E. M. 107
Bryant, R. L. 592
Bryson, Bethany 349–62, 571, 574, 575
Bryson, N. 376, 380
Bull, Michael 545
Bulmer, M. 238, 239–40
bureaucracies 351
Burgess, Ernest 239–40
Burke, Peter 437
Burt, Ronald 289, 555
Burtynsky, Edward 328
Butler, Judith 336, 544

Caldwell, M. L. 149
Caliskan, Koray 557, 559
Callois, R. 364
Callon, Michel 131–5, 137, 139, 325, 557, 559
Campbell, Colin 228, 593
Campbell, R. 450
capitalism
  architecture 470
  brands 580–1
  citizenship 404, 409, 411
  poetry 16
  spirits 161
  Weber's work 29, 34, 36–7, 41
Carnap, R. 243
Carroll, Patrick 216
Castoriadis, Cornelius 404
Caudwell, Christopher 16
censorship 200
centrality, social network analysis 287
Cerulo, Karen A. 116–30
Champy, Florent 472
Chaney, David 317, 318, 374, 375, 376
charisma 37–40
*Charlie Hebdo* attack 367, 368
Charrad, Mounira 215
Charters, W. W. 483, 484
Chatterjee, Partha 435
Chaves, M. 368, 370
Chiapello, E. 161, 164
Chicago School 197, 205, 237–40, 239–42, 242, 247, 249, 294–5
  everyday life 378
  subsequent eras 243
Chomsky, Noam 117

Cibois, Philippe 263, 264
Cicourel, Aaron 117
cinema 481–95
circuit model 201
circuits of culture 106–7
citizenship 403–13, 459
Clark, T. M. 229
Clarke, John 298
class 69
  Bourdieu's work 93–4, 99
  cinema 482
  citizenship 408
  fair-trade 595
  fashion 511, 512–13, 518–19
  Mannheim's work 67
  MCA 256–9, 263, 265, 268
  media audiences 447
  omnivorousness 570–1, 574
  symbolic boundaries 350–1
  voting 229–30
  Weber's work 31–2
Classen, Constance 547
classification 365
  historical sociology 217
  MCA 263
  symbolic boundaries 350, 351, 353–4, 355
Cloutier, Charlotte 167
cognition
  culturally mediated 232–3
  inside and outside of thought 116–30
Cohen, J. 19
collective action 414, 416, 418, 420–1, 423, 424
collective effervescence 63, 65–6, 350, 370, 397, 457
collective identity 422
collective intelligence 341
collective memory 66, 218, 220, 456–7
collective plagiarism 468–9
collective representations 62
collective selection 512
Collier, John Jr 248
Columbia School 197, 204–5, 240
comedy 120
commodification 582, 585, 592
commodity fetishism 579, 591, 592
common culture 299
communication
  in action perspective 391, 393–5, 397
  brands 580
  hypodermic model 486
  museums 500–1
  music 393
  organizational 120
  systems theory 179, 185–90
communicative democracy 302
communicative knowledge 52–3, 53
*ComparetheMarket.com* mascot 122–3
computer aided design (CAD) 475
Comte, Auguste 226, 481

concrete boundaries 355–6
condensed meaning 189, 190
conjunctive knowledge 52–3
conjunctural analysis 16
Connell, R. W. 337
Conquergood, D. 105, 110–12
conservation dilemmas 502
conservatism 53–4
constructivist institutionalism 145
consumer markets 200, 201
consumerism
  citizenship 407, 409
  music 527
consumption 565–98
  boundaries 358
  brands 578–89
  conspicuous 511–12
  ethics 590–8
  fashion 517
  markets 561–2
  omnivorousness 567–77
  symbolic interactionism 106–7, 108, 112–13
content analysis 486
context, hermeneutics 276
controller, culture as 181–2
controlling myths 417
convergence culture 341
conversation analysis 246, 248
Cooley, Charles 241, 520
copyright law 200
Corbin, J. 242
core-periphery analysis 285, 287, 292
Cormack, P. 584
corporate social responsibility (CSR) 325, 585–6
Correspondence Analysis (CA) 255
Coser, Lewis 197, 239
cosmopolitan memory 459
Coulangeon, Philippe 265
counter-branding 585, 587
Crane, A. 591
Crane, Diana 3, 197, 357, 512–13, 517, 518, 519, 520
Cressey, Paul G. 484, 485, 486–7
crisis of sociology 226, 233
Critcher, C. 17
critical discourse 448
critique, Marxian 15
Crossley, Nick 282–93
Cuff, Dana 470–1
'cult of the individual' 62
cultivated culture 53
cultivation, culture as 83–4
cultural artifacts 416, 423–4
cultural attachments 218–19
cultural capital 91, 92–4, 98–9, 99–100, 230, 351
cultural citizenship 403–13
cultural commons 377–8
cultural consumer 112–13

cultural diamond 201
cultural economy 581–2
cultural festivals 102
cultural intermediaries 582–3
cultural legitimacy model 265
cultural materialism 375
cultural memory 455–62
cultural orientation 180
cultural pragmatics 74, 278
cultural radicalism 296
cultural studies, sociology relationship 307–21
cultural turn 2, 182, 226–7, 246–7, 273, 274, 374, 375, 390, 531–2
cultural voting 230
cuteness 121–3
cybernetics 181, 184

Darmon, I. 43–4
Davies, I. A. 591, 593
Davis, Alexander 356
Davis, Fred 512
Davis, M. S. 78, 79, 88
Davis, Vaginal 342
Davis, Whitney 322
de Certeau, M. 316
de la Fuente, Eduardo 2, 6, 43, 78–90, 83, 85, 140, 301, 339
De Nooy, W. 284
de Saint-Martin, Monique 258
de-traditionalisation 458
Debray, Regis 549
decision-making 123
  neoinstitutionalism 145
Delanty, Gerard 467
democratisation 512
demographics, music 530
Denisoff, R. S. 529
DeNora, Tia 6, 390–9, 504, 531
Denord, François 268
Dentler, Robert 350
Denzin, Norman K. 105–15
Descartes, Rene 185
deviance 242
Diawara, M. 108, 110–11
Diaz Pedregal, V. 592, 594
Dickens, Charles 297
difference, historical sociology 217
diffusion 149, 151, 152, 154
diffusion theory 512
digital media 249
  hermeneutics 279
  iconicity 549
  music 527, 532–3
  social movements 424
  *see also* Internet; technology
digital networks 340–2
digital photography 329
Dilthey, Wilhelm 237, 273–4, 275

DiMaggio, Paul 98–9, 118, 144, 146, 194, 196, 199, 201, 202, 203, 205, 282
  museums 499, 501, 503
  Nadel's paradox 556
  symbolic boundaries 351, 357
discursive formation 110
discursive institutionalism 148, 152, 154
disenchantment 366
'disenchantment of the world' 39
disidentification 342
displacement 52
dispositionalist theory of action 98
Dissanayake, E. 397
dissonance 264
distantiation 56
'distinction effect' 263
distortion 118–21
Dobbin, Frank 215–16, 555
Dobrenko, Evgeny 468
domain violations 119–20
domestication 149–50, 154
dominant ethnicity 434
Dominguez-Rubio, Fernando 220
Donnat, O. 265
double-consciousness 406
doughnut theory of culture 84
Douglas, Mary 230–1, 350, 365, 380, 382
Douglass, Frederick 352
dramaturgy, symbolic boundaries 356
du Gay, Paul 201
dualisms 365
Dubois, Sébastien 266
Dubois, Vincent 266
DuBois, W.E.B. 352, 403, 405–6, 411
Duchamp, Marcel 496–7
Dudrah, R. K. 489
During, S. 311, 314
Durkheim, Émile 32, 60–77, 226, 227, 481
  citizenship 405
  collective effervescence 397
  economics 560–1
  everyday life 379, 380, 382
  experimental research 230–1
  markets 557
  memory 456–7
  morality 162
  qualitative sociology 239
  religion 363–6, 367–8, 369
  symbolic boundaries 350, 350–1, 353
  totems 541–2
Durkheimian Cultural Sociologies 60–77
Dutton, Thomas 472–3
Duval, Julien 255–71, 266
dwelling-oriented spirituality 369
dyadic level of analysis 287–8

Eagleton, Terry 17
eastern nationalism 432
Easternization 369–70
eating disorders 340
Eberle, Thomas S. 237–54, 248
eclectic 570
ecology, and aesthetics 397
economics
  brands 581–2
  historical sociology 217
  markets 553–64
  neoinstitutionalism 144–9
economies of worth 159–77
economy of symbolic goods 91–104
Edelman, Lee 338
edenic discourse 592
Edensor, Tim 436
Edles, Laura D. 363–71
education
  citizenship 410
  museums 503
Edwards, Elizabeth 326
ego-net density 287
ego-nets 283, 289–90
Egypt 50–1
eighth moment of inquiry 105, 108–9, 112, 113
Eisenberg, Eric M. 120
Ekelund, Bo G. 268
elective affinities 36–7
Eley, G. 437
Elias, Norbert 43
Eliasoph, N. 419
Eliot, 485
elites 69
embeddedness, ethical consumption 595
embodied ethnography 300–1
embodiment 126–7
Emirbayer, M. 60, 62, 63, 556
enactment 56
enchantment 366
'Energy Exploration' exhibition 323–30
energy humanities 323–4
Engels, F. 12–13, 374, 377
Enlightenment 225, 366, 404, 408, 410
  museums 498
entry points 125
Entwistle, J. 139, 515–16
*episteme* 500
epistemic governance 153
epistemology, symbolic interactionism 108–9
epochal reductivism 16
*Erfahrung* 498
Erikson, Kai 219, 350
Espeland, Wendy 217, 351
ethics
  brands 586
  consumption 590–8
  fashion 517
  religion 366
  symbolic interactionism 108–9

ethno-nationalist movements 423
ethno-symbolism 432–4, 436
ethnographic capital 556
ethnographic imagination 373
ethnographic praxis 112
ethnography 242–3, 247, 249–50, 294–303
  in action perspective 390
  everyday life 373, 378
  museums 504
  news 446
  symbolic boundaries 353, 354
  visual 502
ethnomethodology 160, 163, 190, 246, 248, 250, 379
ethnophenomenology 246
etiquettes 419
Evans, Mel 325
Everett, M. 292
everyday life 372–88, 457
  fashion 517–18
*Everyman* 376
exclusive boundaries 357
exhibitions 496–509
existentially connectedness 55
experimental research 226, 230–3, 234
exploration 241
Exponential Random Graph Models (ERGMs) 288
expressive culture 147–8
Eyerman, Ron 21, 71
Ezzell, Matthew 356

fair-trade 590–6
Falasca-Zamponi, Simonetta 217
Farkhatdinov, Nail 496–509, 504
fascism 217
fashion 510–26
fashion systems 511, 512, 513–14, 516–17, 521–2
Faure, Sylvia 266
Featherstone, M. 81
Febvre, Lucien 66
Feld, Steven 397
feminism
  art and culture 335–45
  performance art 335–6, 342
festivals 102
field theory 265–6, 268, 451, 556
  cinema 491–2
field work 239–40
fields
  of cultural production 93, 94–6, 98, 101–2
  organizational 201
Fierro, Annette 475
film theory 488
  feminist 339
films
  cinema sociology 481–95
  nationalism 436
  *see also* media

Fine, B. 517
Fine, Gary Alan 242, 242–3, 458
Fiske, John 231
Flacks, R. 423
*flaneur* 81, 374
Flinders, Carol Lee 368
formal rationality 37–8, 41
formalism 13–14, 18–19, 20
  trap 19, 20, 21
Forman, Henry James 484, 485
Foucault, Michel 66
  ANT influence 132
  citizenship 408
  ethics 593
  governance 153
  historical sociology 214
  museums 499
  power/knowledge 154
  visual culture 323
Fourcade, Marion 217
Fowler, Bridget 473
frame analysis 117
framing 202, 232
  museums 502, 503
  social movements 420–2
François, Pierre 266
Frankfurt School 12, 13, 15, 16, 445, 528
  omnivorousness 567
free association 132, 135
French pragmatic sociology 159–77
Friedan, Betty 337
Friedland, R. 226–7, 317
Frisby, D. 81, 83, 84, 85
Frith, Simon 527, 529
Frye, Northrop 20, 73
functionalism 144, 145, 146, 378
fundamentalism 366–8
Fustel de Coulanges, Numa Denis 60–1, 75
Futurism 13
Fyfe, Gordon 497

Gadamer, Hans-Georg 272
Galinsky, Adam D. 121
Gallery Tally project 335–6
Gane, Nick 27
Gans, H. 446, 472, 530, 568
Ganz, M. 419
Garber, J. 518–19
Garfinkel, H. 160, 190, 246, 378–9
Garland, D. 375
Garnham, Nicholas 299–300
Gayo, Modesto 267
gaze 339
Geddes, Patrick 377–8
Geertz, Clifford 19, 73, 161, 180, 190, 203, 227, 247, 298, 363, 545
  hermeneutics 273, 275–6, 278, 280
  memory 459

*Geico* gecko 122
*Geist* 30, 49, 50, 431
*Geisteswissenschaften* 30, 83, 237, 273–4
Gellner, Ernest 429
gender
　architecture 473
　cinema 482–3, 490
　fashion 515–16, 518–20
　historical sociology 217
　lindyhop 300–1
　media convergence 335–45
　nationalism 436–7
　religion 367
　ritual protests 458
　symbolic boundaries 352, 353, 355, 356, 356–7
genealogy 218
generalized meaning 180–1, 190
geodesic distance 286
geological imagery 328
geometric data analysis 268
geometric data analysis (GDA) 268
*Gerber* baby 122
*Gesellschaft* 49
Gibson, J. J. 86, 87
Giddens, Anthony 435, 458
Gieryn, T. 356, 474, 475
Giesen, B. 499
gift exchange 364–5
Gillett, C. 528
Gilroy, Paul 406
Giroux, Henry 410
Gitlin, T. 444
Glaeser, Andreas 216
Glaser, Barney 241–2, 242
globalisation, fair-trade 591–2
globalization 458
　architecture 470
　brands 584, 586
　fashion 521–2
　nationalism 435–6
　neoinstitutionalism 151–2, 154
Godart, F. 513
Godwin, Fay 326
Goethe, Johann Wolfgang Von 36
Goffman, Alice 375
Goffman, Erving 117, 242, 287, 339–40, 381, 382, 421, 520
Goldberg, David Theo 405, 407
Goldmann, Lucien 15
Gomart, E. 133, 137–8
Goodman, M. K. 592
Goodwin, J. 556
Gould, N. J. 594
Gould, Stephen J. 122
Gouldner, Alvin 182, 196, 197, 204, 226, 240
governance, neoinstitutionalism 152–4
Graeber, D. 365
Gramsci, Antonio 16, 17, 19

grand theory 240
Granovetter, Mark 554, 555, 559–60, 561, 562
graph theory 283, 285
Green, B. 82, 533
Greenberg, M. 579, 581, 582, 584–5, 587
Greenfeld, L. 501
Greiling, Meredith 326
Grindstaff, L. 447
Griswold, Wendy 201, 218, 504
Grossberg, Lawrence 310, 312, 313
Ground Zero reconstruction 469
grounded aesthetic 112
grounded aesthetics 299, 301
grounded theory 241–2
Grubbauer, Monika 470
Guerilla Girls 335–6, 342
Guggenheim, Michael 474
Guo, Yingjie 434
Gutman, Robert 467, 472
Guy, Simon 475

Habermas, Jürgen 12, 15, 21, 81, 179, 190, 245, 302, 448, 458, 467
habilitation 53
habituation 118–21
*habitus* 62, 67, 91, 93, 94, 99, 101, 257
　bodily 301
　cinema 490–2
　ethnography 299–301
　mind-body 117
　music 300, 301, 573
Halbwachs, Maurice 66, 68, 456–7
Hall, Stuart 17, 17–18, 19, 20, 21, 107, 108, 201, 231, 312, 313, 340, 446
Halsey, A. H. 572
Halton, Eugene 84
Hamlin, J. 118–19
Hammersley, Martin 294, 295
Handel, Leo A. 487–8
Hannan, M. T. 354
Hannerz, Ulf 539, 543
haptic experience 249, 250
Haraway, Donna 315–16, 323
*Hard Times* 297
Harding, David 353
Hardt, M. 405, 409, 411
Hariman, R. 540, 543, 549
Harper, Douglas 248
Harrington, A. 231
Harrisson, Tom 378
Harvard School 240
Harvey, David 409
Hay, Colin 145
Hays, S. 310, 317
Heath, C. 248, 504, 505
Heavy Metal music 574–5
Hebdige, Dick 197, 199, 298, 518
Hebron, Micol 335

Heinich, N. 3, 502, 505
Heise, Tatiana S. 481–95
Hennion, Antoine 6, 133, 137–9, 218, 391, 395, 531
Henrich, J. 234
Herder, Johann Gottfried 430–2, 432
hermeneutics 112, 203, 246, 272–81
Herrero, M. 139
Hertz, Robert 364, 365
heterarchy 167
heterodoxy 349–50
Hetherington, K. 497, 498
Highmore, Ben 327
Higson, Andrew 436
Hinde, John 327
Hirsch, E. D. 275
Hirst, Paul 470
historical institutionalism 145–6
historical sociology 214–22, 274
history, cultural 437–8
Hobbes, T. 132
Hobsbawm, Eric 429, 457
Hochschild, Arlie 242
Hodder, Ian 547, 548, 549–50
Hodkinson, P. 518, 533
Hoggart, Richard 295, 312, 407–8
Holloway, John 411
Holt, Douglas 99, 542, 578–80, 581, 583, 584, 586, 587
Holt, Richard 296
home school movement 419
homology 15, 21, 529–30
homophily 287–8
homosexuality 340, 342, 516
    citizenship 408
    collective identity 422
Honneth, Axel 410
hooks, bell 340
Horkheimer, Max 12, 485
Hout, M. 229
Houtman, Dick 225–36
Howes, David 546, 549
Hroch, Miroslav 433
Hsu, G. 354
Huaco, G. A. 488
Huang, Li 121
Hughes, E. 197, 241–2, 378, 382
Hughey, M. W. 490
Hughson, John 294–303
Hugo, Gustav 54
human rights 410–11, 458
humanism 295
Hunt, L. 316
Hunt, S. 421
Hurdley, Rachel 372–88
Husserl, Edmund 188, 243–4, 379
Hutchinson, John 430, 433–4, 436, 438
hybrid organizations 167
hybridity 435

Hyde, Lewis 411
hydrogen technology 232, 232–3
hypodermic model 486

iconic brands 580
iconic objects 499
iconic turn 540, 548–9
iconicity 538–52
iconography, ethics 592
ideal factors 34–6
ideal-type 274
ideation 414–16, 417, 420–2
identity
    brands 580, 581, 583
    collective 422
    fashion 517, 520–1
    narratives 422
    nationalism 434
    politics 408
    value 580
identity work 356
Ignatow, Gabriel 120, 124, 125, 126
immediacy, turn to 323, 324, 329–30
immortal ordinary society 379
imperialism, citizenship 404, 405, 406, 409
Impressionism, French 195, 197
Imrie, Rob 474
in action perspective 390–9
inarticulacy 219–20
incidence matrix 291
inclusive boundaries 357
incongruities 120
individualism 62, 70
    methodological 274
inference statistics, MCA 268
Information Technology, charisma 40
Inglis, David 26–47, 60–77, 307–21, 329, 374, 376, 499
inspection 241
institutional logics 161, 167
institutionalism
    constructivist 145
    discursive 148, 152, 154
    historical 145–6
    rational choice 145–6, 154
    Scandinavian 149
    sociological 145, 146, 151
    *see also* neoinstitutionalist sociology
institutionalization 182
    high art 499
instrumental culture 147–8
intellectualism 50
intelligentsia 52, 55–7
interaction rituals 120
interactionist studies 242–3
intermediaries 582–3
Internet
    citizenship 411–12

hermeneutics 279
music 532
qualitative research 249
social movements 424
zines 342
*see also* digital media; technology
interpretive paradigm 237, 240–3, 243, 247, 248
intersecting social circles 290
interviews 247
isomorphism 148, 150–1, 152, 155, 288

Jack, Anthony 358
Jacobs, Ronald N. 442–54
Jakobson, Roman 14
Jamison, A. 21
jamming 120–1
Jenkins, Henry 341
Jennings, Humphrey 378
Jhally, Sut 340
Johnson, Paul 528
Johnson, Richard 309
Johnson, Victoria 219
Johnston, H. 414–28, 415, 423, 424
Jolls, Christine 557–8
Jones, Paul 11–25, 302, 465–80
Jowett, G. S. 484, 485, 492
Joyce, Patrick 216
Julier, G. 587
Jusdanis, Gregory 430

Kadushin, Charles 197
Kaika, Monika 470
Kaiser, S. B. 520–1
Kaluli people 397
Kant, Immanuel 62, 318, 376, 391
Karenga, M. 109–10
Katz, E. 445, 447
Kaufmann, Eric 434
Kawamura, Y. 514, 517
Keane, Webb 543, 544–5, 547
Kemple, T. M. 28–9, 41–2
Killborne, Jean 340
kinesis 111
King, Anthony D. 468
Kirchberg, V. 503
Klandermans, B. 415
Klein, Naomi 578, 579
Klimova, S. 417
Knoblauch, H. 246, 248
knowledge deficit 232
Kohn, Hans 432, 433
Kolegar, F. 29, 37
Kopf, David 435
Kosut, Mary 335–45
Kozinets, R. V. 249
Kracauer, S. 486
Krippner, G. R. 555, 559, 560
*Kulturwissenschaften see Geisteswissenschaften*

Lacan, Jacques 540
Laermans, Rudi 178–92
Lahire, Bernard 99, 264, 573
Lamont, Michèle 99, 164, 167, 267, 349, 351–2, 353, 354, 354–5
Lan, Pei-Chia 355
Langley, Ann 167
language 539
  film 485, 486, 487, 488
  iconicity 546
  immediacy 330
  nationalism 431
  Saussure 275
  systems theory 180, 188–9
  *see also* textuality
Lareau, A. 351, 355
Larson, Magali Safuri 471
Lasch, Christopher 62
Lash, S. 580
latent pattern maintenance 181, 183, 188
Latour, Bruno 6, 131–7, 319, 324, 325, 328, 473–4, 503, 549, 557
Law, John 131–5, 137
law and regulation, six-facets model 200
laws of form 184, 188, 189
Lazarsfeld, Paul 197, 240, 265, 288, 445, 487
Le Play, F. 377
Le Roux, Brigitte 268
Le Velly, R. 594
Leahy, H. R. 499
*Learning to Labour* 297–8, 299, 300
Leavis, F. R. 295–7, 485
Lebart, Ludovic 255
Leclair, M. S. 592
Lederer, Emil 52
Leerssen, Joep 430, 431, 436, 437–8, 439
Leibler, Anat 217
Leites, N. 486
Lenin, V. 14
Lenoir, Remi 266
Leopold, E. 517
Lessig, Lawrence 279
Lester, M. 445–6
Lévi-Strauss, Claude 14, 15–16, 20, 92, 275, 365, 541
Levy, D. 459
Levy, P. 341
Lewis, George H. 530
liberalism 54, 405
Libeskind, Daniel 469
Lichterman, P. 419
Liebes, T. 447
life-world analysis 238, 239, 243–4, 245–6, 249, 379
Lifshitz-Assaf, Hila 356
limited effects 445
lindyhop 300–1
linear regression analysis 262
Linebaugh, Peter 412
Lipovetsky, G. 511, 512, 513

Lipset, S. M. 229
Lipstadt, Hélène 471
literary analysis 417
lived experience 244, 249
  ethnography 302
  visual culture 324
lived religion 370
Lizardo, O. 570, 571, 573
Loader, Colin 48–59
local culture 584
local knowledge 276
Loiperdinger, M. 482
London Fashion Week (LFW) 515
Long, Elizabeth 217, 317
Lorber, Judith 336
Lorenz, Konrad 121
Löw, Martina 469, 470, 475
Lowenthal, Leo 12, 195, 196, 197
Lucaites, J. L. 540, 543, 549
Luckmann, Thomas 117, 163, 244–6, 318, 376, 377
Luhmann, Niklas 41, 178–92
Lukács, György 13, 48, 50, 52, 54, 80–1, 82
Lury, Celia 85, 138–9, 580, 581, 582, 583
Lynd, H. M. 486
Lynd, R. S. 486
Lyon, S. 592, 595

McCarthy, John 418
McClellan, A. 499–500, 503
McCoy, C. 358
McDonald, Christopher 435
McDonaldization 40, 149, 584
McDonnell, Terrence 547
McGuigan, Jim 299
McKernan, B. 449
McLennan, G. 308, 309, 311, 316, 317, 319
MacLeod, Suzanne 474–5
McLuhan, M. 498
macro-cultural analysis 160–1, 164, 165
McRobbie, A. 514, 517, 518–19
macrosociological study 239, 247
Madge, Charles 378
Madison, D. S. 110, 112
magazines, fashion 516
Makdisi, Saree 368
Malinowski, Bronislaw 294
Maman, D. 148–9
Manchester School 283
Manet, Édouard 95, 97–8
Mannheim, Karl 48–59, 67, 117
manufacture, fashion 513–14
maps, geological 328
Marcuse, Herbert 12
Margalit, A. 459
marketing
  cuteness 122–3
  *see also* brands
markets 553–64

Márkus, G. 11, 13, 15, 16
Markus, Thomas 469–70
Marx, Karl 226, 318
  cultural materialism 375
  everyday life 374
  ideology 329
  symbolic boundaries 351
Marxism 2, 54, 67, 312, 313
  architecture 470
  Bourdieu's work 93, 94
  citizenship 405
  fair-trade 594
  Geertz's critique 276
  Weber's opposition 27, 31, 31–2, 34
Marxist Cultural Sociology 11–25
Mäs, M. 357
mascots 122–3, *123*
mass consumption 567
mass culture 485–8, 487
mass fashion 512
mass media *see* media
Mass Observation project 378
mass society 445, 485–8
material factors 34–6
materialism 375
materiality 521
  ANT 139–40
  iconicity 540, 541, 545–8
Maturana, Humberto 179
Mauss, Marcel 62, 364–5
Mayer, J. P. 487, 488
Mazzini, Giuseppe 431
Mead, George Herbert 116–17, 219, 241, 520
Mead, M. 248
meaning
  boundaries 354, 355
  historical sociology 216–17
  markets 553–4
  meaning of 188–9
  phenomenology 243
  webs 548
meaning-kernel 189
meaning-making 237, 247
  everyday life 372, 381–2
  iconicity 538–9
  museums 500, 501
  social movements 417, 419, 424
Mears, A. 515–16
media 567
  aesthetic public sphere 302
  age of convergence 335–45
  brands 582
  convergence 335–45
  domestication 150
  fashion 514–15
  nationalism 436
  news 442–54
  omnivorousness 574

sequencing 124
symbolic interactionism 108
mediation 138–40
  fashion 514–15
  museums 500–1, 502, 503, 505
mediatization 582
Medvedev, P. 14
megalography 376
Meinecke, Friedrich 432
memorialization 66
memory
  collective 66, 218, 220, 456–7
  cosmopolitan 459
  cultural 455–62
  film 489–90
  music 534
mentalities 66
Merleau-Ponty, Maurice 125
Merton, Robert K. 194, 195, 197, 240, 288
Metallinos, Nikos 119
*methodenstreit* 273–4
methodological individualism 274
Meuleman, Roza 267
Meyer, John W. 146–8, 151, 154
Micheletti, M. 590, 594
micro-sociology 160–1, 164
  museums 504, 505
Mies van der Rohe, Ludwig 469
Milgram, Stanley 284
Miller, Daniel 547
Miller, Toby 409
Mills, C. Wright 197, 379–80, 486
mimesis 111
mind–body dissonance/consonance 121
mind–body link 116–18
minority 296
Mirzoeff, Nicholas 323
Mische, A. 418, 419–20
Mitchell, W. J. T. 322, 323, 540, 544
mobilizing structures 418–20
modelling, fashion 514–15
modernity
  architecture 467, 469
  cinema 483
  everyday life 374–6
  fashion 511
  gender 437
  mass society/culture 485
  memory 457
  multiple 370
  museums 500
  nationalism 434
  second-order observation 185
  Simmel 81
  Weber's work 27, 35, 40
modernization 225
modular cultural theory 163–6
Moeran, B. 516

Mohr, J. 226–7, 317, 351
Molnár, V. 352, 354, 469
Molotch, H. 301, 445–6
Moor, L. 578–9, 580, 582–3, 585, 586
Mora, E. 514
moral boundary 350
moral consensus 182
moral criticism 109–10
moral judgements 124
morality
  cinema 483–4
  markets 558
  pragmatic sociology 162, 164, 168
Moretti, Franco 437
Morley, D. 446–7
Morrison, James 517
Möser, Justus 54
Mosse, George 437
Mouzelis, N. 316
Muggleton, D. 518
Mühlichen, Andreas 267
Mukařovský, J. 18
Mukerji, Chandra 214–22, 220
Mulcahy, , Linda 475
Mulgan, Geoff 407
Müller, Adam 54
Multi-Dimensional Scaling 357
multimethod approach 240
Multiple Correspondence Analysis 99, 255–71
multiple modernities 370
Mulvey, Laura 339
Muñoz, J. E. 342
museums 496–509
  visual culture 323–30
music 74–5, 527–37
  in action perspective 390–9
  cultural attachments 218–19
  deviance 242
  ethno-nationalist movements 423
  *habitus* 300, 301, 573
  lindyhop 300–1
  new monkey 300
  omnivorousness 569–75
  pop-rockization 147–8, 155
  production of culture 196, 199, 201
  Weber's work 43–4

Nadel's paradox 556
narrative performance 417–18
narrative performance turn 110–11
narrative theory 14
nationalism 429–41
Negri, A. 405, 409, 411
Negroponte, N. 341
Negus, K. 535
Neo-Durkheimian Cultural Sociologies 60–77
neo-Fordism 586
neoinstitutionalist sociology 144–58, 161, 202

neoliberalism 409–11
netnography 249
network analysis 268, 282–93, 418–19, 556
networks
 domains (net doms) 290
 dynamics 288
 markets 555–6
news media 442–54
Newsroom Studies 445–6
Nietzsche, Friedrich 30, 318
Nieuwbeerta, Paul 229, 230
Nippert-Eng, Christina 356
Nochlin, Linda 335, 338–9
nodes
 ego-nets 289–90
 properties 287
 set 283–4, 290
 *see also* social network analysis
Noël, Sophie 266
nominalist view 33
Nora, Pierre 457
normative order 182
noumena 318
Nowak, Raphaël 533
nurturing response 121–2
Nussbaum, Martha 544, 545
Nye, David 327

object agency 219–20
objectification 49, 52
objective culture 84, 85
objectivity
 media 448, 450
 news 445
occupational careers 200, 201
Occupy movement 411, 412
O'Doherty, B. 499, 503
Olick, Jeffrey 218
Ollivier, M. 570, 572, 573
omnivorism 99, 193, 202, 265, 267, 567–77
oppositional readings 447
orders of worth 164
Organisation for Economic Co-operation and
 Development (OECD) 153, 569
 PISA 150
organizational aesthetics 82
organizational communication 120
organizational fields 201
organizational sociology 196
organizational structures 200–1
Orwell, George 297
'other-worldly' orientation 369
over-socialized approaches 554

Palmer, Vivian 240
Park, Robert E. 239–40, 294, 377, 443–4
Parsons, Talcott 28, 29, 30, 39, 67–8, 71, 178–92, 240,
 243, 337, 378

participant observation 241, 300–1
patrimonial state 215
patterns of cultural choice 199
Patterson, O. 5, 217
Payne Fund Studies 483–5, 486
Peel, John 435
Peirce, Charles 540, 542
Pereira, José Virgílio Borges 267
performance 74–5
 call to 111–12
 hermeneutics 278
 memory 458
 narrative turn 110–11
 social movements 416–18
 symbolic boundaries 356
performative turn 278
performativity 110–11
 ANT 134–5, 139
perspective 125
Peters, B. Guy 145
Peterson, Richard A. 31, 99, 193–205, 267, 529, 532,
 567, 568–72, 574
phenomenal side 318
phenomenological hermeneutics 246
phenomenological sociology 163, 188, 249–50
phenomenology 243–6, 247, 379
photo elicitation techniques 248
photography 381
 fashion 514–15, 516
 visual culture 326–9
picture theory 544
Pike, C. 13
Pillsbury dough boy 122, *123*
Pinney, Christopher 548
Piper Alpha disaster 326–7
placebo effects 231, 234
plagiarism, collective 468–9
pluralism 51, 52, 53, 54, 178
plurality, pragmatic sociology 163–6
poiesis 111
point-horizon structure 125
Polanyi, Karl 560
polarization 357
*The Polish Peasant* 238–9
political economy 106, 579, 582
political performers 278
politics 401–62
 ANT 133
 anti- 411, 412
 class voting 229–30
 cultural citizenship 403–13
 cultural memory 455–62
 ethics 594
 hermeneutics 278–9
 historical sociology 214–20
 music 530
 nationalism 429–41
 neoinstitutionalism 149–50

New Left 377
  production of culture 204
  social movement 414–28
  sociology and cultural studies 313–14
Polletta, F. 415, 417–18
Pollock, D. 111
Pool, I. de Sola 341
Popper, Karl 240
popular culture 18
  artifacts 423
  cinema 485–6, 491
  music 527–37
  religion 370
populism 299
Porter, Gaby 326
positivism 226, 230, 233, 247
  POC 203
postcolonialism 434–5
postmodernism 247
  ANT 136
  fashion 518
  memory 457–8
postpositivism 203
poststructuralism 203, 323
Powdermaker, H. 486–8, 492
Powell, W. W. 144, 146
power, neoinstitutionalism 152–4
pragmatic sociology 241
  French 159–77
Prague Circle 14
Presley, Elvis 528, 534
Press, A. 447
Prieur, A. 99, 100, 267
primacy effects 123–4
Principle Correspondence Analysis (PCA) 255, 260–2
print revolution 431
Prior, N. 138, 139
Pritchard, Sarah 216
privatization 409
process-oriented approach 432, 434
producer image 592–3
production
  brands 586
  of fashion 513–14
  in meaning 298
  paradigm 16
  turn 197
production of culture (POC) 31, 40, 42, 44, 193–213
  aesthetics 301
  gender 338
  MCA 259
  omnivorousness 574
Propp, Vladimir 14
prosopographic database 259
protest studies 416
Protestantism 34, 35, 36, 39
psychoanalysis 339
public sphere 15, 21, 166–8, 279, 302, 405–6, 554–5

media 442, 448–51
  memory 458
Pugh, Allison 546
punctualization 134
Purhonen, Semi 268
Purser, Gretchen 355
*pyrtaneum* 61

qualitative cultural sociology 237–54
qualitative research
  omnivorousness 569, 571–4
  theory 78–90
  *see also* survey research
quantification, historical sociology 217
quantitative analysis
  symbolic boundaries 352
  why and how 225–36
queer studies 337–8, 343
queer theory 352
queercore scene 342

Raab, Jürgen 248
race
  cinema 490
  citizenship 405–7
  fashion 515, 519–20, 521–2
  historical sociology 217
  symbolic boundaries 352, 353, 354, 355, 357, 358
  symbolic interactionism 109–10, 113
  *see also* nationalism
radical performance 110
Radway, Janice 340
Ragone, G. 512
Raisborough, J. 591, 594, 595
Rancière, Jacques 330, 572
Ranger, Terrence 429
Rank, J. Arthur 487
rape 437
rational choice institutionalism 145–6, 154
rational choice theory 144, 145, 148
rational discourse 448
rationalisation 366
  Weber's work 27, 28, 29, 29–30, 33, 34, 35, 37–40, 37–41, 43, 43–4, 44
recency effects 123–4
reception 340
Reckwitz, Andreas 543
Regev, Motti 147–8, 155
regime power 215–16
regimes of justification 160–1, 163, 165–7
regression analysis 268
Reich, C. A. 528–9
reification 13
reification of the visible 328
relational accounting 559
relational realism 419
relational sociology 419, 422, 574
relationism 55

religion 363–71
  Alfred Weber's work 49, 51
  Bellah's work 70–1
  charisma 38–9
  distortion 119–20
  Durkheim 62, 63–6
  economic sociology 560–1
  Fustel 61
  Shils' work 68–9
  socio-historical analysis 274
  survey research 232–3
  systems theory 180
  Weber's work 34–5, 38–40, 228
  *see also* Protestantism
religious market model 367
Rembrandt Harmenszoon van Rijn 79
repertoire theory 160, 161–3, 167, 415, 416, 418, 419
representation 340
  collective 62
  everyday life 381–2
  historical sociology 216–17
  symbolic interactionism 105, 106, 107, 112–13
  textual 296
reputational entrepreneurs 458
resistance
  citizenship 411
  fashion 518
  symbolic interactionism 108, 109, 110, 111, 112
  *see also* social movement research
resource mobilization perspective (RM) 414, 418
responsibilization 586
Revers, M. 451
reversed economy 96–7
Reyes, D. 353
rhopography 376
Rickert, Heinrich 237
Ricoeur, Paul 19, 20, 21, 273, 274–6, 277, 280
Riesman, David 197
Riis, J. 372, 377
Rimmer, M. 300, 301, 573
riot grrrl movement 341–2
risk theory 231
rites 364
ritual 416, 498, 561
  commitments 558–9
  protests 458
  symbolic boundaries 356
Ritzer, G. 29, 39, 40
Robbins, Joyce 218
Roberge, Jonathan 272–81
Robertson, R. 79
Robnett, B. 422
Rocamora, A. 513, 515, 516
Rogers, Laura 358
Rojek, Chris 315, 316
Romantic nationalism 430
Romanticism
  citizenship 404

museums 498
Roose, Henk 267
Rosaldo, Renato 408
Roselund, Lennart 267–8
Rosenhek, Z. 148–9
Rosenthal, B. 423
Rossi, Alice 337
Rosten, L. C. 486–7, 488, 492
Rouanet, Henry 268
Rousseau, Jean-Jacques 404, 432
routine, charismaticisation 40
routinisation 37–40
Rubio, F. D. 325
Rudofsky, B. 473
Rudwick, Martin 328
Ruskin, John 404
Rutherford, Jonathan 404

sacred centre 68–9
Saguy, Abigail 355
Sahlin-Andersson, K. 149
Said, Edward 352, 404, 408
Santoro, Marco 193–213
Sapiro, Gisèle 91–104, 266
sartorial fashion 510–26
Sartre, Jean-Paul 94, 95
Sassen, Saskia 330
Sauder, M. 351
Saussure, Ferdinand de 73, 275, 318, 538, 539
Savage, M. 99, 100, 267
Savigny, Friedrich von 54
Scandinavian institutionalists 149
scapegoating 66
Scarborough, R. C. 358
Schafer, Murray R. 248
Schatzki, Theodore 543
Scheler, Max 53, 244
Schiller, F. 12
Schmidt, Leigh Eric 368
Schmidt, Vivien 148, 152
Schor, Naomi 327
Schroeder, R. 27, 30, 32, 34, 39, 41
Schudson, M. 218, 315–16, 450, 459
Schütz, Alfred 117, 163, 237–8, 243, 244, 245–6, 378–9
Schwartz, B. 218, 459
Science and Technology Studies (STS) 43, 44, 216, 219
  architecture 473, 474–6
scientism, Althusserian 13–14
scopic regime 328
scopophilia 339
Scott, James 215, 558
second-class citizens 408
second-order observation 185, 190
secularization 366–7, 368
seeking-oriented spirituality 369
Seidman, Steven 307, 308, 314, 317, 408
self 520–1
  music 531

self-reference 179, 185, 186
semantic structure 188
Semantic Web 279
semantics 275
semiotics 17, 247
   historical sociology 216, 218
   structural 275, 277
sensitizing concepts 241, 378, 379, 382, 555
sensory ethnography 249
sequencing 123–5
serial position effects 123–4
Serres, Michel 132, 325
Sewell, William 215
Sherwood, S. 20, 227, 231
Shibutani, Tom 242
Shields, Mary 80
Shils, Edward 68–71, 459
Short, William Harrison 483–4
Shostakovitch, Dmitri 14
Shove, Elisabeth 475
Silber, Ilana F. 159–77
Silva, E. 267, 325
Simmel, Georg 28, 29, 52, 78–90, 290, 329, 405, 511, 512, 539, 543, 545
Simpson, Mark 327
six-facets model 199–201
Skiles, S. 570, 571, 573
Sklair, Leslie 470
Slater, D. 139
slavery 406
slow culture 85
Sluga, Glenda 436
Small, Mario 353
smells 249, 250
Smelser, Neil J. 488
Smilde, D. 370
Smith, Anthony D. 433–4, 436, 436–7
Smith, Philip 19, 20, 21, 71, 247, 445, 448
Snow, D. A. 420, 421–2
social action 353, 356–7
social biography 327
social boundaries 354
social constructionism 204, 244–6
   gender 339, 343
   social movements 419
social constructions 376
   iconicity 539, 541
   museums 502
social constructivism 408
social contract 432
social democratic era 406–7, 409
social facts 230–2
'social life' of buildings 474
social media 341, 451, 532
social movement organizations (SMOs) 418–19
social movement research 414–28
social network analysis 282–93
social order 179

social stratification 32
social theory of the image 248
social world 242, 243, 512
sociobiology 337
sociological institutionalism 145, 146, 151
sociological poetics 14
sociology of the arts 339
sociology of knowledge 53–6, 245, 248
sociology of translation 325
sociology of valuation and evaluation (SVE) 167
sociology/cultural studies relationship 307–21
Solanas, V. 335
solidarity, nationalism 434
Somers, M. 418
soteriology 366
soul 49–50, 52
sound studies 248, 250
Spencer, Herbert 511
Spencer-Brown, George 184, 188, 189
Spiegelberg, Herbert 244
Spillman, Lyn 218, 237, 246–7, 555
sponsorship 325
sport, ethnography 295–6
stabilization of objects 504
Stanford school 145, 154
status homophily 288
Steets, Silke 469, 470, 475
Steinmetz, George 215, 216, 556
Stevens, Garry 466, 471, 472–3
Stevens, M. 351, 419
Stevenson, Nick 403–13
stewardship 232, 233
Stewart, James 322–34
Stolle, D. 590, 594
Stoller, Paul 249
Strati, Antonio 82
Strauss, Anselm 241–2, 242
Straw, W. 530
Strong, C. 534
'Strong Program' (SP) 17, 19–20, 21, 60, 71–3, 87, 136, 203, 247
   economic sociology 557–9
   everyday life 375
   film 490
   French pragmatic sociology 160
   hermeneutics 277–8
   pragmatic sociology 165–6
structural causality 264
structural coupling 189, 190
structural functionalism 179, 240, 243
structuralism 13–14, 16
   Bourdieu's work 93–4
   hermeneutics 19, 20, 275, 277
Sturken, M. 458
subgroups, social network analysis 286–7
subject-positioning theory 488
substantive rationality 37, 39–40
suicide 382

Suny, R. 437
supplementary variables 257–8
Surak, Kristin 438
surrender rituals 216
Survey of Public Participation in the Arts (SPPA) 569, 572
survey research 226, 228–30, 232–3, 233–4, 240, 267
  ego-nets 290
  omnivorousness 571–4, 576
Swedberg, R. 27, 29, 35, 42
Swidler, Ann 162, 414–15, 545
Swindle, Jeffrey 353
'switchmen' metaphor 35
symbolic approaches, brands 579–80, 583
symbolic boundaries 349–62
Symbolic Boundaries Research Network 351
symbolic creativity 299
symbolic generalization 183–4, 187
symbolic goods 91–104
symbolic interactionism 105–15, 240–1, 249–50
  everyday life 378
  fashion 512, 520
  social movements 418–19, 422
symbolic meanings 520–1, 539–40
symbolic revolution 95, 97–8, 100
symbolic value, fashion 513–17
symbolic violence 92, 93
symbols, religion 364
symmetry
  ANT 132, 133, 135, 136–7, 139
  Simmel 85, 87, 88
symptomatic reading 14, 18
synaesthetics 249, 250
synchronization, neoinstitutionalism 151–2, 154
systematisation 32
systems theory 178–92
systems-equilibrium 179, 182
Szeman, I. 324
Sznaider, N. 459

taboos 65, 365
Tancred, Petra 473
Tanner, J. 82
Tarde, Gabriel 132–3
taste 138, 530, 531
  ethics 593
  *see also* omnivorism
Taylor, C. 370
Taylor, Sue Jane 327
Taylor, V. 422
techno-utopianism 324
technology
  architecture 475
  computer aided design 475
  everyday life 375–6
  experimental research 232
  hermeneutics 279
  iconicity 542
  music 532–3

six-facets model 200
video games 449
*see also* digital media; Science and Technology Studies (STS)
television
  news 446, 448, 450
  reality TV 447
  *Supergirl* 449
  *see also* media
temporality 391
Ténédos, J. 502
territory 431
textual analysis 247, 529
textual representation 296
textuality
  hermeneutics 273, 275–6, 277, 279
  iconicity 540
  social movements 423–4
textural analysis 80
theology 366
Therborn, Göran 467
Thévenot, Laurent 159, 160, 163–4, 165–7
thick description 19, 227, 276, 277, 298, 539, 545–8
Thielen, Korinna 470
Thiesse, Anne-Marie 436
thin model of culture 445–6
'this-worldly' orientation 369
Thomas, D. S. 239
Thomas theorem 239, 243
Thomas, William Isaac 238–9
Thompson, E. P. 312, 377, 404
Thoreau, H. 374
Thorne, Barrie 352
Thorp, Margaret Farrand 486, 488
Thrift, Nigel 547
Till, Jeremy 472
Tilly, Charles 215, 353, 415, 416, 419, 422
Tocqueville, Alexis de 70
Todorov, Tzvetan 410
tolerance 571
Tombesi, Paolo 475
Tönnies, Ferdinand 48
tool-box 414–15
tool-kit, pragmatic sociology 162
totalitarianism 410
totem 65, 364, 541–2
touch 249, 250
trade associations 555
tradition, memory 457, 459
traditionalism 54
transgender studies 338
transitivity 288
translation 132, 134, 325
  neoinstitutionalism 149
transposition 15, 16
Trevor-Roper, H. 457
triadic level of analysis 287–8
Trigilia, Carlo 560

Tröndle, M. 503
'truth spot' 474
Tuchman, G. 445–6
Tudor, Andrew 481–95
Turner, Bryan S. 315, 316
Turner, Graeme 308, 309, 310, 313, 314
Turner, Stephen 548–9
Turner, Victor 365–6, 438, 542–3
Twigg, J. 520
Twitter 451
two-mode networks 282, 283, 290–2

Universal Design movement 474
univorism 99, 570
urban brands 579, 584–5, 586–7
Urry, J. 134
utilitarianism 404
utopia 54–5
utopianism 112

Vale, Lawrence J. 468
validation 275
value creation 579–80
value homophily 288
value spheres 40–2
value-principle 184, 187
Van Bohemen, S. 232
van Gennep, Arnold 365
Varela, Francisco 179
Varul, Matthias 590–8
Veblen, Thorstein 511–12
*Verdichtung* 543
Verger, Annie 266
*Verstehen* 29, 33, 238, 243, 273–4, 379
victimisation, fashion models 515
video games 125, 449
videography 246, 248
Vidler, Anthony 468
virtual data 249
virtual music 532
visitor behavior studies 503–4
visual anthropology 248
visual culture studies 322–34
visual ethnography 502
visual sociology 248, 250
visual turn 247–8
visuality 322, 323
vitalism 49, 52, 54
Vološinov, V. 14, 17
vom Lehn, Dirk 504
von Foerster, Heinz 184
voraciousness 570

Wade, L. 300–1
Wagner-Pacifici, R. 216, 353
Walzer, Michael 369
Warde, A. 570, 571, 573, 575, 584, 595
Waridel, L. 594

Watergate scandal 73
Watkinson, Gareth 327
Watson, Cate 120
Watt, Ian 195
'weak program' 445, 554, 555–7
Weaver, Simon 120
Weber, Alfred 48–59, 482
Weber, Max 26–47, 71, 78, 95, 227–8, 244, 273, 318, 443, 481
  and brother Alfred 48, 50
  citizenship 405
  everyday life 374, 379
  qualitative sociology 237
  religion 363, 366, 369, 561
  sociology definition 243, 274
  symbolic boundaries 350–1, 351, 356, 357
webs of meaning 548
*Wechselwirkung* 543
Weibel, P. 324
Weingartner, R. H. 79
West, B. 455–62, 458, 459
West, Cornel 405
western nationalism 432
westernisation 520, 521
Whannel, Paddy 18
Wherry, Frederick F. 553–64
Whimster, S. 28
White, C. 195, 197
White, Harrison C. 195, 197, 290, 419
Whittier, N. 422
Whittock, Trevor 119
whole networks 283–8
Wicca 370
Wilde, M. 370
Williams, Raymond 2, 12, 13, 15, 16–17, 17–19, 20, 21, 84, 197, 295–7, 312
  art 498–9
  citizenship 403, 404, 407–8, 411
  common culture 299
  ethnography 299–300, 301–2, 302
  everyday life 377
Willis, Paul 17, 197, 199, 296, 297–9, 300, 301, 309, 310, 373, 529–30
Wilson, E. O. 337
Wilson, Fiona 473
Wilson, Thomas 241
wind band world 266
*Wirkungsgeschichte* 272
wisdom 109
Wissinger, E. 515
Wittgenstein, Ludwig 189, 373
Wolfenstein, M. 486
Wolff, Janet 6, 317, 323, 324, 326, 329–30
Wolff, K. H. 78
Woods, Eric Taylor 429–41
world culture 146
world polity theory (WPT) 62, 146, 148, 151, 152
Worpole, Ken 407

Worringer, W. 80
Wright, C. 592
Wright, David 267, 268, 567–77
Wu, J. 449
Wuthnow, Robert 119–20, 369

Yale School 3, 273, 276–8
　*see also* Alexander, Jeffrey C.
Yaneva, Albana 473–4, 502
Yoshino, Kosaku 434, 438
Young, M. 422
Yuval-Davis, Nira 408, 437

Zald, Mayer 418
Zelizer, Viviana 217, 219, 554, 558, 559, 562
Zerubavel, E. 81–2, 86, 87, 117, 355, 356
Zhang, T. 459
Zimmer, Oliver 432, 434
zines 336, 340–2
Znaniecki, Florian 197, 238–9
Zobl, E. 336, 341, 342
Zolberg, Vera 99
Zubrzycki, Geneviève 220
Zukin, S. 584, 585